D0891530

CONCORDANCE TO VAUGHAN'S *SILEX SCINTILLANS*

CONCORDANCE TO VAUGHAN'S
SILEX SCINTILLANS

Imilda Tuttle

THE PENNSYLVANIA STATE UNIVERSITY PRESS

University Park and London

Standard Book Number 271-00095-3
Copyright © 1969 by The Pennsylvania State University
Library of Congress Catalog Card No. 75-79843
Printed in the United States of America

INTRODUCTION

In his introduction to the first concordance to be prepared on a computer, **A Concordance to the Poems of Matthew Arnold** (Ithaca, 1959), Steven Maxfield Parrish details the history of concordances. He describes the extraordinary amount of time and energy formerly invested in good hand concordances, and compares those monumental efforts to the relative ease with which his own concordance was completed with the aid of a computer. The present Vaughan concordance was begun and completed in three months with the aid of an IBM 704 computer.

By now most readers are familiar with the form, the weaknesses, and the strengths of a concordance prepared by such means. The major advantage is that the computer completes the job expeditiously. The major disadvantage is that editorial decisions cannot be individualized, or else the major advantage is canceled. In the present case, these editorial decisions deal mainly with choice of omissions and with inconsistent spellings. In deciding omissions, I was guided by the choices of others in the same situation — that is, those concordances completed under the general direction of Parrish, beginning with the Matthew Arnold mentioned above. Many choices of omission are obvious — for example, the personal pronouns, the auxiliary verbs, the articles. A frequency count of these omitted words was not taken as it was in the other concordances prepared by the computer. For certain types of comparative, time-change linguistic studies, omissions of any sort are regrettable.

In making choices of words to be omitted, homographs present a peculiar kind of problem, because individual evaluation is impossible. Despite the loss of a few nouns in "doe," "may," "might," "till," "will," and adjectives in "wilt," the decision was made to omit these words altogether, for otherwise the length of the concordance and the endless pages of meaningless entries would make the book useless. An error in the final typing of the program is a good example of the case in point. The pronoun "thou" was selected for omission, but was inadvertently retained in the final typing. As a result, the machine printed all the "thou's." As the concordance now stands, there are three "thou's" on the bottom of page 206, and seventy-three "thou's" on the top of page 207, and yet three full pages of "thou's" were deleted after printout. The full list of omitted words, alphabetically arranged, appears at the end of the introduction.

The aberrant spelling of the seventeenth century is another editorial problem. A general principle followed is that if the variant spelling is not a consecutive entry with the standard spelling, or if there are so few of the sample in question as to be insignificant, the standard spelling is adopted.

Because of the space limitation of IBM cards, on which the verse was originally typed, the titles of individual poems had to be reduced to ten characters. Generally the obvious has been done in this reduction. Unnecessary vowels have been removed — e.g.,, "Unprofitableness" becomes "Unprftblns." If the reader is uncertain about the title abbreviation, he can check the page number listed in the concordance against the text. The text used is **The Complete Poetry of Henry**

Vaughan, edited by French Fogle (Garden City, 1964). Although only the **Silex Scintillans** — Vaughan's most important and pertinent collection — is here reproduced in concordance form, if the need and opportunity arise for a complete concordance to Vaughan this will simply be a matter of merging the present tape with the new.

Imilda Tuttle

Pittsburgh, Pa.
March 1969

OMITTED WORDS

a	ere	mightest	such	up
about	ev'n	mine	sure	upon
after	even	more	surely	us
again	ever	much	t'	very
agen	every	must	th	was
ah	for	my	th'	wast
al	for't	myself	than	was't
all	forth	nay	th'art	we
all's	from	ne'	that	wee
also	had	ne'r	that's	wee'l
am	hadst	neither	thats	were
amidst	hark	never	the	wert
among	has	no	thee	what
an	hast	non	their	what's
and	hath	none	them	whats
another	have	nor	then	when
any	having	not	thence	whence
are	he	now	theirs	whensoe're
as	heark	o	there	where
aswee	hee	of	there's	which
at	hee'll	off	these	while
awhile	he'll	oft	they	who
ay	hence	often	they'l	whom
aye	her	oh	they'r	whose
be	here	on	th'hast	why
because	hers	once	thine	sil
been	herself	one	this	wilbe
before	him	onely	thither	wilt
behind	himself	only	tho	with
beside	his	onto	those	within
between	hither	o'r	thou*	without
betwixt	how	or	thou'dst	would
bin	howe'r	o're	thou'lt	ye
but	however	ore	though	yet
by	I	other	through	you
can	I'de	our	thus	you'l
canst	if	ours	thy	you'll
cans't	I'm	ourself	til	your
cannot	Ime	ourselves	'til	yours
'cause	into	over	till	
could	is	put	'till	
couldst	it	rather	tis	
did	its	same	'tis	
didst	i'th	self	to	
do	I've	selves	to't	
doe	less	shal	toward	
doest	lest	shall	towards	
dost	mai'st	shalt	twixt	
doth	maiest	she	'twixt	
down	maist	she'l	twas	
either	many	shou'd	'twas	
els	may	should	under	
else	me	since	unless	
elsewhere	'midst	so	until	
e'r	midst	stil	untill	
e're	might	still	unto	

---

*See note on "thou" in the Introduction.

CONCORDANCE TO VAUGHAN'S *SILEX SCINTILLANS*

		PAGE	TITLE	LINE
'BIDE				
AS 'BIDE THE TOUCH		230	LAW + GOSP	16
'STEAD				
AND 'STEAD OF PHISICK, A DISEASE		150	RELIGION	44
'TWILL				
'TWILL MAKE THE LAND OF DARKNESS LIGHT.		299	JESUS WP B	51
'WHOSE				
'WHOSE SERVICE MAKES EV'N CAPTIVES FREE)		300	PROVIDENCE	14
ABEAR				
WHO NOTING WELL MY VAIN ABEAR		282	GARLAND	27
ABEL				
THEN ABELS DOTH. MAY ABEL BE		326	ABELS BLOD	41
ABELS				
THEN ABELS DOTH. MAY ABEL BE		326	ABELS BLOD	41
JUST ABELS BLOOD		338	DEATH B	2
ABIDE				
WHO IN THIS WINDY WORLD ABIDE.		298	JESUS WP B	21
THAT HEAVEN WITHIN HIM MIGHT ABIDE		166	THE CALL	60
MY LAMP, AND LIFE, BOTH SHALL IN THEE ABIDE.		177	MRNG-WTCH	33
SEEING THY SEED ABIDES IN ME		277	COCK-CRWNG	23
ABODE				
THE WAY WHICH FROM THIS DEAD AND DARK ABODE		233	THE WORLD	53
HONOUR AND MAJESTY HAVE THEIR ABODE		284	PSALM 104	3
HEAV'NS SECRET SOLITUDE, THOSE FAIR ABODES		327	RIGHTSNESS	6
ABOUNDS				
THY UPPER RIVER, WHICH ABOUNDS		336	PSALM 65	29
ABOVE				
THE ONELY DAY DEALT FROM ABOVE.		334	JUDGEMENT	2
THAT CANDLE GIVEN ME FROM ABOVE.		333	AGREEMENT	42
THE EVERLASTING DOORS AROVE		325	ABELS BLOD	19
THE THINGS ABOVE		327	RIGHTSNESS	14
THOU FROM THY UPPER SPRINGS ABOVE, FROM THOSE		285	PSALM 104	37
ABOVE THE MOUNTAINS STEEP.		285	PSALM 104	20
ABOVE THEM THE COOL MOON HER KNOWN COURSE HOLDS		286	PSALM 104	51
DIRT IN HER WAY, WILL KEEP ABOVE THE SKIE.		291	THE TIMBER	56
HATH KEPT ABOVE		291	THE JEWS	10
BLEST SHOWERS THEY ARE, AND STREAMS SENT FROM ABOVE		291	THE TIMBER	49
TYE ME TO FAITH, THOUGH ABOVE REASON		318	THE ASS	19
ABOVE ALL, MAKE ME LOVE THE POOR		319	THE ASS	33
YET WOULD NOT PLACE ONE PEECE ABOVE, BUT LIVES		232	THE WORLD	34
AS THERE ABOVE		226	RETIREMENT	37
AND BETHLEMS HUMBLE COTTS ABOVE THEM STEPT		238	SHEPHEARDS	21
NOW BENEATH, AND NOW ABOVE		235	CONSTLATN	6
AS THOSE CLEAR HEIGHTS WHICH ABOVE TEMPESTS SHINE.		281	JOY	16
SHOWN, AND BUT SHOWN ME FROM ABOVE.		281	THE FAVOUR	2
THIS IS THE LIFE WHICH HID ABOVE WITH CHRIST		280	PALM-TREE	13
WHOSE HEIGHT ABOVE ALL AGES SHINES		273	WHT SUNDAY	46
HIGH AS THE HEAVENS ABOVE.		271	ALL GONE	14
WHEN HEAV'N ABOVE THEM SHIN'D LIKE MOLTEN GLASS		268	ASCN-DAY A	45
LEAD ME ABOVE		248	I WALKT	58
ABOVE THE MORNING-STARRE		225	RETIREMENT	3
AND CHIEF ACQUAINTANCE BE ABOVE.		212	DAWNING	44
TWO FLOWRES THAT GREW WITH THEE ABOVE.		216	DRESSING	26
WE CLIMB ABOVE ALL AGES, LAMPS THAT LIGHT		2	SON-DAYES	6
YET ARE ABOVE		177	MRNG-WTCH	28
ME FROM ABOVE.		174	JOY OF LIF	4
WHEN YET I HAD NOT WALKT ABOVE		169	RETREATE	7
THE GOD ABOVE.		179	CHRCH-SVC	2
THERE ABOVE NOISE, AND DANGER		184	PEACE	5
LIKE THOSE ABOVE		182	CHRFLNESS	5
ABOVE THE STARS, A TRACK UNKNOWN, AND HIGH		155	ISAACS M.	50
OF STARS, ABOVE INFIRMITY.		204	DSRDR + FR	49
ABOVE THIS INNE		199	NTVTY 1	15
ABOVE ARE RESTLES MOTIONS, RUNNING LIGHTS		194	RLS + LSNS	89
ABR'AMS				
THAT SERV'D THE CALF, NOT ABR'AMS SEED		296	JESUS WP A	6
ABR'HAMS				
IN ABR'HAMS TENT THE WINGED GUESTS		149	RELIGION	13
ABRAM				
WHEN TERAH, NAHOR, HARAN, ABRAM, LOT		306	RAIN-BOW	5
ABROAD				
RETIRE INTO THEIR DENS. MAN GOES ABROAD		286	PSALM 104	62
I STOLE ABROAD		139	RGNRTN	11
WHEN THE WORLDS UP, AND EV'RY SWARM ABROAD		192	RLS + LSNS	31
WHETHER ABROAD, AMIDST THE CROWD		221	PSALM 121	17
GREATER THAN THOSE THAT GAD ABROAD.		214	MISERY	70
ABSENCE				
YET WITH THY LOVE THAT ABSENCE WINS		213	ADMISSION	23
HOW IN THY ABSENCE THOU DOST STEERE		174	JOY OF LIF	3
MY SOULS BRIGHT FOOD, THY ABSENCE KILLS.		308	THE SEED	6
ABSENT				
THAT, ABSENT, HE MAY SEE		216	DRESSING	15
ABSENTS				
ABSENTS WITHIN THE LINE CONSPIRE, AND SENSE		183	THRS A TYE	9
ABUS'D				
TILL HIS ABUS'D, DESPISED FLAME		305	ST MARY MN	53
ABUSE				
THY CREATURES BONDAGE AND ABUSE.		335	JUDGEMENT	32
SHALL I THY MERCIES STILL ABUSE		187	NO DO THEY	33
ABUSE NOT, SHUN NOT HOLY FIRE		266	VAIN WITS	3

	PAGE	TITLE	LINE
ACCENTS			
HE WEIGHS NOT YOUR FORC'D ACCENTS, WHO CAN HAVE • •	280	JOY	7
ACCEPT			
MY GOD, ACCEPT OF MY CONFESSION. • • • • •	207	REPENTANCE	26
ACCEPT, DREAD LORD, AND THE PCOR OBLATION • • •	190	THE MATCH	13
ON THOSE THAT KEEP THEM, O ACCEPT • • • • •	326	ABELS BLOD	27
ACCEPTATION			
OF NO MORE ACCEPTATION. • • • • • • •	200	NTVTY 2	8
ACCESSE			
PIERC'D NOT, LOVE ONLY CAN WITH QUICK ACCESSE • •	160	THE SHOWRE	9
ACCESSE ADMIT • • • • • • • • •	215	PRAISE	37
ACCESSIONS			
THY SICK ACCESSIONS INTC SETLED HEALTH • • • •	221	AFFLICTION	3
ACCIDENTS			
THE PAST DAIES ACCIDENTS DO SUMME • • • • •	228	PILGRIMAGE	3
ACCOUNT			
THAT KEEP'ST ACCOUNT, TILL HE RETURNE • • • •	165	THE CALL	32
ACCOUNTS			
THY ACCOUNTS THUS MADE, SPEND IN THE GRAVE ONE HOURE •	195	RLS + LSNS	121
NEW FRESH ACCOUNTS OF BLOOD AND LUST. • • • •	297	HERODIAS	8
ACCURSED			
AND BLOOD BY AN ACCURSED DEATH • • • • •	220	HOLY COMM.	42
ACCUSETH			
HE THAT ACCUSETH NONE, SO STEERS • • • • •	314	THE STONE	29
ACKNOWLEDGE			
MUST NEEDS ACKNOWLEDGE TO BE JUST. • • • •	314	THE STONE	36
ACQUAINTANCE			
AND CHIEF ACQUAINTANCE BE ABOVE. • • • • •	212	DAWNING	44
ACQUAINTED			
AND THOUGH HERE BORN, YET IS ACQUAINTED • • • •	212	DAWNING	35
ACT			
SHARES IN THE ACT, AND PUTS ME TO'T. • • •	319	THE ASS	31
THESE TWO GRAND SINS WE JOYN AND ACT TOGETHER • •	307	RAIN-BOW	25
BUT WHERE TO ACT, THAT NONE SHALL KNOW • • •	313	THE STONE	2
AND EVERY ACT SHE DOTH COMMENCE • • • • •	311	FAIR+YONG	19
TO ACT AS WELL AS TO CONCEIVE. • • • • •	329	ANGUISH	18
THEY SEEM'D TO QUARREL WITH HIM, FOR THAT ACT • •	196	CORRUPTION	13
ACTED			
WITHOUT COMMAND YOU NEVER ACTED OUGHT • • • •	236	CONSTLATN	35
ACTION			
ACTION AND BLOUD NOW GET THE GAME • • • •	214	MISERY	67
FOR THINGS THUS CENTER'D, WITHOUT BEAMES, OR ACTION •	183	THRS A TYE	5
BUSINESS AND WEIGHTY ACTION ALL • • • • •	322	CHILDEHOOD	28
ACTIONS			
TO THEE THEREFORE MY THOUGHTS, WORDS, ACTIONS • •	191	THE MATCH	25
THROUGH ALL THY ACTIONS, COUNSELS, AND DISCOURSE •	193	RLS + LSNS	37
ACTIVE			
HADST THOU GIVEN TO THIS ACTIVE DUST • • • •	162	PURSUITE	9
ACTIVE BRIGHTNES • • • • • • • •	172	MIDNIGHT	28
WHOSE ACTIVE ZEAL AND TRIED FAITH WERE TO THEE • •	156	ISAACS M.	65
AND THY ASPIRING, ACTIVE FIRES REVEALE • • •	158	THE LAMPE	12
WHILE ACTIVE WINDS AND STREAMS BOTH RUN AND SPEAK •	288	THE BIRD	15
ACTIVE AS LIGHT, AND CALM WITHOUT ALL NOISE • •	244	MT. OLV. B	2
ACTS			
AND AFTER ALL THY ACTS OF GRACE DOTH KICK • • •	230	LAW + GOSP	22
WHOSE ACTS, WORDS AND PRETENCE • • • • •	327	RIGHTSNESS	19
MET IN THY FLAMES, ALL ACTS OF PIETY. • • •	158	THE LAMPE	10
ACTUATE			
AND ACTUATE SUCH SPIRITS AS ARE SHED • • • •	244	THE SAP	33
ADAM			
AND WHAT ADAM MARR'D, IS MENDED. • • • • •	218	EASTER HYM	4
ADAMANT			
WEPT BLOUD, THAT BROKE THIS ADAMANT, AND GAVE • •	159	MANS FALL	25
ADDE			
AND ADDE UNTO THAT DAY HE WENT • • • • •	165	THE CALL	36
AND FOOLISH THOUGHTS ADDE TO MY BIL • • • •	204	DSRDR + FR	51
ADDITION			
WITHOUT ADDITION TO OUR WOES • • • • •	312	FAIR+YONG	43
ADDS			
HIS ART ADDS STILL (THOUGH HE BE DEAD) • • •	297	HERODIAS	7
ADJOURNS			
BREAKS, NIGHT ADJOURNS • • • • • • •	210	FAITH	18
ADMIRATION			
YET STONES ARE DEEP IN ADMIRATION. • • • •	288	THE BIRD	16
ADMIRE			
LET ME ADMIRE THOSE, AND BE KINDE • • • •	319	THE ASS	35
AND THEN BE THANKFUL, O ADMIRE HIS WAYS • • •	195	RLS + LSNS	99
SPEAK'ST THERE SO MUCH, THAT I ADMIRE • • •	149	RELIGION	19
ADMIRING			
HOW BRIGH WERT THOU, WHEN SHEM'S ADMIRING EYE • •	306	RAIN-BOW	3
ADMIT			
LOVE THAT SHAL NOT ADMIT • • • • • •	216	DRESSING	27
ACCESSE ADMIT • • • • • • • •	215	PRAISE	37
A STATE, THAT NO REDRESS ADMITS • • • • •	273	WHT SUNDAY	34
ADORE			
THAT LAMB OF GOD ADORE • • • • • •	239	SHEPHEARDS	48
TO BUY, THE POOR CAME TO ADORE. • • • • •	302	ORNAMENT	4
ADORE HIM IN THEIR KINDS • • • • • •	176	MRNG-WTCH	15
ADORES			
ADORES DEAD DUST, SETS HEART ON CORNE AND GRASS • •	236	CONSTLATN	19

	PAGE	TITLE	LINE
ADORING			
WITH PROSTRATE SOULS ADORING THEE • • • • •	351	L'ENVOY	61
ADORN			
ADORN THE PLACE • • • • • • • •	339	THE FEAST	5
ADORNMENTS			
WEAR FRESH ADORNMENTS ON EACH SIDE. • • • •	337	PSALM 65	44
ADVANCE			
QUICK TO ADVANCE, AND TO RETREAT MOST SLOW. • • •	327	RIGHTSNESS	18
AND BY HIS BLOOD DID US ADVANCE • • • •	218	EASTER HYM	15
ADVANTAGE			
NONE COULD WITH MORE ADVANTAGE USE, THEN I. • •	320	HIDDN TRSR	18
ADVIS'D			
ADVIS'D THY SERVANT WHAT TO DO, AND SAY. • • •	155	ISAACS M.	28
AFFECTIONS			
COLD AFFECTIONS • • • • • • • •	172	MIDNIGHT	15
OF WILD AFFECTIONS, RID • • • • • •	282	GARLAND	10
AFFLICT			
MOVES IN DISGUISE, AND SIGHS AFFLICT THE AIR. • • •	280	JOY	4
THOSE SECRET SEARCHES, WHICH AFFLICT THE WISE • •	320	HIDDN TRSR	11
AFFLICTIONS			
SINCE TWO AFFLICTIONS MAY NOT REIGN • • •	298	JESUS WP B	16
AFFLICTION IS A MOTHER • • • • •	167	THE CALL	75
AFFLICTION THUS, MEERE PLEASURE IS • • • •	182	CHRFLNESS	9
STILL MORE AFFLICTIONS LEND • • • • •	147	DAY OF JDG	34
AFFORD			
AFFORD ME LIFE • • • • • • •	190	THE MATCH	17
AFFORDED			
AFFORDED VISITS, AND STILL PARADISE LAY • •	197	CORRUPTION	23
AFRAID			
LINGRING, AND WERE OF THIS STEEP PLACE AFRAID • •	343	WATER-FALL	6
AGE			
IN THAT DEAD AGE, ONE BEAM I'TH' DARK OUTVIES • •	196	RLS + LSNS	134
AGE MADE THEM REV'REND, AND A SNOWIE HEAD • •	156	ISAACS M.	69
TEACH AGE, THE HOLY WAY. • • • • •	310	THE SEED	64
SINCE ALL THAT AGE DOTH TEACH, IS ILL • • •	321	CHILDEHOOD	19
DEAR, HARMLESS AGE. THE SHORT, SWIFT SPAN • •	322	CHILDEHOOD	31
AN AGE OF MYSTERIES. WHICH HE • • • •	322	CHILDEHOOD	35
WHEN FIRST MY YOUTHFULL, SINFULL AGE • • •	282	GARLAND	5
SO IN THIS LAST AND LEWDEST AGE • • • •	273	WHT SUNDAY	39
SO LET ME ALL MY BUSIE AGE • • • • •	212	DAWNING	37
THE AGE, THE PRESENT TIMES ARE NOT • • • •	214	MISERY	65
AGED			
THE WEAK, AND AGED TIR'D, WITH LENGTH • • •	218	EASTER HYM	9
A COVERING O'RE THIS AGED BOOK • • • •	347	THE BOOK	19
AGES			
THE ROCK OF AGES IN WHOSE SHADE • • •	346	THE BOOK	3
WE CLIMB ABOVE ALL AGES, LAMPS THAT LIGHT • •	2	SON-DAYES	6
WHOSE HEIGHT ABOVE ALL AGES SHINES • • •	273	WHT SUNDAY	46
SO MANY AGES FROM ME) IS SO PROV'D • • •	267	ASCN-DAY A	6
WHERE THOU MAY'ST SLEEP WHOLE AGES, LIFES POOR FLOWR •	195	RLS + LSNS	123
ALL AGES UP. WHO DREW THIS CIRCLE, EVEN • • •	178	EVNG-WTCH	13
AGO			
OR BETTER, BUT THOU LONG AGO • • • • •	273	WHT SUNDAY	27
SOMTHING I HAD, WHICH LONG AGO • • • •	308	THE SEED	9
BUT SEEING SOLDIERS LONG AGO • • • •	317	MEN OF WAR	29
AGONIE			
IDAEA'S OF HIS AGONIE • • • • • •	152	THE SEARCH	38
AGONIES			
WHERE THROUGH THICK PANGS, HIGH AGONIES • • •	310	THE SEED	65
AGONY			
HIS AGONY, AND BLOUDY THROWS. • • • • •	208	REPENTANCE	62
AGREE			
AND SAY, WHERE GOD IS, ALL AGREE. • • • •	237	CONSTLATN	60
STILL SINGLE HEARD, WHILE THESE AGREE • • •	326	ABELS BLOD	42
JOINTLY AGREE • • • • • • •	180	CHRCH-SVC	18
A STATE AGREEING WITH THY MINDE • • • •	350	L'ENVOY	19
AID			
AND GIVES FULL AID • • • • • • •	328	RIGHTSNESS	41
AND BROUGHT US SAVING AID. • • • • •	302	THE KNOT	4
AIM			
ONE AIM AND END, WHO WALKS NOT BY HIS SIGHT. • •	327	RIGHTSNESS	21
THEE ONLY AIM, AND MEAN. • • • • •	187	NO DO THEY	24
YET LET MY COURSE, MY AIM, MY LOVE • • •	212	DAWNING	43
AIMING			
AND STRETCH TO THEE, AIMING AT ALL • • • •	203	DSRDR + FR	21
AIR			
THUS THE ENLARG'D, INRAGED AIR • • • •	176	THE STORM	13
THE FLOWRES TO AIR DRAW NEER, AND SUBTILTIE •	223	TEMPEST	35
SUCH A RICH AIR OF SWEETS, AS EVENING SHOWRS • •	244	MT. OLV. B	4
I SEE THEM WALKING IN AN AIR OF GLORY • • •	271	ALL GONE	9
SUCH LOSSES AS BEFEL HIM IN THIS AIR • • •	247	I WALKT	26
MOVES IN DISGUISE, AND SIGHS AFFLICT THE AIR. • •	280	JOY	4
AND AIR OF EDEN, LIKE A MALE-CONTENT • • •	279	PALM-TREE	6
PLEASING AND INNOCENT AN AIR • • • • •	303	ST MARY MN	6
STORMS TURN TO MUSICK, CLOUDS TO SMILES AND AIR. •	306	RAIN-BOW	10
O AIR, AND SEA, AND LAND. • • • • • •	284	PSALM 104	8
AIRE			
WATER'S REFIN'D TO MOTION , AIRE TO LIGHT • • •	223	TEMPEST	31
WITH AIRE DISGUIS'D. • • • • • •	162	PURSUITE	8
HE DOTH COMPRISE. BUT IN THIS AIRE • • • •	163	MT. OLVS A	29

		PAGE	TITLE	LINE
AIRE	**(CON'T)**			
AND IN THE OPEN AIRE		147	DAY OF JDG	22
AND THROUGH THE DARK AIRE SPIN A FIRIE SHREAD		157	THE LAMPE	3
THE AIRE WAS ALL IN SPICE		140	RGNRTN	54
AIRES				
AND SWEETER AIRES STREAME FROM A GRONE		167	THE CALL	80
AIRS				
ERRE IN LOOSE AIRS BEYOND HER BOUNDS.		297	HERODIAS	4
AKE				
TWO IN THE DAY, THEN FROM THE DAMPS, AND AKE		196	RLS + LSNS	135
OR THAT A SOUL COULD AKE.		282	GARLAND	16
THIS BALM FOR SOULS THAT AKE		244	THE SAP	44
AT LENGTH I FEEL MY HEAD TO AKE		214	MISERY	61
ALAS				
SLEEPS AT THE LADDERS FOOT, ALAS. WHAT CAN		224	TEMPEST	39
ALAS, FRAIL WEED.		203	DSRDR + FR	30
ALAS, MY GOD. THY BIRTH NOW HERE		200	NTVTY 2	17
ALAS, THY LOVE.		203	DSRDR + FR	15
AND MANY YEARES (ALAS)		166	THE CALL	47
BUT I (ALAS)		340	RGNRTN	6
ALAS. MY GOD. TAKE HOME THY SHEEP.		312	FAIR+YONG	51
BUT I (ALAS)		313	THE STONE	18
ALIVE				
WERE STILL ALIVE) THOU DOST GREAT STORMS RESENT		289	THE TIMBER	15
WERE NOW THAT CHRONICLE ALIVE		321	CHILDEHOOD	3
THE BLACE GROWS UP ALIVE AND GREEN.		337	PSALM 65	38
BUT LIFT THEM UP, WHERE STILL ALIVE		339	DEATH B	29
THY DEATH MAY KEEP MY SOUL ALIVE.		343	OBSEQUIES	32
ALL-HEALING				
BLOOD, IS THE WORLDS ALL-HEALING BALM.		304	ST MARY MN	40
ALL-QUICKNING				
SOME DROPS OF THY ALL-QUICKNING BLOOD		264	INTRO. 1	5
ALL-SEEING				
(THOUGH BOTH ALL-SEEING AND ALL RIGHT)		314	THE STONE	33
ALL-SURPRIZING				
OR WIL THY ALL-SURPRIZING LIGHT		211	DAWNING	5
ALLAY				
AND NOTHING DOTH THY LOVE ALLAY		274	WHT SUNDAY	51
IF SHOWERS THEN FALL, WILL SHOWERS ALLAY		298	JESUS WP B	19
ALLIE				
GOD IS MADE OUR ALLIE		302	THE KNOT	6
ALLOW				
MY SAVIOUR SATE, SHALL I ALLOW		162	MT. OLVS A	2
THAT GILD RANK POYSON, AND ALLOW		205	IDLE VERSE	11
ALLOW YOUR JOYES RELIGION, THAT DONE, SPEED		194	RLS + LSNS	81
ALLURING				
BUT WHILE EACH GAY, ALLURING WEAR		303	ORNAMENT	9
ALMIGHTY				
'TWAS NOT THAT VAST, ALMIGHTY MEASURE		299	JESUS WP B	26
MY DEAR, ALMIGHTY LORD. WHY DOST THOU WEEP.		298	JESUS WP B	1
ALMIGHTY JUDGE.		326	ABELS BLOD	23
ALMIGHTY LOVE. WHERE ART THOU NOW. MAD MAN		197	CORRUPTION	29
BUT O THY LOVE. THY RICH, ALMIGHTY LOVE		188	RELAPSE	5
ALMOST				
ALMOST TO HELL		188	RELAPSE	2
ALMOST OUTLIVE OUR NAME.		166	THE CALL	57
AND ALMOST REACH'D, BECAUSE 'TIS SURE		317	MEN OF WAR	39
AND ALMOST FAMISH'D, EVER WILL CONSENT		275	PROFFER	21
ALONE				
HEE ALONE		270	ASCSN-HYMN	37
AND I ALONE SIT LINGRING HERE.		270	ALL GONE	2
I SAW THE WARM RECLUSE ALONE TO LIE		247	I WALKT	19
MY SINS ALONE OUTWEIGH'D THEM ALL.		208	REPENTANCE	46
I SATE ALONE, AND TAKING UP		207	REPENTANCE	29
HOW IS IT THAT THE SUN TO THEE ALONE		224	TEMPEST	54
HE IS ALONE MY HELP, AND HOPE		220	PSALM 121	5
O HEAR. YET NOT MY TEARS ALONE		214	ADMISSION	29
(FOR TEARS ALONE ARE OFTEN FOUL)		242	MISERY	108
(NOT THINE ALONE BUT MINE TOO) THAT WHEN ALL		234	MUTINIE	15
AND LODGE ALONE.		323	THE NIGHT	22
MAN TO HIS DUTY. THOU ALONE		336	PSALM 65	15
AND ALL ALONE FULL EARLY RUN		295	PALM-SUNDY	36
LEST LEFT ALONE TOO LONG		161	DSTRQCTION	31
THY HAND ALONE DOTH TAME		179	CHRCH-SVC	15
BE GODS ALONE, AND CHOOSE THE BETTER PART.		192	RLS + LSNS	36
ALONG				
DARKEN'D ALONG, AS THEIR SCRIBES BE		332	AGREEMENT	27
ALREADY				
THOU HAS CROWND HIM ALREADY.		167	THE CALL	93
TO WHAT'S ALREADY GROWN TOO HIGH		240	MISERY	18
ALTAR				
WHERE SOULS BEHIND THE ALTAR MOVE		325	ABELS BLOD	20
ALTARS				
CHURCHES AND ALTARS FED HIM, PERJURIES		232	THE WORLD	27
VEILES BECAME USELES, ALTARS FEL		210	FAITH	25
ALTHOUGH				
ALTHOUGH THEIR DIFT MAY BE FINE		228	PILGRIMAGE	18
ALTHOUGH THE FIRST MUST SURELY FALL		302	ORNAMENT	7
ALWAYS				
IN GOD, DOTH ALWAYS (HIDDEN) MULTIPLY		280	PALM-TREE	14

                                                          PAGE   TITLE   LINE
AMAZ'D
   (AMAZ'D TO SEE'T)   140   RGNRTN   47
AMBUSH'D
   NOTHING BUT MAN, WHEN AMBUSH'D THERE.   313   THE STONE   17
AMEN
   AMEN. BUT HARK, E'R WE TWO STRAY   178   EVNG-WTCH   9
AMEND
   ONE SINNER DOTH AMEND   200   NTVTY 2   2
ANCIENT
   AN ANCIENT WAY   189   RESOLVE   22
   AND TREAD AGAIN THAT ANCIENT TRACK.   170   RETREATE   22
   DEAR LORD. RESTORE THY ANCIENT PEACE   294   BEGGING B   21
ANGEL
   THE ANGEL SHEWD THAT HOLY WELL   300   PROVIDENCE   3
   AND LOVE OF THEE, EACH WILLING ANGEL IS   .   .   .   284   PSALM 104   15
   AT LENGTH, MY LIFES KINDE ANGEL CAME   .   .   .   332   AGREEMENT   7
   BUT HARK. WHAT TRUMPETS THAT. WHAT ANGEL CRIES   .   .   197   CORRUPTION   39
   THIS MADE THE ANGEL CALL AT REEDS AND THATCH   .   .   238   SHEPHEARDS   27
ANGELL
   AN ANGELL TALKING WITH A MAN.   148   RELIGION   4
   ANOTHER TIME BY TH' ANGELL, WHERE   149   RELIGION   11
ANGELL-INFANCY
   SHIN'D IN MY ANGELL-INFANCY   169   RETREATE   2
ANGELS
   YET, HADST THOU NOBLER GUESTS. ANGELS DID WIND   .   .   155   ISAACS M.   25
   ANGELS LAY LEIGER HERE, EACH BUSH, AND CEL   .   .   197   CORRUPTION   25
   THAT BLEST INCLOSURE, WHERE THE ANGELS GAVE   .   .   267   ASCN-DAY A   16
   OF SAINTS AND ANGELS GLORIFIE THE EARTH.   .   .   .   267   ASCN-DAY A   26
   AND YET, AS ANGELS IN SOME BRIGHTER DREAMS   .   .   271   ALL GONE   25
   ANGELS DESCENDING, THE RETURNS OF TRUST.   .   .   .   2   SON-DAYES   15
   WHO DOEST THINE ANGELS CHARGE WITH FOLLY.   .   .   .   208   REPENTANCE   68
   AND, WITH THY ANGELS IN THE VAN   212   DAWNING   27
   IF SAINTS, AND ANGELS FAL DOWN, MUCH MORE THOU.   .   217   DRESSING   42
   WHICH ANGELS GUARD, AND WITH IT PLAY   .   .   .   322   CHILDEHOOD   37
   ANGELS. WHICH FOUL MEN DRIVE AWAY.   322   CHILDEHOOD   38
   WHOSE PEACE BUT BY SOME ANGELS WING OR VOICE   .   .   324   THE NIGHT   39
   AND THEIR OWN ANGELS SHINE AND SING   .   .   .   295   PALM-SUNDY   22
   YOUR HEARTS SHALL THAW. WHEN ANGELS HERE   .   .   291   THE JEWS   4
ANGER
   ANGER FOR ONE SHORT FIT   216   DRESSING   28
ANGER'D
   NE'R MARR'D WITH FLOODS, NOR ANGER'D WITH A SHOWRE.   .   268   ASCN-DAY A   48
ANGRY
   IN SPIRES, GLOBES, ANGRY CURLS AND COY   .   .   .   304   ST MARY MN   18
   THE ANGRY SPRING IN BUBBLES SWELL'D   .   .   .   151   THE SEARCH   29
ANGUISH
   IN WHAT DEEP ANGUISH   185   PASSION   22
ANGUISHMENTS
   AND MOVING ANGUISHMENTS THAT SET   152   THE SEARCH   39
ANIMATE
   THUS SOULES THEIR BODIES ANIMATE   218   HOLY COMM.   5
ANOINT
   AND WITH HIS HEALING BLOUD ANOINT THINE EYES   .   .   217   EASTER-DAY   14
ANSWER
   DOTH ANSWER, LIVE.   211   FAITH   44
   WAS THINE OWN ANSWER TO THE STUBBORN JEW.   .   .   268   ASCN-DAY A   60
ANSWERS
   BY EACH, HE ANSWERS ALL   161   DSTRQCTION   13
ANTEDATE
   COME, ANTEDATE   339   THE FEAST   16
ANTIENT
   MANS ANTIENT WEAR.   269   ASCSN-HYMN   2
   THY ANTIENT LOVE ON SOME MAY SHINE.   273   WHT SUNDAY   40
   THEN KEEP THE ANTIENT WAY.   276   PROFFER   43
ANTIK
   THOU HADST NO POMPOUS TRAIN, NOR ANTIK CROWD   .   .   154   ISAACS M.   21
ANTIPHONES
   IN ANTIPHONES SING TO THY NAME.   336   PSALM 65   26
ANTIQUITY
   A PEECE OF MUCH ANTIQUITY   168   VNTY SPRIT   22
ANTY-TYPES
   SO LET THE ANTY-TYPES IN ME   284   TRINITY-SN   7
APACE
   OF THEIR LORDS THUNDER THEY RETIR'D APACE.   .   .   285   PSALM 104   22
APOSTLES
   THOSE FLAMES WHICH ON THE APOSTLES RUSH'D   .   .   272   WHT SUNDAY   5
APPEALES
   AND BY APPEALES FROM HIM DECREE.   149   RELIGION   24
APPEAR
   DID ONCE APPEAR   210   FAITH   22
   EXPECT STIL WHEN THOU WILT APPEAR   228   PILGRIMAGE   11
   AND IN THE SKY THE STARS APPEAR   228   PILGRIMAGE   2
   SHALL YET TO MAN APPEAR   291   THE JEWS   5
APPEAR'D
   AND IN THOSE CRANIES LIGHT APPEAR'D   .   .   .   143   DEATH   24
APPEARE
   AND WHY THESE TEARES APPEARE   165   THE CALL   31
APPEARETH
   APPEARETH PLAIN.   178   SILENCE   20
APPEARING
   TO WATCH FOR THY APPEARING HOUR.   276   COCK-CRWNG   16

                                                              PAGE   TITLE   LINE
APPETITES
    MANS FAVORITE SINS, THOSE TAINTING APPETITES   .   .   .   320   HIDDN TRSR   19
APPOINT
    THEIR MEAT FROM THEE, WHO DOEST APPOINT THE PREY   .   .   286   PSALM 104   59
APPOINTED
    APPOINTED FOR MY SECOND RACE   169   RETREATE   4
APPOINTING
    APPOINTING ÉRROUR FOR MY PAGE   282   GARLAND   7
APPOINTMENTS
    TO HIS DIVINE APPOINTMENTS EVER CLEAVE   245   MAN   10
APPROACH
    MAY NOT APPROACH THEE (FOR AT NIGHT   168   VNTY SPRIT   31
    SHALL DARE APPROACH US. WE SHALL THERE NO MORE   .   .   146   RSRCTN +IM   65
    AT HIS APPROACH, THAT DID THE BODY KILL.   .   .   .   289   THE TIMBER   24
ARBOURS
    IN SUDDAIN FLOWRES AND ARBOURS TO MY EYES   .   .   245   MT. OLV. B   18
ARCH
    THY BURNISHT, FLAMING ARCH DID FIRST DESCRY.   .   .   306   RAIN-BOW   4
ARCHIVES
    LAID UP ALL HER ARCHIVES AND BOOKS)   303   ORNAMENT   12
ARDOUR
    WITH THE LIKE ARDOUR SHIN'D   172   MIDNIGHT   10
ARGUES
    WHO ARGUES, FOLLOWS HIS OWN HEAD.   318   THE ASS   24
ARGUMENTS
    WHAT EVER ARGUMENTS, OR SKILL   338   THE THRONE   8
ARIGHT
    WHO SO RETURNS NOT, CANNOT PRAY ARIGHT   .   .   .   194   RLS + LSNS   83
ARISE
    ARISE. THRUST IN THY SICKLE.   197   CORRUPTION   40
    AND MAKE THE DEAD, LIKE FLOWERS, ARISE   .   .   .   334   JUDGEMENT   5
    O COME, ARISE, SHINE, DO NOT STAY   334   JUDGEMENT   11
    ARISE, ARISE   217   EASTER-DAY   13
    ARISE, ARISE   217   EASTER-DAY   13
    ARISE, ARISE   349   L'ENVOY   7
    ARISE, ARISE   349   L'ENVOY   7
ARK
    THAT SECRET ARK, WHERE THE MILDE DOVE DOTH DWELL   .   .   330   JACOBS PLW   28
ARM
    WITH HIS STRONG ARM TURNS OUR CAPTIVITY.   .   .   .   331   JACOBS PLW   40
    THY ARM DID FIRST THE MOUNTAINS LAY   336   PSALM 65   21
    THY ARM DOTH SLEEP, BUT WRITE THIS DAY   .   .   .   335   JUDGEMENT   44
    TO THY BRIGHT ARM, WHICH WAS MY LIGHT   .   .   .   326   ABELS BLOD   31
    AND SUCH A KNOT, WHAT ARM DARES LOOSE   .   .   .   302   THE KNOT   13
    SINCE THOU HAST MADE THY ARM MY FOLD   .   .   .   301   PROVIDENCE   48
    THE ARM OF GOD, GLORIOUS AND TRUE   292   THE JEWS   40
    UNTO THAT PROVIDENCE, WHOSE UNSEEN ARM   .   .   .   288   THE BIRD   9
    THY ARM UNMOVEABLE FOR EVER LAID   285   PSALM 104   17
    IS NOTHING TO THY GLORIOUS ARM   299   JESUS WP B   41
    WHOSE ARM SUPPLY'D THEE, TAKE WHAT MAY SUFFICE   .   .   195   RLS + LSNS   98
ARMIES
    ARMIES THOU HAST IN HEAVEN, WHICH FIGHT   .   .   .   316   MEN OF WAR   21
ARMS
    DRY UP THEIR ARMS, WHO VEX THY SPOUSE   .   .   .   350   L'ENVOY   33
ARRAIGN
    WILL BY LOOSE DUST THAT MAN ARRAIGN   315   THE STONE   58
    WHAT THUNDERS SHALL THOSE MEN ARRAIGN   .   .   .   325   ABELS BLOD   11
ARRAY
    WHEN IN HIS NAKED, PURE ARRAY.   303   ST MARY MN   2
    PUT ON, PUT ON YOUR BEST ARRAY.   294   PALM-SUNDY   7
    AND MY SOUL IN NEW ARRAY   214   PRAISE   15
    IN PERFUMES, OR ARRAY   226   RETIREMENT   41
    BLUSHING, AND IN MEEK WEEDS ARRAY'D   303   ORNAMENT   14
ARREARS
    AND LEST I SHOULD LACK FOR ARREARS   208   REPENTANCE   43
ARRIVE
    UNSEEN BY HIM, TILL THEY ARRIVE   300   PROVIDENCE   10
ARROWS
    STILL LODGED, WHERE ALL THY UNSEEN ARROWS SHROWD   .   .   307   RAIN-BOW   34
ART
    HOW ART THOU CHANG'D. HOW LIVELY-FAIR   .   .   .   303   ST MARY MN   5
    THOU ART THE TRUE LOVES-KNOW, BY THEE   .   .   .   302   THE KNOT   5
    WHICH ONCE THY CARE AND ART DID SHOW.   .   .   .   304   ST MARY MN   16
    WHY ART THOU HUMBLED THUS, AND LOW   .   .   .   304   ST MARY MN   25
    LEARN MARYS ART OF TEARS, AND THEN   305   ST MARY MN   47
    CHEAP, MIGHTY ART. HER ART OF LOVE   305   ST MARY MN   49
    CHEAP, MIGHTY ART. HER ART OF LOVE   305   ST MARY MN   49
    HER ART. WHOSE MEMORY MUST LAST   305   ST MARY MN   51
    HER ART. WHOSE PENSIVE, WEEPING EYES   .   .   .   305   ST MARY MN   57
    YET, THOU SO FULL OF PITY ART   299   JESUS WP B   38
    BUT STILL UNKINDE. ART THIS DAY NOTHING MOV'D.   .   .   296   JESUS WP A   2
    ART SENSELESS STILL. O CAN'ST THOU SLEEP   .   .   .   296   JESUS WP A   3
    DEAR LORD. THOU ART ALL GRIEF AND LOVE   .   .   .   298   JESUS WP B   22
    BUT WHICH THOU ART MOST, NONE CAN PROVE.   .   .   .   298   JESUS WP B   23
    VAIN, SINFUL ART. WHO FIRST DID FIT   .   .   .   297   HERODIAS   1
    HIS ART ADDS STILL (THOUGH HE BE DEAD)   .   .   .   297   HERODIAS   7
    AND TO THY WORKS ART TRUE.   287   PSALM 104   84
    MY GOD, HOW GREAT, HOW VERY GREAT ART THOU.   .   .   284   PSALM 104   ?
    THESE MOUNTAINS OF COLD ICE IN ME. THOU ART   .   .   283   LOVE-SICK   12
    MY FOUL, FOUL HEART. THOU ART IMMORTALL HEAT   .   .   283   LOVE-SICK   14

ART   (CON'T)

ASSE
ASSE
ASS
ASS
ASS
ASSU
ASTO
ASTR
ASWE
ATTI
ATTI
ATTE
ATTI
ATTI
ATTI
ATTI
AUTH
AW
AWA
AWA
AWA
AWE
AWE
AY
AZ
BA
BA

	PAGE	TITLE	LINE
HERE THE WILDE ASSES SWALLOW THE COOL SPRING.	285	PSALM 104	34
N'D			
HIS BUSIE RAY THOU HAST ASSIGN'D.	276	COCK-CRWNG	4
NED			
SSIGNED THINE.	226	RETIREMENT	28
TING			
Y WHOSE ASSISTING, SWIFT COMMAND	300	PROVIDENCE	2
ES			
ND ONE WHO DRANK IT THUS, ASSURES THAT YOU	244	THE SAP	45
ISH'D			
T THY GREAT WORKS ASTONISH'D BE.	336	PSALM 65	24
Y			
HEN I WENT QUITE ASTRAY	225	RETIREMENT	8
ARLY, ASWEL AS LATE	245	MAN	6
PTS			
E TRAVELL'D IN, OUR FIRST ATTEMPTS	143	DEATH	16
D			
TTEND AND WIND THE CLUE	236	CONSTLATN	14
ET NIGHTINGALES ATTEND THE SPRING	205	IDLE VERSE	23
OLD STORMS, AND SIMPLY DOST ATTEND ON RAIN	307	RAIN-BOW	40
DED			
AS ATTENDED.	163	MT. OLVS A	24
T			
WO AND NO MORE. WHAT TWO ATTEST, IS TRUE	268	ASCN-DAY A	59
TING			
ITH ONE ATTESTING VOICE DETECT	314	THE STONE	40
CTS			
TTRACTS THEE THUS AND MAKES THEE STREAM AND FLOW	278	THE STARRE	2
BUTE			
HE GREATEST ATTRIBUTE WE SEE	335	JUDGEMENT	40
IR			
ND AUTHOR OF MY FAITH, SO SHEW ME HOME	234	MUTINIE	22
ND LET THESE LONG, SHARP JUDGEMENTS AW	351	L'ENVOY	54
AWAK, AWAK. HEARK, HOW TH' WOOD RINGS	199	NTVTY 1	7
AWAK, AWAK. HEARK, HOW TH' WOOD RINGS	199	NTVTY 1	7
E			
AWAKE, GLAD HEART. GET UP, AND SING	199	NTVTY 1	1
AWAKE. AWAKE.	199	NTVTY 1	3
AWAKE. AWAKE.	199	NTVTY 1	3
AWAKE. AWAKE.	199	NTVTY 1	10
AWAKE. AWAKE.	199	NTVTY 1	10
O GODS OWN BLOOD AWAKE THEE. HE BIDS BEWARE	202	THE CHECK	41
AWAKE, AWAKE	164	THE CALL	5
AWAKE, AWAKE	164	THE CALL	5
AND (O MY SOUL AWAKE)	184	PEACE	10
AWAKE, AND THEN REFINE THE WHOLE.	151	THE SEARCH	20
AND KEEP US STILL AWAKE	219	HOLY COMM.	37
AWAKE, AWAKE	217	EASTER-DAY	5
AWAKE, AWAKE	217	EASTER-DAY	5
AWAKE, AWAKE. AND, LIKE THE SUN, DISPERSE	217	EASTER-DAY	9
AWAKE, AWAKE. AND, LIKE THE SUN, DISPERSE	217	EASTER-DAY	9
IF PIOUS GRIEFS HEAVENS JOYS AWAKE	308	THE SEED	15
AWAKES, AND SINGS.	176	MRNG-WTCH	11
SHE WING'D AWAY	144	RSRCTN +IM	10
AND VANISH CLEANE AWAY	147	DAY OF JDG	14
WITH THAT, SOME CRYED, AWAY. STRAIGHT I	140	RGNRTN	34
THY LINES, THY LOVE. AWAY	202	THE CHECK	44
AND MIND IT NOT, PLAY NOT AWAY	201	THE CHECK	23
THEE OTHER THOUGHTS, AWAY WITH FRIENDS, AND MIRTH.	195	RLS + LSNS	104
O PURGE THEM, PURGE THEM ALL AWAY.	336	PSALM 65	8
O COME AWAY	339	THE FEAST	1
BUT GRAVELY CAST THEMSELVES AWAY.	322	CHILDEHOOD	30
ANGELS. WHICH FOUL MEN DRIVE AWAY.	322	CHILDEHOOD	38
CAST BY THE HUSBAND-MAN AWAY.	292	THE JEWS	19
DROVE THEE AWAY	213	ADMISSION	22
STARS SHUT UP SHOP, MISTS PACK AWAY	210	FAITH	19
I FLUNG AWAY, AND WITH FULL CRIE	282	GARLAND	9
NOW CAST AT NIGHT MY CROWN AWAY.	275	PROFFER	30
I'VE READ, WHO 'TWAS, DROVE YOU AWAY.	275	PROFFER	18
BOTH FAITH, AND AWE.	230	LAW + GOSP	28
GUILTS, TRESPASSES, AND ALL THIS INWARD AWE	159	MANS FALL	19
L			
DAWN WITH THE DAY, THERE ARE SET, AWFUL HOURS	192	RLS + LSNS	8
A HEART IS THAT DREAD PLACE, THAT AWFUL CELL	330	JACOBS PLW	27
AND IN HER PIERCING FLIGHT PERFUM'D THE AYER	155	ISAACS M.	51
E			
AND HEAVEN ITS AZURE DID UNFOLD	140	RGNRTN	52
VAST CIRCLING AZURE, GIDDY CLOUDS, DAYS, NIGHTS.	194	RLS + LSNS	90
WHO ON YON THRONE OF AZURE SITS	225	RETIREMENT	1
L-WEIGHT			
THAT BABEL-WEIGHT	234	MUTINIE	17
S			
BUT EVEN IN BABES DOEST TRIUMPH STILL AND WIN.	216	DRESSING	12

		PAGE	TITLE	LINE
BABES	**(CON'T)**			
	HAD NOT THE BABES HOSANNA CRYED	296	JESUS WP A	7
BACK				
	AND SOON AS LEFT, SHRINKS BACK TO ILL.	308	THE SEED	18
	AND BRING THE SAME MAN BACK. THOU WERT AT FIRST	194	RLS + LSNS	82
	HER YEARLY NURSE, CAME BACK, ENQUIR'D	151	THE SEARCH	13
	AND LOOKING BACK (AT THAT SHORT SPACE)	169	RETREATE	9
	O HOW I LONG TO TRAVELL BACK	170	RETREATE	21
	BACK TO HIS DAY	178	SILENCE	12
	OR SINCE THOSE DROPS ARE ALL SENT BACK	343	WATER-FALL	19
BACKWARD				
	BUT I BY BACKWARD STEPS WOULD MOVE	170	RETREATE	30
BAD				
	AND BAD THE LAZIE SUNNE MAKE HASTE	143	DEATH	21
	WHAT'S GOOD SCORE UP FOR JOY, THE BAD WEL SCANN'D	195	RLS + LSNS	119
	LASTS NOT A NIGHT SOMETIMES. BAD SPIRITS FEAR	195	RLS + LSNS	124
	TO CHECK BAD MOTIONS, KEEP ME STILL	318	THE ASS	25
	SO THOSE BAD DAUGHTERS, WHICH GOD SAV'D FROM FIRE	307	RAIN-BOW	31
	INLARG'D THAT LIGHT, AND TO THE BAD WAS KINDE.	330	JACOBS PLW	14
	WITH BAD, OR WITH NEGLECT, AND HEAPS NOT WRATH	328	RIGHTSNESS	51
BAGS				
	BAGS THAT WAX OLD MAY PLUNDERED BE	300	PROVIDENCE	21
BAIT				
	LET GLORY BE THEIR BAIT, WHOSE MINDES	309	THE SEED	33
BALAAMS				
	LET NOT THY STARS FOR BALAAMS HIRE	274	WHT SUNDAY	63
BALL				
	HE SEES (LIKE PYRAMIDS) SHOOT FROM THIS BALL	224	TEMPEST	43
	BEING THERE, THIS SPACIOUS BALL	163	MT. OLVS A	25
BALM				
	THIS BALM FOR SOULS THAT AKE	244	THE SAP	44
	ODORS, AND MYRRH, AND BALM IN ONE RICH FLOUD	244	MT. OLV. B	7
	BALM ON THE CLEFT EARTH, MILK ON GRASS AND FLOWERS.	306	RAIN-BOW	12
	BLOOD, IS THE WORLDS ALL-HEALING BALM.	304	ST MARY MN	40
BALSAM				
	BALSAM OF SOULES, THE BODYES BLISSE.	152	THE SEARCH	44
BANISH'D				
	NOR BOLD-FAC'D CUSTOME BANISH'D INNOCENCE.	154	ISAACS M.	20
BANK				
	ON SOME PARCH'D BANK, CROWN'D WITH A FLOWRIE WREATH.	244	MT. OLV. B	6
	DEAR STREAM. DEAR BANK, WHERE OFTEN I	343	WATER-FALL	13
	WHICH REACH BY COURSE THE BANK, AND THEN	344	WATER-FALL	35
BANKE				
	IT WAS A BANKE OF FLOWERS, WHERE I DESCRIED	141	RGNRTN	74
BANKS				
	UNTO THE BANKS, WHERE, STORMING AT THOSE BOUNDS	234	MUTINIE	8
BARE				
	WENT BLEAK AND BARE IN BODY AS IN MIND	245	MT. OLV. B	13
	BUT THE BARE ROOT	203	DSRDR + FR	28
	STOOD BARE BEFORE UNPRACTIC'D EYES	311	FAIR+YONG	18
BARK				
	NOR ANY THOUGHT OF GREENNESS, LEAF OR BARK.	289	THE TIMBER	12
BARRE				
	SO BARRE ME IN, THAT I AM STILL AT WARRE	283	LOVE-SICK	8
	THESE NARROW SKIES (NARROW TO ME) THAT BARRE	283	LOVE-SICK	7
	MUST TO THY BARRE REPAIRE.	147	DAY OF JUG	24
BARREN				
	AND TAME PROUD WAVES, IF YET THESE BARREN GROUNDS	234	MUTINIE	12
	SINCE IN A LAND NOT BARREN STIL	227	LV + DSPLN	1
	FROM THOSE RUDE, BARREN HOURS.	345	THE WREATH	4
BASE				
	IN JUDGEMENT AGAINST LEWDNESS, THAT'S BASE WIT	194	RLS + LSNS	74
BATH				
	WHO BATH NOT IN A SHALLOW FLOOD	325	ABELS BLOD	13
BAYS				
	TWIST NOT MY CYPRESSE WITH YOU BAYS	205	IDLE VERSE	19
BEAD				
	THER'S ONE SUN MORE STRUNG ON MY BEAD OF DAYS.	195	RLS + LSNS	118
BEAM				
	IN THAT DEAD AGE, ONE BEAM I'TH' DARK OUTVIES	196	RLS + LSNS	134
	OR BEAM PASSE BY	171	COME, COME	12
	NOT ONE BEAM TRIUMPHS, BUT FROM FAR	212	DAWNING	23
BEAME				
	BRIGHT, AND BLEST BEAME. WHOSE STRONG PROJECTION	210	FAITH	1
	AND WISH EACH BEAME	171	MIDNIGHT	8
	AND WATER IN ONE BEAME	172	MIDNIGHT	23
	FIRST OUT. THIS BEAME	175	JOY OF LIF	31
	HATH ONE BEAME FROM THY EYES.	198	UNPRFTBLNS	12
	ONE SULLEN BEAME, WHOSE CHARGE IS TO DISPENSE	159	MANS FALL	13
	THE BEAMES I THEN HAD SHOT	161	DSTRQCTION	7
	IS LIKE A CLOUDED STARRE, WHOSE BEAMES THOUGH SED	177	MRNG-WTCH	25
	WEAKE BEAMES, AND FIRES FLASH'D TO MY SIGHT	168	VNTY SPRIT	19
	FOR THINGS THUS CENTER'D, WITHOUT BEAMES, OR ACTION	183	THRS A TYE	5
BEAMS				
	THOSE BEAMS AGAIN	178	SILENCE	18
	THEIR BEAMS, AND LIGHT	175	JOY OF LIF	23
	RAY'D INTO THEE, LIKE BEAMS INTO A GLASSE	154	ISAACS M.	8
	(WHICH WAK'D BY HEAT, AND BEAMS, MAKES UP	203	DSRDR + FR	32
	TURNING THEIR MISTS TO BEAMS, THEIR DAMPS TO DAY	202	THE CHECK	31
	THE SUN NOW STOOPS, AND HASTS HIS BEAMS TO HIDE	195	RLS + LSNS	105

		PAGE	TITLE	LINE
BEAMS	**(CCN'T)**			
THY BEAMS HOME WITH THEE. TRIM THY LAMP, BUY OYL		195	RLS + LSNS	110
FRESH, SPICIE MORNINGS, AND ETERNAL BEAMS		188	RELAPSE	27
THE BEAMS THEY WARM THEM AT I'TH' LIGHT		207	REPENTANCE	40
THE BEAMS, AND BRIGHTNES OF THY FACE		217	DRESSING	32
NAY, THOSE BRIGHT BEAMS SHOT FROM THY EYES		242	MISERY	85
OR THOSE FAINT BEAMS IN WHICH THIS HILL IS DREST		270	ALL GONE	7
BEFORE BRIGHT STARS, AND GODS OWN BEAMS.		321	CHILDEHOOD	12
THE BEAMS OF THY BRIGHT CHAMBERS THOU DOST LAY		284	PSALM 104	9
BEAMY				
O BEAMY BOOK. O MY MID-DAY		332	AGREEMENT	13
THE HIVE OF BEAMY, LIVING LIGHTS		333	AGREEMENT	32
SO BY ONE BEAMY LINE		310	THE SEED	69
BEAR				
KEEP CLEAN, BEAR FRUIT, EARN LIFE AND WATCH		309	THE SEED	47
WHAT HALLOW'D SOLITARY GROUND DID BEAR		323	THE NIGHT	15
MIGHT LIVE, AND SEE THE OLIVE BEAR		292	THE JEWS	15
ORDAIN'D, AND MADE TO BEAR HIS MAKER.		295	PALM-SUNDY	29
THEN LIKE THE PALM, THOUGH WRONG, I'LE BEAR		295	PALM-SUNDY	38
DEARE FRIEND SIT DOWN, AND BEAR AWHILE THIS SHADE		279	PALM-TREE	1
I KNOW, THOU'LT BEAR		230	LAW + GOSP	38
TO ALL THAT SEEK THEE, BEAR AN OPEN HEART.		193	RLS + LSNS	55
SHOULD I NOT EVER BEAR IN MINDE		342	OBSEQUIES	11
BEARE				
NEVER DID TREE BEARE FRUIT LIKE THIS		152	THE SEARCH	43
WHEN HE DID STAY TO BEARE OUR ILL		163	MT. OLVS A	30
BEARS				
THY DOVE TOO BEARS US ON HER SACRED WINGS.		230	LAW + GOSP	20
WHO SITS AT HOME TOO BEARS A LOADE		214	MISERY	69
WHICH IN THY MUSICK BEARS NO PART		214	MISERY	82
WHO BEARS HIS CROSS WITH JOY		328	RIGHTSNESS	37
THY QUICKNING BREATH, WHICH GLADLY BEARS		345	THE WREATH	16
BEAST				
THOU KNEW'ST THIS HARMLESS BEAST, WHEN HE		347	THE BOOK	15
IN WHOSE THICK SHADES AND SILENCE EACH WILDE BEAST		286	PSALM 104	54
THAT NEVER LIKE A BEAST		217	DRESSING	33
IF NO A VERY DEVILL, WORSE THAN A BEAST.		194	RLS + LSNS	78
BIRDS SING, BEASTS FEED, FISH LEAP, AND TH'EARTH STANDS FAST		194	RLS + LSNS	88
TAKE THEIR LEAVE, AND DIE. BIRDS, BEASTS, EACH TREE		201	THE CHECK	27
THOSE BEASTS WERE CLEANE, THAT CHEW'D THE CUD.		165	THE CALL	29
BIRDS, BEASTS, ALL THINGS		176	MRNG-WTCH	14
FIND BEASTS MORE MERCIFULL THEN MAN		152	THE SEARCH	54
THESE TO THE BEASTS OF EVERY FIELD GIVE DRINK.		285	PSALM 104	33
TREES, FLOWERS AND HERBS. BIRDS, BEASTS AND STONES		294	PALM-SUNDY	11
JERUSALEM, WITH BLOOD OF BEASTS, AND FAT.		330	JACOBS PLW	26
THOU SHALT RESTORE TREES, BEASTS AND MEN		347	THE BOOK	26
BEAT				
HEAT MOTION GIVES. THEN WARM IT, TILL IT BEAT		283	LOVE-SICK	15
SO BEAT FOR THEE, TILL THOU IN MERCY HEAR		283	LOVE-SICK	16
BEAT THROUGH, AND STAIN		180	BURIALL	14
LIKE WAVES BEAT ON MY RESOLUTIONS		214	MISERY	76
AND BEAT ABOUT YOUR ENDLES LINE.		235	CONSTLATN	12
BEATE				
THY SIX-DAYES BUILDINGS BEATE		147	DAY OF JDG	12
WITH ECCHOES BEATEN FROM TH' ETERNALL HILLS.		168	VNTY SPRIT	18
BEATETH				
OF MANY WATERS, BEATETH AT		325	ABELS BLOD	18
BEATS				
BEATS THEM QUITE OFF, AND IN AN HOUR		203	DSRDR + FR	26
AS RAIN HERE AT OUR WINDOWS BEATS		213	ADMISSION	7
AND HEARTS, WHOSE PULSE BEATS STILL FOR LIGHT		277	COCK-CRWNG	32
BEAUTEOUS				
AS BEAUTEOUS SHAPES, WE KNOW NOT WHY		278	THE STARRE	23
DEAR, BEAUTEOUS DEATH. THE JEWEL OF THE JUST		271	ALL GONE	17
SO HAVE I KNOWN SOME BEAUTEOUS PAISAGE RISE		245	MT. OLV. B	17
COMMANDS THE BEAUTEOUS FILES		184	PEACE	8
DEAR, BEAUTEOUS SAINT. MORE WHITE THEN DAY		303	ST MARY MN	1
BEAUTY				
WHOSE BEAUTY TYED LIFE TO THY HOUSE		302	THE KNOT	3
MAKES BEAUTY LASTING, FRESH AND PURE.		305	ST MARY MN	46
BUT SINCE THY BEAUTY DOTH STILL KEEP		303	ST MARY MN	9
A BEAUTY FAR MORE BRIGHT		310	THE SEED	81
DID NOT A GREATER BEAUTY RULE MINE EYES		320	HIDDN TRSR	23
THEIR YOUTH, AND BEAUTY, COLD SHOWRES NIPT, AND WRUNG		198	UNPRFTBLNS	5
TELL YOUTH, AND BEAUTY THEY MUST ROT		189	RESOLVE	11
WHEN FIRST I SAW TRUE BEAUTY, AND THY JOYS		244	MT. OLV. B	1
BEAUTY AND HOLINESS		237	CONSTLATN	58
THAT BY THE BEAUTY OF THE SEAT		277	COCK-CRWNG	21
WHAT EVER 'TIS, WHOSE BEAUTY HERE BELOW		278	THE STARRE	1
OR SOME FRAIL BEAUTY MAKES THE BRAVEST SHEW		282	GARLAND	3
SEEKS IN THEE FOR PERFECT BEAUTY		218	EASTER HYM	8
THEY, BY THY WORD, THEIR BEAUTY HAD, AND DATE.		218	HOLY COMM.	8
HEAVEN HATH LESS BEAUTY THAN THE DUST HE SPIES		224	TEMPEST	47
BEAUTY CONSISTS IN COLOURS, AND THAT'S BEST		222	AFFLICTION	25
BECAM'ST				
BECAM'ST THY SELF, BOTH GUIDE, AND SCOUT.		202	DSRDR + FR	4
AND BECAM'ST A WOFULL STORY.		163	INCARNATN	4
BECAME				
VEILES BECAME USELES, ALTARS FEL		210	FAITH	25
BECKEN				
AND WOMB OF DARKNES BECKEN OUT		202	DSRDR + FR	2

		PAGE	TITLE	LINE
BECKEN'D				
BECKEN'D BY THEE, THOUGH HIGH AND FAR	. . . .	315	DWELLNG-PL	8
BECOME				
WHEN HE FROM WILDE IS BECOME WISE	. . . .	319	THE ASS	47
BECOME BOTH FOOD, AND SHEPHEARD TO THY SHEEP.	. .	220	HOLY COMM.	52
BECOME AN HUMBLE, HOLY NATION.	. . . . .	237	CONSTLATN	56
BECOMES				
TILL ALL BECOMES THY CLOUDLESS GLASS	. . . .	349	L'ENVOY	12
BED				
O PAINFLL CROSS, MY BED OF REST.	. . . . .	341	THE FEAST	63
QUIT THEIR FIRST BED AND MOUNT. TREES, HERBS, FLOWRES, ALL		223	TEMPEST	27
UPON HIS BED	. . . .	247	I WALKT	32
O CALM AND SACRED BED WHERE LIES	. . . .	310	THE SEED	79
THAT VOICE, WHICH TO EACH SECRET BED	. . .	335	JUDGEMENT	19
RAIN'D ON THY BED	. . . . . .	287	THE BIRD	5
ON MY FIRST BED	. . . . . .	203	DSRDR + FR	43
WITHIN OUR FIRST FAIRE BED	. . . . .	166	THE CALL	67
WHERE ALL HER SECRETS LAY A BED	. . . .	168	VNTY SPRIT	12
AND THEIR DARK BED	. . . . .	180	BURIALL	2
SO IN MY BED	. . . .	177	MRNG-WTCH	31
US INTO BED.	. . . .	175	JOY OF LIF	24
A BED, AND SLEEP	. . . . .	171	COME, COME	29
ME FROM SO DARKE, AND SAD A BED	. . .	142	DEATH	10
CREATURES A BED	. . . . .	144	RSRCTN +IM	4
SOME CALL'D IT, JACOBS BED	. . . .	140	RGNRTN	37
A SMALL BRIGHT SPARKLE WAS A BED	. . .	151	THE SEARCH	18
SUCH AS DOTH GILD THE LAZIE GLOW-WORMS BED.	. . .	157	THE LAMPE	4
BEDS				
ERECT PEEP FROM THEIR BEDS.	. . . .	187	NO DO THEY	27
THORNS IN THE BEDS	. . . . .	327	RIGHTSNESS	26
GRAVES ARE BEDS NOW FOR THE WEARY	. . .	218	EASTER HYM	5
BEE				
THE POOR BEE IN HER HIVE MUST SWEL.	. . . .	309	THE SEED	36
BEES				
WHICH KILLS THY BEES, AND EATS THY HONEY.	. .	300	PROVIDENCE	12
WHERE BEES AT NIGHT GET HOME AND HIVE, AND FLOWRS	. .	245	MAN	5
LIKE BEES IN STORMS UNTO THEIR HIVE	. . .	343	OBSEQUIES	30
BEFEL				
SUCH LOSSES AS BEFEL HIM IN THIS AIR	. . .	247	I WALKT	26
BEG				
BEG, THOU WOULDST TAKE THY TENANTS RENT.	. .	264	INTRO. 1	14
TO THEE EACH HOURE, BEG AT THY DOOR	. . .	230	LAW + GOSP	25
I BEG, MY FAITH MAY NEVER FAIL.	. . .	334	AGREEMENT	62
LORD, GOD. I BEG NOR FRIENDS, NOR WEALTH	. .	148	DAY OF JDG	37
(O NOT IN VAIN) NOW BEG THY BREATH.	. .	345	THE WREATH	15
BEG'D				
I BEG'D HERE LONG, AND GRON'D TO KNOW	. . .	167	VNTY SPRIT	3
BEGAN				
THUS UNTO ME BEGAN	. . . . .	282	GARLAND	28
BEGETTING				
BEGETTING VIRGINS WHERE THEY USE TO FLOW.	. .	291	THE TIMBER	50
BEGGER				
AND LET THY BEGGER LIE	. . . .	213	ADMISSION	10
THY BEGGER GLAD	. . . . .	215	PRAISE	52
BEGGERS				
AND SHOULD THOSE SPEECHLESS BEGGERS FAIL	. .	338	THE THRONE	12
THOU HAST MADE BEGGERS RICH.	. . . .	329	TEARS	16
BEGGING				
AND TURN'D TO SMILES THE BEGGING TEARS	. .	300	PROVIDENCE	5
THY WRETCH COMES BEGGING	. . . .	215	PRAISE	47
BEGIN				
SOME NEW IMPLOYMENT, I BEGIN	. . .	214	MISERY	63
AND SETS, WILL FEW HOURS HENCE BEGIN	. .	292	THE JEWS	29
SO THOU, WHO DIDST THE WORK BEGIN	. .	334	AGREEMENT	67
AND SERIOUS THOUGHTS BEGIN TO TAME	. .	166	THE CALL	64
AND LET ME NOW BEGIN	. . .	147	DAY OF JDG	30
AND WHERE THOU MAD'ST AN END, THERE I'LE BEGIN.	.	158	THE LAMPE	26
BEGINS EVEN AT THE BRINK.	. . . .	166	THE CALL	45
BEGS				
HE BEGS, AND CALLS. O THAT IN THESE THY DAYS	. .	202	THE CHECK	38
BEGUN				
PERFECT WHAT THOU HAST BEGUN	. . .	249	BEGGING A	3
BEHELD				
THE FIRST LIGHT THEY BEHELD WAS BRIGHT AND GAY	.	239	SHEPHEARDS	51
BEHOLD				
HAVING LOST THEE, BEHOLD TWO MEN IN WHITE.	.	268	ASCN-DAY A	58
THINE EYES BEHOLD THE EARTH, AND THE WHOLE STAGE	.	287	PSALM 104	85
WHEN I BEHOLD THEE, THOUGH MY LIGHT BE DIM	.	306	RAIN-BOW	15
BEING				
BEING AND LIFE, BUT IS DEAD THRALL.	.	319	THE ASS	56
ALL THINGS IN BEING) THEY CONSUME AND MOURN.	.	287	PSALM 104	78
WHICH ONCE HAD NEITHER BEING, FORME, NOR NAME	.	248	I WALKT	47
BEING LAID, AND DREST FOR SLEEP, CLOSE NOT THY EYES	.	195	RLS + LSNS	127
BEING THERE, THIS SPACIOUS BALL	. . .	163	MT. OLVS A	25
HIS INNE, AND CRADLE, BEING THERE	. .	151	THE SEARCH	7
BUT BEING FOR A BRIDE, PRAYER WAS SUCH	. .	154	ISAACS M.	11
THE FOOD OF MANS IMMORTAL BEING.	. .	340	THE FEAST	39
THUS FED BY THEE, WHO DOST ALL BEINGS NOURISH	. .	245	MT. OLV. B	21
BELIEV'D				
SIMPLY BELIEV'D, 'TWAS NOT MY QUILL.	. .	320	RGNRTN	8

		PAGE	TITLE	LINE
BELIEV'D (CON'T)				
SIMPLY BELIEV'D, 'TWAS NOT MY QUILL.	. . . .	332	AGREEMENT	6
BELIEVE				
WHAT THOU DIDST HOPF FOR AND PELIEVE, WE FINDE	. .	331	JACOBS PLW	51
BE SURE, NOT TO BELIEVE.	. .	183	THRS A TYE	24
AND YET, HOW FEW BELIEVE SUCH DOCTRINE SPRINGS	. .	248	I WALKT	36
I DO PELIEVE	. . . .	211	FAITH	42
BELIEVED				
THIS I BELIEVED. AND THOUGH A FRIEND	. . .	207	REPENTANCE	15
RELIEVER				
MOST BLEST BELIEVER HE.	. . . . .	323	THE NIGHT	7
BELONG				
STRONG HOLDS SHOULD BELONG TO THEF	. . .	249	BEGGING A	16
BELOVED				
AND GUARDETH HIS BELOVED.	. . .	220	PSALM 121	8
WOUND THY BELOVED, MORE THEN SWORDS.	. . .	350	L'ENVOY	42
BELOW				
ROCK HIM ASLEEP BELOW.	. . . .	247	I WALKT	35
THY STEPS TRACK HERE BELOW	. . . .	248	I WALKT	49
SHINE HERE BELOW WITHIN THY ROCK	. . .	272	WHT SUNDAY	18
THOU, WHO DOST FLOW AND FLOURISH HERE BELOW	. .	282	GARLAND	1
WHAT EVER 'TIS, WHOSE BFAUTY HERE BELOW	. .	278	THE STARRE	1
OF SOME MEAN THINGS WHICH HERE BELOW RESIDE	. .	245	MAN	2
THAT SERVE HIM HERE BELOW	. . .	238	SHEPHEARDS	14
AND WE HERE TAST SOMETIMES BELOW)	. . .	235	CONSTLATN	4
NOW HERE BELOW WHERE YET UNTAM'D	. .	226	RETIREMENT	34
DEAR, SECRET GREENNESS. NURST BELOW	. .	309	THE SEED	25
OF HALLELUJAHS HERE BELOW.	. . .	182	CHRFLNESS	24
TO HEAV'N, OR EARTH BELOW	. . . .	146	RSRCTN +IM	58
SIN TRIUMPHS STILL, AND MAN IS SUNK BELOW	. .	197	CORRUPTION	35
BEND				
FOR COALESCENT BY THAT PEND	. . . .	302	THE KNOT	9
BENDS				
WHERE LOVE WITHOUT LUST DWELLS, AND BENDS	. . .	322	CHILDEHOOD	33
BENEATH				
BENEATH HIS BLEST FEET THOU DIDST CAST	. .	304	ST MARY MN	30
BENEATH THE OKE AND JUNIPER.	. .	291	THE JEWS	7
THUS PRAISE AND PRAYER HERE BENEATH THE SUN	. .	288	THE BIRD	17
BUT THOU BENEATH THE SAD AND HEAVY LINE	. .	289	THE TIMBER	9
WHICH WOULD ONE DAY (BENEATH THE POLE)	. .	151	THE SEARCH	19
OTHERS BENEATH AN OAKES GREENE BOUGHS	. .	148	RELIGION	7
IN QUICK BLASTS SIGH BENEATH THESE SHROUDS	. .	176	THE STORM	19
AND ROUND BENEATH IT, TIME IN HOURS, DAYS, YEARS	. .	231	THE WORLD	4
NOW BENEATH, AND NOW ABOVE	. .	235	CONSTLATN	6
HE GROPS BENEATH HERE, AND WITH RFSTLESS CARE	. .	236	CONSTLATN	17
BENT				
IN POST FOR PLEASURES, BENT TO TRIE	. .	282	GARLAND	11
AND SIN) HANG AT HIM, FOR THE MORE HE'S BENT	. .	279	PALM-TREE	8
BUT LORD, I HAVE EXPELL'D THEM, AND SO BENT	. .	264	INTRO. 1	13
WHO BENT THE SPHERES, AND CIRCLED IN	. . .	167	VNTY SPRIT	5
BENUM				
SUCH THOUGHTS BENUM.	. . . .	171	COME, COME	26
AND THAT LONG FROST WHICH NOW BENUMS	. . .	291	THE JEWS	3
BEQUEATH				
THE ODOUR I BEQUEATH.	. . . .	198	UNPRFTBLNS	18
BEQUEATHED				
TO JACOBS WEL, BEQUEATHED SINCE	. . . .	151	THE SEARCH	22
BEREAVE				
TO US THAT DID BEREAVE	. . . .	220	HOLY COMM.	44
BESIEGE				
AND THEN BESIEGE THE HEART.	. . . .	183	THRS A TYE	20
BEST				
THE BEST OF US EXCELL	. . . .	166	THE CALL	53
I WOULD I HAD IN MY BEST PART	. . . .	199	NTVTY 1	19
WHICH THRIVES IN STORMS, AND SMELS BEST AFTER SHOWRES.	.	193	RLS + LSNS	60
BEAUTY CONSISTS IN COLOURS, AND THAT'S BEST	. .	222	AFFLICTION	25
THAT WITH THY GLORY DOTH BEST CHIME	. .	211	DAWNING	14
AND STILL THE LESSER BY THE BEST	. . .	278	THE STARRE	7
AND OUR BEST NOTE AND HIGHEST EASE	. . .	273	WHT SUNDAY	42
MY DAYS, WHICH ARE AT BEST BUT DULL AND HOARY	. .	271	ALL GONE	11
WHEN IT WERE BEST TO SLEEP	. . .	236	CONSTLATN	26
IN BOTH THOU WORK'ST UNTO THE BEST.	. .	227	LV + DSPLN	12
SO THRIVE I BEST, 'TWIXT JOYES, AND TEARS	. .	227	LV + DSPLN	17
POOR BIRDS SING BEST, AND PRETTIEST SHOW	. .	294	BEGGING B	19
PUT ON, PUT ON YOUR BEST ARRAY.	. .	294	PALM-SUNDY	7
AS THOU IN TEARS DOST, BEST IN DEW.	. .	303	ST MARY MN	4
AND BUILD ON IT, BECAUSE THE PEST.	. .	318	THE ASS	14
THY PILLOW WAS BUT TYPE AND SHADE AT BEST	. .	331	JACOBS PLW	53
O THY WORST STATE, MY ONELY BEST.	. . .	341	THE FEAST	66
BESTOW				
DIDST THEN BESTOW	. . . .	161	DSTROCTION	20
BESTOW'D				
HOW ILL HAVE WE OUR SELVES BESTOW'D	. .	165	THE CALL	18
BETHANI				
I WALK THE FIELDS OF BETHANI WHICH SHINE	. .	268	ASCN-DAY A	37
BETHEL				
YEA BETHEL SHALL HAVE TITHES (SAITH ISRAELS STONE)	. .	331	JACOBS PLW	33
BETHLEM				
ALL TOWARDS BETHLEM WALK	. . . .	239	SHEPHEARDS	44
AS FAR AS BETHLEM, AND HAVE SEEN	. . .	151	THE SEARCH	6

	PAGE	TITLE	LINE
BETHLEMS			
AND BETHLEMS HUMBLE COTTS ABOVE THEM STEPT	238	SHEPHEARDS	21
BETRAY'D			
WRIT IN HIS BOOK, WHO NE'R BETRAY'D MANS TRUST.	177	EVNG-WTCH	8
BETROTH			
THOU DOST UNTO THY SELF BETROTH	219	HOLY COMM.	30
BETTER			
AND MONEY BETTER MUSICK THAN THE SPHERES.	224	TEMPEST	48
YET LOOK I FOR FAR BETTER BREAD	228	PILGRIMAGE	23
OR THY GREAT MERCIES BETTER PRIZE.	214	MISERY	56
SPEAKS MORE AND BETTER FOR MY GOOD.	242	MISERY	106
OR BETTER, BUT THOU LONG AGO	273	WHT SUNDAY	27
GROWES STILL FROM BETTER UNTO WORSE	150	RELIGION	35
BE GODS ALONE, AND CHOOSE THE BETTER PART.	192	RLS + LSNS	36
SHALL (WHEN THEY RISE) SPEAK BETTER THINGS	326	ABFLS BLOD	40
ALL BETTER FAR THEN 'TWAS BEFORE.	299	JESUS WP B	37
BETTER, THE POOLS SHOULD FLOW WITH RAIN AND FLOODS	290	THE TIMBER	47
BEWARE			
O GODS OWN BLOUD AWAKE THEE. HE BIDS BEWARE	202	THE CHECK	41
BEYOND			
BEYOND A CURLED LOCK, OR PAITED FACE.	155	ISAACS M.	38
BEYOND THAT MISTIE SHROWD.	177	MRNG-WTCH	30
FAR BEYOND THE STARS	184	PEACE	2
BEYOND ALL EYES	181	BURIALL	28
ERRE IN LOOSE AIRS BEYOND HER BOUNDS.	297	HERODIAS	4
WHAT MYSTERIES DO LIE BEYOND THY DUST.	271	ALL GONE	19
THERE IS BEYOND THE STARS AN HIL OF MYRRH	243	THE SAP	11
BID			
TO MAKE MAN GOOD, AS BID HIM BE	242	MISERY	94
ALL GAMESTERS THAT WOULD BID.	282	GARLAND	12
WHAT EVER THOU DOST BID, LET FAITH MAKE GOOD	216	DRESSING	23
WHAT THOUGH SOME CLOUDS DEFIANCE BID	294	BEGGING B	15
AND PRECIPICE IT LEADS TO, BID ME FLIE	320	HIDDN TRSR	17
BID THY POOR ASS (WITH TEARS I CRAVE)	329	TEARS	11
BID ME, BY VERTUE FROM HIM, CHALENGE HERE	188	RELAPSE	23
BIDS			
O GODS OWN BLOUD AWAKE THEE. HE BIDS BEWARE	202	THE CHECK	41
BUT BIDS THE THREAD BE SPUN.	197	CORRUPTION	32
BIDST			
BUT WHAT THOU BIDST, AND SHEW'ST, AND TEACHEST ME.	321	HIDDN TRSR	32
BIL			
AND FOOLISH THOUGHTS ADDE TO MY BIL	204	DSRDR + FR	51
BILLOW			
BUT WHEN HIS WATERS BILLOW THUS	175	THE STORM	9
BIND			
CAN NEITHER LOVE, NOR SUFF'RINGS BIND.	200	NTVTY 2	13
I WIL BIND THEE.	214	PRAISE	20
CHERISH, AND BIND THY POW'RS	221	AFFLICTION	14
LORD, BIND ME UP, AND LET ME LYE	239	MISERY	1
BINDS			
THAT BINDS, AND LOOSENS DEATH	144	RSRCTN +IM	2
BIRD			
I WOULD I WERE SOME BIRD, OR STAR	199	NTVTY 1	13
THEN EITHER STAR, OR BIRD, SHOULD BE	199	NTVTY 1	17
TO FLOW, OR BIRD TO SING	187	NO DO THEY	14
INTO THIS BIRD. TO ALL THE BREED	276	COCK-CRWNG	3
AT FIRST SIGHT, IF THE BIRD BE FLOWN.	271	ALL GONE	22
BIRDS			
HE THAT HATH FOUND SOME FLEDG'D BIRDS NEST, MAY KNOW	271	ALL GONE	21
ARE GIVEN TO BIRDS, WHO, BUT THEE KNOWS	277	COCK-CRWNG	33
WHERE BIRDS LIKE WATCHFUL CLOCKS THE NOISELESS DATE	245	MAN	3
THE BIRDS NOR SOW, NOR REAP, YET SUP AND DINE	245	MAN	12
AS BIRDS ROB'D OF THEIR NATIVE WOOD	228	PILGRIMAGE	17
THY LAWS BUT NETS, WHERE SOME SMALL BIRDS	207	REPENTANCE	11
BIRDS, BEASTS, ALL THINGS	176	MRNG-WTCH	14
TAKE THEIR LEAVE, AND DIE. BIRDS, BEASTS, EACH TREE	201	THE CHECK	27
BIRDS SING, BEASTS FEED, FISH LEAP, AND TH'EARTH STANDS FAST	194	RLS + LSNS	88
POOR BIRDS SING BEST, AND PRETTIEST SHOW	294	BEGGING B	19
BUT AS THESE BIRDS OF LIGHT MAKE A LAND GLAD	288	THE BIRD	23
POOR BIRDS THIS DOCTRINE SING	301	PROVIDENCE	25
TREES, FLOWERS AND HERBS. BIRDS, BEASTS AND STONES	294	PALM-SUNDY	11
AND BIRDS AMONGST THE BRANCHES ON THEIR BRINK	285	PSALM 104	35
THE BIRDS THEIR NESTS BUILD, THOUGH THE STORK DOTH CHOOSE	286	PSALM 104	47
BIRTH			
AT THEIR LORDS FOOT-STOOL HAVE THEIR BIRTH.	304	ST MARY MN	28
HAD SOME GLIMPSE OF HIS BIRTH.	196	CORRUPTION	4
AND LET ONCE MORE BY MYSTICK BIRTH	200	NTVTY 1	29
NOR ONE DAY BLESSE HIS BIRTH.	200	NTVTY 2	16
ALAS, MY GOD. THY BIRTH NOW HERE	200	NTVTY 2	17
OTHERS, WHOSE BIRTH IS IN THE TOMB	187	NO DO THEY	26
'TWAS SO. I SAW THY BIRTH. THAT DROWSIE LAKE	160	THE SHOWRE	1
DERIVES HER BIRTH, AND THENCE DOTH BRING	150	RELIGION	31
UNTO A SECOND BIRTH	147	DAY OF JDG	20
FORGETTING THY FIRST BIRTH.	243	THE SAP	2
A STATE THY BIRTH, AND DEATH DESIGN'D.	350	L'ENVOY	20
IT IS THE BIRTH-DAY OF THY KING	199	NTVTY 1	2
BIRTHS			
SHROWD IN THEIR BIRTHS. THE CROWN OF LIFE, LIGHT, TRUTH	192	RLS + LSNS	27
NOR ARE THOSE BIRTHS WHICH WE	145	RSRCTN +IM	35
BIT			
BY WINDS, AND BIT WITH FROST	202	DSRDR + FR	7

		PAGE	TITLE	LINE

BITING
AND SINCE THESE BITING FROSTS BUT KIL . . . . 227 LV + DSPLN 4
BITTER
THE BITTER CUP . . . . 207 REPENTANCE 30
AND BITTER FIGHTS . . . . 211 FAITH 30
THAT PILL, THOUGH BITTER, IS MOST DEARE . . . 147 DAY OF JDG 35
O BITTER CURS'D DELIGHTS OF MEN. . . . . . 311 FAIR+YONG 11
BITTER AND SAD . . . . 327 RIGHTSNESS 29
BLACK
OR HAD THE BLACK ART TO DISPENCE . . . . . 169 RETREATE 17
NOT BREAK THY FENCE, AND BY A BLACK EXCESS . . . 230 LAW + GOSP 32
WHICH FOR THESE MISTS, AND BLACK DAYS WERE RESERV'D . 237 CONSTLATN 47
BUT HERE COMMISSION'D BY A BLACK SELF-WIL . . . 237 CONSTLATN 37
THOUGH SEEN AT ONCE, WERE BLACK TO THEE. . . . 272 WHT SUNDAY 2
BE STILL BLACK PARASITES . . . . 274 PROFFER 1
BLACKEST
ENTIRE STILL, WEARS OUT BLACKEST NIGHTS. . . . 333 AGREEMENT 34
BLACKNESS
AND BLACKNESS SITS . . . . 219 HOLY COMM. 18
BLADE
THE BLADE GROWS UP ALIVE AND GREEN. . . . 337 PSALM 65 38
THEM ALL, AND THIS THE EARTH, AND EVERY BLADE . . 286 PSALM 104 67
THE BLADES OF GRASSE, THY CREATURES FEEDING . . 207 REPENTANCE 33
BLAME
BLESS THEE, AND BLAME UNTHANKFUL MAN. . . . 334 AGREEMENT 72
BLAST
LIFE'S BUT A BLAST, HE KNOWS IT, WHAT. SHAL STRAW . 224 TEMPEST 49
IF A MEER BLAST SO FILL THE SAIL . . . . 276 COCK-CRWNG 17
WHEN ONE LOWD BLAST SHALL REND THE DEEPE . . . 147 DAY OF JDG 17
HERE UNDER CLOUDS, WHERE STORMES, AND TEMPESTS BLAST . 158 MANS FALL 2
EACH SNARLING BLAST SHOT THROUGH ME, AND DID SHARE . 198 UNPRFTBLNS 4
POYSON, AND BLAST . . . . 203 DSRDR + FR 24
A GIDDY BLAST EACH WAY . . . . . . 187 NO DO THEY 18
BLASTED
BLASTED MY INFANT BUDS, AND SINNE . . . . 139 RGNRTN 16
BLASTS
IN QUICK BLASTS SIGH BENEATH THOSE SHROUDS . . 176 THE STORM 19
IN BLASTS . . . . 181 BURIALL 26
THOSE BLASTS, AND KNIT MY FRAME . . . . 179 CHRCH-SVC 16
THOSE BLASTS, WHICH O'R OUR HEADS HERE STRAY . . 298 JESUS WP B 18
BLEAK
'TWAS BUT JUST NOW MY BLEAK LEAVES HOPELES HUNG . 198 UNPRFTBLNS 2
WENT BLEAK AND BARE IN BODY AS IN MIND . . . 245 MT. OLV. B 13
BLEAT
THE SHEEP BLEAT THEE A SILLY LAY . . . . 163 MT. OLVS A 14
BLEED
HE MUST BE FOUND, WHERE HE DID BLEED. . . . 152 THE SEARCH 36
O THINK ON THIS, THY SON DID BLEED. . . . . 208 REPENTANCE 60
THOU WOULDST NO LEGIONS, BUT WOULDST BLEED. . . 316 MEN OF WAR 24
WHY THOU DIDST BLEED . . . . 341 THE FEAST 77
BLEMISH
AND WITHOUT BLEMISH OR DECAY . . . . . 349 L'ENVOY 14
BLENDS
WHILE THE MANS ZEAL LAYS OUT AND BLENDS . . 332 AGREEMENT 29
THE THANKFUL EARTH UNLOCKS HER SELF, AND BLENDS . 156 ISAACS M. 59
BLESS
BLESS THEE, AND BLAME UNTHANKFUL MAN. . . . 334 AGREEMENT 72
FOR THOU DOST EVEN THE DESARTS BLESS . . . 337 PSALM 65 42
THEN BLESS THY SECRET GROWTH, NOR CATCH . . 309 THE SEED 45
SHALL BE CONSUM'D. O MY SOUL, BLESS THY LORD. . 287 PSALM 104 95
FORCE DOWN A JUST CURSE, WHEN THY HANDS WOULD BLESS. . 230 LAW + GOSP 33
THY BLESSED HANDS TO BLESS, THESE THOU DOST LEAVE. . 268 ASCN-DAY A 56
I WILL BLESSE THEE . . . . 214 PRAISE 14
YEA, BLESSE THOU HIM FOR EVER. . . . . . 287 PSALM 104 96
UP, O MY SOUL, AND BLESSE THE LORD. O GOD . . 284 PSALM 104 1
BUT NOW SINCE THOU DIDST BLESSE . . . . 161 DSTRQCTION 24
NOR ONE DAY BLESSE HIS BIRTH. . . . . 200 NTVTY 2 16
BLESSED
LORD JESU, THOU DIDST BOW THY BLESSED HEAD . . 191 THE MATCH 31
TO WRENCH, AND RACK THY BLESSED LIMBES. . . . 185 PASSION 33
O BLESSED LAMB. . . . . 186 PASSION 44
MOST BLESSED VINE. . . . . 185 PASSION 16
O HOLY, BLESSED, GLORIOUS THREE . . . . 284 TRINITY-SN 1
BLESSED, UNHAPPY CITY. DEARLY LOV'D . . . 296 JESUS WP A 1
WELL FARE THOSE BLESSED DAYS OF OLD . . . 293 BEGGING B 11
SLEEP HAPPY ASHES (BLESSED SLEEP) . . . 311 THE SEED 84
BUT THE BLOOD OF THE BLESSED LAMB. . . . 317 MEN OF WAR 52
THE GLAD WORLDS BLESSED MAID. . . . . 302 THE KNOT 2
TO SERVE THEE IN THY BLESSED HOUSE. . . . 336 PSALM 65 10
BUT BLESSED JACOB, THOUGH THY SAD DISTRESS . . 331 JACOBS PLW 41
FAIR, SOLITARY PATH. WHOSE BLESSED SHADES . . 326 RIGHTSNESS 1
WHOSE BLESSED, SWEET COMMANDS DO POUR . . . 326 ABELS BLOD 25
MOST BLESSED LAMB. AND MILDEST DOVE. . . . 208 REPENTANCE 48
THY BLESSED HANDS TO BLESS, THESE THOU DOST LEAVE. . 268 ASCN-DAY A 56
OR NAIL THOSE BLESSED LIMBS AGAIN . . . 230 LAW + GOSP 35
WAS IT BECAUSE THOSE FIRST AND BLESSED SWAINS . . 238 SHEPHEARDS 9
BLESSING
UNTIL THOU HAS A BLESSING, THEN RESIGNE . . . 192 RLS + LSNS 20
BLESSINGS
THREE BLESSINGS WAIT UPON THEM, TWO OF WHICH . . 192 RLS + LSNS 29

		PAGE	TITLE	LINE
BLESSINGS	**(CCN'T)**			
BUT GRACE, AND BLESSINGS CAME WITH THEE SO RIFE	• •	218	HOLY COMM.	3
SIT REGENT YET, AND BLESSINGS FLOW	• • •	351	L'ENVOY	57
BLEST				
IN HIS BLEST HEART	• • • •	340	THE FEAST	32
OR THE DREAD MYSTERIES CF THY BLEST BLOUD	• •	217	DRESSING	35
BLEST INFANT BUD, WHOSE BLOSSCME-LIFE	• • •	209	THE BURIAL	1
BRIGHT, AND BLEST BEAME. WHOSE STRONG PROJECTICN	•	210	FAITH	1
MY LOTT IS FALN, BLEST BE THY WILL.	• • • •	227	LV + DSPLN	3
THAT SEED THOU SOW'ST, BLEST BE THY SKIL.	• •	227	LV + DSPLN	6
BLEST BE THY DEW, AND BLEST THY FROST	• • •	227	LV + DSPLN	7
BLEST BE THY DEW, AND BLEST THY FROST	• • •	227	LV + DSPLN	7
AND HIGHEST GOOD IS BLEST.	• • • • •	278	THE STARRE	8
THAT BLEST INCLOSURE, WHERE THE ANGELS GAVE	•	267	ASCN-DAY A	16
WHEN THY BLEST BLOUD	• • • •	184	PASSION	3
BLEST BE THE GOD OF HARMONY, AND LOVE.	• •	179	CHRCH-SVC	1
HIS BLEST FACE IN A BLOUDY SWEAT.	• • •	152	THE SEARCH	40
MOST BLEST BELIEVER HE.	• • •	323	THE NIGHT	7
BENEATH HIS BLEST FEET THOU DIDST CAST	• •	304	ST MARY MN	30
HOW BLEST HAD MEN BEEN, HAD THEIR SIRE	• •	312	FAIR+YONG	27
BLEST SHOWERS THEY ARE, AND STREAMS SENT FROM ABCVE	•	291	THE TIMBER	49
THIS LAND, THOUGH WITH THY HEARTS BLEST EXTRACT FED	•	296	JESUS WP A	17
THOU MAK'ST TC GROW. THESE (BLEST BY THEE) THE EARTH	•	285	PSALM 104	42
BLEW				
BLEW THROUGH THY LODGING, WHERE THY OWN WARM WING	•	287	THE BIRD	2
EACH STIRRING WIND AND STORM BLEW THROUGH THEIR COTS	•	239	SHEPHEARDS	33
BLIND				
THY EYES, AND BLIND THEE STILL	• • • •	226	RETIREMENT	52
THE STARS TO WHICH I AM STARK BLIND	• • •	207	REPENTANCE	38
WHOSE SPITTLE ONLY COULD RESTCRE THE BLIND.	•	217	EASTER-DAY	16
WOULD SHINE ELSEWHERE, SINCE YOU WERE BLIND	•	292	THE JEWS	24
WERE DULL, AND BLIND, BUT CUSTCME STRAIGHT	•	143	DEATH	17
BLIND , DESP'RATE FITS, THAT STUDY HOW	• • •	205	IDLE VERSE	9
BLINDE				
SELF-ROASTING PHARISEE. HOW BLINDE	• • •	305	ST MARY MN	61
TC BLINDE THE EYES OF LOOKERS-BACK, AND I	•	320	HIDDN TRSR	9
WHO IN THAT LAND CF DARKNESS AND BLINDE EYES	•	323	THE NIGHT	8
AND MIX AN EYE-SALVEFCR THE BLINDE	• • •	266	VAIN WITS	6
AND MIX AN EYE-SALVE FOR THE BLINDE.	• • •	266	VAIN WITS	7
THEY NEVER SHALL SO BLINDE MY SIGHT	• •	272	WHT SUNDAY	19
THOU ART A MOON-LIKE TOIL, A BLINDE	• • •	344	QUICKNESS	5
BLINDS				
HE FILS IT. DAYES, AND HOURS ARE BLINDS.	• • •	178	EVNG-WTCH	14
BLISS				
LIES SUCH A HEAV'N OF BLISS	• • • •	243	THE SAP	28
NO BLISS HERE LENT	• • • • •	339	THE FEAST	7
WHICH MAKES THE HIGH TRANSCENDENT BLISS	• •	346	THE QUEER	15
IMMORTAL SHAPE, WHO WROUGHT THEIR BLISS	• •	349	L'ENVOY	6
FAITH SPANS UP BLISSE, WHAT SIN, AND DEATH	•	211	FAITH	37
BRIGHT SHADOWS OF TRUE REST. SCME SHOOTS OF BLISSE	•	205	SON-DAYES	1
WHOSE ECCHO IS HEAV'NS BLISSE.	• • • •	177	MRNG-WTCH	22
FCR WHEN ALL FAILES TC BRING TO BLISSE	• •	162	PURSUITE	15
BALSAM CF SOULES, THE BODYES BLISSE.	• • •	152	THE SEARCH	44
BLISSES				
EXALTED PLEASURES, CROWNING BLISSES	• • • •	348	HOLY BIBLE	30
BLISSFUL				
'TIS SUCH A BLISSFUL THING, THAT STILL	• •	345	QUICKNESS	13
'TIS SUCH A BLISSFUL THING, THAT STILL	• • •	320	RGNRTN	7
BLOCK				
'TWIXT HEAVEN, AND THEE, BLOCK IT NOT WITH DELAYS	• •	195	RLS + LSNS	116
BLOOD				
TO MANY, AND HAVE CHECKT MY BLCOD	• • •	190	THE MATCH	3
MY FIERCE, WILD BLOOD THAT STILL HEAVES, AND INCLINES	•	190	THE MATCH	4
AND BY HIS BLOOD DID US ADVANCE	• • •	218	EASTER HYM	15
BREAD FCR THY BODY, AND WINE FCR THY BLOOD.	• •	216	DRESSING	24
AFTER THY BLOOD	• • • • •	219	HOLY COMM.	26
AND BLOOD BY AN ACCURSED DEATH	• • •	220	HOLY COMM.	42
THE FULLER, WHOSE PURE BLOOD DID FLOW	• •	270	ASCSN-HYMN	35
SCME DROPS OF THY ALL-QUICKNING BLOOD	• •	264	INTRO. 1	5
WHILE THY BLOOD WASH'D ME WHITE AS HEAVEN.	• •	265	INTRO. 2	28
JUST ABELS BLOOD	• • • •	338	DEATH B	2
THAT PROUDLY SPILT AND DESPIS'D BLOOD	• •	326	ABELS BLOD	34
BUT WHAT (LIKE HIS, WHOSE BLOOD PEACE BRINGS)	•	326	ABELS BLOD	39
WITH HIS MILDE BLOOD IN VOICE AND WILL	• •	326	ABELS BLOD	43
BUT IN A DEEP, WIDE SEA OF BLOOD	• • •	325	ABELS BLOD	14
WHO SPILLS NO BLOOD, NOR SPREDS	• • •	327	RIGHTSNESS	25
MY GOD, COULD I WEEP BLCOD	• • • •	328	ANGUISH	7
JERUSALEM, WITH BLOOD OF BEASTS, AND FAT.	• •	330	JACOBS PLW	26
OF FLESH AND BLOOD, WHERE TWO WAYS MEET.	• •	318	THE ASS	2
A SWORD SHALL HIS BLOOD LIKEWISE SPILL.	• • •	316	MEN OF WAR	6
BY THY BLOOD, AND THEIR MARTYRDOM.	• • •	317	MEN OF WAR	28
WHO BY NO BLOOD (HERE) OVERCAME	• • •	317	MEN OF WAR	51
BUT THE BLOOD OF THE BLESSED LAMB.	• • •	317	MEN OF WAR	52
AS LOUD AS BLOOD. NOT THAT GOD NEEDS	• • •	314	THE STONE	24
BLOOD, IS THE WORLDS ALL-HEALING BALM.	• •	304	ST MARY MN	40
AFTER THE FALL, THE FIRST SIN WAS IN BLOOD	•	307	RAIN-BOW	21
THOUGH BLOOD AND DRUNKENNESS MAKE BUT FOUL, FOUL WEATHER.	307	RAIN-BOW	26
COULD NCT REFORM US, AND BLOOD (IN DESPIGHT)	• •	307	RAIN-BOW	29
YEA GODS OWN BLOOD WE TREAD UPCN AND SLIGHT.	• •	307	RAIN-BOW	30
AND HIS BLOOD FREEZ'D, KEEPS IN THE CENTER STILL	•	289	THE TIMBER	22

		PAGE	TITLE	LINE
BLOOD	(CON'T)			
SOME SECRET SENSE, WHICH MAKES THE DEAD BLOOD RUN		289	THE TIMBER	23
MINE WITH THY BLOOD, THY BLOOD WHICH MAKES THEE MINE		283	LOVE-SICK	21
MINE WITH THY BLOOD, THY BLOOD WHICH MAKES THEE MINE		283	LOVE-SICK	21
THE SPIRIT, WATER, AND THE BLOOD		284	TRINITY-SN	5
NEW FRESH ACCOUNTS OF BLOOD AND LUST.		297	HERODIAS	8
SHE TEMPTS TO INCEST, THOU TO BLOOD.		297	HERODIAS	20
THEY WILL DRINK BLOOD, THAT DESPISE TEARS.		296	JESUS WP A	12
OF MY LORDS BLOOD		341	THE FEAST	52
AND CEMENT US WITH THY SONS BLOOD		350	L'ENVOY	46
FOR THOU A BROTHER, AND BLOOD-THIRSTY TOO		331	JACOBS PLW	43
BLOODY				
OF BLOODY CAIN		325	ABELS BLOD	4
FROM BLOODY MEN. AND GRANT, I MAY		326	ABELS BLOD	29
BLOOM				
LET MY YOUTH, MY BLOOM OF DAYES		249	BEGGING A	7
BLOOMY				
BLOOMY AND FRESH, WHY DOST THOU WEEP.		303	ST MARY MN	10
BLOSSOM				
COME SAPLESS BLOSSOM, CREEP NOT STIL ON EARTH	←	243	THE SAP	1
BLOSSOME				
THAT ONE POOR BLOSSOME.		215	PRAISE	56
BLOSSOME-LIFE				
BLEST INFANT BUD, WHOSE BLOSSOME-LIFE		209	THE BURIAL	1
BLOT				
EITHER DISPERSE THESE MISTS, WHICH BLOT AND FILL		271	ALL GONE	37
THESE GOOD DEEDS BLOT		328	RIGHTSNESS	50
AND QUITE BLOT OUT THEIR NAMES		147	DAY OF JDG	8
BLOTS				
MOST MODERN BOOKS ARE BLOTS ON THEE		332	AGREEMENT	25
COUNT BUT THE BLOTS OF A VAIN PEN.		335	JUDGEMENT	26
BLOUD				
THY BLOUD TO ICE, AND THOU MUST STAY		142	DEATH	3
'MIDST SO MUCH BLOUD, AND CRUELTIE.		152	THE SEARCH	52
TOGETHER WITH HIS BLOUD, THY FATHERS SPIRIT		156	ISAACS M.	64
WEPT BLOUD, THAT BROKE THIS ADAMANT, AND GAVE		159	MANS FALL	25
O BROOK IT NOT. THY BLOUD IS MINE		187	NO DO THEY	35
BUT HE THAT WITH HIS BLOUD (A PRICE TOO DEERE)		188	RELAPSE	21
INJURE NOT MODEST BLOUD, WHOSE SPIRITS RISE		194	RLS + LSNS	73
THE PURLES OF YOUTHFULL BLOUD, AND BOWLES		205	IDLE VERSE	13
TOUCH'D BY THY FIRE, AND BREATH. THY BLOUD		203	DSRDR + FR	18
THEIR SPICINESS, AND BLOUD.		198	UNPRFTBLNS	6
SHALL NOT THE CRYS OF BLOUD		202	THE CHECK	40
O GODS OWN BLOUD AWAKE THEE. HE BIDS BEWARE		202	THE CHECK	41
TO SLIGHT THY PRECIOUS BLOUD, AND BREATH.		164	INCARNATN	18
BREEDS TEMPESTS IN MY BLOUD.		176	THE STORM	16
I SEE THE USE. AND KNOW MY BLOUD		175	THE STORM	1
SHINE ON THIS BLOUD		172	MIDNIGHT	22
AND IN THIS MUSICK BY THY MARTYRS BLOUD		180	CHRCH-SVC	20
WHEN THY BLEST BLOUD		184	PASSION	3
BUT THY FAIRE BRANCHES FELT AS BLOUD		185	PASSION	19
WHAT SPRINGS OF SWEAT, AND BLOUD DID DROWN THEE.		185	PASSION	24
AND WITH HIS HEALING BLOUD ANOINT THINE EYES		217	EASTER-DAY	14
THY INWARD EYES, HIS BLOUD WILL CURE THY MIND		217	EASTER-DAY	15
OR THE DREAD MYSTERIES OF THY BLEST BLOUD		217	DRESSING	35
MY SAVIOURS BLOUD.		214	ADMISSION	32
HE GAVE HIS SACRED BLOUD		243	THE SAP	26
O'R-RAN MY HEART, AND SPIRITED MY BLOUD		244	MT. OLV. B	109
O HEAR MY GOD. HEAR HIM, WHOSE BLOUD		242	MISERY	105
BUT WITH THE BLOUD OF ALL MY SOUL		242	MISERY	109
ACTION AND BLOUD NOW GET THE GAME		214	MISERY	67
LET ME NOT SPIL, BUT DRINK THY BLOUD		230	LAW + GOSP	31
AND THROUGH THY BLOUD THY GLORY SEE		229	LAW + GOSP	12
IT RAIN'D ABOUT HIM BLOUD AND TEARS, BUT HE		232	THE WORLD	29
THEN CAST HER BLOUD, AND TEARS UPON THY BOOK		237	CONSTLATN	41
HOW PALE, AND BLOUDIE		185	PASSION	34
BLOUDS				
O HOW IT BLOUDS		176	MRNG-WTCH	8
BLOUDY				
NEITHER HIS BLOUDY PASSIONS MIND		200	NTVTY 2	15
HIS BLEST FACE IN A BLOUDY SWEAT.		152	THE SEARCH	40
AND THY BLOUDY WOUNDS, AND STRIFE		215	PRAISE	27
HIS AGONY, AND BLOUDY THROWS.		208	REPENTANCE	62
BLOW				
YET DOTH IT BLOW STIL WHERE IS LIST		239	MISERY	6
THAT BUZ IN EVERY EAR, AND BLOW ON SOULS		275	PROFFER	15
FEEL IN EACH BLOW.		184	PASSION	6
O FEED THAT LIFE, WHICH MAKES HIM BLOW		308	THE SEED	19
BLOW'N				
AND WAS BLOW'N THROUGH BY EV'RY STORM AND WIND		245	MT. OLV. B	14
BLOWES				
WHICH THY SPIRIT BLOWES.		172	MIDNIGHT	32
BLOWN				
BLOWN FROM THE TREE OF LIFE TO US		332	AGREEMENT	21
BLUBBER'D				
(THOUGH OF THEMSELVES BUT A SAD BLUBBER'D STORY)		290	THE TIMBER	42
BLUSH				
BUT IN A VIRGINS NATIVE BLUSH AND FEARS		155	ISAACS M.	35
PEACH, PEACE. I BLUSH TO HEAR THEE. WHEN THOU ART		201	THE CHECK	1
AND WITH THEIR BLUSH OF LIGHT DESCRY		211	DAWNING	11

		PAGE	TITLE	LINE
BLUSHES				
TEARS ONELY AND MY BLUSHES STILL	• • • • • •	338	THE THRONE	10
BLUSHING				
BLUSHING, AND IN MEEK WEEDS ARRAY'D	• • • •	303	ORNAMENT	14
WE BREATH'D STILL FOR A BLUSHING EAST	• • •	143	DEATH	20
BOARD				
WHEN TO THY BOARD	• • • • • • •	215	PRAISE	46
BOAST				
THOUGH THEN SCME BOAST THAT FIRE EACH DAY	• •	272	WHT SUNDAY	13
SET FCRTH TO FOOL AND FOIL THEE, DO NOT BOAST.	•	320	HIDDN TRSR	5
BOASTS IT THIS DAY, THOUGH NOT IN STORY	• • •	315	DWELLNG-PL	4
BODIES				
OUR BODIES, POYSONS THAT INTREAT	• •	311	FAIR+YONG	13
IS WELL DISPOSED, FOR BODIES ONCE INFECTED	•	278	THE STARRE	14
THUS SOULES THEIR BODIES ANIMATE	• • •	218	HOLY COMM.	5
OUR SOULS, AND BODIES BOTH	• • • •	219	HOLY COMM.	31
TO DO THE LIKE. OUR BODIES BUT FORERUN	• •	191	RLS + LSNS	2
BODY				
LOOKT THY BODY.	• • • • • •	185	PASSION	35
THY BODY AS THEIR COMMON MEAT	• • •	217	DRESSING	38
THEN KNEEL MY SOUL, AND BODY. KNEEL, AND BOW.	•	217	DRESSING	41
BREAD FOR THY BODY, AND WINE FOR THY BLOOD.	•	216	DRESSING	24
POLLUTIONS ALL MY BODY WED	• • • •	209	REPENTANCE	77
BOTH SOUL, AND BODY ARE WELL DREST	• •	209	REPENTANCE	80
WENT BLEAK AND BARE IN BODY AS IN MIND	• •	245	MT. OLV. B	13
WE ARE HIS BODY GROWN	• • • •	302	THE KNOT	10
AT HIS APPROACH, THAT DID THE BODY KILL.	• •	289	THE TIMBER	24
BODYES				
SURE, THERE'S A TYE OF BODYES. AND AS THEY	• •	183	THRS A TYE	1
BALSAM OF SOULES, THE BODYES BLISSE.	• •	152	THE SEARCH	44
BOLD				
BOLD STORMS, AND SIMPLY DOST ATTEND ON RAIN	• •	307	RAIN-BOW	40
THOSE GUSTS MIGHT QUARREL AND GROW BOLD.	• •	240	MISERY	8
BOLD-FAC'D				
NOR BOLD-FAC'D CUSTOME BANISH'D INNOCENCE.	• •	154	ISAACS M.	20
BOND				
OF BOND, OR FREE	• • • •	210	FAITH	10
BONDAGE				
THY CREATURES BONDAGE AND ABUSE.	• • •	335	JUDGEMENT	32
BONDS				
THAT I TERM'D THEN MEER BONDS AND THRALL	• •	311	FAIR+YONG	8
THESE BONDS, THIS SAD CAPTIVITY	• • •	319	THE ASS	54
A WARD, AND STILL IN BONDS, ONE DAY	• •	139	RGNRTN	10
BONE				
BRING BONE TO BONE	• • • •	270	ASCSN-HYMN	39
BRING BONE TO BONE	• • • •	270	ASCSN-HYMN	39
BONES				
AND BONES REJOYCE, WHICH ONCE WERE BROKEN.	• •	319	THE ASS	65
CAN MAKE MANS DEAD AND SCATTER'D BONES	• •	298	JESUS WP B	7
BOOK				
MY SPRING AND FALL ARE IN THY BOOK.	• •	293	BEGGING B	2
THAT BY THY BOOK MUST NOT BE SOUGHT	• •	319	THE ASS	38
AND SPYED HIS CURIOUS BOOK	• •	309	THE SEED	52
I DID ONCE READ IN AN OLD BOOK	• •	312	FAIR+YONG	31
A COMET, THE SAD WORLDS ILL-BODING BOOK.	• •	307	RAIN-BOW	36
O BEAMY BOOK. O MY MID-DAY	• •	332	AGREEMENT	13
SHINE HERE BELOW WITHIN THY BOCK	• •	272	WHT SUNDAY	18
O'R THE SULLYED, SINFUL BOOK	• •	249	BEGGING A	10
ALL UNREGARDED, AND THY BOOK	• •	240	MISERY	27
THEN CAST HER BLOUD, AND TEARS UPON THY BOOK	•	237	CONSTLATN	41
WRIT IN HIS BOOK, WHO NE'R BETRAY'D MANS TRUST.	•	177	EVNG-WTCH	8
WELCOME DEAR BOOK, SOULS JOY, AND FOOD. THE FEAST	•	197	SCRIPTURES	1
READ HERE, MY FAULTS ARE THINE. THIS BOOK, AND I	•	198	SCRIPTURES	13
FAREWEL O BOOK OF GOD. FAREWELL.	• •	348	HOLY BIBLE	36
A COVERING O'RE THIS AGED BOOK	• •	347	THE BOOK	19
O BOOK. LIFES GUIDE. HOW SHALL WE PART	•	348	HOLY BIBLE	1
MY FIRST CHEAP BOOK HAD ALL I SOUGHT.	•	348	HOLY BIBLE	16
BOOKES				
WRITE IN THY BOOKES	• • • •	157	BRT. CHRCH	15
BOOKS				
AND BURN THY BOOKS.	• • • • •	187	NO DO THEY	10
MOST MODERN BOOKS ARE BLOTS ON THEE	• •	332	AGREEMENT	25
LAID UP ALL HER ARCHIVES AND BOOKS)	• •	303	ORNAMENT	12
BOOTH				
AND EV'RY BUSH IS SOMETHINGS BOOTH.	• • •	313	THE STONE	15
BORDER				
IN SUCH A DARK, EGYPTIAN BORDER	• • •	277	COCK-CRWNG	29
BORDERING				
THY EDGES, AND THY BORDERING LIGHT.	• • •	322	CHILDEHOOD	42
BORE				
YET LIV'D HE HERE SOMETIMES, AND BORE FOR THEE	•	243	THE SAP	17
WHICH BORE MY PAIN.	• • • • •	230	LAW + GOSP	36
BORN				
AND HAVING BORN THE BURTHEN ALL THE DAY	• •	275	PROFFER	29
AND THOUGH HERE BORN, YET IS ACQUAINTED	• •	212	DAWNING	35
(FOR WHICH COURSE MAN SEEMS MUCH THE FITTER BORN)	•	287	THE BIRD	4
AND ONE BORN IN A MANGER	• • • •	184	PEACE	7
BORNE				
THE LORD OF LIFE BE BORNE IN EARTH.	• • •	200	NTVTY 1	30
BORROW				
YOUR SHADES AND FRESHNESS COMES TO BORROW.	• •	294	PALM-SUNDY	6

	PAGE	TITLE	LINE
BORROWED			
WHOSE LIGHT, THOUGH FETCHT AND BORROWED FROM FAR	288	THE BIRD	21
BOSOME			
WEAR IN MY BOSOME A FULL SUN, SUCH STORE	198	UNPRFTBLNS	11
HER WOMBE, HER BOSOME, AND HER HEAD	168	VNTY SPRIT	11
FROM HER FAINT BOSOME BREATH'D THEE, THE DISEASE	160	THE SHOWRE	2
SHALT IN THY MOTHERS BOSOME SLEEPE	143	DEATH	28
ALL HER PARCHT BOSOME TO NILE'S SHORE	151	THE SEARCH	12
AND FILL'D HIS BOSOME	215	PRAISE	53
WHEN NATURE ON HER BOSOME SAW	222	TEMPEST	5
BOSOMES			
DID IN THEIR BOSOMES PLAY	239	SHEPHEARDS	38
BOTH			
BOTH LIVE AND DIE THY CHILD.	235	MUTINIE	39
BOTH FAITH, AND AWE.	230	LAW + GOSP	28
I WOULD BOTH THINK, AND JUDGE I DID NOT LOVE THEE.	230	LAW + GOSP	40
IN IT MY NAME, AND HONOUR BOTH DO DWELL	226	RETIREMENT	38
IN BOTH THOU WORK'ST UNTO THE BEST.	227	LV + DSPLN	12
TILL THOU BOTH MEND AND MAKE ME THINE.	242	MISERY	113
OUR SOULS, AND BODIES BOTH	219	HOLY COMM.	31
THEE OF THEM BOTH, THESE SEALS THE MEANS	220	HOLY COMM.	45
THAT SHULD BOTH CLEANSE	220	HOLY COMM.	46
BECOME BOTH FOOD, AND SHEPHEARD TO THY SHEEP.	220	HOLY COMM.	52
(UNSEEN) BOTH HEAVEN, AND EARTH.	220	PSALM 121	4
AND PAINTED TRIMMING TAKES DOWN BOTH HIS EYES	224	TEMPEST	46
A FLOUD THAT DROWNS BOTH TEARS, AND GRONES	214	ADMISSION	31
WHERE STARS, AND CLOUDS, BOTH LIGHT, AND SHADE	210	FAITH	15
BOTH SOUL, AND BODY ARE WELL DREST	209	REPENTANCE	80
BOTH GROWTH, AND POWER, CHECKING THE HEALTH	206	REPENTANCE	6
BOTH YOU AND IT, HAD EQUALL LIBERTY	279	PALM-TREE	4
TO PLY BOTH THINE EYES AND BREATH.	281	JOY	22
BOTH LIGHT FROM THEE, AND VIRTUE HAD	265	INTRO. 2	10
THE QUICK, AND DEAD, BOTH SMALL AND GREAT	147	DAY OF JDG	23
AND BOTH HER TASTE, AND COLOUR STAINES	150	RELIGION	36
BUT PRAY AGAINST THEM BOTH	148	DAY OF JDG	38
BOTH STARS AND ELEMENTS CONFOUND	147	DAY OF JDG	7
BOTH LIFE AND YOUTH	145	RSRCTN +IM	30
(BOTH WING'D, AND FREE)	146	RSRCTN +IM	62
IS STILL CUT WITH THY FLAME, AND SO BOTH FAILE.	158	THE LAMPE	24
BUT WHENSCE'RE I'M OUT, BOTH SHALBE IN	158	THE LAMPE	25
COTSWOLD, AND COOPERS BOTH HAVE MET	162	MT. OLVS A	9
THAT HEARD'ST BOTH REED	163	MT. OLVS A	15
SO THAT BOTH STONES, AND DUST, AND ALL OF ME	180	CHRCH-SVC	17
BOTH WASH, AND WING MY SOUL.	176	THE STORM	24
MY LAMP, AND LIFE, BOTH SHALL IN THEE ABIDE.	177	MRNG-WTCH	33
BOTH LIQUORS BURNE, AND STREAME.	172	MIDNIGHT	26
BECAM'ST THY SELF, BOTH GUIDE, AND SCOUT.	202	DSRDR + FR	4
BOTH COST THEE DEER	191	THE MATCH	20
IS BOTH HIS OWN JOY, AND HIS MAKERS TOO.	193	RLS + LSNS	51
WHILE ACTIVE WINDS AND STREAMS BOTH RUN AND SPEAK	288	THE BIRD	15
BOTH MORNINGS MAKES, AND EVENINGS THERE.	288	THE BIRD	22
INNUMERABLE, CREEPING THINGS BOTH SMALL	286	PSALM 104	70
BUT FLOWERS DO BOTH REFRESH AND GRACE	321	CHILDEHOOD	14
WHOSE EYES ARE BOTH PUT OUT	327	RIGHTSNESS	22
QUITE THROUGH THEM BOTH, STILL INFINITE	333	AGREEMENT	51
BOTH SUN AND STARS WOULD HIDE THEIR HEADS.	309	THE SEED	31
WATER (THOUGH BOTH HEAVENS WINDOWS AND THE DEEP	307	RAIN-BOW	27
(THOUGH BOTH ALL-SEEING AND ALL RIGHT)	314	THE STONE	33
TEACH BOTH MINE EYES AND FEET TO MOVE	318	THE ASS	15
BOTTLE			
O FILL HIS BOTTLE. THY CHILDE WEEPS.	308	THE SEED	16
TO FILL MY BOTTLE, THEN I DIE WITH THIRST.	290	THE TIMBER	48
BOTTLES			
CHAMBERS OF RAIN, WHERE HEAV'NS LARGE BOTTLES LIE	285	PSALM 104	38
BOUGHS			
CEDARS IN LEBANON, IN WHOSE THICK BOUGHS	286	PSALM 104	46
I'LE CUT ME BOUGHS OFF MANY A TREE	295	PALM-SUNDY	35
OTHERS BENEATH AN OAKES GREENE BOUGHS	148	RELIGION	7
BOUGHT			
AND IT IS BOUGHT.	160	DSTRQCTION	4
ELECTED, BOUGHT AND SEAL'D FOR FREE	284	TRINITY-SN	8
SERIOUS THEY SEEM'D AND BOUGHT UP ALL	302	ORNAMENT	5
AND DEARLY BOUGHT (WHEN THOU DIDST SEE	304	ST MARY MN	35
BOUND			
FOR THOU TO THEM A BOUND HAST SET, A BOUND	285	PSALM 104	25
FOR THOU TO THEM A BOUND HAST SET, A BOUND	285	PSALM 104	25
O'RE MY HARD HEART, THAT'S BOUND UP, AND ASLEEP	160	THE SHOWRE	15
THAT (FOR REPOSE, AND DARKNES BOUND) HE MIGHT	201	THE CHECK	18
BUT A SHALLOW, BOUNDED FLOUD	175	THE STORM	3
BOUNDLESS			
AND BOUNDLESS EMPYREAN THEMES	346	THE QUEER	6
BOUNDS			
AND AS THY CARE BOUNDS THESE, SO THY RICH LOVE	285	PSALM 104	29
ERRE IN LOOSE AIRS BEYOND HER BOUNDS.	297	HERODIAS	4
WITHIN THOSE BOUNDS SET BY THY LOVE.	318	THE ASS	16
UNTO THE BANKS, WHERE, STORMING AT THOSE BOUNDS	234	MUTINIE	8
BOUNTEOUSNESS			
THEN DRINK AND PRAISE THY BOUNTEOUSNESS.	301	PROVIDENCE	30
THY BOUNTEOUS OPEN HAND HELPS THEM AT NEED	286	PSALM 104	75
BOW			
OR BOW THE HEAVENS. LORD BOW THEM AND DESCEND	283	LOVE-SICK	10

	PAGE	TITLE	LINE
BOW (CON'T)			
OR BOW THE HEAVENS. LORD BOW THEM AND DESCEND	283	LOVE-SICK	10
AS EARTH, THY LOVELY HEAD DOST BOW.	304	ST MARY MN	26
THEN PEACEFUL, SIGNAL BOW, BUT IN A CLOUD	307	RAIN-BOW	33
I BOW MY KNEE	328	ANGUISH	2
I BOW MY TROUBLED SOUL, AND GREET	328	ANGUISH	3
(UNKNOWN TO US) THE HEAVENS WILT BOW	212	DAWNING	26
THEN KNEEL MY SOUL, AND BODY. KNEEL, AND BOW.	217	DRESSING	41
WHO GAVE THE CLOUDS SO BRAVE A BOW	167	VNTY SPRIT	4
LORD JESU. THOU DIDST BOW THY BLESSED HEAD	191	THE MATCH	31
I SEE, THY CURTAINS ARE CLOSE-DRAWN, THY BOW	197	CORRUPTION	33
BOW'D			
SO PREST AND BOW'D, BEFORE SIN DID DEGRADE	279	PALM-TREE	3
CROWN'D THEE WITH THORNS, AND BOW'D THE KNEE	317	MEN OF WAR	31
BOWELS			
AND ALL MY BOWELS TURN'D	213	ADMISSION	2
BOWELS OF LOVE. AT WHAT LOW RATE	213	ADMISSION	13
BOWER			
THE PULLEYS UNTO HEADLONG MAN, TIMES BOWER	2	SON-DAYES	9
AS LEAFS IN BOWERS	281	JOY	23
WHICH SHADES AND BOWERS DOTH RENT-FREE BRING.	338	DEATH B	10
A SHELTER ALL THE WAY, AND BOWERS TO REST.	326	RIGHTSNESS	4
WHICH NOW ARE DEAD, LODG'D IN THY LIVING BOWERS.	289	THE TIMBER	4
BOWLES			
THE PURLES OF YOUTHFULL BLOUD, AND BOWLES	205	IDLE VERSE	13
BOWRE			
MIGHT HAVE SOME OTHER BOWRE.	247	I WALKT	14
BUT WINTER NOW HAD RUFFLED ALL THE BOWRE	246	I WALKT	5
I SOUGHT CHOICE BOWRES, HAUNTED THE SPRING	282	GARLAND	21
BUT NOW THE DEW AND SUN HAVE WARM'D MY BOWRES	274	PROFFER	5
UNLOCK THY BOWRES.	211	DAWNING	10
WOULD MAKE US BOWRES.	222	AFFLICTION	24
BOWRS			
RISE WITH THE SUN, AND SET IN THE SAME BOWRS.	245	MAN	7
BOWS			
AND TO THY SOFT ARTS STRONGLY BOWS.	297	HERODIAS	16
BOX			
SPLIT, AND THE BOX QUITE BROKE AND MARR'D.	304	ST MARY MN	22
BOXE			
THE WORLD'S THY BOXE. HOW THEN (THERE TOST)	181	BURIALL	31
BOXES			
AND FILLS THE BOXES OF HIS POOR.	209	REPENTANCE	82
BOYL			
THEY MURMUR'D SORE, BUT I, WHO FELT THEM BOYL	234	MUTINIE	9
BOYLING			
AND BOYLING STREMES THAT RAVE	175	THE STORM	6
BRACELET			
AS MY SEAL, AND BRACELET HERE	214	PRAISE	19
BRAG			
ONELY, LET NOT OUR HATERS BRAG	350	L'ENVOY	29
BRAGS			
WITHOUT HIS BRAGS AND CONQUESTS LIES	318	THE ASS	27
BRAINES			
IS THE BRAINES FIT	162	MT. OLVS A	7
BRANCH			
BUT ONE GREEN BRANCH AND A WHITE ROBE.	295	PALM-SUNDY	45
BRANCHES			
FRESH GROVES GROW UP, AND THEIR GREEN BRANCHES SHOOT	289	THE TIMBER	6
HER PROPER BRANCHES. WHICH NOW LIE	292	THE JEWS	16
COME, DROP YOUR BRANCHES, STROW THE WAY	294	PALM-SUNDY	1
AND BIRDS AMONGST THE BRANCHES ON THEIR BRINK	285	PSALM 104	35
FOR WHOSE DRY DUST GREEN BRANCHES BUD	310	THE SEED	83
BUT THY FAIRE BRANCHES FELT AS BLOUD	185	PASSION	19
OF STATELY HEIGHT, WHOSE BRANCHES MET	140	RGNRTN	44
WHERE ARE THY PALMES, THY BRANCHES, AND THY VERSE.	217	EASTER-DAY	11
BRASSE			
TO BRASSE, AND IRON, WHEN MY STOCK LAY DEAD	213	ADMISSION	3
BRAVE			
WHO THINK THEM BRAVE	232	THE WORLD	43
TELL US THE WORLD IS BRAVE	183	THRS A TYE	14
TO BRAVE THE NIGHT	178	SILENCE	8
BRAVE WORMES, AND EARTH. THAT THUS COULD HAVE	164	INCARNATN	9
WHO GAVE THE CLOUDS SO BRAVE A BOW	167	VNTY SPRIT	4
PEACE, PEACE. I KNOW 'TWAS BRAVE	173	CONTENT	1
SET WITH GREEN HERBS, GLAD HOPES AND BRAVE.	310	THE SEED	72
A DAY SO FRESH, SO BRIGHT, SO BRAVE	334	JUDGEMENT	3
TO MAKE ME BRAVE	342	OBSEQUIES	26
RISE TO A LONGER COURSE MORE BRIGHT AND BRAVE.	343	WATER-FALL	12
FOR SHE IS BRAVEST, YOU CONFESS.	303	ORNAMENT	20
OR SOME FRAIL BEAUTY MAKES THE BRAVEST SHEW	282	GARLAND	3
BREACH			
FREQUENT RELAPSE AND WILFUL BREACH	265	INTRO. 2	24
BREACHES			
DOEST WATER THE PARCH'D HILLS, WHOSE BREACHES CLOSE	285	PSALM 104	39
BREAD			
BRINGS FORTH, WITH WINE, OYL, BREAD. ALL WHICH INFUSE	285	PSALM 104	43
THE SOWER DOTH HIS BREAD PROVIDE.	336	PSALM 65	32
YET LOOK I FOR FAR BETTER BREAD.	228	PILGRIMAGE	23
BREAD FOR THY BODY, AND WINE FOR THY BLOOD.	216	DRESSING	24
IS GROWN THICK DARKNESS, AND THY BREAD, A STONE.	224	TEMPEST	55

		PAGE	TITLE	LINE
BREAD	**(CCN'T)**			
HE BRINGS HIM WATER WITH HIS BREAD.		149	RELIGION	12
THE BREAD WE CAST RETURNS IN FRAUGHTS ONE DAY.		193	RLS + LSNS	66
CCME THEN TRUE BREAD		339	THE FEAST	13
O DRINK AND BREAD		340	THE FEAST	37
BREAK				
OF CLAY, AND FRAILTY BREAK, AND BUD		203	DSRDR + FR	17
BREAK, AND THE SHADOWS FLEE, TOUCH WITH ONE COAL		216	DRESSING	3
WATCHING THE BREAK OF THY GREAT DAY.		212	DAWNING	48
BREAK AT MIDNIGHT.		211	DAWNING	6
NCT BREAK THY FENCE, AND BY A BLACK EXCESS		230	LAW + GOSP	32
I BREAK THE FENCE MY CWN HANDS MADE		240	MISERY	21
BLT A STRCNG WIND MUST BREAK THY LOFTY ROCKS.		330	JACOBS PLW	10
SO HILLS AND VALLEYS INTC SINGING BREAK		288	THE BIRD	13
HIS PROMISE STILL, BUT WE BREAK CURS AND SLEEP.		307	RAIN-BOW	20
O THEN, JUST THEN. BREAK CR UNTYE		319	THE ASS	53
AND INTC LOUD DISCOVERIES BREAK		313	THE STONE	23
AND SHOCTS OF GLORY, MY SCUL BREAKES, AND BUDS.		176	MRNG-WTCH	2
BREAKING				
BREAKING THE LINK		* 202	DSRDR + FR	9
BREAKS				
SC POISCN'D, BREAKS FCRTH IN SCME CLIME		150	RELIGION	41
FAITH INTO LIFE BREAKS, AND DEATH DIES.		310	THE SEED	66
WHO BREAKS HIS GLASS TO TAKE MCRE LIGHT		309	THE SEED	43
TILL THE CAY-SPRING BREAKS FORTH AGAIN FROM HIGH.		288	THE BIRD	32
AND NC NEW BUSINESS BREAKS THEIR PEACE.		245	MAN	11
BREAKS, NIGHT ADJCURNS		210	FAITH	18
NCT A THOUGHT, THAT BREAKS MY REST		214	PRAISE	7
WHICH BREAKS FROM THEE		248	I WALKT	53
TILL THE REFINERS FIRE PREAKS FORTH.		270	ASCSN-HYMN	30
BREAKS AS THE CAY DOTH FRCM THE EAST		340	THE FEAST	21
BREAST				
NCT A NCOK IN ALL MY BREAST		214	PRAISE	5
MAKE NOT THY BREAST A LABRYINTH, CR TRAP.		193	RLS + LSNS	56
THIS CEW FELL ON MY BREAST.		176	MRNG-WTCH	7
BREATH				
IS THY FIRST BREATH, AND MANS ETERNALL PRIME.		178	EVNG-WTCH	16
THIS RESTLES BREATH		171	COME, COME	17
TC SLIGHT THY PRECIOUS BLCUD, AND BREATH.		164	INCARNATN	18
WHEN THY LEAST BREATH SUSTAINES MY WING.		182	CHRFLNESS	3
TCUCH'D BY THY FIRE, AND BREATH. THY BLOUD		203	DSRDR + FR	18
BREATH ALL PERFUMES, AND SPICE.		198	UNPRFTBLNS	9
OFT HAVE I SEEN, WHEN THAT RENEWING BREATH		144	RSRCTN +IM	1
LORD, THEN SAID I, ON ME CNE BREATH		141	RGNRTN	90
HEAVEN WITH A LAZIE BREATH, BLT FRUITLES THIS		160	THE SHOWRE	8
AND SLCH IS TRUE REPENTANCE, EV'RY BREATH		158	THE LAMPE	21
WITH THY GRONES MY DAILY BREATH		215	PRAISE	29
LAPT IN THE SWEETS OF THY YOUNG BREATH		209	THE BURIAL	10
LEST WE SHOULD RUN FOR'T CUT CF BREATH		211	FAITH	39
NCTHIN'S MORE VILE THAN IS MY BREATH		208	REPENTANCE	74
WAS'T NCT ENOUGH TO LCSE THY BREATH		220	HOLY COMM.	41
ARE BLT MEER LEAVES TURN'D BY THY BREATH.		219	HOLY COMM.	16
WHEN THE VEYL BROKE WITH THY LAST BREATH		219	HOLY COMM.	22
AMCNGST THE QUICK, SELLING THEIR SOULS AND BREATH		275	PROFFER	39
FCR, THCUGH WE HOURLY BREATH DECAYS		273	WHT SUNDAY	41
MCRE EYES THEN STARS, WHOSE BREATH COULD IT ASPIRE		281	JOY	12
TC PLY BOTH THINE EYES AND BREATH.		281	JOY	22
WITH CTHER TREES. BUT NCW SHUT FROM THE BREATH		279	PALM-TREE	5
SHALL NCT THE BREATH OF GOD PREVAIL.		276	COCK-CRWNG	18
FAND BY A GENTLE GALE CCNVEY AND BREATH		244	MT. OLV. B	5
ME COWN TO BREATH, AND CASTING IN MY HEART		233	MUTINIE	2
ELSE ALL AT REST THOU LYEST, AND THE FIERCE BREATH		289	THE TIMBER	17
WHEN THCU WITH-DRAW'ST THEIR BREATH, THEIR VIGCUR SLEEPS		287	PSALM 104	79
THEREFORE AS LONG AS THCU WILT GIVE ME BREATH		287	PSALM 104	89
SINCE THE SAME SACRED BREATH WHICH THUS		298	JESUS WP B	5
BY HIS BREATH WHOM MY DEAD HEART HEAVES.		332	AGREEMENT	22
EVEN LIFES OWN BREATH.		342	OBSEQUIES	8
(C NOT IN VAIN) NCW BEG THY BREATH.		345	THE WREATH	15
THY QUICKNING BREATH, WHICH GLADLY BEARS		345	THE WREATH	16
BREATH'D				
FROM HER FAINT BOSOME BREATH'C THEE, THE DISEASE		160	THE SHOWRE	2
WE BREATH'D STILL FOR A BLUSHING EAST		143	DEATH	20
BREATHING				
THAT CEW THEY LENT, A BREATHING SACRIFICE.		156	ISAACS M.	62
BREATHING PERFUMES, DOTH SPICE THE DAY		199	NTVTY 1	6
BREATHS				
BUT WHAT EARTH BREATHS AGAINST THY LIGHT.		312	FAIR+YONG	26
BRED				
SKILFLL INCHANTRESS AND TRUE BRED.		297	HERODIAS	17
BRED IN THY GROWTH BETWIXT HIGH WINDS AND THEE		289	THE TIMBER	14
BREED				
STIFF-NECKED JEWS. YOUR FATHERS BREED		296	JESUS WP A	5
DID BREED THIS STRIFE		299	JESUS WP B	29
A GRIEF, WHOSE SILENT DEW SHALL BREED		299	JESUS WP B	48
INTO THIS BIRD. TO ALL THE BRFED		276	COCK-CRWNG	3
O WHAT AM I, THAT I SHOULD BREED		208	REPENTANCE	69
WHICH NATURE BREEDS, AND SOME FINE CLAY INVITES		320	HIDDN TRSR	20
WHICH NE'R BREEDS MCRE.		171	COME, COME	24
BREEDS TEMPESTS IN MY BLOUD.		176	THE STORM	16
WHICH SADNESS BREEDS IN THE MCST VAIN		345	THE WREATH	14

	PAGE	TITLE	LINE

BREST

	PAGE	TITLE	LINE
THE SMOKE, AND EXHALATICNS OF THE BREST.	160	THE SHOWRE	12
OF GRIEF AND PITY IN THY BREST	299	JESUS WP B	30
DEFECTS, AND DARKNES IN MY BREST	209	REPENTANCE	76
TUNING HIS BREST TO RISE, OR FALL.	222	AFFLICTION	37
OPEN MY DESOLATE ROOMS, MY GLOOMIE BREST	216	DRESSING	5
WHOSE CLOUDY BREST COLD DAMPS INVADE	217	EASTER-DAY	2
AS PLEASANT, AS IF WITH THE BREST.	218	EASTER HYM	12
ILL THY BREST WITH HOME. THINK CN THY DREAM.	276	PROFFER	45
IT GLOWS AND GLITTERS IN MY CLOUDY BREST	270	ALL GONE	5
SO SHOCK MY BREST, THAT (SICK AND SORE DISMAI'D)	233	MUTINIE	5
HER BRESTS GROWN CRY.	222	TEMPEST	8
AND FILL'D HER BRESTS.	223	TEMPEST	16

BRIBE

WITHOUT THAT BRIBE WHICH USURERS IMPOSE.	328	RIGHTSNESS	42
MAN I CAN BRIBE, AND WOMAN WILL	313	THE STONE	10

BRICK

AND THIRSTIE BRICK MUST BE (SAID I)	234	MUTINIE	13

BRICAL

WHICH WEARS HEAVEN, LIKE A BRIDAL RING	346	THE QUEER	3

BRIDE

BUT FCR HIS BRIDE.	233	THE WORLD	60
RETINUE, ALL WAS HERE SMOOTH AS THY BRIDE	154	ISAACS M.	23
THESE FETCH'D THEE HOME THY BRIDE, AND ALL THE WAY	155	ISAACS M.	27
LIKE SOME SPRUCE BRIDE	145	RSRCTN +IM	46
BUT BEING FOR A BRIDE, PRAYER WAS SUCH	154	ISAACS M.	11
TO BE THE REFUGE CF HIS BRIDE.	152	THE SEARCH	64
THIS RING THE BRIDE-GROOME DIC FOR NONE PROVIDE	233	THE WORLD	59

BRICEGROOME'S

THE BRICEGROOME'S COMMING. FIL THE SKY.	211	DAWNING	2

BRIEFLY

BRIEFLY, DOE AS THOU WOLLD'ST BE DONE UNTO,	196	RLS + LSNS	139

BRIGH

HOW BRIGH WERT THOU, WHEN SHE'S ADMIRING EYE	306	RAIN-BOW	3

BRIGHT

BRIGHT PLEDGE OF PEACE AND SUN-SHINE. THE SURE TYE	306	RAIN-BOW	13
BRIGHT QUEEN OF HEAVEN. GODS VIRGIN SPOUSE.	302	THE KNOT	1
PLAIN, HARMLESS, FAITHFUL, FAIR AND BRIGHT	312	FAIR+YONG	25
O BRIGHT AND HAPPY KALENDAR.	310	THE SEED	61
FROM THY BRIGHT LAMP DID SHINE	310	THE SEED	70
A BEAUTY FAR MORE BRIGHT	310	THE SEED	81
IF THOSE BRIGHT JCYS HE SINGLY SHEDS	309	THE SEED	29
WHAT NEEDS A CONSCIENCE CALM AND BRIGHT	309	THE SEED	41
MY SOULS BRIGHT FOOD, THY ABSENCE KILLS.	308	THE SEED	6
FOR IN THIS BRIGHT, INSTRUCTING VERSE	316	MEN OF WAR	17
AND GODS BRIGHT MINDE EXPREST IN PRINT.	332	AGREEMENT	24
AND WITH HIS BRIGHT AND BUSIE WING	332	AGREEMENT	8
BEFORE BRIGHT STARS, AND GODS OWN BEAMS.	321	CHILDEHOOD	12
TO THY BRIGHT ARM, WHICH WAS MY LIGHT	326	ABELS BLOD	31
A DAY SC FRESH, SC BRIGHT, SO BRAVE	334	JUDGEMENT	3
DID SOMETIMES RULE. A GRIEF SC BRIGHT	299	JESUS WP B	50
MY DEAR, BRIGHT LORD. MY MORNING-STAR.	296	JESUS WP A	13
THY BRIGHT SOLEMNITIES DID SHEW	295	PALM-SUNDY	32
IN A BRIGHT RING.	295	PALM-SUNDY	23
MANY BRIGHT MCRNINGS, MUCH DEW, MANY SHOWERS	289	THE TIMBER	2
THY QUIKNING FREINDSHIP, MANS BRIGHT WEALTH.	294	BEGGING B	22
WHEN THE BRIGHT DOVE	291	THE JEWS	8
FORERUNNING THE BRIGHT MORNING-STAR	292	THE JEWS	22
THE BEAMS OF THY BRIGHT CHAMBERS THOU DOST LAY	284	PSALM 104	9
AH. WHAT BRIGHT DAYS WERE THOSE.	197	CORRUPTION	20
BY THOSE BRIGHT FIRES WHICH THEE INFLAM'D.	190	THE MATCH	6
BUD IN THE BRIGHT EAST, AND DISCLOSE	151	THE SEARCH	2
A SMALL BRIGHT SPARKLE WAS A BEC	151	THE SEARCH	18
ALL PURE, AND BRIGHT	145	RSRCTN +IM	48
OF DIVERS STONES, SOME BRIGHT, AND ROUND	141	RGNRTN	64
CCULD SEE A GLIMPSE OF HIS BRIGHT FACE.	169	RETREATE	10
BRIGHT SHOOTES OF EVERLASTINGNESSE.	170	RETREATE	20
AND BRIGHT STIRS ARE THERE.	172	MIDNIGHT	13
O WHAT BRIGHT QUICKNES	172	MIDNIGHT	27
BRIGHT, AND BLEST BEAME. WHOSE STRONG PROJECTICN	210	FAITH	1
THE HEAVENS THEMSELVES, THOUGH FAIR AND BRIGHT	208	REPENTANCE	65
BRIGHT SHADOWS OF TRUE REST. SCME SHOOTS OF BLISSE	205	SON-DAYES	1
UP TO THOSE BRIGHT, AND GLADSCME HILS	220	PSALM 121	1
WITH THY BRIGHT ESSENCE)	215	PRAISE	41
MCRE BRIGHT THAN HE.	233	THE WORLD	56
ALL CALM, AND IT WAS BRIGHT	231	THE WORLD	3
NAY, THOSE BRIGHT BEAMS SHOT FROM THY EYES	242	MISERY	85
THE FIRST LIGHT THEY BEHELD WAS BRIGHT AND GAY	239	SHEPHEARDS	51
ALL NAKED, INNOCENT AND BRIGHT	269	ASCSN-HYMN	23
LIKE HEAV'N, ALL BRIGHT.	270	ASCSN-HYMN	34
THEIR VERY MEMORY IS FAIR AND BRIGHT	270	ALL GONE	3
A CALM, BRIGHT DAY.	276	PROFFER	46
AND LONGING FOR THY BRIGHT AND VITALL FIRE	278	THE STARRE	18
O THY BRIGHT LOOKS. THY GLANCE CF LOVE	281	THE FAVOUR	1
THY GLORIOUS, BRIGHT ASCENSION (THOUGH REMOV'D)	267	ASCN-DAY A	5
SUCH WAS THE BRIGHT WORLD, CN THE FIRST SEVENTH DAY	268	ASCN-DAY A	39
WHOSE EASTERN TRAFFIQUE DEALS IN BRIGHT	346	THE QUEER	5
NO CHANCE, OR FIT. BUT EVER BRIGHT	345	QUICKNESS	11
RISE TO A LONGER COURSE MORE BRIGHT AND BRAVE.	343	WATER-FALL	12
THY OWN BRIGHT SELF OVER EACH HEAD	349	L'ENVOY	10

		PAGE	TITLE	LINE
BRIGHTER				
AND YET, AS ANGELS IN SCME BRIGHTER DREAMS	• • •	271	ALL GONE	25
BRIGHTEST				
THE BRIGHTEST DAY.	• • • • • • •	188	RELAPSE	24
BRIGHTNES				
ACTIVE BRIGHTNES	• • • • • •	172	MIDNIGHT	28
THY BRIGHTNESS SOIL'D	• • • • • •	270	ASCSN-HYMN	26
THE BEAMS, AND BRIGHTNES OF THY FACE	• •	217	DRESSING	32
BRIGHTNESS AND MIRTH, AND LOVE AND FAITH, ALL FLYE	• •	288	THE BIRD	31
BRIMSTCNE				
THE PLEASANT LAND TO BRIMSTONE TURNS	• • •	288	THE BIRD	29
OR CHOOSE HELL-FIRE AND BRIMSTCNE STREAMS	• • •	321	CHILDEHOOD	11
BRING				
SHALL BRING TRUE DAY, AND MAKE DUST SEE	• •	335	JUDGEMENT	21
WHICH SPACES AND BOWERS DOTH RENT-FREE BRING.	• •	338	DEATH B	10
THE SWIFT-WING'D RAVEN SHALL BRING ME MEAT	• •	300	PROVIDENCE	16
WHO OUT OF EVIL CAN BRING FORTH GOOD.	• •	297	HERODIAS	18
AND SEND A FIRE DOWN, THAT SHALL BRING	• •	305	ST MARY MN	55
BRING PRAISE, AND INCENSE.	• • • •	215	PRAISE	44
BRING BONE TO BONE	• • • • •	270	ASCSN-HYMN	39
TO BRING ALL STRAGLERS HOME	• • •	239	SHEPHEARDS	46
TO BRING ME HOME, THAN THROUGH A WILDERNES	• •	234	MUTINIE	27
AND BRING NEW TOO. GET THEN THIS SAP, AND GET	• •	244	THE SAP	35
AND IN THE DEPTH AND DEAD OF WINTER BRING	• •	245	MT. OLV. B	19
THEN WOULD I BRING	• • • • •	186	PASSION	51
FOR WHEN ALL FAILES TO BRING TO BLISSE	• •	162	PURSUITE	15
AND THOU UNRAK'ST THY FIRE, THOSE SPARKS WILL BRING	•	195	RLS + LSNS	130
AND BRING THE SAME MAN BACK. THOU WERT AT FIRST	•	194	RLS + LSNS	82
HEALE THEN THESE WATERS, LORD, OR BRING THY FLOCK	•	150	RELIGION	49
AND BRING ME, WHERE I'DE BE.	• • •	148	DAY OF JDG	44
DERIVES HER BIRTH, AND THENCE DOTH BRING	• • •	150	RELIGION	31
THOSE FAMOUS TABLES DID FROM SINAI BRING.	• •	159	MANS FALL	17
TELL ME, O TELL WHO DID THEE BRING	• • •	346	THE QUEER	9
I WILL NOT FOR THY TEMPLES BRING	• • •	345	THE WREATH	7
THIS DAY I BRING FOR ALL THY PAIN	• • •	345	THE WREATH	12
BRINGS				
WHICH BRINGS POOR DUST THE VICTORY.	• • •	339	THE FEAST	18
HE BRINGS HIM WATER WITH HIS BREAD.	• • •	149	RELIGION	12
THAT BRINGS HEALTH IN THE END	• • •	147	DAY OF JDG	36
SUCH TREASURE BRINGS	• • • •	145	RSRCTN +IM	28
A STICK, OR ROD WHICH SCME CHANCE BRINGS	• •	166	THE CALL	52
NAY, THOU TAK'ST CURS, AND (WHICH FUL COMFORT BRINGS)	•	230	LAW + GOSP	19
AND BRINGS MAN HOME, WHEN HE DOTH RANGE	• •	221	AFFLICTION	6
FAITH BRINGS US HOME.	• • • • •	211	FAITH	40
BRINGS FORTH, WITH WINE, CYL, BREAD. ALL WHICH INFUSE	•	285	PSALM 104	43
AND TERRIBLE, THY JUSTICE BRINGS	• •	336	PSALM 65	14
BUT WHAT (LIKE HIS, WHOSE BLOOD PEACE BRINGS)	•	326	ABELS BLOD	39
O WHEN MY GOD, MY GLORY BRINGS	• • •	329	TEARS	1
BRINK				
THERE IS NONE ELSE) DID NOT THE DREADFUL BRINK	•	320	HIDDN TRSR	16
AND BIRDS AMONGST THE BRANCHES ON THEIR BRINK	•	285	PSALM 104	35
NAY, AT THE VERY BRINK	• • •	225	RETIREMENT	19
BUT E'R MY EYES COULD OVERFLOW THEIR BRINK	•	213	ADMISSION	11
BEGINS EVEN AT THE BRINK.	• • • •	166	THE CALL	45
BROACH				
DOTH BROACH THE EARTH, AND LESSER BROOKS LETS FORTH	•	285	PSALM 104	30
BROAD-EYED				
SOME FAST ASLEEPE, OTHERS BROAD-EYED	• • •	141	RGNRTN	76
BROKE				
IS THE TRUCE BROKE. OR 'CAUSE WE HAVE	• •	149	RELIGION	21
WHICH BROKE IN SIGHES STILL, AS THEY FILL'D	•	151	THE SEARCH	30
THE SUN'S BROKE THROUGH TO GUIDE MY WAY.	• •	152	THE SEARCH	66
WEPT BLOOD, THAT BROKE THIS ADAMANT, AND GAVE	•	159	MANS FALL	25
BROKE UP SOME SEALES, WHICH NONE HAD TOUCH'D BEFORE	•	167	VNTY SPRIT	10
HOW BRUIS'D, AND BROKE	• • • •	185	PASSION	36
AND, OATHES ONCE BROKE, THE SOUL CANNOT BE SOUND.	•	193	RLS + LSNS	46
AT THY REBUKE ARE BROKE.	• • •	287	PSALM 104	88
MEANS ONELY THOSE, WHO BROKE (IN LIFE) THY PEACE.	•	289	THE TIMBER	20
SPLIT, AND THE BOX QUITE BROKE AND MARR'D.	•	304	ST MARY MN	22
BE BROKE AGAIN, FOR FLINTS WILL GIVE NO FIRE	•	224	TEMPEST	58
WHEN THE VEYL BROKE WITH THY LAST BREATH	•	219	HOLY COMM.	22
ONELY THIS VEYLE WHICH THOU HAS BROKE	•	277	COCK-CRWNG	37
AND MUST BE BROKEN YET IN ME	• • •	277	COCK-CRWNG	38
CAN TELL THEE WHERE A HEART IS BROKEN.	• •	266	INTRO. 2	32
AND BONES REJOYCE, WHICH ONCE WERE BROKEN.	•	319	THE ASS	65
WHEN THEIR NEST IS FALN AND BROKEN.	• •	294	BEGGING B	20
IF THY SURE MERCIES CAN BE BROKEN	• •	333	AGREEMENT	47
AND BROKEN LETTERS SCARCE REMEMBRED.	• •	168	VNTY SPRIT	24
BROOK				
O BROCK IT NOT. THY BLOOD IS MINE	• •	187	NO DO THEY	35
O BROCK IT NOT. WHY WILT THOU STOP	• •	188	NO DO THEY	37
TOWARDS OLD MAMRE AND ESHCOLS BROOK.	• •	292	THE JEWS	31
WHAT ALL MANKINDE COULD NEVER BROOK	• •	314	THE STONE	53
HOW WILT THOU BROOK'T.	• • • •	142	DEATH	5
BROOKS				
DOTH BROACH THE EARTH, AND LESSER BROOKS LETS FORTH	•	285	PSALM 104	30
AS THIS LOUD BROOKS INCESSANT FALL	• • •	344	WATER-FALL	33
BROTHER				
FOR THOU A BROTHER, AND BLOOD-THIRSTY TOO	• •	331	JACOBS PLW	43
MUST BE THY BROTHER.	• • • • •	179	SILENCE	28

	PAGE	TITLE	LINE
BROUGHT			
AS STRANGE AN OBJECT BROUGHT	141	RGNRTN	73
OUR FEARES, AND FALLS BROUGHT TO CONTEMPT	143	DEATH	18
THESE TAUGHT HIM AT THE WELL, AND THITHER BROUGHT	155	ISAACS M.	29
THIS BROUGHT THEE FORTH, WHERE NOW THOU DIDST UNDRESS	155	ISAACS M.	47
AND BROUGHT US SAVING AID.	302	THE KNOT	4
BEFORE MAN BROUGHT FORTH SIN, AND SIN DECAY.	268	ASCN-DAY A	40
AND HAVING BROUGHT ME HOME, DIDST THERE	348	HOLY BIBLE	25
BROW			
WHO NEVER FEEL'ST THE SUN, NOR SMOOTH'ST THY BROW	217	EASTER-DAY	3
WITH THEE, AND CROWN THY BROW.	284	PSALM 104	4
SITS ON THE SUNS BROW ALL THE YEARE	143	DEATH	13
TWELVE HUNDRED HOURES, AND NOT A BROW	178	SILENCE	3
SWEETE, SACRED HILL. ON WHOSE FAIR BROW	162	MT. OLVS A	1
BRUIS'D			
HOW BRUIS'D, AND BROKE	185	PASSION	36
FOR THY BRUIS'D REED	235	MUTINIE	35
BRUNGS			
BRUNGS TO, AND COMES FROM HEAVEN.	244	THE SAP	50
BRUSH			
BUT BRUSH ME WITH THY LIGHT, THAT I	277	COCK-CRWNG	44
AND LIKE A FIRIE TORRENT BRUSH	146	DAY OF JDG	3
OF CLOVEN TONGUES THEIR HEADS ALL BRUSH'D	272	WHT SUNDAY	7
BRUTE			
YET SINCE MAN IS A VERY BRUTE	230	LAW + GOSP	21
BRUTISH			
IF TRUTH BE THINE, WHAT NEEDS A BRUTISH FORCE.	193	RLS + LSNS	39
MY BRUTISH SOUL, AND TO THY SLAVE	202	DSRDR + FR	3
WITH BRUTISH MEN. THY GIFTS GO ROUND	293	THE JEWS	47
BUBBLES			
THE ANGRY SPRING IN BUBBLES SWELL'D	151	THE SEARCH	29
BUBLING			
OR AT SOME FOUNTAINES BUBLING EYE	148	RELIGION	8
SAD, PURPLE WELL. WHOSE BUBLING EYE	325	ABELS BLOD	1
BUD			
FOR WHOSE DRY DUST GREEN BRANCHES BUD	310	THE SEED	83
BUD IN THE BRIGHT EAST, AND DISCLOSE	151	THE SEARCH	2
OF CLAY, AND FRAILTY BREAK, AND BUD	203	DSRDR + FR	17
MANS RESURRECTION, AND THE FUTURES BUD	192	RLS + LSNS	26
FELL ON MY HEART, THOSE MADE IT BUD	264	INTRO. 1	6
BLEST INFANT BUD, WHOSE BLOSSOME-LIFE	209	THE BURIAL	1
YOU MAKE ROCKS BUD	341	THE FEAST	53
BUDS			
THESE BUDS WILL WITHER	274	PROFFER	8
BLASTED MY INFANT BUDS, AND SINNE	139	RGNRTN	16
AND SHOOTS OF GLORY, MY SOUL BREAKES, AND BUDS.	176	MRNG-WTCH	2
BUILD			
AND BUILD ON IT, BECAUSE THE BEST.	318	THE ASS	14
WHERE TURTLES BUILD, AND CARELESSE SPARROWS MOVE	327	RIGHTSNESS	7
THE BIRDS THEIR NESTS BUILD, THOUGH THE STORK DOTH CHOOSE	286	PSALM 104	47
THY SIX-DAYES BUILDINGS BEATE	147	DAY OF JDG	12
BUILT			
THEIR ARTS AND FORCE ARE BUILT UNTO THE HEIGHT	234	MUTINIE	16
BULRUSH			
AND BULRUSH FETTERS TEMPER HIS SHORT HOUR.	224	TEMPEST	50
BURIED			
AND BURIED IN MY SURFEITS I	240	MISERY	43
BURN			
MY FINGERS ITCH, AND BURN TO TAKE	214	MISERY	62
HER CAPTIVE FLAMES MUST NEEDS BURN THERE.	271	ALL GONE	30
BUT NEVER THOUGHT THAT FIRE WOULD BURN	282	GARLAND	15
AND BURN THY BOOKS.	187	NO DO THEY	10
THERE SHINE, AND BURN.	179	SILENCE	24
AND DIE, THAT BUSH WHERE GOD IS, SHALL NOT BURN.	196	RLS + LSNS	132
BURN'ST			
YET, BURN'ST THOU HERE, A FULL DAY, WHILE I SPEND	157	THE LAMPE	5
STILL AS THOU BURN'ST, AND THE WARME DROPPINGS CREEPE	158	THE LAMPE	14
BURNE			
BOTH LIQUORS BURNE, AND STREAME.	172	MIDNIGHT	26
BURNING			
WITH THY CLEER FIRE REFINE, BURNING TO DUST	216	DRESSING	6
BURNISHT			
THY BURNISHT, FLAMING ARCH DID FIRST DESCRY.	306	RAIN-BOW	4
BURNS			
FROM THEE IT SHIN'D, THOUGH HERE IT BURNS.	265	INTRO. 2	4
NOR WILDLY BURNS, BUT MEEKLY STILL	350	L'ENVOY	37
BURTHEN			
AND HAVING BORN THE BURTHEN ALL THE DAY	275	PROFFER	29
BURTHENS			
THOSE BURTHENS TO THE RICH MANS DOOR	319	THE ASS	34
BUSH			
AND EV'RY BUSH IS SOMETHINGS BOOTH.	313	THE STONE	15
IS ALL THE NOTE WITHIN MY BUSH.	228	PILGRIMAGE	16
AND EVERY BUSH	140	RGNRTN	55
AND DIE, THAT BUSH WHERE GOD IS, SHALL NOT BURN.	196	RLS + LSNS	132
ANGELS LAY LEIGER HERE, EACH BUSH, AND CEL	197	CORRUPTION	25
OR LEAFE BUT HATH HIS MORNING-HYMN. EACH BUSH	192	RLS + LSNS	15
BUSIE			
WINDS WHISPER, AND THE BUSIE SPRINGS	199	NTVTY 1	8
EACH BUSIE RAY	171	MIDNIGHT	6

		PAGE	TITLE	LINE
BUSIE	**(CON'T)**			
WHICH BUSIE THOUGHTS (LIKE WINDS) WOULD SCATTER QUITE	.	179	CHRCH-SVC	12
LORD. WHAT A BUSIE, RESTLES THING	. . .	161	PURSUITE	1
THEY LEAVE THEIR FLOCK, AND IN A BUSIE TALK	. .	239	SHEPHEARDS	43
WHAT SIGHS, WHAT WHISPERS, BUSIE STOPS AND STAYS.	.	268	ASCN-DAY A	27
THIS BUSIE RAY THOU HAST ASSIGN'D.	. .	276	COCK-CRWNG	4
SO LET ME ALL MY BUSIE AGE	. . . .	212	DAWNING	37
THOU. WHO DIDST PLACE ME IN THIS BUSIE STREET	.	318	THE ASS	1
THAT BUSIE COMMERCE KEPT BETWEEN	. . .	313	THE STONE	20
WITH IDLE HEARTS AND BUSIE LOCKS	. . .	303	ORNAMENT	10
HITHER THOU COM'ST. THE BUSIE WIND ALL NIGHT	.	287	THE BIRD	1
THE STOP TO BUSIE FOOLS, CARES CHECK AND CURB.	.	324	THE NIGHT	26
AND WITH HIS BRIGHT AND BUSIE WING	. . .	332	AGREEMENT	8
THICK BUSIE CLOUDS DID MULTIPLY	. . . .	333	AGREEMENT	39
BUSINES				
ALL MUTINOUS THOUGHTS, WHAT BUSINES E'R THOU HAST	.	194	RLS + LSNS	86
BUSINESS				
BUSINESS AND WEIGHTY ACTION ALL	. . . .	322	CHILDEHOOD	28
MY BUSINESS HERE SHALL BE TO GRIEVE.	. . .	299	JESUS WP B	45
AND NO NEW BUSINESS BREAKS THEIR PEACE.	. .	245	MAN	11
BUSTLES				
SO MY FIERCE SOUL BUSTLES ABOUT	. . .	214	MISERY	79
BUY				
AS THOU LONG SINCE WERT PLEAS'D TO BUY	.	274	WHT SUNDAY	53
TO BUY, THE POOR CAME TO ADORE.	. .	302	ORNAMENT	4
THY BEAMS HOME WITH THEE. TRIM THY LAMP, BUY OYL	.	195	RLS + LSNS	110
I'LE DISAPPARELL, AND TO BUY	. . .	168	VNTY SPRIT	33
BUZ				
THAT BUZ IN EVERY EAR, AND BLOW ON SOULS	. .	275	PROFFER	15
CAIN				
OF BLOODY CAIN	. . . .	325	ABELS BLOD	4
CAL				
THUS CAL AND THIRST FOR DEW.	. . .	243	THE SAP	4
CALF				
THAT SERV'D THE CALF, NOT ABR'AMS SEED	. .	296	JESUS WP A	6
CALL				
AND YET THE PRACTICE WORLDLINGS CALL	. .	322	CHILDEHOOD	27
HIS STILL, SOFT CALL.	. . . .	324	THE NIGHT	34
AND LET MEN CALL ME WHAT THEY WILL.	. .	319	THE ASS	44
NEXT DAY I CALL AND CRY FOR THEE	. .	214	MISERY	45
THIS MADE THE ANGEL CALL AT REEDS AND THATCH	.	238	SHEPHEARDS	27
CALL TO THE SOUL, WHEN MAN DOTH SLEEP.	. .	271	ALL GONE	26
TO CALL IT THEIR INHERENT LIGHT.	. .	265	INTRO. 2	6
O CALL TO MIND HIS WOUNDS, HIS WOES	. .	208	REPENTANCE	61
CONCEIT, OR CALL IT WHAT YOU PLEASE	. .	162	MT. OLVS A	6
WHO, WHEN THY SINS CALL FOR'T, CAN FENCE A CURSE.	.	193	RLS + LSNS	64
CALL IN THY POWERS. RUN, AND REACH	. .	189	RESOLVE	17
KNOWS EV'RY NOTE, AND CALL	. . .	161	DSTRQCTION	14
TRAVEL AND GROAN, AND LOOK AND CALL.	. .	350	L'ENVOY	22
MEN CALL GOOD CHEAR	. . . . .	342	OBSEQUIES	14
AND CHIDE, AND CALL	. . . . .	343	WATER-FALL	4
CALL'D				
IS FULL OF VOICES, MAN IS CALL'D, AND HURL'D	.	161	DSTRQCTION	12
SOME CALL'D IT, JACOBS BED	. . .	140	RGNRTN	37
CALL'D FORTH THY TEARS, WHICH RAN IN LIVE	.	305	ST MARY MN	42
CALLETH				
BUT DEEP STILL CALLETH UPON DEEP.	. . .	325	ABELS BLOD	16
CALLING				
I STORM AT THEE, CALLING MY PEACE	. .	242	MISERY	83
CALLOUS				
AND FIRE WILL PURGE YOUR CALLOUS VEYL.	. .	266	VAIN WITS	9
CALLS				
SINCE PLAC'D BY HIM WHO CALLS YOU BY YOUR NAMES	.	236	CONSTLATN	33
HE BEGS, AND CALLS. O THAT IN THESE THY DAYS	.	202	THE CHECK	38
CALM				
SWEET, DOWNIE THOUGHTS, SOFT LILLY-SHADES, CALM STREAMES.		188	RELAPSE	25
AND CALM LIKE HER, OR THAT MILD EVENING-TIDE.	.	154	ISAACS M.	24
YOUR CALM AND WEL-TRAIN'D FLIGHT	. .	236	CONSTLATN	30
THAT CALM AND SILENCE ARE MY JOYS	. .	214	MISERY	59
TO CALM ME IN THESE MUTINIES	. . .	242	MISERY	86
ACTIVE AS LIGHT, AND CALM WITHOUT ALL NOISE	.	244	MT. OLV. B	2
ALL CALM, AND IT WAS BRIGHT	. . .	231	THE WORLD	3
A CALM, BRIGHT DAY.	. . . . .	276	PROFFER	46
WITH CLOUDS AND RAIN, YET FULL AS CALM AND FINE	.	281	JOY	15
SPEECHLESS AND CALM, AS INFANTS SLEEP.	. .	326	ABELS BLOD	35
THE DAY OF SPIRITS, MY SOULS CALM RETREAT	.	324	THE NIGHT	27
CALM AND UNHAUNTED AS IS THY DARK TENT	.	324	THE NIGHT	38
O CHASE IN THAT COLD CALM MY FOES	. .	334	AGREEMENT	65
WHOSE INTERCEDING, MEEK AND CALM	. .	304	ST MARY MN	39
O CALM AND SACRED BED WHERE LIES	. .	310	THE SEED	79
WHAT NEEDS A CONSCIENCE CALM AND BRIGHT	.	309	THE SEED	41
AND CALM AND FULL, YET DOTH NOT CLOY.	. .	345	QUICKNESS	12
CALME				
ROB'D OF YOUR CALME, NOR CAN I EVER MAKE	. .	158	MANS FALL	4
IN THOSE CALME, GOLDEN EVENINGS LAY	. .	151	THE SEARCH	24
CALMES, TEMPESTS, LIGHT, AND DARKNES BY HIS MEANS.	.	194	RLS + LSNS	94
CALMLY				
DO AFTER CALMLY DISAPPEAR	. . . .	339	DEATH B	24
CAME				
(FOR I TILL DRAWN CAME NOT TO THEE)	. . .	334	AGREEMENT	68

	PAGE	TITLE	LINE

CAME   (CON'T)
AT LENGTH, MY LIFES KINDE ANGEL CAME . . . . 332 AGREEMENT 7
HENCE CATHOLICK OR UNIVERSAL CAME . . . . 330 JACOBS PLW 15
RETURN TO HEAVEN, FROM WHENCE IT CAME . . . . 305 ST MARY MN 54
TO BUY, THE POOR CAME TO ADORE. . . . . 302 ORNAMENT 4
CAME THE SHEEP-KEEPING SYRIAN MAID. . . . . 303 ORNAMENT 16
SEEN LONG BEFORE THIS CAME TO PASS . . . . 295 PALM-SUNDY 27
HE CAME (CONDEMNED) HITHER . . . . . 196 CORRUPTION 6
HER YEARLY NURSE, CAME BACK, ENQUIR'D . . . . 151 THE SEARCH 13
(FOR I TILL DRAWN CAME NOT TO THEE) . . . . 340 RGNRTN 4
THROUGH ALL THE CREATURES, CAME AT LAST . . . . 168 VNTY SPRIT 14
IN THAT STATE I CAME RETURN. . . . . 170 RETREATE 32
BUT NOW SINCE WE TO SION CAME . . . . 229 LAW + GOSP 11
BUT WHEN THESE CAME UNTO THE SCALE . . . . 208 REPENTANCE 45
CAME OFT FROM FAR, AND WHISPER'D, NO. . . . . 207 REPENTANCE 16
BUT GRACE, AND BLESSINGS CAME WITH THEE SO RIFE . . . 218 HOLY COMM. 3
WHO CAME (SURE) FROM A SEA OF LIGHT. . . . . 343 WATER-FALL 18
CAMELS
TO DRAW HIM DRINK, AND FOR HIS CAMELS TOO. . . . 155 ISAACS M. 42
CAN'ST
ART SENSELESS STILL. O CAN'ST THOU SLEEP . . . 296 JESUS WP A 3
CANCELL
TO CANCELL ALL THAT E'RE WAS WRIT IN STONE . . . 159 MANS FALL 23
CANCELL'D
ROSE UP, AND CANCELL'D TWO DEATHS DUE TO THEE. . . 217 EASTER-DAY 8
CANCEROUS
FRUSTRATE THOSE CANCEROUS, CLOSE ARTS . . . . 350 L'ENVOY 39
CANDLE
IT SEEMS THEIR CANDLE, HOWE'R DONE . . . . 276 COCK-CRWNG 11
HIS CANDLE SHINES UPON THEIR HEADS. . . . . 272 WHT SUNDAY 16
THE CANDLE SHINING ON SOME HEADS . . . . 265 INTRO. 2 14
THAT CANDLE GIVEN ME FROM ABOVE. . . . . 333 AGREEMENT 42
CANDLE-LIGHT
TO CANDLE-LIGHT UNVEILS. . . . . . 310 THE SEED 68
CANDLES
LIKE CANDLES, SHED . . . . . . 175 JOY OF LIF 22
CANDY
CANDY WITH SUGAR OUR CHOICE FRUITS. . . . . 310 THE SEED 78
CANOPIE
OR THE COOLE MIRTLES CANOPIE . . . . . 148 RELIGION 6
CAPTIVE
LEADS OTHERS, SHALL A CAPTIVE BE. . . . . 316 MEN OF WAR 4
HER CAPTIVE FLAMES MUST NEEDS BURN THERE. . . . 271 ALL GONE 30
CAPTIVES
'WHOSE SERVICE MAKES EV'N CAPTIVES FREE) . . . 300 PROVIDENCE 14
CAPTIVITIE
AND ENTRANCE TO CAPTIVITIE. . . . . . 207 REPENTANCE 10
CAPTIVITY
HE THAT INTO CAPTIVITY . . . . . 316 MEN OF WAR 3
THESE BONDS, THIS SAD CAPTIVITY . . . . 319 THE ASS 54
WITH HIS STRONG ARM TURNS OUR CAPTIVITY. . . . 331 JACOBS PLW 40
WHO TURN'D OUR SAD CAPTIVITY. . . . . 351 L'ENVOY 62
CARE
THY CARE AND LOVE, WHICH JOYNTLY FLOW . . . 333 AGREEMENT 57
ODOROUS OINTMENTS KEPT WITH CARE . . . . 304 ST MARY MN 34
WHICH ONCE THY CARE AND ART DID SHOW. . . . 304 ST MARY MN 16
I CARE NOT, SO I MAY SECURE . . . . . 295 PALM-SUNDY 44
AND AS THY CARE BOUNDS THESE, SO THY RICH LOVE . . 285 PSALM 104 29
HE THAT HATH LEFT LIFES VAIN JOYS AND VAIN CARE . . 290 THE TIMBER 29
AND FROM THIS CARE, WHERE DREAMS AND SORROWS REIGN . 248 I WALKT 57
FALSE, JUGLING SOUNDS, A GRONE WELL DREST, WHERE CARE . 280 JOY 3
MAN HATH STIL EITHER TOYES, OR CARE . . . 246 MAN 15
HE GROPS BENEATH HERE, AND WITH RESTLESS CARE . . 236 CONSTLATN 17
BUT THAT WAS ALL, AND NOW WITH GLADSOME CARE . . 239 SHEPHEARDS 41
BUT NOW 'TIS MONSTROUS, AND THAT PIOUS CARE . . 154 ISAACS M. 2
OF DRUNKNES, SURFEITS, CARE . . . . . 202 THE CHECK 42
CAREIRE
BUT AT THE HEIGHT OF THIS CAREIRE . . . . 282 GARLAND 25
CARELESS
HAVE LEFT US, WHILE WE CARELESS SATE . . . 164 THE CALL 12
DESCEND TO JUDGE POOR CARELESS MAN . . . 212 DAWNING 28
CARELESSE
WHERE TURTLES BUILD, AND CARELESSE SPARROWS MOVE . . 327 RIGHTSNESS 7
CARES
THE STOP TO BUSIE FOOLS, CARES CHECK AND CURB. . . 324 THE NIGHT 26
WHERE OBSCURE CARES THE MEAN DEFEAT . . . 318 THE ASS 7
PERHAPS SOME HARMLESS CARES FOR THE NEXT DAY . . 239 SHEPHEARDS 37
O LEAVE THY CARES, AND FOLLIES. GO THIS WAY . . 192 RLS + LSNS 17
YET KEEP THOSE CARES WITHOUT THEE, LET THE HEART . . 192 RLS + LSNS 35
MY REST IN CARES, AND TO THE DARK WORLD LEND . . 157 THE LAMPE 6
CARRI'D
WHICH MUST BE CARRI'D ON, AND SAFELY MAY. . . 192 RLS + LSNS 34
CARRIED
THUS LAZARUS WAS CARRIED OUT OF TOWN. . . . 183 THRS A TYE 17
CARRIES
WHO CARRIES THEE, IS BY THEE LED . . . . 318 THE ASS 23
CARRY
TO CARRY, NOT SEARCH MYSTERIES. . . . . 318 THE ASS 22
TO CARRY THAT, WHICH SOME WOULD SCORN TO TOUCH. . . 155 ISAACS M. 40
CARV'D
NO DEAD AND DUSTY CHERUB, NOR CARV'D STONE . . . 323 THE NIGHT 20

		PAGE	TITLE	LINE
CARVINGS				
BY FLOWERS AND CARVINGS AND MYSTERIOUS SKILL	. . .	279	PALM-TREE	11
CASE				
THEY'R BUT A CASE.	.	189	RESOLVE	12
CAST				
SHAL HE BE NOW CAST OFF. NO SENSE	. .	200	NTVTY 2	11
THE BREAD WE CAST RETURNS IN FRAUGHTS ONE DAY.	. .	193	RLS + LSNS	66
FAREWELL YOU EVERLASTING HILLS. I'M CAST	. . .	158	MANS FALL	1
CAST IN THEIR LOTS AGAIN	. .	156	BRT. CHRCH	7
WHEN I AM CAST INTO THAT DEEP	. . .	180	BURIALL	3
WHICH SHEW'D ME IN A NOOK CAST BY	. . .	168	VNTY SPRIT	21
NOW CAST AT NIGHT MY CROWN AWAY.	. . .	275	PROFFER	30
THEN CAST HER BLOUD, AND TEARS UPON THY BOOK	. .	237	CONSTLATN	41
HOW DO THEY CAST OFF GROSSNESS. ONLY EARTH	. .	223	TEMPEST	29
SHALL I FROM THENCE CAST DOWN MY SELF	. . .	321	CHILDEHOOD	22
BUT GRAVELY CAST THEMSELVES AWAY.	. . .	322	CHILDEHOOD	30
BUT WERE I ONCE CAST OFF BY THEE	. . .	333	AGREEMENT	59
CAST IT, OR TREAD IT. IT SHALL DO	. . .	328	ANGUISH	5
BENEATH HIS BLEST FEET THOU DIDST CAST	. . .	304	ST MARY MN	30
CAST BY THE HUSBAND-MAN AWAY. . . .	. .	292	THE JEWS	19
WILL THOSE COY SPIRITS CAST ASLEEP	. . .	297	HERODIAS	10
LONG REIGN'D THIS VOGUE, AND THOU CAST BY	. . .	348	HOLY BIBLE	17
CASTING				
ME DOWN TO BREATH, AND CASTING IN MY HEART	. .	233	MUTINIE	2
CATARACTS				
NOT THIS WITH CATARACTS AND CREEKS.	. . .	344	WATER-FALL	40
CATCH				
THEN BLESS THY SECRET GROWTH, NOR CATCH	. .	309	THE SEED	45
WHEN SPIRITS THEIR FAIR KINRED CATCH.	. . .	324	THE NIGHT	36
CATCH AT THE PLACE	. .	189	RESOLVE	10
CATCHES				
(WHILST DEEP SLEEP OTHERS CATCHES)	. . .	171	MIDNIGHT	2
CATHARTICS				
NEW CORDIALS, NEW CATHARTICS DEAL.	. . .	333	AGREEMENT	58
CATHOLICK				
HENCE CATHOLICK OR UNIVERSAL CAME	. . .	330	JACOBS PLW	15
CATTEL				
GRASS FOR THE CATTEL, AND HERBS FOR MANS USE	. .	285	PSALM 104	41
CAUGHT				
(AND THOSE BUT SELDOME TOO) WERE CAUGHT	. .	207	REPENTANCE	12
CAUS'D				
A SINFULL WRETCH, A WRETCH THAT CAUS'D THY WOE	. .	283	LOVE-SICK	18
THY WOE, WHO CAUS'D HIS WEAL, SO FAR HIS WEAL	. .	283	LOVE-SICK	19
CAUSE				
WHERE I SHALL HAVE NO CAUSE TO FEAR	. . .	313	THE STONE	3
WHICH CAUSE SOLUTION IN ALL PARTS	. . .	350	L'ENVOY	40
CAUSELESS				
THY CAUSELESS PAIN. AND SAD AS DEATH.	. .	345	THE WREATH	13
WERE BY MY CAUSELESS ENEMIES . . .	. .	301	PROVIDENCE	39
CAUTIOUS				
THIS CAUTIOUS FOOLS MISTAKE, AND FEAR	. .	313	THE STONE	16
CAVES				
TO LIVE IN GROTS, AND CAVES, AND HATE THE DAY	. .	233	THE WORLD	51
AS HE THAT IN SOME CAVES THICK DAMP . .	. .	178	SILENCE	5
CEAS'D				
BUT THOUGH THUS DEAD UNTO THE WORLD, AND CEAS'D	. .	290	THE TIMBER	33
CEASE				
CEASE THOU THY WRATH.	. .	188	RELAPSE	12
THAT NOW ALL MIRACLES MUST CEASE. . .	. .	149	RELIGION	26
CEDAR				
HER CEDAR, FIRR, HEW'D STONES AND GOLD WERE ALL	. .	238	SHEPHEARDS	23
CEDARS IN LEBANON, IN WHOSE THICK BOUGHS	. .	286	PSALM 104	46
CEL				
EXCLUDE HIM THENCE, WHO OF THAT CEL	. . .	240	MISERY	35
WITHIN THE CIRCLE OF MY CEL . . .	. .	214	MISERY	58
ANGELS LAY LEIGER HERE, EACH BUSH, AND CEL	. .	197	CORRUPTION	25
CELESTIALL				
BUT A WHITE, CELESTIALL THOUGHT	. . .	169	RETREATE	6
AND CELESTIALL FLOWES . . .	. .	172	MIDNIGHT	29
THE MORE HE GROWS. CELESTIALL NATURES STILL	. .	279	PALM-TREE	9
FOR WHERE DESIRE, CELESTIALL, PURE DESIRE	. .	279	THE STARRE	25
IN THY CELESTIALL, GLADSOME MESSAGES	. .	284	PSALM 104	13
CELL				
ARE ALL TOO HIGH FOR A LOW CELL. . .	. .	309	THE SEED	34
A HEART IS THAT DREAD PLACE, THAT AWFUL CELL	. .	330	JACOBS PLW	27
QUITE SPENT WITH THOUGHTS I LEFT MY CELL, AND LAY	. .	167	VNTY SPRIT	1
A GOD ENCLOS'D WITHIN YOUR CELL . .	. .	164	INCARNATN	10
I THREATEN HEAVEN, AND FROM MY CELL . .	. .	203	DSRDR + FR	16
ABOUT HER SILENT CELL	. .	144	RSRCTN +IM	8
CELLS				
WHAT SILENT PATHS, WHAT SHADES, AND CELLS	. .	153	THE SEARCH	69
THE SEATS, AND CELLS WITHIN. . . .	. .	180	BURIALL	15
DROP IN THEIR CELLS.	. .	281	JOY	26
CELS				
IN THOSE THIN CELS COULD LIE . . .	. .	239	SHEPHEARDS	32
CEMENT				
AND CEMENT US WITH THY SONS BLOOD . .	. .	350	L'ENVOY	46
CENTER				
HE IS THE CENTER OF LONG LIFE, AND LIGHT	. . .	209	REPENTANCE	83
NAIL'D TO THE CENTER STOOD . . .	. .	141	RGNRTN	69

		PAGE	TITLE	LINE
CENTER	**(CON'T)**			
THE CENTER, AND HIS SHROWD.	. . . .	197	CORRUPTION	36
O FOR THY CENTER AND MID-DAY.	. . . . . .	322	CHILDEHOOD	43
AND HIS BLOOD FREEZ'D, KEEPS IN THE CENTER STILL	. .	289	THE TIMBER	22
CENTER'D				
FOR THINGS THUS CENTER'D, WITHOUT BEAMES, OR ACTION	.	183	THRS A TYE	5
CENTRIE				
WHERE STANDS A WINGED CENTRIE	. . . . . .	184	PEACE	3
CENTURIES				
TENANT FOR YEARES, AND CENTURIES	. . . . .	142	DEATH	4
CEREMONIES				
THE LAW, AND CEREMONIES MADE	. . . . . .	210	FAITH	13
CHAFF				
PURGING THE FLOOR WHICH CHAFF DISTURBS.	. . . .	221	AFFLICTION	20
THEIR DOCTRINE CHAFF AND WINDY FITS.	. . . .	332	AGREEMENT	26
CHAINS				
FOR CHAINS OF DARKNES, AND ETERNAL NIGHTS.	. . .	196	RLS + LSNS	144
CHAIRE				
WAS THEN HIS CHAIRE.	. . . .	163	MT. OLVS A	32
CHALENGE				
BID ME, BY VERTUE FROM HIM, CHALENGE HERE	. . .	188	RELAPSE	23
CHALKT				
THE MILKY WAY CHALKT OUT WITH SUNS, A CLUE	. . .	2	SON-DAYES	21
CHAMBERS				
NOW SHINES IN ALL THE CHAMBERS OF THE EAST.	. . .	267	ASCN-DAY A	24
THE BEAMS OF THY BRIGHT CHAMBERS THOU DOST LAY	. .	284	PSALM 104	9
CHAMBERS OF RAIN, WHERE HEAV'NS LARGE BOTTLES LIE	. .	285	PSALM 104	38
CHANC'D				
HE HELD, I CHANC'D TO LOOK	. . . . . .	309	THE SEED	51
CHANCE				
A STICK, OR ROD WHICH SOME CHANCE BRINGS	. . .	166	THE CALL	52
NO CHANCE, OR FIT. BUT EVER BRIGHT	. . . .	345	QUICKNESS	11
CHANG'D				
FOUND ALL WAS CHANG'D, AND A NEW SPRING	. . .	140	RGNRTN	48
HOW ART THOU CHANG'D. HOW LIVELY-FAIR	. . .	303	ST MARY MN	5
THAT SCENE WAS CHANG'D, AND A NEW DRESSE	. . .	210	FAITH	23
CHANGE				
THY PHYSICK, PILS THAT CHANGE	. . . . .	221	AFFLICTION	2
AND BY A FRUITFULL CHANGE OF FROSTS, AND SHOWRES	. .	221	AFFLICTION	13
NO MORNING-MEETINGS SINCE THIS CHANGE	. . .	293	BEGGING B	7
AND CHANGE OF SUITS	. . . .	145	RSRCTN +IM	22
THAT CHANGE, AND KNOWS THY CLAY.	. . . .	181	BURIALL	30
THOU CANST NOT CHANGE.	. . . . . .	187	NO DO THEY	20
IF PRIEST, AND PEOPLE CHANGE, KEEP THOU THY GROUND.	.	193	RLS + LSNS	44
O LOSE IT NOT. LOCK UP, WILT CHANGE THOSE LIGHTS	. .	196	RLS + LSNS	143
WHEN SEASONS CHANGE, THEN LAY BEFORE THINE EYES	. .	194	RLS + LSNS	91
CHANGES				
BUT ONE , WHO NEVER CHANGES	. . . . . .	184	PEACE	19
CHANGING				
IS BUT MEER CHANGING OF THE KEYS	. . . . .	273	WHT SUNDAY	43
CHANNEL				
AS THIS DOTH IN HER CHANNEL, FLOW	. . . .	212	DAWNING	42
DID QUIT THEIR TROUBLED CHANNEL, AND RETIRE	. . .	234	MUTINIE	7
THOU ART THE CHANNEL MY SOUL SEEKS	. . . .	344	WATER-FALL	39
CHARACTERS				
THE WORD IN CHARACTERS, GOD IN THE VOICE.	. .	198	SCRIPTURES	8
CHARGE				
ONE SULLEN BEAME, WHOSE CHARGE IS TO DISPENSE	. .	159	MANS FALL	13
WHO DOEST THINE ANGELS CHARGE WITH FOLLY.	. . .	208	REPENTANCE	68
CHARGES				
TILL AT THY CHARGES THEY SHALL BE	. . . .	265	INTRO. 2	15
CHARIOTS				
THE CLOUDS THY CHARIOTS ARE, AND THY PATH-WAY	. .	284	PSALM 104	11
CHARITY				
SO ARE NOW FAITH, HOPE, CHARITY	. . . .	211	FAITH	35
THY LIGHT, IS CHARITY, THY HEAT, IS ZEALE.	. .	158	THE LAMPE	11
CHARMERS				
LULL'D BY THOSE CHARMERS TO A LETHARGY.	. . .	281	JOY	10
CHARTER				
THOU ARE LIFES CHARTER, THE DOVES SPOTLESS NEAST	. .	197	SCRIPTURES	3
CHASE				
THE CHILDREN CHASE THE MOTHER, AND WOULD HEAL	. .	237	CONSTLATN	39
THE LOWER GROUNDS STIL CHASE, AND CHOOSE	. . .	240	MISERY	10
O CHASE IN THAT COLD CALM MY FOES	. . . .	334	AGREEMENT	65
RAN I IN CHASE OF VANITY	. . . . . .	348	HOLY BIBLE	14
CHAST				
OF NIGHT SHUT UP THY LEAVES, BE CHAST, GOD PRYS	.	196	RLS + LSNS	136
WITH WHICH IN MILD, CHAST LANGUAGE SHE DID WOOE	. .	155	ISAACS M.	41
THE CHAST, AND LOVELY OBJECT OF THY THOUGHT.	. .	155	ISAACS M.	30
BUT THESE CHASTE FOUNTAINS FLOW NOT TILL WE DYE.	.	291	THE TIMBER	53
LIV'D STILL IN LEAGUE WITH THY CHASTE FIRE	. .	312	FAIR+YONG	28
CHEAP				
GLORY, THE CROUDS CHEAP TINSEL STILL	. . . .	309	THE SEED	37
CHEAP, MIGHTY ART. HER ART OF LOVE	. . . .	305	ST MARY MN	49
MY FIRST CHEAP BOOK HAD ALL I SOUGHT.	. . .	348	HOLY BIBLE	16
WITH A CHEAP, PLAIN REMEMBRANCE STILL	. . .	342	OBSEQUIES	5
IS ALL DISPERS'D, AND CHEAPE.	. . . . .	160	DSTRQCTION	2
CHEAR				
THOU ART MY CHEAR	. . . .	340	THE FEAST	41
MEN CALL GOOD CHEAR	. . . .	342	OBSEQUIES	14

		PAGE	TITLE	LINE
CHEAR'D	**(CON'T)**			
WERE CHEAR'D, YOUR JEALOUSIE TO MOVE.		293	THE JEWS	45
CHEARFUL				
AND NOW AS FRESH AND CHEARFUL AS THE LIGHT		288	THE BIRD	7
CHEATING				
CHEATING HIMSELF, THAT MAN WALKS IN THIS PATH.		328	RIGHTSNESS	54
CHECK				
THE STOP TO BUSIE FOOLS, CARES CHECK AND CURB.		324	THE NIGHT	26
TO CHECK BAD MOTIONS, KEEP ME STILL		318	THE ASS	25
TO CHECK THE MULE, UNRULY MAN		221	AFFLICTION	18
CHECKING				
BOTH GROWTH, AND POWER, CHECKING THE HEALTH		206	REPENTANCE	6
CHECKING THE POOR CHILDE FOR HIS PLAY		322	CHILDEHOOD	29
CHECKT				
AND CHECKT THEIR FURIE, WHEN I SAW THEM MOVE		188	RELAPSE	7
TO MANY, AND HAVE CHECKT MY BLOOD		190	THE MATCH	3
CHECQUR'D				
CHECQUR'D WITH SNOWIE FLEECES		140	RGNRTN	53
CHEER				
I CHEER THEIR FLOW, GIVING SUPPLY		240	MISERY	17
THE DEW DOTH CHEER WHAT IS DISTREST		227	LV + DSPLN	10
CHEER'D				
THOU HAST CHEER'D ME		214	PRAISE	2
CHERISH				
CHERISH, AND BIND THY POW'RS		221	AFFLICTION	14
CHERUB				
NO DEAD AND DUSTY CHERUB, NOR CARV'D STONE		323	THE NIGHT	20
CHERUBIMS				
OF WINGS, AND CHERUBIMS, AND PALMS FORETOLD.		279	PALM-TREE	12
CHEW'D				
THOSE BEASTS WERE CLEANE, THAT CHEW'D THE CUD.		165	THE CALL	29
CHIDE				
CHIDE, AND FLY UP, MISTS OF CORRUPTEST FOME		223	TEMPEST	26
CHIDE IN THINE EARS.		213	ADMISSION	8
AND CHIDE, AND CALL		343	WATER-FALL	4
CHIEF				
AND CHIEF ACQUAINTANCE BE ABOVE.		212	DAWNING	44
GRANT I MAY, MY CHIEF DESIRE.		249	BEGGING A	5
O MY CHIEF GOOD.		184	PASSION	1
FOR 'TIS OUT FOES CHIEF ART		183	THRS A TYE	18
THREE THINGS I'DE HAVE, MY SOLLES CHIEF HEALTH		148	DAY OF JDG	39
CHILD				
BOTH LIVE AND DIE THY CHILD.		235	MUTINIE	39
CHECKING THE POOR CHILDE FOR HIS PLAY		322	CHILDEHOOD	29
AND SAID, I WAS NO CHILDE OF DAY.		333	AGREEMENT	40
AND PLAIN, AS WHEN I WAS A CHILDE.		317	MEN OF WAR	46
O FILL HIS BOTTLE. THY CHILDE WEEPS.		308	THE SEED	16
YOU WERE THE ELDEST CHILDE, AND WHEN		293	THE JEWS	42
I WILL BE STILL A CHILDE, STILL MEEK		295	PALM-SUNDY	39
CHILDE-HOOD				
WHY SHOULD I NOT LOVE CHILDE-HOOD STILL.		321	CHILDEHOOD	20
CHILDES				
COMES LIKE A CHILDES, SPOTLESS AND FRESH.		306	ST MARY MN	70
CHILDREN				
THOSE WHITE DESIGNS WHICH CHILDREN DRIVE		321	CHILDEHOOD	4
DIDST FLYE, WHOSE CHILDREN WROUGHT THY CHILDRENS WO.		331	JACOBS PLW	44
AND THAT DREAD GLORY, WHICH THY CHILDREN FEAR'D		330	JACOBS PLW	2
HARK. HOW THE CHILDREN SHRIL AND HIGH		295	PALM-SUNDY	18
THE CHILDREN CHASE THE MOTHER, AND WOULD HEAL		237	CONSTLATN	39
WHICH NONE BUT CHILDREN HEARD, OR TAUGHT.		207	REPENTANCE	14
BUT JACOBS CHILDREN WOULD NOT HEARE.		151	THE SEARCH	32
CHILDRENS				
DIDST FLYE, WHOSE CHILDREN WROUGHT THY CHILDRENS WO.		331	JACOBS PLW	44
CHIME				
THE HOURS TO WHICH HIGH HEAVEN DOTH CHIME.		324	THE NIGHT	30
AND IN WEAKE, INFANT HUMMINGS CHIME, AND KNELL		144	RSRCTN +IM	7
IN SACRED HYMNES, AND ORDER, THE GREAT CHIME		177	MRNG-WTCH	17
THAT WITH THY GLORY DOTH BEST CHIME		211	DAWNING	14
CHIRPING				
CHIRPING THEIR SOLEMN MATINS ON EACH TREE.		288	THE BIRD	24
CHOAKT				
AND TARES HAD CHOAKT THE CORNE		166	THE CALL	73
CHOICE				
THAT BY THY EARLY CHOICE FOREWARN'D		166	THE CALL	40
THOU ART THE GREAT ELIXIR, RARE, AND CHOICE.		198	SCRIPTURES	6
CANDY WITH SUGAR OUR CHOICE FRUITS.		310	THE SEED	78
I SOUGHT CHOICE BOWRES, HAUNTED THE SPRING		282	GARLAND	21
CHOKE				
SOME TARES IN ME WHICH CHOKE, OR SPIL		227	LV + DSPLN	5
CHOOSE				
THE LOWER GROUNDS STIL CHASE, AND CHOOSE		240	MISERY	10
THE BIRDS THEIR NESTS BUILD, THOUGH THE STORK DOTH CHOOSE		286	PSALM 104	47
OR CHOOSE HELL-FIRE AND BRIMSTONE STREAMS		321	CHILDEHOOD	11
HAPPY IS HE. WHOM THOU WILT CHOOSE		336	PSALM 65	9
BE GODS ALONE, AND CHOOSE THE BETTER PART.		192	RLS + LSNS	36
WHERE THEY NEW CONSORTS CHOOSE AND STICK		348	HOLY BIBLE	11
CHOSE				
AND WOULD NOT SEE, BUT CHOSE TO WINK		225	RETIREMENT	18
CHOSEN				
THY CHOSEN FLOCK, LIKE LEAFS IN A HIGH WIND		229	LAW + GOSP	9

		PAGE	TITLE	LINE
CHOSEN	**(CON'T)**			
I SEE HIM LEADING OUT HIS CHOSEN TRAIN	• • • •	268	ASCN-DAY A	51
BUT THOU A CHOSEN SACRIFICE WERT GIVEN		154	ISAACS M.	5
YOU WERE THE DEAR AND CHOSEN STOCK.	• • • •	292	THE JEWS	39
AMONGST THAT CHOSEN COMPANY	• • • •	317	MEN OF WAR	50
CHRIST				
BUT SINCE CHRIST DYED (AS IF WE DID DEVISE	• •	307	RAIN-BOW	23
THY COVENANT BY CHRIST EXTENDS.	• • •	333	AGREEMENT	52
THIS IS THE LIFE WHICH HID ABOVE WITH CHRIST	• •	280	PALM-TREE	13
CHRISTS				
AND ON CHRISTS COAT PIT ALL THEIR SHREDS.	• •	272	WHT SUNDAY	14
CHRISTS PROGRESS, AND HIS PRAYER TIME.	• • •	324	THE NIGHT	29
CHRONIC				
LIKE CHRONIC PAINS, WHICH SURELY KILL, THOUGH SLOW.	•	327	RIGHTSNESS	30
CHRONICLE				
WERE NOW THAT CHRONICLE ALIVE	• • • • •	321	CHILDEHOOD	3
CHURCH				
THE TOKENS OF THE CHURCH, AND PEACE	• • • •	149	RELIGION	28
CHURCHES				
CHURCHES AND ALTARS FED HIM, PERJURIES	• • •	232	THE WORLD	27
THE CHURCHES LOVE-FEASTS, TIMES PREROGATIVE	• • •	2	SON-DAYES	17
CIRCLE				
WITHIN THE CIRCLE OF MY CEL	• • • •	214	MISERY	58
ALL AGES UP. WHO DREW THIS CIRCLE, EVEN	• • •	178	EVNG-WTCH	13
CIRCLED				
WHO BENT THE SPHERES, AND CIRCLED IN	• • •	167	VNTY SPRIT	5
CIRCLING				
VAST CIRCLING AZURE, GIDDY CLOUDS, DAYS, NIGHTS.	• •	194	RLS + LSNS	90
CIRCULATIONS				
AND HYMNING CIRCULATIONS THE QUICK WORLD	• • •	176	MRNG-WTCH	10
CISTERNE				
THE CISTERNE FULL	• • • • • •	141	RGNRTN	63
CITIES				
THEY ARE THAT CITIES SHINING SPIRES	• • • •	175	JOY OF LIF	27
CITY				
THAT SHADY CITY OF PALME TREES	• • • •	170	RETREATE	26
BLESSED, UNHAPPY CITY. DEARLY LOV'D	• • •	296	JESUS WP A	1
CLAD				
AND WHERE THE OTHER MOUNT ALL CLAD IN FLAME	• •	229	LAW + GOSP	14
TO THEE WHO WITH TRUE LIGHT ART CLAD	• •	207	REPENTANCE	21
WHEN LIKE A VIRGIN CLAD IN FLOWERS AND GREEN	• •	268	ASCN-DAY A	41
AS THY CLOATHS (WHEN THOU WITH CLOATHS WERE CLAD)	• •	265	INTRO. 2	9
CLAIM				
AND CLAIM IT FOR THEIR MEAT.	• • • •	243	THE SAP	8
AND CLAIM THEIR SHARE	• • • • •	190	THE MATCH	11
CLAIMS				
THY LOVE CLAIMS HIGHEST THANKS, MY SIN	• • •	329	TEARS	13
CLAY				
WHICH NATURE BREEDS, AND SOME FINE CLAY INVITES	• •	320	HIDDN TRSR	20
MAY HIS CROWN, LIKE HIS HOPES, BE CLAY	• •	301	PROVIDENCE	35
KEEP THOU THY TEMPER, MIX NOT WITH EACH CLAY.	•	192	RLS + LSNS	32
AS TO MAKE CLAY	• • • • •	202	THE CHECK	33
OF CLAY, AND FRAILTY BREAK, AND BUD	• • •	203	DSRDR + FR	17
IN THIS IMPURE, REBELLIOUS CLAY	• • •	164	INCARNATN	14
THAT CHANGE, AND KNOWS THY CLAY.	• • •	181	BURIALL	30
DISSOLVE (WITH IT) TO CLAY	• • • •	183	THRS A TYE	2
WEARY OF THIS SAME CLAY, AND STRAW, I LAID	• •	233	MUTINIE	1
THE SAME RESPECT, AND ROOM, WITH EV'RY CLAY.	• •	226	RETIREMENT	44
WE, WHO ARE NOTHING BUT FOUL CLAY	• • •	274	WHT SUNDAY	59
MAKE CLAY ASCEND MORE QUICK THEN LIGHT.	• •	270	ASCSN-HYMN	42
DUST AND CLAY	• • • • • •	269	ASCSN-HYMN	1
LORD, SINCE THOU DIDST IN THIS VILE CLAY	• •	206	REPENTANCE	1
OF DUST, AND CLAY	• • • •	226	RETIREMENT	31
ALL FLESH IS CLAY, THOU KNOW'ST, AND BUT THAT GOD	•	221	AFFLICTION	11
OUR FOUL, CLAY HANDS	• • • • •	215	PRAISE	42
CLEAN				
YET, IF THOU WILT, THOU CANST MAKE CLEAN.	• •	199	NTVTY 1	24
WERE SO CLEAN AS	• • • • •	199	NTVTY 1	21
KEEP CLEAN, BEAR FRUIT, EARN LIFE AND WATCH	• •	309	THE SEED	47
THE CLEAN, PURE HAND, WHICH NEVER MEDLED PITCH.	• •	327	RIGHTSNESS	10
COME WHILE MY HEART IS CLEAN AND STEDDY.	• •	339	THE FEAST	3
BUT NOT SO DRY AND CLEAN AS THIS.	• • •	347	THE BOOK	22
CLEANE				
THOSE BEASTS WERE CLEANE, THAT CHEW'D THE CUD.	• •	165	THE CALL	29
AND VANISH CLEANE AWAY	• • • • •	147	DAY OF JDG	14
CLEANSE				
THAT SHULD BOTH CLEANSE	• • •	220	HOLY COMM.	46
SHAL BE FINE GOLD, WHICH THOU DIDST CLEANSE.	• •	274	WHT SUNDAY	60
TEARS CLEANSE AND SUPPLE WITHOUT FAIL	• • •	266	VAIN WITS	8
CLEANSER				
MY SACRED WASH AND CLEANSER HERE	• • •	344	WATER-FALL	24
CLEAR				
WHERE, CLEAR AS GLASS	• • • •	343	WATER-FALL	8
O USEFUL ELEMENT AND CLEAR.	• • •	344	WATER-FALL	23
THEIR VERY THOUGHTS, THAT BY THEIR CLEAR	• •	351	L'ENVOY	55
AFTER THY DEATH AND FUNERAL, SO CLEAR	• •	268	ASCN-DAY A	34
AND MY SAD THOUGHTS DOTH CLEAR.	• • •	270	ALL GONE	4
AS THOSE CLEAR HEIGHTS WHICH ABOVE TEMPESTS SHINE.	• •	281	JOY	16
NOW WITH CLOUDS, NOW MAKING CLEAR	• • •	281	JOY	20
MAY CLEAR MUCH WAY	• • • • •	174	JOY OF LIF	15

                                                                    PAGE   TITLE   LINE

CLEAR   (CON'T)
    UNTO THOSE CLEAR AND LIVING SPRINGS   329   TEARS   3
    IN MILDE, CLEAR VISIONS, WITHOUT A FROWN   330   JACOBS PLW   3
    HIS LOCKS.ARE WET WITH THE CLEAR DROPS OF NIGHT.   .   .   324   THE NIGHT   33
    SEE NOT ALL CLEAR.   325   THE NIGHT   52
    SOME DROPS MAY FALL BEFORE, BUT A CLEAR SPRING   .   .   291   THE TIMBER   54
CLEAR'D
    HAD CLEAR'D OUR EYES   219   HOLY COMM.   28
CLEARE
    'TIS NOW CLEARE DAY. I SEE A ROSE   151   THE SEARCH   1
CLEAVE
    TO HIS DIVINE APPOINTMENTS EVER CLEAVE   .   .   .   245   MAN   10
CLEER
    WHOSE LEADERS TO THOSE PASTURES, AND CLEER SPRINGS   .   238   SHEPHEARDS   3
    WITHOUT A STEEL, O LET THY POWER CLEER   .   .   .   224   TEMPEST   59
    WITH THY CLEER FIRE REFINE, BURNING TO DUST   .   .   216   DRESSING   6
    MAY MAKE THE FUTURE CLEER.   216   DRESSING   22
    THOU HAS CLEER'D ME.   214   PRAISE   4
CLEFT
    BALM ON THE CLEFT EARTH, MILK ON GRASS AND FLOWERS.   .   306   RAIN-BOW   12
CLIMB
    WE CLIMB ABOVE ALL AGES, LAMPS THAT LIGHT   .   .   .   2   SON-DAYES   6
    WE CLIMB UP THIS, AND HAVE TOO ALL THE WAY   .   .   230   LAW + GOSP   17
    AND BY THOSE HID ASCENTS CLIME TO THAT DAY   .   .   248   I WALKT   52
CLIMB'D
    I CLIMB'D THE HILL, PERUS'D THE CROSSE   .   .   .   152   THE SEARCH   41
CLIMBE
    TO GET THEE WINGS ON, AND DEVOUTLY CLIMBE   .   .   155   ISAACS M.   44
    O LET ME CLIMBE   177   MRNG-WTCH   23
CLIME
    SO POISON'D, BREAKS FORTH IN SOME CLIME   .   .   .   150   RELIGION   41
CLIPT
    YET, HADST THOU CLIPT MY WINGS, WHEN COFFIN'D IN   .   161   DSTRQCTION   17
CLOATH
    AND CLOATH THE MORNING-STARRE WITH DUST   .   .   .   164   INCARNATN   6
    AND PURLING CORN DOTH CLOATH THE VALE.   .   .   .   337   PSALM 65   46
CLOATH'D
    AND FOLLOW THEE ALL CLOATH'D IN WHITE   .   .   .   316   MEN OF WAR   22
    CURB'D THEM, AND CLOATH'D THEE WELL AND WARM.   .   288   THE BIRD   10
    SHALL ONE DAY RISE, AND CLOATH'D WITH SHINING LIGHT   .   145   RSRCTN +IM   47
    CLOATH'D ALL WITH IMMORTALITY.   265   INTRO. 2   16
    CLOATH'D WITH THIS SKIN, WHICH NOW LIES SPREC   .   347   THE BOOK   18
CLOATH'ST
    THOU CLOATH'ST THY SELF WITH LIGHT, AS WITH A ROBE   .   284   PSALM 104   5
CLOATHES
    MADE HIS CLOATHES BE   270   ASCSN-HYMN   33
CLOATHS
    AS THY CLOATHS (WHEN THOU WITH CLOATHS WERE CLAD)   .   265   INTRO. 2   9
    AS THY CLOATHS (WHEN THOU WITH CLOATHS WERE CLAD)   .   265   INTRO. 2   9
    AND LIKE OLD CLOATHS FOLD UP THESE SKIES   .   .   349   L'ENVOY   8
CLOCKS
    WHERE BIRDS LIKE WATCHFUL CLOCKS THE NOISELESS DATE   .   245   MAN   3
CLOD
    BY EV'RY WANDRING CLOD.   248   I WALKT   42
CLOKE
    THIS VEYLE, I SAY, IS ALL THE CLOKE   277   COCK-CRWNG   39
CLOS'D
    WHEN WITH THESE EYES CLOS'D NOW BY THEE   .   .   .   337   THE THRONE   1
CLOSE
    UNTO HIS WORK, AND AT THE CLOSE OF DAY   .   .   286   PSALM 104   63
    DOEST WATER THE PARCH'D HILLS, WHOSE BREACHES CLOSE   .   285   PSALM 104   39
    I'LE JUDGE, WHERE PENAL FLAMES SIT MIXT AND CLOSE.   .   307   RAIN-BOW   38
    FOR WHERE THOU DOST NOT CLOSE THE EYE   .   .   .   277   COCK-CRWNG   27
    THOUGH THY CLOSE COMMERCE NOUGHT AT ALL IMBARRS   .   278   THE STARRE   5
    MAY PROVE THY GLORY, AND THEIR SHAME. SO CLOSE   .   234   MUTINIE   18
    KEEPING CLOSE HOUSE   225   RETIREMENT   2
    AND CLOSE ETERNITIE.   166   THE CALL   61
    BEING LAID, AND DREST FOR SLEEP, CLOSE NOT THY EYES   .   195   RLS + LSNS   127
    FRUSTRATE THOSE CANCEROUS, CLOSE ARTS   .   .   .   350   L'ENVOY   39
    I WILL CLOSE GIRT AND TYED   342   OBSEQUIES   15
CLOSE-DRAWN
    I SEE, THY CURTAINS ARE CLOSE-DRAWN, THY BOW   .   .   197   CORRUPTION   33
CLOSEST
    THE DARKEST NIGHT, AND CLOSEST NOOK.   .   .   .   235   CONSTLATN   8
CLOTHES
    THE FLOWRES WITHOUT CLOTHES LIVE   245   MAN   13
    THIS PAST, I THREW THE CLOTHES QUITE O'R HIS HEAD   .   247   I WALKT   29
CLOUD
    AND CLOUD WHICH SHADOWS THEE FROM ME.   .   .   .   277   COCK-CRWNG   40
    THE CLOUD DOTH NOW RECEIVE THEE, AND THEIR SIGHT   .   268   ASCN-DAY A   57
    HE IS MY PILLAR, AND MY CLOUD   221   PSALM 121   19
    LOOKS DIM TOO IN THE CLOUD   197   CORRUPTION   34
    WHOSE SUNS ARE ALL SET IN A CLOUD.   165   THE CALL   19
    UNDER SOME CLOUD   177   MRNG-WTCH   27
    SHOT O'R SOME CLOUD   174   JOY OF LIF   14
    WHEN ON SOME GILDED CLOUD, OR FLOWRE   .   .   .   169   RETREATE   11
    WHERE SHADOWES THICKEN, AND THE CLOUD   .   .   .   143   DEATH   12
    SO FROM LAHAI-ROIS WELL SOME SPICIE CLOUD   .   .   155   ISAACS M.   53
    UP IN ONE CLOUD, AND SO RETURNS THE SKIES   .   .   156   ISAACS M.   61
    WAS THEN THY DWELLING. DID SOME CLOUD   .   .   .   315   DWELLNG-PL   5

		PAGE	TITLE	LINE
CLOUD (CON'T)				
THEN PEACEFUL, SIGNAL BOW, BUT IN A CLOUD		307	RAIN-BOW	33
HOW IN A MYSTICK CLOUD		300	PROVIDENCE	7
(UNDER THAT STATELY AND MYSTERIOUS CLOUD		330	JACOBS PLW	22
SCATT'RING THAT CLOUD, SHEWD ME THE FLAME		332	AGREEMENT	9
IS LIKE A CLOUDED STARRE, WHOSE BEAMES THOUGH SEO		177	MRNG-WTCH	25
CLOUDIE				
SULLEN, AND SAD ECCLIPSES, CLOUDIE SPHERES		188	RELAPSE	19
AND CLOUDIE RITES.		211	FAITH	32
CLOUDLESS				
THEN THE NOONS CLOUDLESS LIGHT.		310	THE SEED	82
WHERE CLOUDLESS QUIRES SING WITHOUT TEARS		345	THE WREATH	18
TILL ALL BECOMES THY CLOUDLESS GLASS		349	L'ENVOY	12
CLOUDS				
THROUGH SADDEST CLOUDS TO THAT GLAD PLACE		345	THE WREATH	17
AND JOY, LIKE LIGHT, SHINES OFT IN CLOUDS.		342	OBSEQUIES	20
STORMS TURN TO MUSICK, CLOUDS TO SMILES AND AIR.		306	RAIN-BOW	10
THIS MADE HIM PUT ON CLOUDS, AND FIRE AND SMOKE		330	JACOBS PLW	7
THICK BUSIE CLOUDS DID MULTIPLY		333	AGREEMENT	39
LIKE CLOUDS, BEFORE THY GLORIOUS DAWN.		334	JUDGEMENT	10
THE CLOUDS THY CHARIOTS ARE, AND THY PATH-WAY		284	PSALM 104	11
WHAT THOUGH SOME CLOUDS DEFIANCE BID		294	BEGGING B	15
WHERE STARS, AND CLOUDS, BOTH LIGHT, AND SHADE		210	FAITH	15
THE PURSIE CLOUDS DISBAND, AND SCATTER		212	DAWNING	21
UPON THE CLOUDS AGAIN TO JUDGE THIS WORLD.		268	ASCN-DAY A	62
WITH CLOUDS AND RAIN, YET FULL AS CALM AND FINE		281	JOY	15
NOW WITH CLOUDS, NOW MAKING CLEAR		281	JOY	20
AND THREATNING CLOUDS WOULD NOT SO MUCH		230	LAW + GOSP	15
AND CLOUDS OF CRYING WITNESSES WITHOUT		232	THE WORLD	21
VAST CIRCLING AZURE, GIDDY CLOUDS, DAYS, NIGHTS.		194	RLS + LSNS	90
LORD, THEN ROUND ME WITH WEEPING CLOUDS		176	THE STORM	17
OF SLEEP, AND CLOUDS		176	MRNG-WTCH	6
TO PUT ON CLOUDS INSTEAD OF LIGHT		164	INCARNATN	5
BY CLOUDS SURPRIZ'D		161	PURSUITE	5
WHO GAVE THE CLOUDS SO BRAVE A BOW		167	VNTY SPRIT	4
BUT CLOUDS HANG ON.		178	SILENCE	4
OR IF AS YET (UNTIL THESE CLOUDS DEPART		157	BRT. CHRCH	12
HERE UNDER CLOUDS, WHERE STORMES, AND TEMPESTS BLAST		158	MANS FALL	2
BUT WHEN WE SAW THE CLOUDS TO CRACK		143	DEATH	23
THROUGH MELANCHOLLY CLOUDS, AND SAY		146	RSRCTN +IM	67
LIKE CLOUDS ECCLIPS'D MY MIND		139	RGNRTN	17
WHIRLE-WINDS, AND CLOUDS, AND THE SOFT VOICE		149	RELIGION	18
WHEN THOU SHALT MAKE THE CLOUDS THY SEATE		147	DAY OF JDG	21
TRAVELS IN CLOUDS, SEEKS MANNA, WHERE NONE IS.		153	THE SEARCH	95
CLOUDY				
IT GLOWS AND GLITTERS IN MY CLOUDY BREST		270	ALL GONE	5
WHOSE CLOUDY BREST COLD DAMPS INVADE		217	EASTER-DAY	2
CLOVEN				
OF CLOVEN TONGUES THEIR HEADS ALL BRUSH'D		272	WHT SUNDAY	7
CLOY				
AND CALM AND FULL, YET DOTH NOT CLOY.		345	QUICKNESS	12
CLUE				
THE MILKY WAY CHALKT CUT WITH SUNS, A CLUE		2	SON-DAYES	21
ATTEND AND WIND THE CLUE		236	CONSTLATN	14
CLUTCH				
WHERE HE DID CLUTCH HIS PREY, BUT ONE DID SEE		232	THE WORLD	25
CO-HEIRS				
ALL MAY BE NOW CO-HEIRS, NO NOISE		210	FAITH	9
COAL				
BREAK, AND THE SHADOWS FLEE, TOUCH WITH ONE COAL		216	DRESSING	3
COAL-FLAMES				
SUCH COAL-FLAMES SHEW BUT KITCHIN-ROOMS AT MOST.		320	HIDDN TRSR	6
COALESCENT				
FOR COALESCENT BY THAT BEND		302	THE KNOT	9
COASTS				
AND SATANS SEAT, IN ALL HER COASTS HATH LIGHT		331	JACOBS PLW	32
COAT				
AND ON CHRISTS COAT PIT ALL THEIR SHREDS.		272	WHT SUNDAY	14
THAT SEAMLESSE COAT		156	BRT. CHRCH	8
THY SEAMLESS COAT IS GROWN A RAG		350	L'ENVOY	30
COBWEBS				
I WILL NO LONGER COBWEBS SPIN		204	IDLE VERSE	3
COFFIN'D				
YET, HADST THOU CLIPT MY WINGS, WHEN COFFIN'D IN		161	DSTRQCTION	17
COLD				
THEIR YOUTH, AND BEAUTY, COLD SHOWRES NIPT, AND WRUNG		198	UNPRFTBLNS	5
NOR WAS HEAV'D COLD UNTO HIM, FOR EACH DAY		197	CORRUPTION	21
O'R-CAST WITH THAT COLD DUST.		183	THRS A TYE	4
COLD AFFECTIONS		172	MIDNIGHT	15
TO KINDLE MY COLD LOVE		271	ALL GONE	16
BUT OUR HEARTS DEAD AND SINFUL COLD.		274	WHT SUNDAY	52
WHICH, LIKE COLD FRIENDS, SEES US BUT ONCE A YEAR		247	I WALKT	12
WHOSE CLOUDY BREST COLD DAMPS INVADE		217	EASTER-DAY	2
THE COLD BY NIGHT, THE HEAT BY DAY		220	PSALM 121	11
AND WORK ON ME NOW COLD, NOW HOT		227	LV + DSPLN	14
TO MY COLD THOUGHTS A LIVELY SENSE OF SPRING.		245	MT. OLV. B	20
ON STONES DIDST SLEEP AND FOUND'ST BUT COLD RELIEF.		331	JACOBS PLW	46
O CHASE IN THAT COLD CALM MY FOES		334	AGREEMENT	65
THOU DOST BUT COURT COLD RAIN, TILL RAIN TURNS FIRE.		307	RAIN-BOW	42
WHY IS MY GOD THUS SLOW AND COLD		293	BEGGING B	9

		PAGE	TITLE	LINE
COLD	**(CON'T)**			
OF DEATH, DOST WASTE ALL SENSELESS, COLD AND DARK.		289	THE TIMBER	10
THESE MOUNTAINS OF COLD ICE IN ME. THOU ART		283	LOVE-SICK	12
COLOUR				
AND BOTH HER TASTE, AND COLOUR STAINES		150	RELIGION	36
COLOURS				
BEAUTY CONSISTS IN COLOURS, AND THAT'S BEST		222	AFFLICTION	25
COM'ST				
THOU DOST, THOU COM'ST, AND IN A SHOWR		214	MISERY	49
HITHER THOU COM'ST. THE BUSIE WIND ALL NIGHT		287	THE BIRD	1
COMBS				
DEDUCTED FROM THE WHOLE, THE COMBS, AND HIVE		2	SON-DAYES	19
COME				
AH. WHAT-TIME WILT THOU COME. WHEN SHALL THAT CRIE		211	DAWNING	1
SO WHEN THAT DAY, AND HOUR SHAL COME		212	DAWNING	45
WHO SHOULDST NOT THEN COME NEER TO ME		214	MISERY	46
O LET MY CRIE COME TO THY THRONE.		242	MISERY	107
COME SAPLESS BLOSSOM, CREEP NOT STIL ON EARTH		243	THE SAP	1
AS TRAVELLOURS WHEN THE TWILIGHT'S COME		228	PILGRIMAGE	1
THE AFTER-BURTHENS, AND GRIEFS YET TO COME		233	MUTINIE	3
TO SEE THEIR SOULS GREAT SHEPHEARD, WHO WAS COME		239	SHEPHEARDS	45
COME FORTH MOST FAIR AND YOUNG.		247	I WALKT	28
O COME. REFINE US WITH THY FIRE.		274	WHT SUNDAY	61
COME THEN THOU FAITHFUL WITNESS. COME DEAR LORD		268	ASCN-DAY A	61
COME THEN THOU FAITHFUL WITNESS. COME DEAR LORD		268	ASCN-DAY A	61
BEFORE DEATH COME		269	ASCSN-HYMN	9
AT CONSTANT WARRE WITH THEM. O COME AND REND		283	LOVE-SICK	9
BEFORE THEY COME, AND KNOW'ST HOW NEAR THEY BE.		289	THE TIMBER	16
OUR FULNESS TOO IS NOW COME IN		292	THE JEWS	27
COME, DROP YOUR BRANCHES, STROW THE WAY		294	PALM-SUNDY	1
NONE STAIN'D OR WITHER'D SHALL COME NEAR.		308	THE SEED	22
TILL THE WHITE WINGED REAPERS COME.		309	THE SEED	48
BUT I AM SURE, THOU DOST NOW COME		315	DWELLNG-PL	13
O COME, ARISE, SHINE, DO NOT STAY		334	JUDGEMENT	11
MY FELLOW-CREATURES TOO SAY, COME.		335	JUDGEMENT	15
O COME AWAY		339	THE FEAST	1
COME WHILE MY HEART IS CLEAN AND STEDDY.		339	THE FEAST	3
TYR'D HERE, I COME TO SYCHAR, THENCE		151	THE SEARCH	21
ALL WAS PLAIN, MODEST TRUTH, NOR DID SHE COME		155	ISAACS M.	33
COME THEN, MY GOD.		172	MIDNIGHT	21
COME, COME, WHAT DOE I HERE.		170	COME, COME	1
COME, COME, WHAT DOE I HERE.		170	COME, COME	1
COME, COME.		170	COME, COME	5
COME, COME.		170	COME, COME	5
COME, COME.		171	COME, COME	15
COME, COME.		171	COME, COME	15
COME, COME.		171	COME, COME	25
COME, COME.		171	COME, COME	25
O COME LORD JESUS QUICKLY.		181	BURIALL	40
LORD HASTE, LORD COME		181	BURIALL	39
O, YES. THOU KNOW'ST I DOE, COME, AND RELIEVE		161	DSTRQCTION	28
YET, COME, AND LET'S PERUSE THEM ALL.		165	THE CALL	20
COME MY HEART. COME MY HEAD		164	THE CALL	1
COME MY HEART. COME MY HEAD		164	THE CALL	1
TO MEALES WHEN THOU DOEST COME, GIVE HIM THE PRAISE		195	RLS + LSNS	97
SHAL HE THAT DID COME DOWN FROM THENCE		200	NTVTY 2	9
WHEN SHAL THAT TRAVELLER COME HOME		189	RESOLVE	7
IF TRIALS COME, THIS WIL MAKE GOOD THY PART		193	RLS + LSNS	57
FOR HONESTY IS SAFE, COME WHAT CAN HAP.		193	RLS + LSNS	58
THAT WOULD NOT HAVE THE TRUE COME ON.		344	QUICKNESS	4
COME THEN TRUE BREAD		339	THE FEAST	13
COME, ANTEDATE		339	THE FEAST	16
COMELY				
THE COMELY SPACIOUS WHALE.		286	PSALM 104	72
COMES				
A GARLAND, WHERE COMES NEITHER RAIN, NOR WIND.		283	GARLAND	36
THOU DARKNESS, AND THEN COMES THE NIGHT.		286	PSALM 104	53
YOUR SHADES AND FRESHNESS COMES TO BORROW.		294	PALM-SUNDY	6
OF YOUR DELIVERER COMES		291	THE JEWS	2
AND COMES NEXT MORNING FRESH AS HE.		300	PROVIDENCE	24
FOR HERE COMES HE		294	PALM-SUNDY	15
WHERE COMES NO STAIN.		329	TEARS	1
COMES LIKE A CHILDES, SPOTLESS AND FRESH.		306	ST MARY MN	70
WHEN NIGHT COMES, LIST THY DEEDS, MAKE PLAIN THE WAY		195	RLS + LSNS	115
THEN COMES HE.		270	ASCSN-HYMN	31
BUT WHEN THY MASTER COMES, THEY'L FINDE AND SEE		275	PROFFER	41
FOR AFTER THEIR LIGHT, DARKNESS COMES		272	WHT SUNDAY	3
THEN COMES THE LIGHT. WHICH WHEN YOU SPY		266	VAIN WITS	10
BRINGS TO, AND COMES FROM HEAVEN.		244	THE SAP	50
THY WRETCH COMES BEGGING		215	PRAISE	47
EXPECTING TILL THY SAVICUR COMES		209	THE BURIAL	11
COMET				
I WILL ON THEE, AS ON A COMET LOOK		307	RAIN-BOW	35
A COMET, THE SAD WORLDS ILL-BODING BOOK.		307	RAIN-BOW	36
COMFORT				
THEY COULD NOT CURE, NOR COMFORT THEE)		304	ST MARY MN	36
FOR UNTIL THOU DIDST COMFORT ME		333	AGREEMENT	37
THAT YOU'L CONFESS THE COMFORT SUCH, AS EVEN		244	THE SAP	49
NAY, THOU TAK'ST OURS, AND (WHICH FUL COMFORT BRINGS)		230	LAW + GOSP	19
BE MY COMFORT, AND THY PRAISE		249	BEGGING A	8

	PAGE	TITLE	LINE
COMFORT (CON'T)			
O MY SOLE COMFORT, TAKE NO MORE THESE WAYES . . .	188	RELAPSE	9
COMFORTER			
UNTO THAT COMFORTER, THE SUN	203	DSRDR + FR	33
COMFORTS			
WHERE LIGHT, JOY, LEISURE, AND TRUE COMFORTS MOVE . .	248	I WALKT	59
MY THOUGHTS DID SWIM IN COMFORTS, AND MINE EYE . .	244	MT. OLV. B	9
KING OF COMFORTS. KING OF LIFE.	214	PRAISE	1
COMFORTS AND JOYS, AND HOPES EACH HOUR	326	ABELS BLOD	26
GATHER TRUE COMFORTS, BUT THE WICKED LIVER . . .	287	PSALM 104	94
COMING			
AND NOW THOU KNEWEST HER COMING, IT WAS TIME . . .	155	ISAACS M.	43
COMMAND			
BY WHOSE ASSISTING, SWIFT COMMAND	300	PROVIDENCE	2
AND ALL THAT DISTANCE WAS LAW AND COMMAND. . . .	331	JACOBS PLW	48
FINDES THY POOR FOAL AT THY COMMAND	319	THE ASS	46
THE SWORD WHEREWITH THOU DOST COMMAND	316	MEN OF WAR	25
WITHOUT COMMAND YOU NEVER ACTED OUGHT	236	CONSTLATN	35
COMMAND AND GUIDE THE EYE.	278	THE STARRE	24
COMMANDS			
AT THY COMMANDS	215	PRAISE	43
WHOSE BLESSED, SWEET COMMANDS DO POUR	326	ABELS BLOD	25
I'LE SEAL MY EYES UP, AND TO THY COMMANDS . . .	321	HIDDN TRSR	29
COMMANDS THE BEAUTEOUS FILES	184	PEACE	8
COMMENCE			
AND EVERY ACT SHE DOTH COMMENCE	311	FAIR+YONG	19
COMMEND			
SUCCESSFUL WICKEDNESS COMMEND.	316	MEN OF WAR	16
AND WHATSOE'R THOU SHALT COMMEND	167	THE CALL	88
COMMENDS			
THIS TRUTH COMMENDS	174	JOY OF LIF	6
COMMERCE			
WHO CAN HAVE COMMERCE WITH THE LIGHT)	168	VNTY SPRIT	32
HE KEEPES A COMMERCE IN THE NIGHT	162	PURSUITE	7
THAT BUSIE COMMERCE KEPT BETWEEN	313	THE STONE	20
HAVE COMMERCE SOMTIMES WITH POOR DUST	212	DAWNING	40
THERE GOD A COMMERCE STATES, AND SHEDS . . .	279	THE STARRE	27
THOUGH THY CLOSE COMMERCE NOUGHT AT ALL IMBARRS . .	278	THE STARRE	5
THY FORTY DAYS MORE SECRET COMMERCE HERE . . .	268	ASCN-DAY A	33
AND BY THIS LESSER COMMERCE KEEP.	273	WHT SUNDAY	22
COMMING			
THE BRIDEGROOME'S COMMING. FIL THE SKY.	211	DAWNING	2
COMMISSIONS			
HAVE THEIR COMMISSIONS FROM DIVINITIE	278	THE STARRE	10
BUT HERE COMMISSION'D BY A BLACK SELF-WIL . . .	237	CONSTLATN	37
COMMITS			
SIN EVERY DAY COMMITS MORE WASTE	335	JUDGEMENT	28
COMMON			
FOR THIS RICH PEARL, LIKE SOME MORE COMMON STONE . .	330	JACOBS PLW	17
TO BE A COMMON RACK.	238	SHEPHEARDS	30
MADE LIFE MY COMMON STAKE.	282	GARLAND	14
DISSOLVE INTO THE COMMON CROSS.	274	WHT SUNDAY	64
THY BODY AS THEIR COMMON MEAT	217	DRESSING	38
DEATH TO THE COMMON EYE	166	THE CALL	59
AND COMMON URN	179	SILENCE	22
THEN COMMON PAY	342	OBSEQUIES	2
THE COMMON PASS	343	WATER-FALL	7
COMMONWEALTH			
WITH YOUR COMMONWEALTH AND GLORY.	275	PROFFER	36
COMMUNION			
THY MYSTICALL COMMUNION	216	DRESSING	14
COMPANIONS			
THY YOUTHS COMPANIONS	201	THE CHECK	26
COMPANY			
HIM COMPANY ALL DAY, AND IN HIM SLEEP.	191	RLS + LSNS	6
AMONGST THAT CHOSEN COMPANY	317	MEN OF WAR	50
COMPAR'D			
ALL OTHER DAYS, COMPAR'D TO THEE	334	JUDGEMENT	7
COMPARE			
O LET NO STAR COMPARE WITH THEE.	281	THE FAVOUR	9
COMPASSIONS			
BUT THY COMPASSIONS CANNOT FAIL.	333	AGREEMENT	46
COMPLAIN			
WHOSE STREAMS STILL VOCAL, STILL COMPLAIN . . .	325	ABELS BLOD	3
DID THEIR COMPLAIN	231	THE WORLD	9
COMPLEAT			
THROUGH HIM COMPLEAT.	211	FAITH	36
COMPLEMENT			
BUT HERE WAS NE'R A COMPLEMENT, NOT ONE . . .	155	ISAACS M.	31
HAD'ST NE'R AN OATH, NOR COMPLEMENT. THOU WERT . .	154	ISAACS M.	13
NEW SEV'RAL OATHES, AND COMPLEMENTS (TOO) PLENTY. . .	154	ISAACS M.	16
COMPLY			
PLANTS IN THE ROOT WITH EARTH DO MOST COMPLY . .	223	TEMPEST	33
WHO SEES INVISIBLES, AND DOTH COMPLY	327	RIGHTSNESS	11
COMPLYING			
OR BY COMPLYING WITH THE WORLD	322	CHILDEHOOD	23
COMPRISE			
HE DOTH COMPRISE. BUT IN THIS AIRE	163	MT. OLVS A	29
CONCEAL			
WILL NOR CONCEAL NOR ASSENT TO	313	THE STONE	8

	PAGE	TITLE	LINE
CONCEAL'D			
INTO A PILLAR, AND CONCEAL'D FROM MEN.	331	JACOBS PLW	36
CONCEALS			
ALL THAT MAN DOTH, CONCEALS OR SHOWS	314	THE STONE	31
CONCEIT			
CONCEIT, OR CALL IT WHAT YOU PLEASE	162	MT. OLVS A	6
CONCEIVE			
TO ACT AS WELL AS TO CONCEIVE.	329	ANGUISH	18
CONCERNING			
CONCERNING THEE, MUST PASSE.	166	THE CALL	49
CONDEMN			
CONDEMN MEN. BUT WILL TRY THEM BY	314	THE STONE	34
CONDEMNED			
HE CAME (CONDEMNED) HITHER	196	CORRUPTION	6
CONDEMNING			
CONDEMNING THOUGHTS (LIKE SAD ECCLIPSES) SCOWL	232	THE WORLD	19
CONF'RENCE			
WE HAVE NO CONF'RENCE IN THESE DAIES	149	RELIGION	20
CONFER			
AND FAMILIARLY CONFER	291	THE JEWS	6
CONFESS			
FOR SHE IS BRAVEST, YOU CONFESS.	303	ORNAMENT	20
O GOD. I KNOW AND DO CONFESS	333	AGREEMENT	43
THAT YOU'L CONFESS THE COMFORT SUCH, AS EVEN	244	THE SAP	49
CONFESSE			
WHICH I CONFESSE WITH ALL MY SOUL	207	REPENTANCE	25
LORD, I CONFESSE THE HEYNOUS SCORE	208	REPENTANCE	57
CONFESSION			
MY GOD, ACCEPT OF MY CONFESSION.	207	REPENTANCE	26
CONFEST			
CONFEST, THE WORLD DID ONLY PAINT AND LIE.	244	MT. OLV. B	10
CONFIDENCE			
WITH FILIAL CONFIDENCE WE TOUCH EV'N THEE.	229	LAW + GOSP	13
TO SINNERS CONFIDENCE, LIFE TO THE GRAVE.	159	MANS FALL	26
CONFIN'D			
WHAT GLANCE OF DAY HAST THOU CONFIN'D	276	COCK-CRWNG	2
IF A STAR WERE CONFIN'D INTO A TOMB	271	ALL GONE	29
CONFINE			
O LET THY JUSTICE THEN IN HIM CONFINE	209	REPENTANCE	85
CONFORMABLE			
AND MADE CONFORMABLE TO HIS	349	L'ENVOY	5
CONFOUND			
BOTH STARS AND ELEMENTS CONFOUND	147	DAY OF JDG	7
CONFUSED			
FALSE ECCHOES, AND CONFUSED SOUNDS	150	RELIGION	38
CONFUSIONS			
THSES DARK CONFUSIONS, THAT WITHIN ME NEST	216	DRESSING	7
CONIES			
THE ROCKS GIVE CONIES A RETYRING PLACE.	286	PSALM 104	50
CONJUNCTION			
BE IN CONJUNCTION WITH TRUE LIGHT.	332	AGREEMENT	16
CONQUERERS			
THY SAINTS ARE NOT THE CONQUERERS.	316	MEN OF WAR	18
CONQUERORS			
THESE CONQUERORS BEFORE IT FALL	317	MEN OF WAR	48
CONQUEST			
WHOSE GLORIOUS CONQUEST NOTHING CAN RESIST	216	DRESSING	11
CONQUESTS			
WITHOUT HIS BRAGS AND CONQUESTS LIES	318	THE ASS	27
CONSCIENCE			
WHAT NEEDS A CONSCIENCE CALM AND BRIGHT	309	THE SEED	41
AND HEALTH OF CONSCIENCE IT IS TO BE HAD.	327	RIGHTSNESS	36
WHEN CONSCIENCE BY LEW'D USE HAD NOT LOST SENSE	154	ISAACS M.	19
A DARTING CONSCIENCE FULL OF STABS, AND FEARS.	188	RELAPSE	17
WRONG NOT THY CONSCIENCE FOR A ROTTEN STICK	193	RLS + LSNS	41
MY CONSCIENCE WITH A SINFUL SOUND	169	RETREATE	16
CONSENT			
THEMSELVES AND OTHERS, I CONSENT AND RUN	324	THE NIGHT	45
CONSENT TO ANY GAINFUL ILL	313	THE STONE	11
AND ALMOST FAMISH'D, EVER WILL CONSENT	275	PROFFER	21
CONSEQUENCE			
HAD WRIT DOWN ITS SAD CONSEQUENCE	311	FAIR+YONG	20
CONSIDER'D			
I HAVE CONSIDER'D IT. AND FIND	189	RESOLVE	1
CONSIGNER			
MY FIRST CONSIGNER UNTO THOSE	344	WATER-FALL	25
CONSISTS			
BEAUTY CONSISTS IN COLOURS, AND THAT'S BEST	222	AFFLICTION	25
CONSORT			
A CONSORT MAKE.	199	NTVTY 1	9
A CONSORT RAISE	182	CHRFLNESS	23
CONSORTS			
WHERE THEY NEW CONSORTS CHOOSE AND STICK	348	HOLY BIBLE	11
CONSPIRE			
ABSENTS WITHIN THE LINE CONSPIRE, AND SENSE	183	THRS A TYE	9
CONSTANT			
ONE CONSTANT SPRING.	186	PASSION	50
TO THY SURE TROT, A CONSTANT, HUMBLE MIND	193	RLS + LSNS	50
WERE ALL THE YEAR ONE CONSTANT SUN-SHINE, WEE	222	AFFLICTION	21
AT CONSTANT WARRE WITH THEM. O COME AND REND	283	LOVE-SICK	9

	PAGE	TITLE	LINE
CONSTELLATION			
THE SACRED CONSTELLATION OF THY MIND.	154	ISAACS M.	10
CONSUM'D			
SHALL BE CONSUM'D. O MY SOUL, BLESS THY LORD.	287	PSALM 104	95
CONSUME			
ALL THINGS IN BEING) THEY CONSUME AND MOURN.	287	PSALM 104	78
CONSUMPTION			
AND A CONSUMPTION THAT DOTH PLEASE.	273	WHT SUNDAY	44
CONTACTION			
NOR GIVE, NOR TAKE CONTACTION	183	THRS A TYE	6
CONTEMPT			
OUR FEARES, AND FALLS BROUGHT TO CONTEMPT	143	DEATH	18
EVEN TO CONTEMPT THY KINGDOME DOWN	218	EASTER HYM	14
BUT IN CONTEMPT, AS STILL WE SEE	317	MEN OF WAR	32
CONTEND			
IN MUSICK DOTH CONTEND.	200	NTVTY 2	4
CONTENT			
WITH THEIR CONTENT TOO IN MY POW'R	321	CHILDEHOOD	6
ONLY CONTENT, AND LOVE, AND HUMBLE JOYS	239	SHEPHEARDS	35
CONTENTED			
WHO IS CONTENTED, THAT THIS HOLY FLAME	331	JACOBS PLW	38
CONTENTED THOUGHTS, INNOXIOUS EASE	317	MEN OF WAR	42
CONTEST			
AND INFANTS WITH THY PANGS CONTEST	218	EASTER HYM	11
A DARK CONTEST OF WAVES AND WINDE.	344	QUICKNESS	7
CONTRACTION			
SCARCE WARMS, BUT BY CONTRACTION	189	RESOLVE	15
CONTROUL			
DOTH ALL THEIR PLOTS CONTROUL	220	PSALM 121	14
CONVERSATION			
THIS CONVERSATION, BUT THE GOOD MAN LYES	195	RLS + LSNS	125
CONVERTS			
I SEE THAT MORNING IN THY CONVERTS TEARS	267	ASCN-DAY A	19
CONVEY			
FAND BY A GENTLE GALE CONVEY AND BREATH	244	MT. OLV. B	5
DOEST THOU CONVEY MAN FOOD AND MONEY	300	PROVIDENCE	9
AND OFT LEFT OPEN WOULD'ST CONVEY	348	HOLY BIBLE	19
COOL			
DOTH THY TRANSPARENT, COOL AND WATRY WEALTH	343	WATER-FALL	2
ABOVE THEM THE COOL MOON HER KNOWN COURSE HOLDS	286	PSALM 104	51
THERE THE WILDE ASSES SWALLOW THE COOL SPRING.	285	PSALM 104	34
THE COOL O'TH DAY.	2	SON-DAYES	12
COOL TO A GLORIOUS EVENING, AND EXPIRE.	195	RLS + LSNS	114
COOL'D			
COOL'D BY THE DAMPS OF NIGHT, DESCENDS	203	DSRDR + FR	36
COOLD			
AND SOMETHING COOLD THE PARCH'D, AND THIRSTIE ISLE	156	ISAACS M.	58
COOLE			
UNTILL THE COOLE, AND SHACY EVEN.	149	RELIGION	16
OR THE COOLE MIRTLES CANOPIE	148	RELIGION	6
COOPERS			
COTSWOLD, AND COOPERS BOTH HAVE MET	162	MT. OLVS A	9
COPYED			
THAT COPYED IT, PRESENTS IT THEE.	265	INTRO. 2	2
CORDIAL			
BY WIL OUR SAP, AND CORDIAL. NOW IN THIS	243	THE SAP	27
CORDIALS			
CORDIALS IN EVERY DROP, AND WINE.	150	RELIGION	32
NEW CORDIALS, NEW CATHARTICS DEAL.	333	AGREEMENT	58
CORN			
AND PURLING CORN DOTH CLOATH THE VALE.	337	PSALM 65	46
WHITHER GOOD CORN, OR FRUITLESS WEEDS.	347	THE BOOK	10
CORNE			
AND TARES HAD CHOAKT THE CORNE	166	THE CALL	73
ADORES DEAD DUST, SETS HEART ON CORNE AND GRASS	236	CONSTLATN	19
CORNER-STONE			
BUT THERE WAS NOT THE CORNER-STONE.	152	THE SEARCH	48
CORRODE			
WHICH NEITHER TYRES, NOR DOTH CORRODE	318	THE ASS	11
CORRUPT			
IN A CORRUPT SECURITIE	212	DAWNING	30
CORRUPTEST			
CHIDE, AND FLY UP, MISTS OF CORRUPTEST FOME	223	TEMPEST	26
CORRUPTION			
CORRUPTION WITH THIS GLORIOUS RING	167	VNTY SPRIT	6
CORSE			
BUT THIS CORSE FLEECE	173	CONTENT	2
COST			
(UNTO MY COST)	159	MANS FALL	12
BOTH COST THEE DEER	191	THE MATCH	20
AND CUR'D BY CROSSES AT THY COST.	227	LV + DSPLN	9
COSTLY			
NO COSTLY PRICE, NO SOFT-CLOATH'D LUXURIE	239	SHEPHEARDS	31
COT			
TO SNUDGE IN, AND EMBRACE A COT	214	MISERY	66
COTS			
EACH STIRRING WIND AND STORM BLEW THROUGH THEIR COTS	239	SHEPHEARDS	33
COTSWOLD			
COTSWOLD, AND COOPERS BOTH HAVE MET	162	MT. OLVS A	9
COTT			
AND IN THIS COTT	180	BURIALL	18

		PAGE	TITLE	LINE

COTTAGE
HIS COTTAGE FAILES, WHOSE NARROW SPAN   •   •   •   •   166   THE CALL   44
HIS PASSIVE COTTAGE, WHICH (THOUGH LAID ASIDE)   •   •   145   RSRCTN +IM   45
THE SMALL, STILL VOICE, AT SOME LOW COTTAGE KNOCKS   •   •   330   JACOBS PLW   9
COTTS
AND BETHLEMS HUMBLE COTTS ABOVE THEM STEPT   •   •   •   238   SHEPHEARDS   21
COUNSELL
I PLAYED WITH FIRE, DID COUNSELL SPURN   •   •   •   •   282   GARLAND   13
COUNSELS
THROUGH ALL THY ACTIONS, COUNSELS, AND DISCOURSE   •   •   193   RLS + LSNS   37
COUNT
HAVE YET MORE DAYS, MORE NIGHTS TO COUNT   •   •   •   229   PILGRIMAGE   26
COUNT BUT THE BLOTS OF A VAIN PEN.   •   •   •   •   335   JUDGEMENT   26
WHO CANNOT COUNT THOSE THEY HAVE SLAIN   •   •   •   325   ABELS BLOD   12
COUNTING
AND POOR, DESPISED TRUTH SATE COUNTING BY   •   •   •   232   THE WORLD   44
COUNTRIE
TO GOD, THY COUNTRIE, AND THY FRIEND BE TRUE   •   •   193   RLS + LSNS   43
MY SOUL, THERE IS A COUNTRIE   •   •   •   •   •   184   PEACE   1
COUNTRY
THERE IS THY COUNTRY, AND HE IS THE WAY   •   •   •   243   THE SAP   15
COURAGE
LORD, WITH WHAT COURAGE, AND DELIGHT   •   •   •   182   CHRFLNESS   1
COURSE
AND COURSE OF THINGS   •   •   •   •   •   146   RSRCTN +IM   54
A DECRYED COURSE, SURE IT PREVAIL'D NOT MUCH.   •   •   154   ISAACS M.   12
BUT IN HER LONG, AND HIDDEN COURSE   •   •   •   150   RELIGION   33
AND WHERE BEFORE I DID NO SAFE COURSE STEER   •   •   244   MT. OLV. B   11
BE DUMB COURSE MEASURES, JAR NO MORE. TO ME   •   •   280   JOY   1
YET LET MY COURSE, MY AIM, MY LOVE   •   •   •   212   DAWNING   43
HIS RIGHTEOUS COURSE, THAT THOUGH HE KNOWS   •   •   314   THE STONE   30
ABOVE THEM THE COOL MOON HER KNOWN COURSE HOLDS   •   286   PSALM 104   51
(FOR WHICH COURSE MAN SEEMS MUCH THE FITTER BORN)   •   287   THE BIRD   4
RISE TO A LONGER COURSE MORE BRIGHT AND BRAVE.   •   343   WATER-FALL   12
WHICH REACH BY COURSE THE BANK, AND THEN   •   •   •   344   WATER-FALL   35
COURSES
AND THEN YOU IN YOUR COURSES FOUGHT.   •   •   •   236   CONSTLATN   36
COURT
WOULD MAKE A COURT, SHOULD HE THERE DWEL.   •   •   240   MISERY   36
THOU DOST BUT COURT COLD RAIN, TILL RAIN TURNS FIRE.   •   307   RAIN-BOW   42
COURTS
OF A FULL FEAST, AND THE OUT COURTS OF GLORY.   •   •   •   2   SON-DAYES   24
COVENANT
AND MINDES THE COVENANT 'TWIXT ALL AND ONE.   •   •   306   RAIN-BOW   18
THY COVENANT BY CHRIST EXTENDS.   •   •   •   •   333   AGREEMENT   52
WHO KEEPS HIS COVENANT EVEN WITH OUR DUST.   •   •   144   RSRCTN +IM   18
COVER
COVER'D IT, SINCE A COVER MADE   •   •   •   •   347   THE BOOK   12
COVER'D
COVER'D IT, SINCE A COVER MADE   •   •   •   •   347   THE BOOK   12
COVERING
A COVERING O'RE THIS AGED BOOK   •   •   •   •   347   THE BOOK   19
COVERT
ROAR IN THE COVERT OF THE WOODS, AND SEEK   •   •   286   PSALM 104   58
COY
WILL THOSE COY SPIRITS CAST ASLEEP   •   •   •   297   HERODIAS   10
IN SPIRES, GLOBES, ANGRY CURLS AND COY   •   •   304   ST MARY MN   18
AS WITHOUT WOOING WINS THE COY   •   •   •   281   THE FAVOUR   4
COYL
AND KNEW THEIR COYL   •   •   •   •   •   •   234   MUTINIE   10
COYN'D
OF THESE OUR DAYES, THOU COULDST HAVE COYN'D THEE TWENTY   154   ISAACS M.   15
CRACK
BUT WHEN WE SAW THE CLOUDS TO CRACK   •   •   •   143   DEATH   23
HE DREW THE CURSE UPON THE WORLD, AND CRACKT   •   •   197   CORRUPTION   15
CRADLE
HIS INNE, AND CRADLE, BEING THERE   •   •   •   151   THE SEARCH   7
CRANIES
AND IN THOSE CRANIES LIGHT APPEAR'D   •   •   •   143   DEATH   24
CRAVE
NOR MUST WE FOR THE KERNELL CRAVE   •   •   •   150   RELIGION   47
WHERE, IF A TRAVELLER WATER CRAVE   •   •   •   212   DAWNING   31
BID THY POOR ASS (WITH TEARS I CRAVE)   •   •   •   329   TEARS   11
SINCE DYING FOR ME, THOU DIDST CRAVE NO MORE   •   •   342   OBSEQUIES   1
CRAVES
THIS IS THE HEART HE CRAVES, AND WHO SO WILL   •   •   279   THE STARRE   29
CREATED
CREATED GLORIES UNDER THEE.   •   •   •   •   271   ALL GONE   34
CREATION
THE WHOLE CREATION SHAKES OFF NIGHT   •   •   •   212   DAWNING   17
IN THE CREATION SHED, AND SLAV'D TO SENCE   •   •   223   TEMPEST   19
AND TAUGHT OBEDIENCE BY THE WHOLE CREATION   •   •   237   CONSTLATN   55
CREATOR
WITH WHICH THEIR GREAT CREATOR HAD THEM DREST.   •   •   268   ASCN-DAY A   44
CREATURE
OF THIS POOR CREATURE, BY A GRACIOUS ART   •   •   •   223   TEMPEST   22
CREATURES
THE CREATURES JUBILE, GODS PARLE WITH DUST.   •   •   •   2   SON-DAYES   13
THE BLADES OF GRASSE, THY CREATURES FEEDING   •   •   207   REPENTANCE   33
THY CREATURES BONDAGE AND ABUSE.   •   •   •   335   JUDGEMENT   32

		PAGE	TITLE	LINE
CREATURES	(CON'T)			
BUT THESE DUMB CREATURES ARE SO TRUE	. . . .	313	THE STONE	12
GOD AND HIS CREATURES, THOUGH UNSEEN.	. . .	313	THE STONE	21
CREATURES A BED	. . .	144	RSRCTN +IM	4
THY OTHER CREATURES IN THIS SCENE	. . .	187	NO DO THEY	23
VIEW THY FORE-RUNNERS. CREATURES GIV'N TO BE	. . .	201	THE CHECK	25
THROUGH ALL THE CREATURES, CAME AT LAST	. . .	168	VNTY SPRIT	14
AND THROUGH THY CREATURES PIERCE AND PASS	. . .	349	L'ENVOY	11
A STATE FOR WHICH THY CREATURES ALL . . .	. .	350	L'ENVOY	21
CREEK				
AND SEARCH OUT EV'RY HOLE, AND CREEK.	. . .	240	MISERY	12
NOT THIS WITH CATARACTS AND CREEKS.	. . .	344	WATER-FALL	40
CREEP				
COME SAPLESS BLOSSOM, CREEP NOT STIL ON EARTH	. . .	243	THE SAP	1
OR FROM THEE CREEP	. . .	219	HOLY COMM.	39
'TWIXT THEE, AND ME, AND OFTIMES CREEP	. . .	203	DSRDR + FR	10
BUT OUT OF PARADISE MUST CREEPE . . .	. . .	166	THE CALL	68
SOME DROWSIE SILK-WORME CREEPE	. . .	144	RSRCTN +IM	5
'TIS DEAD NIGHT ROUND ABOUT. HORROR DOTH CREEPE	. .	157	THE LAMPE	1
STILL AS THOU BURN'ST, AND THE WARME DROPPINGS CREEPE	.	158	THE LAMPE	14
CREEPES				
HOW NEERE REDEMPTION CREEPES.	. . .	143	DEATH	30
CREEPING				
INNUMERABLE, CREEPING THINGS BOTH SMALL	. . .	286	PSALM 104	70
CREEPS				
CREEPS FORTH, AND PINCH'D FOR FOOD, WITH SCENT AND SIGHT		286	PSALM 104	55
CREEPT				
MY FORWARD FLESH CREEPT ON, AND SUBTLY STOLE	. .	206	REPENTANCE	5
CRIE				
AH. WHAT TIME WILT THOU COME. WHEN SHALL THAT CRIE	. .	211	DAWNING	1
WITH THESE I CRIE, AND CRYING PINE . . .	. .	242	MISERY	112
O LET MY CRIE COME TO THY THRONE. . . .	. .	242	MISERY	107
I FLUNG AWAY, AND WITH FULL CRIE . . .	. .	282	GARLAND	9
CRIES				
AND STIL OUR CRIES	. . .	213	ADMISSION	16
FOR THOSE THAT SPILT IT. MAY NO CRIES	. . .	326	ABELS BLOD	37
BUT HARK. WHAT TRUMPETS THAT. WHAT ANGEL CRIES	. .	197	CORRUPTION	39
CRIMES				
AND PENALTIES SPREAD TO OUR CRIMES.	. . .	273	WHT SUNDAY	32
CRINGE				
SPRUCE, SUPPLE CRINGE, OR STUDY'D LOOK PUT ON	. .	155	ISAACS M.	32
CROSS				
THEN FROM THY CROSS UNTO THESE DAYS . .	. . .	273	WHT SUNDAY	35
FIX'D LATELY ON THE CROSS, NOW ON THE SKIES.	. .	268	ASCN-DAY A	54
WHO BEARS HIS CROSS WITH JOY . . .	. . .	328	RIGHTSNESS	37
AND WOULD BE CROSS, WHEN GOD WAS KINDE.	. .	292	THE JEWS	25
O PAINFUL CROSS, MY BED OF REST. . .	. . .	341	THE FEAST	63
I CLIMB'D THE HILL, PERUS'D THE CROSSE . .	. .	152	THE SEARCH	41
THUS BY THE CROSSE SALVATION RUNNES . .	. .	167	THE CALL	74
BUT CROSSE TO THOSE	. . .	174	CONTENT	23
CROSSES				
GIVE ME, O GIVE ME CROSSES HERE . . .	. .	147	DAY OF JDG	33
SICKNESS IS WHOLSOME, AND CROSSES ARE BUT CURBS	. .	221	AFFLICTION	17
AND CUR'D BY CROSSES AT THY COST. . .	. .	227	LV + DSPLN	9
CROST				
AND HAPPY I TO BE SO CROST	. .	227	LV + DSPLN	8
CROUD				
AND GLIDE A CROUD.	. . .	174	JOY OF LIF	16
GLORY, THE CROUDS CHEAP TINSEL STILL . .	. .	309	THE SEED	37
CROWD				
THIS GOD FORESAW. AND WHEN SLAIN BY THE CROWD	. .	330	JACOBS PLW	21
CROWD, AND GATHER	. . .	185	PASSION	28
THOU HADST NO POMPOUS TRAIN, NOR ANTIK CROWD	. .	154	ISAACS M.	21
SEEK NOT THE SAME STEPS WITH THE CROWD, STICK THOU	. .	193	RLS + LSNS	49
WHETHER ABROAD, AMIDST THE CROWD . .	. .	221	PSALM 121	17
CROWN				
TO CROWN HIS TEMPLES. SEAL DREAMS BE HIS LAW.	. .	224	TEMPEST	52
NOW CAST AT NIGHT MY CROWN AWAY. . . .	. .	275	PROFFER	30
SHROWD IN THEIR BIRTHS. THE CROWN OF LIFE, LIGHT, TRUTH	.	192	RLS + LSNS	27
WHAT PLEASURES SHOULD MY JOIRNEY CROWN	. .	152	THE SEARCH	68
ON THEE, WERE ALL MET IN ONE CROWN . .	. .	309	THE SEED	30
AND FAITH TO SEE MY CROWN AS NEAR . .	. .	317	MEN OF WAR	38
MAY HIS CROWN, LIKE HIS HOPES, BE CLAY . .	. .	301	PROVIDENCE	35
WITH THEE, AND CROWN THY BROW. . . .	. .	284	PSALM 104	4
AND CROWN DRY HILS WITH WELLS AND FLOWERS.	. .	341	THE FEAST	54
O THORNY CROWN	. . .	341	THE FEAST	61
AND CROWN'D MY HEAD WITH ROSES. . . .	. .	282	GARLAND	24
CROWN'D THEE WITH THORNS, AND BOW'D THE KNEE	. .	317	MEN OF WAR	31
THE YEAR IS WITH THY GOODNESS CROWN'D . .	. .	337	PSALM 65	39
SWEET PEACE SITS CROWN'D WITH SMILES . .	. .	184	PEACE	6
AND CROWN'D THEM WITH PROPHETIC FIRE. . .	. .	272	WHT SUNDAY	8
OF WORMWOOD, AND A DEATHS-HEAD CROWN'D WITH ROSES.	. .	280	JOY	6
THY LOCKS CROWN'D WITH ETERNITIE. . .	. .	211	DAWNING	12
ON SOME PARCH'D BANK, CROWN'D WITH A FLOWRIE WREATH.	.	244	MT. OLV. B	6
ALL CROWN'D WITH VICTORY	. .	237	CONSTLATN	50
CROWND				
THOU HAS CROWND HIM ALREADY. . . .	. .	167	THE CALL	93
CROWNE				
AND DECK ME , LORD, WITH THE SAME CROWNE	. . .	167	THE CALL	92
CROWNING				
EXALTED PLEASURES, CROWNING BLISSES . .	. .	348	HOLY BIBLE	30

		PAGE	TITLE	LINE
CROWNS				
THEIR MASTERS WILL, MEET TO RECEIVE THEIR CRCWNS.		280	PALM-TREE	20
GLORY, ANC GOLD, AND CRCWNS AND THRONES		308	THE SEED	3
CRUDE				
DARK, VCID, AND CRUDE		218	HOLY COMM.	7
CRUELL				
WHAT CRUELL SMART		185	PASSION	10
CRUELTIE				
'MIDST SO MUCH BLCUD, AND CRUELTIE.		152	THE SEARCH	52
CRUM				
AND CRUM OF LIFE, NOW READY TC DISBAND		275	PROFFER	27
CRUMBLED				
O KNIT ME, THAT AM CRUMBLED DUST. THE HEAPE		160	DSTRQCTION	1
CRUMM'D				
THOUGH THEN (THUS CRUMM'D) I STRAY		181	BURIALL	25
CRUSH				
OR THE NEXT FCOT TO CRUSH		201	THE CHECK	9
CRY				
FOLLOW THE CRY NO MORE. THERE IS		189	RESOLVE	21
HOW DIDST THOU CRY		185	PASSION	39
TO CRY TO THEE		180	CHRCH-SVC	19
NEXT CAY I CALL AND CRY FCR THEE		214	MISERY	45
WITH EARNEST GROANS FCR FREEDCM CRY		335	JUDGEMENT	14
O MY GOD, HEAR MY CRY.		329	ANGUISH	19
DID FIRST AGAINST A MURTH'RER CRY.		325	ABELS BLOD	2
COULD'ST SUCH A SPRILL AND LCNG CRY REAR		325	ABELS BLOD	9
AND WITH ONE STRONG, INCESSANT CRY		326	ABELS BLOD	21
HOSANNA CRY		295	PALM-SUNDY	19
CRYE				
AND VCWS AND VISICNS, THOUGH HER FOES CRYE, NCNE.		331	JACOBS PLW	34
CRYED				
HAD NCT THE BABES HOSANNA CRYED		296	JESUS WP A	7
WHILE ONE CRYED OUT, WE ARE DISGRAC'D.		303	ORNAMENT	19
WITH THAT, SOME CRYED, AWAY. STRAIGHT I		140	RGNRTN	34
CRYED DROSS FCR GOLD, AND NEVER THOUGHT		348	HOLY BIBLE	15
CRYING				
WITH THESE I CRIE, AND CRYING PINE		242	MISERY	112
THE WCUNDS THEY GIVE, BY CRYING, ZEALE.		237	CONSTLATN	40
AND CLOUDS OF CRYING WITNESSES WITHOUT		232	THE WORLD	21
CRYS				
SHALL NCT THE CRYS OF BLOUD		202	THE CHECK	40
CUD				
THOSE BEASTS WERE CLEANE, THAT CHEW'D THE CUD.		165	THE CALL	29
CUE				
A TASTE OF HEAV'N CN EARTH, THE PLEDGE, AND CUE		2	SON-DAYES	23
CULD				
O THAT MAN CULD DO SO. THAT HE WOULD HEAR		223	TEMPEST	17
CULL				
TO CULL THIS PRIM-RCSE CUT		166	THE CALL	39
CULL'D				
CULL'D FLCWRES AND MADE ME POSIES.		282	GARLAND	22
CUP				
THE BITTER CUP		207	REPENTANCE	30
CUR'D				
AND CLR'D BY CROSSES AT THY CCST.		227	LV + DSPLN	9
CURB				
THE STOP TO BUSIE FOOLS, CARES CHECK AND CURB.		324	THE NIGHT	26
CURB'D				
CURB'D THEM, AND CLOATH'D THEE WELL AND WARM.		288	THE BIRD	10
CURBS				
WHICH (THOUGH BUT SANC) KEEPS IN A CURBS WHOLE SEAS.		285	PSALM 104	26
SICKNESS IS WHOLSCME, AND CROSSES ARE BUT CURBS		221	AFFLICTION	17
CURE				
THY INWARC EYES, HIS BLCUD WILL CURE THY MIND		217	EASTER-DAY	15
KILL AND CURE THE TENDER FLOWERS		281	JOY	18
THAT, THOUGH THE CURE OF ALL MANS HARM		299	JESUS WP B	40
YET CANST NOT THOU THAT FREE CURE DO		299	JESUS WP B	42
THEY COULD NOT CURE, NCR COMFCRT THEE)		304	ST MARY MN	36
LEARN, LADIES, HERE THE FAITHFUL CURE		305	ST MARY MN	45
THY GOD, THY LIFE, THY CURE.		184	PEACE	20
CURE HIM, EASE HIM		200	NTVTY 1	27
CURIOUS				
THY CLRIOUS VANITIES ANC RARE.		304	ST MARY MN	33
ABOUT THY CURIOUS, WILDE, YONG HEAD.		304	ST MARY MN	20
AND SPYED HIS CURIOUS BCOK		309	THE SEED	52
AND CLRIOUS STORE		246	I WALKT	6
CURL'D				
WHY THEN THESE CURL'D, PUFF'D PCINTS		173	CONTENT	17
CURLE				
AND WIND AND CURLE, AND WINK ANC SMILE		278	THE STARRE	3
BEYOND A CURLED LCCK, OR PAITED FACE.		155	ISAACS M.	38
CURLES				
IN ROWLES AND CURLES, MINCING AND STATELY DUMB		155	ISAACS M.	34
CURLING				
WITH THE SAME CURLING FCRCE, ANC HISSE		175	THE STORM	7
CURLS				
IN SPIRES, GLCBES, ANGRY CURLS AND COY		304	ST MARY MN	18
CURS'D				
O BITTER CURS'D DELIGHTS CF MEN.		311	FAIR+YONG	11
LILIES AND MYRRHE, WHERE THE CLRS'D SEED		299	JESUS WP B	49

	PAGE	TITLE	LINE
CURSE			
HE DREW THE CURSE UPON THE WORLD, AND CRACKT	197	CORRUPTION	15
WHO, WHEN THY SINS CALL FOR'T, CAN FENCE A CURSE.	193	RLS + LSNS	64
OUR DROWN'D ESTATE, TAKING THE CURSE	274	WHT SUNDAY	54
FORCE DOWN A JUST CURSE, WHEN THY HANDS WOULD BLESS.	230	LAW + GOSP	33
WHY SHOULD THE CURSE REIGN ANY MORE.	350	L'ENVOY	24
CURST			
THE GROUND WAS CURST, AND VOID OF STORE.	264	INTRO. 1	8
WHERE ALL THE LAND WITH SCORCHING HEAT IS CURST.	290	THE TIMBER	46
CURTAIN'D			
THAT CURTAIN'D GRAVE, THOUGH SLEEP, LIKE ASHES, HIDE	177	MRNG-WTCH	32
CURTAINES			
I'LE WISH MY CURTAINES OFF TO FREE	142	DEATH	9
CURTAINS			
I SEE, THY CURTAINS ARE CLOSE-DRAWN, THY BOW	197	CORRUPTION	33
UP WITH THY CURTAINS, GIVE THY SOUL THE WING	195	RLS + LSNS	128
DOTH SPREAD LIKE CURTAINS ROUND ABOUT THIS GLOBE	284	PSALM 104	7
CUSTOME			
WERE DULL, AND BLIND, BUT CUSTOME STRAIGHT	143	DEATH	17
NOR BOLD-FAC'D CUSTOME PANISH'D INNOCENCE.	154	ISAACS M.	20
USE, WITH LIKE CUSTOME, AS MY KITCHEN FOOD.	217	DRESSING	36
CUT			
CUT ME NOT OFF FOR MY TRANSGRESSIONS	208	REPENTANCE	53
NOT BUT I KNOW THOU HAST A SHORTER CUT	234	MUTINIE	26
O THAT I HAD DEEP CUT IN MY HARD HEART	198	SCRIPTURES	9
CUT OFF THE SUM	170	COME, COME	6
WHAT THOU HAST CUT TO DAY	283	GARLAND	30
I'LE CUT ME BOUGHS OFF MANY A TREE	295	PALM-SUNDY	35
CUTS			
CUTS THROUGH THE HEAVY MISTS IN HASTE	178	SILENCE	11
HEALINGS, AND CUTS	219	HOLY COMM.	14
CUTT			
CUTT THEN THE SUMME	181	BURIALL	38
CYPERS			
THEY ARE BUT VEILS, AND CYPERS DRAWN	334	JUDGEMENT	9
CYPRESSE			
TWIST NOT MY CYPRESSE WITH YOU BAYS	205	IDLE VERSE	19
DAIES			
WE HAVE NO CONF'RENCE IN THESE DAIES	149	RELIGION	20
OF DAIES, FROM THEE LOOK FOR NEW STRENGTH	218	EASTER HYM	10
FROM THIS, UNTO THE LAST OF DAIES.	218	EASTER HYM	18
THAT LAMB WHOSE DAIES GREAT KINGS AND PROPHETS WISH'D	239	SHEPHEARDS	49
THE PAST DAIES ACCIDENTS DO SUMME	228	PILGRIMAGE	3
DAILY			
WITH THY GRONES MY DAILY BREATH	215	PRAISE	29
AND DAILY DIDST MY YONG EYES LEAD	348	HOLY BIBLE	7
DALE			
THE FRUITFUL FLOCKS FILL EVERY DALE	337	PSALM 65	45
DAMNATION			
O THOU. THAT CANST NOT WISH MY SOULS DAMNATION	190	THE MATCH	16
DAMP			
I HAVE DESERV'D A THICK, EGYPTIAN DAMP	188	RELAPSE	13
AS HE THAT IN SOME CAVES THICK DAMP	178	SILENCE	5
HUNT OUT EACH DAMP	340	THE FEAST	47
DAMPS			
COOL'D BY THE DAMPS OF NIGHT, DESCENDS	203	DSRDR + FR	36
TURNING THEIR MISTS TO BEAMS, THEIR DAMPS TO DAY	202	THE CHECK	31
TWO IN THE DAY, THEN FROM THE DAMPS, AND AKE	196	RLS + LSNS	135
WHOSE CLOUDY BREST COLD DAMPS INVADE	217	EASTER-DAY	2
DANC'D			
DANC'D THROUGH THE FLOUD	141	RGNRTN	67
DANGER			
THERE ABOVE NOISE, AND DANGER	184	PEACE	5
DANGERS			
SUGRING ALL DANGERS WITH SUCCESSE	153	THE SEARCH	73
DARE			
SHALL DARE APPROACH US. WE SHALL THERE NO MORE	146	RSRCTN +IM	65
THESE DARE DIVIDE, AND STAIN	156	BRT. CHRCH	10
I DARE NOT THINK SUCH VILLANY.	316	MEN OF WAR	14
DARES			
AND SUCH A KNOT, WHAT ARM DARES LOOSE	302	THE KNOT	13
TIE UP HIS HANDS, THAT DARES MOCK GOD, AND MAN.	193	RLS + LSNS	48
DARES KNOW EFFECTS, AND JUDGE THEM LONG BEFORE	236	CONSTLATN	27
DARES OWN THE TRUTH, AND SHEW THE ILL.	350	L'ENVOY	38
DARK			
A DARK CONTEST OF WAVES AND WINDE.	344	QUICKNESS	7
THEIR DAY WAS DARK, AND DIM.	239	SHEPHEARDS	54
O FOOLS (SAID I) THUS TO PREFER DARK NIGHT	233	THE WORLD	49
THE WAY WHICH FROM THIS DEAD AND DARK ABODE	233	THE WORLD	53
DARK, VOID, AND CRUDE	218	HOLY COMM.	7
THSES DARK CONFUSIONS, THAT WITHIN ME NEST	216	DRESSING	7
ARE DARK, AND UNCLEAN IN THY SIGHT	208	REPENTANCE	66
MAN THROUGH HIS HEAP OF DARK DAYS, AND THE RICH	2	SON-DAYES	7
WHEN EITHER SLEEP, OR SOME DARK PLEASURE	211	DAWNING	7
BUT DARK AND DEEP PANGS TO THY SIGHT.	264	INTRO. 1	4
ALL DARK AND SPOIL'D	270	ASCSN-HYMN	28
SHINING NO WHERE, BUT IN THE DARK.	271	ALL GONE	18
IN SUCH A DARK, EGYPTIAN BORDER	277	COCK-CRWNG	29
AND ON THE VERGE OF THAT DARK, DREADFUL PIT	188	RELAPSE	3
DARK AS MY DEEDS	188	RELAPSE	14

	PAGE	TITLE	LINE
DARK (CON'T)			
IN THAT DEAD AGE, ONE BEAM I'TH' DARK OUTVIES	196	RLS + LSNS	134
UNDER THE DARK, AND MELANCHOLY EARTH.	195	RLS + LSNS	106
AND THROUGH THE DARK AIRE SPIN A FIRIE SHREAD	157	THE LAMPE	3
MY REST IN CARES, AND TO THE DARK WORLD LEND	157	THE LAMPE	6
THAT DARK, AND DEAD SLEEPS IN ITS KNOWN	179	SILENCE	21
AND THY DARK BED	180	BURIALL	2
BUT A DARK AND SEAL'D UP WOMBE	171	COME, COME	23
O'RE DARK HILLS, SWIFT STREAMES, AND STEEEP WAYS	174	JOY OF LIF	19
DARK STORMS, AND WIND	175	THE STORM	10
IS DARK, AND LONG.	174	JOY OF LIF	10
HELPS SUCH DARK STRAGLERS TO THEIR SIGHT.	305	ST MARY MN	60
MY DARK DESIGNS, WHAT SHALL I DO.	313	THE STONE	9
IN DEATHS DARK MYSTERIES	310	THE SEED	80
TO THY DARK LAND THESE FEEDLESS GO.	338	DEATH B	11
ALL THY DARK WAY.	338	DEATH B	17
CALM AND UNHAUNTED AS IS THY DARK TENT	324	THE NIGHT	38
FROM YOUR DARK HEARTS THIS VEIL REMOVE.	292	THE JEWS	37
OF DEATH, DOST WASTE ALL SENSELESS, COLD AND DARK.	289	THE TIMBER	10
SO IN THE SHADES OF NIGHT SOME DARK FOWLS BE	288	THE BIRD	25
DARKE			
ME FROM SO DARKE, AND SAD A BED	142	DEATH	10
PASSING THROUGH THE EARTHS DARKE VEINES	150	RELIGION	34
DARKEN'D			
DARKEN'D ALONG, AS THEIR SCRIBES BE	332	AGREEMENT	27
DARKEST			
THE DARKEST NIGHT, AND CLOSEST NOOK.	235	CONSTLATN	8
WHICH IN THE DARKEST NIGHTS POINT TO THEIR HOMES	246	MAN	24
DARKLY			
THEN I THAT HERE SAW DARKLY IN A GLASSE	146	RSRCTN +IM	51
DARKNES			
FOR CHAINS OF DARKNES, AND ETERNAL NIGHTS.	196	RLS + LSNS	144
ALL'S IN DEEP SLEEP, AND NIGHT. THICK DARKNES LYES	197	CORRUPTION	37
CALMES, TEMPESTS, LIGHT, AND DARKNES BY HIS MEANS.	194	RLS + LSNS	94
THAT (FOR REPOSE, AND DARKNES BOUND) HE MIGHT	201	THE CHECK	18
AND WOMB OF DARKNES BECKEN OUT	202	DSRDR + FR	2
SO GUIDE US THROUGH THIS DARKNES, THAT WE MAY	237	CONSTLATN	51
DEFECTS, AND DARKNES IN MY BREST	209	REPENTANCE	76
DARKNESS			
DEATH, AND DARKNESS GET YOU PACKING	218	EASTER HYM	1
DARKNESS, AND DAY-LIGHT, LIFE, AND DEATH	219	HOLY COMM.	15
BUT THAT GREAT DARKNESS AT THY DEATH	219	HOLY COMM.	21
IS GROWN THICK DARKNESS, AND THY BREAD, A STONE.	224	TEMPEST	55
THUS GROVELING IN THE SHADE, AND DARKNESS, HE	224	TEMPEST	41
FOR AFTER THEIR LIGHT, DARKNESS COMES	272	WHT SUNDAY	3
WHO IN THAT LAND OF DARKNESS AND BLINDE EYES	323	THE NIGHT	8
A DEEP, BUT DAZLING DARKNESS. AS MEN HERE	325	THE NIGHT	50
'TWILL MAKE THE LAND OF DARKNESS LIGHT.	299	JESUS WP B	51
THOU MAKEST DARKNESS, AND THEN COMES THE NIGHT.	286	PSALM 104	53
WANDRED THROUGH DARKNESS, DENS AND MIRE.	311	FAIR+YONG	6
WHEN THOU DOST SHINE DARKNESS LOOKS WHITE AND FAIR	306	RAIN-BOW	9
DARKNESSE			
AND DARKNESSE FOR MY DAYES.	282	GARLAND	8
DARKSOME			
THE DARKSOME STATES-MAN HUNG WITH WEIGHTS AND WOE	231	THE WORLD	16
DARTING			
A DARTING CONSCIENCE FULL OF STABS, AND FEARS.	188	RELAPSE	17
DASH			
DASH NOT THY FRIEND, NOR HEAV'N, O SMOTHER	194	RLS + LSNS	69
DATE			
ALL DAY EXPECT MY DATE.	187	NO DO THEY	16
REPENTANCE THERE IS OUT OF DATE	147	DAY OF JDG	27
THOUGH OF OUR SELVES, IS SO MUCH OUT OF DATE,	154	ISAACS M.	3
WHERE BIRDS LIKE WATCHFUL CLOCKS THE NOISELESS DATE	245	MAN	3
THEY, BY THY WORD, THEIR BEAUTY HAD, AND DATE.	218	HOLY COMM.	8
DAUGHTERS			
SO THOSE BAD DAUGHTERS, WHICH GOD SAV'D FROM FIRE	307	RAIN-BOW	31
DAWN			
WHOSE FRUITFUL DAWN SHEDS HOPES AND LIGHTS.	295	PALM-SUNDY	31
LIKE CLOUDS, BEFORE THY GLORIOUS DAWN.	334	JUDGEMENT	10
THE OUTGOINGS OF THE EVEN AND DAWN	336	PSALM 65	25
DAWN WITH THE DAY, THERE ARE SET, AWFUL HOURS	192	RLS + LSNS	8
DAWNING			
FRESH AS THE DEW, WHICH BUT THIS DAWNING WEARS.	267	ASCN-DAY A	20
DAY			
LEAVING THE WORLD THEIR DAY	267	ASCN-DAY A	11
THEY PASS AS AT THE LAST GREAT DAY, AND RUN	268	ASCN-DAY A	29
SUCH WAS THE BRIGHT WORLD, ON THE FIRST SEVENTH DAY	268	ASCN-DAY A	39
AND BY THOSE HID ASCENTS CLIMB TO THAT DAY	248	I WALKT	52
MAY SHINE UNTO A PERFECT DAY	277	COCK-CRWNG	45
WHAT GLANCE OF DAY HAST THOU CONFIN'D	276	COCK-CRWNG	2
WELLCOME WHITE DAY. A THOUSAND SUNS	272	WHT SUNDAY	1
THOUGH THEN SOME BOAST THAT FIRE EACH DAY	272	WHT SUNDAY	13
SINCE THEN THOU ART THE SAME THIS DAY	274	WHT SUNDAY	49
AND HAVING BORN THE BURTHEN ALL THE DAY	275	PROFFER	29
A CALM, BRIGHT DAY.	276	PROFFER	46
WHO ON THIS DAY (THAT THOU MIGHT'ST RISE AS HE)	217	EASTER-DAY	7
ALL MISTS THAT WOULD USURP THIS DAY.	217	EASTER-DAY	10
THAT FEEDST AMONG THE LILLIES, 'TILL THE DAY	216	DRESSING	2
DAY, AND NIGHT, NOT ONCE A DAY	214	PRAISE	13

DAY	(CCN'T)	PAGE	TITLE	LINE
DAY, AND NIGHT, NCT ONCE A DAY		214	PRAISE	13
ALL DAY, AND NIGHT DOTH RLN, ANC SING		212	DAWNING	34
SC WHEN THAT DAY, AND HCUR SHAL CCME		212	DAWNING	45
WATCHING THE BREAK OF THY GREAT DAY.		212	DAWNING	48
PART CF HIS MANSICN. HE CNE DAY		225	RETIREMENT	7
STILL THY OWN FOE, AND MINE, FCR TC THIS CAY		225	RETIREMENT	16
DID NCT HE, WHC ORDAIN'C THE CAY		221	AFFLICTION	7
THE CCLC BY NIGHT, THE HEAT BY CAY		220	PSALM 121	11
BLT, AS IN NATURE, WHEN THE CAY		210	FAITH	17
A DAY TC SEEK.		205	SON-DAYES	4
THE CCOL C'TH DAY.		2	SON-DAYES	12
IT WAS LAST DAY		207	REPENTANCE	27
I WALKT THE OTHER DAY (TO SPENC MY HOUR)		246	I WALKT	1
NEXT CAY I CALL AND CRY FCR THEE		214	MISERY	45
TC LIVE IN GRCTS, AND CAVES, ANC HATE THE DAY		233	THE WORLD	51
WHERE TILL THE DAY RESTCRE THE RACE		228	PILGRIMAGE	7
BE MORE AND MCRE IN LCVE WITH CAY.		237	CONSTLATN	52
PERHAPS SCME HARMLESS CARES FCR THE NEXT DAY		239	SHEPHEARDS	37
WITHOLT ONE THOUGHT OF CAY.		238	SHEPHEARDS	8
AND TURN'C THEIR NIGHT TO DAY		239	SHEPHEARDS	52
THEIR DAY WAS CARK, AND DIM.		239	SHEPHEARDS	54
TAKE LP MY DAY, WHILE THOU COST SHINE		240	MISERY	26
HIM CCMPANY ALL DAY, ANC IN HIM SLEEP.		191	RLS + LSNS	6
DAWN WITH THE DAY, THERE ARE SET, AWFUL HCURS		192	RLS + LSNS	8
ALL DAY EXPECT MY DATE.		187	NO DO THEY	16
THE BRIGHTEST DAY.		188	RELAPSE	24
AND THOU ART SURE TC PRCSPER ALL THE DAY.		192	RLS + LSNS	18
THE BREAD WE CAST RETURNS IN FRAUGHTS ONE DAY.		193	RLS + LSNS	66
NCR WAS HEAV'C COLC UNTC HIM, FCR EACH DAY		197	CORRUPTION	21
TWO IN THE DAY, THEN FRCM THE CAMPS, AND AKE		196	RLS + LSNS	135
DC THCU THE WCRKS OF DAY, AND RISE A STAR.		196	RLS + LSNS	138
MAN IS A SUMMERS CAY, WHCSE YCUTH, AND FIRE		195	RLS + LSNS	113
IN SOME GCOC THCUGHTS, SO WHEN THE DAY SHALL RISE		195	RLS + LSNS	129
THE DAY THAT GIVES NO CRSERVATICN		202	THE CHECK	46
RECEEM THE DAY		202	THE CHECK	45
ALL THE LCNG CAY		203	DSRDR + FR	13
AS HE THAT IN THE MIDST OF CAY EXPECTS		201	THE CHECK	13
PAYING THE DAY ITS DEBTS.		201	THE CHECK	17
TURNING THEIR MISTS TC BEAMS, THEIR DAMPS TO DAY		202	THE CHECK	31
NCR CNE DAY BLESSE HIS BIRTH.		200	NTVTY 2	16
BREATHING PERFUMES, DOTH SPICE THE DAY		199	NTVTY 1	6
I SMELL A DEW LIKE MYRRH, AND ALL THE DAY		198	UNPRFTBLNS	10
THUS THCU ALL DAY A THANKLESS WEED DOES DRESS		198	UNPRFTBLNS	16
I'LE THITHER THEN, SEE, IT IS CAY		152	THE SEARCH	65
WHICH HELC UP NIGHT, ANC DAY		147	DAY OF JDG	16
'TIS NOW CLEARE DAY. I SEE A ROSE		151	THE SEARCH	1
WHICH WCULD ONE DAY (BENEATH THE POLE)		151	THE SEARCH	19
SHALL ONE DAY RISE, AND CLOATH'C WITH SHINING LICHT		145	RSRCTN +IM	47
WCULD IT WERE DAY.		146	RSRCTN +IM	68
WE THOUGHT THE DAY THEN WAS NCT SLACK		143	DEATH	25
'TIS A SAC LAND, THAT IN CNE CAY		142	DEATH	1
A WARC, AND STILL IN BONDS, CNE DAY		139	RGNRTN	10
YET, BURN'ST THOU HERE, A FULL CAY, WHILE I SPENC		157	THE LAMPE	5
AND THE DAY SPRINGS)		157	BRT. CHRCH	13
EACH CAY IS GROWN A DCZEN YEAR		170	COME, COME	3
HCW MANY HOURS DO'ST THINK 'TILL CAY.		178	EVNG-WTCH	10
BACK TC HIS DAY		178	SILENCE	12
AND ACDE UNTO THAT DAY HE WENT		165	THE CALL	36
FCR THOSE THAT KILL THEE EVERY DAY.		164	INCARNATN	16
WHERE A SHRILL SPRING TLN'D TC THE EARLY DAY.		167	VNTY SPRIT	2
EACH CAY, AND HOURE HE IS CN WING		161	PURSUITE	3
AND GIRCS THEIR ROCKY HEACS THIS DAY.		336	PSALM 65	22
SIN EVERY DAY COMMITS MCRE WASTE		335	JUDGEMENT	28
THY ARM DCTH SLEEP, BUT WRITE THIS DAY		335	JUDGEMENT	44
TRANSGRESSIONS MAKE ME FOUL EACH CAY		336	PSALM 65	7
DEARLY LOV'D DAY.		334	JUDGEMENT	12
SHALL BRING TRUE CAY, AND MAKE CUST SEE		335	JUDGEMENT	21
AND SAIC, I WAS NC CHILCE CF CAY.		333	AGREEMENT	40
O DAY OF LIFE, OF LIGHT, CF LCVE.		334	JUDGEMENT	1
THE ONELY DAY DEALT FROM ABOVE.		334	JUDGEMENT	2
A DAY SC FRESH, SO BRIGHT, SC BRAVE		334	JUDGEMENT	3
MISTS MAKE BUT TRIUMPHS FOR THE DAY.		338	DEATH B	20
THE DAY OF SPIRITS, MY SOULS CALM RETREAT		324	THE NIGHT	27
EV'N THCSE, WHO BY THEM WCULD FINDE OUT THE CAY		321	HIDDN TRSR	28
BUT WE A HEALING SUN BY DAY ANC NIGHT		331	JACOBS PLW	49
THE THIRD GLAD DAY THROLGH TWC SAC NIGHTS.		295	PALM-SUNDY	33
BUT STILL UNKINDE. ART THIS DAY NOTHING MOV'C.		296	JESUS WP A	2
WHAT THCU HAST CUT TO DAY		283	GARLAND	30
THAT GIFT OF THINE, AND TO MY DAY OF DEATH		287	PSALM 104	91
UNTC HIS WORK, AND AT THE CLOSE OF DAY		286	PSALM 104	63
PLANTS CF THE DAY.		294	PALM-SUNDY	2
AND ALL HIS LIFE A RAINY, WEEPING DAY.		290	THE TIMBER	36
SAY, YOU HAVE GOT THE DAY FROM MEN		305	ST MARY MN	48
THE LUCKY WORLD SHEWD ME CNE CAY		302	ORNAMENT	1
DEAR, BEAUTEOUS SAINT. MORE WHITE THEN DAY		303	ST MARY MN	1
THY SERVICE, NOR HIS SOUL CNE DAY.		301	PROVIDENCE	34
AS TIME ONE DAY BY ME DID PASS		309	THE SEED	49
AS SOME MEEK NIGHT-PIECE WHICH CAY QUAILS		310	THE SEED	67
WAS SHOWN ONE DAY IN A STRANGE GLASS		313	THE STONE	19

		PAGE	TITLE	LINE
DAY	**(CON'T)**			
BOASTS IT THIS DAY, THOUGH NOT IN STORY	. . . .	315	DWELLNG-PL	4
THIS DAY I BRING FOR ALL THY PAIN	. . . .	345	THE WREATH	12
BREAKS AS THE DAY DOTH FROM THE EAST	. . . .	340	THE FEAST	21
TRANSPARENT AS THE PUREST DAY	. . . .	349	L'ENVOY	13
DAY-LIGHT				
DARKNESS, AND DAY-LIGHT, LIFE, AND DEATH	. . . .	219	HOLY COMM.	15
DAY-SPRING				
TILL THE DAY-SPRING BREAKS FORTH AGAIN FROM HIGH.	. .	288	THE BIRD	32
FRESH AS THOSE ROSES, WHICH THE DAY-SPRING WEARS.	. .	155	ISAACS M.	36
DAY-STAR				
THE DAY-STAR SPRINGS, I'LE WAKE AGEN.	. .	177	EVNG-WTCH	2
THOU FROM THE DAY-STAR A LONG WAY DIDST STAND	. .	331	JACOBS PLW	47
THE DAY-STAR SMILES, AND LIGHT WITH DECEAST	. .	267	ASCN-DAY A	23
DAY-STARS				
MOUNTAINS OF SPICE, DAY-STARS AND LIGHT	. . . .	346	THE QUEER	7
DAYES				
LET MY YOUTH, MY BLOOM OF DAYES	. . . .	249	BEGGING A	7
AND DARKNESSE FOR MY DAYES.	. . . .	282	GARLAND	8
TO WHOM A FALLING STAR AND NINE DAYES GLORY	. .	282	GARLAND	2
HE FILS IT. DAYES, AND HOURS ARE BLINDS.	. .	178	EVNG-WTCH	14
DAYES ARE MY FEARES.	. . . .	170	COME, COME	10
HAPPY THOSE EARLY DAYES. WHEN I	. .	169	RETREATE	1
OF DAYES, AND YEARES	. . . .	165	THE CALL	15
SILENCE, AND STEALTH OF DAYES. 'TIS NOW	. .	178	SILENCE	1
MAKE ME FAIRE DAYES OF EVERY NIGHT.	. . . .	182	CHRFLNESS	8
IN SUNNIE DAYES	. . . .	182	CHRFLNESS	13
A TRAINE OF LIGHTS, WHICH IN THOSE SUN-SHINE DAYES	.	159	MANS FALL	10
THOSE WHITE DAYES, DROVE HOME TO THE TENT	. .	151	THE SEARCH	26
AND FORTY DAYES WITHSTOOD THE FELL	. .	152	THE SEARCH	57
OF THESE OUR DAYES, THOU COULDST HAVE COYN'D THEE TWENTY		154	ISAACS M.	15
WHITE DAYES, THAT DURST NO IMPIOUS MIRTH EXPOSE.	.	154	ISAACS M.	18
DAYS				
HE BEGS, AND CALLS. O THAT IN THESE THY DAYS	.	202	THE CHECK	38
LET IT SUFFICE MY WARMER DAYS	. . . .	205	IDLE VERSE	17
THER'S ONE SUN MORE STRUNG ON MY BEAD OF DAYS.	.	195	RLS + LSNS	118
INTOMBED MANY DAYS BEFORE HE DYES	. .	195	RLS + LSNS'	126
SURE, IT WAS SO. MAN IN THOSE EARLY DAYS	. .	196	CORRUPTION	1
AH. WHAT BRIGHT DAYS WERE THOSE.	. .	197	CORRUPTION	20
VAST CIRCLING AZURE, GIDDY CLOUDS, DAYS, NIGHTS.	.	194	RLS + LSNS	90
SUCH NUMBERS TELL THEIR DAYS, WHOSE SPIRITS BE	.	281	JOY	9
THY FORTY DAYS MORE SECRET COMMERCE HERE	. .	268	ASCN-DAY A	33
AS THE SUN DOTH, WHICH TO THOSE DAYS GAVE LICHT.	.	268	ASCN-DAY A	36
THEN FROM THY CROSS UNTO THESE DAYS	. .	273	WHT SUNDAY	35
WHOSE LIGHT DOTH TRAMPLE ON MY DAYS.	. .	271	ALL GONE	10
MY DAYS, WHICH ARE AT BEST BUT DULL AND HOARY	.	271	ALL GONE	11
MAN THROUGH HIS HEAP OF DARK DAYS, AND THE RICH	.	2	SON-DAYES	7
WHICH FOR THESE MISTS, AND BLACK DAYS WERE RESERV'D	.	237	CONSTLATN	47
HAVE YET MORE DAYS, MORE NIGHTS TO COUNT	. .	229	PILGRIMAGE	26
AND ROUND BENEATH IT, TIME IN HOURS, DAYS, YEARS	.	231	THE WORLD	4
WERE ALL MY LOUD, EVIL DAYS	. . . .	324	THE NIGHT	37
ALL OTHER DAYS, COMPAR'D TO THEE	. .	334	JUDGEMENT	7
WELL FARE THOSE BLESSED DAYS OF OLD	. .	293	BEGGING B	11
THY NAME WAS WRIT, AND ALL THY DAYS.	. .	310	THE SEED	60
OF PAST DAYS, WHERE SAD HEAV'N DID SHED	.	309	THE SEED	53
FULL FORTY DAYS O'R THE DROWN'D WORLD DID WEEP)		307	RAIN-BOW	28
SHINING WITH JOY, LIKE DEWY DAYS	. . .	345	THE WREATH	11
DAZLES				
DAZLES AT IT, AS AT ETERNITY.	. . . .	321	CHILDEHOOD	2
DAZLING				
A DEEP, BUT DAZLING DARKNESS. AS MEN HERE	. .	325	THE NIGHT	50
DEAD				
ARE WHEN DEAD, MEDICINAL THEN.	. . .	321	CHILDEHOOD	16
HE FOUND THEE AT THAT DEAD AND SILENT HOUR.	.	323	THE NIGHT	14
NO DEAD AND DUSTY CHERUB, NOR CARV'D STONE	.	323	THE NIGHT	20
OF MY LORDS DEAD	. . . .	335	JUDGEMENT	20
AND MAKE THE DEAD, LIKE FLOWERS, ARISE	.	334	JUDGEMENT	5
BY HIS BREATH WHOM MY DEAD HEART HEAVES.	.	332	AGREEMENT	22
A MOURNING LIGHT UPON THE DEAD.	.	309	THE SEED	54
THOUGH LIFE BE DEAD, AND MY JOYS GONE.	.	311	THE SEED	89
FOR HE THAT'S DEAD, IS FREED FROM SIN.	.	312	FAIR+YONG	46
WHICH SOME THINK DEAD, SHALL ALL AT ONCE	.	314	THE STONE	39
AMONGST THE DEAD, WHERE THRIVING ILL	.	318	THE ASS	26
BEING AT LIFE, BUT IS DEAD THRALL.	. .	319	THE ASS	56
WHICH NOW ARE DEAD, LODG'D IN THY LIVING BOWERS.	.	289	THE TIMBER	4
SOME SECRET SENSE, WHICH MAKES THE DEAD BLOOD RUN	.	289	THE TIMBER	23
BUT THOUGH THUS DEAD UNTO THE WORLD, AND CEAS'D		290	THE TIMBER	33
AS MEER A STRANGER, AS MEN LONG SINCE DEAD.	.	290	THE TIMBER	38
TO MAKE DRIE DUST, AND DEAD TREES GROW.	.	291	THE JEWS	13
THE FROZEN EARTHS DEAD FACE THOU DOST RENEW.	.	287	PSALM 104	82
I MET WITH A DEAD MAN	. . .	282	GARLAND	26
ON THEIR DEAD HEARTS, BUT (O MY FEARS)	.	296	JESUS WP A	11
HIS ART ADDS STILL (THOUGH HE BE DEAD)	.	297	HERODIAS	7
CAN MAKE MANS DEAD AND SCATTER'D BONES	.	298	JESUS WP B	7
DEW OF THE DEAD WHICH MAKES DUST MOVE	.	298	JESUS WP B	11
WHERE DEAD MEN PREACH, WHO CAN TURN FEASTS, AND MIRTH		226	RETIREMENT	49
THE WAY WHICH FROM THIS DEAD AND DARK ABODE	.	233	THE WORLD	53
HOW HAPPEND IT THAT IN THE DEAD OF NIGHT	.	238	SHEPHEARDS	5
ADORES DEAD DUST, SETS HEART ON CORNE AND GRASS	.	236	CONSTLATN	19
AND IN THE DEPTH AND DEAD OF WINTER BRING	.	245	MT. OLV. B	19

		PAGE	TITLE	LINE
DEAD	**(CCN'T)**			
OR READY TO BE DEAD	. . . .	244	THE SAP	34
AND EVEN MY SOUL TO THEE IS DEAD	. . . .	209	REPENTANCE	78
SINKS TC A DEAD OBLIVIOUN, AND THCUGH ALL	.	224	TEMPEST	42
TC BRASSE, AND IRCN, WHEN MY STCCK LAY DEAD	.	213	ADMISSION	3
HE FINDS IT DEAD, AND IN A GRAVE.	. . . .	212	DAWNING	32
DEAD I WAS, AND DEEP IN TROUBLE.	. . . .	218	HOLY COMM.	2
BUT OUR HEARTS DEAD AND SINFUL CCLD.	. . .	274	WHT SUNDAY	52
AND WARM THE DEAD	. . . .	248	I WALKT	44
THEN SIGHING WHISPER'D, HAPPY ARE THE DEAD.	.	247	I WALKT	33
DEPRAV'C OR DEAD, CAN HAVE WITH THEE	. .	278	THE STARRE	15
IN THAT DEAD AGE, CNE BEAM I'TH' DARK OUTVIES		196	RLS + LSNS	134
LEAVING ME DEAD	. . . .	203	DSRDR + FR	42
INTO TH' CLD SILENCE, AND DEAC SLEEP	. .	203	DSRDR + FR	11
THOUGH DEAD, AND SICK	. . . . . .	191	THE MATCH	40
LIKE THAT SAMARITANS CEAD WELL	. . . .	150	RELIGION	46
THE QLICK, AND DEAD, BOTH SMALL AND GREAT	.	147	DAY OF JDG	23
'TIS DEAD NIGHT ROUND APOLT. FCRRCR DCTH CREEPE		157	THE LAMPE	1
AND SCMETHING STILL BE LEFT THE DEAD	. .	142	DEATH	8
INSPIR'C A QUICKNING POWER THRCUGH THE CEAD	.	144	RSRCTN +IM	3
THAT DARK, AND DEAC SLEEPS IN ITS KNOWN	. .	179	SILENCE	21
O THOU. THE FIRST FRUITS CF THE DEAD	. .	180	BURIALL	1
O HEAR, AND HEAL THY SERVANT. LCRD STRIKE DEAD		185	PASSION	14
THEY WERE ALL DULL, AND DEAD	. . . .	187	NO DO THEY	6
'TIS NOW, SINCE YCU HAVE LAINE THUS DEAD	. .	164	THE CALL	3
WITH QUICK, OR DEAD	. . . . . .	174	JOY OF LIF	7
QUICKNING THE DEAC	. . . . . .	339	THE FEAST	14
PCOR DUST THOUGH DEAD	. . . . . .	340	THE FEAST	35
WHICH STRIKES DEATH DEAC	. . . . .	340	THE FEAST	38
AS IF IT NEVER SHOULD BE DEAD.	. . . .	347	THE BOOK	14
DEAL				
EARNEST, AND SIGN, THY CIFTS SC DEAL	. .	216	DRESSING	20
THUS, RIGHTEOUS FATHER. DCEST THOU DEAL	. .	293	THE JEWS	46
NEW CCRDIALS, NEW CATHARTICS CEAL.	. . .	333	AGREEMENT	58
DEALS				
CN IT THE PRINCE CF SALEM SITS, WHO DEALS	.	243	THE SAP	13
WHCSE EASTERN TRAFFIQUE DEALS IN BRIGHT	. .	346	THE QUEER	5
DEALT				
PRAISE HIM, WHO DEALT HIS GIFTS SC FREE	. .	266	VAIN WITS	12
THE CNELY DAY CEALT FROM ABOVE.	. . .	334	JUDGEMENT	2
DEAR				
DEAR LORD. MAKE HASTE	. . . . .	335	JUDGEMENT	27
DEAR NIGHT. THIS WORLCS DEFEAT.	. . .	324	THE NIGHT	25
DEAR, HARMLESS AGE. THE SHORT, SWIFT SPAN	.	322	CHILDEHOOD	31
HATE NOT THINE OWN DEAR GIFT AND TCKEN.	. .	294	BEGGING B	18
DEAR LORD. RESTORE THY ANCIENT PEACE	. .	294	BEGGING B	21
YCU WERE THE DEAR AND CHOSEN STCCK.	. .	292	THE JEWS	39
DEAR LORD. THCU ART ALL GRIEF AND LOVE	. .	298	JESUS WP B	22
MY DEAR, ALMIGHTY LORD. WHY DCST THOU WEEP.	.	298	JESUS WP B	1
DEAR JESUS WEEP ON. PCUR THIS LATTER	. .	296	JESUS WP A	9
MY DEAR, BRIGHT LCRD. MY MORNING-STAR.	. .	296	JESUS WP A	13
CEAR FEAST OF PALMS, CF FLOWERS AND DEW.	. .	295	PALM-SUNDY	30
AND ONELY MY DEAR JESUS SEEK.	. . . .	295	PALM-SUNDY	41
(THCUGH PURCHAS'D WITH THY HEARTS DEAR TREASLRE)		299	JESUS WP B	28
MY DEAR, CEAR GOD. I DO NCT KNCW	. . .	315	DWELLNG-PL	11
MY DEAR, CEAR GOD. I CO NOT KNCW	. . .	315	CWELLNG-PL	11
WERE NOT THY WORD (DEAR LCRD) MY LIGHT	. .	316	MEN OF WAR	9
DEAR JESUS GIVE MY PATIENCE HERE	. . .	317	MEN OF WAR	37
HERE SLEPT MY THOUGHTS CEAR MARK. WHICH DUST		310	THE SEED	73
DEAR, SECRET GREENNESS. NURST BELOW	. .	309	THE SEED	25
DEAR, BEAUTEOUS SAINT. MORE WHITE THEN DAY	.	303	ST MARY MN	1
DEAR SOUL. THOU KNEW'ST, FLOWERS HERE ON EARTH		304	ST MARY MN	27
DEAR LORD, 'TIS FINISHED. AND NCW HE	. .	265	INTRO. 2	1
MY DEAR REDEEMER, THE WCRLDS LIGHT	. . .	265	INTRO. 2	17
DEAR, BEAUTEOUS DEATH. THE JEWEL OF THE JUST	.	271	ALL GONE	17
COME THEN THOU FAITHFUL WITNESS. COME DEAR LCRD		268	ASCN-DAY A	61
THY OWN DEAR PEOPLE PENS CUR TIMES	. . .	273	WHT SUNDAY	30
EXCLUCE MY DEAR GCD FROM MY MIND	. . .	240	MISERY	34
YET HIS DEAR TREASURE	. . . . .	231	THE WORLD	13
O MY DEAR GOD. MY LIFE, MY LOVE.	. . .	208	REPENTANCE	47
MY DEAR, CEAR GOD.	. . . . . .	184	PASSION	2
MY DEAR, CEAR GOD.	. . . . . .	184	PASSION	2
HASTE, HAST MY DEAR	. . . . . .	156	BRT. CHRCH	5
DEAR FRIEND. WHOSE HOLY, EVER-LIVING LINES	.	190	THE MATCH	1
AND HUMBLE DUST, TELL THEN DEAR FLESH	. .	201	THE CHECK	11
WELCCME DEAR BOOK, SOULS JOY, AND FOOD. THE FEAST		197	SCRIPTURES	1
DEAR STREAM. DEAR BANK, WHERE CFTEN I	. .	343	WATER-FALL	13
DEAR STREAM. DEAR BANK, WHERE CFTEN I	. .	343	WATER-FALL	13
DEAR LORD, DO THIS. AND THEN LET GRACE	. .	350	L'ENVOY	43
DEARE				
THAT PILL, THCUGH BITTER, IS MOST DEARE	. .	147	DAY OF JDG	35
WHERE MY DEARE LORD DID OFTEN TREAD	. .	153	THE SEARCH	72
AH, MY CEARE LORD. WHAT COULDST THOU SPYE	.	164	INCARNATN	13
DEARE FRIEND SIT DOWN, AND BEAR AWHILE THIS SHADE		279	PALM-TREE	1
DEAREST				
FOR, CEAREST JESUS, 'TIS ALL THINE.	. . .	265	INTRO. 2	8
DEARLY				
AND DEARLY BOUGHT (WHEN THOU CIDST SEE	. .	304	ST MARY MN	35
BLESSED, UNHAPPY CITY. CEARLY LCV'D	. .	296	JESUS WP A	1
DEARLY LOV'D DAY.	. . . .	334	JUDGEMENT	12

	PAGE	TITLE	LINE
DEATH			
AND WHEN IN DEATH MY SPEECH IS SPENT	334	AGREEMENT	63
AND SINCE HIS DEATH, WE THROUGHLY SEE	338	DEATH B	16
AND LEADER THROUGH THICK DEATH AND NIGHT.	326	ABELS BLOD	32
WHICH HIS DEATH SCATTER'D) HE FORETOLD THE PLACE	330	JACOBS PLW	23
WHOSE DEATH WILL BE	294	PALM-SUNDY	16
FOR THOUGH DEATH CANNOT SO UNDO	299	JESUS WP B	34
OF DEATH, DOST WASTE ALL SENSELESS, COLD AND DARK.	289	THE TIMBER	10
BUT THIS THY STRANGE RESENTMENT AFTER DEATH	289	THE TIMBER	19
THAT GIFT OF THINE, AND TO MY DAY OF DEATH	287	PSALM 104	91
WHAT LIFE, WHAT DEATH CAN SEVER.	302	THE KNOT	14
FAITH INTO LIFE BREAKS, AND DEATH DIES.	310	THE SEED	66
THE OTHER OF DEATH, SIN AND STRIFE.	318	THE ASS	4
WHERE DEATH AND FRAILTY ARE FORGOTTEN	319	THE ASS	64
DEATH THAT TO ME WAS LIFE AND LIGHT	264	INTRO. 1	3
AFTER THY DEATH AND FUNERAL, SO CLEAR	268	ASCN-DAY A	34
IT THRIVES NO WHERE. THIS MAKES THESE WEIGHTS (LIKE DEATH	279	PALM-TREE	7
BE SURE UNDER PAINS OF DEATH	281	JOY	21
YEA, 'TIS A DEATH PARTAKES OF HELL.	277	COCK-CRWNG	26
THE SHADES OF DEATH DWELL AND DISORDER.	277	COCK-CRWNG	30
BEFORE DEATH COME	269	ASCSN-HYMN	9
DEAR, BEAUTEOUS DEATH. THE JEWEL OF THE JUST	271	ALL GONE	17
AND SCATTER DEATH	275	PROFFER	38
IN ALL THIS ROUND OF LIFE AND DEATH	208	REPENTANCE	73
SCATTER THESE SHADES OF DEATH, AND GIVE	208	REPENTANCE	51
DEATH WEAN'D THEE FROM THE WORLD, AND SIN.	209	THE BURIAL	8
TO DRESSE THEM, AND UNSWADLE DEATH.	209	THE BURIAL	12
FAITH SPANS UP BLISSE, WHAT SIN, AND DEATH	211	FAITH	37
AND MY LIFE HID IN THY DEATH	215	PRAISE	31
DEATH, AND DARKNESS GET YOU PACKING	218	EASTER HYM	1
DEATH A NAP, TO WAKE MORE MERRY.	218	EASTER HYM	6
DARKNESS, AND DAY-LIGHT, LIFE, AND DEATH	219	HOLY COMM.	15
BUT THAT GREAT DARKNESS AT THY DEATH	219	HOLY COMM.	21
AND BLOOD BY AN ACCURSED DEATH	220	HOLY COMM.	42
OF SIN, AND DEATH I SOJOURN, YET ONE EYE	234	MUTINIE	20
LIFE LOCKT IN DEATH, HEAV'N IN A SHELL.	164	INCARNATN	12
IS ONLY STRONGER FAR THAN DEATH.	164	INCARNATN	20
DEATH TO THE COMMON EYE	166	THE CALL	59
TO WEEP, TO SING, THY DEATH, MY LIFE.	186	PASSION	57
AND DEATH UNITE	185	PASSION	32
DEATH SETS ALL OUT OF JOINT	173	CONTENT	19
UNTILL IN DEATH.	171	COME, COME	20
WE SPEND IN SIGHES, IS TREASURE AFTER DEATH.	158	THE LAMPE	22
THAT BINDS, AND LOOSENS DEATH	144	RSRCTN +IM	2
JUST SO IT IS IN DEATH. BUT THOU	143	DEATH	27
AND LET ME DYE BEFORE MY DEATH.	141	RGNRTN	91
HATH DULL'D THEE THUS, WHEN DEATH SHALL FREEZE	142	DEATH	2
AND HOW OF DEATH WE MAKE	145	RSRCTN +IM	23
FURTHERS HIS GLORY, AND GIVES DEATH THE FOYL.	195	RLS + LSNS	112
HAVE ONE LARGE LANGUAGE, DEATH.	201	THE CHECK	28
A STATE THY BIRTH, AND DEATH DESIGN'D.	350	L'ENVOY	20
DESTROYING ONELY DEATH AND PAIN	347	THE BOOK	28
THY DEATH MAY KEEP MY SOUL ALIVE.	343	OBSEQUIES	32
THY CAUSLESS PAIN. AND SAD AS DEATH.	345	THE WREATH	13
WHICH STRIKES DEATH DEAD	340	THE FEAST	38
OF THY SAD DEATH	342	OBSEQUIES	6
TWO DEATHS HAD BIN THY DUE.	243	THE SAP	22
ROSE UP, AND CANCELL'D TWO DEATHS DUE TO THEE.	217	EASTER-DAY	8
THESE THY DEATHS FRUITS I OFFER THEE	264	INTRO. 1	2
IN DEATHS DARK MYSTERIES	310	THE SEED	80
DEATHS-HEAD			
OF WORMWOOD, AND A DEATHS-HEAD CROWN'D WITH ROSES.	280	JOY	6
BUT I WILL BE MY OWN DEATHS-HEAD. AND THOUGH	183	THRS A TYE	21
DEBATE			
A MEER TEMPESTUOUS DEBATE.	344	QUICKNESS	8
DEBTS			
PAYING THE DAY ITS DEBTS.	201	THE CHECK	17
DECAY			
BEFORE MAN BROUGHT FORTH SIN, AND SIN DECAY.	268	ASCN-DAY A	40
THAT, WHO BUT TRULY TASTS IT, NO DECAY	244	THE SAP	29
THAT NO DECAY SHAL TOUCH ME. O BE PLEAS'D	234	MUTINIE	32
QUITE VANISH AND DECAY.	283	GARLAND	32
AND WITHOUT ROOT AND SAP DECAY	292	THE JEWS	18
AND WITHOUT BLEMISH OR DECAY	349	L'ENVOY	14
FOR AS YOUR FAST AND FOUL DECAYS	292	THE JEWS	21
THY GREAT DECAYS RESTOR'D MIGHT BE.	304	ST MARY MN	32
MEER GLIMERING AND DECAYS.	271	ALL GONE	12
FOR, THOUGH WE HOURLY BREATH DECAYS	273	WHT SUNDAY	41
THEIR SAD DECAYS, I FLOURISH, AND ONCE MORE	198	UNPRFTBLNS	8
HIGH-NOON THUS PAST, THY TIME DECAYS, PROVIDE	195	RLS + LSNS	103
DECEAST			
THE DAY-STAR SMILES, AND LIGHT WITH DECEAST	267	ASCN-DAY A	23
DECEITFUL			
O FOUL, DECEITFUL MEN. MY GOD DOTH KEEP	307	RAIN-BOW	19
DECEITS			
FALSE STARS AND FIRE-DRAKES, THE DECEITS OF NIGHT	320	HIDDN TRSR	4
DECEPTIONS			
GLORIOUS DECEPTIONS, GILDED MISTS	282	GARLAND	17
THOU FOUL DECEPTION OF ALL MEN	344	QUICKNESS	3
DECIDE			
I SUMMON'D TO DECIDE THIS STRIFE	207	REPENTANCE	42

		PAGE	TITLE	LINE

DECK
AND DECK ME , LORD, WITH THE SAME CROWNE • • • • 167 THE CALL 92
TO DECK THEIR OWN, THEN GIVE THY SAINTS • • • • 350 L'ENVOY 35
DECLARE
OF GRASS, WE TREAD, DECLARE. • • • • • 286 PSALM 104 68
DECLINES
AND THE SAME SUN WHICH HERE DECLINES • • • • 292 THE JEWS 28
DECREASE
MUST LANGUISH AND DECREASE. • • • • • 285 PSALM 104 28
DECREE
AND BY APPEALES FROM HIM DECREE. • • • • 149 RELIGION 24
DID LIVE AND FEED BY THY DECREE • • • • 347 THE BOOK 16
DECREED
AND HERE A FRESH SEARCH IS DECREED • • • • 152 THE SEARCH 35
THY SACRED AND ETERNAL WIL DECREED • • • • 235 MUTINIE 34
DECRYED
A DECRYED COURSE, SURE IT PREVAIL'D NOT MUCH. • • 154 ISAACS M. 12
DEDUCTED
DEDUCTED FROM THE WHOLE, THE COMBS, AND HIVE • • • 2 SON-DAYES 19
DEED
INTO THY DEED • • • • • • 190 THE MATCH 8
PERFORMANCE, WILL FOR THAT SAME DEED • • • • 314 THE STONE 48
DEEDS
THESE GOOD DEEDS BLOT • • • • • • 328 RIGHTSNESS 50
DARK AS MY DEEDS • • • • • • 188 RELAPSE 14
WHEN NIGHT COMES, LIST THY DEEDS, MAKE PLAIN THE WAY • 195 RLS + LSNS 115
WHAT WERE THEIR LIFES, THEIR THOUGHTS AND DEEDS • • 347 THE BOOK 9
DEEP
LODGE IN THY MYSTICAL, DEEP STREAMS. • • • 344 WATER-FALL 28
WITH WHAT DEEP MURMURS THROUGH TIMES SILENT STEALTH • 343 WATER-FALL 1
BUT QUICKNED BY THIS DEEP AND ROCKY GRAVE • • 343 WATER-FALL 11
O THAT I HAD DEEP CUT IN MY HARD HEART • • • 198 SCRIPTURES 9
ALL'S IN DEEP SLEEP, AND NIGHT. THICK DARKNES LYES • 197 CORRUPTION 37
IN WHAT DEEP ANGUISH • • • • • 185 PASSION 22
WHEN I AM CAST INTO THAT DEEP • • • • 180 BURIALL 3
(WHILST DEEP SLEEP OTHERS CATCHES) • • • • 171 MIDNIGHT 2
BUT DEEP STILL CALLETH UPON DEEP. • • • 325 ABELS BLOD 16
BUT DEEP STILL CALLETH UPON DEEP. • • • 325 ABELS BLOD 16
A DEEP, BUT DAZLING DARKNESS. AS MEN HERE • • 325 THE NIGHT 50
BUT IN A DEEP, WIDE SEA OF BLOOD • • • 325 ABELS BLOD 14
WATER (THOUGH BOTH HEAVENS WINDOWS AND THE DEEP • 307 RAIN-BOW 27
IN THE DEEP WATERS, WHICH NO EYE CAN FIND. • • 284 PSALM 104 10
AND FOUNDED THE FIRM EARTH. THEN WITH THE DEEP • 285 PSALM 104 18
SO DOTH THE DEEP AND WIDE SEA, WHEREIN ARE • • 286 PSALM 104 69
AND YET (AS IF SOME DEEP HATE AND DISSENT • • 289 THE TIMBER 13
YET STONES ARE DEEP IN ADMIRATION. • • • 288 THE BIRD 16
AND WITH SUCH DEEP • • • • • 298 JESUS WP B 3
DEAD I WAS, AND DEEP IN TROUBLE. • • • 218 HOLY COMM. 2
BUT DARK AND DEEP PANGS TO THY SIGHT. • • 264 INTRO. 1 4
DEEPE
BUT THOU SLEEP'ST IN A DEEPE NEGLECT • • • 163 MT. OLVS A 12
WHEN ONE LOWD BLAST SHALL REND THE DEEPE • • 147 DAY OF JDG 17
DEER
BOTH COST THEE DEER • • • • • • 191 THE MATCH 20
DEERE
BUT HE THAT WITH HIS BLOOD (A PRICE TOO DEERE) • 188 RELAPSE 21
DEFEAT
WHICH SHEW'D THEE LAST, BUT DID DEFEAT • • • 178 SILENCE 15
WHERE OBSCURE CARES THE MEAN DEFEAT • • • 318 THE ASS 7
DEAR NIGHT. THIS WORLDS DEFEAT. • • • 324 THE NIGHT 25
DEFECTS
DEFECTS, AND DARKNES IN MY BREST • • • • 209 REPENTANCE 76
DEFENSE
IF NOT THY MIGHTY LOVE, MY OWN DEFENSE. • • 342 OBSEQUIES 12
DEFIANCE
WHAT THOUGH SOME CLOUDS DEFIANCE BID • • • 294 BEGGING B 15
DEGENERATE
THAT TO RENEW'T WERE TO DEGENERATE. • • • 154 ISAACS M. 4
DEGRADE
SO PREST AND BOW'D, BEFORE SIN DID DEGRADE • • 279 PALM-TREE 3
DEITY
THE FULNESS OF THE DEITY. • • • • 323 THE NIGHT 18
DEJECTION
REACHETH AS WELL THINGS OF DEJECTION • • • 210 FAITH 3
DELAY
I DID DELAY • • • • • • 225 RETIREMENT 17
O TAKE IT OFF. MAKE NO DELAY • • • • 277 COCK-CRWNG 43
MAKE NO DELAY • • • • • • 339 THE FEAST 2
THE LYONS WHELPS IMPATIENT OF DELAY • • • 286 PSALM 104 57
BUT THE DELAY IS ALL. TYME NOW • • • • 181 BURIALL 33
DELAYES
AND I WIL MEND MY OWN WITHOUT DELAYES • • • 188 RELAPSE 11
DELAYS
'TWIXT HEAVEN, AND THEE, BLOCK IT NOT WITH DELAYS • 195 RLS + LSNS 116
DELIGHT
LORD, WITH WHAT COURAGE, AND DELIGHT • • • 182 CHRFLNESS 1
AND LIFE TOO, AND MY HEARTS DELIGHT. • • • 265 INTRO. 2 18
AND MAN (LIKE ISSACHAR) IN LODES DELIGHT • • 223 TEMPEST 30
AND FOR THAT HOUR TH'ART MY DELIGHT • • • 214 MISERY 54
ALL THY DELIGHT (WHAT E'R THEY BE) • • • 242 MISERY 99

	PAGE	TITLE	LINE
DELIGHTS			
WITS SOUR DELIGHTS	231	THE WORLD	11
LORD JESUS. WITH WHAT SWEETNESS AND DELIGHTS	267	ASCN-DAY A	1
THESE WERE MY PRIME DELIGHTS.	282	GARLAND	20
BUT HEARTS ARE NOT SO KIND. FALSE, SHORT DELIGHTS	183	THRS A TYE	13
ENDEAR DELIGHTS	339	THE FEAST	11
O BITTER CURS'D DELIGHTS OF MEN.	311	FAIR+YONG	11
THEREFORE, THOSE LOOSE DELIGHTS AND LUSTS, WHICH HERE	342	OBSEQUIES	13
DELIVERED			
THE LAW DELIVERED TO THE JEWS	314	THE STONE	46
DELIVERER			
OF YOUR DELIVERER COMES	291	THE JEWS	2
DENIES			
THIS VEYLE THY FULL-EYED LOVE DENIES	277	COCK-CRWNG	41
DENS			
RETIRE INTO THEIR DENS. MAN GOES ABROAD	286	PSALM 104	62
WANDRED THROUGH DARKNESS, DENS AND MIRE.	311	FAIR+YONG	6
DENY			
OR, IF THOU GOEST, DO NOT DENY	.293	BEGGING B	3
DENYED			
THE STONES HAD SPOKE, WHAT YOU DENYED.	296	JESUS WP A	8
DEPART			
OR IF AS YET (UNTIL THESE CLOUDS DEPART	157	BRT. CHRCH	12
DEPRAV'D			
DEPRAV'D OR DEAD, CAN HAVE WITH THEE	278	THE STARRE	15
DEPRAVE			
THEIR SUBSTANCE DOTH DEPRAVE	145	RSRCTN +IM	38
DEPTH			
AND IN THE DEPTH AND DEAD OF WINTER BRING	245	MT. OLV. B	19
DERIVES			
DERIVES HER BIRTH, AND THENCE DOTH BRING	150	RELIGION	31
DESART			
THOUGH IN THIS DESART I WERE WHOLY SHUT	234	MUTINIE	30
DESARTS			
FOR THOU DOST EVEN THE DESARTS BLESS	337	PSALM 65	42
DESCEND			
THY JUDGING ONE, DESCEND, DESCEND.	335	JUDGEMENT	45
THY JUDGING ONE, DESCEND, DESCEND.	335	JUDGEMENT	45
DESCEND, AND LIVING WATERS FLOW	291	THE JEWS	12
OR BOW THE HEAVENS. LORD BOW THEM AND DESCEND	283	LOVE-SICK	10
FIX'D TO A TENT, DESCEND AND SHROWD	315	DWELLNG-PL	6
AND ROT, DESCEND NOT HERE, NOR THINK TO STAY	275	PROFFER	17
DESCEND TO JUDGE POOR CARELESS MAN	212	DAWNING	28
THY JUDGING ONE. DESCEND, DESCEND.	340	RGNRTN	5
THY JUDGING ONE. DESCEND, DESCEND.	340	RGNRTN	5
DID IN PURE LOVE DESCEND	184	PEACE	11
ALL MUST DESCEND	343	WATER-FALL	9
DESCEND, AND HALLOW ALL THE PLACE.	350	L'ENVOY	44
DESCENDING			
ANGELS DESCENDING, THE RETURNS OF TRUST.	2	SON-DAYES	15
DESCENDS			
COOL'D BY THE DAMPS OF NIGHT, DESCENDS	203	DSRDR + FR	36
DESCENT			
WHOSE RISE, HEIGHT, AND DESCENT IS BUT A SPAN.	195	RLS + LSNS	108
THY TRUE DESCENT.	226	RETIREMENT	48
DESCENTS			
NOR MADE LIFE THROUGH HER LONG DESCENTS	312	FAIR+YONG	29
DESCRIED			
IT WAS A BANKE OF FLOWERS, WHERE I DESCRIED	141	RGNRTN	74
DESCRIES			
DESCRIES	153	THE SEARCH	79
DESCRIEST			
IS BUT ONE DRAMME, AND WHAT THOU NOW DESCRIEST	177	EVNG-WTCH	5
DESCRY			
DESCRY SOME PART OF HIS GREAT LIGHT.	167	VNTY SPRIT	8
THY BURNISHT, FLAMING ARCH DID FIRST DESCRY.	306	RAIN-BOW	4
AND WITH THEIR BLUSH OF LIGHT DESCRY	211	DAWNING	11
DESCRYED			
A GROVE DESCRYED	140	RGNRTN	43
DESERT			
THUS WAS THE DESERT SANCTIFIED	152	THE SEARCH	63
DESERTS			
IF MY WAY LIES THROUGH DESERTS AND WILDE WOODS.	290	THE TIMBER	45
DESERV'D			
I HAVE DESERV'D A THICK, EGYPTIAN DAMP	188	RELAPSE	13
DESIGN'D			
A STATE THY BIRTH, AND DEATH DESIGN'D.	350	L'ENVOY	20
DESIGNS			
MY DARK DESIGNS, WHAT SHALL I DO.	313	THE STONE	9
WITH ALL DETESTABLE DESIGNS	335	JUDGEMENT	37
THOSE WHITE DESIGNS WHICH CHILDREN DRIVE	321	CHILDEHOOD	4
FOR ALL DESIGNS MEANT AGAINST THEE	265	INTRO. 2	25
DESIR'D			
AMONGST THE DOCTORS, AND DESIR'D	151	THE SEARCH	14
MY RESTLESS EYE THAT STILL DESIR'D	141	RGNRTN	72
NOR HOME DESIR'D.	162	PURSUITE	12
DESIRE			
WHICH LONG RESISTED THY DESIRE	264	INTRO. 1	10
GRANT I MAY, MY CHIEF DESIRE.	249	BEGGING A	5
NEXT, THERE'S IN IT A RESTLESS, PURE DESIRE	278	THE STARRE	17

			PAGE	TITLE	LINE
DESIRE (CON'T)					
DESIRE THAT NEVER WILL BE QUENCH'D	.	. . . .	278	THE STARRE	19
FOR WHERE DESIRE, CELESTIALL, PURE DESIRE		. . .	279	THE STARRE	25
FOR WHERE DESIRE, CELESTIALL, PURE DESIRE		. . .	279	THE STARRE	25
DISPATCH'D TO HOLY SOULS, SICK WITH DESIRE		. . .	284	PSALM 104	14
DESIST					
DESIST FOND FOOL, BE NOT UNDONE		. . . .	283	GARLAND	29
DESOLATE					
OPEN MY DESOLATE ROOMS, MY GLOOMIE BREST		. . .	216	DRESSING	5
DESP'RATE					
BLIND , DESP'RATE FITS, THAT STUDY HOW		. . .	205	IDLE VERSE	9
DESPAIR					
MY MEER DESPAIR	. . . . .	. . .	153	THE SEARCH	86
AND TRAMPLES ON DOUBTS AND DESPAIR.	.	. . .	346	THE QUEER	4
DESPIGHT					
THE VILE DESPIGHT DONE TO THY NAME.	.	. . .	335	JUDGEMENT	34
COULD NOT REFORM US, AND BLOOD (IN DESPIGHT)		. . .	307	RAIN-BOW	29
DESPIS'D					
THAT PROUDLY SPILT AND DESPIS'D BLOOD		. . .	326	ABELS BLOD	34
DESPISE					
DO NOT DESPISE A LOVE-SICK HEART.		. . .	294	BEGGING B	14
THEY WILL DRINK BLOOD, THAT DESPISE TEARS.		. . .	296	JESUS WP A	12
LET ME NOT SCATTER, AND DESPISE MY FOOD		. . .	230	LAW + GOSP	34
NO MAN CAN MORE THE WORLD DESPISE		. . .	214	MISERY	55
DESPISED					
AND POOR, DESPISED TRUTH SATE COUNTING BY		. . .	232	THE WORLD	44
YOUR STONY HEARTS DESPISED LOVE		. . .	293	THE JEWS	43
WHY LIES THIS HAIR DESPISED NOW		. . .	304	ST MARY MN	15
TILL HIS ABUS'D, DESPISED FLAME		. . .	305	ST MARY MN	53
DESTINIE					
AND THIRSTIE BRICK MUST BE (SAID I)	.	. . .	234	MUTINIE	13
DESTROY					
UPON THY SELF, SO TO DESTROY	.	. . .	274	WHT SUNDAY	55
HOW ARTFULLY DO YOU DESTROY	.	. . .	311	FAIR+YONG	15
DESTROY'D					
DESTROY'D AT ALL, BUT WHEN TIMES RESTLES WAVE		. . .	145	RSRCTN +IM	37
DESTROYING					
DESTROYING ONELY DEATH AND PAIN		. . .	347	THE BOOK	28
DESTROYS					
AND SPLENDID VICE DESTROYS THE GREAT.		. . .	318	THE ASS	8
DESTRUCTION					
DESTRUCTION ON HIS RUDDY WING.	.	. . .	305	ST MARY MN	56
DETAIN'D					
AND TRULY HATES TO BE DETAIN'D ON EARTH		. . .	290	THE TIMBER	30
DETECT					
WITH ONE ATTESTING VOICE DETECT		. . .	314	THE STONE	40
DETER					
HOW IN THIS WORLD SHOULD THEY DETER		. . .	312	FAIR+YONG	39
DETESTABLE					
WITH ALL DETESTABLE DESIGNS		. . .	335	JUDGEMENT	37
DEVEST					
BUT I GO ON, HASTE TO DEVEST		. . .	240	MISERY	41
DEVIL					
THE PERJURER'S A DEVIL LET LOOSE. WHAT CAN		. . .	193	RLS + LSNS	47
DEVILL					
IF NO A VERY DEVILL, WORSE THAN A BEAST.		. . .	194	RLS + LSNS	78
DEVISE					
SOME FIG-LEAFS STIL I DO DEVISE		. . .	240	MISERY	23
BUT SINCE CHRIST DYED (AS IF HE DID DEVISE		. . .	307	RAIN-BOW	23
DEVOTION					
DEVOTION STILL ON WING, THEN, THOU DOST WEEPE		. . .	158	THE LAMPE	13
DEVOTIONS					
TO HEIGHTEN THY DEVOTIONS, AND KEEP LOW		. . .	194	RLS + LSNS	85
DEVOUR					
SEEM'D TO DEVOUR, LIKE RUST.	.	. . .	310	THE SEED	74
DEVOUTLY					
TO GET THEE WINGS ON, AND DEVOUTLY CLIMBE		. . .	155	ISAACS M.	44
DEW					
THAT DEW THEY LENT, A BREATHING SACRIFICE.		. . .	156	ISAACS M.	62
TOO, IS MY DEW, AND SPRINGING WEL.		. . .	203	DSRDR + FR	19
I SMELL A DEW LIKE MYRRH, AND ALL THE DAY		. . .	198	UNPRFTBLNS	10
THIS DEW FELL ON MY BREAST.	.	. . .	176	MRNG-WTCH	7
MY DEW, MY DEW, MY EARLY LOVE	.	. . .	308	THE SEED	5
MY DEW, MY DEW. MY EARLY LOVE	.	. . .	308	THE SEED	5
AS THOU IN TEARS DOST, REST IN DEW.	.	. .	303	ST MARY MN	4
WHEN MY LORDS HEAD IS FILL'D WITH DEW, AND ALL		. . .	324	THE NIGHT	32
MANY BRIGHT MORNINGS, MUCH DEW, MANY SHOWERS		. . .	289	THE TIMBER	2
DEAR FEAST OF PALMS, OF FLOWERS AND DEW.		. . .	295	PALM-SUNDY	30
DEW OF THE DEAD WHICH MAKES DUST MOVE		. . .	298	JESUS WP B	11
A GRIEF, WHOSE SILENT DEW SHALL BREED		. . .	299	JESUS WP B	48
BLEST BE THY DEW, AND BLEST THY FROST		. . .	227	LV + DSPLN	7
THE DEW DOTH CHEER WHAT IS DISTREST		. . .	227	LV + DSPLN	10
A POWERFUL, RARE DEW	. . .	. . .	244	THE SAP	40
THUS CAL AND THIRST FOR DEW.		. . .	243	THE SAP	4
BUT NOW THE DEW AND SUN HAVE WARM'D MY BOWRES		. . .	274	PROFFER	5
WITH DEW BY NIGHT, BUT ONE YOU CANNOT SEE		. . .	280	PALM-TREE	23
FRESH AS THE DEW, WHICH BUT THIS DAWNING WEARS.		. . .	267	ASCN-DAY A	20
THE DEW THY HERBS DRINK UP BY NIGHT		. . .	207	REPENTANCE	39
WHEN THE SPILT DEW	. . . .	. . .	340	THE FEAST	22
DEWY					
SHINING WITH JOY, LIKE DEWY DAYS		. . .	345	THE WREATH	11

	PAGE	TITLE	LINE
DEWY (CON'T)			
DO KNOW THY DEWY MORNING-HOURS	301	PROVIDENCE	28
DIDDST			
DIDDST THY SWIFT YEERS IN PIETY CUT-GROW	156	ISAACS M.	68
DIE			
TO DIE HERE FOR THY SAKE	184	PEACE	12
SO SHOULD WE TOO. ALL THINGS TEACH US TO DIE	201	THE CHECK	20
TAKE THEIR LEAVE, AND DIE. BIRDS, BEASTS, EACH TREE	201	THE CHECK	27
AND DIE, THAT BUSH WHERE GOD IS, SHALL NOT BURN.	196	RLS + LSNS	132
TO FILL MY BOTTLE, THEN I DIE WITH THIRST.	290	THE TIMBER	48
FLOWRES GATHER'D IN THIS WORLD, DIE HERE. IF THOU	283	GARLAND	33
FIRES SMOKING DIE.	210	FAITH	26
LIVE, DIE, AND RISE WITH THEE.	216	DRESSING	18
HER INFANTS DIE	222	TEMPEST	6
SPIRITS WITHOUT THEE DIE	219	HOLY COMM.	17
TO SLEEP WITHOUT THEE, IS TO DIE.	277	COCK-CRWNG	25
THAT KNOW TO DIE	269	ASCSN-HYMN	8
THEN WOULD GO TRAVEL, FIGHT OR DIE.	214	MISERY	74
BOTH LIVE AND DIE THY CHILD.	235	MUTINIE	39
DIED			
NOW LANGUISHED AND DIED	238	SHEPHEARDS	20
WHO DIED TO STAKE	204	DSRDR + FR	58
DIES			
FAITH INTO LIFE BREAKS, AND DEATH DIES.	310	THE SEED	66
DIET			
ALTHOUGH THEIR DIET MAY BE FINE	228	PILGRIMAGE	18
WHOSE DIET IS DIVINE AND FAIR	346	THE QUEER	2
DIFFER			
WHERE, THOUGH THE GLORY DIFFER IN EACH STAR	236	CONSTLATN	31
DIFFUS'D			
EVER THE SAME, WHOSE DIFFUS'D STOCK	333	AGREEMENT	33
DIG'D			
YET DIG'D THE MOLE, AND LEST HIS WAYS BE FOUND	232	THE WORLD	23
DIGG'D			
I DIGG'D ABOUT	247	I WALKT	16
WHEN SIX YEARS THENCE DIGG'D UP, SOME YOUTHFULL EYE	201	THE CHECK	6
DIGNIFIE			
WITH HIS DID DIGNIFIE.	302	THE KNOT	8
DIM			
WHEN I BEHOLD THEE, THOUGH MY LIGHT BE DIM	306	RAIN-BOW	15
MIGHT LIVE INVISIBLE AND DIM.	325	THE NIGHT	54
LOOKS DIM TOO IN THE CLOUD	197	CORRUPTION	34
THEIR DAY WAS DARK, AND DIM.	239	SHEPHEARDS	54
DIMME			
DUST THAT WOULD RISE, AND DIMME MY SIGHT	161	DSTRQCTION	30
DINE			
THE BIRDS NOR SOW, NOR REAP, YET SUP AND DINE	245	MAN	12
DINNER			
AND SATE THERE NONE SUCH AT THY DINNER.	305	ST MARY MN	68
DIRT			
DIRT IN HER WAY, WILL KEEP ABOVE THE SKIE.	291	THE TIMBER	56
DISAPPARELL			
I'LE DISAPPARELL, AND TO BUY	168	VNTY SPRIT	33
DISAPPEAR			
DO AFTER CALMLY DISAPPEAR	339	DEATH B	24
DISBAND			
AND CRUM OF LIFE, NOW READY TO DISBAND	275	PROFFER	27
THE PURSIE CLOUDS DISBAND, AND SCATTER	212	DAWNING	21
DISCENT			
SURE, MIGHTY LOVE FORESEEING THE DISCENT	223	TEMPEST	21
DISCERN			
I CAN DISCERN WOLVES FROM THE SHEEP.	273	WHT SUNDAY	24
DISCERNING			
LIFE IS A FIX'D, DISCERNING LIGHT	345	QUICKNESS	9
DISCLOSE			
SOMETHING OF SICKNESS WOULD DISCLOSE.	222	AFFLICTION	28
HIS LOVE THERE FIRST DISCLOSE.	238	SHEPHEARDS	16
BUD IN THE BRIGHT EAST, AND DISCLOSE	151	THE SEARCH	2
DISCOMPOSE			
MIGHT HIS FRIENDS DISCOMPOSE	243	THE SAP	24
DISCORD			
THERE IS NO DISCORD, BUT YOUR HARMONY.	280	JOY	2
DISCOURSE			
EATE, DRINKE, DISCOURSE, SIT DOWNE, AND REST	149	RELIGION	15
THROUGH ALL THY ACTIONS, COUNSELS, AND DISCOURSE	193	RLS + LSNS	37
DISCOVER'D			
DISCOVER'D ALL, THAT THERE IS DONE.	338	DEATH B	15
DISCOVERIES			
AND INTO LOUD DISCOVERIES BREAK	313	THE STONE	23
THESE NEW DISCOVERIES DO, EXCEPT THEY DROWN.	224	TEMPEST	40
DISCUSSE			
BUT AS I DID THEIR MADNES SO DISCUSSE	233	THE WORLD	57
E'RE WE CAN LISP, OR OUGHT DISCUSSE	166	THE CALL	48
INCITE THEM TO THAT FIERCE DISCUSSE	175	THE STORM	11
DISDAIN			
BUT MEER DISDAIN, LET NOT MAN SAY	335	JUDGEMENT	43
DISDEIN			
DISDEIN TREADS ON THE PEACEFUL NAME	214	MISERY	68
DISEASE			
A LETHARGY, AND MEER DISEASE	242	MISERY	84

			PAGE	TITLE	LINE
DISEASE	(CON'T)				
SHUT OUT ALL PAIN AND EACH DISEASE.	. . . . .	319	THE ASS	63
AND MEERE DISEASE	. . . . . .	162	MT. OLVS A	8
AND 'STEAD OF PHISICK, A DISEASE	. . . .	150	RELIGION	44
FROM HER FAINT BOSOME BREATH'D THEE, THE DISEASE	. .	160	THE SHOWRE	2
DISEASES					
OUR SOULS DISEASES FIRST, AND THEN	. . .	311	FAIR+YONG	12
THY ROOT SUCKS BUT DISEASES, WORMS THERE SEAT	. .	243	THE SAP	7
DISGRAC'D					
WHILE ONE CRYED OUT, WE ARE DISGRAC'D.	. . .	303	ORNAMENT	19
DISGUIS'D					
WITH AIRE DISGUIS'D.	. . . . . .	162	PURSUITE	8
DISGUISE					
MOVES IN DISGUISE, AND SIGHS AFFLICT THE AIR.	. .	280	JOY	4
DISHONOR					
THAT MAY DISHONOR THOSE PURE LINES.	. . . .	335	JUDGEMENT	38
DISMAI'D					
SO SHOOK MY BREST, THAT (SICK AND SORE DISMAI'D)	.	233	MUTINIE	5
DISMEMBRED					
WITH HYEROGLIPHICKS QUITE DISMEMBRED	. . .	168	VNTY SPRIT	23
DISORDER					
THE SPACES OF DEATH DWELL AND DISORDER.	. . .	277	COCK-CRWNG	30
DISORDER'D					
THUS BY OUR LUSTS DISORDER'D INTO WARS	. .	237	CONSTLATN	45
THUS DOTH GOD KEY DISORDER'D MAN	. . . .	222	AFFLICTION	35
DISORDERED					
MANY DISORDERED LIVES I SAW	. . . .	310	THE SEED	55
DISPATCH					
THAT HOURE, WHICH MUST THY LIFE, AND MINE DISPATCH.	.	157	THE LAMPE	8
DISPATCH NECESSITIES, LIFE HATH A LOAD	.	192	RLS + LSNS	33
DISPATCH'D					
DISPATCH'D AN EYE	. . . . . .	141	RGNRTN	83
DISPATCH'D TO HOLY SOULS, SICK WITH DESIRE	. .	284	PSALM 104	14
DISPENCE					
OR HAD THE BLACK ART TO DISPENCE	. . . .	169	RETREATE	17
DISPENSE					
ONE SULLEN BEAME, WHOSE CHARGE IS TO DISPENSE	. .	159	MANS FALL	13
RARE LOOKS, THAT CAN DISPENSE SUCH JOY	. .	281	THE FAVOUR	3
DISPERS'D					
IS ALL DISPERS'D, AND CHEAPE.	. . . .	160	DSTROCTION	2
DISPERSE					
EITHER DISPERSE THESE MISTS, WHICH BLOT AND FILL	.	271	ALL GONE	37
THOU WOULDST TO WEEDS, AND THISTLES QUITE DISPERSE	.	221	AFFLICTION	15
AWAKE, AWAKE. AND, LIKE THE SUN, DISPERSE	. .	217	EASTER-DAY	9
IS VERY HARD. O GOD, DISPERSE	. . . .	329	ANGUISH	16
DISPLAY					
AND IN THE GREATER WORLD DISPLAY	. . .	221	AFFLICTION	9
DISPLEAS'D					
BE NOT DISPLEAS'D, IF I, WHO HAVE A SUTE	.	230	LAW + GOSP	24
YET GRIEF AND OLD WOUNDS MAKE HIM SORE DISPLEAS'D	.	290	THE TIMBER	35
DISPOSE					
UNTO MY DISPOSE OR LOT	. . . .	249	BEGGING A	18
DISPOSED					
IS WELL DISPOSED, FOR BODIES ONCE INFECTED	. .	278	THE STARRE	14
DISPUTE					
WHICH OTHERS ONELY GROPE FOR AND DISPUTE.	. .	320	HIDDN TRSR	14
DISSENT					
AND YET (AS IF SOME DEEP HATE AND DISSENT	. .	289	THE TIMBER	13
DISSOLV'D					
AND SPRINGS, LIKE DISSOLV'D PEARLS THEIR STREAMS DID POUR		268	ASCN-DAY A	47
DISSOLV'ST					
AS THOU DISSOLV'ST TO THEM, AND THEY DISTILL	. . .	158	THE LAMPE	18
DISSOLVE					
DISSOLVE (WITH IT) TO CLAY	. . . . .	183	THRS A TYE	2
DISSOLVE INTO THE COMMON DROSS.	. . . .	274	WHT SUNDAY	64
DIST					
NO QUIET COULDST THOU HAVE, NOR DIST THOU WINK	.	213	ADMISSION	9
WHEN FIRST THOU DIST EVEN FROM THE GRAVE	. . .	202	DSRDR + FR	1
DISTANCE					
BY DISTANCE ALL GOOD OBJECTS FIRST TO DROWN	. .	183	THRS A TYE	19
I SAW AT DISTANCE, AND WHERE GROWS THAT FRUIT	. .	320	HIDDN TRSR	13
AND ALL THAT DISTANCE WAS LAW AND COMMAND.	. .	331	JACOBS PLW	48
DISTANT					
THEIR JOYS PROVOKE THE DISTANT SKIE	. . .	295	PALM-SUNDY	20
DISTANT AND LOW, I CAN IN THINE SEE HIM	. . .	306	RAIN-BOW	16
THINGS DISTANT DOTH UNITE	. . . .	183	THRS A TYE	10
DISTIL					
(BECAUSE THOU DOST THY GRACE DISTIL)	. . .	227	LV + DSPLN	2
DISTILL					
AS THOU DISSOLV'ST TO THEM, AND THEY DISTILL	. . .	158	THE LAMPE	18
DISTRACTIONS					
SETTLE MY HOUSE, AND SHUT OUT ALL DISTRACTIONS	.	191	THE MATCH	28
DISTRESS					
BUT BLESSED JACOB, THOUGH THY SAD DISTRESS	. .	331	JACOBS PLW	41
DISTRESSED					
OF YONG, DISTRESSED ISHMAEL.	. . . .	300	PROVIDENCE	6
DISTREST					
OF THE DISTREST, HASTING THEIR OVERTHROW.	. .	327	RIGHTSNESS	27
MY DISTREST LORD. OR DID A STAR	. . .	315	DWELLNG-PL	7
THE DEW DOTH CHEER WHAT IS DISTREST	. . .	227	LV + DSPLN	10

	PAGE	TITLE	LINE
DISTURB			
WHICH NCNE DISTURB.	324	THE NIGHT	28
OF TEMPESTS CAN NC MORE DISTURB THY EASE.	289	THE TIMBER	18
DISTURBS			
PURGING THE FLOOR WHICH CHAFF DISTURBS.	221	AFFLICTION	20
DIVERS			
OF DIVERS STONES, SCME BRIGHT, AND ROUND	141	RGNRTN	64
DIVIDE			
THESE DARE DIVIDE, AND STAIN	156	BRT. CHRCH	10
AND INTERCOURSE OF TIMES DIVIDE	245	MAN	4
DIVINE			
TO HIS DIVINE APPCINTMENTS EVER CLEAVE	245	MAN	10
AND PITTY OF SUCH A DIVINE EXTENT	216	DRESSING	29
O SWEET, DIVINE SIMPLICITY. O GRACE	155	ISAACS M.	37
THIS, THIS DIVINE RESTORATIVE	305	ST MARY MN	41
WHCSE DIET IS DIVINE ANC FAIR	346	THE QUEER	2
DIVINELY			
WHICH THOU DIVINELY HAST FORGIVEN	265	INTRO. 2	27
DIVINEST			
ON THE DIVINEST WITS	219	HOLY COMM.	19
DIVINITIE			
HAVE THEIR COMMISSIONS FRCM DIVINITIE	278	THE STARRE	10
DO'ST			
HOW MANY HOURS DO'ST THINK 'TILL DAY.	178	EVNG-WTCH	10
DO'T			
AND IF NOT THCU, LET NOT ME DC'T.	319	THE ASS	32
DOCTORS			
AMONGST THE DOCTORS, ANC DESIR'D	151	THE SEARCH	14
DOCTRINE			
PCOR BIRDS THIS DOCTRINE SING	301	PROVIDENCE	25
THEIR DOCTRINE CHAFF AND WINDY FITS.	332	AGREEMENT	26
AND YET, HOW FEW BELIEVE SUCH DOCTRINE SPRINGS	248	I WALKT	36
DOES			
THUS THOU ALL DAY A THANKLESS WEED DOES DRESS	198	UNPRFTBLNS	16
DONE			
AND WHEN TH'HAST CONE, A STENCH, CR FOG IS ALL	198	UNPRFTBLNS	17
THY WILL IN ALL BE DONE, NOT MINE.	191	THE MATCH	27
HAVE CONE MUCH GOOD	190	THE MATCH	2
BRIEFLY, DOE AS THOU WOULD'ST BE CONE UNTO,	196	RLS + LSNS	139
ALLCW YOUR JOYES RELIGICN, THAT DONE, SPEED	194	RLS + LSNS	81
THE MYSTERY, BUT THIS NFER DONE	168	VNTY SPRIT	27
THAT CONE, WE SHALBE SAFE, AND GOOD	165	THE CALL	28
IT SEEMS THEIR CANDLE, HOWE'R CCNE	276	COCK-CRWNG	11
WHEN CUR WORDS AND WORKS ARE CCNE.	211	DAWNING	4
AND HAD NOT HE SO DONE, IT IS MCST TRUE	243	THE SAP	21
AND WCRK, AND WIND TIL ALL BE CCNE	214	MISERY	78
AND WHAT CAN NEVER MORE BE DONE	323	THE NIGHT	11
THE VILE DESPIGHT DONE TO THY NAME.	335	JUDGEMENT	34
AND SAY, THY WILL BE DCNE.	338	THE THRONE	15
DISCOVER'D ALL, THAT THERE IS DCNE.	338	DEATH B	15
WHAT THOU HAST DONE (BUT THOUGH MAN TOO	299	JESUS WP B	35
SC MURTHERED MAN, WHEN LOVELY LIFE IS DONE	289	THE TIMBER	21
MAKE LESSER MORNINGS, WHEN THE GREAT ARE DONE.	288	THE BIRD	18
EVEN WHAT WAS DCNE BEFORE, ANC NO NEW THING.	320	HIDDN TRSR	2
NCW ALL IS DCNE, FINDE ALL IS VANITY.	320	HIDDN TRSR	10
EVER THE SAME, AND NEVER CONE.	349	L'ENVOY	2
DOOR			
BY EACH MANS DOOR, AND CUICKLY WILL	351	L'ENVOY	51
THOSE BURTHENS TC THE RICH MANS COOR	319	THE ASS	34
TO THEE EACH HOURE, BEG AT THY DOOR	230	LAW + GOSP	25
OR ELS WITHIN MY CCOR	221	PSALM 121	18
STROW AT THY DOOR	215	PRAISE	55
BUT SHUTS HIS DOOR, AND LEAVES GOOD OUT ALL NIGHT.	194	RLS + LSNS	84
THIS LEPER HAUNT, AND SCYL THY DCCR	200	NTVTY 1	26
SHADOW NO MORE MY DOOR.	204	IDLE VERSE	2
DOORES			
STILL OUT OF COORES	153	THE SEARCH	78
DOORS			
THERE DUST THAT OUT OF COORS MIGHT FILL	226	RETIREMENT	51
WITHIN THOSE COORS (MY CCORS) DCST HEAR. I WILL.	226	RETIREMENT	55
WITHIN THOSE DOORS (MY CCORS) DCST HEAR. I WILL.	226	RETIREMENT	55
HE KNCCKS AT ALL COORS, STRAYS AND ROAMS	246	MAN	22
THE EVERLASTING DOORS ABOVE	325	ABELS BLOD	19
DOSIS			
SCRROWS IN WHITE, GRIEFS TUN'C, A SUGERD DOSIS	280	JOY	5
DOTAGE			
FRESH DCTAGE TEMPTS, CR OLD USURPS HIS WILL.	161	DSTRQCTION	16
DOTE			
NONE WOULD MORE DCTE ON, NOR SC SCON ENTICE.	320	HIDDN TRSR	24
DOTING			
THE DCTING LOVER IN HIS QUEINTEST STRAIN	231	THE WORLD	8
DOUBLE			
US DOUBLE PAY.	213	ADMISSION	24
UNBITTED TONGUES ARE IN THEIR PENANCE DOUBLE	194	RLS + LSNS	71
DOUBLING			
DOUBLING THY GRIEFS, WHEN NCNE WCULD OWN THEE.	185	PASSION	29
DOUBT			
WHY SHOULC FRAIL FLESH COUBT ANY MORE	343	WATER-FALL	21
DOUBTS			
AND TRAMPLES CN DCUBTS AND DESPAIR.	346	THE QUEER	4

		PAGE	TITLE	LINE
DOUBTS	(CON'T)			
AND WHEN FEARS, AND DOUBTS WERE RIFE		214	PRAISE	3
DOVE				
BY HIS MILD DOVE		225	RETIREMENT	10
MOST BLESSED LAMB. AND MILDEST DOVE.		208	REPENTANCE	48
THY DOVE TOO BEARS US ON HER SACRED WINGS.		230	LAW + GOSP	20
NOR GRIEVE THY DOVE, BUT SOFT AND MILD		235	MUTINIE	38
THESE LIGHTS OF SERPENTS LIKE THE DOVE.		272	WHT SUNDAY	10
AND HOLY DOVE.		179	CHRCH-SVC	3
A WOLF, MORE THEN A LAMB OR DOVE.		321	CHILDEHOOD	10
THAT SECRET ARK, WHERE THE MILDE DOVE DOTH DWELL		330	JACOBS PLW	28
HOVER NOT LONG, ETERNAL DOVE.		308	THE SEED	7
WHEN THE BRIGHT DOVE		291	THE JEWS	8
O HOLY GROANS. GROANS OF THE DOVE.		298	JESUS WP B	9
THE SECRET FAVORS OF THE DOVE		348	HOLY BIBLE	28
DOVES				
THOU ARE LIFES CHARTER, THE DOVES SPOTLESS NEAST		197	SCRIPTURES	3
DOWN				
WALK BUT THE FIELDS, OR SIT DOWN AT SOME WEL		197	CORRUPTION	27
SITS DOWN, AND FREEZETH ON		197	CORRUPTION	30
SHAL HE THAT DID COME DOWN FROM THENCE		200	NTVTY 2	9
WHEN I LYE DOWN. THE PICUS SOLL BY NIGHT		177	MRNG-WTCH	24
BUT AS I URG'D THUS, AND WRIT DOWN		152	THE SEARCH	67
AND MOONS, THOUGH FULL, WOULD GET THEM DOWN.		309	THE SEED	32
HAD WRIT DOWN ITS SAD CONSEQUENCE		311	FAIR+YONG	20
IN SPARKLING SMILES HASTE GLADLY DOWN		315	DWELLNG-PL	9
AND SEND A FIRE DOWN, THAT SHALL BRING		305	ST MARY MN	55
AND SETS UP LAWS TO PULL HIS HONOR DOWN.		330	JACOBS PLW	20
I WROTE IT DOWN. BUT ONE THAT SAW		332	AGREEMENT	1
SHALL I FROM THENCE CAST DOWN MY SELF		321	CHILDEHOOD	22
OUR STORIES ARE IN THEIRS SET DOWN		273	WHT SUNDAY	31
DEARE FRIEND SIT DOWN, AND BEAR AWHILE THIS SHADE		279	PALM-TREE	1
OF MY OWN FRAILTY DROPT DOWN MANY A TEAR		247	I WALKT	31
AND FROTHIE NOISE WHICH UP AND DOWN DOTH FLIE		234	MUTINIE	24
FORCE DOWN A JUST CURSE, WHEN THY HANDS WOULD BLESS.		230	LAW + GOSP	33
(A PLACE, AND NO MORE, IS SET DOWN)		228	PILGRIMAGE	6
ME DOWN TO BREATH, AND CASTING IN MY HEART		233	MUTINIE	2
AND PAINTED TRIMMING TAKES DOWN BOTH HIS EYES		224	TEMPEST	46
IF SAINTS, AND ANGELS FAL DOWN, MUCH MORE THOU.		217	DRESSING	42
EVEN TO CONTEMPT THY KINGDOME DOWN		218	EASTER HYM	14
BECAUSE WE FORC'D THY JUDGEMENTS DOWN.		350	L'ENVOY	32
AND LOVE THE LURE, THAT WOOS THEE DOWN.		346	THE QUEER	14
KNEEL DOWN AND FALL		341	THE FEAST	59
MORE SOFT THEN DOWN.		341	THE FEAST	62
DOWN-RIGHT				
THE DOWN-RIGHT EPICURE PLAC'D HEAV'N IN SENSE		232	THE WORLD	38
DOWN-RODE				
TAKE THE DOWN-RODE TO VANITIE		240	MISERY	14
DOWNE				
LOOKE DOWNE GREAT MASTER OF THE FEAST, O SHINE		150	RELIGION	51
EATE, DRINKE, DISCOURSE, SIT DOWNE, AND REST		149	RELIGION	15
AND TAME, AND KEEPE DOWNE WITH THY LIGHT		161	DSTROCTION	29
DOWNIE				
SWEET, DOWNIE THOUGHTS, SOFT LILLY-SHADES, CALM STREAMES.		188	RELAPSE	25
DOWNWARDS				
SOME DOWNWARDS TO THEIR PLACE.		285	PSALM 104	24
DOZEN				
EACH DAY IS GROWN A DOZEN YEAR		170	COME, COME	3
DRAGONS				
AND LIKE THAT LAMB WHICH HAD THE DRAGONS VOICE		237	CONSTLATN	43
DRAMME				
IS BUT ONE DRAMME, AND WHAT THOU NOW DESCRIEST		177	EVNG-WTCH	5
DRANK				
DRANK THEM AS FREE.		232	THE WORLD	30
AND ONE WHO DRANK IT THUS, ASSURES THAT YOU		244	THE SAP	45
DRAW				
THE FLOWRES TO AIR DRAW NEER, AND SUBTILTIE		223	TEMPEST	35
TO DRAW HIM DRINK, AND FOR HIS CAMELS TOO.		155	ISAACS M.	42
SUCH A MIST OVER MY MINDE DRAW		332	AGREEMENT	3
DRAWN				
THAT SACRED VAIL DRAWN O'R THY GLORIOUS NOON		323	THE NIGHT	2
(FOR I TILL DRAWN CAME NOT TO THEE)		334	AGREEMENT	68
THEY ARE BUT VEILS, AND CYPERS DRAWN		334	JUDGEMENT	9
(FOR I TILL DRAWN CAME NOT TO THEE)		340	RGNRTN	4
DRAWS				
AND, AS FIRST LOVE DRAWS STRONGEST, SO FROM HENCE		196	CORRUPTION	7
DREAD				
ACCEPT, DREAD LORD, AND THE POOR OBLATION		190	THE MATCH	13
OF MY DREAD LORD.		337	THE THRONE	4
A HEART IS THAT DREAD PLACE, THAT AWFUL CELL		330	JACOBS PLW	27
AND THAT DREAD GLORY, WHICH THY CHILDREN FEAR'D		330	JACOBS PLW	2
OR THE DREAD MYSTERIES OF THY BLEST BLOUD		217	DRESSING	35
IF THEN, DREAD LORD		215	PRAISE	45
DREADFUL				
THERE IS NONE ELSE) DID NOT THE DREADFUL BRINK		320	HIDDN TRSR	16
AND ON THE VERGE OF THAT DARK, DREADFUL PIT		188	RELAPSE	3
THAT GAIN IS DREADFUL, WHICH MAKES SPIRITS SICK.		193	RLS + LSNS	42
DREAM				
THEY REST AND DREAM HOMES OF THEIR OWN.		228	PILGRIMAGE	8
ILL THY BREST WITH HOME. THINK ON THY DREAM.		276	PROFFER	45

		PAGE	TITLE	LINE
DREAMES	**(CCN'T)**			
HERE JACOB DREAMES, AND WRESTLES, THERE	• • • •	149	RELIGION	9
DREAMS				
AND YET, AS ANGELS IN SCME BRIGHTER DREAMS	• • •	271	ALL GONE	25
AND FRCM THIS CARE, WHERE DREAMS AND SORROWS REIGN	• •	248	I WALKT	57
AND DREAMS OF PARADISE AND LIGHT.	• • • •	276	COCK-CRWNG	6
TC CRCWN HIS TEMPLES. SHAL DREAMS BE HIS LAW.	• • •	224	TEMPEST	52
WHERE NCT SO MUCH AS CREAMS OF LIGHT MAY SHINE	• •	289	THE TIMBER	11
DRESS				
WHO THEN DID CRESS THE MUCH LCV'D TOY	• • • •	304	ST MARY MN	17
FCRC'D BY HER ARTLESS LCCKS AND DRESS	• • • •	303	ORNAMENT	18
AND AFTER FALL, FOR IN HER DRESS	• • • •	269	ASCSN-HYMN	17
GIVE TO THY SPOUSE HER PERFECT, AND PURE DRESS	• •	237	CONSTLATN	57
THUS THCU ALL DAY A THANKLESS WEED DOES DRESS	• •	198	UNPRFTBLNS	16
AND DRESS THIS EARTH FOR NEXT YEARS MEAT.	• •	341	THE FEAST	75
DRESSE				
BUT DRESSE, AND WATER WITH THY GRACE	• • • •	204	DSRDR + FR	55
TC DRESSE, AND TRIM OUR SHAME	• • • •	205	IDLE VERSE	10
BUT FELT THROUGH ALL THIS FLESHLY DRESSE	• • •	170	RETREATE	19
I WILL CRESSE THEE.	• • • •	214	PRAISE	16
THAT SCENE WAS CHANG'D, AND A NEW DRESSE	• • •	210	FAITH	23
TC DRESSE THEM, AND UNSWADLE DEATH.	• • • •	209	THE BURIAL	12
DRESSINGS				
THE SCFTER DRESSINGS CF THE SPRING	• • • •	345	THE WREATH	5
DREST				
BEFORE 'TWAS CREST OR SPUN, AND WHEN	• • •	347	THE BOOK	7
SHALL ALL BE CREST IN SHINING WHITE	• • •	349	L'ENVOY	4
BOTH SOUL, AND BODY ARE WELL CREST	• • •	209	REPENTANCE	80
THOU'LT FIND ME DREST AND CN MY WAY	• • •	212	DAWNING	47
YET SCLCMCN WAS NEVER DREST SC FINE.	• • •	245	MAN	14
OR THCSE FAINT BEAMS IN WHICH THIS HILL IS DREST	• •	270	ALL GONE	7
THAT GLASS OF SOULS AND SPIRITS, WHERE WELL CREST	•	275	PROFFER	23
FALSE, JUGLING SOUNDS, A GRONE WELL DREST, WHERE CARE	•	280	JOY	3
WITH WHICH THEIR GREAT CREATOR HAD THEM DREST.	• •	268	ASCN-DAY A	44
IN THE SAME LIVERY DREST	• • • •	201	THE CHECK	4
AND THEN SET FORTH, WHO IS THUS DREST, THE FALL	• •	195	RLS + LSNS	111
BEING LAID, AND DREST FCR SLEEP, CLOSE NOT THY EYES	•	195	RLS + LSNS	127
THE OLD, WHITE PRCPHETS PLANTED FIRST AND DREST.	• •	326	RIGHTSNESS	2
DREW				
HE CREW THE CURSE UPON THE WORLD, AND CRACKT	• •	197	CORRUPTION	15
ALL AGES UP. WHO CREW THIS CIRCLE, EVEN	• • •	178	EVNG-WTCH	13
I DREW HER NEERE, AND FCUND	• • • •	141	RGNRTN	62
EXTENT, AND END, FOR MY HANDS CREW THE LINE	• •	226	RETIREMENT	27
DRIE				
THAT THEY HAVE CUICKEN'D EVEN DRIE STUBBLE.	• •	218	HOLY COMM.	4
TC MAKE DRIE CUST, AND DEAD TREES GROW.	• • •	291	THE JEWS	13
DRILLING				
THEN DRILLING ON, LEARNES TO ENCREASE	• • • •	150	RELIGION	37
DRILLS				
HERE CF THIS MIGHTY SPRING, I FOUND SOME CRILLS	• •	168	VNTY SPRIT	17
DRINK				
TO DRAW HIM DRINK, AND FOR HIS CAMELS TOO.	• • •	155	ISAACS M.	42
THESE TO THE BEASTS OF EVERY FIELC GIVE DRINK.	• •	285	PSALM 104	33
THEN DRINK AND PRAISE THY BCUNTECUSNESS.	• • •	301	PROVIDENCE	30
THEY WILL DRINK BLOOD, THAT DESPISE TEARS.	• • •	296	JESUS WP A	12
DRINK AFTER THEM.	• • • •	329	TEARS	12
THE DEW THY HERBS DRINK UP BY NIGHT	• • •	207	REPENTANCE	39
LET ME NOT SPIL, BUT CRINK THY BLOOD	• • •	230	LAW + GOSP	31
O DRINK AND BREAD	• • • • • •	340	THE FEAST	37
DRINKE				
EATE, DRINKE, DISCOURSE, SIT DCWNE, AND REST	• •	149	RELIGION	15
DRIV'N				
DRIV'N BY THE SPHERES	• • • • •	231	THE WORLD	5
DRIVE				
DRIVE THEE FRCM ME	• • • • •	181	BURIALL	22
THOSE WHITE DESIGNS WHICH CHILDREN DRIVE	• •	321	CHILDEHOOD	4
ANGELS. WHICH FOUL MEN CRIVE AWAY.	• • •	322	CHILDEHOOD	38
THUS THOU THY GLORY THRCUGH THE WORLD DOST DRIVE	• •	287	PSALM 104	83
DROOPS				
HE SLEEPES, AND CROOPS, AND IN THIS DROWSIE STATE	• •	158	MANS FALL	7
DROP				
CCRDIALS IN EVERY CROP, AND WINE.	• • • •	150	RELIGION	32
AFTER WHOLE SHOWRES ONE CROP.	• • • •	188	NO DO THEY	38
CCME, DROP YOUR BRANCHES, STRCW THE WAY	• •	294	PALM-SUNDY	1
AND ALL THY PATHS DROP FATNESS RCUND	• • •	337	PSALM 65	40
THEY CROP UPON THE WILDERNESS	• • • •	337	PSALM 65	41
CNE LIVING DRCP. CNE DRCP LIFE KEEPS.	• • •	308	THE SEED	14
CNE LIVING DRCP. CNE DRCP LIFE KEEPS.	• • •	308	THE SEED	14
DIOST TC EACH DROP REPLY.	• • • •	213	ADMISSION	12
DROP IN THEIR CELLS.	• • • •	281	JOY	26
WHY, SINCE EACH DROP CF THY QUICK STORY	• • •	343	WATER-FALL	15
DROPPINGS				
STILL AS THOU BURN'ST, AND THE WARME DROPPINGS CREEPE	•	158	THE LAMPE	14
DROPS				
OF DRCPS MAKE SCFT THE EARTH, MY EYES COULD WEEP	•	160	THE SHOWRE	14
THEN CRCPS, AND RAINS FCR GRIEFE	• • • •	139	RGNRTN	25
IN SILENT DROPS STEAL FROM THEIR HOLY EYES	• •	268	ASCN-DAY A	53
SCME DRCPS OF THY ALL-QLICKNING BLOOD	• • •	264	INTRO. 1	5
THEN DID THESE DRCPS (FCR MARBLE SWEATS	• •	213	ADMISSION	5
THE DROPS OF RAIN, THE SIGHS CF THE WIND	• • •	207	REPENTANCE	37

		PAGE	TITLE	LINE
DROPS	(CCN'T)			
FROM WHICH SOME DROPS FAL HERE	. . . . . .	243	THE SAP	12
AND HASTY DROPS, AS IF THEY HAD	. . . .	305	ST MARY MN	43
HIS LCCKS ARE WET WITH THE CLEAR DROPS OF NIGHT.	. .	324	THE NIGHT	33
SCME DRCPS MAY FALL BEFCRE, BLT A CLEAR SPRING	. .	291	THE TIMBER	54
OR SINCE THOSE DRCPS ARE ALL SENT BACK	. . .	343	WATER-FALL	19
DROPT				
OF MY OWN FRAILTY CROPT DCWN MANY A TEAR	. . .	247	I WALKT	31
DROSS				
DISSOLVE INTO THE COMMON CROSS.	. . .	274	WHT SUNDAY	64
CRYED DROSS FCR GCLD, AND NEVER THOUGHT	. .	348	HOLY BIBLE	15
DROUGHT				
ALL WOULD BE DROUGHT, AND LEANNESS, NCT A TREE	. .	222	AFFLICTION	23
DROVE				
DROVE THEE AWAY	. . . .	213	ADMISSION	22
I'VE READ, WHC 'TWAS, DROVE YCL AWAY.	. . .	275	PROFFER	18
THOSE WHITE DAYES, DRCVE HOME TC THE TENT	. .	151	THE SEARCH	26
DROWN				
AND DROWN MY EYES	. . . . .	191	THE MATCH	37
WHAT SPRINGS CF SWEAT, AND BLCCD CID DROWN THEE.	. .	185	PASSION	24
THEN WOULD I DROWN	. . . . .	182	CHRFLNESS	20
BY DISTANCE ALL GCOD CBJECTS FIRST TO DROWN	. .	183	THRS A TYE	19
THESE NEW DISCOVERIES DC, EXCEPT THEY DROWN.	. .	224	TEMPEST	40
OUR DROWN'D ESTATE, TAKING THE CURSE	. .	274	WHT SUNDAY	54
FULL FORTY DAYS O'R THE DRCWN'D WORLD DID WEEP)	. .	307	RAIN-BOW	28
DROWNS				
A FLOUD THAT CROWNS BCTH TEARS, AND GRONES	. .	214	ADMISSION	31
DROWSIE				
SCME DRCWSIE SILK-WCRME CREEPE	. . .	144	RSRCTN +IM	5
'TWAS SC. I SAW THY BIRTH. THAT CROWSIE LAKE	. .	160	THE SHOWRE	1
HE SLEEPES, AND DROCPS, AND IN THIS DROWSIE STATE	. .	158	MANS FALL	7
DRUDGE				
TC WHAT MCST TAKES THEM, IS A CRUDGE.	. . .	309	THE SEED	38
DRUNK				
DRUNK OF THY LIVING STREAM	. . . .	329	TEARS	10
BUT DRUNK, IS PUDDLE, CR MEERE SLIME	. . .	150	RELIGION	43
IS DRUNK, AND STAGGERS IN THE WAY.	. . .	170	RETREATE	28
THOUGH BLCOD AND DRUNKENNESS MAKE BUT FOUL, FCLL WEATHER.		307	RAIN-BOW	26
AND DRUNKENNESS CUICKLY DID SLCCEED THE FLOOD.	. .	307	RAIN-BOW	22
DRUNKNES				
OF DRLNKNES, SURFFITS, CARE	. . . .	202	THE CHECK	42
DRY				
FCR WHOSE DRY DUST GREEN BRANCHES BUD	. . .	310	THE SEED	83
AND HERBS WHICH ON DRY HILLS DC SPRING	. .	301	PROVIDENCE	26
HER BRESTS GROWN DRY.	. . . .	222	TEMPEST	8
BUT NCT SC DRY AND CLEAN AS THIS.	. .	347	THE BOOK	22
DRY UP THEIR ARMS, WHC VEX THY SPCUSE	. .	350	L'ENVOY	33
AND CROWN DRY HILS WITH WELLS AND FLOWERS.	. .	341	THE FEAST	54
DUE				
RCSE UP, AND CANCELL'D TWC DEATHS DUE TO THEE.	. .	217	EASTER-DAY	8
TWO DEATHS HAD BIN THY CUE.	. . . .	243	THE SAP	22
THEM IN DUE SEASON. WHAT THCU GIV'ST, THEY TAKE.	. .	286	PSALM 104	74
THESE ARE MY CUE	. . . . . .	188	RELAPSE	20
THESE ARE HIS DUE.	. . . . . .	188	RELAPSE	28
DULL				
HIS WINGS ARE DULL, AND SICKLY.	. . .	181	BURIALL	35
THEY WERE ALL DULL, AND DEAD	. . .	187	ND DO THEY	6
DULL, WRETCHED WORMES. THAT WCULD NOT KEEPE	. .	166	THE CALL	66
AN ODDE DULL SUTOR, HADST THOU BUT THE ART	. .	154	ISAACS M.	14
WERE DULL, AND BLIND, BLT CUSTCME STRAIGHT	. .	143	DEATH	17
OTHERS ILL-SHAP'D, AND DULL	. . .	141	RGNRTN	65
THE SETTLED RED IS DULL, AND WHITES THAT REST	. .	222	AFFLICTION	27
MY DAYS, WHICH ARE AT BEST BUT DULL AND HOARY	. .	271	ALL GONE	11
SUCH AS DULL MAN CAN NEVER FINDE	. . .	344	WATER-FALL	29
DULL'D				
HATH DULL'D THEE THUS, WHEN DEATH SHALL FREEZE	. .	142	DEATH	2
DULNESS				
FROM DUST AND DULNESS.	. . . . .	215	PRAISE	38
DULY				
THAT SWCRN MEMORIAL DULY PAY	. . . .	326	ABELS BLOD	30
DUMB				
HIS KNOCKING TIME, THE SOULS DUMB WATCH	. .	324	THE NIGHT	35
AND STCNES, THOUGH SPEECHLESS, ARE NOT DUMB.	. .	335	JUDGEMENT	16
AT NOISE, BUT THRIVE UNSEEN AND DUMB.	. .	309	THE SEED	46
BUT THESE DUMB CREATURES ARE SC TRUE	. .	313	THE STONE	12
LIKE THEE, WHEN SET AT NAUGHT AND DUMB.	. .	316	MEN OF WAR	20
BE DUMB CCURSE MEASURES, JAR NC MCRE. TO ME	. .	280	JOY	1
IN ROWLES AND CURLES, MINCING AND STATELY DUMB	. .	155	ISAACS M.	34
STRIKE THESE LIPS DUMB.	. . . .	171	COME, COME	16
AND STRIKE THEM DUMB, WHC FOR MEER WORDS	. .	350	L'ENVOY	41
WITH MEEK, DUMB LCCKS DIDST WCC MINE EYE	. .	348	HOLY BIBLE	18
DUMBE				
AND CN THE DUMBE SHADES LANGUAGE SPENT	. .	141	RGNRTN	60
AT WHCSE DUMBE URN	. . . . . .	248	I WALKT	62
DURST				
WHITE DAYES, THAT DURST NC IMPICUS MIRTH EXPCSE.	. .	154	ISAACS M.	18
DURST NCT LOCK ON THOSE SMILING YEARS	. .	303	ST MARY MN	12
DURT				
YET HUGS HE STIL HIS CURT. THE STUFFE HE WEARS	. .	224	TEMPEST	45
DUSKY				
THIS DUSKY STATE CF SIGHS AND TEARS	. . .	303	ST MARY MN	11

		PAGE	TITLE	LINE
DUSKY	(CON'T)			
THROUGH A LARGE DUSKY GLASSE		309	THE SEED	50
SAY IT IS LATE AND DUSKY, BECAUSE THEY		325	THE NIGHT	51
DUST				
SHALL BRING TRUE DAY, AND MAKE DUST SEE		335	JUDGEMENT	21
THEN LET NOT DUST YOUR EYES OBSCURE		339	DEATH B	28
MAKING DUST AND ASHES READY.		339	THE FEAST	6
BE TA'N IN DUST		328	RIGHTSNESS	47
FOR WHOSE DRY DUST GREEN BRANCHES BUD . .		310	THE SEED	83
HERE SLEPT MY THOUGHTS DEAR MARK. WHICH DUST . .		310	THE SEED	73
BUT DUST (I DID OBSERVE)		310	THE SEED	75
AND THE LAST IS MOST LOATHSOME DUST. . . .		302	ORNAMENT	8
HENCE SAND AND DUST		314	THE STONE	37
WILL BY LOOSE DUST THAT MAN ARRAIGN . . .		315	THE STONE	58
AS ONE THEN DUST MORE VILE AND VAIN. . .		315	THE STONE	59
AND THEY TO DUST RETURN.		287	PSALM 104	80
DEW OF THE DEAD WHICH MAKES DUST MOVE . .		298	JESUS WP B	11
TO MAKE DRIE DUST, AND DEAD TREES GROW. . .		291	THE JEWS	13
HEAVEN HATH LESS BEAUTY THAN THE DUST HE SPIES .		224	TEMPEST	47
OF DUST, AND CLAY		226	RETIREMENT	31
THY GIFT ONCE MORE, AND GRIND THIS FLINT TO DUST.		224	TEMPEST	60
FROM DUST AND DULNESS.		215	PRAISE	38
WITH THY CLEER FIRE REFINE, BURNING TO DUST .		216	DRESSING	6
POOR DUST SHOULD LY STILL LOW		217	DRESSING	40
HAVE COMMERCE SOMTIMES WITH POOR DUST . .		212	DAWNING	40
THE DUST, OF WHICH I AM A PART		207	REPENTANCE	35
THE CREATURES JUBILE, GODS PARLE WITH DUST. .		2	SON-DAYES	13
WHAT MYSTERIES DO LIE BEYOND THY DUST. . .		271	ALL GONE	19
DUST AND CLAY		269	ASCSN-HYMN	1
'TIS NOT FROM DUST, OR IF SO, WHY DOST THOU .		243	THE SAP	3
DUST LIES WITH DUST		226	RETIREMENT	42
DUST LIES WITH DUST		226	RETIREMENT	42
THERE DUST THAT OUT OF COOKS MIGHT FILL . .		226	RETIREMENT	51
HIS OWN HANDS WITH THE DUST		232	THE WORLD	33
'TIS TRUE, HE LOVES THAT DUST WHEREON THEY GO .		238	SHEPHEARDS	13
DOTH GRIEVE FOR DUST, AND DUST DOTH SING. .		240	MISERY	40
DOTH GRIEVE FOR DUST, AND DUST DOTH SING. .		240	MISERY	40
ADDRES DEAD DUST, SETS HEART ON CORNE AND GRASS .		236	CONSTLATN	19
OR DUST		153	THE SEARCH	89
A LITTLE DUST, AND FOR THE TOWN . . .		151	THE SEARCH	16
WHO KEEPS HIS COVENANT EVEN WITH OUR DUST. .		144	RSRCTN +IM	18
O KNIT ME, THAT AM CRUMBLED DUST. THE HEAPE .		160	DSTROCTION	1
AND WHEN THIS DUST FALLS TO THE URN . .		170	RETREATE	31
UNNUMBER'D IN THY DUST, WHEN ALL THIS FRAME .		177	EVNG-WTCH	4
THEN MAY HIS PEACE BE WTIH THEE, AND EACH DUST .		177	EVNG-WTCH	7
DUST THAT WOULD RISE, AND DIMME MY SIGHT .		161	DSTROCTION	30
HADST THOU GIVEN TO-THIS ACTIVE DUST . .		162	PURSUITE	9
AND CLOATH THE MORNING-STARRE WITH DUST .		164	INCARNATN	6
OF ALL HIS DUST LEFT HERE.		165	THE CALL	33
HOW SHALL THY DUST THY PRAISES SING. . .		186	PASSION	47
IN LIFE, OR DUST.		181	BURIALL	24
O'R-CAST WITH THAT COLD DUST.		183	THRS A TYE	4
AND NOW THE SPIRIT, NOT THE DUST . . .		179	SILENCE	27
FOR DUST, AND STONES		179	CHRCH-SVC	6
FOR DUST IN EVERY PART		179	CHRCH-SVC	7
SO THAT BOTH STONES, AND DUST, AND ALL OF ME .		180	CHRCH-SVC	17
SUFFER NO MORE THIS DUST TO OVERFLOW . .		191	THE MATCH	36
LET FOLLY DUST IT ON, OR LAG BEHIND. . .		193	RLS + LSNS	52
AND HUMBLE DUST, TELL THEN DEAR FLESH . .		201	THE CHECK	11
IN DUST, AND STONES.		202	THE CHECK	35
SULLYED WITH DUST AND MUD.		198	UNPRFTBLNS	3
ON MY OWN DUST, MEER DUST IT IS . . .		347	THE BOOK	21
ON MY OWN DUST, MEER DUST IT IS . . .		347	THE BOOK	21
WHICH BRINGS POOR DUST THE VICTORY. . .		339	THE FEAST	18
POOR DUST THOUGH DEAD		340	THE FEAST	35
DUSTY				
A DUSTY STORY		201	THE CHECK	2
NO DEAD AND DUSTY CHERUB, NOR CARV'D STONE .		323	THE NIGHT	20
DUTIES				
THERE FROM NO DUTIES TO BE FREED . . .		190	THE MATCH	9
DUTY				
THE SPIRITS DUTY, TRUE HEARTS SPREAD, AND HEAVE		191	RLS + LSNS	3
MAN TO HIS DUTY. THOU ALONE		336	PSALM 65	15
AND TEACH US DUTY, I WILL SEE		278	THE STARRE	11
YOUTH NOW, FULL OF PIOUS DUTY		218	EASTER HYM	7
DWEL				
WOULD MAKE A COURT, SHOULD HE THERE DWEL. .		240	MISERY	36
I SCHOOL MY EYES, AND STRICTLY DWEL . .		214	MISERY	57
WHERE FREED SOULS DWEL BY LIVING FOUNTAINS .		312	FAIR+YONG	49
DWELL				
THAT SECRET ARK, WHERE THE MILDE DOVE DOTH DWELL		330	JACOBS PLW	28
IN IT MY NAME, AND HONOUR BOTH DO DWELL .		226	RETIREMENT	38
DWELL THOU IN IT, AND I IN THEE. . . .		277	COCK-CRWNG	24
THE SHADES OF DEATH DWELL AND DISORDER. .		277	COCK-CRWNG	30
A SPIRIT, AND TRUE GLORY DWELL . . .		202	THE CHECK	34
MY GAZING SOUL WOULD DWELL AN HOURE . .		169	RETREATE	12
DWELLING				
WAS THEN THY DWELLING. DID SOME CLOUD . .		315	DWELLNG-PL	5
DWELLINGS				
THEIR DWELLINGS HAVE AND SING. . . .		285	PSALM 104	36

	PAGE	TITLE	LINE

DWELLS

A FRESH, IMMORTAL GREEN THERE DWELLS	308	THE SEED	23
WHO IN THY HOLY TEMPLE DWELLS	336	PSALM 65	11
WHERE LOVE WITHOUT LUST DWELLS, AND BENDS	322	CHILDEHOOD	33

DYE

SO DYE HIS SERVANTS, AND AS SURE	339	DEATH B	26
OR LET ME DYE.	329	ANGUISH	20
SO THAT FAM'D FRUIT WHICH MADE ALL DYE	312	FAIR+YONG	35
BUT THESE CHASTE FOUNTAINS FLOW NOT TILL WE DYE.	291	THE TIMBER	53
I, DO NOT GO. THOU KNOW'ST, I'LE DYE.	293	BEGGING B	1
MAY HE FOR EVER DYE	301	PROVIDENCE	31
BUT ONE HALF GLAUNCE, MOST GLADLY DYE.	168	VNTY SPRIT	34
I DYE TO MAKE MY FOES INHERIT.	185	PASSION	43
THAT MADE THEE THUS RESOLVE TO DYE	164	INCARNATN	15
STRIVING TO SAVE THE WHOLE, BY PARCELLS DYE	161	DSTRQCTION	34
WILL TELL THEE SO, SWEET SAVIOUR THOU DIDST DYE.	198	SCRIPTURES	14
AND LET ME DYE BEFORE MY DEATH.	141	RGNRTN	91
AND MAKES HIM MOURN, AND PINE AND DYE	281	THE FAVOUR	5
MY GOD. THOU THAT DIDST DYE FOR ME	264	INTRO. 1	1
WHOSE EATER SHALL NOT, CANNOT DYE	339	THE FEAST	15

DYED

NOR DID THOSE LAST, BUT (LIKE HIMSELF) DYED STILL	196	CORRUPTION	11
UNITE, AND RAISE UP ALL THAT DYED, AT ONCE.	298	JESUS WP B	8
BUT SINCE CHRIST DYED (AS IF WE DID DEVISE	307	RAIN+BOW	23
AND GOD HIMSELF DYED BY THE MULTITUDE.	330	JACOBS PLW	6

DYES

INTOMED MANY DAYS BEFORE HE DYES	195	RLS + LSNS	126

DYING

SINCE DYING FOR ME, THOU DIDST CRAVE NO MORE	342	OBSEQUIES	1
AND DYING MAK'ST ME GO IN PEACE.	348	HOLY BIBLE	34

EACH

ON EACH GREEN THING. THEN SLEPT (WELL FED)	347	THE BOOK	17
INCLINE EACH HARD HEART TO DO GOOD	350	L'ENVOY	45
BY EACH MANS DOOR, AND QUICKLY WILL	351	L'ENVOY	51
THY OWN BRIGHT SELF OVER EACH HEAD	349	L'ENVOY	10
HUNT OUT EACH DAMP	340	THE FEAST	47
WHY, SINCE EACH DROP OF THY QUICK STORY	343	WATER-FALL	15
NOR WAS HEAV'D COLD UNTO HIM, FOR EACH DAY	197	CORRUPTION	21
EACH LINE IN THEE. THEN WOULD I PLEAD IN GROANS	198	SCRIPTURES	10
ANGELS LAY LEIGER HERE, EACH BUSH, AND CEL	197	CORRUPTION	25
EACH OAKE, AND HIGH-WAY KNEW THEM	197	CORRUPTION	26
THOU CANST NOT MISSE HIS PRAISE, EACH TREE, HERB, FLOWRE	194	RLS + LSNS	95
TAKE THEIR LEAVE, AND DIE. BIRDS, BEASTS, EACH TREE	201	THE CHECK	27
EACH SNARLING BLAST SHOT THROUGH ME, AND DID SHARE	198	UNPRFTBLNS	4
EACH FLY DOTH TAST	203	DSRDR + FR	23
KEEP THOU THY TEMPER, MIX NOT WITH EACH CLAY.	192	RLS + LSNS	32
OR LEAFE BUT HATH HIS MORNING-HYMN. EACH BUSH	192	RLS + LSNS	15
A GIDDY BLAST EACH WAY	187	NO DO THEY	18
I TURN'D ME ROUND, AND TO EACH SHADE	141	RGNRTN	82
WHILST I EACH MINUTE GRONE TO KNOW	143	DEATH	29
BY EACH, HE ANSWERS ALL	161	DSTRQCTION	13
WHICH, SCATTER'D IN A THOUSAND PEARLS, EACH FLOWRE	155	ISAACS M.	56
I SEE IN EACH SHADE THAT THERE GROWES	148	RELIGION	3
EACH DAY, AND HOURE HE IS ON WING	161	PURSUITE	3
EACH FAIRER THAN THE OTHER.	167	THE CALL	77
FEEL IN EACH BLOW.	184	PASSION	6
WOULDST MAKE EACH PART	182	CHRFLNESS	18
I DOE EACH THING	182	CHRFLNESS	2
EACH DAY IS GROWN A DOZEN YEAR	170	COME, COME	3
AND EACH HOURE, ONE.	170	COME, COME	4
EACH BUSIE RAY	171	MIDNIGHT	6
AND WISH EACH BEAME	171	MIDNIGHT	8
THEN MAY HIS PEACE BE WTIH THEE, AND EACH DUST	177	EVNG-WTCH	7
EACH PAGE OF THINE HATH TRUE LIFE IN'T	332	AGREEMENT	23
WEAR FRESH ADORNMENTS ON EACH SIDE.	337	PSALM 65	44
TRANSGRESSIONS MAKE ME FOUL EACH DAY	336	PSALM 65	7
THAT VOICE, WHICH TO EACH SECRET BED	335	JUDGEMENT	19
TWILL SHEW US EACH FORGOTTEN GRAVE	334	JUDGEMENT	4
COMFORTS AND JOYS, AND HOPES EACH HOUR	326	ABELS BLOD	26
AND THE THOUGHTS OF EACH HARMLESS HOUR	321	CHILDEHOOD	5
FOR THY NEW LIGHT, AND TREMBLED AT EACH SHOWER.	306	RAIN-BOW	8
BUT WHILE EACH GAY, ALLURING WEAR	303	ORNAMENT	9
THE MEASURE GIVEN BY THEE EACH YEAR	301	PROVIDENCE	38
EACH THING TURNS SCRIBE AND REGISTER	314	THE STONE	43
SHUT OUT ALL PAIN AND EACH DISEASE.	319	THE ASS	63
SCATTERED EACH WHERE	292	THE JEWS	17
FOR EACH INCLOSED SPIRIT IS A STAR	288	THE BIRD	19
CHIRPING THEIR SOLEMN MATINS ON EACH TREE.	288	THE BIRD	24
AND LOVE OF THEE, EACH WILLING ANGEL IS	284	PSALM 104	15
IN WHOSE THICK SHADES AND SILENCE EACH WILDE BEAST	286	PSALM 104	54
FOR ALL MY SECRET FAULTS, AND EACH	265	INTRO. 2	23
THOUGH THEN SOME BOAST THAT FIRE EACH DAY	272	WHT SUNDAY	13
AND HUG'D EACH ONE HIS PELF	232	THE WORLD	37
TO THEE EACH HOURE, BEG AT THY DOOR	230	LAW + GOSP	25
WHERE, THOUGH THE GLORY DIFFER IN EACH STAR	236	CONSTLATN	31
EACH STIRRING WIND AND STORM BLEW THROUGH THEIR COTS	239	SHEPHEARDS	33
DIDST TO EACH DROP REPLY.	213	ADMISSION	12
AND LAYD SURPRIZES IN EACH ELEMENT.	223	TEMPEST	24

EAGER

HUNTS IN AN EAGER QUEST.	286	PSALM 104	56

	PAGE	TITLE	LINE
EAGLES			
MY PRESENT SEARCH, FOR EAGLES EYE NOT STARRS	278	THE STARRE	6
EAGLET			
LIKE A STARV'D EAGLET, FOR THINE EYE.	281	THE FAVOUR	6
EAR			
THAT BUZ IN EVERY EAR, AND BLCW CN SOULS	275	PROFFER	15
MAKES UP BUT LECTURES FCR HIS EYE, AND EAR.	223	TEMPEST	20
IF ANY HAVE AN EAR	316	MEN OF WAR	1
AN EYE CR EAR	313	THE STONE	4
AS SPEAKS STILL IN THY MAKERS EAR	325	ABELS BLOD	10
EARE			
BUT ALL THE EARE LAY HUSH	140	RGNRTN	57
EARES			
SCME USE FOR EARES	141	RGNRTN	59
STOLE BY CUR EARES	165	THE CALL	17
EARLY			
THAT BY THY EARLY CHOICE FOREWARN'D	166	THE CALL	40
WHERE A SHRILL SPRING TUN'D TC THE EARLY DAY.	167	VNTY SPRIT	2
HAPPY THOSE EARLY DAYES. WHEN I	169	RETREATE	1
AND OFFER'D UP SO EARLY UNTO HEAVEN	154	ISAACS M.	6
SURE, IT WAS SO. MAN IN THOSE EARLY DAYS	196	CORRUPTION	1
MY DEW, MY DEW. MY EARLY LOVE	308	THE SEED	5
LIKE A WISE, EARLY PENITENT	304	ST MARY MN	37
THY LITTLE HEART IN EARLY HYMNS DOTH SING	288	THE BIRD	8
AND ALL ALONE FULL EARLY RUN	295	PALM—SUNDY	36
OR SHAL THESE EARLY, FRAGRANT HCURS	211	DAWNING	9
THE FIRST GLAD TICINGS CF THY EARLY LIGHT	267	ASCN—DAY A	17
EARLY, ASWEL AS LATE	245	MAN	6
EARN			
KEEP CLEAN, BEAR FRUIT, EARN LIFE AND WATCH	309	THE SEED	47
BUT THOU, WHO DIDST MANS WHOLE LIFE EARN	342	OBSEQUIES	21
EARNEST			
WITH EARNEST GROANS FOR FREEDCM CRY	335	JUDGEMENT	14
WITH SPIRIT—SIGHS, AND EARNEST GRONES	242	MISERY	110
THIS IS THE EARNEST THY LOVE SHEDS	265	INTRU. 2	13
IF JOYES, AND HOPES, AND EARNEST THROWS	277	COCK—CRWNG	31
HER EARNEST SIGHES PROCUR'D HER TEARS	223	TEMPEST	15
EARNEST, AND SIGN, THY CIFTS SC DEAL	216	DRESSING	20
EARS			
CHIDE IN THINE EARS.	213	ADMISSION	8
AS IF THOU HADST NOR EARS, NOR EYES.	240	MISERY	24
AND ALL THE YEAR HAVE SCME GREAN EARS	227	LV + DSPLN	18
HEDGES HAVE EARS, SAIC THE OLC SOOTH	313	THE STONE	14
EARTH			
BUT WHAT EARTH BREATHS AGAINST THY LIGHT.	312	FAIR+YONG	26
DEAR SOUL. THCU KNEW'ST, FLOWERS HERE ON EARTH	304	ST MARY MN	27
AS EARTH, THY LOVELY HEAD DOST BOW.	304	ST MARY MN	26
BALM ON THE CLEFT EARTH, MILK CN GRASS AND FLOWERS.	306	RAIN—BOW	12
BUT HERE CN EARTH (THCUGH THCU HAST NEED)	316	MEN OF WAR	23
THOU VISIT'ST THE LOW EARTH, AND THEN	336	PSALM 65	27
FROM THE LOW EARTH TO HIGH HEAVEN RISE	326	ABELS BLOD	38
WHO KNOWS EARTH NCTHING HATH	327	RIGHTSNESS	31
MAKES HEAVEN AND EARTH	295	PALM—SUNDY	25
WHERE THE STARV'D EARTH GROANS FOR ONE TEAR.	296	JESUS WP A	16
THIS PAST, THE SUN SHINES ON THE EARTH, AND THY	286	PSALM 104	61
THEM ALL, AND THIS THE EARTH, AND EVERY BLADE	286	PSALM 104	67
THINE EYES BEHOLD THE EARTH, ANC THE WHOLE STAGE	287	PSALM 104	85
THOU MAK'ST TO GROW. THESE (BLEST BY THEE) THE EARTH	285	PSALM 104	42
AND FCUNDED THE FIRM EARTH. THEN WITH THE DEEP	285	PSALM 104	18
DCTH BROACH THE EARTH, ANC LESSER BROOKS LETS FORTH	285	PSALM 104	30
AS HERE ON EARTH (WHEN MEN WITH—STCOD)	284	TRINITY—SN	4
AND TRULY HATES TC BE DETAIN'C CN EARTH	290	THE TIMBER	30
FAITH SCJOURN'D FIRST CN EARTH IN YCU	292	THE JEWS	38
OF STCNES, ANC SPEECHLESS EARTH	226	RETIREMENT	47
AND KINDLY TEL ME, I AM EARTH	240	MISERY	30
ABOUT THIS EARTH DOTH RUN AND RIDE	246	MAN	18
CCME SAPLESS BLOSSCM, CREEP NCT STIL ON EARTH	243	THE SAP	1
SHE MADE THE EARTH THEIR NURSE, AND TOMB	222	TEMPEST	9
HOW DO THEY CAST CFF CRCSSNESS. ONLY EARTH	223	TEMPEST	29
PLANTS IN THE ROOT WITH EARTH CC MOST COMPLY	223	TEMPEST	33
(UNSEEN) BOTH HEAVEN, AND EARTH.	220	PSALM 121	4
A TASTE OF HEAV'N CN EARTH, THE PLEDGE, AND CUE	2	SON—DAYES	23
AND RESURRECTION FRCM THE EARTH AND NIGHT.	267	ASCN—DAY A	18
THE PURE EARTH SAT, AND THE FAIR WOODS HAC SEEN	268	ASCN—DAY A	42
OF SAINTS AND ANGELS GLCRIFIE THE EARTH.	267	ASCN—DAY A	26
WAS NCT ALL STONE, AND EARTH	196	CORRUPTION	2
UNDER THE DARK, AND MELANCHOLY EARTH.	195	RLS + LSNS	106
OUT—RUNS THE EARTH, AND LINES THE UTMCST POLE.	193	RLS + LSNS	54
THE LCRC OF LIFE BE BCRNE IN EARTH.	200	NTVTY 1	30
ARE WE ALL STONE, AND EARTH.	200	NTVTY 2	14
AND FROM THE WOMBE OF EARTH	147	DAY OF JDG	18
TC HEAV'N, OR EARTH BELCW	146	RSRCTN +IM	58
THE THANKFUL EARTH UNLOCKS HER SELF, AND BLENDS	156	ISAACS M.	59
OF DRCPS MAKE SOFT THE EARTH, MY EYES COULD KEEP	160	THE SHOWRE	14
AND SPIRITS ALL MY EARTH. HEARK. IN WHAT RINCS	176	MRNG—WTCH	9
BRAVE WCRMES, ANC EARTH. THAT THUS COULD HAVE	164	INCARNATN	9
AND IN THE HEART CF EARTH, ANC NIGHT	179	SILENCE	31
AND DRESS THIS EARTH FOR NEXT YEARS MEAT.	341	THE FEAST	75
EARTHS			
PASSING THROUGH THE EARTHS DARKE VEINES	150	RELIGION	34

		PAGE	TITLE	LINE
EARTHS	**(CON'T)**			
THE FROZEN EARTHS DEAD FACE THOU COST RENEW.		287	PSALM 104	82
EASE				
AND IF THOU WILT NOT GIVE ME EASE		294	BEGGING B	23
OF TEMPESTS CAN NO MORE DISTURB THY EASE.		289	THE TIMBER	18
WHEN WITH THE EASE		327	RIGHTSNESS	35
WE TALK AND NAME THEE WITH MUCH EASE		338	DEATH B	6
CONTENTED THOUGHTS, INNOXIOUS EASE		317	MEN OF WAR	42
OF HER SICK WATERS, AND INFECTIOUS EASE.		160	THE SHOWRE	3
MY MIND TO EASE		141	RGNRTN	87
THY FORTRESSE, AND THY EASE.		184	PEACE	16
WHICH SINFULL EASE MADE FOUL		176	THE STORM	22
CURE HIM, EASE HIM		200	NTVTY 1	27
THY MERCY, LOVE, AND EASE		248	I WALKT	56
AND OUR BEST NOTE AND HIGHEST EASE		273	WHT SUNDAY	42
THEY WIL EASE ME.		215	PRAISE	28
SUCH PERFECT EASE, AND SUCH A LIVELY SENSE		244	THE SAP	47
FOR THIS TRUE EASE		341	THE FEAST	55
LIVING, THOU WERT MY SOULS SURE EASE		348	HOLY BIBLE	33
THY SERVICE TO BE OUR SOLE EASE		351	L'ENVOY	60
EASIE				
YET SINCE AS EASIE 'TIS FOR THEE		242	MISERY	93
HIS EASIE YOKE REJECTS OR SLIGHTS		315	THE STONE	55
THY EASIE HANDS TO DO THIS WASTE.		304	ST MARY MN	24
O. 'TIS AN EASIE THING		329	ANGUISH	13
WITH ALL THEIR SOFT, KINDE ARTS AND EASIE STRAINS		320	HIDDN TRSR	21
EASILY				
AS EASILY THOU MIGHTST PREVENT		165	THE CALL	34
EAST				
LIKE A YOUNG EAST, OR MOONE-SHINE NIGHT		168	VNTY SPRIT	20
HERBS SLEEP UNTO THE EAST, AND SOME FOWLES THENCE		183	THRS A TYE	11
WE BREATH'D STILL FOR A BLUSHING EAST		143	DEATH	20
AND ROWLE INTO THE EAST		146	DAY OF JDG	2
FULL EAST, A FAIRE, FRESH FIELD COULD SPY		140	RGNRTN	36
BUD IN THE BRIGHT EAST, AND DISCLOSE		151	THE SEARCH	2
SOME NIGHTS I SEE YOU IN THE GLADSOME EAST		235	CONSTLATN	9
NOW SHINES IN ALL THE CHAMBERS OF THE EAST.		267	ASCN-DAY A	24
BREAKS AS THE DAY DOTH FROM THE EAST		340	THE FEAST	21
EASTERN				
WHOSE EASTERN TRAFFIQUE DEALS IN BRIGHT		346	THE QUEER	5
EAT				
AND WHAT IN THE NEXT WORLD TO EAT.		341	THE FEAST	78
SOME SIT TO THEE, AND EAT		217	DRESSING	37
WITH FATAL SWEETNESS, TILL WE EAT.		311	FAIR+YONG	14
EATE				
EATE, DRINKE, DISCOURSE, SIT DOWNE, AND REST		149	RELIGION	15
EATER				
WHOSE EATER SHALL NOT, CANNOT DYE		339	THE FEAST	15
EATS				
WHICH KILLS THY BEES, AND EATS THY HONEY.		300	PROVIDENCE	12
ECCHO				
THE ECCHO OF THESE STONES		180	CHRCH-SVC	23
WITH LEARNED SWAINES, AND ECCHO YET		162	MT. OLVS A	10
WHOSE ECCHO IS HEAV'NS BLISSE.		177	MRNG-WTCH	22
ECCHOES				
WITH ECCHOES BEATEN FROM TH' ETERNALL HILLS.		168	VNTY SPRIT	18
FALSE ECCHOES, AND CONFUSED SOUNDS		150	RELIGION	38
ECCLIPS'D				
LIKE CLOUDS ECCLIPS'D MY MIND		139	RGNRTN	17
SINCE IN THESE VEYLS MY ECCLIPS'D EYE		168	VNTY SPRIT	30
ECCLIPSES				
SULLEN, AND SAD ECCLIPSES, CLOUDIE SPHERES		188	RELAPSE	19
AS ON THE SUN ECCLIPSES LIE.		219	HOLY COMM.	20
CONDEMNING THOUGHTS (LIKE SAD ECCLIPSES) SCOWL		232	THE WORLD	19
EDEN				
ALL NEW AS FRESH AS EDEN, AND AS FINE.		268	ASCN-DAY A	38
OF EDEN COULD		269	ASCSN-HYMN	21
AND AIR OF EDEN, LIKE A MALE-CONTENT		279	PALM-TREE	6
HE SIGH'D FOR EDEN, AND WOULD OFTEN SAY		197	CORRUPTION	19
EDGE				
AND EDGE OF ALL		225	RETIREMENT	20
EDGES				
THY EDGES, AND THY BORDERING LIGHT.		322	CHILDEHOOD	42
EFFECTS				
DARES KNOW EFFECTS, AND JUDGE THEM LONG BEFORE		236	CONSTLATN	27
THY NEXT EFFECTS NO TONGUE CAN TELL.		348	HOLY BIBLE	35
EGYPT				
TO EGYPT HENCE I FLED, RAN O'RE		151	THE SEARCH	11
EGYPTIAN				
I HAVE DESERV'D A THICK, EGYPTIAN DAMP		188	RELAPSE	13
IN SUCH A DARK, EGYPTIAN BORDER		277	COCK-CRWNG	29
EJECTIONS				
WHAT THIN EJECTIONS		172	MIDNIGHT	14
ELDEST				
YOU WERE THE ELDEST CHILDE, AND WHEN		293	THE JEWS	42
ELECTED				
ELECTED, BOUGHT AND SEAL'D FOR FREE		284	TRINITY-SN	8
ELEMENT				
AND LAYD SURPRIZES IN EACH ELEMENT.		223	TEMPEST	24
O USEFUL ELEMENT AND CLEAR.		344	WATER-FALL	23

		PAGE	TITLE	LINE
ELEMENTS				
A SLAVE TO LUSTFUL ELEMENTS.		312	FAIR+YONG	30
TO RACK OLD ELEMENTS		153	THE SEARCH	88
BOTH STARS AND ELEMENTS CONFOUND		147	DAY OF JDG	7
ESTEEM'D (VAINE THINGS) OF TWO WHOLE ELEMENTS		144	RSRCTN +IM	13
ELIAS				
ELIAS BY A RAVEN IS FED		149	RELIGION	10
ELIXIR				
THOU ART THE GREAT ELIXIR, RARE, AND CHOICE.		198	SCRIPTURES	6
THIS IS THE GREAT ELIXIR THAT TURNS GALL		221	AFFLICTION	4
EMANATIONS				
WHAT EMANATIONS		172	MIDNIGHT	11
EMBRACE				
TO SNUDGE IN, AND EMBRACE A COT		214	MISERY	66
EMPTINESS				
MEER EMPTINESS AND SHOW		238	SHEPHEARDS	26
EMPTY				
THY PROMISES BUT EMPTY WORDS		207	REPENTANCE	13
AND EMPTY HOUSE		180	BURIALL	9
EMPYREAN				
AND BOUNDLESS EMPYREAN THEMES		346	THE QUEER	6
ENACT				
ENACT FOR SAINTS MY SELF AND MINE.		316	MEN OF WAR	12
ENCLOS'D				
A GOD ENCLOS'D WITHIN YOUR CELL		164	INCARNATN	10
ENCREASE				
THEN DRILLING ON, LEARNES TO ENCREASE		150	RELIGION	37
END				
THAT BRINGS HEALTH IN THE END		147	DAY OF JDG	36
AND WHERE THOU MAD'ST AN END, THERE I'LE BEGIN.		158	THE LAMPE	26
O LET ME (LIKE HIM) KNOW MY END.		167	THE CALL	86
ALL BUT PRELUDES THY END. THOU ART THE MAN		195	RLS + LSNS	107
ONE AIM AND END, WHO WALKS NOT BY HIS SIGHT.		327	RIGHTSNESS	21
MAKE ALL THINGS NEW. AND WITHOUT END.		335	JUDGEMENT	46
YET THAT NOT SORTING TO MY END		207	REPENTANCE	17
EXTENT, AND END, FOR MY HANDS DREW THE LINE		226	RETIREMENT	27
LET HIM SO FOLLOW HERE, THAT IN THE END		216	DRESSING	17
NOT TO AN END.		343	WATER-FALL	10
ENDEAR				
ENDEAR DELIGHTS		339	THE FEAST	11
ENDED				
AS IF IT ENDED IN A SPRING		338	DEATH B	9
ALL YOUR TRIUMPHS NOW ARE ENDED		218	EASTER HYM	3
AND FROM THENCE (HIS SUFF'RINGS ENDED)		163	MT. OLVS A	22
ENDLES				
AND BEAT ABOUT YOUR ENDLES LINE.		235	CONSTLATN	12
ENDLESS				
LIKE A GREAT RING OF PURE AND ENDLESS LIGHT		231	THE WORLD	2
AND ENDLESS IS		191	THE MATCH	23
HOW WOULD I RUN TO ENDLESS NIGHT		316	MEN OF WAR	10
ENDS				
ETERNITY, WHICH NEVER ENDS		333	AGREEMENT	50
AND, WHENCE IT SPRUNG, THERE ENDS)		203	DSRDR + FR	37
IT NEVER ENDS.		174	JOY OF LIF	8
ENDURE				
OR THAT HE CAN ENDURE TO BE UNJUST		144	RSRCTN +IM	17
IF I LOSE ALL, AND MUST ENDURE		295	PALM-SUNDY	42
ENDURING				
TOWARDS THE OLD AND STILL ENDURING SKIES		289	THE TIMBER	7
ENEMIE				
THE WORLD AN ENEMIE		148	DAY OF JDG	42
ENEMIES				
WERE BY MY CAUSLESS ENEMIES		301	PROVIDENCE	39
ENEMY				
AND THY OLD ENEMY, WHICH KNOWS		335	JUDGEMENT	29
ENLARG'D				
THUS THE ENLARG'D, INRACED AIR		176	THE STORM	13
ENLIGHTEN'D				
BUT NOW ENLIGHTEN'D THUS BY THEE		316	MEN OF WAR	13
ENOUGH				
WHOSE SUBSTANCE, THOUGH 'TIS HARD ENOUGH		314	THE STONE	50
WAS'T NOT ENOUGH THAT THOU HADST PAYD THE PRICE		219	HOLY COMM.	33
WAS'T NOT ENOUGH TO LOSE THY BREATH		220	HOLY COMM.	41
ENQUIR'D				
HER YEARLY NURSE, CAME BACK, ENQUIR'D		151	THE SEARCH	13
ENSUING				
HARK, AND MAKE USE OF THIS ENSUING STORY.		282	GARLAND	4
ENTER				
SO NONE MAY ENTER THERE BUT THEE.		242	MISERY	104
ENTICE				
NONE WOULD MORE DOTE ON, NOR SO SOON ENTICE.		320	HIDDN TRSR	24
ENTIRE				
ENTIRE STILL, WEARS OUT BLACKEST NIGHTS.		333	AGREEMENT	34
ENTRANCE				
THOUGH SINCE THY FIRST SAD ENTRANCE BY		338	DEATH B	1
AND ENTRANCE TO CAPTIVITIE.		207	REPENTANCE	10
ENTRED				
I ENTRED, AND ONCE IN		140	RGNRTN	46
ENVYED				
AND ENVYED THAT RECORD, DID SINCE		332	AGREEMENT	2

	PAGE	TITLE	LINE

EPICURE
THE DOWN-RIGHT EPICURE PLAC'D HEAV'N IN SENSE . . . 232 THE WORLD 38
EQUAL
HAD EQUAL RIGHT. . . . . 210 FAITH 16
TO EQUAL WINDS. WOULD PROVE TOO SHORT. THOU HAST . . 281 JOY 13
EQUALL
BOTH YOU AND IT, HAD EQUALL LIBERTY . . . . 279 PALM-TREE 4
EQUALL TO ALL . . . . 210 FAITH 2
ERECT
ERECT PEEP FROM THEIR BEDS. . . . . . . 187 NO DO THEY 27
ERRE
ERRE MORE THEN I CAN DO BY NIGHT. . . . . 324 THE NIGHT 48
FOR KNOW, WILDE MEN, THAT WHEN YOU ERRE . . . . 314 THE STONE 42
ERRE IN LOOSE AIRS BEYOND HER BOUNDS. . . . . 297 HERODIAS 4
ERRING
THAT GUIDES THROUGH ERRING HOURS, AND IN FULL STORY . 2 SON-DAYES 22
ERROUR
APPOINTING ERROUR FOR MY PAGE . . . . . . 282 GARLAND 7
ESCAPES
ONLY, ONE POINT ESCAPES THEE. THAT THY OILE . . . 158 THE LAMPE 23
ESHCOLS
TOWARDS OLD MAMRE AND ESHCOLS BROOK. . . . . 292 THE JEWS 31
ESSENCE
AND MANS INFERIOR ESSENCE HE . . . . . 302 THE KNOT 7
AND THE MORE NOBLE ESSENCE FINDS HIS HOUSE . . . 145 RSRCTN +IM 39
WITH THY BRIGHT ESSENCE) . . . . . . 215 PRAISE 41
ESTATE
OUR DROWN'D ESTATE, TAKING THE CURSE . . . . 274 WHT SUNDAY 54
DOE BUT SEE YOUR SAD ESTATE . . . . . 164 THE CALL 10
O MY INVISIBLE ESTATE . . . . . . 344 WATER-FALL 37
ESTATES
TO LOW ESTATES, AND A LOW MINDE. . . . . 319 THE ASS 36
ESTEEM'D
WHEN ONCE MADE PUBLIQUE, IS ESTEEM'D BY NONE. . . 330 JACOBS PLW 18
ESTEEM'D (VAINE THINGS) OF TWO WHOLE ELEMENTS . . 144 RSRCTN +IM 13
ETERNAL
FRESH, SPICIE MORNINGS, AND ETERNAL BEAMS . . . 188 RELAPSE 27
FOR CHAINS OF DARKNES, AND ETERNAL NIGHTS. . . 196 RLS + LSNS 144
AND GLORY BE TO HIS ETERNAL NAME. . . . . 331 JACOBS PLW 37
GLORY TO THE ETERNAL KING. . . . . . 337 PSALM 65 48
HOVER NOT LONG, ETERNAL DOVE. . . . . 308 THE SEED 7
FOR THY ETERNAL, LIVING WELLS . . . . . 308 THE SEED 21
AND KEEPS HIS SOUL UNTO ETERNAL MIRTH. . . . 290 THE TIMBER 32
YET THOU THE GREAT ETERNAL ROCK . . . . 273 WHT SUNDAY 45
O FATHER OF ETERNAL LIFE, AND ALL . . . . 271 ALL GONE 33
AND NOW (ETERNAL JESUS) THOU COST HEAVE . . . 268 ASCN-DAY A 55
THY SACRED AND ETERNAL WIL DECREED . . . . 235 MUTINIE 34
THE MIGHTY GOD, TH' ETERNAL KING . . . . 240 MISERY 39
ETERNAL GOD. MAKER OF ALL . . . . . 346 THE BOOK 1
ETERNALL
ETERNALL WITNESSES THAT BE . . . . . 284 TRINITY-SN 2
ROVE IN THAT MIGHT, AND ETERNALL LIGHT . . . 146 RSRCTN +IM 63
WITH ECCHOES BEATEN FROM TH' ETERNALL HILLS. . . 168 VNTY SPRIT 18
IS THY FIRST BREATH, AND MANS ETERNALL PRIME. . . 178 EVNG-WTCH 16
ETERNITIE
PLEASURES HAD FOIL'D ETERNITIE . . . . . 166 THE CALL 72
AND CLOSE ETERNITIE. . . . . . . 166 THE CALL 61
WHERE SOULS ARE HATCH'D UNTO ETERNITIE. . . . 197 SCRIPTURES 4
THY LOCKS CROWN'D WITH ETERNITIE. . . . . 211 DAWNING 12
ETERNITY
, SAW ETERNITY THE OTHER NIGHT . . . . . 231 THE WORLD 1
BUT THINE SHINES TO ETERNITY. . . . . . 272 WHT SUNDAY 4
SOME SHADOWS OF ETERNITY . . . . . 169 RETREATE 14
ETERNITY, WHICH NEVER ENDS . . . . . 333 AGREEMENT 50
DAZLES AT IT, AS AT ETERNITY. . . . . 321 CHILDEHOOD 2
TO PLEASE WITHOUT ETERNITY. . . . . . 345 QUICKNESS 16
EV'RY
TO EV'RY MYRE . . . . 324 THE NIGHT 46
AND EV'RY BUSH IS SOMETHINGS BOOTH. . . . . 313 THE STONE 15
A SEV'RALL SINNE TO EV'RY SENCE . . . . 169 RETREATE 18
FOR EV'RY FOOTE TO TREAD. . . . . . 166 THE CALL 69
WHEN THE WORLDS UP, AND EV'RY SWARM ABROAD . . . 192 RLS + LSNS 31
STRAIT THERE IS JOY, AND EV'RY SPHERE . . . 200 NTVTY 2 3
AND SUCH IS TRUE REPENTANCE, EV'RY BREATH . . . 158 THE LAMPE 21
BUT EV'RY HOURE . . . . 158 MANS FALL 6
KNOWS EV'RY NOTE, AND CALL . . . . . 161 DSTRQCTION 14
BY EV'RY WANDRING CLOD. . . . . . 248 I WALKT 42
AND EV'RY PUBLISH'D VANITY . . . . . 265 INTRO. 2 26
THE SAME RESPECT, AND ROOM, WITH EV'RY CLAY. . . 226 RETIREMENT 44
AND SEARCH OUT EV'RY HOLE, AND CREEK. . . . 240 MISERY 12
AND WAS BLOW'N THROUGH BY EV'RY STORM AND WIND . . 245 MT. OLV. B 14
ALL NOW ARE STIRRING, EV'RY FIELD . . . . 212 DAWNING 15
SO AFTER THINE, THAT ALL, AND EV'RY PART . . . 213 ADMISSION 27
LIKE STRINGS, STRETCH EV'RY PART . . . . 222 AFFLICTION 39
HOW IS MAN PARCELL'D OUT. HOW EV'RY HOUR . . . 222 TEMPEST 1
EVENING
SHALL IT IN THE EVENING RUN . . . . . 211 DAWNING 3
SUCH A RICH AIR OF SWEETS, AS EVENING SHOWRS . . 244 MT. OLV. B 4
COOL TO A GLORIOUS EVENING, AND EXPIRE. . . . 195 RLS + LSNS 114
AND NOW AT EVENING ARE AS RED . . . . . 325 ABELS BLOD 5

	PAGE	TITLE	LINE
EVENING-TIDE			
AND CALM LIKE HER, OR THAT MILD EVENING-TIDE.	154	ISAACS M.	24
EVENING-WALKS			
NOR EVENING-WALKS HAVE I WITH THEE.	293	BEGGING B	8
EVENINGS			
BOTH MORNINGS MAKES, AND EVENINGS THERE.	288	THE BIRD	22
IN THOSE CALME, GOLDEN EVENINGS LAY	151	THE SEARCH	24
EVER-LIVING			
DEAR FRIEND. WHOSE HOLY, EVER-LIVING LINES	190	THE MATCH	1
EVERLASTING			
FAREWELL YOU EVERLASTING HILLS. I'M CAST	158	MANS FALL	1
ONE EVERLASTING SABOTH THERE SHALL RUNNE	146	RSRCTN +IM	69
BRIGHT SHOOTES OF EVERLASTINGNESSE.	170	RETREATE	20
THE EVERLASTING DOORS ABOVE	325	ABELS BLOD	19
ON EVERLASTING, SPICY MOUNTAINS.	312	FAIR+YONG	50
IN EVERLASTING LIGHT.	219	HOLY COMM.	32
EVERMORE			
NOW, AND FOR EVERMORE.	221	PSALM 121	20
FOR EVERMORE IMMACULATE.	349	L'ENVOY	16
EVIL			
WERE ALL MY LOUD, EVIL DAYS	324	THE NIGHT	37
WHO OUT OF EVIL CAN BRING FORTH GOOD.	297	HERODIAS	18
EVILS			
WITHOUT TO MORROWS EVILS AND FUTURE LOADS.	327	RIGHTSNESS	8
EXACT			
WITH WHAT EXACT OBEDIENCE DO YOU MOVE	235	CONSTLATN	5
EXALT			
IT WIL EXALT AND RISE	244	THE SAP	32
EXALTED			
A LOVE-SICK SOULS EXALTED FLIGHT.	277	COCK-CRWNG	34
EXALTED PLEASURES, CROWNING BLISSES	348	HOLY BIBLE	30
EXCEED			
THOUGH THEN ALL SINNERS I EXCEED	208	REPENTANCE	59
EXCELL			
THE BEST OF US EXCELL	166	THE CALL	53
WHOSE POW'R DOTH SO EXCELL	202	THE CHECK	32
EXCEPT			
THESE NEW DISCOVERIES DO, EXCEPT THEY DROWN.	224	TEMPEST	40
EXCEPTION			
THE RULE WITHOUT EXCEPTION FITS.	273	WHT SUNDAY	36
EXCESS			
NOT BREAK THY FENCE, AND BY A BLACK EXCESS	230	LAW + GOSP	32
EXCESSE			
WHILE OTHERS SLIPT INTO A WIDE EXCESSE	232	THE WORLD	40
EXCESSE OF FRIENDS, OF WORDS, AND WINE	240	MISERY	25
O SAD, AND WILDE EXCESSE. AND HAPPY THOSE	154	ISAACS M.	17
EXCHANGE			
EXCHANGE THEIR PEACE, AND FURRS.	222	AFFLICTION	34
EXCLUDE			
EXCLUDE MY DEAR GOD FROM MY MIND	240	MISERY	34
EXCLUDE HIM THENCE, WHO OF THAT CEL	240	MISERY	35
EXCUS'D			
IS BUT EXCUS'D NEGLECT. TO MIND	189	RESOLVE	3
EXHALATION			
THUS LIKE SOME SLEEPING EXHALATION	203	DSRDR + FR	31
THE SMOKE, AND EXHALATIONS OF THE BREST.	160	THE SHOWRE	12
OR EXHALATIONS, AND WASTS	181	BURIALL	27
EXHAUST			
I WILL EXHAUST IT ALL, AND MAKE	328	ANGUISH	11
EXPECT			
THAT SINCE MAN FELL, EXPECT WITH GROANS	294	PALM-SUNDY	12
CAN THEY THEIR HEADS LIFT, AND EXPECT	186	NO DO THEY	3
ALL DAY EXPECT MY DATE.	187	NO DO THEY	16
EXPECT STIL WHEN THOU WILT APPEAR	228	PILGRIMAGE	11
ALL EXPECT SOME SUDDEN MATTER	212	DAWNING	22
EXPECTED			
THY LONG EXPECTED HEALING WINGS COULD SEE	323	THE NIGHT	9
EXPECTING			
EXPECTING TILL THY SAVIOUR COMES	209	THE BURIAL	11
EXPECTS			
AS HE THAT IN THE MIDST OF DAY EXPECTS	201	THE CHECK	13
EXPEDIENT			
PROVE NOT EXPEDIENT FOR THY WAY.	319	THE ASS	40
EXPELL'D			
BUT LORD, I HAVE EXPELL'D THEM, AND SO BENT	264	INTRO. 1	13
EXPELLING			
THEIR LITTLE GRAIN EXPELLING NIGHT	276	COCK-CRWNG	8
EXPENCE			
THE WORLD READ TO HIM. ALL THE VAST EXPENCE	223	TEMPEST	18
HEAV'NS RICH EXPENCE	144	RSRCTN +IM	12
EXPERIENCE			
AND LONG EXPERIENCE SHOLLD MAKE WISE.	321	CHILDEHOOD	18
EXPIRATIONS			
IN SICKLY EXPIRATIONS TAMES	203	DSRDR + FR	41
EXPIRE			
COOL TO A GLORIOUS EVENING, AND EXPIRE.	195	RLS + LSNS	114
SWEETLY DIDST THOU EXPIRE. THY SOUL	209	THE BURIAL	5
EXPOSE			
WHITE DAYES, THAT DURST NO IMPIOUS MIRTH EXPOSE.	154	ISAACS M.	18
EXPRESS			
BUT LIFE IS, WHAT NONE CAN EXPRESS	345	QUICKNESS	19

	PAGE	TITLE	LINE
EXPREST			
AS, BUT IN THEE, WAS NE'R EXPREST.	164	INCARNATN	8
AND GODS BRIGHT MINDE EXPREST IN PRINT.	332	AGREEMENT	24
EXTASIE			
SPENT IN A ROVING EXTASIE	151	THE SEARCH	4
EXTENDS			
THY COVENANT BY CHRIST EXTENDS.	333	AGREEMENT	52
EXTENT			
EXTENT, AND END, FOR MY HANDS DREW THE LINE	226	RETIREMENT	27
AND PITTY OF SUCH A DIVINE EXTENT	216	DRESSING	29
EXTERIOR			
GUIDED BY FAITH, NOT BY EXTERIOR LIGHT.	327	RIGHTSNESS	24
EXTERMINATING			
EXTERMINATING FEARS AND NIGHT.	332	AGREEMENT	14
EXTORT			
BUT ALL I COULD EXTORT WAS, THAT HE NOW	247	I WALKT	24
EXTRACT			
AND WHAT YOU NOW EXTRACT, IN HARDER WEATHER	274	PROFFER	9
WHICH ONLY GRIEF AND LOVE EXTRACT. WITH THIS	244	THE SAP	41
THIS LAND, THOUGH WITH THY HEARTS BLEST EXTRACT FED	296	JESUS WP A	17
EXTRACTED			
OF SPIRITS, HEAV'N EXTRACTED LYES IN THEE.	197	SCRIPTURES	2
EYE			
WHEN SIX YEARS THENCE DIGG'D UP, SOME YOUTHFULL EYE	201	THE CHECK	6
THEN JOURNEY ON, AND HAVE AN EYE TO HEAV'N.	192	RLS + LSNS	24
OR AT SOME FOUNTAINES BUBLING EYE	148	RELIGION	8
DISPATCH'D AN EYE	141	RGNRTN	83
AND AS A PILGRIMS EYE	139	RGNRTN	22
MY RESTLESS EYE THAT STILL DESIR'D	141	RGNRTN	72
DEATH TO THE COMMON EYE	166	THE CALL	59
SINCE IN THESE VEYLS MY ECCLIPS'D EYE	168	VNTY SPRIT	30
MY HEART, OR EYE	186	PASSION	54
IN THE DEEP WATERS, WHICH NO EYE CAN FIND.	284	PSALM 104	10
WHO HATH THE UPRIGHT HEART, THE SINGLE EYE	327	RIGHTSNESS	9
I CANNOT REACH IT. AND MY STRIVING EYE	321	CHILDEHOOD	1
SAD, PURPLE WELL. WHOSE BUBLING EYE	325	ABELS BLOD	1
A PROCESS, WHICH EV'N MANS OWN EYE	314	THE STONE	35
AN EYE OR EAR	313	THE STONE	4
SEEM'D FAIR UNTO THE WOMANS EYE.	312	FAIR+YONG	36
OF THY LORDS HAND, THE OBJECT OF HIS EYE.	306	RAIN-BOW	14
BY THAT FOUL RHEUM THY FALSE EYE WEARS.	305	ST MARY MN	66
HOW BRIGH WERT THOU, WHEN SHEMS ADMIRING EYE	306	RAIN-BOW	3
MY THOUGHTS DID SWIM IN COMFORTS, AND MINE EYE	244	MT. OLV. B	9
OF SIN, AND DEATH I SOJOURN, YET ONE EYE	234	MUTINIE	20
FOR WHERE THOU DOST NOT CLOSE THE EYE	277	COCK-CRWNG	27
CAN SOULS BE TRACK'D BY ANY EYE	277	COCK-CRWNG	35
AND WARME ME AT THY GLORIOUS EYE.	277	COCK-CRWNG	46
MY PRESENT SEARCH, FOR EAGLES EYE NOT STARRS	278	THE STARRE	6
LIKE A STARV'D EAGLET, FOR THINE EYE.	281	THE FAVOUR	6
COMMAND AND GUIDE THE EYE.	278	THE STARRE	24
MAKES UP BUT LECTURES FOR HIS EYE, AND EAR.	223	TEMPEST	20
HIS WATCHFUL EYE IS EVER OPE	220	PSALM 121	7
HAVE SATE, AND PLEAS'D MY PENSIVE EYE	343	WATER-FALL	14
WHICH FROM THINE EYE	340	THE FEAST	20
WITH MEEK, DUMB LOOKS DIDST WOO MINE EYE	348	HOLY BIBLE	18
IMMEDIATE, PURE AND UNVEIL'D EYE	349	L'ENVOY	18
EYE-SALVEFOR			
AND MIX AN EYE-SALVEFOR THE BLINDE	266	VAIN WITS	6
AND MIX AN EYE-SALVE FOR THE BLINDE.	266	VAIN WITS	7
EYES			
VAIN WITS AND EYES	266	VAIN WITS	1
IN SILENT DROPS STEAL FROM THEIR HOLY EYES	268	ASCN-DAY A	53
MORE EYES THEN STARS, WHOSE BREATH COULD IT ASPIRE	281	JOY	12
TO PLY BOTH THINE EYES AND BREATH.	281	JOY	22
THEIR EYES WATCH FOR THE MORNING-HUE	276	COCK-CRWNG	7
THINK YOU THESE LONGING EYES	275	PROFFER	19
HAD CLEAR'D OUR EYES	219	HOLY COMM.	28
AND GIVEN US EYES	219	HOLY COMM.	34
AND PAINTED TRIMMING TAKES DOWN BOTH HIS EYES	224	TEMPEST	46
AND WITH HIS HEALING BLOOD ANOINT THINE EYES	217	EASTER-DAY	14
THY INWARD EYES, HIS BLOOD WILL CURE THY MIND	217	EASTER-DAY	15
BUT E'R MY EYES COULD OVERFLOW THEIR BRINK	213	ADMISSION	11
AS IF THOU HADST NOR EARS, NOR EYES.	240	MISERY	24
IN SUDDAIN FLOWRES AND ARBOURS TO MY EYES	245	MT. OLV. B	18
NAY, THOSE BRIGHT BEAMS SHOT FROM THY EYES	242	MISERY	85
I SCHOOL MY EYES, AND STRICTLY DWEL	214	MISERY	57
THY EYES, AND BLIND THEE STILL	226	RETIREMENT	52
ALL SCATTER'D LAY, WHILE HE HIS EYES DID POUR	231	THE WORLD	14
WHOSE HANDS ARE OPEN AS THINE EYES.	301	PROVIDENCE	42
HER ART. WHOSE PENSIVE, WEEPING EYES	305	ST MARY MN	57
STOOD BARE BEFORE UNPRACTIC'D EYES	311	FAIR+YONG	18
MY KINDE EYES STILL, BUT IN	310	THE SEED	57
ALL THINGS WITH LIFE, BEFORE WHOSE EYES	314	THE STONE	26
TO BLINDE THE EYES OF LOOKERS-BACK, AND I	320	HIDDN TRSR	9
TEACH BOTH MINE EYES AND FEET TO MOVE	318	THE ASS	15
I'LE SEAL MY EYES UP, AND TO THY COMMANDS	321	HIDDN TRSR	29
IF SEEING MUCH SHOULD MAKE STAID EYES	321	CHILDEHOOD	17
PATHS THAT ARE HIDDEN FROM THE VULTURS EYES	320	HIDDN TRSR	12
DID NOT A GREATER BEAUTY RULE MINE EYES	320	HIDDN TRSR	23
WHO IN THAT LAND OF DARKNESS AND BLINDE EYES	323	THE NIGHT	8

		PAGE	TITLE	LINE
EYES	(CON'T)			
WHOSE EYES ARE BOTH PUT OUT	. . . . . .	327	RIGHTSNESS	22
WHICH THROUGH THE EYES POURS CUT THE HEART	. . .	328	ANGUISH	10
WHEN WITH THESE EYES CLCS'D NCW BY THEE	. . .	337	THE THRONE	1
THEN LET NOT DUST YOUR EYES OBSCURE	. . .	339	DEATH B	28
THINE EYES BEHOLD THE EARTH, AND THE WHOLE STAGE	.	287	PSALM 104	85
WHICH TEACH THEE NOW TO PLEASE HIS EYES	. .	297	HERODIAS	11
MADE THINE EYES MELT, AND THY HEART HEAVE.	.	299	JESUS WP B	33
BEYOND ALL EYES	. . . .	181	BURIALL	28
NOT WORTH THY EYES	. . . .	180	BURIALL	12
HOW LIKE THE EYES QUICK WINKE	. . . .	166	THE CALL	43
WHEN TO MY EYES	. . . .	171	MIDNIGHT	1
A GARLAND WORE. THUS FED MY EYES	. . .	140	RGNRTN	56
BUT WITH THE FOUNTAIN IN MY EYES	. . .	152	THE SEARCH	34
HE HEAV'ND THEIR WALKS, AND WITH HIS EYES	.	152	THE SEARCH	61
OF DROPS MAKE SOFT THE EARTH, MY EYES COULD WEEP	.	160	THE SHOWRE	14
SMILE AT FAIR EYES	. . . . . .	189	RESOLVE	26
AND DROWN MY EYES	. . . .	191	THE MATCH	37
WHEN FIRST THY EYES UNVEIL, GIVE THY SOUL LEAVE	.	191	RLS + LSNS	1
HATH ONE BEAME FROM THY EYES.	. . . .	198	UNPRFTBLNS	12
BEING LAID, AND DREST FOR SLEEP, CLOSE NOT THY EYES		195	RLS + LSNS	127
WHEN SEASONS CHANGE, THEN LAY BEFORE THINE EYES	.	194	RLS + LSNS	91
SEAL NOT THY EYES UP FRCM THE POOR, BUT GIVE	.	193	RLS + LSNS	61
AND DAILY DIDST MY YONG EYES LEAD	. . .	348	HOLY BIBLE	7
A WING WITH EYES, AND EYES THAT TASTE.	. .	346	THE QUEER	12
A WING WITH EYES, AND EYES THAT TASTE.	. .	346	THE QUEER	12
FAC'D				
WHOM STRAIT THE SHINING ROW ALL FAC'D	. . .	303	ORNAMENT	17
FACE				
WHEN THOU DOEST HIDE THY FACE (THY FACE WHICH KEEPS	.	287	PSALM 104	77
WHEN THOU DOEST HIDE THY FACE (THY FACE WHICH KEEPS	.	287	PSALM 104	77
THE FROZEN EARTHS DEAD FACE THOU DOST RENEW.	. .	287	PSALM 104	82
WHICH ALL THE YEAR SEES THE SUNS FACE.	. .	332	AGREEMENT	12
MUST LIVE TWICE, THAT WOULD GODS FACE SEE.	.	322	CHILDEHOOD	36
AND FACE THE MOON.	. . . . . .	323	THE NIGHT	4
WHO KISSETH THORNS, WILL HURT HIS FACE	. .	321	CHILDEHOOD	13
BEYOND A CURLED LCCK, OR PAITED FACE.	. .	155	ISAACS M.	38
HIS BLEST FACE IN A BLOUDY SWEAT.	. . .	152	THE SEARCH	40
COULD SEE A GLIMPSE OF HIS BRIGHT FACE.	. .	169	RETREATE	10
I'TH' FACE OF THINGS	. . . . .	247	I WALKT	9
BUT HIDE, OR TURN THY FACE	. . . .	213	ADMISSION	18
THE BEAMS, AND BRIGHTNES CF THY FACE	. .	217	DRESSING	32
SING THY JUST PRAISE, AND SEE THY FACE.	. .	345	THE WREATH	19
WHICH FIRST UPON THY FACE DID MCVE	. . .	344	WATER—FALL	31
WHO IN THEM LOV'D AND SCUGHT THY FACE.	. .	347	THE BOOK	30
FADE				
THEY LIVE UNSEEN, WHEN HERE THEY FADE.	. .	346	THE BOOK	4
AND MARK HOW THEY DO FAIL, ANC FADE	. . .	208	REPENTANCE	64
WILL FADE AT NIGHT, AND WITH THIS SUN	. .	283	GARLAND	31
OF PARADISE, COULD MAKE MAN FADE	. . .	312	FAIR+YONG	38
FADES				
WOULDST HAVE A WREATH THAT FADES NOT, LET THEM GROW		283	GARLAND	34
LEAVING FOR US (WHOSE GCODNESS QUICKLY FADES)	. .	326	RIGHTSNESS	3
FAIL				
AND SHOULD THOSE SPEECHLESS BEGGERS FAIL	. .	338	THE THRONE	12
BUT THY COMPASSIONS CANNOT FAIL.	. . .	333	AGREEMENT	46
I BEG, MY FAITH MAY NEVER FAIL.	. . .	334	AGREEMENT	62
LET ME NOT FAIL TC QUESTION, WHO	. . .	319	THE ASS	30
AND MARK HOW THEY DO FAIL, ANC FADE	. . .	208	REPENTANCE	64
TEARS CLEANSE AND SUPPLE WITHCUT FAIL	. .	266	VAIN WITS	8
FAILE				
IS STILL OUT WITH THY FLAME, ANC SO BOTH FAILE.	. .	158	THE LAMPE	24
HIS COTTAGE FALLS, WHOSE NARROW SPAN	. . .	166	THE CALL	44
FOR WHEN ALL FAILES TC BRING TC BLISSE	. .	162	PURSUITE	15
FAILINGS				
FOR MY SAD FAILINGS AND MY WILDE	. . .	265	INTRO. 2	21
FAINT				
OR THOSE FAINT BEAMS IN WHICH THIS HILL IS DREST	.	270	ALL GONE	7
AND FAINT REQUESTS	. . . . . .	223	TEMPEST	14
THEN FAINT, AND FEAR.	. . . . .	229	LAW + GOSP	8
FROM HER FAINT BOSOME BREATH'C THEE, THE DISEASE	.	160	THE SHOWRE	2
FAINTS				
AND THE TRUE FAITH, WHICH NEVER FAINTS.	. .	316	MEN OF WAR	8
THAT FAITHFUL ZEAL, WHICH NEITHER FAINTS	. .	350	L'ENVOY	36
FAIR				
WHOSE DIET IS DIVINE AND FAIR	. . . .	346	THE QUEER	2
FAIR SHADE, OR MOUNTAIN	. . . . .	315	DWELLNG-PL	2
SEEM'D FAIR UNTO THE WOMANS EYE.	. . .	312	FAIR+YONG	36
HOME BY OUR FIRST FAIR PUNISHMENT	. . .	312	FAIR+YONG	42
PLAIN, HARMLESS, FAITHFUL, FAIR AND BRIGHT	. .	312	FAIR+YONG	25
A FAIR, WHITE PAGE OF THIN	. . . .	310	THE SEED	58
FAIR AND YONG LIGHT. MY GUIDE TC HOLY	. .	311	FAIR+YONG	1
WHEN THOU DOST SHINE DARKNESS LCCKS WHITE ANC FAIR	.	306	RAIN-BOW	9
YOUTHFUL AND FAIR TO SEE NEW SKIES.	. . .	334	JUDGEMENT	6
FAIR, SOLITARY PATH. WHCSE BLESSED SHADES	. .	326	RIGHTSNESS	1
HEAV'NS SECRET SOLITUDE, THOSE FAIR ABODES	. .	327	RIGHTSNESS	6
WHEN SPIRITS THEIR FAIR KINRED CATCH.	. .	324	THE NIGHT	36
A MOST FAIR NOTION, BUT A VERY NAME.	. .	330	JACOBS PLW	16
WHEN THE FAIR YEAR	. . . . . .	291	THE JEWS	1
SWEETE, SACRED HILL. CN WHOSE FAIR BROW	. .	162	MT. OLVS A	1

		PAGE	TITLE	LINE

FAIR   (CON'T)

BUT STILL THE WEATHER THAT'S MOST FAIR	• • • •	176	THE STORM	15
SMILE AT FAIR EYES	• • • • • • • •	189	RESOLVE	26
FAIR, ORDER'D LIGHT (WHOSE MOTION WITHOUT NOISE	• •	235	CONSTLATN	1
THE HEAVENS THEMSELVES, THOUGH FAIR AND BRIGHT	• •	208	REPENTANCE	65
THROUGH ALL THY FAIR, AND VARIOUS STORY	• • • •	207	REPENTANCE	31
BUT WHAT FAIR WELL, OR GROVE HE SINGS IN NOW	• •	271	ALL GONE	23
THEIR VERY MEMORY IS FAIR AND BRIGHT	• • • •	270	ALL GONE	3
THE PURE EARTH SAT, AND THE FAIR WOODS HAD SEEN	•	268	ASCN-DAY A	42
WITH THESE FAIR THOUGHTS I MOVE IN THIS FAIR PLACE	•	268	ASCN-DAY A	49
WITH THESE FAIR THOUGHTS I MOVE IN THIS FAIR PLACE	•	268	ASCN-DAY A	49
COME FORTH MOST FAIR AND YOUNG.	• • • •	247	I WALKT	28
IF THESE BE FAIR, O WHAT IS HEAVEN.	• • • •	276	PROFFER	48

FAIRE

A FAIRE SUPPLY OF YEARES.	• • • • • •	165	THE CALL	37
WITHIN OUR FIRST FAIRE BED	• • • • •	166	THE CALL	67
MAKE ME FAIRE DAYES OF EVERY NIGHT.	• • • •	182	CHRFLNESS	8
BUT THY FAIRE BRANCHES FELT AS BLOUD	• • •	185	PASSION	19
MY FATHERS JOURNEYS, AND IN ONE FAIRE STEP	• •	159	MANS FALL	28
FAIRE, VIRGIN-FLOWERS, AND HALLOW'D WELLS	• •	153	THE SEARCH	70
THOUGH FAIRE	• • • • • • • •	153	THE SEARCH	82
FULL EAST, A FAIRE, FRESH FIELD COULD SPY	• •	140	RGNRTN	36
A FAIRE-COMPACTED FRAME	• • • • •	166	THE CALL	55

FAIRER

| EACH FAIRER THAN THE OTHER. | • • • • • | 167 | THE CALL | 77 |
| VICE IN A FAIRER NAME. | • • • • • • | 205 | IDLE VERSE | 12 |

FAITH

MY FAITH AS PURE, AND STEDDY	• • • • •	167	THE CALL	91
A LIVING FAITH, A HEART OF FLESH	• • • •	148	DAY OF JDG	41
REDUC'D TH'EXTENT OF WORKS OF FAITH, SO MADE	•	159	MANS FALL	31
WHOSE ACTIVE ZEAL AND TRIED FAITH WERE TO THEE	•	156	ISAACS M.	65
HERE IS THEIR FAITH TOO, WHICH IF YOU WILL KEEP	•	280	PALM-TREE	24
AMONGST THEM, WITH THEM, WING'D WITH FAITH AND LOVE.	•	268	ASCN-DAY A	32
SO ARE NOW FAITH, HOPE, CHARITY	• • • •	211	FAITH	35
FAITH SPANS UP BLISSE, WHAT SIN, AND DEATH	• •	211	FAITH	37
FAITH BRINGS US HOME.	• • • • • •	211	FAITH	40
WHAT EVER THOU DOST BID, LET FAITH MAKE GOOD	•	216	DRESSING	23
AND AUTHOR OF MY FAITH, SO SHEW ME HOME	• •	234	MUTINIE	22
BOTH FAITH, AND AWE.	• • • • • •	230	LAW + GOSP	28
BRIGHTNESS AND MIRTH, AND LOVE AND FAITH, ALL FLYE	•	288	THE BIRD	31
FAITH SOJOURN'D FIRST ON EARTH IN YOU	• • •	292	THE JEWS	38
GUIDED BY FAITH, NOT BY EXTERIOR LIGHT.	• •	327	RIGHTSNESS	24
I BEG, MY FAITH MAY NEVER FAIL.	• • • •	334	AGREEMENT	62
WHILE FAITH AND GRACE	• • • • • •	339	THE FEAST	4
FAITH INTO LIFE BREAKS, AND DEATH DIES.	• •	310	THE SEED	66
AND THE TRUE FAITH, WHICH NEVER FAINTS.	• •	316	MEN OF WAR	8
AND FAITH TO SEE MY CROWN AS NEAR	• • •	317	MEN OF WAR	38
TYE ME TO FAITH, THOUGH ABOVE REASON	• • •	318	THE ASS	19
PLAIN, HARMLESS, FAITHFUL, FAIR AND BRIGHT	• •	312	FAIR+YONG	25
IS'T JUST TO JUDGE HER FAITHFUL TEARS	• • •	305	ST MARY MN	65
LEARN, LADIES, HERE THE FAITHFUL CURE	• • •	305	ST MARY MN	45
THOU ART THE FAITHFUL, PEARLY ROCK	• • •	333	AGREEMENT	31
A FAITHFUL SCHOOL WHERE THOU MAIST SEE	• •	226	RETIREMENT	45
FAITHFUL AND MOST REPENTING MONES	• • •	242	MISERY	111
COME THEN THOU FAITHFUL WITNESS. COME DEAR LORD	•	268	ASCN-DAY A	61
THAT FAITHFUL ZEAL, WHICH NEITHER FAINTS	• •	350	L'ENVOY	36

FAITHFULL

| WIDE OF A FAITHFULL GRAVE. | • • • • • | 183 | THRS A TYE | 16 |
| THOU ART THE SAME, FAITHFULL, AND JUST | • • | 181 | BURIALL | 23 |

FAL

FROM WHICH SOME DROPS FAL HERE	• • •	243	THE SAP	12
FOR THEE, WHO IN THE FIRST MANS LOYNS DIDST FAL	•	243	THE SAP	19
FIND OUT THE FIRST AND STEEPEST FAL.	• •	240	MISERY	16
IF SAINTS, AND ANGELS FAL DOWN, MUCH MORE THOU.	•	217	DRESSING	42
DID ONLY LOOK ABOUT, AND FAL	• • • •	209	THE BURIAL	2

FAL'ST

| THOU ONLY FAL'ST TO BE REFIN'D AGAINE | • • • | 145 | RSRCTN +IM | 50 |

FALL

FOR NO THING CAN TO NOTHING FALL BUT STILL	• •	145	RSRCTN +IM	25
THAT TO IT FALL	• • • • • •	145	RSRCTN +IM	34
WHAT SINS ON EVERY MINUTE FALL	• • •	165	THE CALL	22
HID UNDER GROUND SURVIVES THE FALL.	• •	203	DSRDR + FR	29
WHAT ONE POOR LEAF DID EVER I YET FALL	• •	198	UNPRFTBLNS	14
AND THEN SET FORTH, WHO IS THUS DREST, THE FALL	•	195	RLS + LSNS	111
THE WHOLE FRAME WITH HIS FALL.	• • •	197	CORRUPTION	16
THEN DID HE SHINE FORTH, WHOSE SAD FALL	• •	210	FAITH	29
TUNING HIS BREST TO RISE, OR FALL.	• • •	222	AFFLICTION	37
ALL THINGS HERE SHEW HIM HEAVEN, WATERS THAT FALL	•	223	TEMPEST	25
WHEN THOU WOULDST FALL	• • • • •	225	RETIREMENT	21
POLLUTED THROUGH THEIR FALL	• • • •	238	SHEPHEARDS	24
AND AFTER FALL, FOR IN HER DRESS	• • •	269	ASCSN-HYMN	17
AFTER THE FALL, THE FIRST SIN WAS IN BLOOD	•	307	RAIN-BOW	21
ALTHOUGH THE FIRST MUST SURELY FALL	• •	302	ORNAMENT	7
THAT THESE THREE THOUSAND YEARS TIME DID LET FALL	•	320	HIDDN TRSR	8
THESE CONQUERORS BEFORE IT FALL	• • •	317	MEN OF WAR	48
MY SPRING AND FALL ARE IN THY BOOK.	• •	293	BEGGING B	2
SOME CROPS MAY FALL BEFORE, BUT A CLEAR SPRING	•	291	THE TIMBER	54
IF SHOWERS THEN FALL, WILL SHOWERS ALLAY	•	298	JESUS WP B	19
THAT HAVE LIV'D HERE, SINCE THE MANS FALL.	•	346	THE BOOK	2
AS THIS LOUD BROOKS INCESSANT FALL	• •	344	WATER-FALL	33

		PAGE	TITLE	LINE
FALL	**(CON'T)**			
HERE FLOWING FALL	. . . .	343	WATER-FALL	3
KNEEL DOWN AND FALL	. . . .	341	THE FEAST	59
FALL'ST				
THOU FALL'ST IN TEARES, AND WEEP'ST FOR THY MISTAKE.	.	160	THE SHOWRE	6
FALLING				
POOR, FALLING STAR.	. . . .	203	DSRDR + FR	45
AND FALLING SPRINGS	. . . . . .	176	MRNG-WTCH	13
TO WHOM A FALLING STAR AND NINE DAYES GLORY	. .	282	GARLAND	2
FALLS				
AND WHEN THIS DUST FALLS TO THE URN	. . . .	170	RETREATE	31
'TWIXT STEPS, AND FALLS	. . . .	139	RGNRTN	27
OUR FEARES, AND FALLS BROUGHT TO CONTEMPT	. .	143	DEATH	18
FALN				
MY LOTT IS FALN, BLEST BE THY WILL.	. . . .	227	LV + DSPLN	3
WHEN THEIR NEST IS FALN AND BROKEN.	. . .	294	BEGGING B	20
FALSE				
FALSE STARS AND FIRE-DRAKES, THE DECEITS OF NIGHT	.	320	HIDDN TRSR	4
BY THAT FOUL RHEUM THY FALSE EYE WEARS.	. .	305	ST MARY MN	66
WHO WERT ALL FALSE, SHOULD'ST TRUE GRIEF KNOW.	.	305	ST MARY MN	64
LODGED IN THOSE FALSE LOOKS, TILL TOO LATE.	. .	311	FAIR+YONG	22
FALSE JOYES, PHANTASTICK FLIGHTS	. . . . .	282	GARLAND	18
FALSE, JUGLING SOUNDS, A GRONE WELL DREST, WHERE CARE		280	JOY	3
I SKILL NOT YOUR FINE TINSEL, AND FALSE HAIR	. .	275	PROFFER	33
FALSE ECCHOES, AND CONFUSED SOUNDS	. . .	150	RELIGION	38
BUT HEARTS ARE NOT SO KIND. FALSE, SHORT DELIGHTS	.	183	THRS A TYE	13
FALSE LIFE. A FOIL AND NO MORE. WHEN	. . .	344	QUICKNESS	1
THAT FROM THE MURD'RING WORLDS FALSE LOVE	. .	343	OBSEQUIES	31
FAM'D				
SO THAT FAM'D FRUIT WHICH MADE ALL DYE	. . .	312	FAIR+YONG	35
FAMILIAR				
MAN SLIGHTS HIS MAKER, WHEN FAMILIAR GROWN	. .	330	JACOBS PLW	19
(O HOW FAMILIAR THEN WAS HEAVEN)	. . . .	149	RELIGION	14
FAMILIAR EVER SINCE THY INFANCIE.	. . . .	156	ISAACS M.	66
FAMILIARLY				
AND FAMILIARLY CONFER	. . . . . .	291	THE JEWS	6
FAMILIE				
AND OF A PRIVATE FAMILIE	. . . . . .	210	FAITH	7
FAMISH'D				
AND ALMOST FAMISH'D, EVER WILL CONSENT	. . .	275	PROFFER	21
FAMOUS				
THEY ARE HEAVENS HUSBANDRY, THE FAMOUS FAN	. .	221	AFFLICTION	19
THOSE FAMOUS TABLES DID FROM SINAI BRING.	. .	159	MANS FALL	17
FAN				
AND LEAVES THY SPIRIT DOTH STILL FAN	. .	148	RELIGION	2
HE RAVES, AND SWEARS TO STIR NOR FIRE, NOR FAN	.	197	CORRUPTION	31
THEY ARE HEAVENS HUSBANDRY, THE FAMOUS FAN	.	221	AFFLICTION	19
FANCIES				
WITH FANCIES, FRIENDS, OR NEWES.	. . . .	187	NO DO THEY	34
FANCY				
OR TAUGHT MY SOUL TO FANCY OUGHT	. . . .	169	RETREATE	5
NEER HIM, HIS LUTE, HIS FANCY, AND HIS FLIGHTS	.	231	THE WORLD	10
FAND				
FAND BY A GENTLE GALE CONVEY AND BREATH	. .	244	MT. OLV. B	5
FAR				
HE SAYES IT IS SO FAR	. . . . .	246	MAN	20
YET LOOK I FOR FAR BETTER BREAD	. . . .	228	PILGRIMAGE	23
CAME OFT FROM FAR, AND WHISPER'D, NO.	. .	207	REPENTANCE	16
NOT ONE BEAM TRIUMPHS, BUT FROM FAR	. . .	212	DAWNING	23
SOME KINDE HERBS HERE, THOUGH LOW AND FAR	.	281	THE FAVOUR	7
BUT STRAIT I THINK (THOUGH FAR)	. . . .	171	COME, COME	13
FAR BEYOND THE STARS	. . . . .	184	PEACE	2
IS ONLY STRONGER FAR THAN DEATH.	. .	164	INCARNATN	20
THROUGH THICKEST NIGHTS, THOUGH THEN THE SUN BE FAR	.	196	RLS + LSNS	137
FLUTT'RING IN WOODS, OR LIFTED FAR	. . .	199	NTVTY 1	14
AS FAR AS BETHLEM, AND HAVE SEEN	. . .	151	THE SEARCH	6
FAR FROM RELIEFE	. . . . .	139	RGNRTN	23
AND SURE IT IS NOT FAR.	. . .	292	THE JEWS	20
FAR GREATER, AND SO SPEAK MY SAVIORS GLORY.	.	290	THE TIMBER	44
TO LEND ME, THOUGH FROM FAR, ONE LOOK.	. .	293	BEGGING B	4
WHOSE LIGHT, THOUGH FETCHT AND BORROWED FROM FAR	.	288	THE BIRD	21
SHED THIS LIVE-DEW ON FIELDS WHICH FAR	. .	296	JESUS WP A	14
ALL BETTER FAR THEN 'TWAS BEFORE.	. .	299	JESUS WP B	37
THY WOE, WHO CAUS'D HIS WEAL, SO FAR HIS WEAL	.	283	LOVE-SICK	19
A BEAUTY FAR MORE BRIGHT	. . . .	310	THE SEED	81
BECKEN'D BY THEE, THOUGH HIGH AND FAR	. .	315	DWELLNG-PL	8
FAR-DAY				
AFTER SUN-RISING, FAR-DAY SULLIES FLOWRES.	. .	192	RLS + LSNS	10
FARE				
WELL FARE THOSE BLESSED DAYS OF OLD	. . .	293	BEGGING B	11
FAREWEL				
THEN FAREWEL JOYS. FOR WHILE I LIVE	. .	299	JESUS WP B	44
FAREWEL O BOOK OF GOD. FAREWELL.	. . .	348	HOLY BIBLE	36
FAREWELL				
FAREWEL O BOOK OF GOD. FAREWELL.	. .	348	HOLY BIBLE	36
FAREWELL YOU EVERLASTING HILLS. I'M CAST	. .	158	MANS FALL	1
FAREWELL. I GOE TO SLEEP. BUT WHEN	. .	177	EVNG-WTCH	1
FARR				
THAT THOU WERT PLEAS'D TO SHED THY GRACE SO FARR,	.	283	LOVE-SICK	3
FASHION				
WHERE THEY FOR FASHION LOOK	. . . .	237	CONSTLATN	42

	PAGE	TITLE	LINE
FASHIONING			
NINE MONTHS THY HANDS ARE FASHIONING US	166	THE CALL	46
FAST			
SOME FAST ASLEEPE, OTHERS BROAD-EYED	141	RGNRTN	76
BIRDS SING, BEASTS FEED, FISH LEAP, AND TH'EARTH STANDS FAST	194	RLS + LSNS	88
WHILE PALESTINE WAS FAST A SLEEP, AND LAY	238	SHEPHEARDS	7
IS FAST ASLEEP.	226	RETIREMENT	53
FOR AS YOUR FAST AND FOUL DECAYS	292	THE JEWS	21
IF I HOLD FAST AND SLIGHT THE LURE.	317	MEN OF WAR	40
AS FAST, AS PERSECUTIONS NOW.	351	L'ENVOY	58
FASTENS			
SIGHS MAKE JOY SURE, AND SHAKING FASTENS THEE.	281	JOY	30
FAT			
JERUSALEM, WITH BLOOD OF BEASTS, AND FAT.	330	JACOBS PLW	26
FATAL			
WITH FATAL SWEETNESS, TILL WE EAT.	311	FAIR+YONG	14
FATE			
YET WOULD NOT MEN GRANT, THEIR ILL FATE	311	FAIR+YONG	21
LEAVES ME A SLAVE TO PASSIONS, AND MY FATE.	158	MANS FALL	8
THEIR WELL-FLEEC'D TRAINE) AND HERE (O FATE)	151	THE SEARCH	27
FATHER			
OF THY GREAT FATHER	185	PASSION	27
FATHER FORGIVE	185	PASSION	41
THUS, RIGHTEOUS FATHER. DOEST THOU DEAL	293	THE JEWS	46
FATHER OF LIGHTS. WHAT SUNNIE SEED	276	COCK-CRWNG	1
O FATHER OF ETERNAL LIFE, AND ALL	271	ALL GONE	33
THE SONS THE FATHER KIL	237	CONSTLATN	38
FATHERS			
STIFF-NECKED JEWS. YOUR FATHERS BREED	296	JESUS WP A	5
THE YOUTHFUL WORLDS GRAY FATHERS IN ONE KNOT	306	RAIN-BOW	6
TO FEELE MY LOVING FATHERS ROD	147	DAY OF JDG	31
HIS FATHERS FLAMING MINISTRIE	152	THE SEARCH	60
MY FATHERS JOURNEYS, AND IN ONE FAIRE STEP	159	MANS FALL	28
TOGETHER WITH HIS BLOUD, THY FATHERS SPIRIT	156	ISAACS M.	64
FATNESS			
AND ALL THY PATHS DROP FATNESS ROUND	337	PSALM 65	40
FAULTS			
READ HERE, MY FAULTS ARE THINE. THIS BOOK, AND I	198	SCRIPTURES	13
BUT AS FOR THEE, WHOSE FAULTS LONG SINCE REQUIRE	281	JOY	11
FOR ALL MY SECRET FAULTS, AND EACH	265	INTRO. 2	23
FAVORITE			
MANS FAVORITE SINS, THOSE TAINTING APPETITES	320	HIDDN TRSR	19
FAVORS			
NOURISHED WITH FAVORS FROM HIS HAND	302	THE KNOT	11
THE SECRET FAVORS OF THE DOVE	348	HOLY BIBLE	28
FEAR			
SHOULD POOR SOULS FEAR A SHADE OR NIGHT	343	WATER-FALL	17
WHERE I SHALL HAVE NO CAUSE TO FEAR	313	THE STONE	3
THIS CAUTIOUS FOOLS MISTAKE, AND FEAR	313	THE STONE	16
AND NEITHER GRIEVE, REPINE, NOR FEAR.	339	DEATH B	25
I WILL NOT FEAR WHAT MAN	300	PROVIDENCE	19
AND GREAT. THERE SHIPS GO, AND THE SHIPMENS FEAR	286	PSALM 104	71
AND STUNG WITH FEAR	247	I WALKT	30
I MAY AS WEL AS LOVE, FIND TOO THY FEAR.	230	LAW + GOSP	30
SO SHALL THY MERCIES FLOW. FOR WHILE I FEAR	230	LAW + GOSP	37
THEN FAINT, AND FEAR.	229	LAW + GOSP	8
LASTS NOT A NIGHT SOMETIMES. BAD SPIRITS FEAR	195	RLS + LSNS	124
FEAR'D			
AND WON THE FIGHT, AND HAVE NOT FEAR'D THE FROWNS	280	PALM-TREE	18
AND THAT DREAD GLORY, WHICH THY CHILDREN FEAR'D	330	JACOBS PLW	2
FEARD			
AND PLEAS'D OURSELVES WITH WHAT WE FEARD	143	DEATH	26
FEARE			
I FEARE	161	DSTRQCTION	21
IN FEARE OF THEEVES.	232	THE WORLD	35
FEARES			
THESE SWELL'D MY FEARES	159	MANS FALL	18
OUR FEARES, AND FALLS BROUGHT TO CONTEMPT	143	DEATH	19
O THOU, WHOM MY SOUL LOVES, AND FEARES.	185	PASSION	15
DAYES ARE MY FEARES.	170	COME, COME	10
FEARFUL			
FEARFUL AND WAN	328	RIGHTSNESS	44
FEARFULL			
THE FEARFULL MISER ON A HEAP OF RUST	232	THE WORLD	31
FEARS			
AND WHEN FEARS, AND DOUBTS WERE RIFE	214	PRAISE	3
SO IN THE MIDST OF ALL HER FEARS	223	TEMPEST	13
EXTERMINATING FEARS AND NIGHT.	332	AGREEMENT	14
WHICH FREED POOR HAGAR FROM HER FEARS	300	PROVIDENCE	4
ON THEIR DEAD HEARTS, BUT (O MY FEARS)	296	JESUS WP A	11
BUT IN A VIRGINS NATIVE BLUSH AND FEARS	155	ISAACS M.	35
A DARTING CONSCIENCE FULL OF STABS, AND FEARS.	188	RELAPSE	17
REST FROM THE FEARS I'TH' NIGHT.	201	THE CHECK	19
FEAST			
IT IS THE GOOD MANS FEAST, THE PRINCE OF FLOWRES	193	RLS + LSNS	59
WELCOME DEAR BOOK, SOULS JOY, AND FOOD. THE FEAST	197	SCRIPTURES	1
A THANKLES FEEDER IS A THIEF, HIS FEAST	195	RLS + LSNS	101
AND ON SURE HOPES, THOUGH LONG, DID FEAST.	143	DEATH	22
LOOKE DOWNE GREAT MASTER OF THE FEAST, O SHINE	150	RELIGION	51
TO BE MY FEAST.	185	PASSION	21

	PAGE	TITLE	LINE
FEAST (CON'T)			
DEAR FEAST OF PALMS, OF FLOWERS AND DEW.	295	PALM-SUNDY	30
I TAKE THY SACRED FEAST	217	DRESSING	34
WELCOME SWEET, AND SACRED FEAST. WELCOME LIFE.	218	HOLY COMM.	1
THERE SHALL FEAST ME.	214	PRAISE	24
OF A FULL FEAST, AND THE OUT COURTS OF GLORY.	2	SON-DAYES	24
ONLY IN HIM, ON WHOM I FEAST	209	REPENTANCE	79
AT THIS GREAT FEAST, AND IN A TYRE	272	WHT SUNDAY	6
WHERE DEAD MEN PREACH, WHO CAN TURN FEASTS, AND MIRTH	226	RETIREMENT	49
FEAT			
'TIS NOT TH'APPLOUSE, AND FEAT	226	RETIREMENT	30
FEATHER			
A FEATHER, OR A SHELL	166	THE CALL	51
FEAV'RISH			
THE IDLE TALK OF FEAV'RISH SOULS	205	IDLE VERSE	15
FED			
ELIAS BY A RAVEN IS FED	149	RELIGION	10
A GARLAND WORE. THUS FED MY EYES	140	RGNRTN	56
CHURCHES AND ALTARS FED HIM, PERJURIES	232	THE WORLD	27
THUS FED BY THEE, WHO DOST ALL BEINGS NOURISH	245	MT. OLV. B	21
IS WATER'D BY THEIR TEARS, AS FLOWERS ARE FED	280	PALM-TREE	22
AND BY A SACRED INCUBATION FED	248	I WALKT	45
THIS LAND, THOUGH WITH THY HEARTS BLEST EXTRACT FED	296	JESUS WP A	17
AND WHEN THEY ALL ARE FED, AND HAVE	329	TEARS	9
TO LIVING SPRINGS, AND THERE BE FED	319	THE ASS	60
TO LIVING SPRINGS, AND THERE BE FED	319	THE ASS	61
THAT WITH I FED	340	THE FEAST	34
ON EACH GREEN THING. THEN SLEPT (WELL FED)	347	THE BOOK	17
WE MAY BE FED, AND ONE MINDE HOLD.	350	L'ENVOY	48
FEED			
DID LIVE AND FEED BY THY DECREE	347	THE BOOK	16
O FEED THAT LIFE, WHICH MAKES HIM BLOW	308	THE SEED	19
THESE ALL UPON THEE WAIT, THAT THOU MAIST FEED	286	PSALM 104	73
DOST THOU FEED THINE. O THOU. THE HAND THAT LIFTS	267	ASCN-DAY A	3
O FEED ME THEN. AND SINCE I MAY	229	PILGRIMAGE	25
FEED ON THOSE VOMITS OF MY HEART.	240	MISERY	20
BIRDS SING, BEASTS FEED, FISH LEAP, AND TH'EARTH STANDS FAST	194	RLS + LSNS	88
FEED'ST			
AND FEED'ST THEM ALL THE WEEK.	286	PSALM 104	60
FEEDER			
A THANKLES FEEDER IS A THIEF, HIS FEAST	195	RLS + LSNS	101
FEEDING			
THE BLADES OF GRASSE, THY CREATURES FEEDING	207	REPENTANCE	33
FEEDS			
THY SPIRIT FEEDS.	188	RELAPSE	16
INTELLIGENCE, WHOSE SPIRIT FEEDS	314	THE STONE	25
BY SECRET FILTH, NOR FEEDS	328	RIGHTSNESS	52
THAT FEEDST AMONG THE LILLIES, 'TILL THE DAY	216	DRESSING	2
FEEL			
THAT, MIDST ALL STORMS I FEEL A RAY OF THEE.	245	MT. OLV. B	16
AT LENGTH I FEEL MY HEAD TO AKE	214	MISERY	61
FEEL ME A SHARER IN THY VICTORY.	267	ASCN-DAY A	8
BUT GIVE IT HIM, AND GRUDGE NOT. HE SHALL FEEL	279	THE STARRE	30
AND FEEL A FRIEND MOST READY, SURE AND KINDE.	331	JACOBS PLW	52
(UNSEEN) SUCH JOYS I FEEL.	337	THE THRONE	7
WHAT SOME POOR MAN MAY OFTEN FEEL	308	THE SEED	2
I FEEL AS WINE	185	PASSION	18
FEEL IN EACH BLOW.	184	PASSION	6
FEEL'ST			
WHO NEVER FEEL'ST THE SUN, NOR SMOOTH'ST THY BROW	217	EASTER-DAY	3
FEELE			
TO FEELE MY LOVING FATHERS ROD	147	DAY OF JDG	31
FEET			
RUDE FEET ERE TROD	140	RGNRTN	39
TEACH BOTH MINE EYES AND FEET TO MOVE	318	THE ASS	15
BENEATH HIS BLEST FEET THOU DIDST CAST	304	ST MARY MN	30
WITH MY FOUL HEART THY HOLY FEET.	328	ANGUISH	4
FEIGN			
IN ONE AT ONE TIME, AS SOME FEIGN.	298	JESUS WP B	17
FEL			
THAT FEL HIM, FOYL'D THEM ALL	196	CORRUPTION	14
VEILES BECAME USELES, ALTARS FEL	210	FAITH	25
FELL			
FELL ON MY HEART, THOSE MADE IT BUD	264	INTRO. 1	6
AND FORTY DAYES WITHSTOOD THE FELL	152	THE SEARCH	57
THIS DEW FELL ON MY BREAST.	176	MRNG-WTCH	7
THAT SINCE MAN FELL, EXPECT WITH GROANS	294	PALM-SUNDY	12
FELLOW-CREATURE			
MY FELLOW-CREATURES TOO SAY, COME.	335	JUDGEMENT	15
WALK WITH THY FELLOW-CREATURES. NOTE THE HUSH	192	RLS + LSNS	13
FELLOW-MURTHERE			
THIS WORLD, THEIR FELLOW-MURTHERER.	312	FAIR+YONG	40
FELLOWSHIP			
SUCH MUSICK SPOILS GOOD FELLOWSHIP.	240	MISERY	32
FELT			
SHIN'D ON MY SOUL, I FELT THROUGH ALL MY POWR'S	244	MT. OLV. B	3
THEY MURMUR'D SORE, BUT I, WHO FELT THEM BOYL	234	MUTINIE	9
BUT FELT THROUGH ALL THIS FLESHLY DRESSE	170	RETREATE	19
BUT THY FAIRE BRANCHES FELT AS BLOUD	185	PASSION	19
FENCE			
WHO, WHEN THY SINS CALL FOR'T, CAN FENCE A CURSE.	193	RLS + LSNS	64

	PAGE	TITLE	LINE
FENCE (CON'T)			
NOT BREAK THY FENCE, AND BY A BLACK EXCESS	230	LAW + GOSP	32
I BREAK THE FENCE MY OWN HANDS MADE	240	MISERY	21
FERTIL			
WITH FERTIL STREAMS, MAKES RICH ALL GROUNDS	336	PSALM 65	30
FETCH'D			
'TIL TO THOSE SIGHES FETCH'D FROM HER WOMB	222	TEMPEST	11
THESE FETCH'D THEE HOME THY BRIDE, AND ALL THE WAY	155	ISAACS M.	27
FETCHT			
WHOSE LIGHT, THOUGH FETCHT AND BORROWED FROM FAR	288	THE BIRD	21
FETTERS			
AND BULRUSH FETTERS TEMPER HIS SHORT HOUR.	224	TEMPEST	50
FEW			
AND YET, HOW FEW BELIEVE SUCH DOCTRINE SPRINGS	248	I WALKT	36
AND SETS, WILL FEW HOURS HENCE BEGIN	292	THE JEWS	29
SOME FEW TRUE TEARS, AND THOSE SHED FOR	342	OBSEQUIES	3
FIE			
AND SWEETLY LIVING (FIE ON MEN)	321	CHILDEHOOD	15
FIELD			
THESE TO THE BEASTS OF EVERY FIELD GIVE DRINK.	285	PSALM 104	33
ALL NOW ARE STIRRING, EV'RY FIELD	212	DAWNING	15
INTO A FIELD	246	I WALKT	2
FULL EAST, A FAIRE, FRESH FIELD COULD SPY	140	RGNRTN	36
FIELDS			
WALK BUT THE FIELDS, OR SIT DOWN AT SOME WEL	197	CORRUPTION	27
AS RICH A SCENT AS THE NOW PRIMROS'D FIELDS	267	ASCN-DAY A	22
I WALK THE FIELDS OF BETHANI WHICH SHINE	268	ASCN-DAY A	37
AND FLOWERS THAT INTO FIELDS DO STRAY,	294	PALM-SUNDY	9
SHED THIS LIVE-DEW ON FIELDS WHICH FAR	296	JESUS WP A	14
THE FIELDS ARE LONG SINCE WHITE, AND I	334	JUDGEMENT	13
FIERCE			
ELSE ALL AT REST THOU LYEST, AND THE FIERCE BREATH	289	THE TIMBER	17
SO MY FIERCE SOUL BUSTLES ABOUT	214	MISERY	79
MY FIERCE, WILD BLOOD THAT STILL HEAVES, AND INCLINES	190	THE MATCH	4
FROM THE FIERCE JEW, AND HEROCS HEAT	152	THE SEARCH	56
INCITE THEM TO THAT FIERCE DISCUSSE	175	THE STORM	11
FIG-LEAFS			
SOME FIG-LEAFS STIL I DO DEVISE	240	MISERY	23
FIGHT			
THEN WOULD GO TRAVEL, FIGHT OR DIE.	214	MISERY	74
AND WON THE FIGHT, AND HAVE NOT FEAR'D THE FROWNS	280	PALM-TREE	18
ARMIES THOU HAST IN HEAVEN, WHICH FIGHT	316	MEN OF WAR	21
AND BITTER FIGHTS	211	FAITH	30
FIGS			
FIGS ON A THORNE, FLOWRES ON A WEED.	208	REPENTANCE	70
FIGUR'D			
WERE FIGUR'D IN THOSE MYSTICAL	211	FAITH	31
FIGURES			
IS A PLAIN WATCH, AND WITHOUT FIGURES WINDS	178	EVNG-WTCH	12
FIL			
THE BRIDEGROOME'S COMMING. FIL THE SKY.	211	DAWNING	2
OPEN MY ROCKIE HEART, AND FIL	242	MISERY	101
FILE			
QUITE THROUGH THEIR PROUD AND POMPOUS FILE	303	ORNAMENT	13
FILES			
COMMANDS THE BEAUTEOUS FILES	184	PEACE	8
FILIAL			
WITH FILIAL CONFIDENCE WE TOUCH EV'N THEE.	229	LAW + GOSP	13
FILL			
THERE DUST THAT OUT OF COCKS MIGHT FILL	226	RETIREMENT	51
IF A MEER BLAST SO FILL THE SAIL	276	COCK-CRWNG	17
PRIVATE AND HOLY TALK FILL ALL THE WAYS.	268	ASCN-DAY A	28
EITHER DISPERSE THESE MISTS, WHICH BLOT AND FILL	271	ALL GONE	37
THE GLASSE WITH TEARES YOU FILL.	165	THE CALL	27
O FILL HIS BOTTLE. THY CHILDE WEEPS.	308	THE SEED	16
TO FILL MY BOTTLE, THEN I DIE WITH THIRST.	290	THE TIMBER	48
THE FRUITFUL FLOCKS FILL EVERY DALE	337	PSALM 65	45
FILL'D			
AND FILL'D WITH JOY, THY GOODNESS TELLS.	336	PSALM 65	12
WHEN MY LORDS HEAD IS FILL'D WITH DEW, AND ALL	324	THE NIGHT	32
WHICH BROKE IN SIGHES STILL, AS THEY FILL'D	151	THE SEARCH	30
AND FILL'D HER BRESTS.	223	TEMPEST	16
AND FILL'D HIS BOSOME	215	PRAISE	53
FILL'ST			
BUT THOU FILL'ST IT	214	PRAISE	6
FILLS			
AND FILLS THE BOXES OF HIS POOR.	209	REPENTANCE	82
FILS			
I LOOK, AND SIGH FOR HIM, WHO FILS	220	PSALM 121	3
(I KNOW IT WEL) FILS ALL THE PLACE.	214	MISERY	52
HE FILS IT. DAYES, AND HOURS ARE BLINDS.	178	EVNG-WTCH	14
WHO FILS THE WORLDS UNEMPTY'D GRANARIES.	195	RLS + LSNS	100
FILTH			
THAT VOYDS BUT FILTH, AND STENCH. HAST THOU NO PRIZE	194	RLS + LSNS	75
BUT I AM ALL FILTH, AND OBSCENE	199	NTVTY 1	23
ALL FILTH, AND SPOTT	180	BURIALL	19
BY SECRET FILTH, NOR FEEDS	328	RIGHTSNESS	52
FIND			
IN THE DEEP WATERS, WHICH NO EYE CAN FIND.	284	PSALM 104	10
AND GROW FOR THEE, WHO SPARES THEM HERE, SHALL FIND	283	GARLAND	35

	PAGE	TITLE	LINE
FIND (CON'T)			
FIND HEAVEN, AND THEE.	179	SILENCE	32
AND BE AS GLAD TO FIND IT	167	THE CALL	87
TO SEARCH MY SELFE, WHERE I DID FIND	168	VNTY SPRIT	15
T' UNITE THOSE PEECES, HOPING TO FIND OUT	168	VNTY SPRIT	26
THEY SHALL FIND THOU ART THEIR HILL	163	MT. OLVS A	18
I HAVE CONSIDER'D IT. AND FIND	189	RESOLVE	1
TO FIND MY SAVIOUR, I HAVE BEEN	151	THE SEARCH	5
FIND BEASTS MORE MERCIFULL THEN MAN	152	THE SEARCH	54
NO WHERE I COULD NOT FIND	141	RGNRTN	81
I FIND MY SELFE THE LESSE, THE MORE I GROW.	161	DSTRQCTION	10
SHAL FIND A JOY SO TRUE	244	THE SAP	46
I MAY AS WEL AS LOVE, FIND TOO THY FEAR.	230	LAW + GOSP	30
FIND OUT THE FIRST AND STEEPEST FAL.	240	MISERY	16
WHERE NOW THEY FIND HIM OUT, AND TAUGHT BEFORE	239	SHEPHEARDS	47
THESE FIND THEE OUT, AND THOUGH OUR SINS	213	ADMISSION	21
THOU'LT FIND ME DREST AND ON MY WAY	212	DAWNING	47
I MAY FIND THY HAND THEREIN	249	BEGGING A	11
FINDE			
BUT WHEN THY MASTER COMES, THEY'L FINDE AND SEE	275	PROFFER	41
WHAT THOU DIDST HOPE FOR AND BELIEVE, WE FINDE	331	JACOBS PLW	51
EV'N THOSE, WHO BY THEM WOULD FINDE OUT THE DAY	321	HIDDN TRSR	28
AND THIS I HOURLY FINDE, FOR THOU	333	AGREEMENT	55
AND PRESENT THINGS FINDE MEN MOST KINDE.	318	THE ASS	6
NOW ALL IS DONE, FINDE ALL IS VANITY.	320	HIDDN TRSR	10
I CANNOT FINDE, BUT WHERE THY HEAD	342	OBSEQUIES	27
SUCH AS DULL MAN CAN NEVER FINDE	344	WATER-FALL	29
FINDES THY POOR FOAL AT THY COMMAND	319	THE ASS	46
FINDING			
BUT FINDING NONE, SHAL LEAVE THEE TO THE WIND	201	THE CHECK	8
FINDS			
AND THE MORE NOBLE ESSENCE FINDS HIS HOUSE	145	RSRCTN +IM	39
HE FINDS IT DEAD, AND IN A GRAVE.	212	DAWNING	32
FINE			
I SKILL NOT YOUR FINE TINSEL, AND FALSE HAIR	275	PROFFER	33
SHAL BE FINE GOLD, WHICH THOU DIDST CLEANSE.	274	WHT SUNDAY	60
ALL NOW AS FRESH AS EDEN, AND AS FINE.	268	ASCN-DAY A	38
WITH CLOUDS AND RAIN, YET FULL AS CALM AND FINE	281	JOY	15
ALTHOUGH THEIR DIET MAY BE FINE	228	PILGRIMAGE	18
YET SOLOMON WAS NEVER DREST SO FINE.	245	MAN	14
HADST THOU BIN RICH, OR FINE	173	CONTENT	14
STILL YONG AND FINE. BUT WHAT IS STILL IN VIEW	306	RAIN-BOW	1
WHICH NATURE BREEDS, AND SOME FINE CLAY INVITES	320	HIDDN TRSR	20
FINEST			
THE FINEST THINGS THAT ARE, TO SEE.	312	FAIR+YONG	34
FINGERS			
MY FINGERS ITCH, AND BURN TO TAKE	214	MISERY	62
FINISH			
WILT FINISH IT, AND BY NO SIN	334	AGREEMENT	69
FINISHED			
DEAR LORD, 'TIS FINISHED. AND NOW HE	265	INTRO. 2	1
FINISHER			
MAY LOOK TO THEE, TO THEE THE FINISHER	234	MUTINIE	21
FINITE			
I AM BUT FINITE, HE IS INFINITE.	209	REPENTANCE	84
FIR-TREES			
THE FIR-TREES FOR HER HOUSE.	286	PSALM 104	48
FIRE			
THY MINISTER IN FIRE.	284	PSALM 104	16
REFINING FIRE, O THEN REFINE MY HEART	283	LOVE-SICK	13
THIS MADE HIM PUT ON CLOUDS, AND FIRE AND SMOKE	330	JACOBS PLW	7
LIV'D STILL IN LEAGUE WITH THY CHASTE FIRE	312	FAIR+YONG	28
THOU DOST BUT COURT COLD RAIN, TILL RAIN TURNS FIRE.	307	RAIN-BOW	42
AND LEAD BY MY OWN FOOLISH FIRE	311	FAIR+YONG	5
SO THOSE BAD DAUGHTERS, WHICH GOD SAV'D FROM FIRE	307	RAIN-BOW	31
AND SEND A FIRE DOWN, THAT SHALL BRING	305	ST MARY MN	55
WITH THY CLEER FIRE REFINE, BURNING TO DUST	216	DRESSING	6
FIRE TO ALL THREE, BUT MAN HATH NO SUCH MIRTH.	223	TEMPEST	32
BE BROKE AGAIN, FOR FLINTS WILL GIVE NO FIRE	224	TEMPEST	58
AND SEEDS A KINRED FIRE HAVE WITH THE SKY.	223	TEMPEST	36
ABUSE NOT, SHUN NOT HOLY FIRE	266	VAIN WITS	3
AND FIRE WILL PURGE YOUR CALLOUS VEYL.	266	VAIN WITS	9
IN TEARS TO YOU, IN FIRE TO ME.	266	VAIN WITS	13
I PLAYED WITH FIRE, DID COUNSELL SPURN	282	GARLAND	13
BUT NEVER THOUGHT THAT FIRE WOULD BURN	282	GARLAND	15
AND LONGING FOR THY BRIGHT AND VITALL FIRE	278	THE STARRE	18
O COME. REFINE US WITH THY FIRE.	274	WHT SUNDAY	61
AND CROWN'D THEM WITH PROPHETIC FIRE.	272	WHT SUNDAY	8
THOUGH THEN SOME BOAST THAT FIRE EACH DAY	272	WHT SUNDAY	13
TILL THE REFINERS FIRE BREAKS FORTH.	270	ASCSN-HYMN	30
WHEN THROUGH THE NORTH A FIRE SHALL RUSH	146	DAY OF JDG	1
NAY THOU THY SELFE, MY GOD, IN FIRE	149	RELIGION	17
DOTH MY WEAK FIRE	203	DSRDR + FR	38
O, IS. BUT GIVE WINGS TO MY FIRE	204	DSRDR + FR	46
TOUCH'D BY THY FIRE, AND BREATH. THY BLOUD	203	DSRDR + FR	18
HE RAVES, AND SWEARS TO STIR NOR FIRE, NOR FAN	197	CORRUPTION	31
AND THOU UNRAK'ST THY FIRE, THOSE SPARKS WILL BRING	195	RLS + LSNS	130
WHEN THY NAP'S OVER, STIR THY FIRE, UNRAKE	196	RLS + LSNS	133
MAN IS A SUMMERS DAY, WHOSE YOUTH, AND FIRE	195	RLS + LSNS	113
FIRE-DRAKES			
FALSE STARS AND FIRE-DRAKES, THE DECEITS OF NIGHT	320	HIDDN TRSR	4

	PAGE	TITLE	LINE
FIRES			
WHAT FIRES HATH HE HEAP'D ON HIS HEAD.	297	HERODIAS	5
BY THOSE BRIGHT FIRES WHICH THEE INFLAM'D.	190	THE MATCH	6
AND THY ASPIRING, ACTIVE FIRES REVEALE	158	THE LAMPE	12
WEAKE BEAMES, AND FIRES FLASH'D TO MY SIGHT	168	VNTY SPRIT	19
FIRES SMOKING DIE.	210	FAITH	26
FIRIE			
AND SHINE FROM PARAN, WHEN A FIRIE LAW	229	LAW + GOSP	2
AND THROUGH THE DARK AIRE SPIN A FIRIE SHREAD	157	THE LAMPE	3
AND LIKE A FIRIE TORRENT BRUSH	146	DAY OF JDG	3
FIRIE-LIQUID			
ARE A FIRIE-LIQUID LIGHT	172	MIDNIGHT	18
FIRM			
SO FIRM A LONGING CAN IMPOWRE	276	COCK-CRWNG	14
AND FOUNDED THE FIRM EARTH. THEN WITH THE DEEP	285	PSALM 104	18
STAND FIRM BY THEE, AND HAVE SURE PEACE.	336	PSALM 65	18
FIRMLY			
BUT FIRMLY TRUSTS IN GOD, THE GREAT MANS MEASURE	328	RIGHTSNESS	45
FIRR			
HER CEDAR, FIRR, HEW'D STONES AND GOLD WERE ALL	238	SHEPHEARDS	23
FIRST			
WHAT TIME WE FROM OUR FIRST LOVE SWERV'D.	237	CONSTLATN	48
WAS IT BECAUSE THOSE FIRST AND BLESSED SWAINS	238	SHEPHEARDS	9
'TWAS THERE FIRST SHOWN TO YOU.	238	SHEPHEARDS	12
HIS LOVE THERE FIRST DISCLOSE.	238	SHEPHEARDS	16
FIRST MAKES, THEN HUGS A SNARE	236	CONSTLATN	18
THE FIRST LIGHT THEY BEHELD WAS BRIGHT AND GAY	239	SHEPHEARDS	51
FIND OUT THE FIRST AND STEEPEST FAL.	240	MISERY	16
WHEN FIRST I SAW TRUE BEAUTY, AND THY JOYS	244	MT. OLV. B	1
FORGETTING THY FIRST BIRTH.	243	THE SAP	2
FOR THEE, WHO IN THE FIRST MANS LOYNS DIDST FAL	243	THE SAP	19
FIRST, I AM SURE, THE SUBJECT SO RESPECTED	278	THE STARRE	13
WHEN FIRST MY YOUTHFULL, SINFULL AGE	282	GARLAND	5
SHE MUST FIRST MAR	269	ASCSN-HYMN	15
AT FIRST SIGHT, IF THE BIRD BE FLOWN.	271	ALL GONE	22
AND PRAY, THESE LAST MAY BE AS FIRST	273	WHT SUNDAY	26
'TWAS THINE FIRST, AND TO THEE RETURNS	265	INTRO. 2	3
SUCH WAS THE BRIGHT WORLD, ON THE FIRST SEVENTH DAY	268	ASCN-DAY A	39
THE FIRST GLAD TIDINGS OF THY EARLY LIGHT	267	ASCN-DAY A	17
O THOU, WHOSE SPIRIT DID AT FIRST INFLAME	248	I WALKT	43
QUIT THEIR FIRST BED AND MOUNT. TREES, HERBS, FLOWRES, ALL	223	TEMPEST	27
AND THUS, AT FIRST, WHEN THINGS WERE RUDE	218	HOLY COMM.	6
THE FIRST TRUE WORSHIP OF THE WORLDS GREAT KING	330	JACOBS PLW	11
THY ARM DID FIRST THE MOUNTAINS LAY	336	PSALM 65	21
WHEN SHALL THOSE FIRST WHITE PILGRIMS RISE	335	JUDGEMENT	23
WHICH HIS FIRST LOCKS WILL QUICKLY FRAY.	338	DEATH B	19
THOUGH SINCE THY FIRST SAD ENTRANCE BY	338	DEATH B	1
THE OLD, WHITE PROPHETS PLANTED FIRST AND DREST.	326	RIGHTSNESS	2
DID FIRST AGAINST A MURTH'RER CRY.	325	ABELS BLOD	2
AS IN THE MORNING WHEN FIRST SHED.	325	ABELS BLOD	6
VAIN, SINFUL ART, WHO FIRST DID FIT	297	HERODIAS	1
THEIR LESSON TAUGHT THEM, WHEN FIRST MADE.	288	THE BIRD	12
FAITH SOJOURN'D FIRST ON EARTH IN YOU	292	THE JEWS	38
WAS FIRST REVEAL'D TO BE YOUR ROCK.	292	THE JEWS	41
THY BURNISHT, FLAMING ARCH DID FIRST DESCRY.	306	RAIN-BOW	4
AFTER THE FALL, THE FIRST SIN WAS IN BLOOD	307	RAIN-BOW	21
ALTHOUGH THE FIRST MUST SURELY FALL	302	ORNAMENT	7
OUR SOULS DISEASES FIRST, AND THEN	311	FAIR+YONG	12
HOME BY OUR FIRST FAIR PUNISHMENT	312	FAIR+YONG	42
FIRST OUT. THIS BEAME	175	JOY OF LIF	31
IS THY FIRST BREATH, AND MANS ETERNALL PRIME.	178	EVNG-WTCH	16
A MILE, OR TWO, FROM MY FIRST LOVE	169	RETREATE	8
WHERE FIRST I LEFT MY GLORIOUS TRAINE	170	RETREATE	24
WITHIN OUR FIRST FAIRE BED	166	THE CALL	67
HENCE, YOUTH, AND FOLLY (MANS FIRST SHAME)	166	THE CALL	62
O THOU, THE FIRST FRUITS OF THE DEAD	180	BURIALL	1
BY DISTANCE ALL GOOD OBJECTS FIRST TO DROWN	183	THRS A TYE	19
WE TRAVELL'D IN, OUR FIRST ATTEMPTS	143	DEATH	16
THE FIRST (PRAY MARKE) AS QUICK AS LIGHT	141	RGNRTN	66
FIRST, A YOUNG PATRIARCH, THEN A MARRI'D SAINT.	156	ISAACS M.	72
THIS LAST WILL KEEPE THE FIRST TWO FRESH	148	DAY OF JDG	43
AND AT FIRST SIGHT DOTH MANY PLEASE	150	RELIGION	42
WHEN FIRST THY EYES UNVEIL, GIVE THY SOUL LEAVE	191	RLS + LSNS	1
GIVE HIM THY FIRST THOUGHTS THEN, SO SHALT THOU KEEP	191	RLS + LSNS	5
MORNINGS ARE MYSTERIES, THE FIRST WORLDS YOUTH	192	RLS + LSNS	25
AND, AS FIRST LOVE DRAWS STRONGEST, SO FROM HENCE	196	CORRUPTION	7
AND BRING THE SAME MAN BACK. THOU WERT AT FIRST	194	RLS + LSNS	82
ON MY FIRST BED	203	DSRDR + FR	43
WHEN FIRST THOU DIST EVEN FROM THE GRAVE	202	DSRDR + FR	1
MY FIRST CONSIGNER UNTO THOSE	344	WATER-FALL	25
WHICH FIRST UPON THY FACE DID MOVE	344	WATER-FALL	31
THOU WERT THE FIRST PUT IN MY HAND	348	HOLY BIBLE	5
SO WITH THAT FIRST LIGHT GAIN'D FROM THEE	348	HOLY BIBLE	13
MY FIRST CHEAP BOOK HAD ALL I SOUGHT.	348	HOLY BIBLE	16
FISH			
BIRDS SING, BEASTS FEED, FISH LEAP, AND TH'EARTH STANDS FAST	194	RLS + LSNS	88
A FISH SHALL ALL MY TRIBUTE PAY	300	PROVIDENCE	15
FIST			
THE WIND, THOUGH GATHER'D IN THY FIST	239	MISERY	5
FIT			
ANGER FOR ONE SHORT FIT	216	DRESSING	28

	PAGE	TITLE	LINE
FIT (CON'T)			
VAIN, SINFUL ART. WHO FIRST DID FIT	297	HERODIAS	1
FIT ROOMES FOR THEE. OR THAT MY HEART	199	NTVTY 1	20
IS THE BRAINES FIT	162	MT. OLVS A	7
A STATE FIT FOR THE SIGHT OF THY	349	L'ENVOY	17
MAY FULLY FIT THY GLORICUS REIGN.	350	L'ENVOY	28
NO CHANCE, OR FIT. BUT EVER BRIGHT	345	QUICKNESS	11
FITS			
BLIND , DESP'RATE FITS, THAT STUDY HOW	205	IDLE VERSE	9
THEIR DOCTRINE CHAFF AND WINDY FITS.	332	AGREEMENT	26
LET IT SUFFICE AT LENGTH THY FITS	225	RETIREMENT	12
THE RULE WITHOUT EXCEPTION FITS.	273	WHT SUNDAY	36
FITTER			
(FOR WHICH COURSE MAN SEEMS MUCH THE FITTER BORN)	287	THE BIRD	4
FIX			
TO FIX MY STEPS, AND WHATSOEVER PATH	234	MUTINIE	33
SETTLE, AND FIX OUR HEARTS, THAT WE MAY MOVE	237	CONSTLATN	53
FIX'D			
FIX'D LATELY ON THE CROSS, NOW ON THE SKIES.	268	ASCN-DAY A	54
FIX'D TO A TENT, DESCEND AND SHROWD	315	DWELLNG-PL	6
LIFE IS A FIX'D, DISCERNING LIGHT	345	QUICKNESS	9
FIXED			
BUT NOW ARE FIXED STARS, WHOSE LIGHT	305	ST MARY MN	59
FIXETH			
FIXETH A SOLITARY LAMP	178	SILENCE	7
FIXT			
AND FIXT THERE ALL YOUR FLAMES	236	CONSTLATN	34
WHICH IS NOT FIXT, BUT FLIES, AND FLOWES.	222	AFFLICTION	26
FIXT BY THY SPIRIT TO A STATE	349	L'ENVOY	15
FLAME			
AND WHERE THE OTHER MOUNT ALL CLAD IN FLAME	229	LAW + GOSP	14
IS STILL OUT WITH THY FLAME, AND SO BOTH FAILE.	158	THE LAMPE	24
TILL HIS ABUS'D, DESPISED FLAME	305	ST MARY MN	53
WHO IS CONTENTED, THAT THIS HOLY FLAME	331	JACOBS PLW	38
SCATT'RING THAT CLOUD, SHEWD ME THE FLAME	332	AGREEMENT	9
I'LE JUDGE, WHERE PENAL FLAMES SIT MIXT AND CLOSE.	307	RAIN-BOW	38
THESE FLAMES, AS THOU DOST THINE TO ME, I WATCH	157	THE LAMPE	7
MET IN THY FLAMES, ALL ACTS OF PIETY.	158	THE LAMPE	10
THY FLAMES COULD NOT BE OUT, RELIGION WAS	154	ISAACS M.	7
AND WITH SURPRIZING FLAMES	147	DAY OF JDG	6
STREAMES, AND FLAMES THUS TO THE SIGHT	172	MIDNIGHT	20
AND AFTER ALL MY HEIGHT OF FLAMES)	203	DSRDR + FR	40
NEW FLAMES, BESIDES WHERE THESE LODGE VAIN HEARTS MOURN	196	RLS + LSNS	131
AND FIXT THERE ALL YOUR FLAMES	236	CONSTLATN	34
AS FLAMES ABOUT THEIR FUEL RUN	214	MISERY	77
TEARS AND THESE FLAMES WILL SOON GROW KINDE	266	VAIN WITS	5
HER CAPTIVE FLAMES MUST NEEDS BURN THERE.	271	ALL GONE	30
THOSE FLAMES WHICH ON THE APOSTLES RUSH'D	272	WHT SUNDAY	5
FLAMING			
HER FLAMING WEAR	269	ASCSN-HYMN	16
HIS FATHERS FLAMING MINISTRIE	152	THE SEARCH	60
THY BURNISHT, FLAMING ARCH DID FIRST DESCRY.	306	RAIN-BOW	4
FLASH'D			
WEAKE BEAMES, AND FIRES FLASH'D TO MY SIGHT	168	VNTY SPRIT	19
FLATT'RER			
THE FLATT'RER SAY, I LIVE	183	THRS A TYE	22
FLED			
AND MAN IS SUCH A MARYGOLD, THESE FLED	183	THRS A TYE	7
SO O'R FLED MINUTES I RETREAT	178	SILENCE	13
BUT THOSE FLED TO THEIR MAKERS THRONE	179	SILENCE	23
TO EGYPT HENCE I FLED, RAN O'RE	151	THE SEARCH	11
AH. HE IS FLED.	156	BRT. CHRCH	1
THOUGH FLED FROM YOU, THEIR SPIRITS HIVE.	339	DEATH B	30
AT THY REBUKE THEY FLED, AT THE KNOWN VOICE	285	PSALM 104	21
FLEDG'D			
HE THAT HATH FOUND SOME FLEDG'D BIRDS NEST, MAY KNOW	271	ALL GONE	21
FLEE			
O TAKE IT OFF. OR TILL IT FLEE	277	COCK-CRWNG	47
BREAK, AND THE SHADOWS FLEE, TOUCH WITH ONE COAL	216	DRESSING	3
FLEECE			
BUT THIS CORSE FLEECE	173	CONTENT	2
FLEECES			
SLAIN FLOCK, AND PILLAG'D FLEECES	157	BRT. CHRCH	17
CHECQUR'D WITH SNOWIE FLEECES	140	RGNRTN	53
FLESH			
A LIVING FAITH, A HEART OF FLESH	148	DAY OF JDG	41
AND HUMBLE DUST, TELL THEN DEAR FLESH	201	THE CHECK	11
AND IN MY FLESH, THOUGH VILE, AND LOW	212	DAWNING	41
HATH FLESH NO SOFTNESS NOW. MID-DAY NO LIGHT.	224	TEMPEST	56
ALL FLESH IS CLAY, THOU KNOW'ST, AND BUT THAT GOD	221	AFFLICTION	11
MY FORWARD FLESH CREEPT ON, AND SUBTLY STOLE	206	REPENTANCE	5
HOW DID POOR FLESH (WHICH AFTER THOU DIDST WEARE)	229	LAW + GOSP	7
AS TO MAKE MAN ALL PURE LOVE, FLESH A STAR.	283	LOVE-SICK	4
SUCH TRIUMPHS POOR FLESH CANNOT MERIT.	339	THE FEAST	9
ALL FLESH SHALL UNTO THEE REPAIR	336	PSALM 65	3
GO LEPER, GO. WASH TILL THY FLESH	306	ST MARY MN	69
OF FLESH AND BLOOD, WHERE TWO WAYS MEET.	318	THE ASS	2
WHY SHOULD FRAIL FLESH DOUBT ANY MORE	343	WATER-FALL	21
FLESHLY			
BUT FELT THROUGH ALL THIS FLESHLY DRESSE	170	RETREATE	19

	PAGE	TITLE	LINE
FLEW			
FLEW HOME UNSTAIN'D BY HIS NEW KIN	209	THE BURIAL	6
FLIE			
OF THINGS DID FLIE.	210	FAITH	28
AND FROTHIE NOISE WHICH UP AND DOWN DOTH FLIE	234	MUTINIE	24
BUT HIS, WHO GAVE THEM WINGS TO FLIE.	277	COCK-CRWNG	36
YOU FLIE AND FLOCK TO SUCK THE FLOWERS.	274	PROFFER	6
AND PRECIPICE IT LEADS TO, BID ME FLIE	320	HIDDN TRSR	17
FLIES			
STILL HOMEWARDS FLIES	327	RIGHTSNESS	17
AND STILL A NEW SUCCESSION SINGS AND FLIES.	289	THE TIMBER	5
WERE GNATS AND FLIES	232	THE WORLD	28
WHICH IS NOT FIXT, BUT FLIES, AND FLOWES.	222	AFFLICTION	26
FLIGHT			
AND FULL REDEMPTION OF THE WHOLE WEEKS FLIGHT.	2	SON-DAYES	8
YOUR CALM AND WEL-TRAIN'D FLIGHT.	236	CONSTLATN	30
A LOVE-SICK SOULS EXALTED FLIGHT.	277	COCK-CRWNG	34
AND IN MY FLIGHT	267	ASCN-DAY A	12
GODS SILENT, SEARCHING FLIGHT.	324	THE NIGHT	31
AND PUT TO FLIGHT	179	CHRCH-SVC	13
AND IN HER PIERCING FLIGHT PERFUM'D THE AYER	155	ISAACS M.	51
FLIGHTS			
AND WRAP US IN IMAGINARY FLIGHTS	183	THRS A TYE	15
IN SILENT FLIGHTS	165	THE CALL	16
SURE, HOLY HOPES, HIGH JOYS AND QUICKNING FLIGHTS	267	ASCN-DAY A	2
FALSE JOYES, PHANTASTICK FLIGHTS	282	GARLAND	18
YOU'D MAKE NO FLIGHTS.	274	PROFFER	4
NEER HIM, HIS LUTE, HIS FANCY, AND HIS FLIGHTS	231	THE WORLD	10
FLINCH			
REVOLT AND FLINCH	275	PROFFER	28
FLING			
AND EVER RUNNING, TILL HE LEAVE TO FLING	291	THE TIMBER	55
FLINT			
THY GIFT ONCE MORE, AND GRIND THIS FLINT TO DUST.	224	TEMPEST	60
FLINTS			
BE BROKE AGAIN, FOR FLINTS WILL GIVE NO FIRE	224	TEMPEST	58
FLOCK			
HOW ART THOU NOW, THY FLOCK TO KEEP	220	HOLY COMM.	51
YOU FLIE AND FLOCK TO SUCK THE FLOWERS.	274	PROFFER	6
YET BY THESE GLANCES OF THE FLOCK	273	WHT SUNDAY	23
THY CHOSEN FLOCK, LIKE LEAFS IN A HIGH WIND	229	LAW + GOSP	9
THEY LEAVE THEIR FLOCK, AND IN A BUSIE TALK	239	SHEPHEARDS	43
SLAIN FLOCK, AND PILLAG'D FLEECES	157	BRT. CHRCH	17
HEALE THEN THESE WATERS, LORD, OR BRING THY FLOCK	150	RELIGION	49
WATRING THEIR FLOCKS, AND HAVING SPENT	151	THE SEARCH	25
THE FRUITFUL FLOCKS FILL EVERY DALE	337	PSALM 65	45
FLOOD			
WHO BATH NOT IN A SHALLOW FLOOD	325	ABELS BLOD	13
I, MAY THAT FLOOD	326	ABELS BLOD	33
AND DRUNKENNESS QUICKLY DID SUCCEED THE FLOOD.	307	RAIN-BOW	22
BETTER, THE POOLS SHOULD FLOW WITH RAIN AND FLOODS	290	THE TIMBER	47
AS WITH A VAIL THOU HIDST IT, THY FLOODS PLAID	285	PSALM 104	19
NE'R MARR'D WITH FLOODS, NOR ANGER'D WITH A SHOWRE.	268	ASCN-DAY A	48
FLOOR			
PURGING THE FLOOR WHICH CHAFF DISTURBS.	221	AFFLICTION	20
FLOTE			
SAILERS THAT FLOTE ON FLOWING SEAS	336	PSALM 65	17
FLOUD			
HEAR NOT A FLOUD	214	ADMISSION	30
A FLOUD THAT DROWNS BOTH TEARS, AND GRONES	214	ADMISSION	31
ODORS, AND MYRRH, AND BALM IN ONE RICH FLOUD	244	MT. OLV. B	7
DANC'D THROUGH THE FLOUD	141	RGNRTN	67
BUT A SHALLOW, BOUNDED FLOUD	175	THE STORM	3
UNCALMES THESE TO A FLOUD	176	THE STORM	14
FLOURISH			
THEIR SAD DECAYS, I FLOURISH, AND ONCE MORE	198	UNPRFTBLNS	8
MY WITHER'D LEAFS AGAIN LOOK GREEN AND FLOURISH	245	MT. OLV. B	22
THOU, WHO DOST FLOW AND FLOURISH HERE BELOW	282	GARLAND	1
WHERE THE IMPURE SEEDS FLOURISH ALL THE YEAR	321	HIDDN TRSR	26
SURE THOU DIDST FLOURISH ONCE. AND MANY SPRINGS	289	THE TIMBER	1
FLOURISH'D			
NO FROST, BUT FLOURISH'D IN THAT YOUTHFUL VEST	268	ASCN-DAY A	43
AND WHERE IT FLOURISH'D, GREW AND SPREAD	347	THE BOOK	13
FLOW			
SIT REGENT YET, AND BLESSINGS FLOW	351	L'ENVOY	57
THAT WEALTH MAY FLOW	341	THE FEAST	74
THOU, WHO DOST FLOW AND FLOURISH HERE BELOW	282	GARLAND	1
ATTRACTS THEE THUS AND MAKES THEE STREAM AND FLOW	278	THE STARRE	2
THE FULLER, WHOSE PURE BLOOD DID FLOW	270	ASCSN-HYMN	35
I CHEER THEIR FLOW, GIVING SUPPLY	240	MISERY	17
SO SHALL THY MERCIES FLOW. FOR WHILE I FEAR	230	LAW + GOSP	37
AS THIS DOTH IN HER CHANNEL, FLOW	212	DAWNING	42
BETTER, THE POOLS SHOULD FLOW WITH RAIN AND FLOODS	290	THE TIMBER	47
BEGETTING VIRGINS WHERE THEY USE TO FLOW.	291	THE TIMBER	50
BUT THESE CHASTE FOUNTAINS FLOW NOT TILL WE DYE.	291	THE TIMBER	53
DESCEND, AND LIVING WATERS FLOW	291	THE JEWS	12
AND AT THY PRESENCE MAKE THESE MOUNTAINS FLOW	283	LOVE-SICK	11
THY CARE AND LOVE, WHICH JOYNTLY FLOW	333	AGREEMENT	57
OBSERVE GOD IN HIS WORKS, HERE FOUNTAINS FLOW	194	RLS + LSNS	87
TO FLOW, OR BIRD TO SING	187	NO DO THEY	14

		PAGE	TITLE	LINE
FLOW'D				
RUNS THITHER, WHENCE IF FLOW'D BEFORE	. . . .	343	WATER-FALL	16
FLOW'RS				
UNTO THEIR GOD, AS FLOW'RS DO TO THE SUN.	. . . .	191	RLS + LSNS	4
FLOWER				
SO RARE A FLOWER	. . . .	323	THE NIGHT	16
FLOWERS				
BUT FLOWERS DO BOTH REFRESH AND GRACE	. . . .	321	CHILDEHOOD	14
AND MAKE THE DEAD, LIKE FLOWERS, ARISE	. . . .	334	JUDGEMENT	5
WHERE ALL IS LIGHT, AND FLOWERS, AND FRUIT	. . . .	329	TEARS	5
AND I, LIKE FLOWERS SHALL STILL GO NEAT	. . . .	300	PROVIDENCE	17
AND FLOWERS THAT INTO FIELDS DO STRAY,	. . . .	294	PALM-SUNDY	9
TREES, FLOWERS AND HERBS. BIRDS, BEASTS AND STONES	.	294	PALM-SUNDY	11
DEAR FEAST OF PALMS, OF FLOWERS AND DEW.	. . . .	295	PALM-SUNDY	30
TO GATHER FLOWERS TO WELLCOME THEE	. . . .	295	PALM-SUNDY	37
BALM ON THE CLEFT EARTH, MILK ON GRASS AND FLOWERS.	.	306	RAIN-BOW	12
DEAR SOUL. THOU KNEW'ST, FLOWERS HERE ON EARTH	.	304	ST MARY MN	27
IT WAS A BANKE OF FLOWERS, WHERE I DESCRIED	. .	141	RGNRTN	74
YOU FLIE AND FLOCK TO SUCK THE FLOWERS.	. . . .	274	PROFFER	6
A LAND OF FLOWERS AND SPICES. THE WORD GIVEN	.	276	PROFFER	47
KILL AND CURE THE TENDER FLOWERS	. . . .	281	JOY	18
BY FLOWERS AND CARVINGS AND MYSTERIOUS SKILL	.	279	PALM-TREE	11
IS WATER'D BY THEIR TEARS, AS FLOWERS ARE FED	.	280	PALM-TREE	22
WHEN LIKE A VIRGIN CLAD IN FLOWERS AND GREEN	.	268	ASCN-DAY A	41
AND CROWN DRY HILS WITH WELLS AND FLOWERS.	. .	341	THE FEAST	54
AND SELDOM YIELDED FLOWERS	. . . . .	345	THE WREATH	2
FLOWES				
WHICH IS NOT FIXT, BUT FLIES, AND FLOWES.	. .	222	AFFLICTION	26
WHENCE FLOWES MY WEAL, AND MIRTH	. . .	220	PSALM 121	2
AND CELESTIALL FLOWES	. . . . . .	172	MIDNIGHT	29
FLOWING				
ELSEWHERE, AND FLOWING KEEPS UNTAINTED.	. . .	212	DAWNING	36
SAILERS THAT FLOTE ON FLOWING SEAS	. . .	336	PSALM 65	17
HERE FLOWING FALL	. . . .	343	WATER-FALL	3
FLOWN				
AT FIRST SIGHT, IF THE BIRD BE FLOWN.	. . .	271	ALL GONE	22
FLOWR				
MUST HE NOR SIP, NOR SING. GROWS NE'R A FLOWR	. .	224	TEMPEST	51
UPON A FLOWR	. . . .	231	THE WORLD	15
WHERE THOU MAY'ST SLEEP WHOLE AGES, LIFES POOR FLOWR	.	195	RLS + LSNS	123
THOU CANST NOT MISSE HIS PRAISE, EACH TREE, HERB, FLOWRE		194	RLS + LSNS	95
WHEN ON SOME GILDED CLOUD, OR FLOWRE	. . .	169	RETREATE	11
OR FLOWRE BY PEDIGREE	. . . . . .	187	NO DO THEY	12
THERE GROWES THE FLOWRE OF PEACE	. . .	184	PEACE	14
THIS SULLY'D FLOWRE	. . . . . .	158	MANS FALL	3
WHICH, SCATTER'D IN A THOUSAND PEARLS, EACH FLOWRE	.	155	ISAACS M.	56
A GALLANT FLOWRE	. . . .	246	I WALKT	4
HE HATH A FLOWRE	. . . .	215	PRAISE	48
AND SO THE FLOWRE	. . . .	247	I WALKT	13
FLOWRES				
CULL'D FLOWRES AND MADE ME POSIES.	. . .	282	GARLAND	22
TWO FLOWRES THAT GREW WITH THEE ABOVE.	. .	216	DRESSING	26
THE FLOWRES TO AIR DRAW NEER, AND SUBTILTIE	.	223	TEMPEST	35
SHOULD HAVE NO FLOWRES	. . . . .	222	AFFLICTION	22
QUIT THEIR FIRST BED AND MOUNT. TREES, HERBS, FLOWRES, ALL		223	TEMPEST	27
AND ALL HER FLOWRES WITHER'D TO STRAW	. .	222	TEMPEST	7
HEAVEN HERE, MAN ON THOSE HILLS OF MYRRH, AND FLOWRES.	.	2	SON-DAYES	14
FIGS ON A THORNE, FLOWRES ON A WEED.	. . .	208	REPENTANCE	70
THE TREES, THEIR LEAFS, THE FLOWRES, THEIR SEEDING.	.	207	REPENTANCE	34
IN SUDDAIN FLOWRES AND ARBOURS TO MY EYES	. .	245	MT. OLV. B	18
THE FLOWRES WITHOUT CLOTHES LIVE	. . .	245	MAN	13
O JOYES. INFINITE SWEETNESS. WITH WHAT FLOWRES	.	176	MRNG-WTCH	1
AFTER SUN-RISING, FAR-DAY SULLIES FLOWRES.	.	192	RLS + LSNS	10
ALL STREWED WITH FLOWRES, AND HAPPINESS	. .	189	RESOLVE	23
IT IS THE GOOD MANS FEAST, THE PRINCE OF FLOWRES	.	193	RLS + LSNS	59
FLOWRES GATHER'D IN THIS WORLD, DIE HERE. IF THOU	.	283	GARLAND	33
FLOWRIE				
ON SOME PARCH'D BANK, CROWN'D WITH A FLOWRIE WREATH.	.	244	MT. OLV. B	6
FLOWRS				
WHERE BEES AT NIGHT GET HOME AND HIVE, AND FLOWRS	.	245	MAN	5
FLOWS				
YET HAVE I FLOWS, AS STRONG AS HIS	. . . .	175	THE STORM	5
FLUNG				
I FLUNG AWAY, AND WITH FULL CRIE	. . . .	282	GARLAND	9
FLUTT'RING				
FLUTT'RING IN WOODS, OR LIFTED FAR	. . .	199	NTVTY 1	14
FLUTTER				
FLUTTER NO MORE.	. . . .	274	PROFFER	2
FLY				
CHIDE, AND FLY UP, MISTS OF CORRUPTEST FOME	. .	223	TEMPEST	26
AND HATCH MY SOUL, UNTILL IT FLY	. . .	204	DSRDR + FR	47
EACH FLY DOTH TAST	. . . . . .	203	DSRDR + FR	23
YET, FLY NO FRIEND, IF HE BE SUCH INDEED	. .	194	RLS + LSNS	79
FLYE				
HER WEARIED WINGS, WHICH SO RESTOR'D DID FLYE	.	155	ISAACS M.	49
BRIGHTNESS AND MIRTH, AND LOVE AND FAITH, ALL FLYE	.	288	THE BIRD	31
DIDST FLYE, WHOSE CHILDREN WROUGHT THY CHILDRENS WO.	.	331	JACOBS PLW	44
HOW DOST THOU FLYE	. . . . . .	340	THE FEAST	43
FLYE FROM THEIR NURSES TO THE THRONG	. . .	348	HOLY BIBLE	10
FLYES				
THE FLYES OF HELL	. . . .	275	PROFFER	14

		PAGE	TITLE	LINE

FOAL
FINDES THY PCCR FCAL AT THY CCMMAND . . . . . 319 THE ASS 46

FOE
STILL THY OWN FOE, AND MINE, FCR TO THIS DAY . . . 225 RETIREMENT 16
I WHOLY LISTEN'D TO MY FOE. . . . . . 207 REPENTANCE 18
THEN GIVE ME CVER TO MY FCE. . . . . . 242 MISERY 92

FOES
LET ME SO STRIVE AND STRUGGLE WITH THY FOES . . . 234 MUTINIE 14
HE KEEPS ME FRCM THE SPITE OF FCES . . . . 220 PSALM 121 13
THOU HADST NO GALL, EV'N FOR THY FOES . . . . 272 WHT SUNDAY 11
AND WHAT HE SAVES, MAY HIS FOES SPEND. . . . 301 PROVIDENCE 36
AND LINGRING WOUNDS FROM WEAKER FCES. . . . 312 FAIR+YONG 44
AND VCWS AND VISIONS, THOUGH HER FOES CRYE, NCNE. . 331 JACOBS PLW 34
HIS HEART AND TONGUE IN PRAYEPS FCR HIS FOES. . . 328 RIGHTSNESS 39
O CHASE IN THAT CCLD CALM MY FCES . . . . 334 AGREEMENT 65
THEN ALL IS TRUE, MY FOES HAVE SPCKEN. . . . 333 AGREEMENT 48
WITH MURMURERS, AND FOES. . . . . . 197 CORRUPTION 18
I DYE TC MAKE MY FCES INHERIT. . . . . . 185 PASSION 43
FCR 'TIS CUT FOES CHIEF ART . . . . . . 183 THRS A TYE 18

FOG
AND WHEN TH'HAST CONE, A STENCH, OR FOG IS ALL . 198 UNPRFTBLNS 17

FOIL
CAN FCIL HIS MERITS, AND THY TRUTH. . . . . 333 AGREEMENT 54
SET FCRTH TO FOOL AND FCIL THEE, DO NOT BOAST. . 320 HIDDN TRSR 5
FALSE LIFE. A FOIL AND NO MCRE. WHEN . . . 344 QUICKNESS 1

FOIL'D
PLEASLRES HAD FOIL'D ETERNITIE . . . . . 166 THE CALL 72

FOLD
SINCE THOU HAST MADE THY ARM MY FCLD . . . 301 PROVIDENCE 48
AND LIKE CLD CLOATHS FOLD UP THESE SKIES . . . 349 L'ENVOY 8
THAT LIKE TRUE SHEEP, ALL IN CNE FOLD . . . 350 L'ENVOY 47

FOLDED
WITH FOLDED HANDS. . . . . . 164 THE CALL 13

FOLDS
TO THE WILDE GOATS THE HIGH HILLS SERVE FOR FOLDS . 286 PSALM 104 49

FOLIES
GC, GC, QUEINT FOLIES, SUCKED SIN . . . . 204 IDLE VERSE 1

FOLLIES
O LEAVE THY CARES, AND FOLLIES. GC THIS WAY . . 192 RLS + LSNS 17
BUT FROM THOSE FOLLIES A RESOLV'D RETREAT. . . 226 RETIREMENT 33

FOLLOW
LET HIM SC FOLLOW HERE, THAT IN THE END . . 216 DRESSING 17
FCLLOW THE CRY NO MORE. THERE IS . . . . 189 RESOLVE 21
WILL FOLLCW AFTER . . . . . . 172 MIDNIGHT 30
AND FCLLOW THEE ALL CLOATH'C IN WHITE . . . 316 MEN OF WAR 22

FOLLOWS
WHO ARGUES, FCLLOWS HIS CWN HEAD. . . . . 318 THE ASS 24
WHO SEEKS AND FOLLOWS PEACE . . . . . 327 RIGHTSNESS 34

FOLLY
HENCE, YOUTH, AND FCLLY (MANS FIRST SHAME) . . 166 THE CALL 62
AND IF HEREAFTER YOUTH, OR FOLLY THWART . . . 190 THE MATCH 10
LET FCLLY DUST IT CN, OR LAG BEHIND. . . . 193 RLS + LSNS 52
WHO DCEST THINE ANGELS CHARGE WITH FOLLY. . . 208 REPENTANCE 68

FOME
CHIDE, AND FLY UP, MISTS CF CCRRUPTEST FOME . . 223 TEMPEST 26
TO SWEL AND FCME AND FRET WITHIN. . . . 214 MISERY 64
THAT ALL THIS FOME . . . . . . 234 MUTINIE 23
THERE ALL THEIR FLRY, FCME AND HIDEOUS SOUND . . 285 PSALM 104 27

FOND
GAVE MY FCND HUMOURS THEIR FULL WING . . . 282 GARLAND 23
DESIST FOND FCOL, BE NOT UNDCNE . . . . 283 GARLAND 29

FOOD
CREEPS FORTH, AND PINCH'D FOR FOOD, WITH SCENT AND SIGHT 286 PSALM 104 55
DOEST THOU CONVEY MAN FCCC AND MCNEY . . . 300 PROVIDENCE 9
MY SOLLS BRIGHT FCCD, THY ABSENCE KILLS. . . 308 THE SEED 6
YET NEITHER SING, NOR LIKE THEIR FOOD . . . 228 PILGRIMAGE 19
LET ME NOT SCATTER, AND DESPISE MY FOOD . . . 230 LAW + GOSP 34
BECOME BOTH FOOD, AND SHEPHEARC TO THY SHEEP. . 220 HOLY COMM. 52
CF TEARS, AND MILK, THE FCOD CF ALL. . . . 209 THE BURIAL 4
USE, WITH LIKE CUSTOME, AS MY KITCHEN FOOD. . . 217 DRESSING 36
IS STIL'D THEIR STARRE, THE STCNE, AND HIDDEN FCCD. . 192 RLS + LSNS 28
WELCOME DEAR BOOK, SOULS JOY, AND FOOD. THE FEAST . 197 SCRIPTURES 1
THE FCOD OF MANS IMMORTAL BEING. . . . 340 THE FEAST 39

FOOL
SET FCRTH TO FCOL AND FCIL THEE, CC NOT BOAST. . 320 HIDDN TRSR 5
DESIST FOND FCOL, BE NOT UNDCNE . . . . 283 GARLAND 29

FOOLISH
AND LEAD BY MY OWN FOOLISH FIRE . . . . 311 FAIR+YONG 5
AND FCOLISH THOUGHTS ADDE TO MY BIL . . . 204 DSRDR + FR 51
LEAVE THEN THY FOCLISH RANGES. . . . . 184 PEACE 17
O FOOLISH MAN. HOW HAST THOU LOST THY SIGHT. . 224 TEMPEST 53
I WERE MOST FCOLISH AND UNKINDE . . . . 342 OBSEQUIES 9

FOOLS
O FCOLS (SAID I) THUS TC PREFER DARK NIGHT . . 233 THE WORLD 49
THIS CAUTIOUS FOOLS MISTAKE, AND FEAR . . . 313 THE STONE 16
THE STOP TO BUSIE FOOLS, CARES CHECK AND CURB. . 324 THE NIGHT 26

FOOT
SLEEPS AT THE LADDERS FCCT, ALAS. WHAT CAN . . 224 TEMPEST 39
WHICH ALL THE WINTER SLEEPS HERE UNDER FOOT . . 248 I WALKT 38
OR THE NEXT FCCT TO CRUSH . . . . . 201 THE CHECK 9

	PAGE	TITLE	LINE

FOOT-STCOL
AT THEIR LORDS FOCT-STOCL HAVE THEIR BIRTH. . . . 304 ST MARY MN 28
FOCTE
FCR EV'RY FOCTE TC TREAC. . . . . 166 THE CALL 69
FOOTSTOCLE
IS BUT HIS NARROW FOOTSTOCLE ALL . . . . . 163 MT. OLVS A 26
FORBEARE
I SHOLLC HAVE SPURN'D, ANC SAIC THOU CIDST FCRBEARE. . 161 DSTROCTION 22
FORC'D
BUT 'TWAS MY SINNE THAT FCRC'C THY HAND . . . 166 THE CALL 38
DID ISSUE FORTH FCRC'D BY THE RCC . . . . . 184 PASSION 4
FCRC'C BY HER ARTLESS LCCKS ANC DRESS . . . . 303 ORNAMENT 18
HE WEIGHS NOT YOUR FORC'D ACCENTS, WHO CAN HAVE . . 280 JOY 7
BECAUSE WE FORC'D THY JUDGEMENTS COWN. . . . . 350 L'ENVOY 32
FORCE
AND THOUGH (WHILE HERE) OF FCRCE I MUST . . . . 212 DAWNING 39
THEIR ARTS AND FORCE ARE BUILT UNTO THE HEIGHT . . 234 MUTINIE 16
FCRCE DCWN A JUST CURSE, WHEN THY HANDS WOULC BLESS. . 230 LAW + GOSP 33
AND PCWER FORCE CN HOLY WRIT . . . . . . 335 JUDGEMENT 36
WITH THE SAME CURLING FCRCE, AND HISSE . . . . 175 THE STORM 7
IF TRUTH BE THINE, WHAT NEEDS A BRUTISH FORCE. . . 193 RLS + LSNS 39
FORE-RUNNERS
VIEW THY FORE-RUNNERS. CREATURES GIV'N TC BE . . . 201 THE CHECK 25
FORERUN
TC CO THE LIKE. OUR BCDIES BUT FORERUN . . . . 191 RLS + LSNS 2
FORERUNNERS
THAT THESE FORERUNNERS HERE . . . . . . 216 DRESSING 21
FORERUNNING
FCRERUNNING THE BRIGHT MORNING-STAR . . . . . 292 THE JEWS 27
FORESAW
THIS COD FORESAW. AND WHEN SLAIN BY THE CRCWC . . 330 JACOBS PLW 21
FORESEEING
SURE, MIGHTY LOVE FORESEEING THE CISCENT . . . 223 TEMPEST 21
FORETOLC
OF WINGS, AND CHERUBIMS, AND PALMS FORETOLD. . . 279 PALM-TREE 12
WHICH HIS DEATH SCATTER'D) HE FCRETOLD THE PLACE . . 330 JACOBS PLW 23
FOREWARN'C
THAT BY THY EARLY CHOICE FOREWARN'C . . . . 166 THE CALL 40
FORGERIES
THE FCRGERIES, WHICH IMPICUS WIT . . . . . 335 JUDGEMENT 35
FORGETFULNESS
BECAUSE FCRGETFULNESS WCULD KILL . . . . . 342 OBSEQUIES 7
FORGETTING
FORGETTING THY FIRST BIRTH. . . . . . . 243 THE SAP 2
FORGIVE
FCRGIVE YCUR PENITENT OFFENDER . . . . . 208 REPENTANCE 49
OR IF IT WATCH, FCRGIVE ANC WEEP . . . . . 326 ABELS BLOD 36
FATHER FORGIVE . . . . 185 PASSION 41
FORGIVEN
WHICH THOU DIVINELY HAST FORGIVEN . . . . . 265 INTRO. 2 27
FORGOT
THAT HE HATH QUITE FORGCT HOW TC GO THERE. . . 246 MAN 21
IT QUITE FORGCT THAT PURPCS'D GLIMPSE. . . . . 332 AGREEMENT 4
FORGOTT'ST
THAT THOU FORGOTT'ST THINE CWN, FCR THOU CIDST SEAL . 283 LOVE-SICK 20
FORGOTTEN
TWILL SHEW US EACH FORGCTTEN CRAVE . . . . 334 JUDGEMENT 4
WHERE DEATH AND FRAILTY ARE FCRGCTTEN . . . . 319 THE ASS 64
FORM
AND FCRM TO SERVE HIM IN, SHOLLC BE TRUE GRACE . . 330 JACOBS PLW 24
FORME
WHICH ONCE HAC NEITHER BEING, FCRME, NOR NAME . . 248 I WALKT 47
FORSAKE
FCR THOUGH HE SHOULD FORSAKE THE WORLD, AND LIVE . 290 THE TIMBER 37
FORTRESSE
THY FCRTRESSE, AND THY EASE. . . . . . . 184 PEACE 16
FORTUNATES
MAKES MCST UNHAPPY, OR MCST FCRTUNATES. . . . 155 ISAACS M. 46
FORTY
AND FCRTY DAYES WITHSTCCD THE FELL . . . . 152 THE SEARCH 57
FULL FORTY CAYS O'R THE DROWN'C WORLD DID WEEP) . . 307 RAIN-BOW 28
THY FCRTY DAYS MORE SECRET COMMERCE HERE . . . 268 ASCN-DAY A 33
FORWARD
MY FORWARD FLESH CREEPT CN, ANC SUBTLY STCLE . . 206 REPENTANCE 5
SCME MEN A FORWARD MOTICN LOVE . . . . . 170 RETREATE 29
OF FORWARC SINS, ANC KIL . . . . 204 DSRDR + FR 52
FOSTS
THE FCSTS ILL WEECS NIP, AND MCLEST . . . . 227 LV + DSPLN 11
FOUGHT
AND THEN YOU IN YCUR CCURSES FCUGHT. . . . 236 CONSTLATN 36
HERE SPIRITS THAT HAVE RUN THEIR RACE AND FOLGHT . . 280 PALM-TREE 17
FOUL
WE, WHO ARE NCTHING BUT FCUL CLAY . . . . 274 WHT SUNDAY 59
(FCR TEARS ALCNE ARE CFTEN FOUL) . . . . . 242 MISERY 108
FCR ERE THOU KNEW'ST HOW TO BE FOUL . . . . 209 THE BURIAL 7
OUR FCUL, CLAY HANDS . . . . 215 PRAISE 42
THE RCDE FOUL, AND WHERE ONE GOES RIGHT . . . 174 JOY OF LIF 11
WHICH SINFULL EASE MACE FOUL . . . . . . 176 THE STORM 22
THOUGH BLCOD AND CRUNKENNESS MAKE BUT FOUL, FOLL WEATHER. 307 RAIN-BOW 26
THOUGH BLCOD AND CRUNKENNESS MAKE BUT FOUL, FOLL WEATHER. 307 RAIN-BOW 26

		PAGE	TITLE	LINE
FOUL	(CCN'T)			
O FCUL, DECEITFUL MEN. MY GOD DCTH KEEP	. . . .	307	RAIN-BOW	19
BY THAT FCUL RHEUM THY FALSE EYE WEARS.	. . . .	305	ST MARY MN	66
THAT THE SEEDS OF FOUL SCRROWS BE	. . . .	312	FAIR+YONG	33
AND FCUL RECCRDS WHICH THAW	. . . .	310	THE SEED	56
FCR AS YOUR FAST AND FOUL DECAYS	. . . .	292	THE JEWS	21
AND ALL HER STREAMS GROW FOUL.	. . . .	288	THE BIRD	30
OR ANY STCRMS MORE FOUL THEN A LEWD LIFE.	. . .	290	THE TIMBER	26
MY FOLL, FOUL HEART. THCU ART IMMORTALL HEAT	. .	283	LOVE-SICK	14
MY FOLL, FOUL HEART. THCU ART IMMORTALL HEAT	. .	283	LOVE-SICK	14
WITH THCSE FOLL STCRMS, WHEN THEY WERE WRIT.	. .	332	AGREEMENT	28
WITH MY FOUL HEART THY HCLY FELT.	. . . .	328	ANGUISH	4
TRANSGRESSICNS MAKE ME FOUL EACH CAY	. . . .	336	PSALM 65	7
ANGELS. WHICH FOUL MEN CRIVE AWAY.	. . . .	322	CHILDEHOOD	38
THCSE OBSERVATIONS ARE BUT FOLL	. . . .	322	CHILDEHGOD	25
THOU FOLL DECEPTICN OF ALL MEN	. . . .	344	QUICKNESS	3
FOUND				
HE FOUND THEE AT THAT DEAD AND SILENT HOUR.	. .	323	THE NIGHT	14
THE LCST SON BY THE NEWLY FOUND.	. . .	293	THE JEWS	49
I MAY BE FOUNC (PRESERV'D BY THEE)	. . .	317	MEN OF WAR	49
HERE CF THIS MIGHTY SPRING, I FOUND SCME DRILLS	.	168	VNTY SPRIT	17
HEE'LE NOT BE FOUND, WHERE HE WAS SLAINE	. .	152	THE SEARCH	50
HE MUST BE FOUND, WHERE HE DIC BLEED.	. . .	152	THE SEARCH	36
HE MIGHT BE FCUND, OR WHAT STARRE CAN	. . .	151	THE SEARCH	9
YET HAVE I FOUND	. . . . . .	159	MANS FALL	21
I DREW HER NEERE, AND FCUND	. . . . .	141	RGNRTN	62
I FCUND A PAIRE CF SCALES	. . . .	139	RGNRTN	29
FCUND ALL WAS CHANG'D, AND A NEW SPRING	. .	140	RGNRTN	48
YET DIG'D THE MCLE, AND LEST HIS WAYS BE FOUND	.	232	THE WORLD	23
HE THAT HATH FOUND SOME FLEDG'D BIRDS NEST, MAY KNCW	.	271	ALL GONE	21
FOUND'ST				
CN STCNES DIDST SLEEP AND FOUNC'ST BUT CCLD RELIEF.	.	331	JACOBS PLW	46
FOUNDED				
AND FCUNDED THE FIRM EARTH. THEN WITH THE DEEP	. .	285	PSALM 104	18
FOUNTAIN				
WHAT HAPPY, SECRET FOUNTAIN	. . . .	315	DWELLNG-PL	1
CNLY A LITTLE FOUNTAIN LENT	. . . .	141	RGNRTN	58
BUT WITH THE FOUNTAIN IN MY EYES	. . . .	152	THE SEARCH	34
IN SOME GREEN SHADE, CR FCUNTAIN.	. . . .	197	CORRUPTION	24
FOUNTAINES				
OR AT SCME FCUNTAINES BLBLING EYE	. . . .	148	RELIGION	8
AND FCUNTAINE TOO	. . . . .	163	MT. OLVS A	19
FOUNTAINS				
OBSERVE GCD IN HIS WORKS, HERE FCUNTAINS FLOW	. .	194	RLS + LSNS	87
WHERE FREED SCULS DWEL BY LIVING FOUNTAINS	. .	312	FAIR+YONG	49
BLT THESE CHASTE FOUNTAINS FLCW NCT TILL WE DYE.	.	291	THE TIMBER	53
FCUNTAINS OF LIFE, WHERE THE LAMB GOES.	. .	344	WATER-FALL	26
FOWLES				
HERBS SLEEP UNTO THE EAST, AND SOME FOWLES THENCE	.	183	THRS A TYE	11
FOWLS				
SC IN THE SHADES CF NIGHT SOME DARK FCWLS BE	. .	288	THE BIRD	25
O POYS'NOUS, SUBTILE FOWLS.	. . .	275	PROFFER	13
FOYL				
FURTHERS HIS GLORY, AND GIVES DEATH THE FOYL.	. .	195	RLS + LSNS	112
FOYL'D				
THAT FEL HIM, FOYL'D THEM ALL	. . .	196	CORRUPTION	14
FRACTICNS				
AND CNELY GLEAMS AND FRACTIONS SPIES.	. .	277	COCK-CRWNG	42
FRAGRANT				
OR SHAL THESE EARLY, FRAGRANT HCURS	. . .	211	DAWNING	9
AND FROM HIS MOIST WOMBE WEEPS A FRAGRANT SHCWRE	.	155	ISAACS M.	55
FRAIL				
ALAS, FRAIL WEED.	. . . . .	203	DSRDR + FR	30
OR SOME FRAIL BEAUTY MAKES THE BRAVEST SHEW	. .	282	GARLAND	3
WHERE FRAIL VISIBLES RULE THE MINDE	. .	318	THE ASS	5
WHY SHOULD FRAIL FLESH DOUBT ANY MORE	. .	343	WATER-FALL	21
FRAILTY				
WHERE DEATH AND FRAILTY ARE FCRGCTTEN	. .	319	THE ASS	64
NO SINS OF FRAILTY, NCR OF YOUTH	. . .	333	AGREEMENT	53
OF MY OWN FRAILTY DROPT DCWN MANY A TEAR	. .	247	I WALKT	31
OF CLAY, AND FRAILTY BREAK, AND BUD	. .	203	DSRDR + FR	17
FRAM'D				
I KNOW THEE WELL, FOR I HAVE FRAM'D	. . .	225	RETIREMENT	23
FRAME				
WITH LIFE THIS FRAME	. . . . .	248	I WALKT	46
WHOSE HAND SO SHINES THROUGH ALL THIS FRAME	. .	277	COCK-CRWNG	20
THE WHOLE FRAME WITH HIS FALL.	. . .	197	CORRUPTION	16
OF THIS PCOR, SINFULL FRAME PURE HEART.	. .	182	CHRFLNESS	19
THOSE BLASTS, AND KNIT MY FRAME	. . .	179	CHRCH-SVC	16
A FAIRE-CCMPACTED FRAME	. . . .	166	THE CALL	55
UNNUMBER'D IN THY DUST, WHEN ALL THIS FRAME	. .	177	EVNG-WTCH	4
FRANTICK				
THOUSANDS THERE WERE AS FRANTICK AS HIMSELF	. .	232	THE WORLD	36
FRAUGHTS				
THE BREAD WE CAST RETURNS IN FRAUGHTS ONE DAY.	.	193	RLS + LSNS	66
FRAY				
WHICH HIS FIRST LCCKS WILL QUICKLY FRAY.	. .	338	DEATH B	19
FREE				
WILL THY FREE MERCIES HINDRED BE.	. . . .	334	AGREEMENT	70
AND WHEN (O GCD) THE ASS IS FREE	. . . .	319	THE ASS	57

	PAGE	TITLE	LINE
FREE (CCN'T)			
O THAT I WERE WINGED AND FREE	312	FAIR+YONG	47
NOT TLTOR'D BY THY GLASS, BUT FREE	303	ST MARY MN	7
HIS ONELY SON TO MAKE IT FREE	292	THE JEWS	34
ELECTED, BOUGHT AND SEAL'D FOR FREE	284	TRINITY-SN	8
'WHOSE SERVICE MAKES EV'N CAPTIVES FREE)	300	PROVIDENCE	14
YET CANST NOT THOU THAT FREE CURE DO	299	JESUS WP B	42
YET, HAD OUR PILGRIMAGE BIN FREE	166	THE CALL	70
I'LE WISH MY CURTAINES CFF TO FREE	142	DEATH	9
(BOTH WING'D, AND FREE)	146	RSRCTN +IM	62
DRANK THEM AS FREE.	232	THE WORLD	30
PRAISE HIM, WHO DEALT HIS GIFTS SO FREE	266	VAIN WITS	12
OF BOND, CR FREE	210	FAITH	10
IN THY FREE SERVICES INGAGE	212	DAWNING	38
FREED			
THERE FROM NO DUTIES TO BE FREED	190	THE MATCH	9
WHICH FREED PCOR HAGAR FROM HER FEARS	300	PROVIDENCE	4
FOR HE THAT'S DEAD, IS FREED FROM SIN.	312	FAIR+YONG	46
WHERE FREED SOULS DWEL BY LIVING FOUNTAINS	312	FAIR+YONG	49
FREEDOM			
SINCE THAT DOTH QUICKLY FREEDOM WIN	312	FAIR+YONG	45
WITH EARNEST GROANS FOR FREEDOM CRY	335	JUDGEMENT	14
FREELY			
AND SAVED THAT LIGHT, WHICH FREELY THOU	161	DSTRQCTION	19
AND FREELY SPEND	182	CHRFLNESS	15
FREEZ'D			
AND HIS BLOOD FREEZ'D, KEEPS IN THE CENTER STILL	289	THE TIMBER	22
FREEZE			
HATH DULL'D THEE THUS, WHEN DEATH SHALL FREEZE	142	DEATH	2
LOOSE, PARCELL'D HEARTS WIL FREEZE. THE SUN	189	RESOLVE	13
FREEZETH			
SITS DOWN, AND FREEZETH ON	197	CORRUPTION	30
IT SNOWS , AND FREEZETH HERE.	205	IDLE VERSE	22
FREINDSHIP			
THY QUIKNING FREINDSHIP, MANS BRIGHT WEALTH.	294	BEGGING B	22
FREQUENT			
FREQUENT RELAPSE AND WILFUL BREACH	265	INTRO. 2	24
FRESH			
WHERE FRESH AND GREEN	247	I WALKT	20
ALL NOW AS FRESH AS EDEN, AND AS FINE.	268	ASCN-DAY A	38
FRESH AS THE DEW, WHICH BUT THIS DAWNING WEARS.	267	ASCN-DAY A	20
FRESH GROVES GROW UP, AND THEIR GREEN BRANCHES SHOOT	289	THE TIMBER	6
AND COMES NEXT MORNING FRESH AS HE.	300	PROVIDENCE	24
NEW FRESH ACCOUNTS CF BLOOD AND LUST.	297	HERODIAS	8
AND NOW AS FRESH AND CHEARFUL AS THE LIGHT	288	THE BIRD	7
A DAY SO FRESH, SO BRIGHT, SO BRAVE	334	JUDGEMENT	3
WEAR FRESH ADORNMENTS ON EACH SIDE.	337	PSALM 65	44
A FRESH, IMMORTAL GREEN THERE DWELLS	308	THE SEED	23
COMES LIKE A CHILDES, SPOTLESS AND FRESH.	306	ST MARY MN	70
WE SLIGHT AS OLD AND SOIL'D, THOUGH FRESH AND NEW.	306	RAIN-BOW	2
MAKES BEAUTY LASTING, FRESH AND PURE.	305	ST MARY MN	46
BLOOMY AND FRESH, WHY DOST THOU WEEP.	303	ST MARY MN	10
HOW RICH, O LORD. HOW FRESH THY VISITS ARE.	198	UNPRFTBLNS	1
FRESH, SPICIE MORNINGS, AND ETERNAL BEAMS	188	RELAPSE	27
AND FRESH AS MAY.	189	RESOLVE	24
FULL EAST, A FAIRE, FRESH FIELD COULD SPY	140	RGNKTN	36
FRESH DOTAGE TEMPTS, CR OLD USURPS HIS WILL.	161	DSTRQCTION	16
FRESH AS THOSE ROSES, WHICH THE DAY-SPRING WEARS.	155	ISAACS M.	36
THIS LAST WILL KEEPE THE FIRST TWO FRESH	148	DAY OF JDG	43
AND HERE A FRESH SEARCH IS DECREED	152	THE SEARCH	35
FRESHER			
FRESHER THEN MORNING-FLOWERS WHICH SHEW	303	ST MARY MN	3
FRESHNESS			
YCUR SHADES AND FRESHNESS COMES TO BORROW.	294	PALM-SUNDY	6
FRET			
DOTH FRET AND WRANGLE, PINE AND WASTE.	308	THE SEED	12
TO SWEL AND FOME AND FRET WITHIN.	214	MISERY	64
FRIEND			
DEARE FRIEND SIT DOWN, AND BEAR AWHILE THIS SHADE	279	PALM-TREE	1
THIS I BELIEVED. AND THOUGH A FRIEND	207	REPENTANCE	15
AND FEEL A FRIEND MOST READY, SURE AND KINDE.	331	JACOBS PLW	52
LESSE FRIEND TO ME.	144	RSRCTN +IM	16
DEAR FRIEND. WHOSE HOLY, EVER-LIVING LINES	190	THE MATCH	1
TO GOD, THY COUNTRIE, AND THY FRIEND BE TRUE	193	RLS + LSNS	43
DASH NOT THY FRIEND, NOR HEAV'N, C SMOTHER	194	RLS + LSNS	69
YET, FLY NO FRIEND, IF HE BE SUCH INDEED	194	RLS + LSNS	79
HE IS THY GRACIOUS FRIEND	184	PEACE	9
TO FRIEND, OR SONNE	173	CONTENT	7
FRIENDS			
THEE OTHER THOUGHTS, AWAY WITH FRIENDS, AND MIRTH.	195	RLS + LSNS	104
WITH FANCIES, FRIENDS, CR NEWES.	187	NO DO THEY	34
PROPHETS, AND FRIENDS OF GOD	140	RGNRTN	41
LORD, GOD. I BEG NOR FRIENDS, NOR WEALTH	148	DAY OF JDG	37
THE WORLDS LOV'D WISDOM (FOR THE WORLDS FRIENDS THINK	320	HIDDN TRSR	15
IF THIS WORLDS FRIENDS MIGHT SEE BUT ONCE	308	THE SEED	1
WHICH, LIKE COLD FRIENDS, SEES US BUT ONCE A YEAR	247	I WALKT	12
MIGHT HIS FRIENDS DISCOMPOSE	243	THE SAP	24
EXCESSE OF FRIENDS, OF WORDS, AND WINE	240	MISERY	25
FRO			
AND FULL CF TOSSINGS TOO AND FRO	228	PILGRIMAGE	10

		PAGE	TITLE	LINE
FRO (CCN'T)				
WHO SEARCH'D IT QUITE THRCUGH TC AND FRO	. . . .	338	DEATH B	13
FROST				
AND THAT LONG FROST WHICH NCW BENUMS	. . . .	291	THE JEWS	3
BLEST BE THY DEW, AND BLEST THY FROST	. . . .	227	LV + DSPLN	7
NO FRCST, BUT FLOURISH'C IN THAT YCUTHFUL VEST	. .	268	ASCN-DAY A	43
YET, WAS IT FROST WITHIN	. . . . .	139	RGNRTN	14
BY WINDS, AND BIT WITH FRCST	. . . .	202	DSRDR + FR	7
AND SINCE THESE BITING FRCSTS BLT KIL	. .	227	LV + DSPLN	4
AND BY A FRUITFULL CHANGE CF FRCSTS, AND SHOWRES	. .	221	AFFLICTION	13
FROTHIE				
AND FROTHIE NCISE WHICH UP AND DCWN DOTH FLIE	. . .	234	MUTINIE	24
FROWARD				
WHO WCULD'ST NCT HATE MY FRCWARD YCUTH	. . .	301	PROVIDENCE	44
FROWN				
IN MILDE, CLEAR VISICNS, WITHCLT A FROWN	. . .	330	JACOBS PLW	3
AND WCN THE FIGHT, AND HAVE NCT FEAR'D THE FROWNS	. .	280	PALM-TREE	18
FROZEN				
MY FRCZEN HEART, AND WITH THY SECRET KEY	. . .	216	DRESSING	4
THE FROZEN EARTHS DEAD FACE THCU DUST RENEW.	. .	287	PSALM 104	82
FRUIT				
WHERE ALL IS LIGHT, AND FLOWERS, AND FRUIT	. .	329	TEARS	5
I SAW AT DISTANCE, AND WHERE GRCWS THAT FRUIT	. .	320	HIDDN TRSR	13
SC THAT FAM'D FRUIT WHICH MADE ALL DYE	. .	312	FAIR+YONG	35
KEEP CLEAN, BEAR FRUIT, EARN LIFE AND WATCH	. .	309	THE SEED	47
A TREE, WHOSE FRUIT IS IMMCRTALITY.	. . .	280	PALM-TREE	16
BUT, AH, MY GCD, WHAT FRUIT HAS THOU OF THIS.	. .	198	UNPRFTBLNS	13
NEVER DID TREE BEARE FRUIT LIKE THIS	. . .	152	THE SEARCH	43
FRUITFUL				
THE FRUITFUL FLOCKS FILL EVERY DALE	. . .	337	PSALM 65	45
WHOSE FRUITFUL DAWN SHECS HOPES AND LIGHTS.	. .	295	PALM-SUNDY	31
FRUITFULL				
AND BY A FRUITFULL CHANGE OF FRCSTS, AND SHOWRES	. .	221	AFFLICTION	13
FRUITION				
FRUITION, UNICN, GLORY, LIFE	. . . .	348	HOLY BIBLE	31
FRUITLES				
HEAVEN WITH A LAZIE BREATH, BLT FRUITLES THIS	. .	160	THE SHOWRE	8
FRUITLESS				
WHITHER GCOD CCRN, OR FRUITLESS WEEDS.	. . .	347	THE BOOK	10
FRUITS				
O THOU, THE FIRST FRUITS CF THE DEAD	. . .	180	BURIALL	1
THESE THY DEATHS FRUITS I OFFER THEE	. . .	264	INTRO. 1	2
CANDY WITH SUGAR CUR CHCICE FRUITS.	. . . .	310	THE SEED	78
FRUSTRATE				
FRUSTRATE THOSE CANCEROUS, CLCSE ARTS	. . .	350	L'ENVOY	39
FUEL				
AS FLAMES ABOLT THEIR FUEL RUN	. . . . .	214	MISERY	77
FUL				
O GIVE IT FUL OBEDIENCE, THAT SC SEIZ'D	. . .	235	MUTINIE	36
NAY, THCU TAK'ST CURS, AND (WHICH FUL COMFORT BRINGS)	.	230	LAW + GOSP	19
THE PERFECT, FUL CBLATION FOR ALL SIN	. . .	216	DRESSING	10
FUL HYMNS DCTH YIELD	. . . . .	212	DAWNING	16
FULFIL				
SC MUCH OF STRENGTH, AS MY FULFIL	. . . .	242	MISERY	98
FULL				
AND FULL CF TCSSINGS TOC AND FRC	. . . .	228	PILGRIMAGE	10
THAT GUIDES THROUGH ERRING HOLRS, AND IN FULL STCRY	.	2	SON-DAYES	22
OF A FULL FEAST, AND THE CUT CCURTS OF GLCRY.	. .	2	SON-DAYES	24
AND FULL REDEMPTICN OF THE WHCLE WEEKS FLIGHT.	. .	2	SON-DAYES	8
YCUTH NCW, FULL OF PICUS DUTY	. . . .	218	EASTER HYM	7
I FLUNG AWAY, AND WITH FULL CRIE	. . . .	282	GARLAND	9
WITH CLCUDS AND RAIN, YET FULL AS CALM AND FINE	. .	281	JOY	15
AND MCONS, THOUGH FULL, WCULD GET THEM DCWN.	. .	309	THE SEED	32
FLLL FORTY DAYS O'R THE DRCWN'D WCRLD DID WEEP)	. .	307	RAIN-BOW	28
AND ALL ALONE FULL EARLY RUN	. . . .	295	PALM-SUNDY	36
MANS LIFE, AND YOUR FULL LIBERTY.	. . .	294	PALM-SUNDY	17
YET, THCU SO FULL OF PITY ART	. . . .	299	JESUS WP B	38
GAVE MY FCND HUMCURS THEIR FULL WING	. . .	282	GARLAND	23
AND HILLS FULL OF SPRINGING PRICE	. . .	337	PSALM 65	43
AND GIVES FULL AID	. . . . .	328	RIGHTSNESS	41
DID THE FULL WRATH	. . . . .	185	PASSION	26
SUCH, THOUGH NO PROUD, NOR FULL	. . .	173	CONTENT	9
IS FULL OF VCICES, MAN IS CALL'D, AND HURL'D	. .	161	DSTRQCTION	12
YET, BURN'ST THCU HERE, A FULL DAY, WHILE I SPEND	. .	157	THE LAMPE	5
FULL EAST, A FAIRE, FRESH FIELD COULD SPY	. .	140	RGNRTN	36
THE CISTERNE FULL	. . . . .	141	RGNRTN	63
UNTILL AT LAST FULL WITH THE VITALL RAY	. .	144	RSRCTN +IM	9
WEAR IN MY BOSOME A FULL SUN, SLCH STORE	. .	198	UNPRFTBLNS	11
JCYES FULL, AND TRUE.	. . . .	188	RELAPSE	26
A DARTING CONSCIENCE FULL CF STABS, AND FEARS.	. .	188	RELAPSE	17
AND CALM AND FULL, YET DOTH NCT CLOY.	. .	345	QUICKNESS	12
FULL-EYED				
THIS VEYLE THY FULL-EYED LOVE DENIES	. . .	277	COCK-CRWNG	41
FULLER				
THE FULLER, WHCSE PURE BLCCD DIC FLOW	. . .	270	ASCSN-HYMN	35
FULLNES				
AND THOUGH THCU DOST ME FULLNES GIVE	. . .	228	PILGRIMAGE	22
FULLY				
MAY FLLLY FIT THY GLORICUS REIGN.	. . . .	350	L'ENVOY	28
FULNESS				
ALL PERFECT FULNESS	. . . . . .	215	PRAISE	35

		PAGE	TITLE	LINE
FULNESS	**(CON'T)**			
THE FULNESS OF THE DEITY.		323	THE NIGHT	18
OUR FULNESS TOO IS NOW COME IN		292	THE JEWS	27
FUNERAL				
AFTER THY DEATH AND FUNERAL, SO CLEAR		268	ASCN-DAY A	34
FUNERALS				
TO FUNERALS, AND LENT.		226	RETIREMENT	50
FURIE				
AND CHECKT THEIR FURIE, WHEN I SAW THEM MOVE		188	RELAPSE	7
FURROWS				
THE FURROWS OF IT, THEN THY WARM		337	PSALM 65	35
FURRS				
EXCHANGE THEIR PEACE, AND FURRS.		222	AFFLICTION	34
FURTHERS				
FURTHERS HIS GLORY, AND GIVES DEATH THE FOYL.		195	RLS + LSNS	112
FURY				
THERE ALL THEIR FURY, FOME AND HIDEOUS SOUND		285	PSALM 104	27
FUTURE				
WITHOUT TO MORROWS EVILS AND FUTURE LOADS.		327	RIGHTSNESS	8
MAY MAKE THE FUTURE CLEER.		216	DRESSING	22
FUTURES				
MANS RESURRECTION, AND THE FUTURES BUD		192	RLS + LSNS	26
GAD				
GREATER THAN THOSE THAT GAD ABROAD.		214	MISERY	70
GADDING				
LEAVE, LEAVE, THY GADDING THOUGHTS.		153	THE SEARCH	75
GAIN				
THAT GAIN IS DREADFUL, WHICH MAKES SPIRITS SICK.		193	RLS + LSNS	42
AND WITH ONE GLAUNCE (COULD HE THAT GAIN)		242	MISERY	95
HID IN THESE LOW THINGS SNARES TO GAIN HIS HEART		223	TEMPEST	23
GAIN'D				
SO WITH THAT FIRST LIGHT GAIN'D FROM THEE		348	HOLY BIBLE	13
GAINE				
HUNG WITH MY GAINE, AND HIS GREAT LOSSE		152	THE SEARCH	42
THUS, LORD, I SEE MY GAINE IS GREAT		167	THE CALL	82
GAINFUL				
CONSENT TO ANY GAINFUL ILL		313	THE STONE'	11
GALE				
FAND BY A GENTLE GALE CONVEY AND BREATH		244	MT. OLV. B	5
GALL				
THIS IS THE GREAT ELIXIR THAT TURNS GALL		221	AFFLICTION	4
THOU HADST NO GALL, EV'N FOR THY FOES		272	WHT SUNDAY	11
GALLANT				
A GALLANT FLOWRE		246	I WALKT	4
GAME				
ACTION AND BLOUD NOW GET THE GAME		214	MISERY	67
VICISSITUDE PLAIES ALL THE GAME		222	AFFLICTION	29
GAMESTERS				
ALL GAMESTERS THAT WOULD BID.		282	GARLAND	12
GARDEN				
I WALKE THE GARDEN, AND THERE SEE		152	THE SEARCH	37
GARLAND				
A GARLAND WORE. THUS FED MY EYES		140	RGNRTN	56
TO PLUCK A GARLAND HENCE, WHILE YOU DO SLEEP		280	PALM-TREE	26
A GARLAND, WHERE COMES NEITHER RAIN, NOR WIND.		283	GARLAND	36
GARMENTS				
HIS GARMENTS BE		270	ASCSN-HYMN	27
GASP				
YET, THIS TAKE WITH THEE. THE LAST GASP OF TIME		178	EVNG-WTCH	15
GASTLY				
THEN, WHEN THE GASTLY TWELVE WAS PAST		143	DEATH	19
GATE				
AND HEAV'NS GATE OPENS, WHEN THIS WORLDS IS SHUT.		192	RLS + LSNS	12
SHIFTING THY GATE AND GUILE.		278	THE STARRE	4
DOST THOU RELIEVE US AT THY GATE		213	ADMISSION	15
AND HEAT OF THINE. THAT LITTLE GATE		207	REPENTANCE	7
GATHER				
CROWD, AND GATHER		185	PASSION	28
GATHER TRUE COMFORTS, BUT THE WICKED LIVER		287	PSALM 104	94
TO GATHER FLOWERS TO WELLCOME THEE		295	PALM-SUNDY	37
GATHER'D				
FLOWRES GATHER'D IN THIS WORLD, DIE HERE. IF THOU		283	GARLAND	33
THE WIND, THOUGH GATHER'D IN THY FIST		239	MISERY	5
GAV'ST				
SLIGHTING THAT HEALTH THOU GAV'ST, WHEN HE WAS SICK		230	LAW + GOSP	23
LOOK WHAT THOU GAV'ST, ALL THAT I DO RESTORE		321	HIDDN TRSR	33
GAVE				
GAVE MY FOND HUMOURS THEIR FULL WING		282	GARLAND	23
BY SOME HID SENSE THEIR MAKER GAVE		246	MAN	25
HE GAVE HIS SACRED BLOUD		243	THE SAP	26
BUT HIS, WHO GAVE THEM WINGS TO FLIE.		277	COCK-CRWNG	36
AS THE SUN DOTH, WHICH TO THOSE DAYS GAVE LIGHT.		268	ASCN-DAY A	36
THAT BLEST INCLOSURE, WHERE THE ANGELS GAVE		267	ASCN-DAY A	16
WHO GAVE THE CLOUDS SO BRAVE A BOW		167	VNTY SPRIT	4
WEPT BLOUD, THAT BROKE THIS ADAMANT, AND GAVE		159	MANS FALL	25
GAY				
OF YOUNG, GAY SWEARERS, WITH THEIR NEEDLESSE, LOWD		154	ISAACS M.	22
I MAKE ALL NEW. THERE NOTHING GAY		226	RETIREMENT	40
THE FIRST LIGHT THEY BEHELD WAS BRIGHT AND GAY		239	SHEPHEARDS	51
WHOM SUFFERINGS MAKE MOST GREEN AND GAY.		294	PALM-SUNDY	3

	PAGE	TITLE	LINE
GAY (CCN'T)			
BUT WHILE EACH GAY, ALLURING WEAR	303	ORNAMENT	9
GAZING			
MY GAZING SOUL WOULD DWELL AN HOURE	169	RETREATE	12
GENTILES			
THE YOUNGEST, EV'N THE GENTILES THEN	293	THE JEWS	44
GENTLE			
FAND BY A GENTLE GALE CONVEY AND BREATH	244	MT. OLV. B	5
GENTLY			
RAIN GENTLY SPENDS HIS HONEY-DROPS, AND POURS	306	RAIN-BOW	11
GET			
AND MOONS, THOUGH FULL, WOULD GET THEM DOWN.	309	THE SEED	32
I'LE GET ME UP BEFORE THE SUN	295	PALM-SUNDY	34
AND BRING NEW TOO. GET THEN THIS SAP, AND GET	244	THE SAP	35
AND BRING NEW TOO. GET THEN THIS SAP, AND GET	244	THE SAP	35
WHERE BEES AT NIGHT GET HOME AND HIVE, AND FLOWRS	245	MAN	5
ACTION AND BLOOD NOW GET THE GAME	214	MISERY	67
THAT I MAY GET ME UP, AND GO.	228	PILGRIMAGE	12
DEATH, AND DARKNESS GET YOU PACKING	218	EASTER HYM	1
IF THOU CANST GET BUT THITHER	184	PEACE	13
TO GET THEE WINGS ON, AND DEVOUTLY CLIMBE	155	ISAACS M.	44
O GET THEE WINGS.	157	BRT. CHRCH	11
WASH OFF WITH TEARS, AND GET THY MASTERS HAND.	195	RLS + LSNS	120
AWAKE, GLAD HEART. GET UP, AND SING	199	NTVTY 1	1
HOW SHALL I GET A WREATH FOR THEE	345	THE WREATH	3
TILL THOU DIDST GROW AND GET A WING	346	THE QUEER	11
GETS			
AND TRUTH (OPPREST HERE) GETS THE PRIZE.	318	THE ASS	28
GIDDY			
VAST CIRCLING AZURE, GIDDY CLOUDS, DAYS, NIGHTS.	194	RLS + LSNS	90
A GIDDY BLAST EACH WAY	187	NO DO THEY	18
GIFT			
NOT WORTH OUR THANKS. IS LIFE A GIFT	200	NTVTY 2	7
HATE NOT THINE OWN DEAR GIFT AND TOKEN.	294	BEGGING B	18
THAT GIFT OF THINE, AND TO MY DAY OF DEATH	287	PSALM 104	91
THY GIFT ONCE MORE, AND GRIND THIS FLINT TO DUST.	224	TEMPEST	60
BUT THIS THY OWN GIFT, GIVEN TO ME.	266	INTRO. 2	30
GIFTS			
PRAISE HIM, WHO DEALT HIS GIFTS SO FREE	266	VAIN WITS	12
TO HIM, WHO GIVES ALL GOOD AND PERFECT GIFTS.	267	ASCN-DAY A	4
EARNEST, AND SIGN, THY GIFTS SO DEAL	216	DRESSING	20
THUS DO I MAKE THY GIFTS GIV'N ME	214	MISERY	71
WITH BRUTISH MEN. THY GIFTS GO ROUND	293	THE JEWS	47
NO GOLD NOR GIFTS CAN THEM SUBDUE.	313	THE STONE	13
GILD			
THAT GILD RANK POYSON, AND ALLOW	205	IDLE VERSE	11
SUCH AS DOTH GILD THE LAZIE GLOW-WORMS BED.	157	THE LAMPE	4
GILDED			
WHEN ON SOME GILDED CLOUD, OR FLOWRE	169	RETREATE	11
GLORIOUS DECEPTIONS, GILDED MISTS	282	GARLAND	17
GIRDS			
AND GIRDS THEIR ROCKY HEADS THIS DAY.	336	PSALM 65	22
GIRT			
I WILL CLOSE GIRT AND TYED	342	OBSEQUIES	15
GIV'N			
THUS DO I MAKE THY GIFTS GIV'N ME	214	MISERY	71
VIEW THY FORE-RUNNERS. CREATURES GIV'N TO BE	201	THE CHECK	25
GIV'ST			
FOR TEARS ARE NOT THINE OWN. IF THOU GIV'ST WORDS	194	RLS + LSNS	68
AND AS THOU GIV'ST LINE, AND LENGTH	214	PRAISE	11
THEM IN DUE SEASON. WHAT THOU GIV'ST, THEY TAKE.	286	PSALM 104	74
THOU GIV'ST THE TREES THEIR GREENNESS, EV'N TO THOSE	286	PSALM 104	45
GIVE			
THE ROCKS GIVE CONIES A RETYRING PLACE.	286	PSALM 104	50
THESE TO THE BEASTS OF EVERY FIELD GIVE DRINK.	285	PSALM 104	33
THEREFORE AS LONG AS THOU WILT GIVE ME BREATH	287	PSALM 104	89
AND IF THOU WILT NOT GIVE ME EASE	294	BEGGING B	23
FROM SICKNESSE, GIVE MY SPIRIT HEALTH.	294	BEGGING B	24
WHO LOV'D THE WORLD SO, AS TO GIVE	292	THE JEWS	33
AS HARMLESS VIOLETS, WHICH GIVE	339	DEATH B	21
OR IF THOU WILT GIVE ME THAT ART	328	ANGUISH	9
THESE WEIGHTS, AND GIVE MY SPIRIT LEAVE	329	ANGUISH	17
SO GIVE ME GRACE EVER TO REST	318	THE ASS	13
DEAR JESUS GIVE ME PATIENCE HERE	317	MEN OF WAR	37
GIVE ME HUMILITY AND PEACE	317	MEN OF WAR	41
GIVE ME, MY GOD. A HEART AS MILDE	317	MEN OF WAR	45
GIVE TO THY WRETCHED ONE	216	DRESSING	13
GIVE HIM THY PRIVATE SEAL	216	DRESSING	19
GIVE HIM (WITH PITTY) LOVE	216	DRESSING	25
GIVE ME, MY GOD. THY GRACE	217	DRESSING	31
O GIVE ME THEN A THANKFUL HEART. A HEART	213	ADMISSION	25
BE BROKE AGAIN, FOR FLINTS WILL GIVE NO FIRE	224	TEMPEST	58
SCATTER THESE SHADES OF DEATH, AND GIVE	208	REPENTANCE	51
BUT GIVE THEM IN THOSE STREAMS A PART	208	REPENTANCE	55
THEN GIVE ME OVER TO MY FOE.	242	MISERY	92
THOU MUST (AND DOST) GIVE HIM HIS MEASURE.	214	MISERY	48
I WOULD (SAID I) MY GOD WOULD GIVE	245	MAN	8
AND THOUGH THOU DOST ME FULLNES GIVE	228	PILGRIMAGE	22
O GIVE IT FUL OBEDIENCE, THAT SO SEIZ'D	235	MUTINIE	36
THE WOUNDS THEY GIVE, BY CRYING, ZEALE.	237	CONSTLATN	40

	PAGE	TITLE	LINE
GIVE (CCN'T)			
GIVE TO THY SPCUSE HER PERFECT, AND PURE CRESS	237	CONSTLATN	57
BUT GIVE IT HIM, AND GRUDGE NCT. HE SHALL FEEL	279	THE STARRE	30
THOU TO PCOR RAGS DOST STILL GIVE GRACE.	265	INTRO. 2	12
I NCTHING HAVE TC GIVE TO THEE	266	INTRO. 2	29
SEAL NOT THY EYES UP FRCM THE PCOR, BUT GIVE	193	RLS + LSNS	61
TC MEALES WHEN THOU DOEST COME, GIVE HIM THE PRAISE	195	RLS + LSNS	97
UP WITH THY CURTAINS, GIVE THY SCUL THE WING	195	RLS + LSNS	128
O, IS. BUT GIVE WINGS TC MY FIRE	204	DSRDK + FR	46
WHEN FIRST THY EYES UNVEIL, GIVE THY SOUL LEAVE	191	RLS + LSNS	1
GIVE HIM THY FIRST THOUGHTS THEN, SO SHALT THOU KEEP	191	RLS + LSNS	5
NCR GIVE, NOR TAKE CONTACTICN	183	THRS A TYE	6
MY GOC WOLLD CIVE A SUN-SHINE AFTER RAINE.	160	THE SHOWRE	18
GIVE FOR A HANDFULL, RUT A THCLGHT	160	DSTRCCTION	3
GIVE ME, C GIVE ME CRCSSES HERE	147	DAY OF JDG	33
GIVE ME, C GIVE ME CROSSES HERE	147	DAY OF JDG	33
GIVE HIM AMONGST THY WORKS A PLACE	347	THE BOOK	29
TC DECK THEIR OWN, THEN GIVE THY SAINTS	350	L'ENVOY	35
GIVE WATCHFUL SPIRITS TC CUR GUIDES.	350	L'ENVOY	49
GIVEN			
BUT THOU A CHOSEN SACRIFICE WERT GIVEN	154	ISAACS M.	5
HADST THOU GIVEN TO THIS ACTIVE DUST	162	PURSUITE	9
BUT THIS THY OWN GIFT, GIVEN TC ME.	266	INTRU. 2	30
ARE GIVEN TC BIRDS, WHO, BUT THEE KNOWS	277	COCK-CRWNG	33
A LAND OF FLOWERS AND SPICES. THE WCRD GIVEN	276	PROFFER	47
AND GIVEN US SIGHT.	219	HOLY COMM.	29
AND GIVEN US EYES	219	HOLY COMM.	34
THE MEASURE GIVEN BY THEE EACH YEAR	301	PROVIDENCE	38
THAT CANDLE GIVEN ME FRCM ABOVE.	333	AGREEMENT	42
GIVES			
AND GIVES FULL AID	328	RIGHTSNESS	41
HEAT MOTICN GIVES. THEN WARM IT, TILL IT BEAT	283	LOVE-SICK	15
TC HIM, WHO GIVES ALL GCOD AND PERFECT GIFTS.	267	ASCN-DAY A	4
BUT WHEN THE HAND THAT LOCKT HER UP, GIVES RCOM	271	ALL GONE	31
THE DAY THAT GIVES NO OBSERVATION	202	THE CHECK	46
FURTHERS HIS GLORY, AND GIVES CEATH THE FOYL.	195	RLS + LSNS	112
GIVING			
I CHEER THEIR FLOW, GIVING SUPPLY	240	MISERY	17
GLAD			
THE FIRST GLAC TIDINGS CF THY EARLY LIGHT	267	ASCN-DAY A	17
THY BEGGER GLAD	215	PRAISE	52
AWAKE, GLAD HEART. GET LP, AND SING	199	NTVTY 1	1
AND BE AS GLAC TO FIND IT	167	THE CALL	87
BUT AS THESE BIRDS OF LIGHT MAKE A LAND GLAD	288	THE BIRD	23
THE THIRD GLAC DAY THROLGH TWC SAD NIGHTS.	295	PALM-SUNDY	33
BUT IN HIS HOPE AND ROCK IS EVER GLAD.	327	RIGHTSNESS	33
THE GLAC WORLDS BLESSED MAID.	302	THE KNOT	2
(THEIR LORD SO NEAR) SENSE TO BE GLAD.	305	ST MARY MN	44
SET WITH GREEN HERBS, GLAC HOPES AND BRAVE.	310	THE SEED	72
THRCUGH SADDEST CLOUDS TO THAT GLAD PLACE	345	THE WREATH	17
WITH SOME GLAD MESSAGE FROM HIS HEART	340	THE FEAST	27
GLADLY			
THY QUICKNING BREATH, WHICH GLADLY BEARS	345	THE WREATH	16
UNFINISH'D, WE SHALL GLADLY SIT	350	L'ENVOY	26
GLADLY WILL I, LIKE PCNTICK SHEEP	301	PROVIDENCE	46
IN SPARKLING SMILES HASTE GLADLY DOWN	315	DWELLNG-PL	9
GLADLY I WOULC.	328	ANGUISH	8
BUT ONE HALF GLAUNCE, MCST GLADLY DYE.	168	VNTY SPRIT	34
GLADNES			
THE NEXT WORLDS GLADNES PREPOSSEST IN THIS.	205	SON-DAYES	3
GLADNESS			
GLADNESS, AND PEACE, AND HOPE, AND LOVE	348	HOLY BIBLE	27
GLADNESSE			
AND (WITH MUCH GLADNESSE	182	CHRFLNESS	6
GLADSOME			
UP TO THOSE BRIGHT, AND GLADSOME HILS	220	PSALM 121	1
BUT THAT WAS ALL, AND NCW WITH GLADSOME CARE	239	SHEPHEARDS	41
SCME NIGHTS I SEE YOU IN THE GLADSOME EAST	235	CONSTLATN	9
IN THY CELESTIALL, GLADSOME MESSAGES	284	PSALM 104	13
GLANCE			
I AM SO WARM'D NOW BY THIS GLANCE ON ME	245	MT. OLV. B	15
WHAT GLANCE OF DAY HAST THOU CCNFIN'D	276	COCK-CRWNG	2
O THY BRIGHT LOOKS. THY GLANCE CF LOVE	281	THE FAVOUR	1
BUT SINCE THOU DIDST IN ONE SWEET GLANCE SURVEY	198	UNPRFTBLNS	7
GLANCES			
YET BY THESE GLANCES OF THE FLCCK	273	WHT SUNDAY	23
GLAS			
WHERE I SHALL NEED NO GLAS.	271	ALL GONE	40
GLASS			
THAT GLASS OF SOULS AND SPIRITS, WHERE WELL DREST	275	PROFFER	23
WHEN HEAV'N ABOVE THEM SHIN'D LIKE MOLTEN GLASS	268	ASCN-DAY A	45
BUT SELDOM DOTH MAKE HEAV'N HIS GLASS.	236	CONSTLATN	20
WAS SHOWN ONE DAY IN A STRANGE GLASS	313	THE STONE	19
NCT TUTCR'D BY THY GLASS, BUT FREE	303	ST MARY MN	7
WHO BREAKS HIS GLASS TO TAKE MCRE LIGHT	309	THE SEED	43
TILL ALL BECOMES THY CLCUDLESS GLASS	349	L'ENVOY	12
WHERE, CLEAR AS GLASS	343	WATER-FALL	8
THRCUGH A LARGE DUSKY GLASSE	309	THE SEED	50
AS SMCOTH AS GLASSE.	174	JOY OF LIF	20
SCORE ON THE GLASSE.	165	THE CALL	23

	PAGE	TITLE	LINE
GLASSE (CON'T)			
THE GLASSE WITH TEARES YOU FILL.	165	THE CALL	27
RAY'D INTO THEE, LIKE BEAMS INTO A GLASSE	154	ISAACS M.	8
THEN I THAT HERE SAW DARKLY IN A GLASSE	146	RSRCTN +IM	51
GLAUNCE			
BUT ONE HALF GLAUNCE, MOST GLADLY DYE.	168	VNTY SPRIT	34
AND WITH ONE GLAUNCE (COULD HE THAT GAIN)	242	MISERY	95
GLEAM			
A GLEAM OF GLORY, AFTER SIX-DAYS SHOWRES.	2	SON-DAYES	16
GLEAME			
A SWORDLIKE GLEAME	175	JOY OF LIF	29
GLEAMS			
AND ONELY GLEAMS AND FRACTIONS SPIES.	277	COCK-CRWNG	42
GLIDES			
FOR SIN (LIKE WATER) HOURLY GLIDES	350	L'ENVOY	50
GLIM'RING			
THAT GLIM'RING RAY	178	SILENCE	10
GLIMERING			
MEER GLIMERING AND DECAYS.	271	ALL GONE	12
GLIMPSE			
COULD SEE A GLIMPSE OF HIS BRIGHT FACE.	169	RETREATE	10
THY GLIMPSE OF LIGHT.	201	THE CHECK	24
HAD SOME GLIMPSE OF HIS BIRTH.	196	CORRUPTION	4
IT QUITE FORGOT THAT PURPOS'D GLIMPSE.	332	AGREEMENT	4
GLITTER			
GLITTER AND KINDLE WITH THY LOVE.	332	AGREEMENT	18
GLITTERING			
HER GORGEOUS MART AND GLITTERING STORE	302	ORNAMENT	2
GLITTERS			
IT GLOWS AND GLITTERS IN MY CLOUDY BREST	270	ALL GONE	5
GLO-WORMS			
THAT MEN MIGHT LOOK AND LIVE AS GLO-WORMS SHINE	323	THE NIGHT	3
GLOBE			
DOTH SPREAD LIKE CURTAINS ROUND ABOUT THIS GLOBE	284	PSALM 104	7
IN SPIRES, GLOBES, ANGRY CURLS AND COY	304	ST MARY MN	18
GLOOMIE			
OPEN MY DESOLATE ROOMS, MY GLOOMIE BREST	216	DRESSING	5
A NEAST OF NIGHTS, A GLOOMIE SPHERE	143	DEATH	11
GLOOMY			
LIKE STARS UPON SOME GLOOMY GROVE	270	ALL GONE	6
AND YET, AS IN NIGHTS GLOOMY PAGE	273	WHT SUNDAY	37
GLORIE			
UNTO GLORIE	163	MT. OLVS A	23
GLORIES			
AND IN THESE WEAKER GLORIES SPY	169	RETREATE	13
CREATED GLORIES UNDER THEE.	271	ALL GONE	34
AND OUTWARD UTENSILS THESE GLORIES ARE	225	RETIREMENT	5
GLORIFIE			
OF SAINTS AND ANGELS GLORIFIE THE EARTH.	267	ASCN-DAY A	26
GLORIOUS			
THY GLORIOUS, BRIGHT ASCENSION (THOUGH REMOV'D	267	ASCN-DAY A	5
AND WARME ME AT THY GLORIOUS EYE.	277	COCK-CRWNG	46
GLORIOUS DECEPTIONS, GILDED MISTS	282	GARLAND	17
THE GLORIOUS GOD IS MY SOLE STAY	220	PSALM 121	9
WHOSE GLORIOUS CONQUEST NOTHING CAN RESIST	216	DRESSING	11
A GLORIOUS NIGHT	210	FAITH	14
THY GLORIOUS NAME. WHICH GRANT I MAY SO DO	245	MT. OLV. B	25
WHERE FIRST I LEFT MY GLORIOUS TRAINE	170	RETREATE	24
CORRUPTION WITH THIS GLORIOUS RING	167	VNTY SPRIT	6
MY GLORIOUS HEAD	156	BRT. CHRCH	3
COOL TO A GLORIOUS EVENING, AND EXPIRE.	195	RLS + LSNS	114
WHO LOOKS UPON THEE FROM HIS GLORIOUS THRONE	306	RAIN-BOW	17
O HOLY, BLESSED, GLORIOUS THREE	284	TRINITY-SN	1
AND THE HIGH, GLORIOUS HEAV'NS THY MIGHTY HAND	284	PSALM 104	6
IS NOTHING TO THY GLORIOUS ARM	299	JESUS WP B	41
THE ARM OF GOD, GLORIOUS AND TRUE	292	THE JEWS	40
THAT SACRED VAIL DRAWN O'R THY GLORIOUS NOON	323	THE NIGHT	2
LIKE CLOUDS, BEFORE THY GLORIOUS DAWN.	334	JUDGEMENT	10
WHEN SHALL WE HEAR THAT GLORIOUS VOICE	335	JUDGEMENT	17
SIGNS TRUE, GLORIOUS GOD. ON THEE	336	PSALM 65	1
MAY FULLY FIT THY GLORIOUS REIGN.	350	L'ENVOY	28
O KNOWING, GLORIOUS SPIRIT. WHEN	347	THE BOOK	25
MY GLORIOUS LIBERTY, STILL LATE.	344	WATER-FALL	38
GLORY			
FOR THIS TASTE OF LIVING GLORY	341	THE FEAST	57
FRUITION, UNION, GLORY, LIFE	348	HOLY BIBLE	31
AND TAKE THE GLORY OF THY HOUSE	350	L'ENVOY	34
GLORY TO THE ETERNAL KING.	337	PSALM 65	48
O WHEN MY GOD, MY GLORY BRINGS	329	TEARS	1
AND THAT DREAD GLORY, WHICH THY CHILDREN FEAR'D	330	JACOBS PLW	2
AND GLORY BE TO HIS ETERNAL NAME.	331	JACOBS PLW	37
FAR GREATER, AND SO SPEAK MY SAVIORS GLORY.	290	THE TIMBER	44
THUS THOU THY GLORY THROUGH THE WORLD DOST DRIVE	287	PSALM 104	83
LET GLORY BE THEIR BAIT, WHOSE MINDES	309	THE SEED	33
GLORY, THE CROUDS CHEAP TINSEL STILL	309	THE SEED	37
GLORY, AND GOLD, AND CROWNS AND THRONES	308	THE SEED	3
WHOSE UNDISCOVER'D VIRGIN GLORY	315	DWELLNG-PL	3
FURTHERS HIS GLORY, AND GIVES DEATH THE FOYL.	195	RLS + LSNS	112
A SPIRIT, AND TRUE GLORY DWELL	202	THE CHECK	34
WHERE IS THY GLORY.	201	THE CHECK	12

	PAGE	TITLE	LINE
GLORY (CON'T)			
LAYING BY THY ROBES OF GLORY	163	INCARNATN	2
AND SCORNES THEIR GLORY.	173	CONTENT	20
AND SHOOTS OF GLORY, MY SOUL BREAKES, AND BUDS.	176	MRNG-WTCH	2
WHERE, THOUGH THE GLORY DIFFER IN EACH STAR	236	CONSTLATN	31
MAY PROVE THY GLORY, AND THEIR SHAME. SO CLOSE	234	MUTINIE	18
AND THROUGH THY BLOUD THY GLORY SEE	229	LAW + GOSP	12
THAT WITH THY GLORY DOTH BEST CHIME	211	DAWNING	14
A GLEAM OF GLORY, AFTER SIX-DAYS SHOWRES.	2	SON-DAYES	16
OF A FULL FEAST, AND THE OUT COURTS OF GLORY.	2	SON-DAYES	24
TO HIM BE GLORY, POWER, PRAISE	218	EASTER HYM	17
TO WHOM A FALLING STAR AND NINE DAYES GLORY	282	GARLAND	2
AND INTO GLORY PEEP.	271	ALL GONE	28
I SEE THEM WALKING IN AN AIR OF GLORY	271	ALL GONE	9
OF GLORY, SHE CANNOT TRANSGRESS.	269	ASCSN-HYMN	18
WITH YOUR COMMONWEALTH AND GLORY.	275	PROFFER	36
GLOVE			
SICK WITH A SCARF, OR GLOVE.	205	IDLE VERSE	16
WITH GLOVES, AND KNOTS THE SILLY SNARES OF PLEASURE	231	THE WORLD	12
GLOW-WORMS			
SUCH AS DOTH GILD THE LAZIE GLOW-WORMS BED.	157	THE LAMPE	4
GLOWS			
IT GLOWS AND GLITTERS IN MY CLOUDY BREST	270	ALL GONE	5
GLUT			
RISE TO PREVENT THE SUN, SLEEP DOTH SINS GLUT	192	RLS + LSNS	11
GNATS			
WERE GNATS AND FLIES	232	THE WORLD	28
GO			
HE DID NOR STAY, NOR GO.	231	THE WORLD	18
THAT I MAY GET ME UP, AND GO.	228	PILGRIMAGE	12
AND YET SHOULDST THOU LET GO THY HOLD	240	MISERY	7
BUT I GO ON, HASTE TO DEVEST	240	MISERY	41
'TIS TRUE, HE LOVES THAT DUST WHEREON THEY GO	238	SHEPHEARDS	13
THAT HE HATH QUITE FORGOT HOW TO GO THERE.	246	MAN	21
THEN WOULD GO TRAVEL, FIGHT OR DIE.	214	MISERY	74
GO SEEK ELSEWHERE.	275	PROFFER	32
GO SEEKING ALL THE WAY.	267	ASCN-DAY A	14
BECAUSE WHERE THOU ART, YET, HE CANNOT GO	213	ADMISSION	19
BUT WHAT'S NOT GOOD, AND JUST NE'R GO ABOUT.	193	RLS + LSNS	40
O LEAVE THY CARES, AND FOLLIES. GO THIS WAY	192	RLS + LSNS	17
SERVE GOD BEFORE THE WORLD. LET HIM NOT GO	192	RLS + LSNS	19
GO, GO, SEEK OUT SOME GREENER THING	205	IDLE VERSE	21
GO, GO, SEEK OUT SOME GREENER THING	205	IDLE VERSE	21
GO, GO, QUEINT FOLIES, SUGRED SIN	204	IDLE VERSE	1
GO, GO, QUEINT FOLIES, SUGRED SIN	204	IDLE VERSE	1
WHERE (SINCE HE STEPT THERE) ONLY GO	140	RGNRTN	40
AH. GO. TH'ART WEAK, AND SLEEPIE. HEAV'N	178	EVNG-WTCH	11
SIX MAY GO WRONG.	174	JOY OF LIF	12
SEEN AS WE GO	175	JOY OF LIF	26
GO, GO, SEAL UP THY LOOKS	187	NO DO THEY	9
GO, GO, SEAL UP THY LOOKS	187	NO DO THEY	9
GO LEPER, GO. WASH TILL THY FLESH	306	ST MARY MN	69
GO LEPER, GO. WASH TILL THY FLESH	306	ST MARY MN	69
AND GREAT. THERE SHIPS GO, AND THE SHIPMENS FEAR	286	PSALM 104	71
WITH BRUTISH MEN. THY GIFTS GO BEYOND	293	THE JEWS	47
I, DO NOT GO. THOU KNOW'ST, I'LE DYE.	293	BEGGING B	1
AND I, LIKE FLOWERS SHALL STILL GO NEAT	300	PROVIDENCE	17
TO THY DARK LAND THESE FEEDLESS GO.	338	DEATH B	11
AND BY MEER PLAYING GO TO HEAVEN.	321	CHILDEHOOD	8
AND DYING MAK'ST ME GO IN PEACE.	348	HOLY BIBLE	34
GOATS			
TO THE WILDE GOATS THE HIGH HILLS SERVE FOR FOLDS	286	PSALM 104	49
GOD			
O LORD MY GOD, HOW MANY AND HOW RARE	286	PSALM 104	65
IN HEAVEN, ONE GOD IN TRINITIE.	284	TRINITY-SN	3
MY GOD, HOW GREAT, HOW VERY GREAT ART THOU.	284	PSALM 104	2
UP, O MY SOUL, AND BLESSE THE LORD. O GOD	284	PSALM 104	1
WHEN GOD HIMSELF FOR THEE DOTH WEEP.	296	JESUS WP A	4
WHY IS MY GOD THUS SLOW AND COLD	293	BEGGING B	9
AND WOULD BE CROSS, WHEN GOD WAS KINDE.	292	THE JEWS	25
THE ARM OF GOD, GLORIOUS AND TRUE	292	THE JEWS	40
AS MADE HIM KNOW HIS GOD BY NIGHT.	323	THE NIGHT	6
THERE IS IN GOD (SOME SAY)	325	THE NIGHT	49
SIGNS TRUE, GLORIOUS GOD. ON THEE	336	PSALM 65	1
O GOD. THOUGH MERCY BE IN THEE	335	JUDGEMENT	39
O GOD. I KNOW AND DO CONFESS	333	AGREEMENT	43
I KNOW (MY GOD) THIS WOULD NOT BE.	333	AGREEMENT	60
FOR WHICH, O GOD, I ONELY CAN	334	AGREEMENT	71
AND GOD HIMSELF DYED BY THE MULTITUDE.	330	JACOBS PLW	6
THIS GOD FORESAW. AND WHEN SLAIN BY THE CROWD	330	JACOBS PLW	21
MY GOD AND KING. TO THEE	328	ANGUISH	1
MY GOD, COULD I WEEP BLOOD	328	ANGUISH	7
IS VERY HARD. O GOD, DISPERSE	329	ANGUISH	16
O MY GOD, HEAR MY CRY.	329	ANGUISH	19
O WHEN MY GOD, MY GLORY BRINGS	329	TEARS	1
BUT FIRMLY TRUSTS IN GOD, THE GREAT MANS MEASURE	328	RIGHTSNESS	45
O FOUL, DECEITFUL MEN. MY GOD DOTH KEEP	307	RAIN-BOW	19
SO THOSE BAD DAUGHTERS, WHICH GOD SAV'D FROM FIRE	307	RAIN-BOW	31
GOD IS MADE OUR ALLIE	302	THE KNOT	6
MY DEAR, DEAR GOD. I DO NOT KNOW	315	DWELLNG-PL	11

		PAGE	TITLE	LINE
GOD	(CCN'T)			
MY COC, I MEAN MY SINFUL HEART.		315	DWELLNG-PL	16
GCD AND HIS CREATURES, THOUGH LNSEEN.		313	THE STONE	21
AS LOUD AS BLCOD. NCT THAT GOC NEEDS		314	THE STONE	24
BUT NCW, SINCE GOC CN HIMSELF TCCK		314	THE STONE	52
GIVE ME, MY GCC. A HEART AS MILDE		317	MEN OF WAR	45
AND WHEN (O GCD) THE ASS IS FREE		319	THE ASS	57
ALAS. MY COD. TAKE HCME THY SHEEP.		312	FAIR+YONG	51
THY GCD, THY LIFE, THY CURE.		184	PEACE	20
MY DEAR, CEAR GOD.		184	PASSION	2
PRESENT, C GOC.		180	CHRCH-SVC	22
BLEST BE THE GOD CF HARMCNY, ANC LOVE.		179	CHRCH-SVC	1
THE GCD ABOVE.		179	CHRCH-SVC	2
CCME THEN, MY GOD.		172	MIDNIGHT	21
A GOD ENCLOS'C WITHIN YCUR CELL		164	INCARNATN	10
I GRIEVE, MY GOD. THAT THCU HAS MADE ME SUCH.		161	DSTRQCTION	26
PRCPHETS, AND FRIENDS CF GCC		140	RGNRTN	41
WHAT (O GCD) BUT A SILENT TEAR		320	RGNRTN	9
MY GOC WOULD GIVE A SUN-SHINE AFTER RAINE.		160	THE SHOWRE	18
FCR GCD (MACE MAN,)		159	MANS FALL	30
UNTC THY GOD, FCR MARRIAGE CF ALL STATES		155	ISAACS M.	45
PREPARE, PREPARE ME THEN, C GCC		147	DAY OF JDG	29
LCRC, GCD. I BEG NOR FRIENDS, NCR WEALTH		148	DAY OF JDG	37
MY GOC, WHEN I WALKE IN THOSE GROVES		148	RELIGION	1
NAY THOL THY SELFE, MY COC, IN FIRE		149	RELIGION	17
YET, SURE, MY GOD. I LOVE THEE MOST		203	DSRDR + FR	14
BLT, AH, MY GOD. WHAT FRUIT HAS THOU OF THIS.		198	UNPRFTBLNS	13
ALAS, MY GOD. THY BIRTH NCW HERE		200	NTVTY 2	17
SERVE GCD BEFCRE THE WORLC. LET HIM NCT GO		192	RLS + LSNS	19
TC GOC, THY CCUNTRIE, AND THY FRIEND BE TRUE		193	RLS + LSNS	43
TIE UP HIS HANDS, THAT CARES MCCK GOD, AND MAN.		193	RLS + LSNS	48
UNTC THEIR GOD, AS FLCW'RS CO TC THE SUN.		191	RLS + LSNS	4
MY GOC, HCW GRACICUS ART THCU. I HAC SLIPT		188	RELAPSE	1
AND DIE, THAT BUSH WHERE GOD IS, SHALL NOT BLRN.		196	RLS + LSNS	132
OF NIGHT SHUT UP THY LEAVES, BE CHAST, GOC PRYS		196	RLS + LSNS	136
LOVE GOD, AND LOVE THY NEIGHBCUR, WATCH, AND PRAY.		196	RLS + LSNS	140
THE WCRC IN CHARACTERS, GOD IN THE VOICE.		198	SCRIPTURES	8
OBSERVE GCD IN HIS WORKS, HERE FCUNTAINS FLOW		194	RLS + LSNS	87
GIVE ME, MY GCD. THY GRACE		217	DRFSSING	31
MY GOD, ACCEPT OF MY CONFESSICN.		207	REPENTANCE	26
HCW HATH MY GCC BY RAYING THEE		210	FAITH	5
O MY CEAR GOD. MY LIFE, MY LOVE.		208	REPENTANCE	47
THE GLORIOUS GOD IS MY SOLE STAY		220	PSALM 121	9
ALL FLESH IS CLAY, THOU KNOW'ST, AND BUT THAT COC		221	AFFLICTION	11
THUS COTH GOD KEY DISCRCER'D MAN		222	AFFLICTION	35
O MY GOC, LET IT BE THINE.		249	BEGGING A	20
MY GOC. THOU THAT DIDST DYE FCR ME		264	INTRO. 1	1
SHALL NCT THE BREATH OF GCC PREVAIL.		276	COCK-CRWNG	18
THERE GCD A CCMMERCE STATES, ANC SHEDS		279	THE STARRE	27
THAT GOC IS TRUE, AS HERBS UNSEEN		279	THE STARRE	31
IN GOC, DCTH ALWAYS (HICDEN) MULTIPLY		280	PALM-TREE	14
O HEAR MY GOD. HEAR HIM, WHOSE BLCUD		242	MISERY	105
GCC ORDER'D MCTION, BUT ORDAIN'C NO REST.		246	MAN	28
I WOULD (SAID I) MY GCD WOULD GIVE		245	MAN	8
AND SAY, WHERE GOD IS, ALL AGREE.		237	CONSTLATN	60
EXCLUCE MY DEAR GCD FROM MY MINC		240	MISERY	34
THE MICHTY GOC, TH' ETERNAL KING		240	MISERY	39
THAT LAMB OF GOD ADORE		239	SHEPHEARDS	48
LEACS UP TO GOD		233	THE WORLD	54
FAREWEL O BOCK OF GOD. FAREWELL.		348	HOLY BIBLE	36
WHAT (O GCD) BUT A SILENT TEAR.		341	THE FEAST	72
THAT WHAT GOD TAKES, HEE'L NOT RESTORE.		343	WATER-FALL	22
ETERNAL GCD. MAKER OF ALL		346	THE BOOK	1
A QUICKNESS, WHICH MY GCD HATH KIST.		345	QUICKNESS	20
GODS				
AND GCDS CWN LODGING (THOUGH HE CCULD NOT LACK)		238	SHEPHEARDS	29
TRANSPLANTED PARACISE, GODS WALKING HOUR.		2	SON-DAYES	11
THE CREATURES JUBILE, GCDS PARLE WITH DUST.		2	SON-DAYES	13
BE GODS ALONE, AND CHCOSE THE BETTER PART.		192	RLS + LSNS	36
O GODS CWN BLCOD AWAKE THEE. HE BIDS BEWARE		202	THE CHECK	41
GCDS SAINTS ARE SHINING LIGHTS. WHO STAYS		174	JOY OF LIF	17
BRIGHT QUEEN CF HEAVEN. GODS VIRGIN SPOUSE.		302	THE KNOT	1
YEA GCDS CWN BLOOC WE TREAD UPCN AND SLIGHT.		307	RAIN-BOW	30
BLT THE GOOD MAN IS GCDS PECULIAR TREASURE.		328	RIGHTSNESS	48
BY GOCS PERMISSICN, AND MAN TURNS A MULE.		330	JACOBS PLW	30
AND GCDS BRIGHT MINDE EXPREST IN PRINT.		332	AGREEMENT	24
MUST LIVE TWICE, THAT WCULD GCDS FACE SEE.		322	CHILDEHOOD	36
GCDS SILENT, SEARCHING FLIGHT.		324	THE NIGHT	31
BEFCRE BRIGHT STARS, ANC GODS CWN BEAMS.		321	CHILDEHOOD	12
GOE				
FAREWELL. I GCE TC SLEEP. BUT WHEN		177	EVNG-WTCH	1
GCE, SLEEP IN PEACE. ANC WHEN THOU LYEST		177	EVNG-WTCH	3
AND AS THOU SAW'ST, I IN A THCUGHT COULD GOE		146	RSRCTN +IM	57
GOES				
THE RODE FOUL, AND WHERE ONE GCES RIGHT		174	JOY OF LIF	11
AND GOES ABOUT		327	RIGHTSNESS	23
PASTURES CF LIFE, WHERE THE LAMB GOES.		319	THE ASS	52
RETIRE INTO THEIR DENS. MAN GCES ABROAD		286	PSALM 104	62
HE GOES, HE YIELDS, AND TROUBLEC SORE		240	MISERY	37
THE WCRK GOES CN, AND SLACKETH NOT		227	LV + DSPLN	15

                                                              PAGE   TITLE   LINE
GOES   (CCN'T)
    FCUNTAINS OF LIFE, WHERE THE LAMB GOES.   .   .   .   .   344 WATER-FALL   26
GOFST
    CR, IF THCU GCEST, DO NCT DENY   .   .   .   .   .   .   293 BEGGING B   3
GUING
    BLT GCING HENCE, AND KNCWING WEL WHAT WOES   .   .   .   243 THE SAP   23
    ANC GCING HENCE, LEAVE WRITTEN CN SCME TREE   .   .   .   281 JOY   29
GOLD
    SHAL BE FINE GOLD, WHICH THCU DIDST CLEANSE.   .   .   .   274 WHT SUNDAY   60
    HER CEDAR, FIRR, HEW'D STCNES ANC GOLD WERE ALL   .   .   .   238 SHEPHEARDS   23
    HUNTS GCLD ANC WEALTH, AND WILL NCT LEND   .   .   .   .   301 PROVIDENCE   33
    NC GOLD NCR GIFTS CAN THEM SUBDLE.   .   .   .   .   .   313 THE STONE   13
    GLORY, AND GOLD, AND CRCWNS ANC THRCNES   .   .   .   .   308 THE SEED   3
    NC MERCY-SEAT CF GOLD   .   .   .   .   323 THE NIGHT   19
    THE UNTHRIFT SUNNE SHCT VITALL GOLD   .   .   .   .   .   140 RGNRTN   50
    CRYED DROSS FCR GCLD, AND NEVER THCUGHT   .   .   .   .   348 HOLY BIBLE   15
GOLCEN
    THAT FRCM SOME SECRET, COLDEN MINE   .   .   .   .   .   150 RELIGION   30
    IN THCSE CALME, GCLDEN EVENINGS LAY   .   .   .   .   .   151 THE SEARCH   24
GONE
    WHEN I AM GONE   .   .   .   .   173 CONTENT   5
    SINCE HE IS GCNE .   .   .   .   170 COME, COME   2
    THAT LITTLE LIGHT I HAD WAS GCNE.   .   .   .   .   .   168 VNTY SPRIT   29
    SINCE THOU ART GONE   .   .   .   .   178 SILENCE   2
    THOUGH LIFE BE DEAD, ANC MY JCYS GONE.   .   .   .   .   311 THE SEED   89
    THEY ARE ALL GONE INTC THE WORLD CF LIGHT.   .   .   .   270 ALL GONE   1
    GRCWING O'R NIGHT, AND GCNE TCMCRROW .   .   .   .   .   208 REPENTANCE   72
    WILT THCU BE GONE.   .   .   .   .   344 QUICKNESS   2
GOOD
    MEN CALL GOOD CHEAR   .   .   .   .   342 OBSEQUIES   14
    WHITHER GCOD CORN, CR FRUITLESS WEEDS.   .   .   .   .   347 THE BOOK   10
    INCLINE EACH HARD HEART TO DO GCOD   .   .   .   .   .   350 L'ENVOY   45
    (CUR SOV'RAIN GOOC)   .   .   .   .   219 HOLY COMM.   27
    WHAT EVER THOU COST BID, LET FAITH MAKE GOOD   .   .   .   216 DRESSING   23
    AND HIGHEST GCOD IS BLEST.   .   .   .   .   .   .   278 THE STARRE   8
    TO HIM, WHO GIVES ALL GCOC ANC PERFECT GIFTS.   .   .   .   267 ASCN-DAY A   4
    SLCH MUSICK SPOILS GOCD FELLOWSHIP.   .   .   .   .   .   240 MISERY   32
    TC SHEW WHAT STRANGE LOVE HE HAD TO OUR GOOD   .   .   .   243 THE SAP   25
    GOOD STCRE OF IT, BUT LET   .   .   .   .   .   .   244 THE SAP   36
    TC MAKE MAN GOOD, AS BIC HIM BE   .   .   .   .   .   242 MISERY   94
    SPEAKS MORE AND BETTER FOR MY GCOD.   .   .   .   .   .   242 MISERY   106
    AND THEY TOO CFT TAKE GCOD FOR ILL   .   .   .   .   .   309 THE SEED   39
    BUT THE GOOD MAN IS GODS PECULIAR TREASURE.   .   .   .   328 RIGHTSNESS   48
    THESE GCOD DEEDS BLOT .   .   .   .   328 RIGHTSNESS   50
    AND STILL THY SOV'RAINTY HOLDS GCOD. .   .   .   .   .   338 DEATH B   4
    WHO OUT OF EVIL CAN BRING FORTH GOOD. .   .   .   .   .   297 HERODIAS   18
    MADE MY LCRDS INCARNATICN GOOC.   .   .   .   .   .   284 TRINITY-SN   6
    SEAL'D , AND MADE GOOD   .   .   .   .   .   .   180 CHRCH-SVC   21
    O MY CHIEF GCOD. .   .   .   .   184 PASSION   1
    WHOSE JLICE SC GOCD   .   .   .   .   185 PASSION   17
    BY CISTANCE ALL GOOD CBJECTS FIRST TO DROWN   .   .   .   183 THRS A TYE   19
    THAT CONE, WE SHALBE SAFE, AND GCCD   .   .   .   .   .   165 THE CALL   28
    THOU THINK'ST IT GOOD TC TARRY WHERE THOU ART   .   .   .   157 BRT. CHRCH   14
    THOU KNEW'ST BUT THY CWN GOOD.   .   .   .   .   .   202 THE CHECK   39
    BUT WHAT'S NOT GOOD, ANC JUST NE'R GO ABOUT.   .   .   .   193 RLS + LSNS   40
    IF TRIALS COME, THIS WIL MAKE GCOD THY PART   .   .   .   193 RLS + LSNS   57
    IT IS THE GOOD MANS FEAST, THE PRINCE OF FLOWRES .   .   .   193 RLS + LSNS   59
    'TWIXT HEAVEN, AND US, THE MANNA WAS NOT GCOC   .   .   .   192 RLS + LSNS   9
    HAVE CONE MUCH GOCD   .   .   .   .   190 THE MATCH   2
    BUT SHUTS HIS DOOR, AND LEAVES GOCD OUT ALL NIGHT.   .   .   194 RLS + LSNS   84
    WHAT'S GOCD SCORE UP FOR JOY, THE BAD WEL SCANN'C   .   .   195 RLS + LSNS   119
    THIS CONVERSATION, BUT THE GOCC MAN LYES   .   .   .   .   195 RLS + LSNS   125
    IN SOME GCOD THOUGHTS, SO WHEN THE DAY SHALL RISE   .   .   195 RLS + LSNS   129
GOOD-NIGHT
    'TIS LAST GOOD-NIGHT, CUR SUNNE SHALL NEVER SET. .   .   143 DEATH   32
GOODNESS
    THE YEAR IS WITH THY GOCDNESS CROWN'D   .   .   .   .   337 PSALM 65   39
    AND FILL'D WITH JOY, THY GOODNESS TELLS.   .   .   .   .   336 PSALM 65   12
    LEAVING FCR US (WHOSE GCODNESS CUICKLY FACES)   .   .   .   326 RIGHTSNESS   3
    THE ONE OF GOODNESS, PEACE ANC LIFE   .   .   .   .   .   318 THE ASS   3
GORGECUS
    HER GCRGECUS MART AND GLITTERING STORE   .   .   .   .   302 ORNAMENT   2
GOSHEN
    THIS LITTLE GCSHEN, IN THE MICST OF NIGHT .   .   .   .   331 JACOBS PLW   31
GOSPEL
    THE GCSPEL THEN (FOR 'TIS HIS WCRD   .   .   .   .   .   315 THE STONE   56
    O PLANT IN ME THY GOSPEL, AND THY LAW .   .   .   .   .   230 LAW + GOSP   27
GOT
    HCW SHRIL ARE SILENT TEARS. WHEN SIN GOT HEAC   .   .   .   213 ADMISSION   1
    SAY, YOU HAVE GOT THE DAY FROM MEN   .   .   .   .   .   305 ST MARY MN   48
    HATH GOT AN HCUSE WHERE MANY MANSIONS ARE .   .   .   .   290 THE TIMBER   31
    BUT GOT   .   .   .   .   153 THE SEARCH   85
    HATH GOT THE PRIZE.   .   .   .   .   189 RESOLVE   28
GOTST
    THOU GOTST MY HEART, ANC THOUGH HERE TOST .   .   .   202 DSRDR + FR   6
GOURD
    I AM THE GOURD OF SIN, AND SORRCW   .   .   .   .   208 REPENTANCE   71
GRACE
    GIVE ME, MY GCD. THY GRACE   .   .   .   .   .   217 DRESSING   31
    BUT GRACE, AND BLESSINGS CAME WITH THEE SO RIFE .   .   .   218 HOLY COMM.   3

	PAGE	TITLE	LINE
GRACE (CCN'T)			
AND AFTER ALL THY ACTS CF GRACE DCTH KICK	230	LAW + GOSP	22
(BECALSE THOU DOST THY CRACE CISTIL)	227	LV + DSPLN	2
AT SOME SET TIMES, BUT ARE THY CRACE.	242	MISERY	88
INTC MY WCUNDS, AND NCW THY GRACE	214	MISERY	51
OF GRACE AGAINST ALL SINS	244	THE SAP	48
THOU TO PCOR RAGS DOST STILL CIVE GRACE.	265	INTRO. 2	12
SC LET THY GRACE NCW MAKE THE WAY	274	WHT SUNDAY	57
BLT DRESSE, AND WATER WITH THY GRACE	204	DSRDR + FR	55
O SWEET, CIVINE SIMPLICITY. O GRACE	155	ISAACS M.	37
THAT THCU WERT PLEAS'C TO SHEC THY GRACE SO FARR,	283	LOVE-SICK	3
SC CIVE ME GRACE EVER TC REST	318	THE ASS	13
TC SHLN THAT PERIL, LET THY GRACE	319	THE ASS	41
AND FCRM TO SERVE HIM IN, SHOLLC BE TRUE GRACE	330	JACOBS PLW	24
BLT FLOWERS DC BOTH REFRESH AND GRACE	321	CHILDEHOOD	14
WHILE FAITH AND GRACE	339	THE FEAST	4
DEAR LORD, DO THIS, AND THEN LET GRACE	350	L'ENVOY	43
GRACIOUS			
TWO LIFES I HCLD FRCM THEE, MY GRACICUS LORD	191	THE MATCH	19
MY GOC, HCW GRACICUS ART THOU. I HAD SLIPT	188	RELAPSE	1
HE IS THY GRACICUS FRIEND	184	PEACE	9
OF THIS PCOR CREATURE, BY A GRACICUS ART	223	TEMPEST	22
GRAIN			
THEIR LITTLE CRAIN EXPELLING NIGHT	276	COCK-CRWNG	8
AND LET THIS GRAIN WHICH HERE IN TEARS I SOW	191	THE MATCH	39
WHO SHEWS ME BUT CNE GRAIN OF SINCERE LIGHT.	320	HIDDN TRSR	3
GRAINES			
BLT PROV'C THE HEAVIER CRAINES	139	RGNRTN	33
GRAINS			
WITH THAT ONE GRAINS INFUSED WEALTH	206	REPENTANCE	4
GRANARIES			
WHC FILS THE WORLCS UNEMPTY'C CRANARIES.	195	RLS + LSNS	100
GRAND			
THESE TWO GRAND SINS WE JOYN AND ACT TOGETHER	307	RAIN-BOW	25
GRANT			
GRANT I MAY SCFT AND LOWLY BE	318	THE ASS	17
YET WCULD NOT MEN GRANT, THEIR ILL FATE	311	FAIR+YONG	21
FROM BLCOCY MEN. AND GRANT, I MAY	326	ABELS BLOD	29
GRANT, I MAY NCT LIKE PLDDLE LIE	212	DAWNING	29
GRANT I MAY, MY CHIEF DESIRE.	249	BEGGING A	5
GRANT I MAY SO	248	I WALKT	48
THY GLORICUS NAME. WHICH GRANT I MAY SO DO	245	MT. OLV. B	25
GRASS			
ADORES DEAD DUST, SETS HEART CN CORNE AND GRASS	236	CONSTLATN	19
BALM CN THE CLEFT EARTH, MILK CN GRASS AND FLOWERS.	306	RAIN-BOW	12
OF GRASS, WE TREAC, DECLARE.	286	PSALM 104	68
GRASS FCR THE CATTEL, AND HERBS FCR MANS USE	285	PSALM 104	41
MEER SEED, AND AFTER THAT BUT GRASS.	347	THE BOOK	6
THE BLADES OF GRASSE, THY CREATURES FEEDING	207	REPENTANCE	33
GRATE			
THE PASSAGE IS, HE TERM'D A GRATE	207	REPENTANCE	9
GRATIFIES			
AND GRATIFIES THY SIN WITH VOWS.	297	HERODIAS	14
GRAVE			
AND MADE CRAVE MUSICUE LIKE WILDE WIT	297	HERODIAS	3
IN THE SAME PAGE THY HUMBLE GRAVE	310	THE SEED	71
TWILL SHEW US EACH FORGCTTEN GRAVE	334	JUDGEMENT	4
HE FINDS IT DEAD, AND IN A GRAVE.	212	DAWNING	32
I GREET THY SEPULCHRE, SALUTE THY GRAVE	267	ASCN-DAY A	15
THY ACCCUNTS THUS MADE, SPENC IN THE GRAVE ONE HCLRE	195	RLS + LSNS	121
WHEN FIRST THCU DIST EVEN FROM THE GRAVE	202	DSRDR + FR	1
TO SINNERS CONFIDENCE, LIFE TC THE GRAVE.	159	MANS FALL	26
BLT, C HIS GRAVE. WHERE I SAW LENT	152	THE SEARCH	45
WIDE CF A FAITHFULL GRAVE	183	THRS A TYE	16
YOUR MAKER PENT UP IN A GRAVE	164	INCARNATN	11
THAT CURTAIN'C GRAVE, THOUGH SLEEP, LIKE ASHES, HIDE	177	MRNG-WTCH	32
FCR SCME WORE WHITE EV'N IN THY GRAVE	342	OBSEQUIES	19
WAS ONCE LAID FCR ME IN THY GRAVE.	342	OBSEQUIES	28
THY GRAVE. TO WHICH MY THCUGHTS SHAL MOVE	343	OBSEQUIES	29
BLT QUICKNED BY THIS CEEP AND RCCKY GRAVE	343	WATER-FALL	11
BLT GRAVELY CAST THEMSELVES AWAY.	322	CHILDEHOOD	30
GRAVES			
GRAVES ARE BECS NOW FCR THE WEARY	218	EASTER HYM	5
GRAY			
THE YCUTHFUL WORLDS GRAY FATHERS IN ONE KNCT	306	RAIN-BOW	6
GREAN			
AND ALL THE YEAR HAVE SCME GREAN EARS	227	LV + DSPLN	18
GREAT			
LIKE A GREAT RING OF PURE AND ENCLESS LIGHT	231	THE WORLD	2
TC SEE THEIR SOULS GREAT SHEPHEARD, WHO WAS COME	239	SHEPHEARDS	45
THAT LAMB WHOSE DAIES GREAT KINGS AND PROPHETS WISH'D	239	SHEPHEARDS	49
OR THY GREAT MERCIES BETTER PRIZE.	214	MISERY	56
WATCHING THE BREAK OF THY GREAT DAY.	212	DAWNING	48
BLT THAT GREAT DARKNESS AT THY DEATH	219	HOLY COMM.	21
THIS IS THE GREAT ELIXIR THAT TURNS GALL	221	AFFLICTION	4
WITH WHICH THEIR GREAT CREATOR HAD THEM CREST.	268	ASCN-DAY A	44
THEY PASS AS AT THE LAST GREAT DAY, AND RUN	268	ASCN-DAY A	29
YET THOU THE GREAT ETERNAL ROCK	273	WHT SUNDAY	45
AT THIS GREAT FEAST, AND IN A TYRE	272	WHT SUNDAY	6
YET WHILE SOME RAYS OF THAT GREAT LIGHT	272	WHT SUNDAY	17

		PAGE	TITLE	LINE
GREAT (CON'T)				
FOR THOUGH THOU DOEST THAT GREAT LIGHT LOCK	• • •	273	WHT SUNDAY	21
THY GREAT DECAYS RESTOR'D MIGHT BE.	• • •	304	ST MARY MN	32
GREAT KING OF LOVE AND TRUTH.	• • •	301	PROVIDENCE	43
AND SPLENDID VICE DESTROYS THE GREAT.	• • •	318	THE ASS	8
MY SINS ARE GREAT AND STILL PREVAIL	• • •	333	AGREEMENT	44
THE GREAT AND WHITE THRONE I SHALL SEE	• • •	337	THE THRONE	3
AT THY GREAT WORKS ASTONISH'D BE.	• • •	336	PSALM 65	24
THE FIRST TRUE WORSHIP OF THE WORLDS GREAT KING	• •	330	JACOBS PLW	11
BUT FIRMLY TRUSTS IN GOD, THE GREAT MANS MEASURE	• •	328	RIGHTSNESS	45
ARE THY GREAT WORKS. IN WISDOM HAST THOU MADE	• •	286	PSALM 104	66
AND GREAT. THERE SHIPS GO, AND THE SHIPMENS FEAR	• •	286	PSALM 104	71
I WILL IN SONGS TO THY GREAT NAME IMPLOY	• • •	287	PSALM 104	90
MY GOD, HOW GREAT, HOW VERY GREAT ART THOU.	• • •	284	PSALM 104	2
MY GOD, HOW GREAT, HOW VERY GREAT ART THOU.	• • •	284	PSALM 104	2
BY SHEWING THE SIN GREAT, SHEW THE RELIEF	• • •	290	THE TIMBER	43
MAKE LESSER MORNINGS, WHEN THE GREAT ARE CONF.	• •	288	THE BIRD	18
WERE STILL ALIVE) THOU DOST GREAT STORMS RESENT	• •	289	THE TIMBER	15
IN SACRED HYMNES, AND ORDER, THE GREAT CHIME	• •	177	MRNG-WTCH	17
DESCRY SOME PART OF HIS GREAT LIGHT.	• • •	167	VNTY SPRIT	8
THUS, LORD, I SEE MY GAINE IS GREAT	• • •	167	THE CALL	82
OF THY GREAT FATHER	• • •	185	PASSION	27
THOU GREAT PRESERVER OF ALL MEN.	• • •	180	BURIALL	7
HUNG WITH MY GAINE, AND HIS GREAT LOSSE	• • •	152	THE SEARCH	42
LOOKE DOWNE GREAT MASTER OF THE FEAST, O SHINE	• •	150	RELIGION	51
THE QUICK, AND DEAD, BOTH SMALL AND GREAT	• •	147	DAY OF JDG	23
MY GREAT PRESERVER SMILES	• • •	205	IDLE VERSE	6
THOU ART THE GREAT ELIXIR, RARE, AND CHOICE.	• •	198	SCRIPTURES	6
GREATER				
FAR GREATER, AND SO SPEAK MY SAVIORS GLORY.	• • •	290	THE TIMBER	44
DID NOT A GREATER BEAUTY RULE MINE EYES	• • •	320	HIDDN TRSR	23
AND IN THE GREATER WORLD DISPLAY	• • •	221	AFFLICTION	9
GREATER THAN THOSE THAT GAD ABROAD.	• • •	214	MISERY	70
GREATEST				
THE GREATEST ATTRIBUTE WE SEE	• • •	335	JUDGEMENT	40
AND TO MY GREATEST HATERS KINDE.	• • •	317	MEN OF WAR	44
GREATNESS				
NOR LOV'D THE SMILES OF GREATNESS, BUT HAVE WROUGHT	•	280	PALM-TREE	19
GREEN				
PUT ON THEIR YOUTH AND GREEN.	• • •	279	THE STARRE	32
WHEN LIKE A VIRGIN CLAD IN FLOWERS AND GREEN	• •	268	ASCN-DAY A	41
WHERE FRESH AND GREEN	• • •	247	I WALKT	20
MY WITHER'D LEAFS AGAIN LOOK GREEN AND FLOURISH	• •	245	MT. OLV. B	22
THAT AT THE ROOT OF THIS GREEN TREE	• • •	304	ST MARY MN	31
SET WITH GREEN HERBS, GLAD HOPES AND BRAVE.	• •	310	THE SEED	72
FOR WHOSE DRY DUST GREEN BRANCHES BUD	• • •	310	THE SEED	83
A FRESH, IMMORTAL GREEN THERE DWELLS	• • •	308	THE SEED	23
THE BLADE GROWS UP ALIVE AND GREEN.	• • •	337	PSALM 65	38
FRESH GROVES GROW UP, AND THEIR GREEN BRANCHES SHOOT	•	289	THE TIMBER	6
WHOM SUFFERINGS MAKE MOST GREEN AND GAY.	• • •	294	PALM-SUNDY	3
BUT ONE GREEN BRANCH AND A WHITE ROBE.	• • •	295	PALM-SUNDY	45
IN SOME GREEN SHADE, OR FOUNTAIN.	• • •	197	CORRUPTION	24
OR IS'T SO, AS SOME GREEN HEADS SAY	• • •	149	RELIGION	25
GREEN TREES OF LIFE, AND LIVING STREAMS.	• • •	346	THE QUEER	8
THOU KNEW'ST THIS TREE, WHEN A GREEN SHADE	• •	347	THE BOOK	11
ON EACH GREEN THING. THEN SLEPT (WELL FED)	• •	347	THE BOOK	17
GREENE				
OTHERS BENEATH AN OAKES GREENE BOUGHS	• • •	148	RELIGION	7
GREENER				
GO, GO, SEEK OUT SOME GREENER THING	• • •	205	IDLE VERSE	21
GREENNESS				
NOR ANY THOUGHT OF GREENNESS, LEAF OR BARK.	•	289	THE TIMBER	12
THOU GIV'ST THE TREES THEIR GREENNESS, EV'N TO THOSE	•	286	PSALM 104	45
DEAR, SECRET GREENNESS. NURST BELOW	• • •	309	THE SEED	25
GREET				
I BOW MY TROUBLED SOUL, AND GREET	• •	328	ANGUISH	3
DID ALL MY SENSES GREET	• • •	140	RGNRTN	49
I GREET THY SEPULCHRE, SALUTE THY GRAVE	• •	267	ASCN-DAY A	15
GREW				
GREW MASTER OF MY WAYES	• • •	282	GARLAND	6
TWO FLOWRES THAT GREW WITH THEE ABOVE.	• •	216	DRESSING	26
AND WHERE IT FLOURISH'D, GREW AND SPREAD	• •	347	THE BOOK	13
GREWST				
WHERE, AS THOU GREWST, IT MULTIPLI'D AND SHIN'D	• •	154	ISAACS M.	9
GRIEF				
WHEREFORE, PIERC'D THROUGH WITH GRIEF, MY SAD	• •	207	REPENTANCE	19
AND THY TWO WINGS WERE GRIEF AND LOVE.	• •	272	WHT SUNDAY	12
WHICH ONLY GRIEF AND LOVE EXTRACT. WITH THIS	•	244	THE SAP	41
YET THOU IN ALL THY SOLITUDE AND GRIEF	• •	331	JACOBS PLW	45
GRIEF AND SOUL-CURING MELANCHOLY.	• • •	311	FAIR+YONG	2
WHO WERT ALL FALSE, SHOULD'ST TRUE GRIEF KNOW.	•	305	ST MARY MN	64
THE KING OF GRIEF, THE MAN OF SORROW	• •	294	PALM-SUNDY	4
BUT AS SHADES SET OFF LIGHT, SO TEARS AND GRIEF	•	290	THE TIMBER	41
YET GRIEF AND OLD WOUNDS MAKE HIM SORE DISPLEAS'D	•	290	THE TIMBER	35
DEAR LORD. THOU ART ALL GRIEF AND LOVE	• •	298	JESUS WP B	22
OF GRIEF AND PITY IN THY BREST	• • •	299	JESUS WP B	30
A GRIEF THAT SHALL OUTSHINE ALL JOYS	• • •	299	JESUS WP B	46
A GRIEF, WHOSE SILENT DEW SHALL BREED	• • •	299	JESUS WP B	48
DID SOMETIMES RULE. A GRIEF SO BRIGHT	• • •	299	JESUS WP B	50
BUT A TWIN'D WREATH OF GRIEF AND PRAISE	• • •	345	THE WREATH	9

	PAGE	TITLE	LINE
GRIEFE			
THEN CROPS, AND RAINS FOR GRIEFE	139	RGNRTN	25
GRIEFS			
DOUBLING THY GRIEFS, WHEN NONE WOULD OWN THEE. . .	185	PASSION	29
THE PROVERB'D GRIEFS OF HOLY JOB	295	PALM-SUNDY	43
IF PIOUS GRIEFS HEAVENS JOYS AWAKE	308	THE SEED	15
THE AFTER-BURTHENS, AND GRIEFS YET TO COME . . .	233	MUTINIE	3
SORROWS IN WHITE, GRIEFS TUN'D, A SUGERD DOSIS .	280	JOY	5
OH. ALL THY GRIEFS	341	THE FEAST	67
GRIEV'D			
IT GRIEV'D ME MUCH. AT LAST, SAID I . . .	168	VNTY SPRIT	29
GRIEV'ST			
THOU GRIEV'ST, MAN SHOULD HIMSELF UNDO . . .	298	JESUS WP B	24
GRIEVE			
AND SPRING, HOW IS'T THAT YOU SO SADLY GRIEVE . .	298	JESUS WP B	12
MY BUSINESS HERE SHALL BE TO GRIEVE. . . .	299	JESUS WP B	45
YET JOY IT SELF WILL MAKE A RIGHT SOUL GRIEVE . . .	290	THE TIMBER	39
WHOSE SPIRIT TOO DOTH MOURN AND GRIEVE . . .	292	THE JEWS	35
AND WHY THEN GRIEVE WE TO BE SENT	312	FAIR+YONG	41
USURP'D. IT NEVER SHOULD ME GRIEVE	301	PROVIDENCE	40
AND NEITHER GRIEVE, REPINE, NOR FEAR. . . .	339	DEATH B	25
I GRIEVE, MY GOD. THAT THOU HAS MADE ME SUCH. .	161	DSTRQCTION	26
I GRIEVE.	161	DSTRQCTION	27
I LONG, AND GRONE, AND GRIEVE FOR THEE . . .	228	PILGRIMAGE	13
DOTH GRIEVE FOR DUST, AND DUST DOTH SING. . .	240	MISERY	40
NOR GRIEVE THY DOVE, BUT SOFT AND MILD . . .	235	MUTINIE	38
GRIEVES			
HIS HOLY SPIRIT GRIEVES THEREFORE	240	MISERY	38
GRIND			
THY GIFT ONCE MORE, AND GRIND THIS FLINT TO DUST. . .	224	TEMPEST	60
GROAN			
WHY DOST THOU GROAN AND GROAN AGAIN . . .	298	JESUS WP B	2
WHY DOST THOU GROAN AND GROAN AGAIN . . .	298	JESUS WP B	2
TRAVEL AND GROAN, AND LOOK AND CALL. . . .	350	L'ENVOY	22
O HOLY GROANS. GROANS OF THE DOVE. . . .	298	JESUS WP B	9
O HOLY GROANS. GROANS OF THE DOVE. . . .	298	JESUS WP B	9
WHERE THE STARV'D EARTH GROANS FOR ONE TEAR. .	296	JESUS WP A	16
THAT SINCE MAN FELL, EXPECT WITH GROANS . . .	294	PALM-SUNDY	12
WITH EARNEST GROANS FOR FREEDOM CRY . . .	335	JUDGEMENT	14
EACH LINE IN THEE. THEN WOULD I PLEAD IN GROANS .	198	SCRIPTURES	10
GRON'D			
I BEG'D HERE LONG, AND GRON'D TO KNOW . . .	167	VNTY SPRIT	3
GRONE			
AND SWEETER AIRES STREAME FROM A GRONE . . .	167	THE CALL	80
WHO NEVER WAKE TO GRONE, NOR WEEPE . . .	164	THE CALL	8
AND GRONE ON HIGH	185	PASSION	40
HOW DIDST THOU GRONE IT	185	PASSION	12
AND GRONE TOO. WHY TH'ELECT	186	NO DO THEY	4
SIGH THERE, AND GRONE FOR THEE	187	NO DO THEY	29
WHILST I EACH MINUTE GRONE TO KNOW . . .	143	DEATH	29
I LONG, AND GRONE, AND GRIEVE FOR THEE . . .	228	PILGRIMAGE	13
FALSE, JUGLING SOUNDS, A GRONE WELL DREST, WHERE CARE .	280	JOY	3
GRONES			
WITH SPIRIT-SIGHS, AND EARNEST GRONES . . .	242	MISERY	110
WITH THY GRONES MY DAILY BREATH	215	PRAISE	29
A FLOUD THAT DROWNS BOTH TEARS, AND GRONES . .	214	ADMISSION	31
MY SICHES, AND GRONES.	180	CHRCH-SVC	24
WHOSE INTERCEDING, SPIRITUALL GRONES . . .	179	CHRCH-SVC	4
GROPE			
WHICH OTHERS ONELY GROPE FOR AND DISPUTE. . .	320	HIDDN TRSR	14
GROPS			
HE GROPS BENEATH HERE, AND WITH RESTLESS CARE . .	236	CONSTLATN	17
GROSSE			
TOO GROSSE FOR HEAVEN	160	THE SHOWRE	5
GROSSNESS			
HOW DO THEY CAST OFF GROSSNESS. ONLY EARTH . .	223	TEMPEST	29
GROTS			
TO LIVE IN GROTS, AND CAVES, AND HATE THE DAY . .	233	THE WORLD	51
GROUND			
WORKT UNDER GROUND	232	THE WORLD	24
THE GROUND WAS CURST, AND VOID OF STORE. . .	264	INTRO. 1	8
ON VEINES OF SULPHUR UNDER GROUND. . . .	150	RELIGION	40
IF PRIEST, AND PEOPLE CHANGE, KEEP THOU THY GROUND. .	193	RLS + LSNS	44
HID UNDER GROUND SURVIVES THE FALL. . . .	203	DSRDR + FR	29
WHAT FALLOW'D SOLITARY GROUND DID BEAR . . .	323	THE NIGHT	15
GROUNDS			
WITH FERTIL STREAMS, MAKES RICH ALL GROUNDS . .	336	PSALM 65	30
AND TAME PROUD WAVES, IF YET THESE BARREN GROUNDS .	234	MUTINIE	12
THE LOWER GROUNDS STIL CHASE, AND CHOOSE . .	240	MISERY	10
GROVE			
LIKE STARS UPON SOME GLOOMY GROVE . . .	270	ALL GONE	6
BUT WHAT FAIR WELL, OR GROVE HE SINGS IN NOW . .	271	ALL GONE	23
A GROVE DESCRYED	140	RGNRTN	43
AND IDOLIZE SOME SHADE, OR GROVE	162	MT. OLVS A	4
THUS GROVELING IN THE SHADE, AND DARKNESS, HE .	224	TEMPEST	41
GROVES			
MY GOD, WHEN I WALKE IN THOSE GROVES . . .	148	RELIGION	1
OR SECRET GROVES, KEEP THE HIGH-WAY. . . .	294	PALM-SUNDY	10
FRESH GROVES GROW UP, AND THEIR GREEN BRANCHES SHOOT .	289	THE TIMBER	6
GROW			
AND ALL HER STREAMS GROW FOUL.	288	THE BIRD	30

	PAGE	TITLE	LINE
GROW (CON'T)			
FRESH GROVES GROW UP, AND THEIR GREEN BRANCHES SHOOT	289	THE TIMBER	6
THESE UPPER SPRINGS AND NONE ELSE MAKE THEM GROW.	291	THE TIMBER	52
TO MAKE DRIE CUST, AND CEAD TREES GROW.	291	THE JEWS	13
THOU MAK'ST TO GROW. THESE (BLEST BY THEE) THE EARTH	285	PSALM 104	42
WOULDST HAVE A WREATH THAT FADES NOT, LET THEM GROW	283	GARLAND	34
AND GROW FOR THEE, WHO SPARES THEM HERE, SHALL FIND	283	GARLAND	35
SLOWLY AND·SADLY DOTH HE GROW	308	THE SEED	17
VEX NOT, THAT BUT ONE SEES THEE GROW	309	THE SEED	27
I FIND MY SELFE THE LESSE, THE MORE I GROW.	161	DSTRQCTION	10
BUT WHILE I GROW	203	DSRDR + FR	20
THROUGH THY INCREASE GROW NEW, AND QUICK.	191	THE MATCH	41
AND LESS'NING STILL GROW UP INVISIBLY	224	TEMPEST	44
TEARS AND THESE FLAMES WILL SOON GROW KINDE	266	VAIN WITS	5
THAT PLACE WHERE I HAD SEEN HIM TO GROW OUT	247	I WALKT	17
AND SPRING, AND GROW, A TREE NE'R TO BE PRIC'D	280	PALM-TREE	15
THOSE GUSTS MIGHT QUARREL AND GROW BOLD.	240	MISERY	8
WHOSE SPRING IS ON THAT HIL WHERE YOU DO GROW	235	CONSTLATN	3
TILL THOU DIDST GROW AND GET A WING	346	THE QUEER	11
GROWES			
I SEE IN EACH SHADE THAT THERE GROWES	148	RELIGION	3
GROWES STILL FROM BETTER UNTO WORSE	150	RELIGION	35
THERE GROWES THE FLOWRE OF PEACE	184	PEACE	14
GROWING			
GROWING O'R NIGHT, AND GONE TOMORROW	208	REPENTANCE	72
GROWN			
IS GROWN THICK DARKNESS, AND THY BREAD, A STONE.	224	TEMPEST	55
HER BRESTS GROWN DRY.	222	TEMPEST	8
TO WHAT'S ALREADY GROWN TOO HIGH	240	MISERY	18
EACH CAY IS GROWN A DOZEN YEAR	170	COME, COME	3
NOW POINT HIM OUT, GROWN UP A MAN.	151	THE SEARCH	10
BUT NOW GROWN SICKLY, SAD AND SLOW	308	THE SEED	11
AND WILT NOT LEAVE ME, WHEN GROWN OLD.	301	PROVIDENCE	45
WE ARE HIS BODY GROWN	302	THE KNOT	10
MAN SLIGHTS HIS MAKER, WHEN FAMILIAR GROWN	330	JACOBS PLW	19
THY SEAMLESS COAT IS GROWN A RAG	350	L'ENVOY	30
BUT AS RASH YOUTHS, WHEN ONCE GROWN STRONG	348	HOLY BIBLE	9
GROWS			
HIS TIME IS SHORT, MORE RAGING GROWS.	335	JUDGEMENT	30
THE BLADE GROWS UP ALIVE AND GREEN.	337	PSALM 65	38
I SAW AT DISTANCE, AND WHERE GROWS THAT FRUIT	320	HIDDN TRSR	13
MUST HE NOR SIP, NOR SING. GROWS NE'R A FLOWR	224	TEMPEST	51
THE MORE HE GROWS. CELESTIAL NATURES STILL	279	PALM-TREE	9
HATH TAKEN ROOT, AND GROWS, AND DOTH NOT TIRE	279	THE STARRE	26
GROWTH			
BOTH GROWTH, AND POWER, CHECKING THE HEALTH	206	REPENTANCE	6
THIS GROWTH AND STRETCH FOR HEAV'N.	243	THE SAP	6
THEN BLESS THY SECRET GROWTH, NOR CATCH	309	THE SEED	45
BRED IN THY GROWTH BETWIXT HIGH WINDS AND THEE	289	THE TIMBER	14
GRUDGE			
AT WHOSE JUST LAWS NOT JUST MEN GRUDGE.	326	ABELS BLOD	24
BUT GIVE IT HIM, AND GRUDGE NOT. HE SHALL FEEL	279	THE STARRE	30
GUARD			
WHICH ANGELS GUARD, AND WITH IT PLAY	322	CHILDEHOOD	37
AND GUARDETH HIS BELOVED.	220	PSALM 121	8
GUARDIAN			
HAVE OUR SURE GUARDIAN, AND OUR LEADING LIGHT.	331	JACOBS PLW	50
GUARDIANS			
AND ROVE ABOUT THEE, GUARDIANS OF THY MINDE,	155	ISAACS M.	26
GUEST			
A VERY ROBBERY, AND HIM SELF NO GUEST	195	RLS + LSNS	102
YET, HADST THOU NOBLER GUESTS. ANGELS DID WIND	155	ISAACS M.	25
IN ABR'HAMS TENT THE WINGED GUESTS	149	RELIGION	13
GUIDE			
THE SUN'S BROKE THROUGH TO GUIDE MY WAY.	152	THE SEARCH	66
LET MILDNESS, AND RELIGION GUIDE THEE OUT	193	RLS + LSNS	38
BECAM'ST THY SELF, BOTH GUIDE, AND SCOUT.	202	DSRDR + FR	4
AND GUIDE A CROUD.	174	JOY OF LIF	16
WILL GUIDE HIM IN.	175	JOY OF LIF	32
FAIR AND YONG LIGHT. MY GUIDE TO HOLY	311	FAIR+YONG	1
COMMAND AND GUIDE THE EYE.	278	THE STARRE	24
SO GUIDE US THROUGH THIS DARKNES, THAT WE MAY	237	CONSTLATN	51
O BOOK. LIFES GUIDE. HOW SHALL WE PART	348	HOLY BIBLE	1
GUIDED BY FAITH, NOT BY EXTERIOR LIGHT.	327	RIGHTSNESS	24
GUIDES			
OUR GUIDES PROVE WANDRING STARS	237	CONSTLATN	46
THAT GUIDES THROUGH ERRING HOURS, AND IN FULL STORY	2	SON-DAYES	22
WERE MY SURE GUIDES, AND ONLY WITH ME STAYES	159	MANS FALL	11
GIVE WATCHFUL SPIRITS TO OUR GUIDES.	350	L'ENVOY	49
GUILE			
SHIFTING THY GATE AND GUILE.	278	THE STARRE	4
WITH NATIVE LOOKS, WHICH KNEW NO GUILE	303	ORNAMENT	15
GUILT			
(TOUCH'D WITH THE GUILT OF MY OWN WAY)	207	REPENTANCE	28
GUILTS			
GUILTS, TRESPASSES, AND ALL THIS INWARD AWE	159	MANS FALL	19
GUSH			
FOR THEE MY WORDS, MY TEARS DO GUSH	228	PILGRIMAGE	14
GUSTS			
THOSE GUSTS MIGHT QUARREL AND GROW BOLD.	240	MISERY	8

	PAGE	TITLE	LINE

HAD'ST
HAD'ST NE'R AN OATH, NOR COMPLEMENT. THOU WERT · · 154 ISAACS M. 13

HAGAR
WHICH FREED POOR HAGAR FROM HER FEARS · · · · 300 PROVIDENCE 4

HAIL
IN HEAV'N, HAIL, THUNDER, RAIN-BOWS, SNOW, AND ICE · · 194 RLS + LSNS 93

HAIR
WHY LIES THIS HAIR DESPISED NOW · · · · 304 ST MARY MN 15
I SKILL NOT YOUR FINE TINSEL, AND FALSE HAIR · · · 275 PROFFER 33

HALF
BUT ONE HALF GLAUNCE, MOST GLADLY DYE. · · · · 168 VNTY SPRIT 34

HALL
THY STARS, AND SPANGLED HALL · · · · · 203 DSRDR + FR 22

HALLELUJAHS
OF HALLELUJAHS HERE BELOW. · · · · · 182 CHRFLNESS 24

HALLOW
DESCEND, AND HALLOW ALL THE PLACE. · · · · 350 L'ENVOY 44

HALLOW'D
FAIRE, VIRGIN-FLOWERS, AND HALLOW'D WELLS · · · 153 THE SEARCH 70
WHAT HALLOW'D SOLITARY GROUND DID BEAR · · · · 323 THE NIGHT 15

HAND
THE CLEAN, PURE HAND, WHICH NEVER MEDLED PITCH. · · 327 RIGHTSNESS 10
AND SETTLEST WITH THY SECRET HAND · · · · 337 PSALM 65 34
NOURISHED WITH FAVORS FROM HIS HAND · · · · 302 THE KNOT 11
OF THY LORDS HAND, THE OBJECT OF HIS EYE. · · · 306 RAIN-BOW 14
IS IN THY MOUTH, NOT IN THY HAND · · · · 316 MEN OF WAR 26
WHEN THUS THY MILDE, INSTRUCTING HAND · · · · 319 THE ASS 45
SACRED AND SECRET HAND. · · · · · 300 PROVIDENCE 1
AND THE HIGH, GLORIOUS HEAV'NS THY MIGHTY HAND · · 284 PSALM 104 6
THY BOUNTEOUS OPEN HAND HELPS THEM AT NEED · · · 286 PSALM 104 75
(PROPT BY THY HAND) · · · · · · 179 CHRCH-SVC 10
THY HAND ALONE DOTH TAME · · · · · 179 CHRCH-SVC 15
THY HAND IS NIGH. · · · · · · 171 COME, COME 14
IN HAND, SOME IN THE SKIN. · · · · · 174 CONTENT 22
BUT 'TWAS MY SINNE THAT FORC'D THY HAND · · · 166 THE CALL 38
WASH OFF WITH TEARS, AND GET THY MASTERS HAND. · · 195 RLS + LSNS 120
BUT WHEN THE HAND THAT LOCKT HER UP, GIVES ROOM · · 271 ALL GONE 31
WHOSE HAND SO SHINES THROUGH ALL THIS FRAME · · · 277 COCK-CRWNG 20
I MAY FIND THY HAND THEREIN · · · · · 249 BEGGING A 11
DOST THOU FEED THINE. O THOU, THE HAND THAT LIFTS · 267 ASCN-DAY A 3
FOR AS THY HAND THE WEATHER STEERS · · · · 227 LV + DSPLN 16
THY HAND OUR STAY · · · · · · 230 LAW + GOSP 18
AS THY HAND OPES, OR SHUTS. · · · · · 219 HOLY COMM. 13
US BY THE HAND · · · · · · 219 HOLY COMM. 36
THOU WERT THE FIRST PUT IN MY HAND · · · · 348 HOLY BIBLE 5

HANDFULL
GIVE FOR A HANDFULL, BUT A THOUGHT · · · · 160 DSTRQCTION 3
POORE, QUERULOUS HANDFULL WAS'T FOR THIS · · · 145 RSRCTN +IM 19

HANDS
TIE UP HIS HANDS, THAT DARES MOCK GOD, AND MAN. · · 193 RLS + LSNS 48
HERE I JOIN HANDS, AND THRUST MY STUBBORN HEART · · 190 THE MATCH 7
WITH FOLDED HANDS. · · · · · · 164 THE CALL 13
NINE MONTHS THY HANDS ARE FASHIONING US · · · 166 THE CALL 46
EXTENT, AND END, FOR MY HANDS DREW THE LINE · · · 226 RETIREMENT 27
OUR FOUL, CLAY HANDS · · · · · · 215 PRAISE 42
FORCE DOWN A JUST CURSE, WHEN THY HANDS WOULD BLESS. · 230 LAW + GOSP 33
HIS OWN HANDS WITH THE DUST · · · · · 232 THE WORLD 33
I BREAK THE FENCE MY OWN HANDS MADE · · · · 240 MISERY 21
I'D LOOSE THOSE KNOTS THY HANDS DID TIE · · · 214 MISERY 73
THY BLESSED HANDS TO BLESS, THESE THOU DOST LEAVE. · 268 ASCN-DAY A 56
WHOSE HANDS ARE OPEN AS THINE EYES. · · · · 301 PROVIDENCE 42
THY EASIE HANDS TO DO THIS WASTE. · · · · 304 ST MARY MN 24
THEY SAID, MY OWN HANDS DID REMOVE · · · · 333 AGREEMENT 41
SUBMIT MY WILDE HEART, AND RESTRAIN MY HANDS. · · 321 HIDDN TRSR 30

HANG
AND HANG THE HEAD, SIGHING FOR THOSE · · · · 319 THE ASS 51
AND SIN) HANG AT HIM, FOR THE MORE HE'S BENT · · 279 PALM-TREE 8
SO DO I MOURN, AND HANG MY HEAD · · · · 228 PILGRIMAGE 21
BUT CLOUDS HANG ON. · · · · · · 178 SILENCE 4

HANGS
THAT SHUTS, AND HANGS THE HEAD · · · · · 183 THRS A TYE 8

HAP
AND HAP WHAT WILL · · · · · · 182 CHRFLNESS 10
FOR HONESTY IS SAFE, COME WHAT CAN HAP. · · · 193 RLS + LSNS 58

HAPLESSE
WHILE HAPLESSE I STILL WEEP. · · · · · 311 THE SEED 85

HAPPEND
HOW HAPPEND IT THAT IN THE DEAD OF NIGHT · · · 238 SHEPHEARDS 5

HAPPINESS
ALL STREWED WITH FLOWRES, AND HAPPINESS · · · 189 RESOLVE 23

HAPPY
SHOULD MOVE, THEY MAKE US HOLY, HAPPY, RICH. · · 192 RLS + LSNS 30
HAPPY THOSE EARLY DAYES. WHEN I · · · · 169 RETREATE 1
O SAD, AND WILDE EXCESSE. AND HAPPY THOSE · · · 154 ISAACS M. 17
AND HAPPY I TO BE SO CROST · · · · · 227 LV + DSPLN 8
THEN SIGHING WHISPER'D, HAPPY ARE THE DEAD. · · 247 I WALKT 33
SLEEP HAPPY ASHES (BLESSED SLEEP) · · · · 311 THE SEED 84
O BRIGHT AND HAPPY KALENDAR. · · · · · 310 THE SEED 61
O HOLY, HAPPY, HEALTHY HEAVEN · · · · · 312 FAIR+YUNG 23
WHAT HAPPY, SECRET FOUNTAIN · · · · · 315 DWELLNG-PL 1

		PAGE	TITLE	LINE
HAPPY	**(CCN'T)**			
WHOSE HOLY, HAPPY HISTORIES	. . . . . .	335	JUDGEMENT	24
HAPPY IS HE. WHOM THOU WILT CHOOSE	. . . . .	336	PSALM 65	9
HARAN				
WHEN TERAH, NAHOR, HARAN, ABRAM, LOT	. . . . .	306	RAIN-BOW	5
HARBOUR'D				
WHICH NEVER HARBOUR'D PLOTS	. . . . . .	239	SHEPHEARDS	34
HARD				
WHOSE SUBSTANCE, THOUGH 'TIS HARD ENOUGH	. . . .	314	THE STONE	50
IS VERY HARD. O GOD, DISPERSE	. . . . .	329	ANGUISH	16
O'RE MY HARD HEART, THAT'S BOUND UP, AND ASLEEP	. .	160	THE SHOWRE	15
BUT A HARD, STONIE HEART.	. . . . . .	179	CHRCH-SVC	8
O THAT I HAD DEEP CUT IN MY HARD HEART	. . .	198	SCRIPTURES	9
INCLINE EACH HARD HEART TO DO GOOD	. . . .	350	L'ENVOY	45
HARDER				
AND WHAT YOU NOW EXTRACT, IN HARDER WEATHER	. . .	274	PROFFER	9
HARM				
AND OPENING SHOWERS (RESTRAIN'D FROM HARM)	. . .	337	PSALM 65	36
THAT, THOUGH THE CURE OF ALL MANS HARM	. . .	299	JESUS WP B	40
HARMLES				
SWEET, HARMLES LIVES (ON WHOSE HOLY LEISURE	. .	238	SHEPHEARDS	1
WEARYED OUT IN A HARMLES STRIFE	. . . .	209	THE BURIAL	3
HARMLESS				
THOU HOLY, HARMLESS, UNDEFIL'D HIGH-PRIEST.	. . .	216	DRESSING	9
PERHAPS SOME HARMLESS CARES FOR THE NEXT DAY	. .	239	SHEPHEARDS	37
AND HARMLESS HEAD.	. . . . . .	287	THE BIRD	6
AS HARMLESS VIOLETS, WHICH GIVE	. . . .	339	DEATH B	21
AND THE THOUGHTS OF EACH HARMLESS HOUR	. . .	321	CHILDEHOOD	5
DEAR, HARMLESS AGE. THE SHORT, SWIFT SPAN	. .	322	CHILDEHOOD	31
PLAIN, HARMLESS, FAITHFUL, FAIR AND BRIGHT	. .	312	FAIR+YONG	25
THOU KNEW'ST THIS HARMLESS BEAST, WHEN HE	. .	347	THE BOOK	15
HARMONY				
THERE IS NO DISCORD, BUT YOUR HARMONY.	. . .	280	JOY	2
BLEST BE THE GOD OF HARMONY, AND LOVE.	. . .	179	CHRCH-SVC	1
HASTE				
CUTS THROUGH THE HEAVY MISTS IN HASTE	. . .	178	SILENCE	11
LORD HASTE, LORD COME	. . . . . .	181	BURIALL	39
HASTE, HAST MY DEAR	. . . . . .	156	BRT. CHRCH	5
AND BAD THE LAZIE SUNNE MAKE HASTE	. . .	143	DEATH	21
I SEE THEM, HEAR THEM, MARK THEIR HASTE, AND MOVE	.	268	ASCN-DAY A	31
BUT I GO ON, HASTE TO DEVEST	. . . .	240	MISERY	41
IN SPARKLING SMILES HASTE GLADLY DOWN	. . .	315	DWELLNG-PL	9
WHAT PRETTY SULLENNESS DID HASTE	. . . .	304	ST MARY MN	23
THEREFORE THY WITHER'D SELF IN HASTE	. . .	304	ST MARY MN	29
WHERE WITH PROUD HASTE THE RICH MADE WAY	. . .	302	ORNAMENT	3
DEAR LORD. MAKE HASTE	. . . . . .	335	JUDGEMENT	27
HASTING				
OF THE DISTREST, HASTING THEIR OVERTHROW.	. . .	327	RIGHTSNESS	27
HASTS				
THE SUN NOW STOOPS, AND HASTS HIS BEAMS TO HIDE	. .	195	RLS + LSNS	105
HASTY				
AND HASTY DROPS, AS IF THEY HAD	. . . .	305	ST MARY MN	43
HATCH				
AND HATCH MY SOUL, UNTILL IT FLY	. . . .	204	DSRDR + FR	47
AND WHILE THESE HERE THEIR MISTS, AND SHADOWS HATCH,	.	156	BRT. CHRCH	2
WHERE SOULS ARE HATCH'D UNTO ETERNITIE.	. . .	197	SCRIPTURES	4
AND HATCH'D ALL WITH HIS QUICKNING LOVE.	. . .	344	WATER-FALL	32
HATCHETH				
AND HATCHETH O'R THY PEOPLE.	. . . . .	197	CORRUPTION	38
HATE				
WHO WOULD'ST NOT HATE MY FROWARD YOUTH	. . .	301	PROVIDENCE	44
AND YET (AS IF SOME DEEP HATE AND DISSENT	. . .	289	THE TIMBER	13
HATE NOT THINE OWN DEAR GIFT AND TOKEN.	. . .	294	BEGGING B	18
TO LIVE IN GROTS, AND CAVES, AND HATE THE DAY	. .	233	THE WORLD	51
AND HATE THEE NOT	. . . . . .	225	RETIREMENT	24
HATERS				
AND TO MY GREATEST HATERS KINDE.	. . . .	317	MEN OF WAR	44
ONELY, LET NOT OUR HATERS BRAG	. . . .	350	L'ENVOY	29
HATES				
AND TRULY HATES TO BE DETAIN'D ON EARTH	. . .	290	THE TIMBER	30
HAUGHTY				
THOUGH HIGH AND HAUGHTY MUST	. . . . .	328	RIGHTSNESS	46
HAUNT				
THIS LEPER HAUNT, AND SCYL THY DOOR	. . .	200	NTVTY 1	26
I SOUGHT CHOICE BOWRES, HAUNTED THE SPRING	. .	282	GARLAND	21
HAWKS				
THOUGH HAWKS CAN PREY THROUGH STORMS AND WINDS	. .	309	THE SEED	35
HE'S				
AND SIN) HANG AT HIM, FOR THE MORE HE'S BENT	. .	279	PALM-TREE	8
HEAD				
AND WEAVE IT FOR YOUR HEAD AGAINST YOU WAKE.	.	280	PALM-TREE	27
THIS PAST, I THREW THE CLOTHES QUITE O'R HIS HEAD	.	247	I WALKT	29
HOW SHRIL ARE SILENT TEARS. WHEN SIN GOT HEAD	.	213	ADMISSION	1
THOU, WHOSE SAD HEART, AND WEEPING HEAD LYES LOW	.	217	EASTER-DAY	1
SO DO I MOURN, AND HANG MY HEAD	. . . .	228	PILGRIMAGE	21
AT LENGTH I FEEL MY HEAD TO AKE	. . . .	214	MISERY	61
AND HANG THE HEAD, SIGHING FOR THOSE	. . .	319	THE ASS	51
WHO ARGLES, FOLLOWS HIS OWN HEAD.	. . .	318	THE ASS	24
WHOM FOR OUR HEAD WE OWN.	. . . . .	302	THE KNOT	12
ABOUT THY CURIOUS, WILDE, YONG HEAD.	. . .	304	ST MARY MN	20

	PAGE	TITLE	LINE
HEAD (CON'T)			
AS EARTH, THY LOVELY HEAD DOST BOW.	304	ST MARY MN	26
AND OVER-RUN MY HEART AND HEAD.	336	PSALM 65	6
WHEN MY LORDS HEAD IS FILL'D WITH DEW, AND ALL	324	THE NIGHT	32
PAST ORE THY HEAD. MANY LIGHT HEARTS AND WINGS	289	THE TIMBER	3
AND HARMLESS HEAD.	287	THE BIRD	6
AND CROWN'D MY HEAD WITH ROSES.	282	GARLAND	24
WILL NOTHING YIELD BUT THORNS TO WOUND THY HEAD.	296	JESUS WP A	18
WHAT FIRES HATH HE HEAP'D ON HIS HEAD.	297	HERODIAS	5
HE SAW HEAVEN O'R HIS HEAD, AND KNEW FROM WHENCE	196	CORRUPTION	5
LORD JESU. THOU DIDST BOW THY BLESSED HEAD	191	THE MATCH	31
AGE MADE THEM REV'REND, AND A SNOWIE HEAD	156	ISAACS M.	69
MY GLORIOUS HEAD	156	BRT. CHRCH	3
I SHOULD ROVE IN, AND REST MY HEAD	153	THE SEARCH	71
THAT SHUTS, AND HANGS THE HEAD	183	THRS A TYE	8
COME MY HEART. COME MY HEAD	164	THE CALL	1
HER WOMBE, HER BOSOME, AND HER HEAD	168	VNTY SPRIT	11
THY OWN BRIGHT SELF OVER EACH HEAD	349	L'ENVOY	10
I CANNOT FINDE, BUT WHERE THY HEAD	342	OBSEQUIES	27
HEADLONG			
AS WATERS HERE, HEADLONG AND LOOSE	240	MISERY	9
THE PULLEYS UNTO HEADLONG MAN, TIMES BOWER	2	SON-DAYES	9
HEADS			
WHISPER'D OBEDIENCE, AND THEIR HEADS INCLIN'D.	229	LAW + GOSP	10
THE CANDLE SHINING ON SOME HEADS	265	INTRO. 2	14
HIS SECRET ON THEIR HEADS.	279	THE STARRE	28
OF CLOVEN TONGUES THEIR HEADS ALL BRUSH'D	272	WHT SUNDAY	7
HIS CANDLE SHINES UPON THEIR HEADS.	272	WHT SUNDAY	16
CAN THEY THEIR HEADS LIFT, AND EXPECT	186	NO DO THEY	3
OR IS'T SO, AS SOME GREEN HEADS SAY	149	RELIGION	25
SOME RISE TO SEEK THEE, AND WITH HEADS	187	NO DO THEY	25
THOSE BLASTS, WHICH O'R OUR HEADS HERE STRAY	298	JESUS WP B	18
LIFT UP YOUR HEADS AND LEAVE YOUR MOANS.	294	PALM-SUNDY	14
AND GIRDS THEIR ROCKY HEADS THIS DAY.	336	PSALM 65	22
WISE HEADS SHALL USE	338	THE THRONE	9
BOTH SUN AND STARS WOULD HIDE THEIR HEADS.	309	THE SEED	31
HEAL			
DOST STILL RENEW, AND PURGE AND HEAL.	333	AGREEMENT	56
BY TURNS, AND TIMELY, AND SO HEAL	293	THE JEWS	48
O HEAR, AND HEAL THY SERVANT. LORD STRIKE DEAD	185	PASSION	14
THE CHILDREN CHASE THE MOTHER, AND WOULD HEAL	237	CONSTLATN	39
HEAL'D			
HEAL'D BY THE SHOWERS FROM HIGH.	285	PSALM 104	40
HEALE			
HEALE THEN THESE WATERS, LORD, OR BRING THY FLOCK	150	RELIGION	49
HEALING			
DID SADLY NOTE HIS HEALING RAYES	292	THE JEWS	23
O HEALING TEARS. THE TEARS OF LOVE	298	JESUS WP B	10
THY LONG EXPECTED HEALING WINGS COULD SEE	323	THE NIGHT	9
BUT WE A HEALING SUN BY DAY AND NIGHT	331	JACOBS PLW	49
THINE ARE THE PRESENT HEALING LEAVES	332	AGREEMENT	20
THY LEAVES ARE HEALING WINGS HE SPREADS.	333	AGREEMENT	36
OF HEALING SWEETS THY SELF DOST POWR	214	MISERY	50
AND WITH HIS HEALING BLOOD ANCINT THINE EYES	217	EASTER-DAY	14
THIS HEALING PEACE	341	THE FEAST	56
HEALINGS			
HEALINGS, AND CUTS	219	HOLY COMM.	14
HEALTH			
THY SICK ACCESSIONS INTO SETLED HEALTH	221	AFFLICTION	3
BOTH GROWTH, AND POWER, CHECKING THE HEALTH	206	REPENTANCE	6
SLIGHTING THAT HEALTH THOU GAV'ST, WHEN HE WAS SICK	230	LAW + GOSP	23
AND HEALTH OF CONSCIENCE IT IS TO BE HAD.	327	RIGHTSNESS	36
FROM SICKNESSE, GIVE MY SPIRIT HEALTH.	294	BEGGING B	24
WHERE LIGHT, JOY, HEALTH AND PERFECT PEACE	319	THE ASS	62
THREE THINGS I'DE HAVE, MY SOLLES CHIEF HEALTH	148	DAY OF JDG	39
THAT BRINGS HEALTH IN THE END	147	DAY OF JDG	36
HEALTHY			
O HOLY, HAPPY, HEALTHY HEAVEN	312	FAIR+YONG	23
HEAP			
A HEAP OF ASHES, WHERE SOME SEO	151	THE SEARCH	17
A HEAP OF SAND.	179	CHRCH-SVC	11
A SPEECHLESSE HEAP, AND IN THE MIDST MY HEART	201	THE CHECK	3
THE FEARFULL MISER ON A HEAP OF RUST	232	THE WORLD	31
MAN THROUGH HIS HEAP OF DARK DAYS, AND THE RICH	2	SON-DAYES	7
HEAP'D			
WHAT FIRES HATH HE HEAP'D ON HIS HEAD.	297	HERODIAS	5
HEAPE			
O KNIT ME, THAT AM CRUMPLED DUST. THE HEAPE	160	DSTROCTION	1
HEAPS			
WITH BAD, OR WITH NEGLECT, AND HEAPS NOT WRATH	328	RIGHTSNESS	51
HEAR			
O MY GOD, HEAR MY CRY.	329	ANGUISH	19
WHEN SHALL WE HEAR THAT GLORICUS VOICE	335	JUDGEMENT	17
AND HEAR MY HEARTS LAST PRIVATE THROWS.	334	AGREEMENT	66
WHEN THOU DIDST HEAR THE WEEPING LAD.	293	BEGGING B	12
WHOSE HEAVY NOTES MAKE ALL THAT HEAR THEM, SAD.	288	THE BIRD	26
SO HEAR THAT THOU MUST OPEN. OPEN TO	283	LOVE-SICK	17
SO BEAT FOR THEE, TILL THOU IN MERCY HEAR	283	LOVE-SICK	16
SAITH HOLY JOHN, THEN LET HIM HEAR.	316	MEN OF WAR	2
THEY HEAR, SEE, SPEAK	313	THE STONE	22

		PAGE	TITLE	LINE
HEAR	**(CON'T)**			
PEACH, PEACE. I BLUSH TC HEAR THEE. WHEN THOU ART	• •	201	THE CHECK	1
DID HEAR THEM YELL	• • • • • •	188	RELAPSE	4
O HEAR, AND HEAL THY SERVANT. LCRD STRIKE DEAD	• •	185	PASSION	14
O THAT MAN CULD DO SO. THAT HE WOULD HEAR	• •	223	TEMPEST	17
O HEAR. YET NCT MY TEARS ALCNE	• • • •	214	ADMISSION	29
HEAR NOT A FLOUD	• • •	214	ADMISSION	30
WITHIN THCSE DOORS (MY DOCRS) COST HEAR. I WILL.	• •	226	RETIREMENT	55
O HEAR MY GOD. HEAR HIM, WHOSE BLOUD	• •	242	MISERY	105
O HEAR MY GOD. HEAR HIM, WHOSE BLOUD	• •	242	MISERY	105
I SEE THEM, HEAR THEM, MARK THEIR HASTE, AND MOVE	• •	268	ASCN–DAY A	31
AND SCNGS I HEAR. O QUICKNING SHOWERS	• • •	340	THE FEAST	51
HEARD				
WHICH NCNE BUT CHILDREN HEARD, CR TAUGHT.	• •	207	REPENTANCE	14
AND HEARD THEM HOWL.	• • • • •	188	RELAPSE	8
ME THOUGHT I HEARD ONE SINGING THUS.	• • •	153	THE SEARCH	74
HERE MUSING LONG, I HEARD	• • • •	141	RGNRTN	78
STILL SINGLE HEARD, WHILE THESE AGREE	• •	326	ABELS BLOD	42
THAT HEARD'ST BOTH REED	• • • •	163	MT. OLVS A	15
HEARE				
BUT JACCBS CHILDREN WCULD NOT HEARE.	• •	151	THE SEARCH	32
THEY SHAME THEIR CWNERS, AND THE HEARERS TROUBLE.	• •	194	RLS + LSNS	72
HEAREST				
TC THEE, O THOU THAT HEAREST PRAYER.	• • • •	336	PSALM 65	4
HEARS				
BUT HE THAT JUDGETH AS HE HEARS	• • • •	314	THE STONE	28
HEART				
MY GOD, I MEAN MY SINFUL HEART.	• • •	315	DWELLNG–PL	16
GIVE ME, MY GCD. A HEART AS MILDE	• • • •	317	MEN OF WAR	45
AND OVER–RUN MY HEART AND HEAD.	• • •	336	PSALM 65	6
COME WHILE MY HEART IS CLEAN AND STEDDY.	• •	339	THE FEAST	3
OF HIS VOW'D HEART, WHOM THOU HAST KEPT	• •	326	ABELS BLOD	28
SUBMIT MY WILDE HEART, AND RESTRAIN MY HANDS.	• •	321	HIDDN TRSR	30
WITH MY FOUL HEART THY HOLY FEET.	• • •	328	ANGUISH	4
WHICH THROUGH THE EYES POURS CUT THE HEART	• •	328	ANGUISH	10
HIS HEART AND TONGUE IN PRAYERS FOR HIS FOES.	• •	328	RIGHTSNESS	39
WHO HATH THE UPRIGHT HEART, THE SINGLE EYE	• •	327	RIGHTSNESS	9
BY HIS BREATH WHOM MY DEAD HEART HEAVES.	• •	332	AGREEMENT	22
AND THE MEEK HEART, NCT IN A MCUNT, NOR AT	• •	330	JACOBS PLW	25
A HEART IS THAT DREAD PLACE, THAT AWFUL CELL	• •	330	JACOBS PLW	27
REFINING FIRE, O THEN REFINE MY HEART	• •	283	LOVE–SICK	13
MY FOUL, FOUL HEART. THCU ART IMMCRTALL HEAT	• •	283	LOVE–SICK	14
TC MANS HEART STRENGTH AND MIRTH.	• •	285	PSALM 104	44
THY LITTLE HEART IN EARLY HYMNS DOTH SING	• •	288	THE BIRD	8
DC NOT DESPISE A LOVE–SICK HEART.	• •	294	BEGGING B	14
REPEATED SIGHS THY KINDE HEART PAIN	• •	298	JESUS WP B	4
MADE THINE EYES MELT, AND THY HEART HEAVE.	• •	299	JESUS WP B	33
(PITY WHICH OVERFLOWS THY HEART)	• • •	299	JESUS WP B	39
O THAT I HAD DEEP CUT IN MY HARD HEART	• •	198	SCRIPTURES	9
MY HEART, AND THEE PLANTED IN IT.	• • •	191	THE MATCH	30
HERE I JOIN HANDS, AND THRUST MY STUBBORN HEART	• •	190	THE MATCH	7
TC ALL THAT SEEK THEE, BEAR AN CPEN HEART.	• •	193	RLS + LSNS	55
YET KEEP THOSE CARES WITHOUT THEE, LET THE HEART	• •	192	RLS + LSNS	35
A SPEECHLESSE HEAP, AND IN THE MIDST MY HEART	• •	201	THE CHECK	3
THOU GOTST MY HEART, AND THOUGH HERE TOST	• •	202	DSRDR + FR	6
AWAKE, GLAD HEART. GET UP, AND SING	• • •	199	NTVTY 1	1
FIT RCOMES FOR THEE. CR THAT MY HEART	• • •	199	NTVTY 1	20
MY HEART, MY VERSE.	• • • • •	204	DSRDR + FR	60
A LIVING FAITH, A HEART OF FLESH	• • •	148	DAY OF JOG	41
O'RE MY HARD HEART, THAT'S BOUND UP, AND ASLEEP	• •	160	THE SHOWRE	15
COME MY HEART. COME MY HEAD	• • •	164	THE CALL	1
DID TEARE THY HEART.	• • • • •	185	PASSION	11
MY HEART, OR EYE	• • • • •	186	PASSION	54
AND IN THE HEART OF EARTH, AND NIGHT	• •	179	SILENCE	31
BUT A HARD, STONIE HEART.	• • • •	179	CHRCH–SVC	8
OF THIS POOR, SINFULL FRAME PURE HEART.	• •	182	CHRFLNESS	19
AND THEN BESIEGE THE HEART.	• • • •	183	THRS A TYE	20
WHOSE SPRING IS IN MY SAVICURS HEART.	• •	208	REPENTANCE	56
THE STONES MUCH SCFTER THAN MY HEART	• •	207	REPENTANCE	36
O GIVE ME THEN A THANKFLL HEART. A HEART	• •	213	ADMISSION	25
O GIVE ME THEN A THANKFUL HEART. A HEART	• •	213	ADMISSION	25
THOU, WHOSE SAD HEART, AND WEEPING HEAD LYES LCW	• •	217	EASTER–DAY	1
MY FRCZEN HEART, AND WITH THY SECRET KEY	• •	216	DRESSING	4
PAST THCUGHT CF HEART	• • • •	215	PRAISE	34
HID IN THESE LOW THINGS SNARES TC GAIN HIS HEART	• •	223	TEMPEST	23
CAN TELL THEE WHERE A HEART IS BROKEN.	• •	266	INTRO. 2	32
FELL CN MY HEART, THOSE MADE IT BUD	• •	264	INTRO. 1	6
TC REDUCE A STUBBCRN HEART	• • •	249	BEGGING A	14
THIS IS THE HEART HE CRAVES, AND WHO SO WILL	• •	279	THE STARRE	29
OPEN MY RCCKIE HEART, AND FIL	• • •	242	MISERY	101
THUS WILDED BY A PEEVISH HEART	• • •	214	MISERY	81
O'R–RAN MY HEART, AND SPIRITED MY BLOUD	• •	244	MT. OLV. B	8
ME DOWN TC BREATH, AND CASTING IN MY HEART	• •	233	MUTINIE	2
SC TWIST THEM IN MY HEART, THAT EVER THERE	• •	230	LAW + GOSP	29
FEED CN THOSE VOMITS CF MY HEART.	• •	240	MISERY	20
ACCRES DEAD DUST, SETS HEART CN CCRNE AND GRASS	• •	236	CONSTLATN	19
WITH SOME GLAC MESSAGE FRCM HIS HEART	• •	340	THE FEAST	27
IN HIS BLEST HEART	• • • • •	340	THE FEAST	32
INCLINE EACH HARD HEART TC DO GCOD	• •	350	L'ENVOY	45
AND THOU SO LCNG SEIZ'D OF MY HEART.	• •	348	HOLY BIBLE	2

		PAGE	TITLE	LINE
HEARTS	**(CON'T)**			
THEREFORE WRITE IN THEIR HEARTS THY LAW	. . . .	351	L'ENVOY	53
SETTLE, AND FIX OUR HEARTS, THAT WE MAY MOVE	. . .	237	CONSTLATN	53
THY PEOPLES HEARTS, WHEN ALL THY SEEDS WERE RICH	. .	229	LAW + GOSP	4
AND HEARTS, WHOSE PULSE BEATS STILL FOR LIGHT	. . .	277	COCK-CRWNG	32
AND LIFE TOO, AND MY HEARTS DELIGHT.	. . . .	265	INTRO. 2	18
BUT OUR HEARTS DEAD AND SINFUL COLD.	. . .	274	WHT SUNDAY	52
BUT HEARTS ARE NOT SO KIND. FALSE, SHORT DELIGHTS	. .	183	THRS A TYE	13
THE SPIRITS DUTY, TRUE HEARTS SPREAD, AND HEAVE	. .	191	RLS + LSNS	3
LOOSE, PARCELL'D HEARTS WIL FREEZE. THE SUN	. . .	189	RESOLVE	13
NEW FLAMES, BESIDES WHERE THESE LODGE VAIN HEARTS MOURN	.	196	RLS + LSNS	131
(THOUGH PURCHAS'D WITH THY HEARTS DEAR TREASURE)	. .	299	JESUS WP B	28
THIS LAND, THOUGH WITH THY HEARTS BLEST EXTRACT FED	.	296	JESUS WP A	17
ON THEIR DEAD HEARTS, BUT (O MY FEARS)	. . . .	296	JESUS WP A	11
FROM YOUR DARK HEARTS THIS VEIL REMOVE.	. . . .	292	THE JEWS	37
YOUR STONY HEARTS DESPISED LOVE	. . . . .	293	THE JEWS	43
PAST ORE THY HEAD. MANY LIGHT HEARTS AND WINGS	. .	289	THE TIMBER	3
YOUR HEARTS SHALL THAW. WHEN ANGELS HERE	. . .	291	THE JEWS	4
FROM PRIVATE AND SELECTED HEARTS DID SPRING	. . .	330	JACOBS PLW	12
AND HEAR MY HEARTS LAST PRIVATE THROWS.	. . .	334	AGREEMENT	66
HELL AND ALL HEARTS STARK NAKED LYES.	. . .	314	THE STONE	27
WILL PROVE THEIR HEARTS MORE STIFF AND TUFF.	. . .	314	THE STONE	51
WITH IDLE HEARTS AND BUSIE LOCKS	. . . .	303	ORNAMENT	10
HEARTY				
ONE HEARTY TEAR.	. . . .	186	PASSION	49
HEAT				
CAN HEAT ROCKS.	. . . .	189	RESOLVE	16
(WHICH WAK'D BY HEAT, AND BEAMS, MAKES UP	. . .	203	DSRDR + FR	32
THY LIGHT, IS CHARITY, THY HEAT, IS ZEALE.	. . .	158	THE LAMPE	11
FROM THE FIERCE JEW, AND HEROES HEAT	. . .	152	THE SEARCH	56
WHERE ALL THE LAND WITH SCORCHING HEAT IS CURST.	. .	290	THE TIMBER	46
MY FOUL, FOUL HEART. THOU ART IMMORTALL HEAT	. .	283	LOVE-SICK	14
HEAT MOTION GIVES. THEN WARM IT, TILL IT BEAT	. .	283	LOVE-SICK	15
O THOU IMMORTALL LIGHT AND HEAT.	. . . .	277	COCK-CRWNG	19
THIS LATE, LONG HEAT MAY HIS INSTRUCTION BE	. .	222	TEMPEST	1
THE COLD BY NIGHT, THE HEAT BY DAY	. . . .	220	PSALM 121	11
AND HEAT OF THINE. THAT LITTLE GATE	. . . .	207	REPENTANCE	7
LIGHT, MOTION, HEAT	. . . . . .	211	FAITH	34
HEATE				
OF THUNDERS IN THAT HEATE	. . . . . .	147	DAY OF JDG	10
HEATHENS				
WHEN THE PROUD WATERS RAGE. WHEN HEATHENS RULE	. .	330	JACOBS PLW	29
HEAV'D				
NOR WAS HEAV'D COLD UNTO HIM, FOR EACH DAY	. .	197	CORRUPTION	21
HEAV'N				
OF SPIRITS, HEAV'N EXTRACTED LYES IN THEE.	. .	197	SCRIPTURES	2
DASH NOT THY FRIEND, NOR HEAV'N, O SMOTHER	. .	194	RLS + LSNS	69
IN HEAV'N, HAIL, THUNDER, RAIN-BOWS, SNOW, AND ICE	.	194	RLS + LSNS	93
HOW KIND IS HEAV'N TO MAN. IF HERE	. . .	200	NTVTY 2	1
THEN JOURNEY ON, AND HAVE AN EYE TO HEAV'N.	. .	192	RLS + LSNS	24
TO HEAVEN, OR EARTH BELOW	. . . . .	146	RSRCTN +IM	58
LIFE LOCKT IN DEATH, HEAV'N IN A SHELL.	. .	164	INCARNATN	12
AH. GO. TH'ART WEAK, AND SLEEPIE. HEAV'N	. .	178	EVNG-WTCH	11
OF PAST DAYS, WHERE SAD HEAV'N DID SHED	. . .	309	THE SEED	53
A TASTE OF HEAV'N ON EARTH, THE PLEDGE, AND CUE	. .	2	SON-DAYES	23
AND INTIMATE WITH HEAV'N, AS LIGHT.	. . .	269	ASCSN-HYMN	24
LIKE HEAV'N, ALL BRIGHT.	. . . .	270	ASCSN-HYMN	34
WHEN HEAV'N ABOVE THEM SHIN'D LIKE MOLTEN GLASS	.	268	ASCN-DAY A	45
THE DOWN-RIGHT EPICURE PLAC'D HEAV'N IN SENSE	. .	232	THE WORLD	38
BUT SELDOM DOTH MAKE HEAV'N HIS GLASS.	. . .	236	CONSTLATN	20
THIS GROWTH AND STRETCH FOR HEAV'N.	. . .	243	THE SAP	6
LIES SUCH A HEAV'N OF BLISS	. . . .	243	THE SAP	28
HEAV'ND				
HE HEAV'ND THEIR WALKS, AND WITH HIS EYES	. .	152	THE SEARCH	61
HEAV'NS				
HEAV'NS RICH EXPENCE	. . . . . .	144	RSRCTN +IM	12
WHOSE ECCHO IS HEAV'NS BLISSE.	. . . .	177	MRNG-WTCH	22
THY HEAV'NS (SOME SAY)	. . . . .	172	MIDNIGHT	17
AND HEAV'NS GATE OPENS, WHEN THIS WORLDS IS SHUT.	.	192	RLS + LSNS	12
AND LIVE, WHO DOTH NOT THUS, HATH LOST HEAV'NS WAY.	.	196	RLS + LSNS	142
HEAV'NS SECRET SOLITUDE, THOSE FAIR ABODES	.	327	RIGHTSNESS	6
AND THE HIGH, GLORIOUS HEAV'NS THY MIGHTY HAND	.	284	PSALM 104	6
CHAMBERS OF RAIN, WHERE HEAV'NS LARGE BOTTLES LIE	.	285	PSALM 104	38
HEAVE				
MADE THINE EYES MELT, AND THY HEART HEAVE.	. .	299	JESUS WP B	33
THE SPIRITS DUTY, TRUE HEARTS SPREAD, AND HEAVE	. .	191	RLS + LSNS	3
AND NOW (ETERNAL JESUS) THOU DOST HEAVE	. .	268	ASCN-DAY A	55
WHILE THY BLOOD WASH'D ME WHITE AS HEAVEN.	. .	265	INTRO. 2	28
IF THESE BE FAIR, O WHAT IS HEAVEN.	. . .	276	PROFFER	48
BRINGS TO, AND COMES FROM HEAVEN.	. . .	244	THE SAP	50
HEAVEN ONCE A WEEK.	. . . . .	205	SON-DAYES	2
HEAVEN HERE, MAN ON THOSE HILLS OF MYRRH, AND FLOWRES.	.	2	SON-DAYES	14
(UNSEEN) BOTH HEAVEN, AND EARTH.	. . .	220	PSALM 121	4
ALL THINGS HERE SHEW HIM HEAVEN, WATERS THAT FALL	.	223	TEMPEST	25
HEAVEN HATH LESS BEAUTY THAN THE DUST HE SPIES	.	224	TEMPEST	47
IN THY WORD, AS IF IN HEAVEN	. . .	214	PRAISE	21
'TWIXT HEAVEN, AND US, THE MANNA WAS NOT GOOD	.	192	RLS + LSNS	9
'TWIXT HEAVEN, AND THEE, BLOCK IT NOT WITH DELAYS	.	195	RLS + LSNS	116
HE SAW HEAVEN O'R HIS HEAD, AND KNEW FROM WHENCE	.	196	CORRUPTION	5
I THREATEN HEAVEN, AND FROM MY CELL	. . .	203	DSRDR + FR	16

	PAGE	TITLE	LINE
HEAVEN (CON'T)			
THAT HEAVEN WITHIN HIM MIGHT ABIDE	166	THE CALL	60
FIND HEAVEN, AND THEE.	179	SILENCE	32
AND HEAVEN ITS AZURE DID UNFOLD	140	RGNRTN	52
AND OFFER'D UP SO EARLY UNTO HEAVEN	154	ISAACS M.	6
(O HOW FAMILIAR THEN WAS HEAVEN)	149	RELIGION	14
TOO GROSSE FOR HEAVEN	160	THE SHOWRE	5
HEAVEN WITH A·LAZIE BREATH, BUT FRUITLES THIS	160	THE SHOWRE	8
MAKES HEAVEN AND EARTH	295	PALM-SUNDY	25
IN HEAVEN, ONE GOD IN TRINITIE.	284	TRINITY-SN	3
FROM THE LOW EARTH TO HIGH HEAVEN RISE	326	ABELS BLOD	38
AND BY MEER PLAYING GO TO HEAVEN.	321	CHILDEHOOD	8
THE HOURS TO WHICH HIGH HEAVEN DOTH CHIME.	324	THE NIGHT	30
THEN I IN HEAVEN ALL THE LONG YEAR	324	THE NIGHT	41
O HOLY, HAPPY, HEALTHY HEAVEN	312	FAIR+YONG	23
BRIGHT QUEEN OF HEAVEN. GODS VIRGIN SPOUSE.	302	THE KNOT	1
RETURN TO HEAVEN, FROM WHENCE IT CAME	305	ST MARY MN	54
ARMIES THOU HAST IN HEAVEN, WHICH FIGHT	316	MEN OF WAR	21
WHICH WEARS HEAVEN, LIKE A BRIDAL RING	346	THE QUEER	3
HEAVENS			
WATER (THOUGH BOTH HEAVENS WINDOWS AND THE DEEP	307	RAIN-BOW	27
IF PIOUS GRIEFS HEAVENS JOYS AWAKE	308	THE SEED	15
OR BOW THE HEAVENS. LORD BOW THEM AND DESCEND	283	LOVE-SICK	10
WHEN LIKE A SCROWLE THE HEAVENS SHAL PASSE	147	DAY OF JDG	13
(UNKNOWN TO US) THE HEAVENS WILT BOW	212	DAWNING	26
THEY ARE HEAVENS HUSBANDRY, THE FAMOUS FAN	221	AFFLICTION	19
THE HEAVENS THEMSELVES, THOUGH FAIR AND BRIGHT	208	REPENTANCE	65
HIGH AS THE HEAVENS ABOVE.	271	ALL GONE	14
HEAVES			
MY FIERCE, WILD BLOOD THAT STILL HEAVES, AND INCLINES	190	THE MATCH	4
BY HIS BREATH WHOM MY DEAD HEART HEAVES.	332	AGREEMENT	22
HEAVIER			
BUT PROV'D THE HEAVIER GRAINES	139	RGNRTN	33
HEAVY			
BUT, TH'LAST MORE HEAVY THEN THE NIGHT	141	RGNRTN	68
CUTS THROUGH THE HEAVY MISTS IN HASTE	178	SILENCE	11
THEIR HEAVY STATE	165	THE CALL	25
WHOSE HEAVY NOTES MAKE ALL THAT HEAR THEM, SAD.	288	THE BIRD	26
BUT THOU BENEATH THE SAD AND HEAVY LINE	289	THE TIMBER	9
OF HEAVY SINS, MY HIGH TRANSGRESSIONS	207	REPENTANCE	24
THE HEAVY SUM	233	MUTINIE	4
HEDGES			
HEDGES HAVE EARS, SAID THE OLD SOOTH	313	THE STONE	14
HEED			
BUT LET ME HEED	341	THE FEAST	76
HEEDLESS			
TO THY DARK LAND THESE HEEDLESS GO.	338	DEATH B	11
HEIGHT			
BUT AT THE HEIGHT OF THIS CAREIRE	282	GARLAND	25
THEIR ARTS AND FORCE ARE BUILT UNTO THE HEIGHT	234	MUTINIE	16
HER STATELY PILES WITH ALL THEIR HEIGHT AND PRIDE	238	SHEPHEARDS	19
WHOSE HEIGHT ABOVE ALL AGES SHINES	273	WHT SUNDAY	46
WAS A TRANSLATION OF SUCH HEIGHT	164	INCARNATN	7
OF STATELY HEIGHT, WHOSE BRANCHES MET	140	RGNRTN	44
AND AFTER ALL MY HEIGHT OF FLAMES)	203	DSRDR + FR	40
WHOSE RISE, HEIGHT, AND DESCENT IS BUT A SPAN.	195	RLS + LSNS	108
HEIGHTEN			
TO HEIGHTEN THY DEVOTIONS, AND KEEP LOW	194	RLS + LSNS	85
HEIGHTS			
AS THOSE CLEAR HEIGHTS WHICH ABOVE TEMPESTS SHINE.	281	JOY	16
HELD			
MY LOVE-TWIST HELD THEE UP, MY UNSEEN LINK.	225	RETIREMENT	22
WHICH HELD UP NIGHT, AND DAY	147	DAY OF JDG	16
HE HELD, I CHANC'D TO LOOK	309	THE SEED	51
HELL			
HELL AND ALL HEARTS STARK NAKED LYES.	314	THE STONE	27
AND HIGH TEMPTATIONS OF HELL.	152	THE SEARCH	58
ALMOST TO HELL	188	RELAPSE	2
YEA, 'TIS A DEATH PARTAKES OF HELL.	277	COCK-CRWNG	26
THE FLYES OF HELL	275	PROFFER	14
HELL-FIRE			
OR CHOOSE HELL-FIRE AND BRIMSTONE STREAMS	321	CHILDEHOOD	11
HELP			
AND PRIVATE TAPERS WILL BUT HELP TO STRAY	321	HIDDN TRSR	27
SHOULD HELP TO SPOIL) THOU CANST RESTORE	299	JESUS WP B	36
HE IS ALONE MY HELP, AND HOPE	220	PSALM 121	5
HELPS			
THY BOUNTEOUS OPEN HAND HELPS THEM AT NEED	286	PSALM 104	75
HELPS SUCH DARK STRAGLERS TO THEIR SIGHT.	305	ST MARY MN	60
HERALDRIE			
IN HERALDRIE	226	RETIREMENT	46
HERB			
WHEN TH' HERB HE TREADS KNOWS MUCH, MUCH MORE.	236	CONSTLATN	28
NOR ANY HERB OUT-DUTY ME.	281	THE FAVOUR	10
THOU CANST NOT MISSE HIS PRAISE, EACH TREE, HERB, FLOWRE	194	RLS + LSNS	95
AND HERB PARTAKES, WHERE HAVING STOOD AWHILE	155	ISAACS M.	57
OR SOME POOR HIGH-WAY HERB, OR SPRING	187	ND DO THEY	13
HERBS			
HERBS SLEEP UNTO THE EAST, AND SOME FOWLES THENCE	183	THRS A TYE	11
SOME KINDE HERBS HERE, THOUGH LOW AND FAR	281	THE FAVOUR	7

		PAGE	TITLE	LINE
HERBS	(CON'T)			
THAT GOD IS TRUE, AS HERBS UNSEEN	. . . . . .	279	THE STARRE	31
QUIT THEIR FIRST BED AND MOUNT. TREES, HERBS, FLOWRES, ALL		223	TEMPEST	27
THE DEW THY HERBS DRINK UP BY NIGHT	. . . . .	207	REPENTANCE	39
SET WITH GREEN HERBS, GLAD HOPES AND BRAVE.	. . .	310	THE SEED	72
GRASS FOR THE CATTEL, AND HERBS FOR MANS USE	. . .	285	PSALM 104	41
AND HERBS WHICH ON DRY HILLS DO SPRING	. . . .	301	PROVIDENCE	26
TREES, FLOWERS AND HERBS. BIRDS, BEASTS AND STONES	. .	294	PALM-SUNDY	11
WHERE TREES AND HERBS DID WATCH AND PEEP	. . . .	323	THE NIGHT	23
HEREAFTER				
THAT HEREAFTER, WHEN I LOOK	. . . . . .	249	BEGGING A	9
AND IF HEREAFTER YOUTH, OR FOLLY THWART	. . . .	190	THE MATCH	10
HERETOFORE				
I KNEW THERE HERETOFORE.	. . . . . .	246	I WALKT	7
HERMIT-WELLS				
AND HERMIT-WELLS	. . . .	281	JOY	25
HERODS				
FROM THE FIERCE JEW, AND HERODS HEAT	. . . .	152	THE SEARCH	56
HEW'D				
HER CEDAR, FIRR, HEW'D STONES AND GOLD WERE ALL	. .	238	SHEPHEARDS	23
HEYNOUS				
LORD, I CONFESSE THE HEYNOUS SCORE	. . . .	208	REPENTANCE	57
MOST HEYNOUS SINS AND NUMBERLESS.	. . . .	333	AGREEMENT	45
HID				
HID IN THESE LOW THINGS SNARES TO GAIN HIS HEART	. .	223	TEMPEST	23
AND MY LIFE HID IN THY DEATH	. . . . .	215	PRAISE	31
BY SOME HID SENSE THEIR MAKER GAVE	. . . .	246	MAN	25
THIS IS THE LIFE WHICH HID ABOVE WITH CHRIST	. .	280	PALM-TREE	13
AND BY THOSE HID ASCENTS CLIMB TO THAT DAY	. .	248	I WALKT	52
THERE, HID IN THEE, SHEW ME HIS LIFE AGAIN	. .	248	I WALKT	61
HID UNDER GROUND SURVIVES THE FALL.	. . . .	203	DSRDR + FR	29
HIDDEN				
IS STIL'D THEIR STARRE, THE STONE, AND HIDDEN FOOD.	.	192	RLS + LSNS	28
IN THEE THE HIDDEN STONE, THE MANNA LIES	. . .	198	SCRIPTURES	5
BUT IN HER LONG, AND HIDDEN COURSE	. . . .	150	RELIGION	33
IN GOD, DOTH ALWAYS (HIDDEN) MULTIPLY	. . .	280	PALM-TREE	14
PATHS THAT ARE HIDDEN FROM THE VULTURS EYES	. .	320	HIDDN TRSR	12
WITH HIDDEN TREASURES THAT MAKE TRULY RICH.	. .	327	RIGHTSNESS	12
HIDE				
WHEN THOU DOEST HIDE THY FACE (THY FACE WHICH KEEPS	.	287	PSALM 104	77
BOTH SUN AND STARS WOULD HIDE THEIR HEADS.	. .	309	THE SEED	31
BUT HIDE, OR TURN THY FACE	. . . . .	213	ADMISSION	18
THE SUN NOW STOOPS, AND HASTS HIS BEAMS TO HIDE	.	195	RLS + LSNS	105
THAT CURTAIN'D GRAVE, THOUGH SLEEP, LIKE ASHES, HIDE	.	177	MRNG-WTCH	32
HIDEOUS				
THIS HIDEOUS PATH	. . . .	188	RELAPSE	10
THE HIDEOUS NIGHT	. . . . . .	201	THE CHECK	14
THERE ALL THEIR FURY, FOME AND HIDEOUS SOUND	. .	285	PSALM 104	27
HIDING				
BY HIDING DOTH PRESERVE	. . . . . .	310	THE SEED	76
HIDST				
AS WITH A VAIL THOU HIDST IT, THY FLOODS PLAID	. .	285	PSALM 104	19
HIGH				
HEAL'D BY THE SHOWERS FROM HIGH.	. . . .	285	PSALM 104	40
TO THE WILDE GOATS THE HIGH HILLS SERVE FOR FOLDS	.	286	PSALM 104	49
AND THE HIGH, GLORIOUS HEAV'NS THY MIGHTY HAND	.	284	PSALM 104	6
HARK, HOW THE CHILDREN SHRIL AND HIGH	. . .	295	PALM-SUNDY	18
IS IN THESE JOYS AN HIGH PARTAKER	. . . .	295	PALM-SUNDY	28
TILL THE DAY-SPRING BREAKS FORTH AGAIN FROM HIGH.	.	288	THE BIRD	32
BRED IN THY GROWTH BETWIXT HIGH WINDS AND THEE	.	289	THE TIMBER	14
WHERE THROUGH THICK PANGS, HIGH AGONIES	. . .	310	THE SEED	65
ARE ALL TOO HIGH FOR A LOW CELL.	. . . .	309	THE SEED	34
BECKEN'D BY THEE, THOUGH HIGH AND FAR	. . .	315	DWELLNG-PL	8
THOUGH HIGH AND HAUGHTY MUST	. . . . .	328	RIGHTSNESS	46
THE HOURS TO WHICH HIGH HEAVEN DOTH CHIME.	. .	324	THE NIGHT	30
FROM THE LOW EARTH TO HIGH HEAVEN RISE	. . .	326	ABELS BLOD	38
INQUIRE HOW LONG. OF THE MOST HIGH.	. . .	326	ABELS BLOD	22
AND GRONE ON HIGH	. . . . . .	185	PASSION	40
AND HIGH TEMPTATIONS OF HELL.	. . . .	152	THE SEARCH	58
ABOVE THE STARS, A TRACK UNKNOWN, AND HIGH	. .	155	ISAACS M.	50
OF HEAVY SINS, MY HIGH TRANSGRESSIONS	. . .	207	REPENTANCE	24
AS TH' HIGH, AND TALL.	. . . . . .	210	FAITH	4
SURE, HOLY HOPES, HIGH JOYS AND QUICKNING FLIGHTS	.	267	ASCN-DAY A	2
O HOLY HOPE. AND HIGH HUMILITY	. . . .	271	ALL GONE	13
HIGH AS THE HEAVENS ABOVE.	. . . . .	271	ALL GONE	14
TO WHAT'S ALREADY GROWN TOO HIGH	. . . .	240	MISERY	18
THY CHOSEN FLOCK, LIKE LEAFS IN A HIGH WIND	.	229	LAW + GOSP	9
O WHAT HIGH JOYS	. . . . . .	340	THE FEAST	49
WHICH MAKES THE HIGH TRANSCENDENT BLISS	. .	346	THE QUEER	15
HIGH-NOON				
HIGH-NOON THUS PAST, THY TIME DECAYS, PROVIDE	. .	195	RLS + LSNS	103
HIGH-PRIEST				
MAN IS THEIR HIGH-PRIEST, AND SHOULD RISE	. .	199	NTVTY 1	11
THOU HOLY, HARMLESS, UNDEFIL'D HIGH-PRIEST.	. .	216	DRESSING	9
HIGH-SPRING				
IT WAS HIGH-SPRING, AND ALL THE WAY	. . . .	139	RGNRTN	12
HIGH-WAY				
EACH CAKE, AND HIGH-WAY KNEW THEM	. . . .	197	CORRUPTION	26
OR SOME POOR HIGH-WAY HERB, OR SPRING	. . .	187	NO DO THEY	13
OR SECRET GROVES, KEEP THE HIGH-WAY.	. . .	294	PALM-SUNDY	10

		PAGE	TITLE	LINE
HIGHEST				
THY LOVE CLAIMS HIGHEST THANKS, MY SIN	. . . .	329	TEARS	13
BUT WHAT IS HIGHEST SIN AND SHAME	. . . . .	335	JUDGEMENT	33
AND OUR BEST NOTE AND HIGHEST EASE	. . . . .	273	WHT SUNDAY	42
AND HIGHEST GOOD IS BLEST.	. . . . .	278	THE STARRE	8
HIL				
WHOSE SPRING IS ON THAT HIL WHERE YOU DO GROW	. . .	235	CONSTLATN	3
FROM THAT HIL TO THIS VALE	. . . . .	243	THE SAP	20
THERE IS BEYOND THE STARS AN HIL OF MYRRH	. . .	243	THE SAP	11
O SEND ME FROM THY HOLY HIL	. . . . .	242	MISERY	97
HILL				
OR ELSE REMOVE ME HENCE UNTO THAT HILL	. . .	271	ALL GONE	39
OR THOSE FAINT BEAMS IN WHICH THIS HILL IS DREST	. .	270	ALL GONE	7
THEY SHALL FIND THOU ART THEIR HILL	. . . .	163	MT. OLVS A	18
AND SINNE, THIS HILL	. . . . .	163	MT. OLVS A	31
SWEETE, SACRED HILL. ON WHOSE FAIR BROW	. . .	162	MT. OLVS A	1
I CLIMB'D THE HILL, PERUS'D THE CROSSE	. . .	152	THE SEARCH	41
HILLS				
DOTH ON THOSE HILLS OF MIRRHE, AND INCENSE WATCH.	.	156	BRT. CHRCH	4
FAREWELL YOU EVERLASTING HILLS. I'M CAST	. .	158	MANS FALL	1
WITH ECCHOES BEATEN FROM TH' ETERNALL HILLS.	. .	168	VNTY SPRIT	18
O'RE DARK HILLS, SWIFT STREAMES, AND STEEEP WAYS	.	174	JOY OF LIF	19
HEAVEN HERE, MAN ON THOSE HILLS OF MYRRH, AND FLOWRES.	.	2	SON-DAYES	14
AND HILLS FULL OF SPRINGING PRIDE	. . . .	337	PSALM 65	43
AND HERBS WHICH ON DRY HILLS DO SPRING	. . .	301	PROVIDENCE	26
SO HILLS AND VALLEYS INTO SINGING BREAK	. . .	288	THE BIRD	13
TO THE WILDE GOATS THE HIGH HILLS SERVE FOR FOLDS	.	286	PSALM 104	49
WHICH RUN FROM HILLS TO VALLEYS, AND IMPROVE	. .	285	PSALM 104	31
DOEST WATER THE PARCH'D HILLS, WHOSE BREACHES CLOSE	.	285	PSALM 104	39
IS MOV'D AND TREMBLES, THE HILLS MELT AND SMOKE	.	287	PSALM 104	86
HILS				
UP TO THOSE BRIGHT, AND GLADSOME HILS	. . .	220	PSALM 121	1
AND CROWN DRY HILS WITH WELLS AND FLOWERS.	. .	341	THE FEAST	54
HINDRED				
WILL THY FREE MERCIES HINDRED BE.	. . . .	334	AGREEMENT	70
HIRE				
LET NOT THY STARS FOR BALAAMS HIRE	. . . .	274	WHT SUNDAY	63
INDEED I HAD SOME HERE TO HIRE	. . . . .	264	INTRO. 1	9
HISSE				
WITH THE SAME CURLING FORCE, AND HISSE	. . .	175	THE STORM	7
HISTORIES				
WHOSE HOLY, HAPPY HISTORIES	. . . .	335	JUDGEMENT	24
HIVE				
THOUGH FLED FROM YOU, THEIR SPIRITS HIVE.	. .	339	DEATH B	30
THE HIVE OF BEAMY, LIVING LIGHTS	. . . .	333	AGREEMENT	32
JUST AT HIS MOUTH, THAT THANKLESS HIVE	. . .	300	PROVIDENCE	11
THE POOR BEE IN HER HIVE MUST SWEL.	. . .	309	THE SEED	36
DEDUCTED FROM THE WHOLE, THE COMBS, AND HIVE	. .	2	SON-DAYES	19
WHERE BEES AT NIGHT GET HOME AND HIVE, AND FLOWRS	.	245	MAN	5
LIKE BEES IN STORMS UNTO THEIR HIVE	. . .	343	OBSEQUIES	30
HOARY				
MY DAYS, WHICH ARE AT BEST BUT DULL AND HOARY	. .	271	ALL GONE	11
HOLD				
NO HOLD, NOR SYMPATHIE.	. . . .	278	THE STARRE	16
AND YET SHOULDST THOU LET GO THY HOLD	. .	240	MISERY	7
IF I HOLD FAST AND SLIGHT THE LURE.	. . .	317	MEN OF WAR	40
BUT HIS OWN LIVING WORKS DID MY LORD HOLD	. .	323	THE NIGHT	21
TWO LIFES I HOLD FROM THEE, MY GRACIOUS LORD	.	191	THE MATCH	19
WE MAY BE FED, AND ONE MINDE HOLD.	. . .	350	L'ENVOY	48
HOLDS				
AND STILL THY SOV'RAINTY HOLDS GOOD.	. .	338	DEATH B	4
ABOVE THEM THE COOL MOON HER KNOWN COURSE HOLDS	.	286	PSALM 104	51
STRONG HOLDS SHOULD BELONG TO THEE	. . .	249	BEGGING A	16
HOLE				
AND SEARCH OUT EV'RY HOLE, AND CREEK.	. .	240	MISERY	12
HOLINESS				
BEAUTY AND HOLINESS	. . . .	237	CONSTLATN	58
HOLY				
SWEET, HARMLES LIVES (ON WHOSE HOLY LEISURE	. .	238	SHEPHEARDS	1
BECOME AN HUMBLE, HOLY NATION.	. . . .	237	CONSTLATN	56
HIS HOLY SPIRIT GRIEVES THEREFORE	. . .	240	MISERY	38
O SEND ME FROM THY HOLY HIL	. . . .	242	MISERY	97
ABUSE NOT, SHUN NOT HOLY FIRE	. . . .	266	VAIN WITS	3
SURE, HOLY HOPES, HIGH JOYS AND QUICKNING FLIGHTS	.	267	ASCN-DAY A	2
IN SILENT DROPS STEAL FROM THEIR HOLY EYES	. .	268	ASCN-DAY A	53
PRIVATE AND HOLY TALK FILL ALL THE WAYS.	. .	268	ASCN-DAY A	28
O HOLY HOPE. AND HIGH HUMILITY	. . . .	271	ALL GONE	13
HOW THEN, WITH THEE, CAN MAN BE HOLY	. .	208	REPENTANCE	67
THOU HOLY, HARMLESS, UNDEFIL'D HIGH-PRIEST.	. .	216	DRESSING	9
DISPATCH'D TO HOLY SOULS, SICK WITH DESIRE	. .	284	PSALM 104	14
O HOLY, BLESSED, GLORIOUS THREE	. . . .	284	TRINITY-SN	1
THE ANGEL SHEWD THAT HOLY WELL	. . .	300	PROVIDENCE	3
THE PROVERB'D GRIEFS OF HOLY JOB	. . .	295	PALM-SUNDY	43
O HOLY GROANS. GROANS OF THE DOVE.	. . .	298	JESUS WP B	9
WHOSE HOLY, HAPPY HISTORIES	. . . .	335	JUDGEMENT	24
AND POWER FORCE ON HOLY WRIT	. . . .	335	JUDGEMENT	36
WHO IN THY HOLY TEMPLE DWELLS	. . . .	336	PSALM 65	11
WHO IS CONTENTED, THAT THIS HOLY FLAME	. .	331	JACOBS PLW	38
HIS WHITE AND HOLY TRAIN	. . . .	329	TEARS	2
WITH MY FOUL HEART THY HOLY FEET.	. . .	328	ANGUISH	4

		PAGE	TITLE	LINE
HOLY	(CON'T)			
SAITH HOLY JOHN, THEN LET HIM HEAR.		316	MEN OF WAR	2
TEACH AGE, THE HOLY WAY.		310	THE SEED	64
FAIR AND YONG LIGHT. MY GUIDE TO HOLY		311	FAIR+YONG	1
O HOLY, HAPPY, HEALTHY HEAVEN		312	FAIR+YONG	23
DEAR FRIEND. WHOSE HOLY, EVER-LIVING LINES		190	THE MATCH	1
SHOULD MOVE, THEY MAKE US HOLY, HAPPY, RICH.		192	RLS + LSNS	30
AND HOLY DOVE.		179	CHRCH-SVC	3
A PLENTEOUS WAY (THANKS TO THAT HOLY ONE)		159	MANS FALL	22
AND HOLY LIVES, MERCY MAY HERE		351	L'ENVOY	56
HOLY-DAY				
LET THE JOY'D RODE MAKE HOLY-DAY		294	PALM-SUNDY	8
HOLYNESS				
SURE, HOLYNESS THE MAGNET IS		346	THE QUEER	13
HOME				
AND HAVING BROUGHT ME HOME, DIDST THERE		348	HOLY BIBLE	25
SHALL SEND ME (SWAN-LIKE) SINGING HOME.		299	JESUS WP B	53
RETURNS HOME WITH HIS LOAD.		286	PSALM 104	64
ALAS. MY GOD. TAKE HOME THY SHEEP.		312	FAIR+YONG	51
HOME BY OUR FIRST FAIR PUNISHMENT		312	FAIR+YONG	42
THESE FETCH'D THEE HOME THY BRIDE, AND ALL THE WAY		155	ISAACS M.	27
THOSE WHITE DAYES, DROVE HOME TO THE TENT		151	THE SEARCH	26
NOR HOME DESIR'D.		162	PURSUITE	12
WHEN SHAL THAT TRAVELLER COME HOME		189	RESOLVE	7
HOME WITH THE LIGHT		189	RESOLVE	18
THIS MADE HIM LONG FOR HOME, AS LOATH TO STAY		197	CORRUPTION	17
THY BEAMS HOME WITH THEE. TRIM THY LAMP, BUY OYL		195	RLS + LSNS	110
FLEW HOME UNSTAIN'D BY HIS NEW KIN		209	THE BURIAL	6
AND HOME OF REST.		2	SON-DAYES	20
FAITH BRINGS US HOME.		211	FAITH	40
AND BRINGS MAN HOME, WHEN HE DOTH RANGE		221	AFFLICTION	6
STRIVE UPWARDS STIL, AND POINT HIM THE WAY HOME.		223	TEMPEST	28
DID SHEW ME HOME, AND PUT ME IN THE WAY.		225	RETIREMENT	11
ILL THY BREST WITH HOME. THINK ON THY DREAM.		276	PROFFER	45
ASPIRE FOR HOME. THIS SOLOMON OF OLD		279	PALM-TREE	10
WHO SITS AT HOME TOO BEARS A LOADE		214	MISERY	69
WHERE BEES AT NIGHT GET HOME AND HIVE, AND FLOWRS		245	MAN	5
HE KNOWS HE HATH A HOME, BUT SCARCE KNOWS WHERE		246	MAN	19
TO BRING ALL STRAGLERS HOME		239	SHEPHEARDS	46
AND AUTHOR OF MY FAITH, SO SHEW ME HOME		234	MUTINIE	22
TO BRING ME HOME, THAN THROUGH A WILDERNES		234	MUTINIE	27
BUT WITH THE THOUGHT OF HOME DO PINE.		228	PILGRIMAGE	20
HOMELY				
OFT TO A NARROW, HOMELY ROOM		315	DWELLNG-PL	14
HOMES				
THEY REST AND DREAM HOMES OF THEIR OWN.		228	PILGRIMAGE	8
WHICH IN THE DARKEST NIGHTS POINT TO THEIR HOMES		246	MAN	24
BUT WHAT THEIR OWN HOMES WEAVE		173	CONTENT	8
HOMEWARDS				
STILL HOMEWARDS FLIES		327	RIGHTSNESS	17
HONESTY				
FOR HONESTY IS SAFE, COME WHAT CAN HAP.		193	RLS + LSNS	58
HONEY				
WHICH KILLS THY BEES, AND EATS THY HONEY.		300	PROVIDENCE	12
BUT YOU WOULD HONEY MAKE.		274	PROFFER	7
HONEY-DROPS				
RAIN GENTLY SPENDS HIS HONEY-DROPS, AND POURS		306	RAIN-BOW	11
HONOR				
AND SETS UP LAWS TO PULL HIS HONOR DOWN.		330	JACOBS PLW	20
HONOUR				
HONOUR AND MAJESTY HAVE THEIR ABODE		284	PSALM 104	3
IN IT MY NAME, AND HONOUR BOTH DO DWELL		226	RETIREMENT	38
HOPE				
O HOLY HOPE. AND HIGH HUMILITY		271	ALL GONE	13
HE IS ALONE MY HELP, AND HOPE		220	PSALM 121	5
SO ARE NOW FAITH, HOPE, CHARITY		211	FAITH	35
BUT IN HIS HOPE AND ROCK IS EVER GLAD.		327	RIGHTSNESS	33
WHAT THOU DIDST HOPE FOR AND BELIEVE, WE FINDE		331	JACOBS PLW	51
ART THE WORLDS HOPE, AND BUT THEE, NONE.		336	PSALM 65	16
GLADNESS, AND PEACE, AND HOPE, AND LOVE		348	HOLY BIBLE	27
HOPELES				
'TWAS BUT JUST NOW MY BLEAK LEAVES HOPELES HUNG		198	UNPRFTBLNS	2
HOPES				
AND ON SURE HOPES, THOUGH LONG, DID FEAST.		143	DEATH	22
COMFORTS AND JOYS, AND HOPES EACH HOUR		326	ABELS BLOD	26
WHOSE FRUITFUL DAWN SHEDS HOPES AND LIGHTS.		295	PALM-SUNDY	31
MAY HIS CROWN, LIKE HIS HOPES, BE CLAY		301	PROVIDENCE	35
SET WITH GREEN HERBS, GLAD HOPES AND BRAVE.		310	THE SEED	72
IF JOYES, AND HOPES, AND EARNEST THROWS		277	COCK-CRWNG	31
SURE, HOLY HOPES, HIGH JOYS AND QUICKNING FLIGHTS		267	ASCN-DAY A	2
HOPING				
T' UNITE THOSE PEECES, HOPING TO FIND OUT		168	VNTY SPRIT	26
HORROR				
'TIS DEAD NIGHT ROUND ABOUT. HORROR DOTH CREEPE		157	THE LAMPE	1
HOSANNA				
HOSANNA. HEARK, WHY DOEST THOU STAY.		217	EASTER-DAY	12
HOSANNA CRY		295	PALM-SUNDY	19
HAD NOT THE BABES HOSANNA CRYED		296	JESUS WP A	7
HOST				
THINE HOST OF SPYES		171	MIDNIGHT	3

                                                                    PAGE   TITLE   LINE
HOT
    AND WCRK CN ME NOW COLD, NOW HCT   227   LV + DSPLN   14
HOUR
    I WALKT THE OTHER DAY (TO SPEND MY HOUR)   246   I WALKT   1
    AND FCR THAT HOUR TH'ART MY DELIGHT   214   MISERY   54
    SC WHEN THAT DAY, AND HOUR SHAL COME   212   DAWNING   45
    TRANSPLANTED PARACISE, GODS WALKING HOUR.   2   SON-DAYES   11
    AND BULRUSH FETTERS TEMPER HIS SHORT HOUR.   224   TEMPEST   50
    HCW IS MAN PARCELL'D OUT. HOW EV'RY HOUR   222   TEMPEST   1
    TO WATCH FOR THY APPEARING HOUR.   276   COCK-CRWNG   16
    SHALL MY SHORT HOUR, MY INCH   275   PROFFER   25
    UNTO THAT HOUR   178   SILENCE   14
    EVEN FRCM THAT HOUR   202   DSRDR + FR   5
    BEATS THEM QUITE CFF, AND IN AN HOUR   203   DSRDR + FR   26
    AN HOUR, CR SC, THEN VARY.   187   ND DO THEY   22
    SPEND NOT AN HOUR SO, AS TO WEEP ANOTHER   194   RLS + LSNS   67
    DID WITH INTENTIVE LOOKS WATCH EVERY HOUR   306   RAIN-BOW   7
    COMFORTS AND JOYS, AND HOPES EACH HOUR   326   ABELS BLOD   26
    HE FOUND THEE AT THAT DEAD AND SILENT HOUR.   323   THE NIGHT   14
    AND THE THOUGHTS CF EACH HARMLESS HOUR   321   CHILDEHOOD   5
HOURE
    THY ACCOUNTS THUS MADE, SPEND IN THE GRAVE ONE HCURE   .   195   RLS + LSNS   121
    MY GAZING SOUL WOULD DWELL AN HOURE   169   RETREATE   12
    AND EACH HOURE, ONE.   170   COME, COME   4
    EACH CAY, AND HOURE HE IS ON WING   161   PURSUITE   3
    THAT HOURE, WHICH MUST THY LIFE, AND MINE DISPATCH.   .   157   THE LAMPE   8
    BUT EV'RY HOURE   158   MANS FALL   6
    TO THEE EACH HOURE, BEG AT THY DOOR   230   LAW + GOSP   25
    AND NCTHING CAN, I HOURELY SEE   181   BURIALL   21
HOURES
    TWELVE HUNDRED HOURES, AND NOT A BROW   178   SILENCE   3
    ALL THE LCNG HOURES   176   MRNG-WTCH   3
HOURLY
    FOR, THOUGH WE HOURLY BREATH DECAYS   273   WHT SUNDAY   41
    AND THIS I HOURLY FINDE, FOR THCU   333   AGREEMENT   55
    FOR SIN (LIKE WATER) HOURLY GLICES   350   L'ENVOY   50
HOURS
    FROM THOSE RUDE, BARREN HCURS.   345   THE WREATH   4
    THE HCURS TO WHICH HIGH HEAVEN DOTH CHIME.   324   THE NIGHT   30
    AND SETS, WILL FEW HOURS HENCE BEGIN   292   THE JEWS   29
    WHISPER THEIR HOURS   281   JOY   24
    AND ROUND BENEATH IT, TIME IN HCURS, DAYS, YEARS   .   231   THE WORLD   4
    THAT GUIDES THROUGH ERRING HOURS, AND IN FULL STCRY   .   2   SON-DAYES   22
    OR SHAL THESE EARLY, FRAGRANT HOURS   211   DAWNING   9
    HOW MANY HOURS DO'ST THINK 'TILL DAY.   178   EVNG-WTCH   10
    HE FILS IT. DAYES, AND HOURS ARE BLINDS.   178   EVNG-WTCH   14
    DAWN WITH THE DAY, THERE ARE SET, AWFUL HOURS   .   .   192   RLS + LSNS   8
HOUSE
    SETTLE MY HOUSE, AND SHUT OUT ALL DISTRACTIONS   .   .   191   THE MATCH   28
    NO HOUSE CF STORE   171   COME, COME   22
    AND EMPTY HOUSE   180   BURIALL   9
    AND THE MCRE NOBLE ESSENCE FINCS HIS HOUSE   145   RSRCTN +IM   39
    UNDER A JUNIPER, SCME HCUSE   148   RELIGION   5
    MACE CPEN HOUSE.   210   FAITH   8
    KEEPING CLOSE HOUSE   225   RETIREMENT   2
    I HAVE A HOUSE AS WELL   226   RETIREMENT   36
    THE PATH UNTO THE HOUSE OF LIGHT.   276   COCK-CRWNG   10
    HATH GOT AN HCUSE WHERE MANY MANSIONS ARE   290   THE TIMBER   31
    THE FIR-TREES FOR HER HCUSE.   286   PSALM 104   48
    TO SERVE THEE IN THY BLESSED HCUSE.   336   PSALM 65   10
    WHOSE BEAUTY TYED LIFE TO THY HCUSE   302   THE KNOT   3
    AND TAKE THE GLCRY OF THY HOUSE   350   L'ENVOY   34
HOVER
    HCVER NCT LONG, ETERNAL DCVE.   308   THE SEED   7
HOWL
    WHILE OWLS ANC SATYRS HCWL.   288   THE BIRD   28
    AND HEARD THEM HOWL.   188   RELAPSE   8
HOWLING
    OR IN THE HOWLING WILCERNESS   301   PROVIDENCE   27
HUG'D
    AND HUG'D EACH ONE HIS PELF   232   THE WORLD   37
HUGS
    FIRST MAKES, THEN HUGS A SNARE   236   CONSTLATN   18
    YET HUGS HE STIL HIS DURT. THE STUFFE HE WEARS   .   .   224   TEMPEST   45
HUMBLE
    BECOME AN HUMBLE, HOLY NATION.   237   CONSTLATN   56
    AND BETHLEMS HUMBLE COTTS ABOVE THEM STEPT   238   SHEPHEARDS   21
    CNLY CONTENT, AND LOVE, AND HLMBLE JOYS   239   SHEPHEARDS   35
    IN THE SAME PAGE THY HUMBLE GRAVE   .   .   .   .   .   31C   THE SEED   71
    TO THY SURE TROT, A CONSTANT, HUMBLE MIND   193   RLS + LSNS   50
    AND HUMBLE DUST, TELL THEN DEAR FLESH   201   THE CHECK   11
HUMBLED
    WHY ART THOU HUMBLED THLS, ANC LCW   304   ST MARY MN   25
HUMBLY
    TO WASH YCUR VESSEL WEL. THEN HLMBLY TAKF   .   .   .   244   THE SAP   43
HUMICITIE
    THEIR LEAFS WITH WATER, ANC HLMICITIE.   223   TEMPEST   34
HUMILITY
    C HCLY HOPE. AND HIGH HLMILITY   271   ALL GONE   13
    GIVE ME HLMILITY AND PEACE   317   MEN OF WAR   41

		PAGE	TITLE	LINE
HUMILITY	(CON'T)			
PRAISE WAITS IN ALL HUMILITY.	. . . . . .	336	PSALM 65	2
HUMMINGS				
AND IN WEAKE, INFANT HUMMINGS CHIME, AND KNELL	. .	144	RSRCTN +IM	7
HUMOURS				
GAVE MY FOND HUMOURS THEIR FULL WING	. . . .	282	GARLAND	23
HUNDRED				
TWELVE HUNDRED HOURES, AND NOT A BROW	. . . .	178	SILENCE	3
HUNG				
PRIMROS'D, AND HUNG WITH SHADE	. . . .	139	RGNRTN	13
HUNG WITH MY GAINE, AND HIS GREAT LOSSE	. . .	152	THE SEARCH	42
'TWAS BUT JUST NOW MY BLEAK LEAVES HOPELES HUNG	. .	198	UNPRFTBLNS	2
THE DARKSOME STATES-MAN HUNG WITH WEIGHTS AND WOE	. .	231	THE WORLD	16
HUNT				
HUNT OUT EACH DAMP	. . . .	340	THE FEAST	47
HUNTS				
HUNTS IN AN EAGER QUEST.	. . . . .	286	PSALM 104	56
HUNTS GOLD AND WEALTH, AND WILL NOT LEND	. . .	301	PROVIDENCE	33
HURL'D				
FROM THE SAME PRECIPICE BE HURL'D.	. . . .	322	CHILDEHOOD	24
AND ALL HER TRAIN WERE HURL'D.	. . . .	231	THE WORLD	7
IS FULL OF VOICES, MAN IS CALL'D, AND HURL'D	. .	161	DSTRQCTION	12
THUS ALL IS HURL'D	. . . . . .	176	MRNG-WTCH	16
HURT				
WHO KISSETH THORNS, WILL HURT HIS FACE	. . .	321	CHILDEHOOD	13
TO THOSE, TILL EITHER HURT OR SICK.	. . .	348	HOLY BIBLE	12
HUSBAND-MAN				
CAST BY THE HUSBAND-MAN AWAY.	. . . . .	292	THE JEWS	19
HUSBANDRY				
THEY ARE HEAVENS HUSBANDRY, THE FAMOUS FAN	. .	221	AFFLICTION	19
HUSBANDS				
WISE HUSBANDS WILL (YOU SAY) THERE WANTS PREVENT	. .	274	PROFFER	11
HUSH				
BUT ALL THE EARE LAY HUSH	. . . . .	140	RGNRTN	57
WALK WITH THY FELLOW-CREATURES. NOTE THE HUSH	. .	192	RLS + LSNS	13
HUSKE				
THE LOST SONNE HAD NOT LEFT THE HUSKE	. . .	162	PURSUITE	11
HYEROGLIPHICKS				
WITH HYEROGLIPHICKS QUITE DISMEMBRED	. .	168	VNTY SPRIT	23
HYMNES				
IN SACRED HYMNES, AND ORDER, THE GREAT CHIME	. .	177	MRNG-WTCH	17
HYMNING				
AND HYMNING CIRCULATIONS THE QUICK WORLD	. . .	176	MRNG-WTCH	10
HYMNS				
FUL HYMNS DOTH YIELD	. . . . . .	212	DAWNING	16
THY LITTLE HEART IN EARLY HYMNS DOTH SING	. .	288	THE BIRD	8
I'D				
I'D LOOSE THOSE KNOTS THY HANDS DID TIE	. . .	214	MISERY	73
I'L				
BUT I'L MIND THEE	. . . . . .	214	PRAISE	18
I'LE				
AND SMOOTH SEDUCEMENTS. I'LE NOT STUFF MY STORY	. .	275	PROFFER	35
I, DO NOT GO. THOU KNOW'ST, I'LE DYE.	. . .	293	BEGGING B	1
I'LE GET ME UP BEFORE THE SUN	. . .	295	PALM-SUNDY	34
I'LE CUT ME BOUGHS OFF MANY A TREE	. . .	295	PALM-SUNDY	35
THEN LIKE THE PALM, THOUGH WRONG, I'LE BEAR	. .	295	PALM-SUNDY	38
I'LE SEAL MY EYES UP, AND TO THY COMMANDS	. .	321	HIDDN TRSR	29
I'LE MARVEL NOT AT OUGHT THEY DO	. . .	317	MEN OF WAR	33
I'LE JUDGE, WHERE PENAL FLAMES SIT MIXT AND CLOSE.	. .	307	RAIN-BOW	38
THE DAY-STAR SPRINGS, I'LE WAKE AGEN.	. . .	177	EVNG-WTCH	2
I'LE DISAPPARELL, AND TO BUY	. . .	168	VNTY SPRIT	33
I'LE WISH MY CURTAINES OFF TO FREE	. . .	142	DEATH	9
AND WHERE THOU MAD'ST AN END, THERE I'LE BEGIN.	. .	158	THE LAMPE	26
I'LE TO THE WILDERNESS, AND CAN	. . .	152	THE SEARCH	53
I'LE THITHER THEN, SEE, IT IS DAY	. . .	152	THE SEARCH	65
I'TH'				
REST FROM THE FEARS I'TH' NIGHT.	. . . .	201	THE CHECK	19
IN THAT DEAD AGE, ONE BEAM I'TH' DARK OUTVIES	. .	196	RLS + LSNS	134
AND AS I'TH' NATURAL SUN, THESE THREE	. . .	211	FAITH	33
THE BEAMS THEY WARM THEM AT I'TH' LIGHT	. . .	207	REPENTANCE	40
I'TH' FACE OF THINGS	. . . . . .	247	I WALKT	9
ICE				
IN HEAV'N, HAIL, THUNDER, RAIN-BOWS, SNOW, AND ICE	. .	194	RLS + LSNS	93
THY BLOOD TO ICE, AND THOU MUST STAY	. . .	142	DEATH	3
LEAVE THEN YONG SORCERESS. THE ICE	. . .	297	HERODIAS	9
THESE MOUNTAINS OF COLD ICE IN ME. THOU ART	. .	283	LOVE-SICK	12
IDAEA'S				
IDAEA'S OF HIS AGONIE	. . . . .	152	THE SEARCH	38
IDLE				
THE IDLE TALK OF FEAV'RISH SOULS	. . .	205	IDLE VERSE	15
WITH IDLE HEARTS AND BUSIE LOCKS	. . .	303	ORNAMENT	10
IDLENESS				
THEY VIEWD, (FOR IDLENESS HATH THERE	. . .	303	ORNAMENT	11
IDOLIZE				
AND IDOLIZE SOME SHADE, OR GROVE	. . .	162	MT. OLVS A	4
ILE				
ILE SPICE MY THOUGHTS WITH THEE, AND FROM THY WORD	. .	287	PSALM 104	93
ILL				
AND THEY TOO OFT TAKE GOOD FOR ILL	. . .	309	THE SEED	39
AND SOON AS LEFT, SHRINKS BACK TO ILL.	. . .	308	THE SEED	18

                                                              PAGE   TITLE   LINE
ILL   (CON'T)
    CONSENT TO ANY GAINFUL ILL   313   THE STONE   11
    YET WOULD NOT MEN GRANT, THEIR ILL FATE   311   FAIR+YONG   21
    THE SERVANT MUST NOT TAKE IT ILL.   317   MEN OF WAR   36
    AMONGST THE DEAD, WHERE THRIVING ILL   318   THE ASS   26
    SINCE ALL THAT AGE DOTH TEACH, IS ILL   321   CHILDEHOOD   19
    WHEN HE DID STAY TO BEARE OUR ILL   163   MT. OLVS A   30
    HOW ILL HAVE WE OUR SELVES BESTOW'D   165   THE CALL   18
    THE FOSTS ILL WEEDS NIP, AND MOLEST   227   LV + DSPLN   11
    ILL THY BREST WITH HOME. THINK ON THY DREAM.   .   .   .   276   PROFFER   45
    DARES OWN THE TRUTH, AND SHEW THE ILL.   350   L'ENVOY   38
    MY OWN ILL WAY.   342   OBSEQUIES   4
ILL-BODING
    A COMET, THE SAD WORLDS ILL-BODING BOOK.   307   RAIN-BOW   36
ILL-GUIDING
    AND BY THIS WORLDS ILL-GUIDING LIGHT   324   THE NIGHT   47
ILL-PLAC'D
    NEGLECTING THEE. SUCH ILL-PLAC'D WIT   162   MT. OLVS A   5
ILL-SHAP'D
    OTHERS ILL-SHAP'D, AND DULL   141   RGNRTN   65
IMAGE
    SHALL THY OWN IMAGE THINK IT MUCH   276   COCK-CRWNG   15
IMAGINARY
    AND WRAP US IN IMAGINARY FLIGHTS   183   THRS A TYE   15
IMBARRS
    THOUGH THY CLOSE COMMERCE NOUGHT AT ALL IMBARRS .   .   .   278   THE STARRE   5
IMMACULATE
    FOR EVERMORE IMMACULATE.   349   L'ENVOY   16
IMMEDIATE
    IMMEDIATE, PURE AND UNVEIL'D EYE   349   L'ENVOY   18
IMMORTAL
    IMMORTAL SHAPE, WHO WROUGHT THEIR BLISS   349   L'ENVOY   6
    THE FOOD OF MANS IMMORTAL BEING.   340   THE FEAST   39
    A FRESH, IMMORTAL GREEN THERE DWELLS   308   THE SEED   23
IMMORTALITY
    THE WAY TO IMMORTALITY.   335   JUDGEMENT   22
    A TREE, WHOSE FRUIT IS IMMORTALITY.   280   PALM-TREE   16
    CLOATH'D ALL WITH IMMORTALITY.   265   INTRO. 2   16
IMMORTALL
    O THOU IMMORTALL LIGHT AND HEAT.   277   COCK-CRWNG   19
    MY FOUL, FOUL HEART. THOU ART IMMORTALL HEAT   .   .   .   283   LOVE-SICK   14
IMPATIENT
    THE LYONS WHELPS IMPATIENT OF DELAY   286   PSALM 104   57
IMPIOUS
    THE FORGERIES, WHICH IMPIOUS WIT   335   JUDGEMENT   35
    WHITE DAYES, THAT DURST NO IMPIOUS MIRTH EXPOSE.   .   .   154   ISAACS M.   18
IMPLIES
    AGAIN, IF WORST AND WORST IMPLIES   273   WHT SUNDAY   33
IMPLOY
    AND DOTH IMPLOY   328   RIGHTSNESS   38
    I WILL IN SONGS TO THY GREAT NAME IMPLOY   287   PSALM 104   90
IMPLOYMENT
    SOME NEW IMPLOYMENT, I BEGIN   214   MISERY   63
IMPOSE
    WITHOUT THAT BRIBE WHICH USURERS IMPOSE.   328   RIGHTSNESS   42
IMPOSSIBLE
    IT WAS IMPOSSIBLE, THAT THOU   305   ST MARY MN   63
IMPOWRE
    SO FIRM A LONGING CAN IMPOWRE   276   COCK-CRWNG   14
IMPRIS'MENT
    AS AN IMPRIS'MENT SERVING THEE.   239   MISERY   4
IMPROVE
    WHICH RUN FROM HILLS TO VALLEYS, AND IMPROVE   .   .   .   285   PSALM 104   31
IMPURE
    WHERE THE IMPURE SEEDS FLOURISH ALL THE YEAR   .   .   .   321   HIDDN TRSR   26
    IN THIS IMPURE, REBELLIOUS CLAY   164   INCARNATN   14
IN'T
    IF THOU BE IN'T, 'TIS WELCOME STILL.   182   CHRFLNESS   11
    EACH PAGE OF THINE HATH TRUE LIFE IN'T   332   AGREEMENT   23
INACCESSIBLE
    AND INACCESSIBLE FOR LIGHT, ...   229   LAW + GOSP   5
INANIMATE
    WHOLLY INANIMATE.   187   NO DO THEY   8
INCARNATION
    MADE MY LORDS INCARNATION GOOD.   284   TRINITY-SN   6
INCENSE
    DOTH ON THOSE HILLS OF MIRRHE, AND INCENSE WATCH.   .   .   156   BRT. CHRCH   4
    SCATT'RING THE MYRRHE, AND INCENSE OF THY PRAY'R.   .   .   155   ISAACS M.   52
    BRING PRAISE, AND INCENSE.   215   PRAISE   44
INCERTAINTIES
    BECAUSE INCERTAINTIES WE CAN NOT KNOW   183   THRS A TYE   23
INCESSANT
    AND WITH ONE STRONG, INCESSANT CRY   326   ABELS BLOD   21
    AS THIS LOUD BROOKS INCESSANT FALL   344   WATER-FALL   33
INCEST
    SHE TEMPTS TO INCEST, THOU TO BLOOD.   297   HERODIAS   20
INCH
    SHALL MY SHORT HOUR, MY INCH   275   PROFFER   25
INCHANTRESS
    SKILFLL INCHANTRESS AND TRUE BRED.   297   HERODIAS   17

			PAGE	TITLE	LINE
INCITE					
INCITE THEM TO THAT FIERCE DISCUSSE	. . . . .		175	THE STORM	11
INCLIN'D					
ELSE NOT INCLIN'D	. . . .		175	THE STORM	12
WHISPER'D OBEDIENCE, AND THEIR HEADS INCLIN'D.		. .	229	LAW + GOSP	10
INCLINE					
INCLINE EACH HARD HEART TO DO GOOD	. . . .		350	L'ENVOY	45
INCLINES					
MY FIERCE, WILD BLOOD THAT STILL HEAVES, AND INCLINES		.	190	THE MATCH	4
INCLOSED					
FOR EACH INCLOSED SPIRIT IS A STAR	. . . .		288	THE BIRD	19
INCLOSURE					
THAT BLEST INCLOSURE, WHERE THE ANGELS GAVE	. .		267	ASCN-DAY A	16
INCORPORATES					
INCORPORATES BY SKILL	. . . . .		145	RSRCTN +IM	26
INCREAS'D					
WHICH STILL INCREAS'D, BUT WHENCE IT STIRR'D	. .		141	RGNRTN	80
INCREASE					
THROUGH THY INCREASE GROW NEW, AND QUICK.	. .		191	THE MATCH	41
TO LODGE LIGHT, AND INCREASE HER OWN.	. . .		315	DWELLNG-PL	10
INCUBATION					
AND BY A SACRED INCUBATION FED	. . . .		248	I WALKT	45
INDEED					
INDEED I HAD SOME HERE TO HIRE	. . . .		264	INTRO. 1	9
INDEED, IT IS THE ONLY TIME	. . . .		211	DAWNING	13
YET, FLY NO FRIEND, IF HE BE SUCH INDEED	. .		194	RLS + LSNS	79
THEY ARE (INDEED) OUR PILLAR-FIRES	. . .		175	JOY OF LIF	25
INDISPUTABLE					
AND INDISPUTABLE, SHEWS TO MY SIGHT	. . .		268	ASCN-DAY A	35
INFANCIE					
FAMILIAR EVER SINCE THY INFANCIE.	. . .		156	ISAACS M.	66
INFANT					
AND IN WEAKE, INFANT HUMMINGS CHIME, AND KNELL	.		144	RSRCTN +IM	7
BLASTED MY INFANT BUDS, AND SINNE	. . .		139	RGNRTN	16
BLEST INFANT BUD, WHOSE BLOSSOME-LIFE	. . .		209	THE BURIAL	1
INFANTS					
WEE ARE THY INFANTS, AND SUCK THEE, IF THOU	. .		213	ADMISSION	17
AND INFANTS WITH THY PANGS CONTEST	. . .		218	EASTER HYM	11
HER INFANTS DIE	. . . . . .		222	TEMPEST	6
SPEECHLESS AND CALM, AS INFANTS SLEEP.	. .		326	ABELS BLOD	35
INFECTED					
IS WELL DISPOSED, FOR BODIES ONCE INFECTED	. .		278	THE STARRE	14
INFECTION					
BUT SICKNESS, OR INFECTION. STIFLE IT	. .		194	RLS + LSNS	76
INFECTIOUS					
OF HER SICK WATERS, AND INFECTIOUS EASE.	. .		160	THE SHOWRE	3
INFERIOR					
AND MANS INFERIOR ESSENCE HE	. . . .		302	THE KNOT	7
INFINITE					
QUITE THROUGH THEM BOTH, STILL INFINITE	.		333	AGREEMENT	51
O JOYES. INFINITE SWEETNESS. WITH WHAT FLOWRES	.		176	MRNG-WTCH	1
I AM BUT FINITE, HE IS INFINITE.	. . .		209	REPENTANCE	84
INFIRMITY					
OF STARS, ABOVE INFIRMITY.	. . . .		204	DSRDR + FR	49
INFLAM'D					
BY THOSE BRIGHT FIRES WHICH THEE INFLAM'D.			190	THE MATCH	6
INFLAME					
O THOU. WHOSE SPIRIT DID AT FIRST INFLAME	. .		248	I WALKT	43
INFLUENCE					
OF OUGHT BUT INFLUENCE.	. . . . .		186	NO DO THEY	2
INFUSE					
WHO PLAC'D THEE HERE, DID SOMETHING THEN INFUSE	. .		243	THE SAP	9
BRINGS FORTH, WITH WINE, OYL, BREAD. ALL WHICH INFUSE	.		285	PSALM 104	43
INFUSED					
WITH THAT ONE GRAINS INFUSED WEALTH	. . .		206	REPENTANCE	4
INFUSIONS					
THOUSANDS OF WILD AND WASTE INFUSIONS	. . .		214	MISERY	75
INGAGE					
IN THY FREE SERVICES INGAGE	. . . .		212	DAWNING	38
INHERENT					
TO CALL IT THEIR INHERENT LIGHT.	. . .		265	INTRO. 2	6
INHERIT					
I DYE TO MAKE MY FOES INHERIT.	. . . .		185	PASSION	43
THUS SOAR'D THY SOUL, WHO (THOUGH YOUNG) DIDST INHERIT	.		156	ISAACS M.	63
WHO SEEKS FOR MORE, HE WOULD INHERIT.	. . .		339	THE FEAST	12
INHERITANCE					
UNTO HIS OWN INHERITANCE	. . . . .		218	EASTER HYM	16
INJUNCTION					
BUT SHOULD THY MILD INJUNCTION NOTHING MOVE ME	. .		230	LAW + GOSP	39
INJURE					
INJURE NOT MODEST BLOUD, WHOSE SPIRITS RISE	.		194	RLS + LSNS	73
INLARG'D					
INLARG'D HIS SPOUSE	. . . . . .		210	FAITH	6
INLARG'D THAT LIGHT, AND TO THE BAD WAS KINDE.	. .		330	JACOBS PLW	14
INLIGHTEND					
FROM WHENCE TH' INLIGHTEND SPIRIT SEES	. . .		170	RETREATE	25
INLIGHTNED					
SHALL WITH INLIGHTNED RAYES	. . . .		146	RSRCTN +IM	56
INLIGHTNING					
INLIGHTNING HIS OWN LITTLE SPHERE	. . . .		288	THE BIRD	20

		PAGE	TITLE	LINE
INNE				
HIS INNE, AND CRADLE, BEING THERE		151	THE SEARCH	7
DIDST WITH THY SERVANT INNE.		180	BURIALL	20
ABOVE THIS INNE		199	NTVTY 1	15
INNOCENCE				
NOR BOLD-FAC'D CUSTOME BANISH'D INNOCENCE.		154	ISAACS M.	20
WAITS INNOCENCE AND PLEASURE)		238	SHEPHEARDS	2
INNOCENT				
ALL NAKED, INNOCENT AND BRIGHT		269	ASCSN-HYMN	23
PLEASING AND INNOCENT AN AIR		303	ST MARY MN	6
INNOXIOUS				
CONTENTED THOUGHTS, INNOXIOUS EASE		317	MEN OF WAR	42
INNUMERABLE				
INNUMERABLE, CREEPING THINGS BOTH SMALL		286	PSALM 104	70
INQUIRE				
INQUIRE HOW LONG. OF THE MOST HIGH.		326	ABELS BLOD	22
INRAGED				
THUS THE ENLARG'D, INRAGED AIR		176	THE STORM	13
INSLAVE				
THE WEAKER SORT SLIGHT, TRIVIALL WARES INSLAVE		232	THE WORLD	42
INSPIR'D				
INSPIR'D A QUICKNING POWER THROUGH THE DEAD		144	RSRCTN +IM	3
INSTEAD				
TO PUT ON CLOUDS INSTEAD OF LIGHT		164	INCARNATN	5
INSTITUTES				
AND SACRED INSTITUTES IN ME.		242	MISERY	100
INSTRUCTION				
THIS LATE, LONG HEAT MAY HIS INSTRUCTION BE		222	TEMPEST	3
FOR IN THIS BRIGHT, INSTRUCTING VERSE		316	MEN OF WAR	17
WHEN THUS THY MILDE, INSTRUCTING HAND		319	THE ASS	45
INTELLIGENCE				
INTELLIGENCE, WHOSE SPIRIT FEEDS		314	THE STONE	25
INTEND				
HE MAY TAKE THEE, AS THOU DOEST HIM INTEND.		216	DRESSING	16
INTENTIVE				
DID WITH INTENTIVE LOCKS WATCH EVERY HOUR		306	RAIN-BOW	7
INTERCEDING				
WHOSE INTERCEDING, MEEK AND CALM		304	ST MARY MN	39
WHOSE INTERCEDING, SPIRITUALL GRONES		179	CHRCH-SVC	4
INTERCOURSE				
AND INTERCOURSE OF TIMES DIVIDE		245	MAN	4
WHAT STIRS, WHAT POSTING INTERCOURSE AND MIRTH		267	ASCN-DAY A	25
INTERDICT				
CAN INTERDICT US FROM THOSE JOYS		210	FAITH	11
INTEREST				
AND INTEREST		2	SON-DAYES	18
INTERLINE				
ONE SILENT STAR MAY INTERLINE.		273	WHT SUNDAY	38
INTIMATE				
AND INTIMATE WITH HEAV'N, AS LIGHT.		269	ASCSN-HYMN	24
INTOMED				
INTOMED MANY DAYS BEFORE HE DYES		195	RLS + LSNS	126
INTREAT				
OUR BODIES, POYSONS THAT INTREAT		311	FAIR+YONG	13
INTREATE				
YET SOMETHING MORE I MUST INTREATE		167	THE CALL	84
INTRICATE				
MANY A QUESTION INTRICATE AND RARE		247	I WALKT	22
INVADE				
WHOSE CLOUDY BREST COLD DAMPS INVADE		217	EASTER-DAY	2
NEITHER SHALL ME INVADE.		220	PSALM 121	12
INVISIBLE				
MIGHT LIVE INVISIBLE AND DIM.		325	THE NIGHT	54
WHO SEES INVISIBLES, AND DOTH COMPLY		327	RIGHTSNESS	11
O MY INVISIBLE ESTATE		344	WATER-FALL	37
INVISIBLY				
AND LESS'NING STILL GROW UP INVISIBLY		224	TEMPEST	44
WHO ART IN ALL THINGS, THOUGH INVISIBLY.		248	I WALKT	54
INVITE				
HEARK, HOW HE DOTH INVITE THEE. WITH WHAT VOICE		202	THE CHECK	36
DOEST SO INVITE, AND WOO ME STILL		342	OBSEQUIES	22
INVITES				
WHICH NATURE BREEDS, AND SOME FINE CLAY INVITES		320	HIDDN TRSR	20
IF ANY (FOR HE ALL INVITES)		315	THE STONE	54
INWARD				
AND SAVE ME FROM ALL INWARD STRIFE.		190	THE MATCH	18
GUILTS, TRESPASSES, AND ALL THIS INWARD AWE		159	MANS FALL	19
THY INWARD EYES, HIS BLOOD WILL CURE THY MIND		217	EASTER-DAY	15
IRON				
TO BRASSE, AND IRON, WHEN MY STOCK LAY DEAD		213	ADMISSION	3
IRREGULAR				
BUT EVER RESTLESS AND IRREGULAR		246	MAN	17
IS'T				
IF THE SUN RISE ON THE ROCKS, IS'T RIGHT		265	INTRO. 2	5
OR IS'T SO, AS SOME GREEN HEADS SAY		149	RELIGION	25
IS'T JUST TO JUDGE HER FAITHFLL TEARS		305	ST MARY MN	65
AND SPRING, HOW IS'T THAT YOU SO SADLY GRIEVE		298	JESUS WP B	12
ISHMAEL				
OF YONG, DISTRESSED ISHMAEL.		300	PROVIDENCE	6
ISLE				
AND SOMETHING COOLD THE PARCH'D, AND THIRSTIE ISLE		156	ISAACS M.	58

	PAGE	TITLE	LINE

ISRAELS
YEA BETHEL SHALL HAVE TITHES (SAITH ISRAELS STONE) · · 331 JACOBS PLW 33
ISSACHAR
AND MAN (LIKE ISSACHAR) IN LODES DELIGHT · · · · 223 TEMPEST 30
ISSUE
DID ISSUE FORTH FORC'D BY THE ROD · · · · 184 PASSION 4
ITCH
MY FINGERS ITCH, AND BURN TO TAKE · · · · 214 MISERY 62
JABOBS
TO JABOBS WEL, BEQUEATHED SINCE · · · 151 THE SEARCH 27
JACOB
HERE JACOB DREAMES, AND WRESTLES, THERE · · · 149 RELIGION 9
BUT BLESSED JACOB, THOUGH THY SAD DISTRESS · · · 331 JACOBS PLW 41
THEN JACOB-LIKE LODGE IN A PLACE · · · 228 PILGRIMAGE 5
JACOBS
BUT JACOBS CHILDREN WOULD NOT HEARE. · · · 151 THE SEARCH 32
SOME CALL'D IT, JACOBS BED · · · · · 140 RGNRTN 37
JAR
BE DUMB COURSE MEASURES, JAR NO MORE. TO ME · · 280 JOY 1
JEALOUSIE
WERE CHEAR'D, YOUR JEALOUSIE TO MOVE. · · · 293 THE JEWS 45
JEAR
AS THE POOR ASS, WHICH THE PROUD JEAR · · · 295 PALM-SUNDY 40
JERUSALEM
JERUSALEM, WITH BLOOD OF BEASTS, AND FAT. · · · 330 JACOBS PLW 26
JESHURUNS
I SOJOURN'D THUS, AT LAST JESHURUNS KING · · · 159 MANS FALL 16
JESTS
WHO MAKES HIS JESTS OF SINS, MUST BE AT LEAST · · 194 RLS + LSNS 77
JESU
LORD JESU. THOU DIDST BOW THY BLESSED HEAD · · 191 THE MATCH 31
SWEET JESU. WILL THEN. LET NO MORE · · · · 200 NTVTY 1 25
JESUS
AND WHISPER'D, JESUS HAD BEEN THERE · · · 151 THE SEARCH 31
O COME LORD JESUS QUICKLY. · · · · · 181 BURIALL 40
AND ONELY MY DEAR JESUS SEEK. · · · · · 295 PALM-SUNDY 41
DEAR JESUS WEEP ON. POUR THIS LATTER · · · 296 JESUS WP A 9
JESUS, MY LIFE. HOW SHALL I TRULY LOVE THEE. · · 283 LOVE-SICK 1
DEAR JESUS GIVE ME PATIENCE HERE · · · 317 MEN OF WAR 37
FOR, DEAREST JESUS, 'TIS ALL THINE. · · · 265 INTRO. 2 8
LORD JESUS. WITH WHAT SWEETNESS AND DELIGHTS · · 267 ASCN-DAY A 1
AND NOW (ETERNAL JESUS) THOU DOST HEAVE · · 268 ASCN-DAY A 55
JEW
WAS THINE OWN ANSWER TO THE STUBBORN JEW. · · 268 ASCN-DAY A 60
FROM THE FIERCE JEW, AND HERODS HEAT · · · 152 THE SEARCH 56
WHO SELS RELIGION, IS A JUDAS JEW · · · 193 RLS + LSNS 45
JEWEL
DEAR, BEAUTEOUS DEATH. THE JEWEL OF THE JUST · · 271 ALL GONE 17
JEWS
THE JEWS TOUCH'D NOT · · · · · 156 BRT. CHRCH 9
THE LAW DELIVERED TO THE JEWS · · · 314 THE STONE 46
STIFF-NECKED JEWS. YOUR FATHERS BREED · · · 296 JESUS WP A 5
AND WONDER, WHILE THE JEWS DID SLEEP · · · 323 THE NIGHT 24
JOB
THE PROVERB'D GRIEFS OF HOLY JOB · · · 295 PALM-SUNDY 43
JOHN
SAITH HOLY JOHN, THEN LET HIM HEAR. · · · 316 MEN OF WAR 2
JOIN
HERE I JOIN HANDS, AND THRUST MY STUBBORN HEART · · 190 THE MATCH 7
AND JOIN AGAINST THEIR WILES. · · · 205 IDLE VERSE 8
JOINT
DEATH SETS ALL OUT OF JOINT · · · · 173 CONTENT 19
JOINTLY AGREE · · · · · · · 180 CHRCH-SVC 18
JOIRNEY
WHAT PLEASURES SHOULD MY JOIRNEY CROWN · · · 152 THE SEARCH 68
JOURNEY
THEN JOURNEY ON, AND HAVE AN EYE TO HEAV'N. · · 192 RLS + LSNS 24
WHEN WE TWO PART, I WILL A JOURNEY MAKE · · · 280 PALM-TREE 25
JOURNEYS
MY FATHERS JOURNEYS, AND IN ONE FAIRE STEP · · · 159 MANS FALL 28
JOY
IS BOTH HIS OWN JOY, AND HIS MAKERS TOO. · · · 193 RLS + LSNS 51
SURE, THOU WILT JOY TO SEE · · · · · 188 NO DO THEY 39
STRAIT THERE IS JOY, AND EV'RY SPHERE · · · 200 NTVTY 2 3
WHAT'S GOOD SCORE UP FOR JOY, THE BAD WEL SCANN'D · 195 RLS + LSNS 119
WELCOME DEAR BOOK, SOULS JOY, AND FOOD. THE FEAST · 197 SCRIPTURES 1
JOY OF MY LIFE. WHILE LEFT ME HERE · · · 174 JOY OF LIF 1
SIGHS MAKE JOY SURE, AND SHAKING FASTENS THEE. · · 281 JOY 30
RARE LOCKS. THAT CAN DISPENSE SUCH JOY · · · 281 THE FAVOUR 3
WHERE LIGHT, JOY, LEISURE, AND TRUE COMFORTS MOVE · 248 I WALKT 59
THAT THESE MAY BE THY PRAISE, AND MY JOY TOO. · · 245 MT. OLV. B 26
SHAL FIND A JOY SO TRUE · · · · · 244 THE SAP 46
WHERE LIGHT, JOY, HEALTH AND PERFECT PEACE · · 319 THE ASS 62
THAT KILL WITH SMILES AND SEEMING JOY. · · · 311 FAIR+YONG 16
THOU SHALT BE ALL MY JOY. · · · · · 287 PSALM 104 92
YET JOY IT SELF WILL MAKE A RIGHT SOUL GRIEVE · · 290 THE TIMBER 39
AND JOY, AND REST · · · · · · 329 TEARS 6
WHO BEARS HIS CROSS WITH JOY · · · · 328 RIGHTSNESS 37
AND FILL'D WITH JOY, THY GOODNESS TELLS. · · · 336 PSALM 65 12
THEY SHOUT FOR JOY, AND JOYNTLY SING · · · 337 PSALM 65 47

		PAGE	TITLE	LINE
JOY	(CCN'T)			
AND JCY, LIKE LIGHT, SHINES CFT IN CLOUDS.		342	OBSEQUIES	20
A KNOWING JOY.		345	QUICKNESS	10
SHINING WITH JOY, LIKE DEWY DAYS		345	THE WREATH	11
O TELL ME WHENCE THAT JCY DOTH SPRING		346	THE QUEER	1
JOY'D				
LET THE JCY'D RODE MAKE HCLY-DAY		294	PALM-SUNDY	8
I TOOKE THEM UP, AND (MUCH JOY'C) WENT ABOUT		168	VNTY SPRIT	25
JOYES				
WHEN LOWD JOYES WANT A WING		167	THE CALL	79
O JOYES. INFINITE SWEETNESS. WITH WHAT FLOWRES		176	MRNG-WTCH	1
AND VOCALL JOYES		177	MRNG-WTCH	21
ALLOW YOUR JOYES RELIGICN, THAT DONE, SPEED		194	RLS + LSNS	81
JOYES FULL, AND TRUE.		188	RELAPSE	26
SO THRIVE I BEST, 'TWIXT JOYES, AND TEARS		227	LV + DSPLN	17
FALSE JOYES, PHANTASTICK FLIGHTS		282	GARLAND	18
IF JOYES, AND HOPES, AND EARNEST THROWS		277	COCK-CRWNG	31
JOYFUL				
JCYN IN A JOYFUL SYMPHONY		295	PALM-SUNDY	26
JOYN				
JCYN IN A JOYFUL SYMPHONY		295	PALM-SUNDY	26
THESE TWO GRAND SINS WE JCYN AND ACT TOGETHER		307	RAIN-BOW	25
JOYNTLY				
THEY SHOUT FOR JOY, AND JCYNTLY SING		337	PSALM 65	47
THY CARE AND LOVE, WHICH JOYNTLY FLOW		333	AGREEMENT	57
JOYS				
OF LIFE AND JOYS.		335	JUDGEMENT	18
(UNSEEN) SUCH JOYS I FEEL.		337	THE THRONE	7
COMFORTS AND JOYS, AND HOPES EACH HOUR		326	ABELS BLOD	26
IF PIOUS GRIEFS HEAVENS JCYS AWAKE		308	THE SEED	15
IF THOSE BRIGHT JCYS HE SINGLY SHEDS		309	THE SEED	29
THOUGH LIFE BE DEAD, AND MY JCYS GONE.		311	THE SEED	89
THEIR JCYS PROVOKE THE DISTANT SKIE		295	PALM-SUNDY	20
IS IN THESE JCYS AN HIGH PARTAKER		295	PALM-SUNDY	28
THEN FAREWEL JOYS. FOR WHILE I LIVE		299	JESUS WP B	44
A GRIEF THAT SHALL OUTSHINE ALL JCYS		299	JESUS WP B	46
HE THAT HATH LEFT LIFES VAIN JOYS AND VAIN CARE		290	THE TIMBER	29
SURE, HOLY HOPES, HIGH JOYS AND QUICKNING FLIGHTS		267	ASCN-DAY A	2
WHEN FIRST I SAW TRUE BEAUTY, AND THY JOYS		244	MT. OLV. B	1
THAT CALM AND SILENCE ARE MY JCYS		214	MISERY	59
ONLY CONTENT, AND LOVE, AND HUMBLE JOYS		239	SHEPHEARDS	35
RESEMBLES THOSE TRUE JOYS		235	CONSTLATN	2
CAN INTERDICT US FROM THOSE JOYS		210	FAITH	11
O WHAT HIGH JOYS		340	THE FEAST	49
JUBILE				
THE CREATURES JUBILE, GODS PARLE WITH DUST.		2	SON-DAYES	13
JUDAS				
WHO SELS RELIGION, IS A JUDAS JEW		193	RLS + LSNS	45
JUDG'D				
THEY JUDG'D THEM SENSLESSE, AND THEIR STATE		187	NO DO THEY	7
JUDGE				
DESCEND TO JUDGE POOR CARELESS MAN		212	DAWNING	28
DARES KNOW EFFECTS, AND JUDGE THEM LONG BEFORE		236	CONSTLATN	27
I WOULD BOTH THINK, AND JUDGE I DID NOT LOVE THEE.		230	LAW + GOSP	40
UPON THE CLOUDS AGAIN TO JUDGE THIS WORLD.		268	ASCN-DAY A	62
AND THRIVING VICE FOR VERTUE JUDGE.		309	THE SEED	40
I'LE JUDGE, WHERE PENAL FLAMES SIT MIXT AND CLOSE.		307	RAIN-BOW	38
IS'T JUST TO JUDGE HER FAITHFUL TEARS		305	ST MARY MN	65
A JUDGE WERT THOU, AND HOW UNKINDE.		305	ST MARY MN	62
AND NOT HIMSELF SHALL JUDGE THE WORLD)		315	THE STONE	57
ALMIGHTY JUDGE.		326	ABELS BLOD	23
IN JUDGEMENT AGAINST LEWDNESS, THAT'S BASE WIT		194	RLS + LSNS	74
AND LET THESE LONG, SHARP JUDGEMENTS AW		351	L'ENVOY	54
BECAUSE WE FORC'D THY JUDGEMENTS DOWN.		350	L'ENVOY	32
JUDGETH				
BUT HE THAT JUDGETH AS HE HEARS		314	THE STONE	28
JUDGING				
THY JUDGING ONE, DESCEND, DESCEND.		335	JUDGEMENT	45
THY JUDGING ONE. DESCEND, DESCEND.		340	RGNRTN	5
JUGLING				
FALSE, JUGLING SOUNDS, A GRONE WELL DREST, WHERE CARE		280	JOY	3
JUICE				
WHOSE JUICE SO GOOD		185	PASSION	17
JUNIPER				
UNDER A JUNIPER, SOME HOUSE		148	RELIGION	5
BENEATH THE OKE AND JUNIPER.		291	THE JEWS	7
JUST				
JUST AT HIS MOUTH, THAT THANKLESS HIVE		300	PROVIDENCE	11
JUST ABELS BLOOD		338	DEATH B	2
AT WHOSE JUST LAWS NOT JUST MEN GRUDGE.		326	ABELS BLOD	24
AT WHOSE JUST LAWS NOT JUST MEN GRUDGE.		326	ABELS BLOD	24
WAS JUST THE SAME WITH CURS, AND NOTHING LESS		331	JACOBS PLW	42
MUST NEEDS ACKNOWLEDGE TO BE JUST.		314	THE STONE	36
O THEN, JUST THEN. BREAK OR UNTYE		319	THE ASS	53
IS'T JUST TO JUDGE HER FAITHFUL TEARS		305	ST MARY MN	65
AND QUITE UNDREST JUST NOW WITH THEE		312	FAIR+YONG	48
NOR JUST.		153	THE SEARCH	93
JUST SUCH A TAINTED SINK WE HAVE		150	RELIGION	45
JUST SO IT IS IN DEATH. BUT THOU		143	DEATH	27
THOU ART THE SAME, FAITHFULL, AND JUST		181	BURIALL	23

		PAGE	TITLE	LINE
JUST	**(CON'T)**			
BUT WHAT'S NOT GOOD, AND JUST NE'R GO ABOUT.		193	RLS + LSNS	40
'TWAS BUT JUST NOW MY BLEAK LEAVES HOPELES HUNG		198	UNPRFTBLNS	2
DEAR, BEAUTEOUS DEATH. THE JEWEL OF THE JUST		271	ALL GONE	17
FORCE DOWN A JUST CURSE, WHEN THY HANDS WOULD BLESS.		230	LAW + GOSP	33
AND HATH BUT JUST		226	RETIREMENT	43
AND SEEST ALL THINGS JUST AS THEY BE.		207	REPENTANCE	22
SING THY JUST PRAISE, AND SEE THY FACE.		345	THE WREATH	19
ARE NO MORE SEEN, JUST SO PASS MEN.		344	WATER-FALL	36
JUSTICE				
O LET THY JUSTICE THEN IN HIM CONFINE		209	REPENTANCE	85
AND TERRIBLE, THY JUSTICE BRINGS		336	PSALM 65	14
KALENDAR				
O BRIGHT AND HAPPY KALENDAR.		310	THE SEED	61
KEEP				
KEEP CLEAN, BEAR FRUIT, EARN LIFE AND WATCH		309	THE SEED	47
AND TO THY NAME, WHICH STILL I KEEP		311	FAIR+YONG	9
BUT SINCE THY BEAUTY DOTH STILL KEEP		303	ST MARY MN	9
O FOUL, DECEITFUL MEN. MY GOD DOTH KEEP		307	RAIN-BOW	19
UNTO THEIR WORMWOOD-DIET KEEP		301	PROVIDENCE	47
TO CHECK BAD MOTIONS, KEEP ME STILL		318	THE ASS	25
ON THOSE THAT KEEP THEM, O ACCEPT		326	ABELS BLOD	27
WOULD KEEP, AND NEVER WANDER HERE.		324	THE NIGHT	42
OR SECRET GROVES, KEEP THE HIGH-WAY.		294	PALM-SUNDY	10
WHO DOTH THY LOTHSOME MOTHER KEEP.		297	HERODIAS	12
DIRT IN HER WAY, WILL KEEP ABOVE THE SKIE.		291	THE TIMBER	56
AND KEEP US SO		220	HOLY COMM.	47
HOW ART THOU NOW, THY FLOCK TO KEEP		220	HOLY COMM.	51
AND KEEP US STILL AWAKE		219	HOLY COMM.	37
UP THEN, AND KEEP		226	RETIREMENT	54
AND BY THIS LESSER COMMERCE KEEP.		273	WHT SUNDAY	22
THEN KEEP THE ANTIENT WAY.		276	PROFFER	43
HERE IS THEIR FAITH TOO, WHICH IF YOU WILL KEEP		280	PALM-TREE	24
KEEP THOU THY TEMPER, MIX NOT WITH EACH CLAY.		192	RLS + LSNS	32
YET KEEP THOSE CARES WITHOUT THEE, LET THE HEART		192	RLS + LSNS	35
IF PRIEST, AND PEOPLE CHANGE, KEEP THOU THY GROUND.		193	RLS + LSNS	44
GIVE HIM THY FIRST THOUGHTS THEN, SO SHALT THOU KEEP		191	RLS + LSNS	5
TO HEIGHTEN THY DEVOTIONS, AND KEEP LOW		194	RLS + LSNS	85
THY DEATH MAY KEEP MY SOUL ALIVE.		343	OBSEQUIES	32
KEEP'ST				
THAT KEEP'ST ACCOUNT, TILL HE RETURNE		165	THE CALL	32
KEEPE				
DULL, WRETCHED WORMES. THAT WOULD NOT KEEPE		166	THE CALL	66
AND TAME, AND KEEPE DOWNE WITH THY LIGHT		161	DSTRQCTION	29
THIS LAST WILL KEEPE THE FIRST TWO FRESH		148	DAY OF JDG	43
KEEPES				
HE KEEPES A COMMERCE IN THE NIGHT		162	PURSUITE	7
KEEPING				
KEEPING CLOSE HOUSE		225	RETIREMENT	2
KEEPS				
HE KEEPS ME FROM THE SPITE OF FOES		220	PSALM 121	13
ELSEWHERE, AND FLOWING KEEPS UNTAINTED.		212	DAWNING	36
WHO KEEPS HIS COVENANT EVEN WITH OUR DUST.		144	RSRCTN +IM	18
AND KEEPS HIS SOUL UNTO ETERNAL MIRTH.		290	THE TIMBER	32
AND HIS BLOOD FREEZ'D, KEEPS IN THE CENTER STILL		289	THE TIMBER	22
WHEN THOU DOEST HIDE THY FACE (THY FACE WHICH KEEPS		287	PSALM 104	77
WHICH (THOUGH BUT SAND) KEEPS IN A CURBS WHOLE SEAS.		285	PSALM 104	26
UNITED KEEPS FOR EVER.		302	THE KNOT	16
ONE LIVING DROP. ONE DROP LIFE KEEPS.		308	THE SEED	14
KEPT				
ODOROUS OINTMENTS KEPT WITH CARE		304	ST MARY MN	34
THAT BUSIE COMMERCE KEPT BETWEEN		313	THE STONE	20
HATH KEPT ABOVE		291	THE JEWS	10
OF HIS VOW'D HEART, WHOM THOU HAST KEPT		326	ABELS BLOD	28
KEPT MAN FOR SIN		175	JOY OF LIF	30
KERCHIEFS				
BESIDES, THOSE KERCHIEFS SOMETIMES SHED		342	OBSEQUIES	25
KERNELL				
NOR MUST WE FOR THE KERNELL CRAVE		150	RELIGION	47
KEY				
THE KEY THAT OPENS TO ALL MYSTERIES		198	SCRIPTURES	7
MY FROZEN HEART, AND WITH THY SECRET KEY		216	DRESSING	4
THUS DOTH GOD KEY DISORDER'D MAN		222	AFFLICTION	35
AND HATH WITHAL THE KEY.		243	THE SAP	16
O SPEAR, THE KEY		341	THE FEAST	64
KEYES				
ALL HAVE THEIR KEYES, AND SET ASCENTS, BUT MAN		224	TEMPEST	37
KEYS				
IS BUT MEER CHANGING OF THE KEYS		273	WHT SUNDAY	43
KICK				
AND AFTER ALL THY ACTS OF GRACE DOTH KICK		230	LAW + GOSP	22
KIL				
AND SINCE THESE BITING FROSTS BUT KIL		227	LV + DSPLN	4
THE SONS THE FATHER KIL		237	CONSTLATN	38
OF FORWARD SINS, AND KIL		204	DSRDR + FR	52
KILL				
FOR THOSE THAT KILL THEE EVERY DAY.		164	INCARNATN	16
KILL AND CURE THE TENDER FLOWERS		281	JOY	18
WHO PRAY'D FOR THOSE THAT DID HIM KILL.		326	ABELS BLOD	44
LIKE CHRONIC PAINS, WHICH SURELY KILL, THOUGH SLOW.		327	RIGHTSNESS	30

		PAGE	TITLE	LINE
KILL	(CCN'T)			
AT HIS APPROACH, THAT DID THE BODY KILL.		289	THE TIMBER	24
WHO WITH THE SWORD DOTH OTHERS KILL		316	MEN OF WAR	5
THAT KILL WITH SMILES AND SEEMING JOY.		311	FAIR+YONG	16
BECAUSE FORGETFULNESS WOULD KILL		342	OBSEQUIES	7
KILL'ST				
BUT THOU KILL'ST IT.		214	PRAISE	8
KILLING				
KILLING THE MAN OF SINNE		47	DAY OF JDG	32
KILLS				
MY SOULS BRIGHT FOOD, THY ABSENCE KILLS.		308	THE SEED	6
WHICH KILLS THY BEES, AND EATS THY HONEY.		300	PROVIDENCE	12
KIN				
FLEW HOME UNSTAIN'D BY HIS NEW KIN		209	THE BURIAL	6
THESE THINGS ARE KIN TO HIM, AND MUST BE HAD		236	CONSTLATN	23
KIND				
TRACES, AND SOUNDS OF A STRANGE KIND.		168	VNTY SPRIT	16
BUT HEARTS ARE NOT SO KIND. FALSE, SHORT DELIGHTS		183	THRS A TYE	13
HOW KIND IS HEAV'N TO MAN. IF HERE		200	NTVTY 2	1
SCATT'RING THY KIND		201	THE CHECK	10
KINDE				
SCME KINDE HERBS HERE, THOUGH LOW AND FAR		281	THE FAVOUR	7
TEARS AND THESE FLAMES WILL SOON GROW KINDE		266	VAIN WITS	5
REPEATED SIGHS THY KINDE HEART PAIN		298	JESUS WP B	4
AND WOULD BE CROSS, WHEN GOD WAS KINDE.		292	THE JEWS	25
MY KINDE EYES STILL, BUT IN		310	THE SEED	57
LET ME ADMIRE THOSE, AND BE KINDE		319	THE ASS	35
AND TO MY GREATEST HATERS KINDE.		317	MEN OF WAR	44
AND PRESENT THINGS FINDE MEN MOST KINDE.		318	THE ASS	6
AND FEEL A FRIEND MOST READY, SURE AND KINDE.		331	JACOBS PLW	52
AT LENGTH, MY LIFES KINDE ANGEL CAME		332	AGREEMENT	7
INLARG'D THAT LIGHT, AND TO THE BAD WAS KINDE.		330	JACOBS PLW	14
WITH ALL THEIR SOFT, KINDE ARTS AND EASIE STRAINS		320	HIDDN TRSR	21
KINDLE				
GLITTER AND KINDLE WITH THY LOVE.		332	AGREEMENT	18
TO KINDLE MY COLD LOVE		271	ALL GONE	16
KINDLED				
KINDLED BY THEE		172	MIDNIGHT	25
KINDLY				
AND KINDLY TEL ME, I AM EARTH		240	MISERY	30
KINDNESS				
HER QUICKNING KINDNESS, SMILES AND KISSES		348	HOLY BIBLE	29
KINDS				
ADORE HIM IN THEIR KINDS		176	MRNG-WTCH	15
KING				
IT IS THE BIRTH-DAY OF THY KING		199	NTVTY 1	2
I SOJOURN'D THUS, AT LAST JESHURUNS KING		159	MANS FALL	16
THE MIGHTY GOD, TH' ETERNAL KING		240	MISERY	39
KING OF MERCY, KING OF LOVE		249	BEGGING A	1
KING OF MERCY, KING OF LOVE		249	BEGGING A	1
KING OF COMFORTS. KING OF LIFE.		214	PRAISE	1
KING OF COMFORTS. KING OF LIFE.		214	PRAISE	1
THE FIRST TRUE WORSHIP OF THE WORLDS GREAT KING		330	JACOBS PLW	11
MY GOD AND KING. TO THEE		328	ANGUISH	1
KING OF SALVATION. BY STRANGE THINGS		336	PSALM 65	13
GLORY TO THE ETERNAL KING.		337	PSALM 65	48
WHAT CAN THE MAN DO THAT SUCCEEDS THE KING.		320	HIDDN TRSR	1
GREAT KING OF LOVE AND TRUTH.		301	PROVIDENCE	43
THE KING OF GRIEF, THE MAN OF SORROW		294	PALM-SUNDY	4
KINGDOME				
EVEN TO CONTEMPT THY KINGDOME DOWN		218	EASTER HYM	14
KINGDOMES				
KINGDOMES TOO HAVE THEIR PHYSICK, AND FOR STEEL		222	AFFLICTION	33
KINGS				
THAT LAMB WHOSE DAIES GREAT KINGS AND PROPHETS WISH'D		239	SHEPHEARDS	49
WERE PATRIARCH, SAINTS, AND KINGS		238	SHEPHEARDS	4
KINRED				
AND SEEDS A KINRED FIRE HAVE WITH THE SKY.		223	TEMPEST	36
WHEN SPIRITS THEIR FAIR KINRED CATCH.		324	THE NIGHT	36
KISS				
TAKE THIS LAST KISS, AND LET ME WEEP		348	HOLY BIBLE	3
KISSES				
HER QUICKNING KINDNESS, SMILES AND KISSES		348	HOLY BIBLE	29
KISSETH				
WHO KISSETH THORNS, WILL HURT HIS FACE		321	CHILDEHOOD	13
KIST				
A QUICKNESS, WHICH MY GOD HATH KIST.		345	QUICKNESS	20
KITCHEN				
USE, WITH LIKE CUSTOME, AS MY KITCHEN FOOD.		217	DRESSING	36
KITCHIN-ROOMS				
SUCH COAL-FLAMES SHEW BUT KITCHIN-ROOMS AT MOST.		320	HIDDN TRSR	6
KNEE				
CROWN'D THEE WITH THORNS, AND BOW'D THE KNEE		317	MEN OF WAR	31
I BOW MY KNEE		328	ANGUISH	2
KNEEL				
STIFF THEN MUST KNEEL)		337	THE THRONE	6
THEY WOULD SOON QUIT AND LEARN TO KNEEL.		308	THE SEED	4
THEN KNEEL MY SOUL, AND BODY. KNEEL, AND BOW.		217	DRESSING	41
THEN KNEEL MY SOUL, AND BODY. KNEEL, AND BOW.		217	DRESSING	41
KNEEL DOWN AND FALL		341	THE FEAST	59

	PAGE	TITLE	LINE
KNEELING			
AND LCWLY KNEELING (FCR THE MCST	337	THE THRONE	5
KNEELS			
WHO KNEELS, OR SIGHS A LIFE IS MAD.	236	CONSTLATN	24
KNELL			
AND IN WEAKE, INFANT HUMMINGS CHIME, AND KNELL . .	144	RSRCTN +IM	7
KNEW			
HE SAW HEAVEN O'R HIS HEAD, AND KNEW FROM WHENCE .	196	CORRUPTION	5
EACH CAKE, AND HIGH-WAY KNEW THEM	197	CORRUPTION	26
AND KNEW THEIR COYL	234	MUTINIE	10
I KNEW THERE HERETOFORE.	246	I WALKT	7
SO SHINES AND SINGS, AS IF IT KNEW	276	COCK-CRWNG	9
WITH NATIVE LCOKS, WHICH KNEW NC GUILE . . .	303	ORNAMENT	15
AS IF I KNEW NO MONTH BUT MAY.	300	PROVIDENCE	18
KNEW'ST			
DEAR SOUL. THOU KNEW'ST, FLOWERS HERE ON EARTH .	304	ST MARY MN	27
FOR ERE THOU KNEW'ST HOW TO BE FOUL . . .	209	THE BURIAL	7
THOU KNEW'ST BUT THY OWN GOOD.	202	THE CHECK	39
THOU KNEW'ST THIS PAPYR, WHEN IT WAS . . .	347	THE BOOK	5
THOU KNEW'ST THIS TREE, WHEN A GREEN SHADE . .	347	THE BOOK	11
THOU KNEW'ST THIS HARMLESS BEAST, WHEN HE . .	347	THE BOOK	15
THOU KNEW'ST AND SAW'ST THEM ALL AND THOUGH . .	347	THE BOOK	23
KNEWEST			
AND NCW THOU KNEWEST HER COMING, IT WAS TIME . .	155	ISAACS M.	43
KNIT			
O KNIT ME, THAT AM CRUMPLED DUST. THE HEAPE . .	160	DSTRGCTION	1
THOSE BLASTS, AND KNIT MY FRAME	179	CHRCH-SVC	16
AND KNIT ME TO THEE, THAT THOUGH IN THIS VALE .	234	MUTINIE	19
KNOCKING			
HIS KNOCKING TIME, THE SOULS CLIMB WATCH . . .	324	THE NIGHT	35
KNOCKS			
THE SMALL, STILL VOICE, AT SOME LOW COTTAGE KNOCKS .	330	JACOBS PLW	9
HE KNOCKS AT ALL DOORS, STRAYS AND ROAMS . . .	246	MAN	22
KNOT			
AND SUCH A KNOT, WHAT ARM DARES LOOSE . . .	302	THE KNOT	13
THE YOUTHFUL WORLDS GRAY FATHERS IN ONE KNOT . .	306	RAIN-BOW	6
KNOTS			
I'D LOOSE THOSE KNOTS THY HANDS DID TIE . . .	214	MISERY	73
WITH GLOVES, AND KNOTS THE SILLY SNARES OF PLEASURE .	231	THE WORLD	12
THE KNOTS WE TYED UPON THY PURSE	274	WHT SUNDAY	56
KNOW			
HE THAT HATH FOUND SOME FLEDG'D BIRDS NEST, MAY KNOW .	271	ALL GONE	21
THAT KNOW TO DIE	269	ASCSN-HYMN	8
BUT I WILL KNOW WHICH WAY TO LCCK. . . .	272	WHT SUNDAY	20
WATCH FCR, AND KNOW THEIR LOVING STAR. . . .	281	THE FAVOUR	8
AS BEAUTEOUS SHAPES, WE KNOW NOT WHY . . .	278	THE STARRE	23
I KNOW, THOU'LT BEAR	230	LAW + GOSP	38
(I KNEW IT WEL) FILS ALL THE PLACE. . . .	214	MISERY	52
NOT BUT I KNOW THOU HAST A SHORTER CUT . . .	234	MUTINIE	26
DARES KNOW EFFECTS, AND JUDGE THEM LONG BEFORE .	236	CONSTLATN	27
NO VOICE, NOR VISION KNOW	238	SHEPHEARDS	18
I KNOW THEE WELL, FOR I HAVE FRAM'D . . .	225	RETIREMENT	23
I KNOW THY LOT	225	RETIREMENT	26
WHO KNOW, HOW WELL THOU CANST RELIEVE . . .	301	PROVIDENCE	41
WHO WERT ALL FALSE, SHOULD'ST TRUE GRIEF KNOW. .	305	ST MARY MN	64
YET I KNOW WELL, AND SO OUR SINS REQUIRE . .	307	RAIN-BOW	41
BUT WHERE TO ACT, THAT NONE SHALL KNOW . . .	313	THE STONE	2
MY DEAR, DEAR GOD. I DO NOT KNOW	315	DWELLNG-PL	11
FOR KNOW, WILDE MEN, THAT WHEN YOU ERRE . .	314	THE STONE	42
AS MADE HIM KNOW HIS GOD BY NIGHT. . . .	323	THE NIGHT	6
I WILL DO NOTHING, NOTHING KNOW, NOR SEE . .	321	HIDDN TRSR	31
THE MOST REMOTE, WHO KNOW NOT THEE . . .	336	PSALM 65	23
O GOD. I KNOW AND DO CONFESS	333	AGREEMENT	43
I KNOW (MY GOD) THIS WOULD NOT BE. . . .	333	AGREEMENT	60
DO KNOW THY DEWY MORNING-HOURS	301	PROVIDENCE	28
BECAUSE INCERTAINTIES WE CAN NOT KNOW . . .	183	THRS A TYE	23
PEACE, PEACE. I KNOW 'TWAS BRAVE	173	CONTENT	1
I SEE THE USE. AND KNOW MY BLOOD	175	THE STORM	1
O LET ME (LIKE HIM) KNOW MY END. . . .	167	THE CALL	86
I BEG'D HERE LONG, AND GRCN'D TO KNOW . . .	167	VNTY SPRIT	3
TO MEASURE OUT THY LENGTH, AS IF THOU'DST KNOW .	158	THE LAMPE	15
WHILST I EACH MINUTE GRONE TO KNOW . . .	143	DEATH	29
AND OAK DOTH KNOW I AM. CANST THOU NOT SING. . .	192	RLS + LSNS	16
NOW SCATTER'D THUS, DOST KNOW THEM SO. . . .	347	THE BOOK	24
SO SHALL WE KNOW IN WAR AND PEACE	351	L'ENVOY	59
KNOW'ST			
THOU THAT KNOW'ST FOR WHOM I MOURNE . . .	165	THE CALL	30
O, YES. THOU KNOW'ST I DOE, COME, AND RELIEVE .	161	DSTROCTION	28
KNOW'ST TO BE TRUE)	170	COME, COME	9
I, DO NOT GO. THOU KNOW'ST, I'LE DYE. . . .	293	BEGGING B	1
BEFORE THEY COME, AND KNOW'ST HOW NEAR THEY BE. .	289	THE TIMBER	16
ALL FLESH IS CLAY, THOU KNOW'ST, AND BUT THAT GOD .	221	AFFLICTION	11
STIL THINE THOU KNOW'ST, AND IF NOT SO . . .	242	MISERY	91
KNOWING			
BUT GOING HENCE, AND KNOWING WEL WHAT WOES . .	243	THE SAP	23
BY KNOWING, WHERE 'TWAS, OR WHERE NOT . . .	141	RGNRTN	88
O KNOWING, GLORIOUS SPIRIT. WHEN	347	THE BOOK	25
OF KNOWING THEE, SO RARELY KNOWN. . . .	346	THE QUEER	16
A KNOWING JOY.	345	QUICKNESS	10
AND KNOWING LAMP	340	THE FEAST	46

		PAGE	TITLE	LINE
KNOWLEDGE				
AND HERE, WITHOUT MY KNOWLEDGE, PLAC'D	. . . .	346	THE QUEER	10
MORE PUNISHMENT, THAN KNOWLEDGE TO MY SENSE.	. . .	159	MANS FALL	14
KNOWN				
THAT DARK, AND DEAD SLEEPS IN ITS KNOWN	. . .	179	SILENCE	21
SO HAVE I KNOWN SOME BEAUTEOUS PAISAGE RISE	. . .	245	MT. OLV. B	17
SEEM MILD, BUT ARE KNOWN BY THEIR NOISE.	. . .	237	CONSTLATN	44
ABOVE THEM THE COOL MOON HER KNOWN COURSE HOLDS	. .	286	PSALM 104	51
AT THY REBUKE THEY FLED, AT THE KNOWN VOICE	. .	285	PSALM 104	21
IN A STATE KNOWN TO NONE BUT THEE	. . . .	319	THE ASS	58
OF KNOWING THEE, SO RARELY KNOWN.	. . . .	346	THE QUEER	16
OR THAT THY TRUTH WAS NOT HERE KNOWN	. . .	350	L'ENVOY	31
YET HAVE I KNOWNE THY SLIGHTEST THINGS	. . .	166	THE CALL	50
YEA, I HAVE KNOWNE THESE SHREDS CUT LAST	. . .	166	THE CALL	54
KNOWS				
THAT CHANGE, AND KNOWS THY CLAY.	. . . .	181	BURIALL	30
KNOWS EV'RY NOTE, AND CALL	. . . .	161	DSTRCCTION	14
HIS RIGHTEOUS COURSE, THAT THOUGH HE KNOWS	. .	314	THE STONE	30
AND THY OLD ENEMY, WHICH KNOWS	. . . .	335	JUDGEMENT	29
WHO KNOWS EARTH NOTHING HATH	. . . .	327	RIGHTSNESS	31
WHEN TH' HERB HE TREADS KNOWS MUCH, MUCH MORE.	.	236	CONSTLATN	28
HE KNOWS HE HATH A HOME, BUT SCARCE KNOWS WHERE	.	246	MAN	19
HE KNOWS HE HATH A HOME, BUT SCARCE KNOWS WHERE	.	246	MAN	19
THOUGH HE KNOWS THESE, AND HATH MORE OF HIS OWN	.	224	TEMPEST	38
LIFE'S BUT A BLAST, HE KNOWS IT, WHAT. SHAL STRAW	.	224	TEMPEST	49
ARE GIVEN TO BIRDS, WHO, BUT THEE KNOWS	. . .	277	COCK-CRWNG	33
LABOURS				
O'RE ALL THEIR PILGRIMAGE, AND LABOURS LEAP	. .	159	MANS FALL	29
LABRYINTH				
MAKE NOT THY BREAST A LABRYINTH, OR TRAP.	. .	193	RLS + LSNS	56
LACED				
OR A LACED STORY.	. . . .	173	CONTENT	18
LACK				
AND LEST I SHOULD LACK FOR ARREARS	. . .	208	REPENTANCE	43
AND GODS OWN LODGING (THOUGH HE COULD NOT LACK)	.	238	SHEPHEARDS	29
SO SURE TO THEE, THAT NONE DOTH LACK	. .	343	WATER-FALL	20
LACKING				
NOTHING NOW TO MAN IS LACKING	. . . .	218	EASTER HYM	2
LAD				
WHEN THOU DIDST HEAR THE WEEPING LAD.	. .	293	BEGGING B	12
LADDERS				
SLEEPS AT THE LADDERS FOOT, ALAS. WHAT CAN	. .	224	TEMPEST	39
LADIES				
LEARN, LADIES, HERE THE FAITHFUL CURE	. . .	305	ST MARY MN	45
LAG				
LET FOLLY DUST IT ON, OR LAG BEHIND.	. . .	193	RLS + LSNS	52
LAHAI-ROIS				
SO FROM LAHAI-ROIS WELL SOME SPICIE CLOUD	. .	155	ISAACS M.	53
LAID				
HIS PASSIVE COTTAGE, WHICH (THOUGH LAID ASIDE)	.	145	RSRCTN +IM	45
BEING LAID, AND DREST FOR SLEEP, CLOSE NOT THY EYES	.	195	RLS + LSNS	127
LAID UP ALL HER ARCHIVES AND BOOKS)	. . .	303	ORNAMENT	12
THY ARM UNMOVEABLE FOR EVER LAID	. . .	285	PSALM 104	17
WEARY OF THIS SAME CLAY, AND STRAW, I LAID	. .	233	MUTINIE	1
WAS ONCE LAID FOR ME IN THY GRAVE.	. . .	342	OBSEQUIES	28
LAINE				
'TIS NOW, SINCE YOU HAVE LAINE THUS DEAD	. .	164	THE CALL	3
LAKE				
'TWAS SO. I SAW THY BIRTH. THAT DROWSIE LAKE	. .	160	THE SHOWRE	1
MY SELF ALL TEARS, A WEEPING LAKE.	. . .	328	ANGUISH	12
LAMB				
A WOLF, MORE THEN A LAMP OR DOVE.	. . .	321	CHILDEHOOD	10
TO SEE THE LAMB, WHICH ALL AT ONCE	. . .	294	PALM-SUNDY	13
PASTURES OF LIFE, WHERE THE LAMB GOES.	. .	319	THE ASS	52
BUT THE BLOOD OF THE BLESSED LAMB.	. . .	317	MEN OF WAR	52
SO MILD A LAMB CAN NEVER BE	. . . .	152	THE SEARCH	51
O BLESSED LAMB.	. . . . .	186	PASSION	44
AND LIKE THAT LAMB WHICH HAD THE DRAGONS VOICE	.	237	CONSTLATN	43
THAT LAMB OF GOD ADORE	. . . .	239	SHEPHEARDS	48
THAT LAMB WHOSE DAIES GREAT KINGS AND PROPHETS WISH'D	.	239	SHEPHEARDS	49
MOST BLESSED LAMB. AND MILDEST DOVE.	. . .	208	REPENTANCE	48
FOUNTAINS OF LIFE, WHERE THE LAMB GOES.	. .	344	WATER-FALL	26
LAMP				
AND KNOWING LAMP	. . . . .	340	THE FEAST	46
FIXETH A SOLITARY LAMP	. . . .	178	SILENCE	7
MY LAMP, AND LIFE, BOTH SHALL IN THEE ABIDE.	.	177	MRNG-WTCH	33
THY BEAMS HOME WITH THEE. TRIM THY LAMP, BUY OYL	.	195	RLS + LSNS	110
SHOULD MIST WITHIN ME, AND PUT OUT THAT LAMP	.	188	RELAPSE	15
FROM THY BRIGHT LAMP DID SHINE	. . .	310	THE SEED	70
LAMPS				
WE CLIMB ABOVE ALL AGES, LAMPS THAT LIGHT	. .	2	SON-DAYES	6
LAND				
SINCE IN A LAND NOT BARREN STIL	. . .	227	LV + DSPLN	1
A LAND OF FLOWERS AND SPICES. THE WORD GIVEN	.	276	PROFFER	47
'TWILL MAKE THE LAND OF DARKNESS LIGHT.	. .	299	JESUS WP B	51
THIS LAND, THOUGH WITH THY HEARTS BLEST EXTRACT FED	.	296	JESUS WP A	17
O AIR, AND SEA, AND LAND.	. . .	284	PSALM 104	8
BUT AS THESE BIRDS OF LIGHT MAKE A LAND GLAD	.	288	THE BIRD	23
THE PLEASANT LAND TO BRIMSTONE TURNS	. .	288	THE BIRD	29
WHERE ALL THE LAND WITH SCORCHING HEAT IS CURST.	.	290	THE TIMBER	46

		PAGE	TITLE	LINE
LAND	(CCN'T)			
WHO IN THAT LAND CF DARKNESS AND BLINDE EYES		323	THE NIGHT	8
THOU WATER'ST EVERY RIDGE CF LAND		337	PSALM 65	33
TC THY DARK LAND THESE FEEDLESS GC.		338	DEATH B	11
'TIS A SAD LAND, THAT IN CNE DAY		142	DEATH	1
LANGUAGE				
AND ON THE DUMBE SHADES LANGUAGE SPENT		141	RGNRTN	60
WITH WHICH IN MILD, CHAST LANGUAGE SHE DID WCCE		155	ISAACS M.	41
HAVE CNE LARGE LANGUAGE, DEATH.		201	THE CHECK	28
LANGUAGE TO LCVE		162	MT. OLVS A	3
LANGUISH				
DIDST THOU LANGUISH		185	PASSION	23
MUST LANGUISH AND DECREASE.		285	PSALM 104	28
LANGUISHETH				
LCVE LANGUISHETH, AND MEMCRY DCTH RUST		183	THRS A TYE	3
NCW LANGUISHED AND DIED		238	SHEPHEARDS	20
LAPT				
LAPT IN THE SWEETS OF THY YOUNG BREATH		209	THE BURIAL	10
LARGE				
HAVE CNE LARGE LANGUACE, DEATH.		201	THE CHECK	28
CHAMBERS CF RAIN, WHERE HEAV'NS LARGE BOTTLES LIE		285	PSALM 104	38
THROUGH A LARGE DUSKY GLASSE		309	THE SEED	50
LAST				
AND THE LAST IS MCST LOATHSCME DUST.		302	ORNAMENT	8
HER ART. WHOSE MEMORY MUST LAST		305	ST MARY MN	51
AND HEAR MY HEARTS LAST PRIVATE THROWS.		334	AGREEMENT	66
THE LAST CNE, AND THE LEAST.		329	TEARS	8
NCR DID THOSE LAST, BUT (LIKE HIMSELF) DYED STILL		196	CORRUPTION	11
WHICH SHEW'D THEE LAST, BUT DID DEFEAT		178	SILENCE	15
YEA, I HAVE KNOWNE THESE SHREDS CUT LAST		166	THE CALL	54
THROUGH ALL THE CREATURES, CAME AT LAST		168	VNTY SPRIT	14
IT GRIEV'D ME MUCH. AT LAST, SAID I		168	VNTY SPRIT	29
YET, THIS TAKE WITH THEE. THE LAST GASP OF TIME		178	EVNG-WTCH	15
PERHAPS AT LAST		160	THE SHOWRE	16
I SOJCURN'D THUS, AT LAST JESFLRUNS KING		159	MANS FALL	16
WHEN ALL IS SPENT, THY LAST, AND SURE SUPPLY		158	THE LAMPE	20
AT LAST WITH THOUGHT		141	RGNRTN	71
SC SIGH'D I UPWARDS STILL, AT LAST		139	RGNRTN	26
'TIS LAST GOOD-NIGHT, OUR SUNNE SHALL NEVER SET.		143	DEATH	32
UNTILL AT LAST FULL WITH THE VITALL RAY		144	RSRCTN +IM	9
THIS LAST WILL KEEPE THE FIRST TWC FRESH		148	DAY OF JDG	43
LCATH HENCE TC PART, AT LAST I RISE		152	THE SEARCH	33
IT WAS LAST DAY		207	REPENTANCE	27
WHEN THE VEYL BRCKE WITH THY LAST BREATH		219	HOLY COMM.	22
FROM THIS, UNTO THE LAST CF DAIES.		218	EASTER HYM	18
AND PRAY, THESE LAST MAY BE AS FIRST		273	WHT SUNDAY	26
HAST SAID, THESE LAST SHOLLD BE THE WCRST.		273	WHT SUNDAY	28
SC IN THIS LAST AND LEWDEST ACE		273	WHT SUNDAY	39
AND THE LAST STEPS OF MY MILDE MASTER TRACE.		268	ASCN-DAY A	50
THEY PASS AS AT THE LAST GREAT DAY, AND RUN		268	ASCN-DAY A	29
TAKE THIS LAST KISS, AND LET ME WEEP		348	HOLY BIBLE	3
LASTING				
MAKES BEAUTY LASTING, FRESH AND PURE.		305	ST MARY MN	46
LASTS				
LASTS NCT A NIGHT SCMETIMES. BAD SPIRITS FEAR		195	RLS + LSNS	124
LATE				
O THEN IT WILBE ALL TCC LATE		147	DAY OF JDG	25
IN TH'ONE LATE PAINES		139	RGNRTN	31
LCDGED IN THOSE FALSE LCOKS, TILL TCO LATE.		311	FAIR+YONG	22
SAY IT IS LATE AND DUSKY, BECAUSE THEY		325	THE NIGHT	51
WHO DC NOT SO, TCO LATE REPENT		274	PROFFER	12
THIS LATE, LONG HEAT MAY HIS INSTRUCTION BE		222	TEMPEST	3
EARLY, ASWEL AS LATE		245	MAN	6
MY GLCRIOUS LIBERTY, STILL LATE.		344	WATER-FALL	38
LATELY				
FIX'D LATELY CN THE CROSS, NCW CN THE SKIES.		268	ASCN-DAY A	54
LATER				
BUT TC THIS LATER LIGHT THEY SAW IN HIM		239	SHEPHEARDS	53
OF SUMMERS LATER STORE		345	THE WREATH	6
LATEST				
THE LATEST MODES CF PRICE AND LUST		302	ORNAMENT	6
LATTER				
DEAR JESUS WEEP ON. PCUR THIS LATTER		296	JESUS WP A	9
LAUGHS				
THIS WORLD BUT LAUGHS AT THCSE THAT WEEP.		312	FAIR+YONG	52
LAUGHTER				
THE WISE-MANS MADNES LAUGHTER.		166	THE CALL	65
LAW				
FCR SINNE TOCKE STRENGTH, AND VIGCUR FROM THE LAW.		159	MANS FALL	20
RETURN UPON HIMSELF THE LAW, AND STONES.		198	SCRIPTURES	12
AS THOU DIDST SET NO LAW FOR ME		318	THE ASS	9
THE LAW DELIVERED TO THE JEWS		314	THE STONE	46
AND ALL THAT DISTANCE WAS LAW AND COMMAND.		331	JACOBS PLW	48
O PLANT IN ME THY GOSPEL, AND THY LAW		230	LAW + GOSP	27
AND SHINE FROM PARAN, WHEN A FIRIE LAW		229	LAW + GOSP	2
TO CRCWN HIS TEMPLES. SHAL DREAMS BE HIS LAW.		224	TEMPEST	52
THE LAW, AND CEREMCNIES MADE		210	FAITH	13
THEREFORE WRITE IN THEIR HEARTS THY LAW		351	L'ENVOY	53
LAWFUL				
OR THOUGH IT SHOULD BE LAWFUL, MAY		319	THE ASS	39

		PAGE	TITLE	LINE
LAWS				
AND SETS UP LAWS TC PULL HIS FCNCR DOWN.	. . . .	330	JACOBS PLW	20
AT WHCSE JUST LAWS NOT JUST MEN GRUDGE.	. . . .	326	ABELS BLOD	24
THY LAWS BUT NETS, WHERE SOME SMALL BIRCS	. . .	207	REPENTANCE	11
LAY				
TC BRASSE, ANC IRCN, WHEN MY STCCK LAY DEAD	. . .	213	ADMISSION	3
ALL SCATTER'D LAY, WHILE FE HIS EYES DID POUR	. . .	231	THE WORLD	14
THEN LAY THAT TRESPASSE IN THE SHADE	. . .	240	MISERY	22
WHILE PALESTINE WAS FAST A SLEEP, AND LAY	. . .	238	SHEPHEARDS	7
THY ARM DID FIRST THE MCUNTAINS LAY	. . .	336	PSALM 65	21
WFILE SCDCM YET DID SMOKE, LAY WITH THEIR SIRE.	. .	307	RAIN-BOW	32
THE BEAMS OF THY BRIGHT CHAMBERS THOU DOST LAY	.	284	PSALM 104	9
AFFCRCED VISITS, AND STILL PARADISE LAY	. . .	197	CORRUPTION	23
ANGELS LAY LEIGER HERE, EACH BUSH, AND CEL	. . .	197	CORRUPTION	25
WHEN SEASONS CHANGE, THEN LAY BEFCRE THINE EYES	.	194	RLS + LSNS	91
BUT ALL THE EARE LAY HUSH	. . . . .	140	RGNRTN	57
AND LCW AS ERE THEY LAY BEFCRE	. . . .	147	DAY OF JDG	11
IN THCSE CALME, GOLDEN EVENINGS LAY	. . .	151	THE SEARCH	24
QUITE SPENT WITH THOUGHTS I LEFT MY CELL, ANC LAY	.	167	VNTY SPRIT	1
WHERE ALL HER SECRETS LAY A BED	. . . .	168	VNTY SPRIT	12
THE SHEEP BLEAT THEE A SILLY LAY	. . . .	163	MT. OLVS A	14
LAYD				
I TOOKE THEM UP AND LAYC	. . . . .	139	RGNRTN	30
AND LAYC SURPRIZES IN EACH ELEMENT.	. . . .	223	TEMPEST	24
LAYING				
LAYING BY THY ROBES CF GLCRY	. . . . .	163	INCARNA'TN	2
LAYS				
WHILE THE MANS ZEAL LAYS CUT ANC BLENDS	. . .	332	AGREEMENT	29
LAZARUS				
THUS LAZARUS WAS CARRIEC CUT CF TCWN.	. . .	183	THRS A TYE	17
LAZIE				
AND BAC THE LAZIE SUNNE MAKE HASTE	. . .	143	DEATH	21
HEAVEN WITH A LAZIE BREATH, BLT FRUITLES THIS	. .	160	THE SHOWRE	8
SUCH AS DCTH GILD THE LAZIE GLCW-WORMS BED.	. .	157	THE LAMPE	4
LEAD				
A LIFE WELL LEAD	. . . . . .	174	JOY OF LIF	5
TC THINK, HE SHOULD BE SO LCNG VAINLY LEAC.	. .	290	THE TIMBER	40
AND LEAC BY MY OWN FOOLISH FIRE	. . .	311	FAIR+YONG	5
AS WHERE TO LEAD THEIR SHEEP, WHAT SILENT NOCK	.	239	SHEPHEARDS	39
CANST LIGHT AND LEAD ME THERE WITH SUCH REDRESS	.	234	MUTINIE	31
LEAC ME ABOVE	. . . . . .	248	I WALKT	58
AND DAILY DIDST MY YONG EYES LEAC	. . .	348	HOLY BIBLE	7
THOU CIDST LEAD TO, AND STILL ALL STRIFE.	. .	348	HOLY BIBLE	32
UNLESS THAT SPIRIT LEAD HIS MINCE	. . . .	344	WATER-FALL	30
LEADEN				
THIS LEADEN STATE, WHICH MEN MISCAL	. . . .	319	THE ASS	55
LEADER				
AND LEADER THRCUGH THICK DEATH AND NIGHT.	. . .	326	ABELS BLOD	32
LEADERS				
WHOSE LEACERS TO THOSE PASTURES, AND CLEER SPRINGS	.	238	SHEPHEARDS	3
LEADING				
I SEE HIM LEADING OUT HIS CHOSEN TRAIN	. . .	268	ASCN-DAY A	51
HAVE CUR SURE GUARDIAN, AND CLR LEADING LIGHT.	.	331	JACOBS PLW	50
LEADS				
AND PRECIPICE IT LEADS TO, BIC ME FLIE	. . .	320	HIDDN TRSR	17
LEADS OTHERS, SHALL A CAPTIVE BE.	. . .	316	MEN OF WAR	4
LEADS UP TO GCD	. . . .	233	THE WORLD	54
LEADS TO THAT WAY	. . . . . .	226	RETIREMENT	32
LEAF				
NOR ANY THOUGHT OF GREENNESS, LEAF OR BARK.	. .	289	THE TIMBER	12
WHAT CNE POOR LEAF DIC EVER : YET FALL	. .	198	UNPRFTBLNS	14
LEAFE				
OR LEAFE BUT HATH HIS MCRNING-FYMN. EACH BUSF	. .	192	RLS + LSNS	15
TRANSPLANTED THUS, ONE LEAFE CF HIS T'AWAKE	. .	158	MANS FALL	5
TC SEE, IF ANY LEAFE HAD MADE	. . . .	141	RGNRTN	84
LEAFS				
WITHIN WHOSE SACRED LEAFS DID LIE	. . . .	323	THE NIGHT	17
THEIR LEAFS WITH WATER, AND HUMICITIE.	. .	223	TEMPEST	34
THE TREES, THEIR LEAFS, TFE FLCWRES, THEIR SEEDING.	.	207	REPENTANCE	34
THY CHOSEN FLCCK, LIKE LEAFS IN A HIGH WIND	. .	229	LAW + GOSP	9
MY WITHER'D LEAFS AGAIN LCOK GREEN AND FLOURISH	.	245	MT. OLV. B	22
AS LEAFS IN BCWERS	. . . . . .	281	JOY	23
LEAGUE				
LIV'D STILL IN LEAGUE WITF THY CHASTE FIRE	. .	312	FAIR+YONG	28
LEANNESS				
ALL WCULD BE DROUGHT, AND LEANNESS, NOT A TREE	.	222	AFFLICTION	23
LEAP				
O'RE ALL THEIR PILGRIMACE, ANC LABOURS LEAP	. . .	159	MANS FALL	29
BIRDS SING, BEASTS FEED, FISH LEAP, AND TH'EARTH STANDS FAST	194	RLS + LSNS	88
LEARN				
WHAT MAN MAY LEARN FROM THEE.	. . .	278	THE STARRE	12
THEY WOULD SOON QUIT ANC LEARN TO KNEEL.	. .	308	THE SEED	4
DID LEARN TO SUCK, AND SIP, ANC TASTE	. . .	308	THE SEED	10
LEARN MARYS ART OF TEARS, AND THEN	. . .	305	ST MARY MN	47
LEARN, LACIES, HERE THE FAITHFUL CURE	. . .	305	ST MARY MN	45
AND TIME TO LEARN.	. . . . .	342	OBSEQUIES	24
WITH LEARNED SWAINES, AND ECCFC YET	. . .	162	MT. OLVS A	10
LEARNES				
THEN CRILLING ON, LEARNFS TC ENCREASE	. . .	150	RELIGION	37
LEARNT				
TC LETTERS, TILL I LEARNT TO REAC.	. . . .	348	HOLY BIBLE	8

	PAGE	TITLE	LINE
LEASE			
AND EVERY ONE CAN SLIGHT HIS LEASE	338	DEATH B	8
LEAST			
THE LAST CNE, AND THE LEAST.	329	TEARS	8
WHERE THOU TOC HAST BUT THE LEAST PART	315	DWELLNG-PL	15
THOSE SECRET SINS WE LEAST SUSPECT.	314	THE STONE	41
WITH THY LEAST TOUCH, LIGHTNINGS AND WINCS THAT RACE	287	PSALM 104	87
LEAST MOTION, OR REPLY	141	RGNRTN	85
WHEN THY LEAST BREATH SUSTAINES MY WING.	182	CHRFLNESS	3
WHO MAKES HIS JESTS OF SINS, MUST BE AT LEAST	194	RLS + LSNS	77
LEAVE			
WHEN FIRST THY EYES UNVEIL, GIVE THY SOUL LEAVE	191	RLS + LSNS	1
O LEAVE THY CARES, AND FOLLIES. GC THIS WAY	192	RLS + LSNS	17
TAKE THEIR LEAVE, AND CIE. BIRCS, BEASTS, EACH TREE	201	THE CHECK	27
BUT FINCING NCNE, SHAL LEAVE THEE TC THE WINC	201	THE CHECK	8
LEAVE THEN THY FOCLISH RANGES.	184	PEACE	17
I SHALL NC WARD-ROBES LEAVE	173	CONTENT	6
LEAVE, LEAVE, THY GADCINC THOLGHTS.	153	THE SEARCH	75
LEAVE, LEAVE, THY GADCINC THOLGHTS.	153	THE SEARCH	75
AND EVER RUNNING, TILL WE LEAVE TC FLING	291	THE TIMBER	55
LIFT UP YCUR HEADS AND LEAVE YCUR MOANS.	294	PALM-SUNDY	14
LEAVE THEN YONG SCRCERESS. THE ICE	297	HERODIAS	9
BUT 'TWAS THY LOVE THAT (WITHCLT LEAVE)	299	JESUS WP B	32
AND WILT NOT LEAVE ME, WHEN GRCWN OLD.	301	PROVIDENCE	45
THESE WEIGHTS, AND GIVE MY SPIRIT LEAVE	329	ANGUISH	17
AND GCING HENCE, LEAVE WRITTEN CN SCME TREE	281	JOY	29
LORD THEN TAKE IT, LEAVE IT NCT	249	BEGGING A	17
LEAVE, AND BE WISE.	266	VAIN WITS	2
TC LEAVE THOSE SKIES	275	PROFFER	22
THY BLESSED HANDS TO BLESS, THESE THOU DCST LEAVE.	268	ASCN-DAY A	56
LEAVE BEHINDE THEM THE CLD MAN	269	ASCSN-HYMN	12
SHOULC LEAVE THE SPHERE	269	ASCSN-HYMN	14
BUT THOU MUST ALSC LEAVE	220	HOLY COMM.	43
THEY LEAVE THEIR FLOCK, AND IN A BUSIE TALK	239	SHEPHEARDS	43
LEAVES			
ARE BUT MEER LEAVES TURN'C BY THY BREATH.	219	HOLY COMM.	16
THINE ARE THE PRESENT HEALING LEAVES	332	AGREEMENT	20
THY LEAVES ARE HEALING WINGS HE SPREADS.	333	AGREEMENT	36
AND LEAVES THY SPIRIT DCTH STILL FAN	148	RELIGION	2
LEAVES ME A SLAVE TC PASSIONS, AND MY FATE.	158	MANS FALL	8
'TWAS BUT JUST NOW MY BLEAK LEAVES HOPELES HUNG	198	UNPRFTBLNS	2
MY YIELDING LEAVES. SCMETIMES A SHOWR	203	DSRDR + FR	25
BUT SHUTS HIS DOOR, AND LEAVES GOOD OUT ALL NIGHT.	194	RLS + LSNS	84
OF NIGHT SHUT UP THY LEAVES, BE CHAST, GOD PRYS	196	RLS + LSNS	136
LEAVING			
LEAVING ME DEAC	203	DSRDR + FR	42
LEAVING FCR US (WHOSE GCODNESS QUICKLY FADES)	326	RIGHTSNESS	3
LEAVING THE WCRLD THEIR DAY	267	ASCN-DAY A	11
LEBANCN			
CEDARS IN LEBANCN, IN WHOSE THICK BOUGHS	286	PSALM 104	46
LECTURES			
MAKES UP BUT LECTURES FCR HIS EYE, AND EAR.	223	TEMPEST	20
LED			
O LET HIM BY HIS LORD BE LEC	319	THE ASS	59
WHO CARRIES THEE, IS BY THEE LEC	318	THE ASS	23
OBEY'C, AND LEC	140	RGNRTN	35
LED BY THY LOVE WCULDST STCOP THUS LOW	180	BURIALL	17
LEFT			
JCY OF MY LIFE. WHILE LEFT ME HERE	174	JOY OF LIF	1
WHERE FIRST I LEFT MY GLORICUS TRAINE	170	RETREATE	24
LEST LEFT ALONE TCO LCNC	161	DSTROCTION	31
THE LCST SONNE HAC NOT LEFT THE HUSKE	162	PURSUITE	11
QUITE SPENT WITH THOUGHTS I LEFT MY CELL, AND LAY	167	VNTY SPRIT	1
HAVE LEFT US, WHILE WE CARELESS SATE	164	THE CALL	12
OF ALL HIS DUST LEFT HERE.	165	THE CALL	33
AND SCMETHING STILL BE LEFT THE DEAD	142	DEATH	8
WHAT STOCK, AND HOW MUCH TIME WERE LEFT THEE NCW.	158	THE LAMPE	16
AND SCON AS LEFT, SHRINKS BACK TO ILL.	308	THE SEED	18
HE THAT HATH LEFT LIFES VAIN JCYS AND VAIN CARE	290	THE TIMBER	29
LEFT FOR US HERE.	210	FAITH	24
AND HERE ARE LEFT AS NOTHING WCRTH	270	ASCSN-HYMN	29
AND OFT LEFT OPEN WOULD'ST CONVEY	348	HOLY BIBLE	19
LEGICNS			
THOU WOULCST NO LEGIONS, BUT WCLLDST BLEED.	316	MEN OF WAR	24
LEIGER			
ANGELS LAY LEIGER HERE, EACH BUSH, AND CEL	197	CORRUPTION	25
LEISURE			
WHERE LIGHT, JOY, LEISURE, AND TRUE COMFORTS MCVE	248	I WALKT	59
SWEET, HARMLES LIVES (ON WHOSE HCLY LEISURE	238	SHEPHEARDS	1
LEND			
MY REST IN CARES, AND TC THE CARK WORLD LEND	157	THE LAMPE	6
STILL MCRE AFFLICTIONS LEND	147	DAY OF JDG	34
THOU COST THUS LEND	182	CHRFLNESS	14
TO LEND ME, THCUGH FRCM FAR, CNE LOOK.	293	BEGGING B	4
HUNTS GOLD AND WEALTH, AND WILL NOT LEND	301	PROVIDENCE	33
LENDS			
WHO LENDS, NOT TO BE PAID	328	RIGHTSNESS	40
LENGTH			
AT LENGTH, MY LIFES KINDE ANGEL CAME	332	AGREEMENT	7
TC MEASURE OUT THY LENGTH, AS IF THOU'DST KNCW	158	THE LAMPE	15

		PAGE	TITLE	LINE
LENGTH	**(CCN'T)**			
AT LENGTH I FEEL MY HEAD TO AKE		214	MISERY	61
LET IT SUFFICE AT LENGTH THY FITS		225	RETIREMENT	12
THE WEAK, AND AGED TIR'D, WITH LENGTH		218	EASTER HYM	9
AND AS THOU GIV'ST LINE, AND LENGTH		214	PRAISE	11
BY THIS MILDE ART OF LOVE AT LENGTH		348	HOLY BIBLE	23
LENT				
TO FUNERALS, AND LENT.		226	RETIREMENT	50
THAT DEW THEY LENT, A BREATHING SACRIFICE.		156	ISAACS M.	62
BUT, O HIS GRAVE, WHERE I SAW LENT		152	THE SEARCH	45
ONLY A LITTLE FOUNTAIN LENT		141	RGNRTN	58
NO BLISS HERE LENT		339	THE FEAST	7
LEPER				
GO LEPER, GO. WASH TILL THY FLESH		306	ST MARY MN	69
THIS LEPER HAUNT, AND SOYL THY DOOR		200	NTVTY 1	26
LEPROUS				
HE IS STILL LEPROUS, THAT STILL PAINTS.		306	ST MARY MN	71
LESS'NING				
AND LESS'NING STILL GROW UP INVISIBLY		224	TEMPEST	44
LESSE				
SAID LITTLE LESSE.		* 232	THE WORLD	41
O LET NOT ME DO LESSE. SHALL THEY		187	NO DO THEY	31
LESSE FRIEND TO ME.		144	RSRCTN +IM	16
I FIND MY SELFE THE LESSE, THE MORE I GROW.		161	DSTRQCTION	10
OR THAT THY STORE WAS LESSE		161	DSTRQCTION	23
TO MAKE US MORE, THOU WOULDST BE LESSE		163	INCARNATN	3
MY LIGHT HAD LESSEND NOT		161	DSTRQCTION	8
LESSER				
WHAT IN THE LESSER HE WOULD DO.		221	AFFLICTION	10
AND BY THIS LESSER COMMERCE KEEP.		273	WHT SUNDAY	22
AND STILL THE LESSER BY THE BEST		278	THE STARRE	7
THAT ONE MADE ALL THESE LESSER LIGHTS.		309	THE SEED	28
MAKE LESSER MORNINGS, WHEN THE GREAT ARE DONE.		288	THE BIRD	18
DOTH BROACH THE EARTH, AND LESSER BROOKS LETS FORTH		285	PSALM 104	30
LESSON				
THEIR LESSON TAUGHT THEM, WHEN FIRST MADE.		288	THE BIRD	12
A LESSON PLAID HIM BY A WINDE OR WAVE.		280	JOY	8
LET				
O LET NO STAR COMPARE WITH THEE.		281	THE FAVOUR	9
SO LET THY GRACE NOW MAKE THE WAY		274	WHT SUNDAY	57
LET NOT THY STARS FOR BALAAMS HIRE		274	WHT SUNDAY	63
LET NO NIGHT PUT OUT THIS SUN.		249	BEGGING A	4
LET MY YOUTH, MY BLOOM OF DAYES		249	BEGGING A	7
O MY GOD, LET IT BE THINE.		249	BEGGING A	20
LET IT SUFFICE AT LENGTH THY FITS		225	RETIREMENT	12
WITHOUT A STEEL, O LET THY POWER CLEER		224	TEMPEST	59
LET HIM (THOUGH POOR)		215	PRAISE	54
LET HIM SO FOLLOW HERE, THAT IN THE END		216	DRESSING	17
WHAT EVER THOU DOST BID, LET FAITH MAKE GOOD		216	DRESSING	23
O LET NOT ME DO SO.		217	DRESSING	39
YET LET MY COURSE, MY AIM, MY LOVE		212	DAWNING	43
AND LET THY BEGGER LIE		213	ADMISSION	10
SO LET ME ALL MY BUSIE AGE		212	DAWNING	37
O LET THY JUSTICE THEN IN HIM CONFINE		209	REPENTANCE	85
LET ME SO STRIVE AND STRUGGLE WITH THY FOES		234	MUTINIE	14
LET ME NOT SPIL, BUT DRINK THY BLOOD		230	LAW + GOSP	31
LET ME NOT SCATTER, AND DESPISE MY FOOD		230	LAW + GOSP	34
O LET MY CRIE COME TO THY THRONE.		242	MISERY	107
GOOD STORE OF IT, BUT LET		244	THE SAP	36
LORD, BIND ME UP, AND LET ME LYE		239	MISERY	1
AND YET SHOULDST THOU LET GO THY HOLD		240	MISERY	7
I SHUT THEE OUT, AND LET THAT SLIP		240	MISERY	31
WOULDST HAVE A WREATH THAT FADES NOT, LET THEM GROW		283	GARLAND	34
SO LET THE ANTY-TYPES IN ME		284	TRINITY-SN	7
BUT NONE CAN SEQUESTER OR LET		300	PROVIDENCE	22
LET THE JOY'D RODE MAKE HOLY-DAY		294	PALM-SUNDY	8
LET GLORY BE THEIR BAIT, WHOSE MINDES		309	THE SEED	33
LET ME THY ASS BE ONELY WISE		318	THE ASS	21
LET ME NOT FAIL TO QUESTION, WHO		319	THE ASS	30
AND IF NOT THOU, LET NOT ME DO'T.		319	THE ASS	32
LET ME ADMIRE THOSE, AND BE KINDE		319	THE ASS	35
O LET HIM BY HIS LORD BE LED		319	THE ASS	59
THAT THESE THREE THOUSAND YEARS TIME DID LET FALL		320	HIDDN TRSR	8
TO SHUN THAT PERIL, LET THY GRACE		319	THE ASS	41
LET ME BE WISE TO PLEASE THEE STILL		319	THE ASS	43
AND LET MEN CALL ME WHAT THEY WILL.		319	THE ASS	44
SAITH HOLY JOHN, THEN LET HIM HEAR.		316	MEN OF WAR	2
THEN LET NOT DUST YOUR EYES OBSCURE		339	DEATH B	28
BUT MEER DISDAIN, LET NOT MAN SAY		335	JUDGEMENT	43
O LET THAT SILENCE THEN PREVAIL.		334	AGREEMENT	64
OR LET ME DYE.		329	ANGUISH	20
AND LET ME DYE BEFORE MY DEATH.		141	RGNRTN	91
AND LET ME NOW BEGIN		147	DAY OF JDG	30
STILL LET THY SERVANT MIND IT.		167	THE CALL	89
O LET ME (LIKE HIM) KNOW MY END.		167	THE CALL	86
AND LET THEM LIVE		185	PASSION	42
O LET ME CLIMBE		177	MRNG-WTCH	23
AND LET MY MIND		176	THE STORM	18
O LET ME NOT THUS RANGE.		187	NO DO THEY	19
O LET NOT ME DO LESSE. SHALL THEY		187	NO DO THEY	31

		PAGE	TITLE	LINE
LET	(CCN'T)			
SERVE GCD BEFCRE THE WCRLC. LET HIM NCT GC	. . .	192	RLS + LSNS	19
THE PERJURER'S A CEVIL LET LCCSE. WHAT CAN	. .	193	RLS + LSNS	47
LET FCLLY DUST IT CN, OR LAG PEFIND.	. . .	193	RLS + LSNS	52
YET KEEP THCSE CARES WITHCUT THEE, LET THE HEART	. .	192	RLS + LSNS	35
LET MILDNESS, AND RELIGICN GUIDE THEE OUT	. .	193	RLS + LSNS	38
THERE TURN, AND TURN NO MCRE, LET WITS	. . .	189	RESOLVE	25
O LET ME STILL MIND THAT IN THIS.	. .	191	THE MATCH	24
AND LET THIS GRAIN WHICH HERE IN TEARS I SOW	. .	191	THE MATCH	39
SWEET JESU. WILL THEN. LET NO MCRE	. . . .	200	NTVTY 1	25
AND LET ONCE MCRE BY MYSTICK PIRTH	. . .	200	NTVTY 1	29
LET NCT PERVERSE	. . . . .	204	DSRDR + FR	50
LET IT SUFFICE MY WARMER CAYS	. . .	205	IDLE VERSE	17
LET NIGHTINGALES ATTEND THE SPRING	. . .	205	IDLE VERSE	23
TAKE THIS LAST KISS, AND LET ME WEEP	. . .	348	HOLY BIBLE	3
DEAR LORD, DO THIS. AND THEN LET CRACE	. .	350	L'ENVOY	43
AND LET THESE LONG, SHARP JUDGEMENTS AW	. .	351	L'ENVOY	54
CNELY, LET NOT OUR HATERS BRAC	. . .	350	L'ENVOY	29
BUT LET ME HEED	. . . .	341	THE FEAST	76
LET'S				
YET, COME, AND LET'S PERUSE THEM ALL.	. . .	165	THE CALL	20
LETHARGY				
A LETHARGY, AND MEER CISEASE	. . . .	242	MISERY	84
LULL'D BY THOSE CHARMERS TC A LETHARGY.	. . .	281	JOY	10
LETS				
DCTH PRCACH THE EARTH, AND LESSER BROOKS LETS FORTH	.	285	PSALM 104	30
LETTERS				
AND BRCKEN LETTERS SCARCE REMEMBRED.	. . .	168	VNTY SPRIT	24
TC LETTERS, TILL I LEARNT TO READ.	. . . .	348	HOLY BIBLE	8
LEW'D				
WHEN CONSCIENCE BY LEW'C USE HAD NOT LOST SENSE	.	154	ISAACS M.	19
LEWC				
THY LEWC LOATH'C MOTICNS UNTO SCUNDS	. .	297	HERODIAS	2
OR ANY STCRMS MORE FCUL THEN A LEWD LIFE.	. .	290	THE TIMBER	26
LEWDEST				
SC IN THIS LAST AND LEWCEST ACE	. . .	273	WHT SUNDAY	39
LEWDNESS				
IN JUCGEMENT AGAINST LEWCNESS, THAT'S BASE WIT	.	194	RLS + LSNS	74
LIBERTIE				
A PRIS'NER TO MY LIBERTIE	. . . . .	239	MISERY	2
LIBERTY				
INTC TRUE LIBERTY.	. . . .	271	ALL GONE	36
BCTH YOU AND IT, HAD EQUALL LIBERTY	. . .	279	PALM-TREE	4
THEIR LIBERTY.	. . . .	187	NO DO THEY	30
MANS LIFE, AND YOUR FULL LIBERTY.	. . .	294	PALM-SUNDY	17
BUT THAT CF PERFECT LIBERTY	. . . .	318	THE ASS	10
MY GLCRICUS LIBERTY, STILL LATE.	. . .	344	WATER-FALL	38
LIE				
HER PROPER BRANCHES. WHICH NOW LIE	. . .	292	THE JEWS	16
CHAMBERS CF RAIN, WHERE HEAV'NS LARGE BOTTLES LIE	. .	285	PSALM 104	38
WITHIN WHCSE SACRED LEAFS DIC LIE	. . .	323	THE NIGHT	17
WHAT MYSTERIES CO LIE BEYCND THY DUST.	. .	271	ALL GONE	19
I SAW THE WARM RECLUSE ALCNE TC LIE	. . .	247	I WALKT	19
IN THCSE THIN CELS COULC LIE	. . .	239	SHEPHEARDS	32
CCNFEST, THE WCRLC DIC CNLY PAINT AND LIE.	. .	244	MT. OLV. B	10
GRANT, I MAY NCT LIKE PUDCLE LIE	. . .	212	DAWNING	29
AND LET THY BEGGER LIE	. . . .	213	ADMISSION	10
AS CN THE SUN ECCLIPSES LIE.	. . . .	219	HOLY COMM.	20
LIES				
LIES SUCH A HEAV'N OF BLISS	. . .	243	THE SAP	28
SUCH SECRET LIFE, AND VERTUE IN IT LIES	. . .	244	THE SAP	31
DUST LIES WITH DUST	. . . . .	226	RETIREMENT	42
IF MY WAY LIES THROUGH CESERTS AND WILDE WCODS.	.	290	THE TIMBER	45
WITHCUT HIS BRAGS AND CCNQUESTS LIES	. .	318	THE ASS	27
O CALM AND SACRED BED WHERE LIES	. . .	310	THE SEED	79
WHY LIES THIS HAIR DESPISED NCW	. . .	304	ST MARY MN	15
IN THEE THE HIDDEN STCNE, THE MANNA LIES	. .	198	SCRIPTURES	5
CLOATH'C WITH THIS SKIN, WHICH NOW LIES SPREC	. .	347	THE BOOK	18
LIFE				
FRUITICN, UNICN, GLCRY, LIFE	. . . .	348	HOLY BIBLE	31
FCUNTAINS OF LIFE, WHERE THE LAMB GOES.	. .	344	WATER-FALL	26
FALSE LIFE. A FOIL AND NC MCRE. WHEN	. . .	344	QUICKNESS	1
BUT THOU, WHO DIDST MANS WHOLE LIFE EARN	. .	342	OBSEQUIES	21
LIFE IS A FIX'D, CISCERNING LIGHT	. . .	345	QUICKNESS	9
BUT LIFE IS, WHAT NCNE CAN EXPRESS	. . .	345	QUICKNESS	19
GREEN TREES OF LIFE, AND LIVING STREAMS.	. .	346	THE QUEER	8
THESE ARE THE WORDS, AND WORKS CF LIFE, THIS DC	.	196	RLS + LSNS	141
AFFCRC ME LIFE	. . . . . .	190	THE MATCH	17
THE OTHER, THE TRUE LIFE, IN THE NEXT WORLD	. .	191	THE MATCH	22
WHO CNELY WISH LIFE TC SERVE THEE.	. . .	191	THE MATCH	35
DISPATCH NECESSITIES, LIFE HATH A LOAD	. .	192	RLS + LSNS	33
SHRCWC IN THEIR BIRTHS. THE CRCWN OF LIFE, LIGHT, TRUTH	.	192	RLS + LSNS	27
HIS LIFE FOR MINE, TUNE TC THY WILL	. .	204	DSRDR + FR	59
THE LCRD CF LIFE BE BCRNE IN EARTH.	. . .	200	NTVTY 1	30
NCT WCRTH OUR THANKS. IS LIFE A GIFT	. . .	200	NTVTY 2	7
AND PROUD WITH LIFE, AND SENCE	. . .	144	RSRCTN +IM	11
BCTH LIFE AND YOUTH	. . . . .	145	RSRCTN +IM	30
TC SINNERS CONFIDENCE, LIFE TC THE GRAVE.	. .	159	MANS FALL	26
THAT HOURE, WHICH MUST THY LIFE, AND MINE DISPATCH.	.	157	THE LAMPE	8
LIFE LOCKT IN DEATH, HEAV'N IN A SHELL.	. . .	164	INCARNATN	12

	PAGE	TITLE	LINE
LIFE (CCN'T)			
MY LAMP, AND LIFE, BCTH SHALL IN THEE ABICE.	177	MRNG-WTCH	33
JCY OF MY LIFE. WHILE LEFT ME HERE	174	JOY OF LIF	1
A LIFE WELL LEAD	174	JOY OF LIF	5
THY GCD, THY LIFE, THY CURE.	184	PEACE	20
TC WEEP, TO SING, THY DEATH, MY LIFE.	186	PASSION	57
IN LIFE, CR DUST.	181	BURIALL	24
WHOSE BEAUTY TYED LIFE TO THY HCUSE	302	THE KNOT	3
WHAT LIFE, WHAT DEATH CAN SEVER.	302	THE KNOT	14
MY LIFE, AND UNRELIEV'D	311	THE SEED	87
THOUGH LIFE BE DEAD, ANC MY JCYS GONE.	311	THE SEED	89
KEEP CLEAN, BEAR FRUIT, EARN LIFE AND WATCH	309	THE SEED	47
FAITH INTC LIFE BREAKS, ANC DEATH DIES.	310	THE SEED	66
CNE LIVING DRCP. CNE DRCP LIFE KEEPS.	308	THE SEED	14
O FEED THAT LIFE, WHICH MAKES HIM BLCW	308	THE SEED	19
LIFE WITHCUT THEE IS LCCSE AND SPILLS.	308	THE SEED	8
NCR MADE LIFE THRCUGH HER LCNG CESCENTS	312	FAIR+YONG	29
PASTURES CF LIFE, WHERE THE LAMB GOES.	319	THE ASS	52
BEING AND LIFE, BUT IS CEAD TFRALL.	319	THE ASS	56
THE CNE OF GOCDNESS, PEACE ANC LIFE	318	THE ASS	3
ALL THINGS WITH LIFE, BEFCRE WHCSE EYES	*314	THE STONE	26
AND TREES OF LIFE NC CTHER WATERS LCVE	291	THE TIMBER	51
CR ANY STCRMS MORE FCLL THEN A LEWD LIFE.	290	THE TIMBER	26
AND ALL HIS LIFE A RAINY, WEEPING DAY.	290	THE TIMBER	36
MEANS ONELY THCSE, WHC BRCKE (IN LIFE) THY PEACE.	289	THE TIMBER	20
SC MURTHERED MAN, WHEN LCVELY LIFE IS DONE	289	THE TIMBER	21
JESLS, MY LIFE. HCW SHALL I TRULY LCVE THEE.	283	LOVE-SICK	1
MANS LIFE, AND YOUR FULL LIBERTY.	294	PALM-SUNDY	17
WHICH IS REQUIR'D TC MAKE UP LIFE	299	JESUS WP B	27
FCR MIRTH AND LIFE, YET WITHCLT NCISE.	299	JESUS WP B	47
BLCWN FRCM THE TREE CF LIFE TC US	332	AGREEMENT	21
EACH PAGE OF THINE HATH TRUE LIFE IN'T	332	AGREEMENT	23
O CAY OF LIFE, OF LIGHT, CF LCVE.	334	JUDGEMENT	1
OF LIFE AND JCYS.	335	JUDGEMENT	18
SATE PINING ALL HIS LIFE THERE, CID SCARCE TRUST	232	THE WORLD	32
SUCH SECRET LIFE, AND VERTUE IN IT LIES	244	THE SAP	31
SLCH IS MANS LIFE, AND SUCH IS MINE	242	MISERY	89
WFO KNEELS, OR SIGHS A LIFE IS MAC.	236	CONSTLATN	24
DARKNESS, AND DAY-LIGHT, LIFE, AND DEATH	219	HOLY COMM.	15
KING CF CCMFORTS. KING CF LIFE.	214	PRAISE	1
WELCCME SWEET, ANC SACRED FEAST. WELCCME LIFE.	218	HOLY COMM.	1
THEN, THY SAYINGS ALL MY LIFE	215	PRAISE	25
AND MY LIFE HIC IN THY CEATH	215	PRAISE	31
IN ALL THIS RCUND OF LIFE ANC DEATH	208	REPENTANCE	73
HE IS THE CENTER OF LONG LIFE, AND LIGHT	209	REPENTANCE	83
ALL THAT HAVE SIGNATURE OR LIFE	207	REPENTANCE	41
O MY CEAR GOD. MY LIFE, MY LOVE.	208	REPENTANCE	47
THERE, HIC IN THEE, SHEW ME HIS LIFE AGAIN	248	I WALKT	61
DEATH THAT TO ME WAS LIFE AND LIGHT	264	INTRO. 1	3
WITH LIFE THIS FRAME	248	I WALKT	46
AND LIFE TOO, AND MY HEARTS DELIGHT.	265	INTRO. 2	18
EVEN IN THIS LIFE, BUT ALL SUCH CAN	269	ASCSN-HYMN	11
O FATHER CF ETERNAL LIFE, AND ALL	271	ALL GONE	33
AND CRUM CF LIFE, NCW RFACY TC CISBAND	275	PROFFER	27
THIS IS THE LIFE WHICH HIC ABCVE WITH CHRIST	280	PALM-TREE	13
MADE LIFE MY COMMCN STAKE.	282	GARLAND	14
LIFE'S			
LIFE'S BUT A BLAST, HE KNCWS IT, WHAT. SHAL STRAW	224	TEMPEST	49
LIFES			
AT LENGTH, MY LIFES KINCE ANGEL CAME	332	AGREEMENT	7
HE THAT HATH LEFT LIFES VAIN JCYS AND VAIN CARE	290	THE TIMBER	29
TWO LIFES I HOLD FRCM THEE, MY GRACIOUS LORD	191	THE MATCH	19
WHERE THOU MAY'ST SLEEP WHCLE AGES, LIFES PCCR FLCWR	195	RLS + LSNS	123
THOU ARE LIFES CHARTER, THE CCVES SPOTLESS NEAST	197	SCRIPTURES	3
WHAT WERE THEIR LIFES, THEIR THCUGHTS AND DEECS	347	THE BOOK	9
EVEN LIFES OWN BREATH.	342	OBSEQUIES	8
O BCCK. LIFES GUIDE. HCW SHALL WE PART	348	HOLY BIBLE	1
LIFT			
AND SHALL WE THEN NC VOICES LIFT.	200	NTVTY 2	5
CAN THEY THEIR HEACS LIFT, ANC EXPECT	186	NO DO THEY	3
LIFT UP YCUR HEADS AND LEAVE YCUR MCANS.	294	PALM-SUNDY	14
BUT LIFT THEM UP, WHERE STILL ALIVE	339	DEATH B	29
LIFTED			
FLUTT'RING IN WCCDS, CR LIFTEC FAR	199	NTVTY 1	14
LIFTS			
DCST THCU FEEC THINE. O THCU. THE HAND THAT LIFTS	267	ASCN-DAY A	3
LIGHT			
THEN COMES THE LIGHT. WHICH WHEN YOU SPY	266	VAIN WITS	10
MY CEAR REDEEMER, THE WCRLDS LIGHT	265	INTRO. 2	17
TC CALL IT THEIR INHERENT LIGHT.	265	INTRO. 2	6
BCTH LIGHT FROM THEE, AND VIRTUE HAD	265	INTRO. 2	10
TC RAISE IT TO THE TRUTH AND LIGHT OF THINGS	248	I WALKT	40
WHERE LIGHT, JCY, LEISURE, ANC TRUE COMFORTS MCVE	248	I WALKT	59
DEATH THAT TO ME WAS LIFE AND LIGHT	264	INTRO. 1	3
FCR THE TRUE LIGHT	267	ASCN-DAY A	13
THE FIRST GLAD TIDINGS CF THY EARLY LIGHT	267	ASCN-DAY A	17
THE DAY-STAR SMILES, ANC LIGHT WITH DECEAST	267	ASCN-DAY A	23
AS THE SUN DOTH, WHICH TC THOSE DAYS GAVE LIGHT.	268	ASCN-DAY A	36
AND WCRK ALL NIGHT UPCN THY LIGHT AND LOVE	278	THE STARRE	22
BUT BRUSH ME WITH THY LIGHT, THAT I	277	COCK-CRWNG	44

		PAGE	TITLE	LINE
LIGHT	(CCN'T)			
AND DREAMS OF PARADISE AND LIGHT.	. . . .	276	COCK-CRWNG	6
THE PATH UNTO THE HOUSE OF LIGHT.	. . . .	276	COCK-CRWNG	10
O THOU IMMORTALL LIGHT AND HEAT.	. . .	277	COCK-CRWNG	19
AND HEARTS, WHOSE PULSE BEATS STILL FOR LIGHT	. .	277	COCK-CRWNG	32
FOR AFTER THEIR LIGHT, DARKNESS COMES	. . .	272	WHT SUNDAY	3
YET WHILE SOME RAYS OF THAT GREAT LIGHT	. .	272	WHT SUNDAY	17
FOR THOUGH THOU DOEST THAT GREAT LIGHT LOCK	.	273	WHT SUNDAY	21
WHOSE LIGHT DOTH TRAMPLE ON MY DAYS.	. . .	271	ALL GONE	10
AND INTIMATE WITH HEAV'N, AS LIGHT.	. . .	269	ASCSN-HYMN	24
WHOSE MIGHTY LIGHT	. . . .	270	ASCSN-HYMN	32
MAKE CLAY ASCEND MORE QLICK THEN LIGHT.	. .	270	ASCSN-HYMN	42
THEY ARE ALL GONE INTO THE WORLD OF LIGHT.	. .	270	ALL GONE	1
HATH FLESH NO SOFTNESS NOW, MID-DAY NO LIGHT.	.	224	TEMPEST	56
IN EVERLASTING LIGHT.	. . . .	219	HOLY COMM.	32
WATER'S REFIN'D TO MOTION , AIRE TO LIGHT	.	223	TEMPEST	31
THE BEAMS THEY WARM THEM AT I'TH' LIGHT	. .	207	REPENTANCE	40
HE IS THE CENTER OF LONG LIFE, AND LIGHT	.	209	REPENTANCE	83
LIGHT TO MY SOUL, THAT IT MAY LIVE.	. . .	208	REPENTANCE	52
LIGHT, MOTION, HEAT	. . . .	211	FAITH	34
WHERE STARS, AND CLOUDS, BOTH LIGHT, AND SHADE	.	210	FAITH	15
OR WIL THY ALL-SURPRIZING LIGHT	. . .	211	DAWNING	5
AND WITH THEIR BLUSH OF LIGHT DESCRY	. .	211	DAWNING	11
AND FOR THY SHADOW LOCKS THE LIGHT	. .	212	DAWNING	18
TO THEE WHO WITH TRUE LIGHT ART CLAD	. .	207	REPENTANCE	21
WE CLIMB ABOVE ALL AGES, LAMPS THAT LIGHT	. .	2	SON-DAYES	6
BUT SEEKS HE YOUR OBEDIENCE, ORDER, LIGHT	.	236	CONSTLATN	29
CANST LIGHT AND LEAD ME THERE WITH SUCH REDRESS	.	234	MUTINIE	31
FAIR, ORDER'D LIGHT (WHOSE MOTION WITHOUT NOISE	.	235	CONSTLATN	1
SILENCE, AND LIGHT, AND WATCHFULLNESS WITH YOU	.	236	CONSTLATN	13
YOU ONLY SAW TRUE LIGHT	. . . .	238	SHEPHEARDS	6
THE FIRST LIGHT THEY BEHELD WAS BRIGHT AND GAY	.	239	SHEPHEARDS	51
BUT TO THIS LATER LIGHT THEY SAW IN HIM	. .	239	SHEPHEARDS	53
I SIT WITH THEE BY THIS NEW LIGHT	. . .	214	MISERY	53
ACTIVE AS LIGHT, AND CALM WITHOUT ALL NOISE	.	244	MT. OLV. B	2
BEFORE THEIR LIGHT	. . . .	233	THE WORLD	50
AND INACCESSIBLE FOR LIGHT,	. . .	229	LAW + GOSP	5
LIKE A GREAT RING OF PURE AND ENDLESS LIGHT	. .	231	THE WORLD	2
LIGHT FROM HIS LOCKS, AND ALL THE WAY	. .	199	NTVTY 1	5
WEE'L MAKE A MATCH, MY ONLY LIGHT	. . .	205	IDLE VERSE	7
THY GLIMPSE OF LIGHT.	. . .	201	THE CHECK	24
CALMES, TEMPESTS, LIGHT, AND DARKNES BY HIS MEANS.	.	194	RLS + LSNS	94
SHROWD IN THEIR BIRTHS. THE CROWN OF LIFE, LIGHT, TRUTH	.	192	RLS + LSNS	27
HOME WITH THE LIGHT	. . .	189	RESOLVE	18
LOCKT FROM THE LIGHT	. . . .	178	SILENCE	6
THY LIGHT, AND POW'R	. . . .	178	SILENCE	16
YET I HAVE ONE PEARLE BY WHOSE LIGHT	. .	179	SILENCE	29
WATCH THE RETURNS OF LIGHT.	. . .	183	THRS A TYE	12
ARE A FIRIE-LIQUID LIGHT	. . . .	172	MIDNIGHT	18
THEIR BEAMS, AND LIGHT	. . . .	175	JOY OF LIF	23
TO SHED THEIR LIGHT	. . . .	177	MRNG-WTCH	26
TO PUT ON CLOUDS INSTEAD OF LIGHT	. . .	164	INCARNATN	5
AND TAME, AND KEEPE DOWNE WITH THY LIGHT	. .	161	DSTRQCTION	29
THEN HAVING LOST THE SUNNE, AND LIGHT	. .	162	PURSUITE	6
THAT LITTLE LIGHT I HAD WAS GONE.	. . .	168	VNTY SPRIT	28
WHO CAN HAVE COMMERCE WITH THE LIGHT)	. .	168	VNTY SPRIT	32
DESCRY SOME PART OF HIS GREAT LIGHT.	. .	167	VNTY SPRIT	8
THY LIGHT, IS CHARITY, THY HEAT, IS ZEALE.	.	158	THE LAMPE	11
MY LIGHT HAD LESSEND NOT	. .	161	DSTRQCTION	8
AND SAVED THAT LIGHT, WHICH FREELY THOU	. .	161	DSTRQCTION	19
SHALL ONE DAY RISE, AND CLOATH'D WITH SHINING LIGHT	.	145	RSRCTN +IM	47
ROVE IN THAT MIGHT, AND ETERNALL LIGHT	.	146	RSRCTN +IM	63
AND IN THOSE CRANIES LIGHT APPEAR'D	. .	143	DEATH	24
THE FIRST (PRAY MARKE) AS QUICK AS LIGHT	.	141	RGNRTN	66
O DAY OF LIFE, OF LIGHT, OF LOVE.	. . .	334	JUDGEMENT	1
BE IN CONJUNCTION WITH TRUE LIGHT.	. .	332	AGREEMENT	16
HAVE OUR SURE GUARDIAN, AND OUR LEADING LIGHT.	.	331	JACOBS PLW	50
GUIDED BY FAITH, NOT BY EXTERIOR LIGHT.	. .	327	RIGHTSNESS	24
WHERE ALL IS LIGHT, AND FLOWERS, AND FRUIT	.	329	TEARS	5
INLARG'D THAT LIGHT, AND TO THE BAD WAS KINDE.	.	330	JACOBS PLW	14
AND SATANS SEAT, IN ALL HER COASTS HATH LIGHT	.	331	JACOBS PLW	32
THY EDGES, AND THY BORDERING LIGHT.	. .	322	CHILDEHOOD	42
WISE NICODEMUS SAW SUCH LIGHT	. . .	323	THE NIGHT	5
TO THY BRIGHT ARM, WHICH WAS MY LIGHT	. .	326	ABELS BLOD	31
AND BY THIS WORLDS ILL-GUIDING LIGHT	. .	324	THE NIGHT	47
'TWILL MAKE THE LAND OF DARKNESS LIGHT.	. .	299	JESUS WP B	51
BUT AS SHADES SET OFF LIGHT, SO TEARS AND GRIEF	.	290	THE TIMBER	41
WHERE NOT SO MUCH AS DREAMS OF LIGHT MAY SHINE	.	289	THE TIMBER	11
WHOSE LIGHT, THOUGH FETCHT AND BORROWED FROM FAR	.	288	THE BIRD	21
BUT AS THESE BIRDS OF LIGHT MAKE A LAND GLAD	.	288	THE BIRD	23
PAST ORE THY HEAD. MANY LIGHT HEARTS AND WINGS	.	289	THE TIMBER	3
THOU CLOATH'ST THY SELF WITH LIGHT, AS WITH A ROBE	.	284	PSALM 104	5
AND NOW AS FRESH AND CHEARFUL AS THE LIGHT	.	288	THE BIRD	7
YET IS NOT HE BY HIS OWN LIGHT	. . .	314	THE STONE	32
TO LODGE LIGHT, AND INCREASE HER OWN.	. .	315	DWELLNG-PL	10
WERE NOT THY WORD (DEAR LORD) MY LIGHT	.	316	MEN OF WAR	9
WHERE LIGHT, JOY, HEALTH AND PERFECT PEACE	.	319	THE ASS	62
WHO SHEWS ME BUT ONE GRAIN OF SINCERE LIGHT.	.	320	HIDDN TRSR	3
BUT WHAT EARTH BREATHS AGAINST THY LIGHT.	.	312	FAIR+YONG	26
WHO BREAKS HIS GLASS TO TAKE MORE LIGHT	. .	309	THE SEED	43

		PAGE	TITLE	LINE
LIGHT	(CON'T)			
A MOURNING LIGHT UPON THE DEAD.	. . . . .	309	THE SEED	54
THEN THE NOONS CLOUDLESS LIGHT.	. . . . .	310	THE SEED	82
FAIR AND YONG LIGHT. MY GUIDE TO HOLY	. . . .	311	FAIR+YONG	1
BUT NOW ARE FIXED STARS, WHOSE LIGHT	. . .	305	ST MARY MN	59
FOR THY NEW LIGHT, AND TREMBLED AT EACH SHOWER.	. .	306	RAIN-BOW	8
THY LIGHT AS LUCTUAL AND STAIN'D WITH WOES	. .	307	RAIN-BOW	37
WHEN I BEHOLD THEE, THOUGH MY LIGHT BE DIM	. .	306	RAIN-BOW	15
SO WITH THAT FIRST LIGHT GAIN'D FROM THEE	. .	348	HOLY BIBLE	13
THE SEERS OF WHOSE SACRED LIGHT	. . . .	349	L'ENVOY	3
MOUNTAINS OF SPICE, DAY-STARS AND LIGHT	. . .	346	THE QUEER	7
LIFE IS A FIX'D, DISCERNING LIGHT	. . . .	345	QUICKNESS	9
AND JOY, LIKE LIGHT, SHINES OFT IN CLOUDS.	. .	342	OBSEQUIES	20
WHO CAME (SURE) FROM A SEA OF LIGHT.	. . .	343	WATER-FALL	18
WAS TINN'D AND LIGHTED AT THE SUNNE.	. . .	276	COCK-CRWNG	12
LIGHTEN				
WHEN ALL SHALL STREAME, AND LIGHTEN ROUND	. . .	147	DAY OF JDG	5
LIGHTNINGS				
WITH THY LEAST TOUCH, LIGHTNINGS AND WINDS THAT RAGE	.	287	PSALM 104	87
LIGHTS				
WHOSE FRUITFUL DAWN SHEDS HOPES AND LIGHTS.	. .	* 295	PALM-SUNDY	31
THAT ONE MADE ALL THESE LESSER LIGHTS.	. . .	309	THE SEED	28
THE HIVE OF BEAMY, LIVING LIGHTS	. . . .	333	AGREEMENT	32
ARE BUT LIGHTS WEAK MINORITY	. . . . .	334	JUDGEMENT	8
A TRAINE OF LIGHTS, WHICH IN THOSE SUN-SHINE DAYES	. .	159	MANS FALL	10
GODS SAINTS ARE SHINING LIGHTS. WHO STAYS	. .	174	JOY OF LIF	17
ABOVE ARE RESTLES MOTIONS, RUNNING LIGHTS	. .	194	RLS + LSNS	89
O LOSE IT NOT. LOOK UP, WILT CHANGE THOSE LIGHTS	.	196	RLS + LSNS	143
FATHER OF LIGHTS. WHAT SUNNIE SEED	. . .	276	COCK-CRWNG	1
CAN THESE NEW LIGHTS BE LIKE TO THOSE	. . .	272	WHT SUNDAY	9
THESE LIGHTS OF SERPENTS LIKE THE DOVE.	. . .	272	WHT SUNDAY	10
LIKE				
CAN THESE NEW LIGHTS BE LIKE TO THOSE	. . .	272	WHT SUNDAY	9
THESE LIGHTS OF SERPENTS LIKE THE DOVE.	. . .	272	WHT SUNDAY	10
LIKE THE SUN SHINE	. . . . . .	269	ASCSN-HYMN	22
LIKE HEAV'N, ALL BRIGHT.	. . . . .	270	ASCSN-HYMN	34
LIKE STARS UPON SOME GLOOMY GROVE	. . .	270	ALL GONE *	6
THEY SHINE IN WHITE (LIKE STARS) AND REST.	. .	275	PROFFER	24
AND AIR OF EDEN, LIKE A MALE-CONTENT	. . .	279	PALM-TREE	6
IT THRIVES NO WHERE. THIS MAKES THESE WEIGHTS (LIKE DEATH		279	PALM-TREE	7
LIKE A STARV'D EAGLET, FOR THINE EYE.	. . .	281	THE FAVOUR	6
WHEN LIKE A VIRGIN CLAD IN FLOWERS AND GREEN	. .	268	ASCN-DAY A	41
WHEN HEAV'N ABOVE THEM SHIN'D LIKE MOLTEN GLASS	.	268	ASCN-DAY A	45
AND SPRINGS, LIKE DISSOLV'D PEARLS THEIR STREAMS DID POUR		268	ASCN-DAY A	47
ALL SAD WITH TEARS, WHICH LIKE WARM SUMMER RAIN	.	268	ASCN-DAY A	52
WHICH, LIKE COLD FRIENDS, SEES US BUT ONCE A YEAR	.	247	I WALKT	12
LIKE A GREAT RING OF PURE AND ENDLESS LIGHT	. .	231	THE WORLD	2
LIKE A VAST SHADOW MOV'D, IN WHICH THE WORLD	. .	231	THE WORLD	6
LIKE A THICK MIDNIGHT-FOG MOV'D THERE SO SLOW	. .	231	THE WORLD	17
THY CHOSEN FLOCK, LIKE LEAFS IN A HIGH WIND	. .	229	LAW + GOSP	9
CONDEMNING THOUGHTS (LIKE SAD ECCLIPSES) SCOWL	.	232	THE WORLD	19
MY THOUGHTS, LIKE WATER WHICH SOME STONE DOTH START	.	234	MUTINIE	6
YET NEITHER SING, NOR LIKE THEIR FOOD	. . .	228	PILGRIMAGE	19
LIKE WAVES BEAT ON MY RESOLUTIONS	. . .	214	MISERY	76
WHERE BIRDS LIKE WATCHFUL CLOCKS THE NOISELESS DATE	.	245	MAN	3
AND LIKE THAT LAMB WHICH HAD THE DRAGONS VOICE	.	237	CONSTLATN	43
LIKE OTHER TEMPESTS DYE.	. . . . .	234	MUTINIE	25
AND MAN (LIKE ISSACHAR) IN LOOES DELIGHT	. .	223	TEMPEST	30
LIKE STRINGS, STRETCH EV'RY PART	. . . .	222	AFFLICTION	39
HE SEES (LIKE PYRAMIDS) SHOOT FROM THIS BALL	. .	224	TEMPEST	43
THAT NEVER LIKE A BEAST	. . . . .	217	DRESSING	33
USE, WITH LIKE CUSTOME, AS MY KITCHEN FOOD.	. .	217	DRESSING	36
AWAKE, AWAKE. AND, LIKE THE SUN, DISPERSE	. .	217	EASTER-DAY	9
GRANT, I MAY NOT LIKE PUDDLE LIE	. . . .	212	DAWNING	29
NOR DID THOSE LAST, BUT (LIKE HIMSELF) DYED STILL	.	196	CORRUPTION	11
TO DO THE LIKE. OUR BODIES BUT FORERUN	. .	191	RLS + LSNS	2
THUS LIKE SOME SLEEPING EXHALATION	. . .	203	DSRDR + FR	31
I SMELL A DEW LIKE MYRRH, AND ALL THE DAY	. .	198	UNPRFTBLNS	10
LIKE CANDLES, SHED	. . . . . .	175	JOY OF LIF	22
IS LIKE A CLOUDED STARRE, WHOSE BEAMES THOUGH SET	.	177	MRNG-WTCH	25
THAT CURTAIN'D GRAVE, THOUGH SLEEP, LIKE ASHES, HIDE	.	177	MRNG-WTCH	32
WITH THE LIKE ARDOUR SHIN'D	. . . .	172	MIDNIGHT	10
LIKE A YOUNG EAST, OR MOONE-SHINE NIGHT	. .	168	VNTY SPRIT	20
O LET ME (LIKE HIM) KNOW MY END.	. . . .	167	THE CALL	86
HOW LIKE THE EYES QUICK WINKE	. . . .	166	THE CALL	43
LIKE THOSE ABOVE	. . . . . .	182	CHRFLNESS	5
WHICH BUSIE THOUGHTS (LIKE WINDS) WOULD SCATTER QUITE	.	179	CHRCH-SVC	12
AND CALM LIKE HER, OR THAT MILD EVENING-TIDE.	. .	154	ISAACS M.	24
AND LIKE A FIRIE TORRENT BRUSH	. . . .	146	DAY OF JDG	3
WHEN LIKE A SCROWLE THE HEAVENS SHAL PASSE	. .	147	DAY OF JDG	13
LIKE SOME SPRUCE BRIDE	. . . . .	145	RSRCTN +IM	46
LIKE CLOUDS ECCLIPS'D MY MIND	. . . .	139	RGNRTN	17
RAY'D INTO THEE, LIKE BEAMS INTO A GLASSE	. .	154	ISAACS M.	8
LIKE THAT SAMARITANS DEAD WELL	. . . .	150	RELIGION	46
BECAUSE MOST VOICES LIKE THE SHELL	. . .	150	RELIGION	48
NEVER DID TREE BEARE FRUIT LIKE THIS	. . .	152	THE SEARCH	43
LIKE CLOUDS, BEFORE THY GLORIOUS DAWN.	. . .	334	JUDGEMENT	10
AND MAKE THE DEAD, LIKE FLOWERS, ARISE	. . .	334	JUDGEMENT	5
AND THEN RETURNING, LIKE THE SUN	. . . .	338	DEATH B	14
WHICH STRAIT, LIKE MORNING-STARS DID SING	. . .	332	AGREEMENT	10

	PAGE	TITLE	LINE
LIKE (CCN'T)			
FCR THIS RICH PEARL, LIKE SOME MCRE COMMCN STONE	330	JACOBS PLW	17
LIKE CHRONIC PAINS, WHICH SURELY KILL, THOUGH SLCW.	327	RIGHTSNESS	30
WHOSE URGENT SCUNC LIKE UNTC THAT	325	ABELS BLOD	17
BUT WHAT (LIKE HIS, WHOSE ULCCD PEACE BRINGS)	326	ABELS BLOD	39
AND EV'N, SMOCTH LINES, LIKE THE SUNS RAYS	310	THE SEED	59
WHERE YCUTH SHINES LIKE A STAR	310	THE SEED	62
SEEM'C TO DEVCUR, LIKE RUST.	310	THE SEED	74
LIKE THE SURVIVING TURTLE, WEEP	311	FAIR+YONG	10
CCMES LIKE A CHILDES, SPOTLESS AND FRESH.	306	ST MARY MN	70
LIKE A WISE, EARLY PENITENT	304	ST MARY MN	37
MAY HIS CROWN, LIKE HIS HCPES, BE CLAY	301	PROVIDENCE	35
GLACLY WILL I, LIKE PCNTICK SHEEP	301	PROVIDENCE	46
LIKE THEE, WHEN SET AT NAUGHT AND DUMB.	316	MEN OF WAR	20
THEN LIKE THE PALM, THOUGH WRCNG, I'LE BEAR	295	PALM-SUNDY	38
ANC I, LIKE FLCWERS SHALL STILL GC NEAT	300	PROVIDENCE	17
AND MACE GRAVE MUSIQUE LIKE WILCE WIT	297	HERODIAS	3
DCTH SPREAD LIKE CURTAINS RCUND ARCUT THIS GLOBE	284	PSALM 104	7
WEEPING STILL, LIKE THE WET MCRRCW	294	PALM-SUNDY	5
AND JCY, LIKE LIGHT, SHINES OFT IN CLCUDS.	342	OBSEQUIES	20
LIKE BEES IN STORMS UNTC THEIR HIVE	343	OBSEQUIES	30
SHINING WITH JOY, LIKE DEWY DAYS	345	THE WREATH	11
WHICH WEARS HEAVEN, LIKE A BRICAL RING	346	THE QUEER	3
THRCUGH ALL MY PARTS, AND LIKE A QUICK	340	THE FEAST	45
LIKE TEARS DOTH SHEW	340	THE FEAST	23
AND LIKE CLD CLOATHS FOLD UP THESE SKIES	349	L'ENVOY	8
THAT LIKE TRUE SHEEP, ALL IN CNE FOLD	350	L'ENVOY	47
FCR SIN (LIKE WATER) HCURLY GLIDES	350	L'ENVOY	50
LIKEWISE			
A SWORD SHALL HIS BLCCD LIKEWISE SPILL.	316	MEN OF WAR	6
LILIE			
THOUGH WITH NC LILIE, STAY WITH ME.	277	COCK-CRWNG	48
LILIES AND MYRRHE, WHERE THE CLRS'D SEED	299	JESUS WP B	49
LILLIES			
THAT FEEDST AMCNG THE LILLIES, 'TILL THE DAY	216	DRESSING	2
LILLY			
C ROSE CF SHARON. O THE LILLY	220	HOLY COMM.	49
SWEET, COWNIE THOUGHTS, SCFT LILLY-SHADES, CALM STREAMES.	188	RELAPSE	25
LIMBES			
TC WRENCH, AND RACK THY BLESSEC LIMBES.	185	PASSION	33
LIMBS			
OR NAIL THOSE BLESSED LIMBS AGAIN	230	LAW + GOSP	35
LIMNE			
THEN, WHO WOULD TRULY LIMNE THEE CUT, MUST PAINT	156	ISAACS M.	71
LINE			
ABSENTS WITHIN THE LINE CCNSPIRE, AND SENSE	183	THRS A TYE	9
EACH LINE IN THEE. THEN WCULC I PLEAD IN GROANS	198	SCRIPTURES	10
AND BEAT ABOUT YOUR ENDLES LINE.	235	CONSTLATN	12
EXTENT, AND END, FOR MY HANDS CREW THE LINE	226	RETIREMENT	27
AND AS THCU GIV'ST LINE, AND LENGTH	214	PRAISE	11
WITHIN THE LINE	269	ASCSN-HYMN	20
BLT THOU BENEATH THE SAD AND HEAVY LINE	289	THE TIMBER	9
SC BY ONE BEAMY LINE	310	THE SEED	69
LINEN			
MADE LINEN, WHC DIC WEAR IT THEN.	347	THE BOOK	8
LINES			
AND EV'N, SMOCTH LINES, LIKE THE SUNS RAYS	310	THE SEED	59
THY LINES ARE RAYS, THE TRUE SUN SHEDS.	333	AGREEMENT	35
THAT MAY CISHCNOR THOSE PURE LINES.	335	JUDGEMENT	38
DEAR FRIEND. WHOSE HOLY, EVER-LIVING LINES	190	THE MATCH	1
OLT-RLNS THE EARTH, AND LINES THE UTMCST POLE.	193	RLS + LSNS	54
THY LINES, THY LOVE. AWAY	202	THE CHECK	44
LINGER			
IF THCU WCULDST THITHER, LINGER NCT	189	RESOLVE	9
SC FOR THIS NIGHT. I LINGER HERE	228	PILGRIMAGE	9
LINGRING			
ANC I ALONE SIT LINGRINC HERE.	270	ALL GONE	2
AND LINGRING WOUNDS FROM WEAKER FCES.	312	FAIR+YONG	44
LINGRING, AND WERE OF THIS STEEP PLACE AFRAIC	343	WATER-FALL	6
LINK			
MY LOVE-TWIST HELC THEE UP, MY LNSEEN LINK.	225	RETIREMENT	22
BREAKING THE LINK	202	DSRDR + FR	9
LIPS			
OR LIPS, BUT WHO THERE WEEPING SITS	189	RESOLVE	27
STRIKE THESE LIPS DUMB.	171	COME, COME	16
PRICKING HIS LIPS, TILL HE DOTH MOURN	319	THE ASS	50
LIQUID			
AS IF HIS LIQUID, LCOSE RETINUE STAID	343	WATER-FALL	5
LIQUORS			
BCTH LIQUCRS BURNE, AND STREAME.	172	MIDNIGHT	26
LISP			
E'RE WE CAN LISP, OR CUGHT DISCUSSE	166	THE CALL	48
LIST			
WHEN NIGHT COMES, LIST THY CEEDS, MAKE PLAIN THE WAY	195	RLS + LSNS	115
YET DCTH IT BLOW STIL WHERE IS LIST	239	MISERY	6
LISTEN'D			
I WHOLY LISTEN'D TC MY FOE.	207	REPENTANCE	18
LISTNING			
BLT WHILE I LISTNING SOUGHT	141	RGNRTN	86
LITTLE			
CNLY A LITTLE FOUNTAIN LENT	141	RGNRTN	58

	PAGE	TITLE	LINE
LITTLE (CON'T)			
A LITTLE DUST, AND FOR THE TOWN	151	THE SEARCH	16
HE SHIN'D A LITTLE, AND BY THOSE WEAK RAYS	196	CORRUPTION	3
MY LOSSE BUT LITTLE TO IT	167	THE CALL	83
THAT LITTLE LIGHT I HAD WAS GONE.	168	VNTY SPRIT	28
AND HEAT OF THINE. THAT LITTLE GATE	207	REPENTANCE	7
SAID LITTLE LESSE.	232	THE WORLD	41
THEIR LITTLE GRAIN EXPELLING NIGHT	276	COCK-CRWNG	8
THIS LITTLE GOSHEN, IN THE MIDST OF NIGHT	331	JACOBS PLW	31
INLIGHTNING HIS OWN LITTLE SPHERE	288	THE BIRD	20
THY LITTLE HEART IN EARLY HYMNS DOTH SING	288	THE BIRD	8
LIV'D			
LIV'D STILL IN LEAGUE WITH THY CHASTE FIRE	312	FAIR+YONG	28
YET LIV'D HE HERE SOMETIMES, AND BORE FOR THEE	243	THE.SAP	17
WHICH I SOMETIMES LIV'D IN.	180	BURIALL	10
HE LIV'D THERE SAFE, 'TWAS HIS RETREAT	152	THE SEARCH	55
THAT HAVE LIV'D HERE, SINCE THE MANS FALL.	346	THE BOOK	2
LIVE			
THEY LIVE UNSEEN, WHEN HERE THEY FADE.	346	THE BOOK	4
SHALL RISE AGAIN, AND LIVE AND SING.	340	THE FEAST	36
DID LIVE AND FEED BY THY DECREE	347	THE BOOK	16
THE FLATT'RER SAY, I LIVE	183	THRS A TYE	22
AND LET THEM LIVE	185	PASSION	42
AND LIVE, WHO DOTH NOT THUS, HATH LOST HEAV'NS WAY.	196	RLS + LSNS	142
THE FLOWRES WITHOUT CLOTHES LIVE	245	MAN	13
TO LIVE IN GROTS, AND CAVES, AND HATE THE DAY	233	THE WORLD	51
BECAUSE BY THIS MAN CANNOT LIVE	228	PILGRIMAGE	24
BOTH LIVE AND DIE THY CHILD.	235	MUTINIE	39
IN WHOM I LIVE, IN WHOM I MOVE	249	BEGGING A	2
DOTH ANSWER, LIVE.	211	FAITH	44
LIGHT TO MY SOUL, THAT IT MAY LIVE.	208	REPENTANCE	52
LIVE, DIE, AND RISE WITH THEE.	216	DRESSING	18
MUST (SOUL-LESSE SHADOW) SO LIVE ON	311	THE SEED	88
CALL'D FORTH THY TEARS, WHICH RAN IN LIVE	305	ST MARY MN	42
FOR THOUGH HE SHOULD FORSAKE THE WORLD, AND LIVE	290	THE TIMBER	37
MIGHT LIVE, AND SEE THE OLIVE BEAR	292	THE JEWS	15
THEN FAREWEL JOYS. FOR WHILE I LIVE	299	JESUS WP B	44
FOR SALVES AND SYRUPS, WHILE THEY LIVE	339	DEATH B	23
MIGHT LIVE INVISIBLE AND DIM.	325	THE NIGHT	54
MUST LIVE TWICE, THAT WOULD GODS FACE SEE.	322	CHILDEHOOD	36
THAT MEN MIGHT LOOK AND LIVE AS GLO-WORMS SHINE	323	THE NIGHT	3
LIVE-DEW			
SHED THIS LIVE-DEW ON FIELDS WHICH FAR	296	JESUS WP A	14
LIVED			
HE LIVED OF US UNSEEN.	247	I WALKT	21
LIVED THERE WITHOUT ALL NOISE	239	SHEPHEARDS	36
LIVELY			
TO MY COLD THOUGHTS A LIVELY SENSE OF SPRING.	245	MT. OLV. B	20
SUCH PERFECT EASE, AND SUCH A LIVELY SENSE	244	THE SAP	47
LIVELY-FAIR			
HOW ART THOU CHANG'D. HOW LIVELY-FAIR	303	ST MARY MN	5
LIVER			
GATHER TRUE COMFORTS, BUT THE WICKED LIVER	287	PSALM 104	94
IN THE SAME LIVERY DREST	201	THE CHECK	4
LIVES			
MANY DISORDERED LIVES I SAW	310	THE SEED	55
SWEET, HARMLES LIVES (ON WHOSE HOLY LEISURE	238	SHEPHEARDS	1
YET WOULD NOT PLACE ONE PEECE ABOVE, BUT LIVES	232	THE WORLD	34
NOTHING THAT IS, OR LIVES	219	HOLY COMM.	11
AND HOLY LIVES, MERCY MAY HERE	351	L'ENVOY	56
LIVING			
LIVING, THOU WERT MY SOULS SURE EASE	348	HOLY BIBLE	33
THE WELL, WHERE LIVING WATERS SPRING	340	THE FEAST	33
FOR THIS TASTE OF LIVING GLORY	341	THE FEAST	57
GREEN TREES OF LIFE, AND LIVING STREAMS.	346	THE QUEER	8
WHOM LIVING HERE I DID STILL SHUN	311	FAIR+YONG	3
WHERE FREED SOULS DWEL BY LIVING FOUNTAINS	312	FAIR+YONG	49
ONE LIVING DROP. ONE DROP LIFE KEEPS.	308	THE SEED	14
FOR THY ETERNAL, LIVING WELLS	308	THE SEED	21
TO LIVING SPRINGS, AND THERE BE FED	319	THE ASS	60
TO LIVING SPRINGS, AND THERE BE FED	319	THE ASS	61
SOUL-QUICKNING RAIN, THIS LIVING WATER	296	JESUS WP A	10
DESCEND, AND LIVING WATERS FLOW	291	THE JEWS	12
WHICH NOW ARE DEAD, LODG'D IN THY LIVING BOWERS.	289	THE TIMBER	4
BUT HIS OWN LIVING WORKS DID MY LORD HOLD	323	THE NIGHT	21
BUT LIVING WHERE THE SUN	324	THE NIGHT	43
AND SWEETLY LIVING (FIE ON MEN)	321	CHILDEHOOD	15
UNTO THOSE CLEAR AND LIVING SPRINGS	329	TEARS	3
DRUNK OF THY LIVING STREAM	329	TEARS	10
THE HIVE OF BEAMY, LIVING LIGHTS	333	AGREEMENT	32
A LIVING FAITH, A HEART OF FLESH	148	DAY OF JDG	41
LOAD			
DISPATCH NECESSITIES; LIFE HATH A LOAD	192	RLS + LSNS	33
RETURNS HOME WITH HIS LOAD.	286	PSALM 104	64
BUT IS A PILLOW, NOT A LOAD.	318	THE ASS	12
LOADE			
WHO SITS AT HOME TOO BEARS A LOADE	214	MISERY	69
LOADS			
WITHOUT TO MORROWS EVILS AND FUTURE LOADS.	327	RIGHTSNESS	8
LOATH			
THIS MADE HIM LONG FOR HOME, AS LOATH TO STAY	197	CORRUPTION	17

	PAGE	TITLE	LINE
LOATH (CON'T)			
AND ONE OF THESE SEME LOATH	148	DAY OF JDG	40
LOATH HENCE TO PART, AT LAST I RISE	152	THE SEARCH	33
LOATH'D			
THY LEWD LOATH'D MOTIONS UNTO SOUNDS	297	HERODIAS	2
LOATHSOME			
AND THE LAST IS MOST LOATHSOME DUST.	302	ORNAMENT	8
LOCK			
BEYOND A CURLED LOCK, OR PAITED FACE.	155	ISAACS M.	38
FOR THOUGH THOU DOEST THAT GREAT LIGHT LOCK	273	WHT SUNDAY	21
LOCKS			
THY LOCKS CROWN'D WITH ETERNITIE.	211	DAWNING	12
WITH SCATTER'D LOCKS	189	RESOLVE	14
LIGHT FROM HIS LOCKS, AND ALL THE WAY	199	NTVTY 1	5
HIS LOCKS ARE WET WITH THE CLEAR DROPS OF NIGHT.	324	THE NIGHT	33
LOCKT			
LOCKT FROM THE LIGHT	178	SILENCE	6
LIFE LOCKT IN DEATH, HEAV'N IN A SHELL.	164	INCARNATN	12
BUT WHEN THE HAND THAT LOCKT HER UP, GIVES RCOM	271	ALL GONE	31
LODES			
AND MAN (LIKE ISSACHAR) IN LODES DELIGHT	223	TEMPEST	30
LODG'D			
WHICH NOW ARE DEAD, LODG'D IN THY LIVING BOWERS.	289	THE TIMBER	4
LODGD			
WHAT LODGD THEE THEN, NOR WHERE, NOR HOW.	315	DWELLNG-PL	12
LODGE			
TO LODGE LIGHT, AND INCREASE HER OWN.	315	DWELLNG-PL	10
AND LODGE ALONE.	323	THE NIGHT	22
SHALL LODGE IN SUCH A NARROW PIT, TILL HE	331	JACOBS PLW	39
THEN JACOB-LIKE LODGE IN A PLACE	228	PILGRIMAGE	5
NEW FLAMES, BESIDES WHERE THESE LODGE VAIN HEARTS MOURN	196	RLS + LSNS	131
LODGE IN THY MYSTICAL, DEEP STREAMS.	344	WATER-FALL	28
LODGED			
STILL LODGED, WHERE ALL THY UNSEEN ARROWS SHROWD	307	RAIN-BOW	34
LODGED IN THOSE FALSE LOOKS, TILL TOO LATE.	311	FAIR+YONG	22
LODGING			
BLEW THROUGH THY LODGING, WHERE THY OWN WARM WING	287	THE BIRD	2
AND GODS OWN LODGING (THOUGH HE COULD NOT LACK)	238	SHEPHEARDS	29
LOFTY			
BUT A STRONG WIND MUST BREAK THY LOFTY ROCKS.	330	JACOBS PLW	10
LONG			
THOU FROM THE DAY-STAR A LONG WAY DIDST STAND	331	JACOBS PLW	47
THY LONG EXPECTED HEALING WINGS COULD SEE	323	THE NIGHT	9
THEN I IN HEAVEN ALL THE LONG YEAR	324	THE NIGHT	41
AND ONELY SEE THROUGH A LONG NIGHT	322	CHILDEHOOD	41
AND LONG EXPERIENCE SHOULD MAKE WISE.	321	CHILDEHOOD	18
COULD'ST SUCH A SHRILL AND LONG CRY REAR	325	ABELS BLOD	9
INQUIRE HOW LONG. OF THE MOST HIGH.	326	ABELS BLOD	22
THE FIELDS ARE LONG SINCE WHITE, AND I	334	JUDGEMENT	13
(BECAUSE THEY SLEEP SO LONG) SOME MEN	335	JUDGEMENT	25
THEREFORE AS LONG AS THOU WILT GIVE ME BREATH	287	PSALM 104	89
AND THAT LONG FROST WHICH NOW BENUMS	291	THE JEWS	3
AS MEER A STRANGER, AS MEN LONG SINCE DEAD.	290	THE TIMBER	38
TO THINK, HE SHOULD BE SO LONG VAINLY LEAD.	290	THE TIMBER	40
MY SINS LONG SINCE HAVE MADE THEE STRANGE	293	BEGGING B	5
FROM HENCE LONG FOR IT. SHED IT THERE	296	JESUS WP A	15
SEEN LONG BEFORE THIS CAME TO PASS	295	PALM-SUNDY	27
NOR MADE LIFE THROUGH HER LONG DESCENTS	312	FAIR+YONG	29
HOVER NOT LONG, ETERNAL DOVE.	308	THE SEED	7
SOMTHING I HAD, WHICH LONG AGO	308	THE SEED	9
AS WE FOR LONG AND SURE RECRUITS	310	THE SEED	77
BUT SEEING SOLDIERS LONG AGO	317	MEN OF WAR	29
DARES KNOW EFFECTS, AND JUDGE THEM LONG BEFORE	236	CONSTLATN	27
I LONG, AND GRONE, AND GRIEVE FOR THEE	228	PILGRIMAGE	13
THIS LATE, LONG HEAT MAY HIS INSTRUCTION BE	222	TEMPEST	3
HE IS THE CENTER OF LONG LIFE, AND LIGHT	209	REPENTANCE	83
OR BETTER, BUT THOU LONG AGO	273	WHT SUNDAY	27
AS THOU LONG SINCE WERT PLEAS'D TO BUY	274	WHT SUNDAY	53
AND WOULD E'R LONG	247	I WALKT	27
LONG FOR THEE, TO THEE ASPIRE	249	BEGGING A	6
WHICH LONG RESISTED THY DESIRE	264	INTRO. 1	10
BUT AS FOR THEE, WHOSE FAULTS LONG SINCE REQUIRE	281	JOY	11
AS I HAVE YOURS LONG SINCE, THIS PLANT, YOU SEE	279	PALM-TREE	2
THIS MADE HIM LONG FOR HOME, AS LOATH TO STAY	197	CORRUPTION	17
ALL THE LONG DAY	203	DSRDR + FR	13
I BEG'D HERE LONG, AND CRON'D TO KNOW	167	VNTY SPRIT	3
LEST LEFT ALONE TOO LONG	161	DSTRQCTION	31
HERE LONG MUST PASSE	174	JOY OF LIF	18
IS DARK, AND LONG.	174	JOY OF LIF	10
O HOW I LONG TO TRAVELL BACK	170	RETREATE	21
ALL THE LONG HOURES	176	MRNG-WTCH	3
BUT IN HER LONG, AND HIDDEN COURSE	150	RELIGION	33
HERE MUSING LONG, I HEARD	141	RGNRTN	78
AND ON SURE HOPES, THOUGH LONG, DID FEAST.	143	DEATH	22
FROM THAT LONG SLEEPE	144	RSRCTN +IM	6
AND THOU SO LONG SEIZ'D OF MY HEART.	348	HOLY BIBLE	2
LONG REIGN'D THIS VOGUE, AND THOU CAST BY	348	HOLY BIBLE	17
AND LET THESE LONG, SHARP JUDGEMENTS AW	351	L'ENVOY	54
THIS LONG WORN VEYL. THEN SHINE AND SPREAD	349	L'ENVOY	9
LONG'D			
AND LONG'D TO SEE, BUT MISS'D.	239	SHEPHEARDS	50

	PAGE	TITLE	LINE
LONGER			
I WILL NO LONGER COBWEBS SPIN	204	IDLE VERSE	3
A LONGER STAY	189	RESOLVE	2
RISE TO A LONGER COURSE MORE BRIGHT AND BRAVE.	343	WATER-FALL	12
LONGING			
AND LONGING FOR THY BRIGHT AND VITALL FIRE	278	THE STARRE	18
SO FIRM A LONGING CAN IMPOWRE	276	COCK-CRWNG	14
THINK YOU THESE LONGING EYES	275	PROFFER	19
LONGINGS			
BUT MEET TO QUENCH HIS LONGINGS, AND THY THIRST.	194	RLS + LSNS	80
LOOK			
O LOSE IT NOT. LOOK UP, WILT CHANGE THOSE LIGHTS	196	RLS + LSNS	143
SPRUCE, SUPPLE CRINGE, OR STUDY'D LOOK PUT ON	155	ISAACS M.	32
BUT I WILL KNOW WHICH WAY TO LOOK.	272	WHT SUNDAY	20
THAT HEREAFTER, WHEN I LOOK	249	BEGGING A	9
WHAT SPRINGS OR SHADES TO LOOK	239	SHEPHEARDS	40
HATH NOT SO MUCH AS ONE POOR LOOK.	240	MISERY	28
MAY LOOK TO THEE, TO THEE THE FINISHER	234	MUTINIE	21
WHERE THEY FOR FASHION LOOK	237	CONSTLATN	42
YET LOOK I FOR FAR BETTER BREAD	228	PILGRIMAGE	23
TO LOCK HIM OUT OF ALL HIS PAIN	242	MISERY	96
MY WITHER'D LEAFS AGAIN LOOK GREEN AND FLOURISH	245	MT. OLV. B	22
DID ONLY LOOK ABOUT, AND FAL	209	THE BURIAL	2
THEN LOOK ON ALL THAT THOU HAST MADE	208	REPENTANCE	63
LOOK FROM THY THRONE UPON THIS ROWL	207	REPENTANCE	23
I LOOK, AND SIGH FOR HIM, WHO FILS	220	PSALM 121	3
OF DAIES, FROM THEE LOOK FOR NEW STRENGTH	218	EASTER HYM	10
HE HELD, I CHANC'D TO LOOK	309	THE SEED	51
SOIL'D WITH MANY A WEEPING LOCK	312	FAIR+YONG	32
I WILL ON THEE, AS ON A COMET LOOK	307	RAIN-BOW	35
DURST NOT LOOK ON THOSE SMILING YEARS	303	ST MARY MN	12
TO LEND ME, THOUGH FROM FAR, ONE LOOK.	293	BEGGING B	4
TO RISE ON YOU AGAIN, AND LOOK	292	THE JEWS	30
LOOK WHAT THOU GAV'ST, ALL THAT I DO RESTORE	321	HIDDN TRSR	33
THAT MEN MIGHT LOOK AND LIVE AS GLO-WORMS SHINE	323	THE NIGHT	3
TRAVEL AND GROAN, AND LOOK AND CALL.	350	L'ENVOY	22
WHICH MAKES ME WISELY WEEP AND LOOK	347	THE BOOK	20
LOOKE			
LOOKE DOWNE GREAT MASTER OF THE FEAST, O SHINE	150	RELIGION	51
MY SOLLE MIGHT LOCKE ABOUT.	166	THE CALL	41
LOOKERS-BACK			
TO BLINDE THE EYES OF LOOKERS-BACK, AND I	320	HIDDN TRSR	9
LOOKING			
AND LOOKING BACK (AT THAT SHORT SPACE)	169	RETREATE	9
LOOKS			
GO, GO, SEAL UP THY LOOKS	187	NO DO THEY	9
MY RAVISH'D LOOKS	157	BRT. CHRCH	16
LOOKS DIM TOO IN THE CLOUD	197	CORRUPTION	34
DID WITH INTENTIVE LOOKS WATCH EVERY HOUR	306	RAIN-BOW	7
WHEN THOU DOST SHINE DARKNESS LOOKS WHITE AND FAIR	306	RAIN-BOW	9
WHO LOOKS UPON THEE FROM HIS GLORIOUS THRONE	306	RAIN-BOW	17
WITH IDLE HEARTS AND BUSIE LOOKS	303	ORNAMENT	10
WITH NATIVE LOOKS, WHICH KNEW NO GUILE	303	ORNAMENT	15
FORC'D BY HER ARTLESS LOOKS AND DRESS	303	ORNAMENT	18
LODGED IN THOSE FALSE LOOKS, TILL TOO LATE.	311	FAIR+YONG	22
WHICH HIS FIRST LOOKS WILL QUICKLY FRAY.	338	DEATH B	19
WHO NEVER LOOKS ON MAN	328	RIGHTSNESS	43
AND FOR THY SHADOW LOOKS THE LIGHT	212	DAWNING	18
O THY BRIGHT LOOKS. THY GLANCE OF LOVE	281	THE FAVOUR	1
RARE LOOKS. THAT CAN DISPENSE SUCH JOY	281	THE FAVOUR	3
WITH MEEK, DUMB LOOKS DIDST WOO MINE EYE	348	HOLY BIBLE	18
LOOKT			
LOOKT THY BODY.	185	PASSION	35
LOOMS			
AND PASSAGE THROUGH THESE LOOMS	246	MAN	27
LOOSE			
I'D LOOSE THOSE KNOTS THY HANDS DID TIE	214	MISERY	73
AS WATERS HERE, HEADLONG AND LOOSE	240	MISERY	9
WATCH O'RE THAT LOOSE	180	BURIALL	8
LOOSE, PARCELL'D HEARTS WIL FREEZE. THE SUN	189	RESOLVE	13
BUT I AM SADLY LOOSE, AND STRAY	187	NO DO THEY	17
THE PERJURER'S A DEVIL LET LOOSE. WHAT CAN	193	RLS + LSNS	47
SICKLY, AND LOOSE	145	RSRCTN +IM	40
LIFE WITHOUT THEE IS LOOSE AND SPILLS.	308	THE SEED	8
AND SUCH A KNOT, WHAT ARM DARES LOOSE	302	THE KNOT	13
WERE ONCE SINS LOOSE AND TEMPTING SPIES	305	ST MARY MN	58
WILL BY LOOSE DUST THAT MAN ARRAIGN	315	THE STONE	58
ERRE IN LOOSE AIRS BEYOND HER BOUNDS.	297	HERODIAS	4
AS IF HIS LIQUID, LOOSE RETINUE STAID	343	WATER-FALL	5
THEREFORE, THOSE LOOSE DELIGHTS AND LUSTS, WHICH HERE	342	OBSEQUIES	13
LOOSENS			
THAT BINDS, AND LOOSENS DEATH	144	RSRCTN +IM	2
LORD			
LORD, THEN SAID I, ON ME ONE BREATH	141	RGNRTN	90
HEALE THEN THESE WATERS, LORD, OR BRING THY FLOCK	150	RELIGION	49
LORD, GOD. I BEG NOR FRIENDS, NOR WEALTH	148	DAY OF JDG	37
WHERE MY DEARE LORD DID OFTEN TREAD	153	THE SEARCH	72
ACCEPT, DREAD LORD, AND THE POOR OBLATION	190	THE MATCH	13
TWO LIFES I HOLD FROM THEE, MY GRACIOUS LORD	191	THE MATCH	19
LORD JESU. THOU DIDST BOW THY BLESSED HEAD	191	THE MATCH	31

		PAGE	TITLE	LINE
LORD	**(CON'T)**			
HOW RICH, O LORD. HOW FRESH THY VISITS ARE.		198	UNPRFTBLNS	1
THE LORD OF LIFE BE BORNE IN EARTH.		200	NTVTY 1	30
O HEAR, AND HEAL THY SERVANT. LORD STRIKE DEAD		185	PASSION	14
LORD HASTE, LORD COME		181	BURIALL	39
LORD HASTE, LORD COME		181	BURIALL	39
O COME LORD JESUS QUICKLY.		181	BURIALL	40
LORD, WITH WHAT COURAGE, AND DELIGHT		182	CHRFLNESS	1
LORD, THEN ROUND ME WITH WEEPING CLOUDS		176	THE STORM	17
AH, MY DEARE LORD. WHAT COULDST THOU SPYE		164	INCARNATN	13
SURE IT WAS LOVE, MY LORD, FOR LOVE		164	INCARNATN	19
LORD. WHAT A BUSIE, RESTLES THING		161	PURSUITE	1
THEIR LORD WITH THEE HAD MOST TO DOE.		163	MT. OLVS A	20
LORD. WHEN THOU DIDST THY SELFE UNDRESSE		163	INCARNATN	1
AH. LORD. AND WHAT A PURCHASE WILL THAT BE		162	PURSUITE	17
AND DECK ME , LORD, WITH THE SAME CROWNE		167	THE CALL	92
THUS, LORD, I SEE MY GAINE IS GREAT		167	THE CALL	82
DEAR LORD. THOU ART ALL GRIEF AND LOVE		298	JESUS WP B	22
MY DEAR, ALMIGHTY LORD. WHY DOST THOU WEEP.		298	JESUS WP B	1
MY DEAR, BRIGHT LORD. MY MORNING-STAR.		296	JESUS WP A	13
DEAR LORD. RESTORE THY ANCIENT PEACE		294	BEGGING B	21
SHALL BE CONSUM'D. O MY SOUL, BLESS THY LORD.		287	PSALM 104	95
O LORD MY GOD, HOW MANY AND HOW RARE		286	PSALM 104	65
UP, O MY SOUL, AND BLESSE THE LORD. O GOD		284	PSALM 104	1
OR BOW THE HEAVENS. LORD BOW THEM AND DESCEND		283	LOVE-SICK	10
AND IN OBEDIENCE TO HIS LORD		314	THE STONE	44
MY DISTREST LORD. OR DID A STAR		315	DWELLNG-PL	7
O LET HIM BY HIS LORD BE LED		319	THE ASS	59
WERE NOT THY WORD (DEAR LORD) MY LIGHT		316	MEN OF WAR	9
SINCE OF MY LORD THEY HAD THEIR WILL		317	MEN OF WAR	35
(THEIR LORD SO NEAR) SENSE TO BE GLAD.		305	ST MARY MN	44
OF MY DREAD LORD.		337	THE THRONE	4
DEAR LORD. MAKE HASTE		335	JUDGEMENT	27
BUT HIS OWN LIVING WORKS DID MY LORD HOLD		323	THE NIGHT	21
LORD, BIND ME UP, AND LET ME LYE		239	MISERY	1
SO STRENGTHEN ME, LORD, ALL THE WAY		229	PILGRIMAGE	27
LORD, WHEN THOU DIDST ON SINAI PITCH		229	LAW + GOSP	1
LORD THEN TAKE IT, LEAVE IT NOT		249	BEGGING A	17
AND PUT FORTH THUS, THOUGH LORD, BEFORE		264	INTRO. 1	7
BUT LORD, I HAVE EXPELL'D THEM, AND SO BENT		264	INTRO. 1	13
DEAR LORD, 'TIS FINISHED. AND NOW HE		265	INTRO. 2	1
LORD JESUS. WITH WHAT SWEETNESS AND DELIGHTS		267	ASCN-DAY A	1
COME THEN THOU FAITHFUL WITNESS. COME DEAR LORD		268	ASCN-DAY A	61
AND MY MOST LOVING LORD STRAITWAY		211	FAITH	43
LORD, SINCE THOU DIDST IN THIS VILE CLAY		206	REPENTANCE	1
LORD, I CONFESSE THE HEYNOUS SCORE		208	REPENTANCE	57
IF THEN, DREAD LORD		215	PRAISE	45
LORD. THOU DIDST PUT A SOUL HERE. IF I MUST		224	TEMPEST	57
DEAR LORD, DO THIS. AND THEN LET GRACE		350	L'ENVOY	43
LORDS				
OF MY LORDS BLOOD		341	THE FEAST	52
WHEN MY LORDS HEAD IS FILL'D WITH DEW, AND ALL		324	THE NIGHT	32
OF MY LORDS DEAD		335	JUDGEMENT	20
AT THEIR LORDS FOOT-STOOL HAVE THEIR BIRTH.		304	ST MARY MN	28
OF THY LORDS HAND, THE OBJECT OF HIS EYE.		306	RAIN-BOW	14
MADE MY LORDS INCARNATION GOOD.		284	TRINITY-SN	6
OF THEIR LORDS THUNDER THEY RETIR'D APACE.		285	PSALM 104	22
OF MY LORDS PENNING, AND BY SWEETEST ART		198	SCRIPTURES	11
LOSE				
O LOSE IT NOT. LOCK UP, WILT CHANGE THOSE LIGHTS		196	RLS + LSNS	143
THOU SHALT NOT LOSE ONE MITE. THOUGH WATERS STRAY		193	RLS + LSNS	65
IF I LOSE ALL, AND MUST ENDURE		295	PALM-SUNDY	42
TO LOSE HIM TOO, AS WELL AS PARADISE)		307	RAIN-BOW	24
WHICH MAKE ME WISE TO LOSE MY SOUL.		322	CHILDEHOOD	26
WAS'T NOT ENOUGH TO LOSE THY BREATH		220	HOLY COMM.	41
LOSS				
REFINE US. WE ARE AT A LOSS.		274	WHT SUNDAY	62
LOSSE				
MY LOSSE BUT LITTLE TO IT		167	THE CALL	83
HAD MOURN'D THY LOSSE, NOT MINE		173	CONTENT	16
HUNG WITH MY GAINE, AND HIS GREAT LOSSE		152	THE SEARCH	42
SUCH LOSSES AS BEFEL HIM IN THIS AIR		247	I WALKT	26
LOST				
HAVING LOST THEE, BEHOLD TWO MEN IN WHITE.		268	ASCN-DAY A	58
O FOOLISH MAN. HOW HAST THOU LOST THY SIGHT.		224	TEMPEST	53
WHEN CONSCIENCE BY LEW'D USE HAD NOT LOST SENSE		154	ISAACS M.	19
BESIDES I'VE LOST		159	MANS FALL	9
THEN HAVING LOST THE SUNNE, AND LIGHT		162	PURSUITE	6
THE LOST SONNE HAD NOT LEFT THE HUSKE		162	PURSUITE	11
CAN I BE LOST.		181	BURIALL	32
AND LIVE, WHO DOTH NOT THUS, HATH LOST HEAV'NS WAY.		196	RLS + LSNS	142
TO SEE MAN LOST, WILL FOR OLD LOVE		292	THE JEWS	36
THE LOST SON BY THE NEWLY FOUND.		293	THE JEWS	49
LOT				
WHEN TERAH, NAHOR, HARAN, ABRAM, LOT		306	RAIN-BOW	5
AND SOURCE OF SPIRITS, WHERE HE TAKES HIS LOT		145	RSRCTN +IM	43
I KNOW THY LOT		225	RETIREMENT	26
UNTO MY DISPOSE OR LOT		249	BEGGING A	18
LOTHSOME				
WHO DOTH THY LOTHSOME MOTHER KEEP.		297	HERODIAS	12

		PAGE	TITLE	LINE
LOTS				
CAST IN THEIR LOTS AGAIN	. . . .	156	BRT. CHRCH	7
LOTT				
MY LOTT IS FALN, BLEST BE THY WILL.	. . . . .	227	LV + DSPLN	3
LOUD				
AND INTO LOUD DISCOVERIES BREAK	. . .	313	THE STONE	23
AS LOUD AS BLOOD. NOT THAT GOD NEEDS	. . .	314	THE STONE	24
WERE ALL MY LOUD, EVIL DAYS	. . .	324	THE NIGHT	37
THOU STILL'ST THE LOUD WAVES, WHEN MOST WILD	. . .	336	PSALM 65	19
AS THIS LOUD BROOKS INCESSANT FALL	. . . .	344	WATER-FALL	33
LOV'D				
WHO IN THEM LOV'D AND SOUGHT THY FACE.	. . . .	347	THE BOOK	30
DEARLY LOV'D DAY.	. . .	334	JUDGEMENT	12
THE WORLDS LOV'D WISDOM (FOR THE WORLDS FRIENDS THINK	.	320	HIDDN TRSR	15
WHO LOV'D MUCH, AND MUCH MORE COULD MOVE.	. . . .	305	ST MARY MN	50
WHO THEN DID DRESS THE MUCH LOV'D TOY	. . . .	304	ST MARY MN	17
BLESSED, UNHAPPY CITY. DEARLY LOV'D	. . . .	296	JESUS WP A	1
WHO LOV'D THE WORLD SO, AS TO GIVE	. . . .	292	THE JEWS	33
YET I WHOSE SEARCH LOV'D NOT TO PEEP AND PEER	. .	247	I WALKT	8
NOR LOV'D THE SMILES OF GREATNESS, BUT HAVE WROUGHT	.	280	PALM-TREE	19
LOV'ST				
AND LOV'ST HIM, THOUGH HE WORKS THY WO.	. . . .	298	JESUS WP B	25
LOVE				
O HEALING TEARS. THE TEARS OF LOVE	. . . .	298	JESUS WP B	10
DEAR LORD. THOU ART ALL GRIEF AND LOVE	. . . .	298	JESUS WP B	22
BUT 'TWAS THY LOVE THAT (WITHOUT LEAVE)	. . . .	299	JESUS WP B	32
TO SEE MAN LOST, WILL FOR OLD LOVE	. . . .	292	THE JEWS	36
YOUR STONY HEARTS DESPISED LOVE	. . . .	293	THE JEWS	43
AND TREES OF LIFE NO OTHER WATERS LOVE	. . .	291	THE TIMBER	51
BRIGHTNESS AND MIRTH, AND LOVE AND FAITH, ALL FLYE	.	288	THE BIRD	31
AND LOVE OF THEE, EACH WILLING ANGEL IS	. . .	284	PSALM 104	15
AND AS THY CARE BOUNDS THESE, SO THY RICH LOVE	. .	285	PSALM 104	29
JESUS, MY LIFE. HOW SHALL I TRULY LOVE THEE.	. . .	283	LOVE-SICK	1
AS TO MAKE MAN ALL PURE LOVE, FLESH A STAR.	. . .	283	LOVE-SICK	4
CHEAP, MIGHTY ART. HER ART OF LOVE	. . . .	305	ST MARY MN	49
GREAT KING OF LOVE AND TRUTH.	. . . .	301	PROVIDENCE	43
WITHIN THOSE BOUNDS SET BY THY LOVE.	. . . .	318	THE ASS	16
ABOVE ALL, MAKE ME LOVE THE POOR	. . . .	319	THE ASS	33
MY DEW, MY DEW. MY EARLY LOVE	. . . .	308	THE SEED	5
HOW AM I NOW IN LOVE WITH ALL	. . . .	311	FAIR+YONG	7
WHY SHOULD I NOT LOVE CHILDE-HOOD STILL.	. . .	321	CHILDEHOOD	20
WHY SHOULD MEN LOVE	. . . .	321	CHILDEHOOD	9
WHERE LOVE WITHOUT LUST DWELLS, AND BENDS	. . .	322	CHILDEHOOD	33
O DAY OF LIFE, OF LIGHT, OF LOVE.	. . . .	334	JUDGEMENT	1
THY CARE AND LOVE, WHICH JOYNTLY FLOW	. . . .	333	AGREEMENT	57
WORTH LOVE OR WRATH	. . . .	327	RIGHTSNESS	32
HE THAT DOTH SEEK AND LOVE	. . . .	327	RIGHTSNESS	13
GLITTER AND KINDLE WITH THY LOVE.	. . . .	332	AGREEMENT	18
THY LOVE CLAIMS HIGHEST THANKS, MY SIN	. . .	329	TEARS	13
AND WORK ALL NIGHT UPON THY LIGHT AND LOVE	. .	278	THE STARRE	22
O THY BRIGHT LOOKS. THY GLANCE OF LOVE	. . .	281	THE FAVOUR	1
THIS VEYLE THY FULL-EYED LOVE DENIES	. . . .	277	COCK-CRWNG	41
KING OF MERCY, KING OF LOVE	. . . .	249	BEGGING A	1
THY MERCY, LOVE, AND EASE	. . . .	248	I WALKT	56
TO HAVE THE MURTHRED FOR THY LOVE.	. . . .	264	INTRO. 1	12
THIS IS THE EARNEST THY LOVE SHEDS	. . . .	265	INTRO. 2	13
AMONGST THEM, WITH THEM, WING'D WITH FAITH AND LOVE.	.	268	ASCN-DAY A	32
TO KINDLE MY COLD LOVE	. . . .	271	ALL GONE	16
AND NOTHING DOTH THY LOVE ALLAY	. . . .	274	WHT SUNDAY	51
EVEN FOR THY LOVE, FOR BY THAT MEANS	. . . .	274	WHT SUNDAY	58
AND THY TWO WINGS WERE GRIEF AND LOVE.	. . . .	272	WHT SUNDAY	12
THY ANTIENT LOVE ON SOME MAY SHINE.	. . . .	273	WHT SUNDAY	40
WHERE SICK WITH LOVE I STRIVE THY NAME TO SING	. .	245	MT. OLV. B	24
WHICH ONLY GRIEF AND LOVE EXTRACT. WITH THIS	. .	244	THE SAP	41
TO SHEW WHAT STRANGE LOVE HE HAD TO OUR GOOD	. .	243	THE SAP	25
I MAY AS WEL AS LOVE, FIND TOO THY FEAR.	. . .	230	LAW + GOSP	30
I WOULD BOTH THINK, AND JUDGE I DID NOT LOVE THEE.	.	230	LAW + GOSP	40
WHAT TIME WE FROM OUR FIRST LOVE SWERV'D.	. . .	237	CONSTLATN	48
BE MORE AND MORE IN LOVE WITH DAY.	. . . .	237	CONSTLATN	52
IN ORDER, PEACE, AND LOVE	. . . .	237	CONSTLATN	54
ONLY CONTENT, AND LOVE, AND HUMBLE JOYS	. . .	239	SHEPHEARDS	35
HIS LOVE THERE FIRST DISCLOSE.	. . . .	238	SHEPHEARDS	16
BUT WRETCHED SALEM ONCE HIS LOVE, MUST NOW	. .	238	SHEPHEARDS	17
OUT OF MEER LOVE	. . . .	225	RETIREMENT	9
SURE, MIGHTY LOVE FORESEEING THE DISCENT	. . .	223	TEMPEST	21
GIVE HIM (WITH PITTY) LOVE	. . . .	216	DRESSING	25
LOVE THAT SHAL NOT ADMIT	. . . .	216	DRESSING	27
YET WITH THY LOVE THAT ABSENCE WINS	. . . .	213	ADMISSION	23
YET LET MY COURSE, MY AIM, MY LOVE	. . . .	212	DAWNING	43
BOWELS OF LOVE. AT WHAT LOW RATE	. . . .	213	ADMISSION	13
O MY DEAR GOD. MY LIFE, MY LOVE.	. . . .	208	REPENTANCE	47
PIERC'D NOT, LOVE ONLY CAN WITH QUICK ACCESSE	. .	160	THE SHOWRE	9
LOVE GOD, AND LOVE THY NEIGHBOUR, WATCH, AND PRAY.	.	196	RLS + LSNS	140
LOVE GOD, AND LOVE THY NEIGHBOUR, WATCH, AND PRAY.	.	196	RLS + LSNS	140
ALMIGHTY LOVE. WHERE ART THOU NOW. MAD MAN	.	197	CORRUPTION	29
AND, AS FIRST LOVE DRAWS STRONGEST, SO FROM HENCE	.	196	CORRUPTION	7
CAN NEITHER LOVE, NOR SUFF'RINGS BIND.	. . .	200	NTVTY 2	13
LUST IN THE ROBES OF LOVE	. . . .	205	IDLE VERSE	14
THY LINES, THY LOVE. AWAY	. . . .	202	THE CHECK	44
YET, SURE, MY GOD. I LOVE THEE MOST	. . . .	203	DSRDR + FR	14

		PAGE	TITLE	LINE
LOVE	(CCN'T)			
ALAS, THY LOVE.		203	DSRDR + FR	15
OF LOVE, AND SORRCW		202	THE CHECK	37
CANNOT BE LOVE.		189	RESOLVE	6
BUT O THY LOVE. THY RICH, ALMIGHTY LOVE		188	RELAPSE	5
BUT O THY LOVE. THY RICH, ALMIGHTY LOVE		188	RELAPSE	5
YET THY LCVE SPIES		181	BURIALL	29
LCVE LANGUISHETH, AND MEMCRY CCTH RUST		183	THRS A TYE	3
DID IN PURE LCVE CESCEND		184	PEACE	11
LED BY THY LOVE WCULDST STOOP THUS LOW		180	BURIALL	17
BLEST BE THE GOD OF HARMONY, ANC LOVE. . . .		179	CHRCH-SVC	1
LANGUAGE TO LOVE		162	MT. OLVS A	3
SURE IT WAS LOVE, MY LORD, FOR LOVE		164	INCARNATN	19
SURE IT WAS LOVE, MY LORD, FOR LOVE		164	INCARNATN	19
SCME LOVE A ROSE		174	CONTENT	21
AND STILL MY LOVE.		174	JOY OF LIF	2
A MILE, OR TWC, FROM MY FIRST LOVE		169	RETREATE	8
SCME MEN A FORWARD MOTICN LOVE		170	RETREATE	29
BY THIS MILDE ART OF LOVE AT LENGTH		348	HOLY BIBLE	23
GLACNESS, AND PEACE, ANC HOPE, AND LOVE		348	HOLY BIBLE	27
AND HATCH'D ALL WITH HIS QUICKNING LOVE. . . .		344	WATER-FALL	32
THAT FRCM THE MURD'RING WORLDS FALSE LOVE		343	OBSEQUIES	31
IF NOT THY MIGHTY LOVE, MY OWN DEFENSE. . . .		342	OBSEQUIES	12
AND LCVE THE LURE, THAT WCOS THEE DOWN. . . .		346	THE QUEER	14
LOVE-FEASTS				
THE CHURCHES LOVE-FEASTS, TIMES PREROGATIVE . . .		2	SON-DAYES	17
LOVE-SICK				
A LCVE-SICK SCULS EXALTED FLIGHT.		277	COCK-CRWNG	34
CO NOT CESPISE A LOVE-SICK HEART.		294	BEGGING B	14
LOVE-TWIST				
MY LOVE-TWIST HELD THEE UP, MY UNSEEN LINK. . . .		225	RETIREMENT	22
LOVELY				
SC MURTHERED MAN, WHEN LOVELY LIFE IS DONE . . .		289	THE TIMBER	21
AS EARTH, THY LOVELY HEAD DOST BOW.		304	ST MARY MN	26
THE CHAST, AND LOVELY ORJECT CF THY THOUGHT. . .		155	ISAACS M.	30
LOVER				
THE DOTING LOVER IN HIS QUEINTEST STRAIN . . .		231	THE WORLD	8
LOVES				
'TIS TRUE, HE LOVES THAT CUST WHEREON THEY GC .		238	SHEPHEARDS	13
O THOU, WHOM MY SCUL LOVES, ANC FEARES. . .		185	PASSION	15
BUT IF HE PAYS, WHO LOVES MUCH, THEN . .		329	TEARS	15
WHO IS THE MAN THAT WALKS IN THEE. WHO LOVES		327	RIGHTSNESS	5
THOU ART THE TRUE LOVES-KNOW, BY THEE . . .		302	THE KNOT	5
LOVEST				
O THOU THAT LCVEST A PURE, AND WHITEND SOUL./ . .		216	DRESSING	1
LOVING				
AND MY MOST LOVING LORD STRAITWAY		211	FAITH	43
WATCH FCR, AND KNCW THEIR LOVING STAR. . .		281	THE FAVOUR	8
TC FEELE MY LCVING FATHERS ROC		147	DAY OF JDG	31
LOW				
AND LCW AS ERE THEY LAY BEFORE		147	DAY OF JDG	11
LED BY THY LOVE WCULDST STCOP THUS LOW . .		180	BURIALL	17
TC HEIGHTEN THY DEVOTIONS, ANC KEEP LCW . . .		194	RLS + LSNS	85
SOME KINDE HERBS HERE, THOUGH LOW AND FAR . . .		281	THE FAVOUR	7
AND IN MY FLESH, THOUGH VILE, ANC LOW . . .		212	DAWNING	41
BCWELS CF LOVE. AT WHAT LCW RATE . . .		213	ADMISSION	13
PCOR CUST SHOULD LY STILL LOW		217	DRESSING	40
THOU, WHOSE SAD HEART, ANC WEEPING HEAD LYES LCW		217	EASTER-DAY	1
HID IN THESE LOW THINGS SNARES TO GAIN HIS HEART		223	TEMPEST	23
WHY ART THOU HUMBLED THUS, ANC LCW . . .		304	ST MARY MN	25
DISTANT AND LCW, I CAN IN THINE SEE HIM . . .		306	RAIN-BOW	16
ARE ALL TCO HIGH FOR A LOW CELL.		309	THE SEED	34
TC LOW ESTATES, AND A LCW MINCE. . . .		319	THE ASS	36
TC LOW ESTATES, AND A LCW MINCE. . . .		319	THE ASS	36
FRCM THE LOW EARTH TO HIGH HEAVEN RISE . . .		326	ABELS BLOD	38
(THOUGH SINGLE VOICES ARE BUT LOW) . . .		325	ABELS BLOD	8
THE SMALL, STILL VOICE, AT SCME LCW COTTAGE KNCCKS		330	JACOBS PLW	9
WHOSE SPIRIT EVER POOR, IS MEEK ANC LCW. . .		327	RIGHTSNESS	15
THOU VISIT'ST THE LOW EARTH, AND THEN . . .		336	PSALM 65	27
WHILE THE LOW VIOLET THRIVES AT THEIR ROOT. . .		289	THE TIMBER	8
LOWC				
A SEA, WHCSE LCWD WAVES CANNOT SLEEP . . .		325	ABELS BLOD	15
WHEN LOWD JOYES WANT A WING		167	THE CALL	79
WHEN CNE LOWD BLAST SHALL REND THE CEEPE . .		147	DAY OF JDG	17
OF YOUNG, GAY SWEARERS, WITH THEIR NEEDLESSE, LChC		154	ISAACS M.	22
LOWER				
THE LCWER GRCUNDS STIL CHASE, AND CHOOSE . . .		240	MISERY	10
LOWEST				
THE LCWEST PITCH.		329	TEARS	14
LOWLY				
AND LCWLY KNEELING (FCR THE MCST . . .		337	THE THRONE	5
GRANT I MAY SCFT AND LCWLY BE		318	THE ASS	17
LOYNS				
FCR THEE, WHO IN THE FIRST MANS LCYNS DICST FAL .		243	THE SAP	19
LUCKY				
THE LUCKY WORLD SHEWD ME CNE CAY . . .		302	ORNAMENT	1
LUCTUAL				
THY LIGHT AS LUCTUAL ANC STAIN'C WITH WOES . .		307	RAIN-BOW	37
LULL'C				
LULL'C BY THOSE CHARMERS TC A LETHARGY. . . .		281	JOY	10

		PAGE	TITLE	LINE
LURE				
IF I HOLD FAST AND SLIGHT THE LURE.		317	MEN OF WAR	40
AND LOVE THE LURE, THAT WOOS THEE DOWN.		346	THE QUEER	14
LUST				
THE LATEST MODES OF PRIDE AND LUST		302	ORNAMENT	6
WHERE LOVE WITHOUT LUST DWELLS, AND BENDS		322	CHILDEHOOD	33
HIS SHAMELESS LUST IN PUBLICK WEARS		297	HERODIAS	15
NEW FRESH ACCOUNTS OF BLOOD AND LUST.		297	HERODIAS	8
LUST IN THE ROBES OF LOVE		205	IDLE VERSE	14
LUSTFUL				
A SLAVE TO LUSTFUL ELEMENTS.		312	FAIR+YONG	30
LUSTS				
ALL LUSTS IN ME		191	THE MATCH	34
THUS BY OUR LUSTS DISORDER'D INTO WARS		237	CONSTLATN	45
AND LUSTS (SAID HE)		225	RETIREMENT	13
THEREFORE, THOSE LOOSE DELIGHTS AND LUSTS, WHICH HERE		342	OBSEQUIES	13
LUTE				
NEER HIM, HIS LUTE, HIS FANCY, AND HIS FLIGHTS		231	THE WORLD	10
LUXURIE				
NO COSTLY PRIDE, NO SOFT-CLOATH'D LUXURIE		239	SHEPHEARDS	31
LY				
POOR DUST SHOULD LY STILL LOW		217	DRESSING	40
LYE				
LORD, BIND ME UP, AND LET ME LYE		239	MISERY	1
THEY'RE STOR'D UP IN THE SOCKET, WHERE THEY LYE		158	THE LAMPE	19
WHEN I LYE DOWN. THE PIOUS SOUL BY NIGHT		177	MRNG-WTCH	24
LYES				
LYES TAME AS ALL THE REST.		201	THE CHECK	5
ALL'S IN DEEP SLEEP, AND NIGHT. THICK DARKNES LYES		197	CORRUPTION	37
OF SPIRITS, HEAV'N EXTRACTED LYES IN THEE.		197	SCRIPTURES	2
THIS CONVERSATION, BUT THE GOOD MAN LYES		195	RLS + LSNS	125
THOU, WHOSE SAD HEART, AND WEEPING HEAD LYES LOW		217	EASTER-DAY	1
HELL AND ALL HEARTS STARK NAKED LYES.		314	THE STONE	27
LYEST				
ELSE ALL AT REST THOU LYEST, AND THE FIERCE BREATH		289	THE TIMBER	17
GOE, SLEEP IN PEACE. AND WHEN THOU LYEST		177	EVNG-WTCH	3
LYONS				
THE LYONS WHELPS IMPATIENT OF DELAY		286	PSALM 104	57
MAD				
ALMIGHTY LOVE. WHERE ART THOU NOW. MAD MAN		197	CORRUPTION	29
POSSESSETH MAD MAN WITHOUT MEASURE.		211	DAWNING	8
WHO KNEELS, OR SIGHS A LIFE IS MAD.		236	CONSTLATN	24
MAD'ST				
AND WHERE THOU MAD'ST AN END, THERE I'LE BEGIN.		158	THE LAMPE	26
MADE				
AGE MADE THEM REV'REND, AND A SNOWIE HEAD		156	ISAACS M.	69
FOR GOD (MADE MAN,)		159	MANS FALL	30
REDUC'D TH'EXTENT OF WORKS OF FAITH, SO MADE		159	MANS FALL	31
MADE ME A STARRE, A PEARLE, OR A RAIN-BOW		161	DSTRQCTION	6
MADE THOSE WILD SHADES A PARADISE		152	THE SEARCH	62
TO SEE, IF ANY LEAFE HAD MADE		141	RGNRTN	84
THIS MADE HIM LONG FOR HOME, AS LOATH TO STAY		197	CORRUPTION	17
THY ACCOUNTS THUS MADE, SPEND IN THE GRAVE ONE HOURE		195	RLS + LSNS	121
WHICH SINFULL EASE MADE FOUL		176	THE STORM	22
THAT MADE THEE THUS RESOLVE TO DYE		164	INCARNATN	15
I GRIEVE, MY GOD. THAT THOU HAS MADE ME SUCH.		161	DSTRQCTION	26
HAST THOU MADE MAN.		161	PURSUITE	2
SEAL'D , AND MADE GOOD		180	CHRCH-SVC	21
I BREAK THE FENCE MY OWN HANDS MADE		240	MISERY	21
THIS MADE THE ANGEL CALL AT REEDS AND THATCH		238	SHEPHEARDS	27
TURNING TO HIM, WHO MADE POOR SAND TO TIRE		234	MUTINIE	11
MADE OPEN HOUSE.		210	FAITH	8
THE LAW, AND CEREMONIES MADE		210	FAITH	13
THEN LOOK ON ALL THAT THOU HAST MADE		208	REPENTANCE	63
WHEN THOU HAST MADE		215	PRAISE	51
AND THY PROMISE 'TIL MADE EVEN		214	PRAISE	23
SHE MADE THE EARTH THEIR NURSE, AND TOMB		222	TEMPEST	9
MADE LIFE MY COMMON STAKE.		282	GARLAND	14
WE PLAINLY SEE, WHO MADE THE SAME.		277	COCK-CRWNG	22
MADE HIS CLOATHES BE		270	ASCSN-HYMN	33
FELL ON MY HEART, THOSE MADE IT BUD		264	INTRO. 1	6
ARE THY GREAT WORKS. IN WISDOM HAST THOU MADE		286	PSALM 104	66
CULL'D FLOWRES AND MADE ME POSIES.		282	GARLAND	22
MADE MY LORDS INCARNATION GOOD.		284	TRINITY-SN	6
THEIR LESSON TAUGHT THEM, WHEN FIRST MADE.		288	THE BIRD	12
MY SINS LONG SINCE HAVE MADE THEE STRANGE		293	BEGGING B	5
AND MADE GRAVE MUSIQUE LIKE WILDE WIT		297	HERODIAS	3
MADE THINE EYES MELT, AND THY HEART HEAVE.		299	JESUS WP B	33
ORDAIN'D, AND MADE TO BEAR HIS MAKER.		295	PALM-SUNDY	29
NOR MADE LIFE THROUGH HER LONG DESCENTS		312	FAIR+YONG	29
SO THAT FAM'D FRUIT WHICH MADE ALL DYE		312	FAIR+YONG	35
THAT ONE MADE ALL THESE LESSER LIGHTS.		309	THE SEED	28
GOD IS MADE OUR ALLIE		302	THE KNOT	6
WHERE WITH PROUD HASTE THE RICH MADE WAY		302	ORNAMENT	3
SINCE THOU HAST MADE THY ARM MY FOLD		301	PROVIDENCE	48
AS MADE HIM KNOW HIS GOD BY NIGHT.		323	THE NIGHT	6
THOU HAST MADE BEGGERS RICH.		329	TEARS	16
THIS MADE HIM PUT ON CLOUDS, AND FIRE AND SMOKE		330	JACOBS PLW	7
WHEN ONCE MADE PUBLIQUE, IS ESTEEM'D BY NONE.		330	JACOBS PLW	18
MADE LINEN, WHO DID WEAR IT THEN.		347	THE BOOK	8

	PAGE	TITLE	LINE
MADE (CON'T)			
COVER'D IT, SINCE A COVER MADE	347	THE BOOK	12
AND MADE CONFORMABLE TO HIS	349	L'ENVOY	5
MADNES			
BUT AS I DID THEIR MADNES SO DISCUSSE	233	THE WORLD	57
THE WISE-MANS MADNES LAUGHTER.	166	THE CALL	65
MAGDAL-CASTLE			
WHEN MAGDAL-CASTLE WAS THY SEAT	304	ST MARY MN	13
MAGNET			
SURE, HOLYNESS THE MAGNET IS	346	THE QUEER	13
MAGNETISME			
THEIR MAGNETISME WORKS ALL NIGHT	276	COCK-CRWNG	5
MAGNETS			
NO THESE ARE THE MAGNETS WHICH SO STRONGLY MOVE	278	THE STARRE	21
MAID			
THE GLAD WORLDS BLESSED MAID.	302	THE KNOT	2
CAME THE SHEEP-KEEPING SYRIAN MAID.	303	ORNAMENT	16
MAJESTY			
HONOUR AND MAJESTY HAVE THEIR ABODE	284	PSALM 104	3
MAK'ST			
THOU MAK'ST TO GROW. THESE (BLEST BY THEE) THE EARTH	285	PSALM 104	42
AND MAK'ST THE RAGING PEOPLE MILD.	336	PSALM 65	20
AND DYING MAK'ST ME GO IN PEACE.	348	HOLY BIBLE	34
MAKE			
WHEN THOU SHALT MAKE ALL NEW AGAIN	347	THE BOOK	27
YOU MAKE ROCKS BUD	341	THE FEAST	53
TO MAKE ME BRAVE	342	OBSEQUIES	26
DEAR LORD, MAKE HASTE	335	JUDGEMENT	27
MAKE ALL THINGS NEW. AND WITHOUT END.	335	JUDGEMENT	46
TRANSGRESSIONS MAKE ME FOUL EACH DAY	336	PSALM 65	7
MISTS MAKE BUT TRIUMPHS FOR THE DAY.	338	DEATH B	20
MAKE NO DELAY	339	THE FEAST	2
AND MAKE THE DEAD, LIKE FLOWERS, ARISE	334	JUDGEMENT	5
SHALL BRING TRUE DAY, AND MAKE DUST SEE	335	JUDGEMENT	21
MAKE ME AMONGST THEM ('TIS MY SUIT)	329	TEARS	7
WITH HIDDEN TREASURES THAT MAKE TRULY RICH.	327	RIGHTSNESS	12
I WILL EXHAUST IT ALL, AND MAKE	328	ANGUISH	11
QUICKLY WOULD I MAKE MY PATH EVEN	321	CHILDEHOOD	7
IF SEEING MUCH SHOULD MAKE STAID EYES	321	CHILDEHOOD	17
AND LONG EXPERIENCE SHOULD MAKE WISE.	321	CHILDEHOOD	18
WHICH MAKE ME WISE TO LOSE MY SOUL.	322	CHILDEHOOD	26
AS TO MAKE MAN ALL PURE LOVE, FLESH A STAR.	283	LOVE-SICK	4
AND AT THY PRESENCE MAKE THESE MOUNTAINS FLOW	283	LOVE-SICK	11
AND PLENTEOUS MEALS THEY MAKE.	286	PSALM 104	76
LET THE JOY'D RODE MAKE HOLY-DAY	294	PALM-SUNDY	8
'TWILL MAKE THE LAND OF DARKNESS LIGHT.	299	JESUS WP B	51
CAN MAKE MANS DEAD AND SCATTER'D BONES	298	JESUS WP B	7
WHICH IS REQUIR'D TO MAKE UP LIFE	299	JESUS WP B	27
HIS ONELY SON TO MAKE IT FREE	292	THE JEWS	34
WHOM SUFFERINGS MAKE MOST GREEN AND GAY.	294	PALM-SUNDY	3
MAKE LESSER MORNINGS, WHEN THE GREAT ARE DONE.	288	THE BIRD	18
BUT AS THESE BIRDS OF LIGHT MAKE A LAND GLAD	288	THE BIRD	23
WHOSE HEAVY NOTES MAKE ALL THAT HEAR THEM, SAD.	288	THE BIRD	26
THESE UPPER SPRINGS AND NONE ELSE MAKE THEM GROW.	291	THE TIMBER	52
YET GRIEF AND OLD WOUNDS MAKE HIM SORE DISPLEAS'D	290	THE TIMBER	35
YET JOY IT SELF WILL MAKE A RIGHT SOUL GRIEVE	290	THE TIMBER	39
TO MAKE DRIE DUST, AND DEAD TREES GROW.	291	THE TIMBER	13
THOUGH BLOOD AND DRUNKENNESS MAKE BUT FOUL, FOUL WEATHER.	307	RAIN-BOW	26
OF PARADISE, COULD MAKE MAN FADE	312	FAIR+YONG	38
ABOVE ALL, MAKE ME LOVE THE POOR	319	THE ASS	33
WHEN WE TWO PART, I WILL A JOURNEY MAKE	280	PALM-TREE	25
O TAKE IT OFF. MAKE NO DELAY	277	COCK-CRWNG	43
HARK, AND MAKE USE OF THIS ENSUING STORY.	282	GARLAND	4
SIGHS MAKE JOY SURE, AND SHAKING FASTENS THEE.	281	JOY	30
TO MAKE STAIN'D MAN MORE WHITE THEN SNOW.	270	ASCSN-HYMN	36
MAKE CLAY ASCEND MORE QUICK THEN LIGHT.	270	ASCSN-HYMN	42
SO LET THY GRACE NOW MAKE THE WAY	274	WHT SUNDAY	57
YOU'D MAKE NO FLIGHTS.	274	PROFFER	4
BUT YOU WOULD HONEY MAKE.	274	PROFFER	7
I MAKE ALL NEW. THERE NOTHING GAY	226	RETIREMENT	40
WOULD MAKE A COURT, SHOULD HE THERE DWEL.	240	MISERY	36
BUT SELDOM DOTH MAKE HEAV'N HIS GLASS.	236	CONSTLATN	20
TILL THOU BOTH MEND AND MAKE ME THINE.	242	MISERY	113
THUS DO I MAKE THY GIFTS GIV'N ME	214	MISERY	71
TO MAKE MAN GOOD, AS BID HIM BE	242	MISERY	94
WOULD MAKE US BOWRES.	222	AFFLICTION	24
DID MAKE US SEE	219	HOLY COMM.	23
MAY MAKE THE FUTURE CLEER.	216	DRESSING	22
WHAT EVER THOU DOST BID, LET FAITH MAKE GOOD	216	DRESSING	23
AND THROUGH HIS MERITS, MAKE THY MERCY MINE.	209	REPENTANCE	86
TO MAKE US MORE, THOU WOULDST BE LESSE	163	INCARNATN	3
THEN MAKE MY SOULE WHITE AS HIS OWNE	167	THE CALL	90
MAKE RESTLESS MONES	179	CHRCH-SVC	5
I DYE TO MAKE MY FOES INHERIT.	185	PASSION	43
WOULDST MAKE EACH PART	182	CHRFLNESS	18
MAKE ME FAIRE DAYES OF EVERY NIGHT.	182	CHRFLNESS	8
MAY MAKE THEM WEEP	173	CONTENT	10
WHEN NIGHT COMES, LIST THY DEEDS, MAKE PLAIN THE WAY	195	RLS + LSNS	115
MAKE THESE SAD SHADES PURE SUN	202	THE CHECK	30
AS TO MAKE CLAY	202	THE CHECK	33

		PAGE	TITLE	LINE
MAKE	**(CON'T)**			
WEE'L MAKE A MATCH, MY ONLY LIGHT	• • • •	205	IDLE VERSE	7
YET, IF THOU WILT, THOU CANST MAKE CLEAN.	• • •	199	NTVTY 1	24
A CONSORT MAKE.	• • • • •	199	NTVTY 1	9
MAKE NOT THY BREAST A LABRYINTH, OR TRAP.	• • •	193	RLS + LSNS	56
IF TRIALS COME, THIS WIL MAKE GOOD THY PART	• •	193	RLS + LSNS	57
SHOULD MOVE, THEY MAKE US HOLY, HAPPY, RICH.	• •	192	RLS + LSNS	30
AND BAD THE LAZIE SUNNE MAKE HASTE	• • •	143	DEATH	21
AND HOW OF DEATH WE MAKE	• • • • •	145	RSRCTN +IM	23
WHEN THOU SHALT MAKE THE CLOUDS THY SEATE	• •	147	DAY OF JDG	21
OF DROPS MAKE SOFT THE EARTH, MY EYES COULD WEEP	• •	160	THE SHOWRE	14
ROB'D OF YOUR CALME, NOR CAN I EVER MAKE	• • •	158	MANS FALL	4
MAKER				
YOUR MAKER PENT UP IN A GRAVE	• • • •	164	INCARNATN	11
BY SOME HID SENSE THEIR MAKER GAVE	• • •	246	MAN	25
ORDAIN'D, AND MADE TO BEAR HIS MAKER.	• • •	295	PALM-SUNDY	29
MAN SLIGHTS HIS MAKER, WHEN FAMILIAR GROWN	•	330	JACOBS PLW	19
ETERNAL GOD. MAKER OF ALL	• • • • •	346	THE BOOK	1
MAKERS				
AS SPEAKS STILL IN THY MAKERS EAR	• • •	325	ABELS BLOD	10
BUT THOSE FLED TO THEIR MAKERS THRONE	• •	179	SILENCE	23
IS BOTH HIS OWN JOY, AND HIS MAKERS TOO.	• • •	193	RLS + LSNS	51
MAKES				
THAT GAIN IS DREADFUL, WHICH MAKES SPIRITS SICK.	• •	193	RLS + LSNS	42
(WHICH WAK'D BY HEAT, AND BEAMS, MAKES UP	• •	203	DSRDR + FR	32
WHO MAKES HIS JESTS OF SINS, MUST BE AT LEAST	• •	194	RLS + LSNS	77
THIS MAKES ME SPAN	• • • • •	159	MANS FALL	27
MAKES MOST UNHAPPY, OR MOST FORTUNATES.	• •	155	ISAACS M.	46
'TIS NUMBER MAKES A SCHISM. THRONGS ARE RUDE	• •	330	JACOBS PLW	5
WITH FERTIL STREAMS, MAKES RICH ALL GROUNDS	• •	336	PSALM 65	30
MAKES HEAVEN AND EARTH	• • • •	295	PALM-SUNDY	25
DEW OF THE DEAD WHICH MAKES DUST MOVE	• •	298	JESUS WP B	11
'WHOSE SERVICE MAKES EV'N CAPTIVES FREE)	• •	300	PROVIDENCE	14
BOTH MORNINGS MAKES, AND EVENINGS THERE.	• •	288	THE BIRD	22
SOME SECRET SENSE, WHICH MAKES THE DEAD BLOOD RUN	•	289	THE TIMBER	23
MINE WITH THY BLOOD, THY BLOOD WHICH MAKES THEE MINE	•	283	LOVE-SICK	21
O FEED THAT LIFE, WHICH MAKES HIM BLOW	• •	308	THE SEED	19
MAKES WAY FOR STORMS INTO HIS REST.	• • •	309	THE SEED	44
MAKES BEAUTY LASTING, FRESH AND PURE.	• • •	305	ST MARY MN	46
FIRST MAKES, THEN HUGS A SNARE	• • • •	236	CONSTLATN	18
MAKES UP BUT LECTURES FOR HIS EYE, AND EAR.	• •	223	TEMPEST	20
AND MAKES HIM MOURN, AND PINE AND DYE	• •	281	THE FAVOUR	5
OR SOME FRAIL BEAUTY MAKES THE BRAVEST SHEW	• •	282	GARLAND	3
ATTRACTS THEE THUS AND MAKES THEE STREAM AND FLOW	•	278	THE STARRE	2
IT THRIVES NO WHERE. THIS MAKES THESE WEIGHTS (LIKE DEATH	279	PALM-TREE	7
WHICH MAKES THE HIGH TRANSCENDENT BLISS	• • •	346	THE QUEER	15
WHOSE SHADOW MAKES ME SAD OR SICK.	• • •	340	THE FEAST	48
WHICH MAKES ME WISELY WEEP AND LOOK	• • •	347	THE BOOK	20
MAKEST				
THOU MAKEST DARKNESS, AND THEN COMES THE NIGHT.	• •	286	PSALM 104	53
MAKING				
MAKING DUST AND ASHES READY.	• • • •	339	THE FEAST	6
MAKING THE TIME THEY HAD	• • • •	327	RIGHTSNESS	28
NOW WITH CLOUDS, NOW MAKING CLEAR	• • •	281	JOY	20
MAKING THE WHOLE MOST MUSICALL	• • • •	222	AFFLICTION	40
MALE-CONTENT				
AND AIR OF EDEN, LIKE A MALE-CONTENT	• • •	279	PALM-TREE	6
MAMRE				
TOWARDS OLD MAMRE AND ESHCOLS BROOK.	• • • •	292	THE JEWS	31
MAN				
TO SEE MAN LOST, WILL FOR OLD LOVE	• • •	292	THE JEWS	36
THE KING OF GRIEF, THE MAN OF SORROW	• • •	294	PALM-SUNDY	4
SO MURTHERED MAN, WHEN LOVELY LIFE IS DONE	• •	289	THE TIMBER	21
SHALL YET TO MAN APPEAR	• • • • •	291	THE JEWS	5
I MET WITH A DEAD MAN	• • • • •	282	GARLAND	26
AS TO MAKE MAN ALL PURE LOVE, FLESH A STAR.	• •	283	LOVE-SICK	4
RETIRE INTO THEIR DENS. MAN GOES ABROAD	• •	286	PSALM 104	62
(FOR WHICH COURSE MAN SEEMS MUCH THE FITTER BORN)	•	287	THE BIRD	4
I WILL NOT FEAR WHAT MAN	• • • •	300	PROVIDENCE	19
DOEST THOU CONVEY MAN FOOD AND MONEY	• • •	300	PROVIDENCE	9
WHAT THOU HAST DONE (BUT THOUGH MAN TOO	• •	299	JESUS WP B	35
THOU GRIEV'ST, MAN SHOULD HIMSELF UNDO	• •	298	JESUS WP B	24
THAT SINCE MAN FELL, EXPECT WITH GROANS	• •	294	PALM-SUNDY	12
CHEATING HIMSELF, THAT MAN WALKS IN THIS PATH.	• •	328	RIGHTSNESS	54
WHO NEVER LOOKS ON MAN	• • • •	328	RIGHTSNESS	43
BUT THE GOOD MAN IS GODS PECULIAR TREASURE.	• •	328	RIGHTSNESS	48
MAN SLIGHTS HIS MAKER, WHEN FAMILIAR GROWN	• •	330	JACOBS PLW	19
BY GODS PERMISSION, AND MAN TURNS A MULE.	• •	330	JACOBS PLW	30
MAN TO HIS DUTY. THOU ALONE	• • • •	336	PSALM 65	15
BUT MEER DISDAIN, LET NOT MAN SAY	• • •	335	JUDGEMENT	43
BLESS THEE, AND BLAME UNTHANKFUL MAN.	• • •	334	AGREEMENT	72
WHO IS THE MAN THAT WALKS IN THEE. WHO LOVES	•	327	RIGHTSNESS	5
WHERE WEEPING VIRTUE PARTS WITH MAN.	• • •	322	CHILDEHOOD	32
THEE, MORE THEN ERE I STUDYED MAN	• • •	322	CHILDEHOOD	40
WHAT SOME POOR MAN MAY OFTEN FEEL	• • •	308	THE SEED	2
OF PARADISE, COULD MAKE MAN FADE	• • • •	312	FAIR+YONG	38
WHAT MAN WILL SHOW.	• • • • •	313	THE STONE	5
MAN I CAN BRIBE, AND WOMAN WILL	• • • •	313	THE STONE	10
NOTHING BUT MAN, WHEN AMBUSH'D THERE.	• • •	313	THE STONE	17
WHAT CAN THE MAN DO THAT SUCCEEDS THE KING.	• •	320	HIDDN TRSR	1

	PAGE	TITLE	LINE
MAN (CON'T)			
ALL THAT MAN DOTH, CONCEALS OR SHOWS	314	THE STONE	31
WILL BY LOOSE DUST THAT MAN ARRAIGN	315	THE STONE	58
WHAT MAN MAY LEARN FROM THEE.	278	THE STARRE	12
TO MAKE STAIN'D MAN MORE WHITE THEN SNOW.	270	ASCSN-HYMN	36
AND REBUILD MAN	270	ASCSN-HYMN	40
COULD MAN OUTLOOK THAT MARK.	271	ALL GONE	20
LEAVE BEHINDE THEM THE OLD MAN	269	ASCSN-HYMN	12
MAN OF OLD	269	ASCSN-HYMN	19
CALL TO THE SOUL, WHEN MAN DOTH SLEEP.	271	ALL GONE	26
BEFORE MAN BROUGHT FORTH SIN, AND SIN DECAY.	268	ASCN-DAY A	40
HOW IS MAN PARCELL'D OUT, HOW EV'RY HOUR	222	TEMPEST	1
O THAT MAN CULD DO SO, THAT HE WOULD HEAR	223	TEMPEST	17
AND MAN (LIKE ISSACHAR) IN LODES DELIGHT	223	TEMPEST	30
TO CHECK THE MULE, UNRULY MAN	221	AFFLICTION	18
THUS DOTH GOD KEY DISORDER'D MAN	222	AFFLICTION	35
AND BRINGS MAN HOME, WHEN HE DOTH RANGE	221	AFFLICTION	6
O FOOLISH MAN. HOW HAST THOU LOST THY SIGHT.	224	TEMPEST	53
FIRE TO ALL THREE, BUT MAN HATH NO SUCH MIRTH.	223	TEMPEST	32
ALL HAVE THEIR KEYES, AND SET ASCENTS, BUT MAN	224	TEMPEST	37
HOW THEN, WITH THEE, CAN MAN BE HOLY	208	REPENTANCE	67
POSSESSETH MAD MAN WITHOUT MEASURE.	211	DAWNING	8
MAN THROUGH HIS HEAP OF DARK DAYS, AND THE RICH	2	SON-DAYES	7
THE PULLEYS UNTO HEADLONG MAN, TIMES BOWER	2	SON-DAYES	9
HEAVEN HERE, MAN ON THOSE HILLS OF MYRRH, AND FLOWRES. . .	2	SON-DAYES	14
NOTHING NOW TO MAN IS LACKING	218	EASTER HYM	2
DESCEND TO JUDGE POOR CARELESS MAN	212	DAWNING	28
NO SLEEP, NOR SLOTH ASSAILES YOU, BUT POOR MAN	236	CONSTLATN	15
MAN IS THE SHUTTLE, TO WHOSE WINDING QUEST	246	MAN	26
THE STAIDNESS OF THESE THINGS TO MAN. FOR THESE	245	MAN	9
MAN HATH STIL EITHER TOYES, OR CARE	246	MAN	15
TO MAKE MAN GOOD, AS BID HIM BE	242	MISERY	94
NO MAN CAN MORE THE WORLD DESPISE	214	MISERY	55
BECAUSE BY THIS MAN CANNOT LIVE	228	PILGRIMAGE	24
YET SINCE MAN IS A VERY BRUTE	230	LAW + GOSP	21
FOR GOD (MADE MAN,)	159	MANS FALL	30
IS FULL OF VOICES, MAN IS CALL'D, AND HURL'D	161	DSTRQCTION	12
KILLING THE MAN OF SINNE	147	DAY OF JDG	32
AN ANGELL TALKING WITH A MAN.	148	RELIGION	4
FIND BEASTS MORE MERCIFULL THEN MAN	152	THE SEARCH	54
NOW POINT HIM OUT, GROWN UP A MAN.	151	THE SEARCH	10
AND BRING THE SAME MAN BACK. THOU WERT AT FIRST	194	RLS + LSNS	82
ALL BUT PRELUDES THY END. THOU ART THE MAN	195	RLS + LSNS	107
MAN IS A SUMMERS DAY, WHOSE YOUTH, AND FIRE	195	RLS + LSNS	113
THIS CONVERSATION, BUT THE GOOD MAN LYES	195	RLS + LSNS	125
SURE, IT WAS SO. MAN IN THOSE EARLY DAYS	196	CORRUPTION	1
ALMIGHTY LOVE. WHERE ART THOU NOW. MAD MAN	197	CORRUPTION	29
SIN TRIUMPHS STILL, AND MAN IS SUNK BELOW	197	CORRUPTION	35
MAN IS THEIR HIGH-PRIEST, AND SHOULD RISE	199	NTVTY 1	11
HOW KIND IS HEAV'N TO MAN. IF HERE	200	NTVTY 2	1
TIE UP HIS HANDS, THAT DARES MOCK GOD, AND MAN.	193	RLS + LSNS	48
AND MAN IS SUCH A MARYGOLD, THESE FLED	183	THRS A TYE	7
HAST THOU MADE MAN.	161	PURSUITE	2
O WHAT A VANITY IS MAN.	166	THE CALL	42
KEPT MAN FOR SIN	175	JOY OF LIF	30
SUCH AS DULL MAN CAN NEVER FINDE	344	WATER-FALL	29
MANGER			
AND ONE BORN IN A MANGER	184	PEACE	7
THY MANGER WAS.	199	NTVTY 1	22
MANKINDE			
WHAT ALL MANKINDE COULD NEVER BROOK	314	THE STONE	53
BUT HE MOST WILLING TO SAVE ALL MANKINDE	330	JACOBS PLW	13
MANNA			
'TWIXT HEAVEN, AND US, THE MANNA WAS NOT GOOD	192	RLS + LSNS	9
IN THEE THE HIDDEN STONE, THE MANNA LIES	198	SCRIPTURES	5
TRAVELS IN CLOUDS, SEEKS MANNA, WHERE NONE IS.	153	THE SEARCH	95
MANS			
IT IS THE GOOD MANS FEAST, THE PRINCE OF FLOWRES . . .	193	RLS + LSNS	59
MANS RESURRECTION, AND THE FUTURES BUD	192	RLS + LSNS	26
WRIT IN HIS BOOK, WHO NE'R BETRAY'D MANS TRUST.	177	EVNG-WTCH	8
IS THY FIRST BREATH, AND MANS ETERNALL PRIME.	178	EVNG-WTCH	16
THUS HAST THOU PLAC'D IN MANS OUTSIDE	166	THE CALL	58
HENCE, YOUTH, AND FOLLY (MANS FIRST SHAME)	166	THE CALL	62
BUT FIRMLY TRUSTS IN GOD, THE GREAT MANS MEASURE . . .	328	RIGHTSNESS	45
WHILE THE MANS ZEAL LAYS OUT AND BLENDS	332	AGREEMENT	29
MANS FAVORITE SINS, THOSE TAINTING APPETITES	320	HIDDN TRSR	19
A PROCESS, WHICH EV'N MANS OWN EYE	314	THE STONE	35
THOSE BURTHENS TO THE RICH MANS DOOR	319	THE ASS	34
AND MANS INFERIOR ESSENCE HE	302	THE KNOT	7
MANS LIFE, AND YOUR FULL LIBERTY.	294	PALM-SUNDY	17
CAN MAKE MANS DEAD AND SCATTER'D BONES	298	JESUS WP B	7
THAT, THOUGH THE CURE OF ALL MANS HARM	299	JESUS WP B	40
GRASS FOR THE CATTEL, AND HERBS FOR MANS USE	285	PSALM 104	41
TO MANS HEART STRENGTH AND MIRTH.	285	PSALM 104	44
THY QUIKNING FREINDSHIP, MANS BRIGHT WEALTH.	294	BEGGING B	22
SUCH IS MANS LIFE, AND SUCH IS MINE	242	MISERY	89
FOR THEE, WHO IN THE FIRST MANS LOYNS DIDST FAL . . .	243	THE SAP	19
MANS ANTIENT WEAR.	269	ASCSN-HYMN	2
BUT THOU, WHO DIDST MANS WHOLE LIFE EARN	342	OBSEQUIES	21
THE FOOD OF MANS IMMORTAL BEING.	340	THE FEAST	32

		PAGE	TITLE	LINE
MANS	(CON'T)			
THAT HAVE LIV'D HERE, SINCE THE MANS FALL.		346	THE BOOK	2
BY EACH MANS DOOR, AND QUICKLY WILL		351	L'ENVOY	51
MANSION				
PART OF HIS MANSION. HE ONE DAY		225	RETIREMENT	7
MANSIONS				
AND THOSE ONCE SACRED MANSIONS WERE NOW		238	SHEPHEARDS	25
HATH GOT AN HOUSE WHERE MANY MANSIONS ARE		290	THE TIMBER	31
MAR				
SHE MUST FIRST MAR		269	ASCSN-HYMN	15
MARBLE				
THEN DID THESE DROPS (FOR MARBLE SWEATS		213	ADMISSION	5
MARK				
AND MARK HOW THEY DO FAIL, AND FADE		208	REPENTANCE	64
COULD MAN OUTLOOK THAT MARK.		271	ALL GONE	20
I SEE THEM, HEAR THEM, MARK THEIR HASTE, AND MOVE		268	ASCN-DAY A	31
HERE SLEPT MY THOUGHTS DEAR MARK. WHICH DUST		310	THE SEED	73
HIS WONDROUS METHOD, MARK THE VARIOUS SCENES		194	RLS + LSNS	92
MARKE				
THE FIRST (PRAY MARKE) AS QUICK AS LIGHT		141	RGNRTN	66
MARR'D				
SPLIT, AND THE BOX QUITE BROKE AND MARR'D.		304	ST MARY MN	22
NE'R MARR'D WITH FLOODS, NOR ANGER'D WITH A SHOWRE.		268	ASCN-DAY A	48
AND WHAT ADAM MARR'D, IS MENDED.		218	EASTER HYM	4
MARRI'D				
FIRST, A YOUNG PATRIARCH, THEN A MARRI'D SAINT.		156	ISAACS M.	72
MARRIAGE				
UNTO THY GOD, FOR MARRIAGE OF ALL STATES		155	ISAACS M.	45
MARRIED				
PRAYING. AND TO BE MARRIED. IT WAS RARE		154	ISAACS M.	1
MART				
HER GORGEOUS MART AND GLITTERING STORE		302	ORNAMENT	2
MARTYRDOM				
BY THY BLOOD, AND THEIR MARTYRDOM.		317	MEN OF WAR	28
MARTYRS				
AND IN THIS MUSICK BY THY MARTYRS BLOUD		180	CHRCH-SVC	20
MARVEL				
I'LE MARVEL NOT AT OUGHT THEY DO		317	MEN OF WAR	33
MARYGOLD				
AND MAN IS SUCH A MARYGOLD, THESE FLED		183	THRS A TYE	7
MARYS				
LEARN MARYS ART OF TEARS, AND THEN		305	ST MARY MN	47
MASQUES				
THAT IN THESE MASQUES AND SHADOWS I MAY SEE		248	I WALKT	50
MASSE				
THIS QUICKEN'D MASSE OF SINNE		161	DSTRQCTION	18
UNTAINTED THROUGH THIS MASSE		145	RSRCTN +IM	32
MASTER				
LOOKE DOWNE GREAT MASTER OF THE FEAST, O SHINE		150	RELIGION	51
AND THE LAST STEPS OF MY MILDE MASTER TRACE.		268	ASCN-DAY A	50
BUT WHEN THY MASTER COMES, THEY'L FINDE AND SEE		275	PROFFER	41
GREW MASTER OF MY WAYES		282	GARLAND	6
MASTERS				
THEIR MASTERS WILL, MEET TO RECEIVE THEIR CROWNS.		280	PALM-TREE	20
WASH OFF WITH TEARS, AND GET THY MASTERS HAND.		195	RLS + LSNS	120
MATCH				
WEE'L MAKE A MATCH, MY ONLY LIGHT		205	IDLE VERSE	7
MATINS				
CHIRPING THEIR SOLEMN MATINS ON EACH TREE.		288	THE BIRD	24
MATTER				
ALL EXPECT SOME SUDDEN MATTER		212	DAWNING	22
MAY'ST				
WHERE THOU MAY'ST SLEEP WHOLE AGES, LIFES POOR FLOWR		195	RLS + LSNS	123
MEALES				
TO MEALES WHEN THOU DOEST COME, GIVE HIM THE PRAISE		195	RLS + LSNS	97
MEALS				
TO THEE THY SECRET MEALS		243	THE SAP	14
AND PLENTEOUS MEALS THEY MAKE.		286	PSALM 104	76
MEAN				
WHERE OBSCURE CARES THE MEAN DEFEAT		318	THE ASS	7
MY GOD, I MEAN MY SINFUL HEART.		315	DWELLNG-PL	16
OF SOME MEAN THINGS WHICH HERE BELOW RESIDE		245	MAN	2
THEE ONLY AIM, AND MEAN.		187	NO DO THEY	24
MEANE				
AS MEANE, AND SPAN-EXTENTS.		144	RSRCTN +IM	14
WHOSE MEANER SHOWES		225	RETIREMENT	4
MEANS				
THEE OF THEM BOTH, THESE SEALS THE MEANS		220	HOLY COMM.	45
EVEN FOR THY LOVE, FOR BY THAT MEANS		274	WHT SUNDAY	58
CALMES, TEMPESTS, LIGHT, AND DARKNES BY HIS MEANS.		194	RLS + LSNS	94
MEANS ONELY THOSE, WHO BROKE (IN LIFE) THY PEACE.		289	THE TIMBER	20
THESE MEANS ORDAIN		340	THE FEAST	29
MEANT				
FOR ALL DESIGNS MEANT AGAINST THEE		265	INTRO. 2	25
MEASURE				
I WILL MEASURE		215	PRAISE	30
POSSESSETH MAD MAN WITHOUT MEASURE.		211	MISERY	8
THOU MUST (AND DOST) GIVE HIM HIS MEASURE.		214	MISERY	48
'TWAS NOT THAT VAST, ALMIGHTY MEASURE		299	JESUS WP B	26
THE MEASURE GIVEN BY THEE EACH YEAR		301	PROVIDENCE	38

	PAGE	TITLE	LINE
MEASURE (CCN'T)			
BUT FIRMLY TRUSTS IN GOD, THE GREAT MANS MEASURE • •	328	RIGHTSNESS	45
TO MEASURE OUT THY LENGTH, AS IF THOU'DST KNCW • •	158	THE LAMPE	15
MEASURES			
MEASURES THE MELANCHOLY SKYE • • • • • •	139	RGNRTN	24
BE DUMB COURSE MEASURES, JAR NC MORE. TO ME • • •	280	JOY	1
MEAT			
AND CLAIM IT FOR THEIR MEAT. • • • • • •	243	THE SAP	8
THY BODY AS THEIR COMMON MEAT • • • • • •	217	DRESSING	38
THE SWIFT-WING'D RAVEN SHALL BRING ME MEAT • • •	300	PROVIDENCE	16
THEIR MEAT FROM THEE, WHC DOEST APPOINT THE PREY • •	286	PSALM 104	59
AND DRESS THIS EARTH FOR NEXT YEARS. MEAT. • • •	341	THE FEAST	75
MEDIATOUR			
A MEDIATOUR NCW WITH THEE • • • • • •	149	RELIGION	22
MEDICINAL			
ARE WHEN DEAD, MEDICINAL THEN. • • • • •	321	CHILDEHOOD	16
MEDLED			
THE CLEAN, PURE HAND, WHICH NEVER MEDLED PITCH. • •	327	RIGHTSNESS	10
MEEK			
WHOSE SPIRIT EVER POOR, IS MEEK AND LCW. • • •	327	RIGHTSNESS	15
AND THE MEEK HEART, NCT IN A MCUNT, NOR AT • • •	330	JACOBS PLW	25
I WILL BE STILL A CHILDE, STILL MEEK • • • •	295	PALM—SUNDY	39
BLUSHING, AND IN MEEK WEEDS ARRAY'D • • • •	303	ORNAMENT	14
WHOSE INTERCEDING, MEEK AND CALM • • • • •	304	ST MARY MN	39
BUT PATIENT, MEEK, AND CVERCOME • • • • •	316	MEN OF WAR	19
AS SOME MEEK NIGHT—PIECE WHICH DAY QUAILS • • •	310	THE SEED	67
HCW MEEK, AND PATIENT WAS THY SPIRIT. • • • •	185	PASSION	38
WITH MEEK, DUMB LCCKS DIDST WCC MINE EYE • • •	348	HOLY BIBLE	18
MEEKLY			
NCR WILDLY BURNS, BUT MEEKLY STILL • • • •	350	L'ENVOY	37
MEER			
AND STRIKE THEM DUMB, WHO FOR MEER WORDS • • •	350	L'ENVOY	41
CN MY OWN DUST, MEER DUST IT IS • • • • •	347	THE BOOK	21
MEER SEED, AND AFTER THAT BUT GRASS. • • • •	347	THE BOOK	6
A MEER TEMPESTUOUS DEBATE. • • • • • •	344	QUICKNESS	8
MY MEER DESPAIR • • • • • • • •	153	THE SEARCH	86
THAT I TERM'D THEN MEER BONDS AND THRALL • • •	311	FAIR+YONG	8
AS MEER A STRANGER, AS MEN LONG SINCE DEAD. • • •	290	THE TIMBER	38
AND BY MEER PLAYING GC TO HEAVEN. • • • • •	321	CHILDEHOOD	8
BUT MEER DISDAIN, LET NCT MAN SAY • • • • •	335	JUDGEMENT	43
ARE BUT MEER LEAVES TURN'D BY THY BREATH. • • •	219	HOLY COMM.	16
OUT OF MEER LCVE • • • • • • • •	225	RETIREMENT	9
WHICH TC THY PEACE ARE BUT MEER NCISE. • • • •	214	MISERY	60
I STILE MEER TEMPERS, WHICH TAKE PLACE • • • •	242	MISERY	87
A LETHARGY, AND MEER DISEASE • • • • • •	242	MISERY	84
MEER EMPTINESS AND SHCW • • • • • • •	238	SHEPHEARDS	26
IF A MEER BLAST SC FILL THE SAIL • • • • •	276	COCK—CRWNG	17
MEER GLIMERING AND DECAYS. • • • • • •	271	ALL GONE	12
IS BUT MEER CHANGING OF THE KEYS • • • • •	273	WHT SUNDAY	43
MEERE			
BUT DRUNK, IS PUDDLE, CR MEERE SLIME • • • •	150	RELIGION	43
MEERE STAGE, AND SHOW • • • • • • •	139	RGNRTN	19
A MEERE MISTAKE • • • • • • • •	145	RSRCTN +IM	24
AFFLICTION THUS, MEERE PLEASURE IS • • • • •	182	CHRFLNESS	9
AND MEERE DISEASE • • • • • • • •	162	MT. OLVS A	8
MEET			
THEN SHALL WE MEET TO MIXE AGAIN, AND MET • • •	143	DEATH	31
BUT MEET TO QUENCH HIS LCNGINGS, AND THY THIRST. • •	194	RLS + LSNS	80
THEIR MASTERS WILL, MEET TO RECEIVE THEIR CRCWNS. • •	280	PALM—TREE	20
OF FLESH AND BLOOD, WHERE TWO WAYS MEET. • • •	318	THE ASS	2
MELANCHOLY			
GRIEF AND SOUL—CURING MELANCHCLY. • • • • •	311	FAIR+YONG	2
UNDER THE DARK, AND MELANCHOLY EARTH. • • • •	195	RLS + LSNS	106
THROUGH MELANCHOLLY CLOUDS, AND SAY • • • •	146	RSRCTN +IM	67
MEASURES THE MELANCHOLY SKYE • • • • • •	139	RGNRTN	24
MELT			
YET, IF AS THOU DOEST MELT, AND WITH THY TRAINE • •	160	THE SHOWRE	13
MADE THINE EYES MELT, AND THY HEART HEAVE. • • •	299	JESUS WP B	33
IS MOV'D AND TREMBLES, THE HILLS MELT AND SMCKE • •	287	PSALM 104	86
MEMBERS			
THAT MAY THY MEMBERS, MCRE THAN MINE, RESENT. • • •	216	DRESSING	30
MEMCRIAL			
THAT SWCRN MEMORIAL DULY PAY • • • • • •	326	ABELS BLOD	30
MEMCRY			
HER ART. WHOSE MEMORY MUST LAST • • • • •	305	ST MARY MN	51
THEIR VERY MEMCRY IS FAIR AND BRIGHT • • • •	270	ALL GONE	3
AND THEREFORE MIGHT FCR MEMORY CF THOSE • • •	238	SHEPHEARDS	15
LCVE LANGUISHETH, AND MEMCRY DCTH RUST • • • •	183	THRS A TYE	3
MEN			
THOU GREAT PRESERVER CF ALL MEN. • • • • •	180	BURIALL	7
SCME MEN A FORWARD MOTICN LOVE • • • • •	170	RETREATE	29
AND SC REPAIR THESE RENTS, THAT MEN MAY SEE • • •	237	CONSTLATN	59
THE WCRST OF MEN, AND YET STIL THINE • • • •	242	MISERY	90
WHERE DEAD MEN PREACH, WHC CAN TURN FEASTS, AND MIRTH •	226	RETIREMENT	49
HAVING LOST THEE, BEHCLD TWC MEN IN WHITE. • • •	268	ASCN—DAY A	58
SAY, YOU HAVE GOT THE DAY FRCM MEN • • • • •	305	ST MARY MN	48
O FCUL, DECEITFUL MEN. MY GCD DCTH KEEP • • •	307	RAIN—BCW	19
O BITTER CURS'D DELIGHTS CF MEN. • • • • •	311	FAIR+YONG	11
YET WCULD NCT MEN GRANT, THEIR ILL FATE • • •	311	FAIR+YONG	21
HCW BLEST HAD MEN BEEN, HAD THEIR SIRE • • • •	312	FAIR+YONG	27

		PAGE	TITLE	LINE
MEN	**(CON'T)**			
AND PRESENT THINGS FINDE MEN MOST KINDE.		318	THE ASS	6
CONDEMN MEN. BUT WILL TRY THEM BY		314	THE STONE	34
FOR KNOW, WILDE MEN, THAT WHEN YOU ERRE		314	THE STONE	42
AND LET MEN CALL ME WHAT THEY WILL.		319	THE ASS	44
AND SLIGHTS THAT MOST, WHICH MEN MOST PRIZE.		319	THE ASS	48
THIS LEADEN.STATE, WHICH MEN MISCAL		319	THE ASS	55
AT WHOSE JUST LAWS NOT JUST MEN GRUDGE.		326	ABELS BLOD	24
FROM BLOODY MEN. AND GRANT, I MAY		326	ABELS BLOD	29
A DEEP, BUT DAZLING DARKNESS. AS MEN HERE		325	THE NIGHT	50
WHAT THUNDERS SHALL THOSE MEN ARRAIGN		325	ABELS BLOD	11
WHY SHOULD MEN LOVE		321	CHILDEHOOD	9
AND SWEETLY LIVING (FIE ON MEN)		321	CHILDEHOOD	15
ANGELS. WHICH FOUL MEN DRIVE AWAY.		322	CHILDEHOOD	38
THAT MEN MIGHT LOOK AND LIVE AS GLO-WORMS SHINE		323	THE NIGHT	3
(BECAUSE THEY SLEEP SO LONG) SOME MEN		335	JUDGEMENT	25
WATER'ST IT FOR THE SONS OF MEN		336	PSALM 65	28
INTO A PILLAR, AND CONCEAL'D FROM MEN.		331	JACOBS PLW	36
AS HERE ON EARTH (WHEN MEN WITH-STOOD)		284	TRINITY-SN	4
AS MEER A STRANGER, AS MEN LONG SINCE DEAD.		290	THE TIMBER	38
WITH BRUTISH MEN. THY GIFTS GO ROUND		293	THE JEWS	47
MEN CALL GOOD CHEAR		342	OBSEQUIES	14
ARE NO MORE SEEN, JUST SO PASS MEN.		344	WATER-FALL	36
THOU FOUL DECEPTION OF ALL MEN		344	QUICKNESS	3
THOU SHALT RESTORE TREES, BEASTS AND MEN		347	THE BOOK	26
MEND				
TILL THOU BOTH MEND AND MAKE ME THINE.		242	MISERY	113
AND I WIL MEND MY OWN WITHOUT DELAYES		188	RELAPSE	11
MENDED				
AND WHAT ADAM MARR'D, IS MENDED.		218	EASTER HYM	4
MERCIES				
OR THY GREAT MERCIES BETTER PRIZE.		214	MISERY	56
THUS WHILE THY SEV'RAL MERCIES PLOT		227	LV + DSPLN	13
SO SHALL THY MERCIES FLOW. FOR WHILE I FEAR		230	LAW + GOSP	37
FOR ALL THY MERCIES AND THY TRUTH		265	INTRO. 2	19
SHALL I THY MERCIES STILL ABUSE		187	NO DO THEY	33
YET THROUGH THY MERCIES MAY BE MORE.		190	THE MATCH	15
(WHICH DOTH THY STRANGE SURE MERCIES SHROUD)		300	PROVIDENCE	8
AND BY THY MERCIES STILL SUPPLIED		336	PSALM 65	31
WILL THY FREE MERCIES HINDRED BE.		334	AGREEMENT	70
IF THY SURE MERCIES CAN BE BROKEN		333	AGREEMENT	47
MERCIFULL				
FIND BEASTS MORE MERCIFULL THEN MAN		152	THE SEARCH	54
MERCY				
AND SO IS MERCY TOO.		147	DAY OF JDG	28
ARE MERCY, AND SALVATION		200	NTVTY 2	6
THY MERCY TOO		162	PURSUITE	14
O GOD. THOUGH MERCY BE IN THEE		335	JUDGEMENT	39
YET, WHEN THY MERCY NOTHING WINS		335	JUDGEMENT	42
SO BEAT FOR THEE, TILL THOU IN MERCY HEAR		283	LOVE-SICK	16
THY MERCY, LOVE, AND EASE		248	I WALKT	56
KING OF MERCY, KING OF LOVE		249	BEGGING A	1
AND THROUGH HIS MERITS, MAKE THY MERCY MINE.		209	REPENTANCE	86
AND HOLY LIVES, MERCY MAY HERE		351	L'ENVOY	56
MERCY-SEAT				
NO MERCY-SEAT OF GOLD		323	THE NIGHT	19
MERIT				
SUCH TRIUMPHS POOR FLESH CANNOT MERIT.		339	THE FEAST	9
CAN FOIL HIS MERITS, AND THY TRUTH.		333	AGREEMENT	54
AND THROUGH HIS MERITS, MAKE THY MERCY MINE.		209	REPENTANCE	86
PROPORTION TO THEIR MERITS, AND THY PURSE.		193	RLS + LSNS	62
MERRY				
DEATH A NAP, TO WAKE MORE MERRY.		218	EASTER HYM	6
THAT TO BE MERRY I WANT SKILL		342	OBSEQUIES	23
MESSAGE				
WITH SOME GLAD MESSAGE FROM HIS HEART		340	THE FEAST	27
MESSAGES				
IN THY CELESTIALL, GLADSOME MESSAGES		284	PSALM 104	13
MET				
I MET WITH A DEAD MAN		282	GARLAND	26
ON THEE, WERE ALL MET IN ONE CROWN		309	THE SEED	30
COTSWOLD, AND COOPERS BOTH HAVE MET		162	MT. OLVS A	9
I MET THE WISE-MEN, ASKT THEM WHERE		151	THE SEARCH	8
MET IN THY FLAMES, ALL ACTS OF PIETY.		158	THE LAMPE	10
OF STATELY HEIGHT, WHOSE BRANCHES MET		140	RGNRTN	44
THEN SHALL WE MEET TO MIXE AGAIN, AND MET		143	DEATH	31
METHOD				
HIS WONDROUS METHOD, MARK THE VARIOUS SCENES		194	RLS + LSNS	92
BESIDES, THY METHOD WITH THY OWN		273	WHT SUNDAY	29
MIGHTY				
THE MIGHTY GOD, TH' ETERNAL KING		240	MISERY	39
MID-DAY				
HATH FLESH NO SOFTNESS NOW. MID-DAY NO LIGHT.		224	TEMPEST	56
(THOUGH 'TWAS MID-DAY)		141	RGNRTN	75
O FOR THY CENTER AND MID-DAY.		322	CHILDEHOOD	43
O BEAMY BOOK. O MY MID-DAY		332	AGREEMENT	13
MID-NIGHT				
DID AT MID-NIGHT SPEAK WITH THE SUN.		323	THE NIGHT	12
MIDNIGHT				
BREAK AT MIDNIGHT.		211	DAWNING	6

	PAGE	TITLE	LINE
MIDNIGHT-FOG			
LIKE A THICK MIDNIGHT-FOG MOV'D THERE SO SLOW . . .	231	THE WORLD	17
MIDST			
THAT, MIDST ALL STORMS I FEEL A RAY OF THEE. . . .	245	MT. OLV. B	16
SO IN THE MIDST OF ALL HER FEARS	223	TEMPEST	13
THIS LITTLE GOSHEN, IN THE MIDST OF NIGHT . . .	331	JACOBS PLW	31
A SPEECHLESSE HEAP, AND IN THE MIDST MY HEART . .	201	THE CHECK	3
AS HE THAT IN THE MIDST OF DAY EXPECTS	201	THE CHECK	13
MILD			
WITH WHICH IN MILD, CHAST LANGUAGE SHE DID WOOE .	155	ISAACS M.	41
AND CALM LIKE HER, OR THAT MILD EVENING-TIDE. . .	154	ISAACS M.	24
SO MILD A LAMB CAN NEVER BE	152	THE SEARCH	51
AND MAK'ST THE RAGING PEOPLE MILD.	336	PSALM 65	20
BY HIS MILD DOVE	225	RETIREMENT	10
BUT SHOULD THY MILD INJUNCTION NOTHING MOVE ME .	230	LAW + GOSP	39
SEEM MILD, BUT ARE KNOWN BY THEIR NOISE. . . .	237	CONSTLATN	44
NOR GRIEVE THY DOVE, BUT SOFT AND MILD . . .	235	MUTINIE	38
MILDE			
MURMURINGS AT THEE, WHEN MOST MILDE.	265	INTRO. 2	22
AND THE LAST STEPS OF MY MILDE MASTER TRACE. . .	268	ASCN-DAY A	50
THAT SECRET ARK, WHERE THE MILDE DOVE DOTH DWELL .	330	JACOBS PLW	28
IN MILDE, CLEAR VISIONS, WITHOUT A FROWN . . .	330	JACOBS PLW	3
WITH HIS MILDE BLOOD IN VOICE AND WILL . . .	326	ABELS BLOD	43
WHEN THUS THY MILDE, INSTRUCTING HAND . . .	319	THE ASS	45
GIVE ME, MY GOD. A HEART AS MILDE	317	MEN OF WAR	45
BY THIS MILDE ART OF LOVE AT LENGTH	348	HOLY BIBLE	23
MILDEST			
MOST BLESSED LAMB. AND MILDEST DOVE.	208	REPENTANCE	48
MILDNESS			
LET MILDNESS, AND RELIGION GUIDE THEE OUT . . .	193	RLS + LSNS	38
MILE			
A MILE, OR TWO, FROM MY FIRST LOVE	169	RETREATE	8
MILK			
OF TEARS, AND MILK, THE FOOD OF ALL.	209	THE BURIAL	4
BALM ON THE CLEFT EARTH, MILK ON GRASS AND FLOWERS. .	306	RAIN-BOW	12
MILKY			
THE MILKY WAY CHALKT OUT WITH SUNS, A CLUE . . .	2	SON-DAYES	21
MIN'RALL			
TO READE SOME STARRE, OR MIN'RALL, AND IN STATE . .	146	RSRCTN +IM	59
MINCING			
IN ROWLES AND CURLES, MINCING AND STATELY DUMB . .	155	ISAACS M.	34
MIND			
MY MIND TO EASE	141	RGNRTN	87
LIKE CLOUDS ECCLIPS'D MY MIND	139	RGNRTN	17
THE SACRED CONSTELLATION OF THY MIND. . . .	154	ISAACS M.	10
AND LET MY MIND	176	THE STORM	18
YET, IF POETS MIND THEE WELL	163	MT. OLVS A	17
STILL LET THY SERVANT MIND IT.	167	THE CALL	89
TO THY SURE TROT, A CONSTANT, HUMBLE MIND . . .	193	RLS + LSNS	50
O LET ME STILL MIND THAT IN THIS.	191	THE MATCH	24
IS BUT EXCUS'D NEGLECT. TO MIND	189	RESOLVE	3
AND MIND IT NOT, PLAY NOT AWAY	201	THE CHECK	23
NEITHER HIS BLOODY PASSIONS MIND	200	NTVTY 2	15
HIS MIND SURE PROGRESS'D THITHER.	196	CORRUPTION	8
O CALL TO MIND HIS WOUNDS, HIS WOES	208	REPENTANCE	61
THY INWARD EYES, HIS BLOUD WILL CURE THY MIND . .	217	EASTER-DAY	15
BUT I'L MIND THEE	214	PRAISE	18
EXCLUDE MY DEAR GOD FROM MY MIND	240	MISERY	34
WENT BLEAK AND BARE IN BODY AS IN MIND . . .	245	MT. OLV. B	13
MINDE			
AND ROVE ABOUT THEE, GUARDIANS OF THY MINDE, . .	155	ISAACS M.	26
A SWEET, REVENGELESS, QUIET MINDE	317	MEN OF WAR	43
WHERE FRAIL VISIBLES RULE THE MINDE	318	THE ASS	5
AND MINDE THOSE THINGS I CANNOT SEE. . . .	318	THE ASS	18
TO LOW ESTATES, AND A LOW MINDE.	319	THE ASS	36
SUCH A MIST OVER MY MINDE DRAW	332	AGREEMENT	3
AND GODS BRIGHT MINDE EXPREST IN PRINT. . . .	332	AGREEMENT	24
WE MAY BE FED, AND ONE MINDE HOLD.	350	L'ENVOY	48
A STATE AGREEING WITH THY MINDE	350	L'ENVOY	19
SHOULD I NOT EVER BEAR IN MINDE	342	OBSEQUIES	11
UNLESS THAT SPIRIT LEAD HIS MINDE	344	WATER-FALL	30
AND MINDES THE COVENANT 'TWIXT ALL AND ONE. . .	306	RAIN-BOW	18
LET GLORY BE THEIR BAIT, WHOSE MINDES . . .	309	THE SEED	33
MINGLING			
WHICH MINGLING AYE	172	MIDNIGHT	19
MINISTER			
THY MINISTER IN FIRE.	284	PSALM 104	16
MINISTRIE			
HIS FATHERS FLAMING MINISTRIE	152	THE SEARCH	60
MINORITY			
ARE BUT LIGHTS WEAK MINORITY	334	JUDGEMENT	8
MINUTE			
WHILST I EACH MINUTE GRONE TO KNOW	143	DEATH	29
WHAT SINS ON EVERY MINUTE FALL	165	THE CALL	22
NOT ONE MINUTE IN THE YEAR	214	PRAISE	17
MINUTES			
SO O'R FLED MINUTES I RETREAT	178	SILENCE	13
MIRACLES			
THAT NOW ALL MIRACLES MUST CEASE.	149	RELIGION	26
MIRE			
BUT WITH TRUE TEARS WASH OFF YOUR MIRE. . . .	266	VAIN WITS	4

		PAGE	TITLE	LINE
MIRE	(CCN'T)			
WANDRED THROUGH DARKNESS, DENS AND MIRE.	. . . .	311	FAIR+YONG	6
MIRRHE				
DOTH CN THOSE HILLS OF MIRRHE, AND INCENSE WATCH.	. .	156	BRT. CHRCH	4
MIRTH				
WHITE DAYES, THAT DURST NC IMPIOUS MIRTH EXPCSE.	. .	154	ISAACS M.	18
THEE CTHER THOUGHTS, AWAY WITH FRIENDS, AND MIRTH.	.	195	RLS + LSNS	104
TO MANS HEART STRENGTH AND MIRTH.	. . . .	285	PSALM 104	44
FOR MIRTH AND LIFE, YET WITHOUT NCISE.	. . .	299	JESUS WP B	47
SUCH YONG, SWEET MIRTH	. . . . . .	295	PALM-SUNDY	24
AND KEEPS HIS SOUL UNTO ETERNAL MIRTH.	. . .	290	THE TIMBER	32
BRIGHTNESS AND MIRTH, AND LOVE AND FAITH, ALL FLYE	.	288	THE BIRD	31
WHAT STIRS, WHAT POSTING INTERCCURSE AND MIRTH	.	267	ASCN-DAY A	25
ANOTHER MIRTH, A MIRTH THOUGH CVERCAST	. .	281	JOY	14
ANOTHER MIRTH, A MIRTH THOUGH CVERCAST	. . .	281	JOY	14
FIRE TO ALL THREE, BUT MAN HATH NO SUCH MIRTH.	. .	223	TEMPEST	32
WHENCE FLOWES MY WEAL, AND MIRTH	. . . .	220	PSALM 121	2
IF THCU STEAL IN AMIDST THE MIRTH	. . . .	240	MISERY	29
MUSICK AND MIRTH (IF THERE BE MUSICK HERE)	. .	236	CONSTLATN	21
WHERE DEAC MEN PREACH, WHO CAN TURN FEASTS, AND MIRTH	.	226	RETIREMENT	49
MIRTLES				
OR THE COCLE MIRTLES CANOPIE	. . . . .	148	RELIGION	6
MISCAL				
THIS LEADEN STATE, WHICH MEN MISCAL	. . .	319	THE ASS	55
MISCALL				
PEACE, PEACE. IT IS NOT SO. THCU DOEST MISCALL	.	221	AFFLICTION	1
MISER				
THE FEARFULL MISER ON A HEAP CF RUST	. . .	232	THE WORLD	31
MISERIE				
PROVE MY CWN SHAME AND MISERIE.	. . . .	240	MISERY	44
A WORLD OF MISERIE	. . . . . .	243	THE SAP	18
MISS				
BE SURE, AND NEVER MISS	. . . . .	244	THE SAP	42
MISS'C				
AND LCNG'C TO SEE, BUT MISS'D.	. . . . .	239	SHEPHEARDS	50
MISSE				
THOU CANST NOT MISSE HIS PRAISE, EACH TREE, HERB, FLOWRE		194	RLS + LSNS	95
MIST				
SHOULD MIST WITHIN ME, AND PUT CUT THAT LAMP	. .	188	RELAPSE	15
SUCH A MIST OVER MY MINDE DRAW	. . . .	332	AGREEMENT	3
A MCVING MIST.	. . . .	345	QUICKNESS	18
MISTAKE				
THIS CAUTIOUS FOOLS MISTAKE, AND FEAR	. .	313	THE STONE	16
THOU FALL'ST IN TEARES, AND WEEP'ST FOR THY MISTAKE.	.	160	THE SHOWRE	6
A MEERE MISTAKE	. . . .	145	RSRCTN +IM	24
MISTIE				
BEYOND THAT MISTIE SHROWD.	. . . . .	177	MRNG-WTCH	30
MISTS				
CUTS THROUGH THE HEAVY MISTS IN HASTE	. .	178	SILENCE	11
BUT MISTS, AND SHADOWS PASSE	. . . .	146	RSRCTN +IM	52
AND WHILE THESE HERE THEIR MISTS, AND SHADOWS HATCH,	.	156	BRT. CHRCH	2
TURNING THEIR MISTS TO REAMS, THEIR DAMPS TO DAY	.	202	THE CHECK	31
MISTS MAKE BUT TRIUMPHS FCR THE DAY.	. .	338	DEATH B	20
AND WATCH ALL NIGHT FCR MISTS CR SHOWERS	. .	301	PROVIDENCE	29
WHICH FCR THESE MISTS, AND BLACK DAYS WERE RESERV'C	.	237	CONSTLATN	47
CHIDE, AND FLY UP, MISTS CF CCRRUPTEST FOME	. .	223	TEMPEST	26
ALL MISTS THAT WOULD USLRP THIS CAY.	. .	217	EASTER-DAY	10
STARS SHUT UP SHOP, MISTS PACK AWAY	. . .	210	FAITH	19
GLCRIOUS DECEPTIONS, GILDED MISTS	. . .	282	GARLAND	17
EITHER CISPERSE THESE MISTS, WHICH BLCT AND FILL	.	271	ALL GONE	37
MITE				
THOU SHALT NOT LOSE ONE MITE. THCUGH WATERS STRAY	.	193	RLS + LSNS	65
MITES				
THEE TWC SMALL MITES, AND BE AT STRIFE	. .	186	PASSION	52
MIX				
KEEP THCU THY TEMPER, MIX NOT WITH EACH CLAY.	. .	192	RLS + LSNS	32
AND MIX AN EYE-SALVEFCR THE BLINDE	. . .	266	VAIN WITS	6
AND MIX AN EYE-SALVE FOR THE BLINDE.	. . .	266	VAIN WITS	7
DCTH ALL THINGS WAKE, AND WHERE ALL MIX AND TYRE	.	324	THE NIGHT	44
MIXE				
THEN SHALL WE MEET TO MIXE AGAIN, AND MET	. .	143	DEATH	31
MIXT				
AND MIXT CN EVERY SIDE	. . . . .	140	RGNRTN	45
A THOUSAND ODCURS, WHICH (ALL MIXT) SHE SENDS	.	156	ISAACS M.	60
I'LE JUDGE, WHERE PENAL FLAMES SIT MIXT AND CLCSE.	.	307	RAIN-BOW	38
MOAN				
NCR MCAN I ONELY (THOUGH PROFUSE)	. . .	335	JUDGEMENT	31
MOANS				
LIFT UP YCUR HEADS AND LEAVE YCUR MOANS.	. .	294	PALM-SUNDY	14
MOCK				
TIE UP HIS HANDS, THAT CARES MCCK GOD, AND MAN.	.	193	RLS + LSNS	48
MODERN				
MCST MODERN BCOKS ARE BLCTS CN THEE	. . .	332	AGREEMENT	25
MODES				
THE LATEST MOCES CF PRICE AND LUST	. . .	302	ORNAMENT	6
MODEST				
INJURE NOT MOCEST BLOUD, WHOSE SPIRITS RISE	. .	194	RLS + LSNS	73
ALL WAS PLAIN, MODEST TRUTH, NCR DID SHE COME	.	155	ISAACS M.	33
MOIST				
ANC FROM HIS MCIST WOMBE WEEPS A FRAGRANT SHCWRE	. .	155	ISAACS M.	55

	PAGE	TITLE	LINE
MOLE			
YET DIG'D THE MOLE, AND LEST HIS WAYS BE FOUND	232	THE WORLD	23
THOU ART A TOYLSOM MOLE, OR LESS	345	QUICKNESS	17
MOLEST			
THE FOSTS ILL WEEDS NIP, AND MOLEST	227	LV + DSPLN	11
MOLTEN			
WHEN HEAV'N ABOVE THEM SHIN'D LIKE MOLTEN GLASS	268	ASCN-DAY A	45
MONES			
FAITHFUL AND MOST REPENTING MONES	242	MISERY	111
MAKE RESTLESS MONES	179	CHRCH-SVC	5
MONEY			
AND MONEY BETTER MUSICK THAN THE SPHERES.	224	TEMPEST	48
DOEST THOU CONVEY MAN FOOD AND MONEY	300	PROVIDENCE	9
MONSTROUS			
MY WALKE A MONSTROUS, MOUNTAIN'D THING	139	RGNRTN	20
BUT NOW 'TIS MONSTROUS, AND THAT PIOUS CARE	154	ISAACS M.	2
MONTH			
AS IF I KNEW NO MONTH BUT MAY.	300	PROVIDENCE	18
MONTHS			
NINE MONTHS THY HANDS ARE FASHIONING US	166	THE CALL	46
MOON			
ABOVE THEM THE COOL MOON HER KNOWN COURSE HOLDS	286	PSALM 104	51
AND FACE THE MOON.	323	THE NIGHT	4
AND THE MOON MOURNS.	210	FAITH	20
MOON-LIKE			
THOU ART A MOON-LIKE TOIL, A BLINDE	344	QUICKNESS	5
MOONE-SHINE			
LIKE A YOUNG EAST, OR MOONE-SHINE NIGHT	168	VNTY SPRIT	20
MOONS			
AND MOONS, THOUGH FULL, WOULD GET THEM DOWN.	309	THE SEED	32
MORNING			
AS IN THE MORNING WHEN FIRST SHED.	325	ABELS BLOD	6
AND COMES NEXT MORNING FRESH AS HE.	300	PROVIDENCE	24
I SEE THAT MORNING IN THY CONVERTS TEARS	267	ASCN-DAY A	19
MORNING-FLOWERS			
FRESHER THEN MORNING-FLOWERS WHICH SHEW	303	ST MARY MN	3
MORNING-HOURS			
DO KNOW THY DEWY MORNING-HOURS	301	PROVIDENCE	28
THEIR EYES WATCH FOR THE MORNING-HUE	276	COCK-CRWNG	7
OR LEAFE BUT HATH HIS MORNING-HYMN. EACH BUSH	192	RLS + LSNS	15
MORNING-MEETING			
NO MORNING-MEETINGS SINCE THIS CHANGE	293	BEGGING B	7
MORNING-STAR			
FORERUNNING THE BRIGHT MORNING-STAR	292	THE JEWS	22
MY DEAR, BRIGHT LORD. MY MORNING-STAR.	296	JESUS WP A	13
WHICH STRAIT, LIKE MORNING-STARS DID SING	332	AGREEMENT	10
AND CLOATH THE MORNING-STARRE WITH DUST	164	INCARNATN	6
ABOVE THE MORKING-STARRE	225	RETIREMENT	3
THAT MORNING-STAR.	212	DAWNING	24
MORNINGS			
SO SHALL MY NIGHTS AND MORNINGS BE	281	THE FAVOUR	11
MORNINGS ARE MYSTERIES, THE FIRST WORLDS YOUTH	192	RLS + LSNS	25
FRESH, SPICIE MORNINGS, AND ETERNAL BEAMS	188	RELAPSE	27
MANY BRIGHT MORNINGS, MUCH DEW, MANY SHOWERS	289	THE TIMBER	2
MAKE LESSER MORNINGS, WHEN THE GREAT ARE DONE.	288	THE BIRD	18
BOTH MORNINGS MAKES, AND EVENINGS THERE.	288	THE BIRD	22
MORROW			
WEEPING STILL, LIKE THE WET MORROW	294	PALM-SUNDY	5
MORROWS			
WITHOUT TO MORROWS EVILS AND FUTURE LOADS.	327	RIGHTSNESS	8
MORTIFIED			
FOR MOURNING SACK-CLOTH WEAR, ALL MORTIFIED.	342	OBSEQUIES	16
MOST			
SINCE I IN STORMS US'D MOST TO BE	345	THE WREATH	1
WHICH SADNESS BREEDS IN THE MOST VAIN	345	THE WREATH	14
I WERE MOST FOOLISH AND UNKINDE	342	OBSEQUIES	9
A SUDDEN AND MOST SEARCHING RAY	348	HOLY BIBLE	20
INQUIRE HOW LONG. OF THE MOST HIGH.	326	ABELS BLOD	22
MOST BLEST BELIEVER HE.	323	THE NIGHT	7
MOST MODERN BOOKS ARE BLOTS ON THEE	332	AGREEMENT	25
AND FEEL A FRIEND MOST READY, SURE AND KINDE.	331	JACOBS PLW	52
BUT HE MOST WILLING TO SAVE ALL MANKINDE	330	JACOBS PLW	13
A MOST FAIR NOTION, BUT A VERY NAME.	330	JACOBS PLW	16
QUICK TO ADVANCE, AND TO RETREAT MOST SLOW.	327	RIGHTSNESS	18
AND THE MOST NEEDFUL FOR OUR SINS.	335	JUDGEMENT	41
THOU STILL'ST THE LOUD WAVES, WHEN MOST WILD	336	PSALM 65	19
THE MOST REMOTE, WHO KNOW NOT THEE	336	PSALM 65	23
AND LOWLY KNEELING (FOR THE MOST	337	THE THRONE	5
MOST HEYNOUS SINS AND NUMBERLESS.	333	AGREEMENT	45
WHOM SUFFERINGS MAKE MOST GREEN AND GAY.	294	PALM-SUNDY	3
WHEN I AM MOST, MOST SICK AND SAD.	293	BEGGING B	10
WHEN I AM MOST, MOST SICK AND SAD.	293	BEGGING B	10
BUT WHICH THOU ART MOST, NONE CAN PROVE.	298	JESUS WP B	23
AND THE LAST IS MOST LOATHSOME DUST.	302	ORNAMENT	8
TO WHAT MOST TAKES THEM, IS A DRUDGE.	309	THE SEED	38
AND SLIGHTS THAT MOST, WHICH MEN MOST PRIZE.	319	THE ASS	48
AND SLIGHTS THAT MOST, WHICH MEN MOST PRIZE.	319	THE ASS	48
SUCH COAL-FLAMES SHEW BUT KITCHIN-ROOMS AT MOST.	320	HIDDN TRSR	6
AND PRESENT THINGS FINDE MEN MOST KINDE.	318	THE ASS	6
DOTH YOUR MOST PRIVATE SINS RECORD.	314	THE STONE	45

		PAGE	TITLE	LINE
MOST	(CON'T)			
YET, SURE, MY GOD. I LOVE THEE MOST		203	DSRDR + FR	14
THEIR LORD WITH THEE HAD MOST TO DOE.		163	MT. OLVS A	20
WHICH SHOULD MOST VIE		186	PASSION	53
MOST BLESSED VINE.		185	PASSION	16
BUT STILL THE WEATHER THAT'S MOST FAIR		176	THE STORM	15
BUT ONE HALF GLAUNCE, MOST GLADLY DYE.		168	VNTY SPRIT	34
THAT PILL, THOUGH BITTER, IS MOST DEARE		147	DAY OF JDG	35
BECAUSE MOST VOICES LIKE THE SHELL		150	RELIGION	48
RE-MARRY TO THE SOULE, FOR 'TIS MOST PLAINE		145	RSRCTN +IM	49
MAKES MOST UNHAPPY, OR MOST FORTUNATES.		155	ISAACS M.	46
MAKES MOST UNHAPPY, OR MOST FORTUNATES.		155	ISAACS M.	46
MURMURINGS AT THEE, WHEN MOST MILDE.		265	INTRO. 2	22
COME FORTH MOST FAIR AND YOUNG.		247	I WALKT	28
PLANTS IN THE ROOT WITH EARTH DO MOST COMPLY		223	TEMPEST	33
MAKING THE WHOLE MOST MUSICALL		222	AFFLICTION	40
AND MY MOST LOVING LORD STRAITWAY		211	FAITH	43
MOST BLESSED LAMB. AND MILDEST DOVE.		208	REPENTANCE	48
FAITHFUL AND MOST REPENTING MONES		242	MISERY	111
AND HAD NOT HE SO DONE, IT IS MOST TRUE		243	THE SAP	21
TO ALL YOUR POW'R MOST PURE.		244	THE SAP	38
BUT MOST WOULD USE NO WING.		232	THE WORLD	48
THUS WRETCHED I, AND MOST UNKIND		240	MISERY	33
MOTHER				
THE CHILDREN CHASE THE MOTHER, AND WOULD HEAL		237	CONSTLATN	39
AFFLICTION IS A MOTHER		167	THE CALL	75
WHO DOTH THY LOTHSOME MOTHER KEEP.		297	HERODIAS	12
MOTHERS				
THY MOTHERS NETS IN THEE WERE SPRED		297	HERODIAS	19
SHALT IN THY MOTHERS BOSOME SLEEPE		143	DEATH	28
MOTION				
LEAST MOTION, OR REPLY		141	RGNRTN	85
SOME MEN A FORWARD MOTION LOVE		170	RETREATE	29
HEAT MOTION GIVES. THEN WARM IT, TILL IT BEAT		283	LOVE-SICK	15
FAIR, ORDER'D LIGHT (WHOSE MOTION WITHOUT NOISE		235	CONSTLATN	1
GOD ORDER'D MOTION, BUT ORDAIN'D NO REST.		246	MAN	28
LIGHT, MOTION, HEAT		211	FAITH	34
WATER'S REFIN'D TO MOTION , AIRE TO LIGHT		223	TEMPEST	31
MOTIONS				
THY LEWD LOATH'D MOTIONS UNTO SOUNDS		297	HERODIAS	2
TO CHECK BAD MOTIONS, KEEP ME STILL		318	THE ASS	25
AND SLOW MOTIONS HERE		172	MIDNIGHT	16
ABOVE ARE RESTLES MOTIONS, RUNNING LIGHTS		194	RLS + LSNS	89
MOULD				
SOFTEN THE MOULD, WHILE ALL UNSEEN		337	PSALM 65	37
MOUNT				
AND THE MEEK HEART, NOT IN A MOUNT, NOR AT		330	JACOBS PLW	25
THE MOUNT, WHOSE WHITE ASCENDENTS MAY		332	AGREEMENT	15
QUIT THEIR FIRST BED AND MOUNT. TREES, HERBS, FLOWRES, ALL		223	TEMPEST	27
THAT I MAY TRAVEL TO THY MOUNT.		229	PILGRIMAGE	28
AND WHERE THE OTHER MOUNT ALL CLAD IN FLAME		229	LAW + GOSP	14
MOUNTAIN				
FAIR SHADE, OR MOUNTAIN		315	DWELLNG-PL	2
THE VALLY, OR THE MOUNTAIN		197	CORRUPTION	22
MOUNTAIN'D				
AS DOTH THE MOUNTAIN'D WAVE.		175	THE STORM	8
MY WALKE A MONSTROUS, MOUNTAIN'D THING		139	RGNRTN	20
MOUNTAINS				
ON EVERLASTING, SPICY MOUNTAINS.		312	FAIR+YONG	50
THY ARM DID FIRST THE MOUNTAINS LAY		336	PSALM 65	21
AND AT THY PRESENCE MAKE THESE MOUNTAINS FLOW		283	LOVE-SICK	11
THESE MOUNTAINS OF COLD ICE IN ME. THOU ART		283	LOVE-SICK	12
ABOVE THE MOUNTAINS STEEP.		285	PSALM 104	20
SOME UP THE MOUNTAINS PAST BY SECRET WAYS		285	PSALM 104	23
MOUNTAINS OF SPICE, DAY-STARS AND LIGHT		346	THE QUEER	7
MOUNTS				
UPON THE MOUNTS OF SPICES.		157	BRT. CHRCH	20
MOURN				
AND MOURN TO SEE THE WOOLL		173	CONTENT	11
NEW FLAMES, BESIDES WHERE THESE LODGE VAIN HEARTS MOURN		196	RLS + LSNS	131
ALL THINGS IN BEING) THEY CONSUME AND MOURN.		287	PSALM 104	78
DOTH MOURN FOR US		298	JESUS WP B	6
WHOSE SPIRIT TOO DOTH MOURN AND GRIEVE		292	THE JEWS	35
PRICKING HIS LIPS, TILL HE DOTH MOURN		319	THE ASS	50
SO DO I MOURN, AND HANG MY HEAD		228	PILGRIMAGE	21
THUS ALL THE YEAR I MOURN.		248	I WALKT	63
AND MAKES HIM MOURN, AND PINE AND DYE		281	THE FAVOUR	5
AND ALL MY POWERS MOURN'D.		213	ADMISSION	4
HAD MOURN'D THY LOSSE, NOT MINE		173	CONTENT	16
MOURNE				
THOU THAT KNOW'ST FOR WHOM I MOURNE		165	THE CALL	30
MOURNERS				
NOT BUT THAT MOURNERS TOO, CAN HAVE		342	OBSEQUIES	17
MOURNING				
FOR MOURNING SACK-CLOTH WEAR, ALL MORTIFIED.		342	OBSEQUIES	16
A MOURNING LIGHT UPON THE DEAD.		309	THE SEED	54
MOURNS				
THE TURTLE THEN IN PALM-TREES MOURNS		288	THE BIRD	27
AND THE MOON MOURNS.		210	FAITH	20
MOUTH				
JUST AT HIS MOUTH, THAT THANKLESS HIVE		300	PROVIDENCE	11

		PAGE	TITLE	LINE
MOUTH	**(CON'T)**			
IS IN THY MOUTH, NOT IN THY HAND		316	MEN OF WAR	26
MOV'D				
BUT STILL UNKINDE. ART THIS DAY NOTHING MOV'D.		296	JESUS WP A	2
IS MOV'D AND TREMBLES, THE HILLS MELT AND SMOKE		287	PSALM 104	86
LIKE A VAST SHADOW MOV'D, IN WHICH THE WORLD		231	THE WORLD	6
LIKE A THICK MIDNIGHT-FOG MOV'D THERE SO SLOW		231	THE WORLD	17
MOVE				
BUT SHOULD THY MILD INJUNCTION NOTHING MOVE ME		230	LAW + GOSP	39
WITH WHAT EXACT OBEDIENCE DO YOU MOVE		235	CONSTLATN	5
OF ALL I HAVE, I MAY NOR MOVE THY WRATH		235	MUTINIE	37
SETTLE, AND FIX OUR HEARTS, THAT WE MAY MOVE		237	CONSTLATN	53
NO THESE ARE THE MAGNETS WHICH SO STRONGLY MOVE		278	THE STARRE	21
IN WHOM I LIVE, IN WHOM I MOVE		249	BEGGING A	2
WHERE LIGHT, JOY, LEISURE, AND TRUE COMFORTS MOVE		248	I WALKT	59
THAT STON'D THY SERVANTS, AND DID MOVE		264	INTRO. 1	11
WITH THESE FAIR THOUGHTS I MOVE IN THIS FAIR PLACE		268	ASCN-DAY A	49
I SEE THEM, HEAR THEM, MARK THEIR HASTE, AND MOVE		268	ASCN-DAY A	31
O THAT THY SPIRIT WOULD SO STRONGLY MOVE ME		283	LOVE-SICK	2
DEW OF THE DEAD WHICH MAKES DUST MOVE		298	JESUS WP B	11
WERE CHEAR'D, YOUR JEALOUSIE TO MOVE.		293	THE JEWS	45
TEACH BOTH MINE EYES AND FEET TO MOVE		318	THE ASS	15
WHO LOV'D MUCH, AND MUCH MORE COULD MOVE.		305	ST MARY MN	50
MY THOUGHTS, WHEN TOWARDS THEE THEY MOVE		332	AGREEMENT	17
WHERE SOULS BEHIND THE ALTAR MOVE		325	ABELS BLOD	20
WHERE TURTLES BUILD, AND CARELESSE SPARROWS MOVE		327	RIGHTSNESS	7
O WHAT STRANGE WONDERS COULD THEE MOVE		164	INCARNATN	17
BUT I BY BACKWARD STEPS WOULD MOVE		170	RETREATE	30
AND SHINE, AND MOVE		177	MRNG-WTCH	29
I SHINE, AND MOVE		182	CHRFLNESS	4
THAT WILL NOT MOVE.		189	RESOLVE	8
AND CHECKT THEIR FURIE, WHEN I SAW THEM MOVE		188	RELAPSE	7
SHOULD MOVE, THEY MAKE US HOLY, HAPPY, RICH.		192	RLS + LSNS	30
AND MOVE ON WITH THE SHADES, STARS NOT, AND SLEEPE		157	THE LAMPE	2
THY GRAVE. TO WHICH MY THOUGHTS SHAL MOVE		343	OBSEQUIES	29
WHICH FIRST UPON THY FACE DID MOVE		344	WATER-FALL	31
MOVED				
THAT I SHALL NOT BE MOVED		220	PSALM 121	6
MOVES				
MOVES IN DISGUISE, AND SIGHS AFFLICT THE AIR.		280	JOY	4
AND NOTHING MOVES WITHOUT A SHROWD		143	DEATH	14
MOVING				
AND MOVING ANGUISHMENTS THAT SET		152	THE SEARCH	39
A MOVING MIST.		345	QUICKNESS	18
MUD				
SULLYED WITH DUST AND MUD.		198	UNPRFTBLNS	3
MULE				
TO CHECK THE MULE, UNRULY MAN		221	AFFLICTION	18
BY GODS PERMISSION, AND MAN TURNS A MULE.		330	JACOBS PLW	30
MULTIPLI'D				
WHERE, AS THOU GREWST, IT MULTIPLI'D AND SHIN'D		154	ISAACS M.	9
MULTIPLY				
THICK BUSIE CLOUDS DID MULTIPLY		333	AGREEMENT	39
IN GOD, DOTH ALWAYS (HIDDEN) MULTIPLY		280	PALM-TREE	14
MULTITUDE				
AND GOD HIMSELF DYED BY THE MULTITUDE.		330	JACOBS PLW	6
MURD'RING				
THAT FROM THE MURD'RING WORLDS FALSE LOVE		343	OBSEQUIES	31
MURMUR'D				
THEY MURMUR'D SORE, BUT I, WHO FELT THEM BOYL		234	MUTINIE	9
MURMURERS				
WITH MURMURERS, AND FOES.		197	CORRUPTION	18
MURMURINGS				
MURMURINGS AT THEE, WHEN MOST MILDE.		265	INTRO. 2	22
MURMURS				
WITH WHAT DEEP MURMURS THROUGH TIMES SILENT STEALTH		343	WATER-FALL	1
MURTH'RER				
DID FIRST AGAINST A MURTH'RER CRY.		325	ABELS BLOD	2
AND IS THERE ANY MURTH'RER WORSE THEN SIN.		290	THE TIMBER	25
MURTHERED				
SO MURTHERED MAN, WHEN LOVELY LIFE IS DONE		289	THE TIMBER	21
MURTHRED				
TO HAVE THE MURTHRED FOR THY LOVE.		264	INTRO. 1	12
MUSICALL				
MAKING THE WHOLE MOST MUSICALL		222	AFFLICTION	40
MUSICK				
AND MONEY BETTER MUSICK THAN THE SPHERES.		224	TEMPEST	48
MUSICK AND MIRTH (IF THERE BE MUSICK HERE)		236	CONSTLATN	21
MUSICK AND MIRTH (IF THERE BE MUSICK HERE)		236	CONSTLATN	21
SUCH MUSICK SPOILS GOOD FELLOWSHIP.		240	MISERY	32
WHICH IN THY MUSICK BEARS NO PART		214	MISERY	82
STORMS TURN TO MUSICK, CLOUDS TO SMILES AND AIR.		306	RAIN-BOW	10
IN MUSICK DOTH CONTEND.		200	NTVTY 2	4
THE MUSICK OF HER TEARES		141	RGNRTN	61
AND IN THIS MUSICK BY THY MARTYRS BLOUD		180	CHRCH-SVC	20
MUSING				
HERE MUSING LONG, I HEARD		141	RGNRTN	78
MUSIQUE				
AND MADE GRAVE MUSIQUE LIKE WILDE WIT		297	HERODIAS	3
MUTINIES				
TO CALM ME IN THESE MUTINIES		242	MISERY	86

	PAGE	TITLE	LINE

MUTINOUS
ALL MUTINOUS THOUGHTS, WHAT BUSINES E'R THOU HAST . . 194 RLS + LSNS 86
MYRE
TO EV'RY MYRE . . . . 324 THE NIGHT 46
MYRRH
I SMELL A DEW LIKE MYRRH, AND ALL THE DAY . . . 198 UNPRFTBLNS 10
THERE IS BEYOND THE STARS AN HIL OF MYRRH . . . 243 THE SAP 11
ODORS, AND MYRRH, AND BALM IN ONE RICH FLOUD . . . 244 MT. OLV. B 7
HEAVEN HERE, MAN ON THOSE HILLS OF MYRRH, AND FLOWRES. . 2 SON-DAYES 14
SCATT'RING THE MYRRHE, AND INCENSE OF THY PRAY'R. . . 155 ISAACS M. 52
LILIES AND MYRRHE, WHERE THE CURS'D SEED . . . . 299 JESUS WP B 49
MYSTERIES
AN AGE OF MYSTERIES. WHICH HE . . . . . . 322 CHILDEHOOD 35
TO CARRY, NOT SEARCH MYSTERIES. . . . . . 318 THE ASS 22
IN DEATHS DARK MYSTERIES . . . . . . 310 THE -SEED 80
THE KEY THAT OPENS TO ALL MYSTERIES . . . . 198 SCRIPTURES 7
MORNINGS ARE MYSTERIES, THE FIRST WORLDS YOUTH . . 192 RLS + LSNS 25
OR THE DREAD MYSTERIES OF THY BLEST BLOUD . . . 217 DRESSING 35
WHAT MYSTERIES DO LIE BEYOND THY DUST. . . . . 271 ALL GONE 19
MYSTERIOUS
BY FLOWERS AND CARVINGS AND MYSTERIOUS SKILL . . . 279 PALM-TREE 11
(UNDER THAT STATELY AND MYSTERIOUS CLOUD . . . 330 JACOBS PLW 22
MYSTERY
THE MYSTERY, BUT THIS NFER DONE . . . . . 168 VNTY SPRIT 27
MYSTICAL
WERE FIGUR'D IN THOSE MYSTICAL . . . . . 211 FAITH 31
LODGE IN THY MYSTICAL, DEEP STREAMS. . . . . 344 WATER-FALL 28
MYSTICALL
THY MYSTICALL COMMUNION . . . . . . 216 DRESSING 14
MYSTICK
AND LET ONCE MORE BY MYSTICK BIRTH . . . . 200 NTVTY 1 29
HOW IN A MYSTICK CLOUD . . . . . . 300 PROVIDENCE 7
NAHOR
WHEN TERAH, NAHOR, HARAN, ABRAM, LOT . . . . 306 RAIN-BOW 5
NAIL
OR NAIL THOSE BLESSED LIMBS AGAIN . . . . . 230 LAW + GOSP 35
NAIL'D
NAIL'D TO THE CENTER STOOD . . . . . . 141 RGNRTN 69
NAKED
ALL NAKED, INNOCENT AND BRIGHT . . . . . 269 ASCSN-HYMN 23
WHEN IN HIS NAKED, PURE ARRAY. . . . . . 303 ST MARY MN 2
HELL AND ALL HEARTS STARK NAKED LYES. . . . . 314 THE STONE 27
NAKEDNESS
AND SEE YOUR NAKEDNESS THEREBY . . . . . 266 VAIN WITS 11
NAME
WHICH ONCE HAD NEITHER BEING, FORME, NOR NAME . . 248 I WALKT 47
IN IT MY NAME, AND HONOUR BOTH DO DWELL . . . 226 RETIREMENT 38
DISCEIN TREADS ON THE PEACEFUL NAME . . . . 214 MISERY 68
WHERE SICK WITH LOVE I STRIVE THY NAME TO SING . . 245 MT. OLV. B 24
THY GLORIOUS NAME. WHICH GRANT I MAY SO DO . . 245 MT. OLV. B 25
YET TO THY NAME . . . . 215 PRAISE 39
OR HATH A NAME . . . . 222 AFFLICTION 31
AND TO THY NAME, WHICH STILL I KEEP . . . . 311 FAIR+YONG 9
THY NAME WAS WRIT, AND ALL THY DAYS. . . . . 310 THE SEED 60
I WILL IN SONGS TO THY GREAT NAME IMPLOY . . . 287 PSALM 104 90
A MOST FAIR NOTION, BUT A VERY NAME. . . . . 330 JACOBS PLW 16
AND GLORY BE TO HIS ETERNAL NAME. . . . . 331 JACOBS PLW 37
IN ANTIPHONES SING TO THY NAME. . . . . . 336 PSALM 65 26
THE VILE DESPIGHT DONE TO THY NAME. . . . . 335 JUDGEMENT 34
WE TALK AND NAME THEE WITH MUCH EASE . . . . 338 DEATH B 6
VICE IN A FAIRER NAME. . . . . . . 205 IDLE VERSE 12
WHAT IS HIS NAME, AND HOW I MIGHT . . . . 167 VNTY SPRIT 7
ALMOST OUTLIVE OUR NAME. . . . . . . 166 THE CALL 57
IN SEV'RALL PARTS SHALL WANT A NAME . . . . 177 EVNG-WTCH 6
THAT SOILES THY NAME . . . . 171 COME, COME 18
NAMES
AND QUITE BLOT OUT THEIR NAMES . . . . . 147 DAY OF JDG 8
SINCE PLAC'D BY HIM WHO CALLS YOU BY YOUR NAMES . . 236 CONSTLATN 33
NAP
DEATH A NAP, TO WAKE MORE MERRY. . . . . . 218 EASTER HYM 6
NAP'S
WHEN THY NAP'S OVER, STIR THY FIRE, UNRAKE . . . 196 RLS + LSNS 133
NARD
WHY IS THIS RICH, THIS PISTIC NARD . . . . 304 ST MARY MN 21
NARROW
OFT TO A NARROW, HOMELY ROOM . . . . . 315 DWELLNG-PL 14
THY SHADES BUT THIN AND NARROW BE . . . . 338 DEATH B 18
SHALL LODGE IN SUCH A NARROW PIT, TILL HE . . . 331 JACOBS PLW 39
FOR SURE THAT IS THE NARROW WAY. . . . . 322 CHILDEHOOD 44
THESE NARROW SKIES (NARROW TO ME) THAT BARRE . . 283 LOVE-SICK 7
THESE NARROW SKIES (NARROW TO ME) THAT BARRE . . 283 LOVE-SICK 7
FROM SIN, HE WALKS A NARROW, PRIVATE WAY. . . . 290 THE TIMBER 34
HIS COTTAGE FAILES, WHOSE NARROW SPAN . . . . 166 THE CALL 44
IS BUT HIS NARROW FOOTSTOOLE ALL . . . . 163 MT. OLVS A 26
THE NARROW WAY. . . . . 2 SON-DAYES 10
AND NARROW WAY, BY WHICH TO THEE . . . . 207 REPENTANCE 8
NATION
BECOME AN HUMBLE, HOLY NATION. . . . . . 237 CONSTLATN 56
NATIVE
AS BIRDS ROB'D OF THEIR NATIVE WOOD . . . . 228 PILGRIMAGE 17

	PAGE	TITLE	LINE
NATIVE (CCN'T)			
BLT IN A VIRGINS NATIVE BLUSH AND FEARS	155	ISAACS M.	35
WITH NATIVE LCCKS, WHICH KNEW NC GUILE	303	ORNAMENT	15
NATIVE AND PURE SHINES NCW IN THEE	303	ST MARY MN	8
NATURAL			
AND AS I'TH' NATURAL SUN, THESE THREE	211	FAITH	33
NATURE			
BUT, AS IN NATURE, WHEN THE DAY	210	FAITH	17
WHEN NATURE ON HER BOSOME SAW	222	TEMPEST	5
WHICH NATURE BREEDS, AND SCME FINE CLAY INVITES	320	HIDDN TRSR	20
UNROWEL'D NATURE, SHEW'C THEE HER RECRUITS	145	RSRCTN +IM	21
I SUMMON'C NATURE. PIERC'D THRCUGH ALL HER STCRE	167	VNTY SPRIT	9
AND SYMPHCNY CF NATURE. PRAYER IS	177	MRNG-WTCH	18
NATURES			
THE MCRE HE GROWS. CELESTIAL NATURES STILL	279	PALM-TREE	9
NAUGHT			
LIKE THEE, WHEN SET AT NAUGHT AND DUMB.	316	MEN OF WAR	20
ND			
NC DO THEY SO. HAVE THEY A SENSE	186	ND DO THEY	1
NEAR			
AND FAITH TO SEE MY CROWN AS NEAR	317	MEN OF WAR	38
(THEIR LORD SC NEAR) SENSE TO BE GLAD.	305	ST MARY MN	44
NCNE STAIN'D CR WITHER'D SHALL CCME NEAR.	308	THE SEED	22
BEFORE THEY CCME, AND KNCW'ST HCW NEAR THEY BE.	289	THE TIMBER	16
NEAST			
A NEAST OF NIGHTS, A GLCCMIE SPHERE	143	DEATH	11
THOU ARE LIFES CHARTER, THE DCVES SPOTLESS NEAST	197	SCRIPTURES	3
NEAT			
AND I, LIKE FLOWERS SHALL STILL GC NEAT	300	PROVIDENCE	17
WHERE ALL WAS SUMPTUOUS, RARE AND NEAT.	304	ST MARY MN	14
NECESSITIES			
DISPATCH NECESSITIES, LIFE HATH A LOAD	192	RLS + LSNS	33
NEED			
UNTOUCH'D BY ANY, AND WHAT NEED	163	MT. OLVS A	13
BLT HERE CN EARTH (THCUGH THCU HAST NEED)	316	MEN OF WAR	23
THY BOUNTEOUS OPEN HAND HELPS THEM AT NEED	286	PSALM 104	75
WHERE I SHALL NEED NO GLAS.	271	ALL GONE	40
SC THAT I NEED NO MCRE, BUT SAY	211	FAITH	41
NEEDFUL			
AND THE MCST NEEDFUL FOR CUR SINS.	335	JUDGEMENT	41
NEEDFULL			
AND BY A SACRED, NEEDFULL ART	222	AFFLICTION	38
NEEDLESSE			
OF YOUNG, GAY SWEARERS, WITH THEIR NEEDLESSE, LOWD	154	ISAACS M.	22
NEEDS			
SURE HERE HE MUST NEEDS STAY	153	THE SEARCH	91
IF TRLTH BE THINE, WHAT NEEDS A BRUTISH FORCE.	193	RLS + LSNS	39
HER CAPTIVE FLAMES MUST NEEDS BURN THERE.	271	ALL GONE	30
SINCE TC HIS SINS (AS NEEDS IT MUST)	297	HERODIAS	6
AS LOUD AS BLCOD. NOT THAT GOC NEEDS	314	THE STONE	24
MUST NEEDS ACKNOWLEDGE TO BE JUST.	314	THE STONE	36
WHAT NEEDS A CONSCIENCE CALM AND BRIGHT	309	THE SEED	41
NEER			
THE FLCWRES TC AIR DRAW NEER, AND SUBTILTIE	223	TEMPEST	35
NEER HIM, HIS LUTE, HIS FANCY, AND HIS FLIGHTS	231	THE WORLD	10
SOME CTHERS NEER THE WEST	235	CONSTLATN	10
WHO SHOULDST NOT THEN CCME NEER TC ME	214	MISERY	46
THE MYSTERY, BUT THIS NEER CCNE	168	VNTY SPRIT	27
NEERE			
HCW NEERE REDEMPTION CREEPES.	143	DEATH	30
I DREW HER NEERE, AND FCUND	141	RGNRTN	62
THEN TAKING UP WHAT I CCULD NEEREST SPIE	247	I WALKT	15
NEGLECT			
BUT THOU SLEEP'ST IN A DEEPE NEGLECT	163	MT. OLVS A	12
IS BUT EXCUS'D NEGLECT. TC MIND	189	RESOLVE	3
WITH BAC, OR WITH NEGLECT, AND HEAPS NOT WRATH	328	RIGHTSNESS	51
NEGLECTING			
NEGLECTING THEE. SUCH ILL-PLAC'D WIT	162	MT. OLVS A	5
NEGLECTS			
SLEEPS NOT, BUT SHAKING OFF SLCTH, AND NEGLECTS	201	THE CHECK	15
NEGLIGENCE			
WHICH WITH SKILL'D NEGLIGENCE SEEM'D SHED	304	ST MARY MN	19
NEIGHBOUR			
LCVE GOD, AND LOVE THY NEIGHBCUR, WATCH, AND PRAY.	196	RLS + LSNS	140
NEST			
WHEN THEIR NEST IS FALN AND BRCKEN.	294	BEGGING B	20
HE THAT HATH FOUND SOME FLEDG'D BIRDS NEST, MAY KNOW	271	ALL GONE	21
THSES DARK CONFUSIONS, THAT WITHIN ME NEST	216	DRESSING	7
NESTS			
THE BIRDS THEIR NESTS BUILD, THCUGH THE STORK DOTH CHCOSE	286	PSALM 104	47
NETS			
THY MCTHERS NETS IN THEE WERE SPRED	297	HERODIAS	19
THY LAWS BUT NETS, WHERE SCME SMALL BIRDS	207	REPENTANCE	11
NEW			
THAT SCENE WAS CHANG'D, AND A NEW DRESSE	210	FAITH	23
FLEW HOME UNSTAIN'D BY HIS NEW KIN	209	THE BURIAL	6
AND MY SOUL IN NEW ARRAY	214	PRAISE	15
OF DAIES, FROM THEE LCCK FOR NEW STRENGTH	218	EASTER HYM	10
THESE NEW DISCOVERIES DC, EXCEPT THEY DROWN.	224	TEMPEST	40
CAN THESE NEW LIGHTS BE LIKE TC THOSE	272	WHT SUNDAY	9

		PAGE	TITLE	LINE
NEW (CCN'T)				
I SIT WITH THEE BY THIS NEW LIGHT	. . . . .	214	MISERY	53
SCME NEW IMPLCYMENT, I PEGIN	. . . .	214	MISERY	63
AND NC NEW BUSINESS BREAKS THEIR PEACE.	. . .	245	MAN	11
AND BRING NEW TOC. GET THEN THIS SAP, AND GET	. .	244	THE SAP	35
I MAKE ALL NEW. THERE NCTHING GAY	. . .	226	RETIREMENT	40
NEW FRESH ACCCUNTS OF BLOCD AND LUST.	. . .	297	HERODIAS	8
AND STILL A NEW SUCCESSION SINGS AND FLIES.	. .	289	THE TIMBER	5
WE SLIGHT AS CLD AND SOIL'D, THCUGH FRESH AND NEW.	.	306	RAIN-BOW	2
FOR THY NEW LIGHT, AND TREMBLED AT EACH SHOWER.	.	306	RAIN-BOW	8
EVEN WHAT WAS DONE BEFCRE, AND NC NEW THING.	.	320	HIDDN TRSR	2
MAKE ALL THINGS NEW. AND WITHCUT END.	. . .	335	JUDGEMENT	46
NEW CORDIALS, NEW CATHARTICS CEAL.	. . .	333	AGREEMENT	58
NEW CORDIALS, NEW CATHARTICS CEAL.	. . .	333	AGREEMENT	58
YCUTHFUL AND FAIR TO SEE NEW SKIES.	. . .	334	JUDGEMENT	6
NEW FLAMES, BESIDES WHERE THESE LCDGE VAIN HEARTS MCURN	.	196	RLS + LSNS	131
THROUGH THY INCREASE CRCW NEW, AND QUICK.	. .	191	THE MATCH	41
FCUND ALL WAS CHANG'D, AND A NEW SPRING	. .	140	RGNRTN	48
NEW SEV'RAL OATHES, AND CCMPLEMENTS (TOO) PLENTY.	.	154	ISAACS M.	16
THY SCUL, AND WITH NEW PINICNS REFRESH	. .	155	ISAACS M.	48
WHEN THCU SHALT MAKE ALL NEW AGAIN	. .	347	THE BOOK	27
WHERE THEY NEW CONSORTS CHCOSE AND STICK	. .	348	HOLY BIBLE	11
O THE NEW WORLDS NEW, QUICKNING SUN.	. . .	349	L'ENVOY	1
O THE NEW WORLDS NEW, QUICKNING SUN.	. . .	349	L'ENVOY	1
NEW-HEAW'D				
AN UNCEFIL'D AND NEW-HEAW'D CNE	. . .	152	THE SEARCH	47
NEWES				
WITH FANCIES, FRIENDS, CR NEWES.	. . . .	187	NO DO THEY	34
NEWLY				
THE LCST SON BY THE NEWLY FOUND.	. . . .	293	THE JEWS	49
NEWS				
WHICH NOW CAN TEL THEE NEWS.	. . . .	243	THE SAP	10
NEXT				
NEXT CAY I CALL AND CRY FCR THEE	. . .	214	MISERY	45
PERHAPS SCME HARMLESS CARES FCR THE NEXT DAY	.	239	SHEPHEARDS	37
NEXT, THERE'S IN IT A RESTLESS, PURE DESIRE	.	278	THE STARRE	17
THE NEXT WORLDS GLADNES PREPOSSEST IN THIS.	.	205	SON-DAYES	3
AND CCMES NEXT MORNING FRESH AS HE.	. .	300	PROVIDENCE	24
THE OTHER, THE TRUE LIFE, IN THE NEXT WORLD	.	191	THE MATCH	22
OR THE NEXT FCOT TO CRUSH	. . . .	201	THE CHECK	9
THY NEXT EFFECTS NC TCNGUE CAN TELL.	. .	348	HOLY BIBLE	35
AND DRESS THIS EARTH FCR NEXT YEARS MEAT.	.	341	THE FEAST	75
AND WHAT IN THE NEXT WORLC TC EAT.	. .	341	THE FEAST	78
NICCCEMUS				
WISE NICCDEMUS SAW SUCH LIGHT	. . .	323	THE NIGHT	5
NIGH				
'TIS NOW SIX THOUSAND YEARS WELL NIGH	. .	338	DEATH B	3
THY HAND IS NIGH.	. . . .	171	COME, COME	14
NIGHT				
WHEN I LYE DOWN. THE PICUS SOLL BY NIGHT	.	177	MRNG-WTCH	24
OF NIGHT, AND REST	. . . .	176	MRNG-WTCH	4
STARS ARE OF MIGHTY USE, THE NIGHT	. .	174	JOY OF LIF	9
BUT THESE ALL NIGHT	. . .	175	JOY OF LIF	21
HE KEEPES A COMMERCE IN THE NIGHT	. .	162	PURSUITE	7
LIKE A YOUNG EAST, CR MCONE-SHINE NIGHT	.	168	VNTY SPRIT	20
MAY NCT APPROACH THEE (FOR AT NIGHT	.	168	VNTY SPRIT	31
AND IN THE HEART CF EARTH, AND NIGHT	.	179	SILENCE	31
TC BRAVE THE NIGHT	. . .	178	SILENCE	8
MAKE ME FAIRE DAYES OF EVERY NIGHT.	. .	182	CHRFLNESS	8
THE HIDEOLS NIGHT	. . . .	201	THE CHECK	14
REST FROM THE FEARS I'TH' NIGHT.	. .	201	THE CHECK	19
FOR SINCE AMIDST MY YCUTH, AND NIGHT	.	205	IDLE VERSE	5
COOL'C BY THE DAMPS OF NIGHT, CESCENDS	.	203	DSRDK + FR	36
AND SPAN UP NIGHT.	. . .	189	RESOLVE	20
OF NIGHT SHUT UP THY LEAVES, BE CHAST, GOD PRYS	.	196	RLS + LSNS	136
WHEN NIGHT COMES, LIST THY DEEDS, MAKE PLAIN THE WAY	.	195	RLS + LSNS	115
LASTS NOT A NIGHT SOMETIMES. BAD SPIRITS FEAR	.	195	RLS + LSNS	124
ALL'S IN DEEP SLEEP, AND NIGHT. THICK DARKNES LYES	.	197	CORRUPTION	37
BUT SHUTS HIS DOOR, AND LEAVES GCOD OUT ALL NIGHT.	.	194	RLS + LSNS	84
THE PILGRIM-SUNNE, ALL NIGHT HAVE I	. .	151	THE SEARCH	3
WHICH HELD UP NIGHT, AND DAY	. . .	147	DAY OF JDG	16
'TIS CEAD NIGHT RCUND ABOUT. HCRROR DOTH CREEPE	.	157	THE LAMPE	1
BUT, TH'LAST MORE HEAVY THEN THE NIGHT	.	141	RGNRTN	68
'TIS SO. BUT AS THOU SAWEST THAT NIGHT	.	143	DEATH	15
WHERE NO RUDE SHACE, OR NIGHT	. .	146	RSRCTN +IM	64
AND ONELY SEE THROUGH A LONG NIGHT	. .	322	CHILDEHOOD	41
AS MADE HIM KNOW HIS GOC BY NIGHT	. .	323	THE NIGHT	6
HIS LCCKS ARE WET WITH THE CLEAR DROPS OF NIGHT.	.	324	THE NIGHT	33
DEAR NIGHT. THIS WORLDS DEFEAT.	. .	324	THE NIGHT	25
ERRE MORE THEN I CAN DO BY NIGHT.	. .	324	THE NIGHT	48
OF FOR THAT NIGHT. WHERE I IN HIM	. .	325	THE NIGHT	53
AND LEADER THROUGH THICK DEATH AND NIGHT.	.	326	ABELS BLOD	32
BUT WE A HEALING SUN BY DAY AND NIGHT	.	331	JACOBS PLW	49
EXTERMINATING FEARS AND NIGHT.	. .	332	AGREEMENT	14
THIS LITTLE GOSHEN, IN THE MICST OF NIGHT	.	331	JACOBS PLW	31
AND WATCH ALL NIGHT FCR MISTS CR SHOWERS	.	301	PROVIDENCE	29
SO IN THE SHADES OF NIGHT SOME DARK FOWLS BE	.	288	THE BIRD	25
THOU MAKEST DARKNESS, AND THEN COMES THE NIGHT.	.	286	PSALM 104	53
HITHER THCU COM'ST. THE BUSIE WIND ALL NIGHT	.	287	THE BIRD	1
WILL FACE AT NIGHT, AND WITH THIS SUN	.	283	GARLAND	31

	PAGE	TITLE	LINE
NIGHT (CCN'T)			
FALSE STARS AND FIRE-DRAKES, THE DECEITS CF NIGHT . .	320	HIDDN TRSR	4
HOW WCULD I RLN TC ENDLESS NIGHT	316	MEN OF WAR	10
THE DEW THY HERBS DRINK UP BY NIGHT	207	REPENTANCE	39
GROWING O'R NIGHT, AND CONE TOMORROW	208	REPENTANCE	72
A GLORICUS NIGHT	210	FAITH	14
BREAKS, NIGHT ADJOURNS . .	210	FAITH	18
THE WHOLE CREATION SHAKES OFF NIGHT	212	DAWNING	17
THE COLD BY NIGHT, THE HEAT BY DAY	220	PSALM 121	11
ORDAIN NIGHT TOO.	221	AFFLICTION	8
DAY, AND NIGHT, NCT ONCE A DAY	214	PRAISE	13
ALL DAY, AND NIGHT DOTH RUN, AND SING	212	DAWNING	34
AND WCRK ALL NIGHT UPON THY LIGHT AND LOVE	278	THE STARRE	22
WITH DEW BY NIGHT, BUT CNE YOU CANNOT SEE	280	PALM-TREE	23
THEIR MAGNETISME WORKS ALL NIGHT	276	COCK-CRWNG	5
THEIR LITTLE GRAIN EXPELLING NIGHT	276	COCK-CRWNG	8
NCW CAST AT NIGHT MY CRCWN AWAY.	275	PROFFER	30
LET NC NIGHT PUT OUT THIS SUN.	249	BEGGING A	4
AND RESURRECTION FROM THE EARTH AND NIGHT.	267	ASCN-DAY A	18
HOW HAPPEND IT THAT IN THE DEAD OF NIGHT	238	SHEPHEARDS	5
THE DARKEST NIGHT, AND CLOSEST NOCK.	235	CONSTLATN	8
AND TURN'D THEIR NIGHT TO DAY	239	SHEPHEARDS	52
WHERE BEES AT NIGHT GET HOME AND HIVE, AND FLCWRS . . .	245	MAN	5
SC FOR THIS NIGHT. I LINGER HERE	228	PILGRIMAGE	9
I SAW ETERNITY THE OTHER NIGHT	231	THE WORLD	1
O FOOLS (SAID I) THUS TC PREFER DARK NIGHT	233	THE WORLD	49
SHOULD POOR SOULS FEAR A SHADE CR NIGHT	343	WATER-FALL	17
AS SOME MEEK NIGHT-PIECE WHICH DAY QUAILS	310	THE SEED	67
NIGHT-RAVENS			
AS SULLEN NIGHT-RAVENS DO THE SUN	311	FAIR+YONG	4
NIGHTINGALES			
LET NIGHTINGALES ATTEND THE SPRING	205	IDLE VERSE	23
NIGHTS			
VAST CIRCLING AZURE, GIDDY CLOUDS, DAYS, NIGHTS. . . .	194	RLS + LSNS	90
FOR CHAINS OF DARKNES, AND ETERNAL NIGHTS.	196	RLS + LSNS	144
THROUGH THICKEST NIGHTS, THOUGH THEN THE SUN BE FAR . . .	196	RLS + LSNS	137
A NEAST OF NIGHTS, A GLOOMIE SPHERE	143	DEATH	11
HE WEPT ONCE, WALKT WHOLE NIGHTS ON THEE	163	MT. OLVS A	21
WHAT STOCK OF NIGHTS	165	THE CALL	14
IF NIGHTS, AND SHADES, AND SECRET ROOMS	313	THE STONE	6
THE THIRD GLAD DAY THROUGH TWO SAD NIGHTS.	295	PALM-SUNDY	33
ENTIRE STILL, WEARS OUT BLACKEST NIGHTS.	333	AGREEMENT	34
HAVE YET MORE DAYS, MORE NIGHTS TO COUNT	229	PILGRIMAGE	26
WHICH IN THE DARKEST NIGHTS POINT TO THEIR HOMES . . .	246	MAN	24
SOME NIGHTS I SEE YOU IN THE GLADSOME EAST	235	CONSTLATN	9
PERHAPS SOME NIGHTS HEE'L WATCH WITH YOU, AND PEEP . . .	236	CONSTLATN	25
AND YET, AS IN NIGHTS GLOOMY PAGE	273	WHT SUNDAY	37
SC SHALL MY NIGHTS AND MORNINGS BE	281	THE FAVOUR	11
NILE'S			
ALL HER PARCHT BOSOME TC NILE'S SHORE	151	THE SEARCH	12
NINE			
NINE MONTHS THY HANDS ARE FASHIONING US	166	THE CALL	46
TO WHCM A FALLING STAR AND NINE DAYES GLORY	282	GARLAND	2
NIP			
THE FOSTS ILL WEEDS NIP, AND MOLEST	227	LV + DSPLN	11
NIPT			
THEIR YOUTH, AND BEAUTY, COLD SHOWRES NIPT, AND WRUNG . .	198	UNPRFTBLNS	5
NOBLE			
AND THE MORE NOBLE ESSENCE FINDS HIS HOUSE	145	RSRCTN +IM	39
NOBLER			
YET, HADST THCU NOBLER GUESTS. ANGELS DID WIND	155	ISAACS M.	25
NOISE			
AMIDST THE NOISE, AND THRONG	161	DSTRQCTION	32
THERE ABOVE NOISE, AND DANGER	184	PEACE	5
FAIR, ORDER'D LIGHT (WHOSE MOTION WITHOUT NOISE . . .	235	CONSTLATN	1
AND FROTHIE NOISE WHICH UP AND DOWN DOTH FLIE	234	MUTINIE	24
LIVED THERE WITHOUT ALL NOISE	239	SHEPHEARDS	36
SEEM MILD, BUT ARE KNOWN BY THEIR NOISE.	237	CONSTLATN	44
WHICH TO THY PEACE ARE BUT MEEK NOISE.	214	MISERY	60
ACTIVE AS LIGHT, AND CALM WITHOUT ALL NOISE	244	MT. OLV. B	2
ALL MAY BE NOW CO-HEIRS, NO NOISE	210	FAITH	9
FCR MIRTH AND LIFE, YET WITHOUT NOISE.	299	JESUS WP B	47
AT NOISE, BUT THRIVE UNSEEN AND DUMB.	309	THE SEED	46
WHERE BIRDS LIKE WATCHFUL CLOCKS THE NOISELESS DATE . .	245	MAN	3
NOOK			
THE DARKEST NIGHT, AND CLOSEST NOCK.	235	CONSTLATN	8
AS WHERE TO LEAD THEIR SHEEP, WHAT SILENT NOCK . . .	239	SHEPHEARDS	39
NOT A NOOK IN ALL MY BREAST	214	PRAISE	5
WHICH SHEW'D ME IN A NOCK CAST BY	168	VNTY SPRIT	21
NOON			
THAT SACRED VAIL DRAWN O'R THY GLORIOUS NOON	323	THE NIGHT	2
NOONS			
THEN THE NOONS CLOUDLESS LIGHT.	310	THE SEED	82
NORTH			
WHEN THROUGH THE NORTH A FIRE SHALL RUSH	146	DAY OF JDG	1
NOTE			
KNOWS EV'RY NOTE, AND CALL	161	DSTRQCTION	14
WALK WITH THY FELLOW-CREATURES. NOTE THE HUSH . . .	192	RLS + LSNS	13
DID SADLY NOTE HIS HEALING RAYES	292	THE JEWS	23
IS ALL THE NOTE WITHIN MY BUSH.	228	PILGRIMAGE	16

		PAGE	TITLE	LINE
NOTE	(CON'T)			
AND OUR BEST NOTE AND HIGHEST EASE	. . . . .	273	WHT SUNDAY	42
NOTES				
WHOSE HEAVY NOTES MAKE ALL THAT HEAR THEM, SAD.	. .	288	THE BIRD	26
NOTHIN'S				
NOTHIN'S MORE VILE THAN IS MY BREATH	. . . .	208	REPENTANCE	74
NOTHING				
WHOSE GLORIOUS CONQUEST NOTHING CAN RESIST	. . .	216	DRESSING	11
NOTHING THAT IS, OR LIVES .	. . . .	219	HOLY COMM.	11
NOTHING NOW TO MAN IS LACKING	. . . .	218	EASTER HYM	2
NOTHING THAT STIRRS .	. . . .	222	AFFLICTION	30
AND NOTHING DOTH THY LOVE ALLAY	. . . .	274	WHT SUNDAY	51
WE, WHO ARE NOTHING BUT FOUL CLAY	. . . .	274	WHT SUNDAY	59
AND HERE ARE LEFT AS NOTHING WORTH	. . . .	270	ASCSN-HYMN	29
I NOTHING HAVE TO GIVE TO THEE .	. . . .	266	INTRO. 2	29
I MAKE ALL NEW. THERE NOTHING GAY	. . . .	226	RETIREMENT	40
BUT SHOULD THY MILD INJUNCTION NOTHING MOVE ME	. .	230	LAW + GOSP	39
IS NOTHING TO THY GLORIOUS ARM	. . . .	299	JESUS WP B	41
BUT STILL UNKINDE. ART THIS DAY NOTHING MOV'D.	. .	296	JESUS WP A	2
WILL NOTHING YIELD BUT THORNS TO WOUND THY HEAD.	. .	296	JESUS WP A	18
NOTHING BUT MAN, WHEN AMBUSH'D THERE.	. . .	313	THE STONE	17
I WILL DO NOTHING, NOTHING KNOW, NOR SEE	. . .	321	HIDDN TRSR	31
I WILL DO NOTHING, NOTHING KNOW, NOR SEE	. . .	321	HIDDN TRSR	31
WAS JUST THE SAME WITH OURS, AND NOTHING LESS	. .	331	JACOBS PLW	42
WHO KNOWS EARTH NOTHING HATH	. . . .	327	RIGHTSNESS	31
YET, WHEN THY MERCY NOTHING WINS	. . .	335	JUDGEMENT	42
FOR NO THING CAN TO NOTHING FALL BUT STILL	. .	145	RSRCTN +IM	25
AND NOTHING MOVES WITHOUT A SHROWD	. . .	143	DEATH	14
BUT NOTHING BUT THE SNUFF TO ME	. . . .	178	SILENCE	19
AND NOTHING CAN, I HOURELY SEE	. . . .	181	BURIALL	21
NOTING				
WHO NOTING WELL MY VAIN ABEAR	. . . .	282	GARLAND	27
NOTION				
A MOST FAIR NOTION, BUT A VERY NAME.	. . .	330	JACOBS PLW	16
NOUGHT				
AND NOUGHT MUST STAND OF THAT VAST SPACE	. .	147	DAY OF JDG	15
WITHIN THEM NOUGHT	. .	153	THE SEARCH	80
THOUGH THY CLOSE COMMERCE NOUGHT AT ALL IMBARRS	. .	278	THE STARRE	5
NOURISH				
THUS FED BY THEE, WHO DOST ALL BEINGS NOURISH	. .	245	MT. OLV. B	21
NOURISHED				
NOURISHED WITH FAVORS FROM HIS HAND	. . .	302	THE KNOT	11
NUMBER				
'TIS NUMBER MAKES A SCHISM. THRONGS ARE RUDE	. .	330	JACOBS PLW	5
STARS NOW VANISH WITHOUT NUMBER	. . .	212	DAWNING	19
BUT SINCE THY NUMBER IS AS YET .	. . .	350	L'ENVOY	25
NUMBERLESS				
MOST HEYNOUS SINS AND NUMBERLESS.	. . .	333	AGREEMENT	45
NUMBERS				
SUCH NUMBERS TELL THEIR DAYS, WHOSE SPIRITS BE	. .	281	JOY	9
NUMBRED				
MUST NOT BE NUMBRED IN THE YEAR.	. . .	200	NTVTY 2	18
NURSE				
HER YEARLY NURSE, CAME BACK, ENQUIR'D	. . .	151	THE SEARCH	13
SHE MADE THE EARTH THEIR NURSE, AND TOMB	. . .	222	TEMPEST	9
FLYE FROM THEIR NURSES TO THE THRONG	. . .	348	HOLY BIBLE	10
NURST				
DEAR, SECRET GREENNESS. NURST BELOW	. . .	309	THE SEED	25
O'R-CAST				
O'R-CAST WITH THAT COLD DUST. .	. . .	183	THRS A TYE	4
O'R-RAN				
O'R-RAN MY HEART, AND SPIRITED MY BLOUD	. .	244	MT. OLV. B	8
O'TH				
THE COOL O'TH DAY.	. .	2	SON-DAYES	12
OAK				
AND OAK DOTH KNOW I AM. CANST THOU NOT SING.	. .	192	RLS + LSNS	16
OAKE				
EACH OAKE, AND HIGH-WAY KNEW THEM	. . .	197	CORRUPTION	26
OAKES				
OTHERS BENEATH AN OAKES GREENE BOUGHS	. . .	148	RELIGION	7
OATH				
HAD'ST NE'R AN OATH, NOR COMPLEMENT. THOU WERT	. .	154	ISAACS M.	13
OATHES				
NEW SEV'RAL OATHES, AND COMPLEMENTS (TOO) PLENTY.	. .	154	ISAACS M.	16
AND, OATHES ONCE BROKE, THE SOUL CANNOT BE SOUND.	. .	193	RLS + LSNS	46
OBEDIENCE				
IT WITH OBEDIENCE TO THY WIL	. . .	242	MISERY	102
WHISPER'D OBEDIENCE, AND THEIR HEADS INCLIN'D.	. .	229	LAW + GOSP	10
WITH WHAT EXACT OBEDIENCE DO YOU MOVE	. . .	235	CONSTLATN	5
O GIVE IT FUL OBEDIENCE, THAT SO SEIZ'D	. . .	235	MUTINIE	36
BUT SEEKS HE YOUR OBEDIENCE, ORDER, LIGHT	. . .	236	CONSTLATN	29
AND TAUGHT OBEDIENCE BY THE WHOLE CREATION	. .	237	CONSTLATN	55
AND IN OBEDIENCE TO HIS LORD	. . .	314	THE STONE	44
OBEY'D				
OBEY'D, AND LED	. .	140	RGNRTN	35
OBJECT				
AS STRANGE AN OBJECT BROUGHT	. . .	141	RGNRTN	73
THE CHAST, AND LOVELY OBJECT OF THY THOUGHT.	. .	155	ISAACS M.	30
OF THY LORDS HAND, THE OBJECT OF HIS EYE.	. .	306	RAIN-BOW	14
OBJECTS				
BY DISTANCE ALL GOOD OBJECTS FIRST TO DROWN	. .	183	THRS A TYE	19

	PAGE	TITLE	LINE

OBLATION
ACCEPT, DREAD LORD, AND THE POOR OBLATION • • • 190 THE MATCH 13
THE PERFECT, FUL OBLATION FOR ALL SIN • • • 216 DRESSING 10
OBLIVION
SINKS TO A DEAD OBLIVION, AND THOUGH ALL • • • 224 TEMPEST 42
OBSCENE
BUT I AM ALL FILTH, AND OBSCENE • • • • 199 NTVTY 1 23
OBSCURE
WHERE OBSCURE CARES THE MEAN DEFEAT • • • 318 THE ASS 7
THEN LET NOT DUST YOUR EYES OBSCURE • • • 339 DEATH B 28
OBSERVATIONS
THOSE OBSERVATIONS ARE BUT FOLL • • • 322 CHILDEHOOD 25
THE DAY THAT GIVES NO OBSERVATION • • • 202 THE CHECK 46
OBSERVE
OBSERVE GOD IN HIS WORKS, HERE FOUNTAINS FLOW • • • 194 RLS + LSNS 87
BUT DUST (I DID OBSERVE) • • • • 310 THE SEED 75
OBSTRUCTED
TURN IN, IF NOT OBSTRUCTED STILL. • • • 351 L'ENVOY 52
ODDE
AN ODDE DULL SUTOR, HADST THOU BUT THE ART • • • 154 ISAACS M. 14
ODOROUS
ODOROUS OINTMENTS KEPT WITH CARE • • • 304 ST MARY MN 34
ODORS
ODORS, AND MYRRH, AND BALM IN ONE RICH FLOUD • • • 244 MT. OLV. B 7
ODOUR
THE ODOUR I BEQUEATH. • • • • 198 UNPRFTBLNS 18
ODOURS
A THOUSAND ODOURS, WHICH (ALL MIXT) SHE SENDS • • • 156 ISAACS M. 60
OFF-SPRING
HENCE HE IN THUNDER TO THY OFF-SPRING SPOKE. • • • 330 JACOBS PLW 8
OFF'RING
SOME SUCH POOR OFF'RING. • • • • • 215 PRAISE 50
OFFENDER
FORGIVE YOUR PENITENT OFFENDER • • • • 208 REPENTANCE 49
OFFER
THESE THY DEATHS FRUITS I OFFER THEE • • • 264 INTRO. 1 2
TO OFFER UP THE SACRIFICE • • • • 199 NTVTY 1 12
OFFER'D
AND OFFER'D UP SO EARLY UNTO HEAVEN • • • 154 ISAACS M. 6
OFFERS
IF THE WORLD OFFERS TO ME OUGHT • • • • 319 THE ASS 37
OFTIMES
'TWIXT THEE, AND ME, AND OFTIMES CREEP • • • 203 DSRDR + FR 10
OILE
ONLY, ONE POINT ESCAPES THEE. THAT THY OILE • • • 158 THE LAMPE 23
OINTMENT
I SMELL HER SPICES, AND HER OINTMENT YIELDS • • • 267 ASCN-DAY A 21
OINTMENTS
ODOROUS OINTMENTS KEPT WITH CARE • • • 304 ST MARY MN 34
OKE
BENEATH THE OKE AND JUNIPER. • • • • 291 THE JEWS 7
OLD
YET GRIEF AND OLD WOUNDS MAKE HIM SORE DISPLEAS'D • • • 290 THE TIMBER 35
TOWARDS THE OLD AND STILL ENDURING SKIES • • • 289 THE TIMBER 7
WELL FARE THOSE BLESSED DAYS OF OLD • • • 293 BEGGING B 11
TOWARDS OLD MAMRE AND ESHCOLS BROOK. • • • 292 THE JEWS 31
TO SEE MAN LOST, WILL FOR OLD LOVE • • • 292 THE JEWS 36
BAGS THAT WAX OLD MAY PLUNDERED BE • • • 300 PROVIDENCE 21
WE SLIGHT AS OLD AND SOIL'D, THOUGH FRESH AND NEW. • • • 306 RAIN-BOW 2
AND WILT NOT LEAVE ME, WHEN GROWN OLD. • • • 301 PROVIDENCE 45
HEDGES HAVE EARS, SAID THE OLD SOOTH • • • 313 THE STONE 14
I DID ONCE READ IN AN OLD BOOK • • • 312 FAIR+YONG 31
THE OLD, WHITE PROPHETS PLANTED FIRST AND DREST. • • • 326 RIGHTSNESS 2
AND THY OLD ENEMY, WHICH KNOWS • • • 335 JUDGEMENT 29
ASPIRE FOR HOME. THIS SOLOMON OF OLD • • • 279 PALM-TREE 10
MAN OF OLD • • • • • • 269 ASCSN-HYMN 19
LEAVE BEHINDE THEM THE OLD MAN • • • 269 ASCSN-HYMN 12
AND EVER, AS THOU WERT OF OLD • • • 274 WHT SUNDAY 50
FRESH DOTAGE TEMPTS, OR OLD USURPS HIS WILL. • • • 161 DSTRUCTION 16
TO RACK OLD ELEMENTS • • • • • 153 THE SEARCH 88
DOEST THOU THEREFORE OLD TREATIES WAVE • • • 149 RELIGION 23
INTO TH' OLD SILENCE, AND DEAD SLEEP • • • 203 DSRDR + FR 11
IS OLD, AND SLOW • • • • • 181 BURIALL 34
AND LIKE OLD CLOATHS FOLD UP THESE SKIES • • • 349 L'ENVOY 8
OLIVE
MIGHT LIVE, AND SEE THE OLIVE BEAR • • • 292 THE JEWS 15
ONE
TO LEND ME, THOUGH FROM FAR, ONE LOOK. • • • 293 BEGGING B 4
WHERE THE STARV'D EARTH GROANS FOR ONE TEAR. • • • 296 JESUS WP A 16
IN ONE AT ONE TIME, AS SOME FEIGN. • • • 298 JESUS WP B 17
IN ONE AT ONE TIME, AS SOME FEIGN. • • • 298 JESUS WP B 17
BUT ONE GREEN BRANCH AND A WHITE ROBE. • • • 295 PALM-SUNDY 45
IN HEAVEN, ONE GOD IN TRINITIE. • • • 284 TRINITY-SN 3
THY JUDGING ONE, DESCEND, DESCEND. • • • 335 JUDGEMENT 45
AND EVERY ONE CAN SLIGHT HIS LEASE • • • 338 DEATH B 8
BUT THERE WAS ONE • • • • • 338 DEATH B 12
I HAD NOT ONE POOR WORD TO SAY. • • • 333 AGREEMENT 38
AND WITH ONE STRONG, INCESSANT CRY • • • 326 ABELS BLOD 21
BUT FOR ONE THING, THOUGH PURCHAS'D ONCE BEFORE. • • • 321 HIDDN TRSR 34
THE LAST ONE, AND THE LEAST. • • • • 329 TEARS 8

		PAGE	TITLE	LINE
ONE	(CCN'T)			
HAVE ALL CNE SENSE	. . . .	327	RIGHTSNESS	20
ONE AIM AND END, WHC WALKS NOT BY HIS SIGHT.	. . .	327	RIGHTSNESS	21
I WROTE IT DOWN. BUT CNE THAT SAW	. . . .	332	AGREEMENT	1
WAS SHOWN CNE DAY IN A STRANGE CLASS	. . .	313	THE STONE	19
SC BY ONE BEAMY LINE	. . . .	310	THE SEED	69
AS TIME ONE DAY BY ME DID PASS	. . . .	309	THE SEED	49
CNE LIVING DRCP. CNE CRCP LIFE KEEPS.	. . .	308	THE SEED	14
CNE LIVING DRCP. CNE CKCP LIFE KEEPS.	. . .	308	THE SEED	14
VEX NCT, THAT BUT ONE SEES THEE GROW	. . .	309	THE SEED	27
THAT CNE MADE ALL THESE LESSER LIGHTS.	. . .	309	THE SEED	28
CN THEE, WERE ALL MET IN CNE CRCWN	. . .	309	THE SEED	30
THY SERVICE, NOR HIS SOUL ONE DAY.	. . .	301	PROVIDENCE	34
THE LUCKY WORLD SHEWD ME CNE DAY	. . .	302	ORNAMENT	1
WHILE ONE CRYED OUT, WE ARE DISGRAC'D.	. . .	303	ORNAMENT	19
THE YCUTHFUL WORLCS GRAY FATHERS IN ONE KNCT	. . .	306	RAIN-BOW	6
AND MINCES THE COVENANT 'TWIXT ALL AND ONE.	. .	306	RAIN-BOW	18
WHO SHEWS ME BUT CNF GRAIN CF SINCERE LIGHT.	. .	320	HIDDN TRSR	3
THE CNE OF GOCDNESS, PEACE ANC LIFE	. . .	318	THE ASS	3
WITH CNE ATTESTING VOICE DETECT	. . . .	314	THE STONE	40
AS CNE THEN DUST MORE VILE AND VAIN.	. . .	315	THE STONE	59
AND CNE BCRN IN A MANGER	. . . . .	184	PEACE	7
MY SINGLE ONE	. . . .	182	CHRFLNESS	21
TRACK ONE THE CTHER	. . . . . .	179	SILENCE	26
YET I HAVE CNE PEARLE BY WHCSE LIGHT	. . .	179	SILENCE	29
CNE HEARTY TEAR.	. . . .	186	PASSION	49
ONE CCNSTANT SPRING.	. . . . . .	186	PASSION	50
BUT ONE , WHO NEVER CHANGES	. . . .	184	PEACE	19
HCW IN CNE PATH	. . . .	185	PASSION	25
UNSEARCHABLE, NOW WITH CNE WINKE	. . .	163	MT. OLVS A	78
AND FCR ONE TWENTY WE HAVE PAST	. . .	166	THE CALL	56
THE RCDE FOUL, ANC WHERE CNE GCES RIGHT	. .	174	JOY OF LIF	11
CNE TWINKLING RAY	. . . .	174	JOY OF LIF	13
AND WATER IN CNE BEAME	. . . . .	172	MIDNIGHT	23
IS BUT CNE DRAMME, AND WHAT THCU NCW DESCRIEST	.	177	EVNG-WTCH	5
AND EACH HOURE, ONE.	. . . . . .	170	COME, COME	4
BUT ONE HALF GLAUNCE, MCST GLADLY DYE.	. .	168	VNTY SPRIT	34
HAVE CNE LARGE LANGUACE, DEATH.	. . .	201	THE CHECK	28
ONE SINNER DOTH AMEND	. . . . .	200	NTVTY 2	2
NCR CNE DAY BLESSE HIS BIRTH.	. . .	200	NTVTY 2	16
BUT SINCE THOU DICST IN CNE SWEET GLANCE SURVEY	.	198	UNPRFTBLNS	7
HATH CNE BEAME FRCM THY EYES.	. . .	198	UNPRFTBLNS	12
WHAT CNE POOR LEAF DIC EVER I YET FALL	. .	198	UNPRFTBLNS	14
NCT ONE PCOR SHOOT	. . . . . .	203	DSRDR + FR	27
THOU SHALT NOT LOSE ONE MITE. THCUGH WATERS STRAY	.	193	RLS + LSNS	65
THE BREAD WE CAST RETURNS IN FRAUGHTS CNE DAY.	.	193	RLS + LSNS	66
IN THAT DEAD AGE, CNE BEAM I'TH' DARK OUTVIES	.	196	RLS + LSNS	134
THY ACCCUNTS THUS MADE, SPEND IN THE GRAVE ONE HCURE	.	195	RLS + LSNS	121
THER'S CNE SUN MORE STRUNG CN MY BEAD OF DAYS.	.	195	RLS + LSNS	118
FCR ONE, I AM THY TENANT HERE.	. . .	191	THE MATCH	21
THEN SHCULD I (TYED TC CNE SURE STATE)	. .	187	NO DO THEY	15
AFTER WHOLE SHOWRES ONE DROP.	. . .	188	NO DO THEY	38
CNE PATH, AND STRAY	. . . . . .	189	RESOLVE	4
AND ONE OF THESE SEME LCATH	. . . .	148	DAY OF JDG	40
WHEN CNE LOWD BLAST SHALL REND THE DEEPE	. .	147	DAY OF JDG	17
ME THOUGHT I HEARD ONE SINGING THUS.	. .	153	THE SEARCH	74
AN UNDEFIL'D AND NEW-HEAW'D ONE	. . .	152	THE SEARCH	47
WHICH WCULD ONE DAY (BENEATH THE PCLE)	. .	151	THE SEARCH	19
CNE SULLEN BEAME, WHOSE CHARGE IS TO DISPENSE	.	159	MANS FALL	13
A PLENTEOUS WAY (THANKS TC THAT HCLY CNE)	.	159	MANS FALL	22
MY FATHERS JCURNEYS, ANC IN CNE FAIRE STEP	.	159	MANS FALL	28
ONLY, ONE POINT ESCAPES THEE. THAT THY OILE	.	158	THE LAMPE	23
TRANSPLANTED THUS, ONF LEAFE CF HIS T'AWAKE	.	158	MANS FALL	5
NCR DCST THOU SPEND ONE TEARE IN VAIN, FCR STILL	.	158	THE LAMPE	17
UP IN ONE CLOUD, AND SO RETURNS THE SKIES	.	156	ISAACS M.	61
BUT HERE WAS NE'R A CCMPLEMENT, NCT ONE	.	155	ISAACS M.	31
THY JUDGING ONE. DESCENC, DESCEND.	. .	340	RGNRTN	5
A WARD, AND STILL IN BONDS, ONE DAY	. .	139	RGNRTN	10
ONE EVERLASTING SABOTH THERE SHALL RUNNE	. .	146	RSRCTN +IM	69
SHALL ONE DAY RISE, AND CLOATH'D WITH SHINING LIGHT	.	145	RSRCTN +IM	47
LCRD, THEN SAID I, CN ME CNE BREATH	. .	141	RGNRTN	90
'TIS A SAC LAND, THAT IN CNE CAY	. . .	142	DEATH	1
MY ONE PCOR SAND	. . . . . .	275	PROFFER	26
CNE SILENT STAR MAY INTERLINE.	. . .	273	WHT SUNDAY	38
WITH DEW BY NIGHT, BUT CNF YOU CANNOT SEE	.	280	PALM-TREE	23
WITH THAT ONE GRAINS INFUSED WEALTH	. .	206	REPENTANCE	4
THAT CNE POOR BLOSSOME.	. . . .	215	PRAISE	56
BREAK, AND THE SHADCWS FLEE, TCUCH WITH ONE COAL	.	216	DRESSING	3
GIVE TO THY WRETCHED CNE	. . . .	216	DRESSING	13
NCT ONE MINUTE IN THE YEAR	. . . .	214	PRAISE	17
ANGER FCR ONE SHORT FIT	. . . .	216	DRESSING	28
NCT ONE BEAM TRIUMPHS, BUT FRCM FAR	. .	212	DAWNING	23
PART CF HIS MANSICN. HE CNE DAY	. . .	225	RETIREMENT	7
WERE ALL THE YEAR ONE CCNSTANT SUN-SHINE, WEE	.	222	AFFLICTION	21
AND ONE WHO DRANK IT THUS, ASSURES THAT YCU	.	244	THE SAP	45
ODORS, AND MYRRH, AND BALM IN CNE RICH FLOUD	.	244	MT. OLV. B	7
AND WITH CNE GLAUNCE (CCULD HE THAT GAIN)	.	242	MISERY	95
HE HATH NC RCCT, NOR TO ONE PLACE IS TY'D	.	246	MAN	16
WITHOUT ONE THOUGHT CF CAY.	. . .	238	SHEPHEARDS	8
OF SIN, AND DEATH I SCJCURN, YET CNE EYE	.	234	MUTINIE	20

		PAGE	TITLE	LINE
ONE	(CON'T)			
HATH NOT SO MUCH AS ONE POOR LOOK.		240	MISERY	28
FOR THIS ONE MORE.		230	LAW + GOSP	26
ONE WHISPER'D THUS		233	THE WORLD	58
PURSUED HIM WITH ONE SHOUT.		232	THE WORLD	22
WHERE HE DID CLUTCH HIS PREY, BUT ONE DID SEE		232	THE WORLD	25
YET WOULD NOT PLACE ONE PEECE ABOVE, BUT LIVES		232	THE WORLD	34
AND HUG'D EACH ONE HIS PELF		232	THE WORLD	37
THAT LIKE TRUE SHEEP, ALL IN ONE FOLD		350	L'ENVOY	47
WE MAY BE FED, AND ONE MINDE HOLD.		350	L'ENVOY	48
OPE				
HIS WATCHFUL EYE IS EVER OPE		220	PSALM 121	7
OPEN				
OPEN MY DESOLATE ROOMS, MY GLOOMIE BREST		216	DRESSING	5
MADE OPEN HOUSE.		210	FAITH	8
OPEN MY ROCKIE HEART, AND FIL		242	MISERY	101
AND IN THE OPEN AIRE		147	DAY OF JDG	22
TO ALL THAT SEEK THEE, BEAR AN OPEN HEART.		193	RLS + LSNS	55
WHOSE HANDS ARE OPEN AS THINE EYES.		301	PROVIDENCE	42
AND SPRED AND OPEN TO THY WILL.		308	THE SEED	20
SO HEAR THAT THOU MUST OPEN. OPEN TO		283	LOVE-SICK	17
SO HEAR THAT THOU MUST OPEN. OPEN TO		283	LOVE-SICK	17
THY BOUNTEOUS OPEN HAND HELPS THEM AT NEED		286	PSALM 104	75
AND OFT LEFT OPEN WOULD'ST CONVEY		348	HOLY BIBLE	19
OPENING				
OPENING THE WAY.		341	THE FEAST	65
AND OPENING SHOWERS (RESTRAIN'D FROM HARM)		337	PSALM 65	36
OPENLY				
NOT SPARING OPENLY TO SAY		272	WHIT SUNDAY	15
OPENS				
IT NEVER OPENS, I CAN TELL.		277	COCK-CRWNG	28
AND HEAV'NS GATE OPENS, WHEN THIS WORLDS IS SHUT.		192	RLS + LSNS	12
THE KEY THAT OPENS TO ALL MYSTERIES		198	SCRIPTURES	7
OPERATE				
WHICH STRONGLY OPERATE, THOUGH WITHOUT PAINS		320	HIDDN TRSR	22
OPES				
AS THY HAND OPES, OR SHUTS.		219	HOLY COMM.	13
OPPRESSED				
BUT SITT'ST OPPRESSED IN THE SHADE		217	EASTER-DAY	4
OPPRESSED I		161	DSTRCCTION	33
OPPREST				
MY SELF OF REASON, TILL OPPREST		240	MISERY	42
AND TRUTH (OPPREST HERE) GETS THE PRIZE.		318	THE ASS	28
ORDAIN				
ORDAIN NIGHT TOO.		221	AFFLICTION	8
THESE MEANS ORDAIN		340	THE FEAST	29
ORDAIN'D				
DID NOT HE, WHO ORDAIN'D THE DAY		221	AFFLICTION	7
GOD ORDER'D MOTION, BUT ORDAIN'D NO REST.		246	MAN	28
ORDAIN'D, AND MADE TO BEAR HIS MAKER.		295	PALM-SUNDY	29
ORDER				
BUT SEEKS HE YOUR OBEDIENCE, ORDER, LIGHT		236	CONSTLATN	29
IN ORDER, PEACE, AND LOVE		237	CONSTLATN	54
IN SACRED HYMNES, AND ORDER, THE GREAT CHIME		177	MRNG-WTCH	17
FAIR, ORDER'D LIGHT (WHOSE MOTION WITHOUT NOISE		235	CONSTLATN	1
GOD ORDER'D MOTION, BUT ORDAIN'D NO REST.		246	MAN	28
OUGHT				
WITHOUT COMMAND YOU NEVER ACTED OUGHT		236	CONSTLATN	35
OR TAUGHT MY SOUL TO FANCY OUGHT		169	RETREATE	5
E'RE WE CAN LISP, OR OUGHT DISCUSSE		166	THE CALL	48
OF OUGHT BUT INFLUENCE.		186	NO DO THEY	2
IF THE WORLD OFFERS TO ME OUGHT		319	THE ASS	37
I'LE MARVEL NOT AT OUGHT THEY DO		317	MEN OF WAR	33
OUT-DUTY				
NOR ANY HERB OUT-DUTY ME.		281	THE FAVOUR	10
OUT-GOE				
BUT STILL THOU DOEST OUT-GOE ME, I CAN SEE		158	THE LAMPE	9
OUT-GROW				
DIDDST THY SWIFT YEERS IN PIETY OUT-GROW		156	ISAACS M.	68
OUT-LIV'D				
WEEP THAT I HAVE OUT-LIV'D		311	THE SEED	86
OUT-RUN				
SO RISE AND RUN, AS TO OUT-RUN THESE SKIES		283	LOVE-SICK	6
OUT-RUNS				
OUT-RUNS THE EARTH, AND LINES THE UTMOST POLE.		193	RLS + LSNS	54
OUTGOINGS				
THE OUTGOINGS OF THE EVEN AND DAWN		336	PSALM 65	25
OUTLAST				
OUTLAST THE SHEEP		173	CONTENT	12
OUTLIVE				
ALMOST OUTLIVE OUR NAME.		166	THE CALL	57
OUTLOOK				
COULD MAN OUTLOOK THAT MARK.		271	ALL GONE	20
OUTSHINE				
A GRIEF THAT SHALL OUTSHINE ALL JOYS		299	JESUS WP B	46
OUTSIDE				
THUS HAST THOU PLAC'D IN MANS OUTSIDE		166	THE CALL	58
OUTVIE				
SOUGHT OUT WHAT MIGHT OUTVIE MY SCORE.		207	REPENTANCE	32
OUTVIES				
IN THAT DEAD AGE, ONE BEAM I'TH' DARK OUTVIES		196	RLS + LSNS	134

	PAGE	TITLE	LINE
OUTWARD			
AND OUTWARD UTENSILS THESE GLORIES ARE	225	RETIREMENT	5
WITHIN IT SELF AN OUTWARD TEST.	309	THE SEED	42
OUTWEIGH'D			
MY SINS ALONE OUTWEIGH'D THEM ALL.	208	REPENTANCE	46
OVER-RUN			
AND OVER-RUN MY HEART AND HEAD.	336	PSALM 65	6
OVERCAM'ST			
THOU OVERCAM'ST MY SINFUL STRENGTH	348	HOLY BIBLE	24
OVERCAME			
WHO BY NO BLOOD (HERE) OVERCAME	317	MEN OF WAR	51
OVERCAST			
ANOTHER MIRTH, A MIRTH THOUGH OVERCAST	281	JOY	14
OVERCOME			
BUT PATIENT, MEEK, AND OVERCOME	316	MEN OF WAR	19
AND ALL THY SAINTS DO OVERCOME	317	MEN OF WAR	27
OVERFLOW			
BUT E'R MY EYES COULD OVERFLOW THEIR BRINK . . .	213	ADMISSION	11
SUFFER NO MORE THIS DUST TO OVERFLOW . . .	191	THE MATCH	36
OVERFLOWS			
(PITY WHICH OVERFLOWS THY HEART)	299	JESUS WP B	39
OVERLOOK			
AND IN YOUR VAST PROGRESSIONS OVERLOOK . . .	235	CONSTLATN	7
OVERTHROW			
OF THE DISTREST, HASTING THEIR OVERTHROW. . . .	327	RIGHTSNESS	27
OWLS			
WHILE OWLS AND SATYRS HOWL.	288	THE BIRD	28
OWN			
INLIGHTNING HIS OWN LITTLE SPHERE	288	THE BIRD	20
HATE NOT THINE OWN DEAR GIFT AND TOKEN. . . .	294	BEGGING B	18
AND THEIR OWN ANGELS SHINE AND SING	295	PALM-SUNDY	22
THAT THOU FORGOTT'ST THINE OWN, FOR THOU DIDST SEAL .	283	LOVE-SICK	20
BLEW THROUGH THY LODGING, WHERE THY OWN WARM WIND .	287	THE BIRD	2
THEY SAID, MY OWN HANDS DID REMOVE . . .	333	AGREEMENT	41
BEFORE BRIGHT STARS, AND GODS OWN BEAMS. . . .	321	CHILDEHOOD	12
BUT HIS OWN LIVING WORKS DID MY LORD HOLD . . .	323	THE NIGHT	21
WHO ARGUES, FOLLOWS HIS OWN HEAD.	318	THE ASS	24
YET WILL NOT HE BY HIS OWN LIGHT	314	THE STONE	32
A PROCESS, WHICH EV'N MANS OWN EYE	314	THE STONE	35
TO LODGE LIGHT, AND INCREASE HER OWN. . . .	315	DWELLNG-PL	10
AND LEAD BY MY OWN FOOLISH FIRE	311	FAIR+YONG	5
WHOM FOR OUR HEAD WE OWN.	302	THE KNOT	12
YEA GODS OWN BLOOD WE TREAD UPON AND SLIGHT. . .	307	RAIN-BOW	30
AND GODS OWN LODGING (THOUGH HE COULD NOT LACK) . .	238	SHEPHEARDS	29
PROVE MY OWN SHAME AND MISERIE.	240	MISERY	44
I BREAK THE FENCE MY OWN HANDS MADE	240	MISERY	21
HIS OWN HANDS WITH THE DUST	232	THE WORLD	33
THEY REST AND DREAM HOMES OF THEIR OWN. . . .	228	PILGRIMAGE	8
AFTER THY OWN, NOT MINE.	213	ADMISSION	26
UNTO HIS OWN INHERITANCE	218	EASTER HYM	16
(TOUCH'D WITH THE GUILT OF MY OWN WAY) . . .	207	REPENTANCE	28
STILL THY OWN FOE, AND MINE, FOR TO THIS DAY . .	225	RETIREMENT	16
THOUGH HE KNOWS THESE, AND HATH MORE OF HIS OWN .	224	TEMPEST	38
SHALL THY OWN IMAGE THINK IT MUCH	276	COCK-CRWNG	15
WAS THINE OWN ANSWER TO THE STUBBORN JEW. . . .	268	ASCN-DAY A	60
BESIDES, THY METHOD WITH THY OWN	273	WHT SUNDAY	29
THY OWN DEAR PEOPLE PENS OUR TIMES	273	WHT SUNDAY	30
OF MY OWN FRAILTY DROPT DOWN MANY A TEAR . . .	247	I WALKT	31
BUT THIS THY OWN GIFT, GIVEN TO ME.	266	INTRO. 2	30
IS BOTH HIS OWN JOY, AND HIS MAKERS TOO. . . .	193	RLS + LSNS	51
AND I WIL MEND MY OWN WITHOUT DELAYES . . .	188	RELAPSE	11
FOR TEARS ARE NOT THINE OWN. IF THOU GIV'ST WORDS .	194	RLS + LSNS	68
THOU KNEW'ST BUT THY OWN GOOD.	202	THE CHECK	39
O GODS OWN BLOUD AWAKE THEE. HE BIDS BEWARE . .	202	THE CHECK	41
BUT WHAT THEIR OWN HOMES WEAVE	173	CONTENT	8
DOUBLING THY GRIEFS, WHEN NONE WOULD OWN THEE. . .	185	PASSION	29
IN THY OWN PRECIOUS, SAVING TEARES.	184	PASSION	9
BUT I WILL BE MY OWN DEATHS-HEAD. AND THOUGH . .	183	THRS A TYE	21
ON MY OWN DUST, MEER DUST IT IS	347	THE BOOK	21
THY OWN BRIGHT SELF OVER EACH HEAD	349	L'ENVOY	10
TO DECK THEIR OWN, THEN GIVE THY SAINTS . . .	350	L'ENVOY	35
DARES OWN THE TRUTH, AND SHEW THE ILL. . . .	350	L'ENVOY	38
MY OWN ILL WAY.	342	OBSEQUIES	4
EVEN LIFES OWN BREATH.	342	OBSEQUIES	8
IN MY OWN SENSE	342	OBSEQUIES	10
IF NOT THY MIGHTY LOVE, MY OWN DEFENSE. . . .	342	OBSEQUIES	12
OWN'D			
BE OWN'D, SAV'D, SAINTED BY YOU THREE. . . .	284	TRINITY-SN	9
OWNE			
THEN MAKE MY SOULE WHITE AS HIS OWNE	167	THE CALL	90
AND, BY THEIR OWNE WEAKE SHINE, DID SEARCH THE SPRINGS .	146	RSRCTN +IM	53
OWNERS			
THEY SHAME THEIR OWNERS, AND THE HEARERS TROUBLE. . .	194	RLS + LSNS	72
OYL			
THY BEAMS HOME WITH THEE. TRIM THY LAMP, BUY OYL .	195	RLS + LSNS	110
BRINGS FORTH, WITH WINE, OYL, BREAD. ALL WHICH INFUSE .	285	PSALM 104	43
THOU ART THE OYL AND THE WINE-HOUSE. . . .	332	AGREEMENT	19
OYLE			
POURE OYLE UPON THE STONES, WEEP FOR THY SIN . .	192	RLS + LSNS	23
PACK			
STARS SHUT UP SHOP, MISTS PACK AWAY	210	FAITH	19

	PAGE	TITLE	LINE
PACKING			
DEATH, AND DARKNESS GET YCU PACKING	218	EASTER HYM	1
PAGE			
AND YET, AS IN NIGHTS GLCCMY PAGE	273	WHT SUNDAY	37
APPCINTING ERRCUR FCR MY PAGE	282	GARLAND	7
EACH PAGE OF THINE HATH TRUE LIFE IN'T	332	AGREEMENT	23
A FAIR, WHITE PAGE OF THIN	310	THE SEED	59
IN THE SAME PAGE THY HUMBLE GRAVE	310	THE SEED	71
PAID			
WHO LENDS, NOT TO BE PAID	328	RIGHTSNESS	40
O SEEING THOU HAST PAID CUR SCCRE	350	L'ENVOY	23
PAIN			
DESTRCYING CNELY DEATH AND PAIN	347	THE BOOK	28
THIS CAY I BRING FCR ALL THY PAIN	345	THE WREATH	12
THY CAUSLESS PAIN. AND SAC AS DEATH.	345	THE WREATH	13
SHUT CUT ALL PAIN AND EACH CISEASE.	319	THE ASS	63
REPEATED SIGHS THY KINDE HEART PAIN	298	JESUS WP B	4
WITHOLT ALL PAIN	248	I WALKT	60
WHICH BCRE MY PAIN.	230	LAW + GOSP	36
TC LOCK HIM CUT OF ALL HIS PAIN	242	MISERY	96
WHAT PAIN DIDST THOU	184	PASSION	5
PAINEFULL			
WHOSE PAINEFULL THROWS YIELC MANY SCNS	167	THE CALL	76
PAINES			
IN TH'ONE LATE PAINES	139	RGNRTN	31
PAINFLL			
O PAINFLL CRCSS, MY BED OF REST.	341	THE FEAST	63
PAINS			
BE SURE UNDER PAINS OF DEATH	281	JOY	21
LIKE CHRONIC PAINS, WHICH SURELY KILL, THCUGH SLCW.	327	RIGHTSNESS	30
WHICH STRCNGLY OPERATE, THCUGH WITHCUT PAINS	320	HIDDN TRSR	22
PAINT			
CCNFEST, THE WORLC DIC CNLY PAINT AND LIE.	244	MT. CLV. B	10
THEN, WHO WOULD TRULY LIMNE THEE CUT, MUST PAINT	156	ISAACS M.	71
AND PAINTED TRIMMING TAKES DCWN BCTH HIS EYES	224	TEMPEST	46
PAINTS			
HE IS STILL LEPRCUS, THAT STILL PAINTS.	306	ST MARY MN	71
PAIRE			
I FOUND A PAIRE CF SCALES	139	RGNRTN	29
PAISAGE			
SC HAVE I KNOWN SCME BEALTEOUS PAISAGE RISE	245	MT. CLV. B	17
PAITED			
BEYCNC A CURLED LCCK, OR PAITED FACE.	155	ISAACS M.	38
PALE			
HCW PALE, AND BLOUDIE	185	PASSION	34
PALESTINE			
WHILE PALESTINE WAS FAST A SLEEP, AND LAY	238	SHEPHEARDS	7
PALM			
THEN LIKE THE PALM, THCLGH WRCNG, I'LE BEAR	295	PALM-SUNDY	38
PALM-TREES			
THE TLRTLE THEN IN PALM-TREES MCLRNS	288	THE BIRD	27
PALME			
THAT SHADY CITY CF PALME TREES	170	RETREATE	26
PALMES			
WHERE ARE THY PALMES, THY BRANCHES, AND THY VERSE.	217	EASTER-DAY	11
PALMS			
OF WINGS, AND CHERUBIMS, AND PALMS FORETOLD.	279	PALM-TREE	12
DEAR FEAST OF PALMS, CF FLOWERS AND CEW.	295	PALM-SUNDY	30
PANGS			
WHERE THRCUGH THICK PANGS, HIGH AGCNIES	310	THE SEED	65
BLT DARK AND DEEP PANGS TC THY SIGHT.	264	INTRO. 1	4
AND INFANTS WITH THY PANGS CCNTEST	218	EASTER HYM	11
PAPYR			
THCU KNEW'ST THIS PAPYR, WHEN IT WAS	347	THE BOOK	5
PARADISE			
TRANSPLANTED PARADISE, CCDS WALKING HCUR.	2	SON-DAYES	11
AND DREAMS OF PARADISE AND LICHT.	276	COCK-CRWNG	6
OF PARADISE, COULC MAKE MAN FADE	312	FAIR+YONG	38
TC LOSE HIM TCO, AS WELL AS PARADISE)	307	RAIN-BOW	24
BUT OLT OF PARADISE MUST CREEPE	166	THE CALL	68
MADE THCSE WILD SHADES A PARADISE	152	THE SEARCH	62
AFFCRDED VISITS, AND STILL PARADISE LAY	197	CORRUPTION	23
PARAN			
AND SHINE FROM PARAN, WHEN A FIRIE LAW	229	LAW + GOSP	2
PARASITES			
BE STILL BLACK PARASITES	274	PROFFER	1
PARCELL'D			
HCW IS MAN PARCELL'D CUT. HOW EV'RY HCUR	222	TEMPEST	1
LOOSE, PARCELL'D HEARTS WIL FREEZE. THE SUN	189	RESOLVE	13
PARCELLS			
STRIVING TO SAVE THE WHCLE, BY PARCELLS CYE	161	OSTRQCTION	34
PARCH'D			
AND SCMETHING COOLD THE PARCH'C, AND THIRSTIE ISLE	156	ISAACS M.	58
ON SOME PARCH'D BANK, CROWN'D WITH A FLCWRIE WREATH.	244	MT. CLV. B	6
DCEST WATER THE PARCH'D HILLS, WHOSE BREACHES CLCSE	285	PSALM 104	39
PARCHT			
ALL HER PARCHT BOSCME TC NILE'S SHORE	151	THE SEARCH	12
PARLE			
THE CREATLRES JUBILE, GCDS PARLE WITH DUST.	2	SON-DAYES	13
PART			
THE DLST, OF WHICH I AM A PART	207	REPENTANCE	35

		PAGE	TITLE	LINE
PART	**(CON'T)**			
BUT GIVE THEM IN THOSE STREAMS A PART	. . . .	208	REPENTANCE	55
LIKE STRINGS, STRETCH EV'RY PART	. . . .	222	AFFLICTION	39
PART OF HIS MANSION. HE ONE DAY	. . . .	225	RETIREMENT	7
SO AFTER THINE, THAT ALL, AND EV'RY PART	. . . .	213	ADMISSION	27
WHICH IN THY MUSICK BEARS NO PART	. . . .	214	MISERY	82
AND HAVING THUS PERFORM'D THAT PART	. . . .	240	MISERY	19
WHEN WE TWO PART, I WILL A JOURNEY MAKE	. . . .	280	PALM-TREE	25
LOATH HENCE TO PART, AT LAST I RISE	. . . .	152	THE SEARCH	33
DESCRY SOME PART OF HIS GREAT LIGHT.	. . . .	167	VNTY SPRIT	8
WOULDST MAKE EACH PART	. . . .	182	CHRFLNESS	18
FOR DUST IN EVERY PART	. . . .	179	CHRCH-SVC	7
IF TRIALS COME, THIS WIL MAKE GOOD THY PART	. . . .	193	RLS + LSNS	57
BE GODS ALONE, AND CHOOSE THE BETTER PART.	. . . .	192	RLS + LSNS	36
I WOULD I HAD IN MY BEST PART	. . . .	199	NTVTY 1	19
THY SUN MUST SHINE IN EVERY PART.	. . . .	294	BEGGING B	16
WHERE THOU TOO HAST BUT THE LEAST PART	. . . .	315	DWELLNG-PL	15
FOR ME TO HAVE IN HIM A PART.	. . . .	340	THE FEAST	30
SUCH A SURE PART	. . . .	340	THE FEAST	31
O BOOK. LIFES GUIDE. HOW SHALL WE PART	. . . .	348	HOLY BIBLE	1
PARTAKE				
AND IN HIS RESURRECTION PARTAKE	. . . .	217	EASTER-DAY	6
PARTAKER				
IS IN THESE JOYS AN HIGH PARTAKER	. . . .	295	PALM-SUNDY	28
PARTAKES				
YEA, 'TIS A DEATH PARTAKES OF HELL.	. . . .	277	COCK-CRWNG	26
AND HERE PARTAKES, WHERE HAVING STOOD AWHILE	. . . .	155	ISAACS M.	57
PARTS				
IN SEV'RALL PARTS SHALL WANT A NAME	. . . .	177	EVNG-WTCH	6
WHERE WEEPING VIRTUE PARTS WITH MAN.	. . . .	322	CHILDEHOOD	32
WHICH CAUSE SOLUTION IN ALL PARTS	. . . .	350	L'ENVOY	40
THROUGH ALL MY PARTS, AND LIKE A QUICK	. . . .	340	THE FEAST	45
PASS				
THE COMMON PASS	. . . .	343	WATER-FALL	7
ARE NO MORE SEEN, JUST SO PASS MEN.	. . . .	344	WATER-FALL	36
AND THROUGH THY CREATURES PIERCE AND PASS	. . . .	349	L'ENVOY	11
SEEN LONG BEFORE THIS CAME TO PASS	. . . .	295	PALM-SUNDY	27
AS TIME ONE DAY BY ME DID PASS	. . . .	309	THE SEED	49
PASS THY SOLITARY YEARS	. . . .	281	JOY	28
MY PERSPECTIVE (STILL) AS THEY PASS	. . . .	271	ALL GONE	38
THEY PASS AS AT THE LAST GREAT DAY, AND RUN	. . . .	268	ASCN-DAY A	29
WHILE ALL THE PLANETS DID UNCLOUDED PASS.	. . . .	268	ASCN-DAY A	46
PASSAGE				
THE PASSAGE IS, HE TERM'D A GRATE	. . . .	207	REPENTANCE	9
AND PASSAGE THROUGH THESE LOOMS	. . . .	246	MAN	27
PASSE				
OR BEAM PASSE BY	. . . .	171	COME, COME	12
HERE LONG MUST PASSE	. . . .	174	JOY OF LIF	18
CONCERNING THEE, MUST PASSE.	. . . .	166	THE CALL	49
AND AS WE PASSE	. . . .	165	THE CALL	21
BUT MISTS, AND SHADOWS PASSE	. . . .	146	RSRCTN +IM	52
WHEN LIKE A SCROWLE THE HEAVENS SHAL PASSE	. . . .	147	DAY OF JDG	13
FOR A PRESERVING SPIRIT DOTH STILL PASSE	. . . .	145	RSRCTN +IM	31
WHILE WE PASSE BY	. . . .	201	THE CHECK	22
PASSING				
PASSING THROUGH THE EARTHS DARKE VEINES	. . . .	150	RELIGION	34
PASSIONS				
LEAVES ME A SLAVE TO PASSIONS, AND MY FATE.	. . .	158	MANS FALL	8
NEITHER HIS BLOUDY PASSIONS MIND	. . .	200	NTVTY 2	15
PASSIVE				
HIS PASSIVE COTTAGE, WHICH (THOUGH LAID ASIDE)	. .	145	RSRCTN +IM	45
PAST				
THEN, WHEN THE GASTLY TWELVE WAS PAST	. . .	143	DEATH	19
(SOME SUCH SHOWRES PAST)	. . .	160	THE SHOWRE	17
HIGH-NOON THUS PAST, THY TIME DECAYS, PROVIDE	. .	195	RLS + LSNS	103
AND FOR ONE TWENTY WE HAVE PAST	. . .	166	THE CALL	56
I RIFLED QUITE, AND HAVING PAST	. . .	168	VNTY SPRIT	13
AND WALKING FROM HIS SUN, WHEN PAST	. . .	178	SILENCE	9
THE PAST DAIES ACCIDENTS DO SUMME	. . .	228	PILGRIMAGE	3
PAST THOUGHT OF HEART	. . .	215	PRAISE	34
THIS PAST, I THREW THE CLOTHES QUITE O'R HIS HEAD	.	247	I WALKT	29
OF PAST DAYS, WHERE SAD HEAV'N DID SHED	. .	309	THE SEED	53
TILL TRUTH THROUGH ALL THE WORLD BE PAST	. .	305	ST MARY MN	52
PAST ORE THY HEAD. MANY LIGHT HEARTS AND WINGS	.	289	THE TIMBER	3
THEN TRUE REMORSE, WHEN WITH PAST SINS AT STRIFE.	.	290	THE TIMBER	28
SOME UP THE MOUNTAINS PAST BY SECRET WAYS	. .	285	PSALM 104	23
THIS PAST, THE SUN SHINES ON THE EARTH, AND THY	.	286	PSALM 104	61
PASTURES				
PASTURES OF LIFE, WHERE THE LAMB GOES.	. . .	319	THE ASS	52
WHOSE LEADERS TO THOSE PASTURES, AND CLEER SPRINGS	.	238	SHEPHEARDS	3
PATH				
TO FIX MY STEPS, AND WHATSOEVER PATH	. . .	234	MUTINIE	33
THE PATH UNTO THE HOUSE OF LIGHT.	. . .	276	COCK-CRWNG	10
QUICKLY WOULD I MAKE MY PATH EVEN	. . .	321	CHILDEHOOD	7
FAIR, SOLITARY PATH. WHOSE BLESSED SHADES	. .	326	RIGHTSNESS	1
CHEATING HIMSELF, THAT MAN WALKS IN THIS PATH.	.	328	RIGHTSNESS	54
HOW IN ONE PATH	. . .	185	PASSION	25
ONE PATH, AND STRAY	. . .	189	RESOLVE	4
THIS HIDEOUS PATH	. . .	188	RELAPSE	10
PATH-WAY				
THE CLOUDS THY CHARIOTS ARE, AND THY PATH-WAY	. .	284	PSALM 104	11

		PAGE	TITLE	LINE
PATHS				
PATHS THAT ARE HIDDEN FROM THE VULTURS EYES	• • •	320	HIDDN TRSR	12
AND ALL THY PATHS DROP FATNESS ROUND	• • •	337	PSALM 65	40
WHAT SILENT PATHS, WHAT SHADES, AND "CELLS	• • •	153	THE SEARCH	69
PATIENCE				
HERE IS THE PATIENCE OF THE SAINTS	• • •	316	MEN OF WAR	7
DEAR JESUS GIVE ME PATIENCE HERE	• • •	317	MEN OF WAR	37
HERE IS THE PATIENCE OF THE SAINTS. THIS TREE	• • •	280	PALM-TREE	21
PATIENT				
BUT PATIENT, MEEK, AND OVERCOME	• • •	316	MEN OF WAR	19
HOW MEEK, AND PATIENT WAS THY SPIRIT.	• • •	185	PASSION	38
PATRIARCH				
FIRST, A YOUNG PATRIARCH, THEN A MARRI'D SAINT.	• •	156	ISAACS M.	72
WERE PATRIARCH, SAINTS, AND KINGS	• • •	238	SHEPHEARDS	4
PAY				
US DOUBLE PAY.	• • • • • •	213	ADMISSION	24
MY SCORES DID PAY	• • • • •	188	RELAPSE	22
THAT SWORN MEMORIAL DULY PAY	• • •	326	ABELS BLOD	30
A FISH SHALL ALL MY TRIBUTE PAY	• • •	300	PROVIDENCE	15
THEN COMMON PAY	• • • • • •	342	OBSEQUIES	2
PAYD				
WAS'T NOT ENOUGH THAT THOU HADST PAYD THE PRICE	• •	219	HOLY COMM.	33
PAYING				
PAYING THE DAY ITS DEBTS.	• • • • •	201	THE CHECK	17
PAYS				
BUT IF HE PAYS, WHO LOVES MUCH, THEN	• • •	329	TEARS	15
PEACE				
WHO SEEKS AND FOLLOWS PEACE	• • •	327	RIGHTSNESS	34
BUT WHAT (LIKE HIS, WHOSE BLOOD PEACE BRINGS)	• •	326	ABELS BLOD	39
WHOSE PEACE BUT BY SOME ANGELS WING OR VOICE	• •	324	THE NIGHT	39
STAND FIRM BY THEE, AND HAVE SURE PEACE.	• • •	336	PSALM 65	18
THE THRONE WHERE PEACE AND POWER REST.	• • •	299	JESUS WP B	31
MEANS ONELY THOSE, WHO BROKE (IN LIFE) THY PEACE.	• •	289	THE TIMBER	20
DEAR LORD. RESTORE THY ANCIENT PEACE	• • •	294	BEGGING B	21
GIVE ME HUMILITY AND PEACE	• • •	317	MEN OF WAR	41
THE ONE OF GOODNESS, PEACE AND LIFE	• • •	318	THE ASS	3
WHERE LIGHT, JOY, HEALTH AND PERFECT PEACE	• • •	319	THE ASS	62
BRIGHT PLEDGE OF PEACE AND SUN-SHINE. THE SURE TYE	• •	306	RAIN-BOW	13
PEACH, PEACE. I BLUSH TO HEAR THEE. WHEN THOU ART	• •	201	THE CHECK	1
THE TOKENS OF THE CHURCH, AND PEACE	• • •	149	RELIGION	28
THERE GROWES THE FLOWRE OF PEACE	• • •	184	PEACE	14
SWEET PEACE SITS CROWN'D WITH SMILES	• • •	184	PEACE	6
PEACE, PEACE. I KNOW 'TWAS BRAVE	• • •	173	CONTENT	1
PEACE, PEACE. I KNOW 'TWAS BRAVE	• • •	173	CONTENT	1
GOE, SLEEP IN PEACE. AND WHEN THOU LYEST	• • •	177	EVNG-WTCH	3
THEN MAY HIS PEACE BE WTIH THEE, AND EACH DUST	• •	177	EVNG-WTCH	7
PEACE, PEACE. IT IS NOT SO. THOU DOEST MISCALL	• •	221	AFFLICTION	1
PEACE, PEACE. IT IS NOT SO. THOU DOEST MISCALL	• •	221	AFFLICTION	1
EXCHANGE THEIR PEACE, AND FURRS.	• • •	222	AFFLICTION	34
IN ORDER, PEACE, AND LOVE	• • • •	237	CONSTLATN	54
YET IS THERE PEACE STILL, AND NO WAR.	• • •	236	CONSTLATN	32
AND NO NEW BUSINESS BREAKS THEIR PEACE.	• • •	245	MAN	11
I STORM AT THEE, CALLING MY PEACE	• • •	242	MISERY	83
WHICH TO THY PEACE ARE BUT MEER NOISE.	• • •	214	MISERY	60
WHAT PEACE DOTH NOW	• • • •	247	I WALKT	34
SHEW ME THY PEACE	• • • • •	248	I WALKT	55
THIS HEALING PEACE	• • • • •	341	THE FEAST	56
GLADNESS, AND PEACE, AND HOPE, AND LOVE	• • •	348	HOLY BIBLE	27
AND DYING MAK'ST ME GO IN PEACE.	• • •	348	HOLY BIBLE	34
SO SHALL WE KNOW IN WAR AND PEACE	• • •	351	L'ENVOY	59
DISOEIN TREADS ON THE PEACEFUL NAME	• • •	214	MISERY	68
THEN PEACEFUL, SIGNAL BOW, BUT IN A CLOUD	• •	307	RAIN-BOW	33
PEACH				
PEACH, PEACE. I BLUSH TO HEAR THEE. WHEN THOU ART	• •	201	THE CHECK	1
PEARL				
FOR THIS RICH PEARL, LIKE SOME MORE COMMON STONE	• •	330	JACOBS PLW	17
SHEW ME THAT PEARL I SOUGHT ELSEWHERE.	• • •	348	HOLY BIBLE	26
PEARL'D				
ALL PEARL'D WITH TEARS, AND MAY	• • •	310	THE SEED	63
PEARLE				
YET I HAVE ONE PEARLE BY WHOSE LIGHT	• • •	179	SILENCE	29
MADE ME A STARRE, A PEARLE, OR A RAIN-BOW	• •	161	DSTRUCTION	6
PEARLS				
WHICH, SCATTER'D IN A THOUSAND PEARLS, EACH FLOWRE	•	155	ISAACS M.	56
AND SPRINGS, LIKE DISSOLV'D PEARLS THEIR STREAMS DID POUR		268	ASCN-DAY A	47
PEARLY				
THOU ART THE FAITHFUL, PEARLY ROCK	• • •	333	AGREEMENT	31
PECULIAR				
BUT THE GOOD MAN IS GODS PECULIAR TREASURE.	• •	328	RIGHTSNESS	48
PEDIGREE				
OR FLOWRE BY PEDIGREE	• • • • •	187	NO DO THEY	12
PEECE				
IT IS (IN TRUTH) A RUIN'D PEECE	• • •	180	BURIALL	11
TO NO SUCH PEECE.	• • • •	173	CONTENT	4
A PEECE OF MUCH ANTIQUITY	• • • •	168	VNTY SPRIT	22
YET WOULD NOT PLACE ONE PEECE ABOVE, BUT LIVES	• •	232	THE WORLD	34
PEECES				
PEECES OF SACKCLOTH WITH SILK-LISTS	• • •	282	GARLAND	19
T' UNITE THOSE PEECES, HOPING TO FIND OUT	• •	168	VNTY SPRIT	26
A THOUSAND PEECES	• • • • •	140	RGNRTN	51

		PAGE	TITLE	LINE

PEEP
ERECT PEEP FRCM THEIR BECS. . . . . . . 187 NO DO THEY 27
AND INTC GLCRY PEEP. . . . . 271 ALL GONE 28
YET I WHOSE SEARCH LOV'C NCT TC PEEP AND PEER . . 247 I WALKT 8
PERHAPS SCME NIGHTS HEE'L WATCH WITH YOU, ANC PEEP . . 236 CCNSTLATN 25
WHERE TREES AND HERBS DID WATCH AND PEEP . . . . 323 THE NIGHT 23
PEER
YET I WHOSE SEARCH LOV'C NCT TC PEEP AND PEER . . . 247 I WALKT 8
PEEVISH
THUS WILDED BY A PEEVISH HEART . . . . . . 214 MISERY 81
PELF
AND HUG'D EACH CNE HIS PELF . . . . . . 232 THE WORLD 37
PEN
CCUNT BLT THE BLCTS OF A VAIN PEN. . . . . . 335 JUDGEMENT 26
PENAL
I'LE JUDGE, WHERE PENAL FLAMES SIT MIXT AND CLCSE. . . 307 RAIN-BOW 38
PENALTIES
AND PENALTIES SPREAD TC CUR CRIMES. . . . . 273 WHT SUNDAY 32
PENANCE
UNBITTEC TONGLES ARE IN THEIR PENANCE DOUBLE . . . 194 RLS + LSNS 71
PENITENT
FCRGIVE YCUR PENITENT CFFENDER . . . . . 208 REPENTANCE 49
LIKE A WISE, EARLY PENITENT . . . . . . 304 ST MARY MN 37
PENNING
OF MY LCRDS PENNING, ANC BY SWEETEST ART . . . 198 SCRIPTURES 11
PENS
THY OWN DEAR PEOPLE PENS CUR TIMES . . . . 273 WHT SUNDAY 30
PENSIVE
HER ART. WHCSE PENSIVE, WEEPING EYES . . . . 305 ST MARY MN 57
HAVE SATE, AND PLEAS'D MY PENSIVE EYE . . . . 343 WATER-FALL 14
PENT
YCUR MAKER PENT UP IN A GRAVE . . . . . 164 INCARNATN 11
PECPLE
AND HATCHETH C'R THY PECPLE. . . . . . . 197 CORRUPTION 38
IF PRIEST, AND PECPLE CHANGE, KEEP THOU THY GRCUNC. . 193 RLS + LSNS 44
AND MAK'ST THE RACING PEOPLE MILD. . . . . 336 PSALM 65 20
THY OWN DEAR PEOPLE PENS CUR TIMES . . . . 273 WHT SUNDAY 30
PEOPLES
THY PEOPLES HEARTS, WHEN ALL THY SEEDS WERE RICH . . 229 LAW + GOSP 4
PERCEIV'D
STORM'D THUS, I STRAIGHT PERCEIV'D MY SPRING . . . 139 RGNRTN 18
PERFECT
BUT PERFECT ALL BEFORE THCU SLEEP'ST, THEN SAY . . 195 RLS + LSNS 117
SLCH PERFECT EASE, AND SUCH A LIVELY SENSE . . . 244 THE SAP 47
GIVE TO THY SPCUSE HER PERFECT, AND PURE DRESS . . 237 CONSTLATN 57
MAY SHINE UNTC A PERFECT CAY . . . . . . 277 COCK-CRWNG 45
PERFECT WHAT THOU HAST BEGUN . . . . . 249 BEGGING A 3
TC HIM, WHO GIVES ALL GCCD ANC PERFECT GIFTS. . . 267 ASCN-DAY A 4
ALL PERFECT FULNESS . . . . 215 PRAISE 35
THE PERFECT, FUL OBLATICN FOR ALL SIN . . . . 216 DRESSING 10
SEEKS IN THEE FOR PERFECT BEAUTY . . . . . 218 EASTER HYM 8
WHERE LIGHT, JOY, HEALTH ANC PERFECT PEACE . . . 319 THE ASS 62
BUT THAT CF PERFECT LIBERTY . . . . . . 318 THE ASS 10
PERFECTICN
HIS PURE PERFECTICN CUITS ALL SCCRE . . . . 209 REPENTANCE 81
PERFORM'D
AND HAVING THUS PERFORM'D THAT PART . . . . 240 MISERY 19
PERFORMANCE
PERFORMANCE, WILL FOR THAT SAME DEEC . . . . 314 THE STONE 48
PERFUM'D
AND IN HER PIERCING FLIGHT PERFLM'D THE AYER . . . 155 ISAACS M. 51
PERFUMES
BREATHING PERFUMES, DCTH SPICE THE DAY . . . . 199 NTVTY 1 6
BREATH ALL PERFUMES, ANC SPICE. . . . . . 198 UNPRFTBLNS 9
IN PERFLMES, CR ARRAY . . . . 226 RETIREMENT 41
PERHAPS
PERHAPS SCME HARMLESS CARES FCR THE NEXT DAY . . . 239 SHEPHEARDS 37
PERHAPS SCME NIGHTS HEE'L WATCH WITH YOU, ANC PEEP . . 236 CONSTLATN 25
PERHAPS TCMORROW. . . . . 202 THE CHECK 47
PERHAPS AT LAST . . . . 160 THE SHOWRE 16
PERHAPS THAT TEARE . . . . 173 CONTENT 15
PERHAPS SCME THINK A TOMBE . . . . . . 171 COME, COME 21
PERIL
TC SHUN THAT PERIL, LET THY GRACE . . . . . 319 THE ASS 41
PERJURER'S
THE PERJURER'S A DEVIL LET LCCSE. WHAT CAN . . . 193 RLS + LSNS 47
PERJURIES
CHURCHES AND ALTARS FED HIM, PERJURIES . . . . 232 THE WORLD 27
PERMANENT
IS PERMANENT . . . . 339 THE FEAST 8
PERMISSION
BY GOCS PERMISSION, AND MAN TLRNS A MULE. . . . 330 JACOBS PLW 30
PERSECUTING
AND PERSECUTING THEE ANC THINE . . . . . 316 MEN OF WAR 11
AS FAST, AS PERSECUTIONS NCW. . . . . . 351 L'ENVOY 58
PERSPECTIVE
MY PERSPECTIVE (STILL) AS THEY PASS . . . . . 271 ALL GONE 38
PERUS'D
I CLIMB'D THE HILL, PERUS'D THE CROSSE . . . . 152 THE SEARCH 41
PERUSE
YET, CCME, AND LET'S PERUSE THEM ALL. . . . . 165 THE CALL 20

		PAGE	TITLE	LINE
PERVERSE				
LET NCT PERVERSE	. . . .	204	DSRDR + FR	50
PHANTASTICK				
FALSE JCYES, PHANTASTICK FLIGHTS	. . . .	282	GARLAND	18
PHARISEE				
SELF-BOASTING PHARISEE. HCW BLINDE	. . . .	305	ST MARY MN	61
PHENIX-LIKE				
AS PHENIX-LIKE RENEW'TH	. . . . .	145	RSRCTN +IM	29
PHISICK				
AND 'STEAD CF PHISICK, A CISEASE	. . . .	150	RELIGION	44
PHLEGM				
SPIT CUT THEIR PHLEGM	. . . . .	276	PROFFER	44
PHYSICK				
KINGDCMES TOO HAVE THEIR PHYSICK, AND FOR STEEL	. .	222	AFFLICTION	33
THY PHYSICK, PILS THAT CHANGE	. . . . .	221	AFFLICTION	2
PIERC'D				
WHEREFORE, PIERC'D THROLGH WITH GRIEF, MY SAD	. .	207	REPENTANCE	19
PIERC'D NCT, LOVE ONLY CAN WITH QUICK ACCESSE	. .	160	THE SHOWRE	9
I SUMMCN'C NATURE. PIERC'D THRCUGH ALL HER STORE	.	167	VNTY SPRIT	9
PIERCE				
A SILENT TEARE CAN PIERCE THY THRCNE	. .	167	THE CALL	78
PIERCE ALL THEIR WAYES	. . . . .	146	RSRCTN +IM	55
AND THRCUGH THY CREATURES PIERCE AND PASS	. .	349	L'ENVOY	11
PIERCING				
AND IN HER PIERCING FLIGHT PERFUM'D THE AYER	. .	155	ISAACS M.	51
PIETY				
DIDCST THY SWIFT YEERS IN PIETY CUT-GROW	. .	156	ISAACS M.	68
MET IN THY FLAMES, ALL ACTS CF PIETY.	. .	158	THE LAMPE	10
PILES				
HER STATELY PILES WITH ALL THEIR HEIGHT AND PRIDE	. .	238	SHEPHEARDS	19
PILGRIM-SUNNE				
THE PILGRIM-SUNNE, ALL NIGHT HAVE I	. .	151	THE SEARCH	3
PILGRIMAGE				
O'RE ALL THEIR PILGRIMACE, AND LABOURS LEAP	. .	159	MANS FALL	29
YET, HAD CUR PILGRIMAGE BIN FREE	. . .	166	THE CALL	70
PILGRIMS				
AND AS A PILGRIMS EYE	. . . .	139	RGNRTN	22
WERE PILGRIMS ON THOSE PLAINS	. . .	238	SHEPHEARDS	10
WHEN SHALL THCSE FIRST WHITE PILGRIMS RISE	. .	335	JUDGEMENT	23
AS THCSE POOR PILGRIMS CFT HAVE TRYED	. .	298	JESUS WP B	20
PILL				
THAT PILL, THCUGH BITTER, IS MOST DEARE	. .	147	DAY OF JDG	35
PILLAG'D				
SLAIN FLOCK, AND PILLAG'D FLEECES	. . .	157	BRT. CHRCH	17
PILLAR				
INTC A PILLAR, AND CONCEAL'D FRCM MEN.	. .	331	JACOBS PLW	36
I SEE THE TEMPLE IN THY PILLAR REAR'D	. .	330	JACOBS PLW	1
HE IS MY PILLAR, AND MY CLOUD	. . .	221	PSALM 121	19
PILLAR-FIRES				
THEY ARE (INDEED) OUR PILLAR-FIRES	. .	175	JOY OF LIF	25
PILLOW				
THY PILLOW WAS BUT TYPE AND SPACE AT BEST	. .	331	JACOBS PLW	53
THY PILLOW WAS. MANY A SULLEN STORM	. .	287	THE BIRD	3
BUT IS A PILLCW, NCT A LOAD.	. . . .	318	THE ASS	12
PILS				
THY PHYSICK, PILS THAT CHANGE	. . . .	221	AFFLICTION	2
PIN				
BUT SEAL, OR PIN THEM TC THY SKIES.	. . .	191	THE MATCH	38
PINACLE				
I REACH'D THE PINACLE, WHERE PLAC'D	. . .	139	RGNRTN	28
PINCH'D				
CREEPS FORTH, AND PINCH'D FOR FCCD, WITH SCENT AND SIGHT		286	PSALM 104	55
PINE				
DCTH FRET AND WRANGLE, PINE AND WASTE.	. . .	308	THE SEED	12
PINE, AND RETIRE	. . . .	203	DSRDR + FR	39
I PINE, AND SHRINK	. . . . .	202	DSRDR + FR	8
BUT WITH THE THOUGHT OF HCME CC PINE.	. .	228	PILGRIMAGE	20
WITH THESE I CRIE, AND CRYING PINE	. . .	242	MISERY	112
AND MAKES HIM MOURN, AND PINE AND DYE	. .	281	THE FAVOUR	5
PINES				
THY WATERS TC A SCUL THAT PINES.	. . .	273	WHT SUNDAY	48
PINING				
SATE PINING ALL HIS LIFE THERE, DID SCARCE TRUST	.	232	THE WORLD	32
PINICNS				
THY SCUL, AND WITH NEW PINICNS REFRESH	. .	155	ISAACS M.	48
PICUS				
BUT NCW 'TIS MONSTROUS, AND THAT PICUS CARE	.	154	ISAACS M.	2
PCORE, PICUS WEARE.	. . . . . .	173	CONTENT	13
WHEN I LYE DOWN. THE PICUS SOLL BY NIGHT	. .	177	MRNG-WTCH	24
YCUTH NCW, FULL OF PICUS DUTY	. . .	218	EASTER HYM	7
IF PICUS GRIEFS HEAVENS JOYS AWAKE	. .	308	THE SEED	15
PIPES				
THEIR PIPES, AND WIT.	. . . . .	162	MT. OLVS A	11
PISTIC				
WHY IS THIS RICH, THIS PISTIC NARD	. . .	304	ST MARY MN	21
PIT				
SHALL LODGE IN SUCH A NARROW PIT, TILL HE	. .	331	JACOBS PLW	39
AND ON THE VERGE CF THAT DARK, CREADFUL PIT	. .	188	RELAPSE	3
AND ON CHRISTS COAT PIT ALL THEIR SHREDS.	. .	272	WHT SUNDAY	14
PITCH				
LORD, WHEN THCU CIDST ON SINAI PITCH	. . .	229	LAW + GOSP	1

		PAGE	TITLE	LINE
PITCH	(CON'T)			
THE LOWEST PITCH.	. . . .	329	TEARS	14
THE CLEAN, PURE HAND, WHICH NEVER MEDLED PITCH.	. .	327	RIGHTSNESS	10
A PITCHER TOO SHE HAD, NOR THOUGHT IT MUCH	. .	155	ISAACS M.	39
PITTY				
SOME PITTY TAKE	. . . .	164	THE CALL	6
AND PITTY OF SUCH A DIVINE EXTENT	. . . .	216	DRESSING	29
GIVE HIM (WITH PITTY) LOVE	. . . . .	216	DRESSING	25
PITY				
OF GRIEF AND PITY IN THY BREST	. . . .	299	JESUS WP B	30
YET, THOU SO FULL OF PITY ART	. . . .	299	JESUS WP B	38
(PITY WHICH OVERFLOWS THY HEART)	. . . .	299	JESUS WP B	39
PLAC'D				
THE DOWN-RIGHT EPICURE PLAC'D HEAV'N IN SENSE	. .	232	THE WORLD	38
WHO PLAC'D THEE HERE, DID SOMETHING THEN INFUSE	. .	243	THE SAP	9
SINCE PLAC'D BY HIM WHO CALLS YOU BY YOUR NAMES	. .	236	CONSTLATN	33
THUS HAST THOU PLAC'D IN MANS OUTSIDE	. .	166	THE CALL	58
I REACH'D THE PINACLE, WHERE PLAC'D	. .	139	RGNRTN	28
AND HERE, WITHOUT MY KNOWLEDGE, PLAC'D	. .	346	THE QUEER	10
PLACE				
THROUGH SADDEST CLOUDS TO THAT GLAD PLACE	. .	*345	THE WREATH	17
LINGRING, AND WERE OF THIS STEEP PLACE AFRAID	. .	343	WATER-FALL	6
DESCEND, AND HALLOW ALL THE PLACE.	. .	350	L'ENVOY	44
GIVE HIM AMONGST THY WORKS A PLACE	. .	347	THE BOOK	29
BEFORE I UNDERSTOOD THIS PLACE	. . .	169	RETREATE	3
CATCH AT THE PLACE	. . . . .	189	RESOLVE	10
TOGETHER WITH THE SEED, THE PLACE.	. .	204	DSRDR + FR	56
(I KNOW IT WEL) FILS ALL THE PLACE.	. .	214	MISERY	52
I STILE MEER TEMPERS, WHICH TAKE PLACE	. .	242	MISERY	87
HE HATH NO ROOT, NOR TO ONE PLACE IS TY'D	. .	246	MAN	16
YET WOULD NOT PLACE ONE PEECE ABOVE, BUT LIVES	. .	232	THE WORLD	34
THEN JACOB-LIKE LODGE IN A PLACE	. .	228	PILGRIMAGE	5
(A PLACE, AND NO MORE, IS SET DOWN)	. .	228	PILGRIMAGE	6
WE SEND TEARS TO THE PLACE	. .	213	ADMISSION	20
AND NOW (AS THEN WITHIN THIS PLACE)	. .	265	INTRO. 2	11
THAT PLACE WHERE I HAD SEEN HIM TO GROW OUT	. .	247	I WALKT	17
WITH THESE FAIR THOUGHTS I MOVE IN THIS FAIR PLACE	. .	268	ASCN-DAY A	49
SOME DOWNWARDS TO THEIR PLACE.	. . .	285	PSALM 104	24
THE ROCKS GIVE CONIES A RETYRING PLACE.	. .	286	PSALM 104	50
WHICH HIS DEATH SCATTER'D) HE FORETOLD THE PLACE	. .	330	JACOBS PLW	23
A HEART IS THAT DREAD PLACE, THAT AWFUL CELL	. .	330	JACOBS PLW	27
AND SHINE, AND POINT ME TO A PLACE	. .	332	AGREEMENT	11
ADORN THE PLACE	. . . . .	339	THE FEAST	5
THOU, WHO DIDST PLACE ME IN THIS BUSIE STREET	. .	318	THE ASS	1
PREVAIL WITH ME TO SHUN THE PLACE.	. .	319	THE ASS	42
PLAID				
AS WITH A VAIL THOU HIDST IT, THY FLOODS PLAID	. .	285	PSALM 104	19
A LESSON PLAID HIM BY A WINDE OR WAVE.	. .	280	JOY	8
PLAIES				
VICISSITUDE PLAIES ALL THE GAME	. .	222	AFFLICTION	29
PLAIN				
AND PLAIN, AS WHEN I WAS A CHILDE.	. .	317	MEN OF WAR	46
PLAIN, HARMLESS, FAITHFUL, FAIR AND BRIGHT	. .	312	FAIR+YONG	25
WHEN NIGHT COMES, LIST THY DEEDS, MAKE PLAIN THE WAY	.	195	RLS + LSNS	115
IS A PLAIN WATCH, AND WITHOUT FIGURES WINDS	. .	178	EVNG-WTCH	12
APPEARETH PLAIN.	. . . . .	178	SILENCE	20
ALL WAS PLAIN, MODEST TRUTH, NOR DID SHE COME	. .	155	ISAACS M.	33
WITH A CHEAP, PLAIN REMEMBRANCE STILL	. .	342	OBSEQUIES	5
PLAINE				
RE-MARRY TO THE SOULE, FOR 'TIS MOST PLAINE	. .	145	RSRCTN +IM	49
THAT I MIGHT ONCE MORE REACH THAT PLAINE	. .	170	RETREATE	23
PLAINLY				
WE PLAINLY SEE, WHO MADE THE SAME.	. .	277	COCK-CRWNG	22
PLAINS				
WERE PILGRIMS ON THOSE PLAINS	. . .	238	SHEPHEARDS	10
PLANETS				
WHILE ALL THE PLANETS DID UNCLOUDED PASS.	. .	268	ASCN-DAY A	46
SLEEPIE PLANETS SET, AND SLUMBER	. .	212	DAWNING	20
PLANT				
THY SPIRIT PLANT, QUICKNING THE WHOLE	. .	206	REPENTANCE	3
AS I HAVE YOURS LONG SINCE, THIS PLANT, YOU SEE	. .	279	PALM-TREE	2
O PLANT IN ME THY GOSPEL, AND THY LAW	. .	230	LAW + GOSP	27
PLANTED				
MY HEART, AND THEE PLANTED IN IT.	. .	191	THE MATCH	30
THE OLD, WHITE PROPHETS PLANTED FIRST AND DREST.	. .	326	RIGHTSNESS	2
PLANTS				
PLANTS OF THE DAY.	. . . . .	294	PALM-SUNDY	2
PLANTS IN THE ROOT WITH EARTH DO MOST COMPLY	. .	223	TEMPEST	33
PLAY				
DID IN THEIR BOSOMES PLAY	. . .	239	SHEPHEARDS	38
WHICH ANGELS GUARD, AND WITH IT PLAY	. .	322	CHILDEHOOD	37
CHECKING THE POOR CHILDE FOR HIS PLAY	. .	322	CHILDEHOOD	29
WATCH, WHILE I SLEEP, OR PLAY.	. .	187	NO DO THEY	32
AND MIND IT NOT, PLAY NOT AWAY	. .	201	THE CHECK	23
O THEN PLAY NOT, BUT STRIVE TO HIM, WHO CAN	. .	202	THE CHECK	29
AND SHEEPWARD PLAY.	. . . . .	163	MT. OLVS A	16
PLAYED				
I PLAYED WITH FIRE, DID COUNSELL SPURN	. .	282	GARLAND	13
PLAYING				
AND BY MEER PLAYING GO TO HEAVEN.	. .	321	CHILDEHOOD	8

	PAGE	TITLE	LINE
PLEAD			
EACH LINE IN THEE. THEN WOULD I PLEAD IN GROANS	198	SCRIPTURES	10
PLEAS'D			
AND PLEAS'D OURSELVES WITH WHAT WE FEARD	143	DEATH	26
THAT THOU WERT PLEAS'D TO SHED THY GRACE SO FARR,	283	LOVE-SICK	3
BUT THOU HAST PLEAS'D SO WELL, HE SWEARS	297	HERODIAS	13
AS THOU LONG SINCE WERT PLEAS'D TO BUY	274	WHT SUNDAY	53
THAT NO DECAY SHAL TOUCH ME. O BE PLEAS'D	234	MUTINIE	32
HAVE SATE, AND PLEAS'D MY PENSIVE EYE	343	WATER-FALL	14
PLEASANT			
AS PLEASANT, AS IF WITH THE BREST.	218	EASTER HYM	12
THE PLEASANT LAND TO BRIMSTONE TURNS	288	THE BIRD	29
PLEASE			
WHICH TEACH THEE NOW TO PLEASE HIS EYES	297	HERODIAS	11
WHAT WAY WE PLEASE, WITHOUT SELF-ENDS.	322	CHILDEHOOD	34
LET ME BE WISE TO PLEASE THEE STILL	319	THE ASS	43
THEY SHAL PLEASE ME	215	PRAISE	26
AND A CONSUMPTION THAT DOTH PLEASE.	273	WHT SUNDAY	44
IT WHISPER'D, WHERE I PLEASE	141	RGNRTN	89
AND AT FIRST SIGHT DOTH MANY PLEASE	150	RELIGION	42
CONCEIT, OR CALL IT WHAT YOU PLEASE	162	MT. OLVS A	6
TO PLEASE WITHOUT ETERNITY.	345	QUICKNESS	16
PLEASING			
PLEASING AND INNOCENT AN AIR	303	ST MARY MN	6
PLEASURE			
THEIR PLEASURE AND THEIR WORTH.	285	PSALM 104	32
AFFLICTION THUS, MEERE PLEASURE IS	182	CHRFLNESS	9
WHEN EITHER SLEEP, OR SOME DARK PLEASURE	211	DAWNING	7
WAITS INNOCENCE AND PLEASURE)	238	SHEPHEARDS	2
WITH GLOVES, AND KNOTS THE SILLY SNARES OF PLEASURE	231	THE WORLD	12
BUT NOW IT IS THY SERVANTS PLEASURE	214	MISERY	47
PLEASURES			
IN POST FOR PLEASURES, BENT TO TRIE	282	GARLAND	11
PLEASURES HAD FOIL'D ETERNITIE	166	THE CALL	72
WHAT PLEASURES SHOULD MY JOIRNEY CROWN	152	THE SEARCH	68
THE OTHER SMOAKE, AND PLEASURES WEIGH'D	139	RGNRTN	32
EXALTED PLEASURES, CROWNING BLISSES	348	HOLY BIBLE	30
PLEDGE			
A TASTE OF HEAV'N ON EARTH, THE PLEDGE, AND CUE	2	SON-DAYES	23
BRIGHT PLEDGE OF PEACE AND SUN-SHINE. THE SURE TYE	306	RAIN-BOW	13
PLENTEOUS			
AND PLENTEOUS MEALS THEY MAKE.	286	PSALM 104	76
A PLENTEOUS WAY (THANKS TO THAT HOLY ONE)	159	MANS FALL	22
PLENTY			
NEW SEV'RAL OATHES, AND COMPLEMENTS (TOO) PLENTY.	154	ISAACS M.	16
PLOT			
THUS WHILE THY SEV'RAL MERCIES PLOT	227	LV + DSPLN	13
PLOTS			
WHICH NEVER HARBOUR'D PLOTS	239	SHEPHEARDS	34
DOTH ALL THEIR PLOTS CONTROUL	220	PSALM 121	14
WITH ALL HIS PLOTS AND POWER CAN.	300	PROVIDENCE	20
PLUCK			
TO PLUCK A GARLAND HENCE, WHILE YOU DO SLEEP	280	PALM-TREE	26
PLUNDERED			
BAGS THAT WAX OLD MAY PLUNDERED BE	300	PROVIDENCE	21
PLY			
TO PLY BOTH THINE EYES AND BREATH.	281	JOY	22
POETS			
YET, IF POETS MIND THEE WELL	163	MT. OLVS A	17
POINT			
NOW POINT HIM OUT, GROWN UP A MAN.	151	THE SEARCH	10
ONLY, ONE POINT ESCAPES THEE. THAT THY OILE	158	THE LAMPE	23
AND POINT US OUT THE WAY	201	THE CHECK	21
STRIVE UPWARDS STIL, AND POINT HIM THE WAY HOME.	223	TEMPEST	28
WHICH IN THE DARKEST NIGHTS POINT TO THEIR HOMES	246	MAN	24
AND SHINE, AND POINT ME TO A PLACE	332	AGREEMENT	11
POINTS			
WHY THEN THESE CURL'D, PUFF'D POINTS	173	CONTENT	17
POIS'NOUS			
HERE I RENOUNCE THE POIS'NOUS WARE.	190	THE MATCH	12
POISON'D			
SO POISON'D, BREAKS FORTH IN SOME CLIME	150	RELIGION	41
POLE			
WHICH WOULD ONE DAY (BENEATH THE POLE)	151	THE SEARCH	19
OUT-RUNS THE EARTH, AND LINES THE UTMOST POLE.	193	RLS + LSNS	54
POLICIE			
THAT POLICIE	232	THE WORLD	26
POLLUTED			
POLLUTED THROUGH THEIR FALL	238	SHEPHEARDS	24
POLLUTIONS			
POLLUTIONS ALL MY BODY WED	209	REPENTANCE	77
POMP			
AND ALL THAT SACRED POMP, AND SHEL	210	FAITH	27
POMPOUS			
THOU HADST NO POMPOUS TRAIN, NOR ANTIK CROWD	154	ISAACS M.	21
QUITE THROUGH THEIR PROUD AND POMPOUS FILE	303	ORNAMENT	13
PONTICK			
GLADLY WILL I, LIKE PONTICK SHEEP	301	PROVIDENCE	46
POOLS			
BETTER, THE POOLS SHOULD FLOW WITH RAIN AND FLOODS	290	THE TIMBER	47

	PAGE	TITLE	LINE
POOR			
AND THOUGH POOR STONES HAVE NEITHER SPEECH NOR TONGUE	288	THE BIRD	14
POOR BIRDS SING BEST, AND PRETTIEST SHOW	294	BEGGING B	19
POOR BIRDS THIS DOCTRINE SING	301	PROVIDENCE	25
WHICH FREED POOR HAGAR FROM HER FEARS	300	PROVIDENCE	4
AS THOSE POOR PILGRIMS OFT HAVE TRYED	298	JESUS WP B	20
AS THE POOR ASS, WHICH THE PROUD JEAR	295	PALM-SUNDY	40
TO BUY, THE.POOR CAME TO ADORE.	302	ORNAMENT	4
FINDES THY POOR FOAL AT THY COMMAND	319	THE ASS	46
ABOVE ALL, MAKE ME LOVE THE POOR	319	THE ASS	33
WHAT SOME POOR MAN MAY OFTEN FEEL	308	THE SEED	2
THE POOR BEE IN HER HIVE MUST SWEL.	309	THE SEED	36
BID THY POOR ASS (WITH TEARS I CRAVE)	329	TEARS	11
WHOSE SPIRIT EVER POOR, IS MEEK AND LOW.	327	RIGHTSNESS	15
CHECKING THE POOR CHILDE FOR HIS PLAY	322	CHILDEHOOD	29
SUCH TRIUMPHS POOR FLESH CANNOT MERIT.	339	THE FEAST	9
I HAD NOT ONE POOR WORD TO SAY.	333	AGREEMENT	38
ACCEPT, DREAD LORD, AND THE POOR OBLATION	190	THE MATCH	13
POOR, FALLING STAR.	203	DSRDR + FR	45
NOT ONE POOR SHOOT	203	DSRDR + FR	27
WHAT ONE POOR LEAF DID EVER I YET FALL	198	UNPRFTBLNS	14
WHERE THOU MAY'ST SLEEP WHOLE AGES, LIFES POOR FLOWR	195	RLS + LSNS	123
SEAL NOT THY EYES UP FROM THE POOR, BUT GIVE	193	RLS + LSNS	61
OF THIS POOR, SINFULL FRAME PURE HEART.	182	CHRFLNESS	19
OR SOME POOR HIGH-WAY HERB, OR SPRING	187	ND DO THEY	13
AND FILLS THE BOXES OF HIS POOR.	209	REPENTANCE	82
OF THIS POOR CREATURE, BY A GRACIOUS ART	223	TEMPEST	22
SOME SUCH POOR OFF'RING.	215	PRAISE	50
LET HIM (THOUGH POOR)	215	PRAISE	54
THAT ONE POOR BLOSSOME.	215	PRAISE	56
POOR DUST SHOULD LY STILL LOW	217	DRESSING	40
DESCEND TO JUDGE POOR CARELESS MAN	212	DAWNING	28
HAVE COMMERCE SOMTIMES WITH POOR DUST	212	DAWNING	40
NO SLEEP, NOR SLOTH ASSAILES YOU, BUT POOR MAN	236	CONSTLATN	15
HATH NOT SO MUCH AS ONE POOR LOCK.	240	MISERY	28
AND POOR, DESPISED TRUTH SATE COUNTING BY	232	THE WORLD	44
TURNING TO HIM, WHO MADE POOR SAND TO TIRE	234	MUTINIE	11
HOW DID POOR FLESH (WHICH AFTER THOU DIDST WEARE)	229	LAW + GOSP	7
MY ONE POOR SAND	275	PROFFER	26
FROM A POOR ROOT	248	I WALKT	37
THOU TO POOR RAGS DOST STILL GIVE GRACE.	265	INTRO. 2	12
SHOULD POOR SOULS FEAR A SHADE OR NIGHT	343	WATER-FALL	17
WHICH BRINGS POOR DUST THE VICTORY.	339	THE FEAST	18
POOR DUST THOUGH DEAD	340	THE FEAST	35
POORE			
POORE, PIOUS WEARE.	173	CONTENT	13
IT IS BUT POORE	190	THE MATCH	14
POORE, QUERULOUS HANDFULL WAS'T FOR THIS	145	RSRCTN +IM	19
PORE			
WATCH STARS, OR PORE	146	RSRCTN +IM	66
PORES			
WHO PORES	153	THE SEARCH	76
PORTION			
IF ALL MY PORTION HERE	301	PROVIDENCE	37
POSIES			
CULL'D FLOWRES AND MADE ME POSIES.	282	GARLAND	22
POSSESSETH			
POSSESSETH MAD MAN WITHOUT MEASURE.	211	DAWNING	8
POST			
IN POST FOR PLEASURES, BENT TO TRIE	282	GARLAND	11
POSTING			
WHAT STIRS, WHAT POSTING INTERCOURSE AND MIRTH	267	ASCN-DAY A	25
POUR			
AND SPRINGS, LIKE DISSOLV'D PEARLS THEIR STREAMS DID POUR	268	ASCN-DAY A	47
ALL SCATTER'D LAY, WHILE HE HIS EYES DID POUR	231	THE WORLD	14
DEAR JESUS WEEP ON. POUR THIS LATTER	296	JESUS WP A	9
WHOSE BLESSED, SWEET COMMANDS DO POUR	326	ABELS BLOD	25
POURE			
POURE OYLE UPON THE STONES, WEEP FOR THY SIN	192	RLS + LSNS	23
POURS			
WHICH THROUGH THE EYES POURS OUT THE HEART	328	ANGUISH	10
RAIN GENTLY SPENDS HIS HONEY-DROPS, AND POURS	306	RAIN-BOW	11
POVERTY			
TO WINE, AND SWEETNESS. POVERTY TO WEALTH	221	AFFLICTION	5
POW'R			
OR (TO HIS POW'R)	215	PRAISE	49
TO ALL YOUR POW'R MOST PURE.	244	THE SAP	38
WITH THEIR CONTENT TOO IN MY POW'R	321	CHILDEHOOD	6
ARE SHADOWS OF HIS WISEDOME, AND HIS POW'R	194	RLS + LSNS	96
WHOSE POW'R DOTH SO EXCELL	202	THE CHECK	32
THY LIGHT, AND POW'R	178	SILENCE	16
CHERISH, AND BIND THY POW'RS	221	AFFLICTION	14
POWER			
WITHOUT A STEEL, O LET THY POWER CLEER	224	TEMPEST	59
TO HIM BE GLORY, POWER, PRAISE	218	EASTER HYM	17
BOTH GROWTH, AND POWER, CHECKING THE HEALTH	206	REPENTANCE	6
INSPIR'D A QUICKNING POWER THROUGH THE DEAD	144	RSRCTN +IM	3
AND POWER FORCE ON HOLY WRIT	335	JUDGEMENT	36
WHO QUESTION POWER, THEY SPEAK TREASON.	318	THE ASS	20
WITH ALL HIS PLOTS AND POWER CAN.	300	PROVIDENCE	20

		PAGE	TITLE	LINE
POWER	(CCN'T)			
THE THRONE WHERE PEACE AND POWER REST.	• • • •	299	JESUS WP B	31
POWERFUL				
A POWERFUL, RARE DEW • • • • • • • •		244	THE SAP	40
POWERS				
AND ALL MY POWERS MOURN'D. •	• • •	213	ADMISSION	4
CALL IN THY POWERS. RUN, AND REACH •	• • • •	189	RESOLVE	17
POWR				
OF HEALING SWEETS THY SELF DOST POWR	• • • •	214	MISERY	50
POWR'S				
SHIN'D ON MY SOUL, I FELT THROUGH ALL MY POWR'S	• •	244	MT. OLV. B	3
POYS'NOUS				
O POYS'NOUS, SUBTILE FOWLS. • • • • • •		275	PROFFER	13
POYSON				
POYSON, AND BLAST • • • • • •		203	DSRDR + FR	24
THAT GILD RANK POYSON, AND ALLOW • • • •		205	IDLE VERSE	11
POYSON'D				
BUT SINCE THESE SWEETS ARE SOWRE, AND POYSON'D HERE	•	321	HIDDN TRSR	25
POYSONS				
OUR BODIES, POYSONS THAT INTREAT • • • •		311	FAIR+YONG	13
PRACTICE				
AND YET THE PRACTICE WORLDLINGS CALL • • •		322	CHILDEHOOD	27
PRAISE				
PRAISE WAITS IN ALL HUMILITY. • • • •		336	PSALM 65	2
EVEN WHAT THOU WILT, AND PRAISE THEE TOO. • •		328	ANGUISH	6
THEN DRINK AND PRAISE THY BOUNTEOUSNESS. • •		301	PROVIDENCE	30
ALL THINGS THAT BE, PRAISE HIM, AND HAD • • •		288	THE BIRD	11
THUS PRAISE AND PRAYER HERE BENEATH THE SUN • •		288	THE BIRD	17
THOU CANST NOT MISSE HIS PRAISE, EACH TREE, HERB, FLOWRE		194	RLS + LSNS	95
TO MEALES WHEN THOU DOEST COME, GIVE HIM THE PRAISE	•	195	RLS + LSNS	97
AND TO THY PRAISE • • • • • •		182	CHRFLNESS	22
PRAISE HIM, WHO DEALT HIS GIFTS SO FREE • • •		266	VAIN WITS	12
BE MY COMFORT, AND THY PRAISE • • • •		249	BEGGING A	8
THAT THESE MAY BE THY PRAISE, AND MY JOY TOO. • •		245	MT. OLV. B	26
TO HIM BE GLORY, POWER, PRAISE • • • •		218	EASTER HYM	17
BRING PRAISE, AND INCENSE. • • • •		215	PRAISE	44
I WILL PRAISE THEE • • • • • •		214	PRAISE	10
BUT A TWIN'D WREATH OF GRIEF AND PRAISE • •		345	THE WREATH	9
PRAISE SOIL'D WITH TEARS, AND TEARS AGAIN • •		345	THE WREATH	10
SING THY JUST PRAISE, AND SEE THY FACE. • •		345	THE WREATH	19
PRAISES				
HOW SHALL THY DUST THY PRAISES SING. • • •		186	PASSION	47
PRAY				
WHO SO RETURNS NOT, CANNOT PRAY ARIGHT • •		194	RLS + LSNS	83
LOVE GOD, AND LOVE THY NEIGHBOUR, WATCH, AND PRAY. •	•	196	RLS + LSNS	140
THE FIRST (PRAY MARKE) AS QUICK AS LIGHT • •		141	RGNRTN	66
BUT PRAY AGAINST THEM BOTH • • • •		148	DAY OF JDG	38
AND PRAY, I MAY DO SO NO MORE • • • •		208	REPENTANCE	58
AND PRAY, THESE LAST MAY BE AS FIRST • • •		273	WHT SUNDAY	26
PRAY'D				
WHO PRAY'D FOR THOSE THAT DID HIM KILL. • • •		326	ABELS BLOD	44
PRAY'R				
THY WISH, NOR PRAY'R • • • • • •		153	THE SEARCH	84
SCATT'RING THE MYRRHE, AND INCENSE OF THY PRAY'R. •	•	155	ISAACS M.	52
PRAYER				
BUT BEING FOR A BRIDE, PRAYER WAS SUCH • •		154	ISAACS M.	11
YET, NEVER SLEEP THE SUN UP, PRAYER SHOU'D • •		192	RLS + LSNS	7
AND SYMPHONY OF NATURE. PRAYER IS • • •		177	MRNG-WTCH	18
CHRISTS PROGRESS, AND HIS PRAYER TIME. • •		324	THE NIGHT	29
TO THEE, O THOU THAT HEAREST PRAYER. • • •		336	PSALM 65	4
THUS PRAISE AND PRAYER HERE BENEATH THE SUN • •		288	THE BIRD	17
PRAYERS				
HIS HEART AND TONGUE IN PRAYERS FOR HIS FOES. • •		328	RIGHTSNESS	39
PRAYING				
PRAYING. AND TO BE MARRIED. IT WAS RARE • • •		154	ISAACS M.	1
PREACH				
WHERE DEAD MEN PREACH, WHO CAN TURN FEASTS, AND MIRTH	•	226	RETIREMENT	49
PRECIOUS				
IN THY OWN PRECIOUS, SAVING TEARES. • • • •		184	PASSION	9
TO SLIGHT THY PRECIOUS BLOOD, AND BREATH. • • •		164	INCARNATN	18
PRECIPICE				
FROM THE SAME PRECIPICE BE HURL'D. • • • •		322	CHILDEHOOD	24
AND PRECIPICE IT LEADS TO, BID ME FLIE • • •		320	HIDDN TRSR	17
PREFER				
O FOOLS (SAID I) THUS TO PREFER DARK NIGHT • • •		233	THE WORLD	49
PRELUDES				
ALL BUT PRELUDES THY END. THOU ART THE MAN • •		195	RLS + LSNS	107
PREPARE				
PREPARE, PREPARE ME THEN, O GOD • • • •		147	DAY OF JDG	29
PREPARE, PREPARE ME THEN, O GOD • • • •		147	DAY OF JDG	29
THEY FOR THE TOWN PREPARE • • • • •		239	SHEPHEARDS	42
PREPOSSEST				
THE NEXT WORLDS GLADNES PREPOSSEST IN THIS. • •		205	SON-DAYES	3
PREROGATIVE				
THE CHURCHES LOVE-FEASTS, TIMES PREROGATIVE • •	•	2	SON-DAYES	17
PRESENCE				
AND AT THY PRESENCE MAKE THESE MOUNTAINS FLOW •	•	283	LOVE-SICK	11
PRESENT				
THINE ARE THE PRESENT HEALING LEAVES • • • •		332	AGREEMENT	20
AND PRESENT THINGS FINDE MEN MOST KINDE. • • •	•	318	THE ASS	6

		PAGE	TITLE	LINE
PRESENT	**(CCN'T)**			
THOU SADLY DICST TO HIM PRESENT		304	ST MARY MN	38
THE AGE, THE PRESENT TIMES ARE NOT		214	MISERY	65
MY PRESENT SEARCH, FOR EAGLES EYE NOT STARRS		278	THE STARRE	6
PRESENT, O GOC.		180	CHRCH-SVC	22
PRESENT AND SURE WITHOUT MY SEEING.		340	THE FEAST	42
PRESENTS				
THAT COPYED IT, PRESENTS IT THEE.		265	INTRO. 2	2
PRESERV'D				
I MAY BE FOUND (PRESERV'D BY THEE)		317	MEN OF WAR	49
PRESERVE				
BY HICING DOTH PRESERVE		310	THE SEED	76
PRESERVER				
THOU GREAT PRESERVER CF ALL MEN.		180	BURIALL	7
MY GREAT PRESERVER SMILES		205	IDLE VERSE	6
PRESERVING				
FOR A PRESERVING SPIRIT DOTH STILL PASSE		145	RSRCTN +IM	31
PRESSE				
PRESSE NOT TO BE		225	RETIREMENT	15
PREST				
SC PREST AND BOW'C, BEFCRE SIN CIC DEGRADE		279	PALM-TREE	3
AH. IT IS SO WITH ME, OFT HAVE I PREST		160	THE SHOWRE	7
HCW WERT THOU PREST		185	PASSION	20
PRETENCE				
AND SCORND PRETENCE		232	THE WORLD	39
WHOSE ACTS, WCRDS AND PRETENCE		327	RIGHTSNESS	19
PRETTIEST				
POOR BIRDS SING BEST, AND PRETTIEST SHOW		294	BEGGING B	19
PRETTY				
WHAT PRETTY SULLENNESS CID HASTE		304	ST MARY MN	23
PREVAIL				
PREVAIL WITH ME TC SHUN THE PLACE.		319	THE ASS	42
MY SINS ARE GREAT AND STILL PREVAIL		333	AGREEMENT	44
O LET THAT SILENCE THEN PREVAIL.		334	AGREEMENT	64
THEN TAUGHT BY THEE, I WILL PREVAIL		338	THE THRONE	14
SHALL NCT THE BREATH CF GCD PREVAIL.		276	COCK-CRWNG	18
PREVAIL'D				
A DECRYED COURSE, SURE IT PREVAIL'D NOT MUCH.		154	ISAACS M.	12
PREVAIL'D BY WRESTLING ERE THE SUN DID SHINE.		192	RLS + LSNS	22
PREVENT				
RISE TO PREVENT THE SUN, SLEEP DCTH SINS GLUT		192	RLS + LSNS	11
AS EASILY THOU MIGHTST PREVENT		165	THE CALL	34
WISE HUSBANDS WILL (YCU SAY) THERE WANTS PREVENT		274	PROFFER	11
PREY				
WHERE HE DID CLUTCH HIS PREY, BUT ONE DID SEE		232	THE WORLD	25
THOUGH HAWKS CAN PREY THRCUGH STORMS AND WINCS		309	THE SEED	35
THEIR MEAT FROM THEE, WHO DOEST APPOINT THE PREY		286	PSALM 104	59
PRIC'D				
AND SPRING, AND GROW, A TREE NE'R TO BE PRIC'D		280	PALM-TREE	15
PRICE				
WAS'T NOT ENOUGH THAT THOU HACST PAYD THE PRICE		219	HOLY COMM.	33
AND SLIGHT A PRICE		213	ADMISSION	14
BUT HE THAT WITH HIS BLCUD (A PRICE TOO DEERE)		188	RELAPSE	21
PRICKING				
PRICKING HIS LIPS, TILL HE DOTH MCURN		319	THE ASS	50
PRIDE				
THE LATEST MODES CF PRICE AND LUST		302	ORNAMENT	6
AND HILLS FULL OF SPRINGING PRICE		337	PSALM 65	43
HER STATELY PILES WITH ALL THEIR HEIGHT AND PRIDE		238	SHEPHEARDS	19
NC COSTLY PRIDE, NO SCFT-CLOATH'C LUXURIE		239	SHEPHEARDS	31
PRIEST				
IF PRIEST, AND PECPLE CHANGE, KEEP THOU THY GRCUNC.		193	RLS + LSNS	44
PRIM-ROSE				
TO CULL THIS PRIM-ROSE CUT		166	THE CALL	39
PRIME				
IS THY FIRST BREATH, ANC MANS ETERNALL PRIME.		178	EVNG-WTCH	16
THESE WERE MY PRIME DELIGHTS.		282	GARLAND	20
PRIMRCS'D				
AS RICH A SCENT AS THE NCW PRIMROS'D FIELCS		267	ASCN-DAY A	22
PRIMRCS'D, AND HUNG WITH SHADE		139	RGNRTN	13
PRINCE				
IT IS THE GOOD MANS FEAST, THE PRINCE OF FLOWRES		193	RLS + LSNS	59
THOU MAI'ST IN RAGS A MIGHTY PRINCE RELIEVE		193	RLS + LSNS	63
CN IT THE PRINCE CF SALEM SITS, WHO DEALS		243	THE SAP	13
PRINT				
AND GCDS BRIGHT MINDE EXPREST IN PRINT.		332	AGREEMENT	24
PRIS'NER				
A PRIS'NER TO MY LIBERTIE		239	MISERY	2
PRIVATE				
PRIVATE AND HCLY TALK FILL ALL THE WAYS.		268	ASCN-DAY A	28
GIVE HIM THY PRIVATE SEAL		216	DRESSING	19
ANC OF A PRIVATE FAMILIE		210	FAITH	7
FROM PRIVATE AND SELECTFD HEARTS DID SPRING		330	JACOBS PLW	12
AND HEAR MY HEARTS LAST PRIVATE THROWS.		334	AGREEMENT	66
AND PRIVATE TAPERS WILL BUT HELP TC STRAY		321	HIDDN TRSR	27
DCTH YOUR MOST PRIVATE SINS RECCRD.		314	THE STONE	45
FROM SIN, HE WALKS A NARRCW, PRIVATE WAY.		290	THE TIMBER	34
PRIZE				
AND SLIGHTS THAT MOST, WHICH MEN MOST PRIZE.		319	THE ASS	48
AND TRUTH (CPPREST HERE) GETS THE PRIZE.		318	THE ASS	28

		PAGE	TITLE	LINE
PRIZE	(CON'T)			
OR THY GREAT MERCIES BETTER PRIZE.	• • • • •	214	MISERY	56
THAT VOYDS BUT FILTH, AND STENCH. HAST THOU NO PRIZE	•	194	RLS + LSNS	75
HATH GOT THE PRIZE.	• • • • • •	189	RESOLVE	28
PROCEED				
AGAINST THEM BY A STONE PROCEED.	• • • • •	314	THE STONE	49
PROCESS				
A PROCESS, WHICH EV'N MANS OWN EYE	• • • •	314	THE STONE	35
PROCUR'D				
HER EARNEST SIGHES PROCUR'D HER TEARS	• • •	223	TEMPEST	15
PRODUCE				
I WILL PRODUCE.	• • • • • •	338	THE THRONE	11
WHICH DOTH RESOLVE, PRODUCE, AND RIPEN ALL	• •	145	RSRCTN +IM	33
AS NOW PRODUCE THESE TEARES	• • • • •	165	THE CALL	35
PROFANENES				
PROFANENES ON MY TONGUE DOTH REST	• • • •	208	REPENTANCE	75
PROFUSE				
NOR MOAN I ONELY (THOUGH PROFUSE)	• • • •	335	JUDGEMENT	31
PROGRESS				
CHRISTS PROGRESS, AND HIS PRAYER TIME.	• • •	324	THE NIGHT	29
PROGRESS'D				
HIS MIND SURE PROGRESS'D THITHER.	• • • •	196	CORRUPTION	8
PROGRESSIONS				
AND IN YOUR VAST PROGRESSIONS OVERLOOK	• • •	235	CONSTLATN	7
PROJECTION				
BRIGHT, AND BLEST BEAME. WHOSE STRONG PROJECTION	• •	210	FAITH	1
PROMIS'D				
THOUGH THOU HAST PROMIS'D THEY SHOULD STAY	• •	149	RELIGION	27
WHO PROMIS'D MUCH, BUT DID REFUSE	• • • •	314	THE STONE	47
PROMISE				
HIS PROMISE STILL, BUT WE BREAK OURS AND SLEEP.	• •	307	RAIN-BOW	20
AND THY PROMISE 'TIL MADE EVEN	• • • • •	214	PRAISE	23
WHEN THEY RECEIV'D THE PROMISE, FOR WHICH NOW	•	238	SHEPHEARDS	11
PROMISES				
THY PROMISES BUT EMPTY WORDS	• • • • •	207	REPENTANCE	13
PRONOUNC'D				
PRONOUNC'D WITH THUNDER, AND THY THREATS DID THAW	•	229	LAW + GOSP	3
PROPER				
HER PROPER BRANCHES. WHICH NOW LIE	• • • •	292	THE JEWS	16
PROPHETIC				
AND CROWN'D THEM WITH PROPHETIC FIRE.	• • • •	272	WHT SUNDAY	8
PROPHETS				
THAT LAMB WHOSE DAIES GREAT KINGS AND PROPHETS WISH'D		239	SHEPHEARDS	49
THE OLD, WHITE PROPHETS PLANTED FIRST AND DREST.	• •	326	RIGHTSNESS	2
PROPHETS, AND FRIENDS OF GOD	• • • • •	140	RGNRTN	41
PROPORTION				
PROPORTION TO THEIR MERITS, AND THY PURSE.	• •	193	RLS + LSNS	62
PROPT				
(PROPT BY THY HAND)	• • • • • •	179	CHRCH-SVC	10
PROSPER				
AND THOU ART SURE TO PROSPER ALL THE DAY.	• •	192	RLS + LSNS	18
PROSTRATE				
WITH PROSTRATE SOULS ADORING THEE	• • • •	351	L'ENVOY	61
PROTESTATION				
BUT THOU SLEEP'ST ON. WHER'S NOW THY PROTESTATION	•	202	THE CHECK	43
PROUD				
SUCH, THOUGH NO PROUD, NOR FULL	• • • •	173	CONTENT	9
AND PROUD WITH LIFE, AND SENCE	• • • •	144	RSRCTN +IM	11
WHEN THE PROUD WATERS RAGE. WHEN HEATHENS RULE	•	330	JACOBS PLW	29
AS THE POOR ASS, WHICH THE PROUD JEAR	• •	295	PALM-SUNDY	40
WHERE WITH PROUD HASTE THE RICH MADE WAY	• •	302	ORNAMENT	3
QUITE THROUGH THEIR PROUD AND POMPOUS FILE	• •	303	ORNAMENT	13
AND TAME PROUD WAVES, IF YET THESE BARREN GROUNDS	•	234	MUTINIE	12
PROUDLY				
THAT PROUDLY SPILT AND DESPIS'D BLOOD	• • •	326	ABELS BLOD	34
PROV'D				
SO MANY AGES FROM ME) IS SO PROV'D	• • •	267	ASCN-DAY A	6
BUT PROV'D THE HEAVIER GRAINES	• • • •	139	RGNRTN	33
PROVE				
TO EQUAL WINDS. WOULD PROVE TOO SHORT. THOU HAST	• •	281	JOY	13
PROVE MY OWN SHAME AND MISERIE.	• • • •	240	MISERY	44
OUR GUIDES PROVE WANDRING STARS	• • • •	237	CONSTLATN	46
MAY PROVE THY GLORY, AND THEIR SHAME. SO CLOSE	•	234	MUTINIE	18
WILL PROVE THEIR HEARTS MORE STIFF AND TUFF.	• •	314	THE STONE	51
PROVE NOT EXPEDIENT FOR THY WAY.	• • •	319	THE ASS	40
BUT WHICH THOU ART MOST, NONE CAN PROVE.	• •	298	JESUS WP B	23
THE PROVERB'D GRIEFS OF HOLY JOB	• • •	295	PALM-SUNDY	43
PROVIDE				
THE SOWER DOTH HIS BREAD PROVIDE.	• • • •	336	PSALM 65	32
THIS RING THE BRIDE-GROOME DID FOR NONE PROVIDE	•	233	THE WORLD	59
HIGH-NOON THUS PAST, THY TIME DECAYS, PROVIDE	• •	195	RLS + LSNS	103
PROVIDENCE				
SHALL I THEN THINKE SUCH PROVIDENCE WILL BE	• •	144	RSRCTN +IM	15
UNTO THAT PROVIDENCE, WHOSE UNSEEN ARM	• •	288	THE BIRD	9
PROVOKE				
THEIR JOYS PROVOKE THE DISTANT SKIE	• • •	295	PALM-SUNDY	20
OF TEARS, AND NOT PROVOKE TO MORE.	• • •	298	JESUS WP B	15
PRY				
AND SEARCH AND PRY	• • • • • • •	340	THE FEAST	44
PRYS				
OF NIGHT SHUT UP THY LEAVES, BE CHAST, GOD PRYS	• •	196	RLS + LSNS	136

		PAGE	TITLE	LINE
PUBLICK				
HIS SHAMELESS LUST IN PUBLICK WEARS	• • • • •	297	HERODIAS	15
PUBLIQUE				
WHEN ONCE MADE PUBLIQUE, IS ESTEEM'D BY NONE.	• • •	330	JACOBS PLW	18
PUBLISH'D				
AND EV'RY PUBLISH'D VANITY	• • • • •	265	INTRO. 2	26
PUDDLE				
GRANT, I MAY NOT LIKE PUDDLE LIE	• • • • •	212	DAWNING	29
BUT DRUNK, IS PUDDLE, OR MEERE SLIME	• • • •	150	RELIGION	43
PUFF'D				
WHY THEN THESE CURL'D, PUFF'D POINTS	• • • •	173	CONTENT	17
PULL				
AND SETS UP LAWS TO PULL HIS HONOR DOWN.	• • • •	330	JACOBS PLW	20
PULLEYS				
THE PULLEYS UNTO HEADLONG MAN, TIMES BOWER	• • •	2	SON-DAYES	9
PULSE				
AND HEARTS, WHOSE PULSE BEATS STILL FOR LIGHT	• • •	277	COCK-CRWNG	32
PUNISHMENT				
HOME BY OUR FIRST FAIR PUNISHMENT	• • • •	312	FAIR+YONG	42
MORE PUNISHMENT, THAN KNOWLEDGE TO MY SENSE.	• • •	159	MANS FALL	14
PURCHAS'D				
BUT FOR ONE THING, THOUGH PURCHAS'D ONCE BEFORE.	• •	321	HIDDN TRSR	34
(THOUGH PURCHAS'D WITH THY HEARTS DEAR TREASURE)	• •	299	JESUS WP B	28
PURCHASE				
AH. LORD. AND WHAT A PURCHASE WILL THAT BE	• • •	162	PURSUITE	17
PURE				
MY FAITH AS PURE, AND STEDDY	• • • • •	167	THE CALL	91
OF THIS POOR, SINFULL FRAME PURE HEART.	• • • •	182	CHRFLNESS	19
DID IN PURE LOVE DESCEND	• • • • •	184	PEACE	11
ALL PURE, AND BRIGHT	• • • • •	145	RSRCTN +IM	48
MAKE THESE SAD SHADES PURE SUN	• • • •	202	THE CHECK	30
AS TO MAKE MAN ALL PURE LOVE, FLESH A STAR.	• • •	283	LOVE-SICK	4
THROUGH THAT PURE VIRGIN-SHRINE	• • • •	323	THE NIGHT	1
THE CLEAN, PURE HAND, WHICH NEVER MEDLED PITCH.	• •	327	RIGHTSNESS	10
THAT MAY DISHONOR THOSE PURE LINES.	• • • •	335	JUDGEMENT	38
WHERE ALL IS PURE, WHERE ALL IS EVEN	• • • •	312	FAIR+YONG	24
WHEN IN HIS NAKED, PURE ARRAY.	• • • •	303	ST MARY MN	2
NATIVE AND PURE SHINES NOW IN THEE	• • • •	303	ST MARY MN	8
MAKES BEAUTY LASTING, FRESH AND PURE.	• • •	305	ST MARY MN	46
NEXT, THERE'S IN IT A RESTLESS, PURE DESIRE	• • •	278	THE STARRE	17
FOR WHERE DESIRE, CELESTIALL, PURE DESIRE	• • •	279	THE STARRE	25
THE PURE EARTH SAT, AND THE FAIR WOODS HAD SEEN	•	268	ASCN-DAY A	42
THE FULLER, WHOSE PURE BLOOD DID FLOW	• • •	270	ASCSN-HYMN	35
HIS PURE PERFECTION QUITS ALL SCORE	• • • •	209	REPENTANCE	81
O THOU THAT LOVEST A PURE, AND WHITEND SOUL./	• •	216	DRESSING	1
LIKE A GREAT RING OF PURE AND ENDLESS LIGHT	• • •	231	THE WORLD	2
GIVE TO THY SPOUSE HER PERFECT, AND PURE DRESS	• •	237	CONSTLATN	57
TO ALL YOUR POW'R MOST PURE.	• • • •	244	THE SAP	38
IMMEDIATE, PURE AND UNVEIL'D EYE	• • • •	349	L'ENVOY	18
PUREST				
TRANSPARENT AS THE PUREST DAY	• • • • •	349	L'ENVOY	13
PURGE				
AND FIRE WILL PURGE YOUR CALLOUS VEYL.	• • • •	266	VAIN WITS	9
O PURGE THEM, PURGE THEM ALL AWAY.	• • • •	336	PSALM 65	8
O PURGE THEM, PURGE THEM ALL AWAY.	• • • •	336	PSALM 65	8
DOST STILL RENEW, AND PURGE AND HEAL.	• • • •	333	AGREEMENT	56
SO SHALL THAT STORME PURGE THIS RECLUSE	• • •	176	THE STORM	21
PURGING				
PURGING THE FLOOR WHICH CHAFF DISTURBS.	• • •	221	AFFLICTION	20
PURLES				
THE PURLES OF YOUTHFULL BLOUD, AND BOWLES	• • •	205	IDLE VERSE	13
PURLING				
AND PURLING CORN DOTH CLOATH THE VALE.	• • •	337	PSALM 65	46
PURPLE				
SAD, PURPLE WELL. WHOSE BUBLING EYE	• • • •	325	ABELS BLOD	1
PURPOS'D				
IT QUITE FORGOT THAT PURPOS'D GLIMPSE.	• • •	332	AGREEMENT	4
PURSE				
PROPORTION TO THEIR MERITS, AND THY PURSE.	• • •	193	RLS + LSNS	62
THE KNOTS WE TYED UPON THY PURSE	• • • •	274	WHT SUNDAY	56
PURSIE				
THE PURSIE CLOUDS DISBAND, AND SCATTER	• • •	212	DAWNING	21
PURSUED				
PURSUED HIM WITH ONE SHOUT.	• • • • •	232	THE WORLD	22
PUT				
THE VESSEL WHERE YOU PUT IT BE FOR SURE	• • •	244	THE SAP	37
DID SHEW ME HOME, AND PUT ME IN THE WAY.	• • •	225	RETIREMENT	11
LORD. THOU DIDST PUT A SOUL HERE. IF I MUST	• • •	224	TEMPEST	57
PUT US QUITE FROM	• • • • •	211	FAITH	38
AND PUT FORTH THUS, THOUGH LORD, BEFORE	• • •	264	INTRO. 1	7
LET NO NIGHT PUT OUT THIS SUN.	• • • •	249	BEGGING A	4
PUT ON THEIR YOUTH AND GREEN.	• • • •	279	THE STARRE	32
SHOULD MIST WITHIN ME, AND PUT OUT THAT LAMP	• •	188	RELAPSE	15
AND PUT TO FLIGHT	• • • • •	179	CHRCH-SVC	13
TO PUT ON CLOUDS INSTEAD OF LIGHT	• • • •	164	INCARNATN	5
ARE PUT UNTO THE SLAUGHTER	• • • •	166	THE CALL	63
SPRUCE, SUPPLE CRINGE, OR STUDY'D LOOK PUT ON	• •	155	ISAACS M.	32
WHOSE EYES ARE BOTH PUT OUT	• • • •	327	RIGHTSNESS	22
THIS MADE HIM PUT ON CLOUDS, AND FIRE AND SMOKE	•	330	JACOBS PLW	7
PUT ON, PUT ON YOUR BEST ARRAY.	• • • •	294	PALM-SUNDY	7

		PAGE	TITLE	LINE
PUT	(CCN'T)			
PUT ON, PUT CN YOUR BEST ARRAY.		294	PALM-SUNDY	7
THOU WERT THE FIRST PUT IN MY HAND		348	HOLY BIBLE	5
PUTS				
SHARES IN THE ACT, AND PUTS ME TC'T.		319	THE ASS	31
PYRAMIDS				
HE SEES (LIKE PYRAMIDS) SHOOT FROM THIS BALL		224	TEMPEST	43
QUAILS				
AS SOME MEEK NIGHT-PIECE WHICH DAY QUAILS		310	THE SEED	67
QUARREL				
THOSE GUSTS MIGHT QUARREL AND GROW BOLD.		240	MISERY	8
THEY SEEM'D TC QUARREL WITH HIM, FOR THAT ACT		196	CORRUPTION	13
QUARRELLERS				
THE CNLY QUARRELLERS WITH THEE		214	MISERY	72
QUEEN				
BRIGHT QUEEN CF HEAVEN. GCDS VIRGIN SPOUSE.		302	THE KNOT	1
QUEINT				
GO, GO, QUEINT FOLIES, SUGRED SIN		204	IDLE VERSE	1
QUEINTEST				
THE DCTING LOVER IN HIS QUEINTEST STRAIN		231	THE WORLD	8
QUENCH				
BUT MEET TO QUENCH HIS LONGINGS, AND THY THIRST.		194	RLS + LSNS	80
QUENCH'D				
DESIRE THAT NEVER WILL BE QUENCH'D		278	THE STARRE	19
QUERULOUS				
POORE, QUERULCUS HANDFULL WAS'T FOR THIS		145	RSRCTN +IM	19
QUEST				
SURE (THEN SAID I) MY QUEST IS VAINE		152	THE SEARCH	49
MAN IS THE SHUTTLE, TO WHOSE WINDING QUEST		246	MAN	26
HUNTS IN AN EAGER QUEST.		286	PSALM 104	56
WHO QUESTION POWER, THEY SPEAK TREASON.		318	THE ASS	20
LET ME NOT FAIL TC QUESTION, WHO		319	THE ASS	30
MANY A QUESTION INTRICATE AND RARE		247	I WALKT	22
QUICK				
AMONGST THE QUICK, SELLING THEIR SOULS AND BREATH		275	PROFFER	39
MAKE CLAY ASCEND MORE QUICK THEN LIGHT.		270	ASCSN-HYMN	42
THE QUICK, AND TC RETREAT MOST SLOW.		327	RIGHTSNESS	18
THE QUICK, AND DEAD, BOTH SMALL AND GREAT		147	DAY OF JDG	23
THE FIRST (PRAY MARKE) AS QUICK AS LIGHT		141	RGNRTN	66
PIERC'D NOT, LOVE ONLY CAN WITH QUICK ACCESSE		160	THE SHOWRE	9
THROUGH THY INCREASE GRCW NEW, AND QUICK.		191	THE MATCH	41
HCW LIKE THE EYES QUICK WINKE		166	THE CALL	43
IN QUICK BLASTS SIGH BENEATH THCSE SHROUDS		176	THE STORM	19
AND HYMNING CIRCULATICNS THE QUICK WORLD		176	MRNG-WTCH	10
WITH QUICK, OR DEAD		174	JOY OF LIF	7
QUICK VIBRATIONS		172	MIDNIGHT	12
INTO MY SOUL, WITH WHCSE QUICK TCUCH		348	HOLY BIBLE	21
THROUGH ALL MY PARTS, AND LIKE A QUICK		340	THE FEAST	45
WHY, SINCE EACH DROP OF THY QUICK STORY		343	WATER-FALL	15
QUICKEN'D				
THIS QUICKEN'D MASSE OF SINNE		161	DSTRQCTION	18
THAT THEY HAVE QUICKEN'C EVEN CRIE STUBBLE.		218	HOLY COMM.	4
QUICKLY				
O COME LORD JESUS QUICKLY.		181	BURIALL	40
LEAVING FOR US (WHOSE GCCDNESS QUICKLY FADES)		326	RIGHTSNESS	3
QUICKLY WOULD I MAKE MY PATH EVEN		321	CHILDEHOOD	7
WHICH HIS FIRST LOOKS WILL QUICKLY FRAY.		338	DEATH B	19
AND DRUNKENNESS QUICKLY DID SLCCEED THE FLOCD.		307	RAIN-BOW	22
SINCE THAT DOTH QUICKLY FREEDCM WIN		312	FAIR+YONG	45
BY EACH MANS CCOR, AND CUICKLY WILL		351	L'ENVOY	51
QUICKNED				
BUT QUICKNED BY THIS CEEP AND RCCKY GRAVE		343	WATER-FALL	11
QUICKNES				
O WHAT BRIGHT QUICKNES		172	MIDNIGHT	27
QUICKNESS				
A QUICKNESS, WHICH MY GCD HATH KIST.		345	QUICKNESS	20
QUICKNING				
THY QUICKNING BREATH, WHICH GLACLY BEARS		345	THE WREATH	16
AND HATCH'D ALL WITH HIS QUICKNING LOVE.		344	WATER-FALL	32
AND SCNGS I HEAR. O QUICKNING SHOWERS		340	THE FEAST	51
QUICKNING THE DEAD		339	THE FEAST	14
O THE NEW WORLCS NEW, QUICKNING SUN.		349	L'ENVOY	1
HER QUICKNING KINDNESS, SMILES AND KISSES		348	HOLY BIBLE	29
INSPIR'D A QUICKNING PCWER THROUGH THE DEAD		144	RSRCTN +IM	3
BUT HATH HIS QUICKNINGS, AND REPRIEVES		219	HOLY COMM.	12
THY SPIRIT PLANT, QUICKNING THE WHOLE		206	REPENTANCE	3
SURE, HCLY HOPES, HIGH JOYS AND QUICKNING FLIGHTS		267	ASCN-DAY A	2
QUIET				
NC CUIET COULCST THOU HAVE. NCR CIST THOU WINK		213	ADMISSION	9
A SWEET, REVENGELESS, QUIET MINDE		317	MEN OF WAR	43
QUIKNING				
THY QUIKNING FREINDSHIP, MANS BRIGHT WEALTH.		294	BEGGING B	22
QUILL				
SIMPLY BELIEV'D, 'TWAS NCT MY CUILL.		332	AGREEMENT	6
SIMPLY BELIEV'D, 'TWAS NCT MY QUILL.		320	RGNRTN	8
QUIRE				
O HCW IN THIS THY QUIRE OF SOLLS I STAND		179	CHRCH-SVC	9
QUIRES				
WHERE CLOUDLESS QUIRES SING WITHOUT TEARS		345	THE WREATH	18
QUIT				
AND CANNOT QUIT THE WCMB		187	NO DC THEY	28

		PAGE	TITLE	LINE
QUIT	(CON'T)			
THEY WOULD SOON QUIT AND LEARN TO KNEEL.		308	THE SEED	4
QUIT THEIR FIRST BED AND MOUNT. TREES, HERBS, FLOWRES, ALL		223	TEMPEST	27
DID QUIT THEIR TROUBLED CHANNEL, AND RETIRE		234	MUTINIE	7
QUITE				
THAT HE HATH QUITE FORGOT HOW TO GO THERE.		246	MAN	21
THOU WOULDST TO WEEDS, AND THISTLES QUITE DISPERSE		221	AFFLICTION	15
WHEN I WENT QUITE ASTRAY		225	RETIREMENT	8
PUT US QUITE FROM		211	FAITH	38
THIS PAST, I THREW THE CLOTHES QUITE O'R HIS HEAD		247	I WALKT	29
AND QUITE UNDREST JUST NOW WITH THEE		312	FAIR+YONG	48
QUITE THROUGH THEIR PROUD AND POMPOUS FILE		303	ORNAMENT	13
SPLIT, AND THE BOX QUITE BROKE AND MARR'D.		304	ST MARY MN	22
IT QUITE FORGOT THAT PURPOS'D GLIMPSE.		332	AGREEMENT	4
WHO SEARCH'D IT QUITE THROUGH TO AND FRO		338	DEATH B	13
QUITE THROUGH THEM BOTH, STILL INFINITE		333	AGREEMENT	51
QUITE VANISH AND DECAY.		283	GARLAND	32
BEATS THEM QUITE OFF, AND IN AN HOUR		203	DSRDR + FR	26
WHICH BUSIE THOUGHTS (LIKE WINDS) WOULD SCATTER QUITE		179	CHRCH-SVC	12
QUITE SPENT WITH THOUGHTS I LEFT MY CELL, AND LAY		167	VNTY SPRIT	1
I RIFLED QUITE, AND HAVING PAST		168	VNTY SPRIT	13
WITH HYEROGLIPHICKS QUITE DISMEMBRED		168	VNTY SPRIT	23
AND QUITE BLOT OUT THEIR NAMES		147	DAY OF JDG	8
QUITS				
HIS PURE PERFECTION QUITS ALL SCORE		209	REPENTANCE	81
QUITTING				
QUITTING SADNESSE)		182	CHRFLNESS	7
QUITTING THY WAY		203	DSRDR + FR	12
RACE				
APPOINTED FOR MY SECOND RACE		169	RETREATE	4
HERE SPIRITS THAT HAVE RUN THEIR RACE AND FOUGHT		280	PALM-TREE	17
WHERE TILL THE DAY RESTORE THE RACE		228	PILGRIMAGE	7
AND THE SUN RUNS HIS RACE.		286	PSALM 104	52
RACK				
TO BE A COMMON RACK.		238	SHEPHEARDS	30
I SEARCH, AND RACK MY SOUL TO SEE		178	SILENCE	17
TO WRENCH, AND RACK THY BLESSED LIMBES.		185	PASSION	33
TO RACK OLD ELEMENTS		153	THE SEARCH	88
RAG				
THY SEAMLESS COAT IS GROWN A RAG		350	L'ENVOY	30
RAGE				
WITH THY LEAST TOUCH, LIGHTNINGS AND WINDS THAT RAGE		287	PSALM 104	87
WHEN THE PROUD WATERS RAGE. WHEN HEATHENS RULE		330	JACOBS PLW	29
RAGING				
HIS TIME IS SHORT, MORE RAGING GROWS.		335	JUDGEMENT	30
AND MAK'ST THE RAGING PEOPLE MILD.		336	PSALM 65	20
RAGS				
THOU MAI'ST IN RAGS A MIGHTY PRINCE RELIEVE		193	RLS + LSNS	63
THOU TO POOR RAGS DOST STILL GIVE GRACE.		265	INTRO. 2	12
RAIN				
ALL SAD WITH TEARS, WHICH LIKE WARM SUMMER RAIN		268	ASCN-DAY A	52
WITH CLOUDS AND RAIN, YET FULL AS CALM AND FINE		281	JOY	15
THE DROPS OF RAIN, THE SIGHS OF THE WIND		207	REPENTANCE	37
RAIN DID REPLY		222	TEMPEST	12
AS RAIN HERE AT OUR WINDOWS BEATS		213	ADMISSION	7
AND SCARCE A ROOM BUT WIND, AND RAIN		180	BURIALL	13
CHAMBERS OF RAIN, WHERE HEAV'NS LARGE BOTTLES LIE		285	PSALM 104	38
A GARLAND, WHERE COMES NEITHER RAIN, NOR WIND.		283	GARLAND	36
BETTER, THE POOLS SHOULD FLOW WITH RAIN AND FLOODS		290	THE TIMBER	47
SOUL-QUICKNING RAIN, THIS LIVING WATER		296	JESUS WP A	10
RAIN GENTLY SPENDS HIS HONEY-DROPS, AND POURS		306	RAIN-BOW	11
BOLD STORMS, AND SIMPLY DOST ATTEND ON RAIN		307	RAIN-BOW	40
THOU DOST BUT COURT COLD RAIN, TILL RAIN TURNS FIRE.		307	RAIN-BOW	42
THOU DOST BUT COURT COLD RAIN, TILL RAIN TURNS FIRE.		307	RAIN-BOW	42
RAIN-BOW				
MADE ME A STARRE, A PEARLE, OR A RAIN-BOW		161	DSTRQCTION	6
RAIN-BOWS				
IN HEAV'N, HAIL, THUNDER, RAIN-BOWS, SNOW, AND ICE		194	RLS + LSNS	93
RAIN'D				
RAIN'D ON THY BED		287	THE BIRD	5
IT RAIN'D ABOUT HIM BLOUD AND TEARS, BUT HE		232	THE WORLD	29
RAINE				
MY GOD WOULD GIVE A SUN-SHINE AFTER RAINE.		160	THE SHOWRE	18
RAINS				
THEN CROPS, AND RAINS FOR GRIEFE		139	RGNRTN	25
RAINY				
AND ALL HIS LIFE A RAINY, WEEPING DAY.		290	THE TIMBER	36
RAISE				
UNITE, AND RAISE UP ALL THAT DYED, AT ONCE.		298	JESUS WP B	8
A CONSORT RAISE		182	CHRFLNESS	23
I WIL RAISE THEE.		214	PRAISE	12
TO RAISE IT TO THE TRUTH AND LIGHT OF THINGS		248	I WALKT	40
RAN				
A SPRING RAN BY, I TOLD HER TEARS		208	REPENTANCE	44
TO EGYPT HENCE I FLED, RAN O'RE		151	THE SEARCH	11
CALL'D FORTH THY TEARS, WHICH RAN IN LIVE		305	ST MARY MN	42
RAN I IN CHASE OF VANITY		348	HOLY BIBLE	14
RANGE				
O LET ME NOT THUS RANGE.		187	NO DO THEY	19
AND BRINGS MAN HOME, WHEN HE DOTH RANGE		221	AFFLICTION	6

	PAGE	TITLE	LINE
RANGES (CON'T)			
LEAVE THEN THY FOOLISH RANGES.	184	PEACE	17
RANK			
THAT GILD RANK POYSON, AND ALLOW	205	IDLE VERSE	11
RARE			
THOU ART THE GREAT ELIXIR, RARE, AND CHOICE. . . .	198	SCRIPTURES	6
PRAYING. AND TO BE MARRIED. IT WAS RARE	154	ISAACS M.	1
MANY A QUESTION INTRICATE AND RARE	247	I WALKT	22
RARE LOCKS. THAT CAN DISPENSE SUCH JOY	281	THE FAVOUR	3
A POWERFUL, RARE DEW	244	THE SAP	40
THY CURIOUS VANITIES AND RARE.	304	ST MARY MN	33
WHERE ALL WAS SUMPTUOUS, RARE AND NEAT.	304	ST MARY MN	14
O LORD MY GOD, HOW MANY AND HOW RARE	286	PSALM 104	65
SO RARE A FLOWER	323	THE NIGHT	16
RARELY			
OF KNOWING THEE, SO RARELY KNOWN.	346	THE QUEER	16
RASH			
BUT AS RASH YOUTHS, WHEN ONCE GROWN STRONG . . .	348	HOLY BIBLE	9
RATE			
BOWELS OF LOVE. AT WHAT LOW RATE	213	ADMISSION	13
THEN WEIGH, AND RATE	165	THE CALL	24
RAVE			
AND BOYLING STREMES THAT RAVE	175	THE STORM	6
RAVEN			
ELIAS BY A RAVEN IS FED	149	RELIGION	10
THE SWIFT-WING'D RAVEN SHALL BRING ME MEAT . . .	300	PROVIDENCE	16
RAVES			
HE RAVES, AND SWEARS TO STIR NOR FIRE, NOR FAN . .	197	CORRUPTION	31
RAVISH'D			
MY RAVISH'D LOCKS	157	BRT. CHRCH	16
RAY			
UNTILL AT LAST FULL WITH THE VITALL RAY	144	RSRCTN +IM	9
AND TAKING IN THE RAY	141	RGNRTN	77
ONE TWINKLING RAY	174	JOY OF LIF	13
EACH BUSIE RAY	171	MIDNIGHT	6
THAT GLIM'RING RAY	178	SILENCE	10
THAT SACRED RAY	206	REPENTANCE	2
THAT, MIDST ALL STORMS I FEEL A RAY OF THEE. . . .	245	MT. OLV. B	16
THIS BUSIE RAY THOU HAST ASSIGN'D.	276	COCK-CRWNG	4
A SUDDEN AND MOST SEARCHING RAY	348	HOLY BIBLE	20
RAY'D			
RAY'D INTO THEE, LIKE BEAMS INTO A GLASSE . . .	154	ISAACS M.	8
RAYES			
SHALL WITH INLIGHTNED RAYES	146	RSRCTN +IM	56
BUT SINCE THY RAYES	182	CHRFLNESS	12
DID SADLY NOTE HIS HEALING RAYES	292	THE JEWS	23
RAYING			
HOW HATH MY GOD BY RAYING THEE	210	FAITH	5
RAYS			
YET WHILE SOME RAYS OF THAT GREAT LIGHT	272	WHT SUNDAY	17
THY LINES ARE RAYS, THE TRUE SUN SHEDS.	333	AGREEMENT	35
AND EV'N, SMOOTH LINES, LIKE THE SUNS RAYS . . .	310	THE SEED	59
HE SHIN'D A LITTLE, AND BY THOSE WEAK RAYS . . .	196	CORRUPTION	3
RE-MARRY			
RE-MARRY TO THE SOULE, FOR 'TIS MOST PLAINE . . .	145	RSRCTN +IM	49
REACH			
CALL IN THY POWERS. RUN, AND REACH	189	RESOLVE	17
THAT I MIGHT ONCE MORE REACH THAT PLAINE . . .	170	RETREATE	23
I CANNOT REACH IT. AND MY STRIVING EYE	321	CHILDEHOOD	1
WHICH REACH BY COURSE THE BANK, AND THEN . . .	344	WATER-FALL	35
REACH'D			
AND ALMOST REACH'D, BECAUSE 'TIS SURE	317	MEN OF WAR	39
I REACH'D THE PINACLE, WHERE PLAC'D	139	RGNRTN	28
REACHETH			
REACHETH AS WELL THINGS OF DEJECTION	210	FAITH	3
READ			
THE WORLD READ TO HIM. ALL THE VAST EXPENCE . . .	223	TEMPEST	18
I'VE READ, WHO 'TWAS, DROVE YOU AWAY.	275	PROFFER	18
READ HERE, MY FAULTS ARE THINE. THIS BOOK, AND I . .	198	SCRIPTURES	13
I DID ONCE READ IN AN OLD BOOK	312	FAIR+YONG	31
I READ IT SADLY OFT, BUT STILL	332	AGREEMENT	5
TO LETTERS, TILL I LEARNT TO READ.	348	HOLY BIBLE	8
READE			
TO READE SOME STARRE, OR MIN'RALL, AND IN STATE . .	146	RSRCTN +IM	59
READY			
AND FEEL A FRIEND MOST READY, SURE AND KINDE. . . .	331	JACOBS PLW	52
MAKING DUST AND ASHES READY.	339	THE FEAST	6
AND CRUM OF LIFE, NOW READY TO DISBAND	275	PROFFER	27
OR READY TO BE DEAD	244	THE SAP	34
TILL ALL BE READY, THAT THE TRAIN	350	L'ENVOY	27
REAP			
THE BIRDS NOR SOW, NOR REAP, YET SUP AND DINE . .	245	MAN	12
REAPERS			
TILL THE WHITE WINGED REAPERS COME.	309	THE SEED	48
REAR			
COULD'ST SUCH A SHRILL AND LONG CRY REAR . . .	325	ABELS BLOD	9
REAR'D			
I SEE THE TEMPLE IN THY PILLAR REAR'D	330	JACOBS PLW	1
REASON			
TYE ME TO FAITH, THOUGH ABOVE REASON	318	THE ASS	19

		PAGE	TITLE	LINE
REASON (CON'T)				
MY SELF OF REASON, TILL OPPREST	. . . . .	240	MISERY	42
REBELLIONS				
WILFUL REBELLIONS. AND SUPPRESSIONS	. . . . .	208	REPENTANCE	54
REBELLIOUS				
IN THIS IMPURE, REBELLIOUS CLAY	. . . . .	164	INCARNATN	14
REBUILD				
AND REBUILD MAN	. . . . . .	270	ASCSN-HYMN	40
REBUKE				
AT THY REBUKE ARE BROKE.	. . . . .	287	PSALM 104	88
AT THY REBUKE THEY FLED, AT THE KNOWN VOICE	. . .	285	PSALM 104	21
RECEIV'D				
WHEN THEY RECEIV'D THE PROMISE, FOR WHICH NOW	. . .	238	SHEPHEARDS	11
RECEIVE				
THE CLOUD DOTH NOW RECEIVE THEE, AND THEIR SIGHT	. .	268	ASCN-DAY A	57
THEIR MASTERS WILL, MEET TO RECEIVE THEIR CROWNS.	. .	280	PALM-TREE	20
RECKONING				
AND IS A SHIELD (NOT RECKONING THOSE)	. . . .	220	PSALM 121	15
RECLUSE				
I SAW THE WARM RECLUSE ALONE TO LIE	. . . .	247	I WALKT	19
SO SHALL THAT STORME PURGE THIS RECLUSE	. . . .	176	THE STORM	21
RECORD				
DOTH YOUR MOST PRIVATE SINS RECORD.	. . . .	314	THE STONE	45
AND ENVYED THAT RECORD, DID SINCE	. . . .	332	AGREEMENT	2
RECORDS				
AND FOUL RECORDS WHICH THAW	. . . .	310	THE SEED	56
RECRUITS				
AS WE FOR LONG AND SURE RECRUITS	. . . .	310	THE SEED	77
UNBOWEL'D NATURE, SHEW'D THEE HER RECRUITS	. . .	145	RSRCTN +IM	21
RED				
OF THEIR RED SEA, A SPRING, I WASH, THEY WADE	. .	159	MANS FALL	32
THOUGH RED AS HE.	. . . . .	175	THE STORM	4
AND NOW AT EVENING ARE AS RED	. . . .	325	ABELS BLOD	5
THE SETTLED RED IS DULL, AND WHITES THAT REST	. .	222	AFFLICTION	27
REDEEM				
REDEEM THE DAY	. . . .	202	THE CHECK	45
REDEEMER				
MY DEAR REDEEMER, THE WORLDS LIGHT	. . . .	265	INTRO. 2	17
REDEMPTION				
AND FULL REDEMPTION OF THE WHOLE WEEKS FLIGHT.	. .	2	SON-DAYES	8
HOW NEERE REDEMPTION CREEPES.	. . . .	143	DEATH	30
REDRESS				
A STATE, THAT NO REDRESS ADMITS	. . . .	273	WHT SUNDAY	34
CANST LIGHT AND LEAD ME THERE WITH SUCH REDRESS	. .	234	MUTINIE	31
REDUC'D				
REDUC'D TH'EXTENT OF WORKS OF FAITH, SO MADE	. .	159	MANS FALL	31
REDUCE				
TO REDUCE A STUBBORN HEART	. . . . .	249	BEGGING A	14
REED				
FOR THY BRUIS'D REED	. . . . . .	235	MUTINIE	35
THAT HEARD'ST BOTH REED	. . . . .	163	MT. OLVS A	15
REEDS				
THIS MADE THE ANGEL CALL AT REEDS AND THATCH	. . .	238	SHEPHEARDS	27
REFIN'D				
WATER'S REFIN'D TO MOTION , AIRE TO LIGHT	. . .	223	TEMPEST	31
THOU ONLY FAL'ST TO BE REFIN'D AGAINE	. . .	145	RSRCTN +IM	50
REFINE				
AWAKE, AND THEN REFINE THE WHOLE.	. . .	151	THE SEARCH	20
WITH THY CLEER FIRE REFINE, BURNING TO DUST	. . .	216	DRESSING	6
O COME. REFINE US WITH THY FIRE.	. . .	274	WHT SUNDAY	61
REFINE US. WE ARE AT A LOSS.	. . . .	274	WHT SUNDAY	62
REFINING FIRE, O THEN REFINE MY HEART	. . .	283	LOVE-SICK	13
REFINERS				
TILL THE REFINERS FIRE BREAKS FORTH.	. . .	270	ASCSN-HYMN	30
REFINING				
REFINING FIRE, O THEN REFINE MY HEART	. . .	283	LOVE-SICK	13
REFINING STILL, I STRUGLED MUCH.	. . .	348	HOLY BIBLE	22
REFORM				
COULD NOT REFORM US, AND BLOOD (IN DESPIGHT)	. . .	307	RAIN-BOW	29
REFRAIN				
SHOULD NOT THY SIGHS REFRAIN THY STORE	. . .	298	JESUS WP B	14
REFRESH				
BUT FLOWERS DO BOTH REFRESH AND GRACE	. . . .	321	CHILDEHOOD	14
WHILE THE WINDS REFRESH THE YEAR	. . . .	281	JOY	19
THY SOUL, AND WITH NEW PINIONS REFRESH	. . .	155	ISAACS M.	48
REFUGE				
TO BE THE REFUGE OF HIS BRIDE.	. . . .	152	THE SEARCH	64
REFUSE				
REFUSE IT NOT. FOR NOW THY TOKEN	. . . .	266	INTRO. 2	31
WHO PROMIS'D MUCH, BUT DID REFUSE	. . . .	314	THE STONE	47
REGENT				
SIT REGENT YET, AND BLESSINGS FLOW	. . . .	351	L'ENVOY	57
REGISTER				
EACH THING TURNS SCRIBE AND REGISTER	. . .	314	THE STONE	43
REIGN				
SINCE TWO AFFLICTIONS MAY NOT REIGN	. . .	298	JESUS WP B	16
AND FROM THIS CARE, WHERE DREAMS AND SORROWS REIGN	. .	248	I WALKT	57
WHY SHOULD THE CURSE REIGN ANY MORE.	. . .	350	L'ENVOY	24
MAY FULLY FIT THY GLORIOUS REIGN.	. . .	350	L'ENVOY	28
LONG REIGN'D THIS VOGUE, AND THOU CAST BY	. . .	348	HOLY BIBLE	17

	PAGE	TITLE	LINE
REJECTS			
HIS EASIE YOKE REJECTS OR SLIGHTS	315	THE STONE	55
REJOYCE			
AND BONES REJOYCE, WHICH ONCE WERE BROKEN.	319	THE ASS	65
RELAPSE			
FREQUENT RELAPSE AND WILFUL BREACH	265	INTRO. 2	24
RELEASE			
O RELEASE HIM.	200	NTVTY 1	28
RELEAST			
THE SAD WORLD WEPT TO BE RELEAST.	340	THE FEAST	24
RELIEF			
BY SHEWING THE SIN GREAT, SHEW THE RELIEF	290	THE TIMBER	43
ON STONES DIDST SLEEP AND FOUND'ST BUT COLD RELIEF.	331	JACOBS PLW	46
RELIEFE			
FAR FROM RELIEFE	139	RGNRTN	23
RELIEFS			
ARE MY RELIEFS	341	THE FEAST	68
RELIEVE			
THOU MAI'ST IN RAGS A MIGHTY PRINCE RELIEVE	193	RLS + LSNS	63
O, YES. THOU KNOW'ST I COE, CCME, AND RELIEVE	161	DSTRQCTION	28
WHO CAN RELIEVE.	298	JESUS WP B	13
WHO KNOW, HOW WELL THOU CANST RELIEVE	301	PROVIDENCE	41
DOST THOU RELIEVE US AT THY GATE	213	ADMISSION	15
RELIGION			
ALLOW YOUR JOYES RELIGION, THAT DONE, SPEED	194	RLS + LSNS	81
LET MILDNESS, AND RELIGION GUIDE THEE OUT	193	RLS + LSNS	38
WHO SELS RELIGION, IS A JUDAS JEW	193	RLS + LSNS	45
THY FLAMES COULD NOT BE OUT, RELIGION WAS	154	ISAACS M.	7
NO, NO, RELIGION IS A SPRING	150	RELIGION	29
REMAIN			
OF ALL HIS WOES REMAIN.	200	NTVTY 2	12
REMEMBER			
THE WHOLE UNTO HIM, AND REMEMBER WHO	192	RLS + LSNS	21
AND NO MORE HIS SINS REMEMBER	208	REPENTANCE	50
REMEMBRANCE			
WITH A CHEAP, PLAIN REMEMBRANCE STILL	342	OBSEQUIES	5
REMEMBRED			
AND BROKEN LETTERS SCARCE REMEMBRED.	168	VNTY SPRIT	24
REMORSE			
THEN TRUE REMORSE, WHEN WITH PAST SINS AT STRIFE.	290	THE TIMBER	28
REMOTE			
THE MOST REMOTE, WHO KNOW NOT THEE	336	PSALM 65	23
REMOV'D			
THY GLORIOUS, BRIGHT ASCENSION (THOUGH REMOV'D	267	ASCN-DAY A	5
REMOVE			
AFTER THE SUN'S REMOVE.	270	ALL GONE	8
OR ELSE REMOVE ME HENCE UNTO THAT HILL	271	ALL GONE	39
THEY SAID, MY OWN HANDS DID REMOVE	333	AGREEMENT	41
FROM YOUR DARK HEARTS THIS VEIL REMOVE.	292	THE JEWS	37
REND			
AT CONSTANT WARRE WITH THEM. O CCME AND REND	283	LOVE-SICK	9
WHEN ONE LOWD BLAST SHALL REND THE DEEPE	147	DAY OF JDG	17
RENEW			
THE FROZEN EARTHS DEAD FACE THOU DOST RENEW.	287	PSALM 104	82
DOST STILL RENEW, AND PURGE AND HEAL.	333	AGREEMENT	56
THAT TO RENEW'T WERE TO DEGENERATE.	154	ISAACS M.	4
RENEW'TH			
AS PHENIX-LIKE RENEW'TH	145	RSRCTN +IM	29
RENEWING			
OFT HAVE I SEEN, WHEN THAT RENEWING BREATH	144	RSRCTN +IM	1
RENOUNCE			
HERE I RENOUNCE THE POIS'NOUS WARE.	190	THE MATCH	12
RENT			
IS SELDOM RENT.	324	THE NIGHT	40
BEG, THOU WOULDST TAKE THY TENANTS RENT.	264	INTRO. 1	14
RENT-FREE			
WHICH SHADES AND BOWERS DOTH RENT-FREE BRING.	338	DEATH B	10
RENTS			
AND SO REPAIR THESE RENTS, THAT MEN MAY SEE	237	CONSTLATN	59
REPAIR			
AND SO REPAIR THESE RENTS, THAT MEN MAY SEE	237	CONSTLATN	59
DID THERE REPAIR	247	I WALKT	25
ALL FLESH SHALL UNTO THEE REPAIR	336	PSALM 65	3
REPAIRE			
MUST TO THY BARRE REPAIRE.	147	DAY OF JDG	24
REPEATED			
REPEATED SIGHS THY KINDE HEART PAIN	298	JESUS WP B	4
REPENT			
WHO DO NOT SO, TOO LATE REPENT	274	PROFFER	12
REPENTANCE			
REPENTANCE THERE IS OUT OF DATE	147	DAY OF JDG	27
AND SUCH IS TRUE REPENTANCE, EV'RY BREATH	158	THE LAMPE	21
REPENTING			
FAITHFUL AND MOST REPENTING MONES	242	MISERY	111
REPINE			
AND NEITHER GRIEVE, REPINE, NOR FEAR.	339	DEATH B	25
REPLY			
WHERE THRONES AND SERAPHINS REPLY	295	PALM-SUNDY	21
DIDST TO EACH DROP REPLY.	213	ADMISSION	12
RAIN DID REPLY	222	TEMPEST	12

		PAGE	TITLE	LINE
REPLY (CON'T)				
LEAST MOTION, OR REPLY	. . . .	141	RGNRTN	85
TO THIS REPLY.	. . . .	341	THE FEAST	71
REPOS'D				
HERE, I REPOS'D, BUT SCARSE WELL SET	. . . .	140	RGNRTN	42
REPOSE				
THAT (FOR REPOSE, AND DARKNES BOUND) HE MIGHT	. . .	201	THE CHECK	18
REPRIEVES				
BUT HATH HIS QUICKNINGS, AND REPRIEVES	. . . .	219	HOLY COMM.	12
REQUESTS				
AND FAINT REQUESTS	. . . .	223	TEMPEST	14
REQUIR'D				
WHICH IS REQUIR'D TO MAKE UP LIFE	. . . .	299	JESUS WP B	27
REQUIRE				
YET I KNOW WELL, AND SO OUR SINS REQUIRE	. . .	307	RAIN-BOW	41
BUT AS FOR THEE, WHOSE FAULTS LONG SINCE REQUIRE	. .	281	JOY	11
RESEMBLES				
RESEMBLES THOSE TRUE JOYS	. . . . . .	235	CONSTLATN	2
RESENT				
THAT MAY THY MEMBERS, MORE THAN MINE, RESENT.	. .	216	DRESSING	30
WERE STILL ALIVE) THOU DOST GREAT STORMS RESENT	. .	289	THE TIMBER	15
RESENTIENT				
OR WHAT RESENTIENT CAN WORK MORE WITHIN	. . .	290	THE TIMBER	27
RESENTMENT				
BUT THIS THY STRANGE RESENTMENT AFTER DEATH	. . .	289	THE TIMBER	19
RESERV'D				
WHICH FOR THESE MISTS, AND BLACK DAYS WERE RESERV'D	.	237	CONSTLATN	47
RESIDE				
OF SOME MEAN THINGS WHICH HERE BELOW RESIDE	. . .	245	MAN	2
RESIGN				
I DO RESIGN	. . . .	191	THE MATCH	26
RESIGNE				
UNTIL THOU HAS A BLESSING, THEN RESIGNE	. . .	192	RLS + LSNS	20
RESIST				
WHOSE GLORIOUS CONQUEST NOTHING CAN RESIST	. .	216	DRESSING	11
RESISTED				
WHICH LONG RESISTED THY DESIRE	. . . . .	264	INTRO. 1	10
RESOLUTIONS				
LIKE WAVES BEAT ON MY RESOLUTIONS	. . . .	214	MISERY	76
RESOLV'D				
BUT FROM THOSE FOLLIES A RESOLV'D RETREAT.	. . .	226	RETIREMENT	33
RESOLVE				
WHICH DOTH RESOLVE, PRODUCE, AND RIPEN ALL	. .	145	RSRCTN +IM	33
THAT MADE THEE THUS RESOLVE TO DYE	. . . .	164	INCARNATN	15
RESPECT				
THE SAME RESPECT, AND ROOM, WITH EV'RY CLAY.	. .	226	RETIREMENT	44
RESPECTED				
FIRST, I AM SURE, THE SUBJECT SO RESPECTED	. . .	278	THE STARRE	13
REST				
THEY SHINE IN WHITE (LIKE STARS) AND REST.	. . .	275	PROFFER	24
SOULS SOJOURN HERE, BUT MAY NOT REST.	. . .	269	ASCSN-HYMN	5
THEY REST AND DREAM HOMES OF THEIR OWN.	. . .	228	PILGRIMAGE	8
GOD ORDER'D MOTION, BUT ORDAIN'D NO REST.	. . .	246	MAN	28
I WIL REST ME	. . . .	214	PRAISE	22
NOT A THOUGHT, THAT BREAKS MY REST	. . .	214	PRAISE	7
THE SETTLED RED IS DULL, AND WHITES THAT REST	.	222	AFFLICTION	27
PROFANENES ON MY TONGUE DOTH REST	. . .	208	REPENTANCE	75
BRIGHT SHADOWS OF TRUE REST. SOME SHOOTS OF BLISSE	.	205	SON-DAYES	1
AND HOME OF REST.	. . . .	2	SON-DAYES	20
SOFTLY REST ALL THY VIRGIN-CRUMS.	. . .	209	THE BURIAL	9
OF NIGHT, AND REST	. . . .	176	MRNG-WTCH	4
MY REST IN CARES, AND TO THE DARK WORLD LEND	. .	157	THE LAMPE	6
EATE, DRINKE, DISCOURSE, SIT DOWNE, AND REST	. .	149	RELIGION	15
I SHOULD ROVE IN, AND REST MY HEAD	. . .	153	THE SEARCH	71
LYES TAME AS ALL THE REST.	. . . . .	201	THE CHECK	5
REST FROM THE FEARS I'TH' NIGHT.	. . .	201	THE CHECK	19
ELSE ALL AT REST THOU LYEST, AND THE FIERCE BREATH	.	289	THE TIMBER	17
THE THRONE WHERE PEACE AND POWER REST.	. . .	299	JESUS WP B	31
MAKES WAY FOR STORMS INTO HIS REST.	. . .	309	THE SEED	44
SO GIVE ME GRACE EVER TO REST	. . . .	318	THE ASS	13
A SHELTER ALL THE WAY, AND BOWERS TO REST.	. .	326	RIGHTSNESS	4
BUT WE THE SUBSTANCE HAVE, AND ON HIM REST.	. .	331	JACOBS PLW	54
AND JOY, AND REST	. . . .	329	TEARS	6
O PAINFUL CROSS, MY BED OF REST.	. . .	341	THE FEAST	63
RESTAGNATES				
IN STREAMING RINGS RESTAGNATES ALL	. . . .	344	WATER-FALL	34
RESTLES				
ABOVE ARE RESTLES MOTIONS, RUNNING LIGHTS	. .	194	RLS + LSNS	89
DESTROY'D AT ALL, BUT WHEN TIMES RESTLES WAVE	. .	145	RSRCTN +IM	37
THIS RESTLES BREATH	. . . .	171	COME, COME	17
LORD. WHAT A BUSIE, RESTLES THING	. . .	161	PURSUITE	1
RESTLESS				
MAKE RESTLESS MONES	. . . .	179	CHRCH-SVC	5
MY RESTLESS EYE THAT STILL DESIR'D	. . . .	141	RGNRTN	72
BUT AS THIS RESTLESS, VOCALL SPRING	. . .	212	DAWNING	33
BUT EVER RESTLESS AND IRREGULAR	. . . .	246	MAN	17
HE GROPS BENEATH HERE, AND WITH RESTLESS CARE	. .	236	CONSTLATN	17
NEXT, THERE'S IN IT A RESTLESS, PURE DESIRE	. .	278	THE STARRE	17
RESTOR'D				
HER WEARIED WINGS, WHICH SO RESTOR'D DID FLYE	. . .	155	ISAACS M.	49

		PAGE	TITLE	LINE
RESTOR'D	**(CON'T)**			
BUT THEN RESTOR'D	. . . .	337	THE THRONE	2
THY GREAT DECAYS RESTOR'D MIGHT BE.	. . . . . .	304	ST MARY MN	32
RESTORATIVE				
THIS, THIS DIVINE RESTORATIVE	. . . .	305	ST MARY MN	41
RESTORE				
LOOK WHAT THOU GAV'ST, ALL THAT I DO RESTORE	. .	321	HIDDN TRSR	33
SHOULD HELP TO SPOIL) THOU CANST RESTORE	. . .	299	JESUS WP B	36
DEAR LORD. RESTORE THY ANCIENT PEACE	. . .	294	BEGGING B	21
WHERE TILL THE DAY RESTORE THE RACE	. . .	228	PILGRIMAGE	7
WHOSE SPITTLE ONLY COULD RESTORE THE BLIND.	. . .	217	EASTER-DAY	16
THAT WHAT GOD TAKES, HEE'L NOT RESTORE.	. . .	343	WATER-FALL	22
THOU SHALT RESTORE TREES, BEASTS AND MEN	. . .	347	THE BOOK	26
RESTRAIN				
SUBMIT MY WILDE HEART, AND RESTRAIN MY HANDS.	. .	321	HIDDN TRSR	30
FOR THOUGH SOME THINK, THOU SHIN'ST BUT TO RESTRAIN	.	307	RAIN-BOW	39
RESTRAIN'D				
AND OPENING SHOWERS (RESTRAIN'D FROM HARM)	. . .	337	PSALM 65	36
RESTS				
AND NEVER RESTS TIL ALL BE OUT.	. . . .	214	MISERY	80
RESTS NOT A SPAN.	. . . .	161	PURSUITE	4
RESUME				
RESUME THY SPIRIT FROM THIS WORLD OF THRALL	. .	271	ALL GONE	35
RESURRECTION				
AND RESURRECTION FROM THE EARTH AND NIGHT.	. . .	267	ASCN-DAY A	18
AND IN HIS RESURRECTION PARTAKE	. . .	217	EASTER-DAY	6
MANS RESURRECTION, AND THE FUTURES BUD	. . .	192	RLS + LSNS	26
RETINUE				
RETINUE, ALL WAS HERE SMOOTH AS THY BRIDE	. .	154	ISAACS M.	23
AS IF HIS LIQUID, LOOSE RETINUE STAID	. . .	343	WATER-FALL	5
RETIR'D				
OF THEIR LORDS THUNDER THEY RETIR'D APACE.	. .	285	PSALM 104	22
RETIRE				
RETIRE INTO THEIR DENS. MAN GOES ABROAD	. .	286	PSALM 104	62
PINE, AND RETIRE	. . . . . .	203	DSRDR + FR	39
DID QUIT THEIR TROUBLED CHANNEL, AND RETIRE	. .	234	MUTINIE	7
RETREAT				
BUT FROM THOSE FOLLIES A RESOLV'D RETREAT.	. .	226	RETIREMENT	33
HE LIV'D THERE SAFE, 'TWAS HIS RETREAT	. .	152	THE SEARCH	55
SO O'R FLED MINUTES I RETREAT	. . .	178	SILENCE	13
THE DAY OF SPIRITS, MY SOULS CALM RETREAT	. .	324	THE NIGHT	27
QUICK TO ADVANCE, AND TO RETREAT MOST SLOW.	. .	327	RIGHTSNESS	18
RETURN				
AND THEY TO DUST RETURN.	. . . .	287	PSALM 104	80
RETURN TO HEAVEN, FROM WHENCE IT CAME	. .	305	ST MARY MN	54
AH. WHAT SHALL I RETURN FOR THIS.	. .	182	CHRFLNESS	16
IN THAT STATE I CAME RETURN.	. . .	170	RETREATE	32
RETURN UPON HIMSELF THE LAW, AND STONES.	. .	198	SCRIPTURES	12
RETURNE				
THAT KEEP'ST ACCOUNT, TILL HE RETURNE	. . .	165	THE CALL	32
RETURNING				
AND THEN RETURNING, LIKE THE SUN	. . .	338	DEATH B	14
RETURNS				
RETURNS HOME WITH HIS LOAD.	. . . .	286	PSALM 104	64
WATCH THE RETURNS OF LIGHT.	. . . .	183	THRS A TYE	12
WHO SO RETURNS NOT, CANNOT PRAY ARIGHT	.	194	RLS + LSNS	83
THE BREAD WE CAST RETURNS IN FRAUGHTS ONE DAY.	.	193	RLS + LSNS	66
UP IN ONE CLOUD, AND SO RETURNS THE SKIES	.	156	ISAACS M.	61
AND THEN RETURNS, AND FROM THE WOMBE OF THINGS	.	145	RSRCTN +IM	27
ANGELS DESCENDING, THE RETURNS OF TRUST.	. .	2	SON-DAYES	15
'TWAS THINE FIRST, AND TO THEE RETURNS	. .	265	INTRO. 2	3
RETYRING				
THE ROCKS GIVE CONIES A RETYRING PLACE.	. .	286	PSALM 104	50
REV'REND				
AGE MADE THEM REV'REND, AND A SNOWIE HEAD	. .	156	ISAACS M.	69
REVEAL'D				
WAS FIRST REVEAL'D TO BE YOUR ROCK.	. . .	292	THE JEWS	41
REVEALE				
AND THY ASPIRING, ACTIVE FIRES REVEALE	. .	158	THE LAMPE	12
REVENGELESS				
A SWEET, REVENGELESS, QUIET MINDE	. .	317	MEN OF WAR	43
REVIVE				
THOU SEND'ST THY SPIRIT FORTH, AND THEY REVIVE	.	287	PSALM 104	81
SHALL THEY REVIVE.	. . . . . .	339	DEATH B	27
REVOLT				
REVOLT AND FLINCH	. . . . . .	275	PROFFER	28
REWARD				
THERE'S A REWARD FOR THEM AND THEE.	. . .	275	PROFFER	42
RHEUM				
BY THAT FOUL RHEUM THY FALSE EYE WEARS.	. .	305	ST MARY MN	66
RICH				
WHY IS THIS RICH, THIS PISTIC NARD	. .	304	ST MARY MN	21
WHERE WITH PROUD HASTE THE RICH MADE WAY	. .	302	ORNAMENT	3
THOSE BURTHENS TO THE RICH MANS DOOR	. .	319	THE ASS	34
WITH FERTIL STREAMS, MAKES RICH ALL GROUNDS	.	336	PSALM 65	30
WITH HIDDEN TREASURES THAT MAKE TRULY RICH.	.	327	RIGHTSNESS	12
THOU HAST MADE BEGGERS RICH.	. . . .	329	TEARS	16
FOR THIS RICH PEARL, LIKE SOME MORE COMMON STONE	.	330	JACOBS PLW	17
AND AS THY CARE BOUNDS THESE, SO THY RICH LOVE	.	285	PSALM 104	29
AS RICH A SCENT AS THE NOW PRIMROS'D FIELDS	.	267	ASCN-DAY A	22

	PAGE	TITLE	LINE
RICH (CON'T)			
MAN THROUGH HIS HEAP OF DARK DAYS, AND THE RICH	2	SON-DAYES	7
THY PEOPLES HEARTS, WHEN ALL THY SEEDS WERE RICH	229	LAW + GOSP	4
SUCH A RICH AIR OF SWEETS, AS EVENING SHOWRS	244	MT. OLV. B	4
ODORS, AND MYRRH, AND BALM IN ONE RICH FLOUD	244	MT. OLV. B	7
HEAV'NS RICH EXPENCE	144	RSRCTN +IM	12
HOW RICH, O LORD. HOW FRESH THY VISITS ARE.	198	UNPRFTBLNS	1
SHOULD MOVE, THEY MAKE US HOLY, HAPPY, RICH.	192	RLS + LSNS	30
BUT O THY LOVE. THY RICH, ALMIGHTY LOVE	188	RELAPSE	5
HADST THOU BIN RICH, OR FINE	173	CONTENT	14
RICH WEEDS AND SHROUDS.	342	OBSEQUIES	18
RID			
OF WILD AFFECTIONS, RID	282	GARLAND	10
RIDE			
ABOUT THIS EARTH DOTH RUN AND RIDE	246	MAN	18
RIDGE			
THOU WATER'ST EVERY RIDGE OF LAND	337	PSALM 65	33
RIFE			
BUT GRACE, AND BLESSINGS CAME WITH THEE SO RIFE	218	HOLY COMM.	3
AND WHEN FEARS, AND DOUBTS WERE RIFE	214	PRAISE	3
RIFLED			
I RIFLED QUITE, AND HAVING PAST	168	VNTY SPRIT	13
RIGHT			
THE RODE FOUL, AND WHERE ONE GOES RIGHT	174	JOY OF LIF	11
A SWEET SELF-PRIVACY IN A RIGHT SOUL	193	RLS + LSNS	53
HAD EQUAL RIGHT.	210	FAITH	16
IF THE SUN RISE ON THE ROCKS, IS'T RIGHT	265	INTRO. 2	5
YET JOY IT SELF WILL MAKE A RIGHT SOUL GRIEVE	290	THE TIMBER	39
(THOUGH BOTH ALL-SEEING AND ALL RIGHT)	314	THE STONE	33
HIS RIGHTEOUS COURSE, THAT THOUGH HE KNOWS	314	THE STONE	30
THUS, RIGHTEOUS FATHER. DOEST THOU DEAL	293	THE JEWS	46
SO WHEN THE SUN OF RIGHTEOUSNESS	210	FAITH	21
RING			
LIKE A GREAT RING OF PURE AND ENDLESS LIGHT	231	THE WORLD	2
AND SING, AND WEEP, SOAR'D UP INTO THE RING	232	THE WORLD	47
THIS RING THE BRIDE-GROOME DID FOR NONE PROVIDE	233	THE WORLD	59
IN A BRIGHT RING.	295	PALM-SUNDY	23
CORRUPTION WITH THIS GLORIOUS RING	167	VNTY SPRIT	6
WHICH WEARS HEAVEN, LIKE A BRIDAL RING	346	THE QUEER	3
RINGS			
IN STREAMING RINGS RESTAGNATES ALL	344	WATER-FALL	34
AND SPIRITS ALL MY EARTH. HEARK. IN WHAT RINGS	176	MRNG-WTCH	9
AWAK, AWAK. HEARK, HOW TH' WOOD RINGS	199	NTVTY 1	7
RIPEN			
WHICH DOTH RESOLVE, PRODUCE, AND RIPEN ALL	145	RSRCTN +IM	33
RISE			
SHALL ONE DAY RISE, AND CLOATH'D WITH SHINING LIGHT	145	RSRCTN +IM	47
LOATH HENCE TO PART, AT LAST I RISE	152	THE SEARCH	33
MAN IS THEIR HIGH-PRIEST, AND SHOULD RISE	199	NTVTY 1	11
SOME RISE TO SEEK THEE, AND WITH HEADS	187	NO DO THEY	25
RISE TO PREVENT THE SUN, SLEEP DOTH SINS GLUT	192	RLS + LSNS	11
INJURE NOT MODEST BLOUD, WHOSE SPIRITS RISE	194	RLS + LSNS	73
DO THOU THE WORKS OF DAY, AND RISE A STAR.	196	RLS + LSNS	138
WHOSE RISE, HEIGHT, AND DESCENT IS BUT A SPAN.	195	RLS + LSNS	108
IN SOME GOOD THOUGHTS, SO WHEN THE DAY SHALL RISE	195	RLS + LSNS	129
DUST THAT WOULD RISE, AND DIMME MY SIGHT	161	DSTRQCTION	30
TO RISE ON YOU AGAIN, AND LOOK	292	THE JEWS	30
SO RISE AND RUN, AS TO CUT-RUN THESE SKIES	283	LOVE-SICK	6
A STAR THAT WOULD NE'R SET, BUT EVER RISE	283	LOVE-SICK	5
WHEN SHALL THOSE FIRST WHITE PILGRIMS RISE	335	JUDGEMENT	23
WHEN THOU DIDST RISE	323	THE NIGHT	10
FROM THE LOW EARTH TO HIGH HEAVEN RISE	326	ABELS BLOD	38
SHALL (WHEN THEY RISE) SPEAK BETTER THINGS	326	ABELS BLOD	40
RISE WITH THE SUN, AND SET IN THE SAME BOWRS.	245	MAN	7
SO HAVE I KNOWN SOME BEAUTEOUS PAISAGE RISE	245	MT. OLV. B	17
IT WIL EXALT AND RISE	244	THE SAP	32
WHO ON THIS DAY (THAT THOU MIGHT'ST RISE AS HE)	217	EASTER-DAY	7
LIVE, DIE, AND RISE WITH THEE.	216	DRESSING	18
TUNING HIS BREST TO RISE, OR FALL.	222	AFFLICTION	37
IF THE SUN RISE ON THE ROCKS, IS'T RIGHT	265	INTRO. 2	5
I SOAR AND RISE	267	ASCN-DAY A	9
RISE TO A LONGER COURSE MORE BRIGHT AND BRAVE.	343	WATER-FALL	12
SHALL RISE AGAIN, AND LIVE AND SING.	340	THE FEAST	36
RISEN			
IN THEIR WHITE ROBES TO SEEK THE RISEN SUN.	268	ASCN-DAY A	30
RISING			
THE RISING WINDS	176	MRNG-WTCH	12
RITES			
AND CLOUDIE RITES.	211	FAITH	32
RIVER			
THY UPPER RIVER, WHICH ABOUNDS	336	PSALM 65	29
ROAM			
AND WHILE TOO MANY SADLY ROAM	299	JESUS WP B	52
ROAMS			
HE KNOCKS AT ALL DOORS, STRAYS AND ROAMS	246	MAN	22
ROAR			
ROAR IN THE COVERT OF THE WOODS, AND SEEK	286	PSALM 104	58
ROB'D			
AS BIRDS ROB'D OF THEIR NATIVE WOOD	228	PILGRIMAGE	17
ROB'D OF YOUR CALME, NOR CAN I EVER MAKE	158	MANS FALL	4

	PAGE	TITLE	LINE
ROBBERY			
A VERY ROBBERY, AND HIM SELF NO GUEST	195	RLS + LSNS	102
ROBE			
THOU CLOATH'ST THY SELF WITH LIGHT, AS WITH A ROBE	284	PSALM 104	5
BUT ONE GREEN BRANCH AND A WHITE ROBE.	295	PALM-SUNDY	45
ROBES			
LUST IN THE ROBES OF LOVE	205	IDLE VERSE	14
LAYING BY THY ROBES OF GLORY	163	INCARNATN	2
IN THEIR WHITE ROBES TO SEEK THE RISEN SUN.	268	ASCN-DAY A	30
ROCK			
ROCK HIM ASLEEP BELOW.	247	I WALKT	35
YET THOU THE GREAT ETERNAL ROCK	273	WHT SUNDAY	45
SINCE THESE ARE TROUBLED, TO THE SPRINGING ROCK	150	RELIGION	50
WAS FIRST REVEAL'D TO BE YOUR ROCK.	292	THE JEWS	41
WHY IF I SEE A ROCK OR SHELF	321	CHILDEHOOD	21
BUT IN HIS HOPE AND ROCK IS EVER GLAD.	327	RIGHTSNESS	33
THOU ART THE FAITHFUL, PEARLY ROCK	333	AGREEMENT	31
THE ROCK OF AGES IN WHOSE SHADE	346	THE BOOK	3
ROCKIE			
OPEN MY ROCKIE HEART, AND FIL	242	MISERY	101
ROCKS			
IF THE SUN RISE ON THE ROCKS, IS'T RIGHT	265	INTRO. 2	5
AND ROCKS HAVE TEARS)	213	ADMISSION	6
BUT A STRONG WIND MUST BREAK THY LOFTY ROCKS.	330	JACOBS PLW	10
THE ROCKS GIVE CONIES A RETYRING PLACE.	286	PSALM 104	50
ROUGH-CAST WITH ROCKS, AND SNOW	139	RGNRTN	21
CAN HEAT ROCKS.	189	RESOLVE	16
YOU MAKE ROCKS BUD	341	THE FEAST	53
ROCKY			
BUT QUICKNED BY THIS DEEP AND ROCKY GRAVE	343	WATER-FALL	11
AND GIRDS THEIR ROCKY HEADS THIS DAY.	336	PSALM 65	22
ROD			
TO FEELE MY LOVING FATHERS ROD	147	DAY OF JDG	31
A STICK, OR ROD WHICH SOME CHANCE BRINGS	166	THE CALL	52
DID ISSUE FORTH FORC'D BY THE ROD	184	PASSION	4
DOTH USE HIS ROD	221	AFFLICTION	12
RODE			
THE RODE FOUL, AND WHERE ONE GOES RIGHT	174	JOY OF LIF	11
AND RODE OF SIN.	199	NTVTY 1	16
LET THE JOY'D RODE MAKE HOLY-DAY	294	PALM-SUNDY	8
ROE			
AS A YOUNG ROE	157	BRT. CHRCH	19
ROOM			
AND SCARCE A ROOM BUT WIND, AND RAIN	180	BURIALL	13
OFT TO A NARROW, HOMELY ROOM	315	DWELLNG-PL	14
BUT WHEN THE HAND THAT LOCKT HER UP, GIVES ROOM	271	ALL GONE	31
THE SAME RESPECT, AND ROOM, WITH EV'RY CLAY.	226	RETIREMENT	44
ROOMES			
FIT ROOMES FOR THEE. OR THAT MY HEART	199	NTVTY 1	20
ROOMS			
OPEN MY DESOLATE ROOMS, MY GLOOMIE BREST	216	DRESSING	5
IF NIGHTS, AND SHADES, AND SECRET ROOMS	313	THE STONE	6
ROOT			
THAT AT THE ROOT OF THIS GREEN TREE	304	ST MARY MN	31
AND WITHOUT ROOT AND SAP DECAY	292	THE JEWS	18
WHILE THE LOW VIOLET THRIVES AT THEIR ROOT.	289	THE TIMBER	8
PLANTS IN THE ROOT WITH EARTH DO MOST COMPLY	223	TEMPEST	33
HE HATH NO ROOT, NOR TO ONE PLACE IS TY'D	246	MAN	16
THY ROOT SUCKS BUT DISEASES, WORMS THERE SEAT	243	THE SAP	7
FROM A POOR ROOT	248	I WALKT	37
HATH TAKEN ROOT, AND GROWS, AND DOTH NOT TIRE	279	THE STARRE	26
BUT THE BARE ROOT	203	DSRDR + FR	28
ROSE			
THE ROSE THAT CANNOT WITHER	184	PEACE	15
SOME LOVE A ROSE	174	CONTENT	21
'TIS NOW CLEARE DAY. I SEE A ROSE	151	THE SEARCH	1
O ROSE OF SHARON. O THE LILLY	220	HOLY COMM.	49
ROSE UP, AND CANCELL'D TWO DEATHS DUE TO THEE.	217	EASTER-DAY	8
ROSES			
OF WORMWOOD, AND A DEATHS-HEAD CROWN'D WITH ROSES.	280	JOY	6
FRESH AS THOSE ROSES, WHICH THE DAY-SPRING WEARS.	155	ISAACS M.	36
OR ROSES WITH MY YEWGH.	205	IDLE VERSE	20
AND CROWN'D MY HEAD WITH ROSES.	282	GARLAND	24
WHICH THORNS, NOT ROSES WORE.	345	THE WREATH	8
ROT			
TELL YOUTH, AND BEAUTY THEY MUST ROT	189	RESOLVE	11
TILL TIME NO MORE SHALL ROT	145	RSRCTN +IM	44
AND ROT, DESCEND NOT HERE, NOR THINK TO STAY	275	PROFFER	17
ROTTEN			
WRONG NOT THY CONSCIENCE FOR A ROTTEN STICK	193	RLS + LSNS	41
ROUGH-CAST			
ROUGH-CAST WITH ROCKS, AND SNOW	139	RGNRTN	21
ROUND			
OF DIVERS STONES, SOME BRIGHT, AND ROUND	141	RGNRTN	64
WHEN ALL SHALL STREAME, AND LIGHTEN ROUND	147	DAY OF JDG	5
I TURN'D ME ROUND, AND TO EACH SHADE	141	RGNRTN	87
'TIS DEAD NIGHT ROUND ABOUT. HORROR DOTH CREEPE	157	THE LAMPE	1
LORD, THEN ROUND ME WITH WEEPING CLOUDS	176	THE STORM	17
IN ALL THIS ROUND OF LIFE AND DEATH	208	REPENTANCE	73
AND ROUND BENEATH IT, TIME IN HOURS, DAYS, YEARS	231	THE WORLD	4

			PAGE	TITLE	LINE
ROUND	(CON'T)				
DOTH SPREAD LIKE CURTAINS ROUND ABOUT THIS GLOBE	•	•	284	PSALM 104	7
WITH BRUTISH MEN. THY GIFTS GO ROUND	• • • •		293	THE JEWS	47
AND ALL THY PATHS DROP FATNESS ROUND	• • •		337	PSALM 65	40
ROVE					
THOU DOEST THUS ROVE	• • • • • •		226	RETIREMENT	35
AND ROVE ABOUT THEE, GUARDIANS OF THY MINDE,	•	•	155	ISAACS M.	26
ROVE IN THAT MIGHT, AND ETERNALL LIGHT	•	•	146	RSRCTN +IM	63
I SHOULD ROVE IN, AND REST MY HEAD	• • • •		153	THE SEARCH	71
ROVING					
SPENT IN A ROVING EXTASIE	• • • • • •		151	THE SEARCH	4
ROW					
WHOM STRAIT THE SHINING ROW ALL FAC'D	•	•	303	ORNAMENT	17
ROWL					
LOOK FROM THY THRONE UPON THIS ROWL	• • •	•	207	REPENTANCE	23
ROWLE					
AND ROWLE INTO THE EAST	• • • • • •		146	DAY OF JDG	2
ROWLES					
IN ROWLES AND CURLES, MINCING AND STATELY DUMB	•	•	155	ISAACS M.	34
RUDDY					
DESTRUCTION ON HIS RUDDY WING.	• • • •	•	305	ST MARY MN	56
RUDE					
'TIS NUMBER MAKES A SCHISM. THRONGS ARE RUDE	•	•	330	JACOBS PLW	5
WHERE NO RUDE SHADE, OR NIGHT	• • •	•	146	RSRCTN +IM	64
RUDE FEET ERE TROD	• • • • • •		140	RGNRTN	39
AND THUS, AT FIRST, WHEN THINGS WERE RUDE	•	•	218	HOLY COMM.	6
FROM THOSE RUDE, BARREN HOURS.	• • • •	•	345	THE WREATH	4
RUFFLED					
BUT WINTER NOW HAD RUFFLED ALL THE BOWRE	•	•	246	I WALKT	5
RUIN'D					
IT IS (IN TRUTH) A RUIN'D PEECE	• • • •	•	180	BURIALL	11
RULE					
THE RULE WITHOUT EXCEPTION FITS.	• •	•	273	WHT SUNDAY	36
WHEN THE PROUD WATERS RAGE. WHEN HEATHENS RULE	•	•	330	JACOBS PLW	29
DID NOT A GREATER BEAUTY RULE MINE EYES	• •	•	320	HIDDN TRSR	23
WHERE FRAIL VISIBLES RULE THE MINDE	• • •	•	318	THE ASS	5
DID SOMETIMES RULE. A GRIEF SO BRIGHT	• •	•	299	JESUS WP B	50
RUN					
AND ALL ALONE FULL EARLY RUN	• • •	•	295	PALM-SUNDY	36
SOME SECRET SENSE, WHICH MAKES THE DEAD BLOOD RUN	•	•	289	THE TIMBER	23
WHILE ACTIVE WINDS AND STREAMS BOTH RUN AND SPEAK	•	•	288	THE BIRD	15
WHICH RUN FROM HILLS TO VALLEYS, AND IMPROVE	•	•	285	PSALM 104	31
SO RISE AND RUN, AS TO CUT-RUN THESE SKIES	•	•	283	LOVE-SICK	6
HOW WOULD I RUN TO ENDLESS NIGHT	• • •	•	316	MEN OF WAR	10
THEMSELVES AND OTHERS, I CONSENT AND RUN	•	•	324	THE NIGHT	45
HERE SPIRITS THAT HAVE RUN THEIR RACE AND FOUGHT	•	•	280	PALM-TREE	17
THEY PASS AS AT THE LAST GREAT DAY, AND RUN	•	•	268	ASCN-DAY A	29
ABOUT THIS EARTH DOTH RUN AND RIDE	• •	•	246	MAN	18
AS FLAMES ABOUT THEIR FUEL RUN	• • •	•	214	MISERY	77
ALL DAY, AND NIGHT DOTH RUN, AND SING	•	•	212	DAWNING	34
LEST WE SHOULD RUN FOR'T OUT OF BREATH	•	•	211	FAITH	39
SHALL IT IN THE EVENING RUN	• •	•	211	DAWNING	3
CALL IN THY POWERS. RUN, AND REACH	• •	•	189	RESOLVE	17
RUNNE					
ONE EVERLASTING SABOTH THERE SHALL RUNNE	•	•	146	RSRCTN +IM	69
THUS BY THE CROSSE SALVATION RUNNES	• •	•	167	THE CALL	74
RUNNING					
ABOVE ARE RESTLES MOTIONS, RUNNING LIGHTS	•	•	194	RLS + LSNS	89
AND EVER RUNNING, TILL WE LEAVE TO FLING	•	•	291	THE TIMBER	55
RUNS					
AND THE SUN RUNS HIS RACE.	• • •	•	286	PSALM 104	52
BUT WHILE TIME RUNS, AND AFTER IT	•	•	333	AGREEMENT	49
RUNS THITHER, WHENCE IF FLOW'D BEFORE	•	•	343	WATER-FALL	16
RUSH					
WHEN THROUGH THE NORTH A FIRE SHALL RUSH	•	•	146	DAY OF JDG	1
RUSH'D					
THOSE FLAMES WHICH ON THE APOSTLES RUSH'D	•	•	272	WHT SUNDAY	5
RUSHING					
A RUSHING WIND	• • • • • • •		141	RGNRTN	79
RUST					
LOVE LANGUISHETH, AND MEMORY DOTH RUST	•	•	183	THRS A TYE	3
AND SOYL THY TEMPLE WITH A SINFUL RUST.	•	•	216	DRESSING	8
THE FEARFULL MISER ON A HEAP OF RUST	•	•	232	THE WORLD	31
SEEM'D TO DEVOUR, LIKE RUST.	• • •	•	310	THE SEED	74
SABOTH					
ONE EVERLASTING SABOTH THERE SHALL RUNNE	•	•	146	RSRCTN +IM	69
SACK-CLOTH					
FOR MOURNING SACK-CLOTH WEAR, ALL MORTIFIED.	•	•	342	OBSEQUIES	16
SACKCLOTH					
PEECES OF SACKCLOTH WITH SILK-LISTS	• •	•	282	GARLAND	19
SACRED					
AND BY A SACRED INCUBATION FED	• •	•	248	I WALKT	45
THY SACRED WAY	• • • • •	•	248	I WALKT	51
THY DOVE TOO BEARS US ON HER SACRED WINGS.	•	•	230	LAW + GOSP	70
AND SACRED INSTITUTES IN ME.	• •	•	242	MISERY	100
HE GAVE HIS SACRED BLOOD	• • •	•	243	THE SAP	26
THY SACRED AND ETERNAL WIL DECREED	•	•	235	MUTINIE	34
AND THOSE ONCE SACRED MANSIONS WERE NOW	•	•	238	SHEPHEARDS	25
WELCOME SWEET, AND SACRED FEAST. WELCOME LIFE.	•	•	218	HOLY COMM.	1
I TAKE THY SACRED FEAST	• • • •	•	217	DRESSING	34

		PAGE	TITLE	LINE
SACRED	(CON'T)			
AND ALL THAT SACRED POMP, AND SHEL	. . . . .	210	FAITH	27
THAT SACRED RAY	. . . . . .	206	REPENTANCE	2
AND NOW BY THESE SURE, SACRED TIES	. . . . .	219	HOLY COMM.	25
AND BY A SACRED, NEEDFULL ART	. . . . .	222	AFFLICTION	38
WHEN THOU SHALT SPEND THY SACRED STORE	. . . .	147	DAY OF JDG	9
THE SACRED CONSTELLATION OF THY MIND.	. . . .	154	ISAACS M.	10
SWEETE, SACRED HILL. ON WHOSE FAIR BROW	. . . .	162	MT. OLVS A	1
IN SACRED HYMNES, AND ORDER, THE GREAT CHIME	. . .	177	MRNG-WTCH	17
O CALM AND SACRED BED WHERE LIES	. . . . .	310	THE SEED	79
O SPRED THY SACRED WINGS AND SHAKE	. . . .	308	THE SEED	13
WITHIN WHOSE SACRED LEAFS DID LIE	. . . . .	323	THE NIGHT	17
THAT SACRED VAIL DRAWN O'R THY GLORIOUS NOON	. . .	323	THE NIGHT	2
SACRED AND SECRET HAND.	. . . . .	300	PROVIDENCE	1
SINCE THE SAME SACRED BREATH WHICH THUS	. . . .	298	JESUS WP B	5
MY SACRED WASH AND CLEANSER HERE	. . . . .	344	WATER-FALL	24
THE SEERS OF WHOSE SACRED LIGHT	. . . . .	349	L'ENVOY	3
SACRIFICE				
BUT THOU A CHOSEN SACRIFICE WERT GIVEN	. . . .	154	ISAACS M.	5
THAT DEW THEY LENT, A BREATHING SACRIFICE.	. . .	156	ISAACS M.	62
TO OFFER UP THE SACRIFICE	. . . . . .	199	NTVTY 1	12
SAD				
THEIR SAD DECAYS, I FLOURISH, AND ONCE MORE	. . .	198	UNPRFTBLNS	8
MAKE THESE SAD SHADES PURE SUN	. . . . .	202	THE CHECK	30
SULLEN, AND SAD ECCLIPSES, CLOUDIE SPHERES	. . .	188	RELAPSE	19
O SAD, AND WILDE EXCESSE. AND HAPPY THOSE	. . .	154	ISAACS M.	17
'TIS A SAD LAND, THAT IN ONE DAY	. . . .	142	DEATH	1
ME FROM SO DARKE, AND SAD A BED	. . . .	142	DEATH	10
DOE BUT SEE YOUR SAD ESTATE	. . . . .	164	THE CALL	10
THE THIRD GLAD DAY THROUGH TWO SAD NIGHTS.	. . .	295	PALM-SUNDY	33
(THOUGH OF THEMSELVES BUT A SAD BLUBBER'D STORY)	. .	290	THE TIMBER	42
WHOSE HEAVY NOTES MAKE ALL THAT HEAR THEM, SAD.	. .	288	THE BIRD	26
BUT THOU BENEATH THE SAD AND HEAVY LINE	. . .	289	THE TIMBER	9
WHEN I AM MOST, MOST SICK AND SAD.	. . . .	293	BEGGING B	10
SAD, PURPLE WELL. WHOSE BUBLING EYE	. . . .	325	ABELS BLOD	1
THOUGH SINCE THY FIRST SAD ENTRANCE BY	. . .	338	DEATH B	1
BUT BLESSED JACOB, THOUGH THY SAD DISTRESS	. . .	331	JACOBS PLW	41
BITTER AND SAD	. . . . . .	327	RIGHTSNESS	29
BUT NOW GROWN SICKLY, SAD AND SLOW	. . . .	308	THE SEED	11
OF PAST DAYS, WHERE SAD HEAV'N DID SHED	. . .	309	THE SEED	53
HAD WRIT DOWN ITS SAD CONSEQUENCE	. . . .	311	FAIR+YONG	20
THESE BONDS, THIS SAD CAPTIVITY	. . . . .	319	THE ASS	54
A COMET, THE SAD WORLDS ILL-BODING BOOK.	. . .	307	RAIN-BOW	36
WHEREFORE, PIERC'D THROUGH WITH GRIEF, MY SAD	. .	207	REPENTANCE	19
THEN DID HE SHINE FORTH, WHOSE SAD FALL	. . .	210	FAITH	29
THOU, WHOSE SAD HEART, AND WEEPING HEAD LYES LOW	. .	217	EASTER-DAY	1
CONDEMNING THOUGHTS (LIKE SAD ECCLIPSES) SCOWL	. .	232	THE WORLD	19
ALL SAD WITH TEARS, WHICH LIKE WARM SUMMER RAIN	. .	268	ASCN-DAY A	52
FOR MY SAD FAILINGS AND MY WILDE	. . . .	265	INTRO. 2	21
AND MY SAD THOUGHTS DOTH CLEAR.	. . . .	270	ALL GONE	4
WHO TURN'D OUR SAD CAPTIVITY.	. . . .	351	L'ENVOY	62
THY CAUSELESS PAIN. AND SAD AS DEATH.	. . .	345	THE WREATH	13
WHOSE SHADOW MAKES ME SAD OR SICK.	. . . .	340	THE FEAST	48
AND SING HIS SAD VICTORIOUS STORY.	. . . .	341	THE FEAST	60
THE SAD WORLD WEPT TO BE RELEAST.	. . . .	340	THE FEAST	24
OF THY SAD DEATH	. . . . . .	342	OBSEQUIES	6
SADDEST				
THROUGH SADDEST CLOUDS TO THAT GLAD PLACE	. . .	345	THE WREATH	17
SADLY				
THOU SADLY DIDST TO HIM PRESENT	. . . .	304	ST MARY MN	38
SLOWLY AND SADLY DOTH HE GROW	. . . .	308	THE SEED	17
I READ IT SADLY OFT, BUT STILL	. . . .	332	AGREEMENT	5
DID SADLY NOTE HIS HEALING RAYES	. . . .	292	THE JEWS	23
AND SPRING, HOW IS'T THAT YOU SO SADLY GRIEVE	. .	298	JESUS WP B	12
AND WHILE TOO MANY SADLY ROAM	. . . .	299	JESUS WP B	52
BUT I AM SADLY LOOSE, AND STRAY	. . . .	187	NO DO THEY	17
SADNESS				
WHICH SADNESS BREEDS IN THE MOST VAIN	. . . .	345	THE WREATH	14
SADNESSE				
QUITTING SADNESSE)	. . . . . .	182	CHRFLNESS	7
SAFE				
THAT DONE, WE SHALBE SAFE, AND GOOD	. . . .	165	THE CALL	28
FOR HONESTY IS SAFE, COME WHAT CAN HAP.	. . .	193	RLS + LSNS	58
HE LIV'D THERE SAFE, 'TWAS HIS RETREAT	. . .	152	THE SEARCH	55
AND WHERE BEFORE I DID NO SAFE COURSE STEER	. . .	244	MT. OLV. B	11
SAFELY				
WHICH MUST BE CARRI'D ON, AND SAFELY MAY.	. . .	192	RLS + LSNS	34
SAID				
SURE (THEN SAID I) MY QUEST IS VAINE	. . . .	152	THE SEARCH	49
LORD, THEN SAID I, ON ME ONE BREATH	. . . .	141	RGNRTN	90
I SHOULD HAVE SPURN'D, AND SAID THOU DIDST FORBEARE.	.	161	DSTRQCTION	22
IT GRIEV'D ME MUCH. AT LAST, SAID I	. . .	168	VNTY SPRIT	29
I WOULD (SAID I) MY GOD WOULD GIVE	. . . .	245	MAN	8
SAID LITTLE LESSE.	. . . . . .	232	THE WORLD	41
O FOOLS (SAID I) THUS TO PREFER DARK NIGHT	. . .	233	THE WORLD	49
AND THIRSTIE BRICK MUST BE (SAID I)	. . . .	234	MUTINIE	13
HAST SAID, THESE LAST SHOULD BE THE WORST.	. . .	273	WHT SUNDAY	28
AND LUSTS (SAID HE)	. . . . . .	225	RETIREMENT	13
AND SAID, I WAS NO CHILDE OF DAY.	. . . .	333	AGREEMENT	40
THEY SAID, MY OWN HANDS DID REMOVE	. . . .	333	AGREEMENT	41

		PAGE	TITLE	LINE
SAID	**(CCN'T)**			
HEDGES HAVE EARS, SAID THE OLD SCCTH	• • • •	313	THE STONE	14
SAIL				
IF A MEER BLAST SC FILL THE SAIL	• • • • •	276	COCK-CRWNG	17
SAILERS				
SAILERS THAT FLOTE CN FLOWING SEAS	• • • •	336	PSALM 65	17
SAINT				
WHO SAINT THEMSELVES, THEY ARE NC SAINTS.	• • •	306	ST MARY MN	72
DEAR, BEALTEOUS SAINT. MORE WHITE THEN DAY	• •	303	ST MARY MN	1
FIRST, A YOUNG PATRIARCH, THEN A MARRI'D SAINT.	•	156	ISAACS M.	72
BE OWN'C, SAV'C, SAINTED BY YCU THREE.	• • •	284	TRINITY-SN	9
SAINTS				
WHO SAINT THEMSELVES, THEY ARE NC SAINTS.	• • •	306	ST MARY MN	72
HERE IS THE PATIENCE CF THE SAINTS	• • • •	316	MEN CF WAR	7
ENACT FCR SAINTS MY SELF AND MINE.	• • • •	316	MEN OF WAR	12
THY SAINTS ARE NOT THE CONQUERERS.	• • • •	316	MEN OF WAR	18
AND ALL THY SAINTS DO OVERCOME	• • • •	317	MEN OF WAR	27
GCDS SAINTS ARE SHINING LIGHTS. WHO STAYS	• •	174	JOY OF LIF	17
HERE IS THE PATIENCE CF THE SAINTS. THIS TREE	•	280	PALM-TREE	21
OF SAINTS AND ANGELS GLCRIFIE THE EARTH.	• •	267	ASCN-DAY A	26
IF SAINTS, AND ANGELS FAL DCWN, MUCH MORE THCU.	•	217	DRESSING	42
WERE PATRIARCH, SAINTS, AND KINGS	• • • •	238	SHEPHEARDS	4
TO DECK THEIR OWN, THEN GIVE THY SAINTS	• •	350	L'ENVOY	35
SAITH				
SAITH HCLY JOHN, THEN LET HIM FEAR.	• • • •	316	MEN OF WAR	2
YEA BETHEL SHALL HAVE TITHES (SAITH ISRAELS STCNE)	•	331	JACOBS PLW	33
SAKE				
YET O FCR HIS SAKE WHC SITS NCW BY THEE	• • •	237	CONSTLATN	49
TC DIE HERE FCR THY SAKE	• • • • •	184	PEACE	12
AND FCR HIS SAKE	• • • • •	204	DSRDR + FR	57
SALEM				
BLT WRETCHED SALEM ONCE HIS LCVE, MUST NCW	• •	238	SHEPHEARDS	17
CN IT THE PRINCE CF SALEM SITS, WHO DEALS	• •	243	THE SAP	13
SALUTE				
I GREET THY SEPULCHRE, SALUTE THY GRAVE	• •	267	ASCN-DAY A	15
SALVATICN				
ARE MERCY, AND SALVATICN	• • • • •	200	NTVTY 2	6
THUS BY THE CROSSE SALVATION RUNNES	• • •	167	THE CALL	74
KING CF SALVATION. BY STRANGE THINGS	• • •	336	PSALM 65	13
SALVES				
FCR SALVES AND SYRUPS, WHILE THEY LIVE	• •	339	DEATH B	23
SAMARITANS				
LIKE THAT SAMARITANS DEAD WELL	• • • •	150	RELIGION	46
SAME				
AND DECK ME, LORD, WITH THE SAME CROWNE	• •	167	THE CALL	92
THOU ART THE SAME, FAITHFULL, AND JUST	• • •	181	BURIALL	23
WITH THE SAME CURLING FCRCE, AND HISSE	• •	175	THE STORM	7
IN THE SAME LIVERY DREST	• • • •	201	THE CHECK	4
SEEK NOT THE SAME STEPS WITH THE CROWD, STICK THCU	•	193	RLS + LSNS	49
AND BRING THE SAME MAN BACK. THCU WERT AT FIRST	•	194	RLS + LSNS	82
WAS JUST THE SAME WITH CURS, AND NOTHING LESS	•	331	JACOBS PLW	42
EVER THE SAME, WHCSE DIFFLS'D STOCK	• • •	333	AGREEMENT	33
FROM THE SAME PRECIPICE BE HURL'C.	• • •	322	CHILDEHOOD	24
PERFORMANCE, WILL FOR THAT SAME DEED	• •	314	THE STONE	48
IN THE SAME PAGE THY HUMBLE GRAVE	• • •	310	THE SEED	71
SINCE THE SAME SACRED BREATH WHICH THUS	• •	298	JESUS WP B	5
AND THE SAME SUN WHICH HERE DECLINES	• •	292	THE JEWS	28
WE PLAINLY SEE, WHO MADE THE SAME.	• • •	277	COCK-CRWNG	22
ART STILL THE SAME, AND CANST UNLOCK	• •	273	WHT SUNDAY	47
SINCE THEN THCU ART THE SAME THIS DAY	• •	274	WHT SUNDAY	49
RISE WITH THE SUN, AND SET IN THE SAME BCWRS.	•	245	MAN	7
WEARY OF THIS SAME CLAY, AND STRAW, I LAID	•	233	MUTINIE	1
THE SAME RESPECT, AND RCOM, WITH EV'RY CLAY.	•	226	RETIREMENT	44
(AS ALL THE SAME	• • • • •	215	PRAISE	40
EVER THE SAME, AND NEVER DONE.	• • • •	349	L'ENVOY	2
SANCTIFIED				
THUS WAS THE DESERT SANCTIFIED	• • • •	152	THE SEARCH	63
SAND				
A HEAP CF SAND.	• • • • • •	179	CHRCH-SVC	11
TURNING TO HIM, WHO MADE POOR SAND TO TIRE	•	234	MUTINIE	11
MY CNE POOR SAND	• • • • •	275	PROFFER	26
WHICH (THCUGH BUT SAND) KEEPS IN A CURBS WHOLE SEAS.	•	285	PSALM 104	26
HENCE SAND AND DUST	• • • • •	314	THE STONE	37
SANDS				
A SEA, CR SANDS AND SERPENTS, YET SINCE THCU	•	234	MUTINIE	28
HCW MANY SANDS	• • • • •	164	THE CALL	11
SAP				
BY WIL CUR SAP, AND CCRDIAL. NCW IN THIS	•	243	THE SAP	27
AND BRING NEW TOO. GET THEN THIS SAP, AND GET	•	244	THE SAP	35
AND WITHOUT RCOT AND SAP DECAY	• • •	292	THE JEWS	18
SAPLESS				
COME SAPLESS BLOSSCM, CREEP NCT STIL ON EARTH	•	243	THE SAP	1
SAT				
THE PURE EARTH SAT, AND THE FAIR WOODS HAD SEEN	•	268	ASCN-DAY A	42
SATANS				
AND SATANS SEAT, IN ALL HER CCASTS HATH LIGHT	•	331	JACOBS PLW	32
SATE				
AND SATE THERE NCNE SUCH AT THY DINNER.	• •	305	ST MARY MN	68
AND PCOR, DESPISED TRUTH SATE COUNTING BY	•	232	THE WORLD	44
SATE PINING ALL HIS LIFE THERE, DID SCARCE TRUST	•	232	THE WORLD	32

	PAGE	TITLE	LINE
SATE (CON'T)			
I SATE ALCNE, AND TAKING UP	207	REPENTANCE	29
HAVE LEFT US, WHILE WE CARELESS SATE	164	THE CALL	12
MY SAVICUR SATE, SHALL I ALLCW	162	MT. OLVS A	2
I SIT, WHERE CNCE MY SAVICUR SATE.	151	THE SEARCH	28
THERE OFTEN SATE	146	RSRCTN +IM	60
HAVE SATE, AND PLEAS'C MY PENSIVE EYE	343	WATER-FALL	14
SATYRS			
WHILE OWLS AND SATYRS HCWL.	288	THE BIRD	28
SAV'D			
BE CWN'D, SAV'D, SAINTEC BY YCU THREE.	284	TRINITY-SN	9
SC THCSE BAD CAUGHTERS, WHICH GCD SAV'D FROM FIRE	307	RAIN-BOW	31
THAT SAV'C MY SOUL	188	RELAPSE	6
SAVE			
AND SAVE ME FRCM ALL INWARD STRIFE.	190	THE MATCH	18
STRIVING TO SAVE THE WHCLE, BY PARCELLS DYE	161	DSTRQCTION	34
BUT HE MOST WILLING TC SAVE ALL MANKINCE	330	JACOBS PLW	13
SAVEC			
AND SAVED THAT LIGHT, WHICH FREELY THOU	161	DSTRQCTION	19
SAVES			
AND WHAT HE SAVES, MAY HIS FCES SPEND.	301	PROVIDENCE	36
SAVING			
AND BROUGHT US SAVING AID.	302	THE KNOT	4
HIS SAVING WOUND	159	MANS FALL	24
IN THY CWN PRECICUS, SAVING TEARES.	184	PASSION	9
SAVIOR			
BECAUSE THEY US'D MY SAVICR SC.	317	MEN OF WAR	34
SAVIORS			
FAR GREATER, AND SC SPEAK MY SAVICRS GLCRY.	290	THE TIMBER	44
SAVICUR			
MY SAVICUR SATE, SHALL I ALLCW	162	MT. OLVS A	2
I SIT, WHERE CNCE MY SAVICUR SATE.	151	THE SEARCH	28
TO FIND MY SAVIOUR, I HAVE BEEN	151	THE SEARCH	5
WILL TELL THEE SO, SWEET SAVICUR THOU DICST CYE.	198	SCRIPTURES	14
EXPECTING TILL THY SAVICUR COMES	209	THE BURIAL	11
SAVICURS			
WHOSE SPRING IS IN MY SAVICURS HEART.	208	REPENTANCE	56
MY SAVICURS BLCUD.	214	ADMISSION	32
SAW			
WHEN NATURE ON HER BOSOME SAW	222	TEMPEST	5
WITH, THUS WEE SAW THERE, AND THUS HERE.	228	PILGRIMAGE	4
I SAW ETERNITY THE CTHER NIGHT	231	THE WORLD	1
WHEN FIRST I SAW TRUE BEALTY, AND THY JOYS	244	MT. OLV. B	1
YOU ONLY SAW TRUE LIGHT	238	SHEPHEARDS	6
BUT TC THIS LATER LIGHT THEY SAW IN HIM	239	SHEPHEARDS	53
I SAW THE WARM RECLUSE ALCNE TC LIE	247	I WALKT	19
HE SAW HEAVEN O'R HIS HEAC, AND KNEW FROM WHENCE	196	CORRUPTION	5
AND CHECKT THEIR FURIE, WHEN I SAW THEM MCVE	188	RELAPSE	7
BUT, C HIS GRAVE. WHERE I SAW LENT	152	THE SEARCH	45
'TWAS SC. I SAW THY BIRTH. THAT CROWSIE LAKE	160	THE SHOWRE	1
THEN I THAT HERE SAW DARKLY IN A GLASSE	146	RSRCTN +IM	51
BUT WHEN WE SAW THE CLCUDS TO CRACK	143	DEATH	23
AND THOSE I SAW SEARCH'C THRCLGH, YEA THOSE ANC ALL	320	HIDDN TRSR	7
MANY CISORDERED LIVES I SAW	310	THE SEED	55
I WROTE IT DOWN. BUT CNE THAT SAW	332	AGREEMENT	1
I SAW AT DISTANCE, AND WHERE GRCWS THAT FRUIT	320	HIDDN TRSR	13
WISE NICODEMUS SAW SUCH LIGHT	323	THE NIGHT	5
SAW'ST			
AND AS THCU SAW'ST, I IN A THCLGHT COULD GCE	146	RSRCTN +IM	57
THOU KNEW'ST AND SAW'ST THEM ALL AND THOUGH	347	THE BOOK	23
SAWEST			
'TIS SO. BUT AS THCU SAWEST THAT NIGHT	143	DEATH	15
SAY			
THROUGH MELANCHOLLY CLCUDS, ANC SAY	146	RSRCTN +IM	67
ADVIS'D THY SERVANT WHAT TO DC, AND SAY.	155	ISAACS M.	28
AND SAY	153	THE SEARCH	90
TO SAY, WHAT SHALL I DOE.	147	DAY OF JDG	26
OR IS'T SC, AS SOME GREEN HEACS SAY	149	RELIGION	25
HE SIGH'D FOR EDEN, AND WCULD CFTEN SAY	197	CORRUPTION	19
BUT PERFECT ALL BEFORE THOU SLEEP'ST, THEN SAY	195	RLS + LSNS	117
THE FLATT'RER SAY, I LIVE	183	THRS A TYE	22
THY HEAV'NS (SOME SAY)	172	MIDNIGHT	17
THERE IS IN GOD (SOME SAY)	325	THE NIGHT	49
SAY IT IS LATE AND DUSKY, BECAUSE THEY	325	THE NIGHT	51
AND SAY, THY WILL BE DONE.	338	THE THRONE	15
BUT MEER DISDAIN, LET NCT MAN SAY	335	JUDGEMENT	43
I HAD NCT ONE POOR WORD TC SAY.	333	AGREEMENT	38
MY FELLCW-CREATURES TCO SAY, CCME.	335	JUDGEMENT	15
SAY, YOU HAVE GOT THE DAY FROM MEN	305	ST MARY MN	48
NC, NCR CAN I SAY, THIS IS MINE	265	INTRO. 2	7
WISE HUSBANDS WILL (YOU SAY) THERE WANTS PREVENT	274	PROFFER	11
NCT SPARING OPENLY TO SAY	272	WHT SUNDAY	15
THIS VEYLE, I SAY, IS ALL THE CLCKE	277	COCK-CRWNG	39
AND SAY, WHERE GOC IS, ALL AGREE.	237	CONSTLATN	60
SC THAT I NEED NO MORE, BUT SAY	211	FAITH	41
SAY'ST			
THIS WOMAN (SAY'ST THCU) IS A SINNER.	305	ST MARY MN	67
SAYES			
HE SAYES IT IS SO FAR	246	MAN	20
SAYINGS			
THEN, THY SAYINGS ALL MY LIFE	215	PRAISE	25

		PAGE	TITLE	LINE
SCALE				
BUT WHEN THESE CAME UNTO THE SCALE	. . . . .	208	REPENTANCE	45
I FOUND A PAIRE OF SCALFS	. . . . . .	139	RGNRTN	29
SCAN				
HOW DO I STUDY NOW, AND SCAN	. . . . .	322	CHILDEHOOD	39
SCANN'D				
WHAT'S GOOD SCORE UP FOR JOY, THE BAD WEL SCANN'D	. .	195	RLS + LSNS	119
SCARCE				
SCARCE WARMS, BUT BY CONTRACTION	. . . .	189	RESOLVE	15
AND SCARCE A ROOM BUT WIND, AND RAIN	. . .	180	BURIALL	13
AND BROKEN LETTERS SCARCE REMEMBRED.	. . .	168	VNTY SPRIT	24
HE KNOWS HE HATH A HOME, BUT SCARCE KNOWS WHERE	. .	246	MAN	19
SATE PINING ALL HIS LIFE THERE, DID SCARCE TRUST	. .	232	THE WORLD	32
SCARF				
SICK WITH A SCARF, OR GLOVE.	. . . . . .	205	IDLE VERSE	16
SCARSE				
HERE, I REPOS'D, BUT SCARSE WELL SET	. . .	140	RGNRTN	42
SCATT'RING				
SCATT'RING THE MYRRHE, AND INCENSE OF THY PRAY'R.	. .	155	ISAACS M.	52
SCATT'RING THY KIND	. . . . . .	201	THE CHECK	10
SCATT'RING THAT CLOUD, SHEWD ME THE FLAME	. .	332	AGREEMENT	9
SCATTER				
WHICH BUSIE THOUGHTS (LIKE WINDS) WOULD SCATTER QUITE	.	179	CHRCH-SVC	12
LET ME NOT SCATTER, AND DESPISE MY FOOD	. . .	230	LAW + GOSP	34
SCATTER THESE SHADES OF DEATH, AND GIVE	. . .	208	REPENTANCE	51
THE PURSIE CLOUDS DISBAND, AND SCATTER	. . .	212	DAWNING	21
AND SCATTER DEATH	. . . . . .	275	PROFFER	38
SCATTER'D				
ALL SCATTER'D LAY, WHILE HE HIS EYES DID POUR	. .	231	THE WORLD	14
WITH SCATTER'D LOCKS	. . . . . .	189	RESOLVE	14
WHICH, SCATTER'D IN A THOUSAND PEARLS, EACH FLOWRE	.	155	ISAACS M.	56
WHICH HIS DEATH SCATTER'D) HE FORETOLD THE PLACE	.	330	JACOBS PLW	23
CAN MAKE MANS DEAD AND SCATTER'D BONES	. .	298	JESUS WP B	7
NOW SCATTER'D THUS, DOST KNOW THEM SO.	. . .	347	THE BOOK	24
SCATTERED				
SCATTERED EACH WHERE	. . . . . .	292	THE JEWS	17
SCENE				
THY OTHER CREATURES IN THIS SCENE	. . .	187	NO DO THEY	23
THAT SCENE WAS CHANG'D, AND A NEW DRESSE	. .	210	FAITH	23
SCENES				
HIS WONDROUS METHOD, MARK THE VARIOUS SCENES	. .	194	RLS + LSNS	92
SCENT				
AS RICH A SCENT AS THE NOW PRIMROS'D FIELDS	. .	267	ASCN-DAY A	22
CREEPS FORTH, AND PINCH'D FOR FOOD, WITH SCENT AND SIGHT		286	PSALM 104	55
SCHISM				
'TIS NUMBER MAKES A SCHISM. THRONGS ARE RUDE	. .	330	JACOBS PLW	5
SCHOOL				
A FAITHFUL SCHOOL WHERE THOU MAIST SEE	. .	226	RETIREMENT	45
I SCHOOL MY EYES, AND STRICTLY DWEL	. . .	214	MISERY	57
SCORCHING				
WHERE ALL THE LAND WITH SCORCHING HEAT IS CURST.	. .	290	THE TIMBER	46
SCORE				
LORD, I CONFESSE THE HEYNOUS SCORE	. . .	208	REPENTANCE	57
SOUGHT OUT WHAT MIGHT OUTVIE MY SCORE.	. . .	207	REPENTANCE	32
HIS PURE PERFECTION QUITS ALL SCORE	. . .	209	REPENTANCE	81
WHAT'S GOOD SCORE UP FOR JOY, THE BAD WEL SCANN'D	.	195	RLS + LSNS	119
I'M TOO MUCH ON THE SCORE.	. . . . .	204	IDLE VERSE	4
SCORE ON THE GLASSE.	. . . . . .	165	THE CALL	23
O SEEING THOU HAST PAID OUR SCORE	. . .	350	L'ENVOY	23
MY SCORES DID PAY	. . . . . .	188	RELAPSE	22
SCORN				
TO CARRY THAT, WHICH SOME WOULD SCORN TO TOUCH.	. .	155	ISAACS M.	40
SCORND				
AND SCORND PRETENCE	. . . . . .	232	THE WORLD	39
SCORNES				
AND SCORNES THEIR GLORY.	. . . . .	173	CONTENT	20
SCOUT				
BECAM'ST THY SELF, BOTH GUIDE, AND SCOUT.	. .	202	DSRDR + FR	4
SCOWL				
CONCERNING THOUGHTS (LIKE SAD ECCLIPSES) SCOWL	.	232	THE WORLD	19
SCRIBE				
EACH THING TURNS SCRIBE AND REGISTER	. .	314	THE STONE	43
SCRIBES				
DARKEN'D ALONG, AS THEIR SCRIBES BE	. .	332	AGREEMENT	27
SCROWLE				
WHEN LIKE A SCROWLE THE HEAVENS SHAL PASSE	. .	147	DAY OF JDG	13
SEA				
OF THEIR RED SEA, A SPRING, I WASH, THEY WADE	. .	159	MANS FALL	32
IS NOT A SEA	. . . . . .	175	THE STORM	2
BUT IN A DEEP, WIDE SEA OF BLOOD	. . .	325	ABELS BLOD	14
A SEA, WHOSE LOWD WAVES CANNOT SLEEP	. .	325	ABELS BLOD	15
SO DOTH THE DEEP AND WIDE SEA, WHEREIN ARE	. .	286	PSALM 104	69
O AIR, AND SEA, AND LAND.	. . . . .	284	PSALM 104	8
A SEA, OR SANDS AND SERPENTS, YET SINCE THOU	. .	234	MUTINIE	28
WHO CAME (SURE) FROM A SEA OF LIGHT.	. . .	343	WATER-FALL	18
SEAL				
THEN SEAL IT UP, THAT AS NONE SEE	. . .	242	MISERY	103
AS MY SEAL, AND BRACELET HERE	. . . .	214	PRAISE	19
GIVE HIM THY PRIVATE SEAL	. . . . .	216	DRESSING	19
THAT THOU FORGOTT'ST THINE OWN, FOR THOU DIDST SEAL	.	283	LOVE-SICK	20

	PAGE	TITLE	LINE
SEAL (CCN'T)			
I'LE SEAL MY EYES UP, AND TO THY COMMANDS	321	HIDDN TRSR	29
GO, GC, SEAL UP THY LCOKS	187	NO DO THEY	9
BLT SEAL, OR PIN THEM TC THY SKIES.	191	THE MATCH	38
SEAL NOT THY EYES UP FRCM THE PCOR, BLT GIVE	193	RLS + LSNS	61
SEAL'C			
SEAL'C , AND MADE GOOC	180	CHRCH-SVC	21
BUT A DARK AND SEAL'D UP WCMBE	171	COME, COME	23
ELECTED, BOUGHT AND SEAL'D FOR FREE	284	TRINITY-SN	8
AND BY THY SPIRIT SEAL'D TO ME, THAT I	267	ASCN-DAY A	7
SEALES			
BROKE UP SOME SEALES, WHICH NCNE HAD TOUCH'D BEFCRE	167	VNTY SPRIT	10
SEALS			
THEE CF THEM BOTH, THESE SEALS THE MEANS	220	HOLY COMM.	45
SEAMLESS			
THY SEAMLESS COAT IS GRCWN A RAG	350	L'ENVOY	30
SEAMLESSE			
THAT SEAMLESSE COAT	156	BRT. CHRCH	8
SEARCH			
AND, BY THEIR CWNE WEAKE SHINE, DID SEARCH THE SPRINGS	146	RSRCTN +IM	53
SEARCH WELL ANOTHER WORLD, WHC STUDIES THIS	153	THE SEARCH	94
AND HERE A FRESH SEARCH IS DECREED	152	THE SEARCH	35
TC SEARCH MY SELFE, WHERE I CIC FIND	168	VNTY SPRIT	15
I SEARCH, AND RACK MY SCUL TO SEE	178	SILENCE	17
MY PRESENT SEARCH, FOR EAGLES EYE NCT STARRS	278	THE STARRE	6
YET I WHOSE SEARCH LOV'C NOT TC PEEP AND PEER	247	I WALKT	8
AND SEARCH OUT EV'RY HCLE, ANC CREEK.	240	MISERY	17
TC CARRY, NOT SEARCH MYSTERIES.	318	THE ASS	22
AND SEARCH AND PRY	340	THE FEAST	44
SEARCH'D			
AND THOSE I SAW SEARCH'C THROLGH, YEA THOSE ANC ALL	320	HIDDN TRSR	7
WHO SEARCH'D IT QLITE THRCUGH TC AND FRO	338	DEATH B	13
SEARCHES			
THOSE SECRET SEARCHES, WHICH AFFLICT THE WISE	320	HIDDN TRSR	11
SEARCHING			
GCDS SILENT, SEARCHING FLIGHT.	324	THE NIGHT	31
A SLCDEN AND MOST SEARCHING RAY	348	HOLY BIBLE	20
SEAS			
SAILERS THAT FLOTE ON FLCWING SEAS	336	PSALM 65	17
WHICH (THOUGH BUT SANC) KEEPS IN A CURBS WHOLE SEAS.	285	PSALM 104	26
SEASON			
THEM IN DUE SEASON. WHAT THOU GIV'ST, THEY TAKE.	286	PSALM 104	74
SEASCNS			
WHEN SEASCNS CHANGE, THEN LAY BEFCRE THINE EYES	194	RLS + LSNS	91
SEAT			
AND SATANS SEAT, IN ALL HER CCASTS HATH LIGHT	331	JACOBS PLW	32
WHEN MAGDAL-CASTLE WAS THY SEAT	304	ST MARY MN	13
THY RCCT SUCKS BUT DISEASES, WCRMS THERE SEAT	243	THE SAP	7
THAT BY THE BEAUTY OF THE SEAT	277	COCK-CRWNG	21
IF THEN THOU WOULC'ST UNTO MY SEAT	226	RETIREMENT	29
SEATE			
WHEN THOU SHALT MAKE THE CLCUDS THY SEATE	147	DAY OF JDG	21
SEATS			
THE SEATS, AND CELLS WITHIN.	180	BURIALL	15
SECCND			
APPOINTED FOR MY SECCND RACE	169	RETREATE	4
UNTC A SECOND BIRTH	147	DAY OF JDG	20
SECRET			
THAT FROM SOME SECRET, COLDEN MINE	150	RELIGION	30
THAT WAS THY SECRET, ANC IT IS	162	PURSUITE	13
MY FRCZEN HEART, AND WITH THY SECRET KEY	216	DRESSING	4
HIS SECRET ON THEIR HEADS.	279	THE STARRE	28
THY FCRTY DAYS MORE SECRET CCMMERCE HERE	268	ASCN-DAY A	33
FCR ALL MY SECRET FAULTS, AND EACH	265	INTRO. 2	23
TO THEE THY SECRET MEALS	243	THE SAP	14
SLCH SECRET LIFE, AND VERTUE IN IT LIES	244	THE SAP	31
THCSE SECRET SEARCHES, WHICH AFFLICT THE WISE	320	HIDDN TRSR	11
THCSE SECRET SINS WE LEAST SUSPECT.	314	THE STONE	41
WHAT HAPPY, SECRET FOUNTAIN	315	DWELLNG-PL	1
THEN BLESS THY SECRET GROWTH, NCR CATCH	309	THE SEED	45
IF NIGHTS, AND SHADES, ANC SECRET RCOMS	313	THE STONE	6
CEAR, SECRET GREENNESS. NURST BELOW	309	THE SEED	25
THAT SECRET ARK, WHERE THE MILDE DOVE DOTH DWELL	330	JACOBS PLW	28
BY SECRET FILTH, NCR FEFDS	328	RIGHTSNESS	52
AND SETTLEST WITH THY SECRET HAND	337	PSALM 65	34
THAT VOICE, WHICH TO EACH SECRET BED	335	JUDGEMENT	19
HEAV'NS SECRET SOLITUDE, THOSE FAIR ABODES	327	RIGHTSNESS	6
SOME UP THE MCUNTAINS PAST BY SECRET WAYS	285	PSALM 104	23
SCME SECRET SENSE, WHICH MAKES THE DEAD BLOOC RUN	289	THE TIMBER	23
SACREC AND SECRET HAND.	300	PROVIDENCE	1
OR SECRET GROVES, KEEP THE HICH-WAY.	294	PALM-SUNDY	10
THE SECRET FAVORS OF THE COVE	348	HOLY BIBLE	28
SECRETS			
WHERE ALL HER SECRETS LAY A BEC	168	VNTY SPRIT	12
SECURE			
FCR NCNE CAN THEE SECURE	184	PEACE	18
I CARE NOT, SC I MAY SECURE	295	PALM-SUNDY	44
SECURITIE			
IN A CORRUPT SECURITIE	212	DAWNING	30
SED			
CAN DC NO MCRE. MY VOLUMES SEC	187	NO DO THEY	5

		PAGE	TITLE	LINE
SED	(CCN'T)			
IS LIKE A CLOUDED STARRE, WHOSE BEAMES THOUGH SED	• •	177	MRNG-WTCH	25
A HEAP CF ASHES, WHERE SOME SED	• • • • • •	151	THE SEARCH	17
SEDUCED				
SEDUCED SOUL SIGHS UP TC THEE	• • • • • •	207	REPENTANCE	20
SEDUCEMENTS				
AND SMOOTH SEDUCEMENTS. I'LE NCT STUFF MY STCRY	• •	275	PROFFER	35
SEE				
BUT WHEN THY MASTER COMES, THEY'L FINCE ANC SEE	• •	275	PROFFER	41
I SEE THEM WALKING IN AN AIR CF GLORY	• • • •	271	ALL GONE	9
AND SEE YOUR NAKEDNESS THEREBY	• • • • • •	266	VAIN WITS	11
I SEE THEM, HEAR THEM, MARK THEIR HASTE, AND MOVE	• •	268	ASCN-DAY A	31
I SEE THAT MORNING IN THY CONVERTS TEARS	• • • •	267	ASCN-DAY A	19
I SEE HIM LEADING OUT HIS CHOSEN TRAIN	• • • •	268	ASCN-DAY A	51
THAT IN THESE MASQUES AND SHADCWS I MAY SEE	• •	248	I WALKT	50
WITH DEW BY NIGHT, BUT CNE YOU CANNOT SEE	• •	280	PALM-TREE	23
AS I HAVE YOURS LONG SINCE, THIS PLANT, YOU SEE	• •	279	PALM-TREE	2
WE PLAINLY SEE, WHO MADE THE SAME.	• • • • •	277	COCK-CRWNG	22
AND TEACH US DUTY, I WILL SEE	• • • •	278	THE STARRE	11
THY TIME TO SHINE, AND MINE TC SEE.	• • • • •	281	THE FAVOUR	12
THAT, ABSENT, HE MAY SEE	• • • • •	216	DRESSING	15
AND WOULD NOT SEE, BUT CHOSE TO WINK	• • • •	225	RETIREMENT	18
DID MAKE US SEE	• • • • • •	219	HOLY COMM.	23
SHEWS HIM HIMSELF, OR SCMTHING HE SHOULD SEE.	• •	222	TEMPEST	2
THEN SEAL IT UP, THAT AS NONE SEE	• • • • •	242	MISERY	103
TO SEE THEIR SOULS GREAT SHEPHEARD, WHO WAS COME	• •	239	SHEPHEARDS	45
AND LCNG'C TO SEE, BUT MISS'D.	• • • • •	239	SHEPHEARDS	50
SOME NIGHTS I SEE YOU IN THE CLADSOME EAST	• •	235	CONSTLATN	9
AND WHEN I CANNOT SEE, YET DO YCU SHINE	• • • •	235	CONSTLATN	11
AND SC REPAIR THESE RENTS, THAT MEN MAY SEE	• •	237	CONSTLATN	59
WHERE HE DID CLUTCH HIS PREY, BUT ONE DID SEE	• •	232	THE WORLD	25
A FAITHFUL SCHOOL WHERE THOU MAIST SEE	• • • •	226	RETIREMENT	45
O THAT I WERE BUT WHERE I SEE.	• • • • •	228	PILGRIMAGE	15
AND THROUGH THY BLOUD THY GLORY SEE	• • • •	229	LAW + GOSP	12
TC SEE THE TEMPLE, BUT WAS SHCWN	• • • •	151	THE SEARCH	15
I WALKE THE GARDEN, AND THERE SEE	• • • •	152	THE SEARCH	37
'TIS NOW CLEARE DAY. I SEE A ROSE	• • • •	151	THE SEARCH	1
I SEE IN EACH SHADE THAT THERE GROWES	• • • •	148	RELIGION	3
I'LE THITHER THEN, SEE, IT IS DAY	• • • • •	152	THE SEARCH	65
THUS SUFFERING SEE	• • • • •	145	RSRCTN +IM	36
TC SEE, IF ANY LEAFE HAD MADE	• • • • •	141	RGNRTN	84
BUT STILL THOU DOEST OUT-GOE ME, I CAN SEE	• •	158	THE LAMPE	9
CCULD SEE A GLIMPSE OF HIS BRIGHT FACE.	• • • •	169	RETREATE	10
I SEE THE USE. AND KNOW MY BLCCD	• • • •	175	THE STORM	1
AND MCURN TO SEE THE WOCLL	• • • • •	173	CONTENT	11
AND THOU SHALT SEE	• • • • •	172	MIDNIGHT	24
AND NCTHING CAN, I HOURELY SEE	• • • •	181	BURIALL	21
I SEARCH, AND RACK MY SCUL TO SEE	• • • •	178	SILENCE	17
ALL THINGS I SEE	• • • • • •	179	SILENCE	30
THUS, LORD, I SEE MY GAINE IS GREAT	• • • •	167	THE CALL	82
DCE BUT SEE YOUR SAD ESTATE	• • • •	164	THE CALL	10
I SEE, THY CURTAINS ARE CLOSE-CRAWN, THY BOW	• •	197	CORRUPTION	33
SURE, THOU WILT JOY TC SEE	• • • • •	188	NO DO THEY	39
TO SEE THE LAMB, WHICH ALL AT CNCE	• • • •	294	PALM-SUNDY	13
MIGHT LIVE, AND SEE THE OLIVE BEAR	• • • •	292	THE JEWS	15
TO SEE MAN LOST, WILL FCR OLD LOVE	• • • •	292	THE JEWS	36
SEE NCT ALL CLEAR.	• • • • •	325	THE NIGHT	52
MUST LIVE TWICE, THAT WCULD GCDS FACE SEE.	• •	322	CHILDEHOOD	36
AND ONELY SEE THRCUGH A LONG NIGHT	• • • •	322	CHILDEHOOD	41
THY LCNG EXPECTED HEALING WINGS COULD SEE	• •	323	THE NIGHT	9
I WILL DO NOTHING, NOTHING KNCW, NOR SEE	• • • •	321	HIDDN TRSR	31
WHY IF I SEE A ROCK OR SHELF	• • • •	321	CHILDEHOOD	21
YCUTHFUL AND FAIR TO SEE NEW SKIES.	• • • • •	334	JUDGEMENT	6
SHALL BRING TRUE CAY, AND MAKE CUST SEE	• •	335	JUDGEMENT	21
THE GREATEST ATTRIBUTE WE SEE	• • • • •	335	JUDGEMENT	40
AND SINCE HIS DEATH, WE THROUGHLY SEE	• • • •	338	DEATH B	16
THE GREAT AND WHITE THRCNE I SHALL SEE	• •	337	THE THRONE	3
I SEE THE TEMPLE IN THY PILLAR REAR'D	• • • •	330	JACOBS PLW	1
IF THIS WCRLDS FRIENDS MIGHT SEE BUT ONCE	• •	308	THE SEED	1
THE FINEST THINGS THAT ARE, TC SEE.	• • • •	312	FAIR+YONG	34
THEY HEAR, SEE, SPEAK	• • • • •	313	THE STONE	22
BUT IN CONTEMPT, AS STILL WE SEE	• • • •	317	MEN OF WAR	32
AND FAITH TO SEE MY CROWN AS NEAR	• • • •	317	MEN OF WAR	38
AND MINDE THOSE THINGS I CANNCT SEE.	• • • •	318	THE ASS	18
AND DEARLY BOUGHT (WHEN THOU DIDST SEE	• •	304	ST MARY MN	35
DISTANT AND LCW, I CAN IN THINE SEE HIM	• •	306	RAIN-BOW	16
SING THY JUST PRAISE, AND SEE THY FACE.	• • •	345	THE WREATH	19
SEE'T				
(AMAZ'D TC SEE'T)	• • • • • •	140	RGNRTN	47
SEED				
AS SOON AS THEY DID SEED	• • • •	196	CORRUPTION	12
THAT SEED, WHICH THOU	• • • • •	204	DSRDR + FR	53
TCGETHER WITH THE SEED, THE PLACE.	• • • • •	204	DSRDR + FR	56
THAT SERV'D THE CALF, NCT ABR'AMS SEED	• •	296	JESUS WP A	6
LILIES AND MYRRHE, WHERE THE CLRS'D SEED	• •	299	JESUS WP B	49
THAT SEED THOU SOW'ST, BLEST BE THY SKIL.	• •	227	LV + DSPLN	6
SEEING THY SEED ABIDES IN ME	• • • • •	277	COCK-CRWNG	23
FATHER OF LIGHTS. WHAT SUNNIE SEED	• • • •	276	COCK-CRWNG	1
MEER SEED, AND AFTER THAT BUT GRASS.	• • • •	347	THE BOOK	6
SEEDING				
THE TREES, THEIR LEAFS, THE FLCWRES, THEIR SEEDING.	•	207	REPENTANCE	34

	PAGE	TITLE	LINE
SEEDS			
AND SEEDS A KINRED FIRE HAVE WITH THE SKY.	223	TEMPEST	36
THY PEOPLES HEARTS, WHEN ALL THY SEEDS WERE RICH	229	LAW + GOSP	4
THAT THE SEEDS OF FOUL SORROWS BE	312	FAIR+YONG	33
WHERE THE IMPURE SEEDS FLOURISH ALL THE YEAR	321	HIDDN TRSR	26
SEEING			
IF SEEING MUCH SHOULD MAKE STAID EYES	321	CHILDEHOOD	17
BUT SEEING SOLDIERS LONG AGO	317	MEN OF WAR	29
SEEING THY SEED ABIDES IN ME	277	COCK-CRWNG	23
YET, SEEING ALL THINGS THAT SUBSIST AND BE	278	THE STARRE	9
PRESENT AND SURE WITHOUT MY SEEING.	340	THE FEAST	42
O SEEING THOU HAST PAID OUR SCORE	350	L'ENVOY	23
SEEK			
IN THEIR WHITE ROBES TO SEEK THE RISEN SUN.	268	ASCN-DAY A	30
GO SEEK ELSEWHERE.	275	PROFFER	32
WHERE SPREADING ALL THE WAY THEY SEEK	240	MISERY	11
A DAY TO SEEK.	205	SON-DAYES	4
HE THAT DOTH SEEK AND LOVE	327	RIGHTSNESS	13
AND ONELY MY DEAR JESUS SEEK.	295	PALM-SUNDY	41
ROAR IN THE COVERT OF THE WOODS, AND SEEK	286	PSALM 104	58
GO, GO, SEEK OUT SOME GREENER THING	205	IDLE VERSE	21
SOME RISE TO SEEK THEE, AND WITH HEADS	187	ND DO THEY	25
SEEK NOT THE SAME STEPS WITH THE CROWD, STICK THOU	193	RLS + LSNS	49
TO ALL THAT SEEK THEE, BEAR AN OPEN HEART.	193	RLS + LSNS	55
SEEKING			
GO SEEKING ALL THE WAY.	267	ASCN-DAY A	14
SEEKS			
SEEKS IN THEE FOR PERFECT BEAUTY	218	EASTER HYM	8
BUT SEEKS HE YOUR OBEDIENCE, ORDER, LIGHT	236	CONSTLATN	29
SEEKS THERE FOR SYMMETRY	201	THE CHECK	7
TRAVELS IN CLOUDS, SEEKS MANNA, WHERE NONE IS.	153	THE SEARCH	95
WHO SEEKS AND FOLLOWS PEACE	327	RIGHTSNESS	34
WHO SEEKS FOR MORE, HE WOULD INHERIT.	339	THE FEAST	12
THOU ART THE CHANNEL MY SOUL SEEKS	344	WATER-FALL	39
SEEM			
SEEM MILD, BUT ARE KNOWN BY THEIR NOISE.	237	CONSTLATN	44
SEEM'D			
SEEM'D FAIR UNTO THE WOMANS EYE.	312	FAIR+YONG	36
SEEM'D TO DEVOUR, LIKE RUST.	310	THE SEED	74
WHICH WITH SKILL'D NEGLIGENCE SEEM'D SHED	304	ST MARY MN	19
SERIOUS THEY SEEM'D AND BOUGHT UP ALL	302	ORNAMENT	5
THEY SEEM'D TO QUARREL WITH HIM, FOR THAT ACT	196	CORRUPTION	13
SEEMING			
THAT KILL WITH SMILES AND SEEMING JOY.	311	FAIR+YONG	16
SEEMS			
(FOR WHICH COURSE MAN SEEMS MUCH THE FITTER BORN)	287	THE BIRD	4
IT SEEMS THEIR CANDLE, HOWE'R DONE	276	COCK-CRWNG	11
SEEN			
THE PURE EARTH SAT, AND THE FAIR WOODS HAD SEEN	268	ASCN-DAY A	42
THAT PLACE WHERE I HAD SEEN HIM TO GROW OUT	247	I WALKT	17
THOUGH SEEN AT ONCE, WERE BLACK TO THEE.	272	WHT SUNDAY	2
WHERE I SOMETIMES HAD SEEN THE SOIL TO YIELD	246	I WALKT	3
SEEN LONG BEFORE THIS CAME TO PASS	295	PALM-SUNDY	27
AS FAR AS BETHLEM, AND HAVE SEEN	151	THE SEARCH	6
OFT HAVE I SEEN, WHEN THAT RENEWING BREATH	144	RSRCTN +IM	1
SEEN AS WE GO	175	JOY OF LIF	26
ARE NO MORE SEEN, JUST SO PASS MEN.	344	WATER-FALL	36
SEERS			
THE SEERS OF WHOSE SACRED LIGHT	349	L'ENVOY	3
WHILE ALL HER SEERS SLEPT.	238	SHEPHEARDS	22
SEES			
WHICH, LIKE COLD FRIENDS, SEES US BUT ONCE A YEAR	247	I WALKT	12
HE SEES (LIKE PYRAMIDS) SHOOT FROM THIS BALL	224	TEMPEST	43
FROM WHENCE TH' INLIGHTENED SPIRIT SEES	170	RETREATE	25
VEX NOT, THAT BUT ONE SEES THEE GROW	309	THE SEED	27
WHO SEES INVISIBLES, AND DOTH COMPLY	327	RIGHTSNESS	11
WHICH ALL THE YEAR SEES THE SUNS FACE.	332	AGREEMENT	12
SEEST			
AND SEEST ALL THINGS JUST AS THEY BE.	207	REPENTANCE	22
SEIZ'D			
O GIVE IT FUL OBEDIENCE, THAT SO SEIZ'D	235	MUTINIE	36
AND THOU SO LONG SEIZ'D OF MY HEART.	348	HOLY BIBLE	2
SEIZE			
AND UNAWARES DOTH OFTEN SEIZE	150	RELIGION	39
SELDOM			
BUT SELDOM DOTH MAKE HEAV'N HIS GLASS.	236	CONSTLATN	20
IS SELDOM RENT.	324	THE NIGHT	40
AND SELDOM YIELDED FLOWERS	345	THE WREATH	2
SELDOME			
(AND THOSE BUT SELDOME TOO) WERE CAUGHT	207	REPENTANCE	12
SELECTED			
FROM PRIVATE AND SELECTED HEARTS DID SPRING	330	JACOBS PLW	12
SELF-BOASTING			
SELF-BOASTING PHARISEE. HOW BLINDE	305	ST MARY MN	61
SELF-END			
NOR FOR A TEMPORAL SELF-END	316	MEN OF WAR	15
SELF-ENDS			
ONELY SELF-WORSHIP AND SELF-ENDS.	332	AGREEMENT	30
WHAT WAY WE PLEASE, WITHOUT SELF-ENDS.	322	CHILDEHOOD	34
SELF-POSING			
SELF-POSING STATE.	344	QUICKNESS	6

		PAGE	TITLE	LINE

SELF-PRIVACY
A SWEET SELF-PRIVACY IN A RIGHT SOUL ● ● ● ● 193 RLS + LSNS 53

SELF-WIL
BUT HERE COMMISSION'D BY A BLACK SELF-WIL ● ● ● 237 CONSTLATN 37

SELF-WORSHIP
ONELY SELF-WORSHIP AND SELF-ENDS. ● ● ● ● 332 AGREEMENT 39

SELFE
NAY THOU THY SELFE, MY GOD, IN FIRE ● ● ● ● 149 RELIGION 17
I FIND MY SELFE THE LESSE, THE MORE I GROW. ● ● ● 161 DSTRQCTION 10
TO SEARCH MY SELFE, WHERE I DID FIND ● ● ● 168 VNTY SPRIT 15
LORD. WHEN THOU DIDST THY SELFE UNDRESSE ● ● ● ● 163 INCARNATN 1

SELLING
AMONGST THE QUICK, SELLING THEIR SOULS AND BREATH ● ● 275 PROFFER 39

SELS
WHO SELS RELIGION, IS A JUDAS JEW ● ● ● ● 193 RLS + LSNS 45

SEME
AND ONE OF THESE SEME LOATH ● ● ● ● ● 148 DAY OF JDG 40

SENCE
AND PROUD WITH LIFE, AND SENCE ● ● ● ● 144 RSRCTN +IM 11
BUT IF ALL SENCE WINGS NOT WITH THEE ● ● ● 142 DEATH 7
A SEV'RALL SINNE TO EV'RY SENCE ● ● ● ● 169 RETREATE 18
IN THE CREATION SHED, AND SLAV'D TO SENCE ● ● ● 223 TEMPEST 19

SEND
WE SEND TEARS TO THE PLACE ● ● ● ● ● 213 ADMISSION 20
O SEND ME FROM THY HOLY HIL ● ● ● ● 242 MISERY 97
AND SEND A FIRE DOWN, THAT SHALL BRING ● ● ● 305 ST MARY MN 55
SHALL SEND ME (SWAN-LIKE) SINGING HOME. ● ● ● 299 JESUS WP B 53

SEND'ST
THOU SEND'ST THY SPIRIT FORTH, AND THEY REVIVE ● ● 287 PSALM 104 81

SENDS
A THOUSAND ODOURS, WHICH (ALL MIXT) SHE SENDS ● ● 156 ISAACS M. 60

SENSE
MORE PUNISHMENT, THAN KNOWLEDGE TO MY SENSE. ● ● 159 MANS FALL 14
WHEN CONSCIENCE BY LEW'D USE HAD NOT LOST SENSE ● ● 154 ISAACS M. 19
NO DO THEY SO. HAVE THEY A SENSE ● ● ● 186 ND DO THEY 1
ABSENTS WITHIN THE LINE CONSPIRE, AND SENSE ● ● 183 THRS A TYE 9
SHAL HE BE NOW CAST OFF. NO SENSE ● ● ● 200 NTVTY 2 11
SOME SECRET SENSE, WHICH MAKES THE DEAD BLOOD RUN ● 289 THE TIMBER 23
(THEIR LORD SO NEAR) SENSE TO BE GLAD. ● ● ● 305 ST MARY MN 44
HAVE ALL ONE SENSE ● ● ● ● ● 327 RIGHTSNESS 20
BY SOME HID SENSE THEIR MAKER GAVE ● ● ● 246 MAN 25
TO MY COLD THOUGHTS A LIVELY SENSE OF SPRING. ● ● 245 MT. OLV. B 20
SUCH PERFECT EASE, AND SUCH A LIVELY SENSE ● ● 244 THE SAP 47
THE DOWN-RIGHT EPICURE PLAC'D HEAV'N IN SENSE ● ● 232 THE WORLD 38
IN MY OWN SENSE ● ● ● ● ● ● 342 OBSEQUIES 10
OF DEATH, DOST WASTE ALL SENSELESS, COLD AND DARK. ● ● 289 THE TIMBER 10
ART SENSELESS STILL. O CAN'ST THOU SLEEP ● ● ● 296 JESUS WP A 3
AND SENSELESS SLEEP ● ● ● ● ● ● 180 BURIALL 4

SENSES
DID ALL MY SENSES GREET ● ● ● ● ● ● 140 RGNRTN 49

SENSLESSE
THEY JUDG'D THEM SENSLESSE, AND THEIR STATE ● ● 187 ND DO THEY 7

SENT
BLEST SHOWERS THEY ARE, AND STREAMS SENT FROM ABOVE ● 291 THE TIMBER 49
WHEREFORE WITH TEARS (TEARS BY THEE SENT) ● ● ● 334 AGREEMENT 61
AND WHY THEN GRIEVE WE TO BE SENT ● ● ● 312 FAIR+YONG 41
OR SINCE THOSE DROPS ARE ALL SENT BACK ● ● ● 343 WATER-FALL 19

SENTENC'D
SHALL BE SENTENC'D FOR THEIR SLEEPE. ● ● ● ● 164 THE CALL 9

SEPULCHRE
I GREET THY SEPULCHRE, SALUTE THY GRAVE ● ● ● 267 ASCN-DAY A 15

SEQUESTER
BUT NONE CAN SEQUESTER OR LET ● ● ● ● 300 PROVIDENCE 22

SERAPHINS
WHERE THRONES AND SERAPHINS REPLY ● ● ● ● 295 PALM-SUNDY 21
WITH SERAPHINS THERE TALKED HE ● ● ● ● 152 THE SEARCH 59

SERIOUS
AND SERIOUS THOUGHTS BEGIN TO TAME ● ● ● ● 166 THE CALL 64
SERIOUS THEY SEEM'D AND BOUGHT UP ALL ● ● ● 302 ORNAMENT 5

SERPENTS
THESE LIGHTS OF SERPENTS LIKE THE DOVE. ● ● ● 272 WHT SUNDAY 10
A SEA, OR SANDS AND SERPENTS, YET SINCE THOU ● ● 234 MUTINIE 28

SERV'D
THAT SERV'D THE CALF, NOT ABR'AMS SEED ● ● ● 296 JESUS WP A 6

SERVANT
IF I THY SERVANT BE ● ● ● ● ● ● 300 PROVIDENCE 13
THE SERVANT MUST NOT TAKE IT ILL. ● ● ● ● 317 MEN OF WAR 36
STILL LET THY SERVANT MIND IT. ● ● ● ● 167 THE CALL 89
O HEAR, AND HEAL THY SERVANT. LORD STRIKE DEAD ● ● 185 PASSION 14
DIDST WITH THY SERVANT INNE. ● ● ● ● 180 BURIALL 20
THY SERVANT IS, AND WAITS ON THEE ● ● ● ● 181 BURIALL 37
ADVIS'D THY SERVANT WHAT TO DO, AND SAY. ● ● ● 155 ISAACS M. 28

SERVANTS
SO DYE HIS SERVANTS, AND AS SURE ● ● ● ● 339 DEATH B 26
BUT NOW IT IS THY SERVANTS PLEASURE ● ● ● 214 MISERY 47
THAT STON'D THY SERVANTS, AND DID MOVE ● ● ● 264 INTRO. 1 11

SERVE
WILL SERVE TO TAKE. ● ● ● ● ● ● 274 PROFFER 10
THAT SERVE HIM HERE BELOW ● ● ● ● ● 238 SHEPHEARDS 14
TO SERVE THEE IN THY BLESSED HOUSE. ● ● ● ● 336 PSALM 65 10

		PAGE	TITLE	LINE
SERVE	(CCN'T)			
AND FCRM TO SERVE HIM IN, SHOLLD BE TRUE GRACE	. .	330	JACOBS PLW	24
TC THE WILDE CCATS THE HIGH HILLS SERVE FOR FOLDS	. .	286	PSALM 104	49
SERVE GCD BEFCRE THE WORLD. LET HIM NCT GO	. .	192	RLS + LSNS	19
WHO CNELY WISH LIFE TC SERVE THEE.	. .	191	THE MATCH	35
SERVICE				
'WHCSE SERVICE MAKES EV'N CAPTIVES FREE)	. .	300	PROVIDENCE	14
THY SERVICE, NOR HIS SCUL CNE DAY. . . .	. .	301	PROVIDENCE	34
THY SERVICE TC BE OUR SCLE EASE	. .	351	L'ENVOY	60
SERVICES				
IN THY FREE SERVICES INCAGE	. .	212	DAWNING	38
SERVING				
AS AN IMPRIS'MENT SERVING THEE.	. .	239	MISERY	4
SET				
AT SOME SET TIMES, BUT ARE THY GRACE. . .	. .	242	MISERY	88
RISE WITH THE SUN, AND SET IN THE SAME BCWRS. .	. .	245	MAN	7
(A PLACE, AND NO MORE, IS SET DCWN) . . .	. .	228	PILGRIMAGE	6
ALL HAVE THEIR KEYES, AND SET ASCENTS, BLT MAN	. .	224	TEMPEST	37
SLEEPIE PLANETS SET, AND SLUMBER . . .	. .	212	DAWNING	20
OUR STORIES ARE IN THEIRS SET DCWN . . .	. .	273	WHT SUNDAY	31
A STATE THAT WITH THE SLN DOTH SET . . .	. .	300	PROVIDENCE	23
FCR THOU TO THEM A BOUND FAST SET, A BOUND	. .	285	PSALM 104	25
A STAR THAT WCULD NE'R SET, BLT EVER RISE	. .	283	LOVE-SICK	5
BLT AS SHADES SET OFF LIGHT, SC TEARS AND GRIEF	. .	290	THE TIMBER	41
THAT WHEN THY THRCNE IS SET, AND ALL . .	. .	317	MEN OF WAR	47
LIKE THEE, WHEN SET AT NAUGHT AND DUMB. .	. .	316	MEN OF WAR	20
AS THCU DIDST SET NO LAW FCR ME . . .	. .	318	THE ASS	9
WITHIN THCSE BOUNDS SET BY THY LCVE. . .	. .	318	THE ASS	16
SET FCRTH TO FOCL AND FCIL THEE, CO NOT BOAST.	. .	320	HIDDN TRSR	5
SET WITH GREEN HERBS, GLAC HOPES AND BRAVE.	. .	310	THE SEED	72
DAWN WITH THE DAY, THERE ARE SET, AWFUL HCURS	. .	192	RLS + LSNS	8
YET, SET AS HE DOTH, AND 'TIS WELL. HAVE ALL	. .	195	RLS + LSNS	109
AND THEN SET FORTH, WHO IS THLS DREST, THE FALL	. .	195	RLS + LSNS	111
AND MCVING ANGUISHMENTS THAT SET . . .	. .	152	THE SEARCH	39
HERE, I REPOS'D, BUT SCARSE WELL SET . .	. .	140	RGNRTN	42
'TIS LAST GOOC-NIGHT, CLR SUNNE SHALL NEVER SET.	. .	143	DEATH	32
WHOSE SUNS ARE ALL SET IN A CLCUD. . . .	. .	165	THE CALL	19
SETLEC				
THY SICK ACCESSICNS INTC SETLEC HEALTH .	. .	221	AFFLICTION	3
SETS				
ACORES DEAD DUST, SETS HEART CN CCRNE AND GRASS	. .	236	CONSTLATN	19
DEATH SETS ALL CUT OF JCINT	. .	173	CONTENT	19
WCRKS WITH THE SUN, AND SETS	. .	201	THE CHECK	16
AND SETS, WILL FEW HCURS HENCE BEGIN . .	. .	292	THE JEWS	29
AND SETS LP LAWS TO PULL HIS HCNCR DOWN. .	. .	330	JACOBS PLW	20
SETTLE				
SETTLE MY HOUSE, AND SHUT OUT ALL DISTRACTIONS	. .	191	THE MATCH	28
SETTLE, AND FIX OLR HEARTS, THAT WE MAY MCVE	. .	237	CONSTLATN	53
SETTLED				
THE SETTLED RED IS DULL, AND WHITES THAT REST	. .	222	AFFLICTION	27
SETTLEST				
AND SETTLEST WITH THY SECRET HAND . . .	. .	337	PSALM 65	34
SEV'RAL				
THUS WHILE THY SEV'RAL MERCIES PLCT . .	. .	227	LV + DSPLN	13
NEW SEV'RAL OATHES, AND CCMPLEMENTS (TCO) PLENTY.	. .	154	ISAACS M.	16
SEV'RALL				
A SEV'RALL SINNE TC EV'RY SENCE . . .	. .	169	RETREATE	18
IN SEV'RALL PARTS SHALL WANT A NAME . . .	. .	177	EVNG-WTCH	6
SEVENTH				
SLCH WAS THE BRIGHT WCRLD, CN THE FIRST SEVENTH CAY	.	268	ASCN-DAY A	39
SEVER				
WHAT LIFE, WHAT DEATH CAN SEVER. . . .	. .	302	THE KNOT	14
SHADE				
IF THESE SUPPLANTERS IN THE SHADE . .	. .	312	FAIR+YONG	37
FAIR SHADE, OR MOUNTAIN	. .	315	DWELLNG-PL	2
THY PILLOW WAS BUT TYPE AND SHADE AT BEST	. .	331	JACOBS PLW	53
DEARE FRIEND SIT DOWN, AND BEAR AWHILE THIS SHADE	. .	279	PALM-TREE	1
THEN LAY THAT TRESPASSE IN THE SHADE . .	. .	240	MISERY	22
HE IS MY SUN, AND SHADE	. .	220	PSALM 121	10
THUS GRCVELING IN THE SHADE, AND DARKNESS, HE	. .	224	TEMPEST	41
WHERE STARS, AND CLOUDS, BOTH LIGHT, AND SHACE	. .	210	FAITH	15
BUT SITT'ST OPPRESSED IN THE SHADE . . .	. .	217	EASTER-DAY	4
AND ICOLIZE SCME SHADE, CR GRCVE . . .	. .	162	MT. OLVS A	4
I SEE IN EACH SHADE THAT THERE GROWES . .	. .	148	RELIGION	3
I TURN'D ME ROUND, AND TO EACH SHADE . .	. .	141	RGNRTN	82
PRIMRCS'D, AND HUNG WITH SHADE . . .	. .	139	RGNRTN	13
WHERE NC RUDE SHADE, CR NIGHT . . .	. .	146	RSRCTN +IM	64
NO SHADE BUT YEWGH	. .	188	RELAPSE	18
IN SOME GREEN SHADE, CR FCUNTAIN. . . .	. .	197	CORRUPTION	24
THOU KNEW'ST THIS TREE, WHEN A GREEN SHADE	. .	347	THE BOOK	11
SHOULC PCOR SCULS FEAR A SHADE CR NIGHT .	. .	343	WATER-FALL	17
THE RCCK CF AGES IN WHOSE SHADE . . .	. .	346	THE BOOK	3
MAKE THESE SAD SHADES PURE SUN . . .	. .	202	THE CHECK	30
AND ON THE DUMBE SHADES LANGUAGE SPENT .	. .	141	RGNRTN	60
MADE THCSE WILD SHADES A PARADISE . . .	. .	152	THE SEARCH	62
WHAT SILENT PATHS, WHAT SHADES, AND CELLS .	. .	153	THE SEARCH	69
AND MCVE CN WITH THE SHADES, STARS NOT, AND SLEEPE	. .	157	THE LAMPE	2
SCATTER THESE SHACES OF DEATH, AND GIVE .	. .	208	REPENTANCE	51
WHAT SPRINGS CR SHADES TO LOCK . . .	. .	239	SHEPHEARDS	40
THE SHACES OF DEATH DWELL AND DISCRDER. .	. .	277	COCK-CRWNG	30

		PAGE	TITLE	LINE
SHADES	**(CCN'T)**			
WHICH SHADES AND BOWERS DOTH RENT-FREE BRING.	. . . .	338	DEATH B	10
THY SHADES BUT THIN AND NARROW BE	. . . .	338	DEATH B	18
FAIR, SOLITARY PATH. WHOSE BLESSED SHADES	. . .	326	RIGHTSNESS	1
IF NIGHTS, AND SHADES, AND SECRET ROOMS	. . .	313	THE STONE	6
YOUR SHADES AND FRESHNESS COMES TO BORROW.	. .	294	PALM-SUNDY	6
BUT AS SHADES SET OFF LIGHT, SO TEARS AND GRIEF	. .	290	THE TIMBER	41
SO IN THE SHADES OF NIGHT SOME DARK FOWLS BE	. .	288	THE BIRD	25
IN WHOSE THICK SHADES AND SILENCE EACH WILDE BEAST	. .	286	PSALM 104	54
SHADOW				
MUST (SOUL-LESSE SHADOW) SO LIVE ON	. . . .	311	THE SEED	88
LIKE A VAST SHADOW MOV'D, IN. WHICH THE WORLD	. .	231	THE WORLD	6
AND FOR THY SHADOW LOOKS THE LIGHT	. . . .	212	DAWNING	18
SHADOW NO MORE MY DOOR.	. . . . .	204	IDLE 'VERSE	2
WHOSE SHADOW MAKES ME SAD OR SICK.	. . . .	340	THE FEAST	48
SHADOWES				
WHERE SHADOWES THICKEN, AND THE CLOUD	. . .	143	DEATH	12
SHADOWS				
BUT MISTS, AND SHADOWS PASSE	. . . . .	146	RSRCTN +IM	52
AND WHILE THESE HERE THEIR MISTS, AND SHADOWS HATCH,	. .	156	BRT. CHRCH	2
ARE SHADOWS OF HIS WISECOME, AND HIS POW'R	. .	194	RLS + LSNS	96
BE THERE, BEFORE THE SHADOWS STRETCH	. . .	189	RESOLVE	19
SOME SHADOWS OF ETERNITY	. . . . .	169	RETREATE	14
BRIGHT SHADOWS OF TRUE REST. SOME SHOOTS OF BLISSE	.	205	SON-DAYES	1
BREAK, AND THE SHADOWS FLEE, TOUCH WITH ONE COAL	.	216	DRESSING	3
AND CLOUD WHICH SHADOWS THEE FROM ME.	. . .	277	COCK-CRWNG	40
THAT IN THESE MASQUES AND SHADOWS I MAY SEE	. .	248	I WALKT	50
SHADY				
THAT SHADY CITY OF PALME TREES	. . . .	170	RETREATE	26
UNTILL THE COOLE, AND SHADY EVEN.	. . . .	149	RELIGION	16
SHAK'D				
ARE SHAK'D FOR WITNESSES, AND STONES	. . .	314	THE STONE	38
SHAKE				
O SPRED THY SACRED WINGS AND SHAKE	. . . .	308	THE SEED	13
THE SUN DOTH SHAKE	. . . .	199	NTVTY 1	4
THE WHOLE CREATION SHAKES OFF NIGHT	. . .	212	DAWNING	17
SHAKING				
SIGHS MAKE JOY SURE, AND SHAKING FASTENS THEE.	. .	281	JOY	30
SLEEPS NOT, BUT SHAKING OFF SLOTH, AND NEGLECTS	.	201	THE CHECK	15
SHALBE				
BUT WHENSCE'RE I'M OUT, BOTH SHALBE IN	. . .	158	THE LAMPE	25
THAT DONE, WE SHALBE SAFE, AND GOOD	. . .	165	THE CALL	28
SHAME				
HENCE, YOUTH, AND FOLLY (MANS FIRST SHAME)	. .	166	THE CALL	62
THAT TOOK'ST MY SHAME	. . . . .	186	PASSION	46
TO DRESSE, AND TRIM OUR SHAME	. . . .	205	IDLE VERSE	10
THEY SHAME THEIR OWNERS, AND THE HEARERS TROUBLE.	.	194	RLS + LSNS	72
WIPING OUT MY SHAME, AND SIN.	. . . .	249	BEGGING A	12
PROVE MY OWN SHAME AND MISERIE.	. . . .	240	MISERY	44
MAY PROVE THY GLORY, AND THEIR SHAME. SO CLOSE	.	234	MUTINIE	18
BUT WHAT IS HIGHEST SIN AND SHAME	. . .	335	JUDGEMENT	33
HIS SHAMELESS LUST IN PUBLICK WEARS	. . .	297	HERODIAS	15
SHAPE				
IMMORTAL SHAPE, WHO WROUGHT THEIR BLISS	. .	349	L'ENVOY	6
AS BEAUTEOUS SHAPES, WE KNOW NOT WHY	. .	278	THE STARRE	23
SHARE				
THAT SHINE AND SHARE	. . . .	225	RETIREMENT	6
EACH SNARLING BLAST SHOT THROUGH ME, AND DID SHARE	.	198	UNPRFTBLNS	4
AND CLAIM THEIR SHARE	. . . . .	190	THE MATCH	11
FEEL ME A SHARER IN THY VICTORY.	. . . .	267	ASCN-DAY A	8
SHARES				
SHARES IN THE ACT, AND PUTS ME TO'T.	. . .	319	THE ASS	31
SHARON				
O ROSE OF SHARON. O THE LILLY	. . . .	220	HOLY COMM.	49
SHARP				
AND LET THESE LONG, SHARP JUDGEMENTS AW	. . .	351	L'ENVOY	54
SHED				
SOME FEW TRUE TEARS, AND THOSE SHED FOR	. .	342	OBSEQUIES	3
BESIDES, THOSE KERCHIEFS SOMETIMES SHED	. .	342	OBSEQUIES	25
IN THE CREATION SHED, AND SLAV'D TO SENCE	. .	223	TEMPEST	19
AND ACTUATE SUCH SPIRITS AS ARE SHED	. .	244	THE SAP	33
OF PAST DAYS, WHERE SAD HEAV'N DID SHED	. .	309	THE SEED	53
WHICH WITH SKILL'D NEGLIGENCE SEEM'D SHED	. .	304	ST MARY MN	19
FROM HENCE LONG FOR IT. SHED IT THERE	. .	296	JESUS WP A	15
SHED THIS LIVE-DEW ON FIELDS WHICH FAR	. .	296	JESUS WP A	14
THAT THOU WERT PLEAS'D TO SHED THY GRACE SO FARR,	.	283	LOVE-SICK	3
AS IN THE MORNING WHEN FIRST SHED.	. . .	325	ABELS BLOD	6
TO SHED THEIR LIGHT	. . . . .	177	MRNG-WTCH	26
LIKE CANDLES, SHED	. . . . . .	175	JOY OF LIF	22
BUT THOU WERT SO, E'RE TIME HIS SNOW COULD SHED.	.	156	ISAACS M.	70
SHEDS				
THY LINES ARE RAYS, THE TRUE SUN SHEDS.	. .	333	AGREEMENT	35
WHOSE FRUITFUL DAWN SHEDS HOPES AND LIGHTS.	. .	295	PALM-SUNDY	31
IF THOSE BRIGHT JOYS HE SINGLY SHEDS	. .	309	THE SEED	29
THIS IS THE EARNEST THY LOVE SHEDS	. .	265	INTRO. 2	13
THERE GOD A COMMERCE STATES, AND SHEDS	. .	279	THE STARRE	27
SHEEP				
I CAN DISCERN WOLVES FROM THE SHEEP.	. . .	273	WHT SUNDAY	24
AS WHERE TO LEAD THEIR SHEEP, WHAT SILENT NOCK	. .	239	SHEPHEARDS	39
BECOME BOTH FOOD, AND SHEPHEARD TO THY SHEEP.	. .	220	HOLY COMM.	52

	PAGE	TITLE	LINE
SHEEP (CCN'T)			
ALAS, MY GOD, TAKE HOME THY SHEEP.	312	FAIR+YONG	51
GLADLY WILL I, LIKE PONTICK SHEEP	301	PROVIDENCE	46
OUTLAST THE SHEEP	173	CONTENT	12
THE SHEEP BLEAT THEE A SILLY LAY	163	MT. OLVS A	14
THY SHEEP WITH THEE.	188	NO DO THEY	40
THAT LIKE TRUE SHEEP, ALL IN ONE FOLD	350	L'ENVOY	47
CAME THE SHEEP-KEEPING SYRIAN MAID.	303	ORNAMENT	16
SHEEPWARD			
AND SHEEPWARD PLAY.	163	MT. OLVS A	16
SHEL			
AND ALL THAT SACRED POMP, AND SHEL	210	FAITH	27
SHELF			
WHY IF I SEE A ROCK OR SHELF	321	CHILDEHOOD	21
SHELL			
A FEATHER, OR A SHELL	166	THE CALL	51
LIFE LOCKT IN DEATH, HEAV'N IN A SHELL.	164	INCARNATN	12
THE SKINNE, AND SHELL OF THINGS	153	THE SEARCH	81
BECAUSE MOST VOICES LIKE THE SHELL	150	RELIGION	48
SHELTER			
I SHELTER IN, IS SLAVE	173	CONTENT	3
A SHELTER ALL THE WAY, AND BOWERS TO REST.	326	RIGHTSNESS	4
I SHINE AND SHELTER UNDERNEATH THY WING	245	MT. OLV. B	23
SHEMS			
HOW BRIGH WERT THOU, WHEN SHEMS ADMIRING EYE	306	RAIN-BOW	3
SHEPHEARD			
TO SEE THEIR SOULS GREAT SHEPHEARD, WHO WAS COME	239	SHEPHEARDS	45
YET WHERE THE SHEPHEARDS WATCH	238	SHEPHEARDS	28
BECOME BOTH FOOD, AND SHEPHEARD TO THY SHEEP.	220	HOLY COMM.	52
SHEW			
ALL THINGS HERE SHEW HIM HEAVEN, WATERS THAT FALL	223	TEMPEST	25
DID SHEW ME HOME, AND PUT ME IN THE WAY.	225	RETIREMENT	11
AND AUTHOR OF MY FAITH, SO SHEW ME HOME	234	MUTINIE	22
TO SHEW WHAT STRANGE LOVE HE HAD TO OUR GOOD	243	THE SAP	25
OR SOME FRAIL BEAUTY MAKES THE BRAVEST SHEW	282	GARLAND	3
SHEW ME THY PEACE	248	I WALKT	55
THERE, HID IN THEE, SHEW ME HIS LIFE AGAIN	248	I WALKT	61
FRESHER THEN MORNING-FLOWERS WHICH SHEW	303	ST MARY MN	3
SUCH COAL-FLAMES SHEW BUT KITCHIN-ROOMS AT MOST.	320	HIDDN TRSR	6
TWILL SHEW US EACH FORGOTTEN GRAVE	334	JUDGEMENT	4
THY BRIGHT SOLEMNITIES DID SHEW	295	PALM-SUNDY	32
BY SHEWING THE SIN GREAT, SHEW THE RELIEF	290	THE TIMBER	43
DARES OWN THE TRUTH, AND SHEW THE ILL.	350	L'ENVOY	38
SHEW ME THAT PEARL I SOUGHT ELSEWHERE.	348	HOLY BIBLE	26
LIKE TEARS DOTH SHEW	340	THE FEAST	23
SHEW'D			
SHEW'D TO ME IN MY SINFUL YOUTH	265	INTRO. 2	20
THESE ARE YOUR WALKS, AND YOU HAVE SHEW'D THEM ME	271	ALL GONE	15
WHICH SHEW'D ME IN A NOOK CAST BY	168	VNTY SPRIT	21
WHICH SHEW'D THEE LAST, BUT DID DEFEAT	178	SILENCE	15
UNBOWEL'D NATURE, SHEW'D THEE HER RECRUITS	145	RSRCTN +IM	21
SHEW'ST			
BUT WHAT THOU BIDST, AND SHEW'ST, AND TEACHEST ME.	321	HIDDN TRSR	32
SHEWD			
SCATT'RING THAT CLOUD, SHEWD ME THE FLAME	332	AGREEMENT	9
THE ANGEL SHEWD THAT HOLY WELL	300	PROVIDENCE	3
THE LUCKY WORLD SHEWD ME ONE DAY	302	ORNAMENT	1
SHEWING			
BY SHEWING THE SIN GREAT, SHEW THE RELIEF	290	THE TIMBER	43
SHEWS			
WHO SHEWS ME BUT ONE GRAIN OF SINCERE LIGHT.	320	HIDDN TRSR	3
AND INDISPUTABLE, SHEWS TO MY SIGHT	268	ASCN-DAY A	35
BECAUSE IT SHEWS THE WAY	233	THE WORLD	52
SHEWS HIM HIMSELF, OR SOMTHING HE SHOULD SEE.	222	TEMPEST	2
SHIELD			
AND IS A SHIELD (NOT RECKONING THOSE)	220	PSALM 121	15
SHIFTING			
SHIFTING THY GATE AND GUILE.	278	THE STARRE	4
SHIN'D			
WHEN HEAV'N ABOVE THEM SHIN'D LIKE MOLTEN GLASS	268	ASCN-DAY A	45
FROM THEE IT SHIN'D, THOUGH HERE IT BURNS.	265	INTRO. 2	4
SHIN'D ON MY SOUL, I FELT THROUGH ALL MY POWR'S	244	MT. OLV. B	3
WHERE, AS THOU GREWST, IT MULTIPLI'D AND SHIN'D	154	ISAACS M.	9
SHIN'D IN MY ANGELL-INFANCY	169	RETREATE	2
WITH THE LIKE ARDOUR SHIN'D	172	MIDNIGHT	10
SIMPER'D, AND SHIN'D ON YOU	205	IDLE VERSE	18
HE SHIN'D A LITTLE, AND BY THOSE WEAK RAYS	196	CORRUPTION	3
SHIN'ST			
FOR THOUGH SOME THINK, THOU SHIN'ST BUT TO RESTRAIN	307	RAIN-BOW	39
SHINE			
FROM THY BRIGHT LAMP DID SHINE	310	THE SEED	70
WHEN THOU DOST SHINE DARKNESS LOOKS WHITE AND FAIR	306	RAIN-BOW	9
WHERE NOT SO MUCH AS DREAMS OF LIGHT MAY SHINE	289	THE TIMBER	11
THY SUN MUST SHINE IN EVERY PART.	294	BEGGING B	16
WOULD SHINE ELSEWHERE, SINCE YOU WERE BLIND	292	THE JEWS	24
AND THEIR OWN ANGELS SHINE AND SING	295	PALM-SUNDY	22
AND SHINE, AND POINT ME TO A PLACE	332	AGREEMENT	11
THAT MEN MIGHT LOOK AND LIVE AS GLO-WORMS SHINE	323	THE NIGHT	3
O COME, ARISE, SHINE, DO NOT STAY	334	JUDGEMENT	11
PREVAIL'D BY WRESTLING ERE THE SUN DID SHINE.	192	RLS + LSNS	22

	PAGE	TITLE	LINE
SHINE (CON'T)			
THE STARRES SHINE IN THEIR WATCHES	171	MIDNIGHT	4
SHINE ON THIS BLOUD	172	MIDNIGHT	22
AND. SHINE, AND MOVE	177	MRNG-WTCH	29
THERE SHINE, AND BURN.	179	SILENCE	24
I SHINE, AND MOVE	182	CHRFLNESS	4
LOOKE DOWNE GREAT MASTER OF THE FEAST, O SHINE	150	RELIGION	51
AND, BY THEIR OWNE WEAKE SHINE, DID SEARCH THE SPRINGS	146	RSRCTN +IM	53
I SHINE AND SHELTER UNDERNEATH THY WING	245	MT. OLV. B	23
AND SHINE FROM PARAN, WHEN A FIRIE LAW	229	LAW + GOSP	2
AND WHEN I CANNOT SEE, YET DO YOU SHINE	235	CONSTLATN	11
TAKE UP MY DAY, WHILE THOU DOST SHINE	240	MISERY	26
I WALK THE FIELDS OF BETHANI WHICH SHINE	268	ASCN-DAY A	37
MAY SHINE UNTO A PERFECT DAY	277	COCK-CRWNG	45
THY TIME TO SHINE, AND MINE TO SEE.	281	THE FAVOUR	12
AS THOSE CLEAR HEIGHTS WHICH ABOVE TEMPESTS SHINE.	281	JOY	16
LIKE THE SUN SHINE	269	ASCSN-HYMN	22
SHINE HERE BELOW WITHIN THY BOOK	272	WHT SUNDAY	18
THY ANTIENT LOVE ON SOME MAY SHINE.	273	WHT SUNDAY	40
SHE'L SHINE THROUGH ALL THE SPHERE.	271	ALL GONE	32
THEY SHINE IN WHITE (LIKE STARS) AND REST.	275	PROFFER	24
THAT SHINE AND SHARE	225	RETIREMENT	6
THEN DID HE SHINE FORTH, WHOSE SAD FALL	210	FAITH	29
AND SPRINGING SHINE	340	THE FEAST	26
AND SHINE AND SMILE, AND HATH THE SKILL	345	QUICKNESS	15
THIS LONG WORN VEYL. THEN SHINE AND SPREAD	349	L'ENVOY	9
SHINES			
AND JOY, LIKE LIGHT, SHINES OFT IN CLOUDS.	342	OBSEQUIES	20
WHOSE HEIGHT ABOVE ALL AGES SHINES	273	WHT SUNDAY	46
BUT THINE SHINES TO ETERNITY.	272	WHT SUNDAY	4
HIS CANDLE SHINES UPON THEIR HEADS.	272	WHT SUNDAY	16
WHOSE HAND SO SHINES THROUGH ALL THIS FRAME	277	COCK-CRWNG	20
SO SHINES AND SINGS, AS IF IT KNEW	276	COCK-CRWNG	9
NOW SHINES IN ALL THE CHAMBERS OF THE EAST.	267	ASCN-DAY A	24
AND SOARS, AND SHINES, BUT E'R WE SUP	203	DSRDR + FR	34
THIS PAST, THE SUN SHINES ON THE EARTH, AND THY	286	PSALM 104	61
NATIVE AND PURE SHINES NOW IN THEE	303	ST MARY MN	8
WHERE YOUTH SHINES LIKE A STAR	310	THE SEED	62
SHINING			
WHOM STRAIT. THE SHINING ROW ALL FAC'D	303	ORNAMENT	17
SHINING, OR SINGING STILL TO THEE.	199	NTVTY 1	18
SHALL ONE DAY RISE, AND CLOATH'D WITH SHINING LIGHT	145	RSRCTN +IM	47
GODS SAINTS ARE SHINING LIGHTS. WHO STAYS	174	JOY OF LIF	17
THEY ARE THAT CITIES SHINING SPIRES	175	JOY OF LIF	27
THE CANDLE SHINING ON SOME HEADS	265	INTRO. 2	14
SHINING NO WHERE, BUT IN THE DARK.	271	ALL GONE	18
SHINING WITH JOY, LIKE DEWY DAYS	345	THE WREATH	11
SHALL ALL BE DREST IN SHINING WHITE	349	L'ENVOY	4
SHIPMENS			
AND GREAT. THERE SHIPS GO, AND THE SHIPMENS FEAR	286	PSALM 104	71
SHIPS			
AND GREAT. THERE SHIPS GO, AND THE SHIPMENS FEAR	286	PSALM 104	71
SHOOK			
SO SHOOK MY BREST, THAT (SICK AND SORE DISMAI'D)	233	MUTINIE	5
SHOOT			
HE SEES (LIKE PYRAMIDS) SHOOT FROM THIS BALL	224	TEMPEST	43
FRESH GROVES GROW UP, AND THEIR GREEN BRANCHES SHOOT	289	THE TIMBER	6
NOT ONE POOR SHOOT	203	DSRDR + FR	27
BRIGHT SHOOTES OF EVERLASTINGNESSE.	170	RETREATE	20
SHOOTS			
AND SHOOTS OF GLORY, MY SOUL BREAKES, AND BUDS.	176	MRNG-WTCH	2
BRIGHT SHADOWS OF TRUE REST. SOME SHOOTS OF BLISSE	205	SON-DAYES	1
SHOP			
STARS SHUT UP SHOP, MISTS PACK AWAY	210	FAITH	19
SHORE			
ALL HER PARCHT BOSOME TO NILE'S SHORE	151	THE SEARCH	12
SHORT			
AND LOOKING BACK (AT THAT SHORT SPACE)	169	RETREATE	9
BUT HEARTS ARE NOT SO KIND. FALSE, SHORT DELIGHTS	183	THRS A TYE	13
AND BULRUSH FETTERS TEMPER HIS SHORT HOUR.	224	TEMPEST	50
ANGER FOR ONE SHORT FIT	216	DRESSING	28
SHALL MY SHORT HOUR, MY INCH	275	PROFFER	25
TO EQUAL WINDS. WOULD PROVE TOO SHORT. THOU HAST	281	JOY	13
HIS TIME IS SHORT, MORE RAGING GROWS.	335	JUDGEMENT	30
SHORT SIPS AND SIGHTS	339	THE FEAST	10
DEAR, HARMLESS AGE. THE SHORT, SWIFT SPAN	322	CHILDEHOOD	31
NOT BUT I KNOW THOU HAST A SHORTER CUT	234	MUTINIE	26
SHOT			
NAY, THOSE BRIGHT BEAMS SHOT FROM THY EYES	242	MISERY	85
SHOT O'R SOME CLOUD	174	JOY OF LIF	14
THE UNTHRIFT SUNNE SHOT VITALL GOLD	140	RGNRTN	50
THE BEAMES I THEN HAD SHOT	161	DSTROCTION	7
EACH SNARLING BLAST SHOT THROUGH ME, AND DID SHARE	198	UNPRFTBLNS	4
SHOUT			
PURSUED HIM WITH ONE SHOUT.	232	THE WORLD	22
THEY SHOUT FOR JOY, AND JOYNTLY SING	337	PSALM 65	47
SHOW			
POOR BIRDS SING BEST, AND PRETTIEST SHOW	294	BEGGING B	19
WHICH ONCE THY CARE AND ART DID SHOW.	304	ST MARY MN	16
WHAT MAN WILL SHOW.	313	THE STONE	5

	PAGE	TITLE	LINE
SHOW (CON'T)			
(AS THY WORDS SHOW)	234	MUTINIE	29
MEER EMPTINESS AND SHOW	238	SHEPHEARDS	26
MEERE STAGE, AND SHOW	139	RGNRTN	19
SHOWER			
FOR THY NEW LIGHT, AND TREMBLED AT EACH SHOWER.	306	RAIN-BOW	8
SHOWERS			
MANY BRIGHT MORNINGS, MUCH DEW, MANY SHOWERS	289	THE TIMBER	2
BLEST SHOWERS THEY ARE, AND STREAMS SENT FROM ABOVE	291	THE TIMBER	49
HEAL'D BY THE SHOWERS FROM HIGH.	285	PSALM 104	40
AND WATCH ALL NIGHT FOR MISTS OR SHOWERS	301	PROVIDENCE	29
IF SHOWERS THEN FALL, WILL SHOWERS ALLAY	298	JESUS WP B	19
IF SHOWERS THEN FALL, WILL SHOWERS ALLAY	298	JESUS WP B	19
AND OPENING SHOWERS (RESTRAIN'D FROM HARM)	337	PSALM 65	36
THEREFORE WHILE THE VARIOUS SHOWERS	281	JOY	17
AND SONGS I HEAR. O QUICKNING SHOWERS	340	THE FEAST	51
SHOWES			
WHOSE MEANER SHOWES	225	RETIREMENT	4
SHOWN			
SHOWN, AND BUT SHOWN ME FROM ABOVE.	281	THE FAVOUR	2
SHOWN, AND BUT SHOWN ME FROM ABOVE.	281	THE FAVOUR	2
'TWAS THERE FIRST SHOWN TO YOU.	238	SHEPHEARDS	12
UNTO THY SOLITARY SELF IS SHOWN.	330	JACOBS PLW	4
WAS SHOWN ONE DAY IN A STRANGE GLASS	313	THE STONE	19
TO SEE THE TEMPLE, BUT WAS SHOWN	151	THE SEARCH	15
SHOWR			
MY YIELDING LEAVES. SOMETIMES A SHOWR	203	DSRDR + FR	25
THOU DOST, THOU COM'ST, AND IN A SHOWR	214	MISERY	49
AND TEMPESTS HAVE MORE IN THEM THAN A SHOWR.	222	TEMPEST	4
NE'R MARR'D WITH FLOODS, NOR ANGER'D WITH A SHOWRE.	268	ASCN-DAY A	48
AND FROM HIS MOIST WOMBE WEEPS A FRAGRANT SHOWRE	155	ISAACS M.	55
SHOWRES			
(SOME SUCH SHOWRES PAST)	160	THE SHOWRE	17
THEIR YOUTH, AND BEAUTY, COLD SHOWRES NIPT, AND WRUNG	198	UNPRFTBLNS	5
AFTER WHOLE SHOWRES ONE DROP.	188	NO DO THEY	38
WHICH THRIVES IN STORMS, AND SMELS BEST AFTER SHOWRES.	193	RLS + LSNS	60
AND BY A FRUITFULL CHANGE OF FROSTS, AND SHOWRES	221	AFFLICTION	13
A GLEAM OF GLORY, AFTER SIX-DAYS SHOWRES.	2	SON-DAYES	16
SHOWRS			
SUCH A RICH AIR OF SWEETS, AS EVENING SHOWRS	244	MT. OLV. B	4
SHOWS			
ALL THAT MAN DOTH, CONCEALS OR SHOWS	314	THE STONE	31
SHREAD			
AND THROUGH THE DARK AIRE SPIN A FIRIE SHREAD	157	THE LAMPE	3
SHREDS			
YEA, I HAVE KNOWNE THESE SHREDS OUT LAST	166	THE CALL	54
AND ON CHRISTS COAT PIT ALL THEIR SHREDS.	272	WHT SUNDAY	14
SHRIL			
HOW SHRIL ARE SILENT TEARS. WHEN SIN GOT HEAD	213	ADMISSION	1
HARK. HOW THE CHILDREN SHRIL AND HIGH	295	PALM-SUNDY	18
SHRILL			
COULD'ST SUCH A SHRILL AND LONG CRY REAR	325	ABELS BLOD	9
WHERE A SHRILL SPRING TUN'D TO THE EARLY DAY.	167	VNTY SPRIT	2
SHRINK			
I PINE, AND SHRINK	202	DSRDR + FR	8
SHRINKS			
AND SOON AS LEFT, SHRINKS BACK TO ILL.	308	THE SEED	18
SHROUD			
(WHICH DOTH THY STRANGE SURE MERCIES SHROUD)	300	PROVIDENCE	8
SHROUDS			
IN QUICK BLASTS SIGH BENEATH THOSE SHROUDS	176	THE STORM	19
THROUGH THE STILL SHROUDS	176	MRNG-WTCH	5
RICH WEEDS AND SHROUDS.	342	OBSEQUIES	18
SHROWD			
BEYOND THAT MISTIE SHROWD.	177	MRNG-WTCH	30
THE CENTER, AND HIS SHROWD.	197	CORRUPTION	36
SHROWD IN THEIR BIRTHS. THE CROWN OF LIFE, LIGHT, TRUTH	192	RLS + LSNS	27
WOO'D BY THE SUN SWELS UP TO BE HIS SHROWD	155	ISAACS M.	54
AND NOTHING MOVES WITHOUT A SHROWD	143	DEATH	14
FIX'D TO A TENT, DESCEND AND SHROWD	315	DWELLNG-PL	6
STILL LODGED, WHERE ALL THY UNSEEN ARROWS SHROWD	307	RAIN-BOW	34
SHULD			
THAT SHULD BOTH CLEANSE	220	HOLY COMM.	46
SHUN			
ABUSE NOT, SHUN NOT HOLY FIRE	266	VAIN WITS	3
TO SHUN THAT PERIL, LET THY GRACE	319	THE ASS	41
PREVAIL WITH ME TO SHUN THE PLACE.	319	THE ASS	42
WHOM LIVING HERE I DID STILL SHUN	311	FAIR+YONG	3
SHUT			
SHUT OUT ALL PAIN AND EACH DISEASE.	319	THE ASS	63
WITH OTHER TREES. BUT NOW SHUT FROM THE BREATH	279	PALM-TREE	5
STARS SHUT UP SHOP, MISTS PACK AWAY	210	FAITH	19
THERE IS AT ALL TIMES (THOUGH SHUT UP) IN YOU	244	THE SAP	39
THOUGH IN THIS DESART I WERE WHOLY SHUT	234	MUTINIE	30
I SHUT THEE OUT, AND LET THAT SLIP	240	MISERY	31
SETTLE MY HOUSE, AND SHUT OUT ALL DISTRACTIONS	191	THE MATCH	28
AND HEAV'NS GATE OPENS, WHEN THIS WORLDS IS SHUT.	192	RLS + LSNS	12
OF NIGHT SHUT UP THY LEAVES, BE CHAST, GOD PRYS	196	RLS + LSNS	136
SHUTS			
BUT SHUTS HIS DOOR, AND LEAVES GOOD OUT ALL NIGHT.	194	RLS + LSNS	84

		PAGE	TITLE	LINE
SHUTS	(CCN'T)			
THAT SHUTS, AND HANGS THE HEAD	• • • • •	183	THRS A TYE	8
AS THY HAND OPES, OR SHUTS.	• • • • •	219	HOLY COMM.	13
SHUTTLE				
MAN IS THE SHUTTLE, TC WHOSE WINDING QUEST	• • •	246	MAN	26
SICK				
WHERE SICK WITH LOVE I STRIVE THY NAME TO SING	•	245	MT. OLV. B	24
SO SHOOK MY BREST, THAT (SICK AND SORE DISMAI'C)	• •	233	MUTINIE	5
SLIGHTING THAT HEALTH THOU GAV'ST, WHEN HE WAS SICK	•	230	LAW + GOSP	23
THY SICK ACCESSIONS INTC SETLED HEALTH	• • •	221	AFFLICTION	3
THOUGH SICK AND SPENT	• • • •	275	PROFFER	20
TO TAKE US SICK, THAT SCUND WCULD NOT TAKE THEE	•	162	PURSUITE	18
THOUGH DEAD, AND SICK	• • • • • •	191	THE MATCH	40
THAT GAIN IS DREADFUL, WHICH MAKES SPIRITS SICK.	•	193	RLS + LSNS	42
SICK WITH A SCARF, OR GLOVE.	• • • • •	205	IDLE VERSE	16
OF HER SICK WATERS, AND INFECTIOUS EASE.	• • •	160	THE SHOWRE	3
DISPATCH'C TO HOLY SOULS, SICK WITH DESIRE	• •	284	PSALM 104	14
WHEN I AM MOST, MCST SICK AND SAD.	• • • •	293	BEGGING B	10
WHOSE SHADOW MAKES ME SAD OR SICK.	• • •	340	THE FEAST	48
TO THOSE, TILL EITHER HURT OR SICK.	• • • •	348	HOLY BIBLE	12
SICKLE				
ARISE. THRUST IN THY SICKLE.	• • • • •	197	CORRUPTION	40
SICKLY				
IN SICKLY EXPIRATICNS TAMES	• • • • •	203	DSRDR + FR	41
SICKLY, AND LCOSE	• • • • • •	145	RSRCTN +IM	40
HIS WINGS ARE DULL, AND SICKLY.	• • • •	181	BURIALL	35
BUT NCW GROWN SICKLY, SAD AND SLCW	• • • •	308	THE SEED	11
SICKNESS				
BUT SICKNESS, OR INFECTION. STIFLE IT	• • •	194	RLS + LSNS	76
SICKNESS IS WHOLSCME, AND CROSSES ARE BUT CURBS	•	221	AFFLICTION	17
SCMETHING OF SICKNESS WCULD DISCLOSE.	• • •	222	AFFLICTION	28
SICKNESSE				
FROM SICKNESSE, GIVE MY SPIRIT HEALTH.	• • •	294	BEGGING B	24
SIDE				
WEAR FRESH ADCRNMENTS CN EACH SIDE.	• • •	337	PSALM 65	44
AND MIXT CN EVERY SIDE	• • • • • •	140	RGNRTN	45
SIGH				
SIGH THERE, AND GRONE FCR THEE	• • • •	187	NO DO THEY	29
IN QUICK BLASTS SIGH BENEATH THOSE SHROUDS	• •	176	THE STORM	19
SIGH TO THE SKY	• • • • • •	222	TEMPEST	10
I LOOK, AND SIGH FOR HIM, WHO FILS	• • • •	220	PSALM 121	3
SIGH'C				
HE SIGH'D FOR EDEN, AND WCULD CFTEN SAY	• • •	197	CORRUPTION	19
SO SIGH'D I UPWARCS STILL, AT LAST	• • • •	139	RGNRTN	26
SIGHES				
WE SPEND IN SIGHES, IS TREASURE AFTER DEATH.	• •	158	THE LAMPE	22
WHICH BROKE IN SIGHES STILL, AS THEY FILL'D	• •	151	THE SEARCH	30
MY SIGHES, AND GRONES.	• • • • •	180	CHRCH-SVC	24
IN SIGHES, AND TEARES.	• • • • •	164	THE CALL	2
'TIL TO THOSE SIGHES FETCH'D FROM HER WOMB	• •	222	TEMPEST	11
HER EARNEST SIGHES PROCUR'D HER TEARS	• • •	223	TEMPEST	15
SIGHING				
THEN SIGHING WHISPER'D, HAPPY ARE THE DEAD.	• •	247	I WALKT	33
AND HANG THE HEAD, SIGHING FOR THOSE	• • •	319	THE ASS	51
SIGHS				
THIS DUSKY STATE CF SIGHS AND TEARS	• • •	303	ST MARY MN	11
SHOULD NOT THY SIGHS REFRAIN THY STORE	• • •	298	JESUS WP B	14
REPEATED SIGHS THY KINDE HEART PAIN	• • •	298	JESUS WP B	4
WHAT SIGHS, WHAT WHISPERS, BUSIE STOPS AND STAYS.	•	268	ASCN-DAY A	27
MCVES IN DISGUISE, AND SIGHS AFFLICT THE AIR.	•	280	JOY	4
SIGHS MAKE JOY SURE, AND SHAKING FASTENS THEE.	•	281	JOY	30
SO IN SIGHS AND UNSEEN TEARS	• • • •	281	JOY	27
SEDUCED SCUL SIGHS UP TC THEE	• • • •	207	REPENTANCE	20
THE DROPS OF RAIN, THE SIGHS CF THE WIND	• •	207	REPENTANCE	37
WHO KNEELS, OR SIGHS A LIFE IS MAD.	• • •	236	CONSTLATN	24
SIGHT				
ARE DARK, AND UNCLEAN IN THY SIGHT	• • •	208	REPENTANCE	66
AND GIVEN US SIGHT.	• • • • • •	219	HOLY COMM.	29
O FOOLISH MAN. HOW HAST THOU LOST THY SIGHT.	• •	224	TEMPEST	53
AND INDISPUTABLE, SHEWS TO MY SIGHT	• • •	268	ASCN-DAY A	35
BUT DARK AND DEEP PANGS TC THY SIGHT.	• • •	264	INTRO. 1	4
THEY NEVER SHALL SO BLINDE MY SIGHT	• • •	272	WHT SUNDAY	19
AT FIRST SIGHT, IF THE BIRD BE FLOWN.	• • •	271	ALL GONE	22
THE CLOUD DOTH NCW RECEIVE THEE, AND THEIR SIGHT	•	268	ASCN-DAY A	57
CREEPS FORTH, AND PINCH'D FOR FCOD, WITH SCENT AND SIGHT		286	PSALM 104	55
HELPS SUCH DARK STRAGLERS TO THEIR SIGHT.	• •	305	ST MARY MN	60
ONE AIM AND END, WHO WALKS NOT BY HIS SIGHT.	• •	327	RIGHTSNESS	21
DUST THAT WOULD RISE, AND DIMME MY SIGHT	• •	161	DSTRQCTION	30
WEAKE BEAMES, AND FIRES FLASH'D TO MY SIGHT	• •	168	VNTY SPRIT	19
STREAMES, AND FLAMES THUS TO THE SIGHT	• • •	172	MIDNIGHT	20
AND AT FIRST SIGHT DOTH MANY PLEASE	• • •	150	RELIGION	42
A STATE FIT FCR THE SIGHT OF THY	• • • •	349	L'ENVOY	17
SIGHTS				
SHORT SIPS AND SIGHTS	• • • • • •	339	THE FEAST	10
SIGN				
EARNEST, AND SIGN, THY GIFTS SC DEAL	• • •	216	DRESSING	20
SIGNAL				
THEN PEACEFUL, SIGNAL BCW, BUT IN A CLOUD	• •	307	RAIN-BOW	33
SIGNATURE				
ALL THAT HAVE SIGNATURE OR LIFE	• • • •	207	REPENTANCE	41

		PAGE	TITLE	LINE

SIGNS
SO BY ALL SIGNS . . . . 292 THE JEWS 26

SILENCE
IN WHOSE THICK SHADES AND SILENCE EACH WILDE BEAST . . 286 PSALM 104 54
O LET THAT SILENCE THEN PREVAIL. . . . . 334 AGREEMENT 64
SILENCE, AND LIGHT, AND WATCHFULNESS WITH YOU . . 236 CONSTLATN 13
THAT CALM AND SILENCE ARE MY JOYS . . . . 214 MISERY 59
SILENCE, AND STEALTH OF DAYES. 'TIS NOW . . . 178 SILENCE 1
INTO TH' OLD SILENCE, AND DEAD SLEEP . . . 203 DSRDR + FR 11

SILENT
A SILENT TEARE CAN PIERCE THY THRONE . . . 167 THE CALL 78
IN SILENT FLIGHTS . . . . 165 THE CALL 16
WHAT SILENT PATHS, WHAT SHADES, AND CELLS . . 153 THE SEARCH 69
WHAT (O GOD) BUT A SILENT TEAR . . . . 320 RGNRTN 9
ABOUT HER SILENT CELL . . . . . . 144 RSRCTN +IM 8
AS WHERE TO LEAD THEIR SHEEP, WHAT SILENT NOCK . . 239 SHEPHEARDS 39
HOW SHRIL ARE SILENT TEARS. WHEN SIN GOT HEAD . 213 ADMISSION 1
ONE SILENT STAR MAY INTERLINE. . . . . 273 WHT SUNDAY 38
IN SILENT DROPS STEAL FROM THEIR HOLY EYES . . 268 ASCN-DAY A 53
GODS SILENT, SEARCHING FLIGHT. . . . . 324 THE NIGHT 31
HE FOUND THEE AT THAT DEAD AND SILENT HOUR. . . 323 THE NIGHT 14
A GRIEF, WHOSE SILENT DEW SHALL BREED . . . 299 JESUS WP B 48
SILENT AS TOMBS . . . . 313 THE STONE 7
WHAT (O GOD) BUT A SILENT TEAR. . . . . 341 THE FEAST 72
WITH WHAT DEEP MURMURS THROUGH TIMES SILENT STEALTH . 343 WATER-FALL 1

SILK-LISTS
PEECES OF SACKCLOTH WITH SILK-LISTS . . . . 282 GARLAND 19

SILK-WORME
SOME DROWSIE SILK-WORME CREEPE . . . . 144 RSRCTN +IM 5

SILLY
THE SHEEP BLEAT THEE A SILLY LAY . . . . 163 MT. OLVS A 14
WITH GLOVES, AND KNOTS THE SILLY SNARES OF PLEASURE . 231 THE WORLD 12

SIMPER'D
SIMPER'D, AND SHIN'D ON YOU . . . . . 205 IDLE VERSE 18

SIMPLE
WHO SIMPLE STILL AND WISE . . . . . 327 RIGHTSNESS 16

SIMPLICITY
O SWEET, DIVINE SIMPLICITY. O GRACE . . . 155 ISAACS M. 37

SIMPLY
SIMPLY BELIEV'D, 'TWAS NOT MY QUILL. . . . 320 RGNRTN 8
SIMPLY BELIEV'D, 'TWAS NOT MY QUILL. . . . 332 AGREEMENT 6
BOLD STORMS, AND SIMPLY DOST ATTEND ON RAIN . . 307 RAIN-BOW 40

SIN
FOR HE THAT'S DEAD, IS FREED FROM SIN. . . . 312 FAIR+YONG 46
AFTER THE FALL, THE FIRST SIN WAS IN BLOOD . . 307 RAIN-BOW 21
THE OTHER OF DEATH, SIN AND STRIFE. . . . 318 THE ASS 4
THY LOVE CLAIMS HIGHEST THANKS, MY SIN . . . 329 TEARS 13
WILT FINISH IT, AND BY NO SIN . . . . 334 AGREEMENT 69
SIN EVERY DAY COMMITS MORE WASTE . . . . 335 JUDGEMENT 28
BUT WHAT IS HIGHEST SIN AND SHAME . . . . 335 JUDGEMENT 33
AND GRATIFIES THY SIN WITH VOWS. . . . . 297 HERODIAS 14
BY SHEWING THE SIN GREAT, SHEW THE RELIEF . . 290 THE TIMBER 43
FROM SIN, HE WALKS A NARROW, PRIVATE WAY. . . 290 THE TIMBER 34
AND IS THERE ANY MURTH'RER WORSE THEN SIN. . . 290 THE TIMBER 25
GO, GO, QUEINT FOLIES, SUGRED SIN . . . . 204 IDLE VERSE 1
AND RODE OF SIN. . . . . 199 NTVTY 1 16
SIN TRIUMPHS STILL, AND MAN IS SUNK BELOW . . 197 CORRUPTION 35
POURE OYLE UPON THE STONES, WEEP FOR THY SIN . . 192 RLS + LSNS 23
KEPT MAN FOR SIN . . . . 175 JOY OF LIF 30
OF SIN, AND DEATH I SOJOURN, YET ONE EYE . . 234 MUTINIE 20
SO PREST AND BOW'D, BEFORE SIN DID DEGRADE . . 279 PALM-TREE 3
AND SIN) HANG AT HIM, FOR THE MORE HE'S BENT . . 279 PALM-TREE 4
BEFORE MAN BROUGHT FORTH SIN, AND SIN DECAY. . . 268 ASCN-DAY A 40
BEFORE MAN BROUGHT FORTH SIN, AND SIN DECAY. . . 268 ASCN-DAY A 40
WIPING OUT MY SHAME, AND SIN. . . . . 249 BEGGING A 12
HOW SHRIL ARE SILENT TEARS. WHEN SIN GOT HEAD . 213 ADMISSION 1
THE PERFECT, FUL OBLATION FOR ALL SIN . . . 216 DRESSING 10
I AM THE GOURD OF SIN, AND SORROW . . . 208 REPENTANCE 71
DEATH WEAN'D THEE FROM THE WORLD, AND SIN. . . 209 THE BURIAL 8
FAITH SPANS UP BLISSE, WHAT SIN, AND DEATH . . 211 FAITH 37
FOR SIN (LIKE WATER) HOURLY GLIDES . . . 350 L'ENVOY 50

SINAI
LORD, WHEN THOU DIDST ON SINAI PITCH . . . 229 LAW + GOSP 1
THOSE FAMOUS TABLES DID FROM SINAI BRING. . . 159 MANS FALL 17

SINFUL
MY CONSCIENCE WITH A SINFULL SOUND . . . 169 RETREATE 16
AND SOYL THY TEMPLE WITH A SINFULL RUST. . . 216 DRESSING 8
O'R THE SULLYED, SINFUL BOOK . . . . 249 BEGGING A 10
SHEW'D TO ME IN MY SINFUL YOUTH . . . . 265 INTRO. 2 20
BUT OUR HEARTS DEAD AND SINFUL COLD. . . . 274 WHT SUNDAY 52
VAIN, SINFUL ART. WHO FIRST DID FIT . . . 297 HERODIAS 1
BUT SINFUL WORDS AND WORKS STILL SPREAD . . 336 PSALM 65 5
MY GOD, I MEAN MY SINFUL HEART. . . . . 315 DWELLNG-PL 16
THOU OVERCAM'ST MY SINFUL STRENGTH . . . 348 HOLY BIBLE 24

SINFULL
A SINFULL WRETCH, A WRETCH THAT CAUS'D THY WOE . 283 LOVE-SICK 18
WHEN FIRST MY YOUTHFULL, SINFULL AGE . . . 282 GARLAND 5
WHICH SINFULL EASE MADE FOUL . . . . 176 THE STORM 22
OF THIS POOR, SINFULL FRAME PURE HEART. . . . 182 CHRFLNESS 19

SING
HOW SHALL THY DUST THY PRAISES SING. . . . 186 PASSION 47

		PAGE	TITLE	LINE
SING	(CCN'T)			
TC WEEP, TO SING, THY DEATH, MY LIFE.		186	PASSION	57
TC FLCW, CR BIRD TO SINC		187	NO DO THEY	14
AND OAK DCTH KNOW I AM. CANST THOU NOT SING.		192	RLS + LSNS	16
BIRCS SING, BEASTS FEED, FISH LEAP, AND TH'EARTH STANCS FAST		194	RLS + LSNS	88
AWAKE, GLAD HEART. GET LP, ANC SING		199	NTVTY 1	1
ALL DAY, AND NIGHT DOTH RUN, ANC SING		212	DAWNING	34
MLST HE NCR SIP, NOR SING. GRCWS NE'R A FLOWR		224	TEMPEST	51
YET SCME, WHO ALL THIS WHILE CIC WEEP AND SING		232	THE WORLD	46
AND SING, AND WEEP, SCAR'C UP INTC THE RING		232	THE WORLD	47
YET NEITHER SING, NOR LIKE THEIR FOOD		228	PILGRIMAGE	19
DCTH GRIEVE FCR DUST, AND DUST DOTH SING.		240	MISERY	40
WHERE SICK WITH LCVE I STRIVE THY NAME TO SING		245	MT. OLV. B	24
THEIR DWELLINCS HAVE ANC SING.		285	PSALM 104	36
THY LITTLE HEART IN EARLY HYMNS DCTH SING		288	THE BIRD	8
PCCR BIRDS THIS DOCTRINE SING		301	PROVIDENCE	25
AND THEIR OWN ANGELS SHINE ANC SING		295	PALM-SUNDY	22
PCCR BIRDS SING BEST, AND PRETTIEST SHOW		294	BEGGING B	19
IN ANTIPHONES SING TO THY NAME.		336	PSALM 65	26
THEY SHCUT FOR JOY, AND JOYNTLY SING		337	PSALM 65	47
WHICH STRAIT, LIKE MORNING-STARS CID SING		332	AGREEMENT	10
TC WRITE AND SING.		329	ANGUISH	14
AND SING HIS SAD VICTCRIOUS STCRY.		341	THF FEAST	60
SHALL RISE AGAIN, AND LIVE AND SING.		340	THE FEAST	36
WHERE CLOUDLESS QUIRES SING WITHCUT TEARS		345	THE WREATH	18
SING THY JUST PRAISE, AND SEE THY FACE.		345	THE WREATH	19
SINGING				
SC HILLS AND VALLEYS INTO SINCING BREAK		288	THE BIRD	13
SHALL SENC ME (SWAN-LIKE) SINGING HOME.		299	JESUS WP B	53
SHINING, OR SINGING STILL TC THEE.		199	NTVTY 1	18
ME THCUGHT I HEARC CNE SINGING THUS.		153	THE SEARCH	74
SINGLE				
MY SINGLE ONE		182	CHRFLNESS	21
WHO HATH THE UPRIGHT HEART, TFE SINGLE EYE		327	RIGHTSNESS	9
IF SINGLE THOU		325	ABELS BLOD	7
(THOUGH SINGLE VOICES ARE BUT LCW)		325	ABELS BLOD	8
STILL SINGLE HEARC, WHILE THESE ACREE		326	ABELS BLOD	42
SINGLY				
IF THCSE BRIGHT JCYS HE SINGLY SHEDS		309	THE SEED	29
SINGS				
AND STILL A NEW SUCCESSICN SINGS AND FLIES.		289	THE TIMBER	5
AWAKES, AND SINGS.		176	MRNG-WTCH	11
SC SHINES AND SINGS, AS IF IT KNEW		276	COCK-CRWNG	9
BUT WHAT FAIR WELL, CR GROVE HE SINGS IN NOW		271	ALL GONE	23
SINK				
JUST SUCH A TAINTED SINK WE HAVE		150	RELIGION	45
SINKS				
SINKS TC A DEAD OBLIVIOUN, ANC THOUGH ALL		224	TEMPEST	42
SINNE				
KILLING THE MAN OF SINNE		147	DAY OF JDG	32
FCR SINNE TOOKE STRENGTH, AND VIGOUR FROM THE LAW.		159	MANS FALL	20
THIS QUICKEN'D MASSE CF SINNE		161	DSTRQCTION	18
BLASTED MY INFANT BUDS, AND SINNE		139	RGNRTN	16
A SEV'RALL SINNE TO EV'RY SENCE		169	RETREATE	18
THAT TOCK'ST MY SINNE		186	PASSION	45
THE WAGES OF MY SINNE		180	BURIALL	5
AND SINNE, THIS HILL		163	MT. OLVS A	31
BUT 'TWAS MY SINNE THAT FCRC'C THY HAND		166	THE CALL	38
SINNER				
CNE SINNER DCTH AMEND		200	NTVTY 2	2
THIS WOMAN (SAY'ST THCU) IS A SINNER.		305	ST MARY MN	67
SINNERS				
TO SINNERS CONFIDENCE, LIFE TC THE GRAVE.		159	MANS FALL	26
THOUGH THEN ALL SINNERS I EXCEED		208	REPENTANCE	59
SINNES				
OF ALL CUR SINNES		185	PASSION	31
SINS				
WHAT SINS ON EVERY MINUTE FALL		165	THE CALL	22
OF FORWARC SINS, AND KIL		204	DSRDR + FR	52
WHO MAKES HIS JESTS OF SINS, MUST BE AT LEAST		194	RLS + LSNS	77
WHO, WHEN THY SINS CALL FCR'T, CAN FENCE A CURSE.		193	RLS + LSNS	64
RISE TO PREVENT THE SUN, SLEEP DCTH SINS GLUT		192	RLS + LSNS	11
MY SINS ALONE OUTWEIGH'C THEM ALL.		208	REPENTANCE	46
AND NC MORE HIS SINS REMEMBER		208	REPENTANCE	50
OF HEAVY SINS, MY HIGH TRANSGRESSIONS		207	REPENTANCE	24
THESE FIND THEE OUT, ANC THOUGH CUR SINS		213	ADMISSION	21
CF GRACE AGAINST ALL SINS		244	THE SAP	48
THESE TWO GRAND SINS WE JCYN ANC ACT TOGETHER		307	RAIN-BOW	25
WERE CNCE SINS LOOSE ANC TEMPTING SPIES		305	ST MARY MN	58
YET I KNOW WELL, AND SC OUR SINS REQUIRE		307	RAIN-BOW	41
THOSE SECRET SINS WE LEAST SUSPECT.		314	THE STONE	41
DCTH YOUR MOST PRIVATE SINS RECCRC.		314	THE STONE	45
MY SINS LCNG SINCE HAVE MADE TFEE STRANGE		293	BEGGING B	5
THEN TRUE REMCRSE, WHEN WITH PAST SINS AT STRIFE.		290	THE TIMBER	28
SINCE TC HIS SINS (AS NEEDS IT MUST)		297	HERODIAS	6
MANS FAVORITE SINS, THOSE TAINTING APPETITES		320	HIDDN TRSR	19
AND THE MCST NEEDFUL FOR CUR SINS.		335	JUDGEMENT	41
MY SINS ARE GREAT AND STILL PREVAIL		333	AGREEMENT	44
MCST FEYNCUS SINS AND NLMBERLESS.		333	AGREEMENT	45
NC SINS OF FRAILTY, NCR OF YOUTH		333	AGREEMENT	53

		PAGE	TITLE	LINE
SINS	(CON'T)			
AND ALL MY SINS, THY SORROWS WERE.		341	THE FEAST	69
SION				
BUT NOW SINCE WE TO SION CAME		229	LAW + GOSP	11
SIONS				
SIONS TRUE, GLORIOUS GOD. ON THEE		336	PSALM 65	1
SIP				
DID LEARN TO SUCK, AND SIP, AND TASTE		308	THE SEED	10
MUST HE NOR SIP, NOR SING. GROWS NE'R A FLOWR		224	TEMPEST	51
SIPS				
SHORT SIPS AND SIGHTS		339	THE FEAST	10
SIRE				
HOW BLEST HAD MEN BEEN, HAD THEIR SIRE		312	FAIR+YONG	27
WHILE SODOM YET DID SMOKE, LAY WITH THEIR SIRE.		307	RAIN-BOW	32
SIT				
I'LE JUDGE, WHERE PENAL FLAMES SIT MIXT AND CLOSE.		307	RAIN-BOW	38
SOME SIT TO THEE, AND EAT		217	DRESSING	37
I SIT WITH THEE BY THIS NEW LIGHT		214	MISERY	53
AND I ALONE SIT LINGRING HERE.		270	ALL GONE	2
DEARE FRIEND SIT DOWN, AND BEAR AWHILE THIS SHADE		279	PALM-TREE	1
SOMETIMES I SIT WITH THEE, AND TARRY		187	NO DO THEY	21
WALK BUT THE FIELDS, OR SIT DOWN AT SOME WEL		197	CORRUPTION	27
EATE, DRINKE, DISCOURSE, SIT DOWNE, AND REST		149	RELIGION	15
I SIT, WHERE ONCE MY SAVIOUR SATE.		151	THE SEARCH	28
SIT REGENT YET, AND BLESSINGS FLOW		351	L'ENVOY	57
UNFINISH'D, WE SHALL GLADLY SIT		350	L'ENVOY	26
SITS				
SITS ON THE SUNS BROW ALL THE YEARE		143	DEATH	13
SITS DOWN, AND FREEZETH ON		197	CORRUPTION	30
OR LIPS, BUT WHO THERE WEEPING SITS		189	RESOLVE	27
SWEET PEACE SITS CROWN'D WITH SMILES		184	PEACE	6
WHO SITS AT HOME TOO BEARS A LOADE		214	MISERY	69
ON IT THE PRINCE OF SALEM SITS, WHO DEALS		243	THE SAP	13
YET O FOR HIS SAKE WHO SITS NOW BY THEE		237	CONSTLATN	49
WHO ON YON THRONE OF AZURE SITS		225	RETIREMENT	1
AND BLACKNESS SITS		219	HOLY COMM.	18
SITT'ST				
BUT SITT'ST OPPRESSED IN THE SHADE		217	EASTER-DAY	4
SIX				
SIX MAY GO WRONG.		174	JOY OF LIF	12
WHEN SIX YEARS THENCE DIGG'D UP, SOME YOUTHFULL EYE		201	THE CHECK	6
'TIS NOW SIX THOUSAND YEARS WELL NIGH		338	DEATH B	3
SIX-DAYES				
THY SIX-DAYES BUILDINGS BEATE		147	DAY OF JDG	12
SIX-DAYS				
A GLEAM OF GLORY, AFTER SIX-DAYS SHOWRES.		2	SON-DAYES	16
SKIE				
WALK TO THE SKIE		269	ASCSN-HYMN	10
THEIR JOYS PROVOKE THE DISTANT SKIE		295	PALM-SUNDY	20
DIRT IN HER WAY, WILL KEEP ABOVE THE SKIE.		291	THE TIMBER	56
SKIES				
TOWARDS THE OLD AND STILL ENDURING SKIES		289	THE TIMBER	7
SO RISE AND RUN, AS TO CUT-RUN THESE SKIES		283	LOVE-SICK	6
THESE NARROW SKIES (NARROW TO ME) THAT BARRE		283	LOVE-SICK	7
YOUTHFUL AND FAIR TO SEE NEW SKIES.		334	JUDGEMENT	6
TO LEAVE THOSE SKIES		275	PROFFER	22
FIX'D LATELY ON THE CROSS, NOW ON THE SKIES.		268	ASCN-DAY A	54
UP TO THE SKIES		267	ASCN-DAY A	10
UP IN ONE CLOUD, AND SO RETURNS THE SKIES		156	ISAACS M.	61
BUT SEAL, OR PIN THEM TO THY SKIES.		191	THE MATCH	38
AND LIKE OLD CLOATHS FOLD UP THESE SKIES		349	L'ENVOY	8
SKIL				
THAT SEED THOU SOW'ST, BLEST BE THY SKIL.		227	LV + DSPLN	6
SKILFUL				
SKILFUL INCHANTRESS AND TRUE BRED.		297	HERODIAS	17
SKILFULL				
ALL SKILFULL IN THE WARS		184	PEACE	4
SKILL				
INCORPORATES BY SKILL		145	RSRCTN +IM	26
WHAT EVER ARGUMENTS, OR SKILL		338	THE THRONE	8
I SKILL NOT YOUR FINE TINSEL, AND FALSE HAIR		275	PROFFER	33
BY FLOWERS AND CARVINGS AND MYSTERIOUS SKILL		279	PALM-TREE	11
AND SHINE AND SMILE, AND HATH THE SKILL		345	QUICKNESS	15
THAT TO BE MERRY I WANT SKILL		342	OBSEQUIES	23
WHICH WITH SKILL'D NEGLIGENCE SEEM'D SHED		304	ST MARY MN	19
SKIN				
IN HAND, SOME IN THE SKIN.		174	CONTENT	22
CLOATH'D WITH THIS SKIN, WHICH NOW LIES SPRED		347	THE BOOK	18
SKINNE				
THE SKINNE, AND SHELL OF THINGS		153	THE SEARCH	81
SKY				
AND IN THE SKY THE STARS APPEAR		228	PILGRIMAGE	2
THE BRIDEGROOME'S COMMING. FIL THE SKY.		211	DAWNING	2
AND SEEDS A KINRED FIRE HAVE WITH THE SKY.		223	TEMPEST	36
SIGH TO THE SKY		222	TEMPEST	10
SKYE				
MEASURES THE MELANCHOLY SKYE		139	RGNRTN	24
SLACK				
WE THOUGHT THE DAY THEN WAS NOT SLACK		143	DEATH	25
THE WORK GOES ON, AND SLACKETH NOT		227	LV + DSPLN	15

	PAGE	TITLE	LINE
SLAIN			
SLAIN FLOCK, AND PILLAG'D FLEECES	157	BRT. CHRCH	17
AND HERE FOR US WAS SLAIN	200	NTVTY 2	10
WHO CANNOT COUNT THOSE THEY HAVE SLAIN	325	ABELS BLOD	12
THIS GOD FORESAW. AND WHEN SLAIN BY THE CROWD	330	JACOBS PLW	21
WHO DID, WHEN SLAIN	340	THE FEAST	28
HEE'LE NOT BE FOUND, WHERE HE WAS SLAINE	152	THE SEARCH	50
SLAUGHTER			
ARE PUT UNTO THE SLAUGHTER	166	THE CALL	63
SLAV'D			
IN THE CREATION SHED, AND SLAV'D TO SENCE	223	TEMPEST	19
SLAVE			
I SHELTER IN, IS SLAVE	173	CONTENT	3
LEAVES ME A SLAVE TO PASSIONS, AND MY FATE.	158	MANS FALL	8
MY BRUTISH SOUL, AND TO THY SLAVE	202	DSRDR + FR	3
A SLAVE TO LUSTFUL ELEMENTS.	312	FAIR+YONG	30
SLEEP			
SLEEP HAPPY ASHES (BLESSED SLEEP)	311	THE SEED	84
SLEEP HAPPY ASHES (BLESSED SLEEP)	311	THE SEED	84
HIS PROMISE STILL, BUT WE BREAK OURS AND SLEEP.	307	RAIN-BOW	20
ON STONES DIDST SLEEP AND FOUND'ST BUT COLD RELIEF.	331	JACOBS PLW	46
A SEA, WHOSE LOWD WAVES CANNOT SLEEP	325	ABELS BLOD	15
SPEECHLESS AND CALM, AS INFANTS SLEEP.	326	ABELS BLOD	35
AND WONDER, WHILE THE JEWS DID SLEEP	323	THE NIGHT	24
(BECAUSE THEY SLEEP SO LONG) SOME MEN	335	JUDGEMENT	25
THY ARM DOTH SLEEP, BUT WRITE THIS DAY	335	JUDGEMENT	44
ART SENSELESS STILL. O CAN'ST THOU SLEEP	296	JESUS WP A	3
INTO TH' OLD SILENCE, AND DEAD SLEEP	203	DSRDR + FR	11
HIM COMPANY ALL DAY, AND IN HIM SLEEP.	191	RLS + LSNS	6
YET, NEVER SLEEP THE SUN UP, PRAYER SHOU'D	192	RLS + LSNS	7
RISE TO PREVENT THE SUN, SLEEP DOTH SINS GLUT	192	RLS + LSNS	11
WATCH, WHILE I SLEEP, OR PLAY.	187	NO DO THEY	32
ALL'S IN DEEP SLEEP, AND NIGHT. THICK DARKNES LYES	197	CORRUPTION	37
WHERE THOU MAY'ST SLEEP WHOLE AGES, LIFES POOR FLOWR	195	RLS + LSNS	123
BEING LAID, AND DREST FOR SLEEP, CLOSE NOT THY EYES	195	RLS + LSNS	127
A BED, AND SLEEP	171	COME, COME	29
(WHILST DEEP SLEEP OTHERS CATCHES)	171	MIDNIGHT	2
THAT CURTAIN'D GRAVE, THOUGH SLEEP, LIKE ASHES, HIDE	177	MRNG-WTCH	32
OF SLEEP, AND CLOUDS	176	MRNG-WTCH	6
FAREWELL. I GOE TO SLEEP. BUT WHEN	177	EVNG-WTCH	1
GOE, SLEEP IN PEACE. AND WHEN THOU LYEST	177	EVNG-WTCH	3
HERBS SLEEP UNTO THE EAST, AND SOME FOWLES THENCE	183	THRS A TYE	11
AND SENSELESS SLEEP	180	BURIALL	4
WHEN WE WOULD SLEEP	219	HOLY COMM.	38
WHEN EITHER SLEEP, OR SOME DARK PLEASURE	211	DAWNING	7
WHILE PALESTINE WAS FAST A SLEEP, AND LAY	238	SHEPHEARDS	7
NO SLEEP, NOR SLOTH ASSAILES YOU, BUT POOR MAN	236	CONSTLATN	15
WHEN IT WERE BEST TO SLEEP	236	CONSTLATN	26
TO PLUCK A GARLAND HENCE, WHILE YOU DO SLEEP	280	PALM-TREE	26
TO SLEEP WITHOUT THEE, IS TO DIE.	277	COCK-CRWNG	25
CALL TO THE SOUL, WHEN MAN DOTH SLEEP.	271	ALL GONE	26
TRUE THANKS TO THEE, BEFORE I SLEEP.	348	HOLY BIBLE	4
BUT THOU SLEEP'ST IN A DEEPE NEGLECT	163	MT. OLVS A	12
BUT PERFECT ALL BEFORE THOU SLEEP'ST, THEN SAY	195	RLS + LSNS	117
BUT THOU SLEEP'ST ON. WHER'S NOW THY PROTESTATION	202	THE CHECK	43
SLEEPE			
SHALL BE SENTENC'D FOR THEIR SLEEPE.	164	THE CALL	9
AND MOVE ON WITH THE SHADES, STARS NOT, AND SLEEPE	157	THE LAMPE	2
SHALT IN THY MOTHERS BOSOME SLEEPE	143	DEATH	28
FROM THAT LONG SLEEPE	144	RSRCTN +IM	6
SLEEPES			
HE SLEEPES, AND DROOPS, AND IN THIS DROWSIE STATE	158	MANS FALL	7
SLEEPIE			
AH. GO. TH'ART WEAK, AND SLEEPIE. HEAV'N	178	EVNG-WTCH	11
SLEEPIE PLANETS SET, AND SLUMBER	212	DAWNING	20
SLEEPING			
THUS LIKE SOME SLEEPING EXHALATION	203	DSRDR + FR	31
SLEEPS			
SLEEPS NOT, BUT SHAKING OFF SLOTH, AND NEGLECTS	201	THE CHECK	15
THAT DARK, AND DEAD SLEEPS IN ITS KNOWN	179	SILENCE	21
SLEEPS AT THE LADDERS FOOT, ALAS. WHAT CAN	224	TEMPEST	39
WHICH ALL THE WINTER SLEEPS HERE UNDER FOOT	248	I WALKT	38
STILL EITHER SLEEPS, OR SLIPS HIS SPAN.	236	CONSTLATN	16
WHEN THOU WITH-DRAW'ST THEIR BREATH, THEIR VIGOUR SLEEPS	287	PSALM 104	79
SLEPT			
HERE SLEPT MY THOUGHTS DEAR MARK. WHICH DUST	310	THE SEED	73
WHILE ALL HER SEERS SLEPT.	238	SHEPHEARDS	22
ON EACH GREEN THING. THEN SLEPT (WELL FED)	347	THE BOOK	17
SLIGHT			
THE WEAKER SORT SLIGHT, TRIVIALL WARES INSLAVE	232	THE WORLD	42
AND SLIGHT A PRICE	213	ADMISSION	14
YEA GODS OWN BLOOD WE TREAD UPON AND SLIGHT.	307	RAIN-BOW	30
WE SLIGHT AS OLD AND SOIL'D, THOUGH FRESH AND NEW.	306	RAIN-BOW	2
IF I HOLD FAST AND SLIGHT THE LURE.	317	MEN OF WAR	40
AND EVERY ONE CAN SLIGHT HIS LEASE	338	DEATH B	8
TO SLIGHT THY PRECIOUS BLOOD, AND BREATH.	164	INCARNATN	18
SLIGHTEST			
YET HAVE I KNOWNE THY SLIGHTEST THINGS	166	THE CALL	50
SLIGHTING			
SLIGHTING THAT HEALTH THOU GAV'ST, WHEN HE WAS SICK	230	LAW + GOSP	23

		PAGE	TITLE	LINE
SLIGHTS				
MAN SLIGHTS HIS MAKER, WHEN FAMILIAR GROWN	• • •	330	JACOBS PLW	19
HIS EASIE YOKE REJECTS OR SLIGHTS	• • •	315	THE STONE	55
AND SLIGHTS THAT MOST, WHICH MEN MOST PRIZE.	• • •	319	THE ASS	48
SLIME				
BUT DRUNK, IS PUDDLE, OR MEERE SLIME	• • • •	150	RELIGION	43
SLIP				
I SHUT THEE OUT, AND LET THAT SLIP	• • • •	240	MISERY	31
SLIPS				
STILL EITHER SLEEPS, OR SLIPS HIS SPAN.	• • • •	236	CONSTLATN	16
SLIPT				
WHILE OTHERS SLIPT INTO A WIDE EXCESSE	• • •	232	THE WORLD	40
MY GOD, HOW GRACIOUS ART THOU. I HAD SLIPT	• • •	188	RELAPSE	1
SLOTH				
SLEEPS NOT, BUT SHAKING OFF SLOTH, AND NEGLECTS	• •	201	THE CHECK	15
NO SLEEP, NOR SLOTH ASSAILES YOU, BUT POOR MAN	• •	236	CONSTLATN	15
SLOW				
LIKE A THICK MIDNIGHT-FOG MOV'D THERE SO SLOW	• •	231	THE WORLD	17
IS OLD, AND SLOW	• • • • • • •	181	BURIALL	34
AND SLOW MOTIONS HERE	• • • • • •	172	MIDNIGHT	16
BUT NOW GROWN SICKLY, SAD AND SLOW	• • •	308	THE SEED	11
QUICK TO ADVANCE, AND TO RETREAT MOST SLOW.	• •	327	RIGHTSNESS	18
LIKE CHRONIC PAINS, WHICH SURELY KILL, THOUGH SLOW.	•	327	RIGHTSNESS	30
WHY IS MY GOD THUS SLOW AND COLD	• • • •	293	BEGGING B	9
SLOWLY				
SLOWLY AND SADLY DOTH HE GROW	• • • •	308	THE SEED	17
SLUMBER				
SLEEPIE PLANETS SET, AND SLUMBER	• • • •	212	DAWNING	20
SMALL				
THY LAWS BUT NETS, WHERE SOME SMALL BIRDS	• •	207	REPENTANCE	11
INNUMERABLE, CREEPING THINGS BOTH SMALL	• •	286	PSALM 104	70
THE SMALL, STILL VOICE, AT SOME LOW COTTAGE KNOCKS	•	330	JACOBS PLW	9
THEE TWO SMALL MITES, AND BE AT STRIFE	• •	186	PASSION	52
A SMALL BRIGHT SPARKLE WAS A BED	• • •	151	THE SEARCH	18
THE QUICK, AND DEAD, BOTH SMALL AND GREAT	• •	147	DAY OF JDG	23
SMART				
WHAT CRUELL SMART	• • • • • • •	185	PASSION	10
SMELL				
I SMELL A DEW LIKE MYRRH, AND ALL THE DAY	• •	198	UNPRFTBLNS	10
I SMELL HER SPICES, AND HER OINTMENT YIELDS	• •	267	ASCN-DAY A	21
UNTIL THEY SMELL	• • • • • • •	275	PROFFER	16
SMELS				
WHICH THRIVES IN STORMS, AND SMELS BEST AFTER SHOWRES.	•	193	RLS + LSNS	60
SMILE				
SMILE AT FAIR EYES	• • • • • • •	189	RESOLVE	26
AND WIND AND CURLE, AND WINK AND SMILE	• •	278	THE STARRE	3
AND SHINE AND SMILE, AND HATH THE SKILL	• •	345	QUICKNESS	15
HER QUICKNING KINDNESS, SMILES AND KISSES	• •	348	HOLY BIBLE	29
NOR LOV'D THE SMILES OF GREATNESS, BUT HAVE WROUGHT	•	280	PALM-TREE	19
THE DAY-STAR SMILES, AND LIGHT WITH DECEAST	• •	267	ASCN-DAY A	23
MY GREAT PRESERVER SMILES	• • • • •	205	IDLE VERSE	6
IN SMILES, AND TEARS	• • • • • •	186	PASSION	56
SWEET PEACE SITS CROWN'D WITH SMILES	• •	184	PEACE	6
AND TURN'D TO SMILES THE BEGGING TEARS	• •	300	PROVIDENCE	5
THAT KILL WITH SMILES AND SEEMING JOY.	• •	311	FAIR+YONG	16
IN SPARKLING SMILES HASTE GLADLY DOWN	• •	315	DWELLNG-PL	9
STORMS TURN TO MUSICK, CLOUDS TO SMILES AND AIR.	•	306	RAIN-BOW	10
SMILING				
DURST NOT LOOK ON THOSE SMILING YEARS	• •	303	ST MARY MN	12
SMOAKE				
THE OTHER SMOAKE, AND PLEASURES WEIGH'D	• •	139	RGNRTN	32
SMOKE				
THE SMOKE, AND EXHALATIONS OF THE BREST.	• •	160	THE SHOWRE	12
WHILE SODOM YET DID SMOKE, LAY WITH THEIR SIRE.	•	307	RAIN-BOW	32
IS MOV'D AND TREMBLES, THE HILLS MELT AND SMOKE	•	287	PSALM 104	86
THIS MADE HIM PUT ON CLOUDS, AND FIRE AND SMOKE	•	330	JACOBS PLW	7
SMOKING				
FIRES SMOKING DIE.	• • • • • •	210	FAITH	26
SMOOTH				
AND SMOOTH SEDUCEMENTS. I'LE NOT STUFF MY STORY	•	275	PROFFER	35
AND EV'N, SMOOTH LINES, LIKE THE SUNS RAYS	• •	310	THE SEED	59
RETINUE, ALL WAS HERE SMOOTH AS THY BRIDE	• •	154	ISAACS M.	23
AS SMOOTH AS GLASSE.	• • • • • •	174	JOY OF LIF	20
AND SMOOTH WITHOUT A THORNE	• • • •	166	THE CALL	71
SMOOTH'ST				
WHO NEVER FEEL'ST THE SUN, NOR SMOOTH'ST THY BROW	•	217	EASTER-DAY	3
SMOTE				
DID SPIT ON THEE, AND SMOTE THEE TOO.	• • •	317	MEN OF WAR	30
SMOTHER				
DASH NOT THY FRIEND, NOR HEAV'N, O SMOTHER	• •	194	RLS + LSNS	69
SNAKE				
SOME SNAKE, OR WEEDS	• • • • • •	328	RIGHTSNESS	53
SNARE				
FIRST MAKES, THEN HUGS A SNARE	• • • •	236	CONSTLATN	18
WITH GLOVES, AND KNOTS THE SILLY SNARES OF PLEASURE	•	231	THE WORLD	12
HID IN THESE LOW THINGS SNARES TO GAIN HIS HEART	•	223	TEMPEST	23
SNARLING				
EACH SNARLING BLAST SHOT THROUGH ME, AND DID SHARE	•	198	UNPRFTBLNS	4
SNOW				
IN HEAV'N, HAIL, THUNDER, RAIN-BOWS, SNOW, AND ICE	•	194	RLS + LSNS	93

	PAGE	TITLE	LINE
SNOW (CON'T)			
BUT THOU WERT SO, E'RE TIME HIS SNOW COULD SHED.	156	ISAACS M.	70
ROUGH-CAST WITH ROCKS, AND SNOW	139	RGNRTN	21
TO MAKE STAIN'D MAN MORE WHITE THEN SNOW.	270	ASCSN-HYMN	36
SNOWIE			
CHECQUR'D WITH SNOWIE FLEECES	140	RGNRTN	53
AGE MADE THEM REV'REND, AND A SNOWIE HEAD	156	ISAACS M.	69
SNOWS			
IT SNOWS , AND FREEZETH HERE.	205	IDLE VERSE	22
SNUDGE			
TO SNUDGE IN, AND EMBRACE A COT	214	MISERY	66
SNUFF			
BUT NOTHING BUT THE SNUFF TO ME	178	SILENCE	19
SOAR			
I SOAR AND RISE	267	ASCN-DAY A	9
SOAR'D			
AND SING, AND WEEP, SOAR'D UP INTO THE RING	232	THE WORLD	47
THUS SOAR'D THY SOUL, WHO (THOUGH YOUNG) DIDST INHERIT	156	ISAACS M.	63
SOARS			
AND SOARS, AND SHINES, BUT E'R WE SUP	203	DSRDR + FR	34
SOCKET			
THEY'RE STOR'D UP IN THE SOCKET, WHERE THEY LYE	158	THE LAMPE	19
SODOM			
WHILE SODOM YET DID SMOKE, LAY WITH THEIR SIRE.	307	RAIN-BOW	32
SOEVER			
O AT WHAT TIME SOEVER THOU	212	DAWNING	25
SOFT			
NOR GRIEVE THY DOVE, BUT SOFT AND MILD	235	MUTINIE	38
GRANT I MAY SOFT AND LOWLY BE	318	THE ASS	17
HIS STILL, SOFT CALL.	324	THE NIGHT	34
WITH ALL THEIR SOFT, KINDE ARTS AND EASIE STRAINS	320	HIDDN TRSR	21
AND TO THY SOFT ARTS STRONGLY BOWS.	297	HERODIAS	16
OF DROPS MAKE SOFT THE EARTH, MY EYES COULD WEEP	160	THE SHOWRE	14
WHIRLE-WINDS, AND CLOUDS, AND THE SOFT VOICE	149	RELIGION	18
SWEET, DOWNIE THOUGHTS, SOFT LILLY-SHADES, CALM STREAMES.	188	RELAPSE	25
MORE SOFT THEN DOWN.	341	THE FEAST	62
SOFT-CLOATH'D			
NO COSTLY PRIDE, NO SOFT-CLOATH'D LUXURIE	239	SHEPHEARDS	31
SOFTEN			
SOFTEN THE MOULD, WHILE ALL UNSEEN	337	PSALM 65	37
SOFTER			
THE STONES MUCH SOFTER THAN MY HEART	207	REPENTANCE	36
THE SOFTER DRESSINGS OF THE SPRING	345	THE WREATH	5
SOFTLY			
SOFTLY REST ALL THY VIRGIN-CRUMS.	209	THE BURIAL	9
SOFTNESS			
HATH FLESH NO SOFTNESS NOW. MID-DAY NO LIGHT.	224	TEMPEST	56
SOIL			
WHERE I SOMETIMES HAD SEEN THE SOIL TO YIELD	246	I WALKT	3
SOIL'D			
THY BRIGHTNESS SOIL'D	270	ASCSN-HYMN	26
WE SLIGHT AS OLD AND SOIL'D, THOUGH FRESH AND NEW.	306	RAIN-BOW	2
SOIL'D WITH MANY A WEEPING LOCK	312	FAIR+YONG	32
BY THESE SOIL'D TEARES.	170	COME, COME	7
PRAISE SOIL'D WITH TEARS, AND TEARS AGAIN	345	THE WREATH	10
SOILES			
THAT SOILES THY NAME	171	COME, COME	18
SOJOURN			
SOULS SOJOURN HERE, BUT MAY NOT REST.	269	ASCSN-HYMN	5
OF SIN, AND DEATH I SOJOURN, YET ONE EYE	234	MUTINIE	20
SOJOURN'D			
I SOJOURN'D THUS, AT LAST JESHURUNS KING	159	MANS FALL	16
FAITH SOJOURN'D FIRST ON EARTH IN YOU	292	THE JEWS	38
SOLDIERS			
BUT SEEING SOLDIERS LONG AGO	317	MEN OF WAR	29
THE SOLDIERS HERE	156	BRT. CHRCH	6
SOLE			
O MY SOLE COMFORT, TAKE NO MORE THESE WAYES	188	RELAPSE	9
THE GLORIOUS GOD IS MY SOLE STAY	220	PSALM 121	9
THY SERVICE TO BE OUR SOLE EASE	351	L'ENVOY	60
SOLEMN			
CHIRPING THEIR SOLEMN MATINS ON EACH TREE.	288	THE BIRD	24
THUS IS THE SOLEMN TEMPLE SUNK AGEN	331	JACOBS PLW	35
SOLEMNITIES			
THY BRIGHT SOLEMNITIES DID SHEW	295	PALM-SUNDY	32
SOLITARY			
UNTO THY SOLITARY SELF IS SHOWN.	330	JACOBS PLW	4
WHAT HALLOW'D SOLITARY GROUND DID BEAR	323	THE NIGHT	15
FAIR, SOLITARY PATH. WHOSE BLESSED SHADES	326	RIGHTSNESS	1
PASS THY SOLITARY YEARS	281	JOY	28
FIXETH A SOLITARY LAMP	178	SILENCE	7
SOLITUDE			
HEAV'NS SECRET SOLITUDE, THOSE FAIR ABODES	327	RIGHTSNESS	6
YET THOU IN ALL THY SOLITUDE AND GRIEF	331	JACOBS PLW	45
SOLOMON			
ASPIRE FOR HOME. THIS SOLOMON OF OLD	279	PALM-TREE	10
YET SOLOMON WAS NEVER DREST SO FINE.	245	MAN	14
SOLUTION			
WHICH CAUSE SOLUTION IN ALL PARTS	350	L'ENVOY	40
SOMETHING			
WHO PLAC'D THEE HERE, DID SOMETHING THEN INFUSE	243	THE SAP	9

		PAGE	TITLE	LINE
SOMETHING	**(CON'T)**			
SOMETHING OF SICKNESS WOULD DISCLOSE.		222	AFFLICTION	28
AND EV'RY BUSH IS SOMETHINGS BOOTH.		313	THE STONE	15
YET SOMETHING MORE I MUST INTREATE		167	THE CALL	84
AND SOMETHING COOLD THE PARCH'D, AND THIRSTIE ISLE		156	ISAACS M.	58
AND SOMETHING STILL BE LEFT THE DEAD		142	DEATH	8
SOMETIMES				
WHICH I SOMETIMES LIV'D IN.		180	BURIALL	10
SOMETIMES I SIT WITH THEE, AND TARRY		187	NO DO THEY	21
MY YIELDING LEAVES. SOMETIMES A SHOWR		203	DSRDR + FR	25
LASTS NOT A NIGHT SOMETIMES. BAD SPIRITS FEAR		195	RLS + LSNS	124
DID SOMETIMES RULE. A GRIEF SO BRIGHT		299	JESUS WP B	50
YET LIV'D HE HERE SOMETIMES, AND BORE FOR THEE		243	THE SAP	17
WHERE I SOMETIMES HAD SEEN THE SOIL TO YIELD		246	I WALKT	3
AND WE HERE TAST SOMETIMES BELOW)		235	CONSTLATN	4
BESIDES, THOSE KERCHIEFS SOMETIMES SHED		342	OBSEQUIES	25
SOMTHING				
SHEWS HIM HIMSELF, OR SOMTHING HE SHOULD SEE.		222	TEMPEST	2
SOMTHING I HAD, WHICH LONG AGO		308	THE SEED	9
SOMTIMES				
HAVE COMMERCE SOMTIMES WITH POOR DUST		212	DAWNING	40
SON				
O THINK ON THIS, THY SON DID BLEED.		208	REPENTANCE	60
HIS ONELY SON TO MAKE IT FREE		292	THE JEWS	34
THE LOST SON BY THE NEWLY FOUND.		293	THE JEWS	49
SONGS				
I WILL IN SONGS TO THY GREAT NAME IMPLOY		287	PSALM 104	90
AND SONGS I HEAR. O QUICKNING SHOWERS		340	THE FEAST	51
SONNE				
THE LOST SONNE HAD NOT LEFT THE HUSKE		162	PURSUITE	11
TO FRIEND, OR SONNE		173	CONTENT	7
UNTO HIS SONNES, (WHERE OFTEN THEY		151	THE SEARCH	23
SONS				
WHOSE PAINEFULL THROWS YIELD MANY SONS		167	THE CALL	76
WATER'ST IT FOR THE SONS OF MEN		336	PSALM 65	28
THE SONS THE FATHER KIL		237	CONSTLATN	38
AND CEMENT US WITH THY SONS BLOOD		350	L'ENVOY	46
SOON				
TEARS AND THESE FLAMES WILL SOON GROW KINDE		266	VAIN WITS	5
NONE WOULD MORE DOTE ON, NOR SO SOON ENTICE.		320	HIDDN TRSR	24
THEY WOULD SOON QUIT AND LEARN TO KNEEL.		308	THE SEED	4
AND SOON AS LEFT, SHRINKS BACK TO ILL.		308	THE SEED	18
AS SOON AS THEY DID SEED		196	CORRUPTION	12
SOOTH				
HEDGES HAVE EARS, SAID THE OLD SOOTH		313	THE STONE	14
SORCERESS				
LEAVE THEN YONG SORCERESS. THE ICE		297	HERODIAS	9
SORCERY				
YOUR SORCERY		275	PROFFER	34
SORE				
HE GOES, HE YIELDS, AND TROUBLED SORE		240	MISERY	37
SO SHOOK MY BREST, THAT (SICK AND SORE DISMAI'D)		233	MUTINIE	5
THEY MURMUR'D SORE, BUT I, WHO FELT THEM BOYL		234	MUTINIE	9
YET GRIEF AND OLD WOUNDS MAKE HIM SORE DISPLEAS'D		290	THE TIMBER	35
SORROW				
THE KING OF GRIEF, THE MAN OF SORROW		294	PALM-SUNDY	4
BUT THOU MUST SORROW FOR HIM TOO.		299	JESUS WP B	43
I AM THE GOURD OF SIN, AND SORROW		208	REPENTANCE	71
OF LOVE, AND SORROW		202	THE CHECK	37
SORROWS				
AND FROM THIS CARE, WHERE DREAMS AND SORROWS REIGN		248	I WALKT	57
SORROWS IN WHITE, GRIEFS TUN'D, A SUGERD DOSIS		280	JOY	5
THAT THE SEEDS OF FOUL SORROWS BE		312	FAIR+YONG	33
AND ALL MY SINS, THY SORROWS WERE.		341	THE FEAST	69
SORT				
THE WEAKER SORT SLIGHT, TRIVIALL WARES INSLAVE		232	THE WORLD	42
SORTING				
YET THAT NOT SORTING TO MY END		207	REPENTANCE	17
SOUGHT				
SOUGHT OUT WHAT MIGHT OUTVIE MY SCORE.		207	REPENTANCE	32
I SOUGHT CHOICE BOWRES, HAUNTED THE SPRING		282	GARLAND	21
THAT BY THY BOOK MUST NOT BE SOUGHT		319	THE ASS	38
BUT WHILE I LISTNING SOUGHT		141	RGNRTN	86
SHEW ME THAT PEARL I SOUGHT ELSEWHERE.		348	HOLY BIBLE	26
WHO IN THEM LOV'D AND SOUGHT THY FACE.		347	THE BOOK	30
MY FIRST CHEAP BOOK HAD ALL I SOUGHT.		348	HOLY BIBLE	16
SOUL				
INTO MY SOUL, WITH WHOSE QUICK TOUCH		348	HOLY BIBLE	21
MY SOUL AND ALL		341	THE FEAST	58
THY DEATH MAY KEEP MY SOUL ALIVE.		343	OBSEQUIES	32
THOU ART THE CHANNEL MY SOUL SEEKS		344	WATER-FALL	39
THUS SOAR'D THY SOUL, WHO (THOUGH YOUNG) DIDST INHERIT		156	ISAACS M.	63
THY SOUL, AND WITH NEW PINIONS REFRESH		155	ISAACS M.	48
MY BRUTISH SOUL, AND TO THY SLAVE		202	DSRDR + FR	3
AND HATCH MY SOUL, UNTILL IT FLY		204	DSRDR + FR	47
UP WITH THY CURTAINS, GIVE THY SOUL THE WING		195	RLS + LSNS	128
AND MY SOUL SHOULD BE THINE.		187	NO DO THEY	36
THAT SAV'D MY SOUL		188	RELAPSE	6
WHEN FIRST THY EYES UNVEIL, GIVE THY SOUL LEAVE		191	RLS + LSNS	1
AND, CATHES ONCE BROKE, THE SOUL CANNOT BE SOUND.		193	RLS + LSNS	46

		PAGE	TITLE	LINE
SOUL	**(CON'T)**			
A SWEET SELF-PRIVACY IN A RIGHT SOUL		193	RLS + LSNS	53
MY SOUL DOTH STREAME		171	MIDNIGHT	9
BUT (AH) MY SOUL WITH TOO MUCH STAY		170	RETREATE	27
OR TAUGHT MY SOUL TO FANCY OUGHT		169	RETREATE	5
MY GAZING SOUL WOULD DWELL AN HOURE		169	RETREATE	12
BOTH WASH, AND WING MY SOUL.		176	THE STORM	24
AND SHOOTS OF GLORY, MY SOUL BREAKES, AND BUDS.		176	MRNG-WTCH	2
WHEN I LYE DOWN. THE PIOUS SOUL BY NIGHT		177	MRNG-WTCH	24
I SEARCH, AND RACK MY SOUL TO SEE		178	SILENCE	17
MY SOUL, THERE IS A COUNTRIE		184	PEACE	1
AND (O MY SOUL AWAKE)		184	PEACE	10
O THAT I WERE ALL SOUL. THAT THOU		182	CHRFLNESS	17
O THOU, WHOM MY SOUL LOVES, AND FEARES.		185	PASSION	15
DEAR SOUL. THOU KNEW'ST, FLOWERS HERE ON EARTH		304	ST MARY MN	27
THY SERVICE, NOR HIS SOUL ONE DAY.		301	PROVIDENCE	34
AND KEEPS HIS SOUL UNTO ETERNAL MIRTH.		290	THE TIMBER	32
YET JOY IT SELF WILL MAKE A RIGHT SOUL GRIEVE		290	THE TIMBER	39
SHALL BE CONSUM'D. O MY SOUL, BLESS THY LORD.		287	PSALM 104	95
UP, O MY SOUL, AND BLESSE THE LORD. O GOD		284	PSALM 104	1
WHICH MAKE ME WISE TO LOSE MY SOUL.		322	CHILDEHOOD	26
I BOW MY TROUBLED SOUL, AND GREET		328	ANGUISH	3
OR THAT A SOUL COULD AKE.		282	GARLAND	16
THY WATERS TO A SOUL THAT PINES.		273	WHT SUNDAY	48
CALL TO THE SOUL, WHEN MAN DOTH SLEEP.		271	ALL GONE	26
LIGHT TO MY SOUL, THAT IT MAY LIVE.		208	REPENTANCE	52
AND EVEN MY SOUL TO THEE IS DEAD		209	REPENTANCE	78
BOTH SOUL, AND BODY ARE WELL DREST		209	REPENTANCE	80
SWEETLY DIDST THOU EXPIRE. THY SOUL		209	THE BURIAL	5
SEDUCED SOUL SIGHS UP TO THEE		207	REPENTANCE	20
WHICH I CONFESSE WITH ALL MY SOUL		207	REPENTANCE	25
THEN KNEEL MY SOUL, AND BODY. KNEEL, AND BOW.		217	DRESSING	41
O THOU THAT LOVEST A PURE, AND WHITEND SOUL./		216	DRESSING	1
AND MY SOUL IN NEW ARRAY		214	PRAISE	15
UNTO MY VERY SOUL.		220	PSALM 121	16
LORD. THOU DIDST PUT A SOUL HERE. IF I MUST		224	TEMPEST	57
UPON HIS SOUL		232	THE WORLD	20
SHIN'D ON MY SOUL, I FELT THROUGH ALL MY POWR'S		244	MT. OLV. B	3
SO MY FIERCE SOUL BUSTLES ABOUT		214	MISERY	79
BUT WITH THE BLOUD OF ALL MY SOUL		242	MISERY	109
SOUL-CURING				
GRIEF AND SOUL-CURING MELANCHOLY.		311	FAIR+YONG	2
SOUL-LESSE				
MUST (SOUL-LESSE SHADOW) SO LIVE ON		311	THE SEED	88
SOUL-QUICKNING				
SOUL-QUICKNING RAIN, THIS LIVING WATER		296	JESUS WP A	10
SOULE				
THEN MAKE MY SOULE WHITE AS HIS OWNE		167	THE CALL	90
MY SOULE MIGHT LOCKE ABOUT.		166	THE CALL	41
RE-MARRY TO THE SOULE, FOR 'TIS MOST PLAINE		145	RSRCTN +IM	49
BALSAM OF SOULES, THE BODYES BLISSE.		152	THE SEARCH	44
THREE THINGS I'DE HAVE, MY SOULES CHIEF HEALTH		148	DAY OF JDG	39
THUS SOULES THEIR BODIES ANIMATE		218	HOLY COMM.	5
SOULS				
OUR SOULS, AND BODIES BOTH		219	HOLY COMM.	31
THIS BALM FOR SOULS THAT AKE		244	THE SAP	44
TO SEE THEIR SOULS GREAT SHEPHEARD, WHO WAS COME		239	SHEPHEARDS	45
AMONGST THE QUICK, SELLING THEIR SOULS AND BREATH		275	PROFFER	39
THAT BUZ IN EVERY EAR, AND BLOW ON SOULS		275	PROFFER	15
THAT GLASS OF SOULS AND SPIRITS, WHERE WELL DREST		275	PROFFER	23
SOULS SOJOURN HERE, BUT MAY NOT REST.		269	ASCSN-HYMN	5
A LOVE-SICK SOULS EXALTED FLIGHT.		277	COCK-CRWNG	34
CAN SOULS BE TRACK'D BY ANY EYE		277	COCK-CRWNG	35
O COULD I TRACK THEM. BUT SOULS MUST		179	SILENCE	25
O HOW IN THIS THY QUIRE OF SOULS I STAND		179	CHRCH-SVC	9
O THOU. THAT CANST NOT WISH MY SOULS DAMNATION		190	THE MATCH	16
WELCOME DEAR BOOK, SOULS JOY, AND FOOD. THE FEAST		197	SCRIPTURES	1
WHERE SOULS ARE HATCH'D UNTO ETERNITIE.		197	SCRIPTURES	4
THE IDLE TALK OF FEAV'RISH SOULS		205	IDLE VERSE	15
DISPATCH'D TO HOLY SOULS, SICK WITH DESIRE		284	PSALM 104	14
WHERE FREED SOULS DWEL BY LIVING FOUNTAINS		312	FAIR+YONG	49
OUR SOULS DISEASES FIRST, AND THEN		311	FAIR+YONG	12
MY SOULS BRIGHT FOOD, THY ABSENCE KILLS.		308	THE SEED	6
WHERE SOULS BEHIND THE ALTAR MOVE		325	ABELS BLOD	20
THE DAY OF SPIRITS, MY SOULS CALM RETREAT		324	THE NIGHT	27
HIS KNOCKING TIME, THE SOULS DUMB WATCH		324	THE NIGHT	35
SHOULD POOR SOULS FEAR A SHADE OR NIGHT		343	WATER-FALL	17
LIVING, THOU WERT MY SOULS SURE EASE		348	HOLY BIBLE	33
WITH PROSTRATE SOULS ADORING THEE		351	L'ENVOY	61
SOUND				
WHOSE URGENT SOUND LIKE UNTO THAT		325	ABELS BLOD	17
THERE ALL THEIR FURY, FOME AND HIDEOUS SOUND		285	PSALM 104	27
AND, CATHES ONCE BROKE, THE SOUL CANNOT BE SOUND.		193	RLS + LSNS	46
TO TAKE US SICK, THAT SOUND WOULD NOT TAKE THEE		162	PURSUITE	18
MY CONSCIENCE WITH A SINFUL SOUND		169	RETREATE	16
TRACES, AND SOUNDS OF A STRANGE KIND.		168	VNTY SPRIT	16
FALSE ECCHOES, AND CONFUSED SOUNDS		150	RELIGION	38
THY LEWD LOATH'D MOTIONS UNTO SOUNDS		297	HERODIAS	2
FALSE, JUGLING SOUNDS, A GRONE WELL DREST, WHERE CARE		280	JOY	3
SOUR				
WITS SOUR DELIGHTS		231	THE WORLD	11

	PAGE	TITLE	LINE

SOURCE
AND SOURCE OF SPIRITS, WHERE HE TAKES HIS LOT . . . 145 RSRCTN +IM 43
SOUTH
AND SWEEPE UP SOUTH AND WEST . . . . . . 146 DAY OF JDG 4
SOV'RAIN
(OUR SOV'RAIN GOOD) . . . . 219 HOLY COMM. 27
SOV'RAINTY
AND STILL THY SOV'RAINTY HOLDS GOOD. . . . . 338 DEATH B 4
SOW
THE BIRDS NOR SOW, NOR REAP, YET SUP AND DINE . . . 245 MAN 12
THERE ARE, THAT WILL SOW TARES . . . . . . 275 PROFFER 37
AND LET THIS GRAIN WHICH HERE IN TEARS I SOW . . . 191 DSRDR + FR 39
IN ME DIDST SOW . . . . 204 DSRDR + FR 54
SOME TOIL AND SOW . . . . 341 THE FEAST 73
SOW'ST
THAT SEED THOU SOW'ST, BLEST BE THY SKIL. . . . 227 LV + DSPLN 6
SOWER
THE SOWER DOTH HIS BREAD PROVIDE. . . . . 336 PSALM 65 32
SOWRE
BUT SINCE THESE SWEETS ARE SOWRE, AND POYSON'D HERE . 321 HIDDN TRSR 25
SOYL
AND SCYL THY TEMPLE WITH A SINFUL RUST. . . . 216 DRESSING 8
THIS LEPER HAUNT, AND SCYL THY DOOR . . . . 200 NTVTY 1 26
SPACE
AND NOUGHT MUST STAND OF THAT VAST SPACE . . . 147 DAY OF JDG 15
AND LOOKING BACK (AT THAT SHORT SPACE) . . . 169 RETREATE 9
SPACIOUS
BEING THERE, THIS SPACIOUS BALL . . . . 163 MT. OLVS A 25
THE COMELY SPACIOUS WHALE. . . . . . 286 PSALM 104 72
SPAN
DEAR, HARMLESS AGE. THE SHORT, SWIFT SPAN . . . 322 CHILDEHOOD 31
RESTS NOT A SPAN. . . . . . . 161 PURSUITE 4
HIS COTTAGE FAILES, WHOSE NARROW SPAN . . . 166 THE CALL 44
THIS MAKES ME SPAN . . . . . . 159 MANS FALL 27
AND SPAN UP NIGHT. . . . . . . 189 RESOLVE 20
WHOSE RISE, HEIGHT, AND DESCENT IS BUT A SPAN. . . 195 RLS + LSNS 108
STILL EITHER SLEEPS, OR SLIPS HIS SPAN. . . . 236 CONSTLATN 16
SPAN-EXTENTS
AS MEANE, AND SPAN-EXTENTS. . . . . 144 RSRCTN +IM 14
SPANGLED
THY STARS, AND SPANGLED HALL . . . . 203 DSRDR + FR 22
SPANS
FAITH SPANS UP BLISSE, WHAT SIN, AND DEATH . . . 211 FAITH 37
SPARES
AND GROW FOR THEE, WHO SPARES THEM HERE, SHALL FIND . 283 GARLAND 35
SPARING
NOT SPARING OPENLY TO SAY . . . . . 272 WHT SUNDAY 15
SPARKLE
A SMALL BRIGHT SPARKLE WAS A BED . . . . 151 THE SEARCH 18
SPARKLING
IN SPARKLING SMILES HASTE GLADLY DOWN . . . 315 DWELLNG-PL 9
SPARKS
AND THOU UNRAK'ST THY FIRE, THOSE SPARKS WILL BRING . 195 RLS + LSNS 130
SPARROWS
WHERE TURTLES BUILD, AND CARELESSE SPARROWS MOVE . . 327 RIGHTSNESS 7
SPEAK
SHALL (WHEN THEY RISE) SPEAK BETTER THINGS . . . 326 ABELS BLOD 40
DID AT MID-NIGHT SPEAK WITH THE SUN. . . . 323 THE NIGHT 12
THEY HEAR, SEE, SPEAK . . . . . 313 THE STONE 22
WHO QUESTION POWER, THEY SPEAK TREASON. . . . 318 THE ASS 20
FAR GREATER, AND SO SPEAK MY SAVIORS GLORY. . . 290 THE TIMBER 44
WHILE ACTIVE WINDS AND STREAMS BOTH RUN AND SPEAK . . 288 THE BIRD 15
SPEAK'ST THERE SO MUCH, THAT I ADMIRE . . . 149 RELIGION 19
SPEAKS
AS SPEAKS STILL IN THY MAKERS EAR . . . 325 ABELS BLOD 10
SPEAKS MORE AND BETTER FOR MY GOOD. . . . 242 MISERY 106
SPEAR
O SPEAR, THE KEY . . . . . . 341 THE FEAST 64
SPEECH
AND WHEN IN DEATH MY SPEECH IS SPENT . . . 334 AGREEMENT 63
AND THOUGH POOR STONES HAVE NEITHER SPEECH NOR TONGUE . 288 THE BIRD 14
SPEECHLESS
AND STONES, THOUGH SPEECHLESS, ARE NOT DUMB. . . 335 JUDGEMENT 16
AND SHOULD THOSE SPEECHLESS BEGGERS FAIL . . . 338 THE THRONE 12
SPEECHLESS AND CALM, AS INFANTS SLEEP. . . . 326 ABELS BLOD 35
OF STONES, AND SPEECHLESS EARTH . . . 226 RETIREMENT 47
A SPEECHLESSE HEAP, AND IN THE MIDST MY HEART . . 201 THE CHECK 3
SPEED
ALLOW YOUR JOYES RELIGION, THAT DONE, SPEED . . . 194 RLS + LSNS 81
SPEND
SPEND NOT AN HOUR SO, AS TO WEEP ANOTHER . . . 194 RLS + LSNS 67
THY ACCOUNTS THUS MADE, SPEND IN THE GRAVE ONE HOURE . 195 RLS + LSNS 121
WHEN THOU SHALT SPEND THY SACRED STORE . . . 147 DAY OF JDG 9
WE SPEND IN SIGHES, IS TREASURE AFTER DEATH. . . 158 THE LAMPE 22
YET, BURN'ST THOU HERE, A FULL DAY, WHILE I SPEND . . 157 THE LAMPE 5
NOR DOST THOU SPEND ONE TEARE IN VAIN, FOR STILL . . 158 THE LAMPE 17
AND FREELY SPEND . . . . . . 182 CHRFLNESS 15
I WALKT THE OTHER DAY (TO SPEND MY HOUR) . . . 246 I WALKT 1
AND WHAT HE SAVES, MAY HIS FOES SPEND. . . . 301 PROVIDENCE 36
RAIN GENTLY SPENDS HIS HONEY-DROPS, AND POURS . . 306 RAIN-BOW 11

	PAGE	TITLE	LINE
SPENT			
AND WHEN IN DEATH MY SPEECH IS SPENT	334	AGREEMENT	63
THOUGH SICK AND SPENT	275	PROFFER	20
QUITE SPENT WITH THOUGHTS I LEFT MY CELL, AND LAY	167	VNTY SPRIT	1
WHEN ALL IS SPENT, THY LAST, AND SURE SUPPLY	158	THE LAMPE	20
AND ON THE DUMBE SHADES LANGUAGE SPENT	141	RGNRTN	60
SPENT IN A ROVING EXTASIE	151	THE SEARCH	4
WATRING THEIR FLOCKS, AND HAVING SPENT	151	THE SEARCH	25
SPHERE			
A NEAST OF NIGHTS, A GLOOMIE SPHERE	143	DEATH	11
STRAIT THERE IS JOY, AND EV'RY SPHERE	200	NTVTY 2	3
SHE'L SHINE THROUGH ALL THE SPHERE.	271	ALL GONE	32
SHOULD LEAVE THE SPHERE	269	ASCSN-HYMN	14
INLIGHTNING HIS OWN LITTLE SPHERE	288	THE BIRD	20
SPHERES			
DRIV'N BY THE SPHERES	231	THE WORLD	5
AND MONEY BETTER MUSICK THAN THE SPHERES.	224	TEMPEST	48
SULLEN, AND SAD ECCLIPSES, CLOUDIE SPHERES	188	RELAPSE	19
WHO BENT THE SPHERES, AND CIRCLED IN	167	VNTY SPRIT	5
SPICE			
BREATH ALL PERFUMES, AND SPICE.	198	UNPRFTBLNS	9
BREATHING PERFUMES, DOTH SPICE THE DAY	199	NTVTY 1	6
THE AIRE WAS ALL IN SPICE	140	RGNRTN	54
ILE SPICE MY THOUGHTS WITH THEE, AND FROM THY WORD	287	PSALM 104	93
MOUNTAINS OF SPICE, DAY-STARS AND LIGHT	346	THE QUEER	7
UPON THE MOUNTS OF SPICES.	157	BRT. CHRCH	20
A LAND OF FLOWERS AND SPICES. THE WORD GIVEN	276	PROFFER	47
I SMELL HER SPICES, AND HER OINTMENT YIELDS	267	ASCN-DAY A	21
SPICIE			
SO FROM LAHAI-ROIS WELL SOME SPICIE CLOUD	155	ISAACS M.	53
FRESH, SPICIE MORNINGS, AND ETERNAL BEAMS	188	RELAPSE	27
SPICINESS			
THEIR SPICINESS, AND BLOUD.	198	UNPRFTBLNS	6
SPICY			
ON EVERLASTING, SPICY MOUNTAINS.	312	FAIR+YONG	50
SPIE			
THEN TAKING UP WHAT I COULD NEEREST SPIE	247	I WALKT	15
SPIES			
AND ONELY GLEAMS AND FRACTIONS SPIES.	277	COCK-CRWNG	42
HEAVEN HATH LESS BEAUTY THAN THE DUST HE SPIES	224	TEMPEST	47
WERE ONCE SINS LOOSE AND TEMPTING SPIES	305	ST MARY MN	58
AND SPIES	153	THE SEARCH	77
YET THY LOVE SPIES	181	BURIALL	29
SPIL			
LET ME NOT SPIL, BUT DRINK THY BLOUD	230	LAW + GOSP	31
SOME TARES IN ME WHICH CHOKE, OR SPIL	227	LV + DSPLN	5
SPILL			
A SWORD SHALL HIS BLOOD LIKEWISE SPILL.	316	MEN OF WAR	6
LIFE WITHOUT THEE IS LOOSE AND SPILLS.	308	THE SEED	8
WHO SPILLS NO BLOOD, NOR SPREDS	327	RIGHTSNESS	25
SPILT			
THAT PROUDLY SPILT AND DESPIS'D BLOOD	326	ABELS BLOD	34
FOR THOSE THAT SPILT IT. MAY NO CRIES	326	ABELS BLOD	37
SO MY SPILT THOUGHTS WINDING FROM THEE	240	MISERY	13
WHEN THE SPILT DEW	340	THE FEAST	22
SPIN			
AND THROUGH THE DARK AIRE SPIN A FIRIE SHREAD	157	THE LAMPE	3
I WILL NO LONGER COBWEBS SPIN	204	IDLE VERSE	3
SPIRES			
THEY ARE THAT CITIES SHINING SPIRES	175	JOY OF LIF	27
IN SPIRES, GLOBES, ANGRY CURLS AND COY	304	ST MARY MN	18
SPIRIT			
INTELLIGENCE, WHOSE SPIRIT FEEDS	314	THE STONE	25
WHOSE SPIRIT EVER POOR, IS MEEK AND LOW.	327	RIGHTSNESS	15
THESE WEIGHTS, AND GIVE MY SPIRIT LEAVE	329	ANGUISH	17
THOU SEND'ST THY SPIRIT FORTH, AND THEY REVIVE	287	PSALM 104	81
O THAT THY SPIRIT WOULD SO STRONGLY MOVE ME	283	LOVE-SICK	2
THE SPIRIT, WATER, AND THE BLOOD	284	TRINITY-SN	5
FOR EACH INCLOSED SPIRIT IS A STAR	288	THE BIRD	19
FROM SICKNESSE, GIVE MY SPIRIT HEALTH.	294	BEGGING B	24
WHOSE SPIRIT TOO DOTH MOURN AND GRIEVE	292	THE JEWS	35
WHICH THY SPIRIT BLOWES.	172	MIDNIGHT	32
FROM WHENCE TH' INLIGHTEND SPIRIT SEES	170	RETREATE	25
AND NOW THE SPIRIT, NOT THE DUST	179	SILENCE	27
IN THE SPIRIT	185	PASSION	13
HOW MEEK, AND PATIENT WAS THY SPIRIT.	185	PASSION	38
A SPIRIT, AND TRUE GLORY DWELL	202	THE CHECK	34
THY SPIRIT FEEDS.	188	RELAPSE	16
TOGETHER WITH HIS BLOUD, THY FATHERS SPIRIT	156	ISAACS M.	64
AND LEAVES THY SPIRIT DOTH STILL FAN	148	RELIGION	2
FOR A PRESERVING SPIRIT DOTH STILL PASSE	145	RSRCTN +IM	31
HIS HOLY SPIRIT GRIEVES THEREFORE	240	MISERY	38
THY SPIRIT TOO IS MINE.	225	RETIREMENT	25
THY SPIRIT PLANT, QUICKNING THE WHOLE	206	REPENTANCE	3
O THOU. WHOSE SPIRIT DID AT FIRST INFLAME	248	I WALKT	43
AND BY THY SPIRIT SEAL'D TO ME, THAT I	267	ASCN-DAY A	7
RESUME THY SPIRIT FROM THIS WORLD OF THRALL	271	ALL GONE	35
UNLESS THAT SPIRIT LEAD HIS MINCE	344	WATER-FALL	30
O KNOWING, GLORIOUS SPIRIT. WHEN	347	THE BOOK	25
FIXT BY THY SPIRIT TO A STATE	349	L'ENVOY	15

		PAGE	TITLE	LINE
SPIRIT-SIGHS				
WITH SPIRIT-SIGHS, AND EARNEST GRONES	• • • •	242	MISERY	110
SPIRIT-VOYCE				
A SPIRIT-VOYCE • • • • • • • •	•	177	MRNG-WTCH	20
SPIRIT-WIND				
A SPIRIT-WIND • • • • • • • •	•	176	THE STORM	20
SPIRITED				
O'R-RAN MY HEART, AND SPIRITED MY BLOUD	• •	244	MT. OLV. B	8
SPIRITS				
AND ACTUATE SUCH SPIRITS AS ARE SHED	• •	244	THE SAP	33
THAT GLASS OF SOULS AND SPIRITS, WHERE WELL CREST	• •	275	PROFFER	23
HERE SPIRITS THAT HAVE RUN THEIR RACE AND FOUGHT	• •	280	PALM-TREE	17
SUCH NUMBERS TELL THEIR DAYS, WHOSE SPIRITS BE	• •	281	JOY	9
SPIRITS WITHOUT THEE DIE • • • • •	•	219	HOLY COMM.	17
AND SPIRITS ALL MY EARTH. HEARK. IN WHAT RINGS	• •	176	MRNG-WTCH	9
AND SOURCE OF SPIRITS, WHERE HE TAKES HIS LOT	• •	145	RSRCTN +IM	43
THE SPIRITS DUTY, TRUE HEARTS SPREAD, AND HEAVE	•	191	RLS + LSNS	3
THAT GAIN IS DREADFUL, WHICH MAKES SPIRITS SICK.	•	193	RLS + LSNS	42
LASTS NOT A NIGHT SOMETIMES. BAD SPIRITS FEAR	• •	195	RLS + LSNS	124
INJURE NOT MODEST BLOUD, WHOSE SPIRITS RISE	• •	194	RLS + LSNS	73
OF SPIRITS, HEAV'N EXTRACTED LYES IN THEE.	•	197	SCRIPTURES	2
WILL THOSE COY SPIRITS CAST ASLEEP • •	•	297	HERODIAS	10
THE DAY OF SPIRITS, MY SOULS CALM RETREAT	• •	324	THE NIGHT	27
WHEN SPIRITS THEIR FAIR KINRED CATCH. •	•	324	THE NIGHT	36
THOUGH FLED FROM YOU, THEIR SPIRITS HIVE.	• •	339	DEATH B	30
GIVE WATCHFUL SPIRITS TO OUR GUIDES. • •	•	350	L'ENVOY	49
SPIRITUALL				
WHOSE INTERCEDING, SPIRITUALL GRONES	• •	179	CHRCH-SVC	4
SPIT				
DID SPIT ON THEE, AND SMOTE THEE TOO.	• •	317	MEN OF WAR	30
SPIT OUT THEIR PHLEGM • • • • •	•	276	PROFFER	44
SPITE				
HE KEEPS ME FROM THE SPITE OF FOES • •	•	220	PSALM 121	13
SPITTLE				
WHOSE SPITTLE ONLY COULD RESTORE THE BLIND.	• •	217	EASTER-DAY	16
SPLENDID				
AND SPLENDID VICE DESTROYS THE GREAT.	• •	318	THE ASS	8
SPLIT				
SPLIT, AND THE BOX QUITE BROKE AND MARR'D.	•	304	ST MARY MN	22
SPOIL				
SHOULD HELP TO SPOIL) THOU CANST RESTORE	• •	299	JESUS WP B	36
THOUGH I HAVE SPOIL'D, O SPOIL NOT THOU.	•	294	BEGGING B	17
SPOIL'D				
THOUGH I HAVE SPOIL'D, O SPOIL NOT THOU.	•	294	BEGGING B	17
ALL DARK AND SPOIL'D • • • • •	•	270	ASCSN-HYMN	28
SPOILS				
SUCH MUSICK SPOILS GOOD FELLOWSHIP. • •	•	240	MISERY	32
SPOKE				
THE STONES HAD SPOKE, WHAT YOU DENYED.	• •	296	JESUS WP A	8
HENCE HE IN THUNDER TO THY OFF-SPRING SPOKE.	•	330	JACOBS PLW	8
THEN ALL IS TRUE, MY FOES HAVE SPOKEN.	• •	333	AGREEMENT	48
SPOTLESS				
COMES LIKE A CHILDES, SPOTLESS AND FRESH.	• •	306	ST MARY MN	70
AND SPOTLESS WHITE IS ALL THE WEAR. • •	•	308	THE SEED	24
THOU ARE LIFES CHARTER, THE DOVES SPOTLESS NEAST	•	197	SCRIPTURES	3
SPOTT				
ALL FILTH, AND SPOTT • • • • • •	•	180	BURIALL	19
SPOUSE				
BRIGHT QUEEN OF HEAVEN. GODS VIRGIN SPOUSE.	• •	302	THE KNOT	1
GIVE TO THY SPOUSE HER PERFECT, AND PURE DRESS	•	237	CONSTLATN	57
INLARG'D HIS SPOUSE • • • • • •	•	210	FAITH	6
DRY UP THEIR ARMS, WHO VEX THY SPOUSE	• •	350	L'ENVOY	33
SPREAD				
THIS LONG WORN VEYL. THEN SHINE AND SPREAD	• •	349	L'ENVOY	9
AND WHERE IT FLOURISH'D, GREW AND SPREAD	• •	347	THE BOOK	13
AND PENALTIES SPREAD TO OUR CRIMES. •	• •	273	WHT SUNDAY	32
BUT SINFUL WORDS AND WORKS STILL SPREAD	• •	336	PSALM 65	5
SHALL WITH SPREAD WINGS • • • •	•	291	THE JEWS	11
DOTH SPREAD LIKE CURTAINS ROUND ABOUT THIS GLOBE	•	284	PSALM 104	7
THE SPIRITS DUTY, TRUE HEARTS SPREAD, AND HEAVE	•	191	RLS + LSNS	3
SPREADING				
WHERE SPREADING ALL THE WAY THEY SEEK	• •	240	MISERY	11
SPREADS				
THY LEAVES ARE HEALING WINGS HE SPREADS.	• •	333	AGREEMENT	36
SPRED				
THY MOTHERS NETS IN THEE WERE SPRED	• •	297	HERODIAS	19
O SPRED THY SACRED WINGS AND SHAKE	• •	308	THE SEED	13
AND SPRED AND OPEN TO THY WILL.	• •	308	THE SEED	20
CLOATH'D WITH THIS SKIN, WHICH NOW LIES SPRED	•	347	THE BOOK	18
WHO SPILLS NO BLOOD, NOR SPREDS • •	•	327	RIGHTSNESS	25
SPRING				
FROM PRIVATE AND SELECTED HEARTS DID SPRING	• •	330	JACOBS PLW	12
AS IF IT ENDED IN A SPRING • • • •	•	338	DEATH B	9
AND SPRING, HOW IS'T THAT YOU SO SADLY GRIEVE	•	298	JESUS WP B	12
AND HERBS WHICH ON DRY HILLS DO SPRING	• •	301	PROVIDENCE	26
THERE THE WILDE ASSES SWALLOW THE COOL SPRING.	•	285	PSALM 104	34
SOME DROPS MAY FALL BEFORE, BUT A CLEAR SPRING	•	291	THE TIMBER	54
MY SPRING AND FALL ARE IN THY BOOK. • •	•	293	BEGGING B	2
WHOSE SPRING IS ON THAT HIL WHERE YOU DO GROW	•	235	CONSTLATN	3
TO MY COLD THOUGHTS A LIVELY SENSE OF SPRING.	•	245	MT. OLV. B	20

	PAGE	TITLE	LINE
SPRING (CON'T)			
I SOUGHT CHOICE BOWRES, HAUNTED THE SPRING	282	GARLAND	21
AND SPRING, AND GROW, A TREE NE'R TO BE PRIC'D	280	PALM-TREE	15
LET NIGHTINGALES ATTEND THE SPRING	205	IDLE VERSE	23
WHOSE SPRING IS IN MY SAVIOURS HEART.	208	REPENTANCE	56
A SPRING RAN BY, I TOLD HER TEARS	208	REPENTANCE	44
BUT AS THIS RESTLESS, VOCALL SPRING	212	DAWNING	33
AND WHISPERS AMONGST THEM. THERE'S NOT A SPRING	192	RLS + LSNS	14
ONE CONSTANT SPRING.	186	PASSION	50
OR SOME POOR HIGH-WAY HERB, OR SPRING	187	NO DO THEY	13
WHERE A SHRILL SPRING TUN'D TO THE EARLY DAY.	167	VNTY SPRIT	2
HERE OF THIS MIGHTY SPRING, I FOUND SOME DRILLS	168	VNTY SPRIT	17
UNTO THAT SPRING	145	RSRCTN +IM	42
STORM'D THUS, I STRAIGHT PERCEIV'D MY SPRING	139	RGNRTN	18
FOUND ALL WAS CHANG'D, AND A NEW SPRING	140	RGNRTN	48
NO, NO, RELIGION IS A SPRING	150	RELIGION	29
THE ANGRY SPRING IN BUBBLES SWELL'D	151	THE SEARCH	29
OF THEIR RED SEA, A SPRING, I WASH, THEY WADE	159	MANS FALL	32
SPRING UP, O WINE	340	THE FEAST	25
THE WELL, WHERE LIVING WATERS SPRING	340	THE FEAST	33
O TELL ME WHENCE THAT JOY DOTH SPRING	346	THE QUEER	1
THE SOFTER DRESSINGS OF THE SPRING	345	THE WREATH	5
SPRINGING			
AND SPRINGING SHINE	340	THE FEAST	26
SINCE THESE ARE TROUBLED, TO THE SPRINGING ROCK	150	RELIGION	50
TOO, IS MY DEW, AND SPRINGING WEL.	203	DSRDR + FR	19
AND HILLS FULL OF SPRINGING PRIDE	337	PSALM 65	43
SPRINGS			
UNTO THOSE CLEAR AND LIVING SPRINGS	329	TEARS	3
THESE UPPER SPRINGS AND NONE ELSE MAKE THEM GROW.	291	THE TIMBER	52
WHICH NOW THESE MANY, MANY, SPRINGS	291	THE JEWS	9
SURE THOU DIDST FLOURISH ONCE. AND MANY SPRINGS	289	THE TIMBER	1
THOU FROM THY UPPER SPRINGS ABOVE, FROM THOSE	285	PSALM 104	37
TO LIVING SPRINGS, AND THERE BE FED	319	THE ASS	60
TO LIVING SPRINGS, AND THERE BE FED	319	THE ASS	61
WINDS WHISPER, AND THE BUSIE SPRINGS	199	NTVTY 1	8
AND THE DAY SPRINGS)	157	BRT. CHRCH	13
AND, BY THEIR OWNE WEAKE SHINE, DID SEARCH THE SPRINGS	146	RSRCTN +IM	53
WHAT SPRINGS OF SWEAT, AND BLOOD DID DROWN THEE.	185	PASSION	24
AND FALLING SPRINGS	176	MRNG-WTCH	13
THE DAY-STAR SPRINGS, I'LE WAKE AGEN.	177	EVNG-WTCH	2
AND SPRINGS, LIKE DISSOLV'D PEARLS THEIR STREAMS DID POUR	268	ASCN-DAY A	47
THOUGHT WITH MY SELF, THERE MIGHT BE OTHER SPRINGS	247	I WALKT	10
AND YET, HOW FEW BELIEVE SUCH DOCTRINE SPRINGS	248	I WALKT	36
WHAT SPRINGS OR SHADES TO LOOK	239	SHEPHEARDS	40
WHOSE LEADERS TO THOSE PASTURES, AND CLEER SPRINGS	238	SHEPHEARDS	3
SPRUCE			
LIKE SOME SPRUCE BRIDE	145	RSRCTN +IM	46
SPRUCE, SUPPLE CRINGE, OR STUDY'D LOOK PUT ON	155	ISAACS M.	32
SPRUNG			
AND, WHENCE IT SPRUNG, THERE ENDS)	203	DSRDR + FR	37
SPUN			
BUT BIDS THE THREAD BE SPUN.	197	CORRUPTION	32
BEFORE 'TWAS DREST OR SPUN, AND WHEN	347	THE BOOK	7
SPURN			
I PLAYED WITH FIRE, DID COUNSELL SPURN	282	GARLAND	13
I SHOULD HAVE SPURN'D, AND SAID THOU DIDST FORBEARE.	161	DSTRQCTION	22
SPY			
FULL EAST, A FAIRE, FRESH FIELD COULD SPY	140	RGNRTN	36
AND IN THOSE WEAKER GLORIES SPY	169	RETREATE	13
THEN COMES THE LIGHT. WHICH WHEN YOU SPY	266	VAIN WITS	10
SPYE			
AH, MY DEARE LORD. WHAT COULDST THOU SPYE	164	INCARNATN	13
SPYED			
AND SPYED HIS CURIOUS BOOK	309	THE SEED	52
SPYES			
THINE HOST OF SPYES	171	MIDNIGHT	3
STABS			
A DARTING CONSCIENCE FULL OF STABS, AND FEARS.	188	RELAPSE	17
STAGE			
MEERE STAGE, AND SHOW	139	RGNRTN	19
THINE EYES BEHOLD THE EARTH, AND THE WHOLE STAGE	287	PSALM 104	85
STAGGERS			
IS DRUNK, AND STAGGERS IN THE WAY.	170	RETREATE	28
STAID			
IF SEEING MUCH SHOULD MAKE STAID EYES	321	CHILDEHOOD	17
AS IF HIS LIQUID, LOOSE RETINUE STAID	343	WATER-FALL	5
THE STAIDNESS OF THESE THINGS TO MAN. FOR THESE	245	MAN	9
STAIN			
WHERE COMES NO STAIN.	329	TEARS	4
BEAT THROUGH, AND STAIN	180	BURIALL	14
THESE DARE DIVIDE, AND STAIN	156	BRT. CHRCH	10
NONE STAIN'D OR WITHER'D SHALL COME NEAR.	308	THE SEED	22
THY LIGHT AS LUCTUAL AND STAIN'D WITH WOES	307	RAIN-BOW	37
TO MAKE STAIN'D MAN MORE WHITE THEN SNOW.	270	ASCSN-HYMN	36
STAINES			
AND BOTH HER TASTE, AND COLOUR STAINES	150	RELIGION	36
STAKE			
WHO DIED TO STAKE	204	DSRDR + FR	58
MADE LIFE MY COMMON STAKE.	282	GARLAND	14

	PAGE	TITLE	LINE
STAND			
WHO WITHOUT THEE CANNOT STAND.	219	HOLY COMM.	40
AND NOUGHT MUST STAND OF THAT VAST SPACE	147	DAY OF JDG	15
O HOW IN THIS THY QUIRE OF SOULS I STAND	179	CHRCH-SVC	9
THOU FROM THE DAY-STAR A LONG WAY DIDST STAND	331	JACOBS PLW	47
STAND FIRM BY THEE, AND HAVE SURE PEACE.	336	PSALM 65	18
STANDS			
WHERE STANDS A WINGED CENTRIE	184	PEACE	3
BIRDS SING, BEASTS FEED, FISH LEAP, AND TH'EARTH STANDS FAST	194	RLS + LSNS	88
STAR			
DO THOU THE WORKS OF DAY, AND RISE A STAR.	196	RLS + LSNS	138
POOR, FALLING STAR.	203	DSRDR + FR	45
I WOULD I WERE SOME BIRD, OR STAR	199	NTVTY 1	13
THEN EITHER STAR, OR BIRD, SHOULD BE	199	NTVTY 1	17
WHERE YOUTH SHINES LIKE A STAR	310	THE SEED	62
MY DISTREST LORD. OR DID A STAR	315	DWELLNG-PL	7
AS TO MAKE MAN ALL PURE LOVE, FLESH A STAR.	283	LOVE-SICK	4
A STAR THAT WOULD NE'R SET, BUT EVER RISE	283	LOVE-SICK	5
FOR EACH INCLOSED SPIRIT IS A STAR	288	THE BIRD	19
WATCH FOR, AND KNOW THEIR LOVING STAR.	281	THE FAVOUR	8
O LET NO STAR COMPARE WITH THEE.	281	THE FAVOUR	9
TO WHOM A FALLING STAR AND NINE DAYES GLORY	282	GARLAND	2
IF A STAR	269	ASCSN-HYMN	13
ONE SILENT STAR MAY INTERLINE.	273	WHT SUNDAY	38
IF A STAR WERE CONFIN'D INTO A TOMB	271	ALL GONE	29
WHERE, THOUGH THE GLORY DIFFER IN EACH STAR	236	CONSTLATN	31
STARK			
THE STARS TO WHICH I AM STARK BLIND	207	REPENTANCE	38
HELL AND ALL HEARTS STARK NAKED LYES.	314	THE STONE	27
STARRE			
IS STIL'D THEIR STARRE, THE STONE, AND HIDDEN FOOD.	192	RLS + LSNS	28
IS LIKE A CLOUDED STARRE, WHOSE BEAMES THOUGH SEE	177	MRNG-WTCH	25
TO READE SOME STARRE, OR MIN'RALL, AND IN STATE	146	RSRCTN +IM	59
HE MIGHT BE FOUND, OR WHAT STARRE CAN	151	THE SEARCH	9
MADE ME A STARRE, A PEARLE, OR A RAIN-BOW	161	DSTRQCTION	6
STARRES			
THE STARRES SHINE IN THEIR WATCHES	171	MIDNIGHT	4
STARRS			
MY PRESENT SEARCH, FOR EAGLES EYE NOT STARRS	278	THE STARRE	6
STARS			
MORE EYES THEN STARS, WHOSE BREATH COULD IT ASPIRE	281	JOY	12
LIKE STARS UPON SOME GLOOMY GROVE	270	ALL GONE	6
THEY SHINE IN WHITE (LIKE STARS) AND REST.	275	PROFFER	24
LET NOT THY STARS FOR BALAAMS HIRE	274	WHT SUNDAY	63
THE STARS TO WHICH I AM STARK BLIND	207	REPENTANCE	38
WHERE STARS, AND CLOUDS, BOTH LIGHT, AND SHADE	210	FAITH	15
STARS SHUT UP SHOP, MISTS PACK AWAY	210	FAITH	19
STARS NOW VANISH WITHOUT NUMBER	212	DAWNING	19
OUR GUIDES PROVE WANDRING STARS	237	CONSTLATN	46
THERE IS BEYOND THE STARS AN HIL OF MYRRH	243	THE SAP	11
AND IN THE SKY THE STARS APPEAR	228	PILGRIMAGE	2
STARS ARE OF MIGHTY USE, THE NIGHT	174	JOY OF LIF	9
FAR BEYOND THE STARS	184	PEACE	2
AND MOVE ON WITH THE SHADES, STARS NOT, AND SLEEPE	157	THE LAMPE	2
ABOVE THE STARS, A TRACK UNKNOWN, AND HIGH	155	ISAACS M.	50
WATCH STARS, OR PORE	146	RSRCTN +IM	66
BOTH STARS AND ELEMENTS CONFOUND	147	DAY OF JDG	7
OF STARS, ABOVE INFIRMITY.	204	DSRDR + FR	49
THY STARS, AND SPANGLED HALL	203	DSRDR + FR	22
FALSE STARS AND FIRE-DRAKES, THE DECEITS OF NIGHT	320	HIDDN TRSR	4
BOTH SUN AND STARS WOULD HIDE THEIR HEADS.	309	THE SEED	31
BUT NOW ARE FIXED STARS, WHOSE LIGHT	305	ST MARY MN	59
BEFORE BRIGHT STARS, AND GODS OWN BEAMS.	321	CHILDEHOOD	12
START			
MY THOUGHTS, LIKE WATER WHICH SOME STONE DOTH START	234	MUTINIE	6
STARV'D			
LIKE A STARV'D EAGLET, FOR THINE EYE.	281	THE FAVOUR	6
WHERE THE STARV'D EARTH GROANS FOR ONE TEAR.	296	JESUS WP A	16
STATE			
A STATE THAT WITH THE SUN DOTH SET	300	PROVIDENCE	23
THIS DUSKY STATE OF SIGHS AND TEARS	303	ST MARY MN	11
THIS LEADEN STATE, WHICH MEN MISCAL	319	THE ASS	55
IN A STATE KNOWN TO NONE BUT THEE	319	THE ASS	58
A STATE, THAT NO REDRESS ADMITS	273	WHT SUNDAY	34
WEIGHING THE STEDFASTNESS AND STATE	245	MAN	1
IF SUCH A STATE AT ALL CAN BE	239	MISERY	3
THEN SHOULD I (TYED TO ONE SURE STATE)	187	NO DO THEY	15
TO READE SOME STARRE, OR MIN'RALL, AND IN STATE	146	RSRCTN +IM	59
HE SLEEPES, AND DROOPS, AND IN THIS DROWSIE STATE	158	MANS FALL	7
THEY JUDG'D THEM SENSLESSE, AND THEIR STATE	187	NO DO THEY	7
IN THAT STATE I CAME RETURN.	170	RETREATE	32
THEIR HEAVY STATE	165	THE CALL	25
A STATE UNTIR'D	162	PURSUITE	10
SELF-POSING STATE.	344	QUICKNESS	6
ON ME THAT STATE	339	THE FEAST	17
O THY WORST STATE, MY ONELY BEST.	341	THE FEAST	66
FIXT BY THY SPIRIT TO A STATE	349	L'ENVOY	15
A STATE FIT FOR THE SIGHT OF THY	349	L'ENVOY	17
A STATE AGREEING WITH THY MINDE	350	L'ENVOY	19
A STATE THY BIRTH, AND DEATH DESIGN'D.	350	L'ENVOY	20

		PAGE	TITLE	LINE
STATE (CON'T)				
A STATE FOR WHICH THY CREATURES ALL		350	L'ENVOY	21
STATELY				
IN ROWLES AND CURLES, MINCING AND STATELY DUMB	. .	155	ISAACS M.	34
OF STATELY HEIGHT, WHOSE BRANCHES MET .	. .	140	RGNRTN	44
HER STATELY PILES WITH ALL THEIR HEIGHT AND PRIDE	. .	238	SHEPHEARDS	19
(UNDER THAT STATELY AND MYSTERIOUS CLOUD . .	. .	330	JACOBS PLW	22
STATES				
THERE GOD A COMMERCE STATES, AND SHEDS .	. .	279	THE STARRE	27
UNTO THY GOD, FOR MARRIAGE OF ALL STATES .	. .	155	ISAACS M.	45
STATES-MAN				
THE DARKSOME STATES-MAN HUNG WITH WEIGHTS AND WOE	. .	231	THE WORLD	16
STAY				
THY HAND OUR STAY	.	230	LAW + GOSP	18
HE DID NOR STAY, NOR GO.	.	231	THE WORLD	18
THOUGH WITH NO LILIE, STAY WITH ME. . . .	.	277	COCK-CRWNG	48
AND ROT, DESCEND NOT HERE, NOR THINK TO STAY	. .	275	PROFFER	17
HERE YOU MUST STAY	.	269	ASCSN-HYMN	3
THE GLORIOUS GOD IS MY SOLE STAY . .	. .	220	PSALM 121	9
HOSANNA. HEARK, WHY DOEST THOU STAY. . .	. .	217	EASTER-DAY	12
THY BLOUD TO ICE, AND THOU MUST STAY .	. .	142	DEATH	3
THOUGH THOU HAST PROMIS'D THEY SHOULD STAY .	. .	149	RELIGION	27
SURE HERE HE MUST NEEDS STAY . . .	. .	153	THE SEARCH	91
WHEN HE DID STAY TO BEARE OUR ILL . .	. .	163	MT. OLVS A	30
BUT (AH) MY SOUL WITH TOO MUCH STAY . .	. .	170	RETREATE	27
A LONGER STAY	. .	189	RESOLVE	2
THIS MADE HIM LONG FOR HOME, AS LOATH TO STAY	. .	197	CORRUPTION	17
O COME, ARISE, SHINE, DO NOT STAY . . .	. .	334	JUDGEMENT	11
STAYES				
WERE MY SURE GUIDES, AND ONLY WITH ME STAYES	. .	159	MANS FALL	11
STAYS				
GODS SAINTS ARE SHINING LIGHTS. WHO STAYS .	. .	174	JOY OF LIF	17
WHAT SIGHS, WHAT WHISPERS, BUSIE STOPS AND STAYS.	. .	268	ASCN-DAY A	27
STEAL				
IN SILENT DROPS STEAL FROM THEIR HOLY EYES .	. .	268	ASCN-DAY A	53
IF THOU STEAL IN AMIDST THE MIRTH . . .	. .	240	MISERY	29
STEALTH				
SILENCE, AND STEALTH OF DAYES. 'TIS NOW . .	.	178	SILENCE	1
WITH WHAT DEEP MURMURS THROUGH TIMES SILENT STEALTH	.	343	WATER-FALL	1
STEDDY				
MY FAITH AS PURE, AND STEDDY . . .	. .	167	THE CALL	91
COME WHILE MY HEART IS CLEAN AND STEDDY. . .	.	339	THE FEAST	3
STEDFASTNESS				
WEIGHING THE STEDFASTNESS AND STATE . .	. .	245	MAN	1
STEEEP				
O'RE DARK HILLS, SWIFT STREAMES, AND STEEEP WAYS	. .	174	JOY OF LIF	19
STEEL				
WITHOUT A STEEL, O LET THY POWER CLEER .	. .	224	TEMPEST	59
KINGDOMES TOO HAVE THEIR PHYSICK, AND FOR STEEL	. .	222	AFFLICTION	33
STEEP				
AND THY SELF STEEP . . .	. .	184	PASSION	8
ABOVE THE MOUNTAINS STEEP. . . .	. .	285	PSALM 104	20
LINGRING, AND WERE OF THIS STEEP PLACE AFRAID	. .	343	WATER-FALL	6
STEEPEST				
FIND OUT THE FIRST AND STEEPEST FAL. .	. .	240	MISERY	16
STEER				
AND WHERE BEFORE I DID NO SAFE COURSE STEER .	. .	244	MT. OLV. B	11
HOW IN THY ABSENCE THOU DOST STEERE . .	. .	174	JOY OF LIF	3
STEERS				
FOR AS THY HAND THE WEATHER STEERS . .	. .	227	LV + DSPLN	16
HE THAT ACCUSETH NONE, SO STEERS . .	. .	314	THE STONE	29
STENCH				
THAT VOYDS BUT FILTH, AND STENCH. HAST THOU NO PRIZE	.	194	RLS + LSNS	75
AND WHEN TH'HAST DONE, A STENCH, OR FOG IS ALL	.	198	UNPRFTBLNS	17
STEP				
MY FATHERS JOURNEYS, AND IN ONE FAIRE STEP .	. .	159	MANS FALL	28
STEPS				
'TWIXT STEPS, AND FALLS	. .	139	RGNRTN	27
AND WALK TWO STEPS	. .	203	DSRDR + FR	35
SEEK NOT THE SAME STEPS WITH THE CROWD, STICK THOU	.	193	RLS + LSNS	49
BUT I BY BACKWARD STEPS WOULD MOVE .	. .	170	RETREATE	30
TO FIX MY STEPS, AND WHATSOEVER PATH .	. .	234	MUTINIE	33
ETERNITY IN TIME, THE STEPS BY WHICH .	. .	2	SON-DAYES	5
AND THE LAST STEPS OF MY MILDE MASTER TRACE.	. .	268	ASCN-DAY A	50
THY STEPS TRACK HERE BELOW . .	. .	248	I WALKT	49
STEPT				
AND BETHLEMS HUMBLE COTTS ABOVE THEM STEPT	. .	238	SHEPHEARDS	21
WHERE (SINCE HE STEPT THERE) ONLY GO . .	. .	140	RGNRTN	40
STICK				
A STICK, OR ROD WHICH SOME CHANCE BRINGS .	. .	166	THE CALL	52
SEEK NOT THE SAME STEPS WITH THE CROWD, STICK THOU	.	193	RLS + LSNS	49
WRONG NOT THY CONSCIENCE FOR A ROTTEN STICK	. .	193	RLS + LSNS	41
WHERE THEY NEW CONSORTS CHOOSE AND STICK .	. .	348	HOLY BIBLE	11
STIFF				
WILL PROVE THEIR HEARTS MORE STIFF AND TUFF.	. .	314	THE STONE	51
STIFF THEN MUST KNEEL)	. .	337	THE THRONE	6
STIFF-NECKED				
STIFF-NECKED JEWS. YOUR FATHERS BREED . .	. .	296	JESUS WP A	5
STIFLE				
BUT SICKNESS, OR INFECTION. STIFLE IT . .	. .	194	RLS + LSNS	76

	PAGE	TITLE	LINE

STIL'D
IS STIL'D THEIR STARRE, THE STCNE, AND HIDDEN FOCD.   192   RLS + LSNS   28
STILE
I STILE MEER TEMPERS, WHICH TAKE PLACE   242   MISERY   87
STIR
HE RAVES, AND SWEARS TO STIR NCR FIRE, NOR FAN   197   CORRUPTION   31
WHEN THY NAP'S OVER, STIR THY FIRE, UNRAKE   196   RLS + LSNS   133
THER'S NOT A WIND CAN STIR   171   COME, COME   11
STIRR'D
WHICH STILL INCREAS'D, BUT WHENCE IT STIRR'D   141   RGNRTN   80
STIRRING
EACH STIRRING WIND AND STORM BLEW THROUGH THEIR COTS   239   SHEPHEARDS   33
ALL NCW ARE STIRRING, EV'RY FIELD   212   DAWNING   15
STIRRS
NOTHING THAT STIRRS   222   AFFLICTION   30
STIRS
WHAT STIRS, WHAT POSTING INTERCOURSE AND MIRTH   267   ASCN-DAY A   25
AND BRIGHT STIRS ARE THERE.   172   MIDNIGHT   13
STOCK
WHAT STOCK OF NIGHTS   165   THE CALL   14
WHAT STOCK, AND HOW MUCH TIME WERE LEFT THEE NCW.   158   THE LAMPE   16
TC BRASSE, AND IRCN, WHEN MY STOCK LAY DEAD   213   ADMISSION   3
YOU WERE THE DEAR AND CHOSEN STOCK.   292   THE JEWS   39
EVER THE SAME, WHOSE DIFFUS'D STOCK   333   AGREEMENT   33
STOLE
MY FORWARD FLESH CREEPT CN, AND SUBTLY STOLE   206   REPENTANCE   5
I STOLE ABROAC   139   RGNRTN   11
STOLE BY OUR EARES   165   THE CALL   17
STON'D
THAT STON'D THY SERVANTS, AND DID MOVE   264   INTRO. 1   11
STONE
IS GROWN THICK DARKNESS, AND THY BREAD, A STCNE.   224   TEMPEST   55
MY THCUGHTS, LIKE WATER WHICH SOME STONE DOTH START   234   MUTINIE   6
I WOULD I WERE A STONE, OR TREE   187   NO DO THEY   11
TO CANCELL ALL THAT E'RE WAS WRIT IN STONE   159   MANS FALL   23
WAS NCT ALL STONE, AND EARTH   196   CORRUPTION   2
IN THEE THE HIDDEN STONE, THE MANNA LIES   198   SCRIPTURES   5
IS STIL'D THEIR STARRE, THE STCNE, AND HIDDEN FOCD.   192   RLS + LSNS   28
ARE WE ALL STONE, AND EARTH.   200   NTVTY 2   14
YEA BETHEL SHALL HAVE TITHES (SAITH ISRAELS STCNE)   331   JACOBS PLW   33
FOR THIS RICH PEARL, LIKE SOME MORE COMMON STONE   330   JACOBS PLW   17
NO DEAD AND DUSTY CHERUB, NOR CARV'D STONE   323   THE NIGHT   20
AGAINST THEM BY A STONE PROCEED.   314   THE STONE   49
STONES
ARE SHAK'C FOR WITNESSES, AND STONES   314   THE STONE   38
ON STONES DIDST SLEEP AND FOUNC'ST BUT COLD RELIEF.   331   JACOBS PLW   46
AND STONES, THOUGH SPEECHLESS, ARE NOT DUMB.   335   JUDGEMENT   16
AND THOUGH POOR STONES HAVE NEITHER SPEECH NCR TCNGUE   288   THE BIRD   14
YET STONES ARE DEEP IN ADMIRATICN.   288   THE BIRD   16
THE STONES HAC SPOKE, WHAT YOU DENYED.   296   JESUS WP A   8
TREES, FLCWERS AND HERBS. BIRCS, BEASTS AND STCNES   294   PALM-SUNDY   11
IN CUST, AND STONES.   202   THE CHECK   35
POURE OYLE UPCN THE STONES, WEEP FOR THY SIN   192   RLS + LSNS   23
RETURN UPCN HIMSELF THE LAW, AND STONES.   198   SCRIPTURES   12
OF DIVERS STONES, SOME BRIGHT, AND ROUND   141   RGNRTN   64
FOR DUST, AND STONES   179   CHRCH-SVC   6
SO THAT BOTH STONES, ANC DUST, AND ALL OF ME   180   CHRCH-SVC   17
THE ECCHO OF THESE STCNES   180   CHRCH-SVC   23
OF STONES, AND SPEECHLESS EARTH   226   RETIREMENT   47
HER CEDAR, FIRR, HEW'D STONES AND GOLD WERE ALL   238   SHEPHEARDS   23
NAY HATH NOT SO MUCH WIT AS SCME STONES HAVE   246   MAN   23
THE STONES MUCH SCFTER THAN MY HEART   207   REPENTANCE   36
STCNIE
BUT A HARD, STONIE HEART.   179   CHRCH-SVC   8
STCNY
YCUR STCNY HEARTS DESPISED LOVE   293   THE JEWS   43
STOCD
STOCD BARE BEFORE UNPRACTIC'D EYES   311   FAIR+YONG   18
NAIL'C TO THE CENTER STCOD   141   RGNRTN   69
AND HERB PARTAKES, WHERE HAVING STOOD AWHILE   155   ISAACS M.   57
STOOP
LED BY THY LOVE WCULDST STOOP THUS LOW   180   BURIALL   17
STOOPS
THE SLN NCW STOOPS, AND HASTS HIS BEAMS TO HIDE   195   RLS + LSNS   105
STOP
O BROCK IT NOT. WHY WILT THOU STOP   188   NO DO THEY   37
THE STOP TO BUSIE FOOLS, CARES CHECK AND CURB.   324   THE NIGHT   26
STOPS
WHAT SIGHS, WHAT WHISPERS, BUSIE STOPS AND STAYS.   268   ASCN-DAY A   27
STOR'C
THEY'RE STOR'C UP IN THE SOCKET, WHERE THEY LYE   158   THE LAMPE   19
STORE
OR THAT THY STORE WAS LESSE   161   DSTRQCTION   23
WHEN THCU SHALT SPEND THY SACREC STORE   147   DAY OF JDG   9
WEAR IN MY BOSCME A FULL SUN, SLCH STORE   198   UNPRFTBLNS   11
I SUMMON'D NATURE. PIERC'D THRCUGH ALL HER STORE   167   VNTY SPRIT   9
NC HOLSE CF STORE   171   COME, COME   22
THE GROUND WAS CURST, AND VOIC OF STORE.   264   INTRO. 1   8

	PAGE	TITLE	LINE
STORE (CON'T)			
AND CURIOUS STORE	246	I WALKT	6
GOOD STORE OF IT, BUT LET	244	THE SAP	36
HER GORGEOUS MART AND GLITTERING STORE	302	ORNAMENT	2
SHOULD NOT THY SIGHS REFRAIN THY STORE	298	JESUS WP B	14
OF SUMMERS LATER STORE	345	THE WREATH	6
STORIES			
OUR STORIES ARE IN THEIRS SET DOWN	273	WHT SUNDAY	31
STORK			
THE BIRDS THEIR NESTS BUILD, THOUGH THE STORK DOTH CHOOSE	286	PSALM 104	47
STORM			
THY PILLOW WAS. MANY A SULLEN STORM	287	THE BIRD	3
AND WAS BLOW'N THROUGH BY EV'RY STORM AND WIND	245	MT. OLV. B	14
I STORM AT THEE, CALLING MY PEACE	242	MISERY	83
EACH STIRRING WIND AND STORM BLEW THROUGH THEIR COTS	239	SHEPHEARDS	33
STORM'D			
STORM'D THUS, I STRAIGHT PERCEIV'D MY SPRING	139	RGNRTN	18
STORME			
SO SHALL THAT STORME PURGE THIS RECLUSE	176	THE STORM	21
STORMES			
HERE UNDER CLOUDS, WHERE STORMES, AND TEMPESTS BLAST	158	MANS FALL	2
STORMING			
UNTO THE BANKS, WHERE, STORMING AT THOSE BOUNDS	234	MUTINIE	8
STORMS			
THAT, MIDST ALL STORMS I FEEL A RAY OF THEE.	245	MT. OLV. B	16
DARK STORMS, AND WIND	175	THE STORM	10
WHICH THRIVES IN STORMS, AND SMELS BEST AFTER SHOWRES.	193	RLS + LSNS	60
WERE STILL ALIVE) THOU COST GREAT STORMS RESENT	289	THE TIMBER	15
OR ANY STORMS MORE FOUL THEN A LEWD LIFE.	290	THE TIMBER	26
STORMS TURN TO MUSICK, CLOUDS TO SMILES AND AIR.	306	RAIN-BOW	10
THOUGH HAWKS CAN PREY THROUGH STORMS AND WINDS	309	THE SEED	35
BOLD STORMS, AND SIMPLY DOST ATTEND ON RAIN	307	RAIN-BOW	40
MAKES WAY FOR STORMS INTO HIS REST.	309	THE SEED	44
WITH THOSE FOUL STORMS, WHEN THEY WERE WRIT.	332	AGREEMENT	28
SINCE I IN STORMS US'D MOST TO BE	345	THE WREATH	1
LIKE BEES IN STORMS UNTO THEIR HIVE	343	OBSEQUIES	30
STORY			
WHY, SINCE EACH DROP OF THY QUICK STORY	343	WATER-FALL	15
AND SING HIS SAD VICTORIOUS STORY.	341	THE FEAST	60
BOASTS IT THIS DAY, THOUGH NOT IN STORY	315	DWELLNG-PL	4
(THOUGH OF THEMSELVES BUT A SAD BLUBBER'D STORY)	290	THE TIMBER	42
A DUSTY STORY	201	THE CHECK	2
OR A LACED STORY.	173	CONTENT	18
AND BECAM'ST A WOFULL STORY.	163	INCARNATN	4
AND SMOOTH SEDUCEMENTS. I'LE NOT STUFF MY STORY	275	PROFFER	35
HARK, AND MAKE USE OF THIS ENSUING STORY.	282	GARLAND	4
THROUGH ALL THY FAIR, AND VARIOUS STORY	207	REPENTANCE	31
THAT GUIDES THROUGH ERRING HOURS, AND IN FULL STORY	2	SON-DAYES	22
STRAGLERS			
TO BRING ALL STRAGLERS HOME	239	SHEPHEARDS	46
HELPS SUCH DARK STRAGLERS TO THEIR SIGHT.	305	ST MARY MN	60
STRAIGHT			
STORM'D THUS, I STRAIGHT PERCEIV'D MY SPRING	139	RGNRTN	18
WITH THAT, SOME CRYED, AWAY. STRAIGHT I	140	RGNRTN	34
WERE DULL, AND BLIND, BUT CUSTOME STRAIGHT	143	DEATH	17
STRAIN			
THE DOTING LOVER IN HIS QUEINTEST STRAIN	231	THE WORLD	8
STRAINS			
WITH ALL THEIR SOFT, KINDE ARTS AND EASIE STRAINS	320	HIDDN TRSR	21
STRAIT			
WHICH STRAIT, LIKE MORNING-STARS DID SING	332	AGREEMENT	10
WHOM STRAIT THE SHINING ROW ALL FAC'D	303	ORNAMENT	17
BUT STRAIT I THINK (THOUGH FAR)	171	COME, COME	13
STRAIT THERE IS JOY, AND EV'RY SPHERE	200	NTVTY 2	3
STRAITWAY			
AND MY MOST LOVING LORD STRAITWAY	211	FAITH	43
STRANGE			
TO SHEW WHAT STRANGE LOVE HE HAD TO OUR GOOD	243	THE SAP	25
SO SOME STRANGE THOUGHTS TRENSCEND OUR WONTED THEAMS	271	ALL GONE	27
THINGS HERE WERE STRANGE UNTO HIM. SWET, AND TILL	196	CORRUPTION	9
TRACES, AND SOUNDS OF A STRANGE KIND.	168	VNTY SPRIT	16
O WHAT STRANGE WONDERS COULD THEE MOVE	164	INCARNATN	17
AS STRANGE AN OBJECT BROUGHT	141	RGNRTN	73
WAS SHOWN ONE DAY IN A STRANGE GLASS	313	THE STONE	19
KING OF SALVATION. BY STRANGE THINGS	336	PSALM 65	13
BUT THIS THY STRANGE RESENTMENT AFTER DEATH	289	THE TIMBER	19
MY SINS LONG SINCE HAVE MADE THEE STRANGE	293	BEGGING B	5
(WHICH DOTH THY STRANGE SURE MERCIES SHROUD)	300	PROVIDENCE	8
STRANGER			
A VERY STRANGER UNTO ME.	293	BEGGING B	6
AS MEER A STRANGER, AS MEN LONG SINCE DEAD.	290	THE TIMBER	38
BEFORE THY TIME, BE NOT A STRANGER THERE	195	RLS + LSNS	122
STRAW			
WEARY OF THIS SAME CLAY, AND STRAW, I LAID	233	MUTINIE	1
LIFE'S BUT A BLAST, HE KNOWS IT, WHAT. SHAL STRAW	224	TEMPEST	49
AND ALL HER FLOWRES WITHER'D TO STRAW	222	TEMPEST	7
STRAY			
WHERE THEY ALL STRAY AND STRIVE, WHICH SHAL	240	MISERY	15
THOU SHALT NOT LOSE ONE MITE. THOUGH WATERS STRAY	193	RLS + LSNS	65
BUT I AM SADLY LOOSE, AND STRAY	187	NO DO THEY	17

	PAGE	TITLE	LINE
STRAY (CON'T)			
ONE PATH, AND STRAY	189	RESOLVE	4
WHEN ALL ELSE STRAY	160	THE SHOWRE	11
AMEN. BUT HARK, E'R WE TWC STRAY	178	EVNG-WTCH	9
THOUGH THEN (THUS CRUMM'D) I STRAY	181	BURIALL	25
THOSE BLASTS, WHICH O'R OUR HEADS HERE STRAY	298	JESUS WP B	18
AND FLOWERS THAT INTO FIELDS DO STRAY,	294	PALM-SUNDY	9
AND PRIVATE TAPERS WILL BUT HELP TO STRAY	321	HIDDN TRSR	27
HE KNOCKS AT ALL DOORS, STRAYS AND ROAMS	246	MAN	22
STREAM			
ATTRACTS THEE THUS AND MAKES THEE STREAM AND FLOW	278	THE STARRE	2
DRUNK OF THY LIVING STREAM	329	TEARS	10
DEAR STREAM. DEAR BANK, WHERE OFTEN I	343	WATER-FALL	13
STREAME			
MY SOUL DOTH STREAME	171	MIDNIGHT	9
BOTH LIQUORS BURNE, AND STREAME.	172	MIDNIGHT	26
AND SWEETER AIRES STREAME FROM A GRONE	167	THE CALL	80
WHEN ALL SHALL STREAME, AND LIGHTEN ROUND	147	DAY OF JDG	5
STREAMES			
STREAMES, AND FLAMES THUS TO THE SIGHT	172	MIDNIGHT	20
O'RE DARK HILLS, SWIFT STREAMES, AND STEEEP WAYS	174	JOY OF LIF	19
SWEET, DOWNIE THOUGHTS, SOFT LILLY-SHADES, CALM STREAMES.	188	RELAPSE	25
STREAMING			
IN STREAMING RINGS RESTAGNATES ALL	344	WATER-FALL	34
STREAMS			
LODGE IN THY MYSTICAL, DEEP STREAMS.	344	WATER-FALL	28
GREEN TREES OF LIFE, AND LIVING STREAMS.	346	THE QUEER	8
OR CHOOSE HELL-FIRE AND BRIMSTONE STREAMS	321	CHILDEHOOD	11
WHOSE STREAMS STILL VOCAL, STILL COMPLAIN	325	ABELS BLOD	3
WITH FERTIL STREAMS, MAKES RICH ALL GROUNDS	336	PSALM 65	30
BLEST SHOWERS THEY ARE, AND STREAMS SENT FROM ABOVE	291	THE TIMBER	49
WHILE ACTIVE WINDS AND STREAMS BOTH RUN AND SPEAK	288	THE BIRD	15
AND ALL HER STREAMS GROW FOUL.	288	THE BIRD	30
AND SPRINGS, LIKE DISSOLV'D PEARLS THEIR STREAMS DID POUR	268	ASCN-DAY A	47
BUT GIVE THEM IN THOSE STREAMS A PART	208	REPENTANCE	55
STREET			
THOU. WHO DIDST PLACE ME IN THIS BUSIE STREET	318	THE ASS	1
STREMES			
AND BOYLING STREMES THAT RAVE	175	THE STORM	6
STRENGTH			
FOR SINNE TOOKE STRENGTH, AND VIGOUR FROM THE LAW.	159	MANS FALL	20
TO MANS HEART STRENGTH AND MIRTH.	285	PSALM 104	44
OF DAIES, FROM THEE LOOK FOR NEW STRENGTH	218	EASTER HYM	10
WHEREFORE WITH MY UTMOST STRENGTH	214	PRAISE	9
SO MUCH OF STRENGTH, AS MY FULFIL	242	MISERY	98
THOU OVERCAM'ST MY SINFUL STRENGTH	348	HOLY BIBLE	24
STRENGTHEN			
SO STRENGTHEN ME, LORD, ALL THE WAY	229	PILGRIMAGE	27
STRETCH			
THIS GROWTH AND STRETCH FOR HEAV'N.	243	THE SAP	6
LIKE STRINGS, STRETCH EV'RY PART	222	AFFLICTION	39
BE THERE, BEFORE THE SHADOWS STRETCH	189	RESOLVE	19
AND STRETCH TO THEE, AIMING AT ALL	203	DSRDR + FR	21
STREWED			
ALL STREWED WITH FLOWRES, AND HAPPINESS	189	RESOLVE	23
STRICTLY			
I SCHOOL MY EYES, AND STRICTLY DWEL	214	MISERY	57
STRIFE			
AND SAVE ME FROM ALL INWARD STRIFE.	190	THE MATCH	18
THEE TWO SMALL MITES, AND BE AT STRIFE	186	PASSION	52
AND THY BLOUDY WOUNDS, AND STRIFE	215	PRAISE	27
I SUMMON'D TO DECIDE THIS STRIFE	207	REPENTANCE	42
WEARYED OUT IN A HARMLES STRIFE	209	THE BURIAL	3
THEN TRUE REMORSE, WHEN WITH PAST SINS AT STRIFE.	290	THE TIMBER	28
DID BREED THIS STRIFE	299	JESUS WP B	29
THE OTHER OF DEATH, SIN AND STRIFE.	318	THE ASS	4
THOU DIDST LEAD TO, AND STILL ALL STRIFE.	348	HOLY BIBLE	32
STRIKE			
AND STRIKE THEM DUMB, WHO FOR MEER WORDS	350	L'ENVOY	41
O HEAR, AND HEAL THY SERVANT. LORD STRIKE DEAD	185	PASSION	14
STRIKE THESE LIPS DUMB.	171	COME, COME	16
STRIKES			
WHICH STRIKES DEATH DEAD	340	THE FEAST	38
STRING			
THAN ANY ARTED STRING.	167	THE CALL	81
STRINGS			
LIKE STRINGS, STRETCH EV'RY PART	222	AFFLICTION	39
STRIVE			
STRIVE UPWARDS STIL, AND POINT HIM THE WAY HOME.	223	TEMPEST	28
WHERE SICK WITH LOVE I STRIVE THY NAME TO SING	245	MT. OLV. B	24
LET ME SO STRIVE AND STRUGGLE WITH THY FOES	234	MUTINIE	14
WHERE THEY ALL STRAY AND STRIVE, WHICH SHAL	240	MISERY	15
O THEN PLAY NOT. BUT STRIVE TO HIM, WHO CAN	202	THE CHECK	29
STRIVING			
STRIVING TO SAVE THE WHOLE, BY PARCELLS DYE	161	DSTRQCTION	34
I CANNOT REACH IT. AND MY STRIVING EYE	321	CHILDEHOOD	1
STROKE			
WITH EVERY STROKE.	185	PASSION	37
STRONG			
YET HAVE I FLOWS, AS STRONG AS HIS	175	THE STORM	5
AND WITH ONE STRONG, INCESSANT CRY	326	ABELS BLOD	21
BUT A STRONG WIND MUST BREAK THY LOFTY ROCKS.	330	JACOBS PLW	10

	PAGE	TITLE	LINE
STRONG (CON'T)			
WITH HIS STRONG ARM TURNS OUR CAPTIVITY.	331	JACOBS PLW	40
BRIGHT, AND BLEST BEAME. WHOSE STRONG PROJECTION	210	FAITH	1
STRONG HOLDS SHOULD BELONG TO THEE	249	BEGGING A	16
BUT AS RASH YOUTHS, WHEN ONCE GROWN STRONG	348	HOLY BIBLE	9
STRONGER			
IS ONLY STRONGER FAR THAN DEATH.	164	INCARNATN	20
STRONGEST			
AND, AS FIRST LOVE DRAWS STRONGEST, SO FROM HENCE	196	CORRUPTION	7
STRONGLY			
NO THESE ARE THE MAGNETS WHICH SO STRONGLY MOVE	278	THE STARRE	21
WHICH STRONGLY OPERATE, THOUGH WITHOUT PAINS	320	HIDDN TRSR	22
AND TO THY SOFT ARTS STRONGLY BOWS.	297	HERODIAS	16
O THAT THY SPIRIT WOULD SO STRONGLY MOVE ME	283	LOVE-SICK	2
STROW			
COME, DROP YOUR BRANCHES, STROW THE WAY	294	PALM-SUNDY	1
DID I THERE STROW	247	I WALKT	23
STROW AT THY DOOR	215	PRAISE	55
STRUGGLE			
LET ME SO STRIVE AND STRUGGLE WITH THY FOES	234	MUTINIE	14
STRUGLED			
REFINING STILL, I STRUGLED MUCH.	348	HOLY BIBLE	22
STRUNG			
THER'S ONE SUN MORE STRUNG ON MY BEAD OF DAYS.	195	RLS + LSNS	118
STUBBLE			
THAT THEY HAVE QUICKEN'D EVEN DRIE STUBBLE.	218	HOLY COMM.	4
STUBBORN			
TO REDUCE A STUBBORN HEART	249	BEGGING A	14
WAS THINE OWN ANSWER TO THE STUBBORN JEW.	268	ASCN-DAY A	60
HERE I JOIN HANDS, AND THRUST MY STUBBORN HEART	190	THE MATCH	7
STUDIES			
SEARCH WELL ANOTHER WORLD, WHO STUDIES THIS	153	THE SEARCH	94
STUDY			
BLIND , DESP'RATE FITS, THAT STUDY HOW	205	IDLE VERSE	9
HOW DO I STUDY NOW, AND SCAN	322	CHILDEHOOD	39
STUDY'D			
SPRUCE, SUPPLE CRINGE, OR STUDY'D LOOK PUT ON	155	ISAACS M.	32
STUDYED			
THEE, MORE THEN ERE I STUDYED MAN	322	CHILDEHOOD	40
STUFF			
AND SMOOTH SEDUCEMENTS. I'LE NOT STUFF MY STORY	275	PROFFER	35
STUFFE			
YET HUGS HE STIL HIS DURT. THE STUFFE HE WEARS	224	TEMPEST	45
STUNG			
AND STUNG WITH FEAR	247	I WALKT	30
SUBDUE			
NO GOLD NOR GIFTS CAN THEM SUBDUE.	313	THE STONE	13
SUBDUING			
AND BY HIS ALL SUBDUING MIGHT	270	ASCSN-HYMN	41
SUBJECT			
FIRST, I AM SURE, THE SUBJECT SO RESPECTED	278	THE STARRE	13
SUBLIME			
WHAT SUBLIME TRUTHS, AND WHOLESOME THEMES	344	WATER-FALL	27
SUBMIT			
SUBMIT MY WILDE HEART, AND RESTRAIN MY HANDS.	321	HIDDN TRSR	30
SUBSIST			
YET, SEEING ALL THINGS THAT SUBSIST AND BE	278	THE STARRE	9
SUBSTANCE			
BUT WE THE SUBSTANCE HAVE, AND ON HIM REST.	331	JACOBS PLW	54
WHOSE SUBSTANCE, THOUGH 'TIS HARD ENOUGH	314	THE STONE	50
THEIR SUBSTANCE DOTH DEPRAVE	145	RSRCTN +IM	38
SUBTILE			
O POYS'NOUS, SUBTILE FOWLS.	275	PROFFER	13
SUBTILTIE			
THE FLOWRES TO AIR DRAW NEER, AND SUBTILTIE	223	TEMPEST	35
IF ALL THE SUBTILTIES OF VICE	311	FAIR+YONG	17
SUBTLY			
MY FORWARD FLESH CREEPT ON, AND SUBTLY STOLE	206	REPENTANCE	5
SUCCEED			
AND DRUNKENNESS QUICKLY DID SUCCEED THE FLOOD.	307	RAIN-BOW	22
SUCCEEDS			
WHAT CAN THE MAN DO THAT SUCCEEDS THE KING.	320	HIDDN TRSR	1
SUCCESSE			
SUGRING ALL DANGERS WITH SUCCESSE	153	THE SEARCH	73
SUCCESSFUL			
SUCCESSFUL WICKEDNESS COMMEND.	316	MEN OF WAR	16
SUCCESSION			
AND STILL A NEW SUCCESSION SINGS AND FLIES.	289	THE TIMBER	5
WITHOUT SUCCESSION, AND WITHOUT A SUNNE	146	RSRCTN +IM	70
SUCK			
DID LEARN TO SUCK, AND SIP, AND TASTE	308	THE SEED	10
WEE ARE THY INFANTS, AND SUCK THEE, IF THOU	213	ADMISSION	17
YOU FLIE AND FLOCK TO SUCK THE FLOWERS.	274	PROFFER	6
SUCKS			
THY ROOT SUCKS BUT DISEASES, WORMS THERE SEAT	243	THE SAP	7
SUDDAIN			
IN SUDDAIN FLOWRES AND ARBOURS TO MY EYES	245	MT. OLV. B	18
SUDDEN			
ALL EXPECT SOME SUDDEN MATTER	212	DAWNING	22
A SUDDEN AND MOST SEARCHING RAY	348	HOLY BIBLE	20

	PAGE	TITLE	LINE
SUFF'RINGS			
CAN NEITHER LOVE, NOR SUFF'RINGS BIND.	200	NTVTY 2	13
AND FROM THENCE (HIS SUFF'RINGS ENDED)	163	MT. OLVS A	22
SUFFER			
SUFFER NO MORE THIS DUST TO OVERFLOW	191	THE MATCH	36
SUFFERING			
THUS SUFFERING SEE	145	RSRCTN +IM	36
WHOM SUFFERINGS MAKE MOST GREEN AND GAY.	294	PALM-SUNDY	3
SUFFICE			
LET IT SUFFICE MY WARMER DAYS	205	IDLE VERSE	17
WHOSE ARM SUPPLY'D THEE, TAKE WHAT MAY SUFFICE	195	RLS + LSNS	98
LET IT SUFFICE AT LENGTH THY FITS	225	RETIREMENT	12
SUGAR			
CANDY WITH SUGAR OUR CHOICE FRUITS.	310	THE SEED	78
SUGERD			
SORROWS IN WHITE, GRIEFS TUN'D, A SUGERD DOSIS	280	JOY	5
SUGRED			
GO, GO, QUEINT FOLIES, SUGRED SIN	204	IDLE VERSE	1
SUGRING			
SUGRING ALL DANGERS WITH SUCCESSE	153	THE SEARCH	73
SUIT			
MAKE ME AMONGST THEM ('TIS MY SUIT)	329	TEARS	7
SUITS			
AND CHANGE OF SUITS	145	RSRCTN +IM	22
SULLEN			
ONE SULLEN BEAME, WHOSE CHARGE IS TO DISPENSE	159	MANS FALL	13
SULLEN, AND SAD ECCLIPSES, CLOUDIE SPHERES	188	RELAPSE	19
AS SULLEN NIGHT-RAVENS DO THE SUN	311	FAIR+YONG	4
THY PILLOW WAS. MANY A SULLEN STORM	287	THE BIRD	3
SULLENNESS			
WHAT PRETTY SULLENNESS DID HASTE	304	ST MARY MN	23
SULLIES			
AFTER SUN-RISING, FAR-DAY SULLIES FLOWRES.	192	RLS + LSNS	10
SULLY'D			
THIS SULLY'D FLOWRE	158	MANS FALL	3
SULLYED			
SULLYED WITH DUST AND MUD.	198	UNPRFTBLNS	3
O'R THE SULLYED, SINFUL BOOK	249	BEGGING A	10
SULPHUR			
ON VEINES OF SULPHUR UNDER GROUND.	150	RELIGION	40
SUM			
CUT OFF THE SUM	170	COME, COME	6
THE HEAVY SUM	233	MUTINIE	4
SUMME			
THE PAST DAIES ACCIDENTS DO SUMME	228	PILGRIMAGE	3
CUTT THEN THE SUMME	181	BURIALL	38
ALL SAD WITH TEARS, WHICH LIKE WARM SUMMER RAIN	268	ASCN-DAY A	52
SUMMERS			
MAN IS A SUMMERS DAY, WHOSE YOUTH, AND FIRE	195	RLS + LSNS	113
OF SUMMERS LATER STORE	345	THE WREATH	6
SUMMON			
SUMMON UP ALL THAT ARE ASLEEPE	147	DAY OF JDG	19
SUMMON'D			
I SUMMON'D NATURE. PIERC'D THROUGH ALL HER STORE	167	VNTY SPRIT	9
I SUMMON'D TO DECIDE THIS STRIFE	207	REPENTANCE	42
SUMPTUOUS			
WHERE ALL WAS SUMPTUOUS, RARE AND NEAT.	304	ST MARY MN	14
SUN			
AS SULLEN NIGHT-RAVENS DO THE SUN	311	FAIR+YONG	4
BOTH SUN AND STARS WOULD HIDE THEIR HEADS.	309	THE SEED	31
THIS PAST, THE SUN SHINES ON THE EARTH, AND THY	286	PSALM 104	61
WILL FADE AT NIGHT, AND WITH THIS SUN	283	GARLAND	31
AND THE SUN RUNS HIS RACE.	286	PSALM 104	52
THY SUN MUST SHINE IN EVERY PART.	294	BEGGING B	16
AND THE SAME SUN WHICH HERE DECLINES	292	THE JEWS	28
THUS PRAISE AND PRAYER HERE BENEATH THE SUN	288	THE BIRD	17
A STATE THAT WITH THE SUN DOTH SET	300	PROVIDENCE	23
I'LE GET ME UP BEFORE THE SUN	295	PALM-SUNDY	34
BUT WE A HEALING SUN BY DAY AND NIGHT	331	JACOBS PLW	49
THY LINES ARE RAYS, THE TRUE SUN SHEDS.	333	AGREFMENT	35
DID AT MID-NIGHT SPEAK WITH THE SUN.	323	THE NIGHT	12
BUT LIVING WHERE THE SUN	324	THE NIGHT	43
AND THEN RETURNING, LIKE THE SUN	338	DEATH B	14
SO WHEN THE SUN OF RIGHTEOUSNESS	210	FAITH	21
AND AS I'TH' NATURAL SUN, THESE THREE	211	FAITH	33
HOW IS IT THAT THE SUN TO THEE ALONE	224	TEMPEST	54
HE IS MY SUN, AND SHADE	220	PSALM 121	10
AS ON THE SUN ECCLIPSES LIE.	219	HOLY COMM.	20
IN WHICH THY SELF WIL BE THE SUN	212	DAWNING	46
WHO NEVER FEEL'ST THE SUN, NOR SMOOTH'ST THY BROW	217	EASTER-DAY	3
AWAKE, AWAKE. AND, LIKE THE SUN, DISPERSE	217	EASTER-DAY	9
IN THEIR WHITE ROBES TO SEEK THE RISEN SUN.	268	ASCN-DAY A	30
AS THE SUN DOTH, WHICH TO THOSE DAYS GAVE LIGHT.	268	ASCN-DAY A	36
LET NO NIGHT PUT OUT THIS SUN.	249	BEGGING A	4
IF THE SUNNE RISE ON THE ROCKS, IS'T RIGHT	265	INTRO. 2	5
BUT NOW THE DEW AND SUN HAVE WARM'D MY BOWRES	274	PROFFER	5
LIKE THE SUN SHINE	269	ASCSN-HYMN	22
A WAY WHERE YOU MIGHT TREAD THE SUN, AND BE	233	THE WORLD	55
RISE WITH THE SUN, AND SET IN THE SAME BOWRS.	245	MAN	7
AND WALKING FROM HIS SUN, WHEN PAST	178	SILENCE	9

	PAGE	TITLE	LINE
SUN (CON'T)			
WOO'D BY THE SUN SWELS UP TO BE HIS SHROWD	155	ISAACS M.	54
THE SUN NOW STOOPS, AND HASTS HIS BEAMS TO HIDE	195	RLS + LSNS	105
THER'S ONE SUN MORE STRUNG ON MY BEAD OF DAYS.	195	RLS + LSNS	118
THROUGH THICKEST NIGHTS, THOUGH THEN THE SUN BE FAR	196	RLS + LSNS	137
WEAR IN MY BOSOME A FULL SUN, SUCH STORE	198	UNPRFTBLNS	11
THE SUN DOTH SHAKE	199	NTVTY 1	4
UNTILL THY SUN AGAIN ASCENDS.	203	DSRDR + FR	44
UNTO THAT COMFORTER, THE SUN	203	DSRDR + FR	33
MAKE THESE SAD SHADES PURE SUN	202	THE CHECK	30
WORKS WITH THE SUN, AND SETS	201	THE CHECK	16
UNTO THEIR GOD, AS FLOW'RS DO TO THE SUN.	191	RLS + LSNS	4
YET, NEVER SLEEP THE SUN UP, PRAYER SHOU'D	192	RLS + LSNS	7
RISE TO PREVENT THE SUN, SLEEP DOTH SINS GLUT	192	RLS + LSNS	11
LOOSE, PARCELL'D HEARTS WIL FREEZE. THE SUN	189	RESOLVE	13
PREVAIL'D BY WRESTLING ERE THE SUN DID SHINE.	192	RLS + LSNS	22
O THE NEW WORLDS NEW, QUICKNING SUN.	349	L'ENVOY	1
SUN-RISING			
AFTER SUN-RISING, FAR-DAY SULLIES FLOWRES.	192	RLS + LSNS	10
SUN-SHINE			
A TRAINE OF LIGHTS, WHICH IN THOSE SUN-SHINE DAYES	159	MANS FALL	10
MY GOD WOULD GIVE A SUN-SHINE AFTER RAINE.	160	THE SHOWRE	18
WERE ALL THE YEAR ONE CONSTANT SUN-SHINE, WEE	222	AFFLICTION	21
BRIGHT PLEDGE OF PEACE AND SUN-SHINE. THE SURE TYE	306	RAIN-BOW	13
SUN'S			
AFTER THE SUN'S REMOVE.	270	ALL GONE	8
THE SUN'S BROKE THROUGH TO GUIDE MY WAY.	152	THE SEARCH	66
SUNK			
SIN TRIUMPHS STILL, AND MAN IS SUNK BELOW	197	CORRUPTION	35
THUS IS THE SOLEMN TEMPLE SUNK AGEN	331	JACOBS PLW	35
SUNNE			
WITHOUT SUCCESSION, AND WITHOUT A SUNNE	146	RSRCTN +IM	70
THE UNTHRIFT SUNNE SHOT VITALL GOLD	140	RGNRTN	50
AND BAD THE LAZIE SUNNE MAKE HASTE	143	DEATH	21
'TIS LAST GOOD-NIGHT, OUR SUNNE SHALL NEVER SET.	143	DEATH	32
THEN HAVING LOST THE SUNNE, AND LIGHT	162	PURSUITE	6
WAS TINN'D AND LIGHTED AT THE SUNNE.	276	COCK-CRWNG	12
SUNNIE			
FATHER OF LIGHTS. WHAT SUNNIE SEED	276	COCK-CRWNG	1
IN SUNNIE DAYES	182	CHRFLNESS	13
SUNS			
WHOSE SUNS ARE ALL SET IN A CLOUD.	165	THE CALL	19
SITS ON THE SUNS BROW ALL THE YEARE	143	DEATH	13
WELLCOME WHITE DAY. A THOUSAND SUNS	272	WHT SUNDAY	1
THE MILKY WAY CHALKT CUT WITH SUNS, A CLUE	2	SON-DAYES	21
WHICH ALL THE YEAR SEES THE SUNS FACE.	332	AGREEMENT	12
AND EV'N, SMOOTH LINES, LIKE THE SUNS RAYS	310	THE SEED	59
SUP			
THE BIRDS NOR SOW, NOR REAP, YET SUP AND DINE	245	MAN	12
AND SCARS, AND SHINES, BUT E'R WE SUP	203	DSRDR + FR	34
SUPPLANTERS			
IF THESE SUPPLANTERS IN THE SHADE	312	FAIR+YONG	37
SUPPLE			
SPRUCE, SUPPLE CRINGE, OR STUDY'D LOOK PUT ON	155	ISAACS M.	32
TEARS CLEANSE AND SUPPLE WITHOUT FAIL	266	VAIN WITS	8
SUPPLIED			
AND BY THY MERCIES STILL SUPPLIED	336	PSALM 65	31
SUPPLY			
I CHEER THEIR FLOW, GIVING SUPPLY	240	MISERY	17
WHEN ALL IS SPENT, THY LAST, AND SURE SUPPLY	158	THE LAMPE	20
A FAIRE SUPPLY OF YEARES.	165	THE CALL	37
SUPPLY'D			
WHOSE ARM SUPPLY'D THEE, TAKE WHAT MAY SUFFICE	195	RLS + LSNS	98
SUPPRESSIONS			
WILFUL REBELLIONS. AND SUPPRESSIONS	208	REPENTANCE	54
SURFEITS			
AND BURIED IN MY SURFEITS I	240	MISERY	43
OF DRUNKNES, SURFEITS, CARE	202	THE CHECK	42
SURLY			
AND SURLY WINDS	139	RGNRTN	15
SURPRIZ'D			
BY CLOUDS SURPRIZ'D	161	PURSUITE	5
SURPRIZES			
AND LAYD SURPRIZES IN EACH ELEMENT.	223	TEMPEST	24
SURPRIZING			
AND WITH SURPRIZING FLAMES	147	DAY OF JDG	6
SURVEY			
I DOE SURVEY	171	MIDNIGHT	5
BUT SINCE THOU DIDST IN ONE SWEET GLANCE SURVEY	198	UNPRFTBLNS	7
SURVIVES			
HID UNDER GROUND SURVIVES THE FALL.	203	DSRDR + FR	29
SURVIVING			
LIKE THE SURVIVING TURTLE, WEEP	311	FAIR+YONG	10
SUSPECT			
THOSE SECRET SINS WE LEAST SUSPECT.	314	THE STONE	41
SUSTAINES			
WHEN THY LEAST BREATH SUSTAINES MY WING.	182	CHRFLNESS	3
SUTE			
BE NOT DISPLEAS'D, IF I, WHO HAVE A SUTE	230	LAW + GOSP	24
SUTOR			
AN ODDE DULL SUTOR, HADST THOU BUT THE ART	154	ISAACS M.	14

	PAGE	TITLE	LINE
SWAINES			
WITH LEARNED SWAINES, AND ECCHO YET	162	MT. OLVS A	10
SWAINS			
WAS IT BECAUSE THOSE FIRST AND BLESSED SWAINS . . .	238	SHEPHEARDS	9
SWALLOW			
THERE THE WILDE ASSES SWALLOW THE COOL SPRING. . .	285	PSALM 104	34
SWAN-LIKE			
SHALL SEND ME (SWAN-LIKE) SINGING HOME.	299	JESUS WP B	53
SWARM			
WHEN THE WORLDS UP, AND EV'RY SWARM ABROAD . .	192	RLS + LSNS	31
SWEARERS			
OF YOUNG, GAY SWEARERS, WITH THEIR NEEDLESSE, LOWD . .	154	ISAACS M.	22
SWEARS			
HE RAVES, AND SWEARS TO STIR NOR FIRE, NOR FAN . .	197	CORRUPTION	31
BUT THOU HAST PLEAS'D SO WELL, HE SWEARS	297	HERODIAS	13
SWEAT			
HIS BLEST FACE IN A BLODDY SWEAT.	152	THE SEARCH	40
WHAT SPRINGS OF SWEAT, AND BLOUD DID DROWN THEE. .	185	PASSION	24
THEN DID THESE DROPS (FOR MARPLE SWEATS	213	ADMISSION	5
SWEEPE			
AND SWEEPE UP SOUTH AND WEST	146	DAY OF JDG	4
SWEET			
O SWEET, DIVINE SIMPLICITY. O GRACE	155	ISAACS M.	37
SWEET PEACE SITS CROWN'D WITH SMILES	184	PEACE	6
WILL TELL THEE SO, SWEET SAVIOUR THOU DIDST DYE. .	198	SCRIPTURES	14
A SWEET SELF-PRIVACY IN A RIGHT SOUL	193	RLS + LSNS	53
SWEET, DOWNIE THOUGHTS, SOFT LILLY-SHADES, CALM STREAMES.	188	RELAPSE	25
BUT SINCE THOU DIDST IN ONE SWEET GLANCE SURVEY . .	198	UNPRFTBLNS	7
SWEET JESU. WILL THEN. LET NO MORE	200	NTVTY 1	25
WELCOME SWEET, AND SACRED FEAST. WELCOME LIFE. .	218	HOLY COMM.	1
SWEET, HARMLES LIVES (ON WHOSE HOLY LEISURE . .	238	SHEPHEARDS	1
SUCH YONG, SWEET MIRTH	295	PALM-SUNDY	24
A SWEET, REVENGELESS, QUIET MINDE	317	MEN OF WAR	43
WHOSE BLESSED, SWEET COMMANDS DO POUR . . .	326	ABELS BLOD	25
SWEETE			
SWEETE, SACRED HILL. ON WHOSE FAIR BROW . . .	162	MT. OLVS A	1
SWEETER			
AND SWEETER AIRES STREAME FROM A GRONE . . .	167	THE CALL	80
SWEETEST			
OF MY LORDS PENNING, AND BY SWEETEST ART . . .	198	SCRIPTURES	11
SWEETLY			
AND SWEETLY LIVING (FIE ON MEN)	321	CHILDEHOOD	15
SWEETLY DIDST THOU EXPIRE. THY SOUL	209	THE BURIAL	5
SWEETNESS			
TO WINE, AND SWEETNESS. POVERTY TO WEALTH . .	221	AFFLICTION	5
LORD JESUS. WITH WHAT SWEETNESS AND DELIGHTS . .	267	ASCN-DAY A	1
WITH FATAL SWEETNESS, TILL WE EAT.	311	FAIR+YONG	14
O JOYES. INFINITE SWEETNESS. WITH WHAT FLOWRES .	176	MRNG-WTCH	1
SWEETS			
BUT SINCE THESE SWEETS ARE SOWRE, AND POYSON'D HERE .	321	HIDDN TRSR	25
LAPT IN THE SWEETS OF THY YOUNG BREATH . . .	209	THE BURIAL	10
SUCH A RICH AIR OF SWEETS, AS EVENING SHOWRS . .	244	MT. OLV. B	4
OF HEALING SWEETS THY SELF DOST POWR . . .	214	MISERY	50
SWEL			
TO SWEL AND FOME AND FRET WITHIN.	214	MISERY	64
THE POOR BEE IN HER HIVE MUST SWEL.	309	THE SEED	36
SWELL'D			
THESE SWELL'D MY FEARES	159	MANS FALL	18
THE ANGRY SPRING IN BUBBLES SWELL'D	151	THE SEARCH	29
SWELS			
WOO'D BY THE SUN SWELS UP TO BE HIS SHROWD . .	155	ISAACS M.	54
SWERV'D			
WHAT TIME WE FROM OUR FIRST LOVE SWERV'D. . .	237	CONSTLATN	48
SWET			
THINGS HERE WERE STRANGE UNTO HIM. SWET, AND TILL .	196	CORRUPTION	9
SWIFT			
DIDDST THY SWIFT YEERS IN PIETY OUT-GROW . . .	156	ISAACS M.	68
O'RE DARK HILLS, SWIFT STREAMES, AND STEEEP WAYS .	174	JOY OF LIF	19
DEAR, HARMLESS AGE. THE SHORT, SWIFT SPAN . .	322	CHILDEHOOD	31
BY WHOSE ASSISTING, SWIFT COMMAND	300	PROVIDENCE	2
THE WINGS OF THE SWIFT WIND.	284	PSALM 104	12
SWIFT-WING'D			
THE SWIFT-WING'D RAVEN SHALL BRING ME MEAT . .	300	PROVIDENCE	16
SWIM			
MY THOUGHTS DID SWIM IN COMFORTS, AND MINE EYE . .	244	MT. OLV. B	9
SWORD			
THE SWORD WHEREWITH THOU DOST COMMAND . . .	316	MEN OF WAR	25
WHO WITH THE SWORD DOTH OTHERS KILL	316	MEN OF WAR	5
A SWORD SHALL HIS BLOOD LIKEWISE SPILL. . . .	316	MEN OF WAR	6
SWORDLIKE			
A SWORDLIKE GLEAME	175	JOY OF LIF	29
SWORDS			
A VIP'ROUS THOUGHT, SOME SYLLABLES ARE SWORDS. .	194	RLS + LSNS	70
WOUND THY BELOVED, MORE THEN SWORDS. . . .	350	L'ENVOY	42
SWORN			
THAT SWORN MEMORIAL DULY PAY	326	ABELS BLOD	30
SYCHAR			
TYR'D HERE, I COME TO SYCHAR, THENCE . . .	151	THE SEARCH	21
SYLLABLES			
A VIP'ROUS THOUGHT, SOME SYLLABLES ARE SWORDS. .	194	RLS + LSNS	70

	PAGE	TITLE	LINE
SYMMETRY			
SEEKS THERE FOR SYMMETRY	201	THE CHECK	7
SYMPATHIE			
NO HOLD, NOR SYMPATHIE.	278	THE STARRE	16
SYMPHONY			
AND SYMPHONY OF NATURE. PRAYER IS	177	MRNG-WTCH	18
JOYN IN A JOYFUL SYMPHONY	295	PALM-SUNDY	26
SYRIAN			
CAME THE SHEEP-KEEPING SYRIAN MAID.	303	ORNAMENT	16
SYRUPS			
FOR SALVES AND SYRUPS, WHILE THEY LIVE . . .	339	DEATH B	23
T'AWAKE			
TRANSPLANTED THUS, ONE LEAFE OF HIS T'AWAKE . .	158	MANS FALL	5
TA'N			
BE TA'N IN DUST	328	RIGHTSNESS	47
TABLES			
THOSE FAMOUS TABLES DID FROM SINAI BRING. . .	159	MANS FALL	17
TAINTED			
JUST SUCH A TAINTED SINK WE HAVE	150	RELIGION	45
TAINTING			
MANS FAVORITE SINS, THOSE TAINTING APPETITES . . .	320	HIDDN TRSR	19
TAK'ST			
NAY, THOU TAK'ST OURS, AND (WHICH FUL COMFORT BRINGS) .	230	LAW + GOSP	19
TAKE			
MY FINGERS ITCH, AND BURN TO TAKE	214	MISERY	62
I STILE MEER TEMPERS, WHICH TAKE PLACE . . .	242	MISERY	87
TO WASH YOUR VESSEL WEL. THEN HUMBLY TAKE . .	244	THE SAP	43
TAKE UP MY DAY, WHILE THOU DOST SHINE . . .	240	MISERY	26
TAKE THE DOWN-RODE TO VANITIE	240	MISERY	14
TAKE UP, AND TUNE HIS YEAR	236	CONSTLATN	22
O TAKE IT OFF. MAKE NO DELAY	277	COCK-CRWNG	43
O TAKE IT OFF. OR TILL IT FLEE	277	COCK-CRWNG	47
BEG, THOU WOULDST TAKE THY TENANTS RENT. . .	264	INTRO. 1	14
LORD THEN TAKE IT, LEAVE IT NOT	249	BEGGING A	17
WILL SERVE TO TAKE.	274	PROFFER	10
WHEN WE HAD NONE, BUT THOU MUST ALSO TAKE . .	219	HOLY COMM.	35
I TAKE THY SACRED FEAST	217	DRESSING	34
HE MAY TAKE THEE, AS THOU DOEST HIM INTEND. . .	216	DRESSING	16
THE SERVANT MUST NOT TAKE IT ILL. . . .	317	MEN OF WAR	36
AND THEY TOO OFT TAKE GOOD FOR ILL . . .	309	THE SEED	39
ALAS. MY GOD. TAKE HOME THY SHEEP. . . .	312	FAIR+YONG	51
WHO BREAKS HIS GLASS TO TAKE MORE LIGHT . .	309	THE SEED	43
THEM IN DUE SEASON. WHAT THOU GIV'ST, THEY TAKE. .	286	PSALM 104	74
YET, THIS TAKE WITH THEE. THE LAST GASP OF TIME .	178	EVNG-WTCH	15
TO TAKE US SICK, THAT SOUND WOULD NOT TAKE THEE .	162	PURSUITE	18
TO TAKE US SICK, THAT SOUND WOULD NOT TAKE THEE .	162	PURSUITE	18
SOME PITTY TAKE	164	THE CALL	6
NOR GIVE, NOR TAKE CONTACTION	183	THRS A TYE	6
TAKE THEIR LEAVE, AND DIE. BIRDS, BEASTS, EACH TREE .	201	THE CHECK	27
WHOSE ARM SUPPLY'D THEE, TAKE WHAT MAY SUFFICE .	195	RLS + LSNS	98
O MY SOLE COMFORT, TAKE NO MORE THESE WAYES .	188	RELAPSE	9
AND TAKE THE GLORY OF THY HOUSE . . .	350	L'ENVOY	34
TAKE THIS LAST KISS, AND LET ME WEEP . . .	348	HOLY BIBLE	3
TAKEN			
HATH TAKEN ROOT, AND GROWS, AND DOTH NOT TIRE . .	279	THE STARRE	26
TAKES			
AND PAINTED TRIMMING TAKES DOWN BOTH HIS EYES .	224	TEMPEST	46
AND SOURCE OF SPIRITS, WHERE HE TAKES HIS LOT .	145	RSRCTN +IM	43
TO WHAT MOST TAKES THEM, IS A DRUDGE. . .	309	THE SEED	38
THAT WHAT GOD TAKES, HEE'L NOT RESTORE. . .	343	WATER-FALL	22
TAKING			
AND TAKING IN THE RAY	141	RGNRTN	77
I SATE ALONE, AND TAKING UP . . .	207	REPENTANCE	29
OUR DROWN'D ESTATE, TAKING THE CURSE . .	274	WHT SUNDAY	54
THEN TAKING UP WHAT I COULD NEEREST SPIE .	247	I WALKT	15
TALK			
PRIVATE AND HOLY TALK FILL ALL THE WAYS. . .	268	ASCN-DAY A	28
THEY LEAVE THEIR FLOCK, AND IN A BUSIE TALK . .	239	SHEPHEARDS	43
THE IDLE TALK OF FEAV'RISH SOULS . . .	205	IDLE VERSE	15
WE TALK AND NAME THEE WITH MUCH EASE . .	338	DEATH B	6
TALKED			
WITH SERAPHINS THERE TALKED HE	152	THE SEARCH	59
TALKING			
AN ANGELL TALKING WITH A MAN. . . .	148	RELIGION	4
TALL			
AS TH' HIGH, AND TALL.	210	FAITH	4
TAM'D			
BUT IS STILL TAM'D	190	THE MATCH	5
TAME			
LYES TAME AS ALL THE REST.	201	THE CHECK	5
THY HAND ALONE DOTH TAME	179	CHRCH-SVC	15
AND SERIOUS THOUGHTS BEGIN TO TAME . . .	166	THE CALL	64
AND TAME, AND KEEPE DOWNE WITH THY LIGHT . .	161	COME, COME	29
WILL NE'R BE TAME	171	COME, COME	19
AND TAME PROUD WAVES, IF YET THESE BARREN GROUNDS .	234	MUTINIE	12
TAMES			
IN SICKLY EXPIRATIONS TAMES	203	DSRDR + FR	41
TAPERS			
AND PRIVATE TAPERS WILL BUT HELP TO STRAY . .	321	HIDDN TRSR	27
TARES			
AND TARES HAD CHOAKT THE CORNE	166	THE CALL	73

		PAGE	TITLE	LINE
TARES	(CCN'T)			
SCME TARES IN ME WHICH CHCKE, CR SPIL		227	LV + DSPLN	5
THERE ARE, THAT WILL SOW TARES		275	PROFFER	37
TARRY				
SCMETIMES I SIT WITH THEE, ANC TARRY		187	NO DO THEY	21
THOU THINK'ST IT GOOD TC TARRY WHERE THOU ART		157	BRT. CHRCH	14
TASKE				
AND THIRSTIE BRICK MUST BE (SAIC I)		234	MUTINIE	13
TAST				
AND WE HERE TAST SCMETIMES BELCW)		235	CONSTLATN	4
EACH FLY COTH TAST		203	DSRDR + FR	23
TASTE				
AND BCTH HER TASTE, AND CCLOUR STAINES		150	RELIGION	36
A TASTE OF HEAV'N ON EARTH, THE PLEDGE, AND CUE		2	SON-DAYES	23
DID LEARN TO SUCK, ANC SIP, ANC TASTE		308	THE SEED	10
A WING WITH EYES, AND EYES THAT TASTE.		346	THE QUEER	12
FCR THIS TASTE OF LIVING GLCRY		341	THE FEAST	57
TASTS				
THAT, WHO BUT TRULY TASTS IT, NO DECAY		244	THE SAP	29
TAUGHT				
WHERE NCW THEY FIND HIM CUT, ANC TAUGHT BEFORE		239	SHEPHEARDS	47
AND TAUGHT OBECIENCE BY THE WHCLE CREATION		237	CONSTLATN	55
WHICH NCNE BUT CHILDREN HEARD, CR TAUGHT.		207	REPENTANCE	14
THEN TALGHT BY THEE, I WILL PREVAIL		338	THE THRONE	14
THEIR LESSON TAUGHT THEM, WHEN FIRST MADE.		288	THE BIRD	12
THESE TAUGHT HIM AT THE WELL, AND THITHER BROLGHT		155	ISAACS M.	29
I TAUGHT THEE ALL THAT IS.		145	RSRCTN +IM	20
OR TALGHT MY SOUL TO FANCY OUGHT		169	RETREATE	5
BEFCRE I TAUGHT MY TONGUE TC WCUNC		169	RETREATE	15
TEACH				
SC SHCULD WE TOO. ALL THINGS TEACH US TO DIE		201	THE CHECK	20
WHICH TEACH THEE NCW TC PLEASE HIS EYES		297	HERODIAS	11
SINCE ALL THAT AGE DOTH TEACH, IS ILL		321	CHILDEHOOD	19
TEACH AGE, THE HOLY WAY.		310	THE SEED	64
TEACH BCTH MINE EYES ANC FEET TC MCVE		318	THE ASS	15
AND TEACH US CUTY, I WILL SEE		278	THE STARRE	11
TEACHEST				
BUT WHAT THOU BIDST, ANC SHEW'ST, AND TEACHEST ME.		321	HIDDN TRSR	32
TEACHING				
TEACHING MY YEARS		186	PASSION	55
TEAR				
CNE HEARTY TEAR.		186	PASSION	49
WHAT (O GCO) BUT A SILENT TEAR		320	RGNRTN	9
WHERE THE STARV'C EARTH GROANS FCR CNE TEAR.		296	JESUS WP A	16
OF MY OWN FRAILTY DROPT DCWN MANY A TEAR		247	I WALKT	31
WHAT (O GCD) BUT A SILENT TEAR.		341	THE FEAST	72
TEARE				
NCR DCST THOU SPEND CNE TEARE IN VAIN, FOR STILL		158	THE LAMPE	17
DID TEARE THY HEART.		185	PASSION	11
PERHAPS THAT TEARE		173	CONTENT	15
A SILENT TEARE CAN PIERCE THY THRCNE		167	THE CALL	78
TEARES				
IN SIGHES, AND TEARES.		164	THE CALL	2
THE GLASSE WITH TEARES YOU FILL.		165	THE CALL	27
AND WHY THESE TEARES APPEARE		165	THE CALL	31
AS NCW PRCDUCE THESE TEARES		165	THE CALL	35
BY THESE SOIL'D TEARES.		170	COME, COME	7
IN THY CWN PRECIOUS, SAVING TEARES.		184	PASSION	9
THOU FALL'ST IN TEARES, AND WEEP'ST FCR THY MISTAKE.		160	THE SHOWRE	6
THE MUSICK OF HER TEARES		141	RGNRTN	61
TEARS				
IN SMILES, AND TEARS		186	PASSION	56
AND LET THIS GRAIN WHICH HERE IN TEARS I SOW		191	THE MATCH	39
FCR TEARS ARE NOT THINE OWN. IF THOU GIV'ST WORDS		194	RLS + LSNS	68
WASH CFF WITH TEARS, ANC GET THY MASTERS HANC.		195	RLS + LSNS	120
ALL SAD WITH TEARS, WHICH LIKE WARM SUMMER RAIN		268	ASCN-DAY A	52
I SEE THAT MORNING IN THY CONVERTS TEARS		267	ASCN-DAY A	19
BUT WITH TRUE TEARS WASH OFF YCUR MIRE.		266	VAIN WITS	4
TEARS AND THESE FLAMES WILL SCCN GROW KINDE		266	VAIN WITS	5
TEARS CLEANSE AND SUPPLE WITHCLT FAIL		266	VAIN WITS	8
IN TEARS TO YOU, IN FIRE TO ME.		266	VAIN WITS	13
IS WATER'C BY THEIR TEARS, AS FLCWERS ARE FEC		280	PALM-TREE	22
SC IN SIGHS ANC UNSEEN TEARS		281	JOY	27
OF TEARS, AND MILK, THE FOOD CF ALL.		209	THE BURIAL	4
A SPRING RAN BY, I TOLD HER TEARS		208	REPENTANCE	44
HER EARNEST SIGHES PROCLR'D HER TEARS		223	TEMPEST	15
HCW SHRIL ARE SILENT TEARS. WHEN SIN GOT HEAC		213	ADMISSION	1
AND RCCKS HAVE TEARS)		213	ADMISSION	6
WE SEND TEARS TO THE PLACE		213	ADMISSION	20
O HEAR. YET NCT MY TEARS ALONE		214	ADMISSION	29
A FLOUD THAT CROWNS BCTH TEARS, AND GRONES		214	ADMISSION	31
THEN CAST HER BLOUD, ANC TEARS UPON THY BOOK		237	CONSTLATN	41
(FOR TEARS ALCNE ARE OFTEN FOUL)		242	MISERY	108
IT RAIN'D ABOUT HIM BLOUD AND TEARS, BUT HE		232	THE WORLD	29
SC THRIVE I BEST, 'TWIXT JOYES, AND TEARS		227	LV + DSPLN	17
FOR THEE MY WORDS, MY TEARS DC GUSH		228	PILGRIMAGE	14
O HEALING TEARS. THE TEARS OF LCVE		298	JESUS WP B	10
O HEALING TEARS. THE TEARS OF LOVE		298	JESUS WP B	10
OF TEARS, AND NOT PROVOKE TO MCRE.		298	JESUS WP B	15
THEY WILL DRINK BLOOD, THAT DESPISE TEARS.		296	JESUS WP A	12

		PAGE	TITLE	LINE
TEARS	**(CON'T)**			
AND TLRN'D TO SMILES THE BEGGING TEARS		300	PROVIDENCE	5
BUT AS SHADES SFT OFF LIGHT, SO TEARS AND GRIEF		290	THE TIMBER	41
TEARS ONELY AND MY BLUSHES STILL		338	THE THRONE	10
WHEREFORE WITH TEARS (TEARS BY THEE SENT)		334	AGREEMENT	61
WHEREFORE WITH TEARS (TEARS BY THEE SENT)		334	AGREEMENT	61
MY SELF ALL TEARS, A WEEPING LAKE.		328	ANGUISH	12
BID THY POOR ASS (WITH TEARS I CRAVE)		329	TEARS	11
ALL PEARL'D WITH TEARS, AND MAY		310	THE SEED	63
AS THOU IN TEARS DOST, REST IN DEW.		303	ST MARY MN	4
IS'T JUST TO JUDGE HER FAITHFLL TEARS		305	ST MARY MN	65
THIS DUSKY STATE CF SIGHS AND TEARS		303	ST MARY MN	11
LEARN MARYS ART OF TEARS, AND THEN		305	ST MARY MN	47
CALL'D FORTH THY TEARS, WHICH RAN IN LIVE		305	ST MARY MN	42
SOME FEW TRUE TEARS, AND THOSE SHED FOR		342	OBSEQUIES	3
LIKE TEARS DOTH SHEW		340	THE FEAST	23
PRAISE SOIL'D WITH TEARS, AND TEARS AGAIN		345	THE WREATH	10
PRAISE SOIL'D WITH TEARS, AND TEARS AGAIN		345	THE WREATH	10
WHERE CLOUDLESS QUIRES SING WITHOUT TEARS		345	THE WREATH	18
TEL				
WHICH NOW CAN TEL THEE NEWS.		243	THE SAP	10
AND KINDLY TEL ME, I AM EARTH		240	MISERY	30
TELL				
SLCH NUMBERS TELL THEIR DAYS, WHOSE SPIRITS BE		281	JOY	9
IT NEVER OPENS, I CAN TELL.		277	COCK-CRWNG	28
CAN TELL THEE WHERE A HEART IS BROKEN.		266	INTRO. 2	32
O WHO WILL TELL ME, WHERE		323	THE NIGHT	13
WILL TELL THEE SO, SWEET SAVICUR THOU DIDST DYE.		198	SCRIPTURES	14
TELL YOUTH, AND BEAUTY THEY MUST ROT		189	RESOLVE	11
AND HUMBLE DUST, TELL THEN DEAR FLESH		201	THE CHECK	11
TELL US THE WORLD IS BRAVE		193	THRS A TYE	14
I CANNOT TELL		142	DEATH	6
O TELL ME WHENCE THAT JOY DOTH SPRING		346	THE QUEER	1
TELL ME, O TELL WHO DID THEE BRING		346	THE QUEER	9
TELL ME, O TELL WHO DID THEE BRING		346	THE QUEER	9
THY NEXT EFFECTS NO TONGUE CAN TELL.		348	HOLY BIBLE	35
TELLS				
AND FILL'D WITH JOY, THY GOODNESS TELLS.		336	PSALM 65	12
TEMPER				
KEEP THOU THY TEMPER, MIX NOT WITH EACH CLAY.		192	RLS + LSNS	32
AND BULRUSH FETTERS TEMPER HIS SHORT HOUR.		224	TEMPEST	50
TEMPERS				
I STILE MEER TEMPERS, WHICH TAKE PLACE		242	MISERY	87
TEMPESTS				
BUT WANDER'D UNDER TEMPESTS ALL THE YEAR		244	MT. OLV. B	12
LIKE OTHER TEMPESTS BY.		234	MUTINIE	25
AND TEMPESTS HAVE MORE IN THEM THAN A SHOWR.		222	TEMPEST	4
AS THOSE CLEAR HEIGHTS WHICH ABOVE TEMPESTS SHINE.		281	JOY	16
CALMES, TEMPESTS, LIGHT, AND DARKNES BY HIS MEANS.		194	RLS + LSNS	94
HERE UNDER CLOUDS, WHERE STORMES, AND TEMPESTS BLAST		158	MANS FALL	2
BREEDS TEMPESTS IN MY BLOUD.		176	THE STORM	16
TEMPESTS AND WINDES, AND WINTER-NIGHTS		309	THE SEED	26
OF TEMPESTS CAN NO MORE DISTURB THY EASE.		289	THE TIMBER	18
TEMPESTUOUS				
A MEER TEMPESTUOUS DEBATE.		344	QUICKNESS	8
TEMPLE				
WHO IN THY HOLY TEMPLE DWELLS		336	PSALM 65	11
I SEE THE TEMPLE IN THY PILLAR REAR'D		330	JACOBS PLW	1
THUS IS THE SOLEMN TEMPLE SUNK AGEN		331	JACOBS PLW	35
TO SEE THE TEMPLE, BUT WAS SHOWN		151	THE SEARCH	15
AND SOYL THY TEMPLE WITH A SINFUL RUST.		216	DRESSING	8
TEMPLES				
TO CROWN HIS TEMPLES. SHAL DREAMS BE HIS LAW.		224	TEMPEST	52
I WILL NOT FOR THY TEMPLES BRING		345	THE WREATH	7
TEMPORAL				
NOR FOR A TEMPORAL SELF-END		316	MEN OF WAR	15
TEMPTATIONS				
AND HIGH TEMPTATIONS OF HELL.		152	THE SEARCH	58
TEMPTING				
WERE ONCE SINS LOOSE AND TEMPTING SPIES		305	ST MARY MN	58
TEMPTS				
SHE TEMPTS TO INCEST, THOU TO BLOOD.		297	HERODIAS	20
FRESH DOTAGE TEMPTS, OR OLD USURPS HIS WILL.		161	DSTROCTION	16
TENANT				
TENANT FOR YEARES, AND CENTURIES		142	DEATH	4
FOR ONE, I AM THY TENANT HERE.		191	THE MATCH	21
TENANTS				
BEG, THOU WOULDST TAKE THY TENANTS RENT.		264	INTRO. 1	14
TENDER				
KILL AND CURE THE TENDER FLOWERS		281	JOY	18
TENDS				
IT TENDS NOT THITHER, IF IT DOTH, WHY THEN		243	THE SAP	5
TENT				
THOSE WHITE DAYES, DROVE HOME TO THE TENT		151	THE SEARCH	26
IN ABR'HAMS TENT THE WINGED GUESTS		149	RELIGION	13
FIX'D TO A TENT, DESCEND AND SHROWD		315	DWELLNG-PL	6
CALM AND UNHAUNTED AS IS THY DARK TENT		324	THE NIGHT	38
TERAH				
WHEN TERAH, NAHOR, HARAN, ABRAM, LOT		306	RAIN-BOW	5
TERM'D				
THAT I TERM'D THEN MEER BONDS AND THRALL		311	FAIR+YONG	8

		PAGE	TITLE	LINE
TERM'D (CON'T)				
THE PASSAGE IS, HE TERM'D A GRATE	. . . . .	207	REPENTANCE	9
TERRIBLE				
AND TERRIBLE, THY JUSTICE BRINGS	. . . . .	336	PSALM 65	14
TERROUR				
TERROUR, AND MIGHT	. . . . .	229	LAW + GOSP	6
TEST				
WITHIN IT SELF AN OUTWARD TEST.	. . . .	309	THE SEED	42
TH'APPLOUSE				
'TIS NOT TH'APPLOUSE, AND FEAT	. . . .	226	RETIREMENT	30
TH'EARTH				
BIRDS SING, BEASTS FEED, FISH LEAP, AND TH'EARTH STANDS FAST		194	RLS + LSNS	88
TH'ELECT				
AND GRONE TOO. WHY TH'ELECT	. . . . .	186	NO DO THEY	4
TH'EXTENT				
REDUC'D TH'EXTENT OF WORKS OF FAITH, SO MADE	. . .	159	MANS FALL	31
TH'LAST				
BUT, TH'LAST MORE HEAVY THEN THE NIGHT	. . .	141	RGNRTN	68
TH'ONE				
IN TH'ONE LATE PAINES	. . . . .	139	RGNRTN	31
THANKFUL				
THE THANKFUL EARTH UNLOCKS HER SELF, AND BLENDS	. .	156	ISAACS M.	59
AND THEN BE THANKFUL, O ADMIRE HIS WAYS	. . .	195	RLS + LSNS	99
O GIVE ME THEN A THANKFUL HEART. A HEART	. . .	213	ADMISSION	25
THANKLES				
A THANKLES FEEDER IS A THIEF, HIS FEAST	. . .	195	RLS + LSNS	101
THANKLESS				
THUS THOU ALL DAY A THANKLESS WEED DOES DRESS	. .	198	UNPRFTBLNS	16
JUST AT HIS MOUTH, THAT THANKLESS HIVE	. . .	300	PROVIDENCE	11
THANKS				
THY LOVE CLAIMS HIGHEST THANKS, MY SIN	. . .	329	TEARS	13
NOT WORTH OUR THANKS. IS LIFE A GIFT	. . .	200	NTVTY 2	7
A PLENTEOUS WAY (THANKS TO THAT HOLY ONE)	. . .	159	MANS FALL	22
TRUE THANKS TO THEE, BEFORE I SLEEP.	. . .	348	HOLY BIBLE	4
THATCH				
THIS MADE THE ANGEL CALL AT REEDS AND THATCH	. .	238	SHEPHEARDS	27
THAW				
PRONOUNC'D WITH THUNDER, AND THY THREATS DID THAW	.	229	LAW + GOSP	3
YOUR HEARTS SHALL THAW. WHEN ANGELS HERE	. .	291	THE JEWS	4
AND FOUL RECORDS WHICH THAW	. . .	310	THE SEED	56
THEAMS				
SO SOME STRANGE THOUGHTS TRENSCEND OUR WONTED THEAMS	.	271	ALL GONE	27
THEEVES				
IN FEARE OF THEEVES.	. . . . .	232	THE WORLD	35
THEMES				
AND BOUNDLESS EMPYREAN THEMES	. . . .	346	THE QUEER	6
WHAT SUBLIME TRUTHS, AND WHOLFSOME THEMES	. .	344	WATER-FALL	27
THEMSELVES				
THE HEAVENS THEMSELVES, THOUGH FAIR AND BRIGHT	.	208	REPENTANCE	65
WHO SAINT THEMSELVES, THEY ARE NO SAINTS.	. .	306	ST MARY MN	72
(THOUGH OF THEMSELVES BUT A SAD BLUBBER'D STORY)	.	290	THE TIMBER	42
THEMSELVES AND OTHERS, I CONSENT AND RUN	. .	324	THE NIGHT	45
BUT GRAVELY CAST THEMSELVES AWAY.	. . .	322	CHILDEHOOD	30
THER'S				
THER'S ONE SUN MORE STRUNG ON MY BEAD OF DAYS.	.	195	RLS + LSNS	118
THER'S NOT A WIND CAN STIR	. . .	171	COME, COME	11
THICK				
AS HE THAT IN SOME CAVES THICK DAMP	. . .	178	SILENCE	5
ALL'S IN DEEP SLEEP, AND NIGHT. THICK DARKNES LYES	.	197	CORRUPTION	37
I HAVE DESERV'D A THICK, EGYPTIAN DAMP	. .	188	RELAPSE	13
AND LEADER THROUGH THICK DEATH AND NIGHT.	. .	326	ABELS BLOD	32
THICK BUSIE CLOUDS DID MULTIPLY	. . .	333	AGREEMENT	39
CEDARS IN LEBANON, IN WHOSE THICK BOUGHS	. .	286	PSALM 104	46
IN WHOSE THICK SHADES AND SILENCE EACH WILDE BEAST	.	286	PSALM 104	54
WHERE THROUGH THICK PANGS, HIGH AGONIES	. .	310	THE SEED	65
IS GROWN THICK DARKNESS, AND THY BREAD, A STONE.	.	224	TEMPEST	55
LIKE A THICK MIDNIGHT-FOG MOV'D THERE SO SLOW	.	231	THE WORLD	17
THICKEN				
WHERE SHADOWES THICKEN, AND THE CLOUD	. . .	143	DEATH	12
THICKEST				
THROUGH THICKEST NIGHTS, THOUGH THEN THE SUN BE FAR	.	196	RLS + LSNS	137
THIEF				
A THANKLES FEEDER IS A THIEF, HIS FEAST	. . .	195	RLS + LSNS	101
THIN				
WHAT THIN EJECTIONS	. . . . .	172	MIDNIGHT	14
IN THOSE THIN CELS COULD LIE	. . .	239	SHEPHEARDS	32
A FAIR, WHITE PAGE OF THIN	. . .	310	THE SEED	58
THY SPACES BUT THIN AND NARROW BE	. . .	338	DEATH B	18
THING				
AS A TRYED THING	. . . . .	338	DEATH B	7
BUT FOR ONE THING, THOUGH PURCHAS'D ONCE BEFORE.	.	321	HIDDN TRSR	34
O. 'TIS AN EASIE THING	. . . . .	329	ANGUISH	13
EACH THING TURNS SCRIBE AND REGISTER	. . .	314	THE STONE	43
EVEN WHAT WAS DONE BEFORE, AND NO NEW THING.	. .	320	HIDDN TRSR	2
I DOE EACH THING	. . .	182	CHRFLNESS	2
LORD. WHAT A BUSIE, RESTLES THING	. . .	161	PURSUITE	1
GO, GO, SEEK OUT SOME GREENER THING	. . .	205	IDLE VERSE	21
'TIS SUCH A BLISSFUL THING, THAT STILL	. . .	320	RGNRTN	7
MY WALKE A MONSTROUS, MOUNTAIN'D THING	. . .	139	RGNRTN	20
FOR NO THING CAN TO NOTHING FALL BUT STILL	. .	145	RSRCTN +IM	25

	PAGE	TITLE	LINE
THING (CCN'T)			
'TIS SUCH A BLISSFUL THING, THAT STILL	345	QUICKNESS	13
ON EACH GREEN THING. THEN SLEPT (WELL FED)	347	THE BOOK	17
AND THEN RETURNS, AND FROM THE WOMBE OF THINGS	145	RSRCTN +IM	27
AND COURSE OF THINGS	146	RSRCTN +IM	54
ESTEEM'C (VAINE THINGS) OF TWC WHOLE ELEMENTS	144	RSRCTN +IM	13
THREE THINGS I'DE HAVE, MY SOLLES CHIEF HEALTH	148	DAY OF JDG	39
THE SKINNE, AND SHELL OF THINGS	153	THE SEARCH	81
SC SHOULD WE TOC. ALL THINGS TEACH US TO DIE	201	THE CHECK	20
THINGS HERE WERE STRANGE UNTO HIM. SWET, AND TILL	196	CORRUPTION	9
YET HAVE I KNOWNE THY SLIGHTEST THINGS	166	THE CALL	50
FCR THINGS THUS CENTER'C, WITHOUT BEAMES, OR ACTION	183	THRS A TYE	5
THINGS CISTANT DOTH UNITE	183	THRS A TYE	10
ALL THINGS I SEE	179	SILENCE	30
BIRDS, BEASTS, ALL THINGS	176	MRNG-WTCH	14
WHEN ALL THINGS HERE TO THISTLES TURN	319	THE ASS	49
ALL THINGS WITH LIFE, BEFORE WHOSE EYES	314	THE STONE	26
AND PRESENT THINGS FINDE MEN MOST KINDE.	318	THE ASS	6
AND MINDE THOSE THINGS I CANNCT SEE.	318	THE ASS	18
THE FINEST THINGS THAT ARE, TC SEE.	312	FAIR+YONG	34
THE THINGS ABCVE	327	RIGHTSNESS	14
SHALL (WHEN THEY RISE) SPEAK BETTER THINGS	326	ABELS BLOD	40
DCTH ALL THINGS WAKE, AND WHERE ALL MIX AND TYRE	324	THE NIGHT	44
MAKE ALL THINGS NEW. AND WITHOUT END.	335	JUDGEMENT	46
KING CF SALVATION. BY STRANGE THINGS	336	PSALM 65	13
ALL THINGS IN BEING) THEY CONSUME AND MOURN.	287	PSALM 104	78
INNUMERABLE, CREEPING THINGS BCTH SMALL	286	PSALM 104	70
ALL THINGS THAT BE, PRAISE HIM, AND HAD	288	THE BIRD	11
THESE THINGS ARE KIN TO HIM, AND MUST BE HAD	236	CONSTLATN	23
OF SOME MEAN THINGS WHICH HERE BELOW RESIDE	245	MAN	2
THE STAIDNESS OF THESE THINGS TC MAN. FOR THESE	245	MAN	9
I'TH' FACE OF THINGS	247	I WALKT	9
HID IN THESE LOW THINGS SNARES TO GAIN HIS HEART	223	TEMPEST	23
ALL THINGS HERE SHEW HIM HEAVEN, WATERS THAT FALL	223	TEMPEST	25
AND SEEST ALL THINGS JUST AS THEY BE.	207	REPENTANCE	22
REACHETH AS WELL THINGS OF DEJECTION	210	FAITH	3
OF THINGS DID FLIE.	210	FAITH	28
AND THUS, AT FIRST, WHEN THINGS WERE RUDE	218	HOLY COMM.	6
YET, SEEING ALL THINGS THAT SUBSIST AND BE	278	THE STARRE	9
TO RAISE IT TO THE TRUTH AND LIGHT OF THINGS	248	I WALKT	40
WHO ART IN ALL THINGS, THOUGH INVISIBLY.	248	I WALKT	54
THINK			
SHALL THY OWN IMAGE THINK IT MUCH	276	COCK-CRWNG	15
ILL THY BREST WITH HOME. THINK CN THY DREAM.	276	PROFFER	45
AND RCT, CESCEND NOT HERE, NOR THINK TO STAY	275	PROFFER	17
THINK YOU THESE LCNGING EYES	275	PROFFER	19
O THINK ON THIS, THY SCN DID BLEED.	208	REPENTANCE	60
I WOULD BOTH THINK, AND JUDGE I DID NOT LCVE THEE.	230	LAW + GOSP	40
WHO THINK THEM BRAVE	232	THE WORLD	43
TO THINK, HE SHOULD BE SO LONG VAINLY LEAD.	290	THE TIMBER	40
THE WORLDS LOV'D WISDCM (FCR THE WORLDS FRIENDS THINK	320	HIDDN TRSR	15
FOR THOUGH SOME THINK, THOU SHIN'ST BUT TC RESTRAIN	307	RAIN-BOW	39
I DARE NOT THINK SUCH VILLANY.	316	MEN OF WAR	14
WHICH SCME THINK DEAD, SHALL ALL AT ONCE	314	THE STONE	39
HCW MANY HOURS DO'ST THINK 'TILL CAY.	178	EVNG-WTCH	10
BUT STRAIT I THINK (THOUGH FAR)	171	COME, COME	13
PERHAPS SCME THINK A TOMBE	171	COME, COME	21
THINK'ST			
THOU THINK'ST IT GOOD TC TARRY WHERE THOU ART	157	BRT. CHRCH	14
THINKE			
SHALL I THEN THINKE SUCH PROVIDENCE WILL BE	144	RSRCTN +IM	15
AND WHAT WE THINKE	163	MT. OLVS A	27
THIRD			
THE THIRD GLAD DAY THROUGH TWC SAD NIGHTS.	295	PALM-SUNDY	33
THIRST			
TC FILL MY BOTTLE, THEN I DIE WITH THIRST.	290	THE TIMBER	48
BUT MEET TO QUENCH HIS LONGINGS, AND THY THIRST.	194	RLS + LSNS	80
THUS CAL AND THIRST FCR DEW.	243	THE SAP	4
THIRSTIE			
AND THIRSTIE BRICK MUST BE (SAIC I)	234	MUTINIE	13
AND SCMETHING COOLD THE PARCH'C, AND THIRSTIE ISLE	156	ISAACS M.	58
THISTLES			
THOU WOULDST TO WEEDS, AND THISTLES QUITE DISPERSE	221	AFFLICTION	15
WHEN ALL THINGS HERE TO THISTLES TURN	319	THE ASS	49
THORN			
ALL WAS A THORN, CR WEED	196	CORRUPTION	10
AND SMOOTH WITHOUT A THCRNE.	166	THE CALL	71
FIGS CN A THORNE, FLOWRES ON A WEED.	208	REPENTANCE	70
THORNS			
CROWN'D THEE WITH THORNS, AND BCW'D THE KNEE	317	MEN OF WAR	31
WILL NOTHING YIELD BUT THCRNS TC WOUND THY HEAC.	296	JESUS WP A	18
WHO KISSETH THORNS, WILL HURT HIS FACE	321	CHILDEHOOD	13
THORNS IN THE BEDS	327	RIGHTSNESS	26
WHICH THORNS, NOT ROSES WCRE.	345	THE WREATH	8
THORNY			
O THORNY CROWN	341	THE FEAST	61
THOU			
THOU ART MY CHEAR	340	THE FEAST	41
HOW DCST THOU FLYE	340	THE FEAST	43
WHY THOU CIDST BLEED	341	THE FEAST	77

		PAGE	TITLE	LINE
THOU	(CCN'T)			
BRIEFLY, CUE AS THCU WOLLC'ST EE CONE UNTO,	. . .	196	RLS + LSNS	139
ALL BLT PRELUCES THY ENC. THOL ART THE MAN	. .	195	RLS + LSNS	107
BUT PERFECT ALL BEFORE THOU SLEEP'ST, THEN SAY	.	195	RLS + LSNS	117
WHERE THOU MAY'ST SLEEP WHCLE ACES, LIFES POCR FLCWR	.	195	RLS + LSNS	123
AND THOU UNRAK'ST THY FIRE, THCSE SPARKS WILL BRING	.	195	RLS + LSNS	130
PEACH, PEACE. I BLUSH TC HEAR THEE. WHEN THOL ART	.	201	THE CHECK	1
THOU KNEW'ST BUT THY CWN GOOD.	. . .	202	THE CHECK	39
BLT THOL SLEEP'ST CN. WHER'S NCW THY PROTESTATICN	.	202	THE CHECK	43
WHEN FIRST THCU DIST EVEN FROM THE GRAVE	. .	202	DSRDR + FR	1
THOU GOTST MY HEART, ANC THOUGH HERE TOST	. .	202	DSRDR + FR	6
UP WHERE THOU ART, AMCNGST THY TIRE	. . .	204	DSRDR + FR	48
THAT SEED, WHICH THOU	. . . .	204	DSRDR + FR	53
YET, IF THOU WILT, THCU CANST MAKE CLEAN.	. .	199	NTVTY 1	24
BUT SINCE THOU DIDST IN CNE SWEET GLANCE SLRVEY	.	198	UNPRFTBLNS	7
BUT, AH, MY GOC. WHAT FRUIT HAS THCU CF THIS.	. .	198	UNPRFTBLNS	13
THUS THCU ALL DAY A THANKLESS WEEC CCES DRESS	.	198	UNPRFTBLNS	16
YET, IF THOU WILT, THCU CANST MAKE CLEAN.	. .	199	NTVTY 1	24
MY GOC, HCW GRACIOUS ART THOU. I HAD SLIPT	. .	188	RELAPSE	1
CEASE THOU THY WRATH.	. . . .	188	RELAPSE	12
IF THCU WOULDST THITHER, LINGER NCT	. . .	189	RESOLVE	9
THOU CANST NOT CHANGE.	. . .	187	NO DO THEY	20
O BROCK IT NOT. WHY WILT THOU STOP	. . .	188	NO DO THEY	37
SURE, THOU WILT JCY TC SEE	. . .	188	NO DO THEY	39
O THOL. THAT CANST NOT WISH MY SCULS DAMNATICN	.	190	THE MATCH	16
LORD JESU. THOU DIDST BCW THY BLESSED HEAD	. .	191	THE MATCH	31
GIVE HIM THY FIRST THCUGHTS THEN, SO SHALT THOU KEEP	.	191	RLS + LSNS	5
KEEP THCU THY TEMPER, MIX NOT WITH EACH CLAY.	. .	192	RLS + LSNS	32
IF PRIEST, ANC PECPLE CHANGE, KEEP THOU THY GRCUND.	.	193	RLS + LSNS	44
SEEK NOT THE SAME STEPS WITH THE CROWD, STICK THCU	.	193	RLS + LSNS	49
AND OAK DCTH KNOW I AM. CANST THOU NOT SING.	.	192	RLS + LSNS	16
AND THOL ART SURE TC PRCSPER ALL THE DAY.	. .	192	RLS + LSNS	18
UNTIL THOU HAS A BLESSING, THEN RESIGNE	. .	192	RLS + LSNS	20
OTHERS WERE TYM'D AND TRAIN'D UP TO'T BUT THCU	.	156	ISAACS M.	67
THOU HACST NO POMPOUS TRAIN, NCR ANTIK CROWD	.	154	ISAACS M.	21
YET, HACST THOU NOBLER GUESTS. ANGELS DID WIND	.	155	ISAACS M.	25
AND NCW THOU KNEWEST HER COMING, IT WAS TIME	.	155	ISAACS M.	43
THIS BRCUGHT THEE FORTH, WHERE NCW THOU DIDST UNCRESS	.	155	ISAACS M.	47
BUT THOU WERT SO, E'RE TIME HIS SNOW COULD SPEC.	.	156	ISAACS M.	70
THOU THINK'ST IT GOOD TC TARRY WHERE THOU ART	.	157	BRT. CHRCH	14
THOU THINK'ST IT GOOD TC TARRY WHERE THOU ART	.	157	BRT. CHRCH	14
AS THCU DISSOLV'ST TO THEM, ANC THEY DISTILL	.	158	THE LAMPE	18
AND WHERE THOU MAC'ST AN END, THERE I'LE BEGIN.	.	158	THE LAMPE	26
YET, BURN'ST THOU HERE, A FULL CAY, WHILE I SPEND	.	157	THE LAMPE	5
THESE FLAMES, AS THOU DCST THINE TO ME, I WATCH	.	157	THE LAMPE	7
BLT STILL THOU DOEST CUT-GOE ME, I CAN SEE	.	158	THE LAMPE	9
DEVOTION STILL CN WING, THEN, THCU DOST WEEPE	.	158	THE LAMPE	13
STILL AS THOU BURN'ST, AND THE WARME DROPPINCS CREEPE	.	158	THE LAMPE	14
NCR DCST THOU SPEND ONE TEARE IN VAIN, FOR STILL	.	158	THE LAMPE	17
THOU FALL'ST IN TEARES, AND WEEP'ST FOR THY MISTAKE.	.	160	THE SHOWRE	6
YET, IF AS THCU DOEST MELT, AND WITH THY TRAINE	.	160	THE SHOWRE	13
HACST THOU	. . . .	160	DSTRQCTION	5
YET, HADST THCU CLIPT MY WINGS, WHEN COFFIN'C IN	.	161	DSTRQCTION	17
AND SAVED THAT LIGHT, WHICH FREELY THOU	. .	161	DSTRQCTION	19
I SHOULD HAVE SPURN'C, AND SAIC THOU DIDST FCRBEARE.	.	161	DSTRQCTION	22
BUT NCW SINCE THOU DIDST BLESSE	. . .	161	DSTRQCTION	24
JUST SO IT IS IN CEATH. BUT THCU	. . .	143	DEATH	27
'TIS SO. BUT AS THOU SAWEST THAT NIGHT	. .	143	DEATH	15
THY BLOUD TO ICE, AND THOU MUST STAY	. .	142	DEATH	3
HCW WILT THOU BROCK'T.	. . .	142	DEATH	5
THOU CNLY FAL'ST TO BE REFIN'D AGAINE	. .	145	RSRCTN +IM	50
AND AS THOU SAW'ST, I IN A THCUGHT COULD GOE	.	146	RSRCTN +IM	57
SC SHALT THOU THEN WITH ME	. . .	146	RSRCTN +IM	61
WHEN THCU SHALT SPEND THY SACREC STORE	. .	147	DAY OF JDG	9
BUT THOL A CHOSEN SACRIFICE WERT GIVEN	. .	154	ISAACS M.	5
WHERE, AS THCU GREWST, IT MULTIPLI'D AND SHIN'D	.	154	ISAACS M.	9
HAD'ST NE'R AN OATH, NOR COMPLEMENT. THOU WERT	.	154	ISAACS M.	13
AN ODDE DULL SUTOR, HADST THOU BUT THE ART	.	154	ISAACS M.	14
OF THESE CUR CAYES, THOL COULCST HAVE COYN'D THEE TWENTY	.	154	ISAACS M.	15
NAY THOU THY SELFE, MY GOD, IN FIRE	. . .	149	RELIGION	17
DCEST THOU THEREFCRE CLC TREATIES WAVE	. .	149	RELIGION	23
THOUGH THOU HAST PROMIS'D THEY SHCULD STAY	. .	149	RELIGION	27
WHEN THOU SHALT MAKE THE CLOUDS THY SEATE	.	147	DAY OF JDG	21
THOUGH				
THAT PILL, THOUGH BITTER, IS MCST DEARE	. .	147	DAY OF JDG	35
THOUGH THOU HAST PROMIS'D THEY SHOULD STAY	. .	149	RELIGION	27
THOUGH FAIRE	. . . .	153	THE SEARCH	82
THOUGH OF OUR SELVES, IS SO MUCH OUT OF DATE,	.	154	ISAACS M.	3
HIS PASSIVE CCTTAGE, WHICH (THCUGH LAID ASIDE)	.	145	RSRCTN +IM	45
(THOUGH 'TWAS MID-DAY)	. . . .	141	RGNRTN	75
AND ON SURE HCPES, THOUGH LONG, DID FEAST.	.	143	DEATH	22
THUS SOAR'D THY SCUL, WHO (THCUGH YOUNG) DIDST INHERIT	.	156	ISAACS M.	63
THOUGH DEAD, AND SICK	. . . .	191	THE MATCH	40
THOU GOTST MY HEART, ANC THOUGH HERE TOST	. .	202	DSRDR + FR	6
THROUGH THICKEST NIGHTS, THOUGH THEN THE SUN BE FAR	.	196	RLS + LSNS	137
THOU SHALT NOT LOSE ONE MITE. THOUGH WATERS STRAY	.	193	RLS + LSNS	65
THOUGH THEN (THUS CRUMM'D) I STRAY	. .	181	BURIALL	25
BUT I WILL BE MY CWN DEATHS-HEAD. AND THOUGH	. .	183	THRS A TYE	21
SUCH, THOUGH NO PROUD, NOR FULL	. . .	173	CONTENT	9
THOUGH RED AS HE.	. . . .	175	THE STORM	4

	PAGE	TITLE	LINE
THOUGH (CON'T)			
IS LIKE A CLOUDED STARRE, WHOSE BEAMES THOUGH SEC	177	MRNG-WTCH	25
THAT CURTAIN'D GRAVE, THOUGH SLEEP, LIKE ASHES, HIDE	177	MRNG-WTCH	32
BUT STRAIT I THINK (THOUGH FAR)	171	COME, COME	13
THY GLORIOUS, BRIGHT ASCENSION (THOUGH REMOV'D	267	ASCN-DAY A	5
AND PUT FORTH THUS, THOUGH LORD, BEFORE	264	INTRO. 1	7
FROM THEE IT SHIN'D, THOUGH HERE IT BURNS.	265	INTRO. 2	4
WHO ART IN ALL THINGS, THOUGH INVISIBLY.	248	I WALKT	54
SOME KINDE HERBS HERE, THOUGH LOW AND FAR	281	THE FAVOUR	7
ANOTHER MIRTH, A MIRTH THOUGH OVERCAST	281	JOY	14
THOUGH WITH NO LILIE, STAY WITH ME.	277	COCK-CRWNG	48
THOUGH THY CLOSE COMMERCE NOUGHT AT ALL IMBARRS	278	THE STARRE	5
THOUGH THEN SOME BOAST THAT FIRE EACH DAY	272	WHT SUNDAY	13
FOR THOUGH THOU DOEST THAT GREAT LIGHT LOCK	273	WHT SUNDAY	21
FOR, THOUGH WE HOURLY BREATH DECAYS	273	WHT SUNDAY	41
THOUGH SEEN AT ONCE, WERE BLACK TO THEE.	272	WHT SUNDAY	2
THOUGH SICK AND SPENT	275	PROFFER	20
THE WIND, THOUGH GATHER'D IN THY FIST	239	MISERY	5
AND KNIT ME TO THEE, THAT THOUGH IN THIS VALE	234	MUTINIE	19
THOUGH IN THIS DESERT I WERE WHOLY SHUT	234	MUTINIE	30
WHERE, THOUGH THE GLORY DIFFER IN EACH STAR	236	CONSTLATN	31
AND GODS OWN LODGING (THOUGH HE COULD NOT LACK)	238	SHEPHEARDS	29
THERE IS AT ALL TIMES (THOUGH SHUT UP) IN YOU	244	THE SAP	39
AND THOUGH THOU DOST ME FULLNES GIVE	228	PILGRIMAGE	22
THOUGH THEN THOU ART	215	PRAISE	33
LET HIM (THOUGH POOR)	215	PRAISE	54
AND THOUGH HERE BORN, YET IS ACQUAINTED	212	DAWNING	35
AND THOUGH (WHILE HERE) OF FORCE I MUST	212	DAWNING	39
AND IN MY FLESH, THOUGH VILE, AND LOW	212	DAWNING	41
THESE FIND THEE OUT, AND THOUGH OUR SINS	213	ADMISSION	21
THOUGH HE KNOWS THESE, AND HATH MORE OF HIS OWN	224	TEMPEST	38
SINKS TO A DEAD OBLIVIOUN, AND THOUGH ALL	224	TEMPEST	42
THIS I BELIEVED. AND THOUGH A FRIEND	207	REPENTANCE	15
THOUGH THEN ALL SINNERS I EXCEED	208	REPENTANCE	59
THE HEAVENS THEMSELVES, THOUGH FAIR AND BRIGHT	208	REPENTANCE	65
WHEN I BEHOLD THEE, THOUGH MY LIGHT BE DIM	306	RAIN-BOW	15
WE SLIGHT AS OLD AND SOIL'D, THOUGH FRESH AND NEW.	306	RAIN-BOW	2
THOUGH BLOOD AND DRUNKENNESS MAKE BUT FOUL, FOUL WEATHER.	307	RAIN-BOW	26
WATER (THOUGH BOTH HEAVENS WINDOWS AND THE DEEP	307	RAIN-BOW	27
FOR THOUGH SOME THINK, THOU SHIN'ST BUT TO RESTRAIN	307	RAIN-BOW	39
AND MOONS, THOUGH FULL, WOULD GET THEM DOWN.	309	THE SEED	32
THOUGH HAWKS CAN PREY THROUGH STORMS AND WINDS	309	THE SEED	35
THOUGH LIFE BE DEAD, AND MY JOYS GONE.	311	THE SEED	89
BOASTS IT THIS DAY, THOUGH NOT IN STORY	315	DWELLNG-PL	4
BECKEN'D BY THEE, THOUGH HIGH AND FAR	315	DWELLNG-PL	8
GOD AND HIS CREATURES, THOUGH UNSEEN.	313	THE STONE	21
HIS RIGHTEOUS COURSE, THAT THOUGH HE KNOWS	314	THE STONE	30
(THOUGH ALL-SEEING AND ALL RIGHT)	314	THE STONE	33
WHOSE SUBSTANCE, THOUGH 'TIS HARD ENOUGH	314	THE STONE	50
TYE ME TO FAITH, THOUGH ABOVE REASON	318	THE ASS	19
OR THOUGH IT SHOULD BE LAWFUL, MAY	319	THE ASS	39
BUT HERE ON EARTH (THOUGH THOU HAST NEED)	316	MEN OF WAR	23
WHICH (THOUGH BUT SAND) KEEPS IN A CURBS WHOLE SEAS.	285	PSALM 104	26
THE BIRDS THEIR NESTS BUILD, THOUGH THE STORK DOTH CHOOSE	286	PSALM 104	47
TO LEND ME, THOUGH FROM FAR, ONE LOOK.	293	BEGGING B	4
WHAT THOUGH SOME CLOUDS DEFIANCE BID	294	BEGGING B	15
THOUGH I HAVE SPOIL'D, O SPOIL NOT THOU.	294	BEGGING B	17
AND THOUGH POOR STONES HAVE NEITHER SPEECH NOR TONGUE	288	THE BIRD	14
WHOSE LIGHT, THOUGH FETCHT AND BORROWED FROM FAR	288	THE BIRD	21
(THOUGH OF THEMSELVES BUT A SAD BLUBBER'D STORY)	290	THE TIMBER	42
BUT THOUGH THUS DEAD UNTO THE WORLD, AND CEAS'D	290	THE TIMBER	33
FOR THOUGH HE SHOULD FORSAKE THE WORLD, AND LIVE	290	THE TIMBER	37
FOR THOUGH DEATH CANNOT SO UNDO	299	JESUS WP B	34
WHAT THOU HAST DONE (BUT THOUGH MAN TOO	299	JESUS WP B	35
THAT, THOUGH THE CURE OF ALL MANS HARM	299	JESUS WP B	40
THEN LIKE THE PALM, THOUGH WRONG, I'LE BEAR	295	PALM-SUNDY	38
AND LOV'ST HIM, THOUGH HE WORKS THY WO.	298	JESUS WP B	25
(THOUGH PURCHAS'D WITH THY HEARTS DEAR TREASURE)	299	JESUS WP B	28
THIS LAND, THOUGH WITH THY HEARTS BLEST EXTRACT FED	296	JESUS WP A	17
HIS ART ADDS STILL (THOUGH HE BE DEAD)	297	HERODIAS	7
AND STONES, THOUGH SPEECHLESS, ARE NOT DUMB.	335	JUDGEMENT	16
THOUGH SINCE THY FIRST SAD ENTRANCE BY	338	DEATH B	1
THOUGH FLED FROM YOU, THEIR SPIRITS HIVE.	339	DEATH B	30
NOR MOAN I ONELY (THOUGH PROFUSE)	335	JUDGEMENT	31
O GOD. THOUGH MERCY BE IN THEE	335	JUDGEMENT	39
(THOUGH SINGLE VOICES ARE BUT LOW)	325	ABELS BLOD	8
BUT FOR ONE THING, THOUGH PURCHAS'D ONCE BEFORE.	321	HIDDN TRSR	34
WHICH STRONGLY OPERATE, THOUGH WITHOUT PAINS	320	HIDDN TRSR	22
BUT BLESSED JACOB, THOUGH THY SAD DISTRESS	331	JACOBS PLW	41
AND VOWS AND VISIONS, THOUGH HER FOES CRYE, NONE.	331	JACOBS PLW	34
LIKE CHRONIC PAINS, WHICH SURELY KILL, THOUGH SLOW.	327	RIGHTSNESS	30
THOUGH HIGH AND HAUGHTY MUST	328	RIGHTSNESS	46
THOU KNEW'ST AND SAW'ST THEM ALL AND THOUGH	347	THE BOOK	23
POOR DUST THOUGH DEAD	340	THE FEAST	35
THOUGHT			
CRYED DROSS FOR GOLD, AND NEVER THOUGHT	348	HOLY BIBLE	15
NOR ANY THOUGHT OF GREENNESS, LEAF OR BARK.	289	THE TIMBER	12
NOT A THOUGHT, THAT BREAKS MY REST	214	PRAISE	7
PAST THOUGHT OF HEART	215	PRAISE	34
BUT WITH THE THOUGHT OF HOME DO PINE.	228	PILGRIMAGE	20

	PAGE	TITLE	LINE
THOUGHT (CON'T)			
THOUGHT WITH MY SELF, THERE MIGHT BE OTHER SPRINGS	247	I WALKT	10
WITHOUT ONE THOUGHT OF DAY.	238	SHEPHEARDS	8
BUT NEVER THOUGHT THAT FIRE WOULD BURN	282	GARLAND	15
BUT A WHITE, CELESTIALL THOUGHT	169	RETREATE	6
A VIP'ROUS THOUGHT, SOME SYLLABLES ARE SWORDS.	194	RLS + LSNS	70
A PITCHER TOO SHE HAD, NOR THOUGHT IT MUCH	155	ISAACS M.	39
THE CHAST, AND LOVELY OBJECT OF THY THOUGHT.	155	ISAACS M.	30
GIVE FOR A HANDFULL, BUT A THOUGHT	160	DSTRQCTION	3
WE THOUGHT THE DAY THEN WAS NOT SLACK	143	DEATH	25
AND AS THOU SAW'ST, I IN A THOUGHT COULD GOE	146	RSRCTN +IM	57
AT LAST WITH THOUGHT	141	RGNRTN	71
ME THOUGHT I HEARD ONE SINGING THUS.	153	THE SEARCH	74
THOUGHTS			
LEAVE, LEAVE, THY GADDING THOUGHTS.	153	THE SEARCH	75
ALL MUTINOUS THOUGHTS, WHAT BUSINES E'R THOU HAST	194	RLS + LSNS	86
IN SOME GOOD THOUGHTS, SO WHEN THE DAY SHALL RISE	195	RLS + LSNS	129
THEE OTHER THOUGHTS, AWAY WITH FRIENDS, AND MIRTH.	195	RLS + LSNS	104
AND FOOLISH THOUGHTS ADDE TO MY BIL	204	DSRDR + FR	51
TO THEE THEREFORE MY THOUGHTS, WORDS, ACTIONS	191	THE MATCH	25
GIVE HIM THY FIRST THOUGHTS THEN, SO SHALT THOU KEEP	191	RLS + LSNS	5
SWEET, DOWNIE THOUGHTS, SOFT LILLY-SHADES, CALM STREAMES.	188	RELAPSE	25
SUCH THOUGHTS BENUM.	171	COME, COME	26
WHICH BUSIE THOUGHTS (LIKE WINDS) WOULD SCATTER QUITE	179	CHRCH-SVC	12
AND SERIOUS THOUGHTS BEGIN TO TAME	166	THE CALL	64
QUITE SPENT WITH THOUGHTS I LEFT MY CELL, AND LAY	167	VNTY SPRIT	1
SO SOME STRANGE THOUGHTS TRENSCEND OUR WONTED THEAMS	271	ALL GONE	27
AND MY SAD THOUGHTS DOTH CLEAR.	270	ALL GONE	4
WITH THESE FAIR THOUGHTS I MOVE IN THIS FAIR PLACE	268	ASCN-DAY A	49
SO MY SPILT THOUGHTS WINDING FROM THEE	240	MISERY	13
MY THOUGHTS DID SWIM IN COMFORTS, AND MINE EYE	244	MT. OLV. B	9
TO MY COLD THOUGHTS A LIVELY SENSE OF SPRING.	245	MT. OLV. B	20
MY THOUGHTS, LIKE WATER WHICH SOME STONE DOTH START	234	MUTINIE	6
CONDEMNING THOUGHTS (LIKE SAD ECCLIPSES) SCOWL	232	THE WORLD	19
ILE SPICE MY THOUGHTS WITH THEE, AND FROM THY WORD	287	PSALM 104	93
MY THOUGHTS, WHEN TOWARDS THEE THEY MOVE	332	AGREEMENT	17
AND THE THOUGHTS OF EACH HARMLESS HOUR	321	CHILDEHOOD	5
CONTENTED THOUGHTS, INNOXIOUS EASE	317	MEN OF WAR	42
HERE SLEPT MY THOUGHTS DEAR MARK. WHICH DUST	310	THE SEED	73
THEIR VERY THOUGHTS, THAT BY THEIR CLEAR	351	L'ENVOY	55
THY GRAVE. TO WHICH MY THOUGHTS SHAL MOVE	343	OBSEQUIES	29
WHAT WERE THEIR LIFES, THEIR THOUGHTS AND DEEDS	347	THE BOOK	9
THOUSAND			
THAT THESE THREE THOUSAND YEARS TIME DID LET FALL	320	HIDDN TRSR	8
'TIS NOW SIX THOUSAND YEARS WELL NIGH	338	DEATH B	3
WELLCOME WHITE DAY. A THOUSAND SUNS	272	WHT SUNDAY	1
A THOUSAND PEECES	140	RGNRTN	51
TWO THOUSAND YEARES	159	MANS FALL	15
WHICH, SCATTER'D IN A THOUSAND PEARLS, EACH FLOWRE	155	ISAACS M.	56
A THOUSAND ODOURS, WHICH (ALL MIXT) SHE SENDS	156	ISAACS M.	60
THOUSANDS			
THOUSANDS THERE WERE AS FRANTICK AS HIMSELF	232	THE WORLD	36
THOUSANDS OF WILD AND WASTE INFUSIONS	214	MISERY	75
THRALL			
RESUME THY SPIRIT FROM THIS WORLD OF THRALL	271	ALL GONE	35
BEING AND LIFE, BUT IS DEAD THRALL.	319	THE ASS	56
THAT I TERM'D THEN MEER BONDS AND THRALL	311	FAIR+YONG	8
THREAD			
BUT BIDS THE THREAD BE SPUN.	197	CORRUPTION	32
THREATEN			
I THREATEN HEAVEN, AND FROM MY CELL	203	DSRDR + FR	16
THREATNING			
AND THREATNING CLOUDS WOULD NOT SO MUCH	230	LAW + GOSP	15
THREATS			
PRONOUNC'D WITH THUNDER, AND THY THREATS DID THAW	229	LAW + GOSP	3
THREE			
AND AS I'TH' NATURAL SUN, THESE THREE	211	FAITH	33
FIRE TO ALL THREE, BUT MAN HATH NO SUCH MIRTH.	223	TEMPEST	32
THREE BLESSINGS WAIT UPON THEM, TWO OF WHICH	192	RLS + LSNS	29
THREE THINGS I'DE HAVE, MY SOULES CHIEF HEALTH	148	DAY OF JDG	39
THAT THESE THREE THOUSAND YEARS TIME DID LET FALL	320	HIDDN TRSR	8
O HOLY, BLESSED, GLORIOUS THREE	284	TRINITY-SN	1
BE OWN'D, SAV'D, SAINTED BY YOU THREE.	284	TRINITY-SN	9
THREW			
THIS PAST, I THREW THE CLOTHES QUITE O'R HIS HEAD	247	I WALKT	29
THRIVE			
SO THRIVE I BEST, 'TWIXT JOYES, AND TEARS	227	LV + DSPLN	17
AT NOISE, BUT THRIVE UNSEEN AND DUMB.	309	THE SEED	46
THRIVES			
WHILE THE LOW VIOLET THRIVES AT THEIR ROOT.	289	THE TIMBER	8
IT THRIVES NO WHERE. THIS MAKES THESE WEIGHTS (LIKE DEATH	279	PALM-TREE	7
WHICH THRIVES IN STORMS, AND SMELS BEST AFTER SHOWRES.	193	RLS + LSNS	60
THRIVING			
AND THRIVING VICE FOR VERTUE JUDGE.	309	THE SEED	40
AMONGST THE DEAD, WHERE THRIVING ILL	318	THE ASS	26
THRONE			
THAT WHEN THY THRONE IS SET, AND ALL	317	MEN OF WAR	47
WHO LOOKS UPON THEE FROM HIS GLORIOUS THRONE	306	RAIN-BOW	17
THE THRONE WHERE PEACE AND POWER REST.	299	JESUS WP B	31
THE GREAT AND WHITE THRONE I SHALL SEE	337	THE THRONE	3

			PAGE	TITLE	LINE
THRONE	**(CON'T)**				
A SILENT TEARE CAN PIERCE THY THRONE	. . . .		167	THE CALL	78
BUT THOSE FLED TO THEIR MAKERS THRONE			179	SILENCE	23
O LET MY CRIE COME TO THY THRONE.	. . . .		242	MISERY	107
WHO ON YON THRONE OF AZURE SITS	. . . .		225	RETIREMENT	1
LOOK FROM THY THRONE UPON THIS ROWL	. . . .		207	REPENTANCE	23
THRONES					
WHERE THRONES AND SERAPHINS REPLY	. . . .		295	PALM-SUNDY	21
GLORY, AND GOLD, AND CROWNS AND THRONES	. . . .		308	THE SEED	3
THRONG					
AMIDST THE NOISE, AND THRONG	. . . .		161	DSTRQCTION	32
FLYE FROM THEIR NURSES TO THE THRONG	. . . .		348	HOLY BIBLE	10
THRONGS					
'TIS NUMBER MAKES A SCHISM. THRONGS ARE RUDE	. .		330	JACOBS PLW	5
THROWN					
THEN, UNTO HIM, WHO THUS HATH THROWN	. . . .		218	EASTER HYM	13
THROWS					
HIS AGONY, AND BLOUDY THROWS.	. . . .		208	REPENTANCE	62
IF JOYES, AND HOPES, AND EARNEST THROWS	. . . .		277	COCK-CRWNG	31
AND HEAR MY HEARTS LAST PRIVATE THROWS.	. . . .		334	AGREEMENT	66
WHOSE PAINEFULL THROWS YIELD MANY SONS	. . . .		167	THE CALL	76
THRUST					
HERE I JOIN HANDS, AND THRUST MY STUBBORN HEART	. .		190	THE MATCH	7
ARISE. THRUST IN THY SICKLE.	. . . .		197	CORRUPTION	40
THSES					
THSES DARK CONFUSIONS, THAT WITHIN ME NEST	. .		216	DRESSING	7
THUNDER					
PRONOUNC'D WITH THUNDER, AND THY THREATS DID THAW	.		229	LAW + GOSP	3
IN HEAV'N, HAIL, THUNDER, RAIN-BOWS, SNOW, AND ICE	.		194	RLS + LSNS	93
HENCE HE IN THUNDER TO THY OFF-SPRING SPOKE.	. .		330	JACOBS PLW	8
OF THEIR LORDS THUNDER THEY RETIR'D APACE.	. .		285	PSALM 104	22
THUNDERS					
WHAT THUNDERS SHALL THOSE MEN ARRAIGN	. . .		325	ABELS BLOD	11
OF THUNDERS IN THAT HEATE	. . . . .		147	DAY OF JDG	10
THWART					
AND IF HEREAFTER YOUTH, OR FOLLY THWART	. .		190	THE MATCH	10
TIDINGS					
THE FIRST GLAD TIDINGS OF THY EARLY LIGHT	. .		267	ASCN-DAY A	17
TIE					
I'D LOOSE THOSE KNOTS THY HANDS DID TIE	. .		214	MISERY	73
TIE UP HIS HANDS, THAT CARES MOCK GOD, AND MAN.	.		193	RLS + LSNS	48
TIES					
AND NOW BY THESE SURE, SACRED TIES	. . .		219	HOLY COMM.	25
TIME					
O AT WHAT TIME SOEVER THOU	. . . .		212	DAWNING	25
ETERNITY IN TIME, THE STEPS BY WHICH	. .		2	SON-DAYES	5
AH. WHAT TIME WILT THOU COME. WHEN SHALL THAT CRIE	.		211	DAWNING	1
INDEED, IT IS THE ONLY TIME	. . . .		211	DAWNING	13
AND ROUND BENEATH IT, TIME IN HOURS, DAYS, YEARS	.		231	THE WORLD	4
WHAT TIME WE FROM OUR FIRST LOVE SWERV'D.	.		237	CONSTLATN	48
THY TIME TO SHINE, AND MINE TO SEE.	.		281	THE FAVOUR	12
HIGH-NOON THUS PAST, THY TIME DECAYS, PROVIDE	.		195	RLS + LSNS	103
BEFORE THY TIME, BE NOT A STRANGER THERE	.		195	RLS + LSNS	122
TILL TIME NO MORE SHALL ROT	. . .		145	RSRCTN +IM	44
ANOTHER TIME BY TH' ANGELL, WHERE	. .		149	RELIGION	11
AND NOW THOU KNEWEST HER COMING, IT WAS TIME	.		155	ISAACS M.	43
WHAT STOCK, AND HOW MUCH TIME WERE LEFT THEE NOW.	.		158	THE LAMPE	16
BUT THOU WERT SO, E'RE TIME HIS SNOW COULD SHED.	.		156	ISAACS M.	70
YET, THIS TAKE WITH THEE. THE LAST GASP OF TIME	.		178	EVNG-WTCH	15
CHRISTS PROGRESS, AND HIS PRAYER TIME.	.		324	THE NIGHT	29
HIS KNOCKING TIME, THE SOULS DUMB WATCH	.		324	THE NIGHT	35
MAKING THE TIME THEY HAD	. . . .		327	RIGHTSNESS	28
BUT WHILE TIME RUNS, AND AFTER IT	. .		333	AGREEMENT	49
HIS TIME IS SHORT, MORE RAGING GROWS.	.		335	JUDGEMENT	30
IN ONE AT ONE TIME, AS SOME FEIGN.	.		298	JESUS WP B	17
AS TIME ONE DAY BY ME DID PASS	. . .		309	THE SEED	49
THAT THESE THREE THOUSAND YEARS TIME DID LET FALL	.		320	HIDDN TRSR	8
AND TIME TO LEARN.	. . . . .		342	OBSEQUIES	24
TIMELY					
BY TURNS, AND TIMELY, AND SO HEAL	. . .		293	THE JEWS	48
TIMES					
AT ALL TIMES, WHATSO'R I DO	. . .		319	THE ASS	29
DESTROY'D AT ALL, BUT WHEN TIMES RESTLES WAVE	.		145	RSRCTN +IM	37
THY OWN DEAR PEOPLE PENS OUR TIMES	. . .		273	WHT SUNDAY	30
THE AGE, THE PRESENT TIMES ARE NOT	. .		214	MISERY	65
AT SOME SET TIMES, BUT ARE THY GRACE.	.		242	MISERY	88
AND INTERCOURSE OF TIMES DIVIDE	. . .		245	MAN	4
THERE IS AT ALL TIMES (THOUGH SHUT UP) IN YOU	.		244	THE SAP	39
THE PULLEYS UNTO HEADLONG MAN, TIMES BOWER	.		2	SON-DAYES	9
THE CHURCHES LOVE-FEASTS, TIMES PREROGATIVE	.		2	SON-DAYES	17
WITH WHAT DEEP MURMURS THROUGH TIMES SILENT STEALTH	.		343	WATER-FALL	1
TINCTURE					
IF SUCH A TINCTURE, SUCH A TOUCH	. . .		276	COCK-CRWNG	13
TINN'D					
WAS TINN'D AND LIGHTED AT THE SUNNE.	. . .		276	COCK-CRWNG	12
TINSEL					
I SKILL NOT YOUR FINE TINSEL, AND FALSE HAIR	.		275	PROFFER	33
GLORY, THE CROUDS CHEAP TINSEL STILL	. . .		309	THE SEED	37
TIR'D					
THE WEAK, AND AGED TIR'D, WITH LENGTH	. .		218	EASTER HYM	9

	PAGE	TITLE	LINE
TIRE			
HATH TAKEN ROOT, AND GROWS, AND DOTH NOT TIRE . . .	279	THE STARRE	26
TURNING TO HIM, WHO MADE POOR SAND TO TIRE . . .	234	MUTINIE	11
UP WHERE THOU ART, AMONGST THY TIRE	204	DSRDR + FR	48
TITHES			
YEA BETHEL SHALL HAVE TITHES (SAITH ISRAELS STONE) . .	331	JACOBS PLW	33
TOGETHER			
THESE TWO GRAND SINS WE JOYN AND ACT TOGETHER . .	307	RAIN-BOW	25
TOGETHER WITH THE SEED, THE PLACE.	204	DSRDR + FR	56
TOGETHER WITH HIS BLOOD, THY FATHERS SPIRIT . . .	156	ISAACS M.	64
TOIL			
THOU ART A MOON-LIKE TOIL, A BLINDE	344	QUICKNESS	5
SOME TOIL AND SOW	341	THE FEAST	73
TOKEN			
HATE NOT THINE OWN DEAR GIFT AND TOKEN. . . .	294	BEGGING B	18
REFUSE IT NOT. FOR NOW THY TOKEN	266	INTRO. 2	31
THE TOKENS OF THE CHURCH, AND PEACE	149	RELIGION	28
TOLD			
A SPRING RAN BY, I TOLD HER TEARS	208	REPENTANCE	44
TOMB			
SHE MADE THE EARTH THEIR NURSE, AND TOMB . . .	222	TEMPEST	9
IF A STAR WERE CONFIN'D INTO A TOMB	271	ALL GONE	29
OTHERS, WHOSE BIRTH IS IN THE TOMB	187	ND DO THEY	26
TOMBE			
PERHAPS SOME THINK A TOMBE	171	COME, COME	21
TOMBS			
SILENT AS TOMBS	313	THE STONE	7
TOMORROW			
PERHAPS TOMORROW.	202	THE CHECK	47
GROWING O'R NIGHT, AND GONE TOMORROW	208	REPENTANCE	72
TONGUE			
PROFANENES ON MY TONGUE DOTH REST	208	REPENTANCE	75
BEFORE I TAUGHT MY TONGUE TO WOUND	169	RETREATE	15
AND THOUGH POOR STONES HAVE NEITHER SPEECH NOR TONGUE .	288	THE BIRD	14
HIS HEART AND TONGUE IN PRAYERS FOR HIS FOES. . .	328	RIGHTSNESS	39
THY NEXT EFFECTS NO TONGUE CAN TELL.	348	HOLY BIBLE	35
TONGUES			
UNBITTED TONGUES ARE IN THEIR PENANCE DOUBLE . .	194	RLS + LSNS	71
OF CLOVEN TONGUES THEIR HEADS ALL BRUSH'D . . .	272	WHT SUNDAY	7
TOO			
NOT, BUT THAT I HAVE WISHES TOO	273	WHT SUNDAY	25
WHO DO NOT SO, TOO LATE REPENT	274	PROFFER	12
AND LIFE TOO, AND MY HEARTS DELIGHT.	265	INTRO. 2	18
HERE IS THEIR FAITH TOO, WHICH IF YOU WILL KEEP . .	280	PALM-TREE	24
TO EQUAL WINDS. WOULD PROVE TOO SHORT. THOU HAST .	281	JOY	13
(AND THOSE BUT SELDOME TOO) WERE CAUGHT . . .	207	REPENTANCE	12
KINGDOMES TOO HAVE THEIR PHYSICK, AND FOR STEEL . .	222	AFFLICTION	33
ORDAIN NIGHT TOO.	221	AFFLICTION	8
THY SPIRIT TOO IS MINE.	225	RETIREMENT	25
(NOT THINE ALONE BUT MINE TOO) THAT WHEN ALL . .	234	MUTINIE	15
WE CLIMB UP THIS, AND HAVE TOO ALL THE WAY . .	230	LAW + GOSP	17
THY DOVE TOO BEARS US ON HER SACRED WINGS. . .	230	LAW + GOSP	20
I MAY AS WEL AS LOVE, FIND TOO THY FEAR. . . .	230	LAW + GOSP	30
AND FULL OF TOSSINGS TOO AND FRO	228	PILGRIMAGE	10
AND BRING NEW TOO. GET THEN THIS SAP, AND GET . .	244	THE SAP	35
THAT THESE MAY BE THY PRAISE, AND MY JOY TOO. . .	245	MT. OLV. B	26
WHO SITS AT HOME TOO BEARS A LOADE	214	MISERY	69
TO WHAT'S ALREADY GROWN TOO HIGH	240	MISERY	18
LOOKS DIM TOO IN THE CLOUD	197	CORRUPTION	34
SO SHOULD WE TOO. ALL THINGS TEACH US TO DIE . .	201	THE CHECK	20
I'M TOO MUCH ON THE SCORE.	204	IDLE VERSE	4
TOO, IS MY DEW, AND SPRINGING WEL.	203	DSRDR + FR	19
BUT HE THAT WITH HIS BLOOD (A PRICE TOO DEERE) . .	188	RELAPSE	21
IS BOTH HIS OWN JOY, AND HIS MAKERS TOO. . . .	193	RLS + LSNS	51
BUT (AH) MY SOUL WITH TOO MUCH STAY	170	RETREATE	27
WE TRAVELL TOO.	175	JOY OF LIF	28
LEST LEFT ALONE TOO LONG	161	DSTRUCTION	31
THY MERCY TOO	162	PURSUITE	14
AND FOUNTAINE TOO	163	MT. OLVS A	19
AND GRONE TOO. WHY TH'ELECT	186	ND DO THEY	4
O THEN IT WILBE ALL TOO LATE	147	DAY OF JDG	25
AND SO IS MERCY TOO.	147	DAY OF JDG	28
NEW SEV'RAL OATHES, AND COMPLEMENTS (TOO) PLENTY. .	154	ISAACS M.	16
A PITCHER TOO SHE HAD, NOR THOUGHT IT MUCH . .	155	ISAACS M.	39
TO DRAW HIM DRINK, AND FOR HIS CAMELS TOO. . . .	155	ISAACS M.	42
TOO GROSSE FOR HEAVEN	160	THE SHOWRE	5
EVEN WHAT THOU WILT, AND PRAISE THEE TOO. . . .	328	ANGUISH	6
FOR THOU A BROTHER, AND BLOOD-THIRSTY TOO . . .	331	JACOBS PLW	43
MY FELLOW-CREATURES TOO SAY, COME.	335	JUDGEMENT	15
WITH THEIR CONTENT TOO IN MY POW'R	321	CHILDEHOOD	6
OUR FULNESS TOO IS NOW COME IN	292	THE JEWS	27
WHOSE SPIRIT TOO DOTH MOURN AND GRIEVE . . .	292	THE JEWS	35
WHAT THOU HAST DONE (BUT THOUGH MAN TOO . . .	299	JESUS WP B	35
BUT THOU MUST SORROW FOR HIM TOO.	299	JESUS WP B	43
AND WHILE TOO MANY SADLY ROAM	299	JESUS WP B	52
LODGED IN THOSE FALSE LOOKS, TILL TOO LATE. . .	311	FAIR+YONG	22
ARE ALL TOO HIGH FOR A LOW CELL.	309	THE SEED	34
AND THEY TOO OFT TAKE GOOD FOR ILL	309	THE SEED	39
TO LOSE HIM TOO, AS WELL AS PARADISE)	307	RAIN-BOW	24
DID SPIT ON THEE, AND SMOTE THEE TOO. . . .	317	MEN OF WAR	30

	PAGE	TITLE	LINE
TOO (CCN'T)			
WHERE THOU TOO HAST BUT THE LEAST PART	315	DWELLNG-PL	15
NCT BLT THAT MOURNERS TCC, CAN HAVE	342	OBSEQUIES	17
TOOK			
BUT NCW, SINCE GOD ON HIMSELF TCCK	314	THE STONE	52
TOOK'ST			
THAT TOOK'ST MY SINNE	186	PASSION	45
THAT TOOK'ST MY SHAME	186	PASSION	46
TOOKE			
I TCOKE THEM LP, ANC (MUCH JOY'C) WENT ABOUT	168	VNTY SPRIT	25
FOR SINNE TOCKE STRENGTH, ANC VIGOUR FROM THE LAW.	159	MANS FALL	20
I TOOKE THEM UP AND LAYC	139	RGNRTN	30
TORRENT			
AND LIKE A FIRIE TORRENT BRUSH	146	DAY OF JDG	3
TOSSINGS			
AND FULL CF TCSSINGS TOC AND FRC	228	PILGRIMAGE	10
TOST			
THE WCRLD'S THY BOXE. HCW THEN (THERE TOST)	181	BURIALL	31
THOL GOTST MY HEART, ANC THOUGH HERE TOST	202	DSRDR + FR	6
TOUCH			
TC CARRY THAT, WHICH SOME WOULD SCORN TO TOUCH.	155	ISAACS M.	40
WITH FILIAL CONFIDENCE WE TOUCH EV'N THEE.	229	LAW + GOSP	13
AS 'BIDE THE TOUCH	230	LAW + GOSP	16
THAT NO DECAY SHAL TOUCH ME. C BE PLEAS'D	234	MUTINIE	32
CAN TCUCH HIM ANY WAY	244	THE SAP	30
BREAK, AND THE SHADOWS FLEE, TCLCH WITH ONE CGAL	216	DRESSING	3
IF SUCH A TINCTURE, SUCH A TOUCH	276	COCK-CRWNG	13
WITH THY LEAST TOLCH, LIGHTNINGS AND WINDS THAT RAGE	287	PSALM 104	87
INTO MY SOUL, WITH WHCSF CUICK TCUCH	348	HOLY BIBLE	21
(TOUCH'D WITH THE GUILT CF MY CWN WAY)	207	REPENTANCE	28
THE JEWS TOUCH'D NCT	156	BRT. CHRCH	9
TCUCH'D BY THY FIRE, ANC BREATH. THY BLOUD	203	DSRDR + FR	18
BROKE UP SOME SEALES, WHICH NCNE HAD TOUCH'D BEFCRE	167	VNTY SPRIT	10
TOWN			
THUS LAZARUS WAS CARRIEC CUT CF TOWN.	183	THRS A TYE	17
A LITTLE DUST, AND FOR THE TOWN	151	THE SEARCH	16
THEY FOR THE TCWN PREPARE	239	SHEPHEARDS	42
TOY			
WHO THEN DID CRESS THE MUCH LCV'D TOY	304	ST MARY MN	17
TOYES			
MAN HATH STIL EITHER TOYES, OR CARE	246	MAN	15
TOYLSOM			
THCU ART A TOYLSOM MOLE, CR LESS	345	QUICKNESS	17
TRACE			
AND THE LAST STEPS OF MY MILDE MASTER TRACE.	268	ASCN-DAY A	50
TRACES, AND SOUNDS OF A STRANGE KIND.	168	VNTY SPRIT	16
TRACK			
O CCULD I TRACK THEM. BLT SOULS MUST	179	SILENCE	25
TRACK ONE THE OTHER	179	SILENCE	26
AND TREAD AGAIN THAT ANCIENT TRACK.	170	RETREATE	22
ABCVE THE STARS, A TRACK UNKNCWN, AND HIGH	155	ISAACS M.	50
THY STEPS TRACK HERE BELOW	248	I WALKT	49
TRACK'D			
CAN SCULS BE TRACK'C BY ANY EYE	277	COCK-CRWNG	35
TRAFFIQUE			
WHOSE EASTERN TRAFFIQUE DEALS IN BRIGHT	346	THE QUEER	5
TRAIN			
TILL ALL BE READY, THAT THE TRAIN	350	L'ENVOY	27
I SEE HIM LEACING OUT HIS CHOSEN TRAIN	268	ASCN-DAY A	51
AND ALL HER TRAIN WERE FURL'D.	231	THE WORLD	7
THCU HACST NO POMPOUS TRAIN, NCR ANTIK CROWD	154	ISAACS M.	21
HIS WHITE AND HOLY TRAIN	329	TEARS	2
CTHERS WERE TYM'D AND TRAIN'D LP TO'T BUT THCU	156	ISAACS M.	67
TRAINE			
A TRAINE CF LIGHTS, WHICH IN THCSE SUN-SHINE CAYES	159	MANS FALL	10
YET, IF AS THOU DCEST MELT, AND WITH THY TRAINE	160	THE SHOWRE	13
THEIR WELL-FLEEC'D TRAINE) AND HERE (C FATE)	151	THE SEARCH	27
WHERE FIRST I LEFT MY GLCRIOUS TRAINE	170	RETREATE	24
TRAMPLE			
WHOSE LIGHT DCTH TRAMPLE CN MY CAYS.	271	ALL GONE	10
TRAMPLES			
AND TRAMPLES CN DOUBTS AND DESPAIR.	346	THE QUEER	4
TRANSCENDENT			
WHICH MAKES THE HIGH TRANSCENCENT BLISS	346	THE QUEER	15
TRANSGRESS			
OF GLCRY, SHE CANNCT TRANSGRESS.	269	ASCSN-HYMN	18
OF HEAVY SINS, MY HIGH TRANSGRESSIONS	207	REPENTANCE	24
CUT ME NOT OFF FOR MY TRANSGRESSICNS	208	REPENTANCE	53
TRANSGRESSIONS MAKE ME FOUL EACH DAY	336	PSALM 65	7
TRANSLATICN			
WAS A TRANSLATION CF SUCH HEIGHT	164	INCARNATN	7
TRANSPARENT			
DCTH THY TRANSPARENT, CCOL AND WATRY WEALTH	343	WATER-FALL	2
TRANSPARENT AS THE PUREST DAY	349	L'ENVOY	13
TRANSPLANTED			
TRANSPLANTED THUS, ONE LEAFE CF HIS T'AWAKE	158	MANS FALL	5
TRANSPLANTEC PARACISE, GCDS WALKING HCUR.	2	SON-DAYES	11
TRAP			
MAKE NCT THY BREAST A LABRYINTH, CR TRAP.	193	RLS + LSNS	56
TRAVEL			
THAT I MAY TRAVEL TO THY MOUNT.	229	PILGRIMAGE	28

		PAGE	TITLE	LINE
TRAVEL	(CON'T)			
THEN WOULD GO TRAVEL, FIGHT OR DIE.		214	MISERY	74
TRAVEL AND GROAN, AND LOOK AND CALL.		350	L'ENVOY	22
TRAVELL				
O HOW I LONG TO TRAVELL BACK		170	RETREATE	21
WE TRAVELL TOO.		175	JOY OF LIF	28
TRAVELL'D				
WE TRAVELL'D IN, OUR FIRST ATTEMPTS		143	DEATH	16
TRAVELLER				
WHEN SHAL THAT TRAVELLER COME HOME		189	RESOLVE	7
WHERE, IF A TRAVELLER WATER CRAVE		212	DAWNING	31
TRAVELLOURS				
AS TRAVELLOURS WHEN THE TWILIGHT'S COME		228	PILGRIMAGE	1
TRAVELS				
TRAVELS IN CLOUDS, SEEKS MANNA, WHERE NONE IS.		153	THE SEARCH	95
TREAD				
WHERE MY DEARE LORD DID OFTEN TREAD		153	THE SEARCH	72
AND TREAD AGAIN THAT ANCIENT TRACK.		170	RETREATE	22
FOR EV'RY FOOTE TO TREAD.		166	THE CALL	69
A WAY WHERE YOU MIGHT TREAD THE SUN, AND BE		233	THE WORLD	55
CAST IT, OR TREAD IT. IT SHALL DO		328	ANGUISH	5
YEA GODS OWN BLOOD WE TREAD UPON AND SLIGHT.		307	RAIN-BOW	30
OF GRASS, WE TREAD, DECLARE.		286	PSALM 104	68
DISDEIN TREADS ON THE PEACEFUL NAME		214	MISERY	68
WHEN TH' HERB HE TREADS KNOWS MUCH, MUCH MORE.		236	CONSTLATN	28
TREASON				
WHO QUESTION POWER, THEY SPEAK TREASON.		318	THE ASS	20
TREASURE				
(THOUGH PURCHAS'D WITH THY HEARTS DEAR TREASURE)		299	JESUS WP B	28
BUT THE GOOD MAN IS GODS PECULIAR TREASURE.		328	RIGHTSNESS	48
YET HIS DEAR TREASURE		231	THE WORLD	13
I WILL TREASURE.		215	PRAISE	32
SUCH TREASURE BRINGS		145	RSRCTN +IM	28
WE SPEND IN SIGHES, IS TREASURE AFTER DEATH.		158	THE LAMPE	22
TREASURES				
WITH HIDDEN TREASURES THAT MAKE TRULY RICH.		327	RIGHTSNESS	12
TREATIES				
DOEST THOU THEREFORE OLD TREATIES WAVE		149	RELIGION	23
TREE				
NEVER DID TREE BEARE FRUIT LIKE THIS		152	THE SEARCH	43
I WOULD I WERE A STONE, OR TREE		187	NO DO THEY	11
UPON A TREE		191	THE MATCH	32
TAKE THEIR LEAVE, AND DIE. BIRDS, BEASTS, EACH TREE		201	THE CHECK	27
THOU CANST NOT MISSE HIS PRAISE, EACH TREE, HERB, FLOWRE		194	RLS + LSNS	95
BLOWN FROM THE TREE OF LIFE TO US		332	AGREEMENT	21
I'LE CUT ME BOUGHS OFF MANY A TREE		295	PALM-SUNDY	35
CHIRPING THEIR SOLEMN MATINS ON EACH TREE.		288	THE BIRD	24
THAT AT THE ROOT OF THIS GREEN TREE		304	ST MARY MN	31
ALL WOULD BE DROUGHT, AND LEANNESS, NOT A TREE		222	AFFLICTION	23
AND GOING HENCE, LEAVE WRITTEN ON SOME TREE		281	JOY	29
HERE IS THE PATIENCE OF THE SAINTS. THIS TREE		280	PALM-TREE	21
AND SPRING, AND GROW, A TREE NE'R TO BE PRIC'D		280	PALM-TREE	15
A TREE, WHOSE FRUIT IS IMMORTALITY.		280	PALM-TREE	16
THOU KNEW'ST THIS TREE, WHEN A GREEN SHADE		347	THE BOOK	11
TREES				
THOU SHALT RESTORE TREES, BEASTS AND MEN		347	THE BOOK	26
GREEN TREES OF LIFE, AND LIVING STREAMS.		346	THE QUEER	8
WITH OTHER TREES. BUT NOW SHUT FROM THE BREATH		279	PALM-TREE	5
QUIT THEIR FIRST BED AND MOUNT. TREES, HERBS, FLOWRES, ALL		223	TEMPEST	27
THE TREES, THEIR LEAFS, THE FLOWRES, THEIR SEEDING.		207	REPENTANCE	34
AND TREES OF LIFE NO OTHER WATERS LOVE		291	THE TIMBER	51
TO MAKE DRIE DUST, AND DEAD TREES GROW.		291	THE JEWS	13
TREES, FLOWERS AND HERBS. BIRDS, BEASTS AND STONES		294	PALM-SUNDY	11
THOU GIV'ST THE TREES THEIR GREENNESS, EV'N TO THOSE		286	PSALM 104	45
WHERE TREES AND HERBS DID WATCH AND PEEP		323	THE NIGHT	23
THAT SHADY CITY OF PALME TREES		170	RETREATE	26
TREMBLED				
FOR THY NEW LIGHT, AND TREMBLED AT EACH SHOWER.		306	RAIN-BOW	8
TREMBLES				
IS MOV'D AND TREMBLES, THE HILLS MELT AND SMOKE		287	PSALM 104	86
TRENSCEND				
SO SOME STRANGE THOUGHTS TRENSCEND OUR WONTED THEAMS		271	ALL GONE	27
TRESPASSE				
THEN LAY THAT TRESPASSE IN THE SHADE		240	MISERY	22
GUILTS, TRESPASSES, AND ALL THIS INWARD AWE		159	MANS FALL	19
TRIALS				
IF TRIALS COME, THIS WIL MAKE GOOD THY PART		193	RLS + LSNS	57
TRIBUTE				
A FISH SHALL ALL MY TRIBUTE PAY		300	PROVIDENCE	15
TRIE				
IN POST FOR PLEASURES, BENT TO TRIE		282	GARLAND	11
TRIED				
WHOSE ACTIVE ZEAL AND TRIED FAITH WERE TO THEE		156	ISAACS M.	65
TRIM				
THY BEAMS HOME WITH THEE. TRIM THY LAMP, BUY OYL		195	RLS + LSNS	110
TO DRESSE, AND TRIM OUR SHAME		205	IDLE VERSE	10
TRIMMING				
AND PAINTED TRIMMING TAKES DOWN BOTH HIS EYES		224	TEMPEST	46
TRINITIE				
IN HEAVEN, ONE GOD IN TRINITIE.		284	TRINITY-SN	3

	PAGE	TITLE	LINE
TRIUMPH			
BUT EVEN IN BABES DOEST TRIUMPH STILL AND WIN.	216	DRESSING	12
TRIUMPHS			
NOT ONE BEAM TRIUMPHS, BUT FROM FAR	212	DAWNING	23
ALL YOUR TRIUMPHS NOW ARE ENDED	218	EASTER HYM	3
MISTS MAKE BUT TRIUMPHS FOR THE DAY.	338	DEATH B	20
SUCH TRIUMPHS POOR FLESH CANNOT MERIT.	339	THE FEAST	9
SIN TRIUMPHS STILL, AND MAN IS SUNK BELOW	197	CORRUPTION	35
TRIVIALL			
THE WEAKER SORT SLIGHT, TRIVIALL WARES INSLAVE	232	THE WORLD	42
TROD			
BUT IS STIL TROD	248	I WALKT	41
RUDE FEET ERE TROD	140	RGNRTN	39
TROT			
TO THY SURE TROT, A CONSTANT, HUMBLE MIND	193	RLS + LSNS	50
TROUBLE			
THEY SHAME THEIR OWNERS, AND THE HEARERS TROUBLE.	194	RLS + LSNS	72
DEAD I WAS, AND DEEP IN TROUBLE.	218	HOLY COMM.	2
TROUBLED			
DID QUIT THEIR TROUBLED CHANNEL, AND RETIRE	234	MUTINIE	7
HE GOES, HE YIELDS, AND TROUBLED SORE	240	MISERY	37
SINCE THESE ARE TROUBLED, TO THE SPRINGING ROCK	150	RELIGION	50
I BOW MY TROUBLED SOUL, AND GREET	328	ANGUISH	3
TRUCE			
IS THE TRUCE BROKE. OR 'CAUSE WE HAVE	149	RELIGION	21
TRUE			
AND SUCH IS TRUE REPENTANCE, EV'RY BREATH	158	THE LAMPE	21
TO GOD, THY COUNTRIE, AND THY FRIEND BE TRUE	193	RLS + LSNS	43
THE OTHER, THE TRUE LIFF, IN THE NEXT WORLD	191	THE MATCH	22
THE SPIRITS DUTY, TRUE HEARTS SPREAD, AND HEAVE	191	RLS + LSNS	3
JOYES FULL, AND TRUE.	188	RELAPSE	26
A SPIRIT, AND TRUE GLORY DWELL	202	THE CHECK	34
KNOW'ST TO BE TRUE)	170	COME, COME	9
BUT TO WRITE TRUE, UNFEIGNED VERSE	329	ANGUISH	15
EACH PAGE OF THINE HATH TRUE LIFE IN'T	332	AGREEMENT	23
THY LINES ARE RAYS, THE TRUE SUN SHEDS.	333	AGREEMENT	35
BE IN CONJUNCTION WITH TRUE LIGHT.	332	AGREEMENT	16
AND FORM TO SERVE HIM IN, SHOULD BE TRUE GRACE	330	JACOBS PLW	24
THE FIRST TRUE WORSHIP OF THE WORLDS GREAT KING	330	JACOBS PLW	11
SIONS TRUE, GLORIOUS GOD. ON THEE	336	PSALM 65	1
SHALL BRING TRUE DAY, AND MAKE DUST SEE	335	JUDGEMENT	21
THEN ALL IS TRUE, MY FOES HAVE SPOKEN.	333	AGREEMENT	48
AND TO THY WORKS ART TRUE.	287	PSALM 104	84
GATHER TRUE COMFORTS, BUT THE WICKED LIVER	287	PSALM 104	94
SKILFUL INCHANTRESS AND TRUE BRED.	297	HERODIAS	17
THEN TRUE REMORSE, WHEN WITH PAST SINS AT STRIFE.	290	THE TIMBER	28
THE ARM OF GOD, GLORIOUS AND TRUE	292	THE JEWS	40
WHO WERT ALL FALSE, SHOULD'ST TRUE GRIEF KNOW.	305	ST MARY MN	64
THOU ART THE TRUE LOVES-KNOW, BY THEE	302	THE KNOT	5
AND THE TRUE FAITH, WHICH NEVER FAINTS.	316	MEN OF WAR	8
BUT THESE DUMB CREATURES ARE SO TRUE	313	THE STONE	12
RESEMBLES THOSE TRUE JOYS	235	CONSTLATN	2
YOU ONLY SAW TRUE LIGHT	238	SHEPHEARDS	6
'TIS TRUE, HE LOVES THAT DUST WHEREON THEY GO	238	SHEPHEARDS	13
BEFORE TRUE LIGHT	233	THE WORLD	50
THY TRUE DESCENT.	226	RETIREMENT	48
AND HAD NOT HE SO DONE, IT IS MOST TRUE	243	THE SAP	21
SHAL FIND A JOY SO TRUE	244	THE SAP	46
WHEN FIRST I SAW TRUE BEAUTY, AND THY JOYS	244	MT. OLV. B	1
BRIGHT SHADOWS OF TRUE REST. SOME SHOOTS OF BLISSE	205	SON-DAYES	1
TO THEE WHO WITH TRUE LIGHT ART CLAD	207	REPENTANCE	21
WHERE LIGHT, JOY, LEISURE, AND TRUE COMFORTS MOVE	248	I WALKT	59
FOR THE TRUE LIGHT	267	ASCN-DAY A	13
BUT WITH TRUE TEARS WASH OFF YOUR MIRE.	266	VAIN WITS	4
THAT GOD IS TRUE, AS HERBS UNSEEN	279	THE STARRE	31
INTO TRUE LIBERTY.	271	ALL GONE	36
TWO AND NO MORE. WHAT TWO ATTEST, IS TRUE	268	ASCN-DAY A	59
THAT WOULD NOT HAVE THE TRUE COME ON.	344	QUICKNESS	4
SOME FEW TRUE TEARS, AND THOSE SHED FOR	342	OBSEQUIES	3
COME THEN TRUE BREAD	339	THE FEAST	13
FOR THIS TRUE EASE	341	THE FEAST	55
TRUE THANKS TO THEE, BEFORE I SLEEP.	348	HOLY BIBLE	4
THAT LIKE TRUE SHEEP, ALL IN ONE FOLD	350	L'ENVOY	47
TRULY			
THAT, WHO BUT TRULY TASTS IT, NO DECAY	244	THE SAP	29
AND TRULY HATES TO BE DETAIN'D ON EARTH	290	THE TIMBER	30
JESUS, MY LIFE. HOW SHALL I TRULY LOVE THEE.	283	LOVE-SICK	1
WITH HIDDEN TREASURES THAT MAKE TRULY RICH.	327	RIGHTSNESS	12
THEN, WHO WOULD TRULY LIMNE THEE OUT, MUST PAINT	156	ISAACS M.	71
TRUMPETS			
BUT HARK. WHAT TRUMPETS THAT. WHAT ANGEL CRIES	197	CORRUPTION	39
TRUST			
WRIT IN HIS BOOK, WHO NE'R BETRAY'D MANS TRUST.	177	EVNG-WTCH	8
SATE PINING ALL HIS LIFE THERE, DID SCARCE TRUST	232	THE WORLD	32
ANGELS DESCENDING, THE RETURNS OF TRUST.	2	SON-DAYES	15
BUT FIRMLY TRUSTS IN GOD, THE GREAT MANS MEASURE	328	RIGHTSNESS	45
WHO TRUSTS NOT THEE. BUT WRETCHEDLY	301	PROVIDENCE	32
TRUTH			
CAN FOIL HIS MERITS, AND THY TRUTH.	333	AGREEMENT	54
AND TRUTH (OPPREST HERE) GETS THE PRIZE.	318	THE ASS	28

		PAGE	TITLE	LINE
TRUTH	(CON'T)			
GREAT KING OF LOVE AND TRUTH.	. . . . .	301	PROVIDENCE	43
TILL TRUTH THROUGH ALL THE WORLD BE PAST	. . .	305	ST MARY MN	52
AND POOR, DESPISED TRUTH SATE COUNTING BY	. . .	232	THE WORLD	44
FOR ALL THY MERCIES AND THY TRUTH	. . .	265	INTRO. 2	19
TO RAISE IT TO THE TRUTH AND LIGHT OF THINGS	.	248	I WALKT	40
THIS TRUTH COMMENDS	. . . . .	174	JOY OF LIF	6
IT IS (IN TRUTH) A RUIN'D PEECE	. . .	180	BURIALL	11
IF TRUTH BE THINE, WHAT NEEDS A BRUTISH FORCE.	.	193	RLS + LSNS	39
SHREWD IN THEIR BIRTHS. THE CROWN OF LIFE, LIGHT, TRUTH		192	RLS + LSNS	27
ALL WAS PLAIN, MODEST TRUTH, NOR CID SHE COME	.	155	ISAACS M.	33
OR THAT THY TRUTH WAS NOT HERE KNOWN	. .	350	L'ENVOY	31
DARES OWN THE TRUTH, AND SHEW THE ILL.	. .	350	L'ENVOY	38
WHAT SUBLIME TRUTHS, AND WHOLESOME THEMES	.	344	WATER-FALL	27
TRY				
CONDEMN MEN. BUT WILL TRY THEM BY	. . .	314	THE STONE	34
TRYED				
AS A TRYED THING	. . . . . .	338	DEATH B	7
AS THOSE POOR PILGRIMS OFT HAVE TRYED	. .	298	JESUS WP B	20
TUFF				
WILL PROVE THEIR HEARTS MORE STIFF AND TUFF.	.	314	THE STONE	51
TUN'D				
WHERE A SHRILL SPRING TUN'D TO THE EARLY DAY.	.	167	VNTY SPRIT	2
SORROWS IN WHITE, GRIEFS TUN'D, A SUGERD DOSIS	.	280	JOY	5
TUNE				
TAKE UP, AND TUNE HIS YEAR	. . . .	236	CONSTLATN	22
THE WORLD IN TUNE	. . . . .	177	MRNG-WTCH	19
HIS LIFE FOR MINE, TUNE TO THY WILL	. .	204	DSRDR + FR	59
TUNING				
TUNING HIS BREST TO RISE, OR FALL.	. .	222	AFFLICTION	37
TURN				
BUT HIDE, OR TURN THY FACE	. . . .	213	ADMISSION	18
WHERE DEAD MEN PREACH, WHO CAN TURN FEASTS, AND MIRTH	.	226	RETIREMENT	49
THERE TURN, AND TURN NO MORE, LET WITS	. .	189	RESOLVE	25
THERE TURN, AND TURN NO MORE, LET WITS	. .	189	RESOLVE	25
AND TURN ONCE MORE OUR WATER INTO WINE	.	150	RELIGION	52
WHEN ALL THINGS HERE TO THISTLES TURN	.	319	THE ASS	49
STORMS TURN TO MUSICK, CLOUDS TO SMILES AND AIR.	.	306	RAIN-BOW	10
TURN IN, IF NOT OBSTRUCTED STILL.	. .	351	L'ENVOY	52
TURN'D				
WHO TURN'D OUR SAD CAPTIVITY.	. . .	351	L'ENVOY	62
AND TURN'D TO SMILES THE BEGGING TEARS	. .	300	PROVIDENCE	5
I TURN'D ME ROUND, AND TO EACH SHADE	. .	141	RGNRTN	82
AND TURN'D THEIR NIGHT TO DAY	. . .	239	SHEPHEARDS	52
AND ALL MY BOWELS TURN'D	. . . .	213	ADMISSION	2
ARE BUT MEER LEAVES TURN'D BY THY BREATH.	.	219	HOLY COMM.	16
TURNING				
TURNING TO HIM, WHO MADE POOR SAND TO TIRE	.	234	MUTINIE	11
TURNING THEIR MISTS TO BEAMS, THEIR DAMPS TO DAY	.	202	THE CHECK	31
TURNS				
THIS IS THE GREAT ELIXIR THAT TURNS GALL	. .	221	AFFLICTION	4
BY TURNS, AND TIMELY, AND SO HEAL	. .	293	THE JEWS	48
THE PLEASANT LAND TO BRIMSTONE TURNS	. .	288	THE BIRD	29
EACH THING TURNS SCRIBE AND REGISTER	. .	314	THE STONE	43
THOU DOST BUT COURT COLD RAIN, TILL RAIN TURNS FIRE.	.	307	RAIN-BOW	42
BY GODS PERMISSION, AND MAN TURNS A MULE.	.	330	JACOBS PLW	30
WITH HIS STRONG ARM TURNS OUR CAPTIVITY.	.	331	JACOBS PLW	40
TURTLE				
LIKE THE SURVIVING TURTLE, WEEP	. . .	311	FAIR+YONG	10
THE TURTLE THEN IN PALM-TREES MOURNS	. .	288	THE BIRD	27
TURTLES				
WHERE TURTLES BUILD, AND CARELESSE SPARROWS MOVE	.	327	RIGHTSNESS	7
THE TURTLES VOICE	. . . . .	340	THE FEAST	50
TUTOR'D				
NOT TUTOR'D BY THY GLASS, BUT FREE	. .	303	ST MARY MN	7
TWELVE				
THEN, WHEN THE GASTLY TWELVE WAS PAST	. .	143	DEATH	19
TWELVE HUNDRED HOURES, AND NOT A BROW	. .	178	SILENCE	3
TWENTY				
AND FOR ONE TWENTY WE HAVE PAST	. .	166	THE CALL	56
SOME TWENTY YEARS.	. . . . .	164	THE CALL	4
OF THESE OUR DAYES, THOU COULDST HAVE COYN'D THEE TWENTY		154	ISAACS M.	15
TWICE				
MUST LIVE TWICE, THAT WOULD GODS FACE SEE.	. .	322	CHILDEHOOD	36
TWILIGHT'S				
AS TRAVELLOURS WHEN THE TWILIGHT'S COME	. .	228	PILGRIMAGE	1
TWILL				
TWILL SHEW US EACH FORGOTTEN GRAVE	. .	334	JUDGEMENT	4
TWIN'D				
BUT A TWIN'D WREATH OF GRIEF AND PRAISE	.	345	THE WREATH	9
TWINKLING				
ONE TWINKLING RAY	. . . . .	174	JOY OF LIF	13
TWIST				
TWIST NOT MY CYPRESSE WITH YOU BAYS	. .	205	IDLE VERSE	19
SO TWIST THEM IN MY HEART, THAT EVER THERE	.	230	LAW + GOSP	29
TWO				
TWO DEATHS HAD BIN THY DUE.	. . .	243	THE SAP	22
ROSE UP, AND CANCELL'D TWO DEATHS DUE TO THEE.	.	217	EASTER-DAY	8
TWO FLOWRES THAT GREW WITH THEE ABOVE.	.	216	DRESSING	26
WHEN WE TWO PART, I WILL A JOURNEY MAKE	.	280	PALM-TREE	25

		PAGE	TITLE	LINE
TWO	(CCN'T)			
HAVING LOST THEE, BEHCLC TWO MEN IN WHITE.	. . .	268	ASCN-DAY A	58
TWO AND NC MORE. WHAT TWO ATTEST, IS TRUE	. . .	268	ASCN-DAY A	59
TWO AND NC MORE. WHAT TWO ATTEST, IS TRUE	. . .	268	ASCN-DAY A	59
AND THY TWO WINGS WERE GRIEF AND LCVE.	. . .	272	WHT SUNDAY	12
AND WALK TWO STEPS	. . . .	203	DSRDR + FR	35
TWO LIFES I HCLD FROM THEE, MY GRACIOUS LORD	. . .	191	THE MATCH	19
THREE BLESSINGS WAIT UPCN THEM, TWO CF WHICH	. . .	192	RLS + LSNS	29
TWO IN THE DAY, THEN FRCM THE DAMPS, AND AKE	. . .	196	RLS + LSNS	135
AMEN. BUT HARK, E'R WE TWC STRAY	. . .	178	EVNG-WTCH	9
A MILE, OR TWC, FRCM MY FIRST LCVE	. . .	169	RETREATE	8
THEE TWC SMALL MITES, AND BE AT STRIFE	. . .	186	PASSION	52
THIS LAST WILL KEEPE THE FIRST TWC FRFSH	. . .	148	DAY OF JDG	43
ESTEEM'C (VAINE THINGS) OF TWC WHOLE ELEMENTS	. . .	144	RSRCTN +IM	13
TWO THOUSAND YEARES	. . .	159	MANS FALL	15
THESE TWO GRAND SINS WE JCYN AND ACT TOGETHER	. . .	307	RAIN-BOW	25
OF FLESH AND BLOOD, WHERE TWO WAYS MEFT.	. . .	318	THE ASS	2
SINCE TWO AFFLICTIONS MAY NOT REIGN	. . .	298	JESUS WP B	16
THE THIRD GLAC DAY THROUGH TWC SAD NIGHTS.	. . .	295	PALM-SUNDY	33
TY'D				
HE HATH NC ROCT, NOR TO CNE PLACE IS TY'D	. .	246	MAN	16
TYE				
TYE ME TO FAITH, THOUGH ABOVE REASON	. .	318	THE ASS	19
BRIGHT PLEDGE OF PEACE AND SUN-SHINE. THE SURE TYE	. .	306	RAIN-BOW	13
SURE, THERE'S A TYE OF BODYES. AND AS THEY	. .	183	THRS A TYE	1
TYED				
THEN SHOULD I (TYED TC CNE SURE STATE)	. . .	187	ND DO THEY	15
WHOSE BEAUTY TYED LIFE TO THY HCUSE	. . .	302	THE KNOT	3
THE KNOTS WE TYED UPCN THY PURSE	. . .	274	WHT SUNDAY	56
I WILL CLCSE GIRT AND TYED	. . .	342	OBSEQUIES	15
TYM'D				
OTHERS WERE TYM'D AND TRAIN'D LP IO'T BUT THCU	. .	156	ISAACS M.	67
TYME				
BUT THE DELAY IS ALL. TYME NOW	. . . .	181	BURIALL	33
TYPE				
THY PILLOW WAS BUT TYPE AND SHADE AT BEST	. .	331	JACOBS PLW	53
TYR'D				
I WCNDER'D MUCH, BUT TYR'D	. . .	141	RGNRTN	70
TYR'D HERE, I COME TO SYCHAR, THENCE	. . .	151	THE SEARCH	21
TYRE				
DOTH ALL THINGS WAKE, AND WHERE ALL MIX AND TYRE	. .	324	THE NIGHT	44
AT THIS GREAT FEAST, AND IN A TYRE	. . . .	272	WHT SUNDAY	6
TYRES				
WHICH NEITHER TYRES, NOR DOTH CORRODE	. .	318	THE ASS	11
UNAWARES				
AND UNAWARES DCTH OFTEN SEIZE	. . .	150	RELIGION	39
UNBITTED				
UNBITTED TONGUES ARE IN THEIR PENANCE DOUBLE	. .	194	RLS + LSNS	71
UNBOWEL'D				
UNBOWEL'D NATURE, SHEW'C THEE HER RECRUITS	. .	145	RSRCTN +IM	21
UNCALMES				
UNCALMES THESE TO A FLOUD	. . . .	176	THE STORM	14
UNCLEAN				
ARE DARK, AND UNCLEAN IN THY SIGHT	. . .	208	REPENTANCE	66
UNCLOUDED				
WHILE ALL THE PLANETS DID UNCLCUDED PASS.	. .	268	ASCN-DAY A	46
UNDEFIL'D				
THOU HOLY, HARMLESS, UNCEFIL'C HIGH-PRIEST.	. .	216	DRESSING	9
AN UNCEFIL'D AND NEW-HEAW'D ONE	. . .	152	THE SEARCH	47
UNDISCOVER'D				
WHCSE UNDISCOVER'C VIRGIN GLORY	. .	315	DWELLNG-PL	3
UNDO				
THOU GRIEV'ST, MAN SHOULD HIMSELF UNDO	. . .	298	JESUS WP B	24
FCR THOUGH DEATH CANNOT SC UNDO	. . . .	299	JESUS WP B	34
UNDONE				
DESIST FOND FCOL, BE NOT UNDONE	. . .	283	GARLAND	29
UNDRESS				
THIS BRCUGHT THEE FORTH, WHERE NOW THOU DIDST UNDRESS	.	155	ISAACS M.	47
UNDRESSE				
LCRD. WHEN THCU DIDST THY SELFE UNDRESSE	. .	163	INCARNATN	1
UNDREST				
AND QUITE UNDREST JUST NCW WITH THEE	. . .	312	FAIR+YONG	48
WHO WILL ASCEND, MUST BE UNDREST.	. . .	269	ASCSN-HYMN	6
UNEMPTY'D				
WHO FILS THE WORLDS UNEMPTY'D GRANARIES.	. . .	195	RLS + LSNS	100
UNFEIGNED				
BUT TC WRITE TRUE, UNFEIGNED VERSE	. . .	329	ANGUISH	15
UNFINISH'D				
UNFINISH'D, WE SHALL GLADLY SIT	. . .	350	L'ENVOY	26
UNFOLD				
AND HEAVEN ITS AZURE DIC UNFOLD	. . .	140	RGNRTN	52
UNHAPPY				
MAKES MCST UNHAPPY, OR MOST FCRTUNATES.	. . .	155	ISAACS M.	46
BLESSED, UNHAPPY CITY. DEARLY LCV'D	. . .	296	JESUS WP A	1
UNHAUNTED				
CALM AND UNHAUNTEC AS IS THY DARK TENT	. .	324	THE NIGHT	38
UNION				
FRUITION, UNICN, GLORY, LIFE	. . .	348	HOLY BIBLE	31
UNITE				
UNITE, AND RAISE UP ALL THAT DYED, AT CNCE.	. .	298	JESUS WP B	8

		PAGE	TITLE	LINE

UNITE   (CON'T)
   I' UNITE THOSE PEECES, HOPING TO FIND OUT · · · 168 VNTY SPRIT 26
   THINGS DISTANT DOTH UNITE · · · · · · · 183 THRS A TYE 10
   AND DEATH UNITE · · · · · · · · · 185 PASSION 32
   UNITED KEEPS FOR EVER. · · · · · · · 302 THE KNOT 16
UNIVERSAL
   HENCE CATHOLICK OR UNIVERSAL CAME · · · · 330 JACOBS PLW 15
UNJUST
   OR THAT HE CAN ENDURE TO BE UNJUST · · · · 144 RSRCTN +IM 17
UNKIND
   THUS WRETCHED I, AND MOST UNKIND · · · · 240 MISERY 33
UNKINDE
   A JUDGE WERT THOU, AND HOW UNKINDE. · · · 305 ST MARY MN 62
   BUT STILL UNKINDE. ART THIS DAY NOTHING MOV'D. · · 296 JESUS WP A 2
   I WERE MOST FOOLISH AND UNKINDE · · · · 342 OBSEQUIES 9
UNKNIT
   THAT MAY UNKNIT · · · · · · · · 191 THE MATCH 29
UNKNOWN
   ABOVE THE STARS, A TRACK UNKNOWN, AND HIGH · · 155 ISAACS M. 50
   THAT IS TO HIM UNKNOWN. · · · · · · 271 ALL GONE 24
   (UNKNOWN TO US) THE HEAVENS WILT BOW · · · 212 DAWNING 26
UNLOCK
   UNLOCK THY BOWRES. · · · · · · · 211 DAWNING 10
   ART STILL THE SAME, AND CANST UNLOCK · · · 273 WHT SUNDAY 47
   UNLOCK THE WAY · · · · · · · · 160 THE SHOWRE 10
UNLOCKS
   THE THANKFUL EARTH UNLOCKS HER SELF, AND BLENDS · 156 ISAACS M. 59
UNMOVEABLE
   THY ARM UNMOVEABLE FOR EVER LAID · · · · 285 PSALM 104 17
UNNUMBER'D
   UNNUMBER'D IN THY DUST, WHEN ALL THIS FRAME · · 177 EVNG-WTCH 4
UNPRACTIC'D
   STOOD BARE BEFORE UNPRACTIC'D EYES · · · · 311 FAIR+YONG 18
UNRAK'ST
   AND THOU UNRAK'ST THY FIRE, THOSE SPARKS WILL BRING · 195 RLS + LSNS 130
UNRAKE
   WHEN THY NAP'S OVER, STIR THY FIRE, UNRAKE · · 196 RLS + LSNS 133
UNREGARDED
   ALL UNREGARDED, AND THY BOOK · · · · · 240 MISERY 27
UNRELIEV'D
   MY LIFE, AND UNRELIEV'D · · · · · · 311 THE SEED 87
UNRULY
   TO CHECK THE MULE, UNRULY MAN · · · · 221 AFFLICTION 18
UNSEARCHABLE
   UNSEARCHABLE, NOW WITH ONE WINKE · · · · 163 MT. OLVS A 28
UNSEEN
   (UNSEEN) BOTH HEAVEN, AND EARTH. · · · 220 PSALM 121 4
   MY LOVE-TWIST HELD THEE UP, MY UNSEEN LINK. · · 225 RETIREMENT 22
   HE LIVED OF US UNSEEN. · · · · · · 247 I WALKT 21
   THAT GOD IS TRUE, AS HERBS UNSEEN · · · · 279 THE STARRE 31
   SO IN SIGHS AND UNSEEN TEARS · · · · · 281 JOY 27
   AT NOISE, BUT THRIVE UNSEEN AND DUMB. · · · 309 THE SEED 46
   STILL LODGED, WHERE ALL THY UNSEEN ARROWS SHROWD · 307 RAIN-BOW 34
   GOD AND HIS CREATURES, THOUGH UNSEEN. · · · 313 THE STONE 21
   UNTO THAT PROVIDENCE, WHOSE UNSEEN ARM · · 288 THE BIRD 9
   UNSEEN BY HIM, TILL THEY ARRIVE · · · · 300 PROVIDENCE 10
   SOFTEN THE MOULD, WHILE ALL UNSEEN · · · 337 PSALM 65 37
   (UNSEEN) SUCH JOYS I FEEL. · · · · · 337 THE THRONE 7
   THEY LIVE UNSEEN, WHEN HERE THEY FADE. · · · 346 THE BOOK 4
UNSTAIN'D
   FLEW HOME UNSTAIN'D BY HIS NEW KIN · · · 209 THE BURIAL 6
UNSWADLE
   TO DRESSE THEM, AND UNSWADLE DEATH. · · · 209 THE BURIAL 12
UNTAINTED
   ELSEWHERE, AND FLOWING KEEPS UNTAINTED. · · 212 DAWNING 36
   UNTAINTED THROUGH THIS MASSE · · · · 145 RSRCTN +IM 32
UNTAM'D
   NOW HERE BELOW WHERE YET UNTAM'D · · · 226 RETIREMENT 34
UNTHANKFUL
   BLESS THEE, AND BLAME UNTHANKFUL MAN. · · · 334 AGREEMENT 72
UNTHRIFT
   THE UNTHRIFT SUNNE SHOT VITALL GOLD · · · 140 RGNRTN 50
UNTIR'D
   A STATE UNTIR'D · · · · · · · 162 PURSUITE 10
UNTOUCH'D
   UNTOUCH'D BY ANY, AND WHAT NEED · · · · 163 MT. OLVS A 13
UNTYE
   O THEN, JUST THEN. BREAK OR UNTYE · · · 319 THE ASS 53
UNVEIL
   WHEN FIRST THY EYES UNVEIL, GIVE THY SOUL LEAVE · 191 RLS + LSNS 1
UNVEIL'D
   IMMEDIATE, PURE AND UNVEIL'D EYE · · · · 349 L'ENVOY 18
UNVEILS
   TO CANDLE-LIGHT UNVEILS. · · · · · 310 THE SEED 68
UP
   SERIOUS THEY SEEM'D AND BOUGHT UP ALL · · · 302 ORNAMENT 5
   LAID UP ALL HER ARCHIVES AND BOOKS) · · · 303 ORNAMENT 12
   THE BLADE GROWS UP ALIVE AND GREEN. · · · 337 PSALM 65 38
   BUT LIFT THEM UP, WHERE STILL ALIVE · · · 339 DEATH B 29
   AND SETS UP LAWS TO PULL HIS HONOR DOWN. · · 330 JACOBS PLW 20

		PAGE	TITLE	LINE
UP	(CCN'T)			
I'LE SEAL MY EYES UP, AND TO THY COMMANDS	• • •	321	HIDDN TRSR	29
I'LE GET ME UP BEFORE THE SUN	• • •	295	PALM-SUNDY	34
LIFT UP YOUR HEADS AND LEAVE YOUR MOANS.	• • •	294	PALM-SUNDY	14
UNITE, AND RAISE UP ALL THAT DYED, AT ONCE.	• • •	298	JESUS WP B	8
WHICH IS REQUIR'D TO MAKE UP LIFE	• • •	299	JESUS WP B	27
SCME UP THE MOUNTAINS PAST BY SECRET WAYS	• • •	285	PSALM 104	23
UP, O MY SOUL, AND BLESSE THE LORD. O GOD	• • •	284	PSALM 104	1
FRESH GROVES GROW UP, AND THEIR GREEN BRANCHES SHOOT	•	289	THE TIMBER	6
YET, NEVER SLEEP THE SUN UP, PRAYER SHOU'D	• • •	192	RLS + LSNS	7
AND SPAN UP NIGHT.	• • •	189	RESOLVE	20
WHEN THE WORLDS UP, AND EV'RY SWARM ABROAD	• • •	192	RLS + LSNS	31
TIE UP HIS HANDS, THAT CARES MOCK GOD, AND MAN.	• • •	193	RLS + LSNS	48
OF NIGHT SHUT UP THY LEAVES, BE CHAST, GOD PRYS	• • •	196	RLS + LSNS	136
O LOSE IT NOT. LOCK UP, WILT CHANGE THOSE LIGHTS	• • •	196	RLS + LSNS	143
WHAT'S GOOD SCORE UP FOR JOY, THE BAD WEL SCANN'C	• • •	195	RLS + LSNS	119
UP WITH THY CURTAINS, GIVE THY SOUL THE WING	• • •	195	RLS + LSNS	128
SEAL NOT THY EYES UP FROM THE POOR, BUT GIVE	• • •	193	RLS + LSNS	61
(WHICH WAK'D BY HEAT, AND BEAMS, MAKES UP	• • •	203	DSRDR + FR	32
UP WHERE THOU ART, AMONGST THY TIRE	• • •	204	DSRDR + FR	48
WHEN SIX YEARS THENCE DIGG'D UP, SOME YOUTHFULL EYE	•	201	THE CHECK	6
AWAKE, GLAD HEART. GET UP, AND SING	• • •	199	NTVTY 1	1
TO OFFER UP THE SACRIFICE	• • •	199	NTVTY 1	12
YOUR MAKER PENT UP IN A GRAVE	• • •	164	INCARNATN	11
I TOOKE THEM UP, AND (MUCH JOY'C) WENT ABOUT	• • •	168	VNTY SPRIT	25
BROKE UP SOME SEALES, WHICH NONE HAD TOUCH'D BEFORE	•	167	VNTY SPRIT	10
ALL AGES UP, WHO DREW THIS CIRCLE, EVEN	• • •	178	EVNG-WTCH	13
BUT A DARK AND SEAL'D UP WOMBE	• • •	171	COME, COME	23
GO, GO, SEAL UP THY LOCKS	• • •	187	NO DO THEY	9
I TOOKE THEM UP AND LAYD	• • •	139	RGNRTN	30
AND SWEEPE UP SOUTH AND WEST	• • •	146	DAY OF JDG	4
WOO'D BY THE SUN SWELS UP TO BE HIS SHROWD	• • •	155	ISAACS M.	54
UP IN ONE CLOUD, AND SO RETURNS THE SKIES	• • •	156	ISAACS M.	61
OTHERS WERE TYM'D AND TRAIN'D UP TO'T BUT THOU	• • •	156	ISAACS M.	67
O'RE MY HARD HEART, THAT'S BOUND UP, AND ASLEEP	• • •	160	THE SHOWRE	15
THEY'RE STOR'D UP IN THE SOCKET, WHERE THEY LYE	• • •	158	THE LAMPE	19
AND OFFER'D UP SO EARLY UNTO HEAVEN	• • •	154	ISAACS M.	6
NOW POINT HIM OUT, GROWN UP A MAN.	• • •	151	THE SEARCH	10
WHICH HELD UP NIGHT, AND DAY	• • •	147	DAY OF JDG	16
SUMMON UP ALL THAT ARE ASLEEPE	• • •	147	DAY OF JDG	19
UP THEN, AND KEEP	• • •	226	RETIREMENT	54
THAT I MAY GET ME UP, AND GO.	• • •	228	PILGRIMAGE	12
WE CLIMB UP THIS, AND HAVE TOO ALL THE WAY	• • •	230	LAW + GOSP	17
AND SING, AND WEEP, SOAR'D UP INTO THE RING	• • •	232	THE WORLD	47
LEADS UP TO GOD	• • •	233	THE WORLD	54
TAKE UP MY DAY, WHILE THOU DOST SHINE	• • •	240	MISERY	26
LORD, BIND ME UP, AND LET ME LYE	• • •	239	MISERY	1
TAKE UP, AND TUNE HIS YEAR	• • •	236	CONSTLATN	22
AND FROTHIE NOISE WHICH UP AND DOWN DOTH FLIE	• • •	234	MUTINIE	24
THERE IS AT ALL TIMES (THOUGH SHUT UP) IN YOU	• • •	244	THE SAP	39
THEN SEAL IT UP, THAT AS NONE SEE	• • •	242	MISERY	103
ROSE UP, AND CANCELL'D TWO DEATHS DUE TO THEE.	• • •	217	EASTER-DAY	8
STARS SHUT UP SHOP, MISTS PACK AWAY	• • •	210	FAITH	19
FAITH SPANS UP BLISSE, WHAT SIN, AND DEATH	• • •	211	FAITH	37
THE DEW THY HERBS DRINK UP BY NIGHT	• • •	207	REPENTANCE	39
SEDUCED SOUL SIGHS UP TO THEE	• • •	207	REPENTANCE	20
I SATE ALONE, AND TAKING UP	• • •	207	REPENTANCE	29
MY LOVE-TWIST HELD THEE UP, MY UNSEEN LINK.	• • •	225	RETIREMENT	22
AND LESS'NING STILL GROW UP INVISIBLY	• • •	224	TEMPEST	44
UP TO THOSE BRIGHT, AND GLADSOME HILS	• • •	220	PSALM 121	1
MAKES UP BUT LECTURES FOR HIS EYE, AND EAR.	• • •	223	TEMPEST	20
CHIDE, AND FLY UP, MISTS OF CORRUPTEST FOME	• • •	223	TEMPEST	26
THEN TAKING UP WHAT I COULD NEEREST SPIE	• • •	247	I WALKT	15
UP TO THE SKIES	• • •	267	ASCN-DAY A	10
BUT WHEN THE HAND THAT LOCKT HER UP, GIVES ROOM	• • •	271	ALL GONE	31
AND LIKE OLD CLOATHS FOLD UP THESE SKIES	• • •	349	L'ENVOY	8
DRY UP THEIR ARMS, WHO VEX THY SPOUSE	• • •	350	L'ENVOY	33
SPRING UP, O WINE	• • •	340	THE FEAST	25
UPPER				
THESE UPPER SPRINGS AND NONE ELSE MAKE THEM GROW.	• •	291	THE TIMBER	52
THOU FROM THY UPPER SPRINGS ABOVE, FROM THOSE	• •	285	PSALM 104	37
THY UPPER RIVER, WHICH ABOUNDS	• • •	336	PSALM 65	29
UPRIGHT				
WHO HATH THE UPRIGHT HEART, THE SINGLE EYE	• • •	327	RIGHTSNESS	9
UPWARDS				
STRIVE UPWARDS STIL, AND POINT HIM THE WAY HOME.	• •	223	TEMPEST	28
SO SIGH'D I UPWARDS STILL, AT LAST	• • •	139	RGNRTN	26
URG'D				
BUT AS I URG'D THUS, AND WRIT DOWN	• • •	152	THE SEARCH	67
URGENT				
WHOSE URGENT SOUND LIKE UNTO THAT	• • •	325	ABELS BLOD	17
URN				
AND COMMON URN	• • •	179	SILENCE	22
AND WHEN THIS DUST FALLS TO THE URN	• • •	170	RETREATE	31
AT WHOSE DUMBE URN	• • •	248	I WALKT	62
US'D				
BECAUSE THEY US'D MY SAVIOR SO.	• • •	317	MEN OF WAR	34
SINCE I IN STORMS US'D MOST TO BE	• • •	345	THE WREATH	1
USE				
NONE COULD WITH MORE ADVANTAGE USE, THEN I.	• • •	320	HIDDN TRSR	18

		PAGE	TITLE	LINE
USE	(CON'T)			
WISE HEADS SHALL USE		338	THE THRONE	9
GRASS FOR THE CATTEL, AND HERBS FOR MANS USE		285	PSALM 104	41
BEGETTING VIRGINS WHERE THEY USE TO FLOW.		291	THE TIMBER	50
HARK, AND MAKE USE OF THIS ENSUING STORY.		282	GARLAND	4
DOTH USE HIS ROD		221	AFFLICTION	12
USE, WITH LIKE CUSTOME, AS MY KITCHEN FOOD.		217	DRESSING	36
BUT MOST WOULD USE NO WING.		232	THE WORLD	48
AND WIND, AND WATER TO THY USE		176	THE STORM	23
STARS ARE OF MIGHTY USE, THE NIGHT		174	JOY OF LIF	9
I SEE THE USE. AND KNOW MY BLOOD		175	THE STORM	1
WHEN CONSCIENCE BY LEW'D USE HAD NOT LOST SENSE		154	ISAACS M.	19
SOME USE FOR EARES		141	RGNRTN	59
USEFUL				
O USEFUL ELEMENT AND CLEAR.		344	WATER-FALL	23
USELES				
VEILES BECAME USELES, ALTARS FEL		210	FAITH	25
USURERS				
WITHOUT THAT BRIBE WHICH USURERS IMPOSE.		328	RIGHTSNESS	42
USURP				
ALL MISTS THAT WOULD USURP THIS DAY.		217	EASTER-DAY	10
USURP'D				
USURP'D. IT NEVER SHOULD ME GRIEVE		301	PROVIDENCE	40
USURPS				
FRESH DOTAGE TEMPTS, OR OLD USURPS HIS WILL.		161	DSTRQCTION	16
UTENSILS				
AND OUTWARD UTENSILS THESE GLORIES ARE		225	RETIREMENT	5
UTMOST				
WHEREFORE WITH MY UTMOST STRENGTH		214	PRAISE	9
OUT-RUNS THE EARTH, AND LINES THE UTMOST POLE.		193	RLS + LSNS	54
VAIL				
THAT SACRED VAIL DRAWN O'R THY GLORIOUS NOON		323	THE NIGHT	2
AS WITH A VAIL THOU HIDST IT, THY FLOODS PLAID		285	PSALM 104	19
VAIN				
WHO NOTING WELL MY VAIN ABEAR		282	GARLAND	27
HE THAT HATH LEFT LIFES VAIN JOYS AND VAIN CARE		290	THE TIMBER	29
HE THAT HATH LEFT LIFES VAIN JOYS AND VAIN CARE		290	THE TIMBER	29
VAIN, SINFUL ART. WHO FIRST DID FIT		297	HERODIAS	1
COUNT BUT THE BLOTS OF A VAIN PEN.		335	JUDGEMENT	26
AS ONE THEN DUST MORE VILE AND VAIN.		315	THE STONE	59
NEW FLAMES, BESIDES WHERE THESE LODGE VAIN HEARTS MOURN		196	RLS + LSNS	131
NOR DOST THOU SPEND ONE TEARE IN VAIN, FOR STILL		158	THE LAMPE	17
VAIN WITS AND EYES		266	VAIN WITS	1
WHICH SADNESS BREEDS IN THE MOST VAIN		345	THE WREATH	14
(O NOT IN VAIN) NOW BEG THY BREATH.		345	THE WREATH	15
VAINE				
ESTEEM'D (VAINE THINGS) OF TWO WHOLE ELEMENTS		144	RSRCTN +IM	13
SURE (THEN SAID I) MY QUEST IS VAINE		152	THE SEARCH	49
VAINLY				
TO THINK, HE SHOULD BE SO LONG VAINLY LEAD.		290	THE TIMBER	40
VALE				
AND PURLING CORN DOTH CLOATH THE VALE.		337	PSALM 65	46
FROM THAT HIL TO THIS VALE		243	THE SAP	20
AND KNIT ME TO THEE, THAT THOUGH IN THIS VALE		234	MUTINIE	19
VALLEY				
OF THE VALLEY.		220	HOLY COMM.	50
VALLEYS				
SO HILLS AND VALLEYS INTO SINGING BREAK		288	THE BIRD	13
WHICH RUN FROM HILLS TO VALLEYS, AND IMPROVE		285	PSALM 104	31
VALLY				
THE VALLY, OR THE MOUNTAIN		197	CORRUPTION	22
VAN				
AND, WITH THY ANGELS IN THE VAN		212	DAWNING	27
VANISH				
STARS NOW VANISH WITHOUT NUMBER		212	DAWNING	19
AND VANISH CLEANE AWAY		147	DAY OF JDG	14
QUITE VANISH AND DECAY.		283	GARLAND	32
VANITIE				
TAKE THE DOWN-RODE TO VANITIE		240	MISERY	14
VANITIES				
THY CURIOUS VANITIES AND RARE.		304	ST MARY MN	33
VANITY				
NOW ALL IS DONE, FINDE ALL IS VANITY.		320	HIDDN TRSR	10
AND EV'RY PUBLISH'D VANITY		265	INTRO. 2	26
O WHAT A VANITY IS MAN.		166	THE CALL	42
RAN I IN CHASE OF VANITY		348	HOLY BIBLE	14
VARIOUS				
HIS WONDROUS METHOD, MARK THE VARIOUS SCENES		194	RLS + LSNS	92
THEREFORE WHILE THE VARIOUS SHOWERS		281	JOY	17
THROUGH ALL THY FAIR, AND VARIOUS STORY		207	REPENTANCE	31
VARY				
AN HOUR, OR SO, THEN VARY.		187	NO DO THEY	22
VAST				
VAST CIRCLING AZURE, GIDDY CLOUDS, DAYS, NIGHTS.		194	RLS + LSNS	90
AND NOUGHT MUST STAND OF THAT VAST SPACE		147	DAY OF JDG	15
THE WORLD READ TO HIM. ALL THE VAST EXPENCE		223	TEMPEST	18
AND IN YOUR VAST PROGRESSIONS OVERLOOK		235	CONSTLATN	7
LIKE A VAST SHADOW MOV'D, IN WHICH THE WORLD		231	THE WORLD	6
'TWAS NOT THAT VAST, ALMIGHTY MEASURE		299	JESUS WP B	26
VEIL				
FROM YOUR DARK HEARTS THIS VEIL REMOVE.		292	THE JEWS	37

		PAGE	TITLE	LINE
VEILES				
VEILES BECAME USELES, ALTARS FEL	• • • • •	210	FAITH	25
VEILS				
THEY ARE BUT VEILS, AND CYPERS DRAWN	• • • •	334	JUDGEMENT	9
VEINES				
PASSING THROUGH THE EARTHS DARKE VEINES	• • •	150	RELIGION	34
ON VEINES OF SULPHUR UNDER GROUND.	• • • •	150	RELIGION	40
VERGE				
AND ON THE VERGE OF THAT DARK, DREADFUL PIT	• •	188	RELAPSE	3
VERSE				
MY HEART, MY VERSE. • • • • •	• •	204	DSRDR + FR	60
BUT TO WRITE TRUE, UNFEIGNED VERSE	• • •	329	ANGUISH	15
FOR IN THIS BRIGHT, INSTRUCTING VERSE	• •	316	MEN OF WAR	17
AND BE MORE WILD THAN IS THY VERSE.	• •	221	AFFLICTION	16
WHERE ARE THY PALMES, THY BRANCHES, AND THY VERSE.	•	217	EASTER-DAY	11
VERTUE				
SUCH SECRET LIFE, AND VERTUE IN IT LIES	• •	244	THE SAP	31
AND THRIVING VICE FOR VERTUE JUDGE. •	• •	309	THE SEED	40
BID ME, BY VERTUE FROM HIM, CHALENGE HERE	• •	188	RELAPSE	23
VESSEL				
THE VESSEL WHERE YOU PUT IT BE FOR SURE	• •	244	THE SAP	37
TO WASH YOUR VESSEL WEL. THEN HUMBLY TAKE	• •	244	THE SAP	43
VEST				
NO FROST, BUT FLOURISH'D IN THAT YOUTHFUL VEST	• •	268	ASCN-DAY A	43
VEX				
VEX NOT, THAT BUT ONE SEES THEE GROW	• •	309	THE SEED	27
DRY UP THEIR ARMS, WHO VEX THY SPOUSE	• •	350	L'ENVOY	33
VEYL				
THIS LONG WORN VEYL. THEN SHINE AND SPREAD	• •	349	L'ENVOY	9
AND FIRE WILL PURGE YOUR CALLOUS VEYL.	• •	266	VAIN WITS	9
WHEN THE VEYL BROKE WITH THY LAST BREATH	• •	219	HOLY COMM.	22
VEYLE				
ONELY THIS VEYLE WHICH THOU HAS BROKE	• •	277	COCK-CRWNG	37
THIS VEYLE, I SAY, IS ALL THE CLOKE •	• •	277	COCK-CRWNG	39
THIS VEYLE THY FULL-EYED LOVE DENIES	• •	277	COCK-CRWNG	41
VEYLS				
SINCE IN THESE VEYLS MY ECCLIPS'D EYE	• •	168	VNTY SPRIT	30
UNDER VEYLS HERE • • • • •	• •	340	THE FEAST	40
VIBRATIONS				
QUICK VIBRATIONS • • • • •	• •	172	MIDNIGHT	12
VICE				
VICE IN A FAIRER NAME. • • •	• •	205	IDLE VERSE	12
AND THRIVING VICE FOR VERTUE JUDGE. •	•	309	THE SEED	40
IF ALL THE SUBTILTIES OF VICE • •	• •	311	FAIR+YONG	17
AND SPLENDID VICE DESTROYS THE GREAT.	• •	318	THE ASS	8
VICISSITUDE				
VICISSITUDE PLAIES ALL THE GAME	• • •	222	AFFLICTION	29
VICTORIE				
AND SINCE THINE IS VICTORIE • •	• •	249	BEGGING A	15
VICTORIOUS				
AND SING HIS SAD VICTORIOUS STORY. •	• •	341	THE FEAST	60
VICTORY				
WHICH BRINGS POOR DUST THE VICTORY.	• •	339	THE FEAST	18
I, VICTORY • • • • •	• •	340	THE FEAST	19
FEEL ME A SHARER IN THY VICTORY.	• •	267	ASCN-DAY A	8
THEIR VICTORY • • • •	• •	232	THE WORLD	45
ALL CROWN'D WITH VICTORY • •	• •	237	CONSTLATN	50
I, VICTORY • • • • •	• •	340	RGNRTN	1
VIE				
WHICH SHOULD MOST VIE • • •	• •	186	PASSION	53
VIEW				
VIEW THY FORE-RUNNERS. CREATURES GIV'N TO BE	• •	201	THE CHECK	25
AND HE WAS SURE TO VIEW THEM. • •	• •	197	CORRUPTION	28
STILL YONG AND FINE. BUT WHAT IS STILL IN VIEW	•	306	RAIN-BOW	1
VIEWD				
THEY VIEWD, (FOR IDLENESS HATH THERE	• •	303	ORNAMENT	11
VIGOUR				
WHEN THOU WITH-DRAW'ST THEIR BREATH, THEIR VIGOUR SLEEPS		287	PSALM 104	79
FOR SINNE TOOKE STRENGTH, AND VIGOUR FROM THE LAW.	• •	159	MANS FALL	20
VILE				
AS ONE THEN DUST MORE VILE AND VAIN.	• •	315	THE STONE	59
THE VILE DESPIGHT DONE TO THY NAME. •	• •	335	JUDGEMENT	34
AND IN MY FLESH, THOUGH VILE, AND LOW	• •	212	DAWNING	41
NOTHIN'S MORE VILE THAN IS MY BREATH	• •	208	REPENTANCE	74
LORD, SINCE THOU DIDST IN THIS VILE CLAY	• •	206	REPENTANCE	1
VILLANY				
I DARE NOT THINK SUCH VILLANY. • • •	• •	316	MEN OF WAR	14
VINE				
MOST BLESSED VINE. • • • • •	• •	185	PASSION	16
VIOLET				
WHILE THE LOW VIOLET THRIVES AT THEIR ROOT.	• •	289	THE TIMBER	8
VIOLETS				
AS HARMLESS VIOLETS, WHICH GIVE • •	• •	339	DEATH B	21
VIP'ROUS				
A VIP'ROUS THOUGHT, SOME SYLLABLES ARE SWORDS.	• •	194	RLS + LSNS	70
VIRGIN				
WHOSE UNDISCOVER'D VIRGIN GLORY. • •	• •	315	DWELLNG-PL	3
BRIGHT QUEEN OF HEAVEN. GODS VIRGIN SPOUSE.	• •	302	THE KNOT	1
WHEN LIKE A VIRGIN CLAD IN FLOWERS AND GREEN	• •	268	ASCN-DAY A	41
VIRGIN-CRUMS				
SOFTLY REST ALL THY VIRGIN-CRUMS.	• •	209	THE BURIAL	9

	PAGE	TITLE	LINE
VIRGIN-FLOWERS			
FAIRE, VIRGIN-FLOWERS, AND HALLOW'D WELLS	153	THE SEARCH	70
VIRGIN-SHRINE			
THROUGH THAT PURE VIRGIN-SHRINE	323	THE NIGHT	1
VIRGIN-SOILE			
A VIRGIN-SOILE, WHICH NO	140	RGNRTN	38
VIRGINS			
BUT IN A VIRGINS NATIVE BLUSH AND FEARS	155	ISAACS M.	35
BEGETTING VIRGINS WHERE THEY USE TO FLOW.	291	THE TIMBER	50
VIRTUE			
WHERE WEEPING VIRTUE PARTS WITH MAN.	322	CHILDEHOOD	32
BOTH LIGHT FROM THEE, AND VIRTUE HAD	265	INTRO. 2	10
VIRTUES			
THEIR VIRTUES HERE	339	DEATH B	22
VISIBLES			
WHERE FRAIL VISIBLES RULE THE MINDE	318	THE ASS	5
VISION			
NO VOICE, NOR VISION KNOW	238	SHEPHEARDS	18
VISIONS			
AND VOWS AND VISIONS, THOUGH HER FOES CRYE, NONE.	331	JACOBS PLW	34
IN MILDE, CLEAR VISIONS, WITHOUT A FROWN	330	JACOBS PLW	3
VISIT'ST			
THOU VISIT'ST THE LOW EARTH, AND THEN	336	PSALM 65	27
VISITS			
AFFORDED VISITS, AND STILL PARADISE LAY	197	CORRUPTION	23
HOW RICH, O LORD. HOW FRESH THY VISITS ARE.	198	UNPRFTBLNS	1
VITALL			
THE UNTHRIFT SUNNE SHOT VITALL GOLD	140	RGNRTN	50
UNTILL AT LAST FULL WITH THE VITALL RAY	144	RSRCTN +IM	9
AND LONGING FOR THY BRIGHT AND VITALL FIRE	278	THE STARRE	18
VIVIFIE			
DOTH VIVIFIE	345	QUICKNESS	14
VOCAL			
WHOSE STREAMS STILL VOCAL, STILL COMPLAIN	325	ABELS BLOD	3
BUT AS THIS RESTLESS, VOCALL SPRING	212	DAWNING	33
AND VOCALL JOYES	177	MRNG-WTCH	21
VOGUE			
LONG REIGN'D THIS VOGUE, AND THOU CAST BY	348	HOLY BIBLE	17
VOICE			
THE TURTLES VOICE	340	THE FEAST	50
WHIRLE-WINDS, AND CLOUDS, AND THE SOFT VOICE	149	RELIGION	18
HEARK, HOW HE DOTH INVITE THEE. WITH WHAT VOICE	202	THE CHECK	36
THE WORD IN CHARACTERS, GOD IN THE VOICE.	198	SCRIPTURES	8
NO VOICE, NOR VISION KNOW	238	SHEPHEARDS	18
AND LIKE THAT LAMB WHICH HAD THE DRAGONS VOICE	237	CONSTLATN	43
WITH HIS MILDE BLOOD IN VOICE AND WILL	326	ABELS BLOD	43
WHOSE PEACE BUT BY SOME ANGELS WING OR VOICE	324	THE NIGHT	39
WHEN SHALL WE HEAR THAT GLORIOUS VOICE	335	JUDGEMENT	17
THAT VOICE, WHICH TO EACH SECRET BED	335	JUDGEMENT	19
THE SMALL, STILL VOICE, AT SOME LOW COTTAGE KNOCKS	330	JACOBS PLW	9
WITH ONE ATTESTING VOICE DETECT	314	THE STONE	40
AT THY REBUKE THEY FLED, AT THE KNOWN VOICE	285	PSALM 104	21
(THOUGH SINGLE VOICES ARE BUT LOW)	325	ABELS BLOD	8
AND SHALL WE THEN NO VOICES LIFT.	200	NTVTY 2	5
BECAUSE MOST VOICES LIKE THE SHELL	150	RELIGION	48
IS FULL OF VOICES, MAN IS CALL'D, AND HURL'D	161	DSTRQCTION	12
VOID			
DARK, VOID, AND CRUDE	218	HOLY COMM.	7
THE GROUND WAS CURST, AND VOID OF STORE.	264	INTRO. 1	8
VOLUMES			
CAN DO NO MORE. MY VOLUMES SED	187	NO DO THEY	5
VOMITS			
FEED ON THOSE VOMITS OF MY HEART.	240	MISERY	20
VOW'D			
OF HIS VOW'D HEART, WHOM THOU HAST KEPT	326	ABELS BLOD	28
VOWS			
AND VOWS AND VISIONS, THOUGH HER FOES CRYE, NONE.	331	JACOBS PLW	34
AND GRATIFIES THY SIN WITH VOWS.	297	HERODIAS	14
VOYDS			
THAT VOYDS BUT FILTH, AND STENCH. HAST THOU NO PRIZE	194	RLS + LSNS	75
VULTURS			
PATHS THAT ARE HIDDEN FROM THE VULTURS EYES	320	HIDDN TRSR	12
WADE			
OF THEIR RED SEA, A SPRING, I WASH, THEY WADE	159	MANS FALL	32
WAGES			
THE WAGES OF MY SINNE	180	BURIALL	5
WAIT			
TO WAIT UPON THY WREATH.	198	UNPRFTBLNS	15
THREE BLESSINGS WAIT UPON THEM, TWO OF WHICH	192	RLS + LSNS	29
THESE ALL UPON THEE WAIT, THAT THOU MAIST FEED	286	PSALM 104	73
OF MINE, MAY WAIT ON THINE.	213	ADMISSION	28
THAT WAIT ON THEE	210	FAITH	12
WAITS			
BUT WAITS UPON THIS WHEEL	222	AFFLICTION	32
WAITS INNOCENCE AND PLEASURE)	238	SHEPHEARDS	2
PRAISE WAITS IN ALL HUMILITY.	336	PSALM 65	2
THY SERVANT IS, AND WAITS ON THEE	181	BURIALL	37
WAK'D			
(WHICH WAK'D BY HEAT, AND BEAMS, MAKES UP	203	DSRDR + FR	32
WAKE			
THE DAY-STAR SPRINGS, I'LE WAKE AGEN.	177	EVNG-WTCH	2

		PAGE	TITLE	LINE

WAKE   (CCN'T)
TO WAKE IN THEE.   171   COME, COME   30
WHO NEVER WAKE TO GRONE, NOR WEEPE   164   THE CALL   8
DOTH ALL THINGS WAKE, AND WHERE ALL MIX AND TYRE   324   THE NIGHT   44
DEATH A NAP, TO WAKE MORE MERRY.   218   EASTER HYM   6
AND WEAVE IT FOR YOUR HEAD AGAINST YOU WAKE.   280   PALM-TREE   27
WALK
I WALK THE FIELDS OF BETHANI WHICH SHINE   268   ASCN-DAY A   37
WALK TO THE SKIE   269   ASCN-HYMN   10
ALL TCWARDS BETHLEM WALK   239   SHEPHEARDS   44
AND WALK TWO STEPS   203   DSRDR + FR   35
WALK WITH THY FELLOW-CREATURES. NCTE THE HUSF   192   RLS + LSNS   13
WALK BUT THE FIELCS, CR SIT DCWN AT SCME WEL   197   CORRUPTION   27
WALKE
I WALKE THE GARDEN, AND THERE SEE   152   THE SEARCH   37
MY GOC, WHEN I WALKE IN THOSE GROVES   148   RELIGION   1
MY WALKE A MONSTRCUS, MCUNTAIN'C THING   139   RGNRTN   20
WALKING
AND WALKING FROM HIS SUN, WHEN PAST   178   SILENCE   9
I SEE THEM WALKING IN AN AIR CF GLORY   271   ALL GONE   9
TRANSPLANTED PARACISE, GODS WALKING HOUR.   2   SON-DAYES   11
WALKS
THESE ARE YOUR WALKS, AND YOU HAVE SHEW'D THEM ME   271   ALL GONE   15
HE HEAV'NC THEIR WALKS, ANC WITH HIS EYES   152   THE SEARCH   61
WHO IS THE MAN THAT WALKS IN THEE. WHO LOVES   327   RIGHTSNESS   5
CHEATING HIMSELF, THAT MAN WALKS IN THIS PATH.   328   RIGHTSNESS   54
ONE AIM AND END, WHO WALKS NOT BY HIS SIGHT.   327   RIGHTSNESS   21
FROM SIN, HE WALKS A NARRCW, PRIVATE WAY.   290   THE TIMBER   34
WALKT
HE WEPT ONCE, WALKT WHOLE NIGHTS CN THEE   163   MT. OLVS A   21
WHEN YET I HAD NOT WALKT ABOVE   169   RETREATE   7
I WALKT THE OTHER DAY (TO SPENC MY HOUR)   246   I WALKT   1
WAN
FEARFUL AND WAN   328   RIGHTSNESS   44
WANDER
WOULD KEEP, ANC NEVER WANDER HERE.   324   THE NIGHT   42
WANDER'C
BUT WANDER'D UNDER TEMPESTS ALL THE YEAR   244   MT. OLV. B   12
WANCRED
WANCRED THROUGH DARKNESS, DENS AND MIRE.   311   FAIR+YONG   6
WANDRING
OUR GLIDES PRCVE WANDRING STARS   237   CONSTLATN   46
BY EV'RY WANDRING CLOC.   248   I WALKT   42
WANT
IN SEV'RALL PARTS SHALL WANT A NAME   177   EVNG-WTCH   6
WHEN LOWD JOYES WANT A WING   167   THE CALL   79
THAT TO BE MERRY I WANT SKILL   342   OBSEQUIES   23
WANTS
WISE HUSBANDS WILL (YCU SAY) THERE WANTS PREVENT   274   PROFFER   11
WAR
YET IS THERE PEACE STILL, AND NC WAR.   236   CONSTLATN   32
SC SHALL WE KNOW IN WAR AND PEACE   351   L'ENVOY   59
WARD
A WARC, AND STILL IN BONDS, ONE DAY   139   RGNRTN   10
WARD-ROBES
I SHALL NC WARD-RCBES LEAVE   173   CONTENT   6
WARE
HERE I RENOUNCE THE PCIS'NOUS WARE.   190   THE MATCH   12
WARES
THE WEAKER SORT SLIGHT, TRIVIALL WARES INSLAVE   232   THE WORLD   42
FCR ANY WARES.   275   PROFFER   40
WARM
AND WARM THE DEAD   248   I WALKT   44
I SAW THE WARM RECLUSE ALCNE TC LIE   247   I WALKT   19
ALL SAD WITH TEARS, WHICH LIKE WARM SUMMER RAIN   268   ASCN-DAY A   52
THE BEAMS THEY WARM THEM AT I'TH' LIGHT   207   REPENTANCE   40
THE FURROWS OF IT, THEN THY WARM   337   PSALM 65   35
CURB'C THEM, AND CLOATH'D THEE WELL AND WARM.   288   THE BIRD   10
BLEW THROUGH THY LODGING, WHERE THY OWN WARM WING   287   THE BIRD   2
HEAT MOTION GIVES. THEN WARM IT, TILL IT BEAT   283   LOVE-SICK   15
WARM'C
BUT NCW THE DEW AND SUN HAVE WARM'D MY BOWRES   274   PROFFER   5
I AM SO WARM'C NOW BY THIS GLANCE ON ME   245   MT. OLV. B   15
WARME
AND WARME ME AT THY GLCRICUS EYE.   277   COCK-CRWNG   46
STILL AS THOU BURN'ST, ANC THE WARME DROPPINCS CREEPE 158   THE LAMPE   14
WARMER
LET IT SUFFICE MY WARMER CAYS   205   IDLE VERSE   17
WARMS
SCARCE WARMS, BUT BY CONTRACTICN   189   RESOLVE   15
WARRE
SC BARRE ME IN, THAT I AM STILL AT WARRE   283   LOVE-SICK   8
AT CONSTANT WARRE WITH THEM. C COME AND REND   283   LOVE-SICK   9
WARS
ALL SKILFULL IN THE WARS   184   PEACE   4
THUS BY OUR LUSTS DISCRDER'D INTO WARS   237   CONSTLATN   45
WASH
TO WASH YCUR VESSEL WEL. THEN HUMBLY TAKE   244   THE SAP   43
BUT WITH TRUE TEARS WASH OFF YCUR MIRE.   266   VAIN WITS   4
BOTH WASH, AND WING MY SOUL.   176   THE STORM   24

		PAGE	TITLE	LINE
WASH	(CON'T)			
WASH OFF WITH TEARS, AND GET THY MASTERS HAND.		195	RLS + LSNS	120
OF THEIR RED SEA, A SPRING, I WASH, THEY WADE		159	MANS FALL	32
GO LEPER, GO. WASH TILL THY FLESH		306	ST MARY MN	69
MY SACRED WASH AND CLEANSER HERE		344	WATER-FALL	24
WASH'D				
WHILE THY BLOOD WASH'D ME WHITE AS HEAVEN.		265	INTRO. 2	28
WASTE				
THOUSANDS OF WILD AND WASTE INFUSIONS		214	MISERY	75
THY EASIE HANDS TO DO THIS WASTE.		304	ST MARY MN	24
DOTH FRET AND WRANGLE, PINE AND WASTE.		308	THE SEED	12
OF DEATH, DOST WASTE ALL SENSELESS, COLD AND DARK.		289	THE TIMBER	10
SIN EVERY DAY COMMITS MORE WASTE		335	JUDGEMENT	28
WASTS				
OR EXHALATIONS, AND WASTS		181	BURIALL	27
WATCH				
WATCH THE RETURNS OF LIGHT.		183	THRS A TYE	12
WATCH O'RE THAT LOOSE		180	BURIALL	8
IS A PLAIN WATCH, AND WITHOUT FIGURES WINDS		178	EVNG-WTCH	12
THESE FLAMES, AS THOU DOST THINE TO ME, I WATCH		157	THE LAMPE	7
DOTH ON THOSE HILLS OF MIRRHE, AND INCENSE WATCH.		156	BRT. CHRCH	4
WATCH STARS, OR PORE		146	RSRCTN +IM	66
LOVE GOD, AND LOVE THY NEIGHBOUR, WATCH, AND PRAY.		196	RLS + LSNS	140
WATCH, WHILE I SLEEP, OR PLAY.		187	NO DO THEY	32
HIS KNOCKING TIME, THE SOULS DUMB WATCH		324	THE NIGHT	35
WHERE TREES AND HERBS DID WATCH AND PEEP		323	THE NIGHT	23
OR IF IT WATCH, FORGIVE AND WEEP		326	ABELS BLOD	36
AND WATCH ALL NIGHT FOR MISTS OR SHOWERS		301	PROVIDENCE	29
KEEP CLEAN, BEAR FRUIT, EARN LIFE AND WATCH		309	THE SEED	47
DID WITH INTENTIVE LOCKS WATCH EVERY HOUR		306	RAIN-BOW	7
YET WHERE THE SHEPHEARDS WATCH		238	SHEPHEARDS	28
PERHAPS SOME NIGHTS HEE'L WATCH WITH YOU, AND PEEP		236	CONSTLATN	25
THEIR EYES WATCH FOR THE MORNING-HUE		276	COCK-CRWNG	7
TO WATCH FOR THY APPEARING HOUR.		276	COCK-CRWNG	16
WATCH FOR, AND KNOW THEIR LOVING STAR.		281	THE FAVOUR	8
WATCHES				
THE STARRES SHINE IN THEIR WATCHES		171	MIDNIGHT	4
WATCHFUL				
WHERE BIRDS LIKE WATCHFUL CLOCKS THE NOISELESS DATE		245	MAN	3
HIS WATCHFUL EYE IS EVER OPE		220	PSALM 121	7
GIVE WATCHFUL SPIRITS TO OUR GUIDES.		350	L'ENVOY	49
WATCHFULNESS				
SILENCE, AND LIGHT, AND WATCHFULNESS WITH YOU		236	CONSTLATN	13
WATCHING				
WATCHING THE BREAK OF THY GREAT DAY.		212	DAWNING	48
WATER				
WHERE, IF A TRAVELLER WATER CRAVE		212	DAWNING	31
THEIR LEAFS WITH WATER, AND HUMIDITIE.		223	TEMPEST	34
MY THOUGHTS, LIKE WATER WHICH SOME STONE DOTH START		234	MUTINIE	6
AND WIND, AND WATER TO THY USE		176	THE STORM	23
AND WATER IN ONE BEAME		172	MIDNIGHT	23
ON THAT WATER		172	MIDNIGHT	31
BUT DRESSE, AND WATER WITH THY GRACE		204	DSRDR + FR	55
HE BRINGS HIM WATER WITH HIS BREAD.		149	RELIGION	12
AND TURN ONCE MORE OUR WATER INTO WINE		150	RELIGION	52
WATER (THOUGH BOTH HEAVENS WINDOWS AND THE DEEP		307	RAIN-BOW	27
SOUL-QUICKNING RAIN, THIS LIVING WATER		296	JESUS WP A	10
THE SPIRIT, WATER, AND THE BLOOD		284	TRINITY-SN	5
DOEST WATER THE PARCH'D HILLS, WHOSE BREACHES CLOSE		285	PSALM 104	39
FOR SIN (LIKE WATER) HOURLY GLIDES		350	L'ENVOY	50
IS WATER'D BY THEIR TEARS, AS FLOWERS ARE FED		280	PALM-TREE	22
WATER'S				
WATER'S REFIN'D TO MOTION , AIRE TO LIGHT		223	TEMPEST	31
WATER'ST				
WATER'ST IT FOR THE SONS OF MEN		336	PSALM 65	28
THOU WATER'ST EVERY RIDGE OF LAND		337	PSALM 65	33
WATERS				
OF MANY WATERS, BEATETH AT		325	ABELS BLOD	18
WHEN THE PROUD WATERS RAGE. WHEN HEATHENS RULE		330	JACOBS PLW	29
IN THE DEEP WATERS, WHICH NO EYE CAN FIND.		284	PSALM 104	10
AND TREES OF LIFE NO OTHER WATERS LOVE		291	THE TIMBER	51
DESCEND, AND LIVING WATERS FLOW		291	THE JEWS	12
ALL THINGS HERE SHEW HIM HEAVEN, WATERS THAT FALL		223	TEMPEST	25
THY WATERS TO A SOUL THAT PINES.		273	WHT SUNDAY	48
AS WATERS HERE, HEADLONG AND LOOSE		240	MISERY	9
HEALE THEN THESE WATERS, LORD, OR BRING THY FLOCK		150	RELIGION	49
OF HER SICK WATERS, AND INFECTIOUS EASE.		160	THE SHOWRE	3
THOU SHALT NOT LOSE ONE MITE. THOUGH WATERS STRAY		193	RLS + LSNS	65
BUT WHEN HIS WATERS BILLOW THUS		175	THE STORM	9
THE WELL, WHERE LIVING WATERS SPRING		340	THE FEAST	33
WATRING				
WATRING THEIR FLOCKS, AND HAVING SPENT		151	THE SEARCH	25
WATRY				
DOTH THY TRANSPARENT, COOL AND WATRY WEALTH		343	WATER-FALL	2
WAVE				
DOEST THOU THEREFORE OLD TREATIES WAVE		149	RELIGION	23
DESTROY'D AT ALL, BUT WHEN TIMES RESTLES WAVE		145	RSRCTN +IM	37
AS DOTH THE MOUNTAIN'D WAVE.		175	THE STORM	8
A LESSON PLAID HIM BY A WINDE OR WAVE.		280	JOY	8
WAVES				
AND TAME PROUD WAVES, IF YET THESE BARREN GROUNDS		234	MUTINIE	12

		PAGE	TITLE	LINE
WAVES	**(CON'T)**			
LIKE WAVES BEAT ON MY RESOLUTIONS	• • •	214	MISERY	76
A SEA, WHOSE LOWD WAVES CANNOT SLEEP	• • •	325	ABELS BLOD	15
THOU STILL'ST THE LOUD WAVES, WHEN MOST WILD	• • •	336	PSALM 65	19
A DARK CONTEST OF WAVES AND WINDE.	• • •	344	QUICKNESS	7
WAX				
BAGS THAT WAX OLD MAY PLUNDERED BE	• • •	300	PROVIDENCE	21
WAY				
DIRT IN HER WAY, WILL KEEP ABOVE THE SKIE.	• • •	291	THE TIMBER	56
IF MY WAY LIES THROUGH DESERTS AND WILDE WOODS.	• • •	290	THE TIMBER	45
FROM SIN, HE WALKS A NARROW, PRIVATE WAY.	• • •	290	THE TIMBER	34
COME, DROP YOUR BRANCHES, STROW THE WAY	• • •	294	PALM-SUNDY	1
THE WAY TO IMMORTALITY.	• • •	335	JUDGEMENT	22
ALL THY DARK WAY.	• • •	338	DEATH B	17
A SHELTER ALL THE WAY, AND BOWERS TO REST.	• • •	326	RIGHTSNESS	4
WHAT WAY WE PLEASE, WITHOUT SELF-ENDS.	• • •	322	CHILDEHOOD	34
FOR SURE THAT IS THE NARROW WAY.	• • •	322	CHILDEHOOD	44
THOU FROM THE DAY-STAR A LONG WAY DIDST STAND	• • •	331	JACOBS PLW	47
WHERE WITH PROUD HASTE THE RICH MADE WAY	• • •	302	ORNAMENT	3
MAKES WAY FOR STORMS INTO HIS REST.	• • •	309	THE SEED	44
TEACH AGE, THE HOLY WAY.	• • •	310	THE SEED	64
PROVE NOT EXPEDIENT FOR THY WAY.	• • •	319	THE ASS	40
CAN TOUCH HIM ANY WAY	• • •	244	THE SAP	30
THERE IS THY COUNTRY, AND HE IS THE WAY	• • •	243	THE SAP	15
BECAUSE IT SHEWS THE WAY	• • •	233	THE WORLD	52
THE WAY WHICH FROM THIS DEAD AND DARK ABODE	• • •	233	THE WORLD	53
A WAY WHERE YOU MIGHT TREAD THE SUN, AND BE	• • •	233	THE WORLD	55
SO STRENGTHEN ME, LORD, ALL THE WAY	• • •	229	PILGRIMAGE	27
WE CLIMB UP THIS, AND HAVE TOO ALL THE WAY	• • •	230	LAW + GOSP	17
WHERE SPREADING ALL THE WAY THEY SEEK	• • •	240	MISERY	11
SO LET THY GRACE NOW MAKE THE WAY	• • •	274	WHT SUNDAY	57
THEN KEEP THE ANTIENT WAY.	• • •	276	PROFFER	43
BUT I WILL KNOW WHICH WAY TO LOCK.	• • •	272	WHT SUNDAY	20
GO SEEKING ALL THE WAY.	• • •	267	ASCN-DAY A	14
THY SACRED WAY	• • •	248	I WALKT	51
STRIVE UPWARDS STIL, AND POINT HIM THE WAY HOME.	• •	223	TEMPEST	28
DID SHEW ME HOME, AND PUT ME IN THE WAY.	• • •	225	RETIREMENT	11
HAVE HAD THEIR WISH, AND WAY.	• • •	225	RETIREMENT	14
LEADS TO THAT WAY	• • •	226	RETIREMENT	32
THE WAY TO THEE.	• • •	219	HOLY COMM.	24
THOU'LT FIND ME DREST AND ON MY WAY	• • •	212	DAWNING	47
THE NARROW WAY.	• • •	2	SON-DAYES	10
THE MILKY WAY CHALKT OUT WITH SUNS, A CLUE	• • •	2	SON-DAYES	21
AND NARROW WAY, BY WHICH TO THEE	• • •	207	REPENTANCE	8
(TOUCH'D WITH THE GUILT OF MY OWN WAY)	• • •	207	REPENTANCE	28
MAY CLEAR MUCH WAY	• • •	174	JOY OF LIF	15
IS DRUNK, AND STAGGERS IN THE WAY.	• • •	170	RETREATE	28
IT WAS HIGH-SPRING, AND ALL THE WAY	• • •	139	RGNRTN	12
THE SUN'S BROKE THROUGH TO GUIDE MY WAY.	• • •	152	THE SEARCH	66
IS NOT THE WAY	• • •	153	THE SEARCH	92
UNLOCK THE WAY	• • •	160	THE SHOWRE	10
A PLENTEOUS WAY (THANKS TO THAT HOLY ONE)	• • •	159	MANS FALL	22
THESE FETCH'D THEE HOME THY BRIDE, AND ALL THE WAY	• •	155	ISAACS M.	27
AND LIVE, WHO DOTH NOT THUS, HATH LOST HEAV'NS WAY.	•	196	RLS + LSNS	142
WHEN NIGHT COMES, LIST THY DEEDS, MAKE PLAIN THE WAY	•	195	RLS + LSNS	115
LIGHT FROM HIS LOCKS, AND ALL THE WAY	• • •	199	NTVTY 1	5
AND POINT US OUT THE WAY	• • •	201	THE CHECK	21
QUITTING THY WAY	• • •	203	DSRDR + FR	12
A GIDDY BLAST EACH WAY	• • •	187	NO DO THEY	18
AN ANCIENT WAY	• • •	189	RESOLVE	22
O LEAVE THY CARES, AND FOLLIES. GO THIS WAY	• • •	192	RLS + LSNS	17
OPENING THE WAY.	• • •	341	THE FEAST	65
MY OWN ILL WAY.	• • •	342	OBSEQUIES	4
WAYES				
O MY SOLE COMFORT, TAKE NO MORE THESE WAYES	• • •	188	RELAPSE	9
PIERCE ALL THEIR WAYES	• • •	146	RSRCTN +IM	55
GREW MASTER OF MY WAYES	• • •	282	GARLAND	6
WAYS				
PRIVATE AND HOLY TALK FILL ALL THE WAYS.	• • •	268	ASCN-DAY A	28
YET DIG'D THE MOLE, AND LEST HIS WAYS BE FOUND	• • •	232	THE WORLD	23
AND THEN BE THANKFUL, O ADMIRE HIS WAYS	• • •	195	RLS + LSNS	99
O'RE DARK HILLS, SWIFT STREAMES, AND STEEEP WAYS	• • •	174	JOY OF LIF	19
OF FLESH AND BLOOD, WHERE TWO WAYS MEET.	• • •	318	THE ASS	2
SOME UP THE MOUNTAINS PAST BY SECRET WAYS	• • •	285	PSALM 104	23
WEAK				
ARE BUT LIGHTS WEAK MINORITY	• • •	334	JUDGEMENT	8
AH. GO. TH'ART WEAK, AND SLEEPIE. HEAV'N	• • •	178	EVNG-WTCH	11
HE SHIN'D A LITTLE, AND BY THOSE WEAK RAYS	• • •	196	CORRUPTION	3
DOTH MY WEAK FIRE	• • •	203	DSRDR + FR	38
THE WEAK, AND AGED TIR'D, WITH LENGTH	• • •	218	EASTER HYM	9
WEAKE				
WEAKE BEAMES, AND FIRES FLASH'D TO MY SIGHT	• • •	168	VNTY SPRIT	19
AND, BY THEIR OWNE WEAKE SHINE, DID SEARCH THE SPRINGS	•	146	RSRCTN +IM	53
AND IN WEAKE, INFANT HUMMINGS CHIME, AND KNELL	• •	144	RSRCTN +IM	7
AND IN THOSE WEAKER GLORIES SPY	• • •	169	RETREATE	13
THE WEAKER SORT SLIGHT, TRIVIALL WARES INSLAVE	• • •	232	THE WORLD	42
AND LINGRING WOUNDS FROM WEAKER FOES.	• • •	312	FAIR+YONG	44
WEAL				
THY WOE, WHO CAUS'D HIS WEAL, SO FAR HIS WEAL	• • •	283	LOVE-SICK	19
THY WOE, WHO CAUS'D HIS WEAL, SO FAR HIS WEAL	• • •	283	LOVE-SICK	19

		PAGE	TITLE	LINE
WEAL	**(CON'T)**			
WHENCE FLOWES MY WEAL, AND MIRTH	• • • • •	220	PSALM 121	2
WEALTH				
TO WINE, AND SWEETNESS. POVERTY TO WEALTH	• • •	221	AFFLICTION	5
WITH THAT ONE GRAINS INFUSED WEALTH	• • •	206	REPENTANCE	4
THY QUIKNING FREINDSHIP, MANS BRIGHT WEALTH.	• •	294	BEGGING B	22
HUNTS GOLD AND WEALTH, AND WILL NOT LEND	• •	301	PROVIDENCE	33
LORD, GOD. I BEG NOR FRIENDS, NOR WEALTH	• •	148	DAY OF JDG	37
THAT WEALTH MAY FLOW	• • • • •	341	THE FEAST	74
DOTH THY TRANSPARENT, COOL AND WATRY WEALTH	• •	343	WATER-FALL	2
WEAN'D				
DEATH WEAN'D THEE FROM THE WORLD, AND SIN.	• •	209	THE BURIAL	8
WEAR				
MANS ANTIENT WEAR.	• • • • •	269	ASCSN-HYMN	2
HER FLAMING WEAR	• • • • •	269	ASCSN-HYMN	16
WEAR IN MY BOSOME A FULL SUN, SUCH STORE	• •	198	UNPRFTBLNS	11
AND SPOTLESS WHITE IS ALL THE WEAR.	• •	308	THE SEED	24
BUT WHILE EACH GAY, ALLURING WEAR	• •	303	ORNAMENT	9
WEAR FRESH ADORNMENTS ON EACH SIDE.	• •	337	PSALM 65	44
FOR MOURNING SACK-CLOTH WEAR, ALL MORTIFIED.	• •	342	OBSEQUIES	16
MADE LINEN, WHO DID WEAR IT THEN.	• •	347	THE BOOK	8
WEARE				
POORE, PIOUS WEARE.	• • • • •	173	CONTENT	13
HOW DID POOR FLESH (WHICH AFTER THOU DIDST WEARE)	• •	229	LAW + GOSP	7
WEARIED				
HER WEARIED WINGS, WHICH SO RESTOR'D DID FLYE	• •	155	ISAACS M.	49
WEARS				
FRESH AS THOSE ROSES, WHICH THE DAY-SPRING WEARS.	• •	155	ISAACS M.	36
FRESH AS THE DEW, WHICH BUT THIS DAWNING WEARS.	• •	267	ASCN-DAY A	20
YET HUGS HE STIL HIS DURT. THE STUFFE HE WEARS	• •	224	TEMPEST	45
ENTIRE STILL, WEARS OUT BLACKEST NIGHTS.	• •	333	AGREEMENT	34
BY THAT FOUL RHEUM THY FALSE EYE WEARS.	• •	305	ST MARY MN	66
HIS SHAMELESS LUST IN PUBLICK WEARS	• •	297	HERODIAS	15
WHICH WEARS HEAVEN, LIKE A BRIDAL RING	• •	346	THE QUEER	3
WEARY				
GRAVES ARE BEDS NOW FOR THE WEARY	• •	218	EASTER HYM	5
WEARY OF THIS SAME CLAY, AND STRAW, I LAID	• •	233	MUTINIE	1
WEARYED				
WEARYED OUT IN A HARMLES STRIFE	• • •	209	THE BURIAL	3
WEATHER				
FOR AS THY HAND THE WEATHER STEERS	• •	227	LV + DSPLN	16
AND WHAT YOU NOW EXTRACT, IN HARDER WEATHER	• •	274	PROFFER	9
THOUGH BLOOD AND DRUNKENNESS MAKE BUT FOUL, FOUL WEATHER.		307	RAIN-BOW	26
BUT STILL THE WEATHER THAT'S MOST FAIR	• •	176	THE STORM	15
WEAVE				
BUT WHAT THEIR OWN HOMES WEAVE	• • •	173	CONTENT	8
AND WEAVE IT FOR YOUR HEAD AGAINST YOU WAKE.	• •	280	PALM-TREE	27
WED				
POLLUTIONS ALL MY BODY WED	• • • •	209	REPENTANCE	77
WEED				
FIGS ON A THORNE, FLOWRES ON A WEED.	• •	208	REPENTANCE	70
THUS THOU ALL DAY A THANKLESS WEED DOES DRESS	• •	198	UNPRFTBLNS	16
ALAS, FRAIL WEED.	• • • • •	203	DSRDR + FR	30
ALL WAS A THORN, OR WEED	• • • •	196	CORRUPTION	10
WEEDS				
THOU WOULDST TO WEEDS, AND THISTLES QUITE DISPERSE	• •	221	AFFLICTION	15
THE FOSTS ILL WEEDS NIP, AND MOLEST	• •	227	LV + DSPLN	11
BLUSHING, AND IN MEEK WEEDS ARRAY'D	• •	303	ORNAMENT	14
SOME SNAKE, OR WEEDS	• • • •	328	RIGHTSNESS	53
RICH WEEDS AND SHROUDS.	• • •	342	OBSEQUIES	18
WHITHER GOOD CORN, OR FRUITLESS WEEDS.	• •	347	THE BOOK	10
WEEK				
AND FEED'ST THEM ALL THE WEEK.	• • •	286	PSALM 104	60
HEAVEN ONCE A WEEK.	• • • • •	205	SON-DAYES	2
WEEKS				
AND FULL REDEMPTION OF THE WHOLE WEEKS FLIGHT.	• •	2	SON-DAYES	8
WEEP				
YET SOME, WHO ALL THIS WHILE DID WEEP AND SING	• •	232	THE WORLD	46
AND WEEP, AND WEEP, SOAR'D UP INTO THE RING	• •	232	THE WORLD	47
MY DEAR, ALMIGHTY LORD. WHY DOST THOU WEEP	• •	298	JESUS WP B	1
WHEN GOD HIMSELF FOR THEE DOTH WEEP.	• •	296	JESUS WP A	4
DEAR JESUS WEEP ON. POUR THIS LATTER	• •	296	JESUS WP A	9
MY GOD, COULD I WEEP BLOOD	• • •	328	ANGUISH	7
OR IF IT WATCH, FORGIVE AND WEEP	• •	326	ABELS BLOD	36
FULL FORTY DAYS O'R THE DROWN'D WORLD DID WEEP)	• •	307	RAIN-BOW	28
BLOOMY AND FRESH, WHY DOST THOU WEEP.	• •	303	ST MARY MN	10
LIKE THE SURVIVING TURTLE, WEEP	• •	311	FAIR+YONG	10
THIS WORLD BUT LAUGHS AT THOSE THAT WEEP.	• •	312	FAIR+YONG	52
WHILE HAPLESSE I STILL WEEP.	• • •	311	THE SEED	85
WEEP THAT I HAVE OUT-LIV'D	• • •	311	THE SEED	86
SPEND NOT AN HOUR SO, AS TO WEEP ANOTHER	• •	194	RLS + LSNS	67
POURE OYLE UPON THE STONES, WEEP FOR THY SIN	• •	192	RLS + LSNS	23
MAY MAKE THEM WEEP	• • • • •	173	CONTENT	10
WITH HIM I WEEP	• • • • •	171	COME, COME	28
TO WEEP, TO SING, THY DEATH, MY LIFE.	• •	186	PASSION	57
HOW DIDST THOU WEEP	• • • •	184	PASSION	7
OF DROPS MAKE SOFT THE EARTH, MY EYES COULD WEEP	• •	160	THE SHOWRE	14
WHICH MAKES ME WISELY WEEP AND LOOK	• •	347	THE BOOK	20
TAKE THIS LAST KISS, AND LET ME WEEP	• •	348	HOLY BIBLE	3
WEEP'ST				
THOU FALL'ST IN TEARES, AND WEEP'ST FOR THY MISTAKE.	•	160	THE SHOWRE	6

		PAGE	TITLE	LINE

WEEPE
| DEVOTION STILL ON WING, THEN, THOU DOST WEEPE | . . . | 158 | THE LAMPE | 13 |
| WHO NEVER WAKE TO GRONE, NOR WEEPE | . . . . . | 164 | THE CALL | 8 |

WEEPING
LORD, THEN ROUND ME WITH WEEPING CLOUDS	. . .	176	THE STORM	17
OR LIPS, BUT WHO THERE WEEPING SITS	. . .	189	RESOLVE	27
SOIL'D WITH MANY A WEEPING LOCK	. . .	312	FAIR+YONG	32
HER ART. WHOSE PENSIVE, WEEPING EYES	. . .	305	ST MARY MN	57
WHERE WEEPING VIRTUE PARTS WITH MAN.	. . .	322	CHILDEHOOD	32
MY SELF ALL TEARS, A WEEPING LAKE.	. . .	328	ANGUISH	12
WEEPING STILL, LIKE THE WET MORROW	. . .	294	PALM-SUNDY	5
WHEN THOU DIDST HEAR THE WEEPING LAD.	. . .	293	BEGGING B	12
AND ALL HIS LIFE A RAINY, WEEPING DAY.	. . .	290	THE TIMBER	36
THOU, WHOSE SAD HEART, AND WEEPING HEAD LYES LOW	. .	217	EASTER-DAY	1

WEEPS
| O FILL HIS BOTTLE. THY CHILDE WEEPS. | . . . | 308 | THE SEED | 16 |
| AND FROM HIS MOIST WOMBE WEEPS A FRAGRANT SHOWRE | . | 155 | ISAACS M. | 55 |

WEIGH
| THEN WEIGH, AND RATE | . . . . . | 165 | THE CALL | 24 |
| THE OTHER SMOAKE, AND PLEASURES WEIGH'D | . . . | 139 | RGNRTN | 32 |

WEIGHING
| WEIGHING THE STEDFASTNESS AND STATE | . . . | 245 | MAN | 1 |

WEIGHS
| HE WEIGHS NOT YOUR FORC'D ACCENTS, WHO CAN HAVE | . | 280 | JOY | 7 |

WEIGHT
| HOW DID THE WEIGHT | . . . | 185 | PASSION | 30 |

WEIGHTS
IT THRIVES NO WHERE. THIS MAKES THESE WEIGHTS (LIKE DEATH	279	PALM-TREE	7
THE DARKSOME STATES-MAN HUNG WITH WEIGHTS AND WOE	.	231	THE WORLD	16
THESE WEIGHTS, AND GIVE MY SPIRIT LEAVE	. . .	329	ANGUISH	17

WEIGHTY
| BUSINESS AND WEIGHTY ACTION ALL | . . . . | 322 | CHILDEHOOD | 28 |

WEL
I MAY AS WEL AS LOVE, FIND TOO THY FEAR.	. . .	230	LAW + GOSP	30
BUT GOING HENCE, AND KNOWING WEL WHAT WOES	. .	243	THE SAP	23
TO WASH YOUR VESSEL WEL. THEN HUMBLY TAKE	. .	244	THE SAP	43
(I KNOW IT WEL) FILS ALL THE PLACE.	. . .	214	MISERY	52
TO JABOBS WEL, BEQUEATHED SINCE	. . .	151	THE SEARCH	22
WALK BUT THE FIELDS, OR SIT DOWN AT SOME WEL	. .	197	CORRUPTION	27
WHAT'S GOOD SCORE UP FOR JOY, THE BAD WEL SCANN'D	.	195	RLS + LSNS	119
TOO, IS MY DEW, AND SPRINGING WEL.	. . .	203	DSRDR + FR	19

WEL-TRAIN'D
| YOUR CALM AND WEL-TRAIN'D FLIGHT | . . . | 236 | CONSTLATN | 30 |

WELCOME
WELCOME SWEET, AND SACRED FEAST. WELCOME LIFE.	.	218	HOLY COMM.	1
WELCOME SWEET, AND SACRED FEAST. WELCOME LIFE.	.	218	HOLY COMM.	1
WELCOME DEAR BOOK, SOULS JOY, AND FOOD. THE FEAST	.	197	SCRIPTURES	1
IF THOU BE IN'T, 'TIS WELCOME STILL.	. . .	182	CHRFLNESS	11

WELL-FLEEC'D
| THEIR WELL-FLEEC'D TRAINE) AND HERE (O FATE) | . . | 151 | THE SEARCH | 27 |

WELLCOME
| WELLCOME WHITE DAY. A THOUSAND SUNS | . . . | 272 | WHT SUNDAY | 1 |
| TO GATHER FLOWERS TO WELLCOME THEE | . . . | 295 | PALM-SUNDY | 37 |

WELLS
FOR THY ETERNAL, LIVING WELLS	. . . .	308	THE SEED	21
FAIRE, VIRGIN-FLOWERS, AND HALLOW'D WELLS	. .	153	THE SEARCH	70
AND CROWN DRY HILS WITH WELLS AND FLOWERS.	. .	341	THE FEAST	54

WENT
AND ADDE UNTO THAT DAY HE WENT	. . . .	165	THE CALL	36
I TOOKE THEM UP, AND (MUCH JOY'D) WENT ABOUT	. .	168	VNTY SPRIT	25
WHEN I WENT QUITE ASTRAY	. . .	225	RETIREMENT	8
WENT BLEAK AND BARE IN BODY AS IN MIND	. .	245	MT. OLV. B	13

WEPT
HE WEPT ONCE, WALKT WHOLE NIGHTS ON THEE	. .	163	MT. OLVS A	21
WEPT BLOUD, THAT BROKE THIS ADAMANT, AND GAVE	.	159	MANS FALL	25
THE SAD WORLD WEPT TO BE RELEAST.	. . .	340	THE FEAST	24

WEST
| AND SWEEPE UP SOUTH AND WEST | . . . . | 146 | DAY OF JDG | 4 |
| SOME OTHERS NEER THE WEST | . . . . . | 235 | CONSTLATN | 10 |

WET
| WEEPING STILL, LIKE THE WET MORROW | . . . | 294 | PALM-SUNDY | 5 |
| HIS LOCKS ARE WET WITH THE CLEAR DROPS OF NIGHT. | . | 324 | THE NIGHT | 33 |

WHALE
| THE COMELY SPACIOUS WHALE. | . . . . | 286 | PSALM 104 | 72 |

WHEEL
| BUT WAITS UPON THIS WHEEL | . . . . . | 222 | AFFLICTION | 32 |

WHELPS
| THE LYONS WHELPS IMPATIENT OF DELAY | . . . | 286 | PSALM 104 | 57 |

WHER'S
| BUT THOU SLEEP'ST ON. WHER'S NOW THY PROTESTATION | . | 202 | THE CHECK | 43 |

WHETHER
| WHETHER ABROAD, AMIDST THE CROWD | . . . | 221 | PSALM 121 | 17 |

WHILST
| WHILST I EACH MINUTE GRONE TO KNOW | . . . | 143 | DEATH | 29 |
| (WHILST DEEP SLEEP OTHERS CATCHES) | . . . | 171 | MIDNIGHT | 2 |

WHIRLE-WINDS
| WHIRLE-WINDS, AND CLOUDS, AND THE SOFT VOICE | . . | 149 | RELIGION | 18 |

WHISPER
| WINDS WHISPER, AND THE BUSIE SPRINGS | . . . | 199 | NTVTY 1 | 8 |
| WHISPER THEIR HOURS | . . . . . | 281 | JOY | 24 |

		PAGE	TITLE	LINE
WHISPER'D				
THEN SIGHING WHISPER'D, HAPPY ARE THE DEAD.		247	I WALKT	33
CAME OFT FROM FAR, AND WHISPER'D, NO.		207	REPENTANCE	16
WHISPER'D OBEDIENCE, AND THEIR HEADS INCLIN'D.		229	LAW + GOSP	10
ONE WHISPER'D THUS		233	THE WORLD	58
AND WHISPER'D, JESUS HAD BEEN THERE		151	THE SEARCH	31
IT WHISPER'D, WHERE I PLEASE		141	RGNRTN	89
WHISPERS				
AND WHISPERS AMONGST THEM. THERE'S NOT A SPRING		192	RLS + LSNS	14
WHAT SIGHS, WHAT WHISPERS, BUSIE STOPS AND STAYS.		268	ASCN-DAY A	27
WHIT				
AND CANST NO WHIT		215	PRAISE	36
WHITE				
IN THEIR WHITE ROBES TO SEEK THE RISEN SUN.		268	ASCN-DAY A	30
WHILE THY BLOOD WASH'D ME WHITE AS HEAVEN.		265	INTRO. 2	28
SORROWS IN WHITE, GRIEFS TUN'D, A SUGERD DOSIS		280	JOY	5
WELLCOME WHITE DAY. A THOUSAND SUNS		272	WHT SUNDAY	1
THEY SHINE IN WHITE (LIKE STARS) AND REST.		275	PROFFER	24
HAVING LOST THEE, BEHOLD TWO MEN IN WHITE.		268	ASCN-DAY A	58
TO MAKE STAIN'D MAN MORE WHITE THEN SNOW.		270	ASCSN-HYMN	36
THOSE WHITE DAYES, DROVE HOME TO THE TENT		151	THE SEARCH	26
WHITE DAYES, THAT DURST NO IMPIOUS MIRTH EXPOSE.		154	ISAACS M.	18
BUT A WHITE, CELESTIALL THOUGHT		169	RETREATE	6
THEN MAKE THY SOULE WHITE AS HIS OWNE		167	THE CALL	90
BUT ONE GREEN BRANCH AND A WHITE ROBE.		295	PALM-SUNDY	45
THOSE WHITE DESIGNS WHICH CHILDREN DRIVE		321	CHILDEHOOD	4
THE OLD, WHITE PROPHETS PLANTED FIRST AND DREST.		326	RIGHTSNESS	2
THE MOUNT, WHOSE WHITE ASCENDENTS MAY		332	AGREEMENT	15
HIS WHITE AND HOLY TRAIN		329	TEARS	2
THE GREAT AND WHITE THRONE I SHALL SEE		337	THE THRONE	3
THE FIELDS ARE LONG SINCE WHITE, AND I		334	JUDGEMENT	13
WHEN SHALL THOSE FIRST WHITE PILGRIMS RISE		335	JUDGEMENT	23
AND SPOTLESS WHITE IS ALL THE WEAR.		308	THE SEED	24
TILL THE WHITE WINGED REAPERS COME.		309	THE SEED	48
A FAIR, WHITE PAGE OF THIN		310	THE SEED	58
WHEN THOU DOST SHINE DARKNESS LOOKS WHITE AND FAIR		306	RAIN-BOW	9
DEAR, BEAUTEOUS SAINT. MORE WHITE THEN DAY		303	ST MARY MN	1
AND FOLLOW THEE ALL CLOATH'D IN WHITE		316	MEN OF WAR	22
FOR SOME WORE WHITE EV'N IN THY GRAVE		342	OBSEQUIES	19
SHALL ALL BE DREST IN SHINING WHITE		349	L'ENVOY	4
O THOU THAT LOVEST A PURE, AND WHITEND SOUL./		216	DRESSING	1
WHITES				
THE SETTLED RED IS DULL, AND WHITES THAT REST		222	AFFLICTION	27
WHITHER				
WHITHER GOOD CORN, OR FRUITLESS WEEDS.		347	THE BOOK	10
WHOLE				
BUT THOU, WHO DIDST MANS WHOLE LIFE EARN		342	OBSEQUIES	21
MAKING THE WHOLE MOST MUSICALL		222	AFFLICTION	40
AND FULL REDEMPTION OF THE WHOLE WEEKS FLIGHT.		2	SON-DAYES	8
DEDUCTED FROM THE WHOLE, THE COMBS, AND HIVE		2	SON-DAYES	19
THY SPIRIT PLANT, QUICKNING THE WHOLE		206	REPENTANCE	3
THE WHOLE CREATION SHAKES OFF NIGHT		212	DAWNING	17
AND TAUGHT OBEDIENCE BY THE WHOLE CREATION		237	CONSTLATN	55
THINE EYES BEHOLD THE EARTH, AND THE WHOLE STAGE		287	PSALM 104	85
WHICH (THOUGH BUT SAND) KEEPS IN A CURBS WHOLE SEAS.		285	PSALM 104	26
HE WEPT ONCE, WALKT WHOLE NIGHTS ON THEE		163	MT. OLVS A	21
STRIVING TO SAVE THE WHOLE, BY PARCELLS DYE		161	DSTRQCTION	34
AWAKE, AND THEN REFINE THE WHOLE.		151	THE SEARCH	20
ESTEEM'D (VAINE THINGS) OF TWO WHOLE ELEMENTS		144	RSRCTN +IM	13
THE WHOLE UNTO HIM, AND REMEMBER WHO		192	RLS + LSNS	21
AFTER WHOLE SHOWRES ONE DROP.		188	NO DO THEY	38
THE WHOLE FRAME WITH HIS FALL.		197	CORRUPTION	16
WHERE THOU MAY'ST SLEEP WHOLE AGES, LIFES POOR FLOWR		195	RLS + LSNS	123
WHOLESOME				
WHAT SUBLIME TRUTHS, AND WHOLESOME THEMES		344	WATER-FALL	27
WHOLLY				
WHOLLY INANIMATE.		187	NO DO THEY	8
WHOLSOME				
SICKNESS IS WHOLSOME, AND CROSSES ARE BUT CURBS		221	AFFLICTION	17
WHOLY				
I WHOLY LISTEN'D TO MY FOE.		207	REPENTANCE	18
THOUGH IN THIS DESART I WERE WHOLY SHUT		234	MUTINIE	30
WICKED				
GATHER TRUE COMFORTS, BUT THE WICKED LIVER		287	PSALM 104	94
WICKEDNESS				
SUCCESSFUL WICKEDNESS COMMEND.		316	MEN OF WAR	16
WIDE				
SO DOTH THE DEEP AND WIDE SEA, WHEREIN ARE		286	PSALM 104	69
BUT IN A DEEP, WIDE SEA OF BLOOD		325	ABELS BLOD	14
WHILE OTHERS SLIPT INTO A WIDE EXCESSE		232	THE WORLD	40
WIDE OF A FAITHFULL GRAVE.		183	THRS A TYE	16
WILD				
MY FIERCE, WILD BLOOD THAT STILL HEAVES, AND INCLINES		190	THE MATCH	4
MADE THOSE WILD SHADES A PARADISE		152	THE SEARCH	62
THOUSANDS OF WILD AND WASTE INFUSIONS		214	MISERY	75
AND BE MORE WILD THAN IS THY VERSE.		221	AFFLICTION	16
OF WILD AFFECTIONS, RID		282	GARLAND	10
THOU STILL'ST THE LOUD WAVES, WHEN MOST WILD		336	PSALM 65	19
WILDE				
SUBMIT MY WILDE HEART, AND RESTRAIN MY HANDS.		321	HIDDN TRSR	30

	PAGE	TITLE	LINE
WILDE (CCN'T)			
THERE THE WILDE ASSES SWALLOW THE COOL SPRING.	285	PSALM 104	34
TO THE WILDE GOATS THE HIGH HILLS SERVE FOR FOLDS	286	PSALM 104	49
IN WHOSE THICK SHADES AND SILENCE EACH WILDE BEAST	286	PSALM 104	54
AND MADE GRAVE MUSIQUE LIKE WILDE WIT	297	HERODIAS	3
IF MY WAY LIES THROUGH DESERTS AND WILDE WOODS.	290	THE TIMBER	45
WHEN HE FROM WILDE IS BECOME WISE	319	THE ASS	47
FOR KNOW, WILDE MEN, THAT WHEN YOU ERRE	314	THE STONE	42
ABOUT THY CURIOUS, WILDE, YONG HEAD.	304	ST MARY MN	20
FOR MY SAD FAILINGS AND MY WILDE	265	INTRO. 2	21
O SAD, AND WILDE EXCESSE. AND HAPPY THOSE	154	ISAACS M.	17
WILDED			
THUS WILDED BY A PEEVISH HEART	214	MISERY	81
WILDERNES			
TO BRING ME HOME, THAN THROUGH A WILDERNES	234	MUTINIE	27
I'LE TO THE WILDERNESS, AND CAN	152	THE SEARCH	53
OR IN THE HOWLING WILDERNESS	301	PROVIDENCE	27
THEY DROP UPON THE WILDERNESS	337	PSALM 65	41
WILDLY			
NOR WILDLY BURNS, BUT MEEKLY STILL	350	L'ENVOY	37
WILES			
AND JOIN AGAINST THEIR WILES.	205	IDLE VERSE	8
WILFUL			
FREQUENT RELAPSE AND WILFUL BREACH	265	INTRO. 2	24
WILFUL REBELLIONS. AND SUPPRESSIONS	208	REPENTANCE	54
WILL			
BE BROKE AGAIN, FOR FLINTS WILL GIVE NO FIRE	224	TEMPEST	58
I WILL PRAISE THEE	214	PRAISE	10
I WILL BLESSE THEE	214	PRAISE	14
I WILL DRESSE THEE.	214	PRAISE	16
I WILL MEASURE	215	PRAISE	30
I WILL TREASURE.	215	PRAISE	32
THY INWARD EYES, HIS BLOOD WILL CURE THY MIND	217	EASTER-DAY	15
TEARS AND THESE FLAMES WILL SOON GROW KINDE	266	VAIN WITS	5
AND FIRE WILL PURGE YOUR CALLOUS VEYL.	266	VAIN WITS	9
THEIR MASTERS WILL, MEET TO RECEIVE THEIR CROWNS.	280	PALM-TREE	20
HERE IS THEIR FAITH TOO, WHICH IF YOU WILL KEEP	280	PALM-TREE	24
WHEN WE TWO PART, I WILL A JOURNEY MAKE	280	PALM-TREE	25
DESIRE THAT NEVER WILL BE QUENCH'D	278	THE STARRE	19
THIS IS THE HEART HE CRAVES, AND WHO SO WILL	279	THE STARRE	29
AND TEACH US DUTY, I WILL SEE	278	THE STARRE	11
WHO WILL ASCEND, MUST BE UNDREST.	269	ASCSN-HYMN	6
THESE BUDS WILL WITHER	274	PROFFER	8
WILL SERVE TO TAKE.	274	PROFFER	10
WISE HUSBANDS WILL (YOU SAY) THERE WANTS PREVENT	274	PROFFER	11
AND ALMOST FAMISH'D, EVER WILL CONSENT	275	PROFFER	21
THERE ARE, THAT WILL SOW TARES	275	PROFFER	37
BUT I WILL KNOW WHICH WAY TO LOOK.	272	WHT SUNDAY	20
MY LOTT IS FALN, BLEST BE THY WILL.	227	LV + DSPLN	3
WITHIN THOSE DOORS (MY DOORS) COST HEAR. I WILL.	226	RETIREMENT	55
HIS LIFE FOR MINE, TUNE TO THY WILL	204	DSRDR + FR	59
I WILL NO LONGER COBWEBS SPIN	204	IDLE VERSE	3
SWEET JESU. WILL THEN. LET NO MORE	200	NTVTY 1	25
THY WILL IN ALL BE DONE, NOT MINE.	191	THE MATCH	27
THAT WILL NOT MOVE.	189	RESOLVE	8
AND THOU UNRAK'ST THY FIRE, THOSE SPARKS WILL BRING	195	RLS + LSNS	130
WILL TELL THEE SO, SWEET SAVIOUR THOU DIDST DYE.	198	SCRIPTURES	14
THIS LAST WILL KEEPE THE FIRST TWO FRESH	148	DAY OF JDG	43
SHALL I THEN THINKE SUCH PROVIDENCE WILL BE	144	RSRCTN +IM	15
FRESH DOTAGE TEMPTS, OR OLD USURPS HIS WILL.	161	DSTRQCTION	16
BUT I WILL BE MY OWN DEATHS-HEAD. AND THOUGH	183	THRS A TYE	21
AND HAP WHAT WILL	182	CHRFLNESS	10
AH. LORD. AND WHAT A PURCHASE WILL THAT BE	162	PURSUITE	17
WILL NE'R BE TAME	171	COME, COME	19
WILL FOLLOW AFTER	172	MIDNIGHT	30
WILL GUIDE HIM IN.	175	JOY OF LIF	32
I WILL PRODUCE.	338	THE THRONE	11
THEN TAUGHT BY THEE, I WILL PREVAIL	338	THE THRONE	14
AND SAY, THY WILL BE DONE.	338	THE THRONE	15
WHICH HIS FIRST LOOKS WILL QUICKLY FRAY.	338	DEATH B	19
WILL THY FREE MERCIES HINDRED BE.	334	AGREEMENT	70
I WILL DO NOTHING, NOTHING KNOW, NOR SEE	321	HIDDN TRSR	31
WHO KISSETH THORNS, WILL HURT HIS FACE	321	CHILDEHOOD	13
AND PRIVATE TAPERS WILL BUT HELP TO STRAY	321	HIDDN TRSR	27
WITH HIS WILDE BLOOD IN VOICE AND WILL	326	ABELS BLOD	43
O WHO WILL TELL ME, WHERE	323	THE NIGHT	13
I WILL EXHAUST IT ALL, AND MAKE	328	ANGUISH	11
I WILL NOT FEAR WHAT MAN	300	PROVIDENCE	19
HUNTS GOLD AND WEALTH, AND WILL NOT LEND	301	PROVIDENCE	33
WILL NOTHING YIELD BUT THORNS TO WOUND THY HEAD.	296	JESUS WP A	18
WILL THOSE COY SPIRITS CAST ASLEEP	297	HERODIAS	10
IF SHOWERS THEN FALL, WILL SHOWERS ALLAY	298	JESUS WP B	19
THEY WILL DRINK BLOOD, THAT DESPISE TEARS.	296	JESUS WP A	12
I WILL BE STILL A CHILDE, STILL MEEK	295	PALM-SUNDY	39
WHOSE DEATH WILL BE	294	PALM-SUNDY	16
YET JOY IT SELF WILL MAKE A RIGHT SOUL GRIEVE	290	THE TIMBER	39
DIRT IN HER WAY, WILL KEEP ABOVE THE SKIE.	291	THE TIMBER	56
AND SETS, WILL FEW HOURS HENCE BEGIN	292	THE JEWS	29
TO SEE MAN LOST, WILL FOR OLD LOVE	292	THE JEWS	36
I WILL IN SONGS TO THY GREAT NAME IMPLOY	287	PSALM 104	90

		PAGE	TITLE	LINE
WILL	**(CON'T)**			
WILL FACE AT NIGHT, AND WITH THIS SUN		283	GARLAND	31
GLADLY WILL I, LIKE PONTICK SHEEP		301	PROVIDENCE	46
I WILL ON THEE, AS ON A COMET LOOK		307	RAIN-BOW	35
PERFORMANCE, WILL FOR THAT SAME DEED		314	THE STONE	48
WILL PROVE THEIR HEARTS MORE STIFF AND TUFF.		314	THE STONE	51
WILL BY LOOSE DUST THAT MAN ARRAIGN		315	THE STONE	58
YET WILL NOT HE BY HIS OWN LIGHT		314	THE STONE	32
CONDEMN MEN. BUT WILL TRY THEM BY		314	THE STONE	34
AND LET MEN CALL ME WHAT THEY WILL.		319	THE ASS	44
SINCE OF MY LORD THEY HAD THEIR WILL		317	MEN OF WAR	35
AND SPRED AND OPEN TO THY WILL.		308	THE SEED	20
WHAT MAN WILL SHOW.		313	THE STONE	5
WILL NOR CONCEAL NOR ASSENT TO		313	THE STONE	8
MAN I CAN BRIBE, AND WOMAN WILL		313	THE STONE	10
BY EACH MANS DOOR, AND QUICKLY WILL		351	L'ENVOY	51
I WILL CLOSE GIRT AND TYED		342	OBSEQUIES	15
I WILL NOT FOR THY TEMPLES BRING		345	THE WREATH	7
WILLING				
AND LOVE OF THEE, EACH WILLING ANGEL IS		284	PSALM 104	15
BUT HE MOST WILLING TO SAVE ALL MANKINDE		330	JACOBS PLW	13
WIN				
SINCE THAT DOTH QUICKLY FREEDOM WIN		312	FAIR+YONG	45
BUT EVEN IN BABES DOEST TRIUMPH STILL AND WIN.		216	DRESSING	12
WIND				
THE DROPS OF RAIN, THE SIGHS OF THE WIND		207	REPENTANCE	37
THY CHOSEN FLOCK, LIKE LEAFS IN A HIGH WIND		229	LAW + GOSP	9
ATTEND AND WIND THE CLUE		236	CONSTLATN	14
EACH STIRRING WIND AND STORM BLEW THROUGH THEIR COTS		239	SHEPHEARDS	33
THE WIND, THOUGH GATHER'D IN THY FIST		239	MISERY	5
AND WORK, AND WIND TIL ALL BE DONE		214	MISERY	78
AND WAS BLOW'N THROUGH BY EV'RY STORM AND WIND		245	MT. OLV. B	14
AND WIND AND CURLE, AND WINK AND SMILE		278	THE STARRE	3
BUT A STRONG WIND MUST BREAK THY LOFTY ROCKS.		330	JACOBS PLW	10
THE WINGS OF THE SWIFT WIND.		284	PSALM 104	12
A GARLAND, WHERE COMES NEITHER RAIN, NOR WIND.		283	GARLAND	36
HITHER THOU COM'ST. THE BUSIE WIND ALL NIGHT		287	THE BIRD	1
AND HOW THEY WORK, AND WIND		171	MIDNIGHT	7
THER'S NOT A WIND CAN STIR		171	COME, COME	11
DARK STORMS, AND WIND		175	THE STORM	10
AND WIND, AND WATER TO THY USE		176	THE STORM	23
AND SCARCE A ROOM BUT WIND, AND RAIN		180	BURIALL	13
YET, HADST THOU NOBLER GUESTS. ANGELS DID WIND		155	ISAACS M.	25
A RUSHING WIND		141	RGNRTN	79
BUT FINDING NONE, SHAL LEAVE THEE TO THE WIND		201	THE CHECK	8
WINDE				
A LESSON PLAID HIM BY A WINDE OR WAVE.		280	JOY	8
A DARK CONTEST OF WAVES AND WINDE.		344	QUICKNESS	7
TEMPESTS AND WINDES, AND WINTER-NIGHTS		309	THE SEED	26
WINDING				
MAN IS THE SHUTTLE, TO WHOSE WINDING QUEST		246	MAN	26
SO MY SPILT THOUGHTS WINDING FROM THEE		240	MISERY	13
WINDOWS				
AS RAIN HERE AT OUR WINDOWS BEATS		213	ADMISSION	7
WATER (THOUGH BOTH HEAVENS WINDOWS AND THE DEEP		307	RAIN-BOW	27
WINDS				
THOUGH HAWKS CAN PREY THROUGH STORMS AND WINDS		309	THE SEED	35
WITH THY LEAST TOUCH, LIGHTNINGS AND WINDS THAT RAGE		287	PSALM 104	87
BRED IN THY GROWTH BETWIXT HIGH WINDS AND THEE		289	THE TIMBER	14
WHILE ACTIVE WINDS AND STREAMS BOTH RUN AND SPEAK		288	THE BIRD	15
TO EQUAL WINDS. WOULD PROVE TOO SHORT. THOU HAST		281	JOY	13
WHILE THE WINDS REFRESH THE YEAR		281	JOY	19
BY WINDS, AND BIT WITH FROST		202	DSRDR + FR	7
WINDS WHISPER, AND THE BUSIE SPRINGS		199	NTVTY 1	8
AND SURLY WINDS		139	RGNRTN	15
WHICH BUSIE THOUGHTS (LIKE WINDS) WOULD SCATTER QUITE		179	CHRCH-SVC	12
IS A PLAIN WATCH, AND WITHOUT FIGURES WINDS		178	EVNG-WTCH	12
THE RISING WINDS		176	MRNG-WTCH	12
WINDY				
WHO IN THIS WINDY WORLD ABIDE.		298	JESUS WP B	21
THEIR DOCTRINE CHAFF AND WINDY FITS.		332	AGREEMENT	26
WINE				
BRINGS FORTH, WITH WINE, OYL, BREAD. ALL WHICH INFUSE		285	PSALM 104	43
I FEEL AS WINE		185	PASSION	18
CORDIALS IN EVERY DROP, AND WINE.		150	RELIGION	32
AND TURN ONCE MORE OUR WATER INTO WINE		150	RELIGION	52
BREAD FOR THY BODY, AND WINE FOR THY BLOOD.		216	DRESSING	24
TO WINE, AND SWEETNESS. POVERTY TO WEALTH		221	AFFLICTION	5
EXCESSE OF FRIENDS, OF WORDS, AND WINE		240	MISERY	25
SPRING UP, O WINE		340	THE FEAST	25
WINE-HOUSE				
THOU ART THE OYL AND THE WINE-HOUSE.		332	AGREEMENT	19
WING				
AND WITH HIS BRIGHT AND BUSIE WING		332	AGREEMENT	8
WHOSE PEACE BUT BY SOME ANGELS WING OR VOICE		324	THE NIGHT	39
BLEW THROUGH THY LODGING, WHERE THY OWN WARM WING		287	THE BIRD	2
GAVE MY FOND HUMOURS THEIR FULL WING		282	GARLAND	23
DESTRUCTION ON HIS RUDDY WING.		305	ST MARY MN	56
I SHINE AND SHELTER UNDERNEATH THY WING		245	MT. OLV. B	23
BUT MOST WOULD USE NO WING.		232	THE WORLD	48

		PAGE	TITLE	LINE
WING	**(CON'T)**			
HE, EVER YOUNG, DOTH WING		145	RSRCTN +IM	41
DEVOTION STILL ON WING, THEN, THOU DOST WEEPE		158	THE LAMPE	13
WHEN THY LEAST BREATH SUSTAINES MY WING.		182	CHRFLNESS	3
BOTH WASH, AND WING MY SOUL.		176	THE STORM	24
EACH DAY, AND HOURE HE IS ON WING		161	PURSUITE	3
WHEN LOWD JOYES WANT A WING		167	THE CALL	79
UP WITH THY CURTAINS, GIVE THY SOUL THE WING		195	RLS + LSNS	128
TILL THOU DIDST GROW AND GET A WING		346	THE QUEER	11
A WING WITH EYES, AND EYES THAT TASTE.		346	THE QUEER	12
WING'D				
(BOTH WING'D, AND FREE)		146	RSRCTN +IM	62
SHE WING'D AWAY		144	RSRCTN +IM	10
AMONGST THEM, WITH THEM, WING'D WITH FAITH AND LOVE.		268	ASCN-DAY A	32
WINGED				
IN ABR'HAMS TENT THE WINGED GUESTS		149	RELIGION	13
WHERE STANDS A WINGED CENTRIE		184	PEACE	3
O THAT I WERE WINGED AND FREE		312	FAIR+YONG	47
TILL THE WHITE WINGED REAPERS COME.		309	THE SEED	48
WINGS				
O SPRED THY SACRED WINGS AND SHAKE		308	THE SEED	13
THE WINGS OF THE SWIFT WIND.		284	PSALM 104	12
PAST ORE THY HEAD. MANY LIGHT HEARTS AND WINGS		289	THE TIMBER	3
SHALL WITH SPREAD WINGS		291	THE JEWS	11
THY LONG EXPECTED HEALING WINGS COULD SEE		323	THE NIGHT	9
THY LEAVES ARE HEALING WINGS HE SPREADS.		333	AGREEMENT	36
HIS WINGS ARE DULL, AND SICKLY.		181	BURIALL	35
OF WINGS		153	THE SEARCH	87
BUT IF ALL SENCE WINGS NOT WITH THEE		142	DEATH	7
O GET THEE WINGS.		157	BRT. CHRCH	11
TO GET THEE WINGS ON, AND DEVOUTLY CLIMBE		155	ISAACS M.	44
HER WEARIED WINGS, WHICH SO RESTOR'D DID FLYE		155	ISAACS M.	49
YET, HADST THOU CLIPT MY WINGS, WHEN COFFIN'D IN		161	DSTRQCTION	17
O, IS. BUT GIVE WINGS TO MY FIRE		204	DSRDR + FR	46
AND HATH NO WINGS		248	I WALKT	39
BUT HIS, WHO GAVE THEM WINGS TO FLIE.		277	COCK-CRWNG	36
OF WINGS, AND CHERUBIMS, AND PALMS FORETOLD.		279	PALM-TREE	12
AND THY TWO WINGS WERE GRIEF AND LOVE.		272	WHT SUNDAY	12
THY DOVE TOO BEARS US ON HER SACRED WINGS.		230	LAW + GOSP	20
WINK				
AND WIND AND CURLE, AND WINK AND SMILE		278	THE STARRE	3
AND WOULD NOT SEE, BUT CHOSE TO WINK		225	RETIREMENT	18
NO QUIET COULDST THOU HAVE. NOR DIST THOU WINK		213	ADMISSION	9
WINKE				
UNSEARCHABLE, NOW WITH ONE WINKE		163	MT. OLVS A	28
HOW LIKE THE EYES QUICK WINKE		166	THE CALL	43
WINS				
YET WITH THY LOVE THAT ABSENCE WINS		213	ADMISSION	23
AS WITHOUT WOOING WINS THE COY		281	THE FAVOUR	4
YET, WHEN THY MERCY NOTHING WINS		335	JUDGEMENT	42
WINTER				
WERE IT STILL WINTER, AS IT WAS BEFORE		274	PROFFER	3
WHICH ALL THE WINTER SLEEPS HERE UNDER FOOT		248	I WALKT	38
WINTER IS ALL MY YEAR.		205	IDLE VERSE	24
AND IN THE DEPTH AND DEAD OF WINTER BRING		245	MT. OLV. B	19
BUT WINTER NOW HAD RUFFLED ALL THE BOWRE		246	I WALKT	5
WINTER-NIGHTS				
TEMPESTS AND WINDES, AND WINTER-NIGHTS		309	THE SEED	26
WIPING				
WIPING OUT MY SHAME, AND SIN.		249	BEGGING A	12
WISDOM				
THE WORLDS LOV'D WISDOM (FOR THE WORLDS FRIENDS THINK		320	HIDDN TRSR	15
ARE THY GREAT WORKS. IN WISDOM HAST THOU MADE		286	PSALM 104	66
WISE				
THOSE SECRET SEARCHES, WHICH AFFLICT THE WISE		320	HIDDN TRSR	11
AND LONG EXPERIENCE SHOULD MAKE WISE.		321	CHILDEHOOD	18
WHICH MAKE ME WISE TO LOSE MY SOUL.		322	CHILDEHOOD	26
WISE NICODEMUS SAW SUCH LIGHT		323	THE NIGHT	5
WISE HEADS SHALL USE		338	THE THRONE	9
WHO SIMPLE STILL AND WISE		327	RIGHTSNESS	16
LIKE A WISE, EARLY PENITENT		304	ST MARY MN	37
LET ME BE WISE TO PLEASE THEE STILL		319	THE ASS	43
WHEN HE FROM WILDE IS BECOME WISE		319	THE ASS	47
LET ME THY ASS BE ONELY WISE		318	THE ASS	21
LEAVE, AND BE WISE.		266	VAIN WITS	2
WISE HUSBANDS WILL (YOU SAY) THERE WANTS PREVENT		274	PROFFER	11
WISE-MANS				
THE WISE-MANS MADNES LAUGHTER.		166	THE CALL	65
WISE-MEN				
I MET THE WISE-MEN, ASKT THEM WHERE		151	THE SEARCH	8
WISEDOME				
ARE SHADOWS OF HIS WISEDOME, AND HIS POW'R		194	RLS + LSNS	96
WISELY				
WHICH MAKES ME WISELY WEEP AND LOOK		347	THE BOOK	20
WISH				
O THOU. THAT CANST NOT WISH MY SOULS DAMNATION		190	THE MATCH	16
WHO ONELY WISH LIFE TO SERVE THEE.		191	THE MATCH	35
THY WISH, NOR PRAY'R		153	THE SEARCH	84
I'LE WISH MY CURTAINES OFF TO FREE		142	DEATH	9
AND WISH EACH BEAME		171	MIDNIGHT	8

		PAGE	TITLE	LINE
WISH (CON'T)				
HAVE HAD THEIR WISH, AND WAY.	. . . . . .	225	RETIREMENT	14
WISH'D				
THAT LAMB WHOSE DAIES GREAT KINGS AND PROPHETS WISH'D	.	239	SHEPHEARDS	49
WISHES				
NOT, BUT THAT I HAVE WISHES TOO	. . . .	273	WHT SUNDAY	25
WIT				
NAY HATH NOT SO MUCH WIT AS SOME STONES HAVE	. .	246	MAN	23
NEGLECTING THEE. SUCH ILL-PLAC'D WIT	. .	162	MT. OLVS A	5
THEIR PIPES, AND WIT.	. . . . . .	162	MT. OLVS A	11
IN JUDGEMENT AGAINST LEWDNESS, THAT'S BASE WIT	.	194	RLS + LSNS	74
THE FORGERIES, WHICH IMPIOUS WIT	. . .	335	JUDGEMENT	35
AND MADE GRAVE MUSIQUE LIKE WILDE WIT	. . .	297	HERODIAS	3
WITH-DRAW'ST				
WHEN THOU WITH-DRAW'ST THEIR BREATH, THEIR VIGOUR SLEEPS		287	PSALM 104	79
WITH-STOOD				
AS HERE ON EARTH (WHEN MEN WITH-STOOD)	. . .	284	TRINITY-SN	4
WITHAL				
AND HATH WITHAL THE KEY.	. . . . . .	243	THE SAP	16
WITHER				
THESE BUDS WILL WITHER	. . . . .	274	PROFFER	8
THE ROSE THAT CANNOT WITHER	. . . .	184	PEACE	15
WITHER'D				
MY WITHER'D LEAFS AGAIN LOOK GREEN AND FLOURISH	.	245	MT. OLV. B	22
AND ALL HER FLOWRES WITHER'D TO STRAW	. .	222	TEMPEST	7
THEREFORE THY WITHER'D SELF IN HASTE	. . .	304	ST MARY MN	29
NONE STAIN'D OR WITHER'D SHALL COME NEAR.	. .	308	THE SEED	22
WITHSTOOD				
AND FORTY DAYES WITHSTOOD THE FELL	. . .	152	THE SEARCH	57
WITNESS				
COME THEN THOU FAITHFUL WITNESS. COME DEAR LORD	. .	268	ASCN-DAY A	61
WITNESSES				
AND CLOUDS OF CRYING WITNESSES WITHOUT	. .	232	THE WORLD	21
ARE SHAK'D FOR WITNESSES, AND STONES	. .	314	THE STONE	38
ETERNALL WITNESSES THAT BE	. . . .	284	TRINITY-SN	2
WITS				
WITS SOUR DELIGHTS	. . . .	231	THE WORLD	11
VAIN WITS AND EYES	. . . . . .	266	VAIN WITS	1
ON THE DIVINEST WITS	. . . . .	219	HOLY COMM.	19
THERE TURN, AND TURN NO MORE, LET WITS	. .	189	RESOLVE	25
WO				
WHO WROUGHT THY WO.	. . . . . .	220	HOLY COMM.	48
AND LOV'ST HIM, THOUGH HE WORKS THY WO.	. .	298	JESUS WP B	25
DIDST FLYE, WHOSE CHILDREN WROUGHT THY CHILDRENS WO.	.	331	JACOBS PLW	44
WOE				
A SINFULL WRETCH, A WRETCH THAT CAUS'D THY WOE	. .	283	LOVE-SICK	18
THY WOE, WHO CAUS'D HIS WEAL, SO FAR HIS WEAL	. .	283	LOVE-SICK	19
THE DARKSOME STATES-MAN HUNG WITH WEIGHTS AND WOE	. .	231	THE WORLD	16
WOES				
BUT GOING HENCE, AND KNOWING WEL WHAT WOES	. .	243	THE SAP	23
O CALL TO MIND HIS WOUNDS, HIS WOES	. . . .	208	REPENTANCE	61
THY LIGHT AS LUCTUAL AND STAIN'D WITH WOES	. .	307	RAIN-BOW	37
WITHOUT ADDITION TO OUR WOES	. . . .	312	FAIR+YONG	43
OF ALL HIS WOES REMAIN.	. . . . .	200	NTVTY 2	12
WOFULL				
AND BECAM'ST A WOFULL STORY.	. . . .	163	INCARNATN	4
WOLF				
A WOLF, MORE THEN A LAMB OR DOVE.	. . .	321	CHILDEHOOD	10
WOLVES				
I CAN DISCERN WOLVES FROM THE SHEEP.	. . .	273	WHT SUNDAY	24
WOMAN				
MAN I CAN BRIBE, AND WOMAN WILL	. . .	313	THE STONE	10
THIS WOMAN (SAY'ST THOU) IS A SINNER.	. .	305	ST MARY MN	67
WOMANS				
SEEM'D FAIR UNTO THE WOMANS EYE.	. . .	312	FAIR+YONG	36
WOMB				
'TIL TO THOSE SIGHES FETCH'D FROM HER WOMB	. .	222	TEMPEST	11
AND WOMB OF DARKNES BECKEN OUT	. . .	202	DSRDR + FR	2
AND CANNOT QUIT THE WOMB	. . .	187	NO DO THEY	28
WOMBE				
HER WOMBE, HER BOSOME, AND HER HEAD	. .	168	VNTY SPRIT	11
BUT A DARK AND SEAL'D UP WOMBE	. .	171	COME, COME	23
AND FROM THE WOMBE OF EARTH	. . .	147	DAY OF JDG	18
AND THEN RETURNS, AND FROM THE WOMBE OF THINGS	. .	145	RSRCTN +IM	27
AND FROM HIS MOIST WOMBE WEEPS A FRAGRANT SHOWRE	.	155	ISAACS M.	55
WON				
AND WON THE FIGHT, AND HAVE NOT FEAR'D THE FROWNS	.	280	PALM-TREE	18
WHICH OFT HAVE WON.	. . . . .	338	THE THRONE	13
WONDER				
AND WONDER, WHILE THE JEWS DID SLEEP	. . .	323	THE NIGHT	24
WONDER'D				
I WONDER'D MUCH, BUT TYR'D	. . . .	141	RGNRTN	70
WONDERS				
O WHAT STRANGE WONDERS COULD THEE MOVE	. .	164	INCARNATN	17
WONDROUS				
HIS WONDROUS METHOD, MARK THE VARIOUS SCENES	. .	194	RLS + LSNS	92
WONTED				
SO SOME STRANGE THOUGHTS TRENSCEND OUR WONTED THEAMS	.	271	ALL GONE	27
WOO				
WITH MEEK, DUMB LOOKS DIDST WOO MINE EYE	. . .	348	HOLY BIBLE	18

		PAGE	TITLE	LINE
WOO	(CON'T)			
DOEST SO INVITE, AND WOO ME STILL	• • •	342	OBSEQUIES	22
WOO'D				
WOO'D BY THE SUN SWELS UP TO BE HIS SHROWD	• •	155	ISAACS M.	54
WOOD				
AWAK, AWAK. HEARK, HOW TH' WOOD RINGS	• • •	199	NTVTY 1	7
AS BIRDS ROB'D OF THEIR NATIVE WOOD	• • •	228	PILGRIMAGE	17
WOODS				
THE PURE EARTH SAT, AND THE FAIR WOODS HAD SEEN	• •	268	ASCN-DAY A	42
FLUTT'RING IN WOODS, OR LIFTED FAR	• • •	199	NTVTY 1	14
ROAR IN THE COVERT OF THE WOODS, AND SEEK	• •	286	PSALM 104	58
IF MY WAY LIES THROUGH DESERTS AND WILDE WOODS.	• •	290	THE TIMBER	45
WOOE				
WITH WHICH IN MILD, CHAST LANGUAGE SHE DID WOOE	• •	155	ISAACS M.	41
WOOING				
AS WITHOUT WOOING WINS THE COY	• • •	281	THE FAVOUR	4
WOOLL				
AND MOURN TO SEE THE WOOLL	• • •	173	CONTENT	11
WOOS				
AND LOVE THE LURE, THAT WOOS THEE DOWN.	• • •	346	THE QUEER	14
WORD				
THE WORD IN CHARACTERS, GOD IN THE VOICE.	• •	198	SCRIPTURES	8
A LAND OF FLOWERS AND SPICES. THE WORD GIVEN	• •	276	PROFFER	47
IN THY WORD, AS IF IN HEAVEN	• • •	214	PRAISE	21
THEY, BY THY WORD, THEIR BEAUTY HAD, AND DATE.	• •	218	HOLY COMM.	8
ILE SPICE MY THOUGHTS WITH THEE; AND FROM THY WORD	•	287	PSALM 104	93
I HAD NOT ONE POOR WORD TO SAY.	• • •	333	AGREEMENT	38
THE GOSPEL THEN (FOR 'TIS HIS WORD	• •	315	THE STONE	56
WERE NOT THY WORD (DEAR LORD) MY LIGHT	• •	316	MEN OF WAR	9
WORDS				
BUT SINFUL WORDS AND WORKS STILL SPREAD	• • •	336	PSALM 65	5
WHOSE ACTS, WORDS AND PRETENCE	• • •	327	RIGHTSNESS	19
THY PROMISES BUT EMPTY WORDS	• • •	207	REPENTANCE	13
WHEN OUR WORDS AND WORKS ARE DONE.	• • •	211	DAWNING	4
FOR THEE MY WORDS, MY TEARS DO GUSH	• • •	228	PILGRIMAGE	14
EXCESSE OF FRIENDS, OF WORDS, AND WINE	• • •	240	MISERY	25
(AS THY WORDS SHOW)	• • •	234	MUTINIE	29
FOR TEARS ARE NOT THINE OWN. IF THOU GIV'ST WORDS	•	194	RLS + LSNS	68
THESE ARE THE WORDS, AND WORKS OF LIFE, THIS DO	•	196	RLS + LSNS	141
TO THEE THEREFORE MY THOUGHTS, WORDS, ACTIONS	•	191	THE MATCH	25
AND STRIKE THEM DUMB, WHO FOR MEER WORDS	• •	350	L'ENVOY	41
WORE				
WHICH THORNS, NOT ROSES WORE.	• • •	345	THE WREATH	8
FOR SOME WORE WHITE EV'N IN THY GRAVE	• •	342	OBSEQUIES	19
A GARLAND WORE. THUS FED MY EYES	• • •	140	RGNRTN	56
WORK				
AND HOW THEY WORK, AND WIND	• • • •	171	MIDNIGHT	7
AND WORK ON ME NOW COLD, NOW HOT	• • •	227	LV + DSPLN	14
THE WORK GOES ON, AND SLACKETH NOT	• • •	227	LV + DSPLN	15
AND WORK, AND WIND TIL ALL BE DONE	• • •	214	MISERY	78
AND WORK ALL NIGHT UPON THY LIGHT AND LOVE	• •	278	THE STARRE	22
SO THOU, WHO DIDST THE WORK BEGIN	• • •	334	AGREEMENT	67
UNTO HIS WORK, AND AT THE CLOSE OF DAY	• •	286	PSALM 104	63
OR WHAT RESENTIENT CAN WORK MORE WITHIN	• •	290	THE TIMBER	27
WORK'ST				
IN BOTH THOU WORK'ST UNTO THE BEST.	• • •	227	LV + DSPLN	12
WORKS				
THEIR MAGNETISME WORKS ALL NIGHT	• • •	276	COCK-CRWNG	5
WHEN OUR WORDS AND WORKS ARE DONE.	• • •	211	DAWNING	4
ARE THY GREAT WORKS. IN WISDOM HAST THOU MADE	• •	286	PSALM 104	66
AND TO THY WORKS ART TRUE.	• • •	287	PSALM 104	84
AND LOV'ST HIM, THOUGH HE WORKS THY WO.	• •	298	JESUS WP B	25
BUT SINFUL WORDS AND WORKS STILL SPREAD	• •	336	PSALM 65	5
AT THY GREAT WORKS ASTONISH'D BE.	• •	336	PSALM 65	24
BUT HIS OWN LIVING WORKS DID MY LORD HOLD	• •	323	THE NIGHT	21
REDUC'D TH'EXTENT OF WORKS OF FAITH, SO MADE	•	159	MANS FALL	31
DO THOU THE WORKS OF DAY, AND RISE A STAR.	• •	196	RLS + LSNS	138
THESE ARE THE WORDS, AND WORKS OF LIFE, THIS DO	•	196	RLS + LSNS	141
OBSERVE GOD IN HIS WORKS, HERE FOUNTAINS FLOW	• •	194	RLS + LSNS	87
WORKS WITH THE SUN, AND SETS	• • •	201	THE CHECK	16
GIVE HIM AMONGST THY WORKS A PLACE	• • •	347	THE BOOK	29
WORKT				
WORKT UNDER GROUND	• • • •	232	THE WORLD	24
WORLD				
LIKE A VAST SHADOW MOV'D, IN WHICH THE WORLD	• •	231	THE WORLD	6
NO MAN CAN MORE THE WORLD DESPISE	• • •	214	MISERY	55
A WORLD OF MISERIE	• • •	243	THE SAP	18
CONFEST, THE WORLD DID ONLY PAINT AND LIE.	• •	244	MT. OLV. B	10
DEATH WEAN'D THEE FROM THE WORLD, AND SIN.	• •	209	THE BURIAL	8
THE WORLD READ TO HIM. ALL THE VAST EXPENCE	• •	223	TEMPEST	18
AND IN THE GREATER WORLD DISPLAY	• • •	221	AFFLICTION	9
SUCH WAS THE BRIGHT WORLD, ON THE FIRST SEVENTH DAY	•	268	ASCN-DAY A	39
LEAVING THE WORLD THEIR DAY	• • •	267	ASCN-DAY A	11
RESUME THY SPIRIT FROM THIS WORLD OF THRALL	• •	271	ALL GONE	35
UPON THE CLOUDS AGAIN TO JUDGE THIS WORLD.	• •	268	ASCN-DAY A	62
THEY ARE ALL GONE INTO THE WORLD OF LIGHT.	• •	270	ALL GONE	1
HE DREW THE CURSE UPON THE WORLD, AND CRACKT	• •	197	CORRUPTION	15
THE OTHER, THE TRUE LIFE, IN THE NEXT WORLD	• •	191	THE MATCH	22
SERVE GOD BEFORE THE WORLD. LET HIM NOT GO	• •	192	RLS + LSNS	19
THE WORLD	• • • • • • •	161	DSTRQCTION	11

		PAGE	TITLE	LINE
WORLD	(CON'T)			
MY REST IN CARES, AND TO THE DARK WORLD LEND		157	THE LAMPE	6
THE WORLD AN ENEMIE		148	DAY OF JDG	42
SEARCH WELL ANOTHER WORLD, WHO STUDIES THIS		153	THE SEARCH	94
AND HYMNING CIRCULATIONS THE QUICK WORLD		176	MRNG-WTCH	10
THE WORLD IN TUNE		177	MRNG-WTCH	19
TELL US THE WORLD IS BRAVE		183	THRS A TYE	14
OR BY COMPLYING WITH THE WORLD		322	CHILDEHOOD	23
WHO IN THIS WINDY WORLD ABIDE.		298	JESUS WP B	21
THUS THOU THY GLORY THROUGH THE WORLD DOST DRIVE		287	PSALM 104	83
FLOWRES GATHER'D IN THIS WORLD, DIE HERE. IF THOU		283	GARLAND	33
BUT THOUGH THUS DEAD UNTO THE WORLD, AND CEAS'D		290	THE TIMBER	33
FOR THOUGH HE SHOULD FORSAKE THE WORLD, AND LIVE		290	THE TIMBER	37
WHO LOV'D THE WORLD SO, AS TO GIVE		292	THE JEWS	33
AND NOT HIMSELF SHALL JUDGE THE WORLD)		315	THE STONE	57
IF THE WORLD OFFERS TO ME OUGHT		319	THE ASS	37
HOW IN THIS WORLD SHOULD THEY DETER		312	FAIR+YONG	39
THIS WORLD, THEIR FELLOW-MURTHERER.		312	FAIR+YONG	40
THIS WORLD BUT LAUGHS AT THOSE THAT WEEP.		312	FAIR+YONG	52
FULL FORTY DAYS O'R THE DROWN'D WORLD DID WEEP)		307	RAIN-BOW	28
TILL TRUTH THROUGH ALL THE WORLD BE PAST		305	ST MARY MN	52
THE LUCKY WORLD SHEWD ME ONE DAY		302	ORNAMENT	1
THE SAD WORLD WEPT TO BE RELEAST.		340	THE FEAST	24
AND WHAT IN THE NEXT WORLD TO EAT.		341	THE FEAST	78
WORLD'S				
THE WORLD'S THY BOXE. HOW THEN (THERE TOST)		181	BURIALL	31
WORLDLINGS				
AND YET THE PRACTICE WORLDLINGS CALL		322	CHILDEHOOD	27
WORLDS				
THE WORLDS LOV'D WISDOM (FOR THE WORLDS FRIENDS THINK		320	HIDDN TRSR	15
THE WORLDS LOV'D WISDOM (FOR THE WORLDS FRIENDS THINK		320	HIDDN TRSR	15
DEAR NIGHT. THIS WORLDS DEFEAT.		324	THE NIGHT	25
AND BY THIS WORLDS ILL-GUIDING LIGHT		324	THE NIGHT	47
ART THE WORLDS HOPE, AND BUT THEE, NONE.		336	PSALM 65	16
THE FIRST TRUE WORSHIP OF THE WORLDS GREAT KING		330	JACOBS PLW	11
THE GLAD WORLDS BLESSED MAID.		302	THE KNOT	2
BLOOD, IS THE WORLDS ALL-HEALING BALM.		304	ST MARY MN	40
A COMET, THE SAD WORLDS ILL-BODING BOOK.		307	RAIN-BOW	36
THE YOUTHFUL WORLDS GRAY FATHERS IN ONE KNOT		306	RAIN-BOW	6
IF THIS WORLDS FRIENDS MIGHT SEE BUT ONCE		308	THE SEED	1
MORNINGS ARE MYSTERIES, THE FIRST WORLDS YOUTH		192	RLS + LSNS	25
WHEN THE WORLDS UP, AND EV'RY SWARM ABROAD		192	RLS + LSNS	31
AND HEAV'NS GATE OPENS, WHEN THIS WORLDS IS SHUT.		192	RLS + LSNS	12
WHO FILS THE WORLDS UNEMPTY'D GRANARIES.		195	RLS + LSNS	100
MY DEAR REDEEMER, THE WORLDS LIGHT		265	INTRO. 2	17
THE NEXT WORLDS GLADNES PREPOSSESS IN THIS.		205	SON-DAYES	3
THAT FROM THE MURD'RING WORLDS FALSE LOVE		343	OBSEQUIES	31
O THE NEW WORLDS NEW, QUICKNING SUN.		349	L'ENVOY	1
WORMES				
DULL, WRETCHED WORMES. THAT WOULD NOT KEEPE		166	THE CALL	66
BRAVE WORMES, AND EARTH. THAT THUS COULD HAVE		164	INCARNATN	9
WORMS				
THY ROOT SUCKS BUT DISEASES, WORMS THERE SEAT		243	THE SAP	7
WORMWOOD				
OF WORMWOOD, AND A DEATHS-HEAD CROWN'D WITH ROSES.		280	JOY	6
WORMWOOD-DIET				
UNTO THEIR WORMWOOD-DIET KEEP		301	PROVIDENCE	47
WORN				
THIS LONG WORN VEYL. THEN SHINE AND SPREAD		349	L'ENVOY	9
WORSE				
AND IS THERE ANY MURTH'RER WORSE THEN SIN.		290	THE TIMBER	25
IF NO A VERY DEVILL, WORSE THAN A BEAST.		194	RLS + LSNS	78
GROWES STILL FROM BETTER UNTO WORSE		150	RELIGION	35
WORSHIP				
THE FIRST TRUE WORSHIP OF THE WORLDS GREAT KING		330	JACOBS PLW	11
WORST				
HAST SAID, THESE LAST SHOULD BE THE WORST.		273	WHT SUNDAY	28
AGAIN, IF WORST AND WORST IMPLIES		273	WHT SUNDAY	33
AGAIN, IF WORST AND WORST IMPLIES		273	WHT SUNDAY	33
THE WORST OF MEN, AND YET STIL THINE		242	MISERY	90
O THY WORST STATE, MY ONELY BEST.		341	THE FEAST	66
WORTH				
AND HERE ARE LEFT AS NOTHING WORTH		270	ASCSN-HYMN	29
WORTH LOVE OR WRATH		327	RIGHTSNESS	32
THEIR PLEASURE AND THEIR WORTH.		285	PSALM 104	32
NOT WORTH OUR THANKS. IS LIFE A GIFT		200	NTVTY 2	7
NOT WORTH THY EYES		180	BURIALL	12
WOUND				
BEFORE I TAUGHT MY TONGUE TO WOUND		169	RETREATE	15
HIS SAVING WOUND		159	MANS FALL	24
WILL NOTHING YIELD BUT THORNS TO WOUND THY HEAD.		296	JESUS WP A	18
WOUND THY BELOVED, MORE THEN SWORDS.		350	L'ENVOY	42
WOUNDS				
YET GRIEF AND OLD WOUNDS MAKE HIM SORE DISPLEAS'D		290	THE TIMBER	35
AND LINGRING WOUNDS FROM WEAKER FOES.		312	FAIR+YONG	44
INTO MY WOUNDS, AND NOW THY GRACE		214	MISERY	51
THE WOUNDS THEY GIVE, BY CRYING, ZEALE.		237	CONSTLATN	40
O CALL TO MIND HIS WOUNDS, HIS WOES		208	REPENTANCE	61
AND THY BLOUDY WOUNDS, AND STRIFE		215	PRAISE	27
WRANGLE				
DOTH FRET AND WRANGLE, PINE AND WASTE.		308	THE SEED	12

		PAGE	TITLE	LINE
WRAP				
AND WRAP US IN IMAGINARY FLIGHTS	• • • • •	183	THRS A TYE	15
WRATH				
DID THE FULL WRATH	• • • • •	185	PASSION	26
CEASE THOU THY WRATH.	• • • • •	188	RELAPSE	12
WORTH LOVE OR WRATH	• • • • •	327	RIGHTSNESS	32
WITH BAD, OR WITH NEGLECT, AND HEAPS NOT WRATH	•	328	RIGHTSNESS	51
OF ALL I HAVE, I MAY NOR MOVE THY WRATH	•	235	MUTINIE	37
WREATH				
ON SOME PARCH'D BANK, CROWN'D WITH A FLOWRIE WREATH.	•	244	MT. OLV. B	6
WOULDST HAVE A WREATH THAT FADES NOT, LET THEM GROW	•	283	GARLAND	34
TO WAIT UPON THY WREATH.	• • •	198	UNPRFTBLNS	15
BUT A TWIN'D WREATH OF GRIEF AND PRAISE	• •	345	THE WREATH	9
HOW SHALL I GET A WREATH FOR THEE	• • •	345	THE WREATH	3
WRENCH				
TO WRENCH, AND RACK THY BLESSED LIMBES.	• • •	185	PASSION	33
WRENCH'D				
NOR CAN BE WRITH'D, NOR WRENCH'D.	• • •	278	THE STARRE	20
WRESTLES				
HERE JACOB DREAMES, AND WRESTLES, THERE	• •	149	RELIGION	9
WRESTLING				
PREVAIL'D BY WRESTLING ERE THE SUN DID SHINE.	• •	192	RLS + LSNS	22
WRETCH				
THY WRETCH COMES BEGGING	• • • • •	215	PRAISE	47
A SINFULL WRETCH, A WRETCH THAT CAUS'D THY WOE	•	283	LOVE-SICK	18
A SINFULL WRETCH, A WRETCH THAT CAUS'D THY WOE	•	283	LOVE-SICK	18
WRETCHED				
GIVE TO THY WRETCHED ONE	• • • • •	216	DRESSING	13
BUT WRETCHED SALEM ONCE HIS LOVE, MUST NOW	•	238	SHEPHEARDS	17
THUS WRETCHED I, AND MOST UNKIND	• • •	240	MISERY	33
DULL, WRETCHED WORMES. THAT WOULD NOT KEEPE	•	166	THE CALL	66
WRETCHEDLY				
WHO TRUSTS NOT THEE. BUT WRETCHEDLY	• • •	301	PROVIDENCE	32
WRIT				
WITH THOSE FOUL STORMS, WHEN THEY WERE WRIT.	•	332	AGREEMENT	28
AND POWER FORCE ON HOLY WRIT	• • •	335	JUDGEMENT	36
HAD WRIT DOWN ITS SAD CONSEQUENCE	• • •	311	FAIR+YONG	20
THY NAME WAS WRIT, AND ALL THY DAYS.	• •	310	THE SEED	60
WRIT IN HIS BOOK, WHO NE'R BETRAY'D MANS TRUST.	•	177	EVNG-WTCH	8
BUT AS I URG'D THUS, AND WRIT DOWN	• •	152	THE SEARCH	67
TO CANCELL ALL THAT E'RE WAS WRIT IN STONE	•	159	MANS FALL	23
WRITE				
WRITE IN THY BOOKES	• • • •	157	BRT. CHRCH	15
THY ARM DOTH SLEEP, BUT WRITE THIS DAY	• •	335	JUDGEMENT	44
TO WRITE AND SING.	• • • •	329	ANGUISH	14
BUT TO WRITE TRUE, UNFEIGNED VERSE	• •	329	ANGUISH	15
THEREFORE WRITE IN THEIR HEARTS THY LAW	• •	351	L'ENVOY	53
WRITH'D				
NOR CAN BE WRITH'D, NOR WRENCH'D.	• • •	278	THE STARRE	20
WRITTEN				
AND GOING HENCE, LEAVE WRITTEN ON SOME TREE	•	281	JOY	29
WRONG				
THEN LIKE THE PALM, THOUGH WRONG, I'LE BEAR	•	295	PALM-SUNDY	38
SIX MAY GO WRONG.	• • • • •	174	JOY OF LIF	12
WRONG NOT THY CONSCIENCE FOR A ROTTEN STICK	•	193	RLS + LSNS	41
WROTE				
I WROTE IT DOWN. BUT ONE THAT SAW	• • •	332	AGREEMENT	1
WROUGHT				
DIDST FLYE, WHOSE CHILDREN WROUGHT THY CHILDRENS WO.	•	331	JACOBS PLW	44
NOR LOV'D THE SMILES OF GREATNESS, BUT HAVE WROUGHT	•	280	PALM-TREE	19
WHO WROUGHT THY WO.	• • • •	220	HOLY COMM.	48
IMMORTAL SHAPE, WHO WROUGHT THEIR BLISS	• •	349	L'ENVOY	6
WRUNG				
THEIR YOUTH, AND BEAUTY, COLD SHOWRES NIPT, AND WRUNG	•	198	UNPRFTBLNS	5
WTIH				
THEN MAY HIS PEACE BE WTIH THEE, AND EACH DUST	• •	177	EVNG-WTCH	7
YEA				
YEA, I HAVE KNOWNE THESE SHREDS OUT LAST	• •	166	THE CALL	54
YEA, 'TIS A DEATH PARTAKES OF HELL.	• •	277	COCK-CRWNG	26
YEA BETHEL SHALL HAVE TITHES (SAITH ISRAELS STONE)	•	331	JACOBS PLW	33
YEA, BLESSE THOU HIM FOR EVER.	• • •	287	PSALM 104	96
YEA GODS OWN BLOOD WE TREAD UPON AND SLIGHT.	•	307	RAIN-BOW	30
AND THOSE I SAW SEARCH'D THROUGH, YEA THOSE AND ALL	•	320	HIDDN TRSR	7
YEAR				
THE MEASURE GIVEN BY THEE EACH YEAR	• • •	301	PROVIDENCE	38
WHEN THE FAIR YEAR	• • • • •	291	THE JEWS	1
WHICH ALL THE YEAR SEES THE SUNS FACE.	• •	332	AGREEMENT	12
THE YEAR IS WITH THY GOODNESS CROWN'D	• •	337	PSALM 65	39
THEN I IN HEAVEN ALL THE LONG YEAR	• •	324	THE NIGHT	41
WHERE THE IMPURE SEEDS FLOURISH ALL THE YEAR	•	321	HIDDN TRSR	26
WHILE THE WINDS REFRESH THE YEAR	• • •	281	JOY	19
THUS ALL THE YEAR I MOURN.	• • • •	248	I WALKT	63
WHICH, LIKE COLD FRIENDS, SEES US BUT ONCE A YEAR	•	247	I WALKT	12
WERE ALL THE YEAR ONE CONSTANT SUN-SHINE, WEE	•	222	AFFLICTION	21
NOT ONE MINUTE IN THE YEAR	• • •	214	PRAISE	17
WINTER IS ALL MY YEAR.	• • • •	205	IDLE VERSE	24
TAKE UP, AND TUNE HIS YEAR	• • • •	236	CONSTLATN	22
BUT WANDER'D UNDER TEMPESTS ALL THE YEAR	• •	244	MT. OLV. B	12
AND ALL THE YEAR HAVE SOME GREAN EARS	• •	227	LV + DSPLN	18
EACH DAY IS GROWN A DOZEN YEAR	• • •	170	COME, COME	3

		PAGE	TITLE	LINE
YEAR	(CON'T)			
MUST NOT BE NUMBRED IN THE YEAR.		200	NTVTY 2	18
YEARE				
SITS ON THE SUNS BROW ALL THE YEARE		143	DEATH	13
TENANT FOR YEARES, AND CENTURIES		142	DEATH	4
TWO THOUSAND YEARES		159	MANS FALL	15
AND MANY YEARES (ALAS)		166	THE CALL	47
OF DAYES, AND YEARES		165	THE CALL	15
A FAIRE SUPPLY OF YEARES.		165	THE CALL	37
YEARLY				
HER YEARLY NURSE, CAME BACK, ENQUIR'D		151	THE SEARCH	13
YEARS				
SOME TWENTY YEARS.		164	THE CALL	4
TEACHING MY YEARS		186	PASSION	55
WHEN SIX YEARS THENCE DIGG'D UP, SOME YOUTHFULL EYE		201	THE CHECK	6
AND ROUND BENEATH IT, TIME IN HOURS, DAYS, YEARS		231	THE WORLD	4
PASS THY SOLITARY YEARS		281	JOY	29
'TIS NOW SIX THOUSAND YEARS WELL NIGH		338	DEATH B	3
DURST NOT LOOK ON THOSE SMILING YEARS		303	ST MARY MN	12
THAT THESE THREE THOUSAND YEARS TIME DID LET FALL		320	HIDDN TRSR	8
AND DRESS THIS EARTH FOR NEXT YEARS MEAT.		341	THE FEAST	75
YEERS				
DIDOST THY SWIFT YEERS IN PIETY OUT-GROW		156	ISAACS M.	68
YELL				
DID HEAR THEM YELL		188	RELAPSE	4
YES				
O, YES. THOU KNOW'ST I DOE, COME, AND RELIEVE		161	DSTRQCTION	28
YEWGH				
NO SHADE BUT YEWGH		188	RELAPSE	18
OR ROSES WITH MY YEWGH.		205	IDLE VERSE	20
YIELD				
WHOSE PAINEFULL THROWS YIELD MANY SONS		167	THE CALL	76
WILL NOTHING YIELD BUT THORNS TO WOUND THY HEAD.		296	JESUS WP A	18
WHERE I SOMETIMES HAD SEEN THE SOIL TO YIELD		246	I WALKT	3
FUL HYMNS DOTH YIELD		212	DAWNING	16
AND SELDOM YIELDED FLOWERS		345	THE WREATH	2
YIELDING				
MY YIELDING LEAVES. SOMETIMES A SHOWR		203	DSRDR + FR	25
YIELDS				
HE GOES, HE YIELDS, AND TROUBLED SORE		240	MISERY	37
I SMELL HER SPICES, AND HER OINTMENT YIELDS		267	ASCN-DAY A	21
YOKE				
HIS EASIE YOKE REJECTS OR SLIGHTS		315	THE STONE	55
YON				
WHO ON YON THRONE OF AZURE SITS		225	RETIREMENT	1
YONG				
ABOUT THY CURIOUS, WILDE, YONG HEAD.		304	ST MARY MN	20
STILL YONG AND FINE. BUT WHAT IS STILL IN VIEW		306	RAIN-BOW	1
FAIR AND YONG LIGHT. MY GUIDE TO HOLY		311	FAIR+YONG	1
LEAVE THEN YONG SORCERESS. THE ICE		297	HERODIAS	9
SUCH YONG, SWEET MIRTH		295	PALM-SUNDY	24
OF YONG, DISTRESSED ISHMAEL.		300	PROVIDENCE	6
AND DAILY DIDST MY YONG EYES LEAD		348	HOLY BIBLE	7
YOU'D				
YOU'D MAKE NO FLIGHTS.		274	PROFFER	4
YOUNG				
COME FORTH MOST FAIR AND YOUNG.		247	I WALKT	28
LAPT IN THE SWEETS OF THY YOUNG BREATH		209	THE BURIAL	10
LIKE A YOUNG EAST, OR MOONE-SHINE NIGHT		168	VNTY SPRIT	20
THUS SOAR'D THY SOUL, WHO (THOUGH YOUNG) DIDST INHERIT		156	ISAACS M.	63
OF YONG, GAY SWEARERS, WITH THEIR NEEDLESSE, LOWD		154	ISAACS M.	22
FIRST, A YOUNG PATRIARCH, THEN A MARRI'D SAINT.		156	ISAACS M.	72
AS A YOUNG ROE		157	BRT. CHRCH	19
HE, EVER YOUNG, DOTH WING		145	RSRCTN +IM	41
THE YOUNGEST, EV'N THE GENTILES THEN		293	THE JEWS	44
YOUTH				
WHERE YOUTH SHINES LIKE A STAR		310	THE SEED	62
WHO WOULD'ST NOT HATE MY FROWARD YOUTH		301	PROVIDENCE	44
NO SINS OF FRAILTY, NOR OF YOUTH		333	AGREEMENT	53
BOTH LIFE AND YOUTH		145	RSRCTN +IM	30
HENCE, YOUTH, AND FOLLY (MANS FIRST SHAME)		166	THE CALL	62
FOR SINCE AMIDST MY YOUTH, AND NIGHT		205	IDLE VERSE	5
THEIR YOUTH, AND BEAUTY, COLD SHOWRES NIPT, AND WRUNG		198	UNPRFTBLNS	5
TELL YOUTH, AND BEAUTY THEY MUST ROT		189	RESOLVE	11
MORNINGS ARE MYSTERIES, THE FIRST WORLDS YOUTH		192	RLS + LSNS	25
AND IF HEREAFTER YOUTH, OR FOLLY THWART		190	THE MATCH	10
MAN IS A SUMMERS DAY, WHOSE YOUTH, AND FIRE		195	RLS + LSNS	113
YOUTH NOW, FULL OF PIOUS DUTY		218	EASTER HYM	7
LET MY YOUTH, MY BLOOM OF DAYES		249	BEGGING A	7
SHEW'D TO ME IN MY SINFUL YOUTH		265	INTRO. 2	20
PUT ON THEIR YOUTH AND GREEN.		279	THE STARRE	32
YOUTHFUL				
NO FROST, BUT FLOURISH'D IN THAT YOUTHFUL VEST		268	ASCN-DAY A	43
YOUTHFUL AND FAIR TO SEE NEW SKIES.		334	JUDGEMENT	6
THE YOUTHFUL WORLDS GRAY FATHERS IN ONE KNOT		306	RAIN-BOW	6
YOUTHFULL				
WHEN FIRST MY YOUTHFULL, SINFULL AGE		282	GARLAND	5
THE PURLES OF YOUTHFULL BLOUD, AND BOWLES		205	IDLE VERSE	13
WHEN SIX YEARS THENCE DIGG'D UP, SOME YOUTHFULL EYE		201	THE CHECK	6
YOUTHS				
THY YOUTHS COMPANIONS		201	THE CHECK	26